The Real Cruel Sea

The Real Cruel Sea

The Merchant Navy in the Battle of the Atlantic
1939–1943

RICHARD WOODMAN

Illustrations by John Morris

Pen & Sword
MARITIME

First published in Great Britain in 2004 by John Murray

Published in this format in 2011
and reprinted in 2013 by
PEN & SWORD MARITIME
An imprint of
Pen & Sword Books Ltd
47 Church Street
Barnsley, South Yorkshire
S70 2AS

ISBN 978 1 84884 415 5

A CIP catalogue record for this book is
available from the British Library

Printed and bound in England
By CPI Group (UK) Ltd, Croydon, CR0 4YY

Pen & Sword Books Ltd incorporates the Imprints of Pen & Sword Aviation,
Pen & Sword Family History, Pen & Sword Maritime, Pen & Sword Military,
Pen & Sword Discovery, Pen & Sword Politics, Pen & Sword Atlas,
Pen & Sword Archaeology, Wharncliffe Local History, Wharncliffe True Crime,
Wharncliffe Transport, Pen & Sword Select, Pen & Sword Military Classics,
Leo Cooper, The Praetorian Press, Claymore Press, Remember When,
Seaforth Publishing and Frontline Publishing

For a complete list of Pen & Sword titles please contact
PEN & SWORD BOOKS LIMITED
47 Church Street, Barnsley, South Yorkshire, S70 2AS, England
E-mail: enquiries@pen-and-sword.co.uk
Website: www.pen-and-sword.co.uk

This book is dedicated to the memory of all Allied seafarers
who served in the Atlantic, 1939–1945

'It was forgotten by the British people that the British Merchant Navy
had a war history dating back to a period anterior to the founding of the
Royal Navy.'

Archibald Hurd, 1921

'A useful chapter in naval history and tactics could be written on the defence
of convoys, by which it might perhaps be made manifest, that a determined
bearing, accompanied by a certain degree of force, and a vigorous resolution
to exert that force to the utmost, would, in most cases, save the greater part
of the convoy, even against powerful odds.'

Captain Basil Hall, RN (1788–1844)

CONTENTS

PART THREE

May 1941–December 1941: The Means of Survival

PART FOUR

January 1942–July 1942: Weakness in Defence

PART FIVE

August 1942–May 1943: Grey Dawn Breaking

Inanda

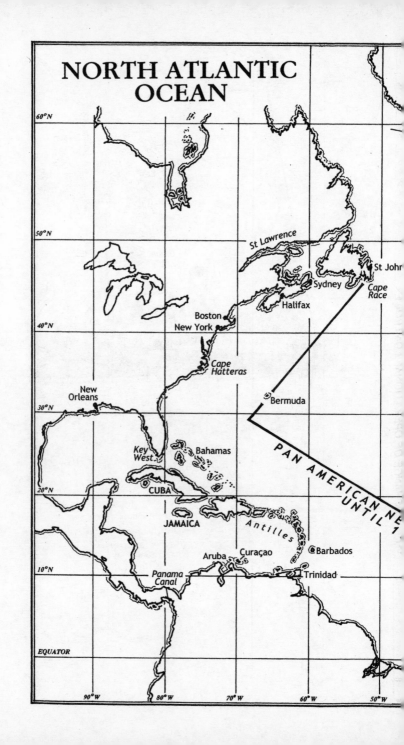

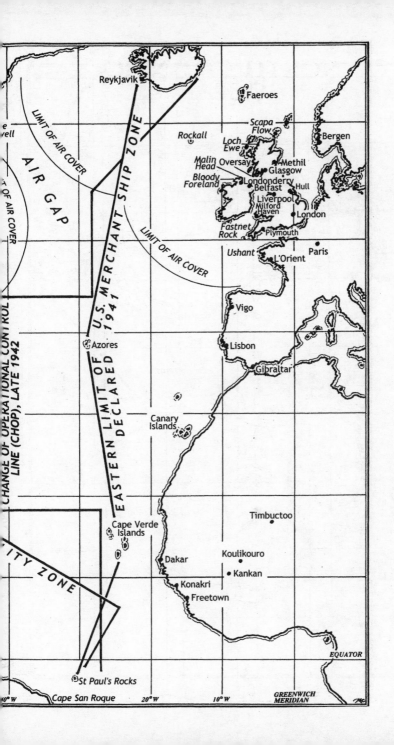

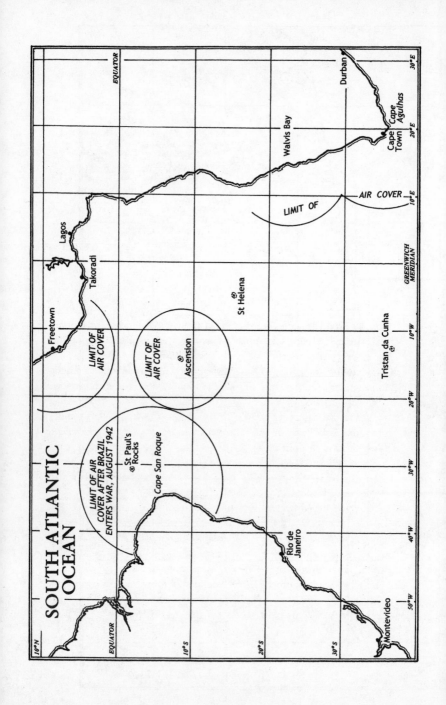

CONVOY SL71

Convoy Escort leaving Freetown: HM Cruiser *Mauritius*, HM Corvettes *Maguerite*, *Cyclamen*, *Clematis* and *Crocus*, with Armed Merchant Cruiser *Cilicia* (ex-Anchor Line).

Cruiser order was changed on 17 April with Commodore B.S. Thesiger leading the Fast Section in the Blue Funnel liner *Rhesus* in position 51 with the fast ships capable of making at least 9.5 knots in positions 11, 12, 13, 14, 15, 21, 22, 23, 24, 25, 31, 32, 33, 34, 35, 41, 42, 43, 44, 45, 51, 52 and 53. Commodore G.W. Jones in the Ellerman City liner *City of Yokohama* led the Slow Section in position 81, with slow ships in positions 61, 62, 63, 64, 71, 72, 73, 74, 81, 82, 83, 84, 91, 92, 93, 94, 95, 101, 103, 104, 111, 112, 113 and 114. At this time the corvettes had returned to Freetown and the Ocean Escort consisted of HM Cruiser *Mauritius* and AMC HMS *Cilicia*. *Mauritius* was relieved by HMS *London* on 23 April off the Azores in Posn. 36°10'N and 023°00'W. On 29 AMC HMS *Malvolian* joined together with destroyers *Campbeltown* and *Sherwood*, whereupon *London* departed. Destroyers *Beagle* and *Eridge*, and corvettes *Sunflower* and *Alisma* also joined, and *Cilicia* left. Other escorts joined that afternoon as at 1515 in 53°N 23°W, Fast and Slow Sections proceeded independently. Slow Section was escorted by *Vanquisher*, *Viscount*, *Rockingham*, *Londonderry*, *Freesia* and the yacht *Philante*, and arrived in the Clyde on 4 May.

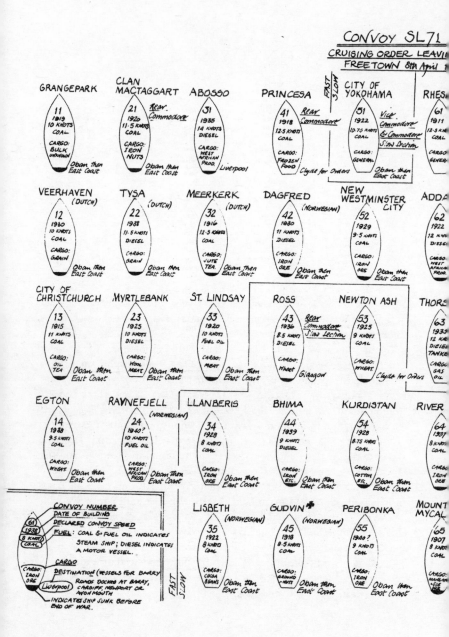

CONVOY SL71 — CRUISING ORDER LEAVING FREETOWN 8th April

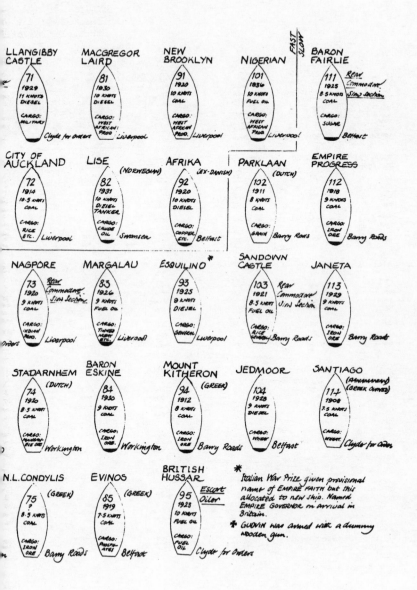

INTRODUCTION

'This nation owes these people a great deal'

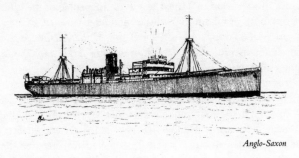

Anglo-Saxon

WHAT HISTORY CALLS the Battle of the Atlantic began a few hours after the declaration of war on Nazi Germany on 3 September 1939 by the then Prime Minister of Great Britain, Neville Chamberlain. It ended on 8 May 1945, the day upon which Hitler's successor as Führer, Grossadmiral Karl Dönitz, surrendered. It was the western arm of the great pincer movement by which the German Third Reich was crushed, complementing the Red Army's war on the eastern front. It was not a battle in the conventional sense, but a series of actions, mostly around slow-moving convoys of merchant ships bearing the sinews of war across the ocean from the manufactories of the United States to the Allies' remaining stronghold in Europe, the beleaguered nation of Great Britain. The outcome of this long Atlantic campaign depended on the resolution of a simple problem: could the Allies build, fill with cargoes and man more merchant ships than the Axis could sink? At first it seemed possible that they could not, although Hitler had committed the Kriegsmarine to hostilities before Germany had the requisite resources. But ultimately the energies unleashed by the ambitions of Hitler proved unable to prevail against the full sea-power of the Western Allies, just as they proved inferior to those of the land-power of Soviet Russia.

The importance of sea-power in the Allies' eventual victory in both the Atlantic and the Pacific theatres can scarcely be exaggerated. The battle was not so much *of* the Atlantic as *for* it, a ceaseless contest in which the enemy might secure a local superiority that, no matter how temporary, could have a cumulative and pivotal effect on events elsewhere. Thus, even when struggling for that mastery, the Allies had to maintain the continuous transport of war material across the North Atlantic.[1]

This book is concerned only with the principal struggle in the Atlantic, only for the first, most critical part of that battle, and largely with only one aspect of it. Although much has already been written on the subject, I believe there is room for another work dedicated to this titanic event. To the British of today, and to a great extent to the people of the United States of America, both of whom know little and understand less of the sea-faring life in peace or in war, study of the Battle of the Atlantic is a matter of singular significance. I believe it epitomises the moral high point of their maritime endeavour.

In this supreme Allied achievement the mustering of manpower and the making of new seamen played a major part; less generally appreciated is the extent to which the outcome was influenced by ship-building on an unprecedented scale in the United States, in Britain and in Canada. Nor must it be forgotten that the Allied fleets included many ships and crews, both naval and mercantile, which had escaped from the German occupation of their own countries; nor that many neutral vessels took shelter within the embrace of Allied convoys. Countries like Sweden suffered substantial losses in men and ships. Moreover, the shelter of convoy was extended by a rapid expansion of the Royal Canadian Navy, whose warships played a major role in the struggle, as did the aircrews of the maritime arms of the principal Allied air forces.

The exhaustion and the fundamental economic changes resulting from the First World War of 1914–1918 had greatly diminished the material resources of the United Kingdom and the British Commonwealth and Empire. Both the Royal Navy and the merchant fleet suffered neglect, and both had consequently declined from their former pre-eminence.[2] Yet from this alarming situation, in response to a new German threat there developed a really remarkable regeneration. The recovery was to be beset by errors, disasters, and the sheer bad management for which the British seem to enjoy a curiously persistent affinity. It was to prove short-lived, but it was to prove crucial. Its successful outcome could not have been secured without the wholehearted support of the United States, a matter by no means certain in 1939, or without that other inexplicable and inveterate British characteristic, a bloody-minded objection to being shoved around too much.

Although there existed in Germany weaknesses equal to British self-conceit and smugness, a curious transfer of sympathy may be discerned in the writing of some British and American historians, perhaps from regard for the greater hurt inevitably inflicted upon the enemy to ensure his defeat. The twilight of a once-great power does not naturally evoke sympathy from those who were not participants in its greatness, nor is it remembered that Britain's imperial decline was largely a consequence of high endeavour, twice in the space of some thirty years, on behalf of the whole community of nations. Britain paid a heavy price for resistance after her principal ally France capitulated to Germany in the spring of 1940. She had to conscript 42 per cent of her peace-time work-force into her armed services, causing a huge reduction in her productive capability which had to be addressed, not merely to re-equip her armed forces[3] but to provide manufactures for export to help pay for the war. Long hours of overtime were worked, while increased numbers of young apprentices were engaged in ship-yards and two million women were recruited to labour in armaments factories. By 1944 British exports, manufactured by plant that had been worked to death in the war, had fallen to 28 per cent of their pre-war level. Even four years *after* the end of the war, in 1949, such was the extent of their debts that the British returned to 'dried eggs, queues and rationing'. By contrast France, although she had suffered a similar fall in the standard of living of her people, had in 1945 'substantial reserves and no indebtedness'.[4]

The consequence of this, it seems to me, has been a wholesale depreciation of the British as the world's greatest exponents of sea-power, an expertise that had not been exhausted by 1939, whatever its considerable material short-comings may have been. Under pressure from a relentless enemy her creaking, over-extended Royal Navy and the leaky bucket of her mercantile marine compelled Britain to seek help from the United States, but her stock of fortitude, resolution, intelligence and seamanship was never insufficient to the long task.

There existed, notwithstanding, a serious, often near-mutinous grumbling among merchant seamen. These theoretical non-combatants enjoyed no special status and lacked even the most primitive 'comforts' that were provided for the regular armed services. During that part of the war in which they suffered most and which is covered in this work, many of them were off pay from the day their ships were sunk. Exposure in a lifeboat or on a raft was an unpaid excursion. Some companies did continue to pay their crews, but they were exemplary exceptions from the norm among the tramp-ship owners whose vessels made up the bulk of Atlantic convoys. The often rough exterior of merchant jacks and the economic vicissitudes that impinged remorselessly upon their entire existence, which was near the subsistence level in universal economic terms, gave them an image perceived by most as one of the lowest social type. That these men bore the brunt of the pre-war Depression was not widely appreciated, the British public being more readily acquainted with the suffering of mill-workers in Lancashire, coal-miners in Yorkshire, or ship-yard workers on Clydeside. Alongside these easily identifiable tribal groups, the British merchant seaman was a mongrel.

For a start he was not necessarily 'British' in the strictest sense. Arabs, Indians, Chinese, Maltese, Somalis and Egyptians, among others, filled berths in British merchant ships, a polyglot mixture that in the social hierarchy of imperial sunset tended to taint the perceptions of the respectable.

While the Royal Navy trained for it, war to the merchant sailor was an imposition added to an already harsh existence, and one that required the swift acquisition of new skills. 'We were able to cope with signals . . . zig-zags and . . . gunnery from the early days but really stormy weather was our worst enemy . . . [because] in bad weather . . . ships in convoy become so widely separated that they often lost touch with each other . . .', one officer recalled. While admiring the 'guts and doggedness' of the small naval escorts which in such weather seemed 'to stand on end at times', shipping 'green seas overall', many merchant masters felt that when sent to round their charges up, the commanders of the escorting warships had no appreciation of their problems. Largely owing to their youth and 'limited sea service . . . [they] could not fully appreciate the problems of handling low powered heavily laden merchant ships'.[5]

An exception existed where escorts were commanded or bore officers from the Royal Naval Reserve, whose members were drawn from the merchant service itself. Their drafting into men-of-war created its own manpower shortage in the ships they had left, just one small knock-on effect of war. The regular naval officers most often forced to confront the realities of life in merchant ships were those superannuated admirals who gallantly returned at the outbreak of war to become convoy commodores. One, Sir Kenelm Creighton, recognised 'the gulf' that in 1939 'still seemed to separate the officers and men of the two services'.[6]

Still less did the Royal Navy understand the merchant jack's psyche. As a generalisation it is true that the navy admired the merchant service's generic self-sacrifice, despaired when it failed to protect its charges in convoy and lost them to the enemy; but it was bewildered when it found itself overwhelmed by unruly survivors, and did not understand the basic situation – that the sodden and oil-soaked human flotsam was not only off-pay, but that their 'Articles' (the contractual agreement between themselves and the master of their ship) were broken by its sinking. Finding these uninvited guests a problem, the navy was often too quick to report on their deficiencies. Drunkenness on the part of survivors was not infrequent, and was usually reported by the rescuing naval officers, particularly if it was found in a master.

Alcohol has always played a large part in the sea-life, as an antidote to loneliness and personal unhappiness. On Foreign-going Articles in peace time, 'merchant seamen' (and under this democratic banner the administering government bureaucracy regulated *all* its members, regardless of their possible substantive ranks as masters, mates, pursers, radio officers or engineers) signed-on a ship for a statutory period of up to two years. On board, 'animosity usually prevailed between the deck and engine departments so that the chief engineer was as isolated as the master. Long voyages, with sea passages as long as three weeks, did not improve a man.'[7] A personal life could be warped by such routine hardships, for they were without palliation by any agency outside the seamen's missions. Undoubtedly there was heavy drinking, which in any situation at sea is reprehensible, but the chance of the offence being noticed and enshrined in an official report arose most notably when a man whose ship was sinking under him raided the stores and sozzled himself before casting himself adrift. Such a scenario needs to be borne in mind, for the reputation for fortitude of the merchant seamen, who were to die in the Battle of the Atlantic in proportionally greater numbers than their naval cousins, has been overshadowed by such pejorative nuances. The truth, expressed by Max Nicholson of the Ministry of War Transport, was that 'This nation owes these people a great deal.'

For all these occasional aberrations, the obligations laid upon masters, mates and engineers were quite specific, and quite different from those laid upon naval officers in a fighting service. From these and other contrasts of style and methodology, the so-called 'Merchant Navy' has suffered greatly. Occasional drunkenness on the part of naval officers was an almost self-confessed feature of naval life, but it took on the character of high jinks because it was most prevalent in port, when a relaxed routine was in operation and unwinding was accepted as a psychological necessity.

As for the poor quality of too many of Britain's merchant ships, one example may suffice here. One 17-year-old radio officer, joining his ship in December 1939, found her to be 'the *Umvoti*, a ship built at the turn of the century with an extra long No. 2 Hold for transporting the field guns for the Boer War. [She had been] torpedoed in the First War in the English Channel, beached on the Isle of Wight and salvaged . . . Our crew consists of the Captain, four mates (the fourth is a Supernumerary, a Mauritian who served his time in sail and has been to London to take his Second Mate's ticket and is going home), two radio officers, a lascar deck crew and Goanese stewards. We have a 4-inch gun on the stern, also a 3-inch anti-aircraft gun . . .'

The highest mortality rate in the Battle of the Atlantic was among the Germans of the Kriegsmarine's submarine arm. This was the price of defeat, a wound inflicted not just by the victors but as a consequence of the inevitable profligate waste of war and the German method of waging it. There has of late emerged a current of opinion mildly disparaging of the British achievement, with a cross-current of increasing admiration for the German submarine service, both in Germany, where it is natural enough, and in the United States, where it lacks a corresponding justification; it is also claimed that the U-boat crews were less tainted by Nazism than other sectors of the German armed forces. Yet to civilian surface sailors, *all* submariners were contemptible, and the losses of American merchant seamen were, as in Britain, proportionately higher than among their fighting services. Even in the great republic merchant seamen were seen as coming low in the pecking order, and many, particularly those volunteers who augmented the peace-time United States' Mercantile Marine, greatly resented their social categorisation as hobos.

Perhaps not surprisingly, the men in the ships which bore the cargoes of raw materials, oil, manufactured hardware, foodstuffs and all the other war supplies, have received little attention from historians. The panorama of technological advantage, of strategy and counter-strategy, of attack and counter-attack, of intelligence coups, of supporting air-power and of leadership, is vastly more glamorous. A fulsome appreciation of the sheer endurance of all those who were engaged in the bitter, five-year campaign can in no circumstances be withheld, yet it remains true that those who were the principal targets of the Kriegsmarine's submarine offensive, those who were in essence *the heart of the matter*, have been curiously sidelined, perhaps because they are simply too ordinary to be clearly perceived. Some authors have sought to redress this imbalance, but it seems to me that the task is not yet completed.

The fortitude of merchant seamen who manned the convoys which in their hundreds ploughed the inhospitable waters of the North Atlantic was central to the issue of the battle; that it should have been found among so diverse, downtrodden, querulous and dour a collection of people who stuck to their guns, both literally and metaphorically, with such marvellous doggedness, seems in retrospect altogether remarkable. There are no war cemeteries for the one in four merchant seamen lost at sea; as the German poem has it, 'There are no roses on a sailor's grave.'

However, my motivation is not simply mere sympathy for the hitherto under-appreciated merchant seamen. In the half-century or so since the Battle of the Atlantic ended, what was then called the British Merchant Navy has almost disappeared. The political and economic reasons for this cannot detain us here, but the fact is that the vast number of ships which were sunk or survived the war were not a 'navy' in any real sense. They were privately-owned vessels commandeered by national necessity and sent to war in the national interest. There was little or no mechanism for formally recording their exploits, and the companies to which they belonged have now largely vanished. These ships were utilitarian and unexceptional – until, that is, the war made them vital.

I have not included statistics available elsewhere and I have omitted such data as individual ships' gross tonnages, which are, in any case, a measure of capacity. Where it has seemed necessary I have denominated a vessel as 'small' if her gross tonnage was less than 2,000 tons, and 'large' if it exceeded 10,000.[8] As a general rule, tramp-ships varied between 3,000 and 5,000 tons, while the more versatile cargo-liner covered a wider spectrum between 5,000 and 12,000 tons, roughly the tonnage of a war-time tanker. Passenger-liners were, of course, larger still. I have, however, indicated the much more relevant tonnages of cargoes lost. To avoid confusion, times in the text, where specified, may be taken as local time on the day in question.

This book deals with only a part of this campaign, the period leading up to the outbreak of war and from then until the climax of May 1943. At this time the Western Allies secured a supremacy at sea which, though it was often challenged, they never afterwards lost. In the succeeding half-century it has been a different matter. One hundred years ago the American naval historian Captain Alfred Mahan wrote that 'Britain . . . will depend as far ahead as we can see, not on the Royal Navy, but on the merchant ships that actually carry [the] basic requirements, both in peace and in war.'

It is something we have forgotten.

Richard Woodman
Harwich, 2004

PART ONE

September 1939–July 1940

THE HEART OF
THE MATTER

I

'We were utterly miserable'

Athenia

AT TWILIGHT ON Sunday 3 September 1939 the 13,600-ton passenger-liner *Athenia* was steaming westwards through a choppy North Atlantic, known to the officers on her bridge, as to countless numbers of British seamen, as 'the Western Ocean'. By about 19.30 hours the *Athenia* was some 220 miles clear of the Irish coast, passing over the Rockall Bank. She was bound on a scheduled service to the Canadian port of Montreal, far up the St Lawrence River. The *Athenia* was an ageing vessel, having been built by Fairfield's on the river Clyde in 1923. Her owners, Donaldson Brothers & Black of Glasgow, were a typical British liner company, possessing a fleet of 21 cargo and passenger vessels engaged in trade with North and South America. As was common among ship-owners, these vessels were divided among a number of subsidiary lines; the *Athenia* and her sister-ship the *Letitia* formed Donaldson & Black's 'Atlantic Line', which with two of Cunard's smaller trans-Atlantic liners maintained a joint weekly service from the Clyde, Liverpool and Belfast to Quebec and Montreal in summer, and Halifax and St John's, Newfoundland in winter. A Donaldson officer recalled that 'This was the world of the Western Ocean where one quickly learnt to treat the elements with a great deal of respect; it was anything but a fine weather trade.' Only four years earlier Donaldson's had lost the 6,000-ton *Vardulia* which, laden with general cargo and coal, had foundered with all hands.[1]

The *Athenia* had left her home port on the Clyde on 2 September and called at Liverpool and Belfast to embark the last of her passengers. These included more than three hundred American tourists anxious to escape the threatening atmosphere of Europe, a large number of children being evacuated from British cities, and some Jewish refugees fleeing Nazi German persecution. 'We were all getting nervous at not getting under way,' wrote John C. Coullie, an American passenger travelling with his wife Isabella.[2] 'We took on an awful lot of people and baggage . . .' During that Sunday the air of apprehension on board was palpable, for war had been declared on Germany at 11.00 that morning by the British Prime Minister, Neville Chamberlain, following the German invasion of Poland a few days earlier. The news had been broadcast on the BBC Home Service, and as Coullie and his wife emerged from attending Matins they saw the bulletin posted on the ship's notice board. They had had a lonely breakfast, for most of their fellow passengers were prostrated by sea-sickness, and as the day wore on Coullie became aware that the ship's company were taking precautions 'so that no lights would show . . . and the lifeboats were uncovered', all of which 'made us very uneasy'.

The *Athenia*'s master, Captain James Cook, was a prudent mariner. He had 1,417 souls in his charge, of whom 1,102 were passengers, and he had held a lifeboat muster of them all before his ship's final departure, as he was bound to do. But although he had assured his passengers that the *Athenia* was protected by international law from submarine attack he was aware that his ship's speed of 15 knots was not high, so once clear of the North Channel he took the precaution of steaming the *Athenia* on a series of erratic zig-zags at varying angles either side of a mean course and in accordance with Admiralty instructions issued to masters of British merchant ships the previous year.

A review of British merchant shipping by the Admiralty had resulted in both the *Athenia* and her sister being selected for conversion to Armed Merchant Cruisers in the event of war.[3] Their speed, though not that of the crack trans-Atlantic liners, would enable them to accompany an 8-knot ocean convoy and still have parity with a naval corvette. The conversion work was to be put in hand as soon as the *Athenia* had completed her present trans-Atlantic passage.

Having dined early, Mr and Mrs Coullie had gone to their lounge, 'to read . . . until bed time'. Other passengers, including a Mr Hugh Stowell Swindley, were still awaiting the call for the third sitting of dinner when at 19.43 the *Athenia* was hit by a torpedo on 'the port side, aft of the midship section. There were two explosions, before the vessel listed to port,' recorded Swindley, who was 'sent sprawling on hands and knees against the port side-rail of the ship. The vessel made a partial recovery, which helped me to regain my feet.'[4] Looking to seaward, Swindley saw 'the deck and conning tower of a submarine about three hundred yards away on the port bow.' He was not the only passenger to sight the U-boat in the offing.

The enemy had struck the liner at the point where a watertight bulk-head separated the engine and boiler rooms, wreaking havoc and disabling the ship's internal domestic power supply. The second explosion heard by Swindley may have been one of the boilers exploding, though other witnesses thought they had been shelled. No one was quite certain. Many of those on duty in the engine room and boiler stokeholds were killed outright, or drowned in the sudden flooding, while the rising force of the detonation wrecked much of the passenger accommodation, the third- and tourist-class dining rooms where many passengers were still eating, and a main compan-ionway leading up to the open deck. Survivors spoke of horribly charred bodies lying about.

In the lounge Isabella Coullie was thrown into her husband's arms, 'the lights all went out' and the ship was plunged into complete and terrifying darkness. Coullie felt dazed and unable to think clearly. 'Everybody rushed for the doors, but I held onto Bella until the rush was over and we made our way out onto the [embarkation] deck: it was not quite dark outside so we made our way to our lifeboat station . . . and what a terrible scene that was[.] People lying all over the deck, women screaming, children crying and the crew keeping the people from rushing the lifeboats . . . Everything was smashed to bits . . .'

The noise persuaded Coullie that the *Athenia* was being shelled; in the dark, 'lots of people were jumping overboard'. Leaving his wife on deck Coullie decided to return to his cabin for their lifebelts, his only illumina-tion 'four matches in a box. I lit one to see my way down stairs, people were jammed [*sic*] tight on the stair and my match lit up the place and let them get clear of our cabin [where] . . . I lit another match and got out lifebelts[.] Women were pulling my coat and asking for a lifebelt, we had three in our cabin so I gave one to a woman then I lit another match and got Bella's red coat and her sweater, then I lit the last one to see my way upstairs again[;] the top of the stairs was badly smashed but I got over all right and soon was back beside Bella.' They donned their lifebelts and Coullie 'went to the other side of the ship and saw the submarine come up about as near as I could judge a quarter mile off.'

Meanwhile, despite the confusion the ship's company were busy launching the boats into a choppy sea. The *Athenia* was settling slowly, and in the hour or so following the attack they succeeded in lowering all the boats into the water, a complicated matter given that several of the pairs of luffing davits serviced two boats, one nested above the other. The upper boat had to be lowered first and then the process reversed before the lower boat could be hooked on, swung out over the side and lowered, first to the embarkation deck where the passengers scrambled in, then to the water.

The second boats on the starboard side caused 'a lot of trouble . . . as the ship had a list of 12°.' But as Mr Copeland, the *Athenia*'s senior surviving officer, afterwards reported, 'Every boat was lowered without accident; only the last one on the starboard side was slightly damaged but was in no way made unseaworthy.'[5]

This seems to have been the boat that Swindley helped to launch, the lower of the pair nested on *Athenia*'s starboard quarter. Curiously, Swindley was no stranger to ship-wreck, having been aboard the Orient liner *Oratava* when she was lost in 1897, and in a small schooner wrecked on the north-west coast of Australia ten years later. Thus he was welcomed, when he appeared on the *Athenia*'s boat deck, when he 'proved he was there to help', for the crew were clearly spread thinly in their efforts to launch all the boats. They found it 'a very difficult task' on account of *Athenia*'s heavy list to port. 'But', Swindley emphasises, 'no man, woman or child was injured in the launching of our two lifeboats and a raft.'

Elsewhere things were less orderly; unfortunately, several boats were over-loaded, which endangered the process of abandonment. Having assisted in launching what proved to be the last lifeboat to leave the *Athenia*, Swindley 'slid [into it] down the falls'. He found about a hundred people crammed into a boat with a designed capacity of forty, and its crew consisted of 'three stewards, a cadet, a seaman and myself . . . I had to use all my strength in getting free the oars [as] passengers were sitting on them.'

The American press subsequently made much of the apparent confusion aboard *Athenia*, picking up 'evidence' from the survivors. Copeland, an experienced passenger-ship officer, made the distinction between the screams and cries of the terrified passengers and real disorder: 'There was no panic at all on board,' he reported. Nevertheless, the passengers' urgent desire to escape meant that many got into the first available boat as soon as it came into view, and many therefore contained a disproportionate number of women and children. Other passengers complained of having to jump over a gap of several feet, doubtless caused by the list and their unwillingness to wait while the ship's company hauled the boats into the rails by means of their bowsing tackles. The desperate impulse to get away from the stricken ship as fast as possible is understandable; a twelve-degree list does not sound much, but it is sufficiently far from the horizontal to frighten, and the vessel's sinking must have seemed imminent.

Several witnesses spoke of boats being 'dropped' into the water, unaware that the release of falls in a choppy sea required the ropes to be let to run at the moment a wave lifted a boat, in order that they could be unhooked quickly and safely as the boat fell into the trough, and the falls ran slack on the next upsurge. Thus the sensation of being 'dropped' would be very real to the inexperienced, and the fear it engendered would be heightened by the darkness, shouted orders, and cries and screams, and the insufficient crew in the boats themselves. With images of the sinking *Lusitania* and *Titanic* vivid in their imaginations, it is not surprising that by the time they had reached the safety of America and were waylaid by eager newshounds, the recollections of survivors had become embellished.

John and Isabella Coullie had a frightening and bruising time abandoning ship, but Coullie implies no wholesale disorder. Having failed to board their lifeboat at their designated embarkation station, they had to board one in the water:

> We went down to the next deck and soon a boat came alongside and I yelled at them to take us off. A fire hose was over the side and a man in the lifeboat got hold of . . . it and told us to slide down. I asked Bella if she could make it, she said she could . . . I helped her over the rail and watched her slide down . . . when a wave washed the boat away, the hose was jerked from the man's hands and Bella fell into the water between the lifeboat and the ship. I thought she would be crushed to bits. I yelled to her to hold on and climbed to the rail and jumped . . . In a minute I was at Bella's side and got her to hold onto the [looped grab-]rope . . . round the lifeboat. I tried and tried to boost her into the boat but oil was pouring from a burst fuel tank and everything was so slippery that [I] quickly realised I had to do something else. I got one leg over the side of the lifeboat and a man held onto me as I reached down and got hold of Bella's foot. Another man came as I yelled for help and he reached down and got hold of Bella's lifebelt strap and we got her into the boat. We were both soaked through to the skin with oil . . . I got an oar and we had a hard time getting clear . . . At one time we were right under another lifeboat that was being lowered but they held it in mid-air until we got clear . . . There were only five men in the boat, all the rest women and children. We got the boat moving and tried to keep it head on to the waves, several times we got broadside on and we shipped a lot of water and also got soaked . . . Bella got sick and then sometime later I was sick, we had swallowed so much oil and the taste was awful, then it got cold and we were utterly miserable.

Now they were able to take stock of their surroundings. Coullie recorded that they observed 'some lights go on, on the *Athenia* they had got an auxiliary dynamo working and were sending an SOS.' In fact the crew had behaved well. As the engineering staff were trying to restore power, all the deck officers and most of the seamen were busy lowering the boats and shepherding the passengers into them, assisted by the stewards and stewardesses who were also searching the accommodation. On the bridge Captain Cook had long since ordered his duty radio officer to transmit the SSSS signal, indicating an attack by a submarine, and the *Athenia*'s position, 56° 44' North, 014° 05' West. The message had been received by Malin Head radio at 2059.

Pulling away, the lifeboats gradually formed an irregular circle of grey-white dots bobbing around the listing *Athenia*, now also well down by the stern. Once waterborne, Swindley's boat's crew had begun to row as best they could, hampered by the numbers of shocked people. In the haste the boat's plug had not been shipped properly, and she was found to be making water. Swindley sacrificed an expensive pair of shoes in order to bail, having 'to be rough in my methods, in order to keep the closely packed passengers from standing in my way.' Order slowly asserted itself. Clearly a man of commanding presence, Swindley was assisted by a quiet, calm Philadelphian passenger who later admitted to being 'only a lieutenant in the Army' and who 'was seasick but . . . game.' Once clear of the ship, they fished up a can of oil from the boat's store, along with a lantern 'which was lighted and held up by a lady passenger'.

Cold, frightened and sea-sick, they bailed for three or four hours as the lifeboat tossed in the darkness on the turbulent sea, until they made contact with another lifeboat, into which they managed to transfer 'a woman and child [who]wished to leave "the sinking boat".' Swindley and the American Army lieutenant had joined the crew members in rowing resolutely, occasionally vomiting over the side.

From his own boat Coullie now saw a faint gleam on the horizon and mistook the rising moon for a ship. By its light they 'could see the other lifeboats many [of which] were burning flares and we could hear children crying and women screaming . . .'

In another boat teenage girls pulled on the looms of oars until their hands blistered, listening to the hacking coughs of those who had swallowed oil and the persistent eructations of the sea-sick. Terror began to give way to a numbing cold and, for some, a hopeless indifference; others bailed relentlessly, submitting to an instinctive, mind-numbing resolve. Swindley related how the monotony of his vital task dulled his perceptions, so that he 'neither heard nor saw anything of any other but that woman and child whom I myself handed over . . . Yet I was told after the rescue, that "10 people", "12 people", and "22 people", transferred from our "sinking lifeboat".'

Fortunately for them all, the *Athenia*'s distress signal had been picked up by a number of vessels. The British destroyers *Fame, Electra* and *Escort*, the Swedish steam yacht *Southern Cross* (owned by the founder of the Electrolux

Company), and the cargo-vessels *City of Flint* and *Knute Nelson* all hurried to the scene.

'At long last,' Coullie recollected, 'we saw a light away in the distance . . . and it proved to be the yacht *Southern Cross*. They put on a searchlight and we saw them pick up some of the lifeboats[' survivors]. We lit our flares and they came towards us, we rowed to meet them and we got alongside, they had a rope ladder over the side and we were pulled up one by one and the lifeboat was allowed to drift away. We were in a dreadful state but they gave us some hot soup and blankets so we just lay on the floor after nine hours in the lifeboat.'

As daylight grew over the bleak grey sea on the morning of the 4th, the stricken *Athenia* still lay wallowing in the swell, heavily down by the stern, surrounded by her lifeboats with their abject cargoes of sea-sick and oil-fouled survivors, among which the rescuing vessels manoeuvred. The survivors were now to be subjected to an ordeal almost as bad as that of abandoning the *Athenia*, for the prospect of rescue only heightened the practical difficulties of effecting it. The Swedish yachtsmen aboard the small, low *Southern Cross* had less difficulty than the seamen aboard the slab-sided freighters. In attempting to come alongside the *Knute Nelson* one lifeboat, containing more than fifty women, ran in under the ship's stern and fell foul of her thrashing propeller: only eight or nine people survived this further tragedy. One, a British seaman cast back into the sea, drifted for a further three hours before he was picked up by the *Southern Cross*. On 4 September 1939 neither the masters of merchantmen nor those cast adrift in lifeboats had much experience of the tricky skills involved in rescue at sea.

In fact the *Knute Nelson* successfully embarked some 430 survivors, ten of whom were injured, leaving about fifty aboard the *Southern Cross*. While *Electra* and *Escort* picked up about five hundred people and their boats assisted with the transfer of passengers and the *Athenia*'s crew between the rescuing vessels, Commander P.N. Walter in *Fame* maintained an anti-submarine sweep around the *Athenia* as she slowly sank deeper into the water.

Swindley and his fellow survivors were also picked up by the *Southern Cross*. They saw the steam yacht approaching at about 06.30, and about fifteen minutes after they were rescued Swindley's boat finally sank. The officers and crew of the *Southern Cross* 'gave up everything for the comfort of *Athenia*'s passengers'. Later HMS *Escort* removed the *Athenia*'s crew members from the neutral yacht; the passengers were offered the choice of continuing the passage and Swindley did so, along with about thirty of his fellow travellers. At about 16.00 that afternoon these were transferred by the destroyer's whaler to the American-owned but Panamanian-flagged freighter *City of Flint*. The Coullies were also among those who boarded this vessel. 'It was terrible to have to get back in the lifeboat again but . . . we all got . . . [aboard] without any more damage . . . We took some bread and water from the yacht. The *City of Flint* was short of food and water so we did not fare so well until we stopped another freighter going the opposite way . . . and got some medical supplies and food.'

The *Athenia* herself did not sink for more than fourteen hours after her torpedoing. Aboard *Electra*, Chief Officer Copeland made enquiries about a woman passenger who had been in the liner's hospital. Shortly after sailing, this unfortunate lady had fallen down a companionway, striking her head and concussing herself. She had been sedated with morphine, and in the aftermath of the torpedo-strike Copeland had instructed two seamen to ensure that she was brought out of the *Athenia*'s hospital. Aboard *Electra* he discovered the men had failed to do so and during that miserable forenoon he was pulled over to the *Athenia* in *Electra*'s whaler with the *Athenia*'s bosun and another seaman, and the injured woman was brought off the ship some thirty minutes before the liner foundered. Sadly, she died after arriving in Greenock Hospital.

Others also died after being rescued, including a ten-year-old Canadian girl, Margaret Hayworth, who had suffered a severe head injury and expired aboard the *City of Flint*. For the Coullies, however, this ship provided a sanctuary. They were soaking, of course, but both managed to secure a change of clothing. Mrs Coullie 'looked terrible but at least she was more comfortable.' Coullie himself wore his oily suit, which dried on his back, until he acquired some shirts, 'a pair of pants and an overall jacket. We were like that until we landed at Halifax nine days later, never had our clothes off day or night and no bath[.] I got a . . . towel, soap and a bucket of cold water so I washed Bella's head and then my own and the engineer who gave me the water let us sit in the engine room till our hair dried. We felt better after this.' But their ordeal was far from over, for 'on Friday Bella fainted in my arms while we were waiting for breakfast. I got her in a cabin, we had been sleeping in bunks which I helped to build down in the hold and it was very cold.' Both suffering from feverish chills, they were finally landed with their fellow survivors in Halifax, Nova Scotia. Here they were taken care of by the Red Cross before a special train carried them all to Montreal, where they arrived on Thursday evening, 14 September.

Once they were back home in Chicago the Coullies 'had an awful time with reporters [who put] our pictures all over the papers and the newsreels. We of course lost everything . . . but we are safe now and gradually getting over the shock . . . I am trying to get something from the Shipping

Co[mpan]y . . . [but] we are so glad we had no broken bones as so many have . . .' Swindley's view of his experience was more positive. Unwell when he joined the *Athenia*, he had lost his medicine and his belongings but also his indisposition by the time he reached Canada.

The British destroyers made for Greenock on the Clyde, and the *Knute Nelson* headed for the Irish port of Galway. Fortunately, one of the survivors aboard the Norwegian ship was a Dr Wilkes, and he was later assisted by two doctors who boarded the ship off the Irish coast. News of the sinking had spread, and when the *Knute Nelson* landed her survivors at Galway they were greeted by a committee led by a bishop and ready with warm clothing. Soon afterwards the American naval attaché arrived from London. News of the sinking had reached the United States at the same time as that of the outbreak of a new European War, and Captain Kirk and his assistant were under instructions from Washington to conduct an investigation. In Greenock the local welcome was equally generous as the destroyers arrived with their abject cargoes, many of the *Athenia*'s passengers still wearing their night-dresses and pyjamas under duffle coats and greatcoats supplied by the naval sailors.

As the men-of-war, the yacht and the two freighters drew away from the scene of the opening act of hostility in the Battle of the Atlantic, they left behind them the remnants of the *Athenia*'s lifeboats, the first wasteful litter of the Second World War. Significantly, perhaps, two of *Athenia*'s stewards, Tom Ritchie and Jake Reid, gave up their civilian status, retrained, and returned to sea in merchant ships as naval gunners.

Despite an inevitable degree of confusion, the loss of life had been moderated by the prompt response of the five vessels and the general discipline and order prevalent in the *Athenia*'s crew and passengers. Most of the 118 lost souls, including sixteen children, had been killed by the torpedo strike. Twenty-two of the dead had been American citizens: while angry outrage greeted the news in the United States, anger of a different temper was raging in Berlin.

Two weeks before war was declared the German Naval Staff, or Seekriegsleitung, had ordered fourteen U-boats to sail from Kiel and Wilhelmshaven towards the North Atlantic Ocean to take up 'waiting stations'. These dispositions were the culmination of Hitler's policies, and initiated in his first war directive. 'The Kriegsmarine', it said, *inter alia*, 'will operate against Merchant Shipping, with England as the focal point . . . [while] the Luftwaffe is to take measures to dislocate English imports . . .'

Two days later, on 21 August, the commerce-raider *Admiral Graf Spee* also left Wilhelmshaven. Earlier her supply tanker, the *Altmark*, had been ordered to an American port to load a full cargo of diesel oil prior to making a rendezvous with the so-called 'pocket-battleship' near her cruising station in the South Atlantic. The following day two more U-boats, including *U-30* commanded by Kapitänleutnant F. J. Lemp, slipped out of Wilhelmshaven along with another supply tanker, the *Westerwald*. The latter was followed by her principal, a second pocket-battleship, the *Deutschland*, bound for a cruising station off Cape Farewell, the southern point of Greenland.[7]

On 25 August the main German radio transmitting station at Norddeich broadcast a warning to all German merchant shipping, alerting them to the possibility of war, and on the 27th transmitted an instruction to make for a German port within four days or, if this was impossible, to head for a friendly or neutral destination.

As three escaping Polish destroyers headed out of the Baltic for the United Kingdom, the British Home Fleet put to sea from Scapa Flow in a show of force, carrying out a sweep through the Iceland–Faeroes Gap to search for German merchant ships heading for the Baltic and North Sea ports of the Reich. At 04.45 on 1 September the German Wehrmacht rolled into Poland.

The British and French governments had both guaranteed the integrity of Poland and sought reassurances from Berlin; these were not forthcoming, and ultimata were presented by London and Paris. When there was no response, a state of war existed and, as Kapitän zur See Karl Dönitz, the commander of the Kriegsmarine's U-boat arm, put it, 'Britain declared war' on Germany. At 12.56 the German navy was ordered to 'Commence hostilities against Britain forthwith'.[8] Others in the German High Command took a less self-exculpatory view than Dönitz: 'Hitler had now landed us unintentionally and against all good counsel in a war on two fronts.'[9]

If that was not enough, the attack on the *Athenia* had embroiled the Reich in further unsought difficulties. Although the Royal Navy had actually been the first to act aggressively, it was within the rules of the Hague Convention. Earlier that same day the destroyer *Somali*, on patrol with the Home Fleet, had intercepted the newly built 2,337-ton Hamburg-owned tramp-ship *Hannah Böge*, but she was not sunk, only captured, and her crew taken prisoner according to the laws governing war against unarmed merchant ships.[10] The case of the *Athenia* was entirely different: she had been sunk without warning, torpedoed with a callous disregard for human life, the Prize Regulations, the Hague Convention, and the orders of Oberkommando der Wehrmacht, the German Armed Forces High Command.

The *Athenia* had been torpedoed by Lemp's *U-30*, one of the few fully commissioned submarines that Dönitz had deployed in the North Atlantic. Of the total of 56 U-boats at his disposal Dönitz had only 26 of the

Types I, VII and IX capable of extended operations,[11] but these were fully operational in every sense of the word, their crews having undergone rigorous training exercises in the Baltic. Their only individual deficiency was in the matter of torpedoes. Both the Germans and the British were to suffer from frustrating failures in the proximity firing mechanisms of these weapons and, given the crucial nature of Germany's war upon British shipping, the woeful performance of the triggers impacted more upon Germany than upon Britain. Once the reports of misfires had been accepted by U-boat command Dönitz was obliged to order contact firing only, until the introduction of a new magnetic pistol in December 1942 again made proximity firing an option.

But this was a detail. The Kriegsmarine's capability had been compromised from the very outset of the war by Hitler's ill-considered and precipitate action against Poland. As German warships were taking up their stations, their Commander-in-Chief Grossadmiral Erich Raeder had written a memorandum: 'At the present moment we are not in the position to play anything like an important part in the war against Britain's commerce.' And two days later, on 3 September, he grumbled: 'Today the war against France and England [meaning Great Britain] broke out, the war which, according to the Führer's previous assertions, we had no need to expect before about 1944.' The previous July Raeder had assembled the senior officers of the U-boat Flotilla aboard Hitler's yacht, the *Grille*, at Swinemünde. He had been approached by Dönitz, then the flotilla's commander, who had tabled a report expressing his own anxiety about the outcome of any future war with Great Britain. Dönitz correctly reasoned that the burden of such a war would fall upon the U-boat arm, then numerically so weak that it would achieve 'little more than a few pin-pricks'. Raeder assured Dönitz and his officers that 'in no circumstances would war with Britain come about. For that would mean *Finis Germaniae*. The officers of the U-boat arm had no cause to worry.'[12]

Raeder was dissembling, or at best buying time, for he had been told by Hitler in May 1938 that Britain must be considered a potential enemy, and that although there would be no immediate war, the naval staff was to study anti-British strategy. Obediently Raeder established an examining committee, which that autumn cut to the heart of the matter: 'The committee laid down the destruction of the British merchant navy as the strategic task of the naval forces.' Raeder consequently recommended to Hitler that 'a well-balanced fleet of great striking power should be built; that this fleet . . . should be allotted the dual task of waging a campaign against British shipping in the Atlantic and against the naval forces protecting it.' This was the so-called 'Z-Plan' and it provided for six large battleships, a dozen large cruisers, four aircraft carriers, an unspecified number of light cruisers, and 233 U-boats. This fleet was to be ready by 1948, by which time the British Royal Navy was expected to have been proportionately weakened by time, lack of investment, and wear-and-tear. Typically, in sanctioning this ambitious programme Hitler cut the lead-time; Raeder was given until 1944.[13]

Realistic, experienced and practical, Dönitz, as commodore of the U-boat arm, wanted 300 submarines, and said so. He was well aware that Great Britain could be defeated by the strangulation of her trade and the interdiction of her vital imports of food, industrial raw materials and, in time of hostilities, the very sinews of war itself. He had himself been a serving officer in the First World War when the Kaiser's submarines brought Britain close to capitulation, and though he had no means of knowing that in 1917 the Admiralty had actually informed the British Government that they had lost the war at sea, he possessed a sufficiently predatory instinct to appreciate how close-run a thing it had been. He knew too that to keep enough U-boats at sea harrying British shipping, he would have to accept a proportion at home undergoing refit and repair while their crews recuperated from arduous patrols. Three hundred boats would enable him to keep a hundred at sea in contact with the enemy, and he wanted three Type VIIs to one Type IX.

Moreover, Dönitz knew, as any thinking strategist did, that Germany was geographically at a disadvantage in waging a maritime war against Great Britain: her warships must run a long gauntlet through waters dominated by the enemy before the broad Atlantic opened out before them. He did not then foresee the great advantage that the fall of France would confer upon his operations after May 1940, an advantage that swung the odds quickly in his favour.

After Raeder's speech aboard the elegant white yacht *Grille*, with her clipper bow and gilded figurehead of the Nazi eagle, Dönitz told his officers that, notwithstanding what they had just heard, 'if at some time or other war comes, we shall find Britain on the side of the enemy. And that, gentlemen,' he added, driving home his point with personal impact, 'is a fact that you would do well to bear in mind!'

As to the number of submarines Dönitz ought to have had at sea on 3 September 1939, Admiral Boehm, commanding the German Fleet, advised Raeder on the very day war broke out that Dönitz's U-boat arm must be extended, and other building programmes set aside in favour of U-boat construction.[14] There is the whiff of panic about this, and it was to grow stronger that same day.

Kapitänleutnant Lemp had done nothing to enhance Germany's position; indeed, by his ill-considered attack on the *Athenia* he had only compounded

Hitler's fatal blunder in embroiling Great Britain. Later in the war he was again to cost his masters and his colleagues dear,[15] but for the moment his blunder simply matched his Führer's folly. When Dönitz sent his submarines to sea, it was to 'wage war against merchant shipping in accordance with the . . . Prize Regulations . . .'[16] Under the strict provisions of this ordinance, which had been reiterated in the London Submarine Agreement of 1936, a submarine had to conform with the same procedures as a surface commerce-raider when stopping a merchant vessel on the high seas. If the flag-state of the merchantman was that of the enemy, then the submarine was entitled to sink her only after having first removed the crew, who were technically non-combatants, to 'a place of safety'. If the flag-state was neutral, then the cargo manifest was to be examined; if the examining officer decided that any part of the neutral vessel's cargo was 'war contraband' consigned to the enemy, she might be sunk after evacuation; otherwise she was free to proceed upon her voyage.

Not surprisingly, there were complications to all this, the first arising from the removal of the merchant ship's crew: their lifeboats were not deemed 'a place of safety', and in theory they were supposed to be taken aboard the commerce-raider herself. In the case of a surface ship this measure spelled potential inconvenience, but it was quite practicable; in the case of a submarine, it was as impracticable as it was undesirable, for its execution would compromise the boat's operational capability on a war patrol. The best a U-boat commander might hope was to arrange the rescue of these helpless non-combatants by another merchant vessel, perhaps belonging to a neutral state. Clearly such a convenient coincidental presence was most unlikely in practice, but no more was it consonant with submarine commerce-raiding for U-boats to swan around seeking a safe refuge for their enemy's nationals.[17] In general, however, in this initial phase U-boat commanders conformed, more or less, with the spirit of the Prize Regulations.

Under these, the master of an apprehended merchant ship was forbidden to transmit any radio signals advertising his plight – but the British Admiralty actively encouraged British masters to do just that. Two years earlier, on 2 December 1937, the Committee of Imperial Defence had concluded it probable that upon the outbreak of war British and Commonwealth shipping would be subjected to unrestricted attack by submarines and from the air, and that the convoy system should therefore be introduced immediately. This became official British policy the following year, when the Admiralty took the precaution of issuing every British-flagged vessel with the *Defence of Merchant Shipping Handbook*. In this, ship-masters were instructed to report the position of any U-boat by radio, 'thus incorporating the merchant service into the warning system of . . . [British] Naval Intelligence'. This, according to Dönitz, proved that 'the British had no intention of adhering to the Submarine Agreement of 1936'.[18]

In truth, both sides realised the impracticality of the Prize Regulations in time of open warfare. At the beginning of the century, during the first naval arms race with Imperial Germany, Admiral 'Jacky' Fisher had declared that 'moderation in war is imbecility', a brutally pragmatic sentiment which quickly found its advocates on both sides of the North Sea during the First World War. Specifically, in January 1914 Fisher had written a memorandum presciently summarising the threat of submarine warfare and its relationship to the Prize Regulations: 'There is nothing the submarine can do except sink her capture, and it must be admitted that (provided it is done, and however inhuman and barbarous it may appear) this submarine menace is a truly terrible one for British commerce and Great Britain.'

To combat German submarines the British had employed disguised merchant ships as Q-ships. A portion of the crew 'abandoned' them to lure the attacking submarine closer, whereupon concealed guns opened fire. Such deceptions were held to be contrary to the laws of war, but German violations of the conventions governing the capture of merchantmen were widely practised, and accusations of atrocities were mutual.

Following the experience of the Great War, the men of both the British merchant service and the Royal Navy knew the consequences of relying upon the Prize Regulations to preserve the life of non-combatants. From the German perspective, the delay inherent in surfacing and boarding a hostile or neutral merchant ship endangered the interdicting submarine by exposing her to possible attack by surface craft in the vicinity or aircraft within range, to which their initial operating dispositions in the Western Approaches and off Gibraltar were particularly vulnerable.

To try to mitigate this danger and to encourage adherence to the protocols of war on commerce, Dönitz ordered his submarines to sink without warning only those merchantmen *excepted* from the protection of the Prize Regulations. These included vessels carrying troops, vessels under the close escort of enemy warships, merchant vessels acting in support of military operations, and vessels deemed to be preparing to resist or to take any action calculated to jeopardise the submarine. This meant not only vessels chartered as naval auxiliaries or those fully fitted out as Armed Merchant Cruisers but also those passing intelligence: and into the category of 'intelligence' fell the seemingly innocent radio transmission of 'SSSS', 'I am being attacked by a submarine'.

Given the natural reluctance of British ship-masters to submit to coercion, the difficulties of identifying ships as troopships, and of sinking such vessels (for which they were personally responsible) without them managing to transmit a distress signal, made the submarine commander's task all but impossible under operational conditions. The Admiralty's desire to learn the whereabouts of predatory U-boats was all very well, but masters with long memories wanted their crews to be picked up, not forced to make long and hazardous voyages under oars and sail.

Nevertheless, in addition to their orders to commence hostilities against Great Britain forthwith at 12.56 on 3 September, Lemp and his colleagues received a second signal transmitted at 14.00: 'U-boat warfare against shipping is at present to be carried out in accordance with international rules': that is to say, the London Protocol of 1936 referred to as the 'Submarine Agreement', and meaning the Prize Regulations. Because of Hitler's initial reluctance to provoke France despite her declaration of war over Poland, the U-boats were only to act defensively in respect of encounters with French *warships*: French merchant ships were not to be stopped, and incidents with France were to be avoided 'at all costs'. Although this situation lasted only a short while, it further complicated the task of the U-boat commander since it meant that a neutral merchant vessel was liable to being stopped, while a nominally hostile French vessel was not. Thus on 30 September *U-3*, Kapitänleutnant Schepke, operating off the Naze of Norway, interdicted the neutral Swedish ship *Gun*. It was a bright, moonlit night and the *Gun* was on a westerly course. She was a small, British-built coal-burning steam vessel owned by Knut Bergqvist, who had acquired her in 1937 when she was already 46 years old. Schepke ordered her master, a Captain J.M. Persson, on board his submarine. Schepke was not satisfied with Persson's papers, nor with the 36 tons of explosives and ammunition consigned to the Belgian Ministry of War by way of Antwerp. Then, while Schepke's prize crew were taking over the merchantman, according to Dönitz, the *Gun* made a sudden attempt to ram *U-3* with the 'rudder hard over [and the engines] at full speed'. The U-boat only escaped 'by immediate and maximum use of [her] diesels'. The *Gun* was then 'scuttled' by the boarding party.[19]

The limitations imposed on the U-boat arm and the consequent risks associated with them so well exemplified by this particular incident were not consonant with Dönitz's notions of waging war, but he had rather Lemp had not sunk the *Athenia*: taking place as it had in the first hours of the war, Lemp's action appeared to the world like an immediate renunciation of the Prize Regulations and a resumption of the methods of 1917.

After the horrors of the First World War attempts had been made to outlaw the submarine. At the Washington Naval Conference of 1921 the British, despite possessing a considerable submarine force, argued that it had proved to be 'a weapon of murder and piracy, involving the drowning of non combatants', while insofar as its use under the Prize Regulations was concerned, 'the submarine was so constructed that it could not be utilized to rescue even women and children from sinking ships'.[20] This declaration carried little weight and by 1935 Great Britain's position had softened: she agreed, infamously and unilaterally, to waive the proscription of German submarine construction contained in the Treaty of Versailles, and, under the provisions of a new Anglo-German Naval Treaty, sanctioned the construction of submarines by Germany. This was appeasement in its most humiliating manifestation, serving merely to legitimise something the Nazi government had long been doing in secret. In 1922 the brilliant naval architectural team originally assembled at Krupp's Germaniawerft at Kiel had been clandestinely reunited in The Netherlands, where the so-called *Ingenieurs scheepsbouwkantoor* built submarines for Finland, Turkey and Spain. Under Hitler's secret instructions, the Kriegsmarine had placed orders for U-boats *before* he repudiated the Treaty of Versailles in March 1935.

As a culmination of deception and bad faith, Lemp's action was deemed appalling. Recalling incidents at sea during the First World War Winston Churchill, as the new First Lord of the Admiralty, rose in Parliament and 'stigmatised [it] as inhumane'. The British press complained of 'pitiless barbarity', 'murder most foul', and of an act that 'at a stroke . . . outrages every human sentiment and breaks the pledged word of the German rulers'. It was all true, of course, but the German rulers, still conscious of their image in the wider world, were having none of it. Berlin was swift to counter-charge. On 4 September an order was transmitted to U-boats at sea that 'The Führer had forbidden attacks on passenger liners sailing independently or in convoy', and the same day Ernst von Weizsaecker, an official of the German Foreign Ministry, went out of his way to assure the United States Chargé d'Affaires in Berlin that no German forces had been involved in the sinking of the *Athenia*. The unfortunate liner had probably detonated a loose-floating British mine, he explained; better still, as the *Volkischer Beobachter* informed its readers on 23 October at the personal instigation of Hitler, the *Athenia* had possibly been sabotaged, blown up by a bomb planted by agents of Churchill to kindle hostility to Germany in America.[21] It was a charge as fanciful as it was unconvincing, evidence of the lengths of improbability to which Hitler would go, but for a while it enjoyed a spurious life in the United States, even after Lemp and *U-30* had returned from their first war patrol and the truth was known for certain in Berlin.

Summoned to explain his actions, Lemp justified his sinking of the Donaldson liner on the grounds that she was steaming without showing lights, on an unusual course, and zig-zagging. On this evidence, Lemp claimed, he could only conclude that the ship he had in his periscope sight must be an armed merchant cruiser, and therefore he attacked. The charge that the *Athenia* was on an unusual course can have been based solely on the fact that Cook had taken his ship wide of the 'traditional' trans-Atlantic rhumb line, for her zig-zag along that unusual course would have made its actual median determination a matter of some complexity for a submarine commander on his first war patrol, at night. Having struck the fatal blow Lemp had surfaced, and when his radio operator intercepted Captain Cook's distress call, had sent two shells from his deck gun into the *Athenia's* super-structure in an attempt to halt her transmissions. Malin Head Radio reported jamming signals which could only have come from Lemp's U-boat. Hearing the *Athenia's* siren blasting out the signal to abandon ship over the heaving black waters, Lemp took *U-30* beneath them, into the still depths of the Atlantic, where he maintained radio silence until 14 September.

The news of the sinking had at first been greeted with incredulity by the staff officers at Seekriegsleitung. Now, in the face of Lemp's mitigating plea of zeal in his first act of war and his explanation that he had opened his orders just a few hours earlier, Dönitz could only severely reprimand him, and order the account of the attack to be erased from *U-30's* War Diary. The original detailed pages were removed and a false page was inserted, putting *U-30* 200 miles west of Rockall. Lemp and his crew were sworn to maintain the strictest secrecy about their part in the sinking. Few German naval officers knew the truth at the time, and it was deliberately concealed from Raeder and his own staff.[22]

To the British, the destruction of the *Athenia* was evidence that the niceties of chivalry enshrined in the Prize Regulations had been flagrantly cast aside. Behind the rhetoric castigating the atrocious behaviour of the Hun, the pragmatic Admiralty staff were sensible that the inherent risk of exposure for a submarine lingering conspicuously on the surface while conducting a charade of examination with a prevaricating ship-master was likely to be avoided by any U-boat commander. In fact Their Lordships were, in a sense, pleased that the Germans should have made this early and fortuitous blunder. Expert in the theory of waging war at sea, they had not forgotten the lesson the submarines of the Kaiser's Imperial Navy had taught them: that of the immediate necessity of convoy.

Despite Britain's declaration of war, Hitler still hoped for an accom-modation. Just as he soft-pedalled on France in those first weeks, so he believed that a maritime war with Great Britain moderately pursued would compel her to institute an overwhelming naval blockade threatening the economies of non-combatant nations such as the Scandinavians, the Soviet

Union, Japan and, most important of all, the United States, and thereby become the perceived aggressor. America was, after all, historically a rival of Britain for sea-power, while Britain's high-handedness was well known and had been a previous cause of war between the two nations. Britain's naval chiefs knew just how unpopular, as well as how necessary, such a blockade would be. Now Lemp had delivered Germany's enemy from the prospect of courting such predictable venom, and he had also murdered American citizens. The sinking of the *Athenia* resonated with the torpedoing-without-warning of the Cunard liner *Lusitania* in May 1915: there had been a significant loss of American lives then, and the incident had been one of the most significant influences on popular opinion in the United States, inclining her to enter the First World War.

The German High Command began to drop the term 'submarine warfare', which had awkward legal implications. Instead they increasingly referred to the 'Siege of England', which reflected the tasks Hitler laid down for the Kriegsmarine and the Luftwaffe in his first War Directive. This was to be carried out, Raeder reported to Hitler on 10 October, 'with the greatest intensity . . . Even the threat of America's entry into the war, which appears certain if the war continues, must *not* give rise to any restrictions. The earlier and more ruthlessly we commence [it], the sooner the effect and the shorter the duration of the war. Any restrictions will lengthen the war.'[23] The Grossadmiral had clearly accepted the inevitable, and now sought the quickest possible resolution.

Lemp's action freed Britain's First Sea Lord, Admiral Sir Dudley Pound, and his staff in London to take the actions they knew would soon prove necessary. Moreover, their political master Winston Churchill, so very recently appointed First Lord of the Admiralty, was an acknowledged hawk. There was much ineptitude, seasoned with over-confidence, yet to come, but the gloves had been cast aside. The fatal torpedo fired from *U-30* initiated the first of the two great battles fought during the Second World War upon which the future of Europe depended.

The second, that terrible fight for supremacy on the Eastern Front, is not to be under-estimated, but it should not be forgotten that as yet it lay in the future, for Nazi Germany and Soviet Russia were for some time to come to be allies in the rape of Poland. When they eventually became enemies, even that titanic clash relied to some extent, both morally and materially, upon the outcome of the first, the Battle of the Atlantic.

'Engaged in a perilous occupation'

Manaar

AFTER HIS BLUNDER Lemp continued his first war patrol off Rockall. On 11 September he sank the outward-bound *Blairlogie* of Glasgow, shelling her and finishing her with a torpedo. Now scrupulous in his observation of the Prize Regulations, Lemp gave the crew ample time to abandon ship and, perhaps galled by conscience or out of disingenuousness, made Captain D.B. McAlpine a memorable gift of gin and cigarettes. McAlpine and his crew were rescued from their boats by the American freighter *American Shipper*. On the 14th Lemp stopped another tramp-ship, the *Fanad Head*, Captain G. Pinckerton, owned by Heyn & Sons of Belfast. She was bound to her home port from Montreal with a bulk cargo of grain. After the crew abandoned her, Lemp was sinking his victim with gunfire and a torpedo when *U-30* was attacked by two aeroplanes from the British aircraft-carrier *Ark Royal*. The Blackburn Skuas attempted to bomb the U-boat but attacked too low, and the detonations of their bombs blew their own tails off. The two aircraft crashed, both tail gunners were killed, and the pilots were rescued by Lemp. A third Skua now appeared and made two bombing runs, but Lemp submerged, resurfacing half an hour later only to be strafed by the circling Skua. The conning tower of *U-30* was damaged and casualties were inflicted, but Lemp escaped with his two prisoners. Meanwhile Pinckerton and his passengers and crew, 42 souls in all, were picked up and landed at Mallaig from the destroyer *Tartar*.

On the 19th Lemp was able to transfer one of his badly wounded sailors to a German cargo ship for medical attention, but effectively the first war patrol of *U-30* was over and on 27 September Lemp reached Wilhelmshaven, and his encounter with Dönitz. With details of the *Athenia*'s destruction expunged, his U-boat was credited with only two sinkings, the *Blairlogie* and the *Fanad Head*. Lemp assured Dönitz that the injured seaman, Adolf Schmidt, who had been landed in Iceland, would keep quiet, for he had made him swear a solemn oath of secrecy before leaving *U-30*. Schmidt became a prisoner of the British when they occupied Iceland in 1940, but despite repeated interrogation he kept his word until after the end of the war and the collapse of the Nazi regime, when, believing his oath to have been nullified, he provided testimony that was used at Nuremberg.

One of the measures now employed to counter the menace of German submarines was centred on an idea discredited in the First World War, when cruisers patrolled the trade routes to deter the Kaiser's submarine and surface commerce-raiders, to small effect compared with sailing merchant ships in convoy. Churchill revived this notion, though he made the significant modification of substituting for the cruisers an escorted aircraft-carrier with its airborne eyes to extend the range, and it was one of these whose aeroplanes attacked Lemp. Churchill's idea was not wholly without merit; a few perceptive young naval officers had noted in 1918 that convoys with rudimentary air cover appeared immune from attack by U-boats.[1] Churchill's instincts were right but his tactic was premature in the closing months of 1939, for where the escort-carrier-based support groups formed later in the war proved highly effective, the early flotillas were a disaster. There were insufficient British aircraft-carriers to cover much of the Western Approaches, and they were large capital ships, far too valuable to commit to such a task, a flaw exposed almost immediately by the loss of HMS *Courageous*.

Complementing *Ark Royal* to the north, *Courageous* had been patrolling off the southern coast of Ireland when she was attacked by *U-29* (Schuhart) and sunk with two torpedoes. Some 518 of her ship's company were lost, including Captain W.T. Makeig-Jones. Schuhart was counter-attacked by the escorting destroyer *Ivanhoe*, but escaped. The *Ark Royal* had herself been similarly caught by *U-39* (Kapitänleutnant G. Glattes) on the 14th, the same day her Skuas attacked *U-30*. Glattes fired three torpedoes, but all exploded harmlessly in the carrier's wake, bringing the wrath of *Ark Royal*'s escort down upon the U-boat (and initiating *Ark Royal*'s extraordinary run of luck, which ended off Gibraltar in November 1941).

Attacked by the destroyers *Faulknor*, *Foxhound* and *Firedrake*, *U-39* was damaged, and ingress of sea-water caused chlorine to be discharged from her batteries. Glattes was forced to surface, whereupon the destroyers opened fire, ceasing only when his crew began to emerge from the conning tower.[2]

In this opening phase of the war, between 3 September 1939 and 28 February 1940, the eager young commanders of Dönitz's U-boats, deployed off the South West Approaches and off Gibraltar, succeeded in sinking 199 ships totalling 701,985 tons. Typical was Otto Schuhart's *U-29*, among the first wave to sail on 19 August. By 8 September he had sunk the tanker *Regent Tiger*, followed on the 13th by the tug *Neptunia*. The tanker's cargo comprised 10,600 tons of motor spirit and 3,400 tons of diesel. Captain W. Roberts and his crew got clear and were rescued by a Belgian vessel. Schuhart gave the *Neptunia's* crew cigarettes and brandy, and they were later picked up by the coaster *Brinkburn* which afterwards landed them at Falmouth. Next day Schuhart sank a second tanker, British Petroleum's *British Influence*, heading for Hull from Abadan with 12,000 tons of fuel and diesel oil. After ordering Captain I.H. McMichael and his crew to abandon ship Schuhart had flares fired to attract the attention of the Norwegian ship *Ide Bakke* to pick up the tanker's crew from their lifeboats. Just before *U-29* left the scene, the U-boat's men and the tanker's crew gave each other three cheers in an apparently spontaneous outburst of goodwill. Schuhart was decorated by Hitler himself when *U-29* returned to Wilhelmshaven on 26 September, but not for observing the Prize Regulations: it was for destroying the *Courageous*, a British capital ship.

Kapitänleutnant Gunther Prien of *U-47*, who was to make his name a few weeks later by penetrating the Home Fleet's anchorage at Scapa Flow and sinking the battleship *Royal Oak* at her moorings, ordered the small Cunard White Star cargo-liner *Bosnia* to heave-to off the Portuguese coast on 6 September. Only when the *Bosnia's* master, Captain W.H. Poole, turned away from the U-boat and thus gave Prien a legal justification for opening fire did he do so. The German shells soon set the vessel on fire, and when the order was given to abandon ship the *Bosnia's* way caused the first boat lowered into the sea to overturn. One of the men, a fireman named Woods, fell into the sea; Cadet Bird dived in after him and kept him afloat for some time until Prien manoeuvred alongside and picked the two men out of the water. As the other lifeboats closed with the U-boat, the survivors saw what they thought was a brutal assault on Woods; in fact, Prien's men were administering artificial respiration. As so many firemen were to do in the coming years, the wretched Woods had run up on deck, grabbed a life-belt and pulled it over the thin trousers and cotton singlet that were the standard garb of men working in the heat of the stokehold. He died from the effects of his immersion in cold water – what was then called exposure but is now known as hypothermia.[3]

Masters were prepared to take a chance by running for it, but once it became clear they could not escape from a pursuing U-boat they generally capitulated. A primary duty laid upon a ship-master was the safety of his crew, and this outweighed any foolhardy notions of misplaced heroics.

Nevertheless, not all masters gave in without a token resistance, as Kapitänleutnant Schultze discovered on 5 September when *U-48* was patrolling off the north-west corner of Spain and sighted Hall Brothers' Newcastle-registered *Royal Sceptre*, homeward bound from Rosario with a cargo of Argentinian grain and maize for Belfast. Her master, Captain J. Gair, resented the interdiction of his voyage. His ship was only two years old and he was almost home, about three hundred miles west of Ushant, approaching the Chops of the Channel. Calculating that he might outrun the U-boat in the rough sea, Gair turned the *Royal Sceptre* away, even after a shot had been put across her bows, while sending out the SSSS distress signal. Schultze intercepted Gair's transmission, which gave him a free hand: he ordered his gunners to shell the *Royal Sceptre*. Captain Gair was killed and others were wounded as Chief Officer Hartley stopped the vessel and ordered the crew to abandon ship. The boats were lowered while Schultze was closing for the kill; at the same time the *Royal Sceptre*'s radio officer, deprived of his aerials after the shelling, appeared on deck as the boats were pulling away from the sinking ship. Seeing this, Schultze directed one of the boats to return and take him off, then gave Hartley an undertaking to send help. A few hours later *U-48* encountered a second British ship, the Lamport & Holt liner *Browning*, and Schultze fired a shot across her bow to bring her to. The *Browning* was outward bound for South America and Schultze quickly extracted an undertaking that she would not transmit an alarm signal, then himself gave an assurance that he would not otherwise interfere with her if her master followed his directions towards the *Royal Sceptre*'s boats. This accomplished, Schultze resumed his patrol.

Three days later, still in the vicinity, *U-48* encountered and sank the *Winkleigh*, a Cardiff tramp owned by the Tatem Steam Navigation Company, laden with grain and timber, homeward bound from Vancouver to Manchester. In the face of the enemy Captain T. Georgeson ordered the transmission of a radio signal and then stopped his ship. In such a location it was just possible that British destroyers might reach the scene before the U-boat departed. Georgeson was summoned on board *U-48*, where as he later recounted Schultze greeted him 'very cordially and said he was sorry he would have to sink my ship . . . He gave me four loaves of bread; then he brought a bottle of Schnapps up, and taking out a packet of cigarettes, offered me one and put the remainder . . . in my hand.'[4] No destroyers appeared, and it was seven hours before the *Winkleigh*'s people were taken from their boats by a Dutch vessel.

Schultze was now running short of fuel and torpedoes. Heading to round Scotland on his return passage to Germany, *U-48* was to the northwards of the pinnacle of Rockall on the 11th when she went in pursuit of Ropner's tramp *Firby*. From her home port of Newcastle the *Firby* was bound for Port Churchill on Hudson Bay, empty and flying light, steaming independently, as were all these early merchant ships before the convoy system had been fully implemented. The *Firby*'s master, Captain T. Prince, was as anxious to reach his destination before the ice formed in the Great Lakes as he was to avoid U-boats. The *Firby* was unarmed; her only concession to hostilities lay in having her boats swung out, ready for lowering. Informed by his officer of the watch that a surfaced submarine was pursuing them, Prince hurried to the bridge and began to zig-zag in an attempt to avoid the shells that Schultze fired after him. Riding high, the slower and slab-sided tramp was an easy target, and began to take punishment as each shell slammed into her. Realising he could not out-run his pursuer, Prince stopped his engines; he had no means of resisting, and already Second Engineer Gidley and Fourth Engineer Lloyd, together with an able seaman and a fireman, were wounded. He rang 'Finished with Engines' on the engine room telegraph. At sea in wartime this could only mean one thing to the men toiling below in the engine room and stokehold: leave your stations, come up on deck and abandon ship. Prince began to destroy his confidential documents as, still under fire, his crew began to lower the boats. Having finished their task, Prince and his radio officer left the bridge and hurried to follow the crew into the boats. Getting clear of the ship, Prince found the enemy submarine approaching, and he was ordered on board. Scrambling over the steel casing he was taken below; here he was given a drink and asked for his papers; he surrendered his master's certificate and his manifest, but nothing else. In return Schultze 'gave him four rolls of bandages and six loaves of bread for the wounded.' Prince was told that Schultze 'would send . . . an SOS . . . to Churchill', a promise he kept and which Churchill acknowledged later in Parliament.

Clambering back into his lifeboat, Prince found that the head wounds of the engineers and Able Seaman Mckeon had been dressed, along with the shrapnel wounds in the back of Fireman Schuff. Having seen these casualties attended to, and with a final promise to inform the British Admiralty of their position, Schultze's U-boat moved away under her diesels, a greasy smudge of smoke from her exhausts trailing over the slight sea. A few moments later a torpedo completed the destruction of the *Firby*, after which *U-48* disappeared and darkness fell.

The onset of night at sea is a bleak moment, arousing primitive apprehensions. The compass of individual perception shrinks as the distant horizon fades; in a small boat filled with wet, cold and anxious men, the threat of the primeval becomes palpable. Some time during the early part of the night one of the lifeboats began to sink and they all scrambled into the remaining boat. Overcrowded as it was, they streamed a sea-anchor and lay head to sea. Then, at about 03.00, they saw a ship. With no thought of its nationality, anxious only that they should attract its attention, they lit flares, and soon the night was stabbed by the powerful beam of a searchlight. Shortly afterwards, greatly relieved, they were picked up by the destroyer *Fearless*.

There were many other examples of the Germans' adherence to the Prize Regulations at this time. On 7 September Captain J. Barnetson of the *Olivegrove* had similarly been taken aboard the attacking submarine, in this case *U-33*. Here he met Kapitänleutnant von Dresky. Having expressed regret that he was duty-bound to sink the *Olivegrove*, von Dresky asked almost plaintively, 'Why does Mr Chamberlain want to make war on us?' With a suitably equivocating regret Barnetson replied that he had no idea, and that he shared the Kapitänleutnant's sorrow over the loss of the *Olivegrove*. Von Dresky then gave Barnetson a course to steer for the Fastnet Rock lighthouse, almost three hundred miles away. Later von Dresky returned to the scene and fired flares to attract the attention of an American ship, which picked up the 33 drifting men.

Other British masters also reported favourably on such ocean encounters: Kapitänleutnant W. Rollmann was described by Captain J.S. Thomson as 'very courteous and anxious that everybody was off [the Common Brothers' steamer *Pukkastan*]'. But after the propaganda 'gift' of the *Athenia's* sinking, these reports were not welcome in London. The first intimation of a U-boat's location was the SSSS signal transmitted by the interdicted merchant ship, and what the Admiralty wanted to do was immediately vector in their dashing destroyers or, better still, Churchill's independent carrier groups, which it was then hoped would, in the First Lord's imaginative phrase, hunt and intimidate U-boats 'like a cavalry division'. Realistically, however, there was little chance of this, even when U-boats obligingly lingered around their victims implementing the Prize Regulations.

The marked success of the German U-boats even under the restrictions of international convention, while it could not last, was an indication of the impossibility of attempting the defence of trade by any method other than convoy. These easy pickings were the inevitable consequence of Britain's widely dispersed mercantile marine, of the remorseless necessity that it should carry out its daily business and proceed upon its lawful occasions regardless of the outbreak of war. Churchill was only too aware of the danger of neutral nations, especially the United States, objecting to interference in *their* trade by the establishment of a British blockade. In the previous war the interdiction of American shipping by British warships had been a red-hot issue, a reminder of the historical antipathies over which, in 1812, the two countries had gone to war.

Churchill highly prized the weapon Lemp had unwittingly placed in his hands. He wanted to rouse international indignation, and especially that of the United States, against the Germans, not feel bound to acknowledge signs of chivalrous compliance, as he did in the case of Schultze. The callous and illegal sinking of the *Athenia* was thus, paradoxically, a godsend, if a grim one, enabling him to attack the Nazis using the very methods they had become so expert in deploying. Unfortunately Churchill as yet lacked an equivalent expertise in this matter of propaganda, and attempted to augment his gift from the gods by seizing on the example of the *Royal Sceptre*, which had not been heard of since the transmission of her SSSS signal on 5 September. In this he had the assistance of the British press.

The master of the *Browning* kept his word to Schultze that he would make no radio transmission after embarking the *Royal Sceptre* survivors. Several neutral vessels subsequently searched the area in response to the initial distress signal from the *Royal Sceptre*, and found nothing; after three weeks it was assumed that she had been lost with all hands, another victim of German aggression. This conclusion was reached at the same time that news of the loss of another vessel reached London. On 24 September *U-31* (Kapitänleutnant Habekost), patrolling off the Fastnet Rock, had sunk the Liverpool-bound Newcastle-owned tramp ship *Hazelside*.[6] Eleven men had been killed in this incident, including Captain C. H. Davis, too many to suggest that the Prize Regulations had been scrupulously observed. Consequently, on 26 September the British press, prompted by the Ministry of Information, had carried an article condemning German barbarity. *The Times*, citing the trio of the *Athenia, Hazelside* and *Royal Sceptre*, thundered that the crew of the *Royal Sceptre* had been the victims of 'a foul act of piracy on the high seas on the part of the German Navy.'

Shortly afterwards, however, the *Browning* arrived at Bahia Blanca in Brazil and landed Mr Hartley and his men, an embarrassing appearance that confounded the British assertion and greatly weakened Britain's position in the eyes of the outside world. To compound this humiliation came the result of an analysis of the first thirty interceptions of British merchant ships by German U-boats. On 21 September the Admiralty concluded that with a few exceptions, of which the *Athenia* was the most prominent, the Kriegsmarine were indeed conforming to the Prize Regulations. Moreover, these encounters had engendered in the non-combatant British mercantile victims 'a somewhat excessive enthusiasm' for the conduct of the enemy.

These first weeks of war are remarkable for their contrast with what followed. The mobilised French armies made no attack across their border with the German Reich, and no air strike was made by any party: while the Germans flew reconnaissance flights over Britain, the Royal Air Force dropped pamphlets on Germany. 'France and Britain remained impassive while Poland was . . . destroyed'. It was therefore unsurprising that this 'Twilight War', later better known by its more popular handle, 'the Phoney War', had its echoes at sea. No one, especially not the aggressive First Lord of the Admiralty and his First Sea Lord, can have expected the situation to remain so quiescent for long, and it grieved Churchill and Pound that by observing the Prize Regulations itself, the Royal Navy had let the Norddeutscher Lloyd liner *Bremen* escape the net spread to catch her by the Home Fleet.[7]

There was much Their Lordships at the Admiralty had to learn about the men and ships of the merchant service whose protection was now their responsibility. There had been considerable pre-war provisions for the defence of commercial shipping, but Their Lordships were not minded to pay over-much attention to the non-combatant status of merchant seamen. In their desire to locate Dönitz's submarines, professional naval officers often forgot what exactly constituted Great Britain's so-called 'Merchant Navy'. Having bound it into their system of intelligence-gathering, they assumed their mercantile marine to be *de facto* an extension of the naval power of the state.

The vague though popular concept of a mercantile 'Navy' had grown out of the First World War when the successes of German submariners almost compelled the British government to sue for terms. The British merchant fleet had grown five-fold in the century since the Napoleonic Wars, so that at the outbreak of hostilities in August 1914 it consisted of 20,938 bottoms, totalling 12 million net tons: but of these, only some four thousand could be regarded as ocean-going carriers.

The experience of the First World War proved beyond doubt that Britain's heavy dependence upon the import of raw materials for her industry and foodstuffs for her population made her vulnerable to any interruption in the flow of these imports. Equally, her economic survival required an outflow of revenue-earning exports, and at the same time her shipping, deployed across the globe, earned 'invisible' income by servicing the economies of other nations, providing carriage in the so-called 'cross trades'. The defence of this mass of shipping had begun to attract the attention of naval planners from about 1880, but there was a general resistance on all sides to the introduction of a convoy system. Despite their success during the Napolenic Wars, escorted convoys were thought to be an anachronism in the modern age of steam-power. Naval pundits opposed the committing of expensive men-of-war to such tedious and *defensive* measures, which were anathema to a fighting service.

Surprising objections were raised elsewhere. Ship-owners were not in favour either, and for a variety of reasons. Steam power enabled their ships to make predictable passages; delay was bad for business. They did not want their vessels held up while convoys were assembled and organised, nor their voyage times and distances increased, measures that would reduce their notoriously narrow profit margins by an increase in fuel and labour costs. In this they found allies among their own ship-masters, who in their turn resented the inevitable naval control of shipping. Such matters rankled with these ruggedly independently-minded men. Moreover, if convoys were to be adopted, it was clear that the ship-owners' increased costs would be passed on to consumers, which would affect the buoyancy of the domestic market. In short, a measure of loss would be acceptable, even if it meant a loss of life among merchant seamen. It was no matter: a century earlier a legal judgment had ruled on a challenge that the impressment of merchant seamen into the Royal Navy was unlawful. Merchant seafarers, it was decided, whose skills were required by the state in war, should have their liberties removed in order to ensure the protection of the liberties of the greater population.

These attitudes derived from a simple, easily overlooked fact: that a merchant ship was (and remains today) a private vessel, designed, built, manned and maintained to carry a cargo for profit. In 1914 the business of doing so was sufficiently regulated by the state to enable the nation to go to war with a fleet of vessels capable, in tonnage and organisational terms, of sustaining its industry and population and acting in support of the national war effort. At that time, no one forced a man to go to sea: when he did so, he voluntarily signed Articles of Agreement. Thus the merchant marine was sufficiently regulated by the State for the private owners to enable the nation to go to war with a fleet of vessels capable of sustaining its industry and population in support of the national war effort.

The defence of this enormous number of ships, widely dispersed throughout the world and still including a significant proportion of sailing vessels, raised concerns within and without the Admiralty. A merchant officer had expressed a prescient opinion in 1905: 'If any naval power decided upon hostilities with Great Britain it will be[,] as far as our mercantile marine is concerned, a war of extermination.'[8] The extent to which this and other more formal naval assessments took into account the then unknown impact of submarine warfare was minimal. It can have been no more than guessed at in 1905, though it doubtless kindled the imagination of the young officers who volunteered for the submarine 'boats' which were just then entering service in the Imperial German Navy (the Royal Navy had acquired its first submarines two years earlier), and Admiral Fisher rang alarm bells nine years later. What really worried naval planners were the potential depredations of cruisers – a once wholly generic term for a commerce-raider of any size which by 1905 meant a specific, long-ranged man-of-war capable of dominating distant waters and terrorising trade routes. Admiral Fisher's assessment of submarine warfare in early 1914 notwithstanding, it was this danger that prevailed. And it lingered in the perception of admirals long after the virtues of convoy had been proved after 1917; in the late 1930s Sir Dudley Pound himself produced a paper on the war-winning capabilities of the big-gun cruiser, especially in the hands of an enemy.

In the event, it was concluded that if the merchant fleet were to be exposed to cruiser warfare it was better *not* to form up the ships in easily targeted, closely packed convoys. To spread the national asset of the merchant fleet's shipping as widely as in normal times was to present only serendipitous targets to the questing enemy, extending and exhausting him, consuming his stores and fuel and buying time to concentrate against him. Unfortunately, the success of the *Unterseeboot* after 1914 changed all this.

This new weapon began to bite, and bite hard, just as Fisher had foreseen. The disguised decoy-vessel or Q-ship achieved some success against the U-boat but not enough to arrest the haemorrhage of merchant ships and merchant seamen, which rapidly became critical.[9] Stocks of food, and especially of grain, grew dangerously low and by 1916 there was a growing air of desperation in the Admiralty, such as had not been known since 1779.[10] A yet more formidable body of opinion arrayed against the introduction of convoys now arose, one that had scant regard for the survival of the nation, let alone that of the unpaid merchant seamen paddling about the ocean in their lifeboats. It was generated by the war-profiteers, many of them ship-owners but even more of them speculative shareholders who reaped huge sums from the insured values of ships sunk, government subsidies, and other dividends paid on sums invested in shipping. In the first two years of the First World War British ship-owners made net profits of £300 millions sterling, according to the assessment of a former Parliamentary Secretary, the aptly named Sir Leo Money. Over the same period the capital value of the British merchant fleet increased by a similar figure.[11]

An Excess Profits Tax was introduced, but such was the nature of this profiteering, helped by government requisitioning of ships to bring in vital materials, that at the very crisis of the war on British trade Mr Bonar Law, then Chancellor of the Exchequer, saw fit to make a tactlessly boastful speech. On 3 July 1917 he enumerated in detail, for the benefit of the House of Commons, his personal gains: 'The sum of money I had invested in shipping, spread over different shipping companies, was £8,100,' he blithely told the House. 'Five per cent interest on that, which in ordinary times I should be glad to get, would be £405, but for 1915 . . . I received £2,624 and for 1916 . . . £3,847 after Excess Profits Duty had been paid. *One of the steamers has either been sunk or sold. I do not know, either way she has been turned into money for me. In that ship I had £200, and after the very handsome dividend I received on liquidation I received a cheque for over £1,000* [my emphasis: RW]. The other day I received a letter from the Managing Owner saying that because the cost of building ships was so high, they were going to make a division of the surplus capital. For that £350 capital of this division I received a cheque for £1,050.'[12] This smug attitude and its widespread extent were to have important repercussions, not least because while Bonar Law and his associates were basking in their good fortune, the men of that inconsequentially disposed-of steamer to the fate of which the Chancellor of the Exchequer showed such indifference had 'their wages stopped and no more money was forthcoming until they got home, if they ever did, and signed on another ship'.[13]

At the end of 1916 David Lloyd George became Prime Minister. When he received the Admiralty's gloomy assessment that they were perilously close to losing the war at sea, and their advice that the Government should therefore seek an accommodation with Germany, Lloyd George ordered the institution of convoys. Characteristically, he personally took the credit for the successful outcome of his decision, although until the United States entered the war the Royal Navy did not have enough escorts capable of shepherding convoys clear of the areas in which German submarines were active.

Much damage had been done by a failure to co-ordinate merchant shipping as a national asset, a matter also addressed at this time, by the formation of a Ministry of Shipping. Representatives of all classes of serving personnel sat on the National Maritime Board, inaugurated the following November, while the different trades and specialisations continued to be represented by trade union and service associations. Only after the US entered the war did convoys have a chance of success, and despite the success they had, Britain, which at the beginning of the war had possessed 42 per cent of the world's ocean-going shipping, had by its end lost one ship in four, some 7.75 million tons.

After the war conditions at sea remained harsh, particularly when the shipping slump that followed a brief post-war boom intensified during the world depression that followed the Wall Street Crash of 1929. Most ruinous for the British bulk-carrying fleet was the fall in exports of coal. Such an economic climate did not encourage investment in new tonnage, particularly in tramp-ships – one of the reasons why the speed of so many of the convoys in 1939 was only 8 knots. For the men at sea in the 1920s and 1930s, far too many tramp-ships were back-breaking, coal-burning relics, just capable of hauling their bulk cargoes of grain, iron ore and coal about the watery wastes of the world. They were also sparsely fitted, and riddled with cockroaches and rats. There were exceptions, for the terrible loss of ships in the Great War had prompted the building of standard war-tonnage, merchant ships built to government specifications in which many of those evils were improved; but by the time war broke out again in 1939, these standard-built ships had in turn deteriorated with age and neglect.

All this had been exacerbated by other factors. While other governments intervened actively to support and promote their national merchant fleets, the British government traditionally remained aloof, content that a significant percentage of the country's trade was borne in foreign ships. The upswing in trade after 1934 again found employment for laid-up, nationally-owned tonnage, but that this was grown old and had further deteriorated from lack of maintenance did not concern the authorities; if elderly vessels remained sea-worthy, in-class and insurable, they were good enough to trade. Eventually the British followed the lead set initially by the Japanese and instituted a 'scrap-and-build' policy, subsidising the building of new vessels and thus revitalising the almost moribund ship-building industry, but even this backfired: British ship-owners deliberately purchased 97 old vessels to obtain the subsidies for new ships; only 50 new bottoms were built, and these provided only half the capacity of the old.

If there was a lack of government investment during the inter-war years, a number of measures were taken in joint initiatives between the government and the ship-owners to improve the industry, most notably the Merchant Shipping Bill of 1921. Not all ship-owners were motivated solely by profit, nor were all the ships tramps; far from it. In addition to passenger liners, there were a large number of cargo and cargo-passenger liners whose owners took a serious view of their responsibilities both as employers and as suppliers of those essential 'shuttles of an Empire's loom'. Some, like Lord Kylsant of the Royal Mail Group, even paid dearly for their higher motivation. Kylsant over-extended himself in a philanthropic attempt to protect jobs during the post-war slump and was driven to over-capitalise his fleet. Ruin followed and he was sent to jail for a year for issuing a false prospectus. Enlightened managers like those of Alfred Holt & Company regarded their employees as assets in their own right and this outlook, though patriarchal, bred a loyalty and efficiency that were to pay dividends in the coming war.

The post-war slump that struck in March 1921 and the poor freight rates which from then on steadily reduced the quality of British shipping had an immediately disastrous effect upon the pay of her merchant seamen. A wholesale reduction in the wages of seamen and firemen of £2 10s. a month was accepted by Havelock Wilson, Liberal MP and ruthless General Secretary of the National Sailors' and Firemen's Union. Wilson was convinced of the rightness of his decision. To organise seafarers in the sense that other working-men were organised was impossible. Merchant crews were dispersed about the globe, and fractured on board individual ships by the cultural schisms arising from the diverse nature of their respective departments: merchant seamen were the least tractable of men. But the Cooks' and Stewards' Union resisted Wilson's high-handed action and precipitated a strike.

In 1923 freight rates had fallen from the £10 per ton for coal in war time to 11 shillings (55 pence). The ship-owners pleaded poverty. Wilson's acquiescence in the owners' successive demands reduced an able seaman's wages from £14 per month to £9, not enough to support a working-class family in the 1920s. A rise of £1 per month was negotiated in early 1925, but in August that year Wilson, without reference to his members, offered the owners a further 10 per cent reduction, which they naturally accepted. This prompted Lord Inchcape of P&O to praise Wilson's sagacity and understanding of economics, claiming that he had 'done better for his men than any other leader', but caused widespread anger among ratings, for it made their very existence impossible. Reduced to absolute beggary, crews walked off their ships in droves, particularly in such friendly ports as Cape Town, and in Australia and New Zealand, receiving support from local people sympathetic to their plight. In New Zealand the striking seamen claimed they were the lowest-paid white workers in the world and were, withal, 'engaged in a perilous occupation'. Yet many of the ships were fast liners fitted with chilled and refrigerated holds for carrying the fruit and mutton of Australasia, and their idleness threatened the very economies of those Dominions.

At home, the cash allotments paid directly to sailors' wives were stopped if their husbands were on ships detained by the strike, while newspapers were full of a 'Red plot'. By invoking the 'Red spectre', the newspapers raised the fear of Bolshevik revolution in the public consciousness, fudged the central issue, and buried the seamen's cause in the same grave as natural justice. Meanwhile, the Trades Union Congress steadfastly refused to support the seamen, claiming their action was an unofficial 'wild-cat' strike.[14]

In the ports where ships were laid up, strike-breaking crews were mustered with cash inducements and marched aboard. Many of these so-called 'black-legs' were desperate strikers eager by then to get home and earn money. The truth was that, despite their vital function, the strikers could wield little industrial muscle. Frustrated ship-masters, their officers and cadets or apprentices, who all owed a more direct loyalty to their employers, occasionally broke the strike and took their under-manned ships to sea. This often hardened the resolve of strikers to hold out, however, and such incidents could misfire badly. The master of the *Sophocles* berthed at Durban locked his

striking crew in their mess-room and with the help of his mates and apprentices took his ship to sea beyond territorial limits, where refusal of duty
could legitimately be construed as mutiny. When ordered back to work the
crew resolutely refused, and the *Sophocles* was compelled to return to port.

In due course, however, the strike lost its momentum and the men drifted
back to work 'under protest'. On 8 October the Union-Castle Line's *Arundel
Castle* arrived at Southampton from the Cape with the first mails for a
month. She also carried £800,000-worth of gold, quantities of oranges and
160 passengers, including a clergyman, a diva, and some undergraduates
bound for British universities who thought it great fun to sail as part of
the crew.[15]

The consequences of the strike were profound. In addition to its effect
upon Dominion and colonial economies, the price of food in Britain had
risen, sharpening the plight of the strikers' own families, and although
exports were shipped out in foreign-flag ships, an inevitable reduction in
outflow damaged already faltering markets for British manufactures. The
world was in the grip of competing fevers arising from the aftermath of
the war and the downturn in the global economy – fascist nationalism, just
then establishing itself firmly in Italy, Bolshevik Communism already
triumphant in Russia, social unrest on the very streets of London, let alone
Berlin – while over all the great shadow of the Depression loomed.
Undoubtedly the merchant seamen's strike of 1925 and the reaction to it
in the press and among the public hardened the government's resolve and
made it easier to break the General Strike the following year.

Despite their different sense of loyalty, the officers of the merchant marine
had fared little better during the post-war period. A short-lived British
Merchant Service League formed in 1919 had quickly foundered, to be
succeeded in 1921 by the Navigators' and General Insurance Company, a
mutual protection society founded by the remarkable Captain W.H. Coombs,
designed to enable officers to insure against loss of their professional certificates of competence (popularly known as 'tickets') following Board of Trade
enquiries into ship-loss, stranding, collision, or any other major accident. In
1932 The Watch Ashore was established for the benefit of officers' wives
and later Coombs campaigned for pensions, for rights to periods of earned
leave and regulated hours, for educational and physical standards for the
entry of cadets and apprentices, and for the establishment of a regular officers' union. In due course the Navigators' and Engineer Officers' Union
was founded, a Merchant Navy Officers' Pension Fund was established, and
representation on the National Maritime Board was achieved. A programme
of formal training for deck officers was introduced, compelling minor and
uninterested small companies, most of which operated tramp-ships, to train

their potential officers with some eye to their future rather than using them as cheap labour. Apprentices were not paid overtime and rarely paid very much at all, what wages they received coming from the premiums stumped up by their parents. The main benefit they enjoyed was their board and lodging, but the undertaking given by the ship-owner when an apprentice took out indentures – to teach him his business if he proved amenable – was observed more rigorously than hitherto. This brought apprentices indentured to such employers more in line with the midshipmen and cadets under training with the crack liner companies and ensured that they would be more interchangeable in time of national emergency. A trained apprentice or cadet, having passed his first professional certificate of competency as a second mate, would nevertheless in the savage conditions of world depression be lucky to find a berth as an officer. During the early 1930s it was far from rare to find officers with master mariner's certificates serving as able seamen, an indignity unheard-of in the Royal Navy.

Between 1929 and 1932 the total of unemployed tonnage world-wide increased fourfold; of this 1.7 million tons were British, and 40,000 British seafarers were unemployed. In 1934 one-third of the British mercantile marine was laid up, 'some vessels having been idle for more than four years[,] and 60,000 merchant seamen were walking the streets'.

At this period a master of a 10,000-ton tramp was earning £24 per month, his chief, second and third mates, the last often a luxury dispensed with, £19, £14 and £10 respectively. Like the seamen, firemen and stewards, who received about £10 a month plus overtime, these officers had to find their bedding, towels and soap, and in addition had to purchase uniform, a sextant, and the nautical tables they needed to navigate their owners' ships; engineers were paid on a similar scale, a chief engineer getting slightly less than a master. Radio officers did rather better, for they were actually employed by a communications company such as Marconi, and were sub-contracted to the shipping company, which was obliged to supply their bedding, towels and soap! Officers were entitled to a fortnight's paid leave per annum, though taking it often cost them their jobs. Generally a senior rating was better off than a junior officer, but without the guaranteed leave.

While these conditions prevailed aboard tramps, first-class liner and cargo-liner companies' officers did a little better, though one deck-officer was told that he need not come back next voyage 'because I had the nerve to ask for the recommended entitlement of leave after serving for fifteen months of 90-hour working weeks. At that time even [Alfred Holt's] Blue Funnel Line, most considerate of shipowners, thought that ten days of leave after a six months' voyage without a weekend in port was enough to keep an officer happy.'

All classes of merchant ships employed large numbers of non-Europeans. Arabs and Somalis commonly served as firemen and greasers in ships' engine rooms, while Chinese and Indians, the latter invariably known as 'lascars', were more often to be found as sailors or stewards. They were all paid less than their white colleagues, lascars, for example, receiving around 30 rupees a month, about £2 5s., while 'their living conditions in many ships were abominable'.[16] These minority members of the nation's seafaring population established their own communities in the poorer quarters of the nation's ports such as Swansea, Cardiff and South Shields, where Arabs and Somalis predominated: considerable Chinese settlements appeared in Liverpool and London.

They might eat in a saloon, waited upon at table, but the officers of a tramp-ship lived, like the crew, in the most primitive and rudimentary accommodation, a marked contrast to the perceptions engendered by the publicity that surrounded the luxurious appointments of every new passenger-liner intended for the prestigious trans-Atlantic route. Few tramps built much before 1935 possessed refrigerators for ship's stores, a sad lack in the extremes of climate through which such a vessel often proceeded, and the food was dull, limited to the scale of minima established by the Board of Trade. They were known as 'pound-and-pint' ships, run by notoriously penurious owners. Lady Astor, the first sitting female Member of Parliament, told the House in 1938 that 'a colleague who had taken a look at the conditions in which seamen lived had said he would not expect ferrets to live in such conditions'. Seamen were three times more likely to die from tuberculosis than the average British male, and nearly three times more likely than a coal-miner to die in an accident.[17]

Nancy Astor's concern did not mean that her regard for merchant seamen was any higher than that of the public at large: she attempted to have them wear yellow armbands, as potential carriers of venereal disease, an insult they never forgave her. The public's attitude towards the merchant jack was one of contempt, for this pitiable creature when seen ashore was often drunk, with every appearance of a social loser.

After 1931 the British government abandoned its cherished belief in free trade and returned to a policy of 'Imperial Preference': exports were despatched to the Dominions and colonies and tariffs were raised against imports from outside the Commonwealth. By 1937 wages in the merchant service had at last begun to rise, working hours had been reduced, and new tonnage was improving living conditions. Rearmament, begun in 1934, had initiated a slow revival in naval ship-building, so that by 1939, despite her decline in exporting power, the weakness of her steel and ship-building industries and the reduction of her navy following the Washington and

London Naval Treaties of the 1920s, Britain remained the world's major maritime power. She still exported £37 millions worth of coal, £42 millions of iron and steel products, £22 millions of chemicals, machinery and vehicles worth £103 millions, and textiles worth £92 millions. Her ocean-going fleet comprised about 2,400 vessels. Of these 1,170 were liners owned by 68 companies and totalling 8.75 million gross tons, in which conditions were perceptibly better than in the 739 tramp-ships which belonged to no fewer than 129 small companies. Each of these owned between one and five ships and the total tonnage of British-flagged tramps was about 3.45 million gross tons. Similar in status and management to cargo-liners were the 498 oil-tankers totalling around 3.45 million tons, usually relatively new compared with the tramps.[18]

This British merchant 'fleet' accounted for something a little less than one-third of the world's total deep-water tonnage, and while it included about half the universal passenger-liner capacity and half its refrigerated vessels, only about a quarter of the world's tankers were British. The Royal Navy pursued an aggressive policy in securing oil supplies for its warships after Admiral Fisher committed it to oil-fired turbines, yet British shipowners had little interest in tankers. The bulk-carrying specialists, the tramp-ship owners, were too short-sighted and mean to invest in the revolutionary new ship-type; they were also resistant to the diesel engine and, since load-line regulations militated against tankers, it was left to major oil companies like British Petroleum and Eagle Oil to establish their own tanker fleets. With their dangerous cargo, tankers required highly-trained officers and crews and consequently rivalled blue-chip liner companies in terms of discipline, pay and conditions. In general, however, the specialised task of hauling bulk cargoes of oil fell largely to countries like Norway, where ship-owning had become almost a cottage industry. Low wages and multiple ownerships with members willing to accept low profit margins as dividends upon their modest investments ensured that numerous large, economic motor-vessels traded under the Norwegian flag. These proved more capable craft than their conservatively built, steam-powered British counterparts. Norwegian multi-owned companies had no trouble securing time or voyage charters from British interests, especially for their tankers.

In addition to this reluctance to invest in tankers, it is equally extraordinary that, having pioneered the marine steam engine, so few British owners embraced the economies offered by the new diesel engine. It found a few advocates: the ill-fated Kylsant of Royal Mail, for example, along with Andrew Weir of the Bank Line and Sir Frederick Lewis of Furness Withy showed an interest, as did Alfred Holt & Co., whose Blue Funnel Line had initiated the long-haul steamship, particularly when they acquired the

run-down Glen Line in 1935 from the wreck of Kylsant's empire and immediately ordered new, fast, diesel-powered tonnage. But even if due allowance
is made for the slow-down resulting from the effects of the Depression,
purblind conservatism and under-investment among ship-owners, combined
with the policy of *laissez-faire* invariably adopted by British governments
where shipping was concerned, resulted in a large sector of the carrying
capacity of the British merchant fleet being obsolete.

The disparate collection of ships run by competing owners was therefore a 'navy' in only the most amorphous sense. Or was it? It was recognised that 'the Navy of Supply has always been the Cinderella, remembered
with loud protestations of undying regard in times of national hardship but
complacently forgotten or ignored when the sun shone again'. And a small
group of influential men consisting of MPs, civil servants and enlightened
ship-owners *had*, since a manning crisis of the 1870s, taken more than a
purely commercial interest in the long-term preservation of what they
perceived to be an essential national asset. They were concerned that it was
being subject to the attrition of economic forces and foresaw that a policy
of non-interference on the part of all interested parties, including government, was not in the long-term interests of Great Britain.

In particular these men had noticed that there was a short-fall developing in the numbers of young men going to sea as aspiring officers.
Owners might be content to man their ships from the four corners of the
Empire, but they wished them to be British-commanded and run. Several
companies therefore dedicated working vessels to the training of cadets,
while a number of training establishments had been set up at home, chief
among them two schools housed in redundant wooden men-of-war, the
Conway on the Mersey and the *Worcester* on the Thames. Both remained
'His Majesty's Ships' and some of their alumni joined the Royal Navy, but
the majority were intended for the merchant service. A number of vessels
were also commissioned to train ratings, often orphans and disadvantaged
boys, in such places as the Hamble, the Thames, where both the Marine
Society's *Warspite* and the Shaftesbury Homes' *Arethusa* lay, and the Mersey,
where the training ship *Indefatigable*, founded by the ship-owner Harold
Bibby, was moored near HMS *Conway*. In addition the ship-owners'
Shipping Federation set up the Gravesend Sea School, and in 1938, when
the old tea clipper *Cutty Sark* became available, she too became part of
the *Worcester* establishment at Greenhithe.[19] By 1938 Devitt & Moore's fine
sail-training ships had been abandoned and they had established a cadet
school at Pangbourne in Berkshire.[20] Cadets from Pangbourne, *Worcester*
and *Conway*, regarded as public schools, generally joined liner companies
and enjoyed the privilege of having obligatory sea-time remitted to qualify

to sit for their first certificate of competency; they were also automatically enrolled into the Royal Naval Reserve. It was, however, still possible for a boy of 16 to go straight to sea under indentures to a shipping company and serve a full four-year apprenticeship. Most small tramp-owners still recruited cheap labour in this way, while other companies preferred it to accepting young men direct from the cadet schools: this was particularly true of oil-tanker owners. By the 1930s few of these young men, and especially those from the major training establishments, regarded the profession into which they were going as a 'Cinderella' service, and many possessed a vague notion of belonging to something greater than the company to which they were bound.

During the First World War King George V had referred to 'my Merchant Navy', a term greeted with some derision in the mercantile marine itself, but hailed by others as a true recognition of this fourth arm of defence. In 1922 the King went further and formally conferred the title 'Merchant Navy' upon the British commercial fleet. Nevertheless, it was clear to many of the officers, and especially to their masters, that if pay and conditions, let alone their social status, were to improve, something more than this nebulous royal condescension was needed. Despite royal approval and all the good work done by Coombs and his campaigners, the image of the merchant mariner, irrespective of rank, remained that of a commercial drudge. Taking matters into their own hands under the leadership of Sir Robert Burton-Chadwick, a number of liner-commanders formed the Honourable Company of Master Mariners, which in 1926 became the first City livery company to be incorporated since medieval times and ensured that the term 'Merchant Navy' grew in common usage.[21] The anomalous position of a merchant shipmaster in time of war had already led to the introduction of a formal uniform for companies without one of their own, under the provisions of the Mercantile Marine (Uniform) Order 1918, authorised by an Order in Council of 13 December 1921. This uniform was intended only for officers however, and although many liner companies had a company livery for some if not all their crews, the fact that the majority of ratings employed in merchant ships lacked a recognised uniform led to some deep humiliations and resentments.

The master of a merchant ship was not simply the commanding officer, charged by the vessel's owners with the business of conducting her safely from port to port and of maintaining their interests in respect of ship, cargo and crew. In addition to these obvious commercial responsibilities he derived his actual authority from another source, that of his ship's flag-state, the national ensign his vessel wore.

In Britain, a government department not only certified a master as a competent person to command a ship, but also regulated his vessel and her crew. In peace-time Britain this was the Board of Trade, which supervised the signing of the contract between a master – not the ship's owner – and all other members of his crew. These so-called 'Articles of Agreement' were the legal contract that stipulated pay for the various ranks and ratings and laid down a scale of provisions and peripheral conditions of employment which bound master and crew for the duration of a voyage, or for two years. Almost invariably the latter period prevailed in the case of tramp-ships, which did not make scheduled voyages like passenger and cargo-liners. The Articles were customarily signed ashore in a Shipping Office under the eye of the Shipping Master, who was a civil servant and the Board of Trade's representative on the spot. This ritual was known as 'signing on' and the reverse process of 'signing off' took place at the end of a voyage or the end of the two-year term. When 'signing off' occurred abroad it was over-seen by a consular officer and was immediately followed by a reopening of the articles, and all hands signed on again so that the ship could continue trading.

Thus, through the agency of the Board of Trade, a master had powers derived from and obligations owed to the State as well as his owners, and by this means the Admiralty could channel to him and demand from him instructions and conduct which were, in effect, rules of engagement. Most masters did not particularly enjoy taking orders from the Admiralty, even by printed instruction, still less from young naval officers in command of small men-of-war. Partly it was the perceived infringement of their liber-ties, but in the latter case there was also an element of social resentment.

The Merchant Service remained during those years between the wars stub-bornly independent, regarding the R[oyal] N[avy] as a snobbish bunch of people taken up with gold lace, strut and ceremony. And the blunt fact was they preferred to have as little contact with us as possible. Perhaps their atti-tude was not so difficult to understand. Inevitably the Merchant Navy life, where a ship only paid her way at sea and where time in harbour was brief, bred a defensive insularity among crews; what is more they were very much aware that they were achieving something solid by carrying goods to every part of the globe in all weathers.

It was small wonder that they were apt to sneer at the peace time RN with its regular life on a station like the Mediterranean, with ships seldom going to sea for more than a few days every year and then ending up with a jaunt to some foreign port where the red carpet was laid down for offi-cers and men alike. The merchant seaman was never fêted . . . had none of this integrated life with football matches and [any] . . . sense of family . . .

The men sailing under the Red Duster felt that they were the only real sailors . . .

Rear-Admiral Creighton, who went back to sea as a convoy commodore at the outbreak of war, was well qualified to make these observations picking up the disparaged image of the merchant service under its 'Red Duster' of an ensign. He concludes: 'One of their pet gibes at the Royal Navy was the fact that a large number of men in smart uniforms were always turned out . . . whenever a ship came to a buoy or went alongside or dropped anchor . . . The Merchant Service considered it far more chic to do the same with one officer and a couple of usually grubby and picturesque characters fore and aft.'

Creighton's recollection is not quite true of the whole of the Merchant Service, for liner companies rose above this shoe-string level of manning and while their employees might be picturesque characters, their masters' daily rounds ensured that personal grubbiness was not tolerated. The masters themselves Creighton at first thought 'ordinary unpretentious people',

> but soon found that there was something which set them apart from their contemporaries ashore – a compact self-contained confidence and calm simplicity. I think it must be [due to] the lonely life they lead with the power and responsibility that is always theirs and which they can seldom put aside . . . Most are kind hearted and generous men . . . [who] uphold discipline by sheer character and personality – for their powers of punishment under Board of Trade Regulations are almost non-existent. A fine of a few shillings is about the maximum.
>
> For more serious offences . . . the master has to take the case to the civil courts . . . These are things that RN officers with the power of the Naval Discipline Act to bolster their position might remember.[22]

Such was the difficult relationship which was to underlie the co-operation between the two sea services in the coming years, one *not* appreciated by Their Lordships in Whitehall as they carried out their analysis on 21 September 1939 and expressed their misgivings about the casual attitude of these men, and the men whom they commanded, towards their German despoilers.

If a master's position aboard his ship depended upon his personality, his situation *vis-à-vis* the orders of a German U-boat commander was far more isolated. Despite the emanations of mutual esteem evinced on certain occasions, the majority of masters deeply resented being told what to do by the enemy. To the merchant ship-master and the majority of his crew, enemy submariners were sneaky war-mongers who hid themselves and attacked by stealth: 'The unchivalrous face of the Kriegsmarine' was what Third Officer A.H. Bird of the *Australind* thought them.

The British Admiralty might know little of the subtleties of the psychology of merchant seafarers in general, but it saw opportunities for capitalising on a master's tacit obligations to his flag-state. Already one British master, Captain C. Shaw of the Brocklebank cargo-liner *Manaar*, had acted, as far as Their Lordships were concerned, with commendable aggression.

The *Manaar* was a 7,200-ton cargo-liner belonging to T. & J. Brocklebank of Liverpool, on her way towards the Suez Canal outward-bound on her regular service to Calcutta and Rangoon. Loaded with a general cargo, she was off Cape Roca, near Lisbon, at dawn on 6 September. Although she was steaming at 12 knots without navigation lights she was not zig-zagging when, quite suddenly, a shot was fired across her bow. The shell came from the gun of *U-38* commanded by Kapitänleutnant H. Liebe, and Shaw responded by slowing the *Manaar* to a stop.[23]

But then, to Liebe's astonishment, as he approached the *Manaar* a gun fitted on her stern opened fire, obliging him to crash-dive and attack the Brocklebank liner with torpedoes. The ship broke in two and swiftly began to sink. Liebe surfaced again to shell her, and hit the bridge and radio room. Considering the *Manaar* to have excluded herself from the protection of the Prize Regulations, Liebe left her crew to fend for themselves. Shaw and 29 of his crew were picked up by the Dutch vessel *Mars*, 16 were rescued by the Portuguese *Carvalho Araujo* and a further 17 by the Italian *Castelbianco*, and all of them were landed at Lisbon, but Shaw had lost seven men in the attack.

Stocks of guns for defence against submarine attack had been maintained since 1918, and at government expense many merchant ships, as they came into dry-dock in the post-Munich period, had been strengthened to accept them; but the actual fitting of the weapons themselves could not be effected before a formal outbreak of hostilities, and it could not be done instantly. In the first days of the war, therefore, ramming was the only means by which a merchant ship, setting aside its legal constraints, could inflict damage on a U-boat. On 1 October the Admiralty issued an addition to the instruction to ship-masters to transmit the vital SSSS signal to indicate a submarine attack, calling upon British merchantmen to turn upon their aggressors and ram them. Even minor damage, Their Lordships knew, would prevent a U-boat from submerging, delay her departure from the scene, and render her vulnerable to reprisal as soon as superior surface or air forces arrived. This instruction put ship-masters in a very difficult position, for such an act was indisputably offensive and would totally demolish a merchant ship's theoretical non-combatant status, instantly removing any protection under the Prize Regulations. There had been, moreover, a disquieting precedent. In 1917 Captain Fryatt, commanding the Great Eastern Railway Company's steam packet *Brussels*, had attempted just such a thing while on passage from The Netherlands to Harwich. Some time later a flotilla of small German naval craft interdicted his ship and took her into Zeebrugge, where after a drum-head court-martial Fryatt was condemned as a *franc-tireur* and summarily shot.

Also during the First World War there had been a brace of actions in which merchant ships armed to defend themselves against submarines had engaged and damaged their attackers. Their masters were awarded the Victoria Cross for their valour, but had to be specially gazetted into the Royal Naval Reserve (in a junior capacity) to receive it.[24] After the war it was established by special warrant that Merchant Navy personnel were not precluded from commendation for the Victoria Cross by their mercantile status; the special warrant has never been invoked. In September 1939 the British State, as opposed to the British Admiralty, announced that the civilian status of merchant shipping would be preserved, and that no military decorations would be awarded; instead, individual acts of courage would be considered for civilian awards. Thus for their action in the first few days of September 1939 Chief Officer Copeland and his boatswain from the *Athenia* were respectively appointed OBE and awarded the BEM.

The most vulnerable post aboard a British merchantman in those first days of war under the Prize Regulations was that of the radio officer, who was compromised the instant he obeyed his master's orders and began transmitting the submarine warning signal. Aboard a U-boat the wireless operator monitored the distress frequency, while on the casing the gun crew laid their weapon on the location of the radio-room, betrayed by the aerial wires rising from it. Upon transmission of the SSSS message the merchant ship was held to have voluntarily abandoned her non-combatant status, and became fair game. Under these circumstances and their inevitable consequences it became common for radio officers to miss the order to abandon ship, and to be forgotten in the rush to get the boats away. Isolated as they were in their 'radio-shacks', headphones clamped to their heads as they transmitted their last desperate signal, often having had to rig an emergency aerial to do so, this was not surprising. The radio officer of the *Manaar* had distinguished himself in this respect, sending out a distress signal as his ship sank under him; for this he too was appointed OBE.

The *Manaar*'s act of defiance gave Dönitz the means with which to counter British allegations of piracy with respect to the *Athenia*.[25] A fortnight afterwards the British Ministry of Information, in the first flushes of its propaganda war, unwisely trumpeted that 'a British merchantman had engaged and driven off a German U-boat'.[26] This was followed on 26 September by Churchill's public announcement of the Admiralty's intention to arm all merchant ships. Although this meant, initially at least, a low-angle 4-inch stern-chase weapon mounted for self-defence such as had been fitted to the *Manaar*, when combined with the Admiralty call for merchantmen to ram it gave Dönitz the pretext he needed to move closer to the opening of unrestricted submarine warfare that he desired. He was in no doubt that the arming of British merchant ships transformed them into a 'navy' with a measure of offensive capability.

The *Manaar* belonged to the oldest British commercial shipping house then in existence, so it was perhaps fitting that her action as the first British merchant ship to resist arrest by a German submarine marked the true genesis of Britain's 'Merchant Navy'. Significantly, this defiance came not at official prompting, but from Captain Campbell Shaw and the men on the spot.

3

'The safety of our trade . . .'

Port Chalmers

An Admiralty assessment of 1921 had concluded that 'in a future war it is safe to assume that no breathing space will be allowed by the enemy and our Mercantile Marine will be subject to the full vigour of attack on the declaration of hostilities'. Regrettably little was done between the wars by way of exercises in the protection of a convoy of merchantmen against submarine or air attack, and in a subsequent strategic appreciation of 1936 the Admiralty thought it 'doubtful whether an enemy would, in fact, adopt unrestricted warfare against our shipping . . .' By 1939 the sonic location device developed by a Frenchman and a Pole, Langouin and Chilowski, fostered by the Anglo-French Allied Submarine Detection Investigation Committee and then called 'asdic' but more commonly known today as 'sonar', had been fitted to two hundred destroyers. Its apparent efficacy led the Admiralty to claim the submarine menace to be rather a thing of the past, and anti-submarine warfare was relegated to what ambitious young naval officers of the day were apt to regard as a naval backwater. At the Admiralty there was no Anti-Submarine Division of the Naval Staff where any such expertise was vested in a single commander until 2 September 1939, the very eve of war, when another officer was added. At no time in the inter-war period had any analytical study been made of the German war on British trade between 1914 and 1918, while such anti-submarine exercises as *were* held were usually fudged, their results massaged in favour of the surface units and the reports 'flogged' to give off a good odour.[1]

Such complacency proved both dangerous, and for many fatal; naval orthodoxy was formidably entrenched. There were individual examples of percipience,[2] but most remained wedded to the perceived virtues of gunnery and Their Lordships continued their preoccupation with the surface commerce-raider as the greatest threat to British merchant shipping. Against these it was considered that defence could be adequately provided to ocean convoys by Armed Merchant Cruisers and obsolete 'R'-class battleships like *Royal Oak*, which on 13 October was sunk at her moorings in Scapa Flow.

Mercifully, the 1936 appreciation, perhaps marking a deep-set anxiety by a hedging of bets, concluded that 'the safety of our trade in war is such a vital matter that in preparing our measures of defence it is only prudent to assume that such attacks may develop, even at the commencement of a war, and our preparations should provide against such a contingency as far as possible.'[3] It was not so much anxieties about submarine attack that lay behind this as appreciation of the relatively unknown danger from aircraft. A row boiled between the Admiralty and the Air Ministry over the vice of a convoy presenting a large aerial target and the virtue of it combining for mutual defence, but the significance of the conclusion lay in the retention of the concept of convoy. Thus, although it went almost unpractised, convoy nevertheless remained central to the naval control of shipping, and in 1937 contingency planning was taken in hand by Admiral Sir Eldon Manisty, the man who had been responsible for convoy introduction in 1917.

The joint Admiralty and Board of Trade Shipping Defence Advisory Committee, incorporating members from prominent shipping companies, had laid plans that ultimately bore fruit in the defensive arming of merchant ships and, prior to that, in the reinforcement of their structures to accept guns. In due course even those ship-owners resentful of any government interference in their affairs lobbied the government through the Chamber of Shipping to expedite the process of 'stiffening' – and to foot the bill. In this context, in the eyes of those mindful of the strategic importance of merchant shipping, Britain's hitherto amorphous collection of mercantile shipping was already a Merchant Navy.

This of course meant a great deal more than simply a collective shift in the imaginations of civil servants. For a Merchant Navy to serve the war effort effectively, its organisation required more than mere gathering into convoys, complex though that was. First the resource had to be secured, then its purpose had to be defined, and the infrastructure to serve and support it had to be established. This was an immense administrative and logistical task, and its driving dynamic was the absolute priority of the supply and flow of imports. During the thirty years prior to 1914, demand for food for the people and raw materials for the industries of Britain had been increasing steadily, at a rate of about 2 per cent per annum, and it was this level of demand that decided the size of the mercantile fleet of the day.

Although the crisis in supply that occurred in 1916–17 was in part due to unrestricted submarine warfare, it could also be attributed to failures in the import system. In essence this centred on departmental fragmentation, leading to a failure to distribute *matériel* properly and efficiently. There was no co-ordinating body in the structure of government (as the national organisational authority), and the privately managed docks and the associated national distribution networks were left to rise miraculously to the occasion. Although merchant shipping was the *only* means of carrying from overseas the commodities essential to the prosecution of the war, it was not shipping alone that was required to expedite the distribution of these commodities beyond the ports at which they arrived. If there was a failure to deliver these commodities to the point of need, whether that was the housewife's shopping-basket or an industrial manufactory, then defeat remained as real a possibility as if the delivering ships had been sunk at sea by enemy action.

In such a case, the provision of merchantmen and their protection by naval escorts, along with all the associated complex efforts to achieve the safe arrival of convoys, was but wasted effort. In short, convoys would prove of only marginal importance if the cargoes still failed to reach their ultimate destination. In April 1937 the Ministry of Transport had been entrusted with the operation of all ports upon the outbreak of a war, but no consideration was given by government to the purchase, discharge or distribution of cargoes. Between the autumn of 1939 and the winter of 1941–2, therefore, history repeated itself. 'The crisis lay in the inability of existing commercial structures to function adequately under war conditions.'[4]

The problems of discharge and distribution by convoy are easily appreciated. A large number of laden ships arriving together in one place created a problem in itself, producing an immediate overload. Demand for berths and services and a rapid congestion of port handling, storage and distribution facilities was followed by a concentrated outflow of goods into road and rail networks geared for the steady pace of peace-time consumption. The docks, a service industry suffering after years of depression, neglect and under-investment, found it extremely difficult to function efficiently. Indeed, it might be asked whether they had ever functioned with true efficiency.[5] Under-capitalised and over-unionised, the docks had always been a focus of industrial unrest. The large casual labour force, having been reduced to a state of truculence by years of cynical neglect on the part of their employers, were in little better mind to bend to the effort necessitated by the war than the weary merchant seamen; but, unlike their floating comrades, the dockers were in a far better position to combine and cause disruption in their own long-overlooked interest.

Matters were not much better when it came to the mechanically-handled bulk cargoes such as iron ore, grain, sugar, and of course oil, which were usually delivered to specialist terminals. These were owned by the companies marketing such materials and generally operated free of industrial dissent while also providing additional facilities for storage and processing prior to onward distribution. They were, however, almost all located in port areas where they could be affected by the congestion caused by contiguous disruption.

In 1939 food and other raw materials were distributed overland throughout Britain by road, rail and canal. The latter two handled both homogeneous commodities and miscellaneous, break-bulk items, while the roads provided the capillaries in the national network, at a time when a significant amount of much road transport was still provided by horse-drawn vehicles. Nor should it be forgotten that a fourth and important artery was then provided by coastal shipping, which also delivered bulk cargoes like coal and oil to remote plant and power stations accessible by river and creek.

Efforts to plan for the handling of shipping in wartime had been instigated by the Committee for Imperial Defence as early as 1933 with the establishment of a Distribution of Imports Committee. On 4 December 1934 the Chiefs of Staff had charged this committee to consider matters in light of the possibility of a war with Germany in five years, a remarkably prescient instruction. The committee's work was complex but flawed, being based not upon rational analysis but entirely upon statistical evaluation, the influences upon which were subjective, conjectural and largely useless. In its prolonged deliberations can be seen the glow of optimism, of a confidence that in the event things would be all right. Although it took four of the allotted five years to report, the committee did however anticipate the closure, or at the least the severe reduction in cargo-handling capacity, of the east-coast ports, of which London was the principal. The theoretical solution to this was that three-quarters of the redirected cargo could be handled by the west-coast ports if an additional third shift was worked by the dockers.

Long before war broke out there were many people, including shipowners whose vessels were frequently affected by delays in port, who appreciated that the docks would prove key choke points. Indeed, 'it seemed that port-capacity and not [a lack of] shipping would set the limit that the United Kingdom would be able to import in time of war'.[6] Clearly, port facilities would attract the attentions of the enemy's air forces; and, given the increasing range of aircraft by 1936, all dock complexes, including those of the west-coast ports of the Bristol Channel and Liverpool, would be vulnerable to air attack. In the event, as well as vastly aiding the Kriegsmarine in advancing Dönitz's U-boat bases to the Atlantic littoral, the capitulation and occupation of France in May 1940 improved the Luftwaffe's access to these British ports, effectively doubling Germany's opportunities to strike at the import flow.

But this was not all; once the north coast of France was in German hands, shipping movements in the English Channel were severely restricted; the commercial port of Southampton was effectively emasculated, further reducing port capacity overall, while the vast amount of shipping based on Southampton had to be diverted to other ports, most notably Liverpool and Birkenhead, exacerbating congestion on the Mersey. Several of the smaller ports along the south coast served important power-stations, and the supply of these throughout the war by coastal colliers coming south from the coal-staithes of the north-east of England is one of the many disregarded elements in Britain's maritime struggle. This 'coal-scuttle brigade' regularly ran the gauntlet of the German guns commanding the Strait of Dover, as well as attack by *Schnellboote* and aircraft. North of the Thames Estuary, with its naval command station at The Nore, these colliers joined other coasters and the larger, ocean-going ships whose terminal ports were not Belfast, Glasgow, Liverpool, Swansea, Cardiff, Newport or Avonmouth, but those of Britain's east coast. Between the Thames Estuary, Leith and Methil, streams of coastal convoys supplemented those coming across the Atlantic, in part to take up otherwise idle port capacity on the east coasts of Scotland and England, but also to avoid overloading the west-coast ports and to mitigate the worst effects of the impaired import chain. However, passages through the North Sea exposed valuable hulls to extra risk and their crews to the stresses of 'E-boat Alley' where, as well as the enemy's fast *Schnellboote*, the colliers had to defend their vessels against air attack, avoid mines, and beat off the occasional sorties made by German destroyers and torpedo boats.[7]

Apart from fulfilling an augmented role as part of the distribution network, these coasters were later called upon for another purpose, attending their larger ocean-going sisters in the 'Emergency Ports' set up in sheltered anchorages such as that on The Tail o' the Bank in the Firth of Clyde. Fitted with derricks, general cargo and cargo-passenger liners were self-sufficient in cargo-handling gear, and by discharging directly into coasters could relieve congestion in the docks, distribute their lading to smaller ports, and avoid exposing themselves to the danger of proceeding down the vulnerable east coast of Britain. Clearly, however, such sensible extempore measures could only be put in place when, from the moment of loading on the far side of the world to the point of delivery in Britain, all parties acted in a co-ordinated manner. Such efficiency took time to develop and establish, and it was not until late 1941, with the merger of the Ministries of Shipping and Transport into the Ministry of War Transport (MoWT), that they became possible.

The coasters' war was as gruelling as that in the Atlantic and complementary to it, for many deep-water merchantmen joined coastal convoys to take their cargoes to their ports of destination. The first coastal convoy between the Thames and the Firth of Forth sailed on 6 September, a day after the very first ocean convoy of the war, which consisted of troopships on passage from the Clyde towards Gibraltar.

In his analysis of Britain's naval strategy, the official naval historian Captain Stephen Roskill divided maritime power into three elements: Strength, or the capable assets which can be sent to sea to fight; Security, or the bases and support available to maintain the first; and Transport, or the merchant shipping necessary to maintain national existence and provide services to the first element. 'Transport' also includes the infrastructures of ship-building and ship-repair which underpin the maintenance of a merchant fleet large enough to fulfil the requirements of the state. It is not a glamorous role, as Roskill acknowledged, but 'without the steady devotion of the men who man those ships the whole structure of maritime power must crumble'.[8]

Whatever their short-comings in respect of pre-war planning, the essence of these elements was well appreciated by the naval staff at the Admiralty who took control of all British merchant shipping on the evening of 26 August 1939. The power by which they did so derived from the decision made by the Cabinet Committee responsible for 'Defence Preparedness' which had, in consultation with the Foreign Office and the Board of Trade, empowered the Admiralty 'to adopt compulsory control of movements of merchant shipping which . . . should include the routeing of ships in the Atlantic'. This was translated to those at sea by Navigation Order No. 1 of 1939, which instructed masters that 'British merchant vessels at all times and Dominion vessels, when in British Territorial Waters, shall comply with any sailing or routeing instructions which may from time to time be issued to them by the Admiralty or by any person authorised by the Admiralty to act under this order.'

Three days later, at 16.38 on 29 August, the Admiralty signalled all naval authorities to mobilise for war with a European power. This was followed on 1 September by a warning message which preceded the signal to commence hostilities against Germany at 11.00 on the 3rd. Thus the mercantile arm of Britain's sea services was swiftly joined to the naval and brought under the executive operational control of the Admiralty.

Within the bailiwick of the First Sea Lord and the Chief of the Naval Staff, Sir Dudley Pound, lay those of the Vice Chief of Naval Staff and the three Assistant Chiefs of Staff, one of whom in due course headed the Trade Division. A new post was created in February 1940, that of the Controller of Merchant Ship-Building and Repairs. From this date, all ship-building and repairing facilities were superintended by him, and he was assisted by an Advisory Committee on Merchant Ship-building, most of the members of which were, of course, drawn from the industry itself. This administration grew in importance as the German submarine offensive began to take its toll and, much later in the war, was pivotal in the build-up to the invasion of Europe and the breaching of Hitler's Atlantic Wall.[9]

But in 1939 it was the Trade Division under Rear Admiral H.M. Burrough which conducted the organisation of convoys. The Trade Division had begun life as a mere section of the Naval Plans Division, but in May 1939 it was reconstituted as a full division in its own right headed by Burrough as Acting Chief of Naval Staff (Trade). In October the hurriedly formed Anti-submarine Warfare Division joined it and from then on anti-submarine warfare analysis and operational research were an integral part of the Trade Division's work. One of its first duties was to initiate the control structure by which convoys would be regulated, and to requisition those liners such as the *Athenia* which it had ear-marked for commissioning as Armed Merchant Cruisers to protect them. As early as February 1938 a rise in the international temperature had led to doubts being expressed as to whether the Naval Control Service Staffs and Armed Merchant Cruisers could be mobilised fast enough, once hostilities broke out. The first step was to appoint as Naval Control of Shipping Officers all naval staff intelligence officers already in post abroad. By this means an embryonic organisation was set up quickly and effectively. As for arming the selected cruisers, the only answer was to put the matter in hand immediately; as many of the vessels had already received structural strengthening, the response was rapid – *Athenia* herself was on her way to Canada for the purpose of conversion.

Situated in the newly built concrete citadel annexed to the old Admiralty building in Whitehall, overlooking Horse Guards Parade, the Trade Division and its Convoy Plot lay next to the Submarine Tracking Plot. Set up in February 1939 with the Operational Intelligence Centre, the Submarine Tracking Plot was maintained by Naval Intelligence, but its influence on, and contact with, the adjacent Trade Plot was intimate. At the outset and for long afterwards this was a simple matter of common-sense co-operation, but became official policy during the crisis of the Battle of the Atlantic in early 1943 on the orders of Rear Admiral J.H. Edelsten, the then Assistant Chief of Naval Staff with specific responsibilities for 'U-boat Warfare and Trade'.[10] His specific purpose was to route convoys clear of known locations of U-boats, knowledge usually derived from Enigma decrypts passed to the Admiralty from the Government Code and Cipher School at Bletchley Park, and vital later in the war when German submarines were concentrated in groups. Thus all routeing and diversion instructions issued by 'the Admiralty' emanated from the combined deliberations of the Trade and Submarine Tracking Plots in the light of the current intelligence picture. Such co-ordination was shaky at first but by the time Edelsten assumed office a series of daily meetings reviewed the summary reports from the Operations and Trade Divisions. The first of these meetings was at 09.30 and was held in the Submarine Tracking Room, chaired by Edelsten. From it emanated orders to redirect convoys and the establishment of the intended route of convoys due to sail. It was followed by a second meeting an hour later headed by the Director Operations Division (Home). At about 15.00 a further review was undertaken by the Head of the Tracking Room in the presence of the ACNS, senior Directors and the naval liaison officer attached to the Royal Air Force's Coastal Command. More senior officers were summoned if the situation demanded it, but this was the most important meeting of the day, dealing with the strategic direction of the naval escort. Later, those who attended the 10.30 meeting reconvened at 18.00 and at 23.00. Sometime after midnight, as his last act of the working day, the First Sea Lord, Sir Dudley Pound, would stump into the Submarine Tracking Plot on the walking-stick he had once waved across the huge wall chart in an arc to the west of the British Isles: 'This is where we shall defeat the enemy,' he had told the assembled staff.[11]

Initially tiny – it numbered some ten people in 1939 – by 1942 the Trade Division employed more than three hundred. The Trade Plot was 'ruled over by a [duty] naval commander and a lieutenant commander, with the help of the glamorous Miss McLeod', while the plot itself was maintained by a group of superannuated master-mariners 'all of whom had started their careers in the days of sail'. These gentlemen sat 'at large tables . . . [and] worked out the estimated daily [08.00 GMT] positions of [independent] merchant ships and convoys . . . In addition three naval lieutenants ruled respectively the Atlantic, Indian Ocean (including the Med) and the Pacific Ocean . . . charts on boards were held vertically and numbered pins with labels represented individual ships, with larger ones for convoys and red stars with black pins for reported U-boats . . . The rest of the staff, except for a few mature ladies and unfit men, were teenagers of at least School Certificate level. Entries were both male and female but of course the lads were called up at eighteen, so girls predominated.'[12]

'Girls' predominated elsewhere in the Admiralty, where by 1942 the volunteer officers intended for junior staff work at the Admiralty had been packed off to sea and replaced, in a moment of inspiration, by young naval officers' wives. These were known as the 'Second Sea Lord's Secret Ladies', and were sufficiently steeped in naval lore and practice to be useful if expedient replacements, requiring little training or induction into the need for confidentiality: it was their husbands and their husbands' colleagues who depended upon their good sense and discretion.[13]

At every port in Great Britain, throughout the Commonwealth and in many neutral and American ports, the Naval Control of Shipping Officers (NCSOs) acted as the Admiralty's 'ambassadors'. Usually retired captains or commanders, or older reservists with intimate knowledge of merchant ship practice, they handled movements in convoy assembly ports and anchorages, issued and checked code books and other instructions making up the 'confidential books', addressed the individual concerns of masters, saw to the provision of special convoy stores, from zig-zag clocks to fog-buoys, made good shortfalls in defence equipment and ammunition, co-ordinated emergency repairs, pilotage and port services, accepted any masters' reports of defects, and made provision for the conference that preceded every convoy. In fact the NCSO supplied the services of agent between the master and the Admiralty for that part of the master's duty that obligated him to the State rather than to the principals interested in his ship's cargo. This therefore meant that the NCSO was responsible for informing the Admiralty of the actual, rather than the planned, constitution of a convoy at the time of its departure. An NCSO was supported by boarding officers who were whisked about between the ships assembling convoy in motor-launches manned by crews which, towards the end of the war, often consisted of young women of the Women's Royal Naval Service (WRNS).

One element of the unsung work of this neglected aspect of the convoy system was the usefulness of the NCSOs' reports in gauging the morale of the merchant seamen, a factor of growing significance as the war dragged on and merchant shipping losses mounted. This was of particular importance in the convoy assembly ports of Canada before the United States entered the war. Much anti-British feeling was generated in the United States, whither many British and Allied merchant ships went to discharge and load for the next east-bound convoy. Given the polyglot nature of many of the crews, it was easy for German agents and sympathisers to peddle the line that 'Britain would fight to the last drop of Polish, Norwegian, Dutch and Danish blood'. There was also a risk of sabotage, and rumours (dangerous in themselves) soon spread, alleging that delayed detonation bombs were being put in cargoes loaded in American ports. There had been a spate of this sort of subversive activity during the First World War, and intelligence suggested that the Germans were investing considerable sums of money in it. Moreover, prior to the German attack on the Soviet Union in the summer of 1941, while Germany and Russia were amicably carving up Poland between them, there was a paranoid conviction that Communist infiltrators were at work against British imperial and capitalist interests, fomenting trouble among the crews of merchant ships, at the very least attempting to increase the wages paid to seamen and firemen by causing unrest and withdrawal of labour. At its worst, crew trouble consisted of drink-related disturbances, deliberate delays, spontaneous sit-down strikes, desertion and, occasionally, deliberate damage to engines and machinery.

In British ports, evidence of disaffection was sought out by officers from MI5, an almost unbelievable piece of crass stupidity: in the Canadian ports this work was left to the officers of Canada's Boarding Service, the active branch of the Royal Canadian Navy's Naval Control of Shipping organisation. Initially the Canadian government in Ottawa tried to adopt the draconian measure of forcibly conscripting British merchant seamen judged guilty of disaffection into the Canadian infantry, and by an Order in Council empowered their Naval Boarding Service to detain and prosecute even foreign seamen found misbehaving aboard ships awaiting convoy. However, the Royal Canadian Naval Reserve's officers and boarding teams adopted instead a policy of gaining the confidence of merchant seamen and distinguishing between trouble-makers and those with genuine and rectifiable grievances. The policy rapidly bore fruit. Free of the rigid class distinctions and cultural divisions between British merchant and naval personnel, the Canadians made a vital contribution in allaying many fears and righting many wrongs at a stage in the war when a wholesale collapse of morale among Allied merchant seamen would have been nothing less than catastrophic. Fortunately, at the Admiralty the Director of the Trade Division, Captain B.B. Schofield, perceived this, and in complimenting the Royal Canadian Naval authorities in Ottawa in 1942 on the excellence of their Boarding Services, candidly admitted that 'nothing is done over here [in Britain] to bolster the morale of our Allied seamen, *or even our own* [my emphasis: RW] and that MI5 provide the wrong sort of security officers. They aren't sailors and the [merchant ships'] masters resent them. Your [Canadian] Naval Boarding Service is . . . much better . . .'

As Admiral Napier had long since pointed out, seamen were 'the devil in harbour'. Drink and unaccustomed liberty ashore played their part, of course, along with fear and apprehension as the ships swung round their anchors and awaited orders to proceed, but poor conditions and bad food contributed, as did the perceptions of the public. In Canada, as elsewhere, civilian-clothed merchant seamen were taunted: like Canadian males who evaded war-service, they were called 'zombies'. Under the circumstances it was an unwarrantable slander.

The concentration of merchant shipping awaiting vital eastbound convoys in such anchorages as Bedford Basin at Halifax in Nova Scotia meant that the officers and ratings of the Canadian Boarding Service became intimately concerned with the business of convoy, and their close association with the masters and crews of the assembling ships led them to make clear distinctions of quality between ships' companies as well as between the vessels themselves. 'Certain nations, and within them certain shipping lines, maintained standards of performance that made them the front line of the maritime community . . .' wrote Commander Frederick Watt. 'With long service under a single house flag, their tradition of seamanship was as jealously guarded as that of any other long-established calling. These were the elite, the men who could be expected to obey . . . [and] to accept casualties . . . There was [also] a type of independent-minded seaman who seemed to prefer a berth lacking spit-and-polish or an ordered future, who yet had his own brand of grainy pride, competence and dependability. But', Watt points out, 'beyond that category were the embittered, the slovenly and the fearful – mariners to whom the sea was an economic fact of life, inescapable because there was nowhere else to turn. They were exploited by their masters [and their owners] on the basis of that hard truth.'[14]

In the larger ports of neutral nations where British or British-chartered shipping might be expected to load or discharge, NCSOs were attached to the consular staff and wore plain clothes.[15] In smaller neutral ports, naval liaison was conducted by the consular officer whose peace-time duties habitually brought him into day-to-day contact with merchant masters.[16]

After its entry into the war, the United States Navy introduced a similar system of Port Directors analogous to, and dovetailing with, the established British *modus operandi*, thus releasing American-based Royal Navy NCSO officers for sea-going duties.

The Admiralty had effectively begun its work in converting the Mercantile Marine into a Merchant Navy in June 1939 with the formation of a section devoted to the defensive arming of British merchantmen and to the training of both reservists and merchant seamen to man the guns once fitted. Initially, and with the co-operation of ship-owners, this meant the structural strengthening already referred to as ships came into dock for routine survey, maintenance or repair work. A few, such as the 11,402-ton Bibby liner *Worcestershire* built in 1930 with government backing because she was intended for trooping, had included integral gun emplacements that wanted only the actual mounting of the weapon to convert them into Armed Merchant Cruisers.

To accomplish all this it was necessary to garner and bring forward from storage sufficient weapons of a low-angle medium calibre for anti-submarine defence, as well as small-calibre anti-aircraft weapons. At this stage of the war the primitive 1916-designed Hotchkiss, Lewis or Marlin machine-guns provided a small measure of anti-aircraft capability, but they were in very short supply and many deep-water merchantmen went without them. The provision of anti-submarine guns was haphazard. Most were of 4-inch calibre, having been removed from scrapped warships: many pre-dated 1900, and not a few of these were of Japanese manufacture. The Blue Funnel cargo-liner *Maron*, for example, requisitioned as an armed Ocean Boarding Vessel, was intended for use in distant-water contraband control and convoy escort as a smaller, supplementary form of merchant cruiser. *Maron* was fitted with two 6-inch guns, one dated 1903, the other 1897. In another of Alfred Holt's ships, the *Glenstrae*, the Japanese 4.7-inch gun 'blew up during a practice shoot, killing two of the gun's crew'.

Once war broke out merchantmen were equipped with impressive speed, but at this early stage not all crew members welcomed defensive armament, clinging with more hope than logic to their non-combatant status. Most submitted to the inevitable and embraced the basic weapons training provided. Supplementary, extemporised devices such as the Holman projector, which used steam power to throw a grenade into the air, or PAC equipment, by which means a parachute and cable were carried upwards by rocket and in slowly subsiding were intended to entangle low-flying aircraft, were also supplied, as were barrage balloons, kites and paravanes. Streamed from either bow from an 'A'-shaped frame, the paravanes were intended to provide minesweeping capabilities. Many merchantmen were degaussed – 'wiped' with a low-voltage current designed to neutralise their inherent magnetic field and render them safe from magnetic mines. Merchantmen already carried lifesaving gear and survival stores in their lifeboats. As the war progressed and the mounting losses of skilled seafarers began to cause serious concern, these basics were improved and augmented by additional flotation devices such as crude rafts, and later the Carley life-raft.

Impressive though these measures might have appeared to many seamen – and on 6 December Churchill, as First Lord of the Admiralty, stated that one thousand merchantmen had been armed for self-defence – they failed to equip all British merchant ships. The situation worsened after Dunkirk, when the British Expeditionary Force abandoned its heavy weapons, tanks and transport in retreating, and subsequently required to be completely re-armed. In terms of priority as well as quality of weaponry the Merchant Navy lost out, though by the end of 1940 approximately 3,400 vessels had received some form of defensive armament. In due course Bofors and Oerlikon guns were fitted to many merchantmen, but it was not until the great ship-building programmes in the United States and Canada got under way that adequate modern armament was provided as standard on merchantmen destined for the Battle of the Atlantic.

In the first instance it was the ships' own crews who were to man these weapons. In the major ports gunnery schools were set up in empty ware-houses where mock weapons were fired at crude models of aircraft descending at speed down taut wires from the roof. These 'defence courses' took two forms: training on the light anti-aircraft weapons, and instruction on the 12-pounder and 4-inch guns, which required a more sophisticated establishment. Many reserve drill halls, conveniently located in ports, were used to process about 150,000 merchant seamen gunners. Aboard ship one of the officers, usually the third mate, was put in charge of the main arma-ment, and he was at the beginning of the war usually assisted by an ex-Royal Navy gunner, a retired man recalled for war service. These two would train up their own team from the raw material to hand, but the professional gunner actually laid and fired the gun in action. As time passed and demand grew, dedicated gun crew cadres were provided from the naval and Royal Marine reserves, and the numbers of servicemen augmenting the merchant crew increased. By the end of the war many thousands had been assigned to serve at sea in merchant ships by the DEMS Organisation, a branch of the Admiralty; the acronym stood for 'Defensively Equipped Merchant Ships', and they were known as 'DEMS ratings'. Shortfalls of personnel trained in the more sophisticated anti-aircraft weapons such as the Oerlikon that came into service later in the war compelled the Admiralty to request help from the War Office, and what became the Maritime Regiment of Royal Artillery was established.[17] The presence of these men had a psycho-logical effect in stiffening the morale of merchant seafarers, which by late 1942 had been much damaged by losses and by a perception that their naval escorts were failing to defend them adequately.

Whether or not an individual merchant seaman thought the defensive armament of his ship was impressive, undesirable or simply inadequate was a matter for him, but as the nature of the war at sea became increasingly bleak, the seriousness with which the Admiralty undertook the arming of merchant ships, despite being long frustrated by lack of *matériel*, may be judged by the fact that in April 1941 it appointed an Inspector of Merchant Navy Gunnery in the person of Admiral Sir Frederick Dreyer, 'a very senior officer of long experience with weapons'. Dreyer put some ginger into the matter; moreover, he had direct access to Churchill.[18]

It might be supposed from the foregoing that the Merchant Navy had in some way been subsumed by its grander and senior service, and that every merchantman had in some way become a naval auxiliary. A number of liners *were* requisitioned to become Armed Merchant Cruisers. Other lesser vessels were taken up and fully converted to auxiliary anti-aircraft cruisers, while not a few fast cargo-liners were also taken over as military transports under naval command with a mixed naval/merchant crew; such vessels became HM Ships and flew the white ensign. Similarly, a number of tankers and some smaller vessels intended as rescue ships were taken up as non-commissioned naval auxiliaries under the blue ensign. There were even isolated cases of a few vessels which had their regular, civilian crews replaced by a naval ship's company. Such were exceptions however, and the general supposition would be wide of the mark.[19]

In fact, 'Naval Control of Shipping' (NCS) had a very limited meaning; effectively, it signified the Admiralty's right and responsibility to direct the movement of British-registered merchant shipping on the high seas. The Admiralty did not dictate where a vessel sailed or, necessarily, unless the vessel had been chartered or requisitioned by the State, what cargo she carried. It *did*, however, decide whether she sailed in convoy or, if she was capable of a speed in excess of 15 knots and thus declared an 'independent', what route she should take in order to avoid anticipated dangers. In short, 'the Admiralty were not concerned with the commerical aspect of the [individual merchant] ship, but with the safety of the vessel itself'.[20]

That said, it must be appreciated that in 1939–40 the British-registered merchant fleet, that is to say all those vessels entitled and obliged to wear the British red ensign, comprised ships owned not only in the United Kingdom of Great Britain and Northern Ireland but also those owned in the Dominions, such as Canada and Australia, or indeed anywhere else in the British Commonwealth and Empire, such as the Crown Colony of Hong Kong where Anglo-Chinese companies owned numerous vessels. After the German occupation of Denmark in April 1940, Danish vessels outside Danish waters were re-registered as British, though they retained their native masters and crews; following the Fall of France in May, Free French vessels were also taken in under the British flag, and in some cases British masters were appointed to them. Polish, Dutch and Belgian ships came over in the same way.

The case of the Norwegian merchant fleet, whose oil-tankers have been mentioned, was most important. By November 1939 an awareness of tanker-tonnage deficiencies in the British merchant fleet had led to the conclusion of an Anglo-Norwegian Shipping Agreement designed to facilitate chartering, especially of tankers. On the invasion of Norway by Germany in early April 1940, one of the first acts of the Norwegian government as it went into exile in Britain was to order all Norwegian merchant ships then on the high seas to proceed to British ports and place themselves under the control of the British authorities. On 25 April a Norwegian Shipping and Trade Mission was established in London; in July another office was opened in New York, and this was followed by fifty more branches throughout the world. By this means all free Norwegian shipping was chartered to the British government.[21] For the purposes of import and, to a lesser extent, export management, all these vessels thus became notionally British, while Polish, Dutch and Belgian ships became so *de facto*.

This was just as well, because insofar as planning for war was concerned, 'the entire bureaucracy functioned at a level of statistical *naïveté* surprising even for its time'.[22] In April 1937 the Mercantile Marine Department of the Board of Trade, the Merchant Navy's regulating authority, had, like the Ministry of Transport in respect of the ports, been empowered and vested with the further task of considering the adequacy of merchant shipping to answer the nation's demands in wartime. The result was close to catastrophic. No proper calculations were made to gauge the effects of war upon the carrying capacity of the British merchant fleet, or the demands that direct support of the armed services in, for example, transporting an expeditionary force to fight abroad would make on its ships. No notice was taken of the effects of routeing which would increase voyage time and therefore affect the speed of the supply chain. Furthermore, there was an astonishing lack of co-ordinated debate between government departments: for instance the Committee of Imperial Defence sub-committee on Food Supply in Time of War had suggested that the civil population could subsist on a lower level of food during hostilities. This led to an assumption by the Mercantile Marine Department of the Board of Trade that a 25 per cent reduction in imports would provide additional capacity for handling the sinews of war. Simultaneously another government department, considering the purchase of foodstuffs in wartime, decided that it would be prudent to increase its demand by one-quarter, on the not unwise assumption that a significant percentage would be destroyed in transit by enemy action. In its own assessment of potential losses of tonnage, the Mercantile Marine Department thought that British shipyards would be able to better peace-time production figures, taking no account in its calculations of diversion to warship production, deficits in raw materials, drains on labour through conscription, let alone direct disruption from enemy bombing! Although it contained the important Sea Transport Organisation which dealt with the formal requisition of merchant ships for military and associated war-related tasks, the Department proved incapable of the lateral thinking necessary to cope with the additional demands of war. Its faulty conclusions and failure to seek advice from ship-owners in the preparation of its analyses must stand as charges against it, particularly as it pronounced magisterially that 'British shipping is adequate for the first year of war'.

These fallacies, falsehoods and follies ultimately resulted in the serious supply crisis of 1941 already alluded to. But long before this the dangers had been exposed, and it was clear that the matter could only be solved by the establishment of a government ministry dedicated to shipping. There was in existence an unactivated provision for reviving the model from the First World War 'should the need arise', and that this was not done is further evidence of the incompetence of the authorities properly to address the very serious matter of national supply. It was not until 13 October 1939, *six weeks after the outbreak of war*, that the Ministry of Shipping was formed, coincidentally with the formation of the Admiralty's Anti-Submarine Warfare Division. The new Ministry immediately subsumed the Mercantile Marine Department of the Board of Trade, including the Sea Transport Organisation. Although the new Minister responsible had himself no direct experience of shipping, the Parliamentary Secretary, Sir Arthur Salter, like the Director-General and the Statistical Adviser, had served in the Ministry's previous incarnation in the First World War.

One of the early tasks of the Ministry was to examine the effects of the first weeks of war, whereupon it made the alarming discovery that imports had been halved. This was largely due to the reduction in foreign-flagged ships delivering cargoes to Britain and the disruption caused by the delays inherent in the convoy system, coinciding with the temporary precautionary closure of the east-coast ports and the Mediterranean. The reopening of the latter would ameliorate the situation, but improvement could only be guaranteed if there was no dramatic change in the strategic situation, a hope that foundered with the capitulation of the French and the opening of the German bombing offensive against British ports.

Thus the situation went from bad to worse as the effects of the Fall of France combined with the inherent inadequacies in the import system, the competing demands of the government purchasing agencies, which had failed to build up stocks of supplies essential in the event of a war, and the significant drain on capacity to provide the Royal Navy with Armed Merchant Cruisers, most of which were soon sunk. With three authorities – the Trade Division of the Admiralty, the Ministry of Shipping and the Ministry of Transport – seeking to cope, not to mention the actual owners of the vessels, largely represented by the Chamber of Shipping in London and the Liverpool Steamship Owners' Association, it was perhaps not surprising that things remained woefully unco-ordinated. The problems seemed likely to remain insuperable unless and until drastic measures were taken to combine responsibility for the *total* movement of all goods, food-stuffs, raw materials and war *matériel* under a single administrative authority. At last, on 9 May 1941, an Order-in-Council amalgamated the Ministries of Shipping and Transport into a single Ministry of War Transport (MoWT) under Mr F. J. Leathers. If this crucial and vastly influential measure did not actually transform matters overnight, it provided the bedrock upon which improvements could be progressively built.

A further complication was the need for the British government itself to acquire raw materials like iron ore and bauxite with which to support the war effort. On the very eve of war the need to safeguard supplies of such commodities had caused furious diplomatic activity which on Saturday 4 November 1939 resulted in President Roosevelt modifying the American Neutrality Act. This act had been intended to keep the United States out of a second European war, but Roosevelt's new clauses excepted Britain and France from its provisions, repealing the embargo on the export of arms supplies and war materials to the two allies on a 'cash and carry' basis, requiring only that their own merchant ships should pick up in North American ports the cargoes of armaments manufactured in the United States. Once France had fallen, the transport of these increasingly varied cargoes, loaded in private merchant ships to the account of the British government, required the chartering of hundreds of merchant ships over and above those required for carrying the normal, everyday trade of goods imported for market distribution and consumption.

The role of government agent responsible for handling the manifold aspects of this task fell in due course upon the Ministry of Shipping and its successor, the MoWT. In addition to vessels from imperial British resources and the associated ships of Norway, Denmark and France, the MoWT began to charter merchantmen from other sources, notably the flags-of-convenience merchant fleets of Panama, Liberia and Honduras, most of which were beneficially owned in the United States, and were clamouring for employment. But other neutral nations, such as Sweden, made tonnage available, and also took advantage of the offered convoy protection to cover their passages.

Most prominent among foreign ship-owners eager to profit from Britain's state of war with Germany were the Greeks, who chartered vessels to Britain and Canada, raising the level of their seamen's wages from a pittance of $30 per month to a staggering $210, an indication of the proportional profits made by the owners themselves. When Greece was itself occupied the Greek government-in-exile, anxious to keep its national fleet employed and earning revenue, reduced their seamen's wage to its former equivalence with the British 'Board of Trade' rate; desertions from Greek ships followed, particularly when they were in North American ports and open to the allure of voyages on charter in the then neutral-flagged vessels of the United States, which could earn a wage of $1,000 per month. Such were the inequities and complexities besetting the merchant seafarer as he plied his embittered trade in wartime.[23]

In due course the Ministry of War Transport also became effectively the 'owner' of the standard war tonnage, the 'Liberty', 'Ocean', 'Park' and 'Fort' type ships, the 'Empires', the 'C'-series fast cargo-vessels and the 'T'-series tankers built variously in the United States, Britain and Canada for the British government. The MoWT was also responsible for those enemy merchant vessels captured at sea or in port and taken into British service.[24] Ships such as these, actually 'owned' by the Ministry of War Transport, became increasingly important as trans-Atlantic lading gradually comprised the increasingly military cargoes that enabled Britain slowly to assume the offensive. Military support of the Russians by way of the Arctic in 1941 and sustaining Malta in the Mediterranean and the Eighth Army in the Western Desert were followed by the three great Allied invasions, that of North Africa in November 1942, Sicily in July 1943 and finally France in June 1944, all of which required shipments of vast quantities of men, arms and armour and the logistic *matériel* without which they could achieve little. Military convoys to Malta and the Western Desert excepted, after the entry of the United States into the war in December 1941, Britain and her European maritime allies shared this enormous burden with the United States Mercantile Marine.

It became usual for the Ministry of War Transport to subcontract the actual management of their vessels to a recognised British shipping company, just one example of the extraordinary synthesis that was eventually successfully established between the commercial shipping industry and a government at war. Final victory owed much to the close, interlinked co-operation between all branches of the commercial shipping industry, from owners to builders, from seafarers to shipping clerks, and its complex but functional integration with the naval administration. It was this, as much as the conversion of hundreds of ships from their individual company liveries to armed and uniformly grey vessels steaming in convoy, which transformed the British Mercantile Marine into a functioning Merchant Navy that also included the exiled merchantmen of Nazi-occupied nations. Arguments may well have raged and personalities clashed inside committee rooms, just as they did over conditions on board or cargo-handling or repair work on the quayside, but where the disagreement could not be resolved a system was developed by which the pros and cons were passed up the chain of command, if necessary to the War Cabinet itself, where the final decision carried all the gravity of absolute authority and was invariably accepted when handed back down the line.

So much for the inefficiencies and bumbling of 18 months from which developed the effective administration behind what became an immense convoy system. At sea some form of equivalent 'official' control was also required to convert a disparate group of merchant vessels into a bound and biddable convoy, and first of all it was vital to have some competent authority able to liaise at sea with the senior officer commanding the naval escort.

Among merchant officers the basic requirements such as conforming to a common speed, being capable of manoeuvring in company and obeying a prescribed zig-zag pattern, of proficiency at inter-ship signalling and so forth, were generally well understood. And while the actual practice of such niceties presented those in charge of unrelated merchant vessels with challenges that only time and practice would or could perfect, it was still necessary to form a command-and-control structure to which all masters owed allegiance and which conveyed authority and discipline to the often extraordinary mixture of vessels making up a typical North Atlantic 'Slow Trade Convoy'. This was provided by a 'Convoy Commodore' and his small signals staff. These peripatetic groups, divided into Ocean or Coastal categories, moved from one convoy to another, often with little remission. Most of those who served as commodores of ocean convoys were retired admirals and captains – some, like Dreyer before his subsequent appointment, of remarkably senior rank – who returned to the colours and served in conditions that contrasted dramatically with their earlier naval experiences; their age – most were over 60 – was a tribute to their hardihood as much as their patriotism; others were senior captains in the Royal Naval Reserve; but all submitted to the exigencies of war and put up with the privations aboard merchant ships, many of which were ill-equipped to support additional personnel of such quondam grandeur. Later in the war officers of the Royal Norwegian and Royal Netherlands Navy joined the ranks of the two hundred or so dogged men who strove for the safe passage of their ocean convoys. Granted the anomalous rank of Commodore 2nd Class in the RNR, these stoic souls were responsible for maintaining a convoy's cohesion, its speed, its course, its general discipline, and its behaviour in the face of the enemy.

Typical of the breed was Admiral Goldsmith, born in 1880, who had suffered several setbacks in his naval career, having on one occasion incurred Their Lordships' 'severe displeasure'. He had nevertheless served in the 9th Destroyer Flotilla at the Battle of Jutland and afterwards made something of a name for himself by sailing his own yacht to Malta in order to take up his appointment as King's Harbour Master at Valletta. By the time he was retired in 1931 he had reached flag-rank, but on 4 September 1939 Goldsmith was back in harness as a mere convoy commodore, sailing on the 7th with the first of the thirty-eight trade convoys he was to conduct across the Atlantic Ocean. He did not rate his new task too highly: 'I hate my job like poison,' he declared at the height of the Battle of the Atlantic, 'it is so dull.'[25]

Occasionally a commodore of the old school could prove difficult. When Convoy HX107 arrived in Barry Roads in February 1941, the commodore announced that he 'did not wish to leave' the *Harmala* 'until 9 a.m.' Such were the constraints of tidal and berthing limitations in the Bristol Channel that this meant a 'twenty four hour delay' before the *Harmala* could pass through the locks at Barry to discharge her cargo.[26]

It was usual to select a suitable vessel for a commodore, a cargo-liner with passenger accommodation if possible, or one of the faster freighters, and she was denominated by flying the commodore's broad pendant, a white, swallow-tailed flag quartered by a blue cross. A commodore was supported by vice and rear commodores, usually experienced masters of proven ability and assiduity who were ready to take over the direction of the convoy should the commodore's ship be sunk. The commodore's vessel was stationed at the head of the centre column of the convoy with his deputies scattered elsewhere within a formation that generally consisted of between 30 and 40 vessels deployed in up to a dozen parallel columns extending on a broad front of up to six or seven miles. Convoys were broader than they were deep, with the outermost, vulnerable columns generally consisting of ships carrying bulk cargoes, the inner columns comprising the more valuable cargoes of oil, munitions or war *matériel*.

A commodore's small personal staff was led by a yeoman of signals, a petty officer specialising in communications, with a telegraphist skilled in the Morse code and three young conscripted 'Hostilities Only' ratings 'trained as signalmen but without the need for experience in Fleet procedures. They carried considerable responsibility and were, without exception, highly efficient visual signallers.'[27] A brace of such paragons was supplied to the vice commodore, and they were also assisted by the regular merchant radio officers attached to the ship, with the young cadets or apprentices providing additional help; it was, of course, their opposite numbers on the other vessels in convoy who were the recipients of and respondents to the commodore's signals. These youngsters became adept signallers. Their biggest problem was reading the coloured hoists of international code flags in damp, windless weather, when they clung to their halliards, or in winds which blew them in inconvenient directions.[28]

Thus ran the threads of control throughout the imperfect fabric of the British Merchant Navy, its exiled allies and chartered, flag-of-convenience and neutral co-habitants, interweaving with the Ministry of War Transport's own ships, those loaded hulls which formed the very 'trade' upon which Britain depended for survival. But while they lay at the heart of the matter, huddled in convoy for mutually passive support, what of those whose duty it was to protect the invaluable assets of these ships and their lading?

4

'The night was monstrous with threat'

Admiral Graf Spee

THE ROYAL NAVY had been cheated of the prestigious prize of the Norddeutscher Lloyd's *Bremen*,[1] but it quickly stifled German overseas trade. Forced to pass through the Denmark Strait or the Iceland–Shetland gap, German merchantmen were intercepted by the British Northern Patrol. In generally poor and often appalling weather, elderly naval cruisers and an increasing number of Armed Merchant Cruisers, plus some trawlers converted to Armed Boarding Vessels, all under the able direction of Admiral Max Horton, stopped ship after ship, both German and neutral, sending the suspect among them into Kirkwall in the Orkneys.[2] Here they were subjected to a formal 'examination' for contraband. Elsewhere other German ships were intercepted and destroyed; many were scuttled by their crews to avoid the ignominy of capture.[3]

One way or another, by the end of September 1939 some 300,000 tons of goods destined for Germany had been seized. Combined with the immobilisation of German merchantmen in foreign ports, amounting to a tonnage of some 750,000, it foreshadowed the end of the German mercantile marine, with the exception of a handful of daring blockade-runners. It was a gratifying start for the British, prompting the Prime Minister, Neville Chamberlain, to make these successes known to the House of Commons. To them Churchill added his claim that a thousand merchant ships had been armed for self-defence, and on 6 December told the House that U-boats were being destroyed at the rate of between two and four a week. The reported sinking of a U-boat by a bomber of the RAF on 18 September and the escape of the Union Castle liner *Warwick Castle* and the cargo-vessel *Chloris* a week earlier, in conjunction with an 'acceptable' loss of 18 vessels during the month of October, seemed to indicate that the Admiralty's provision for the protection of trade was adequate, at least until the implementation of the wholesale movement of merchantmen in convoy could contain the German submarine threat. Indeed, the very paucity of Dönitz's resources made it a fact, at least for the time being. Not only was the number of U-boats well short of what Dönitz needed to prosecute the campaign he had envisaged, but those that were operational were compelled to pass through the same northern seas as their merchant brethren, a gauntlet to be run between the British Home Fleet and its destroyers in the Orkneys and Vice Admiral Horton's cruisers at sea between the string of islands that extended from Scotland to Greenland.

The Admiralty's policy was to contain the Kriegsmarine and German aggression within the North Sea, just as it had in the First World War. To this end, trade protection was to be provided for by the building of general-purpose 'Hunt'-class escort destroyers, short-range 'Flower'-class patrol vessels, and sloops fitted with a predominantly anti-aircraft armament and equipped for mine warfare. None of these were envisaged as trans-Atlantic convoy escorts. Furthermore, in 1939 three-quarters of RAF Coastal Command's strength was deployed to provide air cover over the North Sea and eastern Channel coasts of Britain. Only one air group was intended for service over the Western Approaches.

The escort destroyers and the 'short range patrol vessels' were the result of an appraisal conducted in late 1938 which revealed the lack of convoy escorts. While the escort destroyers were to be built conventionally, the Admiralty sensibly decided that the urgency of their requirements necessitated a quick response, and for the 'short range patrol vessels' accepted a design from Smith's Dock and Engineering Company, on Tees-side in the north-east of England, based on their whale-catcher *Southern Pride*. As a type, the whale-catcher was renowned for its reasonable turn of speed and its ability to respond to sudden helm alterations in its pursuit of cetaceans. It thus lent itself to the Admiralty's basic requirements, and with some modifications the concept was finalised. The construction followed merchant ship-building practice, using standard merchant-ship steam reciprocating engines and the simple scotch boiler; it dispensed with twin screws, reduction gearing, gun-fire control, and a range of sophisticated equipment usually considered indispensable even in a minor man-of-war. The simplicity of the new 'Flower'-class meant that orders could be placed in commercial yards, some of them quite small, which could in turn draw on standard machinery and boilers already in production for the commercial market. This adaptability extended even to auxiliary plant: the 'Flowers', for instance, handled their anchors and forward moorings with a mercantile windlass, rather than naval capstans. In addition to their ease and speed of construction, the 'Flower'-class were relatively cheap and, most importantly, lent themselves to rapid mastery by the inexperienced crews sent to man them.

HMS *Anemone* was ordered in July 1939; by the time her hull was launched on 22 April 1940 it was becoming increasingly obvious that the new vessels *would* be required to serve as convoy escorts in the Atlantic. As their perceived role changed, so did their name. Churchill himself, mindful that the design had been shared with the French navy, advocated the adoption of the French term 'corvette' which had become fashionable at the end of the Napoleonic War for small sloops. 'Sloop' was not available, having been allocated to a number of specialist vessels already building or in service. The most notable of these were the *Black Swan*-class, which were to achieve fame as first-rate anti-submarine vessels.

When *Anemone* left the river Wear that August, she was but the first of almost three hundred sisters, 148 of which were built in Britain for the Royal Navy together with 16 for the Free French, to add to the four they had themselves completed before their defeat. In Canada 130 were built, of which 25 went to the United States Navy when the Americans found themselves desperately short of escorts (see chapter 5). The corvettes' main disadvantage was that they had been designed for the short, steep seas of the tidal North Sea; in the open Atlantic, their round-bilged hulls rolled horribly and pitched badly. Later modifications in *Verbena* and her successors, such as extending the forecastle, made them drier and more comfortable, but their 200-foot hull was simply not long enough for ocean work.

As the Royal Navy gradually subsumed the free navies of occupied countries for operational purposes, corvettes were seen wearing the ensigns of almost every Allied nation. In addition to Britain, Canada and the United States, escaped members of the Belgian pilotage service manned one 'Flower'-class corvette, the Greeks four, the Royal Yugoslavian Navy one and the Dutch another, while along with several Free French corvettes one, *La Malouine*, was under 'joint management' and flew the British white ensign and the French *tricolore* side-by-side. Wartime modifications and alterations continually updated these small men-of-war, and by 1943 they were fitted with a greatly improved anti-aircraft armament and radar. But it was the original fitting of sonar and of depth-charges launched from both mortars and racks which made them a potent anti-submarine weapon. A later addition was the forward-firing 'Hedgehog' anti-submarine 'bomb', which allowed the corvette to attack a submarine located ahead of it, rather than having to wait until it had passed over its quarry and risk losing contact as the U-boat commander took last-minute evasive action in the short but vital hiatus.

An improved corvette type, the 'Castle'-class, was later produced, with a longer hull and forward-firing 'Squid' anti-submarine weapon, but the subsequent larger and faster vessels of the 'Bay'- and 'River'-classes, many of which were built in Canada and served in the Royal Canadian Navy, provided a more effective convoy escort and anti-submarine weapons platform. These later and larger classes of faster escort vessels revived another moribund ship-type and marked their superior status to corvettes by being classified as 'frigates'. Nevertheless, corvettes continued to be built and commissioned as warships up to 1944, and while many last orders were cancelled, a number of hulls were completed as convoy rescue ships, entirely equipped for caring for the crews of torpedoed merchantmen.

With an initial sprinkling of regular naval officers and a greater proportion of regular petty officers, these vessels were largely manned by officers and ratings from the reserves, the Royal Naval Reserve (RNR) and the Royal Naval Volunteer Reserve (RNVR), along with the conscripted 'Hostilities Only' ratings. While the RNR personnel were drawn from the merchant service and adapted to the simple 'Flower'-class with comparative ease, the inexperienced RNVR and HO officers and ratings suffered grievously from sea-sickness in corvettes, which it was asserted would roll upon wet grass.

Despite the immediate attacks of German U-boats and a commensurate lack of action on the part of any German surface commerce-raiders, the Admiralty remained convinced that it was the latter which posed the real threat to British trade. In Berlin, Hitler vacillated over how best to prosecute the naval war, hoping that in the wake of the swift fall of Poland the French and British could be persuaded to seek peace. Since no such overtures were received Grossadmiral Raeder, aware that time favoured the British, persuaded the Führer to relax the restrictions imposed on Dönitz's U-boats, and on 24 September orders were given to commence mercantile war against France and to open fire on any merchantmen, including neutrals, who used their radios to broadcast notice of submarine attack. Two days later, at 17.43 on the 26th, a signal was transmitted to the two *Panzerschiffen* at sea. The *Admiral Graf Spee* had reached the South Atlantic while her sister-ship, the *Deutschland*, remained in the North Atlantic off Greenland.

The *Admiral Graf Spee* was to attack first. Having refuelled from her supply ship *Altmark* she headed south towards the coast of Brazil. Off Pernambuco on the afternoon of 30 September 1939 the *Admiral Graf Spee* intercepted the cargo-liner *Clement*, engaged on the Booth Line's New York-to-Brazil service. Laden with a general cargo which included a large amount of cased petrol and paraffin, the *Clement* had left Pernambuco the previous day on the last part of her outward passage to Bahia. Captain Harris, thinking he was encountering a British cruiser, went below and changed into a clean set of tropical whites, only to have his illusions shattered by the appearance overhead of the *Panzerschiff*'s reconnoitring Arado seaplane with its unmistakable black cross. In contravention of Kapitän zur See Hans Langsdorff's orders the pilot, a Luftwaffe officer, opened fire, whereupon Harris transmitted his position and the RRRR signal indicating attack by a surface raider. There was no hindrance from Langsdorff; indeed, the German commander asked the Brazilian radio station at Pernambuco to send out an 'all ships' request for assistance to be rendered to the lifeboats containing the *Clement*'s people. Cunningly, Langsdorff signed his signal '*Admiral Scheer*', and when Harris and his chief engineer were taken aboard they saw the word 'Admiral' painted over in grey. On the bridge Langsdorff greeted his prisoners with an apology: 'I am sorry, Captain, but I have to sink your ship. We are, you see, at war.'

He failed to sink the Booth liner with two torpedoes and medium-calibre gunfire, however, despite the nature of much of her cargo, and was obliged to use his 11-inch guns. As the main armament opened fire at 16.40, Harris watched the *Clement* catch fire, then sink. She had been built by Cammell Laird on the Mersey only five years earlier; in addition to 25 rounds from the *Panzerschiff*'s 5.9-inch secondary armament, it took five 11-inch shells to despatch her. 'She's a damned tough ship,' he growled.[4]

A few hours later Langsdorff stopped the Greek steamer *Papalemos* for examination and, finding none of her cargo destined for Britain, put Harris and his chief engineer aboard her. As in the case of other captures made by Langsdorff, though the remaining crew members were left to fend for themselves, there was no loss of life from the *Clement*. Some were picked up by the Brazilian steamer *Itatinga* and disembarked at Maceio on 1 October, the rest landed safely on the Brazilian coast the next day. This gloss of chivalry earned Langsdorff a more respectable reputation than other German naval officers of his day among merchant seafarers, recalling that of Count von Lückner of the *Seeadler* in the previous war.[5] While undoubtedly prosecuting what he conceived to be an honourable *guerre de course*, Langsdorff was also playing a serious game of deception, for although he had extracted a promise from the master of the *Papalemos* to maintain radio silence until he reached the Azores, he knew that one way or another Harris would soon inform London that his ship had been sunk by the *Admiral Scheer*. This would raise two questions in the Admiralty: how had the Germans spirited the *Admiral Scheer* from the Schilling Roads, where she had been attacked by RAF Blenheims of 110 Squadron on 4 September, into the South Atlantic? and where were the *Admiral Graf Spee* and the *Deutschland*?

On 5 October Langsdorff struck again, this time south-east of Ascension Island, capturing the *Newton Beech*, a Newcastle tramp on her way to London from South Africa. Her weak RRRR signal was picked up by another merchant ship whose master passed it on to HMS *Cumberland* by lamp when he sighted the British cruiser on her way south, but for some reason it was neither acted upon nor passed on to the Commander-in-Chief, South Atlantic, Vice Admiral D'Oyly Lyon, who remained ignorant of Langsdorff's presence in his bailiwick. Meanwhile the German prize crew captured all the *Newton Beech*'s confidential books, which yielded information of considerable use to the B-Dienst Service operators on board the *Panzerschiff* as well as providing Langsdorff with the Admiralty's routeing instructions to British masters.[6]

Sifting through this material and taking other useful supplies out of the tramp-ship, Langsdorff kept the *Newton Beech* following astern of him as he headed towards another rendezvous with the *Altmark*. On his way he encountered the British tramp *Ashlea* on her way from Durban to Falmouth with a full cargo of sugar, and promptly sent her to the bottom using demolition charges. Two days later, on 9 October, Langsdorff again replenished from the *Altmark*. He was concerned by the amount of smoke the *Newton Beech* made, and as he had taken from her all he could use, she too was scuttled while he filled his bunkers. Before parting from the *Altmark*, Langsdorff sent his prisoners aboard her.

Next day, 10 October, some distance to the west of Ascension and flying the French *tricolore* the *Admiral Graf Spee* approached T. & J. Harrison's cargo-liner *Huntsman*. The French ensign was replaced by the Nazi Swastika as Langsdorff ordered the *Huntsman* to heave-to. Upon the surrender of his ship the master, Captain Brown, was given a receipt by the officer commanding the prize crew before the vessel's general cargo was plundered for supplies.[7]

Once more Langsdorff trailed his captive astern as he returned to another rendezvous with the *Altmark*. In the smooth sea conditions *Huntsman* was brought alongside the *Altmark* and part of her cargo was transferred to the supply ship. Brown and his crew joined the others held in custody by Kapitän H. Dau, while the *Admiral Graf Spee* herself loaded 80 tons of stores from the *Altmark*. Having served her captors well, the *Huntsman* was sunk. The *Admiral Graf Spee* and the *Altmark* now independently headed south-east, for the Cape of Good Hope, where Langsdorff anticipated rich pickings from the concentration of shipping to be found there. Off Walvis Bay on 22 October he sank the Hain tramp *Trevanion*, homeward bound from Port Pirie in Australia with a cargo of concentrates. The master ordered the RRRR signal to be transmitted; Radio-Officer Martinson courageously continued to send it after Langsdorff had opened fire on the *Trevanion*'s superstructure, and carried on until the German prize crew physically removed him from his Morse key. The signal was intercepted by the *Llanstephan Castle* which passed it to D'Oyly Lyon at Freetown, but Langsdorff wasted no time and headed south again after sinking the *Trevanion*.

Clear of the shipping lanes, Langsdorff and Dau had a further rendezvous to transfer fuel, and following an exchange of signals with Berlin Langsdorff decided to make for the Indian Ocean and strike at the Cape-to-Australia route before the inevitable hunt found his scent. To double the Cape of Good Hope he took the *Admiral Graf Spee* deep into the Southern Ocean.

During the same period Kapitän zur See P. Wennecker, moving the *Deustchland* undetected from Cape Farewell to operate on the rhumb line between Bermuda and the Azores, was also ordered to begin operations. On 5 October, the same day that Langsdorff captured the *Newton Beech*, the *Deutschland* was some five hundred miles east of Bermuda when she intercepted Turnbull, Scott's tramp *Stonegate* on her passage from Antofagasta towards Alexandria. As the *Deutschland* approached the RRRR signal stuttered out from the *Stonegate*, only ceasing when Wennecker opened fire. Taking off her crew, Wennecker sank the ship and her cargo of nitrate before heading north at speed, alarmed lest the *Stonegate*'s signal should start a hue and cry. Three days later the *Deutschland* hove in sight of the American freighter *City of Flint*, the same ship that had rendered assistance to the sinking *Athenia* five weeks earlier. Conceiving her cargo to be of use to his enemy, for she was east-bound with a freight consigned to Britain, Wennecker put a prize crew on board and ordered her to be taken first to Murmansk and then later to Germany. The seizure of the Moore, McCormack ship started an international row: Washington issued a strong protest to Berlin and Hitler, anxious to placate America, ordered the prize crew to take the ship into a neutral Norwegian port. Meanwhile the British Admiralty sent the cruiser *Glasgow* and some destroyers to intercept her.[8]

The *City of Flint* eluded them and arrived at Haugesund, where the Norwegian authorities immediately interned the prize crew and released her American company, allowing the vessel to proceed on her lawful occasions.[9] The Norwegians' action infuriated Hitler, but the *Deutschland*'s activities also alarmed him, just as they were alarming the British. The Führer was of a superstitious turn of mind, and the idea of losing Germany's most patriotically-named *Panzerschiff* compelled him to order Raeder to recall Wennecker. In the meantime, on 14 October, about four hundred miles east of Newfoundland, Wennecker had intercepted another neutral ship, the small Norwegian tramp-ship *Lorentz W. Hansen*, and compounded his sins by sinking her; moreover, he left her crew to fend for themselves in their boats. They were afterwards picked up by another ship and landed in the Orkneys on 21 October.

Anxious to continue harrying British trade, Raeder had dodged the issue of recalling Wennecker for three weeks, but now bowed to Hitler's increasingly strident insistence and signalled Wennecker to make his way home. Turning north, the *Deutschland* passed through the Denmark Strait on 8 November and then headed for the Norwegian coast, successfully evading British men-of-war and air patrols. On the 14th the *Panzerschiff* passed through the Skagerrak and the Kattegat heading for Gotenhafen, the new name for the German-occupied Polish port of Gdynia, where she berthed on 15 November. Such was Hitler's relief at the safe return of the *Deutschland* that, without reference to Raeder or the Oberkommando der Kriegsmarine, he immediately ordered her name changed to *Lützow*.

Judged by purely material standards, Wennecker's sortie was an abject failure. Nor did it score any points on the diplomatic front, having roused Norwegian and American ire in a way yet to be equalled by the British blockade. It did however confuse the British Admiralty, whose staff remained unaware of the locations of German raiders in the Atlantic until the *Lorentz W. Hansen*'s crew landed in the Orkneys. Even then they assumed that the *Panzerschiff* in the south was the *Admiral Scheer*, while the Commander-in-Chief of the Home Fleet, Admiral Forbes, once alerted to the danger in the north, had the two 'hunting groups' Force H and Force K, which were destined for the South Atlantic, searching for the *Deutschland* in the north until mid December.

But there was a powerful side-effect, one which continued to influence British naval strategy throughout the war whenever a heavy German warship was concerned. 'The mere presence of this powerful ship upon our main trade route', Churchill wrote afterwards of the *Deutschland*, 'had however imposed, as was intended, a serious strain upon our [convoy] escorts and hunting groups in the North Atlantic.' In this respect Wennecker had successfully implemented Raeder's big-ship policy: 'to maintain strategic pressure on the enemy's North Atlantic sea routes'.[10] Emphasising the desire of the Royal Navy to seek out and destroy the predator, Churchill concluded: 'We should in fact have preferred her activity to the vague menace she embodied.'[11]

Though unaware of the precise disposition of German raiders at sea, the Admiralty had quickly put matters in train to remove them, rapidly concerting plans with the French on 8 October to eliminate the threat to trade posed by the expected and classic actions of commerce-raiders. Now, however, as one sinking followed another, the worst fears of the Naval Staff seemed further emphasised by the news of *Deutschland* from Orkney. The Franco-British response was characteristically global, and several hunting groups, largely made up of cruisers, were soon deployed. In addition to *Cumberland* on her way to join *Exeter* flying the broad pendant of Commodore Harwood off the east coast of South America as Force G, the cruisers *Berwick* and *York* were to patrol between the West Indies and the North American coast as Force F. Force H, the cruisers *Shropshire* and *Sussex*, was to rendezvous off the Cape of Good Hope, with Force I off Ceylon (Sri Lanka) and Force K off Pernambuco. This last consisted of the carrier *Ark Royal* and the battle-cruiser *Renown*.[12] In October, in an operation aimed at cornering the *Deutschland* and protecting Convoy KJ4, the French despatched a *Force de Raide* under Vice Amiral Gensoul consisting of the battleship *Dunkerque*, three cruisers and eight large destroyers. It was a prodigious disposition, evidence of the gravity of the problem as perceived by the Allied admiralties.

At no time during her two and half months' cruise had the *Deutschland* approached, let alone attacked, an ocean convoy, the first of which had set out from Freetown, Sierra Leone on 14 September. Next day Convoy KJF1 sailed from Kingston, Jamaica. As Halifax became a primary convoy terminus, traffic from the West Indies was routed north before setting off across the Western Ocean, and it was from the anchorage at Halifax on the 16th that the first of the HX convoys, 'assembled with rough efficiency and in a surprisingly short time', left Bedford Basin heading east. The 18 merchantmen of Convoy HX1 were escorted out to sea by the Canadian destroyers HMCSs *St Laurent* and *Saguenay*. 'Awaiting them in the open sea were the British cruisers *Berwick* and *York*', yet to be sent south in pursuit of any raiders and providing the 'through ocean escort' as the short-legged Canadian destroyers of the 'local escort' turned back on the afternoon of the 17th, 353 miles east of Halifax. Thereafter Convoy HX1 disappeared into 'the sleety gloom of the Atlantic'.[13]

But Bedford Basin was not empty. Next day, the 17th, the 'fast' convoy HXF1, consisting of eight ships able to steam at a minimum of 15 knots, was escorted offshore by the destroyer HMCS *Fraser*. A week or so later, on the 23rd, HMCS *Skeena* saw the 15 vessels of Convoy HX2 into deep water. Such short-ranged anti-submarine escorts were barely adequate, but were all that could be managed at the time. Ocean escort at this stage was provided by cruisers, AMCs and elderly battleships, which had to combine this duty with the possibility of detaching to hunt down a located raider. On 4 October, for example, the *Berwick* and the Australian cruiser *Perth* were assigned to the escort of the large, 45-strong Convoy KJ3 from Kingston, though the *Perth* turned back on being relieved by the elderly *Effingham* in mid Atlantic. Meanwhile the 28 ships of Convoy HG1 had left for Britain from Gibraltar on the 6th: the system quickly cranked into gear. There were a few fast convoys, but vessels capable of speeds of over 15 knots usually made passages as 'independents', along advised routes. Like the fast ships which could out-run a surfaced U-boat, slow vessels incapable of 9 knots also usually made passage as 'independents', but they were particularly vulnerable and accounted for most of the losses to the enemy in the final months of 1939. In due course, these largely elderly but vitally capacious bottoms were garnered in a series of supplementary slow, 8-knot convoys.

Despite the inadequate escorts supplied, of the 5,756 ships that sailed in these early convoys only four were sunk by U-boats, although several were lost following the dispersal of convoys. In all, 221 vessels were destroyed between September and December. Dönitz's U-boats sank 110 vessels sailing alone, mines sent 78 to the bottom, and aircraft destroyed ten. Of the handful that remain unaccounted for, one was almost certainly torpedoed by a U-boat.[14]

Denied the numbers of U-boats he required, on 1 October Dönitz resolved to concentrate what he had into groups and attack 'those areas in which the enemy sea lines of communication converge and join'. The strength of air and sea patrols in the approaches to the Channel forced him to focus instead on the area north of Gibraltar, and he ordered Korvettenkapitän Hartmann, at 37 a seasoned officer, to take command of this first specially-organised 'Atlantic' group.

In the event, the first 'wolf-pack' attack largely miscarried. Nine boats were assigned to the operation but only six left port, and of these only three made the rendezvous. The first loss incurred was *U-40*, on her passage through the English Channel. She was a Type IX boat, and late leaving Germany; mistakenly believing it to be unmined, Dönitz had sent her down-Channel to catch up with Hartmann. Travelling at speed on the surface, *U-40* was sunk after striking a mine in the Dover Strait during the early hours of 13 October. Nine of her crew escaped, of whom three survived until daylight when they were rescued by British destroyers.[15]

On 4 October, while Hartmann's U-boats were on passage, Hitler gave Dönitz instructions to attack any darkened ship in the vicinity of the British Isles and the French coast, excepting passenger-liners but including neutrals. As a perfunctory nod to the Prize Regulations U-boat commanders were still expected to save the crews but – and it is a significant 'but' – they were not to endanger their submarines in doing so.

At this stage of the war, not all convoys continued in close order across the ocean; many were intended simply to shepherd merchantmen bound for various destinations out to sea and clear of the perceived danger area, beyond which they dispersed and proceeded independently. One such was the outward-bound Convoy OB17, which dispersed in the South West Approaches once its ships from Liverpool and the Bristol Channel were safely out of soundings. On 13 October Kapitänleutnant R. Dau in *U-42*, on his way to join Hartmann, sighted one of its members.

The Ropner tramp *Stonepool* was laden with coal and machinery for the Cape Verde Islands. At 06.15 that morning, over the low south-westerly swell, the chief officer on watch saw *U-42* three miles away on the port beam and immediately informed the master. Captain White reached the bridge and sounded the six short blasts of the ship's whistle that summoned the crew to their action stations. As he did so Dau fired a shot across the *Stonepool*'s bows and then, as the tramp began transmitting the SSSS signal, opened fire in earnest. Hit forward and with water seeping into the coal in the holds, White tried to dodge Dau's fall of shot while his own vintage 4-inch gun barked back from the *Stonepool*'s poop. Supervised by Third Mate Corney, Seaman-Gunner John Hayter and his crew laid their sights on the submarine as White turned his ship away under full starboard helm. In accordance with White's demand for maximum speed, Chief Engineer R. Parsons pressed his firemen as they toiled to feed the boilers.

The *Stonepool*'s port lifeboat, hanging outboard in its davits, was shot away as *U-42* began to overtake the tramp, coming up on her starboard quarter. Dau submerged and fired a salvo of torpedoes, one of which White watched pass ahead of the *Stonepool*, breaking surface for a moment; the others misfired. Frustrated, Dau came back to the surface, and as the gun battle resumed a steel splinter wounded one of the *Stonepool*'s firemen in the head. Next the starboard lifeboat was destroyed as, hampered by the swell, Dau zig-zagged across the *Stonepool*'s wake, trying to steady the roll. At times *U-42* appeared almost broadside to Corney and his gun's crew as they fired at her.

Then, with her fifteenth round, the *Stonepool*'s gunners struck *U-42*'s gun. Dau ordered his boat to dive and then, five minutes later, he surfaced again in roughly the same position. Watching her, Captain White realised that his men had not only hit her gun but inflicted other damage, for 'she came up so high'.[16]

Eager to make good his escape, White held his course and *Stonepool* stood on. The crew were sent forward to get the hatch covers off No. 1 Hold and see how much water was coming into the ship. As they did so two British destroyers approached, *Imogen*, Commander E.B.K. Stevens, and *Ilex*, Lieutenant Commander P.L. Saumarez, both of which had responded to the *Stonepool*'s distress signal while returning home after the dispersal of OB17.

Seeing the rapid approach of the destroyers and despite his damage, Dau dived to 120 metres, but the destroyers' depth-charges soon blew him to the surface, again breaching like a whale. Fire was immediately opened and Saumarez had increased speed to ram, going full astern to minimise damage to his ship, when he realised U-42 was actually sinking. Dau and 16 of his men were picked up by *Imogen*; 32 were lost.

Returning to the *Stonepool*, Stevens signalled 'Good work' to White, then offered to stand by as *Stonepool*, the ingress of water forward proving too serious to be easily stemmed, put back for Barry at 9 knots.

Dau's U-42 was not the only submarine that failed to make the rendezvous.

As Convoy KJF3, the largest to date, approached home waters it was due to meet its inward escort of British destroyers: *Inglefield*, Captain P. Todd, *Intrepid*, Commander J.W. Josselyn, *Ivanhoe*, Commander B. Jones, and *Icarus*, Lieutenant Commander C. Maud. These were to replace the large French submarine *Surcouf* which had provided the ocean escort with her 8-inch guns, but which had detached some time before. On the night of 13/14 October the convoy was without an escort. Informed by B-Dienst of KJF3's whereabouts, Dönitz attempted to direct Hartmann's boats on it, but they were still too dispersed and he was unsuccessful. Two did find it, however.

In the early-morning darkness of 14 October, with KJF3 approaching the south coast of Ireland and some miles to the west and south of the Fastnet Rock, Kapitänleutnant Gelhaar's U-45 came in sight of the convoy. Carefully positioning himself, Gelhaar fired a spread of torpedoes, one of which struck the Royal Mail Liner *Lochavon* on her port side abreast No. 2 Hold. A new ship, *Lochavon* was homeward bound from the Pacific with her master, Captain C.E. Rathkins, acting as convoy commodore of KFJ3. With water pouring into No. 2 Hold and the ship growing sluggish beneath him, Rathkins had no option but to abandon her. He then discovered that his clerk was missing, and Fourth Officer B. W. Meaden reboarded the *Lochavon* and found the man asleep, oblivious of the foundering of his ship. Seeing her reluctant to go, Rathkins twice went back himself, but her end was inevitable.

Meanwhile Gelhaar had gone on to torpedo the Compagnie Générale Transatlantique's passenger-liner *Bretagne*, in breach of Hitler's orders, though she was unlit. Gelhaar's action had by now effectively dispersed the convoy, and as the *Bretagne* began to sink he made his third attack, firing at Shaw, Savill & Albion's cargo-passenger-liner *Karamea*. Frustrated by the failure of his torpedoes, Gelhaar surfaced close to the unarmed *Karamea* as she turned away and opened fire on her. In response Captain E.T. Grayston, an officer of the Royal Naval Reserve, ordered the *Karamea*'s best speed, zig-zagged furiously at 15 knots and skilfully dodged Gelhaar's fall of shot. As she steamed off with *U-45* in hot pursuit, the *Karamea*'s radio was transmitting the news that she was under attack. Over a period of four hours *U-45* fired more than thirty rounds at the British cargo-liner, but at last Grayston's 'act of faith was justified', for his signals had attracted the attention of the approaching escort. *Inglefield, Intrepid, Ivanhoe* and *Icarus* swept down upon Gelhaar, who now submerged, the hunted rather than the hunter. In a flurry of explosions the destroyers counter-attacked with a shower of depth-charges, sending *U-45* to the bottom. There were no survivors.

Todd's destroyers began rounding up the convoy, and early the following afternoon one of them picked up the survivors of the *Lochavon*.

In the same area two days earlier, on the evening of 12 October, also on his way to his rendezvous with Hartmann, Kapitänleutnant Schultze in *U-48* had encountered the French tanker *Émile Miguet*. Having fallen out of Convoy KJ2 with engine trouble, she was stopped when Schultze opened fire and was quickly set ablaze. With a loss of two of their company, her crew took to the boats.

Not far away another Ropner tramp which had also been part of outward-bound OB17 was making her way westwards. The *Heronspool* was loaded with a full cargo of Welsh anthracite, bound from Swansea to Montreal. Her mate, Mr C. Clifford, was on watch when he reported sighting *Émile Miguet*. The master, Captain S. Batson, reached the bridge to see not only a pall of smoke and flicker of flames but a surfaced German submarine silhouetted against the sunset some six miles away. Batson signalled action stations and turned the *Heronspool* away, ordering Radio Officer G. Haresnape to transmit the submarine attack signal, then turned in to the darkening east at his ship's best speed while his gun-crew on the poop stood-to as twilight fell. It was a moonless night; stars began to shine brilliantly in a clear sky as *Heronspool* wallowed in a calm sea and low south-westerly swell at 10 knots. It was not enough; the conditions favoured the faster U-boat. Shortly before 20.00 she came up astern and her signal lamp stabbed the darkness, ordering the *Heronspool* to stop instantly and heave-to.

Doggedly Batson stood on. 'For almost half an hour the tension continued . . . The night was monstrous with threat.' The *U-48* opened fire; from *Heronspool*'s poop Seaman-Gunner J. Pearson retaliated, his inexperienced and amateur crew, with only their extemporised training to call upon, reloading and firing again. Anxiously watching through his glasses on the bridge, Batson saw a flurry in the water astern of them, and then nothing. Schultze had dived.

For two hours they awaited events, then suddenly two fountains of water rose on either side of the ship, after which Schultze held his fire as he sought to overhaul the *Heronspool*. Another hour brought another brief sighting, at which the *Heronspool*'s gun fired again as, in her engine room, Chief Engineer C. Dobson and his firemen laboured to keep up a head of steam. Meanwhile 14-year-old Galley Boy Elders wanted to take a cup of tea to Batson on the bridge, but the steward stopped him: 'No, the Old Man's in a bloody bad temper!'

Then about midnight, after another hiatus, there was a tremendous explosion alongside the ship. The concussion struck her side like a massive hammer-blow and left her company dazed, but the *Heronspool* ploughed doggedly on, undamaged by a torpedo detonating at the end of its run. Intermittent sightings of the U-boat from *Heronspool*'s poop showed her to be still in their wake, moving from side to side as though undecided how best to attack. Pearson kept up a sporadic fire as best he could.

But Schultze had the measure of his opponent, and at about 00.40 succeeded in hitting his target with a torpedo. The explosion blinded and deafened Batson and Clifford; when he could see again, Batson found the whole forepart of his ship had vanished. Quickly he made for the wheelhouse and, seizing the engine-room telegraph, rang 'Finished with Engines' and made the signal to abandon ship. Above his head steam was venting with a loud roar as they ditched the confidential books and grabbed sextant, chronometer and charts from the chart-room. Fortunately the engine room was intact, and with all the crew at action stations no one was posted forward. The *Heronspool* settled slowly; under the direction of the officers the crew had time to lower the boats, and they sat out the night in sight of their ship as she slowly heeled over, still venting steam. From time to time they caught a glimpse of the U-boat above the heaving summits of the swell. Then at 05.00 the *Heronspool* reared her stern into the air and disappeared. Wearily Batson made for the Irish coast; Schultze slunk away.

The dawn brought rescue. Answering the distress call of the *Émile Miguet*, the American passenger-liner *President Harding* appeared out of the dawn, lit up like a small town. Once aboard, Batson and his men were swept westwards, into a storm in which the liner lost a man overboard, a lifeboat was damaged and 68 of her passengers were injured, conscious only that had the weather struck them in their own lifeboats it would have overwhelmed them.

Schultze remained in the vicinity of the Fastnet Rock. The next morning he intercepted and sank by gunfire the French ship *Louisiane*, part of the dispersed outward Convoy OA17 from the Thames Estuary, and on the evening of the 13th, engaging her by torpedo and gunfire, sank the British tramp *Sneaton* on her way from Rio de Janeiro to Cardiff.

Hartmann himself, in *U-37*, had also been effective, sinking three merchantmen on his outward passage round the north of Scotland. These were the small Swedish ship *Vistula*, sunk off the Shetlands on 8 October; the Greek tramp *Aris* sunk with the loss of two lives off the west coast of Ireland on the 12th; and on the 15th, also with two deaths, the French cargo-liner *Vermont*, sent to the bottom in the South West Approaches to the Channel. Finally, on 16 October, Hartmann met his two remaining colleagues, Schultze and Kapitänleutnant Herbert Sohler in *U-46*, on their prearranged rendezvous west of Cape Ortegal. They headed south. It was hardly the wolf-pack Dönitz had envisaged, but he awaited its impact with anxious interest as next day Sohler sighted northbound Convoy HG3. It was unescorted, and the three submarines closed in that afternoon in an attack frustrated by seven torpedo failures. Sohler finally damaged the large Bibby liner *Yorkshire*, homeward bound from Rangoon, leaving Hartmann to administer the *coup de grâce* and send her and her cargo to the bottom with the loss of 58 lives, including her master, Captain V.C.P. Smalley, 24 of her crew and 33 of her 151 passengers.

Seeing the *Yorkshire*'s plight the master of the Ellerman cargo-liner *City of Mandalay*, Captain A.G. Melville, closed to assist and was torpedoed by Sohler, losing seven lives for his pains. This general cargo-liner was homeward bound for Le Havre, London, Dunkirk and Glasgow, having loaded a mixed cargo including tin, coconut products, rice, tea and rubber from Saigon, Singapore, Port Swettenham and India. The survivors from both the *Yorkshire* and the *City of Mandalay* were rescued by the American freighter *Independence Hall* and landed at Bordeaux.

Schultze, meanwhile, attacked and sank another cargo-liner, the *Clan Chisholm*, Captain F.T. Stenson, also on her way home from India with a mixed general cargo including pig-iron, jute and tea. Four of her crew were killed, but Stenson and another 41 crew were picked up by the Swedish motor-vessel *Bardaland*, a further 17 by the small Norwegian steam whaler *Skudd I*, and the remaining 15, after spending four days in their boat, by Union Castle's *Warwick Castle*.

It was not exactly what Dönitz had wanted, nor was a second attempt to assemble a group later the same month. Consequently, 'I decided that for the time being I would despatch each U-boat alone to the Atlantic as soon as it . . . was commissioned for service. It was not until the summer of 1940 that a fresh start could be made with joint operations.'[17]

Meanwhile, on 17 October, again excepting passenger-liners, Hitler ordered the sinking of any British or French ship without observation of Prize Regulations, thus relieving his U-boat commanders of the need to render any kind of assistance to their crews. The gloves were finally removed a month later when, on 17 November, enemy passenger ships were no longer proscribed. The only vessels now protected by the protocol were neutral ships not in convoy and not blacked out, though even these were deemed to be war prizes if they were carrying a contraband cargo. Ships wearing the ensigns of Germany's friends – Italy, Japan, Spain and Ireland – or of her ally Russia were not to be molested, nor for obvious reasons were those of the United States.

Schultze and Sohler, low on fuel and torpedoes, returned home. Hartmann continued south and sank three more tramp-ships in the approaches to Gibraltar, the *Menin Ridge*, laden with iron ore for the steel works at Port Talbot, with the loss of 20 men; the *Ledbury*, with a cargo of bauxite, bound from Toulon to Burntisland; and the *Tafna*, also with iron ore and bound towards London, with the loss of two lives. On his way home, back off the Fastnet Rock, Hartmann sank the Greek tramp *Thrasyvoulos*, ending 23 lives, before returning to Wilhelmshaven with a new record for a single patrol: 35,300 tons of enemy shipping sunk.

As events slowly unwound, the Admiralty's strategy did not seem too wide of the mark. In view of their apprehensions about the depredations of German warships, Their Lordships had reason to be comforted. Most ships lost in convoy had been taken out of one that was unescorted: other losses were the result of attacks on lone ships, though many had been made shortly after dispersal, but even these had given a good account of themselves, particularly the *Stonepool*. White's resistance seemed a complete vindication of Churchill's confidence in the defensive arming of merchantmen, and if the *Imogen* and *Ilex* were credited with 'killing' *U-42*, as seems to have been the case, Their Lordships knew that *Stonepool*'s people had at the very least played the role of *picador*.

There was also the comforting knowledge that the greater part of the losses were occurring to neutral shipping, and while this deprived Britain of cargoes consigned to its shores, it did nothing to endear Germany to those non-belligerent countries whose desire was to continue trading as normal. Not only did these losses contrast badly with the milder disruption inflicted by the British blockade; they drove neutrals into the British camp, persuading them that a living might still be made chartering to Britain or loading for British ports, a judgement given added weight in the coming months as neutral ships availed themselves of the expanding convoy system.

Unaware of the sinisterly experimental nature of the attack on Convoy HG3, Their Lordships continued to focus their anxieties not on defence against U-boats but on the destruction of surface commerce-raiders, whose menacing heavy-calibre guns were what senior officers at the Admiralty best understood and continued therefore to fear most.

As Wennecker manoeuvred the *Deutschland* into her berth in Gotenhafen on the morning of 15 November 1939 his colleague Hans Langsdorff was destroying his next victim, the small tanker *Africa Shell*. Having despaired of intercepting anything in the southern Indian Ocean, Langsdorff was now operating only three hundred miles from the Royal Navy's base at Durban. Moreover he was, according to his victim's master, Captain P. Dove, inside the territorial waters of Portuguese East Africa. Having no radio Dove was unable to alert the authorities and it was his crew, put into their boats and pulling ashore some hours later, who did so on his behalf. He, poor fellow, was a prisoner aboard the *Admiral Graf Spee*. On the following day Langsdorff detained the neutral Dutch liner *Mapia*, allowing her to proceed onwards to Sumatra on condition that she maintain radio silence. After this, concerned that the state of his main engines necessitated a return to Germany, Langsdorff withdrew to a new rendezvous with Dau's *Altmark*. Arriving on station on 23 November, his crew rigged a dummy funnel and a third gun turret from wood and canvas while his engine-room staff overhauled his diesels as best they could. When Dau arrived on the 26th to replenish the *Admiral Graf Spee*'s stores and fuel, Langsdorff collected all the detained ship-masters, chief officers, senior engineers and radio officers aboard his own ship, while the junior officers, seamen and firemen were taken or remained aboard the *Altmark*. Signalling Berlin with his request for a full overhaul, Langsdorff proposed that he should operate off the Rio de la Plata in early December before heading for home. Raeder concurred; he had already initiated a sortie by a battle-group of two heavy battleships to strike at the North Atlantic convoy route, by which he hoped to divert London's attention and cover Langsdorff's return to the Fatherland.

This battle-group left Wilhelmshaven on Tuesday 21 November 1939. Flying his flag in the *Gneisenau*, Vizeadmiral W. Marschall had under his command a second battleship, the *Scharnhorst*, Kapitän zur See K. Hoffmann, the cruisers *Leipzig* and *Köln*, and three destroyers, the *Bernd von Arnim, Karl Glaster* and *Erich Giese*. The cruisers and destroyers turned into the Skagerrak and joined the outward bound and renamed *Lützow* for an unsuccessful sweep against shipping in the Norwegian Sea. Marschall's two capital ships continued north, masked from British reconnaissance by a ferocious northerly gale whose winds occasionally reached hurricane force and compelled Marschall to reduce speed to a crawling 12 knots while in their messdecks his inexperienced young sailors vomited copiously. As an added precaution the Vizeadmiral ordered his ships to hoist the British white ensign as the two grey monsters ploughed north-west, their elegantly sheered bows driving through the heavy seas, throwing the spray high over their towering fore-bridges.

By mid afternoon on the 23rd the two battleships were halfway between the Faeroes and Iceland. The wind had dropped to Force 5 but swept intermittent rain showers down from the north in the gathering dusk. Aboard *Scharnhorst*, Hoffmann was informed of a vessel to the northwards and immediately increased speed and altered course towards the stranger, signalling to Marschall that he had 'Sighted a large steamer on parallel course'.

She was the requisitioned P&O liner, now HMS, *Rawalpindi* with a mixed Royal Naval and P&O crew, commanded by Captain E.C. Kennedy, an officer whose career had been blighted by his sympathy for the 'mutineers' of the Atlantic Fleet at Invergordon in 1931, but whom war had recalled to the service. The *Rawalpindi* was part of Admiral Horton's Northern Patrol, and Kennedy immediately transmitted a signal informing the Admiralty that an enemy battleship was in sight. This, received at 15.51 by Admiral Forbes, C-in-C, Home Fleet, then in the Clyde, was soon followed by a deceptive revision: Kennedy, though uncertain in the squally dusk, decided the enemy was the *Deutschland*, and said so. It was a perfectly plausible mistake.

Units of the Royal Navy were widely scattered about the Norwegian Sea and North Atlantic Ocean and it was unfortunate that the *Scharnhorst* had run into so weakly-armed an exponent of British sea-power. The *Rawalpindi* had been requisitioned on 26 August when the Admiralty first took control of merchant shipping, one of a dozen P&O liners destined to become Armed Merchant Cruisers, of which seven were assigned to the Northern Patrol. Conversions were undertaken in Belfast, Bombay, Calcutta, Cape Town, Glasgow, London and Vancouver. In addition to the fitting of guns, ammunition hoists, extemporised magazines and naval mess-decks, any cargo on board was discharged and the liners were loaded with ballast of pig-iron billets to confer adequate positive stability. Their vacant holds and 'tween-deck spaces were then filled with empty oil drums, to retard sinking should their capacious cargo spaces be breached by enemy shells. With their high freeboard and towering superstructures, these liners made excellent targets.

Having undergone her own metamorphosis the *Rawalpindi* retained about sixty of her peace-time crew, mainly officers and petty officers, plus some key ratings. The officers were granted temporary naval commissions, the others were given temporary naval ranks under special Articles opened under what were called T124 or T124X Agreements, wherein the Admiralty replaced the regular ship-owner as the employer, honouring civilian leave and pension rights. The distinction between the two was that T124 applied to a named ship, whereas under T124X a seafarer could be drafted into another warship. Among the most senior company employees retained aboard *Rawalpindi* was Mr C.C. Sangster, the Chief Engineer, who became a

Temporary Engineer Commander in the Royal Naval Reserve, while the ship's Fourth Officer, Mr A.D. Seabrook, was commissioned a Temporary Sub-Lieutenant, RNR. The *Rawalpindi*'s teeth consisted of eight vintage open-breeched 6-inch and two 3-inch guns. Although she had a service speed of 17 knots the *Rawalpindi* was incapable of out-running the *Scharnhorst* and her as yet unseen consort, or of drawing them onto the guns of British vessels able to deal with them, which would have been the classic tactic had *Rawalpindi* actually been a cruiser in any meaningful sense of the term. Apart from Forbes's main units in the Clyde, Loch Ewe and at Rosyth, the closest warships to her were three of Horton's ageing cruisers and the newer *Newcastle*, patrolling with her between the Faeroes and Iceland. To the south of the Faeroes another trio of Horton's old 'C'-class veterans were on patrol, with *Glasgow* and two destroyers out looking for the *Bremen* to the north-east of the Shetlands. Beyond Iceland in the Denmark Strait were the heavy cruisers *Norfolk* and *Suffolk* and three more Armed Merchant Cruisers, one of which was the former P&O liner *Chitral*. Such 'cruisers' not only made fine targets themselves but were quite inadequate to engage the *Scharnhorst* and the *Gneisenau*, which were the match of any British battleship. The nearest of these to *Rawalpindi* was *Warspite*, and she was many miles away to the SSW, escorting Convoy HX9.

As *Scharnhorst* turned in pursuit and increased speed from 18 to 24 knots a brief exchange occurred between Hoffmann and Marschall. At 15.32, with the sun just set, certain that he had located a British Armed Merchant Cruiser, Hoffmann piped his crew to action stations, and his signalmen to order the AMC to heave-to. She was forbidden the use of her radio, but was to identify herself by lamp; instead the strange ship simply responded with an acknowledgement and, turning to put the *Scharnhorst* on her starboard quarter, increased speed. The pursuit lasted for more than twenty minutes until at 16.02, with the range down to four and a half miles, Hoffmann ordered a shot to be fired across the *Rawalpindi*'s bows. At the same time Kennedy had smoke floats dropped over the stern of the *Rawalpindi* to confuse the enemy's gunlayers. They failed to ignite, and Kennedy then opened fire with his 6-inch guns. Shortly afterwards he sent a chief petty officer round the guns to tell the officers in charge to keep up independent fire for as long as possible.[18]

As the *Rawalpindi*'s gun flashes pierced the gloom Hoffmann ordered his 11-inch radar-controlled guns to respond.[19] It was impossible to miss the high freeboard and elevated superstructure of the liner, and *Scharnhorst*'s shells ripped through her comparatively thin plating, igniting the woodwork in the handsome first-class passenger accommodation and starting several fires. *Scharnhorst*'s second salvo destroyed the *Rawalpindi*'s electrical generating capability, plunging her into total darkness and stopping her ammunition supply hoists. Naval ratings were mustered to form human chains to pass up shells and charges. Emergency power permitted the transmission of a radio signal stating that the *Rawalpindi* was under fire from a single battleship, again amended by Kennedy to read 'Under attack by the *Deutschland*'. As it was transmitted the *Rawalpindi*'s gunners returned the enemy's fire, though their shells were missing the grey shape in the gathering gloom astern of them.

There was a lull as rain and smoke obscured their target and then, at about 16.11, Hoffmann's fourth salvo destroyed the *Rawalpindi*'s bridge and forward superstructure, including the radio room, and killed Kennedy and the officers and ratings in the area. Although fire had now taken serious hold of the liner and two of her six 6-inch guns had been destroyed, the remainder continued firing as ammunition was handed up from below. At this point the *Gneisenau* arrived to fire at *Rawalpindi*'s unengaged port side. Under a very heavy barrage the guns of the British vessel barked defiantly back, their fall of shot short but in line with their vague targets. Night had all but fallen, lit by the blazing liner and an emerging moon. At 16.14 Hoffmann turned *Scharnhorst* to starboard in response to a torpedo alarm, but it was a chimera, and in the following few moments the *Rawalpindi*'s guns began to fall silent one by one as their crews died at their posts. At about this time the order was passed to abandon the *Rawalpindi*. By 16.20 it was all over.

Ten minutes later the Germans heard an explosion from inside the burning vessel as one of her magazines blew up. She appeared to have blown in two. They began to close in, aware that the British had succeeded in launching some of the *Rawalpindi*'s boats. An unknown figure high on the blazing liner's superstructure repeatedly flashed a request to 'Please send boats'.

But it was too late, and the sea conditions precluded proper rescue. As *Rawalpindi* settled, her hull racked by explosions, Kennedy and 270 of his ship's mixed company were dead or dying, among them 58 P&O staff. A handful got away in the lifeboats and a mere 27 men were in course of being recovered from two of these by *Scharnhorst* when at 17.14 Marschall aborted the rescue operation and ordered both battleships to withdraw to the east at high speed: the triangular silhouette of an approaching man-of-war had been seen in the offing from the bridge of the *Gneisenau*. Six and a half miles away the cruiser *Newcastle*, which had occupied the adjacent patrol station to the *Rawalpindi*, was coming up to her support in response to Kennedy's signal.

Having identified and reported two heavy enemy ships to the Admiralty, Captain J. Figgins did not engage. His attempt to shadow in order to vector superior forces onto what were clearly German capital ships rather than risk his own weaker vessel was in conformity with the classic duties of a cruiser, but *Newcastle* had no radar, and the frequent rain squalls were reducing visibility to less than a quarter of a mile, the occasional moonlit interlude notwithstanding. Having failed to regain contact, Figgins sighted and approached the burning *Rawalpindi*. A few minutes later the flames were extinguished as the sea swallowed her forever.

Had Marschall not been so eager to run he might have added *Newcastle* to his bag before drawing down upon his head the hue and cry that her very presence told him was being raised. But Marschall and his colleagues, unlike the gallant Kennedy and his sacrificed crew, were not subscribers to the British dictum that the enemy must always be engaged, and engaged ever more closely. *He* was content to have done enough by his feint to occupy the attentions of the British Home Fleet, an action providing clear evidence, if such were needed, of the ability of a naval force 'in being' to tie down a disproportionately greater force in containing it and guarding against the several options that lay open to it. That alone was a success, and posed a problem that was to dog the Admiralty for much of the war. As for distracting the British in order to allow Langsdorff to make his way home, there Marschall was also partially successful, in that the Admiralty and Forbes were uncertain of the identity of Figgins's reported 'two ships' and still thought one was the *Deutschland*. It was some time before they learned the truth – long after Marschall had reached home, long after the *Deutschland* had been metamorphosed into the *Lützow*, and long after Langsdorff had met his own Nemesis.

In the bleak waters of the Norwegian Sea neither *Newcastle* nor *Delhi*, which soon came up to join her, regained contact with Marschall's battle-group. Both British cruisers left the remaining survivors from the *Rawalpindi* in their wakes as they trailed ineffectually after the huge predators. In that high latitude, not far from the Arctic circle, those wretched men spent the November night huddled in their boats, despairing of rescue. But in addition to *Newcastle* and *Delhi*, the *Chitral*, which a day or so earlier had intercepted the German cargo-ship *Bertha Fisser*, had also heard her sister-ship's signal and had begun steaming towards her.[20] At 10.30 on the 24th the first survivors were found, then *Chitral* passed wreckage and empty or upturned lifeboats. On one her lookouts spotted a single, prone figure which weakly responded to the shriek of *Chitral*'s siren as it competed with the strong and bitterly cold wind. A boat was lowered and picked up the last of the eleven of *Rawalpindi*'s company still living, a P&O cook named Fleming. He and the crew of the *Bertha Fisser* – a pitiful remnant – were landed in Glasgow two days later.[21]

After despatching his weak opponent, the German admiral retired under a smoke screen.[22] Acting with great caution and frustrated by poor visibility and bad weather, Marschall made the best of his way south and succeeded in reaching Wilhemshaven in the early afternoon of 27 November. Here he landed his prisoners and was greeted by press reports claiming a 'Great naval victory', and that 'England has been forced to abandon the North Sea and North Atlantic'. Nothing could have been further from the truth, of course, and the ludicrous propaganda was shortly to backfire, not in the North but in the South Atlantic.

Indeed, it was the British who derived the greater benefit from the victory, for Kennedy's action was the kind of self-sacrificial example that Churchill, with his fine-tuned sense of history and precedent, could mobilise for the greater good. 'They must have known', he growled in the House of Commons on 27 November, '. . . that there was no chance for them, but they had no thought of surrender. They fought their guns till they could be fought no more and they then – many of them – went to their deaths, and thereby carried on the great tradition of the Royal Navy. Their example will be an inspiration . . .'

Naval tradition might attribute much of the credit to the courageous leadership of Captain Kennedy, though he received no supreme posthumous acknowledgement, but Churchill played the democrat and pointed out the plurality of the immolation. And within that great Royal Navy tradition lay the older one of the commoner, mercantile British seafarer, whose ships had always been placed at the service of the state.

As Marschall arrived home, the *Admiral Graf Spee* lay in the vast emptiness of the South Atlantic off Tristan da Cunha, replenishing from the *Altmark* and taking aboard the senior British prisoners, leaving Dau with the junior officers and the ratings. The ships then separated and steamed north, the crew of the *Panzerschiff* removing the false funnel and gun turret that had been intended to make her resemble the British battle-cruiser *Renown*. At noon on 2 December, some 650 miles east of St Helena, Langsdorff catapulted his Arado seaplane off to reconnoitre. Heading up into the South Atlantic, he was aware of an increasing risk to his operations from the vigilance of the Royal Navy. There was no sign of a British man-of-war cruiser, but it was possible that the vessel his Luftwaffe pilot reported having sighted, a 10,000-ton fast cargo-liner, might be an Armed Merchant Cruiser. At 13.00, still hull down and quite unable to determine his quarry's nationality, Langsdorff ordered a shot to be fired at the strange vessel.

Oblivious of having been sighted from the air, the Blue Star liner *Doric Star* was homeward bound from Australia and New Zealand by way of the

Cape of Good Hope. She was loaded 'with a full refrigerated cargo of mutton, lamb, cheese and butter from New Zealand and Australia, with a quantity of wool in bales in her 'tween-decks'. It was a clear day and there was no wind. The sea was calm, although a long swell gave the impression that the ocean was gently respiring. All of a sudden a shell tore through the air, plunging into the sea close to the *Doric Star*. Rushing to the bridge, Captain W. Stubbs reached for his glasses and scanned the horizon. A few minutes later he saw the cause, a distant dark triangle on the *Doric Star*'s port quarter. Immediately Stubbs ordered Radio Officer W. Comber 'to transmit the raider distress call' and ordered the engine room to provide all possible speed. Then, at 13.10, 'a second shell exploded within 200 yards, off the starboard bow'. Identified by her tall forebridge cutting the horizon as she loomed over the rim of the world, 'the overtaking vessel was seen to be a battleship'. Realising that escape was impossible, Stubbs now stopped his engines but 'ordered the wireless operator to amplify the message and state "battleship attacking". By this time,' Stubbs afterwards reported, 'I could read the daylight Morse light from [the] battleship signalling "Stop your wireless", but I took no notice . . .'[23]

Stubbs also prepared to scuttle his ship, and the chief engineer, Mr W. Ray, began preparations to obey. 'A few minutes later,' however, 'the wireless operator reported that our message had been repeated by another British vessel and also a Greek . . . so I countermanded the orders for scuttling, then threw overboard all confidential papers and books, [the] breech of [the] gun, ammunition and rifles, also all papers about [the] cargo.' As she came up hand-over-fist the *Admiral Graf Spee* was displaying a large notice bearing the ominous words STOP YOUR ENGINES OR I WILL OPEN FIRE. Stubbs ordered an end to radio transmissions: 'The *Doric Star*, a 12-knot ship with one anti-submarine gun right aft, had no alternative but to obey.'

Losing way as she closed her victim, the *Admiral Graf Spee* lowered a fast motor-launch and a few moments later the *Doric Star* was boarded by three officers and some thirty armed ratings. The three officers, with drawn revolvers, took parties of sailors to the bridge, the radio room and the engine room. Stubbs was taken to his cabin and questioned, the bridge and radio room were searched for code-books, and Comber was asked whether he had transmitted the *Doric Star*'s position, to which he replied 'Of course.' Stubbs meanwhile was denying that his ship had anything useful on board and maintaining that his cargo was entirely composed of wool. The German sailors ripped off the corners of the hatch tarpaulins and lifted the boards of two hatches. Seeing only bales of wool, they assumed Stubbs to be telling the truth, their interest diverted by a quantity of silver bars in his personal custody. The boarding party were under pressure from Langsdorff to return to their own ship, so the *Doric Star*'s crew were given ten minutes to collect 'lifebelts, blankets, eating utensils and any effects they could carry' before transferring to the *Admiral Graf Spee*. The bridge was looted of its chronometers and the officers' sextants and binoculars before the Germans withdrew.[24]

Langsdorff was impatient to recall his men, for he was in trouble. His B-Dienst operators, monitoring the 500-kilocycles wavelength, knew that Stubbs's distress signal had been received and passed on. The British ship which had received it was the *Port Chalmers*[25] and she passed the information on to Vice Admiral Lyon at Freetown; he in turn informed the Admiralty. That the naval authorities still thought the raider to be the *Admiral Scheer* did not greatly matter; their knowledge that a 'pocket battleship' was at large in the South Atlantic was enough to seal Langsdorff's fate. But Langsdorff had another problem too: having reported the British cargoliner, Oberleutnant Bongard's seaplane had continued her flight, and he now reported that he had run out of fuel and was sitting on the water, miles away. In a hurry to embark his prisoners and the captured silver, then dispatch the *Doric Star*, Langsdorff was already conscious of losing valuable time; now he had the added burden of finding his ditched seaplane. Opening fire on the Blue Star ship with his secondary armament of 5.9-inch guns, he shot a torpedo into her. This was followed by a second, after which the vessel settled, and Langsdorff could go in search of the Arado. The entire day was wasted in this, and it was already twilight when a flare fired by Bongard revealed her wallowing in the swell. By 19.00 the seaplane had been recovered and relocated on its catapult amidships and the *Admiral Graf Spee* was already heading for Langsdorff's next hunting-ground. It lay miles away, in the converging shipping lanes off the Rio de la Plata.

In distant Freetown Vice Admiral Lyon, hearing the relayed signal from the *Port Chalmers*, had ordered a squadron of cruisers to sweep up the West African coast from the Cape of Good Hope, and a second to steam along the Cape-to-St Helena rhumb line.

A third squadron, the cruisers of Force G under Commodore Henry Harwood, was responsible for covering the shipping lanes of eastern South America. Having carried out several exercises, on 2 December Harwood's four ships were dispersed. The heavy cruiser *Exeter* was refitting at Port Stanley in the Falkland Islands, whither the *Cumberland* was on passage. The light cruiser *Achilles* was refuelling in the neutral Uruguayan port of Montevideo, and Harwood himself stood guard alone in his flagship, the light cruiser HMS *Ajax*. On receipt of Lyon's signal concerning the presence of a powerful German raider, he determined to concentrate his force off the Plate. He ordered *Exeter* to leave Port Stanley and the New Zealand-manned

Achilles to sail from Montevideo; *Cumberland* was to continue to her boiler clean in the Falklands, but to rejoin as soon as possible. The British rendezvous was to be 150 miles east of the estuary of the Rio de la Plata on 12 December.

On 3 December the *Admiral Graf Spee* was south-east of St Helena where she intercepted Shaw, Savill & Albion's *Tairoa*, a cargo-liner homeward bound from Melbourne, Australia with a mixed cargo, including wool, lead ingots and frozen butter and meat. The *Tairoa* had left Durban on 27 November, having called for bunkers and mail. On 2 December she had heard the *Doric Star*'s RRRR signal, and Captain W.B.S. Starr had altered course to (as he thought) avoid the likely track of the enemy. In this he had miscalculated, however, and the *Tairoa* and the *Admiral Graf Spee* hove in sight of one another the next morning, Advent Sunday. As the daylight grew and they took a sweep round the horizon, Langsdorff's acute optical range-finder operators saw the smoke of a steamship 13 miles astern. The *Panzerschiff* turned to meet her, Langsdorff reverting to his practice of approaching a potential victim wearing the French ensign.

Unaware of or unimpressed by this ruse, on seeing the sinister silhouette approach Starr sent the raider-attack signal, to Langsdorff's exasperation: British masters simply would not conform and play the game as he wished it to be played. As the *Tairoa*'s signal blasted out into the ether, Langsdorff ordered his small-calibre weapons to open fire. Some sixty shells shattered the port side of the *Tairoa*'s superstructure, destroying the bridge-wing and the lifeboats in their davits.

Boarded by Leutnant B. Kerberg, Starr was compelled to surrender his ship and her cargo, later admitting that Langsdorff had 'used only his smallest [calibre] guns to achieve his purpose [which] helped to keep casualties to a minimum'. Starr and his crew joined the other prisoners aboard the *Admiral Graf Spee* while their ship was sunk. On the evidence of the Chief Officer of the *Huntsman*, 'six shots from 5.9-inch guns and finally a torpedo were fired to sink the *Tairoa* . . . The early firing [of the lighter-calibre 37mm weapons] had been to stop the radio, but the operator had gone on sending until his machine [*sic*] was eventually hit, though he himself escaped injury. Five of the *Tairoa*'s crew were wounded, three deck boys sufficiently to be detained in the hospital on the warship for a week. We were now fifty-one in one small room. Packed, without room to sit, we ate our meals in relays.'

There were now 196 prisoners on board the *Admiral Graf Spee*, the crews of the *Doric Star* and *Tairoa*, separated from their officers, being confined in another part of the raider. It was probably to avoid such congestion and the consequent drain on his resources that Langsdorff arranged for such frequent mid-ocean meetings with his supply ship. Once again he and Dau met, on 6 December, and the crews from the Blue Star and Shaw, Savill ships were transferred aboard the *Altmark*.[26] Along with the three wounded lads from the *Tairoa* 29 masters and officers were retained aboard the *Admiral Graf Spee*, but Brown of the *Huntsman* and Starr of the *Tairoa* were put aboard *Altmark* to tend their apprehensive lascar crews.

Berlin now informed Langsdorff that diplomatic sources in Montevideo had reported HMS *Achilles* still lying alongside there, while the departure from the Plate of two large passenger-cargo-liners, the Royal Mail Line's *Highland Monarch* and Blue Star's *Andalucia Star*, was scheduled between 5 and 8 December. Encouraged by this intelligence Langsdorff headed west, intent on making a lightning strike at the locus of South American trade on about the 10th.

On 7 December the Headlam tramp *Streonshalh* bound from Rosario towards Britain came in sight. Her master did not send a distress signal and Langsdorff, having taken off her crew, had her sunk by his anti-aircraft arma-ment, possibly so as not to broadcast his presence by the concussion of heavier-calibre weapons. The *Streonshalh*'s people told the prisoners they 'were on the South American shipping routes. We now had thirty-one pris-oners in our room, and thirty, the *Streonshalh*'s crew, [were] in a room forward. The three wounded [boys] were in our room.'

For several days the British captives put up with the monotony of their dreary existence, their only relief coming on the morning of the 11th when they realised that the Arado seaplane had cracked a cylinder and become defunct. Langsdorff was thereby deprived of his eyes, for it had flown off every morning and evening to search out prey as well as potential enemy warships. To the bored merchant officers below, this was a gratifying occurrence.

By an odd quirk of fate, Harwood had deliberately not used the perfectly serviceable amphibious aircraft carried by his own cruisers. Had a seaplane been spotted by Langsdorff's lookouts, history might have been different; as it was, Harwood secured the concentration of three of his cruisers 150 miles east of the Rio de la Plata estuary at 07.00 on the morning of 12 December 1939, undetected. Shortly after sunrise the following day, as *Ajax*, *Exeter* and *Achilles* steamed in line ahead, the slight, sulphurous smudge of the *Admiral Graf Spee*'s diesel exhaust smoke could be seen on the horizon. Harwood detached *Exeter* to investigate, and a few minutes later received Captain F. S. Bell's pleasing signal: 'I think it's a pocket-battleship.'

The German range-finders, sweeping the horizon, had seen *Exeter* at 05.52 when she was about twenty miles distant. The alarms sounded 'Action Stations'. The British prisoners heard the steel skylight slamming shut and the dogs being put on the water-tight door of their accommodation, making it feel like an oubliette. They were aware of the *Admiral Graf Spee*'s hull beginning to shudder under the increased thrust of her powerful diesels.

Langsdorff on his bridge correctly identified the reconnoitring *Exeter* as a British cruiser, but mistakenly took the smaller accompanying men-of-war for destroyers. At 06.16 he realised his error. Nevertheless, the German raider's six 11-inch guns possessed a greater range and destructive power than the 8-inch guns of *Exeter* and the 6-inch guns of the two *Leander*-Class light cruisers; moreover, her heavier armour made the *Admiral Graf Spee* almost immune to serious damage from all but well-placed shells from *Exeter*. Her only weakness lay in her speed, which was 6 knots less than that of her opponents, and compelled her to fight. Langsdorff therefore determined to knock out *Exeter* and then deal with her lesser consorts *Ajax* and *Achilles*, meanwhile keeping them tied down with fire from his secondary armament, which at 5.9 inches almost matched the calibre, if not the weight, of their own main armaments.

To the anxious British merchant personnel incarcerated below-decks, what followed was a nightmare of uncertainty and mixed feelings. Hope and fear were in conflict as a desire for the enemy to be defeated warred with the primitive instinct to survive. The sudden heeling of the *Admiral Graf Spee* followed by the tremendous concussion as her guns opened fire shook the massive steel fabric of the all-welded *Panzerschiff*.

Unknown to the anxious men trapped in his cruisers' target, Harwood had disposed his squadron in two divisions, Bell in *Exeter* engaging from the south, *Ajax* and *Achilles* from the east. Langsdorff's main guns were laid on *Exeter* with devastating effect as his 5.9-inch weapons fired at the two light cruisers. The *Exeter* was hit almost immediately, one shell passing through her shell plating without exploding, one landing amidships and another hitting and destroying B-turret. The explosion killed all on the bridge except Bell and two officers. By now Bell's ability to control his ship was seriously compromised, his communications and his main steering having been disabled. Although wounded in the face he quickly manned the alternative steering position aft and wrested command back, using a chain of men to pass orders. As the *Admiral Graf Spee* turned away at 06.36 making smoke, *Exeter* fired a salvo of torpedoes at her from her starboard tubes.

But *Exeter* was undergoing fierce punishment; she continued to be hit and began to fall back, on fire, her forward turret disabled by another 11-inch shell. At 07.30, with only one turret still in action, 61 killed and 23 men wounded, losing boiler pressure and listing heavily to starboard, Bell broke off the action, unable to keep up with the *Admiral Graf Spee*, which was now steering west towards the Plate estuary and the Uruguayan coast.

Nor was all well aboard the *Admiral Graf Spee*. The light cruisers' fire was galling and considerable splinter damage had been sustained on her upper decks, wounding exposed members of her crew. At about this time a shell burst above the prisoners' heads, extinguishing some of the lights and driving down the deck above, fracturing a longitudinal beam, smashing the skylight and sending shards of steel into the crowded room. 'You can imagine our feelings', one master recalled, 'when we felt the shuddering blows of shells striking the ship. We knew it was the intention of the attacking ship to blow our temporary home out of the water. We felt that if she succeeded in doing so it would be good for the country . . . But we felt like rats in a trap shut up in our tiny compartment of twenty feet by seventeen.'

As Langsdorff turned away, *Ajax* and *Achilles* were engaging from the south-east at a range of 13,000 yards, still under fire from the enemy's secondary armament. In swinging, Langsdorff shifted one of his heavy turrets to target *Ajax*, straddling but not hitting her. Using their superior speed and working up from 28 to 31 knots, the two light cruisers followed round, extending the range to 17,000 yards but coming up onto the *Admiral Graf Spee*'s starboard quarter as she headed west making smoke. At 06.40 *Achilles* was hit by a shell which exploded on her waterline, but she escaped serious damage. Harwood ordered Captain C.H.L. Woodhouse to launch the *Ajax*'s Fairey seaplane to assist with spotting the fall of shot, for the range-finding optics were unable to penetrate the enemy's smoke screen and the British gunnery was failing.

For some time the two British light cruisers maintained a running fight with the German warship. Then at 07.16 Langsdorff, keeping the initiative, swung to the south intending to finish off the wounded *Exeter*. Immediately Harwood turned after her and re-engaged to such effect that Langsdorff aborted his attempt to molest *Exeter* and resumed his westwards track, concentrating his fire on *Ajax*. At 07.25 an 11-inch shell knocked out her two after-turrets and a few minutes later a second brought down her topmast. Harwood was now in serious trouble, having apparently made little impression upon the *Panzerschiff*. Ordering Woodhouse to fire torpedoes in the hope that he might cripple the *Admiral Graf Spee*, Harwood turned away to the east and made smoke.

Langsdorff swung, avoided the torpedoes, and launched a Parthian salvo of his own. The torpedoes were spotted and reported by the pilot of the Fairey seaplane, allowing Woodhouse time to put over his helm and to comb their tracks, but Harwood now received the depressing news that not only had his radio aerials been shot away but his stock of ammunition was dangerously low. It must have been a moment of deep despair.

Langsdorff's torpedo salvo had been not just a Parthian but a parting shot: despite having disabled *Exeter* and *Ajax*, thereby effectively defeating Harwood, he withdrew. From their invidious position, the British prisoners had a better idea than Harwood of the situation aboard the German ship as the *Admiral Graf* Spee steamed west at 24 knots. 'Watching the ammunition parties through a small screw hole in the door, the prisoners saw the Germans looked very concerned and glum. Many killed and wounded were carried past during a lull in the action and some of the Germans were physically sick. Most of the *Graf Spee*'s crew were lads of between 17 and 22, with a small sprinkling of older men. Some of the youngest had never been to sea before . . .'[27]

Langsdorff's ship had received a score of direct hits, one of which had gone through her bow. However, although she too had depleted her ammunition, and had 36 of her young company dead, with a further 60 wounded, six severely, she was substantially intact. Harwood, meanwhile, realising that something was amiss, recovered his seaplane and sent a signal to *Cumberland*: Captain Fallowfield was to join him from the Falklands with all despatch. Having then contacted Bell, Harwood concluded that since the *Admiral Graf Spee* was continuing to open up the range as she headed west, she could be doing only one thing – retreating.

Within a few minutes Harwood was in pursuit, with *Ajax* on the *Admiral Graf Spee*'s port quarter, *Achilles* the starboard. It was increasingly clear that Langsdorff was intending to seek shelter in neutral waters, so Harwood alerted the British naval attaché in Buenos Aires, on the Argentinian shore. Harwood's squadron pursued Langsdorff and, in a final exchange of shots allegedly initiated by *Achilles* opening fire just inside Uruguayan territorial waters, also initiated a diplomatic wrangle.[28]

This need not detain us here. Suffice it to say that *Exeter* succeeded in withdrawing to effect temporary repairs in the Falklands before returning home; *Cumberland* reinforced Harwood and, as Lyon also sent the *Devonshire*, the Admiralty added the *Shropshire* to seal the *Admiral Graf Spee*'s fate. Harwood's squadron awaited events offshore.[29]

It was 23.00 on the evening of the 13th before anyone aboard the *Admiral Graf Spee* ascertained the condition of the prisoners. At midnight the anchor was dropped and ten minutes afterwards 'an English-speaking officer came in . . . "Gentlemen," he said, "for you the war is over. We are now in Montevideo harbour. Today you will be free."' The news was received with incredulity which turned swiftly to delight. Astonishingly, not one prisoner had been wounded in the action.

Langsdorff had been superficially wounded in the face, and was concerned about the severe damage to the bow of his ship, but worst of all, by entering neutral waters he had lost control of the situation. He was free to parade his men in their white tropical uniforms and bury his dead with naval pomp, but his luck, and perhaps his resolve, had run out. After protracted posturing on the part of the German and British diplomats, Langmann and Millington-Drake, Langsdorff was compelled to leave. He considered seeking internment across the wide estuary in Anglophobic Argentina, and sought advice from Berlin. Significantly, he does not seem to have considered the alternative of attempting to break out through Harwood's blockade, and in communicating with his superiors he over-emphasised the difficulties confronting him.[30] Hitler thought Langsdorff ought to seek glory, but left it to Raeder to decide. The Grossadmiral advised Langsdorff not to submit to internment in Uruguay and, if he decided to scuttle, to ensure the complete destruction of the *Admiral Graf Spee*. In the event, on the evening of Sunday 17 December, Langsdorff weighed the *Admiral Graf Spee*'s anchor and headed towards the sea.

Offshore the newly promoted and knighted Rear Admiral Sir Henry Harwood, KCB listened to the running commentary broadcast live over the radio by an American reporter named Michael Fowler as the *Admiral Graf Spee*, bedecked in swastika ensigns, increased speed. She had only a skeleton crew on board, Langsdorff having ordered the bulk of his men aboard the German steamship *Tacoma* which followed the *Admiral Graf Spee* downstream. As she entered the wide international waters of the estuary of the Rio de la Plata the *Panzerschiff*, instead of continuing to sea, swung her wounded bow to the west, into the stream, and let go her anchor again.

Hearing this in Fowler's broadcast, Harwood ordered Woodhouse to catapult the *Ajax*'s seaplane off. Meanwhile, the swastikas fluttered to the deck of the *Admiral Graf Spee* and a fast motor-boat ran alongside. A few minutes later it sped away. The sun was setting. It was a Wagnerian moment, the seaplane pilot afterwards recalled: 'The *Graf Spee* was silhouetted against the [setting] sun . . .' At 20.00 the first of a series of explosions began to rip the ship apart. 'The Germans made a very thorough job of it,' another British naval officer wrote. 'She burned fiercely with small explosions every few minutes', and the ship was systematically destroyed 'as the flames reached some new compartment.'

The Argentinians to whom Langsdorff surrendered his ship's company proved unsympathetic, and interned his people for the duration. The popular press on both shores of the Plate thought him a coward. Certainly the Kriegsmarine had no sense of tradition to compare with that of the Royal Navy, and Langsdorff seems not to have been personally imbued with any love of glory. Perhaps the reputation he had among his victims for consideration and the gallantry expected of a gentleman marked, rather, a man incapable of the ruthlessness war demanded. Who knows? One can imagine his isolation and his sense of failure. The former went with his rank and responsibilities, but must have been exacerbated by the latter. Perhaps he had no enthusiasm for the Nazi state; yet in his last letter to the German ambassador in Buenos Aires he wrote hyperbolically of proving by his death 'that the fighting services of the Third Reich were ready to die for the honour of the flag'. In fact, this was also an oxymoron.

Wrapping himself in a German naval ensign, Langsdorff shot himself.

Harwood had stuck to his task and earned the spoils of success, a knighthood and promotion. The future was to reveal his shortcomings;[31] for the present, his victory was timely, reinvigorating the trust Britons traditionally reposed in the Royal Navy; but perhaps most of all, as a reassuring triumph of gunnery over the surface raider, it vindicated Their Lordships. The defeat of Langsdorff was bad for the morale of the Kriegsmarine, and made Hitler even more nervous of exposing his capital ships. Both sides were to suffer from delusions arising from the circumstances of the Battle of the River Plate, for in reality it was no more than a distant curtain-raiser on what was to come. The fact was that the Royal Navy owed its success to the distress signals transmitted in expectant good faith by the *Doric Star* and the *Tairoa*, and relayed by the *Port Chalmers*.

Though the merchant masters and their officers were free, those aboard the *Altmark* were not. Dau had no love for the British, having been a prisoner himself during the First World War. Conditions aboard his ship were poor, the food in particular. 'Black bread, butter substitute, soup composed of fat, salt pork, with tinned and dehydrated vegetables . . . The main hardships were lack of exercise in fresh air . . . and lack of water.'[32]

Although the Admiralty had spread a wide net in anticipation of the *Admiral Graf Spee* breaking out of the Plate, and although this had successfully intercepted almost all the remaining German merchant ships in the Atlantic, Dau evaded British cruisers by remaining for some time in the South Atlantic. It was 11 February 1940 before the *Altmark* was in sight of Iceland, and on the 14th she entered the waters of neutral Norway. She was stopped and boarded by Norwegian naval officers off Trondheim and again off Bergen, Dau repeatedly denying that he had on board any nationals belonging to a belligerent power while the British prisoners did everything they could to attract the attention of the Norwegians. In their pockets most of the deck officers still had their whistles, an item almost as indispensable to them as their sextants, and these were blown, but to no effect.

The Commander-in-Chief of the British Home Fleet, Admiral Forbes, informed Captain P. L. Vian, then conducting a sweep along the Norwegian coast in the destroyer *Cossack* with a cruiser and four other destroyers, that his prime duty was to intercept the *Altmark*. She was eventually located by the British cruiser *Arethusa* and the destroyers *Intrepid* and *Ivanhoe*, part of

Vian's force, but the situation was equivocal: their order to stop was ignored by *Altmark*, and frustrated by the presence of her neutral Norwegian escorts. The attitude of the Norwegian authorities may have been a consequence of the rumpus caused by their detention of the American ship *City of Flint*; from whatever motive, the Norwegian warships saw the *Altmark* in to Jössing Fjord and refused Vian's demand for the release of any prisoners. The *Altmark*, they asserted, was unarmed, and had been examined at Bergen the previous day; she had been cleared to proceed south towards Germany under escort, and had no Britons on board. Vian withdrew, and signalled the situation to the Admiralty. After consultation at the highest level Sir Dudley Pound, over Forbes's head, ordered Vian to intervene. At 22.00 that night, 16 December, *Cossack* returned to Jössing Fjord and entered the narrow defile at speed, brushing aside both the ice floes and the single unco-operative Norwegian torpedo-boat *Kjell*, whose commander remained passive despite the *Cossack*'s violation of his nation's neutrality. Dau attempted to manoeuvre his ship but Vian, undeterred, laid *Cossack* alongside the *Altmark*, and ordered her boarded.

The *Cossack*'s first lieutenant, springing over the gap and catching a turn of steel wire rope round a set of bitts on *Altmark*'s deck, led a party of two officers and thirty men armed with revolvers and cutlasses 'in the old style'. After a vicious skirmish during which one of the boarding party was wounded and eight German seamen were killed, they rounded up the crew and searched the ship. The incarcerated merchant seafarers suddenly heard 'an Englishman shouting down to our hatch "Are you British prisoners?",' to which the answer 'Yes' brought the response, '"Then you're safe. We've come to release you." Then there was a loud burst of cheering.' Shortly afterwards Vian withdrew, the *Cossack* crowded with 299 jubilant merchant officers and seamen whom he landed at Leith the following afternoon. Dau was left fulminating over the British violation of Norwegian waters and the damage to his ship.[33]

Vian's exploit seemed a meet conclusion to the action off the Rio de la Plata. From Uruguay to Norway, it seemed, the traditional writ of the Royal Navy still ran, and the prosaic shout 'Are you British prisoners?' and the laconic response became mythologised into the vastly more rousing and enduring cry of 'The Navy's here!'[34] As far as the merchant seafarers rescued by Lieutenant Commander Bradwell Turner and his boarders were concerned as they joked and sipped their naval 'kye'[35] aboard *Cossack* as she drove seawards down the steep-sided fjord in the moonlight, the Royal Navy had done its splendid bit and restored to them their liberty.

5

'Quite enough disaster'

Karamea

IN THE FIRST quarter of 1940 British cruisers intercepted many of the remaining German merchant ships as they attempted to get home, but as early as 17 January the Minister for Economic Warfare, Mr Ronald Cross, felt able to inform the House of Commons that the British blockade had succeeded in choking German exports. In reprisal, both the Luftwaffe and the Kriegsmarine's light forces had prosecuted vigorous sorties against convoys working their way up and down the North Sea coasts, laid copious mines, all of which caused widespread loss of mercantile shipping, and wantonly strafed lightvessels and lighthouses.

The young U-boat commanders were maddened by the continuing failure of their torpedoes and Dönitz was taking steps to rectify matters, but his submarines continued to be dogged by the problem for some time. The losses of U-boats had also been disconcerting and in the New Year Dönitz was only able to operate a small number, which had little success until the second half of January when Kapitänleutnant Matthes in *U-44* reached the Bay of Biscay. In the early hours of 14 January Matthes was patrolling to the west of Ushant light, an important landfall for vessels entering the English Channel from the south and west. Here he torpedoed the small Tønsberg-registered steam tramp-ship *Fagerheim*, killing 14 Norwegians. He next moved east and sank the new Dutch motor-vessel *Arendskerk*, belonging to the Dutch East Indies Line. The torpedo broke her in two, but the crew escaped unscathed. Matthes then attacked and sank the Greek tramp-steamer *Panachandros*, killing the entire crew, before heading south-west towards the Spanish coast.

During the passage, French radio stations obtained a fix on *U-44*'s radio transmissions to Germany. In their turn the B-Dienst service intercepted the French attempts to vector a response onto Matthes's U-boat, and were comforted by the discovery that the French assumed *U-44* to be some seventy miles from her actual position. On 18 February Matthes arrived off Cape Villano, a focal point for shipping making for Europe from the Mediterranean. Here he sank the Danish Lauritzen refrigerated motor-vessel *Canadian Reefer*, though with no loss of life. Two days later, off Oporto, he despatched the *Ekatontarchos Dracoulis*, killing six men. The Greek tramp had been built as a First World War standard ship and this was her sixth incarnation. Matthes continued to work *U-44* slowly south until he lay off Lisbon, where on the 24th he attacked a French convoy, sinking one ship. Off Cape Mondego next day he caught up with a straggler from the same convoy, and torpedoed her with a loss of eight men dead. Finally, taking a sweep out into the Atlantic before heading home, Matthes found another neutral Greek ship, the *Flora Nomikos*, east of the Azores and promptly sank her.[1]

Following Matthes, Korvettenkapitän Schütze, making his way round the north of Scotland in *U-25*, sank the British tramp-ship *Polzella* of Cardiff. Heavy with iron ore, she sank rapidly, killing Captain J.H. Thompson and all 35 of her crew. That same day, 17 January, he attacked off the Shetlands the small Norwegian short-sea trader *Enid* belonging to Bachke & Co. of Trondheim. Continuing his outward passage he was off the Hebrides next day where he sank another ore-carrier, the Swedish *Pajala*, before heading towards the South Western Approaches. Here, when some 220 miles to the west of the Isles of Scilly on the afternoon of 22 January, Schütze sank his third neutral vessel, the Norwegian *Songa*. He now ran west and then south to refuel from the German supply ship *Thalia* at Cadiz before meeting the southbound Convoy OG16 off Lisbon on 3 February. Schütze neatly picked off the 14-knot British cargo-liner *Armanistan*, owned by F.C. Strick Ltd. There were no dead, but 8,300 tons of British exports, including zinc, sugar, chemicals and steel rails, were lost. As Captain C.R. Knight and his crew wallowed in their lifeboats, Schütze headed home. Knight and his men were rescued by a Spanish ship, the *Monte Abril*, and landed at Tenerife. On his way back, off the Shetlands on 13 February, Schütze hit his fourth neutral target, the Danish tanker *Chastine Maersk*.

Leaving Kiel under Kapitänleutnant Heidel on her first war patrol on 16 January, *U-55* was less fortunate. She is thought to have sunk the Swedish short-sea trader *Foxen* east of the Orkneys on the 19th, and the Norwegian *Telnes* was her next victim that day. Heidel then proceeded to his patrol area west of Ushant and attacked outward bound Convoy OA80G/OG16 on 30 January.[2] This convoy had been disordered by bad weather and had only one escort, the sloop *Fowey*, Commander H.B. Ellison. Heidel succeeded in torpedoing the empty, ballasted Greek tramp *Keramiai*, without loss of life, and the British tanker *Vaclite*, owned by the Standard Transportation Company of Hong Kong. Bound from London to New York, she too was in ballast, and her crew, under Captain G. Legg, were afterwards picked up by the Italian ship *Pollenzo* and landed at Barry. Heidel had, however, succeeded in drawing a hornet's nest about his ears. As soon as the losses of the two ships were signalled to Plymouth, the Commander-in-Chief, Western Approaches, Admiral Sir Martin Dunbar-Nasmith, ordered reinforcements to the scene. As *Fowey* proceeded with the convoy the two warships, the old 'W'-class destroyer *Whitshed*, Commander E.R. Condor, and the French destroyer *Valmy*, located U-55 and subjected her to a punishing but inconclusive depth-charge attack. Heidel dived and made good his escape. They might have lost their quarry, but the continuing presence of the destroyers in the offing kept Heidel's damaged U-boat submerged for too long and, in addition to her leaks, her batteries were soon exhausted. Heidel cautiously surfaced, but Coastal Command had ordered a Sunderland flying-boat of No. 228 Squadron to the area. Commanding a wider horizon than could be seen from the warships' bridges, Flight Lieutenant E.J. Brooks attacked U-55 with anti-submarine bombs, recalling *Whitshed* and *Valmy* to the scene. Once the U-boat was in range of their 4-inch guns *Whitshed* and *Fowey* opened fire, and Heidel determined to scuttle his craft. He lost his life in the process but his crew were picked up to a man and became prisoners-of-war. This first combined use of relentless air and sea power was a foretaste of the fate awaiting many of Heidel's colleagues.

Kapitänleutnant Scheringer in *U-26*, operating off south-west Ireland, sank another Norwegian tramp-ship, the *Nidarholm*, on 12 February. Abandoned by her crew, she broke in two and went down without fatalities. A little further to the north on the 14th *U-26* torpedoed the grain-laden British tramp *Langleeford*,[3] a straggler from Convoy HX18. The four men on watch in the boiler and engine rooms were killed but the remainder, Captain H. Thompson and 29 men, escaped. Scheringer was to have gone south to join Hartmann, but his U-boat had developed a defect and he now headed for Wilhelmshaven. While running north up the west coast of Ireland he sank the Oslo-registered Norwegian general cargo-ship *Steinstad* off the Aran Islands. Thirteen of the *Steinstad*'s crew were lost.

By this time both Schultze in *U-48* and Hartmann in *U-37* were back on their next war patrols. Hartmann left Wilhelmshaven bound for the rich pickings to be had between the Fastnet Rock and the Isles of Scilly. Off the Shetlands on passage to his patrol area he sank a small Norwegian ship, the *Hop*, and the British tramp *Leo Dawson* with the loss of all hands.[4]

Having landed two agents on the shores of Donegal Bay in Eire on 8 February, Hartmann continued south, and off Dingle Bay on the 10th he sank the small Norwegian steamship *Silja*. Rounding Mizen Head he encountered the British trawler *Togimo* which he despatched by gunfire as he headed ESE for the Scillies, where on the 15th he torpedoed the small Danish steamer *Aase*, killing 15 of her crew and leaving just one survivor.

Hartmann was next to rendezvous with Schultze and others. Together *U-26, U-41, U-50, U-53* and *U-54* were going to carry out Dönitz's third attempt at a group attack. Schultze, meanwhile, having laid some mines in the English Channel off Weymouth, was also on his way to the rendezvous. On 10 February, when off the Isles of Scilly, he succeeded in torpedoing the Dutch general cargo-liner *Burgerdijk*. On this occasion he appears to have given the crew time to take to the boats before despatching his quarry.

Schultze remained in this locality for a short period, his next victim the refrigerated cargo-liner *Sultan Star*, owned by F. Leyland & Co., a division of Vestey's Blue Star Line. The twin-screw, 16.5-knot ship was on passage from Buenos Aires to Liverpool loaded with 7,803 tons of frozen meat and 1,000 tons of butter, with an additional 200 tons of deck cargo in barrels. At 06.00 on the morning of 14 February she was about 350 miles to the west and south of Land's End, heading for St George's Channel. During the forenoon she was overhauled by a group of warships centred on the heavy cruiser *Exeter*, then returning from repairing battle-damage in the Falklands after the action off the Rio de la Plata.

At 16.30 the *Sultan Star* was shaken by an explosion in her after-starboard side and immediately began to list. Captain W.H. Bevan ordered First Radio Officer P. Winsor to transmit a distress signal, rang 'Finished with Engines' and ordered the crew to the boats under the direction of the Chief Officer. The ship was sinking rapidly by the stern so Bevan, having seen the confidential books dumped and the boats made ready, ordered the *Sultan Star* abandoned. One man had been killed in the engine room but the rest of the crew mustered in good order and the boats were all launched. Bevan instructed one to hold on alongside, and before leaving the ship himself he checked to see that Winsor had left the radio room. Finding the radio officer still at his post, Bevan told him, 'The ship's sinking fast! You've no time to waste . . .'

Winsor remonstrated, insistent on remaining where he was until he had ensured that his signal had been received. By the time he and the master were ready to leave the radio room the boat-deck was already awash as the bow began to lift high in the air. Finding it difficult to keep his feet and faced with certain death if he delayed further, Bevan dived into the sea, expecting Winsor to follow behind him. The men in the boat left standing-by hauled Bevan out of the water, whereupon the ship finally reared up, the sea pouring into her funnel as her fore-deck cargo of heavy drums broke loose from their lashings, a cascade which caught Winsor as he finally jumped clear. The *Sultan Star* began her final dive, and the displaced water she caused to be thrown up threatened to swamp Bevan's boat. As the ship disappeared and the roar and turmoil of her violent sinking subsided, the men in the lifeboat could hear cries for help. Mindful of the danger of the steamship's boilers bursting as she sank, Bevan ordered them to their oars and they pulled through the floating detritus that, with the barrels, was all that remained of their ship. They found Winsor, guided by 'his groans as he was caught and pounded and crushed between the barrels', and succeeded in lifting him from the water.

Philip Winsor's devotion to duty saved his companions, for his signal had been intercepted by the naval vessels that had passed them that morning. Two of the destroyers escorting *Exeter*, *Vesper* and *Whitshed*, had been sent back, and having rescued the men from the *Sultan Star*'s boats, they sought her executioner. While this was in train Winsor was being worked on by a young surgeon-lieutenant, who saved his life. He was later appointed MBE and awarded Lloyd's War Medal for Bravery at Sea. Bevan, who was himself commended, said of Winsor that he was 'one of the bravest men I have ever met . . .'

Vesper and *Whitshed* found and attacked an echo and confidently reported a kill, a 'fact' revealed in the *London Gazette* of 24 May 1940. Schultze had escaped to fight another day, however, and on the morrow it was the misfortune of the Dutch-flagged motor-tanker *Den Haag* to loom in his attack periscope: he torpedoed her too. The *Den Haag*'s owners were in their turn controlled by the Standard Oil Company of the United States, and complicated chains of ownership like this combined with the damage to neutral parties to earn the German submarine offensive little approval outside the Reich. Particularly was this the case with Schultze's next target, the Helsinki-registered tramp *Wilja*, torpedoed on the 17th, at a time when Finland was locked in battle with Russia.[5] All *Wilja*'s crew survived.

Kapitänleutnant Bauer's *U-50* also struck on her outward passage to co-operate with Hartmann and Schultze, sinking the small Swedish steamer *Orania* about sixty miles north-east of the Shetlands on 11 February and killing 14 of her crew. Stretching out into the Atlantic, on the 13th Bauer fired a salvo of torpedoes at the Norwegian tanker *Albert L. Elsworth*; they exploded prematurely, though close alongside the tanker.[6] Bauer was now approaching Rockall. In the early hours of 15 February he saw the Danish steamer *Maryland*, which he torpedoed with the loss of all hands before heading south for his rendezvous with Hartmann. When well to the westward of Cape Finisterre on the 21st he sank the Dutch tramp *Tara*, with no loss of life. Next day he cut out of Convoy OG19F the empty and ballasted tanker *British Endeavour*, Captain T. Weatherhead. Five men below at the time the torpedoes struck were killed, while 33 survived to be rescued by the British ship *Bodnant* and landed at Funchal in Madeira.

One of Bauer's main diesels now failed and he headed home. In fact *U-50* had already missed the rendezvous, so Dönitz's third group attack was working out no better than the first two. Of the other U-boats, only Korvettenkapitän Grosse's *U-53* was nearing the focal point. Scheringer's *U-26* had aborted her patrol, *U-54* had vanished without trace, and Kapitänleutnant Mugler's *U-41* had been sunk.[7] Having attacked and damaged the Dutch tanker *Ceronia* to the west of the Scillies on 5 February, *U-41* had sunk the Canadian Pacific Steam Ship Company's fast cargo-liner *Beaverburn*. Like many other 15-knot cargo-liners at this period, this fine vessel had been compelled to keep a speed of 9 knots to maintain station in Convoy OB84 when she ought to have been sailing independently. Mugler's torpedo, striking her amidships, broke her in two, and it says much for the seamanship and discipline of Captain T. Jones's crew that they managed to launch their boats and abandon ship in the nine minutes they had before the *Beaverburn* foundered. They were fortunate in that a torpedo-strike amidships killed only one man, and that the 74 survivors were quickly rescued by the American tanker *Narragansett*. Although Convoy OB84 had only the single destroyer *Antelope* as escort, Lieutenant Commander T. White counter-attacked with depth-charges and destroyed Mugler and the crew of *U-41*.

Grosse, meanwhile, had also taken a wide sweep out to the west: *U-53* sank the Norwegian motor-vessel *Snestad* during the forenoon of 11 February and that evening, at about 20.45, torpedoed Houlder Brothers' motor-tanker *Imperial Transport*. The torpedo 'struck the port side in way of No. 6 tanks', creating an explosion of such force that the vessel's back broke just abaft the bridge. Eleven men were killed in the holocaust but, although the hull was irreparably damaged and the forward section began to settle, there was just time for the officers on the bridge or in their cabins in the amidships superstructure to cross to the after section. Such was the subdivision of a tanker that even when empty of a buoyant cargo of oil she could be difficult to sink, and this proved to be the case with the *Imperial Transport*.[8]

The tanker had delivered a cargo of oil to Scapa Flow and was on her way back to Trinidad in ballast. She was not gas-free, however, hence the violence of the blast following the detonation of the torpedo's warhead. As the tanker wallowed in the heavy swell, over which a moderate south-easterly breeze cut up a short sea, Captain W. Smail gave the order to abandon ship. In 'lowering the port boat several men fell into the water, all but two of whom were picked up. The port boat was standing off from the ship until 1 a.m. on the 12th endeavouring to reach the two men who were lost. Whilst searching for these men, the forward half of the ship was found to be drifting [down] on to the boat, and with difficulty the boat crew returned to the after portion which they found to be still afloat.'

Those on board the after part now pumped water ballast to stabilise the remains of the ship while they attempted to recall the starboard boat. This did not return to the *Imperial Transport* until 14.00 the following afternoon, 'having been away nearly 17 hours. Several of the occupants were lightly dressed and in an exhausted condition due to exposure.'

Having failed to attract the attention of two passing vessels, Captain Smail took stock of the situation. Chief Engineer C.J. Swanbrow kept steam on the boilers and they found that with care it was possible to proceed in the after section of the hull at about 2.5 knots. Steering was possible using the emergency hand gear aft and they soon left the forepart of the ship astern. The poop compass had been damaged in the explosion, so Smail navigated with an atlas and ruler, estimating 107 miles made good by noon on the 14th. At 18.00 that evening four British destroyers arrived on the scene. Smail and his crew refused to abandon what was left of their ship, and HMS *Kingston* was assigned to escort them. Smail could now determine the deviation of his magnetic compass and they continued to the eastward, heading for the north coast of Scotland.

By the late evening of 15 February Smail and Swanbrow were becoming increasingly anxious about the state of the forward bulkhead. The *Imperial Transport*'s surviving hull was heavily down by the stern, but twisted steel wreckage and the strain of taking punishment from head seas were weakening the structure forward. As the south-easterly wind freshened an attempt was made to steer stern first, but this failed, as did an attempt at towing by the *Kingston*.

Six of the crew now approached Smail and requested they be put aboard the destroyer. The *Kingston* signalled to ask whether Smail thought the ship 'would hold out until the morning?' If not, all hands would have to be withdrawn, as a gale was imminent. Smail thought the ship's chances poor; moreover, he and Swanbrow were worried that once the pumps were shut off the *Imperial Transport* would fill with water. Caught on the horns of such a bleak dilemma they decided to abandon ship and were taken off in heavy seas by the destroyer's whaler, which was damaged in the process.

At daylight on the 16th the destroyer *Forester* and the naval tug *Buccaneer* arrived, but the conditions were too bad to lower the damaged whaler to put Smail and his men back on board, and 'after consulting with the commanders of the ships present' Smail 'was advised to make port on the *Kingston* and send his crew home.' At 07.00 on 17 February they landed at Lyness in Scapa Flow, where one donkeyman and three seamen were treated for injuries sustained in abandoning ship.[9] In due course, however, the weather moderated, the *Buccaneer* got hold of the *Imperial Transport*, and Smail had the satisfaction of seeing his ship beached in Kilchattan Bay, Bute.[10]

Meanwhile, many miles away to the south, Grosse had sunk three neutral ships, the two Swedish steamers *Dalarö* and *Norna* and the Danish tramp *Martin Goldschmidt*, with some loss of life.

In theory, Hartmann should now have assumed tactical control of a combined attack on an approaching French convoy whose movements B–Dienst had been monitoring. Dönitz believed that although his submarine service belonged to a Germany which in naval terms was an inferior power when compared with Great Britain, in his U-boats Germany possessed a superior force to a British navy lacking in quality and too widespread and weak to contain his planned offensive operations. This bold assumption was to prove flawed. Some U-boat crews were barely trained, and while in due course they sometimes got the better of the fumbling convoy escorts they encountered over the next thirty months, they were not yet battle-hardened and their *current* opponents, though woefully few and far between, were the destroyers of the regular Royal Navy. Dönitz knew that he had no time to waste; to date he had lost a serious number of his submarines to accident and enemy action, and he needed a war-winning tactic without delay.

He had great faith in the application of group or 'wolf-pack' tactics, if and when they could be applied properly. In the autumn of 1937 he had directed the first group exercises from his depot ship at Kiel. The U-boat pack had attacked its simulated convoy 'with complete and impressive success'. Dönitz had next wanted to carry out an exercise in the Atlantic, using the depot ship *Saar* as a target against which to deploy the Type VII U-boats and the large Type Is, *U-25* and *U-56*. Unfortunately, international tensions arising from the Spanish Civil War prompted Hitler to veto the notion of 'a screen of U-boats in the Atlantic'. Then, in the winter of 1938–9, Dönitz had held a *Kriegspiel* 'to examine, with special reference to operations in the Atlantic, the whole question of group tactics: command and organisation, location of enemy convoys and the massing of further U-boats for the final attack. No restrictions were placed on either side and the officer in charge of convoys had the whole of the Atlantic at his disposal and was at liberty to select the courses followed by his various convoys.'[11] From the conclusions drawn by Dönitz and his Chief-of-Staff Godt was derived the optimum U-boat fleet requirement of 300 submarines.

In May 1939 Dönitz had succeeded in holding an exercise off the Iberian coast, with a second in the Baltic in July. But he had meanwhile become increasingly estranged from the Kriegsmarine's heart, not only in his enthusiasm for group tactics but because of his growing conviction that despite Hitler's repudiation of the Anglo–German Naval Agreement of 1935, German naval expansion united with the Führer's policies would inevitably excite British hostility before sufficient U-boats were available to be effective. But as Dönitz, in his own words, 'pressed with increasing vehemence for an acceleration of the German submarine building programme', it was Hitler's judgement that Britain would remain on the fence. Moreover, despite Dönitz's passionate advocacy of group tactics and their proven success, his superiors opposed him, arguing that local radio control would betray the pack's position. They were not wrong. Dönitz, however, argued that this was a reasonable risk, given the likely benefits at stake. With what anxious interest must he then have watched the plot in mid February 1940 when he believed Hartmann capable of mustering six U-boats to attack two French convoys off the Portuguese coast. In the event, only two U-boats found their intended target, and their attack was far from tightly co-ordinated. Hartmann struck first not at the French convoys but at the British Convoy OG18, outward bound towards Gibraltar, sinking the Blue Funnel Liner *Pyrrhus* on 17 February about a hundred miles to the north-west of Cape Ortegal.

The *Pyrrhus* was bound on her regular service to the Far East by way of the Suez Canal, and though she was not particularly fast she could make 13.5 knots and was among the speedier vessels in OG18, the commodore of which had complained that such ships (and there were three other vessels belonging to the same owners in OG18) ought not to be mixed with far slower tramps. However, the sailing of fast independents had not yet been universally adopted, and it was argued that as many ships as could be, should be kept together, in particular on the route to Gibraltar, upon which the enemy seemed to be concentrating. The paucity of escorts did not allow for a greater number of convoys, and a mixture of ships was therefore necessary in order not to limit the volume of trade too seriously. The reasons for this shortage held little comfort for OG18, however, escorted as it was by a French destroyer and a small French naval auxiliary, a quite inadequate defence for a convoy of 44 merchantmen.

The *Pyrrhus* was leading the fifth column and her master, Captain W.T. Spencer, was acting as vice commodore. The notional speed of Convoy OG18 was 8 knots, but on the evening of the 15th a gale came on from the WSW and disrupted its cohesion. By dawn on the 17th OG18 was scattered, and after an exchange of signals the commodore decided to reduce speed to give the laggards time to catch up, while Spencer wanted to increase speed in order to 'contact ships we knew had gone ahead during the night'. Later that afternoon the commodore had second thoughts and ordered his vice commodore to go ahead and round up the faster 'rompers'. This was properly the task of the naval escort, but the French destroyer was not at the time in sight of the commodore's portion of the convoy, and in fact did not rejoin until early on the 18th.

Spencer increased speed to 11.5 knots, and an hour later came in sight of the 17 errant vessels ahead. Fourteen obeyed his signals to put about and rejoin the main body, but three showed a determination to continue forging ahead. Spencer was therefore obliged to chase after them, and had just succeeded in persuading them to fall back on the convoy when at 15.58 'a dull roaring sound occurred in the vicinity of No. 5 Hatch'. Cargo cases, dunnage and débris were thrown high into the air and the *Pyrrhus* was shrouded in a cloud of brown smoke. As he stared aft from his bridge wing it seemed to Spencer that the entire after-part of his ship had disappeared where the mainmast had fallen, bringing down both main and emergency radio aerials. Ordering the engine room abandoned and throwing his confidential books over the side in their prepared weighted bag, Spencer then ordered the boats away, and this was successfully accomplished despite the heavy swell still running after the gale. The muster reported eight men missing and Spencer and his chief officer, having ensured that the ship was empty of the living, descended the ship's side by way of a boarding ladder and scrambled into the same boat. The dead were found to be eight Chinese firemen and greasers, probably those off-duty at the time in their accommodation under the poop. Spencer and his 77 companions were picked up by two other British ships in convoy, the *Uskside* and the *Sinnington Court*, leaving behind them the forward part of the *Pyrrhus*, which remained afloat for two days.[12]

After this success Hartmann withdrew from OG18, but struck again in the early hours of the 18th off Cape Finisterre when he torpedoed the newly-built 10-knot tramp-ship *Ellin*, belonging to S.G. Embiricos Ltd. of Athens and London. The Greek-flagged steamer was proceeding independently, and although she sank, her crew abandoned her without loss of life. A few hours later the same day Hartmann heard a homing transmission from Grosse in *U-53* and finally came in sight of the B-Dienst-targeted Convoy RS10 to the west of El Ferrol, attacked it, and sank a French steamer.

At this time Schultze, so far the most successful U-boat commander and only the second after Prien to be decorated with the *Ritterkreuz*, was miles away and soon to head for home, leaving only Grosse in *U-53* to form with Hartmann the 'group' with which to attack RS10 in which Dönitz had invested so much faith and expectation. To the intense frustration of both Hartmann and Grosse, and afterwards of Dönitz, this third attempt to co-ordinate a group attack on a convoy petered out not so much from lack of U-boats as from the failure of their torpedoes' detonators. One detonator that did function had an unforeseen consequence. Persisting with the attack, Grosse fired at and sank a vessel he thought was from Convoy RS10. In fact it was a neutral Spanish steam-ship, the ancient Mediterranean trader *Banderas* owned by Compañía Naviera Vascongada of Bilbao.[13] Seven of her crew survived but 22 Spanish nationals were killed, and Madrid protested in furious terms to Berlin. In the diplomatic flurry which followed, the Fascist government of El Caudillo refused further permission for Dönitz's U-boats to refuel in mainland Spanish ports. Given the links between Generalissimo Franco's government and Germany, and its sympathies with Nazism, this was a spectacular blow for Dönitz.

Oblivious to the hornet's nest he had created Grosse made a further attack on Convoy RS10, but again his torpedoes failed. Both Grosse and Hartmann now headed for home. Passing north-about round Scotland, Hartmann arrived safely on 27 February, but four days earlier, to the south of the Faeroes, Grosse had been detected by the sonar of HMS *Gurkha*, Commander F.R. Parham. The new 'Tribal'-class destroyer attacked, and in a withering shower of depth-charges sent *U-53* to the bottom. Grosse never had to answer for his misdemeanour, and 41 of his comrades died with him.

Dönitz had suffered more losses elsewhere, particularly in the North Sea, but one was of particular significance. Sent into the Clyde Estuary to lay mines, *U-33* (Dresky) was sunk in shallow water by the minesweeper *Gleaner* on 5 February. From the 17 survivors who were searched and interned after interrogation, three rotors from the U-boat's Enigma encrypting machine were obtained. These included two which helped the Government Code and Cypher School at Bletchley Park break the German naval codes, a coup which later had a significant impact upon the struggle in the Atlantic.[14]

A short uneasy calm now fell upon the North Atlantic as German forces mustered to attack Denmark and Norway. The Danish government capitulated on 9 April, and an ill-conceived Anglo-French operation to invade northern Norway in support of the Norwegians was bogged down and then defeated with considerable losses, particularly among the Royal Navy forces engaged.[15] In the coastal waters of the North Sea and English Channel numerous merchantmen were lost to mines, air attack, surface and submarine attack, but the Western Approaches remained relatively quiet throughout the month of March 1940, with only a handful of British losses. For the time being British Admiralty analysis continued to be content with the war at sea.

Schuhart was the first to revive the German offensive. Having success-fully laid mines in the Bristol Channel, in *U-29* he was heading for Land's End and the English Channel, passing down the rugged north coast of Cornwall.[16] In the pitch dark of the early hours of 4 March he picked up an elderly homeward-bound tramp-ship, the *Thurston*, registered in West Hartlepool and the only ship owned by the Murrell Steamship Company. Laden with a full cargo of manganese ore, she was bound for the Cumbrian port of Workington from Takoradi in West Africa. The explosion of Schuhart's torpedo destroyed her and she sank almost instantly. Captain W.C. Fortune and 25 men went down with her, but three on watch on deck were rescued by the *Moyle* and landed at Cardiff.

A few hours later, further to the south-west, Schuhart sank the Furness Withy general cargo-liner *Pacific Reliance*, apparently separated from her two-score charges while acting as the commodore's ship for Convoy HX19. Captain E.O. Evan and his 47-strong crew, with Commodore R.P. Galer, RNR and his small staff, were rescued by a British ship and landed at Newlyn, Cornwall. Schuhart's torpedoes failed him in his next attack, on the Eagle Oil tanker *San Florentino*, and *U-29*, cheated of so rich a prize, resumed her homeward passage. A similar loss to that of the *Thurston*, a tramp going down with all hands, occurred about three weeks later. Last seen on 25 February, Runciman's *Castlemoor* disappeared without trace when approaching the British Isles after a crossing of the North Atlantic from Halifax, Nova Scotia. The vessel, thought to have been loaded with ore, was not sailing in convoy, and although her loss and that of her 40-strong company cannot be definitively attributed to a U-boat, the suspicion cannot be ruled out.

Despite the preoccupations of the Norwegian Campaign and the desperate need to refit his submarines after its conclusion, Dönitz had not quite with-drawn from the North Atlantic. Under a new commander, Kapitänleutnant V. Oehrn, *U-37* continued to strike at shipping on her fifth war patrol. Oehrn was 'a man with an exceptionally clear and determined mind' and had been on Dönitz's staff. His U-boat's torpedoes had been equipped with improved magnetic firing devices, though it was to gunfire that his first victim succumbed; perhaps Oehrn used his guns because she was a neutral and he wished, on this occasion at least, to display a little chivalry. On 19 May he was off St Kilda when he intercepted and sank the Swedish motor-vessel *Erik Frisell* of Stockholm. There was no loss of life among her crew, who took to their boats and were later picked up.

By the evening of 22 May *U-37* was lying some 150 miles to the south-west of the Isles of Scilly. Shortly before dark that evening, the officer of the watch aboard the homeward-bound Houlder Brothers' *Dunster Grange* was startled by a 'terrific explosion about fifty yards away on the port beam'.

The large general and refrigerated cargo-liner shook from the concussion as Captain R.A. Smiles rushed to the bridge, altering course to starboard and demanding more power from his diesels. Smiles held his new heading at slightly above his vessel's service speed of 15 knots for about ten minutes. It was now almost dark, and as nothing could be seen he resumed his proper course. Disappointed by the poor performance of his modified torpedoes, Oehrn surfaced and pursued, opening fire with his deck gun, the discharge of which further alarmed Smiles and his chief officer, Mr A. Seybold. The shell passed above the bridge, however, and once again the helm was put over and the *Dunster Grange* swung to starboard. The *U-37* was now fine on the starboard quarter and her next shot – aimed at the bridge, Smiles thought – exploded after hitting the starboard engine-room ventilator, spraying the vessel's upperworks with shell splinters and debris, smashing the engine-room skylight and sending a shower of steel shards down below.

The splinters damaged the oil supply pipes to two of the cylinders of one of the ship's two engines, but with commendable skill the chief engineer, Mr G.F. Jones, and his men were able to renew the cut pipes in about twenty minutes, enabling the *Dunster Grange* to work back up to full speed. Meanwhile Seybold had mustered the seamen, the boats were swung out, and the dozen passengers were collected under cover. On the poop the gunners, under the second officer, brought the ship's anti-submarine 4-inch gun into action, aiming at the gun-flashes of the enemy in the darkness. This and the *Dunster Grange*'s speed seem to have deterred Oehrn, whose gunfire became increasingly wide as *U-37* dropped astern. Captain Smiles's SSSS signal was picked up by Land's End radio and a French patrol vessel was informed of the U-boat's presence; when she arrived at the position given by Smiles, Oehrn had disappeared.

It is probable that he went deep and lay quiet, for he was still in the general area the following night, successfully torpedoing the Greek steamer *Kyma* before heading across the Bay of Biscay to operate on the shipping lane running south from Cape Ortegal. He remained in this locality for a week, first sinking the tramp *Sheaf Mead*, owned by Souter's of Newcastle and commanded by Captain A.H. Still, bound from Swansea to Philadelphia, in ballast and flying light. One gunner and 30 of her company perished, though five survived, picked up by a Greek tramp and landed at Cork in Eire.

The same day, 27 May, Oehrn stopped and boarded the Argentinian-flagged *Uruguay*, a 9-knot tramp registered in Buenos Aires. Oehrn judged her cargo to be contraband, and scuttled her after removing her crew and setting charges. Next day he sank the fine French passenger-cargo-liner *Brazza*, operating on the South American service of Chargeurs Réunis of

Le Havre. The ship was sunk by gunfire after her company had been ordered into the boats. Oehrn's next victims were a French fishing vessel and, off Vigo on the 29th, the *Marie José* which ran between Rouen and Algeria.

That same day, also on her way from the Mediterranean to a French port, the loaded British tanker *Telena*, Captain H.F. Gosling, was heading for Pauillac from Syria. She belonged to the Anglo-Saxon Petroleum Company and was carrying 9,368 tons of crude oil. Oehrn attacked on the surface and set her alight by gunfire. Abandoning their ship, the crew were fortunately picked up by two Spanish trawlers. The Spanish maritime authorities seized the *Telena* and had her towed to Bilbao, where she was repaired and renamed, to survive as the *Gerona* until 1975. Oehrn completed his patrol on 3 June off Cape Finisterre, sinking by gunfire a small Greek steamer, the *Ioanna*, and, with the death of one seaman, the Finnish tramp *Snabb*.

Aware that an important British troop convoy, US3, was on its way from Australia, Dönitz attempted to muster a new group under Korvettenkapitän Rösing in *U-48*, but it failed to locate the convoy, which included several liners and a heavy escort, and was dispersed. Among its number was *U-101*, Kapitänleutnant Frauenheim, who was sent to patrol in the mouth of the English Channel. Here, on 30 May, he sank J.A. Billmeir's tramp-steamer *Stanhall* as she made for Liverpool with a full cargo of Australian sugar. One man was killed but the remaining 36, under Captain W.E. Herbert, survived and were landed at Weymouth from the British ship *Temple Moat*. Later that day Frauenheim sank Runciman's *Orangemoor* before withdrawing to the west. The *Orangemoor* had been part of Convoy HGF31 and was full of 8,150 tons of iron ore. She sank rapidly with the loss of 18 of her 40-strong crew, Captain R.E. Richardson and 21 men being rescued by the British ship *Brandenburg*.

On 2 June the steamer *Polycarp*, managed by the Booth Line on behalf of the British Ministry of Shipping, was sunk by *U-101*. The *Polycarp* was routed independently and homeward bound from Para towards Liverpool and Heysham with a general cargo. Fortunately no lives were lost, and Captain A. Allan and his crew were rescued by the French ship *Espiguette*. Frauenheim now made for the Iberian coast, where off Vigo on the 11th he ordered the crew off the Greek tramp *Mount Hymettus*, opened fire and sank her. Off Cape Finisterre on 12 June he torpedoed the British, Glasgow-registered Denholm tramp *Earlspark*, an 'independent' outward bound from Sunderland to Bordeaux with a full cargo of coal. Although 31 men survived to be rescued by Commander A.K. Scott-Moncrieff's sloop *Enchantress*, *Earlspark*'s master Captain E.J. Williams and six seamen were killed. Two days later in the same area *U-101* sank another Greek tramp, the *Antonis Georgandis*, by gunfire.

Keeping company with *U-101* in the Channel Approaches Schuhart's *U-29* had returned from Norway, and during the darkness of 20/21 June she clandestinely refuelled from the German supply-ship *Bessel* at Vigo. Returning to Cape Ortegal Schuhart sank two Greek tramps, the *Dimitris* and the *Adamastos*, before starting his homeward passage. During this he sank a Panamanian freighter by gunfire and the British tanker *Athellaird* by torpedo. The tanker was on her way from Liverpool to the Caribbean in ballast, having been part of Convoy OB176 which had just been dispersed. Fortunately the escorting sloop, HMS *Sandwich*, Commander H.J. Yeatman, was in the offing, able to rescue Captain H. Roberts and his 41 men.

At the end of June Captain George Hopper found himself playing host to a convoy commodore. His ship, another large Blue Star liner, the coal-fired *Avelona Star*, had crossed the Atlantic from Buenos Aires as an 'independent' with a cargo consisting largely of almost 6,000 tons of frozen meat and 1,000 tons of chilled oranges. Ordered to Freetown to join Convoy SL36, a detour which added considerably to the length of her voyage, the *Avelona Star* and her convoy had, by 30 June, reached a position some two hundred miles west of Cape Ortegal. The convoy was zig-zagging, when at 10.00 that morning a submarine alarm was raised as a neutral ship was torpedoed. The convoy executed an emergency turn and continued to zig-zag along the new line of advance. Convoy SL36 had run into the dispersed U-boats of Korvettenkapitän Rösing. After some time it reverted to its original mean course, only to meet *U-43*.

Like Schuhart, Kapitänleutnant W. Ambrosius's *U-43* had topped up her bunkers from the *Bessel*, before trying her luck off Lisbon. Here she had encountered a French convoy and torpedoed and set on fire the British, Hong Kong-registered tanker *Yarraville*, outward bound and in ballast. Captain Beveridge and 44 of his men were rescued by the French anti-submarine trawler *Marie Gilbert* and landed at Gibraltar; the five engine-room staff on duty below lost their lives. Ambrosius had then headed *U-43* for hunting grounds well to the westward, where on 30 June he sighted Convoy SL36. At about 21.00 a large passenger-cargo-liner provided a tempting target, and Ambrosius attacked.

Aboard the *Avelona Star* at 21.30 '[t]here was a dull thud and a huge column of water' rose alongside her starboard side. The ship immediately began to list. With a heave 'she righted herself, and then the foremost boiler blew up with clouds of smoke, ashes and steam which hid everything'. Four men on watch below were killed in the appalling holocaust. Hopper gave the order to abandon ship.

The Blue Star liner did not sink immediately but foundered slowly, left astern of the convoy from which one ship, the steamer *Beignon*, Captain

W.J. Croome, dropped out to pick up the *Avelona Star*'s 80 survivors. As what befell the *Beignon* shows, such acts of humanity could prove rash and they were later prohibited, the business of rescue being left to the escorts until, later still, dedicated rescue ships were commissioned for the purpose. The relief of Hopper's crew was short-lived: at about 03.00 the following morning, as she tried to catch up with SL36 and resume her station, the *Beignon* was hit by a torpedo from *U-30*. A Cardiff tramp, she had been bound for the Tyne with a full cargo of wheat loaded at Fremantle in Western Australia. There were insufficient boats to cope with the number of men now aboard her, and although fine weather and a slight sea meant that all were lowered, many survivors had to cling to an inadequate raft in charge of the *Avelona Star*'s chief officer, Mr G.L. Evans. Three more of the Blue Star ship's crew perished in the darkness, adding to the three lost in *Beignon*'s engine room. Fortunately two of the escorts, the destroyers *Vesper* and *Windsor*, put back at first light and eventually landed some 110 survivors from the two ships at Plymouth.

This was not quite the last of the action surrounding Convoy SL36, for there were other U-boats operating in the South West Approaches on the first day of July 1940. Kapitänleutnant H. von Klot-Heydenfeldt, in *U-102*, succeeded in sinking the straggling *Clearton*, of Newcastle, Captain J.E. Elsdon. She had joined the convoy at Freetown after crossing the Atlantic from Rosario and was bound to Manchester with a cargo of grain. Eight men died in the attack but Elsdon, his single gunner and two dozen of his crew were rescued later that day by the destroyer *Vansittart*. Lieutenant Commander R.G. Knowling searched the area and, obtaining a sonar contact, depth-charged *U-102* to destruction with the loss of all 43 of her company.

Another U-boat lost that day in the same area was *U-26*, temporarily commanded by Korvettenkapitän Fischer. Fischer had sunk a Greek and an Estonian the previous day and on 1 July had located the British ship *Zarian*, one of the dispersed members of Convoy OA175. He failed to sink the *Zarian* but his exploding torpedoes alerted her master, Captain Pelissier, whose signal summoned to the scene HM Corvette *Gladiolus*, one of the first 'Flowers' to enter service. Lieutenant Commander H.M.C. Sanders initiated a depth-charge attack and was soon joined by the sloop *Rochester*, Captain G.F. Renwick and a flying-boat from No. 10 Squadron, Royal Australian Air Force, Coastal Command. Fischer tried to escape but was seen by Flight Lieutenant W.N. Gibson from his Sunderland, and after Gibson had made two bombing runs Fischer was forced to surface and scuttle *U-26*, losing eight men in the process before he surrendered.

Kapitänleutnant F.-J. Lemp's *U-30* had been part of a second group intended by Dönitz to intercept Convoy HX48 in mid June, but this group too had missed its quarry and been dispersed. The U-boats moved south to operate off Cape Finisterre and on 20 June Lemp attacked Convoy HG34F and sunk Ropner's tramp *Otterpool*, commanded by Captain Thomas Prince, formerly of the *Firby*. Though only a 9.5-knot ship, *Otterpool* was in a 'fast' convoy. Carrying 8,180 tons of iron ore from Bona to the river Tees she sank like a stone, drowning 23 of her company, including Prince: her survivors were rescued by the sloop *Scarborough*.

The previous day this convoy had lost the tramp *Baron Loudon*, Captain J.H. Johnson, along with 5,050 tons of iron ore and the three men in her engine room, plus the 11-knot Glasgow-registered tramp *British Monarch* loaded with another 8,200 tons of ore; worse still was the loss of Captain J.F. Scott and all her 39 hands. It did not end there, for that same day Wilhelm Wilhelmsen's fine general cargo-liner *Tudor* had also been sunk after being torpedoed and catching fire. Only one of her Norwegian crew lost his life, but she took with her 4,500 tons of steel. These losses had all been caused by Rösing himself in *U-48*. He had already sunk three British vessels and one Greek on his way to the rendezvous, and on the way back to Kiel torpedoed the Dutch tanker *Moerdrecht*, which had straggled from eastbound Convoy HX49; 25 men were killed.

Ambrosius sank two other British tramp steamers on his way back to Wilhelmshaven, the independently-sailing *Aylesbury*, Captain T. Pryser, and the *Fellside*, Captain J.T. Nelson, which had fallen astern of Convoy OA184. There were no losses, all the survivors being rescued.

The remaining U-boat of the Rösing group was *U-46*, which under Kapitänleutnant E. Endrass sank the former Cunard White Star passenger-liner *Carinthia* off Galway Bay on 6 June. The *Carinthia*, Captain J.F.B. Barrett, was one of three Armed Merchant Cruisers sunk in the Western Approaches during the month; more were to be lost before the year was out. Continuing her passage, *U-46* reached her operational area off Cape Finisterre and on the 9th sank the Finn *Margaretta*. Two days later she damaged but failed to sink the British tanker *Athelprince*. Next day Endrass encounterd Convoy SL34, out of which he torpedoed the *Willowbank* and the *Barbara Marie*. Andrew Weir's *Willowbank* was heading for Hull from Durban, where she had loaded almost 9,000 tons of maize. Captain D. Gillies and his crew were all picked up by the Elder Dempster's general cargo-liner *Swedru* in company within the convoy. The *Swedru* also went to the assistance of the *Barbara Marie*, a tramp-ship belonging to J. Morrison & Company of Newcastle-upon-Tyne which was bound to Workington from Pepel with 7,200 tons of iron ore. Like so many others she paid the tragic penalty of her lading, sinking rapidly as she flooded fast. There were only five survivors out of her 37-man crew, her master, Captain Alfred Smith, going down with his ship.

On 16 June, after the dispersal of the Rösing group, Endrass torpedoed yet another Greek tramp, though her crew abandoned ship safely and she did not sink until the following day. A few days later he failed in an attempt to strike the *Ark Royal* as the aircraft-carrier headed south towards Gibraltar.

Of the group sent out to intercept HX48, Prien's *U-47* sank a single straggler from the convoy, the new British tramp *Balmoralwood*, on the evening of 14 June. With four aircraft as deck cargo she was laden with wheat, and bound for Falmouth from Canada. Captain F.H. Chilton and his 40-strong crew were picked up by the Hull-registered tramp *Germanic*. Failing to catch HX48 Prien withdrew to the Fastnet area, where he located the next incoming convoy, HX49. On 21 June 1940 he torpedoed the Eagle Oil Company's *San Fernando*, Captain A.R. Buckley. The Mersey-bound tanker did not sink immediately, saved for a few hours by her internal sub-division. An attempt to take her in tow and save her valuable cargo succeeded until the following day, when she was seen to be foundering and the tow was cast off. She sank with the loss of 13,500 tons of Venezuelan crude oil and 4,200 tons of furnace-grade fuel-oil. There was no loss of life, and Buckley and his crew were picked up by the escorting sloops *Fowey* and *Sandwich*.

Prien reported torpedo failures in attacks on several vessels, but in the next few days he claimed to have sunk a Panamanian ship, a Dutch tanker, a Greek tramp, and the Norwegian tramp *Lenda*, which he shelled and torpedoed after removing the crew; one man died in the attack. On 29 June he sank the elderly *Empire Toucan*, Captain H.T. Thomas, killing her engine-room crew, though the remainder were picked up by the escorting destroyer *Hurricane*. Thomas's vessel had been outward bound in ballast for Port Sulphur, Louisiana, one of a number of standard vessels built in the United States under programmes begun in the First World War, after which she had been laid up as part of the US War Reserve tonnage. Numbers of these ships were time-chartered or purchased outright by the British Ministry of Shipping, as well as by neutral interests eager to take advantage of the freight rates offered to convey cargoes to Britain. Some of this surplus tonnage had been mothballed by American owners who had found themselves unable to take advantage of the favourable market because of the American Neutrality Act (see chapter 5). There were those however who had got round this problem by registering their ships under flags-of-convenience, particularly that of Panama.

Another of Prien's group, *U-51* commanded by Kapitänleutnant D. Knorr, had fired torpedoes at several ships of Convoy HG34F, including the *Otterpool*, but all his attacks had failed. Moving further north, Knorr located and struck at Convoy OA172, sinking a sister-ship to Constantine's *Balmoralwood*, the *Windsorwood*, on 25 June. She was deeply laden with a full cargo of Tyne coal for Sierra Leone, where the coal was to be held for the bunkers of homeward-bound tramps of her own vintage. Captain G.A. Norton and his crew were rescued without loss by the British ship *Ainderby*, but the four men on duty in the engine room of Knorr's next victim, the tanker *Saranac*, all died. The Anglo-American Oil Company's large tanker was outward bound in ballast from Fawley to Aruba. Captain V.H. Alcock and 30 of his men were rescued by the *Hurricane*, which landed them at Plymouth, and nine by a British trawler, the *Caliph*, which put them ashore at Berehaven, Eire.

On the 29th Knorr attacked an innocent-looking tramp, the *Edgehill*. Owned by Sir William Reardon Smith & Company of Cardiff, the *Willamette Valley* had been requisitioned and renamed by the Admiralty as one of a handful of decoy vessels, better known as Q-ships. These disguised auxiliary men-of-war had been relatively successful in the First World War when their 'merchant crews' would take advantage of the enemy's strict observance of the Prize Regulations by faking a panicky abandonment in the hope that the enemy submarine would close its victim. Once it was in range the mask was cast aside, concealed guns were revealed, and the submarine destroyed. Legal equivocations were raised as to the status of these fake crews who wore no uniform, and they were charged by the Germans with piracy. One incident involving a Q-ship named the *Baralong* had been the subject of recriminations over an alleged 'war-crime'. But the inevitable erosion of respect for the Prize Regulations imposed by the grim imperatives of the current war rendered such a repetition of old tactics questionable. There was no possibility that Knorr or his colleagues would quiz the 'master' of the *Edgehill*; instead, he meted out the fate she would have suffered had she been what she pretended to be. Like the Armed Merchant Cruisers (which in due course were assigned a task more suitable to their immense capacities, carrying cargoes and troops), the 'Decoy' vessels reflected anachronistic practices. Those of the original eight which remained were dismantled in December 1940 and reverted to cargo-work.

The fate of many merchant ships during this phase of the war at sea, a period the wisdom of hindsight judges to have been 'quiet', nevertheless revealed an ominous trend. Generally speaking, loss of life was limited to those whose duty confined them below the water-line in the engine room, but the numbers of deaths among those manning ore-laden tramps were such as to send a frisson of apprehension through merchant seamen likely to be sent aboard such bulk-carriers. Overall, too, the losses were beginning to have a cumulative effect upon the British war effort. Those lost inward consignments of oil, wheat and frozen meat, manganese and iron ore were by no means insignificant; nor were the lost outward cargoes of coal, whether they were bound for the meat-processing plants of the Argentine or the coal hulks of Freetown, Cape Town or Gibraltar, where they would fuel the bottoms that came the other way; nor were the lost contents of those ruptured holds and 'tween-decks in sunken general cargo-liners, with their manufactured wares intended for the money-making markets of the world.

As for the loss of actual hulls from Britain's Merchant Navy, this was already a concern, since the loss of a merchantman was also cumulative in effect, all the cargoes she would have carried in future being forfeit. Although as yet comparatively few ships travelling in convoy had been torpedoed, the ominous threat inherent in the depredations of the German U-boats was something against which individual acts of defiance by merchant crews were no more than heartening. Although a measure of reprisal had been visited on the predators by the Royal Navy, Dönitz seems to have been more concerned with his torpedo failures, and they certainly provided a useful smoke-screen against his critics in the Seekriegsleitung as he waged his political battles on the home front. The Royal Navy itself seems to have suffered from over-confidence, both in its ability to strike back and in its claims of successful anti-submarine operations. Trans-Atlantic convoy escort remained inadequate, and while this weakness was in the process of being corrected, improvements would take time to implement.

Worst hit were the private companies upon whom the Merchant Navy depended. The *Balmoralwood* and *Windsorwood* represented two-thirds of the assets of the Middlesbrough-based, tramp-owning Constantine Shipping Company; by 1943 their final ship had been lost, and two out of the six additional ships owned by the parent company had also been sunk. Though their losses were fewer in terms of numbers, in gross tonnage the liner companies were faring little better, in particular the Blue Star Line, which in addition to the sinkings already described had by the end of July 1940 lost three more ships. One, the *Wellington Star*, was torpedoed on 16 July off Cape Finisterre during the U-boat attacks which followed the dispersal of Rösing's group. The *Wellington Star* was a brand-new, twin-screw, 16-knot motor-vessel, grossing 12,382 tons. At the outbreak of war she had been fitting-out at the Belfast shipyard of Harland & Wolff, from where she had sailed on her maiden voyage under the command of Captain T. Williams. Leaving Melbourne for home on 12 May 1940, she carried a mixed general cargo of frozen lamb and chilled foodstuffs. On 13 June she left Las Palmas in the Canary Islands, sailing independently and relying upon her speed, with Williams taking the added precaution of following Admiralty advice and zig-zagging. Three days later, at 11.02 on a fine, clear morning with a light northerly breeze, she was torpedoed forward, on the starboard bow, in way of Nos 1 and 2 Holds. The ship immediately began to sink by the head and Williams gave orders to abandon her; four boats were successfully lowered, evacuating the entire ship's company of 69. The boats lay off as the *Wellington Star* settled deeper in the water, at which point a second torpedo thundered into her and a U-boat surfaced not far away. Opening fire until the *Wellington Star* was ablaze, the submarine then motored among the lifeboats, seeking the name of her victim and information about her cargo. It was *U-101*, and the *Wellington Star* was Frauenheim's last success before he proceeded towards Kiel.

Withdrawing to base, Prien was off the west coast of Ireland on 2 July when he sighted the *Arandora Star*. Rejected as a possible Armed Merchant Cruiser, this large passenger-cargo-liner had been used by the Admiralty for extensive trials of anti-torpedo netting before taking part in the Norwegian campaign as a troop transport. Following this she had taken part in the evacuation from Western France (see below), returning with her human cargo to Liverpool. Among those on board were German and Italian nationals, both internees and prisoners-of-war, and from Liverpool Captain E. W. Moulton was ordered to convey these wretched people to St John's, Newfoundland, sailing as an 'independent' without escort.

At 06.15 that morning the *Arandora Star* was about 75 miles west of Bloody Foreland, zig-zagging at 15 knots. She had four able seamen closed up as lookouts and two officers, Chief Officer F.B. Brown and Third Officer W.H. Tulip, on watch, while down below were two engineer officers and a full complement of greasers and firemen, when a torpedo from *U-47* struck her starboard side, immediately in way of the after of her two engine rooms. The men tending her furnaces and the two turbines were all killed, either by the blast or by the torrent of sea water that poured into the ruptured hull. Both steam turbines were destroyed and the auxiliary generators failed, darkening the interior of the ship. One starboard lifeboat was destroyed, a second damaged. Brown immediately ordered a distress signal transmitted and rang the alarms for mustering the crew and passengers; switching to battery power, the duty radio officer contacted Malin Head radio station.

The ship's company consisted of 174 officers and ratings, to which were added a military guard of 200 soldiers charged with looking after 86 German prisoners-of-war, 479 interned German males and 734 interned Italian males. Brought on deck, these now terrified men 'greatly hampered the crew in their work of lowering the boats'. Nevertheless, ten of the ship's twelve lifeboats were lowered and half the 90 rigid life-rafts were thrown overboard. None of the prisoners or internees could be persuaded to board the rafts, all of them favouring the lifeboats; as a consequence they caused a dangerous surge of humanity round the davits, swarming over the side down boarding-ladders and life-lines in a wild bid to escape the now dangerously listing ship.

The boats having been launched – all by now overcrowded – the remainder of the rafts were cast loose, but those internees still on board refused to leave the ship as directed and at 07.15, unable to do any more for their charges, Moulton and his senior officers 'walked over the side as the water came up to meet them'. The chief officer later reported that he was picked up after about twenty minutes. 'I saw nothing of the officers who left at the same time as I did.' Brown went on: 'The vessel turned over and sank stern first almost immediately, and I think they must have been trapped as she came over.'

By 07.20, all that remained of the *Arandora Star* was a widening patch of oil, a litter of detritus, bobbing life-rafts, a handful of overloaded boats, and the heads of those left swimming for their lives. The ship had taken with her Captain Moulton, 12 officers and 42 of his crew, 91 soldiers and 713 Germans and Italians.

Two hours later a Sunderland flying-boat of Coastal Command flew over and dropped first aid kits, food and cigarettes in waterproof containers, together with a message that help was on its way. The Sunderland remained overhead until 13.00, when the Canadian destroyer *St Laurent*, Lieutenant Commander H.G. deWolf, arrived. By this time the survivors had spread out, so for five long hours the *St Laurent* and her whalers laboured to recover the human flotsam, many in the last stages of exhaustion and hypothermia. 'Few of the survivors could help themselves or even grasp a rope, because of the scum of oil with which they and the sea were thickly covered.' When the Canadian sailors discovered that most of the people they were rescuing were in fact enemy nationals, they signalled the news to the circling Sunderland. The flying-boat's aircrew expressed the irony of the situation: 'How bloody funny' they winked in reply.

Later the British destroyer *Walker* arrived and, as the grossly overloaded *St Laurent* headed for Greenock, cast about unavailingly for more survivors. The airborne presence of the Sunderland deterred Prien from making any attempt to disrupt the rescue; he slunk away, heading for Kiel. In his wake the 805 dead, many of them his own compatriots, sank into the abyss.

Three weeks later, on 28 July, the *Auckland Star* was sunk as she approached the Irish coast from the Panama Canal, homeward bound from Townsville, Australia with almost 11,000 tons of general cargo. Steaming independently, Captain D.R. MacFarlane's ship was zig-zagging at 16.5 knots when at about 04.00 she was struck by a torpedo on her port side, in way of Nos 5 and

6 Holds, filling and sinking rapidly. The boats were launched, and by 04.55 MacFarlane and his 54 crew had abandoned her. At this point Korvettenkapitän O. Kretschmer of *U-99* fired two more torpedoes into the ship and at about 05.15 she rolled over, her bows reared up and *Auckland Star* vanished.

It was Kretschmer's third war patrol, and the first *U-99* had begun from L'Orient as the Germans shifted their operations into Occupied France (see below). He was to prove himself one of the most successful of Dönitz's young protégés. Following the sinking of the *Auckland Star*, he went on to sink two more British cargo ships, the *Clan Menzies* and *Jamaica Progress*, and damage three tankers before returning to L'Orient.

Although they would have posed little threat to her, one beneficiary of the withdrawal of a number of Dönitz's operational U-boats from the Atlantic to the Norwegian Sea was the brand-new Cunard liner the *Queen Elizabeth*. Conceived to operate a two-ship, high-speed trans-Atlantic service with her half-sister-ship the *Queen Mary*, the *Queen Elizabeth* had been launched on 27 September 1938. As war loomed her builders, John Brown of Clyde Bank, Glasgow, had switched their energies to warship building and her fitting-out had slowed almost to a halt. There was wild talk of selling her, but on 6 February, more or less complete but with her interior finish restricted to essential services, she was ordered out of Britain. It had been deliberately leaked that her fitting-out would be completed at Southampton, and the Luftwaffe had considerably bombed the dock specified for her; in fact she had completed her trials on the 26th and then sailed immediately for New York to join the *Queen Mary*. Both ships afterwards sailed for Sydney, Australia, where they were converted for trooping duties, to re-appear later in the Atlantic.

Despite the ferocious war raging along the coasts of Norway and in the Kattegat and Skagerrak, causing an immense loss of British, Allied and neutral merchant shipping, Grossadmiral Raeder had not taken his eye off the Kriegsmarine's global war against British trade. On 31 March he ordered the first of his auxiliary cruisers, disguised merchant ships intended to raid enemy commerce, to put to sea. The *Atlantis*, commanded by Kapitän zur See B. Rogge, sailed for the South Atlantic, Pacific and Indian Oceans.[17] She was followed by the *Orion*, Fregattenkapitän Kurt Weyher, which put to sea on 6 April. Her cruise was to last until 22 November 1941, when she returned to Germany. Like her sisters *Atlantis, Komet, Kormoran, Michel, Pinguin, Stier, Thor* and *Widder*, *Orion* had little economic impact on the war at sea and virtually none on the Battle of the Atlantic. The effect of these ships sent to operate in the remoter oceans was purely disruptive, both to merchant shipping and to the Royal Navy whose cruisers were obliged to run them down, often in disproportionately large 'hunting groups' which occasionally included an aircraft carrier. On the other hand, these disguised warships required the support of supply vessels and were vulnerable to the interdiction of their replenishment, a fact which caused considerable anxiety both in Berlin and at sea.

Their effectiveness did, however, compare favourably with that of the Kriegsmarine's heavy capital ships. The *Orion* and *Komet*, for example, operating in the southern hemisphere, sank between them 18 ships grossing 115,045 tons; in the North Atlantic the battle-cruisers *Scharnhorst* and *Gneisenau* sank 21 vessels grossing 115,622. Moreover, the combined total of these two magnificent men-of-war, plus the *Admiral Scheer* and the heavy cruiser *Admiral Hipper*, was no more than 48 merchantmen, a total of 270,000 tons, of which only three had been captured. Although they inflicted both material and moral damage on the British Merchant and Royal Navies, they never proved as dangerous a weapon as the British Admiralty had in 1939 feared they might. By the spring of 1941 they had lost their momentum, and in thus faltering surrendered their qualitative edge to British quantity driven by British ruthlessness. Elsewhere, however, German arms had proved triumphant.

On 29 April 1940 the cruiser HMS *Glasgow* embarked the King and Crown Prince of Norway, the Norwegian government and the country's gold reserves from the burning city of Molde. The *Glasgow* remained on the north Norwegian coast for a few days, but by 9 May it was all over. Anglo-French support of Norway ended in débâcle, with the scandalous loss of the carrier *Glorious* and two destroyers sunk off Narvik by the *Scharnhorst* and *Gneisenau*. Aboard *Glasgow*, King Haakon and his government left for exile in London, and it was from this moment that all Norwegian shipping passed to British control.

During the ill-conceived Anglo-French Norwegian campaign, not only the occupied countries but the British merchant fleet had lost a considerable number of fine merchant ships. Many, chartered to convey military cargoes in support of Allied operations in northern Norway, had been mined or torpedoed by the concentration of German submarines in the North and Norwegian Seas.

By mid May the Dutch government too were in exile and, like the Norwegians, soon opened a shipping mission in London to put their free merchant tonnage at the disposal of Great Britain. Belgium fell as the Wehrmacht's tanks rolled westward and drove the British Expeditionary Force back into France, the greater part of it towards the beaches between Dunkirk and the Pas de Calais. Then, between 29 May and 4 June, every available merchantman and naval vessel in home waters and capable of working inshore was mustered for Operation DYNAMO: the rescue of the remnants of the British Expeditionary Force from the collapse of France.

Ten days later the Germans marched into Paris.

Among the officers sent to supervise the evacuation by Admiral Ramsay commanding Operation DYNAMO from Dover was an eccentric retired vice admiral who had been recalled at the outbreak of war to serve as a convoy commodore. Early in 1940 Gilbert Stephenson had then been appointed to organise submarine patrols off Norway, to which end he had had the requisitioned motor-yacht *Philante* commissioned. The German victory overtook events, however, and Stephenson was summoned by Sir Dudley Pound to organise a base for the sea-training of the crews of the new 'Flower'-class corvettes that would shortly be completing and commissioning as escort vessels. Manned largely by amateur-cum-reservist crews, they would require fast working-up in anti-submarine warfare, and the Royal Navy's normal facilities at Portland were unsuitable for this purpose. Initially Pound charged Stephenson with establishing his new Allied, Anglo-French base at Quiberon Bay, on the wild coast of Brittany. It was a measure of the Admiralty's neglect of anti-submarine warfare that Stephenson was considered the Royal Navy's best man for the task largely because when in command of the Otranto Barrage he had applied some rather unorthodox experiments in submarine detection and effectively sealed Austrian submarines in the Adriatic during the First World War. Stephenson requested the services of one of his former colleagues, Lieutenant Commander R.H. Palmer, RNVR as his principal assistant, and then set about acquiring a headquarters ship. This was in train when he was again overtaken by events and hurriedly joined Ramsay's staff, crossing to La Panne to play his part in DYNAMO. On completion of the evacuation and in the wake of the subsequent disaster in France, Stephenson and his headquarters ship, HMS *Western Isles*, were despatched to Tobermory Bay on the Isle of Mull. *Philante* was also sent into Scottish waters to assist, and on 12 July Commodore Stephenson began his new task.[18] He became well known to the officers and ratings not only of Britain's Royal Navy but of all the Allied men-of-war who served on escort duty in the North Atlantic. To the former he was 'The Terror of Tobermory', and his influence on the outcome of the struggle that lay ahead was crucial.

One RNR officer wrote of Stephenson that he was 'the ideal man for the job. He terrified the incompetent and lazy, but was a good friend to those who tried hard. Many commanding officers had cause to be grateful for his help in bringing their ships to peak efficiency before facing the enemy and for the uncompromisingly high standards he insisted on . . .

Nothing that happened in the miniature fleet anchorage off Mull passed unnoticed. From the moment a new ship arrived off the harbour entrance until she departed with his blessing, ready for action, her people were given little rest. There were no shore distractions and no wives to take men's minds off the job.'[19]

As the Germans invaded The Netherlands on 10 May, Winston Churchill succeeded Neville Chamberlain as British Prime Minister. Only a month earlier Chamberlain had confidently told the Conservative Party that Hitler had 'missed the bus'. Now, as the British army abandoned its equipment and the French fell back before the onslaught of Guderian's tanks, the true state of affairs was revealed.

Churchill immediately formed a 'National', coalition government in which he became his own Minister of Defence. Installed in his place as First Lord of the Admiralty was an amiable Labour–Co-operative politician named A. V. Alexander. Alexander had been First Lord at the time when Ramsay MacDonald led a Labour government in 1929, sufficient reason for Churchill to reinstate him, as a paper-worker. Captain Guy Grantham, then naval assistant to the First Sea Lord, thought him 'a pompous little man', but Lieutenant Commander Peter Kemp was kinder: 'He was nothing more than a cipher really . . . a nice, simple man who was brought up on the Co-operative Movement.' Alexander was 'a thick set chunky man with a square face and looked rougher and tougher than he really was.' Known as 'Wide-Mouth' for his indiscretions, he was never informed of the decrypted intelligence known as Ultra which derived from Bletchley Park, but simply expressed surprise whenever naval success ensued.[20]

After the evacuation from the beaches of Dunkirk there yet remained a substantial British force in western France, and on 15 June Operation AERIAL sought to remove them from Cherbourg, St-Malo, Brest, St-Nazaire and La Pallice. 'This time it was hoped to embark transport, guns and ammunition as well as the men.'[21] Large numbers of soldiers and their equipment were successfully evacuated from the French Channel ports, but the operation to recover those trapped against the Atlantic coast was confused and not without loss. Supervised by Admiral Dunbar-Nasmith from Plymouth, this part of the evacuation relied upon several large liners including the *Arandora Star, Strathaird, Otranto, Georgic, Duchess of York, Lancastria, Franconia*, the troopship *Ettrick* and the Polish liners *Batory* and *Sobieski*. Several of these were in Quiberon Bay where they were attacked by German aircraft and the *Franconia* was damaged. On the afternoon of 17 June a heavy air attack was mounted on shipping lying off St-Nazaire in the Loire, and the Cunard White Star liner *Lancastria* was bombed and rapidly caught fire. She had embarked some 5,800 men, and although a number of the many smaller vessels involved in the evacuation rallied to her plight, the anti-submarine trawler *Cambridgeshire* picking up between 900 and 1,000 men, many others in the vicinity did not. Within fifteen minutes of being bombed the *Lancastria* was foundering. 'There were not enough lifebelts for the exceptional numbers embarked, and the waters were covered by a film of burning oil, but the Master of the *Lancastria* has testified that no panic occurred, and small craft were certainly present in some numbers.'[22] In the disaster more than three thousand men perished, and the news was deliberately suppressed by Churchill. 'The newspapers', he growled, 'have got quite enough disaster for today . . .' Afterwards it slipped his mind to release the news, so overwhelmed was he, and it was 'some time before the knowledge of this horror became public'.[23]

The bombers had also damaged the Blue Funnel cargo-liner *Teiresias*. Owned by Alfred Holt & Company, in peace time these ships carried their own insurance and were consequently constructed to the company's own standards, well in excess of the requirements of Lloyd's, the British ship classification society. The immense strength of the *Teiresias* notwithstanding, a succession of near misses had 'cracked the ship right across the deck and down the port side to the waterline'. The engine room and stokehold were flooded and the coal bunkers were shifted. Her master, Captain J.R. Davies, ordered his crew into their boats as a precaution, remaining on board with half a dozen officers and key ratings. Another British vessel, the *Holmside*, offered assistance, but the damage was fatal and Davies was compelled to abandon his ship.

A second of Holt's ships, the *Glenaffric*, entered St-Nazaire 'on an ebb tide', and 'without pilot or tugs the ship was skilfully and safely brought into the quay, where the embarkation of the remaining [4,000] troops was quickly carried out. After a trying night, during which the town was raided twice by enemy aircraft, the ship was brought out of harbour under the most adverse conditions and, the convoy having already departed, the Master [Captain W.G. Harrison] proceeded unescorted to a British port.' The War Office subsequently wrote to the owners expressing a 'glowing tribute to the cheerful manner and quiet confidence displayed by Captain Harrison' and his officers and men.

The evacuation went on for several more days, but by the end of June France had capitulated at Compiègne, the collaboration party retaining Vichy and the south of the country. The new First Lord, Mr Alexander, had headed a delegation to Bordeaux with the aim of persuading the French navy to put itself beyond the grasp of the Germans, but without a decisive outcome. Meanwhile de Gaulle had reached London to raise the Cross of Lorraine and rally the Free French. In Berlin Hermann Goering, chief of the Luftwaffe, had declared that Great Britain was under aerial siege.

As the French made their accommodation with the Germans it was Dönitz who now looked towards Brittany. He moved his command post first to Paris and then, in due course, to Kerneval, near the former French naval base at L'Orient, occupying the adjacent dockyard ports of La Rochelle, St-Nazaire and La Pallice. The strategic advantages of moving the German forward bases from Wilhelmshaven and Helgoland to the Biscayan coast of France were immense. Immediately the loss of Spanish refuelling facilities was offset, and the range of the U-boats was increased in proportion to the time and fuel formerly consumed in steaming round Scotland. In addition, as mentioned earlier, Britain was deprived of the use of the English Channel and her Channel ports. The untimely and unpredictable collapse of France was a disaster for the British, almost overnight shifting the whole strategic balance in favour of the Germans.

In the coming weeks, as the Battle of Britain began, the Battle of the Atlantic intensified. The strategic shift in favour of Germany was likely to have a dire impact upon the war at sea, and the prospect for those involved seemed bleak. And yet, unperceived and vague though they were, the foundations of ultimate victory in the Atlantic had already been laid. On 8 May British troops had pre-emptively occupied Iceland, Commodore Stephenson was on his way to Tobermory, the first of the new corvettes were coming into commission, and on 10 June President Franklin Roosevelt had made a speech in which he had stated that his administration would 'extend to the opponents of force the material resources' of the United States of America.

For the time being, however, Britain stood alone.

PART TWO

July 1940–May 1941

THE LEAKY BUCKET

6

'This is a thing to do now'

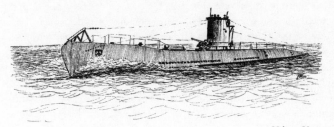

U-boat *U-35*

A S FRANCE FELL apart, Mussolini's Fascist Italy joined Nazi Germany. Hitler's Reich was also allied to the Soviet Union under Stalin and his biddable Politburo, while Spain, although nominally neutral and not entirely happy with German actions, was under the heel of a Fascist dictator and demonstrably favoured the Axis cause at the expense of any accommodation with Britain, holders of Gibraltar. The remnant French power, confined to the Vichy provinces, was minded to collaborate, and equivocated over the use of her powerful navy, a stance that could only lead to the tragic pre-emptive strike launched upon it by Britain. Not only did the greater part of the territory of Britain's late ally now lie under German occupation, but so too did Norway, Denmark and the Low Countries: the entire Atlantic-facing coastline of Europe was in enemy hands, and from it not only submarines but long-range aircraft had ready access to the Atlantic and to hitherto inaccessible targets. On 10 July, in what is generally considered to have been the opening phase of the Battle of Britain, German bombers flying from France struck directly *at the docks* of South Wales.

The collapse of France also wrecked the Anglo-French plan for the defence of the Mediterranean. One reason why the need to neutralise the French fleet was so pressing was that it had been responsible for the domination of the Western Mediterranean, leaving the British Royal Navy to cover the Eastern Mediterranean from its base at Alexandria. Into this lacuna there now moved the Italian navy, an untried but potentially powerful force with a significant fleet of more than a hundred submarines. These were of a high quality and had established a reputation for sinking merchant shipping during the Spanish Civil War. This accession to Dönitz's power ought to have been decisive, but in the event the participation of Italian submarines was to prove a mixed blessing to him.

Although it dominated the Eastern Mediterranean, the Royal Navy could project only temporary power over the Western basin. As a consequence, the Mediterranean became closed to the passage of merchant shipping and everything bound for the Middle East, including *matériel*, had to be carried by way of the Cape of Good Hope, entering the Mediterranean through the Suez Canal from the south. The added burden in terms of time, tonnage, fuel and risk of interdiction was a further example of the transportation difficulties British shipping now had to bear.

Less immediately dramatic consequences of the Fall of France also impinged upon the maintenance of Britain's overseas lifeline. First was the loss of the complementary French convoy organisation and with it many of their escort vessels. A number of French men-of-war came over to England, but not all their crews remained to serve with the Free French forces. The position of the French merchant fleet was more fragmented. All ships in French harbours, like those in Norwegian, Danish, Dutch and Belgian ports, were requisitioned by the Germans. A few stranded abroad, particularly those in the Mediterranean, made their way to Metropolitan France, while others more widely dispersed headed for overseas Vichy possessions. Some came over to the Free French and became *de facto* 'British' merchantmen, usually under British masters and often with all-British crews.

Second, with the failure of the French went supplies of bauxite, the raw material required for the production of aluminium, and thus of aircraft. Before the war France was the world's biggest producer of bauxite; after her submission it went to Germany, a country already capable of producing some 200,000 tons a year on her own account. Third was a sudden loss of hundreds of 20-mm Oerlikon anti-aircraft guns which had been ordered from their Swiss manufacturers.[1] These highly effective weapons, later produced under licence and used in great numbers as anti-aircraft armament in warships as well as merchantmen, had been paid for in gold; now they lay besieged and embargoed by Fascist states. A fourth consequence of the Fall of France was the possibility that the Germans would occupy Vichy French Senegal. Most of the 'Atlantic Narrows' between Dakar and Brazil were well within the capability of long-range German aircraft, while an Axis base at Dakar would prove dangerous to British trade routes. Fortunately the worst possibilities were not realised, though the African coast proved unhappy enough for many British merchant seamen, as will appear.

Then there was the Irish problem. Under the terms of the treaty of 1920 establishing the Irish Free State, the right had been reserved for the Royal Navy to base destroyers at Berehaven and Cobh. Implacably hostile to all things British, the de Valera government had denied this facility, and on 25 April 1938 the British government had voluntarily surrendered the right as a gesture of conciliation. Churchill protested at the folly of it: 'The fact that we cannot use the south and west coasts of Ireland to refuel our flotillas [of destroyers] and aircraft, and thus protect the trade by which Ireland, as well as Great Britain, lives, is a most heavy and grievous burden . . .'

Against these drawbacks there accrued certain small advantages which, though they by no means outweighed the many disadvantages of the French collapse, did mitigate them. The first was psychological. At that nadir in their affairs there was a sense in Britain that rock-bottom meant that all henceforth depended upon the efforts of a single, united nation. In essence it was a distillation of the insular nature of the British: for all their muddling inefficiency they possessed an admirable doggedness that refused to admit defeat. At the point at which Hitler confidently expected the long-awaited overtures seeking an agreement, the British dug in, and Churchill enunciated this perverse determination in a succession of speeches that spoke of self-sacrifice and 'blood and toil', and gave the enemy the prospect of having to battle for every foot of territory, starting on the beaches.

Second was the fact that, although the position of Ireland was different this time, Britain well understood the nature of the war she was called upon to fight. She had resisted the power of Revolutionary and Napoleonic France a century and a half before, and her maritime doctrine was based upon lessons learnt then. A country led by a man whose sense of history was informed by his appreciation and experience of war at sea and supported by an Admiralty which, for all its faults and material inadequacies, comprehended the principles of the business they were embarked upon – a maritime war of sea-power relying upon exterior lines of communication – was set against a pan-European continental power relying upon interior lines. Provided she could tap her resources and sustain her sea-borne communications, the former power had the advantage of the latter because the resources of the latter were constrained by the boundaries of the land mass of Europe. Moreover, sea-power could limit and contain any extension into the Asian continent, so that while Germany might gain access to the Romanian oil fields, she was less likely to reach those of Persia. All therefore depended upon Britain's maintenance of her power at sea.

In addition to these abstract accruals were some small material advantages. Even more spectacular than the slow strangulation of German commerce by the interdiction of her overseas trade and the capture, enforced destruction or neutralisation of her merchant shipping was the swift nemesis visited upon the Italian mercantile marine. In the four days following Mussolini's declaration of war, Italy lost one-sixth of her merchant fleet, 210,855 tons; 80,000 tons were seized in British or British colonial ports, much else was scuttled. Effectively, all Italian vessels outside her own coastal waters were given up, a consequence of Mussolini's abrupt declaration of war.[2] The seizures of Italian bottoms slightly ameliorated Britain's losses at sea.

The stark nature of the British plight had empowered Churchill's new National Government to take other pre-emptive measures in addition to the neutralisation of the French navy. On his first day as Prime Minister, even before the Admiralty was instructed to move against the French battle-squadrons, Churchill ordered the invasion and occupation of Iceland, a former Danish possession. The denial of this European outpost to the Germans was an important move, one only made possible by the British possession of significant sea-power. As an air-base and a convoy mustering port it had an important role to play.

In expectation of the worst, however, Churchill's government shifted a portion of its gold reserves abroad. On 5 July a large shipment amounting to £192 millions sterling left Greenock aboard the two Polish liners *Batory* and *Sobieski*, the British liner *Monarch of Bermuda*, the battleship *Revenge* and the cruiser *Bonaventure*. This fast convoy reached Halifax, Nova Scotia a week later. These events marked the end of the first phase in the war at sea. Britain's sea-communications, so vital to her survival, were attenuated and exposed; her willingness to defend them was unquestioned, but her ability to do so remained in grave doubt. By July 1940 her people had had their food rationed for seven months; she was in grave need of both guns and butter. Encouraged by the amendment to the United States' Neutrality Act of the previous November that enabled Britain and France to buy arms from America, Churchill now sought still greater aid from his own mother's native land.

When Winston Churchill was summoned by Chamberlain immediately after the outbreak of war on 3 September 1939 and sent to the Admiralty as First Lord, a signal immediately went out to the ships of the British fleet deployed around the world: 'Winston is back!' According to Captain Guy Grantham, who initiated it, 'the news shot round the fleet, everyone was cock a-hoop!' More soberly, a Naval Intelligence Officer remembered that 'There was immense relief . . . A do-er was going to take over . . .'[3] Not everyone agreed. Old petty officers in the fleet, recalling the shambles of the Dardanelles, groaned in dismay. Arriving in Whitehall, Churchill convened a meeting of the Board of Admiralty. It was half-past midnight as he took his grand seat at the head of the table. After Pound's welcome, he regarded the assembled members, and addressed them: 'There will be many difficulties ahead, but together we shall overcome them. Gentlemen, to your tasks and duties.'[4]

Churchill was not an advocate of convoys. 'I c[ould]d never be responsible for naval strategy wh[ich] excluded the offensive principle,' he wrote in a memorandum to Pound. During his period as First Lord during the Great War he had opposed them, and they were introduced only after his fall. He saw convoy escort as wholly passive, regarding it, 'quite wrongly, as a defensive practice'.[5] While he did not interfere with the establishment of convoy after his return to office on the outbreak of war in 1939, he remained undeterred by the failure of his carrier-led hunting groups whose premature birth had had such disastrous results, and insisted on a 'loosening up' of the convoy system, with smaller convoys and a division of those merchant ships too slow to sail independently – which meant most cargo-carriers – into 'fast' and 'slow' categories. This was a pragmatic reaction to the very obvious slow-down in both import and export flow which had had its knock-on effect on the economic life of the nation.

But Churchill's penchant for aggression would not rest content with the notion of men-of-war of such dash and offensive spirit as destroyers being tied to the apron-strings of plodding convoys, and he again tried to divert the Royal Navy's limited resources into the formation of small anti-submarine groups to carry out 'sweeps' in waters likely to be the haunt of U-boats. This superficially impressive but wasteful tactic revealed a failure to comprehend the true nature of the enemy's war against trade. There was little passivity about a convoy, for a convoy was where the enemy could be expected to strike, and where he could be counter-attacked, a principle unequivocally laid down by an Admiralty Committee in September 1939 when it stated that 'the best position for anti-submarine vessels is in company with a convoy'.[6] In a sense Churchill was right, however, in that although a convoy was the lure to which the U-boat was drawn, the initiative lay with the enemy submarine until it revealed its hand – and that usually meant the sinking of a laden merchantman.

When Churchill left the Admiralty to become Prime Minister little had changed in the war in the Atlantic and he, like Pound and others on the Admiralty Board, still regarded naval wars as matters to be decided between heavy battle-squadrons.[7] But the crisis in the Battle of the Atlantic was upon them and it was to cause Churchill much anxiety, provoking his later confession that it was the only thing that really worried him during the entire course of the war.

The most pressing concern was the lack of escorts. The new corvettes were coming into service, but it was clear that the time involved in their completion, commissioning and working-up was such that they would not satisfy the immediate need. Practical experience was exposing the realities of applying convoy protection to the actual volume of trade the Admiralty found itself obliged to protect, and also the deficiencies inherent in the system. Broadly, the import flow to Britain was concentrated on four ports of rendezvous from where convoys sailed under the direction of their assigned commodores. Vessels coming from South Africa and South America made for Freetown, Sierre Leone, as did those coming from Australia by way of the Cape of Good Hope, and these formed the SL series of convoys. Vessels from eastern Australia, New Zealand and the Far East by way of the Pacific and the Panama Canal assembled at Kingston, Jamaica and joined KJ convoys. Those from Canadian and United States' ports assembled at Halifax, Nova Scotia to from HX convoys, while those homeward bound from the Mediterranean or the Far East, India and East Africa by way of the Suez Canal made for Gibraltar and the next HG convoy. These Gibraltar-to-home convoys were escorted throughout their passage, as were their recip-rocal outward components. An anti-submarine escort of destroyers or sloops was provided to the other ocean convoys for the part of their passages that lay within the Continental shelf out to longitude 17° West, which in July 1941 was the theoretical limit of submarine operations, but they relied upon the presence of a cruiser or AMC to cover them for the greater part of their passage. Out-going anti-submarine escort groups would transfer from an outward bound (OB) convoy to an inward one and this cycle was run at the assigned time of departure irrespective of what ships were available and ready for convoy.

Approaching home, these convoys broke up into smaller groups, off Land's End for vessels bound up Channel for Southampton and London or into the Irish Sea for the Mersey and Clyde; in the case of the HX series, the convoy divided off Rockall, one part bound for Methil on the Forth and the east coast, the other for the Clyde, Belfast and the Mersey. Some outward convoys, prefixed OA and OB, either merged, if bound for Gibraltar, or dispersed, the ships diverging for their destinations.

After the Fall of France increased the vulnerability of merchantmen using the English Channel and the South West Approaches all convoys had to be routed round the north of Ireland, and for those heading south a westward offing as far as the 19th or 20th meridian had first to be achieved.

Convoys were never delayed, though they might be postponed or cancelled because of extreme weather or particular enemy activity and their regularity could be extended or shortened. Extending the cycle produced large convoys, while shortening it left little time for the crews of the escorts to recuperate. On the other hand, the former made better use of limited escort numbers, while the latter gave a higher escort-to-merchantman ratio and thus a theoretically increased efficiency. For some time the optimum size – and therefore cycle – of convoys remained a matter of debate and analysis.

As circumstances changed, so did the organisation of convoy series. Of the two-letter coding that usually denoted terminal ports, the KJ series disappeared when the Kingston convoys were in due course abandoned; occasionally a third letter indicated convoy speed, while certain convoys, most notably those to the Soviet Union after mid 1941 (PQ, QP, JW and RA), bore the initials of individual naval staff officers. There were more complex denominations when special convoys attached to military operations were involved, such as the WS series denoting 'Winston's Specials', but the several hundred of these lie outside the scope of this work.[8] The principal trans-Atlantic convoys around which the main actions of the Battle of the Atlantic were fought were most commonly those of the HG, HGF, HX, ON, ONS, OS, OSS and SC series.

The prefix HX denoted in the early years a convoy from Halifax to Britain, later one from New York to Britain. The ON convoys, established in 1941, signified Outward North from Liverpool, the Clyde and Northern Ireland, towards North America. These might be suffixed 'F' or 'S', denoting intended average speed; after 1943, ONS meant Outward North Slow between Britain and North America. Ships bound to Freetown from Liverpool and the Clyde formed Outward South, or OS convoys, with those extending southwards from Freetown becoming OSS. It took about nineteen days for the average SL convoy to run between Freetown and Britain; there were some distinctions, some being SLF or SLS convoys, according to speed. From Freetown, as from such ports elsewhere, there radiated subsidiary convoys, such as STW (Freetown, Takoradi, Walvis Bay); or there were convoys like BHX from Bermuda, assigned the same number as the HX convoy with which it would merge at a prescribed rendezvous, or SH, Sydney, Cape Breton Island to Halifax. The last major North Atlantic series were the SC convoys initiated in the late summer of 1940. They ran initially from Sydney, Cape Breton Island to Britain and were intended to relieve the congestion in Bedford Basin at Halifax by providing an alternative assembly port for slower vessels. Sydney was not used during the winter months when loose pack ice complicated navigation, so some convoys mustering in Halifax or New York had the same SC prefix.

The HG series, Britain to Gibraltar, with the suffix 'F' to denote a fast convoy, has already been referred to, as have the OG, Outward to Gibraltar, composed of elements of OA and OB convoys with similar destinations. In response to the increased German access to the South West Approaches, on 11 July all outward convoys from Liverpool, which of course included ships joining from Belfast and the Clyde, were routed by way of the North Channel, so that convoys now debouched into the North Atlantic between the Ulster and the Hebridean coasts, traffic from London and the east-coast ports of Britain steaming north by way of Methil on the Firth of Forth and using Loch Ewe on the north coast of Scotland as an assembly anchorage.

The realisation that much of the world's bulk-carrying tramp shipping was worn out came as something of a shock to the Royal Navy. A slow trans-Atlantic SC convoy was one capable of making 7 knots, while vessels forming HX convoys were at first expected to be able to sustain a speed of 9 knots. Both speeds were raised in the summer of 1941, SC to 7.5 and HX to 10 knots, but these were rarely reached on the average convoy passage. The slowest convoy speed for 1941 was 6.49 knots, and the passage took about two weeks.

The independent routeing of vessels with a service speed of 15 knots or more has already been mentioned. In November 1940 a decision was made, at the highest level but without the benefit of statistical analysis or the input of the Commander-in-Chief, Western Approaches, to reduce this to 13 knots. It produced a staggering increase in losses and the 15-knot minimum was reintroduced on 18 June 1941, with a consequent drop in numbers of ships sunk. As a rigorous application of the convoy system repeatedly proved efficacious in mastering the U-boat, the principle was extended and speedier vessels were often assigned to fast convoys. By 1943 these convoys, usually made up of new tanker tonnage, were running at 15 knots.

But in July 1940, such a comforting ascendancy was nowhere to be divined. The loss of 45 merchant ships in February had been serious enough to alarm the Ministry of Supply, if not the Admiralty. As the collection of data became a tool of war, so the impact upon Britain's economic life of such losses could be statistically perceived as having a cumulative effect: 45 merchantmen seemed a lot when the quantities and substance of their lading were analysed. From this new perspective, the destruction of a number of U-boats seemed less of an achievement. Anxieties about exponential effects mixed with memories of the near-humiliation of 1917 did not recede in the coming months.

As the airborne assault of the Luftwaffe hit Britain, the vulnerability of the nation's infrastructure was thrown into sharp relief. The British and neutral merchantmen dotted about the waters of the globe carrying much-needed goods to and from the United Kingdom looked less like Kipling's 'shuttles of an Empire's loom' and rather more like a chain of leaky buckets. The only proper anti-submarine convoy escorts available to protect this intensity of trade were the pre-war general-purpose sloops, and these were mostly assigned to the Gibraltar convoys. The serious loss of destroyers sustained in the Norwegian campaign was exacerbating the shortfall in escorts, and since they were now needed both for capital-ship protection and to defend the coast against anticipated invasion, the shortage was rapidly becoming acute. To this must be added the necessity now felt to divert Coastal Command's limited resources to fly patrols over the North Sea.

All plans to deploy aircraft capable of providing air cover in the Atlantic were subordinate to what was perceived at the time as the greater priority of ensuring that Bomber Command had enough aircraft to maintain its offensive against the Reich, an offensive now known to have been of dubious value in the material sense, whatever its psychological impact upon either side. The establishment of an air base at Stornoway in the Hebrides and the occupation of the Faeroes and Iceland might have extended Coastal Command's range further west had the aeroplanes been available, but in the summer of 1940 they were not, and any countervailing advantage to mitigate Dönitz's new French bases and reinforcing Italian submarines was thereby missed.[9]

As early as 27 May Churchill was complaining that Britain had received little real help from the United States beyond commercial purchases made there, and by midsummer he was pressing the American government to provide the Royal Navy with the desired escort vessels from the United States Navy's mothballed reserve fleet. General George Strong, chairman of the American War Plans Division, advised the administration that no aid should be given to the British since they would not long be able to withstand Hitler, while private munitions firms should be dissuaded from accepting British orders for fear that the inevitable collapse of Great Britain would result in bad debts; meanwhile, the possessions of the beleaguered Allies in the Americas should be seized to prevent German occupation and thus a German presence within the United States sphere of influence. Such was the trans-Atlantic impact of the Franco-British defeat in Norway, the Low Countries and France, and particularly of the Royal Navy's immense losses off Norway, that even President Roosevelt felt the cold hand of extreme anxiety. He was, however, unimpressed by the Anglophobic attitude of the United States' Ambassador to the Court of St James, Joseph Kennedy, who even before Hitler had launched his *Blitzkrieg* against the west was reporting that Britain had no chance of survival.

Unfortunately Roosevelt's army and naval advisors, General Marshall and Admiral Stark, concurred with Kennedy. Moreover, in replying to Churchill's importunate pleas on 15 June the chairman of the Foreign Affairs Committee, Senator Key Pittman, declared that, since it was 'no secret that Great Britain is totally unprepared for defense and that nothing the United States has to give can do more than delay the result', his committee recommended that a demand be sent to London insisting that the entire British fleet be ordered into American waters to prevent it from being absorbed into the Kriegsmarine; they deprecated any delay, any 'futile encouragement to fight on'.

As things went from bad to worse Joseph Kennedy continued to prophesy Britain's doom while presiding over an embassy which harboured a code-clerk named Tyler G. Kent who was busy passing diplomatic correspondence to Fascists in London; from them it went to the Italians and then, by way of the Nazi ambassador in Rome, to Berlin. As the relationship between Churchill and Roosevelt waxed, Kent ensured that copies of their messages also went to the enemy. Kent later claimed to have been acting from patriotic motives: he wished to expose the President's secret policy of moving towards war in opposition to the will of the United States' people expressed in Congress, and in defiance of the Neutrality Act intended to keep the United States out of a European War. He was imprisoned for seven years upon his apprehension and trial by the British in October.

In Washington there was a growing alarm over the possibility of Germany taking over the British and French navies, partially ameliorated in respect of the latter by the action of the Royal Navy against units of its fallen ally at Dakar and Oran in early July. Henry Morgenthau, Secretary of the Treasury and a close ally of Roosevelt, was almost alone among the president's advisers in sharing his sympathies with the beleaguered British, seeing in American support for them the wisdom of proxy defence in depth. 'Unless we do something to give the English [sic] additional destroyers, it seems to me it is absolutely hopeless to expect them to keep going.' Opposed to Morgenthau's method but sympathetic to Roosevelt's anti-Fascism was Admiral Stark. As the chief naval adviser his opinion was crucial, and he was opposed to handing over any destroyers to Britain on the dual grounds that it would prove a bad move politically, causing hostility in Congress, and that upon the inevitable capitulation of Britain the ships would be required for the defence of the United States. What, Stark postulated, was the point of handing over fifty escorts when in a few months the Kriegsmarine would invade the North Atlantic reinforced with the remains of the French fleet and a Royal Navy itself augmented by fifty American destroyers?[10]

After receiving the American rebuff of 15 June Churchill left the supplications to others, chiefly Lord Lothian, the British ambassador in Washington. On 24 May Lothian had proposed to exchange naval bases in the Americas for the coveted destroyers, an idea Churchill had dismissed. As an 'apostle of the offensive' he was more interested in neutralising the French fleet.

When this had been done, however, on 31 July he once more appealed to Roosevelt's generosity, emphasising the severe losses to the Royal Navy of a further eleven British destroyers. Couched in such terms, it was an appeal likely to misfire in Washington, where no value was set on the gallant self-sacrifice of these ships and of many of their companies: in the light of the myth of an irredeemable lack of moral fibre in the dying and decadent British Empire the Americans, yet to be tried in the crucible of war, were apt to interpret such losses as the result of ineptitude. It was an assumption as false as the one that fondly supposed Japanese men to be afflicted with myopia, rendering them inefficient as fighter pilots. Only the American journalists Ed Murrow and Drew Middleton, reporting from London, seemed willing to point out Britain's pluck as well as her plight, but the hard-nosed analysts in Washington regarded these appeals as sentimental distractions.

Roosevelt was his own man, however; he instructed Stark to select a small team for a fact-finding mission to London. It was headed by Rear Admiral Robert Ghormley, and Churchill, now Prime Minister, extended him a warm welcome. Invited to review British naval planning, Ghormley reported to Roosevelt that it was probable the United States Navy would have actively to assist the Royal Navy in the Atlantic, and that beyond this eventuality it was also possible that in due course the United States would have to 'send large air and land forces to Europe or Africa or both . . .'

Meanwhile Churchill persisted in his desire for American destroyers, informing Roosevelt that 'The Germans have the whole French coastline from which to launch U-boats, dive-bomber attacks upon our trade and food, and in addition we must be constantly prepared to repel by sea-action [the] threatened invasion . . . Mr President, with great respect I must tell you that in the long history of the world, this is a thing to do now.'

For all the constaints placed upon President Roosevelt's administration by the Neutrality Act and other legislation designed to reflect the unwill-ingness of the American people to fight a second war started in Old Europe, in both Washington and Berlin it was clear, following the previous November's relaxation in the law allowing the then Allies Britain and France to buy on a 'cash-and-carry' basis, that American business would respond with alacrity to armaments orders placed by the British. In 1939 the United States Navy, though large, was not capable of fighting a war in the Atlantic and in the Pacific, where it might be confronted by the powerful Imperial Japanese Navy, but secret talks held between the British and Americans in May 1939 had concluded that in the event of an Anglo-German war, the United States Navy would cover the Western and Southern Atlantic. In the event, Washington's diplomacy secured a declaration by 21 American republics that the oceanic waters bordering the Americas constituted a

Pan-American Neutrality Zone in which acts of war would not be toler-ated. To add weight to this, the United States Navy mobilised a powerful deterrent Atlantic Battle Squadron. Then, on 11 September 1939, Roosevelt had taken the personal initiative of offering to the new First Lord of the Admiralty in London a private line of communication. Divining the preda-tory nature of Hitler's Germany, fearful of Chamberlain's intentions with regard to Berlin, the President wished 'to be in touch with the one cabinet member in London who embodied total resistance to Nazism'.[11]

Roosevelt's fear was that any form of British accommodation with Hitler would mean German domination of the Atlantic, bringing with it the menace of German hegemony to the very shores of the United States, a situation which would play into the hands of Fascist interests in South America. He was not the only person in the United States to fear the outcome of capitulation by Great Britain, or to nurse a hatred of Fascism; many young American men volunteered for service in the air force and navy of the country whose institutions their education had taught them to regard as instruments of tyranny. Such men acted in defiance of American statute and risked losing their citizenship, but their action marked a growing perception in the American public of the menace posed by this not-so-distant war.

By the time he received Churchill's eloquent plea to act, Roosevelt had hit upon the expedient of selling some of the mothballed destroyers to Canada 'on condition that they be used in American hemisphere defense'. He now sent for the Secretary of the Navy, Frank Knox, and told him to propose the supply of 50 destroyers in exchange for a long-term lease on Atlantic and Caribbean island bases, an idea he thought might find Congressional favour. The British ambassador Lord Lothian received the proposal warmly. He was emotional in his request to London 'for help, and help quickly', and this time Churchill and the War cabinet acquiesced. As Roosevelt mounted a campaign to sweeten his own contentious pill for the consumption of his countrymen, his lawyers assured him that it lay within his executive power to act without Congressional support. At the same time, on 2 August, Harold Ickes, then Secretary of the Interior, realising that Britain's resources were not infinite and that the problem was not likely to be a short-term one, planted the idea of Lease-Lend, subsequently 'sold' to the American people using the analogy of the good citizen's willingness to lend a neighbour a fire hose if his house were ablaze: in such circumstances, payment was not an immediate issue.

As the fight for air supremacy raged over southern England that beauti-ful summer, Roosevelt made up his courageous mind. On 13 August he signalled his approval for 50 destroyers to be transferred to the Royal Navy in exchange for naval bases at Bermuda, Trinidad, Argentia, Atkinson Field in British Guiana, Jamaica, Antigua, St Lucia and Great Exuma in the Bahamas. The agreement was signed on 2 September 1940, by which time one thousand British naval officers and ratings were already embarked for passage to Halifax.

Of those 50 American 'destroyer escorts', 43 were assigned to the Royal Navy, seven to the Royal Canadian Navy. Those going to the Royal Navy were renamed after towns common to both Britain and America, but all proved to be appalling sea-boats, flush-decked, narrow-gutted and liable to roll, with insufficient buoyancy forward to avoid damage from green seas. With their four 'stacks' their appearance was distinctively antiquated, and they possessed little real operational merit, for space on their quarterdecks was inadequate for anti-submarine depth-charge mortars and the twin screws protruded beyond the line of the ship's side, making them vulnerable to damage when alongside. Their machinery was liable to break down, and their sonar equipment was of primitive, Great War vintage. They all required extensive modification: two had in fact been struck off the United States Navy List, and some were so badly corroded that sea water contaminated the fuel in their double-bottom tanks through leaking rivets. Delivered by American crews to Halifax, Nova Scotia, they all crossed the Atlantic under the white ensign to spend a considerable time in British dockyards being made serviceable. Three needing particularly extensive renovation were selected for conversion to long-range escorts, predating similar conversions of equally elderly British 'V'- and 'W'-class destroyers. Some of what were to be known as the 'Town'-class were manned by exiled Norwegians, and in due course many of them were transferred to the Soviet Union. Stopgaps at best, their chief virtue lay in their effect upon British morale and the fact that their transfer to service under the British ensign demonstrated to the world America's willingness to favour a fellow democracy. They were heartily disliked by their crews, but once in commission in the hands of the Royal Navy they provided an immediate bulwark against Germany's attempt to project Nazi power across the North Atlantic.

After the rigours of Norway, Dönitz refitted his U-boats. Oehrn's patrol had confirmed his misgivings about his submarines' torpedoes, but the return of *U-37* after a 26-day patrol in which more than 40,000 tons of shipping had been sunk encouraged him, as did his new Atlantic bases in Norway and France. Thanks largely to B-Dienst intercepts, Dönitz, as Befelshaber der U-boote, or BdU, gradually became aware of the positions of the meeting-points where British escorting forces left an outward-bound convoy to rendezvous with an incoming one.

The Royal Navy's ability to defend convoys remained poor. Convoy HX55, consisting of 39 vessels deployed in nine short columns, was well within the danger zone, in latitude 56° 10' North and longitude 10° 00' West on the forenoon of 16 July. On an easterly course at 6 knots the convoy had ceased zig-zagging prior to its division, one part to continue east and then south through the North Channel towards Liverpool Bay, with a smaller number of vessels bound north about Scotland for Methil and the east coast. Just prior to this separation the convoy remained in formation, with the Canadian destroyer *Skeena*, Lieutenant J. Hibbard, on its port bow and the senior officer, Lieutenant Commander C.F.H. Churchill in HM Sloop *Folkestone*, on the starboard. The sloop *Winchelsea* and the new corvette *Gardenia* were astern of the convoy. At about 11.35 *Folkestone*'s sonar picked up a contact, only to lose it on her defective equipment. Churchill, confident that the U-boat had passed under the convoy and hoping to catch it in the rear of the mass of merchantmen, ordered *Winchelsea* to investigate. Suddenly, at 11.41, an explosion occurred: the tanker *Scottish Minstrel*, Captain P. Dunn, had been torpedoed, despite her station in the centre of the convoy. Her cargo of 9,200 tons of fuel oil 'immediately caught fire and burned furiously. Blazing oil spread over the calm sea, a fearful sight, as a column of black smoke rose skywards.' All the escorts closed on the scene at full speed while the commodore ordered the tramp-ship *Fiscus* to pick up survivors. This was a mistake, as Churchill afterwards reported, because 'a merchantman is naturally slow and cumbersome on such duty and several men were floating in the water well scattered about. *Gardenia* arrived in the middle of them and stopped and picked up thirty survivors, later transferring two dozen to *Folkestone*. *Fiscus* is believed to have picked up two more.'

Meanwhile *Skeena* and *Winchelsea* began to sweep across the wake of the convoy searching for the perpetrator, Kapitänleutnant Oesten in *U-61*. Two Coastal Command aircraft now arrived overhead and one was signalled to cover the convoy, to which *Fiscus* was ordered to return. Meanwhile HX55 had passed the division position, and had split. At 12.50 Churchill, concerned because the Methil portion was from then on to be regulated by HX55's less experienced vice commodore, told Hibbard to join it as escort while he, in *Folkestone*, remained with the Liverpool section.

At 13.46 *Winchelsea* reported a contact but 'immediately after firing [depth-charges] whales were observed spouting on the surface . . .'[12] At 14.28 *Gardenia*, which had no doctor on board, came alongside *Folkestone* to transfer some badly burned survivors, while in default of concrete results *Winchelsea*'s search was abandoned, though Churchill remained in the area, sending the corvette and sloop after the convoy. The *Scottish Minstrel*, whose hull seemed intact, burned for hours as Churchill waited for the tugs he had summoned to arrive on the scene. Darkness fell, and at 00.34 next morning the *Scottish Minstrel*, listing and down by the head, finally sank, the bright conflagration extinguished by the sea. *Folkestone* headed for the North Channel, meeting the now superfluous tug *Englishman* coming the other way.

Convoy HX55 had had a substantial escort under an experienced regular senior officer, but the defect in *Folkestone*'s sonar had fatally prejudiced the safe arrival of a convoy which had successfully traversed the greater part of the North Atlantic. Oesten had been able to elude location and at periscope depth had boldly torpedoed a tanker within the formation as it passed him, and after his presence had been detected. Nine of *Scottish Minstrel*'s crew were killed. The deficiency in his ship's equipment had compromised poor Churchill, whose escorts were reduced to acting as rescue craft, a role they were to become all too familiar with. 'One result of rescuing survivors,' the first lieutenant of *Folkestone* wrote afterwards, 'was to clean most of our ship's company out of any spare clothing they might have with them . . . [many survivors were] forced by fire to jump into the water and swim for it. Others had escaped hurriedly in the boats, thinly clad in their engine room rig of boiler suit or a singlet and trousers . . . It was not long before a quantity of "survivors'" kits consisting of sacks of old but warm clothing was issued to all escorts for use under such circumstances'.

Oesten's achievement notwithstanding, most of the successes gained by the U-boats at this time were in independent actions against single merchant ships dispersed from OA and OB convoys, although a further unsuccessful attempt was made to mount a group attack of three U-boats, *U-38*, *U-46* and *U-48*, on Convoy HX62.

Having sunk the *Auckland Star*, Kretschmer had gone on to sink the *Clan Menzies* on 29 July, and on the 31st both the *Jamaica Progress* and the *Jersey City*. Thereafter *U-99* fired torpedoes at a further three tankers, the Norwegian-flagged *Strinda*, the *Lucerna* and the *Alexia*. Although he also attacked the last two by gunfire Kretschmer failed to sink any of them; but in destroying the 17-knot Clan liner he had demonstrated the vulnerability of even a fast merchantman to a ruthlessly competent exponent of submarine warfare. Six men were killed in the blast, the two engineers and six lascars on duty in the engine room, but Captain W.J. Hughes and the rest of his 87 crew landed safely on the Irish coast. More than 8,000 tons of general cargo loaded in Australia, which included large consignments of wheat and zinc, were lost with this ship. More than 2,000 tons of fruit, six seamen and a gunner were lost with the *Jamaica Progress*; her master, Captain A. Colm, his four passengers, two dozen crew and a single gunner were picked up by the trawler *Newland* and landed at Fleetwood, while the chief officer and 16 men in a lifeboat landed at Barra in the Hebrides. *Jersey City* was in ballast and most of her crew were picked up by a sister ship, but even so her loss cost two lives.

At the end of July, having sunk several ships, including the British destroyer *Whirlwind*, and replenished his U-boat at L'Orient, Kapitänleutnant Rollman renewed his patrol in *U-34*, sinking the Elder Dempster liner *Accra*, bound from Liverpool to West Africa with 333 passengers in addition to her crew of 163 and a general cargo. She sank slowly and all but 12 crew and 12 passengers were rescued by other merchant and warships. Rollman next despatched Runciman's tramp *Vinemoor* outward bound from Manchester in ballast, followed by the *Sambre* and the tanker *Thiara*. It was *U-34*'s last patrol, and this account only touches upon Rollman's predations, which finished with a flourish: approaching Bergen on 1 August, he sighted and sank the British submarine *Spearfish*.

Eastbound Convoy HX60, consisting of 60 laden vessels, left Halifax on 23 July, escorted by some Canadian destroyers. 'On the second day out the destroyers parted company which left us with the *Ausonia*', an Armed Merchant Cruiser and former Cunard liner, 'for the main leg of the crossing'. As they approached longitude 17° West on the afternoon of 3 August the *Ausonia* parted company in anticipation of the arrival of the close escort during the night, just as they entered the area in which they were most likely to encounter enemy U-boats. Thus far these HX convoys had lost only odd ships, apart from the two sunk in HX55 three weeks earlier.

In the middle watch of the following morning HX60 crossed the 17th meridian and was about 250 miles west of Ireland, the ships ploughing through the dark sea in good order, anticipating their rendezvous with their close escort. In fact HX60 had been trailed by *U-52* for many hours. Kapitänleutnant Salman now seized the opportunity provided by thick cloud covering the moon and made an attack. He fired a salvo of torpedoes and hit the *Gogovale* of London, Captain F.S. Passmore, which had arrived from Montreal with a full cargo of 6,386 tons of London-bound flour to join HX60 assembling in Bedford Basin.

Passmore began to evacuate all his crew, but as they left the *Gogovale* they became aware of another casualty as the *King Alfred*, Captain R. Storm, began to founder, despite her cargo of pit props. The half-dozen men on duty in the engine room were killed as the remainder took to their lifeboats. Some time afterwards the destroyer *Vanoc* arrived on the scene and picked up the combined survivors, some 69 men, from their scattered boats.

Having sunk the two merchantmen almost simultaneously Salman remained in contact, undisturbed by any counter-attack from *Vanoc*, and six hours later he was in a position to strike again. About 06.30 the *Geraldine Mary* (like the *Athenia*, owned by the Donaldson Brothers of Glasgow),

Captain G. McC. Sime, 'was torpedoed on the starboard side amidships'. She 'began to settle and had to be abandoned,' wrote Third Officer Russell. She was loaded with

> a full cargo of 6,112 tons of newsprint and paper pulp, plus 491 tons of sulphite (the salts extracted from sulphuric acid manufacture), all for Manchester. The wreck remained afloat for almost two hours until she broke her back and sank in two halves, leaving many rolls of newsprint . . . not far from where the *Athenia* had sunk eleven months earlier. Two of the engine-room crew and one passenger were killed by the explosion of the torpedo, but the Master, forty-five officers and crew and five passengers were all saved. All four lifeboats and a raft were successfully launched, although not without difficulty due to the heavy list and motion of the ship in the swell. The Master, Chief Officer and some others were on the raft which had been launched from under the port side of the bridge.

Russell and three others in the motor-lifeboat fouled the torpedo damage while clearing away from the ship, damaging their lifeboat. Because of this Russell wisely decided to lay to a sea anchor and thus remain in the vicinity in the hope of being picked up: a Sunderland flying-boat soon arrived overhead and flew around until the destroyer *Vanoc* arrived on the scene. 'Those on the raft and two other boats were picked up by another destroyer and all were landed in Liverpool two days later. The fourth boat had sailed off to the eastward and made the land at the Butt of Lewis seventeen days later, where all the occupants were safely landed at the tiny harbour of Port of Ness. Had they been only a few miles further north, they might well have missed not only Lewis, but also Orkney, Shetland, even the Scottish mainland and ended up in occupied Norway!'

As Salman withdrew to Kiel, Oberleutnant Otto Harms's U-56 lay in ambush for the next OB convoy midway between Malin and Barra Heads. Convoy OB193 consisted of 53 ships, and by 20.30 that night was heading out towards Rockall and the wide ocean beyond. Harms appears to have come to periscope depth inside the convoy and attacked at once, for Elder Dempster's *Boma* lay almost in the convoy's centre. At 20.48 a torpedo tore her hull apart, flooding No. 3 Hold and the engine room, where the duty watch were killed instantly. Flinging the hatch boards and beams high into the air, the searing blast tore through the steel deck and upwards into the superstructure, destroying one of the ship's four lifeboats and igniting gases given off by the 10,000 tons of prime Welsh steam coal the *Boma* had loaded at Cardiff for Lagos. Captain C.E. Anders, two gunners and 47 officers and men took to the remaining boats and were picked up by the Norwegian tanker *Vilja* in the convoy and later transferred to HMS *Viscount*, which took them back to Liverpool. But neither *Viscount* nor a Coastal Command aircraft sent to assist succeeded in locating Harms, who slunk away to lie in wait for further prey.

That night Winston Churchill wrote a Minute to Alexander at the Admiralty: 'The repeated severe losses in the North Western Approaches are most grievous and I wish to feel assured that they are being grappled with . . .' Unfortunately the Royal Navy was just beginning to learn that their early success against German submarines had entailed an element of luck, and that the degree of confidence reposed in the almost miraculous abilities of sonar/asdic had been misplaced. 'Asdic', one experienced regular destroyer commander wrote after the war, 'was never the infallible weapon we cracked it up to be.'[13] A submarine officer remembered 'the failure of the Asdic . . . in the early days . . . not [being] due to any fault in the invention itself but because it had not been energetically developed, nor had the associated tactics been sufficiently understood in the balmy days of peace.' He went on to stigmatise 'those peacetime exercises where hundreds (if not thousands) of records and analyses had been "flogged" to cover inefficiency and to present an outward appearance of smooth competence.'[14]

Salman withdrew, and his next strike pointed up another deficiency in pre-war British naval planning: six days later, on 10 August, the large former Anchor Liner HMS *Transylvania* was struck by a torpedo from *U-56* and sank with the loss of 48 of her company. Part of the 10th Cruiser Squadron, the *Transylvania*, Captain F.N. Miles, was on patrol to the north-west of Malin Head, highly vulnerable to submarine attack by virtue of both her bulk and the predictable nature of her task.

On 28 August Endrass in *U-46* struck at another Armed Merchant Cruiser, HMS *Dunvegan Castle*, Captain H. Adriff, on her station off the west coast of Ireland. The mail and passenger motor-vessel, built as recently as 1936 for the Union Castle Line's London-to-South Africa service, was sunk with the loss of 27 ratings. Six other AMCs were sunk in the North Atlantic by U-boats between June and the end of 1940.[15] Nor were these AMCs much better at engaging their own kidney: on 28 July in the South Atlantic the German auxiliary cruiser *Thor*, a converted cargo-vessel with a far lower profile and a superior armament, out-gunned the British Armed Merchant Cruiser *Alcantara*, a passenger-liner requisitioned by the Admiralty from the Royal Mail Line.

The supposed invulnerability of vessels proceeding independently was also increasingly exposed. At twilight on 7 August, 205 miles due west of Malin Head, *U-38*, Kapitänleutnant H. Liebe, torpedoed the passenger-vessel

Mohamed Ali el-Kebir. Owned in Egypt by the Pharaonic Mail Line of Alexandria but registered in London, the 16-knot ship had been chartered for government service and was on passage from Avonmouth to Gibraltar. In addition to government stores and mail, she had on board 697 troops and 66 Royal Navy personnel. In the sinking ten of her crew, four naval ratings and about 95 soldiers lost their lives, though Captain J.P. Thomson, 153 crew members, one naval gunner and 732 service personnel were rescued by the destroyer *Griffin* and landed at Greenock.

The following day in the same general area Hartmann's *U-37*, while on a relocating passage from Wilhelmshaven to L'Orient, sighted and attacked Houlder Brothers' *Upwey Grange*. Captain W.E. Williams was heading for London from Buenos Aires with 11 passengers and a cargo of 5,500 tons of frozen and tinned meat. Williams's vessel was capable of a service speed of 15 knots but in the late forenoon Hartmann succeeded in hitting her port side with two torpedoes. The effect was devastating. One blasted its way into the engine room, the second hit her aft, in way of No. 6 Hold. Taking a list, the *Upwey Grange* immediately began to settle and list, her after deck being 'under water in 10 to 15 seconds', and there was no time to carry out a formal muster. Under these trying circumstances Williams ordered the ship abandoned, transmitting his distress signal and position by means of the emergency aerial, the main one having been destroyed by blast. The abandonment was carried out 'in a quiet and orderly manner'. On the boat deck, Chief Officer Jones supervised the lowering of the boats. With him was First Officer Ellis, who quickly lowered his No. 3 Boat into the water. The *Upwey Grange* was fitted with relatively new Welin Maclachlan gravity davits which greatly facilitated the speedy lowering of the boats, despite the rough sea and heavy swell then running; unfortunately, the painter was slipped prematurely and Ellis was unable to board. As the *Upwey Grange* still had way upon her, No. 3 Boat was left astern and Ellis joined No. 1 Boat, also on the starboard side. This too was by now also water-borne, but remained towing alongside by her painter, awaiting the master. Men were climbing down into her by way of the boarding ladders, as they were into No. 4 Boat on the port side. There was no No. 2 Boat: when in the London Docks prior to her departure for South America the *Upwey Grange* had lent it for the evacuation of Dunkirk. It had not been returned.

As Williams boarded No. 1 Boat with Ellis and the radio officer the latter reported that the 'in distress' signal had been acknowledged. Then, with the after part of the *Upwey Grange* so low in the water that the ship's poop gun was just awash, they cast off, aware that the submarine had surfaced not far away 'and lay on the water with three men in the conning tower taking photographs. The lifeboat had to pull over very close to her to pick up a man, but the submarine crew ignored them. While the boat was picking up this man the ship went down absolutely vertical and quite slowly, her No. 1 Hatch [forward] burst open [under pressure] and both [anchor] cables came roaring out of her spurling pipes.'

All the boats had got away from the ship safely, though No. 3 was some distance off and No. 1 was contaminated by oily water. Having rescued his man, Williams went alongside No. 3 Boat and put Ellis and an able seaman aboard. Chief Officer Jones's No. 4 Boat had picked up one man from a raft and one from the water with a lifebuoy round him. Jones reported that 'no person was left behind who could possibly have been rescued. There were a number of people in the engine room and possibly some in their quarters who had no chance of escape, but when the boats left the ship no person was in the water. The vessel was practically submerged in under ten minutes although the bow remained above the water quite a while longer.' Jones mentioned the indifference of the U-boat.

Having made his dispositions, Williams ordered them all to hoist sail and make for Ireland. The wind was favourable for this, blowing strongly from the west, but the sea conditions were poor and the speed with which they had had to abandon their ship rendered them vulnerable to hypothermia. There were 25 in Ellis's No. 3 Boat, including three passengers and the stewardess, Mrs Summers. The cooks and stewards, who had so recently been preparing lunch in the galley and saloon, 'wore only singlets', while Apprentice Parker and Assistant Engineer Hurst, who had been bathing when the ship had been struck, were without shoes or socks. 'Fortunately', Ellis reported, 'we had a passenger with us (Mr Stevens) who was one of the most resourceful men I have ever met. Before we entered the danger zone, he had prepared a canvas bag and put in it all the things he thought would be useful if we had to take to the boats. What came out of that bag was amazing. He fitted men out with socks, Balaclava helmets, mufflers, mittens, shirts and even aspirins.' Unfortunately, Ellis also had a wounded man aboard. Engine Room Storekeeper Evett had suffered a bad gash that almost cut off his upper lip below the nose. Despite everything Mrs Summers and Apprentice Parker could do, which included using all the lint in the first aid kit, they were unable to staunch the bleeding. The poor man was 'passed into the bows where he could get his head down'.

With Williams in the lead the boats kept company for a few hours, scudding eastwards before the west wind through a rough sea and swell, making good headway, 'shipping occasional spray, but as it was also raining we did not notice this extra discomfort. Those in the bows and amidships were crouched under the boat cover and able to keep fairly dry, though many were very seasick.' Ellis found Parker a helpful relief on the helm, but at nightfall the wind rose and Ellis prudently handed sail, streamed his sea-anchor and hove-to, head to sea.

Meanwhile Jones's No. 4 Boat had lost contact with the others and the chief officer 'steered in an ENE direction . . . The weather', Jones added with all the understatement characteristic of such reports, 'was not good.' At about 22.00 that night they saw a dark object astern and signalled SOS by torch. The shape manifested itself into a destroyer and, after circling them to ensure that they were indeed a solitary lifeboat, told them to come along-side. They found themselves picked up by HMS *Vanquisher*, on her way to meet Convoy HX61. Lieutenant Commander A.P. Northey remained circling in the area for three hours without sighting the other two boats before heading for his rendezvous.

Next morning the wind had further freshened to a strong breeze from the WSW. First Officer Ellis found No. 3 Boat alone on the ocean. It was a bleak moment. But the mainsail was reefed, then hoisted, and they resumed their easterly course. After this they broke their fast on four small biscuits dipped into condensed milk and half a dipper of water, an amount equiv-alent to an egg-cupful. By mid morning the sea conditions had deterior-ated and Ellis was obliged to lower his mainsail, stream the sea-anchor over the stern and run under jib alone. Nevertheless, No. 3 Boat ran well throughout the day, not shipping any water, until about midnight when, without warning, she broached-to and would not respond to her helm. Mr Stevens offered further proof of his resourcefulness, for it turned out that he was an experienced yachtsman with more expertise than Ellis in handling small craft. After another failed attempt to heave-to, the two men contrived to get the boat before the wind again.

'Things were, by now, very unpleasant; we shipped much water and baled continuously. A very high sea was running with a strong westerly wind; frequent squalls of moderate gale force from NW made a nasty cross sea. As it became light on the Saturday morning [10 August] we could see that our sea anchor had carried away. We hauled the line in and bent an oar to it . . . This . . . made quite an effective sea anchor and eased her a lot. As the morning wore on the squalls became less frequent . . .', so much so that by noon they had hauled in their improvised sea anchor and shaken out the reef.

By now the sun was out, 'drying and warming the men who, although very hungry, became very cheerful, singing and joking. As dusk drew on we served the evening meal, got the boat dried right out and set watches for the night. The lookout had hardly been on [duty] half an hour when he reported a submarine, and it certainly looked like a submarine until, to our relief, it smoked up and we realised it was a trawler and headed towards it.'

Shortly afterwards they were safely aboard the Cardiff steam trawler *Naniwa*. Skipper J. Nightingale gave up his bunk to Mrs Summers, who in Ellis's words 'had gone through a very difficult situation for a woman, with great courage and unflustered throughout.' Nightingale generously abandoned his trawl and made for an Irish port, while his crew tended the survivors and the trawler's cook 'stopped up all night baking bread for us and fed us like lords'.

Ellis's boat had made about 180 miles in three days and two nights and was within 50 miles of Achill Head. He expressed a feeling of disappointment that they had not made it to land under their own sail, but had second thoughts when the *Naniwa* arrived off Berehaven next morning. Here 'the Irish authorities had closed the port and the coastguard station would not take a semaphore message', so Nightingale took his human catch on to Cardiff where on the late afternoon of 13 August they were met by Captain Elliott, Houlder Brothers' Marine Superintendent from Newport, along with representatives from the Shipping Federation and the Shipwrecked Mariners' Association. Soon afterwards they were all on their way home.

The *Naniwa*'s owners refused the compensation offered by Houlder Brothers for the loss of her trawl, expressing their willingness to contribute to the common cause. They also refused a pecuniary grant to Nightingale and his crew, whose earnings depended in part upon the profits from their catch, a by no means indifferent sacrifice when food was scarce. Instead of a cash grant, *Naniwa*'s skipper and hands had to be content with a small memento, Houlders' intended payment of £125 being considered 'far too generous a recognition of any services rendered'.

Jones and his party, which consisted of about twenty of the ship's crew, seven passengers and one Distressed British Seaman (DBS) enjoying a free passage home from South America, had already been landed from the *Vanquisher* on her arrival in Liverpool with Convoy HX61 on 11 August. But of Captain Williams's No. 1 Boat nothing further was heard. The bodies of the *Upwey Grange*'s Chief Engineer Mackrow and Apprentice Butcher, both of whom were known to have been in Williams's lifeboat, were washed up on the Irish coast and provided the only evidence of her fate.[16]

Such ordeals became commonplace, though varying in detail, and scarcely qualified as epic voyages in small boats. Those 'three days and two nights' of Ellis's account seem happily offset by his disappointment at not reaching land under his own resources. Yet when set in context they reveal many horrors; it was August, still within the solstitial period of the northern summer, yet in Jones's words, 'the weather conditions were not good'. There was no time for preparation: the ship's company were rent from their routine tasks, cooks turned up wearing only singlets, others without footwear, and the ship settled in a quarter of an hour.

One master recalled that the greatest ordeal at the time was the waiting for disaster. 'I come and lie down here on the couch [in my cabin] and try and rest, and all the time I'm waiting for the crash. Somehow it's not so bad when it happens.' Yet when it did happen, and a man could fall back on years of self-discipline and a degree of training, matters rarely ran smoothly. The premature slipping of a painter by the bow man of the *Upwey Grange's* No. 3 Boat had cast her adrift without the presence of the officer nominated to board and take charge of her after launching. In the event it was of no great moment, but the lowering of boats was not an easy matter, especially in vessels not fitted with the modern davits boasted by the *Upwey Grange*. It was so easy for things to go wrong; rope falls could part, or slip round a stag-horn, and it required steady and experienced seamen – usually two to a fall, so four to any boat – to lower her safely. Often the rush to board a boat before it left the illusory safety of its elevated station on a boat-deck over-rode common practice and common sense. Occasionally discipline broke down, as in the case of the *Clan MacPhee*.

Part of Convoy OB197, this Clan liner was outward bound for Bombay and the Malabar coast with a valuable general cargo of exports loaded in Glasgow. On 16 August 1940 the convoy was dispersed in the North West Approaches and Captain T.P.B. Cranwell stood away to the south-west before heading south. He could no longer see the ships heading west across the Atlantic, though other vessels were still in sight when a torpedo smashed into the *Clan MacPhee's* engine room, instantly killing those on watch there. When the order to abandon ship was given it was found that the blast had destroyed one of the lifeboats, and those men allotted to it began crowding into another. Chief Officer Chadd remonstrated to little effect, despite taking the rather desperate step of brandishing a revolver. The lascars were not to be persuaded that the loss of their lifeboat meant anything but that they would be left behind, though Chadd made it clear that they would be distributed among the other boats. The *Clan MacPhee* was sinking fast, and in the confusion the overloaded lifeboat was lowered, with inevitable consequences: it fell from the davits, spilling men into the water. While much might be made of the element of panic demonstrated here by the *Clan MacPhee's* lascars, it was not a prevailing feature of mixed-race crews. Most lascars and Chinese behaved with courageous stoicism, just as many British did not. In the case of the *Clan MacPhee*, the panic among her Indian crew was a simple matter of fact. Many paid with their lives, for in addition to Captain Cranwell 66 went down with the ship, which took eight minutes to founder.

Nor was the ordeal over for those in the boats after they were picked up by the Hungarian ship *Kelet* the next morning, for she was torpedoed by another U-boat two days later. The 35 survivors from the Clan liner were finally rescued by the small Norwegian vessel *Vareg* after a further five days adrift.

It was clear that unless she possessed a significantly high speed, such as that of a fast trans-Atlantic passenger-mail-liner, any ship was at risk inside the operational area accessible by German U-boats. Hartmann had continued his voyage to L'Orient but Liebe was still in the area, sinking the Cardiff tramp *Llanfair* with a full cargo of Australian sugar on 11 August. This ship had straggled from Convoy SL41, and was therefore considered to have in some sense placed herself in danger, but the unwise practice of dispersing convoys in predictable areas played into the hands of the increasingly experienced German commanders. Losses from this cause, aided by B-Dienst intelligence and Dönitz's direction, became distressingly commonplace.

Submarine commanders could simply lie in wait in the dispersal areas; or further afield, they could patrol the known shipping lanes. This practice brought the Italians some successes, the *Alessandro Malaspina* being the first of Mussolini's submarines to strike on behalf of the Axis. Based on Bordeaux and on patrol off the Azores, Capitano di Fregata Leoni torpedoed the tanker *British Fame* on her way in ballast from Avonmouth to Abadan by way of Cape Town. The three men on watch below were killed and one man was taken prisoner, but Captain W.G. Knight, the remaining 43 of his crew and their naval gunner were picked up and landed at Lisbon by the Portuguese destroyer *Dao*.

In mid August a third wave of U-boats attacked shipping in the North Western Approaches, in an area bounded by the Hebrides, Ireland and Rockall. Convoy OB 202 sailing from Liverpool on 22 August was dispersed on the 26th, and waiting for its ships off Malin Head was Oberleutnant zur See E. Topp in *U-57*. This was Topp's third war patrol in command, all in the same area. The other two had been short, his first from Bergen of ten days' duration during which he had sunk one Swedish vessel and the Brocklebank liner *Manipur* off Cape Wrath. She was part of the east-coast portion of Convoy HX55 which had been attacked earlier by *U-61*. Though 14 of her crew were lost, Captain R. Mallett and 64 survivors were picked up by the Canadian destroyer *Skeena* and landed at Rosyth. On his second patrol Topp sank a second Swedish vessel, the *Atos*, before moving *U-57* to L'Orient. By midnight on 23/24 August he was off Malin Head. The sky was overcast and the visibility about two miles as he caught sight of Convoy OB202, consisting of 28 vessels escorted by two destroyers, one corvette and two anti-submarine trawlers.

At 23.44 the leading ship of the starboard column, the *St Dunstan*, was hit by Topp's first torpedo on her starboard side. Within a minute the Federal Steam Navigation Company's passenger-cargo-liner *Cumberland* bound for New Zealand with a general cargo including 9,000 tons of steel had been hit. The *Cumberland*'s station was second ship in the sixth column, and the torpedo blew in her starboard side just as the commodore ordered the first of two emergency turns to port. This did not deter Topp, who at 23.46 made his third strike, hitting the brand-new passenger-cargo-vessel *Havildar*, owned by the Asiatic Steam Navigation Company of London and on charter to Brocklebank's with a general cargo for Calcutta.

As with the defence of Convoy HX55, the destroyers swung round to carry out a sonar search across the wake of the convoy. This technique was intended to catch a U-boat which, having delivered its attack, usually allowed the convoy to pass above it, hiding in the disturbed water churned up by the passing ships' propellers. On this occasion a pattern of depth-charges was dropped about an hour later, but Topp had slipped away.

His three victims remained afloat and word was sent for tugs, but the *Cumberland* was settling slowly. Captain E.A.J. Williams had ordered his crew into the boats, and hoped to save his ship if the tugs arrived in time. By the forenoon of the 24th the sea was rising and so they set sail. Four men had been killed by the torpedo, but 53 landed safely at Moville, County Donegal. When the destroyers ran back for survivors an hour later the *Cumberland* had sunk, but tugs arrived in time to assist the *Havildar* and *St Dunstan*. The *St Dunstan* was not taken in tow until the 26th, however, and she slowly foundered and sank next day. The *Havildar*, having been taken in charge by the tugs *Salvonia* and *Englishman*, reached the Clyde on Sunday 25 August and was beached while her cargo was discharged. She was then taken up river to Glasgow and dry-docked for repair.[17]

Topp's final victim before his return to Bergen was the Anglo-Saxon Petroleum Company's tanker *Pecten*, which he torpedoed on the evening of 25 August. The 1927-built tanker was on charter to the Admiralty and bore a full cargo of 9,546 tons of boiler oil bound from the Caribbean to the Clyde. She had fallen astern of Convoy HX65 when Topp caught her and killed Captain H.E. Dale and 15 of his crew. The remaining 44 men were picked up by other vessels and landed safely. Another tanker, the *La Brea*, was torpedoed by Rösing in *U-48* on the 24th. The *La Brea*, which had fallen astern of HX65, was British-flagged but American-owned and had loaded 9,410 tons of fuel oil in Aruba. Next morning Rösing caught up with the main body of Convoy HX65. It consisted of 51 ships and it was suffering a mauling. Attacking a third tanker, the *Athelcrest*, Rösing failed to sink her, but she lost 30 men, was badly damaged, and had to be despatched by gunfire from the corvette *Godetia*. Lieutenant A.H. Pierce also picked up her master, Captain L.V.F. Evans, and five of his crew.

That evening, in the darkness, Kapitänleutnant Wilhelm Schulz in *U-124*, on her first war patrol, stalked and torpedoed J. & C. Harrison's new tramp steamer *Harpalyce*. She had been selected as the convoy commodore's vessel, and among the dead were the ship's master, Captain W.J. Rees, Commodore B.G. Washington, four of his signallers, and 36 members of the ship's crew. Four survivors were rescued by the trawler *Fort Dee* and landed in the Orkneys. With the *Harpalyce* went 8,000 tons of steel loaded in Baltimore, Maryland. Schulz's next stroke was as brutal, though the *Fircrest* was an elderly vessel, having been built as the *Rivoli* in 1907. A London-registered tramp, she was laden with 7,900 tons of iron ore bound for Middlesbrough from Wabana in Newfoundland and she went down rapidly, taking with her Captain R.H. Tuckett and her 38-strong crew.

Schulz failed to sink his next target, the Headlam tramp *Stakesby*, but that was not the end of HX65's ordeal, for Rösing was still in the vicinity and had attacked and sunk the *Empire Merlin*. One of the surplus United States standard ships purchased by the Ministry of War Transport, the *Empire Merlin* had been built in 1919. She had loaded a full cargo at Port Sulphur, Louisiana and joined the assembling ships of Convoy HX65 at Halifax. The 6,830 tons of sulphur submerged the *Empire Merlin* to her marks and at the time of Rösing's attack she appears to have fallen about three miles astern of the convoy. When Rösing's torpedoes hit her she broke in half and sank like a stone in a mere 35 seconds. Captain D.W. Simpson, his 33 officers and men plus a solitary gunner were drowned; only one man, Ordinary Seaman John Lee, survived to be rescued by *Godetia*.

The final losses from Convoy HX65 were caused by aircraft off Kinnaird's Head. The New Zealand Shipping Company's elderly *Remuera*, Captain Robinson, was attacked by four torpedo-carrying Heinkel He115s, one of which caused her to sink, though with no loss of life. She went down with more than 4,800 tons of refrigerated and 1,600 tons of general cargo. The *Cape York*, laden with 3,500 tons of grain and 4,100 tons of timber, was so badly bombed by eight Junkers Ju88s that despite the efforts of her crew she had to be abandoned the next day. All twelve aircraft belonged to Küstenfliegergruppe 506 from Stavanger.

For Dönitz and his submariners, success was charted by the tonnages they grossed. The totals were inevitably coloured by a certain exaggeration, partly from a natural if reprehensible desire to claim each target as significant, but also because exact identification of a torpedoed ship was not always possible. In London, statistical analysis also noted this depletion of bottoms, though with a more rigorous accuracy. In addition to the loss of ships and cargoes a concern was growing, and continued to grow as late summer turned into autumn, as to the erosion of lives, of experience, and of the unspectacular steadfastness that, it was beginning to occur to even the most purblind in the Admiralty, characterised the flower of Britain's Merchant Navy.

And it was going to get worse.

7

'It's only a torpedo'

City of Benares

TOTALS OF MERCHANT tonnage sunk are no more than banal sums, and convey little of the danger that was now beginning to transform a way of life already uncomfortable and estranging. In addition to these events in the Western Approaches, there were the attacks of German aircraft on vessels in the English Channel, and the immense damage inflicted upon coastal and trans-Atlantic shipping once it was on passage in the North Sea, an area of water known in the Kaiser's day, even to English school children, as the 'German Ocean'. Elsewhere, the German auxiliary cruisers *Widder, Thor, Atlantis* and *Pinguin* were active and the slaughter went on. For example, on 21 August 1940 the *Widder* intercepted the steam-ship *Anglo-Saxon*.

The *Anglo-Saxon* was one of five vessels owned by the Nitrate Producers' Steamship Company and managed on their behalf by Lawther, Latta & Company of London. She had been built in 1929, had a service speed of 11.5 knots and was usually employed between the United Kingdom and British Columbia, and from there across the Pacific to Australia. At Newport, Monmouthshire she had loaded a full cargo of coal destined for Bahia Blanca in Argentina, and had sailed in convoy clear of the 17th meridian; thereafter, she was on her own.

By dusk on the 21st she was 810 miles west of the Canary Islands. No one aboard her had spotted the former Hamburg-Amerika Linie vessel that now approached from the starboard bow in the pitch dark. She was the Kriegsmarine's auxiliary cruiser *Widder*, and at 20.20 she opened fire at a range of one mile, rapidly closing to three cables. As the alarms rang and the *Anglo-Saxon*'s crew ran to their action stations, shells hit her poop, destroying the gun and anyone in the accommodation below. As he headed for his station aft 42-year-old ex-Royal Marine seaman-gunner Richard Penny was wounded. Coming out of his cabin, Captain Flynn made for the ship's side to dump his confidential books in the weighted canvas bag provided by the Naval Control of Shipping Organisation; he was riddled with machine-gun bullets as the *Widder* strafed the *Anglo-Saxon*'s accommodation. The ship was raked by fire and it became clear that any attempt to abandon her would prove impossible, for the lifeboats on the boat deck were useless. Chief Officer C.B. Denny, having assured himself that there was no chance of saving the ship, joined an able seaman named Widdicombe who had been on the wheel and together they made for the port side of the lower bridge deck where a small boat hung in her davits, griped into the ship's side. This was the jolly-boat, a working boat intended to provide a means of transport ashore when at anchor, a punt to freshen the ship's draft marks, or a means of running out mooring ropes. She was a transom-sterned open boat, not a double-ended lifeboat, but as a precaution she had been stored with a few essentials and was fitted with yellow-metal buoyancy tanks.

Denny cast off the gripes, and with Widdicombe helping, and hurting his hand in the dark, began to lower the jolly-boat by her rope falls. As they were doing this, men rolled over the maindeck rail into the jolly-boat. Then, with some difficulty, since the ship still had headway and the boat was being dragged through the water, Denny and Widdicombe swung themselves down by way of the falls, searing their hands. Others followed and then they unhooked the falls, slipped the painter and fended off the ship as she sped past. Above them other faces looked over the side, and two more men jumped into the boat. The *Anglo-Saxon*'s stern loomed briefly over them, her propeller thrashing, her poop ablaze; then she disappeared in the darkness, already settling as the *Widder*'s shells slammed into her, their explosions briefly lighting up the night.

The jolly-boat passed within a hundred feet of the blacked-out *Widder* as the raider closed in for the kill, so they began to pull away. The boat was filling with water, and they remembered to ship the plug. After a while the moon rose. Astern of them they could see small lights bobbing on the sea and realised they were the rafts that those left aboard had flung over the side. A searchlight beam and more machine-gun fire raked the water; the lights disappeared. The searchlight beam continued its probing as more streams of high-velocity shot riddled the ship, then there was an explosion as the magazine in the *Anglo-Saxon*'s poop blew up and she made her last dive. The *Widder* disappeared to the east.

Next morning they were alone. Denny's first task was to take stock. The boat had a half-full barricoe of water, some ship's biscuits and a few tins of mutton and condensed milk. The two last induced thirst. In the boat with Denny were Second Radio Officer R.H. Pilcher, Penny the gunner, Third Engineer L. Hawkes, Second Cook L. Morgan, and two young able seamen. Wilbert Widdicombe had just attained his majority; he had been educated and prepared for his career aboard the training ship HMS *Conway*. A tall, bright, but truculent youth, he had failed to complete his time with the Union Castle line so had secured an able seaman's certificate and sailed in that capacity. The other, Robert Tapscott, aged 19, came from a line of Cardiff pilots and had gone to sea at the age of 15. Both had knocked about the world, had been in ships supplying the Republican government during the Spanish Civil War, and had seen action during the present conflict. They cordially disliked one another.

Denny did his best to dress his men's wounds from the small first aid kit. Penny's wounds were severe; he had been hit in the right hip and wrist. Pilcher had had one foot reduced to a bloody pulp. Several, Denny severely, had burned their hands on the ropes when lowering and boarding the jolly-boat. Morgan had a deep flesh wound on his right ankle, and a badly bruised hand. Tapscott had received three minor shrapnel wounds in his back and had broken a tooth, exposing the nerve. He had also been struck by hot shrapnel in the right groin; it had burned but not penetrated the skin.

Hoisting sail they headed west, determined to run to the West Indies if they could. The only advantage to the jolly-boat was that in fair weather it sailed better than a lifeboat. During the daytime the heat exacerbated their condition, and Pilcher's foot quickly putrified. As they had nothing to excrete, they ceased defecating. In the darkness of the second night they saw a ship and burned a flare, but the vessel circled them and they thought from her silhouette that she might have been a German, perhaps their tormentor. They dropped the sail and lay doggo.

On Saturday 24 August Denny recorded: 'Crew's spirits cheerful . . . Issued half a dipper [of water] to each man and half a biscuit. Hoping for rain showers.' The following day it fell calm. They 'dined' on tinned mutton, saucing it with black gallows humour, and afterwards discussed food. Denny was now worried about the gangrene in Pilcher's foot; Morgan's was little better. By Monday the 26th thirst was beginning to dominate their thoughts; their skin began to burn and their mouths dried. There was little wind. They ate more mutton and a little biscuit and took a mouthful of water. Pilcher was now weak, and his swollen foot stank, for which he apologised. But 'everyone else [was] in good spirits and very cheerful . . .' Those fit enough went over the side to cool off. Denny kept up their morale: 'Trusting to make a landfall . . . with God's will and British determination . . .' Later the breeze filled in, and by 22.00 they were 'skimming along fine at about 5 knots'.

Next morning the water ration was lowered. Their throats swelled and their dry tongues began to fill their mouths. By the evening Pilcher was delirious, and they all began to suffer cramps and a profound nausea. Denny was in a bad way himself, and during the day Pilcher died. He was 'committed . . . to the deep with silent prayer.' In the following days the inexorable failing of their bodies produced a breakdown in Denny; the others too began to act irrationally, singing or drinking salt water, their moods swinging from wild optimism to black despair. Widdicombe and Tapscott argued, and Hawkes had to intervene while Denny sought to exert his failing influence. He made his last entry in his log that evening, 2 September, and there followed an argument as to who should succeed him in command. Hawkes, though a time-served engineer, was on his first voyage to sea: Widdicombe was qualified to navigate. Hawkes settled for being in charge of the rations as the boat sailed on towards the west. Morgan's mind, never very stable, was by now wandering, and Penny was debilitated. While at the helm he slipped overboard.

On the dawn of the thirteenth day at sea the boat was sailing well when the rudder carried away. A steering oar was rigged but for Denny, who had thus far saved them, it was the final straw. He asked if anyone else would join him in ending it all; Hawkes agreed. After a sleep the two men rose with surprising energy. Denny gave his signet ring to Widdicombe, asking him, if he survived, to pass it to his mother, then told them to 'keep going west'. He shook hands with Hawkes, the two men went overboard and the boat sailed on. Hawkes's fair, sun-bleached hair could be seen for some time. The three men left aboard tried to pray.

Widdicombe took command and wrote up the log: 'Chief Mate and Third Engineer go over side. No water.'

The three survivors were very weak, and even the nightly heaving-to took an age to perform. Morgan's reason was failing, exacerbated by his drinking large amounts of sea-water. In the failing wind they tried to mitigate the effects of the heat by drenching themselves with sea-water, but their skin blistered and cracked; their mouths grew foul and their tongues swollen as day succeeded day. They could hardly talk, but Morgan began raving, and in an irrational fury Widdicombe threw the empty barricoe overboard. Later he struggled with Morgan. On the evening of 9 September Morgan stood up and quietly announced, 'I'll go down the street for a drink.' Then, thinking himself in Newport, the Welshman stepped over the side. Widdicombe logged the event: 'Cook goes mad; dies. Only two of us left.'

The remaining two young men were now in extremity. Tortured by thirst, they tried drinking their own urine, only to find what little they produced utterly foul. As they lay becalmed, both decided upon suicide and went over the side – but argument saved them, and they clambered back inboard, having benefited a little from their immersion. After a while they removed the plug from the boat's small magnetic compass and drank the alcohol that served to damp the oscillations of the card. In no time they were drunk, and collapsed in the boat's bottom, to be awakened later by rain. As a heavy tropical thunder storm deluged them they had the wit to use the boat's buoyancy tank to catch the rain in, giving them 'water for six days'. Their contracted stomachs rejected the water they gulped down, and they were racked by vomiting.

After the 12th the showers became regular, and they managed to get the boat on course again. They slept better, and slowly their morale began to improve as they eked out the remaining biscuits. On the 20th they thought themselves near land, but four days later the biscuits and the water had all gone. That night it rained again. Day succeeded day, and they began to eat seaweed, clumps of which were now passing the boat. One morning they thought they had run aground, but the stirring of a dark fluke close alongside told another tale. Later they tried fishing; later still they saw a ship, but it passed.

After four more days they ran into heavy weather. Struggling to hold the jolly-boat stern to wind by the steering oar, they ran before it as breaking seas cascaded over the transom. The gale blew for two days and three nights. As the wind and sea abated they were chewing anything – some crabs caught on the seaweed, the remnants of Pilcher's tobacco pouch. They endured this for a week, slowly submitting to bouts of hysteria and dementia. Days merged into weeks as the boat sailed steadily west, her crew taking turns to tend the steering oar in a blur of semi-consciousness. Their skin was now disfigured by lesions and boils. On 27 October they fell out again over the steering, mustering the energy to fight until they collapsed. Tapscott tried apologising; Widdicombe sulked. Later they shared a fish, thinking they had sighted land but unsure, having been deceived before. Then they realised that a reef lay between them and a glistening beach. Tapscott thought he saw a way through the reef and lay in the bow, conning Widdicombe at the steering oar. Shortly afterwards the jolly-boat drove ashore. They clambered out and collapsed, unknowing and uncaring that they had made a remarkable passage of 2,275 miles.[1]

They were found on the morning of Thursday 31 October 1940 in Alabaster Bay at Eleuthera in the Bahamas by two islanders, Mr and Mrs Johnson, and taken to Nassau hospital. Here they were diagnosed as suffering from pellagra, deranged nervous systems and insomnia. Tapscott, the more stolid and less emotional of the two, was now a prey to deep melancholia, a feature of which was a desire to die; Widdicombe, more mercurial by temperament, recovered more rapidly. After eight days they were deemed fit to receive visitors, and found themselves objects of curiosity on the part of the Duke and Duchess of Windsor.[2]

Early in 1941 Widdicombe was passed fit to go home. Sent to New York, he signed on the Furness Withy general cargo-liner *Siamese Prince*, which sailed for Liverpool as an independent. Once again the unwisdom of this practice was exposed. Captain Edgar Litchfield took his 14-knot ship into high latitudes and was some 180 miles north-west of St Kilda on 17 February when his ship was torn apart by a torpedo fired from *U-69*. The U-boat was on her first war patrol and it was Kapitänleutnant J. Metzler's first success. Eight passengers and all hands, including Widdicombe, were killed.

Tapscott joined the Canadian army and survived the war to give evidence against the captain of the *Widder*.[3] Tried by a British Military Court in Hamburg in 1947, Korvettenkapitän H. von Ruckteschell was charged with firing on British seamen clinging to rafts, not making provision for the safety of the crews of the ships he sank, and continuing to shell the ships after they had obeyed radioed instructions. He was found guilty and sentenced to seven years in prison. The ruthlessness he had shown the *Anglo-Saxon* had also been inflicted upon the cargo-liner *Davisian* in July 1940 and, when he was in command of the raider *Michel*, upon the *Empire Dawn* in September 1942.[4] Whether or not the affidavits signed by Tapscott and others exaggerated what they saw, or thought they saw, as has been suggested,[5] it is beyond controversy that in such circumstances there was no refuge for the 'non-combatant' merchant seaman other than his lifeboat – if he was lucky.

As Convoy HX65 suffered its mauling in the North West Approaches, the 51 ships of HX66 were already half-way across the Atlantic and Convoy SC1's 40 vessels were just leaving Sydney, Cape Breton Island. The regularity of this established pattern was inevitable, but until proper anti-submarine escort and air cover could be provided, it played into Dönitz's hands. It was only now that enough warships were becoming available to form Escort Groups. The idea was that by operating in designated groups the ships would develop and reap the rewards of practised co-ordination and team spirit that would enable them to react swiftly when an attack was made upon a convoy. There had been considerable Admiralty opposition to the formation of these groups, but as losses of merchantmen rose it became clear that only an instantaneous seizure of the initiative from the attacker, an immediate turning of the hunter into the hunted, would transform a supine defence into an active and effective deterrent.

The massive influx of untrained personnel into the Royal Navy demanded rapid methods of converting civilians to seamen, and seamen to anti-submarine warriors. Much was accomplished by Stephenson's organisation based at Tobermory and at the other anti-submarine training establishments set up in Scotland. But not even a month's intensive training could fully prepare a green escort for the realities of the war in the North Atlantic, or for the close co-operation needed to achieve success against an enemy who had been active for a year. Nevertheless, it was a start; and, like much else, it was based upon sound principles.

These new Escort Groups operating in the North West Approaches were usually led by a regular naval officer in a destroyer, usually of First World War vintage, supported by an increasing number of corvettes commanded by reservists. Support of a trans-Atlantic convoy remained limited by range, which at this time did not extend beyond the 19th meridian. It was also limited by expertise.

A second important deficiency was the lack of effective air cover, even over those sea areas where the Royal Air Force might have been supposed to enjoy an immediate advantage; but what anti-submarine capability was to the Royal Navy – a poor relation – so in the Royal Air Force was Coastal Command to Fighter and Bomber Commands. Presided over at this time by Air Chief Marshal Sir Frederick Bowhill, Coastal Command was also a victim of Churchill's over-riding desire for the offensive. In 1940 it was 'grievously handicapped by shortage of suitable aircraft, by lack of a lethal weapon with which to attack a U-boat and by the need to achieve a high degree of training in this very specialised work'.[6] Although the foundations of an excellent and developing co-operation between the Admiralty and Coastal Command had already been laid, and the effect of British aircraft was already being felt by U-boats operating too close to the coasts of Britain and Northern Ireland,[7] many merchant seamen were paying with their lives for misdirected effort and neglect.

Convoy SC1's two-score merchantmen arrived in Liverpool on 29 August relatively unscathed, though its losses had been ominous; one ship, the *Blairmore*, laden with pit-props, had been torpedoed by Oehrn's *U-37*. Oehrn had sunk several independently-routed merchantmen before locating SC1 and on the evening of 24 August he had sunk the convoy's sole escort, HM Sloop *Penzance*. Captain H. Campbell had stopped *Blairmore* to pick up Lieutenant Commander A.J. Wavisk and a handful of his sloop's company five hours before Oehrn torpedoed the Clydesdale Navigation Company's tramp with the loss of a further five lives.

Convoy HX66 fared worse, losing four of its number: the *Kyno*, Captain W.A. Thompson, with a general cargo on the 28th to *U-28* (Kuhnke); and on the 30th the *Chelsea*, Captain R. Harrison, *Mill Hill*, Captain R. du Buisson, and the Norwegian *Norne*, all sunk by *U-32* (Jenisch). Almost 8,000 tons of maize and more than 10,000 tons of pig-iron and steel were lost, along with 62 seamen, including both Harrison and du Buisson.

With HX convoys leaving Halifax every four days and a longer, more variable interval between the departures of SC convoys, the opportunities offered to the enemy increased proportionately. No further successes were gained against the faster convoys until two ships were damaged in HX70 and one, the *Tregenna* with a full cargo of 7,000 tons of steel, was sunk in HX71, but the first successful group attack was made, on Convoy SC2. Aided by B-Dienst intercepts obtained on 30 August which revealed the position at which SC2 would meet its escort, Dönitz ordered three U-boats to concentrate on the convoy's track in 19° 15' westerly longitude, due south of Iceland, by 2 September. These were *U-65* (Stockhausen), *U-47* (Prien) and *U-101* (Frauenheim); a fourth submarine, *U-124*, was despatched further west to act as a weather-reporting station, providing information for the projected invasion of Britain, while others lay in the offing.

On 2 September, despite poor weather, the convoy met its escort, consisting of two sloops, *Lowestoft* (Commander Knapp) and *Scarborough*, two destroyers, *Westcott* and *Skeena*, the corvette *Periwinkle* and two anti-submarine trawlers, *Apollo* and *Berkshire*. The *Skeena* was a Canadian destroyer working with the Royal Navy, and the *Periwinkle* was newly commissioned.

Dönitz had stretched his U-boats in line abreast and the most north-easterly, *U-65*, sighted the convoy but was driven off by *Skeena* and *Periwinkle*. Stockhausen maintained contact as the weather worsened, turning into a full gale from the west and preventing an attack, a frustrating experience for the U-boat commanders and their crews.

For those in convoy, bad weather was met with mixed feelings. 'Throughout the war convoy duties were extremely difficult . . . for Masters and watch-keeping officers alike and the regular signals to all ships, "Keep closed up" and "Make less smoke", were almost impossible at times to comply with in many ancient ships with coal-fired boilers and triple expansion engines . . . Repairs of vital parts of machinery by ships' engineers were not unusual, [when the] . . . clanging of heavy hammers on metal when stopped kept one on tenterhooks.' Bearing in mind that merchant ships were never designed to keep close company and that convoys moved on a broad front of several shallow columns, station-keeping in poor visibility or at night was difficult, and keeping in sight the low-wattage blue stern light of the next ship ahead 'entailed constant vigilance'. Changes in speed to keep station often meant that

> the leader of a column of ships would increase speed to keep station on the ship abeam . . . the second in column would see the light disappearing and increase speed. By the time the last ship followed suit she would often have to go flat out to get into station and then suddenly have to cut her speed drastically or the ships piled up on each other. Eventually ships were fitted with fog buoys . . . [which they] towed [and which were] fitted with vanes . . . Trapped water passing under[neath] was scooped up . . . and thrown up vertically . . . [However] keeping the jet of water in sight was much more difficult in thick fog . . .
>
> Confusion could be caused by simple things going wrong such as some of the ships failing to receive a Morse signal that at some specified time during the dark hours the convoy would alter course . . . parts of the convoy would conform, others not, to be rounded up by the escorts in the morning.

Such circumstances sat unhappily with the enthusiastic young volunteer reservist officers now cutting their teeth on North Atlantic escort duties in the new corvettes. That a disorganised convoy was invariably misunderstood by RNVR personnel with 'limited sea service [who] . . . could not fully appreciate the problems of handling low-powered, heavily laden merchant ships' is perhaps worth reiterating. The situation bred much rancour, and soured many hard-bitten and experienced merchant officers.

And always there was the waiting:

> In fine settled weather . . . steaming along, all ships in line and columns correctly spaced . . . life for the moment seemed very pleasant when suddenly . . . a violent explosion [was] followed by another . . . and another, and so it went on . . . One in the starboard column was obviously in trouble and loaded with iron ore . . . [she] continued steaming directly under water and after about one minute nothing could be seen except a few men in the water. We were forbidden to stop and pick up survivors . . . I still recall a raft drifting in between columns of ships as they steamed past with an occupant standing on top sending semaphore . . .
>
> We prayed for bad weather to reduce the prospect of submarine attack and in very bad weather, when hove-to, we prayed for a reduction in the violent conditions to minimise the prospect of unavoidable collision with near-by ships which were often difficult to sight in the poor visibility caused by spindrift from breaking seas.[8]

Such collisions might mean only a glancing blow and superficial damage, accompanied by a robust exchange of views by both parties, or it might prove more serious. That autumn, during a night of squalls, the Canadian destroyer *Margaree* was acting as escort to a small convoy. In the darkness the destroyer found herself close to the leading merchant ship of the port column, the *Port Fairy*. The officer of the watch aboard the *Port Fairy*, seeing the *Margaree* under the starboard bow, rang his engines full astern. Fatally, his opposite number aboard the *Margaree* apparently ordered the helm put over to port, and 'before *Port Fairy*'s full astern order could take effect her bow had crashed into *Margaree* just at the bridge and cut the destroyer in half. The fore part drifted clear, turned over and sank within one minute.' With commendable seamanship, the *Port Fairy* was manoeuvred alongside the after part of the *Margaree*, from which about 30 men scrambled up onto the merchantman, and a further three men were hauled aboard from a raft after the *Port Fairy* and the remnant of *Margaree* had drifted apart, but Commander J.W.R. Roy and 141 men were lost. 'The cause of the disaster was never fully determined': it was one of the hazards of steaming at night in close company before the benefits of radar, and in this case it seems not to have been the experienced merchant officer whose station-keeping was at fault; rather, the evidence suggests an error by his opposite number aboard the *Margaree*.[9]

Such were the conditions under which convoys laboured while their enemies went deep to avoid the violent motion caused by the wind on the sea's surface. In the case of SC2, the gale lasted four days, until the evening of 6 September, when the wind eased and the sea dropped. Stockhausen brought up *U-65* to pursue the convoy and home-in Prien on it. Frauenheim had withdrawn *U-101* to L'Orient with serious engine defects, so as midnight approached only two U-boats were stalking the convoy. Prien had already sunk one Belgian and one British ship on this, his ninth war patrol in command of *U-47*, but he had also lost a man, swept off the casing.[10] Moving in under cover of darkness on the surface Prien rapidly torpedoed the tramps *Neptunian* of Newcastle, *Jose de Larrinaga* of Liverpool and the Norwegian *Gro*, owned by Olsen's of Oslo. Submerging, *U-47* made good her escape undetected by the escorts' sonar. The loss of life was appalling. Captain A.T. Campbell and all 35 of his crew went down with the *Neptunian* and her cargo of sugar, and all 39 hands were lost with Captain A.T. Gass aboard the *Jose de Larrinaga* which sank with 5,000 tons of steel and a large consignment of linseed oil.[11] The *Gro* was broken in half; 21 men were picked up by the escorts, but 11 died.

Stockhausen had no success that night, and during the following day the convoy was met by patrolling Sunderland flying-boats of Coastal Command. Their presence prevented him and Prien from keeping close contact with the convoy, but after dark on the 8th both submarines surfaced and raced after their quarry. By the small hours of the 9th Prien was again in a position to strike, and torpedoed the elderly Greek steamer *Possidon* of Piraeus, with a loss of 17 of her crew. Though she had been built in 1909 and was only just capable of the convoy's speed of 8 knots, her ancient bottom was bearing a useful 5,410 tons of sulphur phosphate towards the United Kingdom.

By now other U-boats had been attracted to the fray. Kuhnke in *U-28* had sighted the convoy during the bad weather of the 6th and in company with Kretschmer in *U-99* made an attack during the remaining hours of darkness. Only *U-28* was successful, sinking the Ellerman & Papayanni cargo ship *Mardinian* with 3,500 tons of pitch. Captain J. Every and all but six of his crew were rescued, most by the *Apollo*, others by the Armed Merchant Cruiser *Aurania*. Kretschmer, meanwhile, had been driven off and, like Stockhausen, secured no trophies from SC2. Nevertheless, the convoy had been badly mauled between the 19th and 9th meridians, and Dönitz was much encouraged by what he saw as the long-awaited justification for his confidence in the group attack – notwithstanding the fact that the achievements had been largely due to Prien's evil genius. *U-47* was down to her last torpedo and Dönitz now sent Prien west, to relieve *U-124* and act as a weather-reporting station for 'our air raids on Britain'.[12]

Meanwhile, closer to the Scottish coast, *U-28, U-65* and *U-99* continued their hunt. On 11 September Kuhnke's *U-28* sighted Convoy OA210, sank a small Dutchman, the *Maas*, and damaged J. & A. Harrison's tramp *Harpenden* of London. Kuhnke, now very low on fuel, retired to L'Orient, but Stockhausen and Kretschmer were joined by six other U-boats, *U-48* (Bleichrodt), *U-58* (Schonder), *U-59* (Matz), *U-61* (Stiebler), *U-100* (Schepke) and *U-138* (Lüth).[13]

This was the prelude to an action against Convoys SC3, OB213 and HX72 which raised the curtain upon what the young men in command of the Kriegsmarine's submarines were pleased to call *Die glückliche Zeit*: The Happy Time. Kapitänleutnant H. Bleichrodt kicked off this orgy of destruction.

Consisting of 47 vessels, Convoy SC3 had left Sydney, Cape Breton Island on 2 September 1940. Making painfully slow progress, almost two weeks later, on the 15th, it was about sixty miles south-west of Rockall and had already met its close escort when the enemy located it. Bleichrodt attacked in *U-48* and sank one of the escorts, HM Sloop *Dundee*, leaving a hole in the convoy's defences. Like the *Penzance*, the sloop had excellent reserves of fuel, and had accompanied her convoy throughout its ocean crossing. Destroyers were now in company, yet Bleichrodt successfully attacked and sank the Greek tramp *Alexandros*, killing five of her 30-man crew, then torpedoed the *Empire Volunteer*. This vessel was the former Italian *Procida*, seized in Cardiff on 10 June when Mussolini declared war and placed by the Ministry of War Transport under the management of the Cardiff tramp owners John Cory & Sons. Although she was loaded with 7,700 tons of iron ore, Captain B. Pearson and most of his crew escaped, being picked up by two Norwegian ships in company, the *Fido* and the *Granli*. Less fortunate were seven men, including the master Captain C.E. Brown, from the small Canadian steamer *Kenordoc*, owned by the Paterson Steamship Company of Ontario. Loaded with 2,000 tons of pit-props, she had dropped astern of the convoy, and loomed in Bleichrodt's sights as he let it pass on above him. He failed to sink her, but she was damaged by *U-48*, whose presence had by now attracted the attention of the escorting destroyers as they criss-crossed the wake of SC3 in a vain attempt to counter-attack. Frustrated, HMCS *St Laurent*, Commander H. de Wolf, and HMS *Amazon*, Lieutenant Commander E.G. Roper, turned instead, as the enemy escaped them, to a duty they were to become only too familiar with. Picking up the survivors from the *Kenordoc*, Roper shelled her until she sank.

Bleichrodt's escape from retribution enabled him two days later to commit an act more heinous in the eyes of the contemporary British press even than Lemp's destruction of the *Athenia*. Essentially it was an episode no more tragic than any other in this increasingly bleak war of attrition, but the heavy loss of life among young and innocent passengers gave it a highly emotive charge and provided ready material for British propagandists.

The Ellerman 'City' liner *City of Benares*, Captain L. Nicoll, had been built in 1936 and had a service speed of 16 knots. She had embarked Commodore E.J.G. Mackinnon and his small staff prior to leaving Liverpool on 13 September in charge of Convoy OB213. The convoy was due to disperse five days later when clear of the danger zone, but on the 17th it was sighted by Bleichrodt, who lay beyond the 21st meridian. In addition to many passengers, the *City of Benares* had on board a large number of children.

Concerned about the effects of the German bombing campaign against British cities, the government had ordered the evacuation of children into the countryside; many were also sent abroad to Canada, under the Children's Overseas Resettlement Scheme. A few weeks earlier the Dutch passenger liner *Volendam* had been westbound in Convoy OB205 with some 230 'mostly working-class' children, aged between six and sixteen, on their way to safety on the far side of the North Atlantic. On 31 August, off Tory Island on the north coast of Ireland, she had been torpedoed by *U-60* (Schnee). Although damaged, she did not sink, and mercifully was towed to safety without loss of life among the young. Despite this near-tragedy, a second group of 231 children, together with fare-paying passengers, had been embarked at Liverpool aboard the *City of Benares*.

Escorted by the destroyer *Anthony* and two sloops, the 20-ship convoy formed up off the Mersey Bar, the Ellerman liner leading the centre of three columns. The superstitious noted the departure date: Friday, 13 September 1940. On board they held boat drills, and everyone was instructed to sleep in their life-jackets. 'An undercurrent of tension ran through the ship . . . The convoy ran at once into squally weather and most of the children were seasick. The escorts were kept hard at work . . .'

During the late afternoon of the 17th the convoy passed 20° West and the escort turned back as they cleared the so-called danger area. 'That evening tension was relaxed. The passengers looked forward to undressing completely, for the first time, when they went to bed . . . The moon was nearly full, but cloud wrack drifted across it and only now and again did it shine out clearly over the sea. On either beam two black shapes, unrelieved by so much as a pinprick of light, showed plainly – the two [merchant] vessels keeping steadily abreast of the *City of Benares*.'

The wind was a strong north-westerly near-gale, kicking up a rough sea, and after dark Mackinnon ordered the convoy to cease zig-zagging to preserve cohesion. By 22.00 the *City of Benares* and her charges were some 250 miles west of the Hebrides, steaming at 8.5 knots, unlit and with lookouts staring apprehensively out over the intermittently gleaming moonlit sea. They were due to part company at daylight on the 18th.

Fourth Officer Ronald Cooper was turned in, expecting to be called at 03.45. Instead, he was awoken 'by a dull explosion and then the sound of the alarm gongs'. As they relaxed the passengers were startled by a 'heavy muffled thud . . . The ship shuddered, and the [internal] lights went out . . .' In the darkness people began running about, and in the centre of the ship there was 'a black abyss . . . The torpedo had struck the after part of the ship, passed just below the children's cabins, and exploded beneath the central row of bathrooms, blowing them to smithereens.' Helped by members of the ship's company, those in charge of them began to extricate the terrified children from the chaos. 'Only one of the children appeared to be seriously hurt. She was unconscious and two of the volunteers, Mary Cornish aided by Mrs Towns, managed . . . to pull her out of her cabin.' Miss Cornish found herself calming the children by saying 'Don't worry, it's only a torpedo', then the emergency lighting came on. Somehow the ship was cleared as people made their way to the embarkation stations at which they had previously mustered in practice. Here the dutiful lascars already had the boats waiting.

Pulling on his sea-boots, Cooper had made his way to No. 12 Life Boat on the port side. The lascar crew were already mustered in good order and he immediately supervised as the boat was cleared away for lowering. The *City of Benares* lost way and broached-to, swinging broadside to the wind, exposing her starboard side and listing to port. Above them shone the fitful moon, below was the black gleam of the heaving and indifferent Atlantic. When Captain Nicoll gave the order to abandon ship at 22.20, Cooper lowered No. 12 Boat from the boat to the promenade deck where the assembled passengers were waiting. Here it was loaded with its human freight, including a quota of six children, one of their attendants, Miss Cornish, and a priest named O'Sullivan. Concerned that there seemed to be too few children, Cooper sent an assistant steward to check their berths; the man returned to say the children's accommodation was wrecked and the water was already up to his waist. With 'eighteen natives . . . and nine Europeans' already in the boat, Cooper hung on for a further quarter of an hour, in case anyone else appeared. Meanwhile the other boats on the port side of the ship were being lowered. A number of children taken into No. 8 Boat were badly burned, and one lifeboat fell from its falls and capsized. The air was filled with shouts and screams and those on deck threw down anything buoyant to hand. On the starboard side the ship's list and the force of the wind were making lowering very difficult.

When No. 12 was the last of the port boats left in the davits, Cooper instructed his lascars on the boat deck above to cast off the bowsing tackles and 'to lower away the boat[,] which was launched in an orderly manner', even if, to those unaccustomed to such a task, the wildly-swinging blocks and the motion of the sea acting upon the small wooden lifeboat alongside the seemingly indestructible mass of the *City of Benares* all seemed dangerously chaotic. With the lifeboat safely in the water the four lascars manning the falls and the assistant steward who had remained on deck in case any further survivors appeared all scrambled down the boarding ladder. Cooper then made a final tour of the deck and clambered down the ship's side himself.

On the starboard, windward side, where the boats in the water were being tossed up and down and flung against the ship's side, the situation was truly hazardous. In the cold and semi-darkness, getting the lowering crews aboard and unhooking the falls with their heavy steel blocks was a frightening and dangerous business.

The *City of Benares*'s boats had no oars but were fitted with Fleming gear, a system of levers designed to be pulled back and forth by those without seafaring skills. The levers operated a simple crankshaft which turned a screw propeller, and by this means Cooper's boat began to edge out from the ship's side. Just as the boat was moving clear four lascars appeared on deck and Cooper returned alongside, allowing these men to climb down the boarding ladder into the boat. Then they lay off until 23.00 when, still a blaze of light from the emergency supply, 'the vessel commenced to go down stern first[;] raising her bow out of the water she appeared to list heavily to port, then disappeared.'

A great ship sinking is an awesome spectacle, and even when she is in her death-throes the massive steel hull can seem a desirable refuge compared with the prospect of sudden isolation promised by her extinction. But Cooper was a professional sea-officer, and he made his crew work, rounding up a number of other survivors from floating rafts until, 'in a rough sea and a heavy swell', his boat contained 'six boys, two escorts one of whom was Father O'Sullivan and the other Miss Cornish, one Polish passenger named Bohdan Nagorski, who was a director of the Gdynia-Amerika Linje, Cadet Critchley, Seaman-Gunner Peards, Assistant Steward Purvis, a naval signaller [from the commodore's staff], thirty-two native ratings' and himself. Two of the boys had brothers who had been on the ship.

Taking stock, Cooper saw a light and headed towards it, only to discover that it marked another lifeboat, though not one from the *City of Benares*. Hailing, Cooper learned that the strange boat belonged to the general cargo-ship *Marina* owned by Kaye, Son & Company, of London. On a voyage from Glasgow to the Rio de la Plata with a mixed cargo of general and coal, she too had been torpedoed – though of course neither Cooper nor Captain Payne of the *Marina* knew they had both been sunk by Bleichrodt's *U-48*. Glad not to be alone in the darkness they kept company until daylight, heading east with the strong wind, sea and swell astern. At daylight Payne made sail, and parted from Cooper's boat.

Cooper decided the weather was too bad to make sail, and that they stood a better chance by remaining near the *City of Benares*'s distress position. He had the two forward Fleming gear handles removed and the 'the canvas hood rigged forward for the children who were quite snugly wrapped in blankets of which there was an ample supply . . . [we] carried on by means of the Fleming gear, setting members of the crew on watch.' At noon he 'put all the occupants . . . on food and water ration, detailing the assist-ant steward to serve out the allotted quantities'. They each dined on a sardine, a ship's biscuit and a dipper full of water.

During the day Miss Cornish tried to alleviate boredom by encouraging the singing of popular songs. That evening, as no rescuing vessel materialised, they began to grasp the vastness of the Atlantic Ocean. They spent a cramped, cold, seemingly endless and very uncomfortable night. The lascars crouched under the doused sail to smoke 'sweet, acrid smelling' cigarettes which they passed 'from mouth to mouth, and as each one drew on it the brief glow lighted up a lean, coppery face'. On Thursday morning the weather had moderated and No. 12 Boat headed east under sail. Washing their faces and their mouths out with sea-water, the lascars chanted their morning prayers and then washed out their clothes. The 'Europeans' maintained an equal stoicism. Peards, the ex-naval gunner, kept their spirits up with a relentless pooh-poohing of their difficulties and an assurance that they would soon be rescued. At noon they ate corned beef and biscuit and the boys played games, led by Miss Cornish. Father O'Sullivan was suffering badly from sea-sickness, but the two then told stories until the evening meal – condensed milk, served by Purvis. The only benefit of their reduced diet was a marked reduction in the need to pass water or defecate. When she detected whimpering, Miss Cornish would brusquely ask, 'Don't you realise that you're the heroes in a *real* adventure story? Did you ever hear of a hero who snivelled?' As the chill of the night set in, she began to massage the boys' limbs. A mood of indifference or resignation fell upon No. 12 Boat. Only Peards maintained his tough cheerfulness.

By the following afternoon the westerly wind had increased 'to gale force with heavy rain and hail squalls'. In order to break the heavy seas before they reached the boat, Cooper decided to run using a sea-anchor and oil bag, by which means they rode out the remainder of the day. 'My object in riding stern to sea', he afterwards reported, 'was to endeavour to keep the children and passengers dry as they were under the hood at the fore end of the boat.'

A mood of disheartened resentment that began to manifest itself between the lascars and the Europeans was quashed by Critchley, the cadet, who spoke a little of the lascar *patois*. The ceaseless motion, the propinquity, the salt that stung in cuts and abrasions, the hunger and thirst, were beginning to make everyone irritable. Immersion or 'Trench' Foot was making its presence known. Cooper worried that some of the lascars were sipping salt water, but by noon on Saturday 21 September the weather had eased again, the sea anchor was hauled aboard and sail was once more set. At 16.00 on Sunday they saw a vessel heading towards them and were convinced they had been seen, but then had to endure the agony of watching her turn away, and Cooper concluded that the unknown ship was zig-zagging. To add to this demoralising encounter the wind now freshened again, bringing with it rain and hail squalls, so Cooper handed his sails and streamed the sea-anchor. Daybreak on Monday brought a light wind and a moderate sea and swell. Sail was again hoisted and they ran on through Tuesday before a moderate westerly breeze, confused by spurious sightings of 'land'. One of the boys, suffering from pain in his feet, was slipping into delirium, while the general condition of the others was deteriorating. Miss Cornish and Cooper were both concerned about the lack of water. A second boy became delirious from thirst that night, but the boat ran on to the east. Peards suppressed complaints from the boys, appealing to their embryonic manhood.

The wind dropped on Wednesday the 25th and although they made slow progress, the lack of motion improved morale. Then, at about 13.00, 'one of the boys sighted a Sunderland flying boat which made towards us and after circling two or three times communicated by means of the Aldis lamp. The naval signalman replied by means of semiphore [sic] . . . The plane dropped a smoke flare with instructions to set it off when the rescue ship was in sight, and he made off.'

Cooper decided it would be prudent to heave-to until rescue arrived, and about 14.00 'the flying boat again appeared and dropped a parcel of food, also a note telling us that assistance was on the way'. It arrived at 16.30 in the form of HMS *Anthony*, which Lieutenant Commander N.J.V. Thew skilfully manoeuvred alongside. Two seamen jumped aboard No. 12 Boat and the survivors were got inboard without much real difficulty, 'with the exception of one lascar who was ill. The destroyer's M[edical] O[fficer] attended him in the life boat but he died shortly after being taken aboard . . . All the children were in good form, having . . . looked upon the whole thing as a picnic, and only one child was suffering from Trench feet. We were all attended to by the officers and men from whom we received every consideration and kindness . . . We were landed at Greenock at 7 p.m. on the . . . 29th September.'

Miss Cornish was subjected to an interview by the Receiver of Wreck while the BBC and the newspapers busily cast this modest woman as a heroine, emphasising the inhumanity of the Germans and provoking a re-action greater than that which had greeted the sinking of the *Athenia*. The survivors were welcomed by the Lord Provost of the city. As a surviving officer of a sunken merchant ship, Cooper was obliged to prepare a report and submit to an interview by staff of the Shipping Casualties Section of the Admiralty's Trade Division. In the continuing effort to glean the smallest crumb of intelligence that might aid the battle, these reports were widely circulated inside the Admiralty, in particular to Naval Intelligence Staff and the Ministry of Shipping (afterwards the MoWT). The officer charged with the duty of conducting these interviews was Commander Norman Holbrook, a First World War submariner and holder of the Victoria Cross who had been recalled from retirement for the purpose, and whose first customer had been *Athenia*'s Chief Officer Copeland. In time the emphasis of Holbrook's debriefings shifted; as well as snippets of information about German tactics, it became clear that there was much to be learned about the survival prospects of a vulnerable asset – merchant seamen. Survival techniques and the understanding of hypothermia became increasingly important secondary weapons in the hideous battle then being waged.

Cooper's report, from which the quotations regarding No. 12 Boat come, was drawn up on 21 October 1940. He was clearly an officer of outstanding competence, unfazed by the departure of Captain Payne in the *Marina*'s boat, content to make a cool assessment of the needs of his own dependants and confident that his lifeboat was well provisioned, itself testimony to Ellerman's, Captain Nicoll's and his officers' foresightedness. Afterwards Cooper deposed that he had no anxiety 'at any time . . . regarding the food supplies . . . as we had plenty of tinned . . . meat, salmon and milk, and there were of course the usual biscuits. However,' he added, 'I realised . . . that if we weren't picked up before reaching land our water . . . would have to be strictly rationed.' They had indeed had very little water, and Cooper was bound to be ruthless in limiting its issue. He went on to say that the children 'behaved splendidly and were looked after very efficiently by Miss Cornish whom I believe massaged them continuously. Throughout I had every assistance from the passengers and crew. I was relieved at the tiller by [Cadet] Critchley, the assistant steward and the naval signalman and the lascar Saloon Boy Ramjan was very good, proving most willing, helpful and keeping the other lascars in good order.

'Everyone behaved very well, and a spirit of loyalty to orders and comparative cheerfulness prevailed throughout the entire seven days and nineteen hours which we were in the boat.'[14]

They were not the only survivors. Unknown to Cooper, the destroyer *Hurricane*, on her way to Greenock, had heard the *City of Benares* put out a distress call and had steamed back to the west, where Lieutenant Commander H.C. Simms had found 105 survivors in boats and clinging to rafts. But that was all. Captain Nicoll and Commodore Mackinnon both went down with the ship, as did 19 other 'European' crew members, while of her 166 lascar sailors the *City of Benares* entombed 101. Afterwards the opinion was once again aired that it was inappropriate to send lascars to sea in these high latitudes. Those who tended the boats on the night of 17 September did their duty, and Cooper's testimony, while it embodies a sense of racial differentiation typical of its time, implies no misconduct. Many officers serving in such ships spoke Hindi, like Cadet Critchley; whether Cooper did is not clear from his factual and unembellished report. That he found the services of Ramjan, whose work in the saloon would have made him proficient in English, useful in communicating with the lascars in No. 12 Boat is certain, but that is all.

In addition to the crew of the *City of Benares*, 51 of her fare-paying passengers drowned, as did 77 children supposedly on their way to safety. There was a terrible irony in all this: the scheme to save them from German bombers had been initiated by newspaper pictures 'of children of the well-to-do posing happily on the country estates of Long Island and Quebec', which had provoked a strong feeling 'that the safety of the nation's children was too vital and too sacred a thing to be bought with gold . . . It was unfair . . .'15 On the same day that Bleichrodt's torpedo shattered that good intention – for its consequence was that no more children were sent abroad by ship and the Children's Overseas Resettlement Scheme was suspended – Hitler abandoned the operation to launch an invasion against Great Britain of which the air assault had been but the preliminary bombardment.

In addition to the survivors from the Ellerman liner, HMS *Hurricane* also rescued 17 crew members and three gunners from the *Marina*. As for Captain R.T. Payne, he and his 16 men were picked up off the Irish coast by the British coaster *Carlingford*. They had been eight days in their boat, and were landed at Londonderry. Payne had exerted himself to the utmost and was awarded the George Medal, as well as Lloyd's War Medal for Bravery. With the exception of two men in her engine room the majority of the *Marina*'s crew had survived, which was more than could be said of Bleichrodt's last victim in this encounter.

As Payne and Cooper went their separate ways on 18 September, not far away the Hartlepool tramp *Magdalena* was also sent to the bottom. A 9-knot steamer belonging to Smith, Hogg & Company of West Hartlepool, she was on a voyage from St John's, New Brunswick to Liverpool. Joining Convoy SC3 at Sydney, she had straggled during the bad weather of the previous day, and fell into *U-48*'s sights. Bleichrodt's torpedo blew a hole in a hull laden with iron ore. Captain F. Allen, his 29 men and their single gunner were drowned in minutes.

Even before the British press had begun their fulminations against the criminal action of Hitler's sea-wolves in sinking the *City of Benares* Bleichrodt's *U-48* had struck again, as part of a new group assembled by Dönitz. It will be recalled that Prien in *U-47*, having exhausted all but one torpedo, was sent west by Dönitz on weather-reporting and reconnaissance duties. On 20 September, as Convoy HX72 hove in sight and almost ran down *U-47*, Prien abandoned his station and began shadowing the convoy, informing Dönitz and transmitting homing signals. Dönitz promptly ordered five more U-boats to concentrate on Prien's.

Convoy HX72 had left Halifax on the 9th and had as its ocean escort the Armed Merchant Cruiser *Jervis Bay*, Captain F. Fegen. Aware of radio activity in the vicinity, the Admiralty ordered the convoy to alter course, briefly throwing Prien off the scent: but HX72 was large, consisting of 47 ships under Commodore H.H. Rogers embarked in the Hain tramp *Tregarthen*, and the evasion was insufficient to avoid Dönitz's converging submarines. Also approaching from the east was the close escort group, led by Commander Knapp in the sloop *Lowestoft*, which had in company three new corvettes, *Calendula, Heartsease* and *La Malouine*. The destroyers *Shikari, Scimitar* and *Skate* were also in the vicinity, but before HX72 reached the rendezvous at what was known as the Mid-Ocean Meeting Point the carnage had begun.

Kretschmer was the first to arrive, on the evening of the 20th. He had already sunk three ships, including the *Crown Arun* off Rockall (she was formerly the *Hannah Boge*, a German war prize), and now he began stalking HX72. Shortly before midnight U-99 torpedoed the tanker *Invershannon*, which was on an Admiralty charter carrying 13,241 tons of boiler oil from Curaçao to Scapa Flow. Captain W.R. Forsyth and the remnant of his ship's company took to the boats, leaving 16 dead who went down with their ship when she sank just after midnight. The survivors were picked up much later by HM Sloop *Flamingo* and the anti-submarine trawler *Fandango*, to be landed in Northern Ireland.

By the early hours of 21 September a formidable pack was assembling to join Kretschmer and Prien, who regained contact that morning. In the coming hours HX72 was to be torn apart.

After sinking *Invershannon* Kretschmer turned on Andrew Weir's *Elmbank*, Captain H.T. Phillips, but failed to sink her in his first attack. He then torpedoed Hogarth's *Baron Blythswood*. Loaded with a full cargo of iron ore bound for the steelworks at Port Talbot, she sank in 40 seconds, killing Captain J.M.R. Davies and his crew of 33.

Bleichrodt arrived in U-48 that forenoon and sank the *Blairangus*, Captain H. Mackinnon, and her cargo of pit-props, causing six deaths.[16] Two hours after his first attack, and after breaking off operations against the convoy, Kretschmer returned to the *Elmbank*, surfaced, and shelled her; in this he was joined by Prien. Phillips and his crew took to their boats with the loss of two men, their ship being finally torpedoed by U-99. The cargo of metal and timber they had brought from the Pacific coast of British Columbia by way of the Panama Canal went to the bottom. In due time Phillips and his boats were picked up by the British ship *Pikepool* and landed at St John's, along with the 28 survivors from the *Blairangus*.

After sending *Elmbank* to the bottom, Prien and Kretschmer headed for

L'Orient. In the late evening *U-48* torpedoed and damaged the *Broompark*. By now Schepke too was on hand, and in a four-hour attack conducted, like those of his colleagues, on the surface, he wrought havoc. During the night of 21/22 September he sank or damaged seven ships. First to go was the *Canonesa*, Captain F. Stephenson, torpedoed with 11,107 tons of general cargo, most of it foodstuffs. The tanker *Torinia* was next to be hit, by a torpedo from *U-100*; damaged, she afterwards had to be sunk by gunfire from the destroyer *Skate* which rescued Captain H. Jackson and his crew. The *Torinia* was also from Curaçao on an Admiralty charter, and with her went 13,815 tons of boiler fuel. Schepke then torpedoed the Tyneside tramp *Dalcairn*, Captain E. Brusby, with no loss of life, but 8,000 tons of wheat went to the bottom. Almost all the crew of the *Empire Airman* were lost when another of *U-100*'s torpedoes tore into the former Italian ship's side. She was filled with iron ore, and only Captain J.B. Raine, the officer of the watch, the helmsman and the lookout survived. Schepke so badly damaged the Harrison liner *Scholar*, Captain W.R. Mackenzie, that although the naval salvage tug *Marauder*, Lieutenant W.J. Hammond, reached her the next day and succeeded in towing her some way east, she could not be saved, and sank with a cargo of cotton, general, steel, timber and wood-pulp loaded at Galveston. Having taken aboard Mackenzie and his men, *Skate*'s guns finished her off too.

Schepke also accounted for a third tanker bound from Curaçao. The Oriental Trade & Transport Company's *Frederick S. Fales*, carrying 13,849 tons of boiler oil for the Admiralty bunkering station in the Clyde, was lost with Captain F. Ramsay, nine of his merchant crew, and his naval gunner. *U-100*'s final victim was the Norwegian general cargo ship *Simla*, owned by Wilhelmsen's of Tønsberg; five of her crew were killed.

Captain Stephenson of the *Canonesa* lost one man, his crew being picked up by *La Malouine*, Lieutenant Commander R.W. Keymer, along with Brusby's, the pathetic handful from the *Empire Airman*, and 32 survivors from the *Frederick S. Fales*. Although the close escort had arrived on the 21st they had been able to do little to stem the haemorrhage, and HX72 had been dispersed. Knapp sent *Shikari, La Malouine* and the other corvettes to recover survivors and, on hearing distress signals from a second Harrison cargo-liner, the *Collegian*, called in the assistance of *Skate* and *Scimitar*.

During the dark hours on the morning of the 22nd the *Collegian* had been attacked by *U-32*, diverted from weather-reporting duties as part of Dönitz's concentration against HX72. Oberleutnant Jenisch's first torpedo had misfired, as had his second; but since the convoy had dispersed and the *Collegian* was alone, Jenisch surfaced and opened fire with his gun, to which the *Collegian* responded in kind, her radio officer transmitting the SSSS signal. Hearing this and seeing the gun flashes in the distance, Knapp now reacted with speed. *Lowestoft, Skate* and *Scimitar* managed to frustrate *U-32*'s attack and drive Jenisch off, but it was scarcely retribution; the depth-charge settings were too deep, and Jenisch escaped.

He did not go away unrewarded, however, for before the end of his patrol he had sunk eight merchant ships. Like two other U-boats which failed to reach Convoy HX72, Schuhart's *U-29* and Ambrosius's *U-43*, Jenisch now operated against dispersing ships from the outward convoys OB216 and OB217, but damaged his submarine's bows by too closely approaching one of his victims, the Dutch steamship *Haulerwijk*. Schuhart succeeded in sinking the Blue Funnel liner *Eurymedon* shortly after the dispersal of OB217 at noon on 25 September. She was bound for Java by way of Cape Town with a general cargo. Schuhart's first torpedo hit the port side and killed all the engine-room watch, while the whipping of the hull destroyed the main radio aerials. Captain J.F. Webster ordered the watertight doors closed and distress signals flashed to other ships from the convoy that remained in sight. The radio officers managed to transmit on the emergency aerial as the crew and passengers mustered on the boat deck and the boats were prepared for lowering. However, the stoutly-built *Eurymedon* remained afloat and Schuhart, circling in *U-29*, fired a second torpedo into her. The explosion wrecked the starboard lifeboats and killed 20 of her crew, ten of whom were Chinese, and nine passengers already either in the boats or attending the davits. Webster, anxious for the safety of his remaining passengers and crew, now ordered the port boats lowered without delay. They were to lie off the ship until he had completed a search; he was also minded to save his ship, for she still seemed reluctant to sink.

Schuhart now surfaced, and again made a circuit of the *Eurymedon* at a distance of about two miles, but at 15.15 he dived, and shortly afterwards the Canadian destroyer *Ottawa* arrived on the scene to embark the 41 crew and 22 passengers from their boats. Webster and his chief officer, Mr W. Stanger, decided to remain in the hope of salvaging the ship, and a properly provisioned lifeboat with a crew of volunteers was left alongside in case of a hurried departure. *Ottawa*'s Captain E.R. Mainguy was committed to his orders and could not wait, so Webster and his mate remained on the *Eurymedon*, inspecting the damage and sounding the hold wells.

That evening four boats from yet another of Donaldson's ships, the *Sulairia*, which had been sunk earlier that day by Ambrosius's *U-43*, came alongside, and Captain R.C. Young and his men clambered aboard to spend the night in a modicum of comfort. By next morning, however, it was clear that the *Eurymedon* was foundering. With the engine room and Nos 3 and 4 Holds full, and water rising in No. 2, the game was up, and the ship was abandoned, the boats lying off to await the end. Mainguy's report led the Admiralty to decide there was a chance of saving *Eurymedon*, and *Ottawa* was ordered to return to her until a corvette arrived to take her in tow. With the *Sulairia*'s people embarked in the destroyer, Webster insisted on remaining in his life-boat for the night, still nursing the hope that his ship could be saved if the corvette arrived in time. In this he was to be disappointed; by dawn on the 27th it was clear that *Eurymedon* had settled deeper in the water, and the corvette was nowhere to be seen. Mainguy was now running short of fuel, and a gale was forecast. Reluctantly Webster concluded that returning to the ship would be 'foolhardy', and boarded *Ottawa*. The *Eurymedon* sank at 20.00 that evening, watched from HM Corvette *Primrose*, which had finally arrived on the scene.[17]

Among the dispersing ships from OB216 was the Ellerman liner *City of Simla*. She was the last of three vessels to be sunk by Oberleutnant Lüth, who fired *U-138*'s final torpedo at her. The *City of Simla* was bound from Glasgow to Cape Town and Bombay with only about three thousand tons of general cargo, but 167 passengers. Captain H. Percival and all but two of his passengers and one of his crew were rescued after taking to the boats, and brought home by the destroyer *Vanquisher* and the Belgian trawler *Van Dyke*. The *City of Simla* sank on 21 September – by one of those curious coincidences that occur from time to time, the same day on which, miles to the west, her Norwegian namesake *Simla* went to the bottom.

In the wake of these actions, British assessments were gloomy. During the month of September, German submarines sank 59 British, Allied and neutral ships, grossing 295,335 tons, the figures only bare indicators of the immense amount of food and raw materials lost. To these must be added a further 15 merchantmen sunk by long-range aircraft, mostly Focke-Wulf FW200 Kondors which in addition to carrying a bomb-load acted as spotters for U-boat headquarters in Paris. Like the U-boats, the aircraft too struck at neutrals: on 25 August 1940 the *Bonita* was bound from Fowey to Norfolk, Virginia with a cargo of china clay when she was bombed and machine-gunned by a Kondor in the South Western Approaches. She had a large Panamanian flag painted on her topsides and her master was a Hungarian, a nation within the Nazi orbit. Captain Herz manoeuvred his ship with great skill, however, aided by the courage of his second engineer, who ordered all hands out of the engine room during the attack and maintained steam despite a leaking feed-pipe and being sprayed with hot oil. That this exemplary individual was a woman, Victoria Drummond, afterwards appointed MBE and awarded Lloyd's War Medal, emphasises both the polyglot composition of a flag-of-convenience tramp-ship, and the fate of a neutral vessel bearing a British cargo. Although the Kondor expended all her bombs fruitlessly and *Bonita* survived the attack, many vessels were not so fortunate.[18]

It was indeed the beginning of *Die glückliche Zeit* for Prien, Kretschmer, Schepke and their colleagues, but it also spelled complete vindication for their Befelshaber der U-boote, Karl Dönitz, and his 'group tactics'. On 22 September 1940 he wrote in his official War Diary: 'The engagement of the last few days shows the principles enunciated in peace time both with regard to the use of radio [homing] in the proximity of the enemy and with regard for U-boat training for offensive action against convoys were correct.'[19]

He was able to crow much louder in the months to come.

8

'Rulers of the sea'

Jervis Bay

THE DAMAGE INFLICTED by German submarines on their enemies' merchant shipping caused Dönitz's U-boat commanders to feel themselves 'the "Rulers of the Sea", more than capable of coping with any defensive measures the enemy might use against them'.[1] They were operating both on the very threshold of Britain's home waters, the majority of U-boats attacking 'close off the Irish coast . . .' in the area to the west of the dispersal points of the outward OA and OB oceanic (and not purely trans-Atlantic) convoys, and just beyond the ocean rendezvous where eastbound trans-Atlantic convoys met their close escort. Early interception of such convoys had a powerful psychological impact, first upon the merchant seafarers involved, who saw how easy it was for an enemy to strike at them beyond the reach of their protectors; and second upon the escorts, who often arrived to find the convoy already under attack. Not only was there no time for convoy and escort to settle down, but the escort and its commanders were at an immediate disadvantage in the face of an enemy in possession of the initiative.

This state of affairs induced a distortion of perception among the mercantile fraternity, promoting images of an ocean swarming with U-boats and merchantmen sinking by the score, not helped by the fact that even after the arrival of the navy, the 'surface escorts were still lamentably weak, no air escort could be provided by night and the type of radar then fitted in aircraft was of little use'. It was a woeful situation that began to cause grave concern in high places. The Trade Protection Committee, assembled weekly to review matters, was soon urging 'that an efficient radar set for anti-submarine surface and air escorts must be developed, that the use of airborne depth

charges [rather than inadequate bombs] should be increased, that radio-
telephony should be developed for rapid communication between escort
vessels and aircraft, and that an experiment should be tried in routeing convoys
along a comparatively narrow avenue of ocean . . .'

Faced with the facts in the Defence Committee, Churchill agreed, and
also approved the return of destroyers from anti-invasion duties on the south-
east coast of England to the North West Approaches off Scotland and
Northern Ireland. 'Thus, in the face of dire necessity, were the escort vessels
returned to their proper function.'² Such measures were the first steps in
defeating the U-boat, but they failed to address the immediate vulnerability
of most convoys, and did nothing to arrest the slow erosion of morale among
merchant seafarers who watched the ineffective dash and splash of their few
escorts with a mounting sense of despair. If Dönitz was sending out his
crack commanders, there was as yet nothing of equal mettle to confront
them.

The lack of experience among the escorts was pitiful. When commissioned at the end of 1940, HM Corvette *Verbena* possessed two distinctions:
she was the first of the 'Flower'-class to be fitted with an extended forecastle (a much-needed alteration which made her and her modified sisters
drier and more comfortable for their crews), and she was the first to be
commanded by an officer of the Royal Naval Volunteer Reserve. Lieutenant
Commander D.A. Rayner had been prevented from joining the Royal Navy
by his flat feet, but in 1925 had done the next best thing for an interested
civilian and joined the Volunteer Reserve. By the end of 1940 he had gained
substantial experience in anti-submarine trawlers, but as the new commander
of *Verbena* he found his watch-keeping officers very green. 'On the morning
of commissioning day the officers arrived. Two Sub-Lieutenants RNVR
and a Midshipman RNVR. They had come straight from HMS *King Alfred*,
the officers' training establishment, and not one of them had a watch-keeping
certificate. They had all been "Hostilities Only" ratings, who had been
selected from their fellows and made officers overnight.' Before the war,
Verbena's two sub-lieutenants had been office clerks, the midshipman a
schoolboy. 'They had each served nine months on the lower deck, and then
three months at *King Alfred*.' Although his ship's company had a sprinkling
of experienced petty officers and artificers, Rayner was concerned that he
had no experienced first lieutenant. The *Verbena* scraped through her ordeal
of pre-operational assessment at Tobermory, but Commodore Stephenson
was adamant that she should have a proper first lieutenant to support Rayner.
On his way back to the Clyde, Rayner was abruptly ordered to fuel and
then join an outward convoy straight away under the orders of the senior
escort in *Velox*. And that was that. A day later, as the *Verbena*'s crew were

prostrated by sea-sickness, these inexperienced young men 'were keeping watch over twenty or thirty merchantmen'.[3]

The conditions aboard a corvette were terrible, and a shock to those 'Hostilities Only' ratings, forced to live cheek-by-jowl with complete strangers. The excoriations of multiple small inconveniences were vividly imprinted: 'the continuing swish of water beneath the bunks is a disturbing sound. Socks fall upon the deck . . . Gumboots fall upon their sides and fill with water. Trousers get soaked and press dankly upon one's legs. Shirts are sodden. Duffel coats are soggy sacks. Life is a mean existence at such times; morale falls swiftly like an ominous barometer, and men move in a stupor of resentment.' Oddly, these ordinary men, dressed as seamen but not yet seasoned or practised in any of the seafaring skills, came through their trials with honour, but it took time, and that time was purchased by the lives of others. And while they struggled to suppress their rising gorges and dragged on soaked socks, wet boots and soggy duffel coats in the communal stench of the mess-decks, dog-tired and unused to undertaking the strains of lookout duty in the black hours of the graveyard watch, the officers tried 'to work out [their] minute plan for war-making within that great framework made by statesmen, politicians and strategists'.

The full complement of a corvette was five officers, three chief petty officers, sixty petty officers, leading hands and ratings, nine sonar and communications staff and about a score in the engine-room department. With inexperienced officers, much of an escort's actual efficiency depended upon the chief petty officers, who were invariably regulars. One RNVR officer commented that 'always one wonders whether the Chiefs will be as good as they can be, and always they are'.[4]

In addition to the Volunteer Reserve, the Admiralty were able to call upon the services of the Royal Naval Reserve itself. Unlike the RNVR, which was made up of enthusiastic amateurs who became sailors at weekends when officers and ratings alike reported to a static drill ship in a major port, the RNR consisted of professional merchant naval officers. The exigencies of war promoted men of ability from both sources, but where the men of the RNVR were characterised by dash and fire-eating, the RNR officers, although universally acknowledged to be competent navigators and first-rate seamen, were often thought dull and unimaginative, in part a consequence of the poor regard in which the service from which they came was held; one RNR officer claimed that 'We were forgotten before and we'll be forgotten again.'

A subsidiary factor in this assessment was that while all the RNR officers were men of wide experience at sea, they were not necessarily at ease in the chummy atmosphere of a naval mess, where they were outshone by the clubby volunteers of the RNVR, for many of whom membership of a naval mess was one of the chief attractions in the first place. By contrast with Rayner of the RNVR, W.J. Moore exemplifies the professional reserve. From a seafaring family with its roots in sail, by 1931 Moore, already holder of an Extra Master Mariner's certificate and so somewhat overqualified for the rank, was undergoing a long period of RNR training as a sub-lieutenant. By training with the Reserve he did however avoid the worst effects of the Depression and the exploitative nature of the mercantile sea-life of the day.[5]

Moore found that, despite his time at sea, he was at rather a disadvantage undergoing training with RNVR officers as they all knew more about the minutiae of the Royal Navy than he did. He deplored the poor quality of the anti-submarine warfare training, which echoed the complacency in the fleet. 'A few sessions on the Asdic (sonar) Teacher, a simulator which gave one the impression that a submarine had little hope of escape once contact had been made. How wrong this impression was, we were all to learn before many months had passed.'

By mid 1940 Moore was first lieutenant of HM Sloop *Folkestone* – shortly to be part of the escort of Convoy OB228 – employed for 'six days, out to 20° West [a later extension from the 17th meridian] with one convoy, and back with another . . . Worrying though the times were, one could only carry on with one's duties as they came to hand . . .'[7] Even the sterling work undertaken by Stephenson and his staff at Tobermory had not resolved the serious problem of the 'poor intership communications and [a] lack of teamwork among escorts'. This latter was of great significance.

Also commissioning at this time was HM Corvette *Bluebell*. Her captain was a Master Mariner with fifteen years' sea-time. Lieutenant Commander R.E. Sherwood, RNR was characterised by confidence and a quick wit; he needed both, for his first lieutenant was an RNVR officer most of whose experience had been as a yachtsman on the east coast of England, while his two RNVR sub-lieutenants were Canadian volunteers. One later recalled that he had received no training whatsoever on how to counter enemy submarine attacks on the surface and within the convoy formation: all emphasis and effort had been concentrated in counter-attack by echo-location. This was another significant fact.

These critical deficiencies were to contribute to German successes in the autumn of 1940. Although several HX and SC convoys traversed the Atlantic unscathed, SC6 lost three ships, two Greek-flagged vessels, the *Delphin* and the *Zannes Gounaris*, and the British tramp *Craigwen*. More than 10,000 tons of maize and wheat and a full cargo of phosphate rock went with them. Dönitz's commanders next struck with great skill at HX77 and SC7. Kapitänleutnant Bleichrodt of *U-48* was the first U-boat commander to make contact with HX77, consisting of 39 deep-laden merchantmen, which had crossed the 17th meridian and by the evening of 11 October was approaching the Rockall Bank. Bleichrodt first attacked the Norwegian tanker *Davanger*, laden with 10,000 tons of fuel oil which caught fire. In the ensuing chaos 17 men died, though a dozen succeeded in escaping. Bleichrodt next hit the cargo-liner *Port Gisbourne*. Although she joined Convoy HX77 she had loaded her cargo of frozen lamb, butter, wool and sheepskin in New Zealand, arriving at Halifax by way of the Panama Canal. Captain T. Kippins lost 26 of his crew in the attack but 38 escaped and were picked up by HM Rescue Tug *Salvonia* and the British cargo ship *Alpera*. Kippins himself earned high praise and a Lloyd's War Medal for his conduct.[8]

Bleichrodt took some time to work into a position from which to make another attack, but before the end of the day he had torpedoed the Bergen-registered Norwegian general cargo motor-vessel *Brändanger*, killing six men and sending 8,000 tons of timber and metals to the bottom.

Kapitänleutnant Matz in *U-59* was stationed a little to the east, and on the following day he struck Furness Withy's *Pacific Ranger* with a torpedo. All hands abandoned ship without loss of life, but a further 8,000 tons of raw materials went down with this ship. Nineteen survivors were picked up by an escort, but the master, Captain W. Evans, and nine men spent nine days in a boat before being rescued by the Icelandic trawler *Thormodur*, while the chief officer and 20 men made it to the Donegal coast near Killybegs.

One straggler from HX77 also fell victim to the Germans. At Halifax in August 1940 the French ship *Saint Malo* had been turned over to the Canadian government. Loaded with 7,274 tons of general cargo she had fallen astern of the convoy and was picked off on 12 October by Frauenheim in *U-101* when still west of Rockall. Twenty-eight men were lost with her, only 16 surviving. Finally, on the 13th, Oehrn's *U-37* concluded a successful patrol by sinking another straggler from HX77, the Billmeir tramp *Stangrant*, an old ship in a deplorable condition; laden with more than 7,000 tons of steel and scrap, she sank quickly.[9] Her hull was wrecked by the explosion and her decks covered by 'steam, fumes and small fires'. As she foundered nine men were killed, but Captain E.D. Rowlands and 29 of his crew took to the two boats. Oehrn surfaced and interrogated the survivors, but soon vanished, leaving the boats tossing about in worsening weather. During the night they became separated from each other, and during the next day most of the survivors were wretchedly seasick until they grew accustomed to the motion. Miserable though they were, they were fortunate enough to be seen by a patrolling Sunderland flying-boat, and although the pilot found it impossible to land at the time, he returned two days later when conditions had improved and picked them up, landing them a mere two hours later at Oban in Scotland.

Slow Convoy SC7 had left Sydney on 5 October, five days after HX77. By the time Bleichrodt had broken off action with HX77 it had still to transit the danger area, and it was Bleichrodt's U-48 that encountered it on the evening of 16 October. Dönitz now directed Frauenheim's U-101, Schepke's U-100, Kretschmer's U-99, Moehle's U-123 and Endrass in U-46 to reposition to form a patrol line across the grain of the convoy's route. Another U-boat, U-38 (Liebe), was thought to be too far north to join the pack.

Again Bleichrodt struck first, sinking two vessels before he was detected by the escorts which had just joined the convoy. He fired at and damaged the tramp Haspenden, but she survived to reach port. His real victims were the British ships Languedoc and Scoresby. The latter, a Whitby-registered, Headlam-owned tramp loaded with pit-props, was sunk with no loss of life. Captain L.Z. Weatherill and his company of 38 were rescued by Sherwood's Bluebell and landed a few days later at Gourock. The Languedoc, formerly a French-registered tanker, had been taken over by the British shipping ministry and re-flagged under the red ensign in the hands of John I. Jacobs's Oil & Molasses Tankers Ltd. '[A] beautiful ship, [with] spotless white painted decks', she was on government service loaded with 13,700 tons of oil fuel for the Clyde when Bleichrodt's torpedoes struck. Captain J. Thomson and his 40-strong crew escaped without loss and were also picked up by Bluebell. Sherwood was obliged to hasten the Languedoc's end by dropping depth-charges close to her.

The remaining escorts, the sloops Scarborough and Fowey, aided by a Sunderland flying-boat, succeeded in driving Bleichrodt away. Ordering Fowey to rejoin the convoy, Scarborough attempted to hunt U-48 for several hours with no success as the convoy drew away from her. In fact Bleichrodt had retired, and later, on 18 October, he pursued and attacked another Headlam steamship, the Sandsend, a straggler out of Convoy OB228. He was too far to the west to regain contact with SC7 but he went on to sink another tanker, the Shirak, which had been damaged in an attack on Convoy HX79.[10]

On the morning of 18 October two more escorts arrived, HM Sloop Leith, Commander R.C. Allen, senior officer of the escort, and HM Corvette Heartsease. Within minutes the advancing front of Convoy SC7, led by Commodore L. MacKinnon at the head of the centre column in the Assyrian, had been spotted by Liebe in U-38 and he attacked and damaged the British tramp Carsbreck. Far from being too far north, Liebe had already sunk a

large Royal Mail liner, the motor-vessel *Highland Patriot*, Captain R.H.
Robinson, and a straggler from SC7, the 3,600-ton Greek steamer *Aenos*,
and now found himself in contact with the main convoy. Liebe was counter-
attacked and driven off by the *Heartsease*, but his report had Dönitz on
tenterhooks in Paris. It was clear that the waiting patrol line needed to be
swiftly repositioned: Dönitz's new orders were transmitted, and Endrass,
Kretschmer, Schepke, Frauenheim and Moehle sped north-east. By the afternoon they had head-reached on SC7, the ships of which could be seen
from the waiting U-boats, breaking the horizon to the west. 'Once again
we had got them!' Dönitz was later able to crow.[11]

There followed three days of exultant slaughter.

Convoy SC7 had been composed of 34 vessels, many of them old or of
dubious reliability. One, the Norwegian tanker *Thorøy*, had been built in
1893 and could make no more than 9 knots; another, the *Empire Miniver*,
was one of the formerly laid-up emergency standard vessels built by the
United States government during the First World War and purchased by the
British for use in the Second. The high cost in dollars of repair work
undertaken in American yards meant that most of these had been loaded
and sent in convoy to be brought up to standard more cheaply in British
shipyards.

Four days out the weather deteriorated into a full gale coming away from
the north-west; several ships began to straggle, among them the small Great
Lakes steamers *Trevisa* and *Eaglescliffe Hall*, incongruously out-of-place on
the wilderness of the Atlantic; then the Greek *Aenos* and the *Empire Miniver*,
whose turbines failed, fell astern. Fortunately the *Empire Miniver* was soon
working up to full speed again, and as this was faster than the convoy's she
soon overhauled another straggler, probably the *Aenos*, showing a bright
light which Captain R. Smith viewed with mixed feelings as he passed
ahead and rejoined the convoy. At this time SC7 had only the sloop
Scarborough as escort and in the early hours of 16 October the convoy lost
its first ship, the *Trevisa*. She was struck by a torpedo from *U-124*, which
had been on weather-reporting duties west of the 20th meridian.
Kapitänleutnant Schulz had missed the main convoy but was able to begin
the offensive part of his war patrol by sinking this small timber-carrier and
killing seven of her company. Sherwood's *Bluebell* was sent to pick up Captain
R.C. Stonehouse and the remainder of his crew.

After Commander Allen joined as Senior Officer in *Leith* and the British
tramp *Carsbreck* reported being damaged, the convoy had steamed on through
the day with a palpable heightening of tension as submarine warnings came
in from the Admiralty. *Heartsease* had had no success against Liebe, and

U-28 (Kuhnke) was also in the area. At 17.45 lookouts aboard *U-101*, lying on the surface, spotted SC7 and flashed a signal by guarded lamp: 'enemy in sight'. Nightfall approached, and the U-boats lurked in the gloom, waiting for moonrise. As SC7 lay silhouetted against the autumnal twilight, the grey hulls submerged, surfacing later to follow and attack.

Such was the carnage that followed that the precise sequence of the action is confused. Careful research and analysis has since revealed the claims made at the time by Dönitz to total more than twice the tonnage actually lost, while exactly which U-boat sank which merchantman remains uncertain; the attributions that follow seem the most likely. As darkness fell and a full, hunter's moon rose it was Endrass in *U-46* who struck first, torpedoing the small Swedish tramp *Convallaria* with no loss of life. A moment later a second torpedo from *U-46* hit the Cardiff-registered *Beatus*. One of her lifeboats was launched prematurely without orders from the bridge, dragged alongside, her bung out, and filled with water; the other was lowered successfully. On the order being given to abandon ship, one of the Indian firemen refused to leave the warmth of the engine room, and Captain W.L. Brett forcibly brought the reluctant man on deck with help of the naval gun-layer, and the crew escaped without loss. As they tossed about on the moonlit sea, one of the hands played his harmonica, until told to desist by the second engineer. '"Knock that off, will you? There's a U-boat on the surface." . . . [They] could hear the engines racing and . . . hear them shouting out in German. They were excited. They were in the chase . . .'

As the *Beatus* and her cargo of steel, timber and crated aircraft on deck settled in the water, the master of the Dutch ship *Boekolo* next astern reduced speed and then came to a stop to pick up the *Beatus*'s people from their boat. While this was in hand, a torpedo from either *U-100* or *U-123* slammed into her port side, No. 4 Hold rapidly filled, causing a heavy list. Incredibly, in all this confusion no one lost his life, and the survivors from all three ships were later picked up by *Bluebell*.

Far less fortunate were the ship's company of the *Creekirk*, a tramp-steamer built in 1912. She was loaded with 5,900 tons of iron ore and received the first of Kretschmer's torpedoes. Captain E. Robilliard and all 36 of his crew were killed. Kretschmer had taken *U-99* inside the convoy, whose escorts he considered useless: they fired star-shell in a hopeless attempt to locate an enemy, instead revealing the state of things to the U-boat commanders in their midst.

At about 22.30 a torpedo fired from Frauenheim's *U-101* hit the timber-laden tramp *Blairspey* of Glasgow. Her master Captain J. Walker, 54 and also from Glasgow, had been chosen as vice commodore. During the attack the convoy had executed a number of emergency turns and Walker had been kept so busy repeating the commodore's signals that, although he heard the torpedo detonate, only when a torrent of water descended upon the *Blairspey*'s deck did he realise it was his own ship that had been hit. The torpedo had struck forward, in No. 1 Hold, and although she staggered under the impact and heeled, *Blairspey* came upright again. The shock had dislodged the packing of the main steam-pipe from the boilers to the engine, however, and with high-pressure steam venting the *Blairspey* came slowly to a halt, falling out of line while the remainder of the convoy passed.

HMS *Leith* came back and circled her, but Allen could do little other than wish Walker luck, for his sloop was wanted with the convoy, not astern of it. For two hours Chief Engineer A. Henderson and his men laboured at shutting off the steam and repacking the joint. Those on the bridge could only wait nervously and watch the flashes of explosions, the distress rockets and the hanging glare of the star-shells drawing slowly away to the east as SC7 lumbered on, its evisceration in progress.

In the confusion and frenzy of the attack, the convoy began to loose its cohesion. Seeing the sudden fate of the *Creekirk* nearby, Captain Smith of the *Empire Miniver* strove to get clear. He too had a cargo of iron and steel, 10,700 tons in total. A moment later 'there was a dull thud, a big flash and a cloud of bluish smoke. Then everything went black; all the lights went out, the engines stopped, the ship shuddered, lay still and lost her way . . . It blew all the hatches off her and the pig-iron was blown into the air . . .' Because Kretschmer's torpedo had hit the engine room, where it killed the duty watch of three men, the speed of the ship's sinking was slowed, allowing Smith and the majority of his crew to take to the boats, from where they watched their ship sink some twenty minutes later. 'There was a terrific explosion amidships. She broke her back and sank immediately.'[12]

Kretschmer dominated what had become an orgy of destruction. Five minutes before midnight *U-99* punched a torpedo into the *Niritos* 'at a range of 750 metres. Hit below foremast.' Kretschmer dictated as he went. 'The explosion of the torpedo immediately followed by a high sheet of flame and an explosion which ripped the ship open as far as the bridge and left a cloud of smoke 200 metres. Ship's forepart apparently shattered . . . burning fiercely, with green flames there is another torpedo explosion.' What his torpedo had ignited was the Greek tramp's full cargo of 5,426 tons of sulphur; astonishingly, only one man lost his life in this holocaust. A little later, as Kretschmer withdrew in the face of 'three destroyers', while 'torpedoes from the other [U-]boats [were] exploding all the time', he commented that 'the destroyers are at their wits' end, shooting off star-shells to comfort themselves and each other . . .'

By now the convoy had passed Kretschmer, and it took him half an hour to regain a station from which he could attack again. His next victim was the *Fiscus*, a sister ship to the *Beatus*, similarly heavily laden with steel, timber and a deck cargo of crated aircraft. She sank rapidly, taking with her Captain E. Williams and his crew of 38.

Waiting for 'the next large vessel', Kretschmer sank the Greek tramp steamer *Thalia*. Carrying steel, lead and spelter (impure zinc), she sank in less than a minute, taking 22 of 24 men to their deaths. She was followed by the *Empire Brigade*, a former Italian ship taken as a prize at Newcastle when Italy had declared war on Great Britain the previous June and placed under the management of Cairns, Noble & Company. Loaded with a mixed cargo of general, 129 tons of ferrous alloys, 750 tons of copper and 980 tons of steel, she caught fire and, hit forward, drove straight under. A precipitate attempt to get the boats launched with the ship under way proved disastrous. Six of her crew were lost, though Captain S. Parkes and 34 men escaped as, with her propellers still turning, *Empire Brigade* kicked her stern into the air and went down. Kretschmer estimated that she sank in less than 50 seconds.

His next target was the Norwegian tramp-ship *Sneffield* of Bergen, from which all hands escaped, and he struck last at the Stag Line tramp *Clintonia*. Although she was damaged, her cargo of timber and wood pulp kept her afloat. Short of torpedoes, Kretschmer briefly engaged her with gunfire, to which the *Clintonia*'s crew responded; but the U-boat commander had no wish to linger to decide the matter. Later Moehle in *U-123*, having expended all his torpedoes, shelled and sank her. One man was killed, but the delay enabled Captain T.H. Irwin and the rest of his crew to escape.

After contributing to the destruction of the *Boekolo*, Moehle had gone on to take a hand in the torpedoing of the *Shekatika*, an almost-new vessel owned by Christian Salvesen of Leith, which had apparently fallen out of the convoy. The ship carried a cargo of 2,003 tons of steel and 6,000 tons of pit-props and, like the *Clintonia*, proved difficult to sink. Moehle sent three torpedoes into her, Schepke then joined in and fired a fourth, but it took a fifth from Moehle's *U-123* to send her to the bottom. Despite this, Captain R. Paterson and his crew got away unscathed. Moehle also sank the *Sedgepool*, yet another Ropner tramp to fall foul of German U-boats. Captain R.B. Witten and two of his crew, including his second mate, were lost as the torpedo blew open the hull and destroyed one side of the bridge. Of the *Sedgepool*'s people, 36 were saved by the rescue tug *Salvonia* as the tramp took 8,720 tons of wheat down with her.

Frauenheim had not pressed his attack on the *Blairspey*, perhaps thinking he had so damaged her that she would sink later. Aboard the Ellerman Papayanni liner *Assyrian* Commodore MacKinnon and his signals staff did what they could to evade the attacks of the U-boats by manoeuvring the convoy while the ship's master Captain R. Kearon was dodging torpedo tracks. At one point he saw a submarine's periscope close on his port bow and altered course to ram, chasing his quarry for seven minutes at all of 9.5 knots before the conning tower rose out of the water and the U-boat, with diesels started, drew rapidly away, leaving only the stink of her fumes in Kearon's nostrils and the wake of a stern-chase torpedo fired from the U-boat for him to comb. This may or may not have been *U-101*, but a few moments later Frauenheim fired first into the *Assyrian*, opening her hull up to the boat deck, and then into the small Dutch freighter *Soesterberg*. Six men were dead as the *Soesterberg's* stern reared up and was struck by the *Assyrian's* stern as they swung. The Dutchman's deck cargo of pit-props was cast loose and tumbled onto the *Assyrian's* boat deck, injuring several of the crew – but by now the *Assyrian* herself was in her death throes, sinking rapidly with her 3,700 tons of general cargo. Commodore MacKinnon, two of his staff, 20 of the ship's crew and her nine passengers floundered amid the wreckage, but Kearon was sucked down as his ship stood vertically before plunging to the sea-bed. Surfacing, Kearon found a spar, and on the other end it he discovered his elderly chief officer. A third and then a fourth man joined them, the last a naval signalman. They discussed their chances of survival as the cold began to penetrate, but were fortunate in being recovered after about an hour by HMS *Leith*. One of the men, though he had swum towards the sloop, subsequently died on board, victim of the irreversible progress of hypothermia. Fifteen merchant seamen and two of MacKinnon's naval staff died with the *Assyrian*. Kearon was afterwards awarded Lloyd's War Medal; Frauenheim received the *Ritterkreuz*.

Allen in HMS *Leith* had been casting about for a sonar contact as one of the U-boats dived to avoid detection, but generally speaking the experience of the night as far as the escorts were concerned bore out Kretschmer's ruthless observations. They felt helpless and frustrated, able only to pick up the survivors as daylight spread across the grey and heaving ocean.

After the *Convallaria* and the *Beatus*, Endrass also sank the small Swedish ship *Gunborg*, but her crew of 23 survived to be picked up by the escorts. He played no part in the later stages of the action. Schepke's *U-100* is thought to have participated in the sinking of the *Shekatina* and the *Boekelo*, but if her contribution to the main battle round SC7 was limited by her late arrival she is also thought to have hit the *Blairspey* at about 01.00 on the 19th. The ship still lay stopped and Schepke's torpedo hit forward, near the gaping hole caused by Frauenheim's. Mercifully the *Blairspey's* cargo was timber, a mass of buoyant material packed into her lower holds and 'tween-decks. Yet Walker knew that his ship was a sitting duck, and that sooner or later the U-boat commander would send a torpedo into the engine room: he gave orders to abandon ship. As was customary, Walker's boat was No. 1, on the starboard side; the chief officer, Mr J. Glasgow, was in charge of No. 2, on the port side. No. 1 had just been launched when an explosion was heard on the far side of the ship, where Glasgow had been lowering No. 2. Walker's crew was pulling away when, looming out of the darkness, he saw the conning towers of two U-boats. As they approached the lifeboat a voice demanded the name of the ship before they motored off, leaving the *Blairspey* to settle of her own accord. Then, to Walker's inexpressible relief, just as he was hoisting sail he saw on a wave crest the outline of No. 2 Boat, which had somehow avoided significant damage in the blast. The wind freshened, separating the boats, but some hours later Walker's men were picked up by *Bluebell* and Glasgow's by the *Salvonia*.

By daylight on the 19th the U-boats had broken off the action. Several had expended most of their torpedoes, Kretschmer, Moehle and Frauenheim their entire stocks. As a second gale struck Convoy SC7 on the 20th they hurried jubilantly back to France to rearm, and a week later, on 30 October, Kretschmer was heading out to sea again.

SC7's escorts had done their best but, lacking any proper, co-ordinated, methodical response to the enemy's tactics, they had been outclassed. Even the procedures for embarking survivors were haphazard. Approaching one lifeboat from the *Beatus*, the *Bluebell* hailed: '"I can't stop, there's a U-boat in the area. I've got nets over the side. When I come alongside you'll have to jump for it and scramble aboard."'[13]

Meanwhile, in the wake of this destruction, the *Blairspey* had not sunk. She was afterwards taken in tow by the tug *Salvonia* and brought safely into the Clyde, repaired, and survived the war. Far astern, the small, straggling and incongruous Great Laker *Eaglescliffe Hall* struggled across the Western Ocean, braving two gales and picking up the Greek survivors from the *Aenos* on her way. It was Trafalgar Day, 21 October, when the surviving half of Convoy SC7 reached Liverpool.

In L'Orient, Dönitz was delighted. His young assassins called the dark hours of 18/19 October 'The Night of the Long Knives', and he claimed the sinking of 30 ships, 197,100 tons; in fact it was 20 ships with a total of 79,646 tons, but that was bad enough. In his assessment Dönitz did however touch on a fundamental weakness: 'Such operations can only be carried out if there are sufficient boats in the operational area. Up to now this has happened only occasionally.' In his conclusion he was more optimistic: 'There will be more of these operations as numbers increase, and there is more likelihood of intercepting convoys with the additional reconnaissance. Moreover, with more U-boats, the British shipping routes will not be left unoccupied after such attacks, as was the case today, when nearly all the boats had to return for torpedoes . . .' Finally, and crucially, he stated that 'The capacity of the individual commanders will always govern results.'[14]

Ultimately, his lack of submarines was to rob Dönitz of victory, for it gave the British and their Allies respite enough. In between the near-successive battles for SC7 and HX79 there were those 32 laden merchantmen of Convoy HX78 that sailed across the North Atlantic unmolested. Alongside Kretschmer's contemptuous disregard for the effectiveness of the British escorts there were already surfacing in L'Orient some disquieting reports about the menace posed by Sunderland flying-boats.[15] And in his remark about 'the capacity of individual commanders' Dönitz touched on an incipient German weakness, that of a strategy reliant not on overwhelming force but upon individual professional skill. The brilliant piracy of Kretschmer and his colleagues was one of the triumphs of warfare, marking a period in which they were exultant and reaped honours for the Reich; but in the event they served only to rouse against themselves powers of overwhelming might which in the end succeeded in crushing the German submarine arm.

As in all the OB series, the merchantmen of Convoy OB228 were at their most vulnerable immediately after the point of dispersal. As they fanned out on their individual courses, whether rhumb line or great-circle, they were close enough together to offer a choice of targets to any waiting U-boats. The only risk the U-boats ran was from the escorts which were generally not far away and, though scheduled to meet and provide a close antisubmarine escort to an incoming HX or SC convoy, would respond to a distress signal. The extent to which this posed a real threat to a U-boat commander is clear from the remarkably candid and graphic account written later by Captain, at the time Lieutenant Commander, C.F.H. Churchill of HM Sloop *Folkestone*, escorting Convoy OB228.

The 47-strong convoy had sailed from Liverpool on 15 October. Early on the 16th some forty miles north-west of Barra Head, the southern extremity of the Outer Hebrides, it was attacked by Oberleutnant Lüth in *U-138*. Lüth succeeded in torpedoing the Rosario-bound Lamport & Holt liner *Bonheur* and the tanker *British Glory*. The latter was only damaged and proceeded on her voyage, but the *Bonheur* sank with 5,200 tons of general cargo, although Captain L.O. Everett and all his 38-man crew were rescued by HM Trawler *Sphene*.

By the 17th OB228 was approaching its dispersal point on the 17th meridian West at a latitude of almost 61° North. It was a clear night with 'visibility 3 to 4 miles depending on the extent of cloud across the full moon'. The sloop *Folkestone* was ahead of the convoy and Churchill was intending to carry out a sweep round the merchant ships at 04.00, but at 02.45 the commodore began signalling that two ships had been torpedoed. As Churchill swung *Folkestone* round to pass through the convoy a third explosion rent the night.

The second ship in the fourth column had been hit 'and ships in the convoy started altering course all over the place . . . The Alarm Gongs [aboard *Folkestone*] were rung and all hands went to Action Stations. One ship of the convoy fired a white rocket [but] no ship indicated the side of [the] attack. Survivors in boats burned red distress flares.

'As we cleared the stern of the convoy, the First Lieutenant, Lieutenant Commander W.J. Moore, RNR reported sighting an object "bigger than a boat and strangely like a submarine", lying stopped close to two rafts in the warter [*sic*] that were burning red distress flares as we closed [them] . . .' These rafts were from the small Norwegian steam tramp *Dokka* which had been torn apart by a torpedo hitting her on the starboard quarter. 'The ship sank stern first in less than one minute,' the master, Captain Pedersen, reported later. 'The Second Officer and Wheelman [*sic*] cut the lashings of the port lifeboat, but were in the same moment washed off the boat deck, the same happened with [the] First Officer and another sailor, who tried the starboard boat. The lookout dived from the top of the bridge. I had left the bridge only fifteen minutes before the explosion occurred, and was in my room on the lower bridge, and getting out on deck there was nothing to do but jump overboard . . .'

A couple of rafts floated clear of the wreck, and onto them Pedersen and seven of his crew scrambled; ten men went down with the ship. A little later, as the men on the raft huddled together for warmth and watched the convoy move away from them, they saw looming out of the darkness the low shape of a submarine. It stopped close to them, wallowing in the swell, the water washing through the steel casing. It was *U-93*, commanded by Kapitänleutnant Korth, on her first war patrol. Since leaving Kiel on 5 October she had sunk the refrigerated cargo ship *Hurunui*, Captain B. Evans, yet another of the New Zealand Shipping Company's vessels and one of several lost from the previous OB convoy.

Pedersen, who later struck Lieutenant Commander Churchill 'as a particularly fine type of man [who] . . . appears to have taken all that he saw under the most adverse circumstances with the utmost calm', was asked by Korth the name of his ship. He gave a false one. By this time Churchill was bearing down towards them.

The U-boat, now aware of her predicament, turned away and made off on the surface in the darkness, leaving a swirl of water which gave a sonar response. Seeing the rafts, Churchill altered course, speeding past them, whereupon Pedersen 'stood up and shouted, "There is the submarine – go and get her!"'

Churchill opened fire but 'the Gunlayer could not see the submarine through his sights, nor could he get sufficient depression on his gun on the . . . bearing. I did not feel inclined to sacrifice speed of approach by altering onto a suitable bearing for the gun. The gun was therefore trained . . . with maximum depression. Five rounds were fired. The fourth round hit the conning tower and a bright flash was seen. The submarine then dived, turning to port . . .'

Churchill ordered depth-charges dropped over the dive position, threw a calcium marker overboard, and started a hunt. His sonar operator found a close contact in the vicinity of the marker and began a 'major attack'. As Churchill ran in and the sonar gave the 'instantaneous echo' that indicated the U-boat close beneath *Folkestone*'s hull, Korth dodged to port and vanished, so Churchill called off the attack and began to stalk his quarry a second time. His operators under Moore soon echo-located Korth and Churchill pressed home, coming close again; but the sloop's speed was insufficient to escape the effects of her own depth-charges and Churchill, worried about the possibility of damaging electrical circuitry in the ship, which would leave him impotent, broke off the attack. Contact was lost and not regained.

Moore, it will be remembered, later recalled that one could 'only get on with the job in hand', while his commanding officer summed up his near despair and frustration in an excoriating and candid self-critique: 'I consider the whole hunt was most unsatisfactory. After it *I was at a loss to know how I could have done better* [my emphasis: RW] . . . I realise that my appreciation of the enemy's movements was at fault. I felt the difficulty in this respect . . . but now think I could have done better had an accurate plot of the whole hunt been kept at the time and propose to try this in the future . . . I received every assistance from officers and men. There was no failure of material throughout . . .'

After picking up the *Dokka*'s survivors and meeting Pedersen, Churchill approached the second casualty. She was the small Newport-owned tramp *Uskbridge*, which as the second vessel in the forth column had been the first to be hit by a torpedo from *U-93*. Captain W.B. Smith had lost two men and abandoned ship. He and his 27 crew were picked up by the Dutch freighter *Katwijk* and later transferred to the British *Cristales*, but *Uskbridge* had not sunk, and lay low in the water astern of the convoy as *Folkestone* steamed back to her station at its head. Churchill launched his sea-boat and sent Moore and a party of men across to assess the situation. Laden with 4,000 tons of anthracite, the *Uskbridge* had been hit in No. 2 Hold, and steam was still raised and the generators running. Moore, an experienced cargo-ship officer, thought she could be saved, and men and gear were being prepared when an explosion rocked the *Uskbridge* and she broke her back and sank immediately.

Abandoning his salvage attempt, Churchill got under way. On *Folkestone*'s bridge, Pedersen expressed the opinion that the explosion had been that of a bulkhead collapsing under immense pressure of water, which was consistent with the *Uskbridge*'s having her forepart full and the after part buoyant. Half an hour later, as *Folkestone* caught up with the convoy, her operators obtained another sonar contact. Having escaped Churchill's attacks, Korth was still shadowing OB228, but he took swift and conclusive evading action and Churchill again lost his quarry.

Korth was the only U-boat in contact with OB228 and had transmitted its position to Dönitz, who was engaged with operations further south, against SC7. He was delighted with their success and that of the attacks against Convoys SC6 and OB227, but piecemeal strikes at outward-bound merchantmen were not enough to satisfy the Befelshaber der U-boote's sanguinary appetites; they were mere tactical triumphs, while the attack on the loaded eastbound ships of SC7 was a victory of strategic significance. He now gathered his ambush for the deep-laden vessels steaming in the columns of Convoy HX79.

The 49 ships of Convoy HX79 had left Halifax on 8 October 1940 under the ocean escort of two Armed Merchant Cruisers, the *Alaunia* and *Montclare*. During the forenoon of 19 October these two ships turned west, handing over HX79 to the protection of the 1st Escort Group. The strength of this group, at least on paper, was a portent of things to come, and a measure of the value attached by the Admiralty to the commodities carried by HX79. Led by the elderly destroyer *Whitehall*, Lieutenant Commander Russell, 1st Escort Group consisted of a second destroyer, *Sturdy*, the minesweeper *Jason*, three corvettes, *Arabis, Coreopsis* and *Hibiscus*, the anti-submarine trawlers *Lady Elsa, Blackfly* and *Angle*, and a Dutch submarine, the *O-21*, which appears to have played no significant part in the action.

Prien's contact report enabled Dönitz to order his remaining operational U-boats in the North West Approaches to concentrate on the 19th, about a hundred and forty miles west of the Rockall Bank. In addition to Prien's *U-47*, *U-38* (Liebe), *U-46* (Endrass), *U-48* (Bleichrodt) and *U-100* (Schepke) were assigned to the forthcoming attack. A number of other U-boats which failed to reach HX79 in time were able to continue sinking ships sailing independently after the dispersal of the outward-bound convoy OB229.

Stationed in the rear of the port column, the British Brocklebank liner

Matheran was the first to be sunk, torpedoed by Liebe from *U-38* outside the convoy. Liebe's torpedo entered No. 3 Hold and the sea flooded into the ship, sinking her in seven minutes, laden as she was with 3,000 tons of iron and 1,200 tons of zinc, grain, machinery and general cargo. Captain J. Greenhall and eight crew lost their lives, while 72, mostly Indian lascars, went over the side in the boats and were picked up later by the *Loch Lomond*, which was acting as a rescue ship.

Having launched his attack on the *Matheran*, Liebe ran on into the convoy and six minutes later fired a second salvo of torpedoes, at the Glaswegian tramp *Uganda* in the third column. Owned by Maclay & McIntyre, she was carrying 2,006 tons of steel and 6,200 of timber. All but one of her boats was destroyed in the blast, yet mercifully no one was killed, and Captain C. Mackinnon and his 39 men were rescued by *Jason*.

The pace of the destruction now increased as Prien engaged, also on the surface, sinking first the Dutch general cargo-vessel *Bilderdijk*, belonging to the Holland–Amerika Lijn. With her went a valuable cargo of 8,640 tons of grain and general cargo, though all 39 of her crew escaped. Having sunk the second vessel in column two, Prien next hit the sixth. A torpedo from *U-47* damaged the British tanker *Shirak*, belonging to the Baltic Trading Company, bound from Aruba for London with 7,771 tons of petroleum products. The damage was not fatal, but the crew abandoned the crippled vessel and all were thereby saved, for as the convoy moved away leaving the *Shirak* on fire astern, Bleichrodt in *U-48* arrived and administered the death-blow. Captain L.R. Morrison and his crew were all rescued by HM Trawler *Blackfly*. Prien's next victim was another Ropner tramp, the *Wandby*, which was homeward bound on her maiden voyage carrying 1,700 tons of lead and zinc and 7,200 tons of timber loaded in Vancouver. Captain Kenny and his entire crew abandoned ship and were rescued by HM Trawler *Angle*. The *Wandby* foundered slowly, and did not actually sink until 21 October.

Endrass had also fired at the *Wandby*, and shortly before midnight he attacked the British tramp *Ruperra* of Cardiff. She contained steel scrap and aircraft, and she sank rapidly; Captain D.T. Davies, 29 crew and a naval gunner were lost with her. Only seven men were rescued by the merchantman *Induna*, which gallantly stopped amid the mayhem.

It was now Schepke's turn in *U-100* and he sank two more tankers, both owned by the British Anglo-Saxon Petroleum Company. The first was the *Caprella*, struck at 23.15. Commanded by Captain P. Prior, she was on her way from Curaçao to Stanlow with 11,300 tons of heavy fuel oil. This failed to ignite, though the torpedo explosion broke the ship's back, hitting her between the bridge superstructure and the engine room. Lifeboats amid-ships and aft were lowered, though without the chief officer, who had been on the bridge and was killed in the blast. As Captain Prior and his crew abandoned ship, the *Shirak* could be seen on fire in the offing. For about an hour or two – 'it was difficult to assess the length of time' – they lay awaiting events in the darkness, and in due course the 52 survivors, all Singapore Chinese apart from the officers, were picked up by the *Lady Elsa*.

Schepke's second target was the *Sitala*, also bound from Curaçao for Stanlow, with 8,444 tons of crude oil. Once again one of the engine-room watch-keepers was killed, while Captain J.L. Morgans and 42 crew escaped to be picked up, like their colleagues, by *Lady Elsa*.

It was now after midnight, and Prien fired at Buries Markes's cargo-vessel *La Estancia*. Again one man below was lost, along with the 8,333 tons of sugar the ship was carrying. Captain J. Meneely, 24 of his crew and one passenger were rescued by HM Corvette *Coreopsis*, Lieutenant Commander A.H. Davies, the remaining seven by the *Induna*. Still on the surface, and picking off targets from the passing columns of zig-zagging merchantmen, Prien next hit the London-registered *Whitford Point* stationed in the rear of the convoy. She was loaded with 7,840 tons of steel and consequently sank quickly, taking with her Captain J.E. Young and 35 of his crew. Only one man was rescued by HMS *Sturdy*.

Having stopped to recover the *Matheran*'s survivors, the *Loch Lomond* now came into Schepke's sights as he caught up with the convoy in *U-100*. Like the *Uganda* and the *Induna*, the *Loch Lomond* was also owned by Maclay & McIntyre. She was only six years old, a 10.5-knot tramp with a low free-board when loaded with a cargo of 6,000 tons of timber and 1,858 tons of steel. Fortunately she did not sink quickly but gave her own crew and the *Matheran*'s survivors time to get away, and Captain W.J. Park, his own 38 and the *Matheran*'s people were all picked up by *Jason*, Lieutenant Commander R.E. Terry.

Further astern of the convoy lagged the laden Swedish Johnson Line's oil-tanker *Janus*, a 1939-built motor-vessel of 9,965 tons. She was Endrass's last victim before he broke off the action and headed *U-46* for Kiel; like his colleagues, he was running short of torpedoes. The *Janus* was the last vessel out of HX79 to be sunk but Prien had also damaged the tanker *Athelmonarch*, though she later made port.

Convoy HX79 was now suffered to continue towards Liverpool, where it arrived without further loss on 23 October, but at the same time as the attack on HX79 began *U-124*, Kapitänleutnant Schulz, operating south of Iceland, had sunk Elders & Fyffe's *Sulaco* and a Norwegian ship, the Wilhelmsen-owned *Cubano*, both out of OB229. Although only two men were lost from the *Cubano*, Captain Henry C. Bower, 62 crew and two gunners died with the *Sulaco*. A single survivor, Chief Cook Harvey, was picked up by the Canadian destroyer *Saguenay*. Schulz was counter-attacked severely but unsuccessfully, and he completed his war patrol by sinking two stragglers from Convoy HX82.[16] One was the small British steamship *Rutland*, owned by the grandly named Leith, Hull and Hamburg Steam Packet Company. She was loaded with bananas, and Captain R.N. Sinclair and his entire ship's company of 24 perished. The second was the *Empire Bison*, another former laid-up American standard ship. Under the management of the MoWT and commanded by Captain W.H. Harland, she was loaded with 6,067 tons of scrap steel and a quantity of trucks. She too sank quickly, Harland and 30 men being lost, and only a handful rescued by the Danish ship *Olga*.

Despite its strength the escort, lacking co-ordinated counter-tactics, had once again proved feeble, only really capable of rescuing the wretched merchant seamen. Although it was vivid moonlight, Russell's ships had failed to locate a single one of the U-boats operating on the surface, while the Admiralty staff did not consider there to be conclusive evidence that they had been doing so. Able Seaman Charles Walker, lookout aboard the *Sitala*, was in no doubt, however: he saw one U-boat pass his ship 'on the surface and . . . so close that I could have hit him with a stone'.[17]

The only success, if success it was, was the bombing of Endrass's *U-46* west of Stavanger on 25 October. One of three Hudsons from No. 233 Squadron succeeded in landing a direct hit and blowing a hole in her stern, killing one man, but this did not prevent *U-46* either reaching Kiel or sailing on her twelfth war patrol in the following February.

This quasi-triumph pointed up the utter inadequacy of the RAF's anti-submarine bombing capability, while the single German casualty stands in mute and terrible contrast to the damage inflicted upon the British and Allied merchant services. There was worse to come in the aftermath of this bitter struggle, for damage to one U-boat was entirely eclipsed by the loss of the destroyer *Sturdy*, driven ashore in bad weather on the coast of the Hebridean island of Tiree on 30 October. She had been part of the escort to Convoy SC8, whose 50 merchant ships arrived in Liverpool Bay the following day.

The problems posed by the sudden arrival of survivors in places as far apart and as different as Methil and Belfast were considerable. For succour these people relied heavily on such charitable institutions as the Anglican Missions to Seamen, the Roman Catholic Apostleship of the Sea, the British Sailors' Society, and the Salvation Army. At a personal level, the fourteen-day survivors' leave and £30 compensation were little enough. One young radio officer spent most of his fortnight 'dashing around getting a new uniform made, collecting shirts, shorts, white suits . . . and, of course, civvy clothes, all of which had been lost . . . There was no compensation for lost money, cameras, radios, glasses [spectacles] . . . Any complaints received the answer, "You shouldn't take any more than is essential to sea with you" . . .'[18] This was all very practical, but the meagre worldly possessions of many indigent seamen who had survived the Depression went everywhere with them, or to the bottom of the Atlantic if their ship was sunk. There was also, of course, that small matter of cessation of pay.

If Dönitz's submarines had scored a triumph in these attacks and the Royal Navy had been tactically defeated, the Merchant Navy had achieved a limited success. It might be argued that there was little else the merchant masters and their ships could do but steam steadfastly on through the carnage, yet the tenacious holding of a position despite suffering loss is in itself a fundamental military virtue. In this respect, Convoy HX79 must be seen as a besieged garrison barely maintaining its integrity while its relief column is out-manoeuvred by a skilful enemy.

The expenditure of their torpedoes compelled most of the U-boats to retire, leaving only two on station, *U-28* and *U-124*; but others were on their way – *U-29*, *U-31* and *U-32* – and Kretschmer was about to sail again in *U-99*. On 26 October Kuhnke's *U-28* attacked Elders & Fyffe's banana-laden *Matina*, on her way from Jamaica to Garston on the river Mersey. The 13-knot vessel was sailing independently and *U-28*'s torpedo failed to sink her. Three days later Kapitänleutnant Prellberg in *U-31* came across her 'abandoned hulk'.[19] Prellberg had been chasing an outbound convoy and was awaiting a reinforcement of seven Italian submarines[20] with which to form a wolf-pack when a gale compelled him to break off the chase. He fired five torpedoes at the drifting *Matina*, three of which missed while the final two sank her. It has to be assumed that Captain D.A. Jack and his 67 men perished in their lifeboats during the gales, for they were not heard of again.

On the day that Kuhnke attacked the *Matina* he had been on his way to join Prellberg and *U-32*, commanded by Oberleutnant zur See Jenisch. The three U-boats had been directed towards a potential prestigious target, the Canadian Pacific liner *Empress of Britain*. The 42,348-ton vessel had been attacked earlier that day, 26 October, by a patrolling Focke-Wulf Kondor from Kampfgeschwader 40 piloted by Oberleutnant Jope and based at Bordeaux-Mérignac. The *Empress of Britain* was about sixty miles north-west of the Aran Islands, homeward bound towards Liverpool by way of Cape Town from Port Tewfik at the south end of the Suez Canal on government service, carrying more than two hundred military personnel and their families as passengers. She also bore 300 tons of sugar, government and military stores, and mail. Many of Captain C.H. Sapsworth's crew of 419 men and women and two naval gunners were fighting the fire Jope's two bombs had caused: the *Empress of Britain* was burning fiercely amidships, and 25 of her crew, largely catering staff, and a score of passengers were already dead.

While Dönitz was vectoring the three U-boats on the disabled liner, the Admiralty was ordering the Polish destroyer *Burza* and two salvage tugs to her support. The *Burza*, which with the *Piorun* had been part of the Clyde escort force, detached from her group and sped to the south. At about 14.00 that Saturday afternoon her lookouts spotted a pall of smoke. An hour later *Burza* was alongside, passing a wire, afterwards handing the tow over to the Admiralty tugs *Marauder* and *Thames. Burza* was now joined by the destroyer *Echo*, and they took up anti-submarine escort positions.[21]

Jenisch, in *U-32*, thought Prellberg's U-boat was nearer the *Empress of Britain* and did not respond to Dönitz's order until it was repeated on the 28th, whereupon he headed towards the liner's position, some sixty miles south of his own, and that afternoon spotted in the distance a Sunderland flying an air patrol, presumably above the liner and her attendant vessels. He submerged, surfaced after dark, and closed with his quarry, taking up a station ahead and to port of the *Empress of Britain*. Holding his fire until the tugs and escorts had passed him, Jenisch then loosed three torpedoes at a range of only 600 yards before turning away and running clear on the surface. Two of his torpedoes proved fatal, and the liner began to sink. The attending vessels rallied and rescued Sapsworth, 390 of his crew, 185 passengers and his two gunners; *U-32* withdrew unimpeded. Not only was the doomed liner possessed of a name that was a gift to German propaganda; she was, as it turned out, the largest British merchantman lost during the war.

But Jenisch's days were numbered; two days later he attacked the Lamport & Holt cargo-liner *Balzac* which was steaming independently after leaving an OB convoy. The torpedo passed beneath the ship and exploded at the end of its run, leading the officer of the watch aboard *Balzac* to conclude that they were under shellfire from a raider. In response to his warning signal the Admiralty ordered the destroyers *Harvester* and *Highlander* to *Balzac's* assistance. Meanwhile Jenisch, frustrated in his first attempt, was trailing the *Balzac* when he was caught by *Harvester's* sonar. Lieutenant Commander M. Thornton began an approach and then spotted *U-32's* periscope ahead as he ran in and dropped six depth-charges. Jensich evaded these by diving, leaving Thornton and his colleague, Commander W.A. Dallmyer, to thrash about while night fell, gaining and losing contact as Jenisch struggled for survival below them. Finally Dallmyer dropped fourteen depth-charges in quick succession and seriously damaged *U-32*, forcing her to surface, whereupon the destroyers opened fire. The wallowing U-boat was at the mercy of her adversaries and Jenisch ordered her scuttled as his men abandoned her under gunfire. Nine of her crew were killed, but Jenisch and 33 others were picked up.

There then followed a ludicrous propaganda battle in which the British crowed over the capture of a *Ritterkreuz*-holding 'ace' while Berlin, cheated of heaping laurels on the man who had accounted for so large a ship, staged a phoney homecoming which included a broadcast account 'by Jenisch' of his sinking of the *Empress of Britain*.

On 2 November, Prellberg's *U-31* was destroyed. After he sank the *Matina* Prellberg sighted a British destroyer, part of the escort of Convoy OB237, which was on the point of dispersal. Intending to attack the warship, Prellberg was frustrated by heavy weather washing over his attack periscope; his target, HMS *Antelope*, detected his presence and counter-attacked. Lieutenant Commander T. White increased speed and raced towards his quarry, signalling his intentions to *Antelope*'s sister-ship, *Achates*. White had to press several attacks, but finally he prevailed, forcing Prellberg to surface. Believing 'an hero's death to be an over-rated gesture', Prellberg ordered the sea-cocks opened and, continuing under way, to the frustration of *Antelope*'s oar-pulled whaler, succeeded in moving off. White closed her and Prellberg swung and rammed *Antelope*, causing considerable damage as the collision threw *U-32* on her beam ends. Her conning tower under water, she sank like a stone. Two men were lost as the U-boat went down, but her commander and 43 German submariners were taken prisoner.[22]

These German losses in early November were soon to be offset by further triumphs. As Dönitz prepared to move his headquarters from Paris to a requisitioned château at Kerneval on the banks of the river Scorff, leading to L'Orient, Kretschmer was at sea again. So too were Convoys HX83 and HX84. Since the attacks on HX79 only a handful of merchant ships had been lost out of Halifax convoys, and these had mostly been stragglers, such as the *Empire Bison* referred to earlier. Kretschmer in *U-99* was lying in wait for HX83 and, late on the afternoon of the 3rd, hove in sight of yet another of Elders & Fyffe's banana-carriers, the *Casanare*, homeward bound from the Cameroons under Captain J.A. Moore.

The German acquisition of bases on the Biscay coast of France had led the Admiralty to establish a Western Patrol using Armed Merchant Cruisers, and the former Cunard White Star liner HMS *Laurentic*, Captain E.P. Vivian, was returning from a patrol when she responded to the *Casanare*'s distress signals. The quondam Blue Funnel liner HMS *Patroclus*, Captain G.C. Wynter, having been relieved from her duty as escort to Convoy HX83, was also in the offing, and also went to the *Casanare*'s assistance. Fatally, Kretschmer too was close by, and as Vivian approached the casualty he fired at the *Laurentic*, hitting her with two torpedoes and missing with a third.

The *Patroclus* went to the assistance of the *Laurentic*, whose crew were already in their boats by the time she arrived. Slowing to manoeuvre, the *Patroclus* was now hit by a torpedo from *U-99*, followed by a second, but both AMCs were loaded with empty barrels and proved difficult to sink. Disdaining the armaments mounted by the AMCs, Kretschmer surfaced and began to shell *Patroclus*, but Wynter responded with 'accurate time-fused shells' which drove him off. He fired another ineffective torpedo, then had to wait for his men to reload. By now, however, a Sunderland flying-boat was approaching, and Kretschmer took *U-99* deep and did not surface until the following morning, when he discovered both liners obdurately afloat. A third torpedo despatched the *Laurentic*, but the *Patroclus*, built to Holt's standards, proved more stubborn, and it took two further torpedoes before serious damage was inflicted to the forward part of her hull and she finally began to founder.

Having been detached from the escort of HX83 the destroyers *Beagle*, Lieutenant Commander C.R.H. Wright, and *Hesperus*, Lieutenant Commander D.G.F.W. Macintyre, were now approaching, but Kretschmer made good his escape, leaving the two destroyers to pick out of the sea Moore and 53 of his crew, along with 368 survivors from the *Lauretic* and 264 from the *Patroclus*. Nine men were lost from the *Casanare*, 49 from the *Laurentic* and 79 from the *Patroclus*.

On 5 November Kretschmer made contact with HX83 and sank the tanker *Scottish Maiden*, Captain J.W.A. Gibson, laden with fuel and diesel oil. Sixteen men were lost with her, 28 were later rescued by the *Beagle*. Kretschmer arrived back at L'Orient on the 8th and was summoned to Berlin, for Hitler wished to meet this paragon of the Kriegsmarine. His *Ritterkreuz* further embellished with oak leaves, he was asked by Hitler what could be done to aid the U-boats in their war. Kretschmer, known to his colleagues as 'Otto the Silent', brusquely told the Führer that proper aerial reconnaissance and many more submarines were required.

The German naval high command held the big-gun cruiser in as great regard as did the British Admiralty. In a memorandum prepared in July 1940, Konteradmiral Fricke, Chief of Operations, had declared that 'The main protagonist in the war against the enemy's communications [i.e., trade] is the battleship itself.' The image of the big ships was seductive, and not only Fricke but Raeder and his Chief-of-Staff, Admiral Schniewind, were among the faithful. Even though most of the German heavy surface vessels were not seaworthy for one reason or another, the abandonment of the invasion of southern England and the acquisition of Atlantic bases had by mid October persuaded Raeder that 'exceptionally favourable possibilities for waging war against the enemy's ocean communications . . .' currently existed for heavy units operating out of Brest or St-Nazaire. The *Admiral*

Scheer was accordingly brought forward, and in early November ordered to sea. The B-Dienst service, monitoring British radio transmissions relating to convoys, indicated an opportunity for the *Admiral Scheer* to make a passage from Gotenhaven to France and attack a Halifax convoy on passage.

Kapitän zur See T. Kranke took his ship to sea on 23 October, two days before the departure of Convoy HX84. The November of 1940 was a cold, miserable month in the North Atlantic. A series of depressions swept across the bleak grey seas, providing cover for the escape of the *Admiral Scheer*, though at the cost of two men swept off her weather deck by green seas. Kranke avoided all contact with other vessels, even independently-sailing merchantmen, using his radar to warn him of their proximity. His objective was an entire convoy, HX84; with the aid of B-Dienst intercepts, its complete destruction was to be accomplished at a stroke.

On 5 November, as Kretschmer was cutting out the *Scottish Maiden* from HX83, Krancke's *Panzerschiff* was athwart the convoy route in mid Atlantic, roughly half-way between Ireland and Labrador, far to the west of the Mid-Ocean Meeting Point where an eastbound convoy could expect to rendezvous with its anti-submarine escort. At about 09.00 Kranke catapulted his Arado seaplane into the air. Its pilot, Leutnant Pietsch, was ordered to locate HX84, keep out of sight and maintain radio silence. Pietsch returned at noon to report that he had located a large convoy; no enemy warships were in sight and, since the weather was reasonable, Krancke decided to attack that same afternoon. The *Admiral Scheer* lay in wait.

Convoy HX84 ploughed its way doggedly eastwards. It consisted of 38 ships in nine columns commanded by Commodore R.H. Maltby, a former rear admiral, aboard the Cardiff-registered tramp *Cornish City*, Captain Isaac, at the head of the fifth column. Indistinguishable from other members of the convoy was its escort, the Armed Merchant Cruiser *Jervis Bay*, an Aberdeen & Commonwealth liner of 14,164 tons armed with seven single-mounted 6-inch and two single 3-inch guns; she was steaming in the centre of the convoy. The *Jervis Bay* was commanded by Acting Captain E.S. Fogarty Fegen, an ascetic-looking bachelor of 48 who had added two decorations from the Royal Humane Society for life-saving in peace time to a fine record in the Great War. He came of a naval family, and was regarded as a fair commander. Among the *Jervis Bay*'s crew were her peace-time Chief Officer, Mr G.L. Roe, Second Officer W. Hill, Third Officer N.E. Wood and Fourth Officer H.G.B. Moss, all of whom held temporary commissions in the Royal Naval Reserve. Her Chief Engineer, Mr J.H.G. Campbell, had been commissioned as a Temporary Commander (E) and most of the engineer officers, having volunteered for naval service, held RNR commissions 'in accordance with their rank in the ship. Purser E.

White was also commissioned as a Paymaster Lieutenant Commander. The naval authorities charged with commissioning the ship as an Armed Merchant Cruiser also engaged a number of ratings under the T124 agreement, augmenting the ship's company with RNVR ratings and a selection of specialist regular naval petty officers, especially in the gunnery department. Nevertheless the proportion of trained naval to former merchant seamen at each gun was one to three.'

From the air the *Jervis Bay* seemed little different in size or appearance from the New Zealand Shipping Company's passenger–cargo-liner *Rangitiki*, which led the sixth column. In addition to a ship's company of 223 souls, the *Rangitiki* carried 75 passengers and a cargo of wool, frozen foodstuffs (mutton, cheese and butter) and a quantity of general cargo, all loaded in New Zealand. She had left Wellington on 7 September under the command of Captain H. Barnett, who had brought her to the rendezvous at Halifax by way of the Panama Canal. Now she joined eleven tankers carrying aviation spirit and fuel oil which were steaming in the inner columns of the convoy. These were the *Athelprincess, Atheltemplar, Cordelia, Delphinula, Erodona, James J. Maguire, Oil Reliance, St Gobain, Solfonn, Sovac*, and the Eagle Oil Company's *San Demetrio*. Under a variety of ensigns an assortment of merchantmen consisting of the *Andalusian, Anna Bulgari, Beaverford, Briarwood, Castilian, Cerus, Danae II, Dan-y-Bryn, Delhi, Emile Franqui, Empire Penguin, Fresno City, Hjalmar Wessel, Kenbane Head, Lancaster Castle, Maidan, Pacific Enterprise, Persier, Puck, Trefusis, Trewellard, Varcy* and two neutral Swedish ships, *Vingaland* and *Stureholm*, carried the usual commodities – food, grain, steel, timber and war materials. The Polish steamship *Morska Wola* had dropped astern three days before (and arrived safely later in the month), but otherwise the convoy was in good order.

Ahead of HX84 lay a complication for Krancke which his Arado pilot had not spotted. In addition to the *Casanare* and the *Matina*, Elders & Fyffe's *Mopan* was also on her way to Garston with a full cargo of bananas. She too was sailing independently, and she threatened to compromise Krancke's plan to strike just before sunset and escape into the darkness. Earlier that day she had come up astern of HX84 and Maltby had signalled her to join the convoy, but her master, another Captain Sapsworth, relished the independence her 14 knots gave him and refused, running on ahead until, at 14.30, he hove in sight of the *Admiral Scheer*.

If the *Mopan* were to transmit the RRRR signal and the Admiralty thereupon diverted HX84, Krancke would at the least lose the initiative; at the worst, he might himself be compromised and become the hunted. To divert around her would carry him too far from HX84 and rule out an attack that day. Resolutely he headed directly for the *Mopan* at 26 knots and fired at her, destroying one of her boats, then signalled her to heave-to and abandon ship at once.

Taken by surprise, his DEMS gunner having reassuringly pronounced the approaching warship to be a British 'R'-class battleship, and suddenly finding himself under the guns of the *Admiral Scheer*, Sapsworth had little alternative. His remaining three boats were lowered and he abandoned the *Mopan* to the secondary armament of the *Admiral Scheer*, which promptly punched 5.9-inch shells into her water-line at close range. Krancke was in the very act of embarking the *Mopan*'s people when wisps of smoke were seen on the western horizon. Leaving the banana-carrier foundering in his wake surrounded by some of the 17,000 hands of fruit in her holds and 'tween-decks, Krancke ordered full speed, well aware that his great grey ship would be indistinct against the looming twilight of the late November afternoon.

The approaching raider was spotted first from the *Rangitiki*, which signalled the *Cornish City*. A moment later the *Empire Penguin* reported the strange vessel, and the *Jervis Bay* was alerted. Fegen saw his enemy at about 16.35 and immediately ordered action stations, full speed and smoke. As his yeomen hoisted battle ensigns, his signallers flashed the challenge 'What ship?' The only reply came when flashes of gunfire sparkled along the length of the strange warship.

Maltby signalled the entire convoy to execute an immediate forty-degree turn to starboard as *Jervis Bay* hauled out towards the 'grey smudge' now visible to her guns' crews as they whipped the canvas covers off the open breeches of their vintage artillery. The two vessels were about ten miles apart, and Krancke now swung the *Admiral Scheer* to open all gun arcs, and fired on the convoy. Fegen turned slightly to port and began to fire *Jervis Bay*'s forward 6-inch guns; their shells fell short and he ordered red rockets, signalling the merchantmen to set off smoke flares to confuse the German gun-laying. It was about 17.10 when Maltby gave the order for Convoy HX84 to scatter.

Fegen's efforts to gall him and draw the *Admiral Scheer*'s fire were successful, and Krancke succumbed to temptation. He ordered his own gunners to shift their target, confident that they would make short work of the *Jervis Bay*, and his shells soon found their mark. As Third Officer J.R. Cooper of the *Castilian* ran aft to man his 4-inch gun, he saw how the 'first salvo landed right ahead of the *Jervis Bay*, the second . . . landed in his wake, the third hit the bridge setting it on fire as she left the convoy'. Fires were started throughout the ship and, like those of *Rawalpindi*, her wooden interior fittings, boats and decks quickly ignited. With his telemotor destroyed Fegen strove to steer using his twin screws, calling for medical attention: he had had one arm torn away by a shell fragment and was severely wounded in the leg. He lost consciousness for a few seconds, but after being crudely bandaged he made his way aft to the docking bridge, where hand-steering was engaged by an emergency party for the few moments the *Jervis Bay* remained manoeuverable.

One by one her guns were knocked out of action. One gunner was blown to pieces when the cartridge he was carrying up to his gun's breech was ignited by a hot fragment and exploded. The ship was riddled with shells and her engines stopped. Fegen could no longer steer and the *Jervis Bay* lay wallowing in the sea; he was last seen on her poop, encouraging the men at an after-gun to keep firing. It took 22 minutes for the *Admiral Scheer*'s guns to destroy this British apology for a man-of-war, at the end of which time she lay inert. Two hours later she rolled over and sank by the stern, her white ensigns still flying but obscured by the darkness, only the sudden extinguishing of the fires signalling her passing. While 68 men escaped by jumping into the sea, Fegen and 186 of his mixed crew perished with their ship.

Krancke had long since pressed on, his secondary armament already concentrating on the *Rangitiki*. Even as the *Admiral Scheer* chased the merchantmen scattering to the south in the fading daylight, Krancke must have sensed that Fegen's sacrifice had cost him the success of his own attack. His guns next engaged the tanker *San Demetrio* and soon, as he thought, both she and the *Rangitiki* were on fire. Captain Waite ordered the burning tanker abandoned, but Barnett had had better luck. Krancke had been deceived by the smoke flares, and all the German shells missed: *Rangitiki* turned north-west and made off at her best speed of 16 knots.

'After dark', Third Officer Cooper of the *Castilian* recalled, 'we thought we were safe[;] around 18.30, after having a sandwich and a mug of tea, we were stood down from the gun platform. The pitch darkness was suddenly broken as his [the *Admiral Scheer*'s]`searchlight was trained on us, we never saw him. Just as suddenly it went off. We had 400 tons of high explosives in magazines in our 'tween-decks. We were lucky he did not shoot at us, but we had just overtaken a tanker called the *San Demetrio* which was his next victim; he put his searchlight on her and put six shells into her. We counted them as they glowed in the darkness.'[23] Krancke's guns also hit a second Ellerman & Papayanni ship, the *Andalusian*, which sustained damage to her amidships accommodation but otherwise escaped.

The *Cornish City* was another of Krancke's targets to escape destruction as the *Admiral Sheer*'s guns were laid upon the Ulsterman *Kenbane Head*, which was illuminated by star-shell at about 18.30 and then hit by a full salvo from the *Admiral Scheer*'s 11-inch guns. She fired back but was entirely wrecked from stem to stern and listed to port in a sinking condition. Of her 45-man crew 23 were killed, and the remainder took to the water. Seeing her predicament, Captain Pettigrew of the Canadian Pacific general cargo-vessel *Beaverford* tried to draw the *Admiral Scheer*'s shells by opening fire himself with his own two anti-submarine guns, a courageous act in view of the fact that while his ship carried food and timber in her 'tween-decks, her holds were full of munitions. Because of the nature of her cargo the *Beaverford* had been astern of the commodore in *Cornish City* in the fifth column and just ahead of Brocklebank's *Maidan*, similarly laden with munitions, though topped off with brass, steel, iron, timber, trucks and tobacco. Both these ships made smoke and, as the convoy scattered, headed south, with the *Admiral Scheer* in pursuit. The *Maidan* was hit by several shells which penetrated her hull and blew her apart, the ammunition counter-mining and destroying the vessel in seconds. Captain Miller and all 89 of his ship's company were consumed inside an intense fire-ball.

Transferring his attention to the Hain tramp *Trewellard*, Captain Daniel, Krancke hit her with overwhelming force. She was carrying pig iron and steel billets, and the crew had just time enough to throw off the falls and get three boats into the water before she sank. Sixteen of her crew were killed, 25 escaped in the boats. Krancke now re-engaged the *Beaverford*, which fought back with a futile gallantry. Pettigrew must have been a dogged commander, for he employed every artifice at his disposal and resisted Krancke for about five hours, using helm and variable speed to try to dodge the fall of shot. But the *Admiral Scheer* was firing star-shell and laying the guns optically in their glare: at about 22.45 the German shells drove deep into the *Beaverford*'s hull and she too exploded, killing all 77 of her company. The second of Reardon Smith's ships in the convoy was not as lucky as the commodore's. The *Fresno City*, Captain Lawson, was shelled by the *Admiral Scheer*'s entire broadside as she steamed on a parallel course two miles abeam. Mercifully only one man lost his life, the remainder escaping in the boats.

Krancke had expended a vast quantity of ammunition in this action, and to that extent Fegen's undoubted gallantry curtailed his enemy's intentions, but that his valorous self-sacrifice 'saved' the convoy is a naval myth. Pettigrew's courage is not to be overlooked, and there were others of equal stature. Aboard the Swedish *Stureholm* that night, Captain Sven Olander mustered his crew, and proposed to unanimous agreement that they should return to search for survivors. The next morning Olander's vessel located one lifeboat and some rafts containing the remnants of the *Jervis Bay*'s crew. Of the 68 men who had escaped the burning vessel, three had died of their wounds in the night. Of her own officers, Third Officer Wood and Fourth Officer Moss survived; Mr Wood was awarded the Distinguished Service

Order. Olander turned back to St John's, Newfoundland, arriving there on 13 November. Sadly, the *Stureholm* was lost with all hands when attempting to recross the Atlantic in Convoy HX92, sunk by *U-96* on 12 December; with her went some of the survivors from a British tanker.

At the time Fegen was attacking the *Admiral Scheer*, almost three hundred miles away to the east the Bristol City Line's *Gloucester City* was heading west after the dispersal of Convoy OB238. At 17.00 that afternoon the duty radio officer had intercepted Maltby's signal that HX84 was under attack by a raider. Informed of this, Captain Smith decided to lay a course through the reported position in anticipation of picking up survivors. That night the *Gloucester City* met strong, storm-force headwinds, but they abated in the small hours and at daylight on 7 November she came in sight of the first of seven boats spread over a wide area. Picking up 25 men from the *Trewellard*, 23 from the *San Demetrio*, 20 from the *Kenbane Head* and 24 from the *Fresno City*, Smith landed them all at St John's on the same day that Olander arrived.

The ordeal of HX84 was far from over. Another Swedish vessel from the convoy, the *Vingaland*, was spotted by an FW200 Kondor three days later and bombed to destruction, taking six men with her to the bottom. Other vessels reached ports on both sides of the Atlantic. When he arrived in Britain Captain Piekarski of the small Polish ship *Puck* expressed his admiration for the courage of Fegen and his crew in a letter to *The Times*, and in due course Edward Fogarty Fegen was awarded a posthumous Victoria Cross. No such honour was accorded the shade of Pettigrew.

Meanwhile, in view of the presence of the *Admiral Scheer* somewhere at large, Convoy HX85 was turned back to Sydney and OB239 to Oban, and all further trade convoys were suspended for twelve days as the Admiralty mustered a force to hunt the raider. Krancke was able to elude his pursuers, however, and cruised for 161 days before being welcomed back to Bergen by Raeder on 1 April, having sunk or captured 17 merchantmen in addition to the *Jervis Bay*, a greater tally than Langsdorff's in the *Admiral Graf Spee*.

There remained the saving of the *San Demetrio*. During the course of the war the longitudinally-framed oil tanker proved herself extraordinarily durable. Provided that her cargo was of a low flashpoint and did not explode, its lighter specific gravity than that of water aided her inherent buoyancy, while the girder-like structure of the long, low hull seemed able to endure all but the worst weather. The survival of the *Imperial Transport* has already been described, and the epic of the *Ohio*, which limped into Malta in August 1942, is well known. Earlier, in August 1940, Convoy OB205 had contained, in addition to the Dutch liner *Volendam* already referred to, the Shell tanker

Anadara of 8,009 tons. Off Bloody Foreland just before midnight on the 30th she was hit by a torpedo from *U-59* (Matz). The tanker was outward bound in ballast but not gas-free, and the night was lit up by a huge sheet of flame, 'thousands of rivets being blown out and landing on the decks like the rattling of machine-gun fire'. She took in about three thousand tons of water and her hull was almost severed, but Captain J.T. Jones managed to bring his wounded ship into the Clyde, where she was temporarily repaired. Despite an immense gash in her side, sixty feet wide, with nothing between the keel and the water-line on one side, she was afterwards rebuilt at Falmouth, only to be lost later in the war.

The *San Demetrio* had sustained similar severe damage from the *Admiral Scheer*'s 11-inch shells. Built for the Eagle Oil Company in 1938 and grossing 8,073 tons with a deadweight of 12,132, she was commanded by Captain G. Waite, 'a ruddy jovial man' who had been torpedoed when in command of the *San Alberto*. The *San Alberto* had broken in half, and the unsuccessful attempt made by Waite and his men to steam the after-part back to Britain had won Waite the OBE. His new command, the *San Demetrio*, had loaded her homeward cargo at Aruba; it consisted of 11,200 tons of petrol.

At 16.30 on Tuesday 5 November, as the *Admiral Scheer* intercepted Convoy HX84, the *San Demetrio* had obeyed Commodore Maltby's order to alter course to starboard and his almost simultaneous order to scatter. Waite had increased speed to the ship's maximum of 13.5 knots and headed away on a course of ESE, unable to 'alter any more to the southward as we were baulked by other ships in the convoy. The weather was fair, moderate sea, and wind Force 4. It was getting dusk when we saw the raider engage the *Jervis Bay*, after which he tackled the *Rangitiki* and then turned his attention to the *Cornish City*. Following this he commenced firing on the *Trewellard* and from what we could see she appeared to take a very heavy hammering,' reported Second Officer A.G. Hawkins, whose station was aft. From here he got off two shots from the 4.7-inch gun on the tanker's poop, but it was growing dark and Waite ordered him to cease firing, so as not to draw attention to his ship. Instead, Hawkins was told to drop six smoke floats overboard, and these 'worked very successfully'.

Waite now altered course to ENE. The *Admiral Scheer* was a 'blurred shape' about eight miles distant, but a moment later the *San Demetrio* was straddled by two successive salvos. A shell in the third salvo struck the tanker's bow about two feet above the water-line, killing the lookout, Able Seaman E. Daines. Another hit her amidships, destroying the radio room and killing the radio officers transmitting Waite's RRRR signal. It was now almost dark, and Waite stopped his engines and ordered the ship abandoned before her cargo could ignite. There were now no direct hits on the *San*

Demetrio, but bursting shell splinters were a danger as Chief Officer Wilson and Hawkins strove to lower the midships boats.

Hawkins 'got nine men into the boat, and then as there didn't appear to be anyone else . . . I climbed in myself and was just about to lower away when someone shouted to me to hold on a moment. I waited and then took another six men on board whom I believe were the overflow from one of the other boats. The Captain, who was still on deck, told me to carry on, and so I lowered away.' The ship, though her engines were stopped, was still moving, but Hawkins managed to get his boat unhooked and sheered off from the *San Demetrio*'s side. 'The shell fire was getting heavier and so we thought it best to get away from the ship and in doing so we lost contact with the other boat and never saw it again.'

From the heaving perspective of the lifeboat Hawkins could see four other ships on fire in the vicinity, and within ten minutes of his boat getting clear the *Admiral Scheer*'s guns 'registered a direct hit on our ship with a really heavy salvo', setting her ablaze. At this point Hawkins was almost run down by an unidentified merchant ship from the convoy. This may have been the *Beaverford*, for she too was on fire within a short space of time.

Krancke fired star-shell for a while but soon retired, leaving the boats of the *San Demetrio* on the heaving ocean. It now came on to blow, and to blow hard. Still within sight of his own burning vessel, Hawkins streamed a sea-anchor and raised a canopy forward; then, at about 01.00 on the 6th, the fires on the *San Demetrio* vanished, extinguished, they assumed, by her sinking. 'Everyone in the boat behaved splendidly, and magnificent assistance was rendered by one member of the crew who had previously been a Shetland fisherman and who knew more about sailing than the rest of us put together.' This was Callum Macneil, who at 26 was the same age as Hawkins.

The following morning they caught sight of what they thought was one of the Swedish ships in the convoy, probably the *Stureholm*, but lost her again in a rain squall. As the hours dragged by the weather eased until, to their amazement, they saw a tanker about six miles away. All hands were put to the oars, and at 17.00 they were close enough to see that she was their own ship. The *San Demetrio* was 'still burning furiously and there was a lot of oil on the water', so Hawkins decided to remain in the boats and heave-to until the following morning, in the hope that the fire would abate. All aboard the lifeboat were now thoroughly seasick, so this was not a decision that found universal favour, but Hawkins was apparently vindicated when at 03.00 the fire suddenly flared up and the vessel seemed to settle more by the head. However, at daybreak the ship had vanished.

With a westerly wind of Force 5 Hawkins decided to hoist sail, and 'about six and a half hours later we sighted our vessel again. We decided to board her immediately, and in drawing alongside we shipped quite a lot of water.' An attempt to secure their only boat failed, and they lost her as she drifted away. While Hawkins and the seamen fought the fires they found still burning in the stern, Chief Engineer Pollard, Third Engineer Mr G. Willey, Storekeeper J. Davies and Greaser J. Boyle went below. Here they found the engine room flooded and the port boiler out of commission, but the auxiliary generators were undamaged. Meanwhile Hawkins found that 'amidships was still smouldering and all the metal work was red hot, so we immediately threw buckets of water on it.' The accommodation here had been gutted by fire, there was extensive shell damage, and petrol lay in pools upon the heat-buckled deck-plating; extraordinarily, it had failed to ignite. Part of the crew accommodation was still burning and they used fire extinguishers, for which they had 36 refills, to attack the flames, which they eventually succeeded in dousing. 'After we had put out the fire we discovered four cases of eggs which had been baked, and a joint of beef which had been cooked. The eggshells were of course blackened by the fire, but they proved to be edible, and after cutting off the outside of the beef we ate that too and enjoyed it. All day long we were exceedingly busy, but everyone worked with a will, and it was surprising how they all adapted themselves.'

By 17.00 that evening Pollard and his team had raised 80 psi on the port boiler, and could therefore run the generators and pumps. The work in the engine room had been Herculean, for the fire raging above the space had made it almost unbearably hot, though 'the shell holes gave us a certain amount of ventilation'. Pollard discovered the main engine to be serviceable, and when the fire-damaged emergency after steering had been repaired a control system was extemporised to enable 'the Engine Room to take orders from the deck'. At 02.30 on 8 November the *San Demetrio* slowly forged ahead, once more under command.

The weather, which had been reasonable during the previous day, now turned foul. A magnetic compass they had hoped to use was found to have been damaged by blast, and Hawkins was compelled to steer by instinct, the wind, and an occasional glimpse of stars through the dense clouds overhead. She was under way, but the *San Demetrio* was labouring, down by the head, and shipping water. 'Every time she rolled petrol came gushing up on deck as the . . . tanks were badly holed. Luckily . . . [Hawkins] had No. 6 Tank empty so decided to run petrol from for'ard and so threw her head up a little.' Pollard and Apprentice Jones went down into the pump rooms 'which were full of gas' to transfer petrol and give the ship a starboard list which 'lifted her head considerably. She rode much better after that and shipped much less water.'

During a slight lull Hawkins sent four of his able seamen to plug the shell- and splinter-holes in the deck above the tanks. The fearsome nature of this task may be judged from the fact that even under the most auspicious of normal conditions a laden tanker's deck will be awash during a winter crossing of the North Atlantic; it possibly explains why the petrol had failed to ignite. One able seaman 'was an American sailor and although he was up to his neck in water most of the time whilst he was plugging the holes he was infectiously cheerful the whole time and did much towards keeping up the spirit of the men.' This man, actually a Canadian named Oswald Preston, had until the disaster occurred done 'no avoidable work . . . and [had] seemed to look on working his passage rather in the light of a pleasure cruise.' Among the other tasks Hawkins's men undertook was the painting of 'SOS' and 'HELP' in large, crude letters on the superstructures.

Apart from the eggs and beef they had been living on tinned food, fearful of lighting the galley range. Pollard, a resourceful man, then cooked a pot-mess of potatoes and onions by injecting steam into a bucket, and with this and a large number of loaves baked the day before the attack the ravenous young and active men assuaged their hunger. One of their number, the greaser John Boyle, then complained of feeling unwell. Hawkins was aware that he had suffered some injury jumping into the lifeboat but had no real idea of his plight until after he expired at 04.00 on Monday 11 November, when they discovered that the poor fellow had been slowly dying of an internal haemorrhage.

Although he was 'steering by the wake and wind' Hawkins estimated making landfall on the evening of the following day. When they did not, the failure cast a gloom over the ship, but the next day they did come in sight of land: the mouth of Blacksod Bay on the coast of Co. Mayo in Eire, within sight of the Black Rock lighthouse. It was night when they closed the coast and tried signalling with a torch, but they received no reply from the lighthouse.[24]

Hawkins decided 'to cruise around the bay', and they buried Boyle beneath its waters. At daybreak the salvage tug *Superman* appeared, but Hawkins declined her offer of a tow. The cost might have been prohibitive, and they were not actually in need of salvaging since they had themselves already achieved that objective and the ship was under her own power. A little later, first a Hudson roared overhead and then the destroyer *Arrow* appeared, signalling that she would escort them to the Clyde. Hawkins indicated that they did not want to proceed that day because of the damage to the fore part of the ship, and because Pollard wanted to carry out some further remedial work on the engines. They accepted the assistance of a naval working party, however, and Pollard took them below, where temporary repairs were effected by men whose adaptability, Pollard thought, was 'simply wonderful. I had an idea they hadn't had much to do with Diesel engines before, but the way they tackled the job was . . . marvellous.' Assistance was also rendered by Second Officer Morfee, Second Engineer Caizley, Third Engineer Drever and Fourth Engineer Semple, survivors from the *Empire Wind* who had been picked up by the destroyer. The *Arrow* 'also sent over watch-keeping officers, Lt Aikin, Sub Lt Curd, and one Merchant Navy Officer RNR in addition to six engine room ratings.'

Led by HMS *Arrow*, the *San Demetrio* entered the Clyde wearing her ensign at half mast in honour of Greaser Boyle, and International Code Flag 'B' indicating that she bore a dangerous cargo. At Rothesay a Dutch salvage tug under British Admiralty orders came alongside and provided auxiliary steam to enable the *San Demetrio* to handle her own cargo, and after berthing at Bowling on the afternoon of Tuesday 19 November she discharged almost 11,000 tons of petrol. In their combined report Hawkins and Pollard singled out Bosun Fletcher, Third Engineer Willey, who had suffered from 'immersion foot' ever since leaving the lifeboat, and the Canadian Preston for particular commendation.

Of the others of the *San Demetrio*'s ship's company who had left the vessel on 5 November, Chief Officer Wilson, Second Engineer Duncan and Fifth Engineer Mockford were among those picked up by Smith's *Gloucester City*. Later they boarded Olander's *Stureholm* for the homeward passage, only to be lost with her. Captain Waite and his boat were also picked up by the *Gloucester City*, and landed at Newfoundland. After the *San Demetrio* had been repaired he returned to command her, but had left her by the time she was finally torpedoed and sunk in the Atlantic in March 1942.

Hawkins, Pollard and their small crew were awarded £14,700 salvage between them following a judgment in the Admiralty Court by Mr Justice Langton assisted by two Elder Brethren from Trinity House. Hawkins transferred to the Royal Naval Reserve, initially as a mere sub-lieutenant, and later in life became a Trinity House pilot. All the rest went back to sea save Preston, who was killed by a bomb when he was in London.

There is one last footnote to the story of HX84 which began with the gallant immolation of Fogarty Fegen's *Jervis Bay*, a requisitioned merchantman that sank with the Royal Navy's white ensign flying from her tall mast trucks, and ended with the quiet arrival in the Clyde of the burnt and twisted petrol-laden *San Demetrio*, her tattered red ensign at half mast and 'B' flag at her foremasthead, and it had nothing to do with either of these epics. Both were possessed of elements of glory, and both belong as much to Britain's maritime mythology as to her documented history.

The footnote is no gallant epic, simply the story of one young man, and of the social obscurity of the merchant seaman as a breed. The young man's name was Warwick Thomas Brookes and he had been a cadet aboard HMS *Conway*, passing out in mid class after being inspected by Earl Jellicoe in August 1929. It was the eve of the Great Depression and he was indentured to the Canadian Pacific Railway Company until November 1932, when he was obliged to sail as an able seaman since the company had no vacancy for a junior officer. At some time he married and tried working ashore for an engineering company as a capstan-hand, but by July 1937 he was back at sea though not on deck, having become a coal-trimmer – at least, that was what he was on the Articles, though his education enabled him to double as 'writer' to the chief engineer of the *Beaverburn*. By December 1939 he was doing this job for Chief Engineer Sinclair of the *Beaverford* when he obtained a pass from the company's marine superintendent generously allowing his wife to visit him 'from 9 a.m. to Noon' on the 1st of that month. ·

Eleven months later she was a widow. She received a cyclostyled message from the King. It read: 'The Queen and I offer you our heartfelt sympathy in your great sorrow. We pray that your country's gratitude for a life so nobly given in its service may bring you some measure of consolation.'

Mrs Brookes's country, in the form of its maritime bureaucracy at least, expressed itself less generously than her King and Queen. The Registrar-General of Shipping and Seamen certified that, according to his records, Warwick Thomas Brookes, aged 28, born Birkenhead and aboard the *Beaverford*, was 'supposed to have died on 5 November 1940 . . .'[25]

It could have been better done.

9

'One of the finest bits of seamanship'

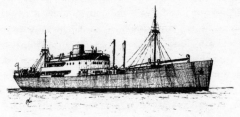

Vaalaren

THE PUBLIC IN Britain remained largely ignorant of both the contribution being made by the lowly merchant seafarer and the losses he was suffering. It was not in the interests either of the Government or of national morale to emphasise such 'noble gifts'; they were too numerous to be publicly aired as patriotic. The same merchant seamen who practised shooting down enemy aircraft in a primitive simulator set up in a warehouse in Liverpool were likely to be charged fares on the country's buses while those in the King's uniform were allowed to travel free by courtesy of the bus conductors. Later, when the dogged and steadfast image of the men who delivered bread and butter to the nation's breakfast tables was deemed to have a propaganda value, merchant seamen were issued with small metal lapel badges showing a knotted rope surrounding the initials 'M.N.' and topped with the naval crown.

Out in the Western Ocean the struggle had become, in the words of the first lieutenant of HM Corvette *Campanula*, Nicholas Monsarrat, 'a private war', one it was impossible to comprehend without personal experience. And if Winston Churchill himself, once so convinced of its efficiency, in due course asked 'Is the Asdic (sonar) any good?', he was not the only one. More pertinent and penetrating was the Prime Minister's second question: 'What do the escorts actually *do* when the convoy is attacked?'

No one seemed to know. Nor were the difficulties under which they laboured much appreciated. For them too, practice was limited to quayside simulation. One escort officer recalled that 'our great difficulty was the lack of opportunities for training . . . The best value we got was from a converted motor bus, which parked alongside the jetty in Liverpool and contained a [mechanical] teacher for representing attacks on submarines. There was great competition for this toy.'

Merchant masters had their own view of how things might be improved. A second mate who went to a convoy conference at Halifax early in 1941 recalled it being 'attended by Captains, navigators and senior radio operators, and addressed by Royal Navy Officers [and . . .] often stormy. Most Captains . . . strongly believed that if the convoy routes showed greater variation, there would be far fewer losses of merchant shipping . . . Nearly all agreed, and there was a lot of noise. The retired Admiral [the convoy commodore] . . . obviously had sympathy with the floor of the meeting and promised to forward our complaints . . .' And while 'merchant seamen were always ready to criticise any action of the Admiralty', the navy's own personnel often crossed swords between themselves.

One sloop commander, Thring of the *Deptford*, experienced difficulties in the early months of the war with a convoy commodore who was 'a very senior officer indeed'. The commodore – it was Dreyer – had expressed his opposition to Thring's intentions. 'I knew I was right,' the latter wrote, 'because the escorts received wireless signals which the Commodore did not get. After a considerable argument by light signal, I finally received the reply "I will obey your orders!" . . . It was much easier when we met [personally] at the [convoy] conference, because it gave an opportunity to work out plans for emergency, and to discuss methods of manoeuvring, zig-zagging and signalling which were not standardised at that time. Meeting a convoy at sea, when one often knew nothing about the character or the methods of the Commodore, was always a little difficult.'

The honest, candid and unembroidered reports of officers like Thring, and Churchill of the *Folkestone*, were raising doubts that spread a chill through the corridors of the Admiralty. There, the notion was gaining ground that in the U-boat the Germans possessed a war-winning weapon, and in Dönitz a man who knew how to wield it. What had once been a heresy was assuming the mantle of orthodoxy; the naval hierarchy were compelled to acknowledge that war was in fact a grubby business, its defeats marked as much by the dry numerical analyses of Professor Frederick Lindemann, head of the Prime Minister's Statistical Branch charged with monitoring the trends of the nation's war economy, as by the *Jervis Bay*'s glorious end. By the end of 1940 Lindemann's staff were demonstrating that stocks of imported food and raw materials were not being sustained by imports, which had fallen by one-quarter from their pre-war levels and currently stood at half what was required. It was a situation exacerbated by delays in the ports; Lindemann also informed Winston Churchill on 21 January 1941 that at the close of 1940 voyage times had increased by 50 per cent.

In addition to the sinkings in the North Atlantic, scores of merchant vessels had been lost to aircraft and mines in home waters. In the wider waters of the world, raiders like the *Komet*, *Pinguin* and *Atlantis* were still at large and busy sinking or capturing a succession of fine cargo-vessels. When the *Atlantis* seized the Blue Funnel liner *Automedon*, her boarding party discovered secret government documents relating to the defence of Singapore in the master's safe. Enemy aircraft were also enjoying successes in the North Atlantic, where on 11 November the small freighter *Balmore* was sunk by German aeroplanes with the loss of all hands. On the 13th the *Empire Wind*, on the 15th the Elder Dempster liner *Apapa*, and on the 18th the tramp *Nestlea* were all lost to patrolling FW200 Kondors.

Repeatedly, ships from the dispersing OB convoys were snapped up as they parted company off the aptly named Bloody Foreland, as were independents, stragglers and rompers passing the headland.[1] Kapitänleutnant Wohlfarth's *U-137* torpedoed the *Cape St Andrew* on the 13th, T. & J. Harrison's *Planter* on the 16th, and the *St Germain* and the Swedish steamship *Veronica* on the 17th. Captain A.R. Bebb of the *Cape St Andrew* and 14 of his men were killed and an attempt to tow the ballasted vessel failed, though the tug *Salvonia* rescued the rest.

Convoy SC11 was waylaid south of Rockall shortly before midnight on 22 November by Schepke in *U-100*. In short and devastating order, within the space of a few hours, he sank five ships. First to go was the British flagged *Justitia*, lost with a cargo of timber, turpentine and steel. Thirteen men died, including the master, Captain D.L. Davies, 26 were picked up by HMS *Enchantress*. Then the British tramp *Bradfyne* was lost with a cargo of grain, her Captain R.G. Vanner and 38 of her hands, though four were picked up by the *Norske King*, a Norwegian ship in convoy. Next the Norwegian ship *Bruse* was torpedoed and broke in two. Sixteen of her crew were killed and about half of her cargo of timber was lost, but her forward part, which remained afloat, was later salvaged and towed to Troon. Another Norwegian vessel, the *Salonica*, was lost with a cargo of pit-props and nine dead shortly before midnight. As the watches changed the Danish crew of the British-flagged *Leise Maersk* was even less fortunate, Captain P.K. Mortensen and 16 of his men being lost as their ship was torpedoed by Schepke; the *Leise Maersk* sank with her cargo of 4,500 tons of grain and general cargo, but a handful of her crew were picked up by a Dutch salvage tug sent out to recover the forward part of the *Bruse*. Finally, having stalked the convoy throughout the day, Schepke made his last attack that evening. The Dutch cargo vessel *Busum* was sent to the bottom with her cargo of 5,200 tons of grain, though her crew escaped with their lives. Convoy SC11 then lost one more vessel, the *Alma Dawson*, when she strayed into a British minefield on 24 November. Once again the escorts, outnumbering Schepke's sole U-boat, were left to pick up the pieces.

The brand-new Cardiff tramp *Daydawn* from Convoy OB244 was sunk by Schütze's *U-103* on 21 November south of Rockall. He next attacked the Greek steam-ship *Victoria* but was driven off by HM Corvette *Rhododendron*, Lieutenant Commander W.N.H. Faichney, which rescued the survivors from both ships. Schütze moved closer to the Irish coast and on the 27th sank the *Glenmoor* from OB248. Captain J. Young and 30 crew members were lost, two survivors were rescued by destroyers. The following morning Schütze torpedoed the Greek steam tramp *Mount Athos* with the loss of 19 lives and that evening the South American Saint Line's *St Elwyn*, killing the master, Captain E.T.A. Daniells, DSC and Bar, and 23 of his crew; 16 men were rescued by the homeward-bound British cargo ship *Leeds City*. Schütze was directed to join a group in an abortive ambush of Convoy SC13 and then headed for L'Orient, but late on 8 December *U-103* encountered the independently-sailing *Empire Jaguar* and torpedoed her. Captain H.T. Thomas and all hands went down with their ship. It proved a bad night and Schütze an efficient executioner, for within hours he also sank the *Calabria*, an Italian war prize under British India's house flag.[2] The 9,515-ton ship was homeward bound from India with a mixed cargo of general, 4,000 tons of iron, 3,050 tons of tea and 1,870 tons of oil-cake. She had joined Convoy SL56 at Freetown, but had apparently straggled when she fell foul of Schütze. In torpedoing her Schütze not only sent Captain D. Lonie and his large crew of 129 men to their deaths but also killed 230 supernumerary lascars being shipped to Britain to make up a crew for the *Varna*. The names of Lonie and his British officers apart, the list of these men, from Serang Fazal Bari x Reazuddin, by way of Tindals, Cassabs, Seacunnies, Bhandaries and Topasses, down through the ranks of the lowlier Lascars and Firemen to Mohammed Nokoo x Ansar Ali, Half General-Service Boy, is a testimony not so much to the British Empire as to India's own history. Among the names are those of Martin and Miranda, D'Silva, Fernandes, Pereira, Cardoze and Gomes. Muslims, Parsees, Hindus, Goan Roman Catholics – the whole spectrum of those from the sub-continent who went to sea under the British ensign is represented.[3]

As Schütze was sinking the *Glenmoor* on 27 November, Kapitänleutnant Jürst was on his first war patrol in *U-104*. That day he sank a straggler from HX88, T. & J. Harrison's liner *Diplomat*, Captain W.A. Hansen, who with 13 seamen lost his life; 40 of the crew were rescued from their boats by a destroyer, HMS *Active*. Jürst also damaged the large Hong Kong-registered tanker *Charles F. Meyer*, but she survived, whereas her attacker did not:

somewhere to the south and east of Rockall *U-104* disappeared. All 49 souls on board perished in a horror one cannot begin to imagine.

Yet another load of bananas was lost when *U-101* sank the *Aracataca* on 30 November in an attack on Convoy HX90. She was the first victim in an assault timed, to perfection, just after the ocean escort, the Armed Merchant Cruiser HMS *Forfar*, had turned north to meet Convoy OB251, but before HX90 had been met by the close escort from Liverpool, not due until noon of 2 December. Thirty-six men were lost with the *Aracataca*, but the rest of her crew were picked up from their boats by two outward-bound British ships. The Royal Mail liner *Potaro* landed Captain Brown and 16 men and a single passenger at Buenos Aires, while the remaining passenger and 15 crew were taken to Newfoundland in the British-operated but former Algerian-registered steamer *Djurdjura*.

Aboard *U-101* Frauenheim had been relieved by Kapitänleutnant Mengersen, and in the time during which he trailed the convoy he was joined by *U-47* (Prien) and *U-52* (Salman). In the small hours of 2 December, having manoeuvred into the convoy, Mengersen sank the motor-tanker *Appalachee*, Captain W. Armstrong, with the loss of seven men and 11,076 tons of aviation spirit and fuel oil. The Glasgow tramp *Loch Ranza* dropped out of her station to pick up Armstrong and his 30 men, and Mengersen fired a torpedo at her. Fortunately she was only damaged, and proceeded on her way, transferring the survivors to the corvette *Heliotrope* when the escort group arrived at about noon. Mengersen now torpedoed the wheat- and timber-laden *Lady Glanely* of Cardiff, sending her down with the loss of Captain A. Hughson and all hands. His last victim was the steamer *Kavak*, belonging to Moss, Hutchinson of Liverpool. A small ship built for the Mediterranean trade, under the exigencies of war she was now homeward bound from Demerara to Newport with a cargo of bauxite and pitch. Captain J. Napier and 24 men were lost, the destroyer *Viscount* picking up the remaining 16 later that day.

Prien had again been on weather-reporting duties when he heard Mengersen's call and joined battle against HX90. He arrived during the early hours of the 2nd and caught a straggler astern of the convoy, sinking her before damaging the Shell tanker *Conch*,[4] then on government service loaded with 11,214 tons of fuel oil for the Royal Navy. Later in the morning *U-95* joined the fray and fired three torpedoes into *Conch*. Under Kapitänleutnant Schreiber, *U-95* was on her first war patrol; on 27 November she had sunk the British-flagged but former Danish tramp *Irene Maria*, killing Captain Evers and his crew, and had also damaged the Norwegian steamer *Ringhorn*, both ships having broken away from Convoy OB248 earlier. Captain Graham and his ship's company abandoned the *Conch*, and were rescued by the Canadian destroyer *St Laurent*; the tanker finally succumbed to a salvo from Kretschmer, who in *U-99* encountered the derelict on the forenoon of 3 December.

The previous day Kretschmer had sunk yet another Armed Merchant Cruiser, HMS *Forfar*, late escort to HX90, and the Norwegian general cargo-ship *Samnanger*. There were no survivors from the latter, but although Acting Captain N.A.C. Walker and 171 officers and ratings were lost from the *Forfar*, the destroyers *Viscount* and *St Laurent* and the British merchant ship *Dursley* picked up between them 309 of her people.[5]

Kapitänleutnant Salman in *U-52* had joined his colleagues hovering around HX90 during the night of 1/2 December. Attacking after midnight he sank the *Tasso*, a small vessel built in 1938 for Ellerman's Wilson Line. She bore a load of 1,300 tons of greenheart logs from South America and all hands escaped, Captain W.A. Thompson and his men being picked up by *Viscount*. Salman had not finished, however, and next sank the *Goodleigh*, like the *Lady Glanely* a two-year-old tramp-ship owned by Tatem's of Cardiff. Like her sister-ship she was carrying spelter and timber, but her Captain W.W. Quaitre and his crew escaped destruction and joined the throng crowding the mess-decks of the elderly *Viscount*. Salman's final thrust at HX90 was an attack on the *Durnsley*, which he damaged but failed to sink, leaving her to continue her passage.

One last U-boat joined the group, *U-94* under Kapitänleutnant Kuppisch, who sank the *Stirlingshire*, Captain C.E. O'Byrne. The ship went down with a cargo of sugar, lead, general and frozen foodstuffs, though all hands were taken up by *Empire Puma*, an ex-American standard ship in the convoy. The last vessel to be lost out of Convoy HX90 was the *Wilhelmina* of Glasgow, carrying 6,400 tons of general cargo, including fish and wood pulp loaded in British Columbia. The corvette *Gentian* rescued Captain J.B. Rue and 33 of his crew, but five men went down with the ship. She too had been sunk by Kuppisch.

Other ships were lost in the Atlantic before the end of the year: the *Oakcrest, King Idwal, Tymeric*, the Greek-flagged *Kolchis* and Swedish *Anten* to *U-123* (Moehle); *Pacific President* and the tanker *Victor Ross* to Lüth's *U-43*, the tanker with all hands; the cargo-liner *Silverpine* to an Italian submarine, the *Argo*; the *Ashcrest* to *U-140*; and north-west of the Hebrides, *U-96* sank the New Zealand Shipping Company's fine cargo-liner the *Rotorua*.

The *Rotorua*, Captain E.R. Kemp, had Commodore J.U.P. Fitzgerald and his staff embarked and was central to Convoy HX92. The order was given to abandon ship, but while 139 of her crew were rescued by the escorts, Fitzgerald and his naval staff, Captain Kemp and 17 of his crew including two naval gunners died. Kemp 'was last seen making his way forward from the gun platform just before the ship sank. There was a heavy sea running at the time . . .' The ship's chief steward survived and reported that when they abandoned ship Kemp 'was then perfectly calm and at his post of duty on the bridge doing all possible to get his crew to the comparative safety of the lifeboats. By doing so he enabled a very large percentage . . . to gain safety . . . We all regret the loss of a gallant and very popular commander.'

Two of the *Rotorua*'s crew were picked up by *U-96*, and that evening, still shadowing the convoy, she torpedoed the Dutch ship *Towa*; it was Kapitänleutnant Lehmann-Willenbrock who also accounted for the sinking of the gallant Olander's *Stureholm* in the early hours of the following morning. He went on to sink the Belgian *Macedonier* before leaving the convoy and attacking west-bound vessels, torpedoing the *Western Prince* and firing at the *Empire Razorbill*, which escaped with damage. Lehmann-Willenbrock fired *U-96*'s last torpedo at the Dutch tanker *Pendrecht*, but she too was only battered.

In mid December, operating between Iceland and Rockall, Schepke, in *U-100*'s fifth war patrol, sank the *Kyleglen, Euphorbia* and *Napier Star* with appalling loss of life from all three ships. The weather was bad, a near SSW'ly gale with a heavy, breaking sea, drizzling rain and a low, racing scud. At 15.55, just as the darkness was gathering, Schepke's torpedo blew in the port side of the *Napier Star*, and in almost total darkness Captain W. Walsh ordered his ship abandoned. By the light of torches and with great difficulty four boats were lowered and were seen to pull away from the ship, into which Schepke now fired another torpedo. The *Napier Star* went down shortly afterwards. The only boat to survive was that of Second Officer J.W. Thompson, who had 20 people on board, six of them passengers, including three women, while the majority of the crew were catering staff. The wind freshened during the night, increasing the seas, which broke on board and 'filled the boat to the thwarts, so that they had to bale for their lives. Everyone was drenched through and the bitter cold was numbing. Nearly everyone was seasick . . . They used what blankets they had for covering the women; but there were not enough to go round.' When the sea-anchor carried away and before an extempore affair of two lashed oars could be got over the side, the boat broached and almost capsized in a breaking sea. Before dawn four men had died of hypothermia, and a fifth expired later that afternoon. All were committed to the deep by Thompson, who recited what he could recall of the burial service. Another night passed, but although they were reduced to a state of extreme privation no further deaths had occurred, and shortly after dawn they saw the lights of a ship. It proved to be the neutral Swedish steam ship *Vaalaren*, which was sailing independently and seeking neither to hide her identity nor take advantage of convoy.

Considerable difficulty was experienced in getting the survivors on board, most being too weak to climb the rope ladders or the cargo nets thrown over the topsides so that they had to be hauled up by rope, an unpleasant experience.

On Christmas Day *U-95* torpedoed Shaw, Savill & Albion's *Waiotira* as she was proceeding independently from Australia to Britain. She was a brand-new, fast, refrigerated cargo-liner, and although attempts were made to save her overnight and her radio officer remained on board to the last, she was despatched next day by Liebe's *U-38*. All except for one passenger were saved by the timely arrival of the destroyer *Mashona*.

Laden with phosphates the tramp *Amicus*, lagging astern of Convoy SC15, was sent to the bottom by Capitano di Fregata Tossoni-Pittoni of the Italian submarine *Alpino Attilio Bagnolini*, while a second Italian submarine, the *Calvi*, sank the tramp *Carlton* and a cargo of coal. A third, the *Enrico Tazzoli*, sank the coal-laden *Ardanbhan* off Iceland. In all cases the loss of life was extensive. Off Freetown on Christmas Eve *U-65* sank the tanker *British Premier*. She contained 8,000 tons of Iraqi crude oil. Captain F. Dalziel and 31 men were killed, a few were picked up by a cruiser, and the rest spent 41 days in a boat before the destroyer *Faulknor* rescued them. After sinking the *British Premier* Stockhausen's *U-65* went on to sink her sister tanker the *British Zeal*, the Norwegian *Risanger* and, on 2 January 1941, the British-India liner *Nalgora*, whose master, Captain A.D. Davies, was rescued along with 101 of her crew and three passengers after spending eight days in their boats.

To this disastrous list for the closing weeks of 1940 must be added the losses by mine and to aircraft, the sinkings in seas and oceans other than the North Atlantic, and the ships damaged or even sunk in port, the fate of Ellerman's Wilson liner the *Silvio*, which was bombed in Alexandra Dock during an air raid on the city of Liverpool. In early December the *W. Hendrik* was sent to the bottom off the west coast of Ireland by an FW200 Kondor. German aircraft also sank the small tanker *Osage* off Wicklow, while off Wexford other enemy aeroplanes, having attacked British lightvessels and their servicing tenders in the North Sea, sank the Liverpool-registered but Irish-manned and Dublin-based lighthouse tender *Isolda*, belonging to the Commissioners of Irish Lights.

Meanwhile the heavy cruiser *Admiral Hipper* had sailed on a sortie and the *Admiral Scheer*, along with the Kriegsmarine's other commerce-raiders, was still busy in her work, taking the cargo-liner *Duquesa* off St Paul's Rocks on 18 December.

If not quite imperceptible, Royal Navy success against this onslaught was certainly poor. A few German blockade-runners had been intercepted; off

Bordeaux the British submarine *Thunderbolt* had sunk the Italian submarine *Tarantini*; but as far as the Atlantic theatre was concerned, the turn of the year marked nothing but continuing losses for the merchant shipping of Britain, her friends and Allies. What minor triumphs there were largely belonged to the merchantmen – those grim struggles for survival of which only the echoes are discernible in the reports made to Commander Holbrook long afterwards at the Admiralty. But there were other triumphs too, such as the saving of the *Orari*.

A 10,350-ton fast diesel-powered cargo-liner belonging to the New Zealand Shipping Company, the *Orari* was homeward bound from Australia with a mixed frozen, chilled and general cargo when on 13 December, about 450 miles west of Cape Clear, she was torpedoed by Lüth's *U-43*.

The weather was poor and the *Orari* emerged from a rain squall to find a submarine on the surface close ahead of her. The general alarms were rung, the water-tight doors were closed, and Captain N. Rice attempted to take evasive action. As he swung *Orari*'s head to starboard, Lüth fired both his bow tubes, which ran towards the liner while she was turning under full helm. *Orari* swung towards the quartering seas and rolled heavily to port, her bow climbing to meet the oncoming wave, her stern sinking into the preceding trough. It was at this point that a torpedo struck her, high up on her port side; the second torpedo counter-mined, its warhead inexplicably detached from the weapon's propulsion system which, even more incredibly, landed on No. 4 Hatch as water poured over the ship's afterdecks. Deluged by water, the gun's crew on the poop loosed off a shot at the surfaced U-boat, which shortly afterwards disappeared, partly hidden when the smoke floats kept aft were activated.

Nursing his stricken ship through the heavy seas and concerned about the difficulty of abandoning her in such conditions, Rice waited for the reports of damage to come in. Already his cargo could be seen, buoyant cases of butter, frozen sheep carcases and granulated cork insulation, bobbing astern in the *Orari*'s wake as the seas washed in and out of her after-holds and 'tween-decks. Rice was informed that the two shaft tunnels were flooded, and the after engine-room bulkhead was leaking. The engineers were covering the auxiliary generators with tarpaulins supplied by the bosun, trying to maintain power for the pumps, which had all been opened up to draw on the after bilge lines. It was found, however, that the dislodged insulation was not all washing astern: a good deal of it was choking the strums. Nevertheless, with frequent stops for clearing the roses pumping went on. Since No. 6 Hold remained intact, the after well deck was soon raised above sea level. Best of all, none of her people had been hurt.

Rice now resolved that since the best lifebelt to hand was *Orari* herself, they should get her home. By means of patient coaxing, and partly hidden by the poor weather and the long hours of gloom or darkness at the winter solstice, Rice and his ship's company made the Clyde with a heavy port list and drawing 45 feet aft, only to find that the defensive boom was closed and that no pilot would board the ship that night. One can only imagine the feelings of those aboard *Orari* as she remained off Ailsa Craig until dawn on 17 December, when she was finally anchored at the Tail of the Bank and, in this 'emergency port', discharged much of her cargo into lighters and puffers.[6]

It was conduct of this kind which moved Sir Alexander Cadogan to note in his diary at the end of the year: 'I am amazed at the courage of my fellow-countrymen. Everything on paper is against us, but we shall live. I don't frankly see how we are going to win, but I am convinced we shall not lose. And if you hang on – like a bulldog – it's funny what things do happen.'[7]

Abstract convictions are one thing; elsewhere brutal facts were prevailing. On 22 December 1940 Admiral Dunbar-Nasmith, Commander-in-Chief, Western Approaches, informed the First Sea Lord that 'the convoy system is now failing'.[8]

The loss of the *Nalgora* on 2 January 1941 set the tone for the New Year. She was the last of eight ships Stockhausen sank on his sixth and last patrol in command in *U-65*. Two of his victims were tankers and he damaged a third, the *British Zeal*, on the last day of 1940. Stockhausen had been operating off Freetown, and was twice replenished by the *Nordmark* off the Cape Verde Islands. The *Nalgora* was outward bound from Leith and Rosyth, where she had loaded government supplies consisting chiefly of boom defence equipment intended for Alexandria Harbour, base of the British Mediterranean Fleet. Although it was dark, the sea was smooth as Captain A.D. Davies ordered all hands into the boats. The purser, who was partially deaf, felt the ship give a 'big lurch' and only realised he was in trouble when his cabin door slammed shut and jammed. This was a commonplace when a ship's hull had been stressed by a torpedo explosion, and 'escape panels' which could be kicked out in an emergency were cut in the bottom of cabin doors.

Stockhausen found that his victim did not sink immediately. Short of torpedoes, he surfaced and fired into the *Nalgora* over the terrified heads of her crew huddling in the boats, and soon set the ship ablaze. Later, survivors reported having been fired at with machine-guns before *U-65* disappeared. The occupants of two of the boats were picked up a couple of days later by two British ships, one outward- and one homeward-bound. The others had a longer ordeal. Captain Davies, meeting the second officer's boat the next day, combined the two parties, which totalled 19 and included the ship's cat. He attempted to set sail for the Cape Verde Islands but found the boat's rudder was inexplicably missing. It was discovered at daylight, having provided a bed for the lascar donkeyman, who produced it with a flourish. The passage lasted eight days, during which they were followed by a shark but nevertheless managed to scoop some tiny fish from the sea for the cat. The shark was finally driven off by a few thrusts of a boathook wielded by Davies, who later reported with admirable detachment that 'in more favourable circumstances' the passage 'would have been very interesting as the water teemed with marine life'. All 105 of *Nalgora's* people survived, but they were scattered between Freetown, Glasgow and São Antonio: a small detail, but one that spelled disruption and difficulty for their employers, and constituted a minor but troublous hampering of the war effort.

Every arm of the German Kriegsmarine was now favoured by fortune, even its uneasy and frequently unco-operative ally the Luftwaffe seemingly blessed after Dönitz had finally persuaded Goering to permit Kapitän Fliegel's Kampfgeschwader 20, operating from the Bordeaux area, to fly under his orders. In the North West Approaches, too, Kondors flying from Norway sank the Blue Funnel liner *Clytoneus* on the 8th, the grain-laden *Temple Mead* on the 21st, the cargo ships *Lurigethan, Langleegorse* and *Mostyn* off Ireland on the 23rd, the *Grelrosa* on the 28th, the *Pandion* the following day, and Andrew Weir's *Rowanbank* on the 31st. Even a rescue ship, the poor little *Beachy*, was sent to the sea-bed by German aircraft in the first weeks of the New Year. Raiders were equally successful during January; in the high latitudes of the South Atlantic the *Pinguin* captured an entire Norwegian whaling fleet, the factory ships *Pelagos* and *Ole Wegger*, the supply-ship *Solglimt* and eleven whale-catchers.[9] Further north a few days later Krancke's *Admiral Scheer* took Billmeir's *Stanpark*, and on the same day the *Komoran* sank two fine cargo-liners, the *Afric Star* and the *Eurylochus*, off the Cape Verde Islands.

The *Kormoran*, Kapitänleutnant Detmers, was the 18-knot cargo-liner *Steiermark* formerly belonging to the Hamburg–Amerika Linie. Built in 1938, she had been constructed from the first with a view to becoming a commerce-raider, and was a faster ship than the Blue Star liner *Afric Star*, homeward bound from Rio de Janeiro with a full cargo of frozen meat, a crew of 72, a pair of gunners and two female passengers. The two ships hove in sight of one another on the morning of 29 January, the *Kormoran*, under Soviet Russian colours and masquerading as the *Vyatcheslav Molotov*, keeping distant company until 14.00, when Detmers increased speed and rapidly closed the *Afric Star*. Captain C.R. Cooper had little option but to take to his boats as Detmers struck the Hammer and Sickle, hoisted the Swastika and unmasked his guns. A brisk fire soon set the *Afric Star* alight and, having abandoned ship, Cooper and his men were taken on board the *Kormoran*.

That same evening the raider came in sight of the Blue Funnel liner *Eurylochus* which was bound towards Suez by way of Takoradi on the then Gold Coast (now Ghana). She was proceeding alone with a cargo of military supplies, the most important items of which were 16 bombers for the Middle East theatre. The *Eurylochus* was not a standard Holt ship, for she had been built in 1912 as the *Indraghiri* and became a Blue Funnel ship when Alfred Holt acquired the Indra Line. One of her crew, a seaman named Frank Laskier, thought the old ship the happiest he ever sailed in.[10]

Laskier was dreaming away his watch beside the gun on the poop. Below him the rumble of the propeller occasionally caused the ship to judder as her stern rose a little on a swell, while the noisy wake boiled out astern. There was an occasional groan as the steering gear shifted the rudder a point or two at the behest of the Chinese quartermaster in the distant wheelhouse. The sunset had been spectacularly tropical, and Laskier had now lost sight of the dolphins which had been gambolling in the old ship's wake, but could hear *The Missouri Waltz* being played on a portable gramophone owned by one of the midshipmen. The chief officer, Mr J.A.C. McGregor, was making his night rounds of the upper deck in accordance with Holt's regulations while on the bridge his watch-mate, Fourth Officer A.C. Sparks, had the con. It was about 18.30 and quite dark when 'suddenly from the starboard beam' there was the detonation of a gun and the *Eurylochus* lay exposed on the black ocean by a star-shell flare.

Sparks hit the alarms, warning the stoke-hold and the engine room. Then he rang the poop. Captain A.M. Caird's large figure loomed on the bridge to order his radio officers to transmit the raider signal and ship's position.[11] The message, monitored by *Kormoran*'s own radio staff, provided Detmers with his pretext to engage; the German 5.9-inch-calibre guns were laid at almost point-blank range and began shelling the *Eurylochus*. On the poop the telephone rang: with a thumping heart Laskier grabbed it and received the order to open fire. Using the third person, Laskier later vividly described his part in the brief but desperate action:

He was at the gun, opened the breech and grabbed the rammer. Smack. His shoulders cracked under the effort as he rammed the shell home. Back to the canister, out with a charge, put it in, slip in a [firing] tube, slam the breach. The ship was being rent and torn . . . Round to the trainer – his shoes split as he braced his feet to the deck and his shoulder to the barrel, and swung the [traversing] wheel. Round she came. The cold, merciless eye of the searchlight came across his sights. Duck under the muzzle, set the range, bring her down. She's there, she's there, she's there . . . and she's there. Pull the trigger. Crash went the gun; and the deck came up in a heave as the recoil gripped the straining girders of the ship.

On the bridge Caird had tried to dodge the fall of shot as the crew of his ancient 4.7-inch weapon joined Laskier and returned fire with four more rounds. Below them the *Eurylochus*'s Chinese crew were spilling out of their accommodation in the poop onto the after well deck, joined by those on watch in the engine room where, although the engineers all mustered, most of the Chinese 'just vanished'. The fourth engineer became the messenger to the bridge, the communications and telegraphs having been destroyed. 'Then the world opened in one great blinding flash . . .', Laskier was flung across the deck and when he picked himself up 'the gun was lying on its side', the ship was on fire and the engine had stopped. The *Kormoran*'s shells and the splinters they threw up had wrought havoc among the Chinese exposed on deck, and the chief officer was also wounded.

As the power failed and the ship slowed, Sparks tried using the battery-powered Aldis lamp to signal to the *Kormoran* that the ship was sinking, lifeboats had been destroyed, and the Germans should cease fire. Although the signal was acknowledged it brought little respite, for the *Eurylochus* was now raked with machine-gun fire so vicious that both Laskier and Caird thought that *Kormoran* was being supported by her supply ship and they were being shot at from two sides. With the *Eurylochus* reduced to a shambles, Caird gave the command to leave her. As the crew mustered at their boat stations he made a round of the upper deck and, finding the chief officer, carried him down to the after well deck, from where access to the boats would be easier for the incapacitated. He then went back to the bridge to reassure himself that the confidential books had been dumped. With the boats gone and the lowering parties in two of them now swimming along-side, Caird saw to it that two rafts were got over the side from the after-deck. Another shell exploded amidships and the *Eurylochus* began to settle quickly. Caird and the last of his men went overboard, and a moment later the ship reared up vertically to sink stern first with a loud submarine deton-ation caused by the boiler exploding.

In the chaos of the sinking Laskier, who had been severely wounded in one leg, made for the after well deck, from where Chief Officer McGregor, 'his clothes torn, his leg shattered, his shoulder broken and his spine hit', was assisted over the side by Mr McDavid, the second engineer. Laskier himself 'leaned his belly over the rail, put his hands over and grabbed the lower bar. Pulled – harder, harder. His legs came down over and he fell with a splash into the water . . .' Laskier was dragged onto one of the two rafts bobbing alongside, where he found Second Steward R. Harvey with a bottle of rum. With the end of his shattered leg hanging in the water, Laskier took a swig. Soon afterwards the raft was cut adrift from the sinking ship and they too watched her go down, venting oil and steam. As 'she mounted high in the air, she bowed to the sky. Then with a roar, as of hatred and vengeance, she slipped under. The huge wave of her sinking rose and engulfed the survivors. The raft overturned.'

In an access of terror at the thought of sharks, the men scrambled back on the two rafts, one of the radio officers being rescued by Midshipman Hay. Soon afterwards the *Kormoran*'s searchlight went off and they were left alone. Caird brought the two rafts together and had them lashed. Daylight showed them to be 28 in number, with McGregor, Laskier and a third man 'in bad shape'. As the sun rose they began to be affected by the heat. They could not take it in turns to hang on the side of the rafts because sharks were circling them. McDavid sat with a small paddle, smacking at the sharks to drive them away as, '[b]lue, green and grey . . . they swept up from the depths of the ocean . . . [making a] rasping . . . sound as they scraped along the bottom of the raft.' Nor could the survivors reach the canisters containing provisions, since the capsize had left them underwater.

The first night passed, and by the second day it was clear the rafts were losing buoyancy. A fact Laskier thought it worth recording was that 'throughout the whole of that time, the Skipper was never referred to as anything other than "Sir".' Another was that '[t]here were no complaints. There were no faintings. We stuck it.'[12] Nevertheless, things were looking very bleak until at 11.00 smoke was sighted, and Midshipman Hay waved his shirt frantically to attract attention. A little later the Spanish tramp *Monte Teide* of Bilbao fell alongside them and they were taken inboard, the wounded hoisted in a large wicker fish basket lowered over the ship's side by a derrick runner. Capitan P. Munecas searched the area but found only wreckage and the two empty lifeboats left by Detmers.

Later that same day the *Monte Teide* came in sight of the Armed Merchant Cruiser *Bulolo*, sent in search of the *Kormoran*. The wounded and eight of the British survivors were transferred aboard her, Laskier to have his leg amputated. Caird and Chief Engineer Mr H. Creech remained in the *Monte Teide* and accompanied the Chinese, 'who were in a bad frame of mind', to Buenos Aires. There was a tendency for Chinese crews to think they were under threat when in lifeboats, which perhaps stemmed from a cultural fear of being abandoned, but although the tone of contemporary reports was often bigoted and their use of language insensitive by today's standards, there is little real evidence to suggest non-Europeans *in extremis* were treated any differently from Europeans.[13]

In his report Caird commended the conduct of Hay for his rescue of the junior radio officer, of Harvey for tending the wounded, and of McGregor. Nor could he 'speak too highly' of the care they received aboard the *Monte Teide*. Characteristically, the senior manager of Alfred Holt & Company, Mr Lawrence Holt, wrote to the *Monte Teide*'s owners, Naviera Aznar SA of Bilbao, expressing how 'profoundly moved he was' by Munecas's 'skilful seamanship and noble humanity.' Holt, head of a company run on patriarchal lines, was worried about the losses of men in boats, and established a training school at Aberdovey in mid Wales where all Blue Funnel officers and men went to hone their small-boat skills. While most deck officers had been instructed in boat-handling during their cadet training aboard HMSs *Conway* and *Worcester* and while in service with the line itself, such skills were not widespread in other departments. As a result of Laurence Holt's initiative, the survival rates in Blue Funnel and Glen Line crews were good, and several lengthy voyages were successfully made in the company's ships' lifeboats.[14]

Detmers later testified that he raked the *Eurylochus* with machine-gun fire because of her continuing radio transmissions and only *after* her crew had abandoned her in two of her four lifeboats. He also claimed to have sent a boarding-party to place detonating charges and, when these did not sink the ship, to have fired a torpedo; too late he then saw a third boat still alongside, and realised the torpedo's explosion would kill the occupants. In fact, only the two lifeboats from the unengaged side could possibly have been launched, and there seems to be no evidence that the *Eurylochus* was ever boarded. Detmers did however pick up some survivors from the two boats, three British and 39 Chinese, though 11 men had been killed in the shelling.[15]

A few days later the prisoners from both the *Eurylochus* and the *Afric Star* were put aboard the *Nordmark*, now masquerading under the Stars and Stripes as the United States merchantman *Dixie* but still loitering in support of Stockhausen and his colleagues as they attacked the southern convoy routes. These men were next transferred to the *Portland*, a captured British ship under the German flag bound from Chile to Bordeaux and now bearing 327 prisoners-of-war. The *Portland* suffered a mysterious fire, thought to have been the work of the prisoners; her crew extinguished it and subsequently shot one passenger and one seaman from the *Afric Star*. The ship arrived at Bordeaux and landed her prisoners for further transfer to Milag Nord, the prison camp for merchant service personnel near Bremerhaven in north-east Germany where most of them sat out the war. One deck boy named King, being a minor, was repatriated by way of Naples, Istanbul, Alexandria and Cape Town.

Three able seamen, Fry, Lynch and Merrett, had indeed attempted to set fire to the *Portland*, hoping in the aftermath to overwhelm the crew and take over the ship. Fry was later sentenced to death by the Germans and the others to long terms of close confinement at Milag Nord, but the death sentence was never carried out and all three survived to be decorated after the war.

As the year drew on, U-boat successes grew; even the Italian submarines enjoyed some of this glory. Also off the Cape Verdes, the *Comandante Cappellini*, Capitano di Fregata Todaro, sank the South American Saint Line's *Shakespear* on 5 January and, having moved east towards Freetown, on the 14th encountered another Blue Funnel liner sailing south independently. This was the *Eumaeus*, whose chief officer spotted a surfaced submarine ahead of the ship at 06.00 that morning. Captain J.E. Watson rang 'Action Stations', increased speed, turned away from the enemy and ordered his radio officers to let Freetown know. As *Eumaeus* swung her stern to the *Comandante Cappellini*, Second Officer Howie opened fire with the poop-mounted 4.7-inch gun. Shortly afterwards the Chinese firemen abandoned the stoke-hold and *Eumaeus* lost boiler pressure. They had had trouble firing since leaving Birkenhead because of the poor quality of the coal, which was not proper 'steam coal'; indeed, Watson was on his way to Freetown to rebunker, for his firemen had been forced to burn extra fuel to maintain speed during the passage. The *Eumaeus* was carrying naval personnel, and Watson now called for volunteers, who came forward to stoke the ship until a direct hit struck the starboard coal bunker and blew open the ship's side. The gun duel had been going on for about a quarter of an hour when a shell hit the bridge and Lieutenant Culmer, the officer in charge of the naval draft, came aft and informed Howie of the fact, suggesting that he relieve Howie at the gun. The second officer went to the bridge, where he found the chief and fourth officers wounded but Watson still in command. After a few more minutes the poop-mounted gun ceased firing and Howie again went aft, to find that the area had been hit by shell splinters which had wounded most of the gun's crew and damaged the gunlayer's sight. He gathered a Royal Marine corporal and one of the ship's own naval gunners and reopened the engagement, replacing the firing pin when it broke. As the *Comandante Cappellini* closed the range Howie was convinced that he had scored at least one hit, but he had to cease fire when the ship's stock of forty rounds of ammunition, a quantity he afterwards reported to be 'totally inadequate', had been expended. Under machine-gun fire, Howie now made his way back to the bridge. The *Eumaeus* was listing heavily and her engines had stopped. With the ship on fire and helpless, Watson gave the order to abandon her, even though her lifeboats were wrecked. Only a sailing dinghy remained, and Howie managed to launch this, while many of the men threw dunnage overboard as they jumped into the sea, or relied upon finding some wreckage. At about 19.30 Todaro closed and fired a torpedo into the *Eumaeus*, and she 'died a gallant death'. As Watson and his men floundered in the water a Walrus amphibian aircraft arrived from Freetown, about 150 miles to the east, and dropped bombs on the *Comandante Cappellini* just after she submerged in the clear water; the Walrus also dropped a life-raft and emergency rations. Both the chief and fourth officers had died, along with the chief engineer and 15 of the naval ratings who had volunteered to stoke the ship.

Todaro retired to the neutral but sympathetic Spanish port of Las Palmas, in the Canaries, claiming he had been engaged by an Armed Merchant Cruiser – for Howie had damaged the submarine's conning tower and killed her second lieutenant. Todaro's colleague Boris, commanding the *Dandolo*, was also successful, sinking MacAndrew's small fruit carrier *Pizaro*, Captain J. Gillanders, with the loss of 21 men. But a third Italian submarine, the *Nani*, was sunk by the corvette *Anemone* in the course of an attack on HX99.

Reporting on the conduct of his own Chinese during an FW200 Kondor attack on the Blue Funnel liner *Clytoneus* which resulted in her sinking, Captain S.G. Goffey said that they had 'behaved splendidly'. The 6,278-ton motor-vessel was closely 'near-missed', the explosions wracking the hull and stopping the engines. On the Kondor's next pass two bombs struck the ship beside No. 2 Hatch and a fire quickly took charge in No. 2 'Tween-deck, fed by tea, kapok, sugar, flour and general cargo. More near misses and a strafing which wounded an able seaman were countered with some anti-aircraft fire from the ship's 12-pounder high-angle gun, but with *Clytoneus* 'burning furiously', Goffey and his ship's company were compelled to take to their boats. Heading for land, they were picked up after a couple of days by British ships.

In the period between 7 January and 4 February, Kondors co-operating with Kerneval and the Axis submarines in the North Atlantic repeated their successes of the pre-Christmas period. In addition to that of the *Nani* on HX99, other attacks were made on outward-bound shipping, both in formation, like the OG convoys heading for Gibraltar, and sailing singly, like the dispersed members of OB convoys. Kondors of Kampfgeschwader 40 sank fifteen ships and damaged five, two of which were subsequently sunk by U-boats which with their Italian allies also destroyed a further 16. The tonnage totals for these weeks made dismal statistics in London: 177,749 tons, including some large vessels.

But at the end of January some fateful conclusions were reached on both sides of the Atlantic, conclusions that were in due course to end *Die glückliche Zeit*.

In the last quarter of 1940 the British imperial merchant service had lost 3,239,190 tons of shipping. Even before Lindemann had compiled his figures, Churchill had written to tell Roosevelt that 'we are passing through an anxious and critical time'. Having instituted neutrality patrols, the United States government were becoming increasingly sensitive to the deteriorating situation of the British in the Atlantic. In their eyes there was little scope for further dispute: the Germans had all but wrested Britannia's trident from her feeble and degenerate grasp.

President Roosevelt had made early and discreet overtures to the Chamberlain government indicating that, the Neutrality Act notwithstanding, he would do everything possible to provide Britain with *matériel*. The culmination came in the President's annual message to Congress in January 1939, in which he spoke of the 'many methods short of war' by which the United States could make a stand against aggression. Congress had refused him a repeal of the arms embargo provisions of the Neutrality Act, echoing the isolationist mood of the American people, but Roosevelt had subtly moved the debate into a more public arena and hinted that, in the event of a war between Great Britain and Germany, he might have to declare certain oceanic areas out of bounds to American shipping and send the United States Navy to impose non-belligerency elsewhere. The implication that this would free the Royal Navy to concentrate its efforts where they were most needed was obvious. Roosevelt had also shared the concern of other Americans over the fate of British warships, anxieties which by the autumn of 1940 had led to the so-called 'destroyers for bases' deal.

Roosevelt was aware of the tendency of political bodies, even and perhaps especially of democratically-elected political bodies, to arrogate to themselves a 'right' to act as if they truly represented the 'common will' of their electorate. Since such bodies are subject to the dynamics of party politics, this is a chimera, but the two great leaders of the Western Powers in those darkest of days, Churchill and Roosevelt, were able to both divine and direct the changing mood of their respective peoples. And where one was able to inspire a nation weakened by material loss, the other was able to outwit Congress and move by subtly devious means to an ethical conclusion.

Moreover, though both men were patriots, they transcended mere national interests, aware that jointly they were much more than the sum of their separate parts. Roosevelt knew that the United States would gain nothing and lose much if Germany were to be victorious over Great Britain, even if the British Empire fought on from its Dominions and Colonies. Churchill and Roosevelt felt themselves to be more than mere national leaders; rather, they saw themselves as custodians of that democratic tradition which had its roots deep in British dissent, in the Revolutions of 1649, 1688 and 1776. Within them, too, the inspiration of history burned fiercely, lighting their way into the future, and both understood the value of their chief weapon, sea-power and its profound 'gleam of steel'.[17]

Hitler, as Dönitz was to discover, was a terrestrial creature, as ignorant of maritime matters as Napoleon. He had plenty of warning of the way the wind was blowing on the far side of the Atlantic, for only eight days after war broke out in Europe the German chargé d'affaires in Washington, Hans Thomsen, cabled Berlin, informing the Führer that 'For the time being, Roosevelt believes himself able to keep the United States out of the war by strengthening the Allies' chance of winning the war through unlimited exportation of arms, military equipment and essential raw materials. But if defeat should threaten the Allies, Roosevelt is determined to go to war against Germany, even in the face of resistance in his own country.'

By January 1941 one of those allies, France, had been subjected to a humiliating defeat, partition and occupation. Now the other was in jeopardy. But in the summer of 1940 fears that the Royal Navy was actually losing its ascendancy over the Atlantic Ocean had prompted the American administration to ask Congress for four billion dollars to build a 'Two Ocean Navy'. The resources of the United States Navy were not immediately adequate to this momentous task, but the Navy Act marked a major shift in national policy. Perhaps, in the long run, it marked the point at which the United States may be seen to have assumed the role of super-power; certainly it meant the establishment of an Atlantic Fleet, and it laid the foundations of a second for service in the Pacific.

The Royal Navy was certainly failing in its primary duty to protect and preserve British trade. At sea, its commanders, officers and men sensed this; ashore, the Admiralty groped for a means to prevent defeat. The immediate emphasis was on more escort vessels: the commissioning of corvettes and the refitting and adaptation of the run-down American destroyers. This, it was felt, would counter the U-boat menace. But in February 1941 half the total escort force of 146 vessels was out of action, a consequence of repair work often falling short of requirements in both quality and speed. It was clear that resources must be conserved and time bargained for. With Plymouth accessible to the enemy's aircraft flying from France, the headquarters of the Commander-in-Chief, Western Approaches was moved to Liverpool, where a bomb-proof command centre had been set up under a block of unremarkable offices known as Derby House, a move initiated by Winston Churchill when First Lord of the Admiralty. Installed in this new command centre was a new Commander-in-Chief, Admiral Sir Percy Noble, and with Noble went Engineer Rear Admiral Sir Henry Wildish, head of an engineering staff whose diligence and organisation was in time to transform Western Approaches command and establish major repair bases and workshops in Londonderry, Liverpool, Greenock, Belfast, and St John's in Newfoundland. Within months these were functioning, and soon had an impact on the serviceability of the warships under Noble's flag. Churchill himself also ordered that thenceforth only the North Channel was to be used, thus removing shipping from danger of transit through the South West Approaches and compelling the enemy to extend his lines of communication.

As Noble took office and the number of serviceable escorts fell, it was Dönitz's misfortune to have only 22 submarines operational. It was also his misfortune that on 15 February Coastal Command was put under the operational control of the Royal Navy, and that Air Vice Marshal Robb commanding No. 15 Air Group joined Noble at Derby House. At the level of grander strategy, moreover, Churchill established a new Cabinet War Committee, the Battle of the Atlantic Committee, which he chaired and which included the First Sea Lord, Sir Dudley Pound. That spring the Admiralty concluded that the Germans would be able to maintain 35 submarines on active service in the Atlantic capable of operating anywhere between Cape Farewell and Freetown. It was clear that with attacks on convoys occurring further and further west – beyond the Mid-Ocean Meeting Point, which had been pushed from the 15th to the 17th meridian in July 1940 and as far as the 19th by October – steps must be taken to increase the range of the close anti-submarine escort.

There was also the question of replacing lost merchant tonnage. British yards were building merchant ships, but the great standard ship-building programmes in Canada and the United States were barely under way, and Britain's own mercantile losses continued to be made good in the short term from America's rusting reserves of standard vessels laid up in the creeks and bayous of the eastern seaboard. The acquisition of the *Braddock* was typical. Mr George Russell, a Donaldson Line officer, was part of 'a complete crew' which early in 1941 'embarked as passengers on the Orient liner *Orontes* at the Tail of the Bank anchorage', sailing west as an independent 'crammed with 3,200 RAF, military and naval personnel'. They reached Halifax safely and without incident eight days later.

Here we were bundled into a train and made our way by various railroads and numerous stops in American towns and cities to the US Gulf port of

Mobile, in Alabama, where at last we found the *Braddock*. This old steamer turned out to be one of a hundred American laid-up ships, built at the end of the First World War, which the Ministry of Shipping [*sic*] had purchased for service under the Red Ensign. Most had been laid-up for 20 years or so, the *Braddock* certainly for 10 years, and we found her completely mothballed, yet it took the local labour only three weeks to prepare her for sea. This was remarkably done by untrained labour, many of whom had hardly seen, never mind been aboard, a ship. We had the odd mistake like trying to fit the starboard sidelight on the port side and vice versa, but otherwise everything worked as it should have done when we finally got to sea.

Like all of her kind the *Braddock* was a three-island ship with five hatches, ten derricks and the old counter stern. She was 6,615 tons gross and 411 feet overall length. However, unlike her British counterparts fitted with [steam reciprocating] engines and coal fired boilers, the *Braddock* was turbine driven and oil fired! We got away from Mobile in the last week of February 1941 and loaded in Tampa a full cargo of cotton, and then steamed up to Halifax to join a homeward convoy, but were delayed there three weeks undergoing boiler repairs. We sailed from Halifax in Convoy HX119 with the AMC *Aurania* (another ex Cunard liner) as Ocean Escort. This was an uneventful crossing which ended at Oban, where we joined a coastal convoy going north-about to Methil Roads, thence to Hull for discharge. The *Braddock* remained in Hull for nearly four weeks having various wartime equipment and armament fitted . . . Also at this time the *Braddock* had her name changed to conform to Ministry nomenclature . . . and became the *Empire Redshank*.[18]

Dunbar-Nasmith had been correct when he informed the Admiralty that the convoy system was failing; more than that, it was playing into the hands of the enemy. The Royal Navy's early destruction of U-boats had become a distant memory, and since Dönitz had insisted on a reversion to the old impact-firing torpedo fuse, a U-boat could almost always pick off ships sailing independently, hence the loss of merchantmen just beyond the dispersal points of OB convoys. But to operate in this way meant relying upon individual attacks, perhaps involving prolonged stalking: and in concentrating against one specific target as the ships parted company, there was always the chance that a second would be lost. Once the German submarine commanders adopted the tactic of surfacing inside the convoy's escort screen at night, the convoy presented target after target in quick succession, a fact men like Kretschmer readily appreciated. The catastrophic potential of the combined effect of several U-boats operating as a group, vectored by aerial reconnaissance, had already been demonstrated, and it is no wonder 'Silent Otto' demanded that Hitler deploy more aircraft and U-boats in the Atlantic.

Despite this failure on the part of the Royal Navy to fulfil its traditional strategic role, morale in the merchant service remained relatively steady, due allowance being made for the merchant seaman's traditional propensity to grumble, and despite the effect of local losses in convoys like SC7. One reason was that the overall scale of the losses was hardly appreciated at a personal level. The members of a torpedoed ship's company might be landed in places as far apart as Brazil, Scotland and the Azores, and this fragmentation of a work force, which had so bedevilled the organisers of the seamen's strike of 1925, now contributed to maintaining its spirit. Memories of deprivation in the very recent past also played their part. When war broke out, most merchant seafarers 'came back to sea to do a job [they] knew rather than go in the army', and once at sea 'developed an armour of indifference to anything with which [they were] not directly concerned'. Against this, however, had to be set the seaman's continual companion: 'It was the stress of war which I remembered most,' wrote Second Mate Patrick Fyrth. 'Some were broken mentally by the struggle, but all of us were changed into more serious and probably less likeable characters. It was the joyousness of living which was the chief casualty.'

Ashore, the merchant jacks 'were not universally popular. The stereotype of the drunken sailor, fighting outside pubs and putting every girl he could lay hands on in the family way, was still a factor in some people's minds. There were some seamen who behaved badly but there were plenty who didn't, both in peace and war. There were lots of women in the dockside pubs giving thanks for a sailor's full pocket book or his pent up urges after a long voyage rather than his heroism.'[19]

In April 1941 the manning of merchant ships came under greater central control with the formation of the Merchant Navy Reserve Pool, to which merchant seamen not on contract to liner or tanker companies signed up for employment. 'Working [for] the Pool meant more shore leave,' recalled Fyrth, 'as one waited to be allocated a fresh ship after each voyage . . .' The disadvantages were that 'some of the ships one signed on were absolutely bloody awful', while masters and shipping companies had less control over the quality of their crews, and were obliged to sign on men whom in peace time they would have rejected.

This was yet to manifest itself to any great extent. During 1941 the experience shared by men of both sea services was working the mystery of symbiosis. Escort commanders like Thring had not only come to appreciate their charges' problems – the difficulties experienced in maintaining station in ageing ships already at their maximum speeds by officers and men 'unused to signalling by lamps or flags . . . [and] unaccustomed to guns . . . called upon to manoeuvre like warships in compact formation in pitch darkness or fog . . .' – but to admire their stoicism. 'Many of these men have had to swim for it more than once or twice; they have known their escorts to be inadequate. They have never failed. The fact that convoys were started at the outbreak of war, with practically no previous training or instruction, and that the ships soon learned the essentials of convoy work, and were soon manoeuvring their unwieldy selves like men of war, speaks volumes for the Merchant Navy.'

At the close of 1940 the heavy cruiser *Admiral Hipper* had sailed on a sortie, but with minimal success and the loss of a supply ship. Then, under the command of Admiral G. Lütjens, the *Scharnhorst* and *Gneisenau* also broke out into the Atlantic, hoping to repeat Krancke's success against an HX convoy by overwhelming its inadequate escort. Having refuelled in Arctic waters they possessed considerable range, and expectations were high in Berlin, where Raeder, Schniewind and Fricke, the German proponents of the dictum that 'the most effective weapon in ocean warfare is the battleship itself', eagerly awaited news of success.

On 8 February Lütjens hove in sight of Convoy HX106, only to discover that it was escorted by the British battleship *Ramillies*. Kapitän zur See K. Hoffman of the *Scharnhorst* wanted to disclose his presence and draw off the ancient *Ramillies*, leaving the convoy to the guns of his colleague Fein in *Gneisenau*, but Lütjens declined to act: any damage even partially disabling his capital ships would leave them vulnerable to the overwhelming force of the British Home Fleet which lay between them and safety. Lütjens knew he had already stirred up the hornet's nest; his hands were effectively tied. Besides, his objective was British merchant ships: 'our job', he declared, 'is to put as many as possible under the water.' In short, it was not the business of the German battle-cruisers to engage British men-of-war voluntarily.

A faulty report from the *Ramillies* persuaded the Admiralty that only one raider was at large and that she was the *Admiral Hipper*, known to be absent from Brest, whither she had gone at the end of her December sortie. Lütjens might after all have scored a major victory for the Kriegsmarine, and for the battleship enthusiasts in Berlin (and perhaps even London). As it was, Admiral Tovey took the British Home Fleet to search for the raider off Iceland, and found nothing.

It was left to Dönitz's twenty-odd U-boats to maintain pressure on the essential flow of British imports. In early February, *U-48*, *U-52*, *U-96*, *U-101*,

U-103, *U-107* and *U-123*, along with a group of Italian submarines, *Barbarigo, Bianchi, Marcello* and *Otaria*, were in the North West Approaches, supported by Petersen's Kondors of Kampfgeschwader 40, and sank stragglers and independently-sailing merchantmen.

As Lütjens was refusing battle with the elderly *Ramillies*, far to the south-east and many miles to the westward of Cape St Vincent *U-37* was on her way south to operate off Freetown. That evening, however, Kapitänleutnant Clausen sighted a northbound convoy and attacked it. Convoy HG53 consisted, with the exception of the commodore's vessel, the *Egyptian Prince*, of 20 small old, slow Mediterranean cargo-ships. To avoid air attack, all HG convoys were routed well west of the Straits of Gibraltar before turning north, a precaution that on this occasion proved almost as pitiful as the escort: Lieutenant Commander G.A. Thring's sloop *Deptford* was stationed ahead of the convoy while the destroyer *Velox* zig-zagged across its rear. At 04.00 on Sunday 9 February, 'just after moonset', two ships on the port side of the convoy, both of which were leading columns, were hit and sank rapidly. The *Deptford* swung round, but her search for any U-boat revealed nothing but wreckage, and at the end of this fruitless pursuit she picked up the four survivors from the Currie Line's *Courland*, which took Captain R.C. Smith and 25 of her crew to the bottom. A second Currie Line ship, 'the *Brandenburg*, a British ship of vast age [she had been built in 1910], filled with iron ore', was stopped by Captain W. Henderson to recover Captain F. Bird and 20 of his men who had, unlike six of their shipmates, escaped the sinking of the *Estrellano*, belonging to Ellerman's Papayanni Line. The *Estrellano* had had among her 3,110 tons of general cargo a large quantity of canned sardines, the destruction of which covered everything with fish-oil.

Having reported the convoy, Clausen was ordered by Dönitz to remain in contact and assist in vectoring onto it a group of Kondors from Kampfgeschwader 40. That afternoon, six flew up the columns from astern at about 150 feet. The escorts took station on either flank of the convoy to deter any possible U-boat attack while 'the merchant ships' AA guns, such as they had,' attempted the defence of the convoy. They 'were not on the top-line. In any case they had so few that it would have made little, if any, difference,' reported Thring. The Kondors bombed and strafed the convoy, damaging the *Varna* so badly that she sank in heavy weather a week later. They also sank outright the ore-laden *Britannic*, the *Jura* and her 2,800 tons of pyrites, the former Danish *Dagmar* and her cargo of oranges and oxide, and the Norwegian *Tejo*. Although only one man lost his life aboard the *Britannic*, 17 from the *Jura*, five from the *Dagmar* and four from the *Tejo* were killed. A sixth ship, the *Raina*, had also been damaged, but laden with pit-props she 'could keep going'. A considerable number of casualties had been caused among the survivors and on other ships, and small fires had broken out after the strafing.

The Kondors' second attack 'was not pressed home . . . [But] the enemy did not get away with it altogether [and] some of the merchant ships put up quite a good show after the initial surprise. It is known that one Fw force-landed in Portugal and burned out . . . The enemy gave up these low level attacks with four-engined aircraft soon after this.'

The commodore being among the casualties, Thring ordered the master of the *Egyptian Prince* to assume the commodore's responsibilities, and the steam-ship *Coxwold* to join *Velox* in picking up survivors. 'We were warned to expect submarine attack, probably from greater numbers, so it was essential that some semblance of order should be restored before dark.' In fact only Clausen was still in touch, but after dark 'the expected occurred. SS *Brandenburg* was hit with two torpedoes from the port side, leaving only one very dazed survivor out of the two crews on board. A real tragedy after her gallant rescue work of the previous night.'

Deptford and *Velox* fired star-shells to expose the U-boat and force it to submerge, and both escorts 'came round the stern of the convoy, hoping to catch him as he retreated, and obtained firm contact. We made three full-pattern attacks before losing contact. It was then pretty dark and impossible to see if there were any results.' Although lookouts aboard *Velox* had seen a torpedo track, the enemy had vanished. Clausen did not re-engage, but he did try to vector the *Admiral Hipper* onto the convoy.

By dawn on the 10th Thring had decided that with *Velox* short of fuel and crowded with survivors, she should return to Gibraltar. He was due to meet SL64, an unescorted convoy coming up from Freetown, at 09.30 on the 12th and combine both groups under *Deptford*'s solo and quite inadequate escort, but before dark on the 11th Convoy HG53 was slowed by bad weather. At 09.30 next morning, the time of the rendezvous, the *Egyptian Prince* signalled that she had received a plain-language radio message that SL64 had scattered on being attacked by a surface raider.

Alarmed by the possibility of the raider attacking HG53, Thring ordered an alteration of course to the north-east and an increase in speed. 'This resulted in black smoke from several ships, which was most undesirable, especially as visibility was improving . . . It was not a very enjoyable day.' They were saved by 'the most monumental gale' and a succession of alterations of course to the north and north-west. By the night of the 13th 'the gale had become very severe, and the sea running was the heaviest I have ever seen.' The convoy became disorganised and Thring received a message from the *Empire Tern* 'that the *Varna*, the ship previously hit by a bomb, had foundered during the night, but that all the crew had been rescued. How *Empire Tern* managed such a feat will always be a mystery to me, it must have been one of the finest bits of seamanship ever carried out.'

Meanwhile, while the *Admiral Hipper* was being sought in vain by the British Home Fleet off Iceland she sank a ship of that name, the *Iceland* belonging to the Currie Line, off the Azores on 10 February. It was dawn on the 12th when she fell upon the 19 unescorted ships making up Convoy SL64. Kapitän zur See W. Meisel sank Ropner's tramp *Warlaby* with the loss of 36 of her 39 crew, the tramps *Westbury* and *Shrewsbury*, both owned by Capper, Alexander & Company, with 52 survivors but a combined loss of 25 men, the Houlder Line's *Oswestry Grange*, and the ore-laden *Derrynane*, which sank instantly, taking all hands down. As German shells began to wreck the *Oswestry Grange*'s port side, Captain E. Stone promptly ordered the starboard lifeboat, on the unengaged side, to be lowered. As the *Admiral Hipper*'s shells burst in his ship they damaged the port boat, a fact Stone and the last of his crew discovered when it capsized under them as they tried to escape in it. In attempting to swim to the starboard boat Stone, Fourth Engineer S.W. Burton and three sailors were drowned. As First Officer A.W. Fuillet pulled away, Meisel closed the stricken ship and fired into her until she capsized and sank.

Since the remainder of the convoy had scattered, Meisel had little option but to head for Brest before the hue-and-cry was raised, for he could not know that the most formidable group of British warships anywhere near, Force H based at Gibraltar, was in fact operating in the Gulf of Lyons. In the event, the gale which caused Thring such anxiety enabled all the ships to escape, those of SLS64 and HG53 from Meisel and the *Admiral Hipper* from further observation.

In due course the gale abated and Thring received 'strong reinforcements' which set about mustering the remnants of the two convoys. During this trying period

the survivors of the *Estrellano* had made themselves most useful. The captain and chief engineer were charming and tactful; they messed with me, were most interesting to talk to and taught me a great deal about the Merchant Navy ... When the [combined] convoy finally split up in the Irish Sea, we embarked the Commodore and other survivors ... [from] the *Coxwold*. They were all very glad of a square meal and a bath, having had no fresh water other than that required for drinking and cooking. There was a Danish stewardess in the party [from the *Dagmar*].

The Commodore and I had a long yarn and came to the conclusion that we were very lucky not to have lost more ships. The voyage [of only 2,300 miles] had taken seventeen days.

On arriving at Liverpool, Thring reported to Derby House and found that 'the arrangements for staff work, and for co-ordinating sea and air effort were vastly superior to those at Devonport (Plymouth); one immediately had a feeling of great confidence in the team-work.' Admiral Noble and his Chief-of-Staff 'listened patiently to the whole story, over a cup of tea in the C-in-C's private room. He made suggestions to AA-arming the merchant ships to force the Condors [sic] higher.'

In a telling and revealing conclusion to his ordeal, Thring stated: 'I was received with the greatest possible consideration, and came away feeling that things had not been so bad after all, and that the C-in-C would do every-thing possible . . . [He] was going down to London that night and my story was of use to him in obtaining priorities. The results of his efforts were almost immediately visible, which was the greatest encouragement we could have.' Chief of these results was the formation of 'regular escort groups under their own commanders'. Another was an increase in air cover, provided by Air Vice Marshal Robb's 15 Group, Coastal Command. But another priority for which both Noble and Robb were arguing was better-equipped aircraft. Shortly after this Thring, who later rose to the rank of rear admiral, was 'appointed to go over to Washington on the British Admiralty staff, which was then starting to talk about convoys with the Americans'.

It was long after Thring had enjoyed his tea with Noble that the last survivor of the combined convoys arrived home. Unable to keep up with SL64 and with his coal consumption soaring from the effort of doing so in the bad weather, Captain G.H. Hyland of the British India liner *Gairsoppa* had been obliged to drop astern at dusk on 14 February. The *Gairsoppa* was on her way home from Calcutta via Freetown with a mixed general cargo, including tea and pig-iron; she was also carrying ingots of silver worth £600,000. On the morning of 17 February she was making up for the Irish coast when she was spotted by a Kondor which circled her; then at 22.30 that evening Kapitänleutnant Mengersen in *U-101* made an attack from her starboard side, hitting her in No. 2 Hold. The destruction of the forepart of the ship brought the foremast, and with it the main radio aerials, down on deck. With the ship settling by the head there was no time to send a distress message, and the order was given to abandon ship. A heavy swell was running and the *Gairsoppa* still had way on her, so great difficulty was experienced in launching the lifeboats. One, in the charge of Second Officer R.H. Ayres, drifted astern, narrowly missed by the ship's propeller, still turning as her stern rose. Ayres reported machine-gun fire from the U-boat and, lying off the ship, observed the *Gairsoppa* on fire forward and aft. He streamed a sea-anchor and awaited daylight, but when it came all that remained of Hyland and his crew of 83 British officers and Indian ratings were eight Britons and 25 lascars, two of whom Ayres had taken off the only other waterlogged boat in sight. This unhappy situation dismayed Ayres but he hoisted a reefed sail and headed due east. He was short of water, for much of it had been lost in launching, and this made the dry biscuit difficult to eat: 'it was found impossible to swallow . . . due to the dryness of mouth and throat.'

As was conventional, the officers were aft in the boat, the lascars forward, where the canopy offered some scanty protection from the cold February weather, and they were also provided with blankets given up by the officers. But within four days hypothermia had begun to take its toll, and from that and the effects of drinking sea-water, at the end of thirteen days there were only three British and four Indians left alive. That day they sighted the Lizard, but were too weak to weather the headland, beyond the lee of which lay the safety of Falmouth. As they attempted to drive the lifeboat into a small bay at the foot of the cliffs she broached, capsizing and flinging the survivors into the water. The boat was righted in the turmoil but the undertow drew her back to seaward, and three of the British, including Ayres, managed to scramble on board again. Another attempt to land was made, but again the boat was capsized in the breakers.

On the cliffs high above them three children, evacuees from London, were gathering firewood and watched in horror before running off to raise the alarm. Once more in the water, the three survivors attempted to swim ashore. One man made the rocks but was washed off with injuries to his head; a second lost his hold on the upturned boat: and the third, Second Officer Ayres, was fortunate in being able to maintain himself until the Lizard lifeboat reached him from its station on the eastern side of the promontory.[21]

Convoy OB287 was sighted by one of Fliegel's Kondors on 19 February. Kerneval ordered *U-48, U-73, U-69, U-96, U-107,* the *Barbarigo, Bianchi* and *Marcello* to intercept it, a concentration which ought to have been assisted by a further air interception by two more Kondors on the 20th. The aircraft bombed three British ships, the *Gracia* (another Donaldson liner) and the tankers *Housatonic* and *Scottish Standard*. The last was not sunk, however, but was hit again early the next day and finally torpedoed by Lehmann-Willenbrock's *U-96*, which had successfully sunk stragglers from HX106 and HX107 a few days earlier.[22] Lehmann-Willenbrock was the only U-boat commander to locate OB287, a poor showing due in part to the inability of the Kondors to transmit a sufficiently accurate position. Dönitz subsequently overcame the frustration this caused by devising a procedure by which the Kondors, having informed Kerneval by short wave that they were in contact with a convoy, thereby enabling his staff to alert all operational U-boats in the area to ready themselves, then transmitted a radio-beacon signal on long wave. This gave the U-boats a bearing towards the convoy, from which they could calculate their own offset for its speed of advance.[23]

OB287's escort had not been idle. The corvette *Periwinkle* and the destroyers *Hurricane* and *Montgomery* had obtained a contact and had depth-charged and destroyed the Italian submarine *Marcello*. Nevertheless, it was a bad day for merchant shipping, for in mid Atlantic Admiral Lütjens had finally found a target to his liking in the form of a group of westbound ships which had earlier dispersed from a convoy. Between them the *Scharnhorst* and *Gneisenau* sank the tramp ships *Trelawney*, *Harlesden* and *A.D. Huff*, the Moss Hutchinson cargo-liner *Kantara* and the tanker *Lustrous*. Loss of life was relatively small, most of the crews being taken prisoners-of-war.

Amid complaints of a lack of Kondors under Fliegel's and his own command and still labouring under the difficulty of obtaining accurate positional information, Dönitz and his staff were beginning to concentrate on a succession of outbound OB convoys. Aerial reconnaissance located Convoy OB288 on 22 February, and the reconnoitring aircraft inflicted some damage. Six German and two Italian submarines were drawn up into a line athwart the convoy's grain, but failed to maintain contact. Only *U-73* (Rosenbaum) sighted it, and Dönitz was compelled to redeploy the submarines. This was partially successful and *U-69*, *U-73* and *U-96* were in contact by the afternoon of the 23rd, when the convoy, warned of the presence of U-boats, turned north and eluded further aerial reconnaissance. Towards midnight *U-69*, *U-95* and *U-96* were in a position to attack, and succeeded in sinking two ships before OB288 dispersed on the morning of 24 February.

Unfortunately the enemy submarines, moving west, now fell upon and sank independent ships loaded with either bunker coal or much needed revenue-earning exports. In summary, during 23 and 24 February Kapitän-leutnant G. Schreiber in *U-95* sank the *Cape Nelson*, the *Anglo-Peruvian* and the *Marslew*; *U-69* (Metzler) torpedoed the *Temple Moat* with the loss of all hands; *U-73* (Rosenbaum) accounted for the *Waynegate*, a tramp which, laden with a cargo of bunker coal for Freetown, sank in four minutes. The coal-laden *Linaria* was lost with all hands as a result of a torpedo from either *U-96* or the Italian *Bianchi*, while the Federal Steam Navigation Company's 10,946-ton liner *Huntingdon* was caught up in the murder and shared a similar fate at the hands of either Giovannini, of the *Bianchi*, or

Lehmann-Willenbrock. A torpedo from *U-96* almost certainly sank the *Sirikrishna*, owned by Christian Salvesen of Leith. She was in ballast, and had served as the commodore's ship for OB288; her master, Captain R. Paterson, Commodore R.R.A. Plowden (a former rear admiral), 25 crew and six naval staff went down with her.

Further east three U-boats were in pursuit of the following convoy, OB289. Korvettenkapitän E. Topp in *U-552*, Korvettenkapitän K. Scholtz in *U-108* and Kapitänleutnant U. Heilmann in *U-97* were all on their submarines' first war patrols. Scholtz had already sunk the small Dutch tanker *Texelstroom* off Iceland, but it was Heilmann who succeeded in attacking OB289 and sinking Ropner's ballasted *Mansepool*, the *Jonathan Holt*, and the tanker *British Gunner* just before they dispersed. Heilmann also torpedoed but did not sink the Norwegian tanker *Brövig*.

In such high latitudes, between 59° 30' North and 61° North, loss of life from all these ships was heavy, though survivors were picked up by other ships which had been among the 46 in the convoy, particularly the *Thomas Holt, Haberton* and *Empire Cheetah*. The escorts *Petunia* and the Free French *Léopard* also saved several lives. OB289 had been supplied with a dedicated rescue ship, the *Copeland*, but her conversion for this work had been minimal and her record on this occasion was poor: she merely managed to recover one of the only three survivors from the *Jonathan Holt*'s crew of 55.

Convoy OB290, which had headed south before dispersing, was the next to be attacked by these U-boats. Giovannini's *Bianchi* sank Strick Line's *Baltistan* on the 27th as the ship laid a course for the South Atlantic and her destination of Cape Town, laden with more than 6,000 tons of military stores and equipment. Forty-seven crew members and four passengers were lost with the ship, but Captain J.H. Hedley, 13 of his crew and four of his passengers were picked up by HMS *Brighton*, one of those 50 four-funnelled ex-American escorts, now fit for Royal Navy service. Topp attacked twice but his torpedoes failed, and while Scholtz was equally unsuccessful against OB289 he did sink the independently-routed *Effna* off Iceland on the 28th. It is not clear why this American ship, chartered and manned by the MoWT, with a cargo of steel and trucks, should have been listed as an idependently-routed ship; she sank quickly, and took Captain R.P. Robertson and all 32 of her hands to the bottom with her.

Convoy OB290, which had sailed from Liverpool on 23 February, was to be the worst hit. Prien spotted it heading west during the 25th but was intimidated by a patrolling Sunderland and withdrew until twilight, when he regained contact and promptly sank the Belgian steam ship *Kasongo*, the Swedish motor-vessel *Rydboholm* and the Norwegian *Borgland*. He also hit but did not sink the British tanker *Diala*, and thereafter homed Kondors onto the convoy.

The Luftwaffe's Focke-Wulf FW200 Kondor derived from a commercial aeroplane designed for Deutsche Lufthansa, and had been adapted for long-range military reconnaissance following a suggestion from Japanese experts impressed by the aircraft's endurance after a propaganda flight to Tokyo in 1938. The air-frame suffered from structural weakness in its after portion but the C-3 variant that entered service in 1941 overcame this problem, while the C-4 of the following year incorporated surface search radar. In all, 263 Kondors were built, and they earned a fearsome reputation as 'the scourge of the Atlantic', largely as a result of their attacks on OB290.

Dönitz strove to vector *U-73*, *U-97*, *U-99*, *Barbarigo* and *Bianchi* to inter-cept, but they failed to catch the convoy. It did not much matter; by noon of the 26th the first of six Kondors from Kampfgeschwader 40 had arrived. During the afternoon they sank two Dutch vessels, the *Amstelland* and *Bursplein*, the Greek *Kyriakoula*, the Norwegian *Solferino* and the British *Llanwern*, all of which were in ballast and, with the exception of the *Llanwern*, went down without great loss of life. The Lamport & Holt liner *Swinburne* was sunk with a cargo of military stores, while Brocklebank's *Mahanada*, with a general cargo, was set on fire and foundered next day. By the following morning the convoy was dispersing, but Prien hung on.

Meanwhile, further east, a Kondor had the previous forenoon located the Blue Funnel liner *Anchises* about 120 miles north-west of Bloody Foreland. On her outward voyage to Australia the *Anchises* had been compelled to surrender her 12-pounder anti-aircraft gun at Cape Town, where it was urgently required for a homeward-bound ship. Now homeward-bound herself, she had in consequence only a pair of Hotchkiss guns, ineffectual weapons with which to ward off a reconnoitring Kondor that flew up from the south, made a pass from stern to stem, and dropped two bombs which straddled the ship and exploded, causing considerable damage. First Radio Officer J. Clarkson succeeded in transmitting an aircraft attack warning just before the ship's power failed, and thereafter switched to emergency supply and maintained contact with Malin Head radio. The Kondor, from Fliegel's Kampfgeschwader based at Bordeaux-Mérignac, made a second pass down the length of the ship from forward to aft, dropping two more bombs and raking the *Anchises* with machine-gun fire. The ship responded on both passes with her Hotchkiss guns, but to no effect. Leaving its victim lying in the trough of a heavy sea and swell, the Kondor flew off. Captain D.W. James had a difficult decision to make; he thought it might be possible to save his ship, but prudence dictated that he evacuate her of all unnecessary personnel. It was, however, blowing hard, with the promise of worse to come. He ordered the engine-room staff on deck and his officers and seamen succeeded in lowering six boats into which 134 people, passengers and crew, and including five women and two children, were safely embarked. James and 33 officers and ratings remained on board, retaining one boat. Because of the leeway made by the immobilised ship it was impossible for the lifeboats to maintain station, and they lost touch with each other during the night.

In the course of the hours of darkness Clarkson and his colleagues contacted several ships, including the corvette *Kingcup*, and at 05.00 on the 28th flares and rockets were burned from the *Anchises*'s bridge and seen by the *Kingcup*, 15 miles away. The weather was now atrocious, and the prospects of saving the foundering ship were negligible. The tug *Superman* was on her way but it was unlikely she would arrive in time or, when she did, be able to do much. While it was possible to lower the last boat in the lee of the drifting hull, the leeway made getting the boat off the ship's side almost impossible. The lifeboat's rudder was carried away and several oars were lost or broken before this difficulty had been overcome, and as he came out from the shelter of his ship James found his boat being torn at by the wind and threatened by the heavy breaking sea. *Kingcup*, manoeuvring to windward, herself drifted down upon the lifeboat, and although a few men scrambled up the boarding nettings over her stern, about a score were thrown into the water as the lifeboat turned turtle. All were rescued except two, a Chinese quartermaster and Captain James himself. *Kingcup* searched the area and without further serious mishap located five of the *Anchises*'s boats; the sixth was found by the Canadian destroyer *Assiniboine*.

Prien's dogged attempt to attack the last dispersing ships from OB290 failed, but on the 28th he surfaced and sank the *Holmelea* by gunfire in the heavy weather afflicting *Anchises*. The *Holmelea* was in fact a straggler from Convoy HX109, which had sailed from Halifax on 13 February. She contained a cargo of grain, linseed and maize. Topp's *U-552* had first made contact with the convoy, blowing up the British tanker *Cadillac*, Captain J.F. Jefferson. She was carrying a few passengers, of whom one, along with four of her crew, escaped from the blazing inferno of 17,000 tons of aviation spirit to be rescued by the destroyer *Malcolm*. The Norwegian vessel *Augvald* was also cut out of HX109, by *U-147*.

Prien now attempted to operate against OB292 and shadowed the convoy for three days, but without success. Fog was now contributing to limit Dönitz's control of the situation, but on 6 March 1941 Prien was ordered to attack OB293, which had been detected from the air and against which Dönitz deployed several U-boats. At 18.00 on the evening of the 6th Prien and Kretschmer met in poor visibility, their U-boats rolling in moderate seas as they shouted at each other through megaphones. Suddenly, with no warning, the destroyers *Wolverine* and *Verity*, zig-zagging ahead of Convoy OB293, guided by radar, tore out of the sea fret and forced the two U-boat 'aces' to crash-dive. Leading the attack in *Wolverine*, Commander J.M. Rowland soon obtained a contact and Prien was subjected to a pounding, while U-99 went deep and avoided further detection. Later, after dark, both boats surfaced and shadowed the convoy. They were joined by Kapitänleutnant J. Matz's U-70, on her first war patrol. Matz fired at the British steam ship *Delilian* and possibly also at the tanker *Athelbeach*, though it may rather have been Prien, hunting for a target worthy of the last of his torpedoes. Sending a position report to Kerneval, Prien then fired at the British whaling factory-ship *Terje Viken*, 20,638 tons and the largest of her type in the world. She had been converted into a tanker and was bound for Aruba to load fuel oil. He failed to sink her but there followed a confused *mêlée* in which he participated with Matz and Kretschmer, their attention focused on the two tankers *Terje Viken* and *Athelbeach*, the latter of which finally succumbed to a torpedo from U-99.

As the first attack took place the convoy was ordered to execute a turn to port while the escorts reacted vigorously. The corvette *Arbutus*, Lieutenant Commander H. Lloyd-Williams, gained a contact astern of the convoy shortly before 05.00, calling up *Camellia*, Lieutenant A.E. Willmot, to assist while the two destroyers steamed back through the columns, forcing Kretschmer, who had briefly engaged *Athelbeach* by gunfire, to crash-dive again.

Submerged, Matz made an approach to the Dutch tanker *Mijdrecht*, but his periscope was seen and the *Mijdrecht's* master altered course and rammed U-70, with little ill-effect to his own ship but damage to the submarine's conning tower. The pressure wave preceding the tanker's hull combined with the way on the submarine to thrust U-70 away, so that the pressure hull nevertheless remained intact. Matz retired to assess the damage, surfacing as soon as he felt it prudent, relying upon the brume to conceal him. Astern of the convoy, still engaged in her hunt in the misty dawn, HM Corvette *Camellia* spotted the wounded U-boat and Willmot headed directly for her, only to find his sonar inoperative at the critical moment. Calling on assistance from *Arbutus*, Willmot delivered a depth-charge attack based on intuition. *Arbutus* arrived and at 09.30 Lloyd-Williams gained a firm contact and attacked, with some eager if ineffectual assistance from *Camellia*. Willmot was ordered off to search for survivors while *Arbutus* pounded her quarry for three hours, until U-70 went out of control. At an angle of 45 degrees, stern first, U-70 descended into the abyss, reaching a depth of some 210 metres before Matz, in desperation, blew all tanks, intending to surface and scuttle.

Seeing the U-boat breach, Lloyd-Williams increased speed and headed for her, his 4-inch gun firing. As Matz threw open the conning tower hatch the compressed air in the submarine forced him and five other men up through the damaged bridge. Fourteen others followed as Lloyd-Williams threw his helm and two life-rafts over, slowing and rounding-to to pick up all but 20 of Matz's crew.

The destroyers *Wolverine* and *Verity*, Commander R.H. Mills, were also busy; Rowland had a contact on *U-99* and he and Mills pounded Kretschmer for nine hours before resuming their stations in support of the convoy. It was late by now, 22.00 on the evening of 7 March, and two other U-boats were coming into contact with the convoy, *U-A* and *U-37*. Shortly after midnight Eckermann, in *U-A*, sank the *Dunaff Head*, but in working up the convoy's starboard flank was spotted by Rowland, who sought to ram her. Unfortunately star-shells fired by *Verity* exposed the pursuer and Eckermann dived, whereupon the two destroyers began a sonar search and a heavy but unsuccessful depth-charging. Eckermann escaped on the surface under electric motors in the dark, *Wolverine* reporting the unmistakable smell of shale oil.

Rowland, himself a former submariner, persisted in his hunt. At about 04.15 on the morning of 8 March the noise of a U-boat's diesels was heard, and Rowland increased speed to run down the assumed line of bearing. After some time a U-boat was seen, but it crash-dived; then Rowland saw bubbles, enhanced by bioluminescence. Convinced that his quarry was nearby, he attacked, but although he saw a mysterious glow under water his sonar still held a contact, and there was no evidence of wreckage to confirm a 'kill'. When 'porpoises were sighted in the vicinity at daylight', Rowland broke off his inconclusive action.

In the aftermath the escorts picked up survivors. The *Terje Viken* remained manned and afloat until 14 March, when she was abandoned and sunk by gunfire from a British salvage tug. Most important was the fact that as British escorts had not sunk a U-boat since the previous November, Matz's *U-70* was a signal victory for the escort group. So was something else: Prien was never heard of again.

The British criteria for crediting U-boat sinkings were strict. There was no sense in making false assumptions without firm evidence, and in the coming months British escorts were duty-bound to pick up the grisly tokens of their grim triumphs. But Prien's loss was of significance in the propaganda war; he had, after all, humiliated the Royal Navy with his claimed destruction of the *Royal Oak* at her moorings in the British Home Fleet anchorage of Scapa Flow. His demise was a success, however it occurred. Modern assessments tend not to support the 'possible kill' attributed to

Rowland and *Wolverine*, favouring a technical or a structural failure following the pounding *U-47* had received earlier, even suggesting that the U-boat was lost to a circular-running torpedo. It did not greatly matter; he was the first of Dönitz's 'aces' to be killed. Their chief mourned them, but from the German perspective the lives of Gunther Prien and his men were a small price to pay for all those other men and *matériel* that had preceded them into the sailors' grave 'upon which no roses grow'.

10

'There was a terrific explosion'

Scharnhorst

THE LOADED SC convoys were relatively unmolested in the winter of
1940/41, though *U-93* sank three ships from SC20 in January and
February.[1] Heavy weather took a greater toll, with the foundering of a
Greek tramp from HX100 in December, two Greek and one British tramps
in SC13, another British ship in SC22, and a scrap-laden Dutchman in
HX100. It was the first of a series of winters characterised by bad weather
– 'The elements seemed to have gone mad,' one U-boat commander reported
– but other forces too were now mustering against the Germans.

As a result of discussions in which Thring participated, the United States
Navy had conceded that 'Owing to the threat to the sea communications
of the United Kingdom, the principal task of the United States naval forces
in the Atlantic will be the protection of shipping of the Associated Powers',
by which was meant vessels under the flags of Britain and the United States,
and shipping belonging to the free mercantile marines of Norway, Denmark,
The Netherlands, Belgium, France and Poland, as well as Greece, and
including any flag-of-convenience vessels chartered by the Allied governments. The Atlantic Fleet was placed under the command of the newly
promoted Admiral Ernest J. King, whose first confidential memorandum
concluded with the words, 'we must all do what we can with what we
have'. The Atlantic Fleet was constituted largely from the naval vessels
deployed in the Neutrality Patrol, but its most important element, insofar
as the immediacy of the hour demanded, was its Support Force, which was
formed on 1 March 1941.

Intended for convoy protection in the North Atlantic, and under the
command of Rear Admiral A. LeR. Bristol, this comprised three destroyer

flotillas under Captains J.L. Kauffman, M.Y. Cohen and W.D. Baker, supported by flying-boat squadrons. Bases in the United Kingdom were assigned to the force, and material necessary for their construction was despatched in British ships, since the United States remained, technically at least, a neutral power. Nevertheless, on 27 March an Anglo-American staff agreement was concluded, providing a strategic plan 'in the event' of the United States being in a state of war with Germany and her allies, while on 30 March all German and Italian merchantmen in American ports were seized.[2]

These developments were to have considerable significance in the months ahead, but a more pressing problem of operational demand for the British was posed by the appearance of U-boats in some force off Sierra Leone. The experimental deployment of single submarines, fuelled en route, had persuaded Dönitz of the benefits to be gained from attacking British trade at this focal point. With the auxiliary *Charlotte Schliemann* stationed at Las Palmas in the Spanish Canary Islands, *U-124, U-105* and *U-106*, all large Type IXB craft, were able to refuel on the nights of 3 to 6 March. Schulz's *U-124* then made a rendezvous on the 6th with Lütjens and the *Scharnhorst* and *Gneisenau* off the Cape Verde Islands. Lütjens soon afterwards alerted Schulz to the approach of Convoy SL67. Once again the presence of a British battleship, in this case HMS *Malaya*, dissuaded Lütjens from committing his capital ships, but Schulz, now supported by Kapitänleutnant G. Schewe in *U-105*, attacked in the early hours of 8 March.

The convoy consisted mainly of medium-sized cargo-liners homeward bound from India escorted by *Malaya*, two destroyers, *Faulknor* and *Forester*, and a corvette. They were sublimely unaware of the danger in their midst, and the impact of the attack was formidable. Schewe struck first, torpedoing the British & South American Steam Navigation Company's cargo-liner *Harmodius*, Captain R.J. Parry, with a general cargo and 2,000 tons of pig-iron. Thereafter Schulz, who appears to have been given the credit for the subsequent carnage, fired all four bow tubes and both stern tubes of *U-124* in quick succession, attacking 'down moon' as it set. According to his encomiasts, Schulz sank British India's *Nardana*, P&O's *Lahore*, Weir's *Tielbank* and Ropner's *Hindpool* in 21 minutes, although the escort counterattacked and drove off the U-boats so that they lost contact with the convoy.

Aboard *Nardana* at 02.50 the senior officer of the watch reported to Captain C.E. White that 'there seemed to be a bit of trouble in the middle of the first column. Lights were flickering.' Just as a rocket was sent up from the *Harmodius*, a shudder ran through the *Nardana*. One of the off-watch officers, Mr A.H. Burfoot, hurriedly drew on uniform jacket and trousers over his pyjamas. He had trouble tying his shoe laces, as his hands were shaking so much. Before leaving he flashed his torch round his cabin. 'There was a fleeting picture of sheets flung back, socks hung on a chair, collar and tie on the table . . . Outside . . . the Old Man called me to tear up the confidential books. We ripped their backs and tore their pages, scattering the bits to the wind. "We'll have some clothes from my cabin," he said. I went inside with him. He opened the wardrobe and passed out coats and mackintoshes . . . I took them to the boat.'

On the boat deck the boats had already been lowered and Burfoot preceded White down a life-line, landing 'in a rush upon the close-packed bodies beneath'. Shoving off from the ship's side, the boat lurched in the swell as they tried to pull to where a man was calling for help, his life-jacket light a faint glow in the dark. 'There was little desperation about it; just "I can't keep up much longer". Then the light went out.' *Nardana* was also no longer visible. The survivors were disoriented: 'here and there the small pinpricks of light flickered in the darkness. A sea anchor steadied us, but we retched our hearts up.'

Daylight revealed 'the bleak waste of the sea . . . The Old Man had decided to steer for the Cape Verde Islands 600 miles off.' Then one of the destroyers was seen approaching. 'We waited, too filled with private thoughts to speak . . . then fear gripped us when she turned away. With hands fumbling in their anxiety we lit a flare which sputtered and burnt with a fierce low light. Slowly it paled, then went out and left only a thick white smoke. We watched the destroyer. After long, dreadful minutes, came back an answering flash and she turned towards us once more. Soon she was close enough to use the loud-hailer and an impeccably accented voice told us to sail in up to the lee quarter.' A week later they were landed at Gibraltar.

The last of the five to be sunk, the *Lahore*, Captain G.S. Stable (SL67's vice commodore), 'took the torpedo on the waterline abreast No. 1 Hatch on the port side and caught fire immediately, for the hatch on the port side contained fifty tons of matches, as well as pig-iron and tea.' With her forepart completely burnt out and the pumps unable to hold the water, the ship was abandoned next morning.[3]

The destroyers rounded up the survivors, but loss of life, particularly from the ore-laden *Hindpool*, had been considerable. Neither Schewe nor Schulz had attempted to sink *Malaya*, therefore Lütjens remained at a distance, constrained by his orders and strangled by a system that admitted no initiative. As *U-124* replenished her torpedoes, food and fuel from the raider *Kormoran* in mid Atlantic, Lütjens also refuelled and headed north-west, back into the North Atlantic. The convoy escort, once it had passed the 50th parallel, was augmented to a powerful force including a cruiser, 14 destroyers, one corvette and a MAC-ship – a 'merchant aircraft carrier', a cargo-laden merchant hull above which a flight deck supported half a dozen Swordfish bi-planes.

After the attacks on SL67 Schewe, now joined by Oesten in *U-106*, sighted and attacked the 59 large ships in Convoy SL68 on 16 March. It had a similar escort to its predecessor, including *Malaya* supported by the Armed Merchant Cruiser *Canton*, with the corvette *Marguerite* and the destroyer *Forester*. Stalking the convoy over four days, the two U-boats sank seven ships, the British merchantmen *Medjerda, Andalusian, Benwyvis, Clan Ogilvy* and *Jhelum*, and two Dutchmen, the *Mandalika* and *Tapanoeli*; they also accounted for an eighth, the *Clan Macnab*, which in the confusion collided with the *Strix* on the 17th and sank the following day. Oesten also hit the *Malaya*, but to no effect.

Several boat-loads of survivors were picked up by ships in the convoy or by the escorts, others made boat passages of varying success. Under Captain H.B. McHugh the *Andalusian*'s crew sailed in their boats to Boavista, in the Cape Verdes. The crew of the *Benwyvis* took to two boats, one of which was capsized by the vessel's sinking, causing five men to drown. It seems incredible that anyone should have survived the forces unleashed by the sinking hull; nevertheless, Second Officer Hardie had 'managed to get to the high side of the engine-room skylight, but found that the boat deck was nearly perpendicular. I hung on waiting for the water to reach me. With much hissing of steam and bubbling of water the ship slid under and I commenced swimming. When I came to the surface it was not difficult to find wreckage to hang on to, and after a time I was picked up . . .'

Hardie was rescued by Captain H.J. Small, *Benwyvis*'s master, and joined him in the single boat; a little later they took aboard eight men from a life-raft. Next morning, as they gave up the search and prepared to make a passage, they spotted boats which turned out to be from the *Clan Ogilvy*. Making common cause, they transferred men more equally between the boats and decided to make for the Cape Verdes. For eleven days they kept company, until both Small and Captain Gough of the *Clan Ogilvy* concluded that they had missed the archipelago. They determined to take their chances alone, each promising that if successful they would send help to the others.

Gough's people were picked up by a Spanish steamer, the *Cabo Villano*, whose master 'spared no effort to locate the other boats . . . but no trace of the missing lifeboats was seen'. In the *Clan Ogilvy*'s second boat Hardie and his opposite number decided to sail east, and improvised an improved rig. Next morning they were picked up by the *King Edgar*, outward bound from home and heading for Freetown. She too searched the area, and heard the signals from the *Cabo Villano* that she had picked up survivors, so they presumed that the rescue was complete. There remained, however, Captain

Small's boat from the *Benwyvis*, which contained 33 British and Chinese men. This lifeboat was provisioned with one 12-gallon barricoe of water, four dozen 12-ounce tins of condensed milk and a drum of biscuits. Small instituted rationing immediately, two thimblefuls of water twice a day; once again, although biscuits were plentiful, 'they were too dry to eat'. The boat was beset by contrary winds, and there was not enough fresh water to enable them to make for the Brazilian coast. No passing shipping save them, and morale sank; 'all the time it was a case of thirst and starvation; cold at night and very hot in the day time . . . the acute strain began to take effect. The Chinese were among the first to lose a grip on themselves, most of them jumping overboard.' When Captain Small died, 17-year-old Cadet John Ross crawled aft and shoved him overboard. 'One by one the survivors were overcome by exposure and thirst,' until Ross was left 'with only one sailor'.

After about two weeks the water supply was exhausted, so I had to mix salt water with condensed milk. Sometimes I mixed sea water with iodine to take the taste of the salt away. A lot of flying-fish flew on board and all the time sharks rubbed against the bottom of the lifeboat. It was impossible to stand up, I could only crawl about the boat. About two days before I was picked up, the sailor went out of his mind, shouting for cigarettes and imagining that he saw water, mountains and trees. He leaned over the side calling to his friends, and then he approached me menacingly. I lifted one of the axes, threatening to kill him. The next morning, saying that he would walk ashore, he jumped overboard.

I was in the boat for twenty-seven days. During this time not a drop of rain fell, and I had to make half a tin of condensed milk do for the last two weeks. On the 17th April I was picked up by the French steamer *Ville de Rouen*. I was yelling and shouting when the French ship came near. The main sail was down at the time, but though I tried desperately I could not get it more than half up. I was too excited to do anything really.

Three Frenchmen rowed up to take me on board, lowering a rope round me and hauling me up. I could not walk. They put me into a cabin and gave me some soup . . . The doctor on board [was] very helpful and everybody was most kind to me. One or two of them could speak English.

The French ship was taking between 2,000 and 3,000 men from Dakar, via the Cape, to Madagascar. Arriving there I was put ashore at Tamatave and later a shipping agent gave me work as an office boy. A number of British people subscribed for my clothing and pocket money. Because of my nationality the French authorities of the Colony refused me a permit to leave, orders from the Vichy Government being that no British national of military age should be granted a visa. However, unofficial arrangements were made and five months later I was helped to stow away on an American Ship, and was taken to Durban. By this time I was feeling well again.[4]

Of the *Benwyvis*'s crew of 55 officers and ratings, almost exactly half British and half Chinese, 34 lost their lives.

The two U-boats responsible for this chaos were resupplied by the *Nordmark* and sent to Rio de Janeiro, where they escorted a German blockade-runner, the *Lech*, through the Pan-American Neutrality Zone, after which they proceeded to the coast of Sierra Leone. As for SL68, it was deprived of its corvettes, which were required elsewhere, and the Admiralty dispersed it on 21 March. Some of its ships made their way to Halifax before crossing the Atlantic under escort.

The same period marked a significant action round Convoy HX112 as it approached the vicinity of Rockall, curving down from the great-circle route that took the ships almost as far north as Cape Farewell, the southern extremity of Greenland. The convoy of 41 merchantmen had left Halifax on 1 March and by the 15th had picked up its ocean escort, the newly formed 5th Escort Group led by Commander D. Macintyre in the destroyer *Walker*. With him were the destroyers *Vanoc, Volunteer, Sturdy, Sardonyx* and *Scimitar*, and the corvettes *Bluebell* and *Hydrangea*. The group, though intended to operate in concert, had had no special joint work-up.

Dönitz was frantically trying to muster a group of U-boats to attack HX112, frustrated by demands for weather reports from the Luftwaffe, under orders from Hitler and pressed by Raeder to intensify their bombing raids on British ports. At one point only Kretschmer's *U-99* and the new *U-74* (Endrass) were available, but by the 15th Lemp had arrived in *U-110*. Hearing the steady rumbling of merchant propellers on his hydrophones, he ran down the bearing and sighted HX112. At about 22.30 on 14 March, by the convoy's time, Lemp reported his sighting to Kerneval and attacked. He hit the tanker *Erodona*, exploding one of her cargo tanks in a flash of intense light: both Lemp and Macintyre thought the ship destroyed, but in fact she was afterwards towed to Iceland. Lemp was forced to dive as Macintyre counter-attacked, leaving *Vanoc* and *Scimitar* to harry *U-110* as the convoy moved on. Lemp's U-boat was also seen from the Shell tanker *Auris* which opened fire with her stern gun but only succeeded in hitting another tanker, the *Franche Comté*, on her starboard bow. 'One shell went across the bridge,' reported Captain L.A. Church, 'another struck us in No. 1 Tank and the next shell fell short of me.' She was loaded with

'13,076.9 tons of Admiralty fuel [but that particular] tank was empty and there was no loss of cargo.'[5]

Lemp's next attack failed because of misfiring torpedoes, but throughout the forenoon of 15 March he continued to shadow HX112, transmitting position signals and enabling Dönitz to summon all available U-boats. He was inhibited by the presence of a Sunderland, which forced him to dive and lose contact, but Clausen in *U-37* now sighted HX112 and homed-in Kretschmer in *U-99* and Schepke in *U-100*. While Lemp and Kentrat in *U-74* were out of touch, *U-37*, *U-99* and *U-100* made an approach after dark. Schepke was seen and counter-attacked, a diversion that allowed Kretschmer to motor into the convoy at speed. The night was dark and the weather fair, with a moderate south-easterly breeze. In a skilful manoeuvre in which he fired all eight of his remaining torpedoes, not all of which ran home, Kretschmer inflicted enormous damage, hitting the British tankers *Venetia* and *Auris*, the Norwegian motor-tankers *Ferm* and *Beduin* and the Canadian cargo-ship *J.B. White*. Like the *Erodona*, the *Auris* did not sink.

Aboard the *Franche Comté*, Captain Church took avoiding action as the *Auris* swung across his bow. Slowing to avoid her, he then rang on full speed and had just worked into the *Auris*'s station when 'there was a terrific explosion . . . A great column of water was thrown up, and there was oil to a depth of about 12 inches all over the bridge . . . Immediately the ship was struck she caught fire . . . The whole of the fore deck had been blown out and was then under water. Sixty five feet of the ship's side was blown away and the plates were buckled outwards. All the bulkheads had been smashed, the deck torn right away and the mast buckled.' Church 'had no option but to order the crew to man the lifeboats, but I gave them instructions to remain alongside.'

With no torpedoes left Kretschmer quietly withdrew, intending to head for L'Orient. Macintyre saw a U-boat ahead of *Walker* and increased speed to ram her; the submarine dived and Macintyre depth-charged her as he passed overhead, inflicting sufficient damage upon Clausen's *U-37* to compel him too to withdraw. Macintyre next attacked a sonar contact, and calling up the assistance of Lieutenant Commander P.R. Ward in *Vanoc* proceeded to hammer Schepke's *U-100*. He broke off once to pick up some survivors, by which time Ward was on the scene and took up the cudgel. Between them the two destroyers wrecked the U-boat, and *U-100* sank stern first to a depth of 250 metres before Schepke ordered the ballast tanks blown. *U-100* breached and was immediately picked up on *Vanoc*'s Type 286M radar. Ward increased speed and headed for the U-boat. Unable to start either his diesels or his electric motors, Schepke's last order was to abandon ship as

Vanoc's bow crushed him on his own conning tower. With her hull pierced *U-100* sank, and Ward informed Macintyre, who was then picking up the survivors of the *J.B. White*. Approaching *Vanoc* and circling her as Ward rescued six men from her victim, Macintyre now received a report that his sonar operator had picked up another contact. At first disinclined to believe that yet another U-boat was in the offing, he was prevailed upon to revise his opinion, broke away and attacked.

His operator had located *U-99*, which had been stealing away on the surface heading for L'Orient when her second watch officer, Leutnant H. Petersen, saw *Walker*'s mass looming in the darkness. Thinking they had been spotted by the British, he ordered *U-99* crash-dived. Kretschmer took over and at 130 metres tried to escape, only to be subjected to a hail of depth-charges. These threw the U-boat about, fractured air, fuel and ballast pipes, and theatened to send her out of control into the abyss. Kretschmer blew his tanks and shot to the surface.

Nine minutes after dropping the last of his charges Macintyre received a signal from Ward that a U-boat had surfaced astern of *Vanoc*. An instant later, illuminated by *Vanoc*'s searchlight, *U-99* was under an ineffective fire from the guns of both destroyers. Like Schepke, Kretschmer found that neither of his power sources functioned; *U-99* was unmanageable, and as he ordered his crew to scuttle the U-boat and then abandon her he sent Dönitz a terse message ending with the words 'Capture. Kretschmer.' His chief received it via Clausen, who intercepted and relayed it. Meanwhile a lamp flickered across the heaving seas to Macintyre informing him that *U-99* was sinking, and with scrambling nets over *Walker*'s side her ship's company rescued 40 men, including 'Silent Otto' himself.

Elsewhere others were struggling. Lemp and Kentrat, having been deceived into thinking the convoy had altered course, saw the distant flames and star-shells and tried to re-engage but were unable to penetrate the escort, the strength of which Lemp had failed to appreciate. Convoy HX112 plodded eastwards, leaving in its wake not only the harrying of the echo-located U-boats but the damaged tankers. All three of these made it, though the *Franche Comté*'s private ordeal was a close-run thing.

Left on deck alone, Captain Church had ordered his port boats to sheer off before they were swamped by the oil pouring out of the tanker's side, then clambered down into his own boat on the starboard side. To his annoyance the painter was precipitately cut, although he had ordered the boat under oars, intending to reboard. At this point HMS *Sturdy* had appeared and 'ordered us aboard'. Church 'went immediately to the Commander . . . and told him I had no intention of leaving my ship until she had sunk. He told me he could not remain with me as he had to rejoin the convoy . . .'

Leaving some of the survivors in their lifeboats, the *Sturdy* then withdrew to make one depth-charge attack before returning to the scene. Church 'then ordered the crew to return to the ship with me, but thirty two refused to do so. I then called for volunteers ... My three Officers, Four Engineers, Chief Steward and three Wireless Operators immediately volunteered ...' Having reboarded their lifeboat, Church and his men found it impossible to reach the *Franche Comté* as she drifted away to leeward in rough seas. Once again the *Sturdy* had withdrawn but now the corvette *Bluebell* arrived, her rail lined with survivors from the *Venetia* and the *Ferm*, six of whom thereupon voluntarily joined Church's forlorn hope. The *Bluebell* towed them into close range of the *Franche Comté*, then left them in order to round up more survivors. Church and his scratch crew found the tanker 'still burning furiously and ... a sad sight.' Unable to persuade the men to reboard, or to pull alongside and allow him to climb back, all he could do was remain in the vicinity until he and his people were picked up by HM Trawler *Northland*. Once again Church informed her commanding officer of his intention to save his ship, and they remained close by overnight.

Next day the fires had been extinguished by the sea, Church and his volunteers boarded, and 'within one and a half hours we had steam on the boilers and proceeded on our passage at a slow speed'. Now the *Northland* left them, but in due course *Bluebell* returned to escort the wounded tanker into safer waters. Church 'had great difficulty in getting my ship to port as she would not steer and she was under water almost up to the bridge. All the compasses had gone, and it was just luck[y] that we were able to reach Rothesay, which I am pleased to say we did on Friday 21st March.'

HMS *Bluebell* was by then herself hard-pressed, crowded with survivors and obliged to beg stores from Church. During the transfer, which was carried out under the lee of the Butt of Lewis, where *Bluebell* could run alongside the *Franche Comté*, a naval gunner named Power from the *Venetia* was put aboard the tanker 'in case of aerial attack'.

Church's recorded interview is a spare, understated document. The ship is 'his' not in any proprietorial sense, but in the full burden of his custodial responsibility. The torpedo-strike was remarkable not for having failed to cause his cargo to explode, but for hitting an empty tank so that no petrol was lost. He makes light of the refusal of his crew to reboard the abandoned ship – the Articles have already been broken and they are off-pay – but his officers are loyal and he finds a handful of men willing to risk their lives for a chance. In his final paragraphs Church expresses his 'admiration for the wonderful manner in which the remaining members of my crew and the volunteers carried out their duties and assisted me to bring my vessel safely back into port.' But then, having discharged his duty both to the Admiralty whose cargo his ship bore and to his 'owners', the Ministry of War Transport, he articulates his concerns. 'I would like to state that in this convoy every ship was capable of a speed of 10 knots. It was supposed to be a 9-knot convoy, but up to the time of the attack it had not done more than 6 knots, and I think that the convoy could be definitely improved by maintaining a faster speed.' Church's implied criticism of the commodore goes on: 'According to convoy regulations you are not supposed to make an emergency turn of more than 40°. On every other day we had been making 90° turns, but at the time of the attack we were proceeding on a straight course.' Nor did Church think much of the Royal Navy monopolising and, in his opinion, abusing the right of communication. 'I think that a great deal of unnecessary signalling takes place in convoys,' he observes trenchantly, a criticism frequently made by other merchant officers, who considered it detrimental to keeping a proper lookout. 'In my own convoy', Church went on, 'we were not allowed to use wireless. The instructions we had received at the conference and also our printed instructions stated that the wireless room was to be kept sealed at all times. We had received no new instructions.'

The struggles attaching to the survival of the *Franche Comté*, *Auris* and *Erodona* were insignificant in the light of the triumphs of Ward and Macintyre. While Dönitz sipped the same bitter draught he had so often forced upon his enemies, Churchill announced to the House of Commons and to the world that Kretschmer had been captured and Schepke killed, forcing Berlin to concede the loss on 20 March. But although debriefings of the prisoners from *U-70*, *U-99* and *U-100* suggested that Prien and *U-47* had also been eliminated, circumstances which encouraged the Admiralty to credit *Wolverine* with the kill, neither London nor Berlin rushed to make this information public. Hitler was particularly concerned about the effect such news would have on German morale, but the German submarine service could not be protected in the same way. To their colleagues, the news that the aces Prien, Schepke and Kretschmer had been lost was devastating and ominous.

Lütjens and his fast battleships were still at large and by the middle of March had succeeded in reaching higher latitudes, having sunk the Greek steamer *Marathon* on 9 March. Two days later Lütjens received orders to cover the movements of the *Admiral Hipper* from Brest to Kiel by way of the Denmark Strait, and to allow Krancke to get back to the Fatherland with the *Admiral Scheer*. With a week's grace before these movements, Lütjens replenished his ships from the *Uckermark* and *Ermland*, which he also used as lookouts. When the latter duly sighted Convoy HX114 south of Cape Race, he ordered the *Scharnhorst* and *Gneisenau* to attack. In the assault on 15 March three tankers were captured, the *San Casimiro, Bianca* and *Polykarp*, and five other vessels were sunk, the tankers *British Strength, Athelfoam* and *Simnia*, and the cargo ships *Royal Crown* and *Rio Dorado*, the last with all hands.[6]

Admiral Tovey, Commander-in-Chief of the British Home Fleet at Scapa Flow in the Orkneys, had deployed extensive cruiser patrols across the North Atlantic and in the southern entrance to the Denmark Strait in an attempt to locate the German battleships, but to no avail. He had also been obliged to direct two of his own battleships, *King George V* and *Rodney*, to cover eastbound convoys, though the *Rodney*, sent to support HX114, failed to arrive in time. Force H based at Gibraltar was kept in hand for any possible diversion into the Atlantic further to the east.

Neither the Admiralty nor Tovey was able to provide protection to the dispersed westbound ships which, having broken away from OB convoys, continued to provide the enemy with easy meat as they 'made a bolt for it . . . radiating on different courses.' By ill-fortune a group of these now ran into Lütjens's squadron, which had been alerted by his auxiliaries. In rapid succession the *Sardinian Prince, Silverfir, Myson, Demeterton, Empire Industry* and the Norwegian *Granli* were sunk, and their crews taken prisoner. The *Myson* was a former French vessel, the *Empire Industry* a German war prize, but both were British-manned and -managed. So too was the former Danish ship the *Chilean Reefer*.

'A smart little passenger ship' originally owned by Lauritzen's, she was placed in the hands of Alfred Holt & Company, owners of the Blue Funnel and Glen lines, and on 16 March she was in ballast from Loch Ewe for Halifax where it was intended she should load 1,500 tons of bacon in her fridge spaces. Captain T. Bell had under his command a crew consisting of 18 Britons, 12 Danes and six Chinese. Capable of 14 knots, the *Chilean Reefer* was routed as an independent, and the previous afternoon her radio operators had intercepted the distress signals indicating attacks by raiders. Bell held his course, 'trusting that by the time we had reached the scene the raider would have moved to another area'. Being a Holt-trained man Bell, while hoping for the best, prepared for the worst. It was as well, for at 16.00 on 16 March his radio operators reported distress signals from the *Demeterton* only 50 miles to the south-east. Bell swung the *Chilean Reefer's* head to the west and waited for the onset of night.

Then, at 17.10, the masthead lookout reported a ship on the port bow. Bell turned away, rang 'Action Stations' and ordered the best speed the engine room could give him. Down below the Danish second engineer was on watch. Mr J. Jacobsen opened up the fuel valve 'to its full extent' while Bell transmitted the raider warning RRRR as the first shells from the *Gneisenau* fell about the *Chilean Reefer*.

Dropping his smoke floats to confuse the enemy's optical gunnery direction, Bell manoeuvred his ship following each fall of shot in order to frustrate his opponents further. This served for a while, but the battleship's superior speed closed the range. When Bell judged her to be within range of his 1914-vintage Japanese 4-inch gun, he ordered his own gunnery officer, Second Mate Collett, to respond. His gun crew kept up this unequal struggle long enough to persuade Kapitän zur See O. Fein that the *Chilean Reefer* might be a decoy vessel or 'Q' ship. Two of the *Gneisenau*'s shells hit their target, starting a fire; the Danish helmsman Ordinary Seaman H. Jensen was wounded but stood to his post, while the 18-year-old junior radio officer, Mr J. Crew, having transmitted the first distress message, took up a position on the bridge as messenger. Bell now stopped the *Chilean Reefer* and ordered her abandoned. He and the officer of the watch dumped the confidential books as the first of the boats was lowered. While it was still clear of the water the naval gunner, presumably used to the Robinson's patent releasing gear common in warships, contrived to disengage one end without orders. The occupants of the boat were thrown into the water, several men thereby needlessly losing their lives.

As *Gneisenau*'s shells continued to hit the burning *Chilean Reefer*, Bell satisfied himself that no one remained aboard and finally went over the side into the port boat. It was now growing dark, and wind and sea were rising. While Bell was preoccupied with picking a number of men out of the water Fein closed the scene, and at close range continued to fire into the *Chilean Reefer*, expending 82 rounds on her. He also hailed the boats and ordered them alongside. Bell responded by claiming that his 'work of rescue was incomplete' and when, with darkness almost upon them, he did attempt to cross the *Gneisenau*'s bow to round-to in her lee, the great grey ship went ahead on her engines. 'No attention was paid to us . . . ,' Bell reported, 'and only by the united efforts of all in the boat were we able to keep sufficiently clear to avoid fatal damage.'

Signalling to the *Scharnhorst*, Fein now swept away, leaving Bell and his boat within sight of the burning *Chilean Reefer*, where they remained until the searchlight of HMS *Rodney* illuminated them. Safe aboard the British battleship, on Sunday 22 March Bell was asked to broadcast to her crew, in the course of which he admitted that in 32 years at sea this was the first time he had been aboard a warship, and shared his frustration with the convoy system. It was, he declared to *Rodney*'s crew, 'tedious to you and always irksome to us'.

Nine officers and men from the *Chilean Reefer*'s crew were killed in the action, and three more died after being rescued. Second Officer C. T. Collett,

Fourth Engineer G. Jones and Ordinary Seaman Hansen, the three men left in the partially upset lifeboat, were taken aboard the *Gneisenau*. Collett was subjected to interrogation and solitary confinement in the expectation of a confession that the *Chilean Reefer* was a Q-ship – a misapprehension which he naturally refused to confirm. After two days he received an apology and was allowed to join the other prisoners-of-war, by which time Lütjens was heading for Brest, leaving Krancke the run of the Atlantic on his home-ward passage in *Admiral Scheer*.

On 20 March aircraft from the British carrier *Ark Royal*, which with the battle-cruiser *Renown*, the cruiser *Sheffield* and a flotilla of destroyers formed Force H, came in sight of two tankers. These were the *San Casimiro* and *Bianca*, which with a third tanker, the *Polykarp*, were on their way to Bordeaux manned by prize crews supplied by *Gneisenau*, which had captured them a week earlier from Convoy HX114. Their own crews were left *in situ*, only the masters and naval gunners being taken aboard the *Gneisenau*. Seeing the aeroplane from the after deck of the *San Casimiro*, Chief Steward Hogget and the cook signalled and attracted the attention of the pilot to their plight. With the approach of Force H the German prize crews scuttled their charges to prevent the ships being recaptured, but now found themselves prisoners. The *Ark Royal*'s Fulmar aircraft also caught sight of Lütjens's distant squadron, but to Admiral James Somerville's intense chagrin Force H was unable to catch them, and the *Scharnhorst* and *Gneisenau* reached Brest on 22 March. Two days later the *Polykarp*, which had also escaped Somerville, entered the Gironde. She was afterwards named *Taifun*, and was sunk in Danish waters on 3 May 1945.[6]

Collett and his colleagues were landed at Brest and paraded through the streets before being loaded into cattle-trucks for a five-day journey across France and the Low Countries to Milag Nord, where they joined other merchant service personnel.

Although much was made of the 'success' of Lütjens's cruise, the admiral had failed in his real objective – 'the annihilation of merchant shipping bound to Britain' – having attacked only one east-bound convoy. Raeder's staff assessment that the sortie of two fast battleships proved a point fell far short of any kind of strategic conclusion, though the Kriegsmarine's determination to 'maintain and increase the effectiveness of such opera-tions by repeating them as often as possible . . . to strike the British supply system a fatal blow' provided the Seekriegsleitung with a neat bureau-cratic *finis* to the operation. *Scharnhorst* and *Gneisenau* were subsequently bombed in Brest and finally, a month later, made their 'Channel dash' eastwards to the Fatherland.[7] Though the British suffered the humilia-tion of failing to intercept and destroy them on their passage, these potent warships were at least removed from the threshold of the North Atlantic.

Nevertheless, Lütjens and the other commanders of Germany's surface raiders had rattled the British Admiralty, and each of the merchantmen sunk or captured, whether loaded or in ballast, represented another hull no longer available to Great Britain. Their crews, whether lost or imprisoned, were also part of a depleting asset.

Among the measures taken to mitigate such losses was the introduction of rescue ships already referred to. There were too few of them during the period when they were most wanted, and their record amid the convoy losses in these months was numerically unimpressive, though this was not the fault of those who manned them. One of the first such vessels in commission was the gallant little *Zamalek*, purchased by the Ministry of War Transport from the Egyptian Khedivial Mail Line of Alexandria and placed under the management of the General Steam Navigation Company.

In March 1941 *Zamalek* sailed in attendance on Convoy OB298 under the command of Captain O.C. Morris.[8] Among the 34 vessels in this convoy was the cargo-liner *Benvorlich*, 8,350 tons, owned by William Thomson of Leith. She was bound for the Far East with a cargo euphemistically described as 'war stores' that included 1,100 tons of cordite and other explosives. Captain E.D. Copeman had completed his lading at Middlesbrough, and proceeding by way of Methil and Oban in coastal convoys joined OB298 in the North Channel where the Clyde and Liverpool portions merged, taking up a rear station. By the 20th the convoy was approaching its dispersal point to the west of Bloody Foreland. Visibility was poor, the sea state rough, and a low scud overcast the sky. At 07.55, hearing aircraft engines, the officer of the watch sounded the alarm. A few moments later, its engines shut off, an FW200 Kondor flew in through the low cloud and dropped a bomb which exploded in No. 1 Upper 'Tween-deck. Before Copeman could reach the bridge the forepart of the *Benvorlich* was burning furiously, and he immediately ordered the ship stopped and abandoned by the after boats. Chief Officer Walker got No. 4 Boat away smartly, but in lowering No. 3 on the starboard side one of the Chinese crew trapped his fingers in the lower block of the falls and was pulled out of the boat.

Having dumped his confidential books Copeman went aft, intending to leave the ship by way of the life-raft in the mainmast rigging, but was knocked unconscious by a second explosion. He did not regain his senses until he was aboard the *Zamalek* almost two hours later, having been rescued by Ordinary Seamen A. Dalziel, who pushed his commander into the sea as the *Benvorlich* sank at 08.20. Dalziel then clung onto Copeman and a piece of timber until he was rescued. The *Zamalek* was joined by the destroyer *Hesperus* and between them they picked up 36 men, four of whom were too badly injured to survive. Copeman had a perforated ear-drum, an injured right leg and a fractured right arm, and like the other badly wounded was attended by the *Zamalek*'s RNVR surgeon-lieutenant. It was fortunate that the rescue ship had been in a station close to the Ben liner – so close, in fact, that a heavy shard of steel from the liner had landed on her bridge.

The *Benvorlich* had been bombed the same day that the *Benwyvis* was torpedoed off the Cape Verdes, and Kondors went on to account for two other vessels in the Atlantic before the end of the month, the fine cargo-liner *Beaverbrae* and the *Empire Mermaid*. And while *Scharnhorst*, *Gneisenau*, *Admiral Scheer* and *Admiral Hipper* reached port, the mercantile raiders *Kormoran* and *Thor* were still at large, the former sinking the British tanker *Agnita* off St Paul's Rocks on 22 March and sending the tanker *Canadolite*, taken off the Cape Verdes three days later, into Bordeaux as a prize.[9] The same day the *Thor*, operating 600 miles off Freetown, encountered the Anchor Line's *Britannia*. The passenger-liner was outward bound with service personnel for the Middle East and India when Kapitän zur See O. Kähler gave chase. The *Britannia* returned fire and transmitted a raider report as she sought to escape. The unequal engagement lasted an hour as the *Thor*'s shells wrecked *Britannia*'s superstructure and boats, until her gun was silenced and in heavy seas her passengers and crew were obliged to take to the boats. Five hundred people tried to escape as the boats heaved up and down along-side while Kähler, concerned by reports that a British warship might be approaching, left the scene. A few hours later he took and scuttled the Swedish merchant ship *Trolleholm*, on the pretext that she was sailing under British charter.

In the bombardment and abandonment of the *Britannia* 122 crew and 127 passengers had been killed, leaving 233 souls at the mercy of the sea. In the ensuing days most of the boats were picked up by passing shipping, but No. 7, in the charge of Third Officer W. McVicar, endured a notable voyage. Unable to make easting against the headwinds, McVicar decided the only remedy was to carry the trade winds west. In the boat were 64 lascars and 18 British, including an unnamed RNR lieutenant and a regular naval officer, Sub-Lieutenant I. McIntosh, both of whom had been passen-gers. The boat's capacity was only 56, and in addition to being grossly over-crowded it was riddled with splinter damage and leaked badly. Extempore tingles were made out of tin lids and pieces of blanket stuffed into the holes by McIntosh, who was hung over the side by his legs. McVicar knew the last position of the *Britannia*, and with the expertise of the RNR lieutenant, who was familiar with the Brazilian coast, a sketch chart was made which enabled them to plot a course. The chief problem was to eke out the 16 gallons of water, four dozen tins of condensed milk and two tins of ship's biscuit on a passage they estimated would take at least 24 days.

In due course they picked up the south-east trades and began to make a passage under 'extremes of heat and cold, drought and rain, hope and disappointment' during which more than half the boat's complement, including the RNR lieutenant, died from privation. After 23 days in which they covered a distance of 1,534 miles they made a landfall on the Brazilian coast near São Luis. Out of the original 82, 'thirty-eight emaciated survivors, one of whom was told that he managed to combine in one body "half the deficiency diseases in the medical dictionary", crawled to land'.[10] Recalling McVicar, McIntosh later remarked: 'You can imagine how valuable it was to have a quiet, undemonstrative, reliable seaman as one's companion in such circumstances.'[11]

Despite the loss of 'three of our most experienced commanders [which] caused me to withdraw my forces from the area [south of Iceland] and concentrate them further to the south-west', Dönitz was proving himself the master in the struggle to 'strike the British supply system a mortal blow', for 'the move turned out to be a good one'. Just how good it 'turned out to be' served to reassure Dönitz that the British had not introduced some new anti-submarine device, and that the loss of Prien, Schepke and Kretschmer 'had been purely fortuitous'. What Dönitz could not know was that while he was reaching this conclusion, the code-breakers at Bletchley Park were working on Enigma codes taken during the boarding of the patrol-vessel *Krebs* in Norwegian waters in early March by a party from the destroyer *Somali*. By the end of April the captured material had yielded nine days' access to German naval signals, but although their suspicions were occasionally aroused, Dönitz, Godt and their staff never became aware of the extent to which their security had been penetrated and their operational orders were being intercepted. This did not, however, give the British an open window on Dönitz's intentions. Routine changes in the codes, upgrades in the Enigma equipment and other factors often occluded the intelligence, a fact that became doubly unfortunate once the Admiralty came to expect and rely upon prompt and accurate decrypts. Furthermore, highly significant though intelligence derived from Enigma interceptions was, it did not do much to improve the merchant seaman's experience in the North Atlantic.

As for Dönitz's assessment that the loss of his three 'aces' was 'purely fortuitous', this was not entirely accurate. Although Macintyre and Ward had had considerable luck, particularly in the capture of Kretschmer, the conclusion could not be avoided that a strong escort made penetration of a convoy difficult, if not impossible, as Lemp and Kentrat had found. If *Walker* and *Vanoc* had lacked finesse in their tactics in defence of Convoy HX112, their energy had paid off. In contrast with Dönitz, who still held the initiative, the job of Admiral Noble and Air Vice Marshal Robb could only be one of patient and, as far as the merchant jack was concerned, painful progress. British anti-submarine tactics were still amateur, *ad hoc*, and unco-ordinated; and while Sir Gilbert Stephenson's induction of the new escorts at Tobermory could scarcely be faulted, it was only *practice* that could make the anti-submarine escort of ocean trade convoys a matter of any efficacy, and such practice was only possible with a large number of trained escorts. Convoy HX112 had had seven men-of-war in attendance, five of which had been destroyers, a fact which surprised Lemp. It was significant.

The Germans too had their difficulties. As yet Dönitz and his staff had been unable to discover the schedule or routes of convoys, a fact at variance with the perception of Captain Church of the *Franche Comté*. Dönitz's decision to move his operational area to the west was shrewd, for it was there that he could rely upon a degree of enemy concentration combined with weak convoy defence. Beginning in April 1941 Dönitz redrew his battle-lines, allocating to the Italian submarines an area closer to Ireland 'where they could not prejudice German operations'.

On 1 April, acting on a report transmitted early in the day by Oberleutnant F. von Hippel, commanding the brand-new *U-76*, he deployed eight boats to intercept Convoy SC26. In addition to *U-76*, these were *U-46*, *U-69*, *U-73*, *U-74*, *U-97*, *U-98* and *U-101*, and during the next four days the group harried the convoy. In fact the convoy had already lost one ship earlier on the 1st, when another Canadian Pacific cargo-liner, the *Beaverdale*, was sunk by Schultze's *U-48* after his attack on HX115.[12] She was lost about four hundred miles east of Cape Discord on the coast of Greenland as the convoy steamed ESE across the Denmark Strait. One boat-load of survivors was picked up by an Icelandic trawler while the other, commanded by Captain C. Draper, landed at Ondverdarnes in Iceland.

On the following nights SC26 received a mauling. Late on the evening of 2 April, escorted by the Armed Merchant Cruiser *Worcestershire*, it passed over the line of U-boats. Suddenly the night's tranquillity was blown apart by the explosion of a torpedo in the hull of the *British Reliance*. The tanker's cargo of refined gas oil from Venzuela caught fire and Captain A. Henney, his passengers and crew rushed to the boats as their ship sank; they were rescued by another British vessel, the *Tennessee*. The *British Reliance* had been hit by Endrass in *U-46*, after which in the early moments of the 3rd he torpedoed Ropner's *Alderpool*, loaded with 7,200 tons of wheat. Captain T.V. Frank got his crew into their lifeboats and they were picked up by another British tramp, the *Thirlby*, at which Endrass unsuccessfully fired a torpedo. He was also thought to have attacked a third tramp, the *Athenic*, but again without success.

Rosenbaum in *U-73* was credited with hitting the *Athenic*, Captain E. W. Agnes, which sank with a full cargo of 8,400 tons of wheat; he also sank another of Ropner's tramps, the scrap-laden *Westpool*, which sank so quickly that only Captain W. Stafford and a handful of his crew were picked up, some by the *Havelock*, which was just then meeting the convoy with the close escort. With Commander E.H. Thomas's destroyer was the corvette *Arbutus*, Lieutenant A.L. Warren, which rescued Agnes and his men, but 35 of the *Westpool*'s people went down with her. Rosenbaum went on to account for a second BP tanker that night, torpedoing the *British Viscount*, Captain W.C. Baikie, who was lost with 27 of his crew. The remaining 20 were also picked up by *Havelock*. The *British Viscount* carried 9,500 tons of boiler oil for the Royal Navy.

There was little HMS *Worcestershire* could do in defence of the convoy in such circumstances, except provide an additional target. Kentrat fired at her from *U-74* and caused some damage, but in the early hours of the 3rd he sank the Greek steamer *Leonidas Z. Cambanis* with her cargo of wheat and the loss of two lives, and the Belgian tramp *Indier*, which with a cargo of 6,300 tons of steel and general sank rapidly, drowning 42 of her 46-strong complement. Nor did the arrival of Thomas's escort group greatly ease the situation.

Close by that morning the inexperienced Oberleutnant Friedrich von Hippel, having first alerted Dönitz to the position of SC26, succeeded in sinking a Finnish steamship, the *Daphne*, which appears to have approached close enough to the convoy to cause confusion. There was considerable loss of life among the hapless Finns. In a final flurry, on the 4th, Kapitänleutnant Kuppisch in *U-96* made contact with SC26 and directed his colleague Gysae in *U-98* onto the target. Gysae sank the small Norwegian steamer *Helle* with no loss of life, and the Pyeman tramp *Wellcombe*. The latter ship, containing almost 8,000 tons of grain, took her master, Captain R.E. Johnson, and half her 41 crew with her into the depths of the Atlantic. Kuppisch sank the last ship out of SC26, J. & C. Harrison's tramp *Harbledown*. She too was full of wheat and took 16 men with her, though Captain G. Jones and 24 men were rescued by the destroyer *Veteran*.

Most of the U-boats had broken off contact by the 4th, however, and some were retiring to their bases. Only von Hippel made another approach, in the small hours of the 5th, and was detected by the sonar operator aboard *Wolverine*. Rowland attacked and damaged *U-76* with a single depth-charge before he was joined by the sloop *Scarborough*, Lieutenant P.A. Northey, who dropped a pattern of charges that forced von Hippel to the surface. *Arbutus* was now approaching, and as the U-boat's crew began pouring out of the conning tower onto the casing Lieutenant Warren sent a boat with a boarding-party. The British sailors were driven out of the sinking U-boat by clouds of chlorine caused by the interaction of sea-water and battery acid, but rounded up and took prisoner all save one man of von Hippel's crew.

Convoy SC26 had departed from Halifax with 23 ships. In these attacks it lost 11, five of which contained grain or wheat, three steel, two large quantities of oil fuel, and one a general cargo. The destruction of von Hippel's *U-76*, though gratifying to the British, was small compensation for the loss of such a quantity of *matériel* and a not inconsiderable number of merchant seamen.

In the attacks Metzler in *U-69* had achieved nothing, nor had Mengersen: *U-101*'s seventh patrol was wholly fruitless. Heilmann in *U-97* had been unable to press home any attack, though on the evening of the 4th he sank the westbound British motor-tanker *Conus* south-east of Cape Farewell; Captain C. Asquith and all hands were lost. Later, on the 9th, Gysae sank the small Dutch steamer *Prins Willem II* which had straggled from HX117, and on his way back to St-Nazaire Rosenbaum in *U-73* sank the *Empire Endurance* off Ireland on 20 April. The ship was loaded with British military stores and passengers and went down with the loss of her master, 63 crew and one passenger. A Canadian corvette, HMCS *Trillium*, and the liner *Highland Brigade* later picked up the remnant; five had by this time been adrift for three weeks.

During that first week in April two other incidents of note occurred upon the broad bosom of the Atlantic, both involving Armed Merchant Cruisers. The first, on the 4th, also involved the raider *Thor* which had abandoned Third Officer McVicar and the *Britannia*'s boats in the central Atlantic west of Sierra Leone when Kähler learned that a British man-of-war was within a hundred miles. Having scuttled the *Trolleholm*, at sunrise on 4 April *Thor* was steaming north-west when she saw to the west the upperworks of a liner. Leaving the rising sun astern Kähler headed towards the stranger, and at 06.45 the *Thor* opened fire. The first salvo hit the target at a range of about six miles, and within three minutes the liner was ablaze. She was in fact the Armed Merchant Cruiser *Voltaire*, a requisitioned Lamport & Holt liner of 13,245 tons built in 1923 for the growing cruising market. Captain J.A.P. Blackburn had had orders to search for commerce-raiders off the Azores, and had been successful. The *Voltaire*'s main armament consisted of eight 6-inch guns, and although these responded to Kähler's salvos for two hours, the outcome was a foregone conclusion. Kähler's first shots had destroyed the *Voltaire*'s aerials, so her fate was something of a mystery at the time, though her destruction was announced from Berlin, and partially confirmed by the sighting of wreckage and an oil slick some time afterwards by the Canadian AMC, HMCS *Saint David*.

According to Kähler, his own radio aerial was carried away by Blackburn's only hit on the *Thor*, and while *Voltaire* turned in slow circles because of her smashed steering gear, *Thor's* rate of fire at a salvo every six seconds systematically reduced her to a blazing shambles. At 07.15 Kähler attempted to torpedo the *Voltaire*, which was burning from end to end, although 'flashes from fore and aft showed that his guns were still firing'. Three out of the four guns on *Thor's* engaged side now overheated and jammed, and at 07.41 Kähler's last three guns failed. The *Thor* now closed to fire a torpedo, but 'the enemy also ceased fire and showed a white flag on the forecastle . . . All the enemy's boats were shot away, or on fire, and [Kähler] began to pick up those of his crew already in the water. The burning ship listed to port still steaming in a circle.'

The action had lasted just under an hour, and the *Voltaire* sank before another had passed. While 75 of her company died with her, Kähler's men fished 197 survivors, including Blackburn, from the water. On 13 April Kähler refuelled from the German supply ship *Ill* and then, sinking another Swedish ship on charter to the British government, the *Sir Ernest Cassel*, the *Thor* headed home. Covered through the Bay of Biscay, she steamed boldly up the English Channel and reached the Elbe by the end of the month. She had sunk or taken eleven ships, a total of more than 83,000 tons.

In war the seaman's ancient enemies lie constantly in wait for him, only adding to the malice of the immediate foe. Indeed, in a blacked-out wartime convoy the risks of collision, even of stranding and foundering, are increased, while fire is an ever-present danger. On the same day that the *Voltaire* was in action, the brand-new *Glenartney* sailed from Birkenhead with a cargo of military stores for the Middle East. One of a very fine class of fast, twin-screw motor-cargo-liners, the *Glenartney* was under the command of Captain D.L.C. Evans, an experienced master who had made a name for himself by bringing the Blue Funnel liner *Phemius* safely through a ferocious West Indian hurricane in November 1932.[13] The *Glenartney* was assigned an escort of the former American destroyer HMS *Lincoln* and an Armed Merchant Cruiser, the former P&O liner HMS *Comorin*, Acting Captain J.I. Hallett, which in addition to her complement was carrying naval personnel out to Freetown, a total of more than four hundred souls. The *Glenartney* met these off Oversay on 5 April and the little convoy headed west into the Atlantic before turning south. On the afternoon of the next day the wind was at gale force from the south-east and a heavy sea was running under a lowering overcast when the alarm was given that a fire had broken out in the *Comorin*'s engine room. At 14.50 Evans received a signal from Hallett: 'Have serious fire on board. Stand by me.'

From his experience in *Phemius* Evans was well aware of the effect of oil on troubled waters, and brought *Glenartney* up close on the *Comorin*'s windward side and pumped oil overboard to flatten the sea. Meanwhile the destroyer *Broke* was on her way to assist at 18 knots. A gallant attempt to fight the fire led by the *Comorin*'s chief engineer Mr W.E. Lee was unsuccessful, and before many minutes had passed it had taken hold. The *Comorin* now lay rolling in the trough of the sea, drifting to leeward with smoke and flames pouring from her funnel, her superstructure ablaze. Her crew and passengers were mustered for abandonment, but their prospects looked poor. Evans's efforts notwithstanding, the sea was extremely rough – some estimates put the wave height at as much as twenty metres – and night was approaching. Against these odds, two lifeboats were lowered and seven rafts launched. The *Comorin* drifted away from them, which enabled Evans to bring *Glenartney* alongside and pick up more than a hundred survivors, even though his own ship was rolling through an arc of sixty degrees. *Lincoln* was also busy, having rigged a line between the *Comorin* and herself by which means a single Carley life-raft was ferried back and forth in a painstaking and often interrupted manner.

The *Broke* arrived after dark to a scene of heaving black waters lit by the glare from the burning ship. She too attempted to withdraw *Comorin*'s men by the same method, but had to give it up. The chances of picking men out of the water were so remote as to render the attempt inadmissible, so with the remaining men aboard the *Comorin* clustered aft *Broke*'s captain, Commander Scurfield, decided he would try to run alongside. Having had every single possible item secured as fenders along her forecastle, including cushions from the wardroom, *Broke* was edged alongside in the lee thrown by *Comorin*'s starboard quarter at about 22.30. On her forecastle Lieutenant P. Scott, RNVR had a party waiting to assist. The vertical movement between the two vessels was enormous: their decks were never level, the quarter of the liner always looming above the destroyer. Both vessels were rolling, and *Broke*'s narrow steel forecastle was wet, slippery, and strewn about with fittings – eyebolts, stanchions, an athwartships breakwater, her capstans and anchor gear, plus her forward gun. The seas, slamming against the *Comorin*'s quarter and heaving in a welter between the two vessels as Scurfield made a succession of patient approaches, threw spray over all. With the flames of the fire almost licking their heels, nine men made it in the first leap; in the second, six jumped but three sustained injuries. Scurfield withdrew and came back. The two hulls made contact, and at first the fendering took the brunt of the impact, but it was soon flattened. Meanwhile lighting had been produced from a streamer of bulbs used in peace time to illuminate the ship on special occasions, and a number of off-watch stokers made up stretcher parties as Scurfield continued his manoeuvres and groups of desperate men leapt aboard. The *Broke's* surgeon, suffering from influenza, turned out to attend the injured, who amounted to about one-third of the rescued. Clearing the casualties from one jump before the next men arrived through the air became a problem, and if Scurfield found positioning his ship tricky, it was just as tricky for the *Comorin's* people to judge the correct moment to jump. One man fell twenty feet, landing across the *Broke's* guardrail, others broke arms and legs.

Scurfield did not rush things. His destroyer was taking a pounding, and periodic damage assessments had to be made by Scott and a chief petty officer. Every time *Broke* went astern it was necessary to ring full speed, the effect of which was to wash down her quarterdeck deck; altogether 15 depth-charges, mooring wires and a rope warp which fouled the port 'A' bracket but did not inhibit its propeller were swept into the sea. Overwhelmed by injured men, *Broke* hailed that they could do with the *Comorin's* doctor. He came forward and jumped, landing flat on his back, where he lay unconscious for a few moments before, to everyone's relief, recovering his wits. By now only about 50 men remained aboard the *Comorin*, 35 of whom were officers, including Hallett, but now two men fell into the sea and just one was hauled back again, clinging onto a scrambling net.

Shortly before midnight the rockets stored on the *Comorin's* bridge roared into the night, then her small-arms ammunition began to detonate, and while this was going on another man mistimed his jump and was left hanging over the side as the two ships threatened to roll together; miraculously they rolled outwards instead, and willing hands dragged the suspended wretch inboard onto *Broke's* deck. Others were not so lucky: one man fell between the ships and was crushed; another landed astride the guardrail, a second astride the barrel of *Broke's* 'B' gun. Both survived. And one P&O steward, a model of *sang froid* 'with his raincoat folded neatly over one arm and a cigarette in his mouth, swung his legs over . . . and stepped casually from one ship to the other.'

The last two to leave were the *Comorin's* executive officer and Captain Hallett. Hallett became 'caught up in a rope which dangled from the deck above and was turned so that he faced his own ship . . . At the same moment *Broke's* forecastle dropped away and began to roll outwards. It was a long fall and the captain's feet went outside the guardrail, so that it seemed certain that he would be deflected overboard. But he landed sitting on the guardrail, balanced there for a moment and then rolled backwards . . . onto the padding of the hammocks. He got to his feet, quite unhurt, and replaced the monocle in his eye.'[14]

At 00.20 on 7 April Scurfield rang full astern for the last time, sending a signal to *Lincoln*: 'Ship now clear of officers and men.' *Lincoln* ended the burning ship's agony, sending a torpedo into her. With her port mess-decks stove in and running with water *Broke*, accompanied by *Lincoln*, ran across the gale to the eastwards, but at sunrise on the 8th the wind died, then chopped round to the west. Steaming at 20 knots, the *Broke* entered the Clyde on 9 April. She had on board 180 of *Comorin*'s people; *Lincoln* had picked up 121 and the Glenartney 109. Incredibly, only 20 had perished.

The *Glenartney* herself proceeded directly to Freetown, where she landed her charges. Evans's report to the Admiralty was terse; the laurels went to the Royal Navy that night, but his comments to his owners are interesting. Writing to Lawrence Holt, he said, 'The Chinese crew were truly excellent, working to the point of exhaustion . . . As an illustration of the spirit prevailing, the Chinese boys made it clear that any attempt on the part of the survivors to offer any reward or gratuity would be most offensive to their feelings, and would be met with disdainful refusal. I can only say with all the sincerity I possess that I am proud to have been in command of such a ship, manned by such excellent officers, midshipmen and crew.'[15] Evans drew particular attention to those of his crew who had gone down pilot ladders to rescue men from the sea, naming in particular Assistant Engineer R. Scott and Quartermaster Chen Siao Chuen.

The Peninsular and Oriental Steam Navigation Company lost another of their liners serving as an Armed Merchant Cruiser a few days later when the *Rajputana*, Captain F.H. Taylor, having handed over the escort of Convoy HX117, was steaming towards Hvalfjord in Iceland to refuel before joining a patrol in the Denmark Strait. Hit at about 06.00, three hours after the sub-Arctic dawn, by two torpedoes from Scholtz in U-108, the *Rajputana* quickly began to settle by the stern. The ship's original master, Captain (Temporary Commander, RNR) C.T.O. Richardson, who was acting as navigator, was lost, along with 39 others. Several of the boats had been launched, despite the speed of the foundering and the heavy sea then running, and these benefited from the oil floating to the surface from the *Rajputana*'s ruptured hull far beneath them. Taylor had had a distress message transmitted, and a Sunderland spotted the boats, so that some hours later 283 of her company were rescued by HM Destroyer *Legion* which arrived from Reykjavik.

Dönitz's submarine commanders could find few targets after the attack on SC26, apart from two westward-bound ships from OB306 which were sunk by Salman in *U-52* and an independent Swedish vessel torpedoed by Moehle in *U-123*.[16] An attempt by Kondors from Kampfgeschwader 40 to locate a predicted convoy in the middle of the month failed, and Dönitz, with several U-boats at his disposal, determined upon a double ambush. A patrol line was extended across the convoy route south of Iceland on the 18th and another was deployed west of Ireland, with Hardegen in *U-147* sent to watch the area south-west of the Faeroes and north-west of the Butt of Lewis known as Bill Bailey's Bank.

In the first of these patrol lines Dönitz had drawn up *U-65, U-95, U-96, U-123* and *U-552*; in the second *U-73, U-101* and *U-110*, together with the Italian submarines *Leonardo da Vinci* and *Comandante Cappellini, Luigi Torelli* and *Alessandro Malaspina.* But even these dispositions failed to yield any fruit, although two British convoys were spotted from the *Luigi Torelli.* Nor did the regular Kondor flights reveal any merchantmen. When Moehle spotted Convoy HX121 on 28 April, the escorts drove him off. Moehle had transmitted his position long enough to alert his colleagues and the first to respond was Lehmann-Willenbrock in *U-96*, who summoned Korvettenkapitän Erich Topp in *U-552*. Topp had already been busy, having sunk HM Trawler *Commander Horton* and Houlder Brothers' *Beacon Grange* in the small hours of the previous day. A little earlier the *Beacon Grange* had been flown over by an aircraft which appeared to be in contact with 'a dark object lying low in the water'. Although the *Beacon Grange* was fitted with a new Bofors gun, her gunners had been unable to secure any hit on the aircraft, and a few minutes later she was torpedoed twice, forward and aft of the engine room.

Captain A.B. Friend ordered all hands to muster at the port boat stations, as the starboard lifeboats had been wrecked. At this point *U-552*, with 'a red devil' painted on her conning tower, 'broke surface on [the] vessel's starboard beam'. An attempt was also made to lower a gig and the Carley liferafts. Topp circled the stricken ship and the wallowing boats while photographs were taken, then fired another torpedo into her, producing 'a remarkable cascade of water which shot high in the air . . . When this had cleared the vessel was seen to have sagged heavily amidships, her bows were up and her propellers were showing. The boats began to pull away . . . as she appeared likely to founder at any moment. The submarine submerged and was not seen again.' As the boats made off to the east, sounds of gunfire and some distant flashes marked the end of the *Beacon Grange.*

During the night the lifeboats became separated. The wind headed them, and it was the afternoon of the 30th before those in the first officer's boat, 39 in all including five soldiers and four boys 'aged fifteen or sixteen', saw a plane. They failed to attract its attention, but early on 1 May a Sunderland flew low overhead, dropping a canister containing 'two loaves of bread, four tins of fruit, two tins of sardines, four tins of Horlick's rations and two tins of RAF emergency rations' plus a note which read: 'Have sent message for help, am looking for a boat which should not be far away. Keep your chins up.' This optimistic message proved premature; they saw a distant ship and continued sailing east, until at daylight on the 3rd it fell a dead calm. Although they were tired, the men decided to get out the oars, and to cut their rations to the bare minimum. But now their luck changed, and at about 10.00 they were seen and picked up by the Belgian trawler *Edward Anseele*, working out of Fleetwood, where Skipper F. Beert landed them late on 5 May. Second Engineer W. Lake, who had suffered a severe facial wound during the attack, conducted himself without complaint, according to the subsequent report, while the first officer's task was 'lightened by the resource and willingness shown by Apprentice John Batchen, and Yesheskell Yarhovsy (A.B.) showed leadership in the execution of all orders which were issued.' The 41 men aboard Captain Friend's boat were picked up by HM Corvette *Gladiolus* on the 29th and later landed at Londonderry.

Topp, meanwhile, had hurried off to the assistance of Lehmann-Willenbrock, who on the night of the 28th attacked HX121 and sank the tankers *Caledonia* and *Oilfield* and the cargo-liner *Port Hardy*. This convoy consisted of 48 ships and included the rescue ship *Zaafaran*, a sister-ship of the *Zamalek*. The Norwegian-flagged *Caledonia* went down with almost 14,000 tons of diesel and fuel oil and a dozen of her crew, which was bad enough, but the *Oilfield*, with 11,700 tons of benzene, lit the night sky like a gigantic torch. Captain R. Andersen, the senior master of Hunting & Sons' fleet, died along with 46 of his men; only eight were picked up by Lieutenant J.K. Craig in HM Trawler *St Zeno*. The most fortunate of *U-96*'s victims was the cargo-liner *Port Hardy*, which with ten passengers was on her way home from New Zealand carrying a general cargo containing 700 tons of zinc, 4,000 tons of frozen lamb and 3,000 tons of cheese. Captain J.G. Lewis, his passengers and all but one of his crew were picked up by Captain C.K. McGowan's *Zaafaran*, which also rescued *Caledonia*'s survivors.

McGowan also picked up many of the survivors from Topp's last victim in this attack, Bowring & Company's tanker *Capulet*, which had been abandoned, her 11,200 tons of refined boiler oil destined for Scapa Flow and the bunkers of the Royal Navy burning fiercely. The others, except for one passenger who lost his life, but including the *Capulet*'s master Captain E.H. Richardson, were rescued by Commander W.E. Banks in the destroyer

Douglas. The tanker continued to burn for several days until she was sent to the bottom by a torpedo from *U-201* (Schnee), which encountered the derelict during a passage from Kiel to France.

One cargo-vessel, the steamer *Nerissa*, had straggled from HX121, and on 1 May she had the misfortune to be seen north-west of Rockall by Topp, nearing the end of his patrol. The Bermudan-registered *Nerissa* was the only ship owned by the Bermuda & West Indies Steamship Company, a subsidiary of the Furness, Withy Group, and she had accommodation for numerous passengers. At the time of the attack she was carrying a great many, and the loss of life was heavy. Captain G.R. Watson, 124 passengers and 82 of his crew were lost with the ship, though her distress calls brought the destroyer *Veteran*, Commander W.T. Couchman, to the scene in time to pick up 51 passengers, 29 crew, including six gunners, and three stowaways. Couchman afterwards transferred his visitors to the corvette *Kingcup*, which landed them at Londonderry.

These losses were severe, but the escort did enjoy one success. Kapitänleutnant Hoppe had taken *U-65* over from Stockhausen after her refit at L'Orient. As he made his approach towards HX121 he was located by Banks and sunk with all hands by *Douglas* and the corvette *Gladiolus*, Lieutenant Commander H.M.C. Sanders.

Of the other boats, *U-95* (Schreiber) took no part in the attack on HX121, but was afterwards directed to the dispersing ships of OB316 following a sighting report by a Kondor. No contact was forthcoming, but off the south-west corner of Iceland Shreiber attacked and sank, by torpedo and gunfire, the independently-sailing Norwegian cargo-liner *Taranger*, a 14-knot motor-vessel owned by Westfal-Larsen & Company of Bergen.

In the aftermath of the assault on HX121 its instigator Lehmann-Willenbrock, on his way back to St-Nazaire, ran across Convoy HG61 some ninety miles west of Bloody Foreland and sank the *Empire Ridge*. She was a newly-built ship, a 2,922-ton, 'three-island' cargo-vessel with a deadweight of about 4,700 tons, a standard 'Scandinavian'-type vessel of which 38 were built. Constructed by Lithgow's at Port Glasgow, she had been placed by the MoWT under the management of a small Newcastle shipping company, Messrs Witherington & Everett, who had appointed Captain E. W. Clark her master. With a cargo of iron ore there was no real chance of survival for either Clark or his crew, and only two men were picked up by the destroyer *Vanquisher*.

It was another miserable story; even those aboard the rescue ship *Zaafaran* had a wretched time of it, for she was grossly overcrowded and her facilities were inadequate to the press of 139 men aboard her. It would hardly have delighted the merchant seamen on their way home to a few weeks of survivors' leave to know that although *U-95, U-96* and *U-123* had been directed to Convoy OB316 by a Kondor, they failed to find it.

But as the summer nights shortened his submarine commanders' opportunities, Dönitz was about to reap a reward that would transform matters in the North Atlantic.

PART THREE

May–December 1941

THE MEANS OF
SURVIVAL

II

'The end was terrible and violent'

Benvenue

THE MONTH OF May 1941 was one of climaxes, though few were perceived as such at the time. From the moment it had detected their move to Bordeaux-Mérignac, British intelligence had kept a close eye upon the strength, operational regularity and deployment of the FW200 Kondors of Kampfgeschwader 40. Its successes, with no more than 15 operational aircraft, both in unilateral attacks and in co-operation with Dönitz's U-boats had prompted Churchill's famous decree of 6 March that the defeat of the enemy's submarines and aircraft over the Atlantic must be accorded priority. By May the anti-shipping strikes by Kondors were past their peak, but in their reconnaissance role these aircraft continued to pose a problem to the defence of trans-Atlantic convoys for a long time to come.

This culmination went unperceived, for the Luftwaffe were successful elsewhere. In a raid on the river Mersey on 3 May, German bombers struck at the docks lining the river and at shipping lying at anchor in the stream. Berthed in Huskisson No. 2 Dock on the Liverpool side, the Brocklebank liner *Malakand* sustained a direct hit and caught fire. Partly discharged, she burned furiously all night, and at 07.00 next morning the fire reached her half-cargo of shells and she blew up. In the Canada Dock, Ellerman's Wilson liner *Domino* was hit and sank at her berth; the former Danish cargo-liner *Europa*, owned by the Østasiatiske Kompagni of Copenhagen, was set on fire and was burnt out, and Houlder Brothers' *Elstree Grange*, which had discharged her cargo and was undergoing some repair work, was also bombed and set on fire. All but two of the crew escaped injury, the two wounded being pulled from the burning ship by Able Seaman G. Wheeler during the raid and passed to three police officers on the quay, a courageous act which won Wheeler the George Medal. In the river another of Houlders' ships, the *Baronesa*, was severely damaged by a near-miss on her starboard quarter, while the small cargo-vessel *Corbet* was hit and sunk. Numerous barges, a tug and a lightvessel were sunk or damaged, and the explosion of the *Malakand* wrecked a mobile grain elevator. In terms of material damage and the delay inherent in clearing the port – for both the *Europa* and the *Elstree Grange* had to be towed away and beached at King's Wharf – the raid was a blow to the already shaky efficiency of Britain's dock system and to the smooth flow of imports. Similar raids impeded work in places as widely separated as Hull, London, Greenock and Belfast.

But Britain was receiving a subtle augmentation of strength from the United States. Contemplating the actions around Convoys SC26 and HX112, Admiral Stark had written (somewhat awkwardly) on 4 April that the situation in the Atlantic was 'hopeless except as we take strong measures to save it. The effect on the British of sinkings with regard both to the food supply and essential material to carry on the war is getting progressively worse.' Stark, hitherto ideologically opposed to assisting the British, courageously decided to weaken American strength in the Pacific Ocean and transfer several powerful task forces to the east. Though perhaps the support they provided was more moral than material at this stage, the presence of an increasing number of American warships in Atlantic waters, most notably at the newly-acquired naval base at Bermuda, inhibited Dönitz's freedom of operation in the far west. Significantly, among the men-of-war assigned to this Central Atlantic Neutrality Patrol were the aircraft-carriers *Ranger* and *Wasp* and, by the end of May, *Yorktown*.

The British occupation of Iceland the year before had prompted Berlin to declare the surrounding waters a war-zone in which neutral shipping would be sunk, a threat honoured faithfully. Then, at about the same time that the British Admiralty decided to use Hvalfjord, near Reykjavik, as a base for convoy escorts, President Roosevelt, in his cautious moves towards entering the war, ordered Stark to consider Iceland as a potential naval and air base. In early April the USS *Niblack*, Lieutenant Commander E.R. Durgin, had sailed for Reykjavik, and on the 10th, as the destroyer approached the coast, she picked up a boatload of survivors from a Dutch merchant ship, the *Saleir*, as noted in chapter 10. As she did so her sonar operator reported a contact and Commander D.L. Ryan, Durgin's Divisional Commander, ordered him to attack with depth-charges. The reliability of the assertion that Durgin and Ryan attacked a U-boat is uncertain – a more likely victim of their aggression was a Greenland Right Whale – but their intent was unambiguous.

*

The British response to the convoy losses of early April was equally un-ambiguous but also, though of more substance, equally uncertain. The Admiralty's decision to use Hvalfjord, 'the whale's fiord', as an escort base arose from the decision to provide convoys with an anti-submarine escort throughout the trans-Atlantic passage. To this end the newly formed Escort Groups B3, B6 and B12 were directed to operate from basic facilities, a depot ship and oiler, anchored in the fiord.[1] Together with these green escort groups went a number of Coastal Command's Sunderland flying-boats and Lockheed Hudsons, the latter an adaptation of the Electra civil air liner. Hudsons of No. 269 Squadron were first based at Kaldadarnes, though they were later transferred to Reykjavik.[2] Even this, however, did not enable aircraft to cover the enormous corridor extending south-east from Cape Farewell, athwart the routes of trans-Atlantic convoys. With a width of approximately 360 to 400 miles, out of reach alike from Northern Ireland, Iceland and Newfoundland, it was known to the strategists as the 'Air Gap', to others as the 'Black Hole'.

In theory at least, all this meant that an east-bound convoy was accom-panied by an escort based on Newfoundland which now, instead of handing over to an AMC at longitude 53° 30' West, extended that cover eastwards to 40° West, at which point an escort group from Iceland took over until it was met by a British-based group on the 20th meridian. The number of available escorts remained a critical factor, however, so in order to gain the greatest benefit it was intended that OB convoys should not be dispersed as early as had been the custom but carry all merchant ships further west, covered by the Iceland-based escorts which would shuttle back and forth, accompanying an OB convoy west from 20° to 40° West and picking up an east-bound HX convoy. At these 'Ocean Meeting Points' the escort groups would transfer from one convoy to the other.

The difficulties inherent in making a worthwhile reality of this theory are not hard to grasp. The North Atlantic is a notoriously tricky ocean across which to navigate. Not only does overcast cloud generally frustrate stellar and solar observations; when it is low, misty and wet, it inhibits visi-bility at sea level, obscuring the horizon for navigational purposes as well as for keeping watch. The increasing introduction of radar in the escorts reduced the risk of a convoy missing its rendezvous, but such conditions did not help. Nor, of course, did the prevalence of gales, never entirely absent from the Western Ocean at any season of the year; nor the presence of icebergs drifting down from the Davis Strait; nor the thick and coiling fogs caused by the Greenland current meeting the warmer waters of the Gulf Stream over the Grand Bank. And while both merchantmen and men-of-war welcomed bad weather as a deterrent to submarine attack, it increased the difficulties of station-keeping, particularly in west-bound hulls 'flying light' in ballast.

To the rigidity of route must be added a complementary rigidity of schedule, which at the so-called East, West or Mid-Ocean Meeting Points provided the enemy with a choice selection of targets conveniently concentrated in a relatively reduced area at an increasingly predictable time. Moreover, although the east and west routes were offset so that the convoys did not pass within sight of one another, these were periods of weak or distracted defence as the corvettes and destroyers swapped charges.

An additional and crucial problem was the need of escorts to fuel, particularly the destroyers, which might burn up unpredictable quantities of oil if diverted to attack sonar contacts, hunts of which often went on for hours. British oiling methods were at the time primitive, and relied upon smooth seas. There was also the duty, limited by the Senior Officer of the Escort's discretion, to stand by or assist stragglers; and always there remained the moral obligation, which usually fell upon the corvettes, to pick up survivors.

Upon these organisational difficulties were imposed those of strategy and quality. Unfortunately it was necessary for the Admiralty to keep 'never less than a dozen' fleet destroyers 'swinging round their moorings' at Scapa Flow, ready to attend the movements of the Home Fleet's capital ships.[3] Even more regrettable was the necessary withdrawal of many of those destroyers assigned to escort Atlantic convoys in order to extricate British forces from Greece at the end of April and from the Cretan débâcle at the end of May. In these 'blue-water' operations many destroyers were irretrievably lost, a severe blow to those struggling in the 'grey-water' theatre.

This unavoidable reduction in the commitment of experienced regular Royal Navy-commanded units to the North Atlantic escorts meant a greater dependence upon the mutating professional Reserve, and upon the green and utterly inexperienced volunteers and conscripted men. That this oddly composed force became as good as it did owed much to its baptism during the two years of adversity and trial to come, for essentially the maritime war fought in defence of trade convoys in the Atlantic became a war waged not by the regular professional Royal Navy, but by its hurriedly-raised auxiliary extensions in both Great Britain and Canada. This is perhaps an over-simplification, but it is a point that needs to be made, because it was for many months a war that was 'lost' by the escorts and 'won', or at least 'held' in the military sense, by the sheer dogged acceptance of punishment by the British and Allied 'Merchant Navies'.

Moreover, these merchantmen and the Royal Navy were about to be ordered to take on another task, a separate campaign which attracted a greater concentration of regular naval units than the Battle of the Atlantic.

In July 1941 Hitler turned on his former ally and invaded Russia; Churchill immediately pledged support to the Soviet Union, and initiated the PQ series of Arctic Convoys.[4]

With the extension of escorts to accompany convoys right across the Atlantic in the summer of 1941, the OB convoys ceased. Their dispersal points had moved steadily west in response to Dönitz's deepening thrusts into the Western Ocean, and towards the end of the series a few remained in formation all the way to Halifax, while a few others swept to the south, detaching ships bound for the Caribbean and South America and actually dispersing off Freetown, where the escorts went to refuel while the merchantmen stood on for the Cape of Good Hope and the Indian Ocean beyond, though this was also a response to Dönitz's concentration of his U-boats in a new operational theatre. They were replaced by the newly designated ON series.

These important developments marked the demise of the Armed Merchant Cruiser, and most of those remaining afloat were gradually withdrawn and converted to troopships. Their apologists claim they filled a gap in the naval inventory; in reality their achievements, though noble, were small. That they added lustre to the glory of the Royal Navy is undisputed, though less widely known is the extent to which their companies were made up of merchant officers and ratings. They were, however, a shining example to the Kriegsmarine: had *its* cruiser commanders been bred in a selfless tradition and, unshackled by restrictive orders, acted with such bold initiative, the outcome of the early stage of the Battle of the Atlantic might have been very different.[5]

Dönitz had his own difficulties, but they were far less than those faced by the British. Defence is inevitably a more costly and complex matter than attack. The attacker may choose his weapon, time and place; he can focus overwhelming resources at a perceived weak point. The defender always has to assume that his position is vulnerable in its entirety and, since his resources are likely to be limited, to concentrate them where the greatest potential weakness lies. In maritime warfare the second-guessing of such points is not difficult, however, and Admiral Dönitz was nothing if not cunning.

With the number of U-boats available to him insufficient for his purpose, Dönitz displayed characteristic flexibility in the spring and summer of 1941. By establishing mid-ocean refuelling and replenishing points from the German supply ships *Nordmark* and *Egerland*, in addition to the *Charlotte Schliemann* and *Corrientes* at Las Palmas, he enabled his U-boats, as mentioned, to proceed to the coast of West Africa and carry out two patrols before returning to base. In company with *U-105* and *U-124*, Oesten's *U-106* had pioneered this, operating against Convoy SL68 as detailed in chapter 10.

On his way south, in March, Oesten had attacked and sunk the Blue Funnel liner *Memnon*, with remarkable consequences. On the afternoon of the 11th the general cargo-liner was about two hundred miles west of Cape Blanco. The weather was clear, but there was a fresh north-westerly breeze cutting up a moderate sea running over a heavy ground swell. The previous autumn the *Memnon* had served the Sea Transport Division of the Ministry of War Transport in an operation to resupply Malta from the east, and having been released from this duty, during which she had been loaded with army stores, had proceeded first to Ceylon and then to Port Pirie in South Australia. Beyond Aden, where she took on bunkers, she had been on her own, arriving in the Spencer Gulf to load 7,629 tons of mixed cargo, principally wheat and zinc concentrates. Now bound for Avonmouth, the 16-knot motor-vessel had bunkered again at Freetown before proceeding independently, passing the port's defensive boom on 7 March.

Built in 1930, the *Memnon* was a well-run vessel, as were all Holt's cargoliners; her deck officers were on double watches of four hours on and four off; her radio officers were working six-hour watches. She was under the command of Captain J.P. Williams, an experienced master, and both his chief and second officers, McCarthy and Hill, were master mariners. Rupert Hill was in nominal charge of the vessel's armament, the usual vintage 4.7-inch low-angle gun mounted on the poop along with five Lewis guns, but the ship's complement of mainly Chinese sailors and greasers was augmented by a sergeant, a corporal and a dozen gunners of the Royal Maritime Regiment.

Four days after leaving Freetown, the *Memnon* was pitching in a heavy swell as she zig-zagged in a strong wind when they passed an empty lifeboat bobbing forlornly in the rough sea. On the bridge Hill had the watch, and at 13.55 Second Radio Officer Peter Le Quesne Johnson entered the radio room at the after end of the boat deck to relieve his chief, Mr G. Whalley. The ship steamed on, Hill ordering the Chinese quartermaster to put the helm over periodically as *Memnon* followed the Admiralty-pattern zig-zag, in which the alterations were timed by the ringing of a programmed alarm clock.

At 14.13 there was a sudden explosion as torpedoes fired from *U-106* struck the *Memnon* aft, one blasting its way into her hull between Nos 5 and 6 holds, demolishing the bulkhead and admitting the sea to the after third of the vessel. Oesten's second torpedo also destroyed *Memnon*'s generators and plunged the engine room into darkness; the concussion stopped the main engines, whereupon the duty engineer, Junior Second Engineer J.H. Berlin, ordered the Chinese greasers on deck and attempted to restore power himself. On the bridge Captain Williams ordered the transmission of a distress message, and this was carried out by the two radio officers.

With the alarms ringing and the crew mustering at their boat stations, Williams ordered the boats lowered. Going to the engine-room door, Chief Engineer A. Jackson called down to Berlin to get out, as the ship was sinking. Despite the poor conditions four of the *Memnon*'s boats were launched, though two were damaged, swept across the after decks as, 'with her poop completely submerged . . . [and] only the tops of the Samson posts and the standing derricks' showing above water, the two radio officers were seen on the boat deck: they had just completed transmitting their distress message from the radio room at the after end of the deck, and it was with consternation that they 'saw the bastards pulling across No. 6 Hatch!'[6]

Berlin also arrived on deck, to find the boats gone and the water almost up to his feet. He dived overboard while others jumped on a Carley life-raft and No. 5 Boat dropped astern to pick them up. Captain Williams, in No. 1 Boat, shouted to Whalley and Johnson to jump, as he considered it too dangerous to take the boat in close to the ship. Neither man needed to be told twice. 'They were . . . very fortunate,' recalled Fourth Mate Eric Casson in No. 1 Boat. 'Mr Whalley was indeed in great danger of being dragged down No. 6 Hatch [the tarpaulin and hatch-boards from which had been blown sky-high by the torpedo], when an uprush swept him clear. We were very fortunate in being able to reach and rescue them both.' Casson then went on to give a vivid description of the *Memnon*'s last moments, which cannot have been very different from those of hundreds of merchant ships.

Then a movement was seen in the ship. A bulkhead had collapsed, her bows lifted higher and higher, and when her deck reached an angle of forty-five degrees she began to slide under. The end was terrible and violent. The rush of water forced oil, air, fumes, etc. in a great cloud out of the funnel. The force must have been enormous. As the funnel was disappearing it collapsed at the base, reared in the air, and fell. The rest of the ship quickly followed, the truck of the foremast barely missing No. 4 Boat (which had just floated off the poop). As the ship vanished the surface of the sea became very confused, and No. 4 Boat was practically swamped. Mr Whalley was picked up in the very nick of time – just as this surge of water reached our boat. The U-boat had meanwhile surfaced and closed first No. 5 Boat, then No. 4 and then ourselves . . . The men in the conning tower shouted and pointed. We pulled in the direction indicated and sighted a Chinese member of the crew hanging onto wreckage. He was picked up.

In his approach Oesten had machine-guns trained on the lifeboats, but he is recorded to have 'behaved properly'. Peter Johnson recalled: 'The German U-boat cruised gently around for some time then, with a wave from her Commander, she began to submerge and was slowly lost to sight.' They were alone on the broad bosom of the ocean; three sadly nameless Chinese passengers and two British seamen, Clements and Herd, had gone down with the ship.

After the U-boat had withdrawn, Captain Williams decided to combine the crews and abandon the two damaged boats. He now had 22 men in No. 1 Boat; there were 44 in No. 5 Boat under the mate, Mr R.J. McCarthy, who had with him Second Mate Hill. The one good piece of news was Whalley's report that their distress message had been acknowledged by a Spanish ship thought to be no more than two hundred miles away. Both boats lay to sea-anchors, awaiting an opportunity to effect another transfer to even things out between them.

'It was necessary', Casson wrote, 'to keep continuous bailing watches. The nearly full moon, which previously we had cursed, now proved a blessing, giving us light until shortly before dawn. The night seemed interminable. Though the boats rode well to the sea, cold spray drenched us all. Flares were burnt every three hours, and threw a lurid light on to an unforgettable scene. We could see No. 5 Boat as a dark silhouette, tossing on the moonlit waters.'

Next day men and stores were transferred from McCarthy's boat to Williams's, and on the 13th, as there was no sign of the Spanish ship, master and mate agreed to take their chances and make a passage south-east towards Dakar. If they made a landfall there, as they hoped, they would then head south, along the coast, towards British territory at Bathurst in The Gambia. At first the boats kept company, No. 1 proving the faster and compelling Williams to heave-to from time to time, until on the evening of the 14th he decided to go ahead, reasoning that once ashore he could the more quickly organise assistance. The night proved stormy, the boat worked, and bailing went on continuously. In the end Williams had to reef his lugsail and heave-to to a sea-anchor. The following afternoon a moderation allowed them to set sail again, but No. 1 Boat was leaking badly and the monotony of bailing, combined with the limited rations and lack of water, was exhausting the men. Johnson recalled that 'after a week all bowel motions had ceased, urine was a dark black fluid and everyone's breath was foetid. All found that any movement was an effort and their legs seemed to be constantly weak.' On the morning of the 16th they were again hove-to under a close-reefed mainsail, and remained so until a drop in the wind allowed them to haul in the sea-anchor, shake out the reefs and head south-east. At 16.00 on 17 March, worried by the state of the men, Williams altered course due east and sought the nearest land. Nothing was seen throughout the following day, but the sea became less blue and the presence of gulls known to forage in coastal waters persuaded them that land could not be far away.

At 09.00 next morning Williams saw land, and recognised it as being near St Louis, on the coast of Senegal. Shortly afterwards they closed with a French steamship, but no notice was taken of their plight. It was a bad omen, and Williams decided to head south for Dakar, the seat of Vichy French government in Senegal. Although enfeebled after a week in the boat, 'they all kept up their spirits wonderfully'. All during the 20th they sailed south parallel to the shore, about six miles off, and at noon the next day, with the water supply exhausted and 'as neither my men nor myself could go on another day', Williams decided enough was enough. He had recognised the shore as being not far from Dakar, so he put in and landed at the small fishing village of Yoff, a native boat acting as pilot.

Both radio officers spoke French, but Johnson was in a bad way, as was Williams. Whalley and Casson went ashore to report to the authorities, whereupon all were placed under armed guard and taken to a military hospital 'where they received food and rest'. Two days later *Memnon*'s bosun and a steward, both of whom had been in McCarthy's boat, arrived in a very poor condition. They had been landed by the French ship *Kilissi*, which had encountered No. 5 Boat and given McCarthy food and water. Her master had very decently advised McCarthy not to land in Vichy territory and so, having accepted food and water and assured himself that the two weakest members of his crew were receiving attention, McCarthy had pressed on to Bathurst, where he arrived safely. He had lost one man during his boat voyage, which brought the total loss of life to five men. He had also had trouble with a steward who attempted to get more than his share of the rations; McCarthy had withheld a ration of corned beef, and this 'quickly reduced him to order'.

At Dakar, the Vichy French authorities released Captain Williams and the older members of his crew, and they were sent to Bathurst as soon as they were fit to travel. The younger men were not treated so kindly, being interned at Koulikoro where a Lieutenant Crabb of the Fleet Air Arm, shot down during Somerville's raid on Dakar the previous September, was senior officer. They were taken to Koulikoro by train, and the French considered it necessary to manacle them in pairs. On the journey, 'the heat was appalling. The sky had assumed a dull leaden colour,' Johnson wrote later, 'which gave the appearance of a solid roof from which the burning ball of the sun shone like burnished copper.'

At Koulikoro they endured a miserable existence in 'four long mud huts with thatched roofs at the foot of a natural rock wall'. They quickly became infected with malaria and dysentery, and also risked being bitten by venomous kraits, the bite of which was fatal within two minutes. The camp was swept by periodic sand-storms, and their sense of isolation was heightened by the occasional sight of a camel caravan setting off for Timbuctoo. After ten weeks they were informed that an exchange had been arranged for them, and they were transported to the Senegal–Gambia border. From there they were taken to Freetown by sea and most were repatriated soon afterwards aboard British destroyers. Not all escaped a lengthy sojourn in Freetown, however; two of those remaining behind were the ill-starred radio officers Whalley and Johnson, of whom there is more to relate.[7]

Having tested the feasibility of engaging the enemy in the area off Sierra Leone with Oesten's *U-106* and Schewe's *U-105*, an experience that sharpened his appetite, Dönitz deployed several U-boats in the approaches to Freetown, a chart of which, it will be recalled, he had already obtained. He also ordered the mining of the waters off Lagos and Takoradi by *U-69*, which resulted in the sinking of several British ships and forced the Admiralty to close the ports until clearance work had been completed. On 21 May, having refuelled *U-69* from the *Egerland*, Kapitänleutnant Metzler headed east for the Nigerian coast and was to the north of St Paul's Rocks when he encountered the American merchantman *Robin Moor*. The ship was lit, but Metzler considered that she might be a 'decoy vessel'. Signalling her, he asked her name, but could find only the American Export Line's *Exmoor* listed in *Lloyd's Register*, a situation further confused when daylight enabled him to read '*Exmoor*' upon her stern. Metzler ordered her to stop, summoning her master in one of his own lifeboats. Captain E.W. Myers explained that the ship had just been renamed upon change of ownership, an answer which failed to satisfy Metzler, who claimed that the ship's manifest indicated a cargo including radio apparatus, guns, and aircraft parts, bound for Cape Town, though Myers insisted that 'the Neutrality Act ensured that *Robin Moor* was neither carrying contraband nor destined for a war zone'. She was in fact bound for Lourenço Marques, Port Elizabeth, Cape Town, Natal and East London with a general cargo which ranged from steel rails to women's brassières. Nevertheless, Metzler chose to consider her a neutral laden with war contraband and, disregarding his explicit orders to avoid tangling with United States vessels, ordered Myers to abandon the *Robin Moor*, giving him twenty minutes to do so. 'You will be sorry if you carry out your threat,' Chief Mate M. Mundy said, adding his own protests that the *Robin Moor* was innocent, to which Metzler is reported to have responded: 'You have supplies for my country's enemies. I must sink you . . .'

After the lifeboats had cleared the ship with 35 passengers and crew, including two elderly British nationals, Metzler sank her with one torpedo and 33 rounds of gunfire. In deference to the Prize Regulations he did give the boats 'food, bread, butter, brandy and medical supplies', then towed them for some time to a position from which 'in a few days they would be driven by the gentle current onto the African shore'. This was a spectacular piece of disingenuousness on the part of a professional seaman: although one boat landed at Cape Town, the 'gentle current' and the prevailing wind condemned eleven of the survivors to 'a terrible ordeal', a 13-day voyage of 'hundreds of miles', not to Africa but to the coast of Brazil.

Roosevelt, as another step in his patient coaxing of the American people towards open war, denounced the sinking of the *Robin Moor* as piracy. In a message to Congress on 20 June, the President stated the American government's belief 'that freedom from cruelty and inhuman treatment is a natural right. It is not a grace to be given or withheld at will by those temporarily in a position to assert force over a defenceless people . . . The sinking of the *Robin Moor* becomes a disclosure of policy as well as an example of methods. Heretofore lawless acts of violence have been preludes to schemes of land conquest. This one appears to be a first step in the assertion of the supreme purpose of the German Reich to seize control of the high seas, the conquest of Great Britain being an indispensable part of that seizure.'

Following this, Roosevelt stopped oil exports from the east coast to all countries except the British Empire and Egypt, turned German consular agents out of the United States, and prepared for the occupation of Greenland. The destruction of the *Robin Moor* also gave impetus to the United States Navy's moves to protect trade in the North Atlantic. This was already being organised on the British model, following Rear Admiral Ghormley's secret visits to London the previous summer. Curiously, the loss of the *Robin Moor* also stimulated a discussion about the arming of American merchantmen, the conclusion of which was that this would rank as a provocation, against the spirit of the Neutrality Act. That same month, 138 American passengers were caught up in the destruction by the *Atlantis* of the Egyptian-registered steamship *Zamzam* in the South Atlantic on a passage from New York to Egypt.

Egyptian-registered ships had been sunk before by the Germans, but the notion that the *Zamzam* was a neutral-flagged vessel was useful to British propagandists, who drew parallels with the *Athenia* and, more evocatively, the *Lusitania*. Although all the passengers were safely repatriated, the outrage nudged American public opinion further in President Roosevelt's favour.

THE MEANS OF SURVIVAL

Metzler had continued his voyage to the Gulf of Guinea and that evening he torpedoed the British ship *Tewkesbury*, homeward bound from Rosario with a general cargo including tinned meat and wheat. While still outward bound and making her way from Blyth to Methil to join a convoy heading for the west coast of Scotland, she had been attacked and bombed. The bomb from the Heinkel HeIII passed through the engine-room skylight and landed on the gratings, from which Second Mate De Neumann (who had signed on under the English name Newman) and the third engineer gingerly prised it, finally getting it hoisted and thrown over the side. Now they were not so lucky, but although they lost their ship Captain T. Pryse and his crew were picked up by two American freighters, one of which transferred Pryse and his boatload to the AMC *Cilicia* for passage to Freetown.

In addition to *U-69*, which after her 'crazy exploits' laying mines continued operations in the Gulf of Guinea, Schewe's *U-105*, Oesten's *U-106* and Schulz's *U-124* were also in the area. Dönitz now reinforced them with Liebe's *U-38*, Schütze's *U-103*, Hessler's *U-107* and two Italian submarines, the *Calvi* and *Enrico Tazzoli*.[8] On the outward passage these U-boats attacked shipping off the Azores and the Canaries. On 8 April Hessler, who was Dönitz's son-in-law, sank the coal-laden *Eskdene* on her way to Buenos Aires, the ballasted *Helena Margareta* bound for Takoradi, and the *Harpathian* heading for Freetown loaded with RAF stores. Most of the survivors were rescued by other British ships but some men were killed, including 27 from the *Helena Margareta* whose master, Captain O.T. Jones, was awarded the Lloyd's War Medal for bravery at sea. Next day *U-107* destroyed the tanker *Duffield*, a sister-ship of the *Oilfield*, on her way to Gibraltar with a cargo of boiler fuel for the Admiralty. Captain M. Manthorpe ordered his men into the boats and succeeded in sailing to Hierro in the Canaries, thus saving half of his crew; his second boat was lost at sea.[9]

Hessler had just begun. His next victim was the Blue Funnel liner *Calchas*, which he torpedoed amidships at 10.30 on 21 April. Seven men in the engine and boiler rooms were killed, though one Chinese fireman scrambled up inside the funnel to safety. Captain W.R.F. Holden had been conducting his daily inspection of the ship, and as the chief engineer reported all power lost he immediately ordered the undamaged boats lowered, into which the passengers and some non-essential members of the crew were told to go. Holden was determined to save his ship and, when he saw Hessler's periscope, equally determined to 'get a shot at him'. Second Mate F.V. Oddly, described by the ship's carpenter, Mr J.H. Frost, as a 'fine officer', went aft to man the gun, only to discover that the percussion tubes had been flung overboard in error. Hessler, having taken *U-107* in a circuit of the stricken *Calchas*, sent a second torpedo into the ship from the opposite beam, killing Holden, Chief Engineer Scott, all the deck officers, and the key men Holden had hoped might save the ship. Carpenter Frost was the only one to escape as the *Calchas* broke in two and sank in about three minutes.

Hessler now surfaced, then 'sailed through the wreckage, and made off at a good speed with many hands on the conning tower waving goodbye to us'. With Holden and his officers dead, 'to our dismay', as a steward recalled, 'we naturally turned to the Bosun for instructions'. The predicament of those who had survived was extreme, for none of them was a navigator. In charge of the six boats left were Bosun H. Thomas, Chief Steward C.W. Harvey, Carpenter Frost, Leading Seaman T. Mason, Able Seaman R. Hughes and Able Seaman J. Vaight. Furthermore, of the six boats only three were properly-provisioned lifeboats; Frost's was a spare boat kept in chocks which had fortuitously broken free of the sinking ship, and the other two were small 22-foot jolly-boats. Radio Officer Harrison advised that after searching for survivors they should remain where they were, in the hope that a response would be forthcoming to his distress message, which he knew had been received and re-broadcast from the Portuguese radio station on the Cape Verde Islands. In Harrison's words, they carried out 'a vain search. All that was seen was the captain's hat and a mutilated body.'

The next day Harvey and Thomas decided they would have to make for the Cape Verdes, which they estimated lay about seven days' sailing to the SSE, for which the only aids to navigation they possessed were their boat compasses. That evening they saw a surfaced submarine. During the coming hours, inevitably, the lifeboats drew apart, broke into smaller groups, or lost contact altogether.

Initially the north-east trade winds were light, but on the third day they blew strongly, cutting up a rough sea, and in all the boats it was found necessary to keep bailing. Thomas's small jolly-boat was in company with Nos 4 and 5 as the weather worsened. Disaster struck Mason's No. 4 Boat when the mast step tore out and she made so much water that her crew 'could not cope with it'. Still in sight of No. 5, Mason hailed Hughes, and with considerable difficulty transferred all his men into No. 5 Boat, which was now well-loaded and included a woman passenger. Thomas's small craft was totally overloaded and she was in some danger of being left behind, so Hughes towed her for two days, until it became plain that those aboard could not cope with the constant danger of being swamped. Her people were also taken aboard Hughes's No. 5 Boat, along with what water and stores they could salvage from the waterlogged craft. This brought the number of persons crowded into No. 5 Boat to 37: 16 British crew, 17 Chinese and four passengers.

On 19 April a merchant ship was seen approaching, a cheerful sight for all those aboard, but she suddenly 'sheered off and proceeded on her way', a particularly heartless act which left the *Calchas's* survivors seriously demoralised. Then, on 1 May, No. 5 Boat's lugsail yard split. This was replaced with an oar, but on the following day the second radio officer, whose mind had been wandering for some time, jumped over the side. This triggered fractious behaviour among the Chinese but after they had been 'threatened with an axe,' reported Second Steward Curtis, '. . . we managed to restore some kind of order [although] our position was none too secure'. On 4 May a passenger died, followed next morning by one of the Chinese firemen. Appetites were somewhat slaked by shaking up condensed milk and water in a sweet-jar to make 'a semi-respectable milk-shake'. On the evening of the 5th they tried to attract the attention of a ship by burning flares, only to find as they approached that it was a surfaced submarine and utterly indifferent to their predicament.

The end, when it came, was unpredictable and savage. At 03.00 on the morning of 6 May, No. 5 Boat suddenly ran aground. Those capable of doing so manned the oars and got the boat off into deeper water, where they lay until daylight. They had grounded on an offshore hump of sand, mercifully clear of the nearby beach upon which beat a heavy and dangerous surf. It was impossible to land, and they began wearily to work along the shore. On the 7th another man died, and others slipped in and out of the unconsciousness that signalled the end. Then, when they were on the point of despair, a fishing boat saw them and assisted them into St Louis, the same place where Captain Williams and the *Memnon's* boat had arrived a few weeks earlier. After landing two more men died, but the 31 survivors from No. 5 Boat were safely repatriated to Bathurst in The Gambia, having made a passage of about 650 miles.

Carpenter Frost's spare lifeboat made a solo voyage, after losing touch with the others on 23 April. He had on board nine British and seven Chinese crew; these included two able seamen and a first-trip midshipman, who assisted Frost with the steering. Frost's main concern was the mood of the Chinese, who became 'full of despair' and required patient humouring. On 5 May they saw land, and were fortunate in running ashore on the island of Sal in the Cape Verdes, where the inhabitants were kind and compassionate. Shortly afterwards they were taken in hand by Captain Crocker, the British consul at São Vicente. Sadly, Frost lost one Chinese fireman, who died after they had landed.

Chief Steward Harvey's No. 6 Boat also landed on Sal. He had remained in company with Vaight's No. 8 until 29 April, when they drew apart. High land was sighted early on 4 May, and after one unsuccessful attempt they made the shore, and in due course were sent to São Vicente. Harvey lost none of his people on the passage. Nor did Vaight lose any of the 21 souls he had in No. 8 Boat. They included the *Calchas*'s Czech doctor, Paul Ederer, nine Chinese and the woman passenger, all of whom landed at Boavista and like Harvey's party were sent to São Vicente before repatriation. Radio Officer Harrison afterwards recorded that 'enough praise cannot be given to . . . A.B. Vaight, who took charge of sailing the boat and seemed to be permanently on duty, and Chief Cook Gray, who took on the unpleasant job of rationing the food and water.' Harvey and Gray, who had served together for many years, were reunited at São Vicente. It was a relief to Harvey, who knew Gray to have a large family.

In the aftermath one passenger, an army officer named Major Boylin, wrote to the *Calchas*'s owners with 'many points of criticism', complaining in particular of the retention on board by Captain Holden of all the deck officers. In response Lawrence Holt, with his typical loyalty to his own employees, said that Holden's decision was 'one that we can only respect, not criticise . . . [Holden and his officers] had put the ship first, their lives second . . .', an obligation their owners would have expected and, for them, a duty equivalent to the soldier's obligation to remain in support of his colours. Until Hessler's second torpedo struck, they might have saved the ship. Equally characteristically, Holt interviewed Ederer and Harrison as soon as they returned home, recording the encounter:

'Who was your navigator?' I [Lawrence Holt] asked.

'A seaman,' one of them [Vaight] replied.

'Did he do the job well?'

'Yes,' was the answer.

'Of course it would have been a help if you had had an officer with you; but I expect you are all proud that they all stayed with the ship, and the gun, to the end.'

'Yes,' the youth answered, looking at me intently, 'they were splendid.'

'Are you ready for sea again?' I concluded.

'Yes, when we've got our papers in order,' both replied.

The radio officer told me that their distress signals were duly acknowledged. but no one came to look for them by sea or air . . .

'Very tragic,' he concluded.[10]

Holt was justifiably annoyed by Boylin's criticism, which included advice on the management of the Chinese. Third Engineer W. Graham pointedly reported that 'All the criticism was by people who were not competent to judge . . . The average Chinese [crew member] . . . must be led not driven.

It is only to be expected that they will ask for more water etc., and shouting at them will not improve matters.' Holt himself was pleased with his own people and took pains to praise them and emphasise their splendid morale and skill. In fact, even in the absence of the deck officers, these unpractised navigators were disciplined enough to 'check the compass morning and night by the rising and setting of the sun'.[11]

Doubtless Major Boylin was an awkward character, but he had a point when it came to their rations, and it was one made repeatedly by survivors who had endured a boat passage of more than a few hours. 'Is it not possible to find something better in the way of biscuits? . . . The food value is very low, and . . . they are so extremely hard as to be quite impossible for many to eat, especially in a hot climate with . . . [a] limited supply of liquid . . .'

Lawrence Holt subsequently took the advice of Second Steward Curtis of the Calchas, whom he also interviewed, and supplemented lifeboat stores in Blue Funnel and Glen Line ships with prunes, raisins and peanuts. Measures were in any case already being taken by the MoWT to improve lifeboat rations generally with the introduction of food concentrates like Horlick's malted milk tablets and Bovril's beef-based 'pemmican', while the confectioners Rowntree and Fry experimented with chocolate that did not induce thirst. An attempt was also made to find a recipe for a better, thinner, fat-enriched biscuit that would keep for a long time. But even after they were adopted by the Ministry, it was a long time before these innovations were distributed to ships dispersed about the globe.[12]

Such improvements were very necessary, and the need went beyond just food and water, including such things as fishing tackle and ocean charts. These last, though it was not until October 1942 that they became official issue, came complete with a protractor, squared paper, and instructions so impressive that the Manchester Guardian reported that it was 'possible for any intelligent non-skilled passenger to undertake navigation . . .' – a cheerfully dismissive journalistic assumption that missed the point that it was essential to know where a ship had sunk, and to have brought a sextant and chronometer off the bridge. These desiderata were not always available, of course, and an attempt made by Fourth Officer Eric Casson of the Memnon to fashion a rough sextant in order to determine latitude by an observation of the Pole Star was 'really very unsatisfactory'.[13]

The truth was that merchant seamen were not universally competent in small boats. In addition to an ability to navigate and some knowledge of seamanship, it was necessary to have an especial sea-sense in order to handle such an inefficient sailer as a ship's lifeboat. Although some if by no means all deck officers might have had a degree of small-craft training in HMS Conway or Worcester, there were many more who had not been to such institutions, or had not practised such skills since leaving. With a few notable exceptions, Holt's among them, shipping companies did not feel any compulsion to develop boat-handling expertise in their employees during peace time, relying instead upon the crude and rudimentary instruction given for 'Board of Trade' certification as 'Lifeboatman', which was reminiscent of a Boy Scout's proficiency badge. For most seafarers forced to take to the boats the only real chance they had was to be picked up within hours; even a few days adrift would swiftly reduce their constitutions. Hypothermia or sunburn, constant wet feet, the impossibility of finding any comfort on wooden thwarts, overcrowding, hunger and thirst all combined to induce physical and moral degeneration, as Peter Johnson graphically recorded. To physical exposure must be added trauma and associated psychological damage. A merchant seaman was conditioned to think of his ship as his dwelling-place, with all the connotations of 'home'. In the vast indifference of the sea, the haziest grasp of the distance from land could be complicated and confounded by the often unfavourable direction of the prevailing wind and currents, as exemplified in the situation of the *Robin Moor*'s crew, and the perception of such difficulties was enough to daunt the staunchest spirit. Occasionally, as in the case of the Hebridean fisherman, the requisite skills were found not among the deck officers or the cadets but in a more unlikely quarter. Cometh the hour, cometh the man: in other cases he was a chief engineer with a penchant for yachting; a West Indian sailor and a bosun born in Latvia, both of whom had spent their youth in small boats; and a lascar greaser who had begun his maritime career in a *malar panshi* on his native Hugli.

To set out on a long passage with a heavy, lug-sail-rigged boat much given to leeway was to take an enormous risk, so that almost any such boat voyage was of itself a minor epic. Most debilitating was the almost universal sea-sickness that was unavoidable when a large ship was exchanged for a small boat. It is significant that while the Royal Navy collectively possessed boat-skills far superior to those of their commercial cousins, few naval personnel were called upon to endure even a modest boat passage of three or four days. If a warship was sunk, the odds were that her personnel would be picked up by another man-of-war whose officers were bound by the ties of the naval *Brüderbond*.

By the summer of 1941, prompted by expectations of greater numbers of active U-boats, losses of merchant seamen as well as their ships were beginning to trouble the Ministry of War Transport, where Colonel J.J. Llewellin, one of two Parliamentary Secretaries and a former Civil Lord of the Admiralty, had special responsibility for their welfare and safety. Analytical projections showed that manpower levels were approaching a crisis point, a situation that could only be exacerbated by the loss of maritime labour from the Indian subcontinent that seemed an increasingly likely consequence of the independence movement there. In 1939 Indians and Chinese made up just over half the manpower of the British merchant service, in a ratio of about four to one, with other nationalities accounting for an additional 5 per cent. By 1940 the attrition rate among merchant seamen had already reached this percentage, but at the same time roughly the same number of French and Danish merchant seamen – about 5,000 – became available for employment in the British Merchant Navy, while a slightly greater number – 6,300 – had been called up into the Royal Naval Reserve. By 1941 there were 'just, but only just, enough men to go round . . . there was no margin to meet emergencies.'[14]

Moreover, there was nothing to prevent an individual seaman, as a civilian, leaving the sea, though the prospect of conscription into the armed services was generally thought to be a deterrent sufficient to maintain loyalty to the red ensign. 'It [was] presumed that no merchant seaman (apart from those who were members of the Royal Naval Reserve) would choose to join a fighting service if they could go to sea in merchant ships.' Under the demands of war production, shore jobs 'were growing progressively more plentiful and remunerative', and by leaving the sea a man relinquished his seaman's card, so that the Registrar-General of Shipping and Seamen lost track of him. Men, even those used to the estrangement of the sea-life, had an understandable desire not to be separated from their families when their homes were being bombed, and 'the sea, who had been an inconstant mistress during the slumps of peace, was becoming an increasingly cruel one in war. The temptation to desert her was very great.'

No one wanted to sign on a tramp destined to load a full cargo of iron ore, for example, and to staunch this slow haemorrhage of men from essential but unappealing work and counter the losses at sea, the Ministry decided upon a form of industrial coercion. In addition to the introduction of the Merchant Navy Pool in April 1941, mentioned in chapter 10, in May the Essential Work (Merchant Navy) Order was imposed by the Ministry of Labour and National Service to prevent seamen finding shore jobs, and to compel former seamen between the ages of 18 and 60 to re-register for possible sea-duty. Of the 53,000 names produced many belonged to the unfit, or those employed in reserved occupations; nevertheless, about 6,000 experienced men were signed on in the second half of 1941, more than 5,000 in 1942. In addition, many stewards made redundant by the decline in ocean travel were retrained as seamen proper, and a small surplus of naval conscripts were offered the choice of the Merchant Navy instead of a draft into the Army. Finally, youth organisations such as the Sea Cadets, Sea Scouts and Boys'

Brigade were encouraged to find volunteer 16-year-olds – as yet too young to serve their country in the armed services – for work on merchant ships.

One scandalous abuse and appalling injustice the new regulations did finally address was that of terminating a seaman's pay the day his ship sank. Under Pool regulations his wages now continued until he was repatriated, thus encouraging an early application to the Pool and return to sea. Since this could hardly be regarded as anything other than a long-overdue reform, it had little effect upon morale at a time when losses were just beginning to awake cynicism in a much-put-upon work force; unfortunately, too, there were many cases of men failing to learn of it, and thus not claiming their new right.

Had the Germans maintained throughout the second half of 1941 and before the United States entered the war the attrition rate on British merchant shipping and seamen that they had established in the first half, Britain might well have been forced out of the war. As midsummer approached, the war at sea had two focal points: the North Atlantic, and the waters off Freetown.

Metzler's *U-69* had completed her patrol off the Gold Coast on 30 May by sinking the Elder Dempster cargo-liner *Sangara* lying at anchor loading off Accra. Metzler then headed for home, unable to refuel from either the *Lothringen* or *Egerland* since they were two of several German supply ships located by the British towards the end of the month after intelligence material was taken from Lemp's captured *U-110* on 9 May.[15] It is worth noting at this point that although German naval messages, and particularly those emanating from Dönitz at Kerneval, were being regularly read and interpreted at the Admiralty by Rodger Winn and Patrick Beesly, the Admiralty were most careful not to initiate any *coup* that would raise enemy suspicions. Operations of entrapment originating from Ultra (the British name for intelligence derived from Engima decrypts) were made to look either circumstantial, or the result of surface searches aided by radar. Fortuitously, disturbing reports of the outstanding efficiency of British radar were reaching Berlin at this time.

Maintaining a slow, economical speed on one engine and exchanging a series of signals with Dönitz, angrily seeking an explanation for his sinking of the *Robin Moor*, Metzler crept north, only to fall in with the 60 ships of Convoy SL76. This convoy had already lost two tramp ships, the British *Djurdjura* and the Greek *Eirini Kyriakidou*, both loaded with iron ore and both sunk with heavy loss of life on 13 June by Capitano di Fregata Longanesi-Cattani in the Italian submarine *Brin*. Now, on the 26th, Metzler torpedoed the *Empire Ability*, a German war prize formerly named the

Uhenfels. She was carrying 44 civilian and military passengers and a mixed cargo of 7,725 tons of sugar, 238 tons of rum and 400 tons of ground-nut kernels. All but two of Captain H. Flowerdew's passengers and crew were rescued by ships in convoy and transferred to the corvette *Burdock*. Lieutenant F.J. Fellowes, an officer of the South African Naval Volunteer Reserve, also picked up six men from the *River Lugar*, a tramp belonging to Mungo Campbell's Ayrshire Navigation. They were all that remained of the 1937-built tramp and her cargo of 9,250 tons of iron ore, also sunk by Metzler. Captain W. Frame, his two passengers and 35 men were killed.

Metzler, now out of torpedoes, reached Las Palmas and refuelled from the *Corrientes*. Clearing the Canaries he fought a gun-duel with the small cargo-liner *Robert L. Holt* of Liverpool, the commodore's ship from the dispersed Convoy OB337. It was a ruthless action in which Captain J.A. Kendall defended his ship with great spirit until she was sunk with the loss of all hands. Metzler described this action as his 'craziest exploit', but the contention of some authorities that it was 'bold' on Metzler's part because the *Robert L. Holt* was 'heavily armed' is unfounded and apologist.

While heading north Metzler heard a broadcast from Berlin crediting him with a bag of successes which appeared to omit the embarrassing destruction of the *Robin Moor*. He arrived at L'Orient on 8 July to the electrifying news of Operation BARBAROSSA, the German invasion of Russia. In the accompanying euphoria, no one seemed inclined to chastise him for his wilful breach of orders; instead Dönitz praised him for his gross tonnage sunk, his mine-laying off Lagos and Accra, and his gun-duel with a civilian merchant ship.

As the numbers of British escorts gradually increased, Freetown, like Gibraltar and Hvalfjord, received its own locally-based escort force. It was not a popular place with Royal Naval personnel. 'Here', recalled one corvette officer, 'we swelter in godawful heat . . . And everyone thinks you're a cissy if you don't have a bout of malaria every fortnight.' While there was some respite in a swim from Lumley Beach, 'the only things free in Freetown were sweat and syph[ilis]!'[16]

Life was even less congenial for merchant survivors landed there. Although some provision had been made for them, such as a gunnery instruction 'school', the Assistant King's Harbour Master was universally disliked. So contemptuously dismissive was he of the plight of merchant survivors that, as one commented, 'One could not believe he was a naval officer.'[17] Most sought to get out of the place as quickly as possible, by volunteering to make up crew deficiencies in other vessels.

*

Dönitz's mid-Atlantic submarines were highly effective during May and June 1941. Still on patrol after attacking SL67, Schewe's *U-105* and Oesten's *U-106* were in the so-called 'Atlantic Narrows', between St Paul's Rocks off the Brazilian coast (where they had been replenished by the *Nordmark*) and Freetown on the bulge of Africa. Schewe sank the outward-bound *Ena de Larrinaga* in early April and the out-bound *Oakdene* late on 6 May.[18] Then in three days in the middle of the month he sank two of Ben Line's fine and valuable cargo-liners, the *Benvrackie* and the *Benvenue*. Both were outward bound with vital revenue-earning general cargoes. *Benvrackie*, heading for Cape Town and coastal ports to Beira in Mozambique, had had a brush with a U-boat off the Azores. Having passed to the south of the Cape Verdes on the afternoon of 9 May, Captain W.E.R. Eyton-Jones altered course towards the sail of a lifeboat and picked up the master, Captain Bibby, and 24 survivors from the *Lassell*, who had been adrift for nine days. 'Four of them, including a woman, had been passengers on the ship. We took them on board and cared for them to the best of our ability.' That evening *Benvrackie*'s radio operator began to intercept the first of several distress and submarine-sighting messages from merchant ships in the vicinity. Eyton-Jones posted extra lookouts, helped by the survivors from the *Lassell*. During the forenoon of the 12th life-rafts were spotted bearing the name *Alfred Olsen*, but they were empty. This Norwegian ship had been shelled and sunk by the Italian submarine *Enrico Tazzoli*, Capitano di Fregata di Cossato, on 9 May, a fact Eyton-Jones learned later when he met her chief officer. These sightings did not augur well, and when at 02.00 on the 13th Eyton-Jones received a report from his gunners aft that they had seen 'two dull flashes', he thought they might be moonlight reflecting off the casing of a submarine. He altered *Benvrackie*'s course a little and pressed on, but at 06.30 he

was hurled off the [chart-room] settee with a terrific crash and a lurch. I was picking myself up when there was a second crash . . . Immediately she listed to port, and even then I could feel she was going down by the stern. I scrambled out to the wing of the bridge and could see the gun platform submerging. The port lifeboat was blown to pieces, and the men were trying to cut away the others. I went back into the wheelhouse, locked the Admiralty weighted box [containing the code books, convoy regulations and special routeing instructions], and threw it over the side.

The afterpart of the ship was now well under water, but I just managed to get to the fore rigging and was letting go the raft, when the ship upended and slid back stern-first. I looked up and saw the bows and windlass above my head, and then was taken down with her.

The time from the first crash to the ship being totally submerged was slightly less than three minutes.

Eyton-Jones found the woman survivor from the *Lassell* without a life-jacket and managed to assist her to cling on to some wreckage until the *Benvrackie*'s only lifeboat picked the pair of them up. It had been saved by the forethought of a Chinese sailor who had cut it free, so that it had floated off its chocks on the boat deck. Eyton-Jones had had 85 souls aboard the *Benvrackie* and the lifeboat spent many hours pulling among the wreckage with 'many sharks swimming around'. During this time 'the enemy submarine surfaced, backed close down towards us, and demanded the name of our ship. He did this twice and finally went away to the northwards, without offering any assistance.'

Eyton-Jones set sail in the overloaded boat. It performed better than anticipated, thanks to the clemency of the weather, but the heat began to burn and blister exposed skin on arms, shoulders and ankles. Rations of half a dipper of water, one biscuit and 'a lick of a stick dipped in condensed milk' were given out at 06.00 and 17.00. A tally of the lost amounted to 15 from the *Lassell* and 12 from the *Benvrackie*. On their second day they came close to a steamer, but it did not see them, and that night one of the Chinese broke down and jumped overboard. With some difficulty he was recovered, but lost when he made a second attempt a few hours later. A week afterwards a second ship failed to see them, a bruising experience, especially since on the eighth day the Chinese cook died from exposure. Although the weather was largely 'unbearably hot', they were also subjected to a series of nocturnal rain squalls so torrential that though they were able to top up their water barricoes they suffered from the accompanying bitter cold, and were obliged to lower the main-sail. However,

> nearly all the light winds were favourable, and we kept to north and easterly courses, checking the boat compass by the Pole Star. This was our only aid to navigation . . . Shortly after 4 p.m. on 26 May we sighted . . . the hospital ship *Oxfordshire* . . . being unable to walk straight, the men were all helped along on each side by stewards, taken to one of the wards, and given a bunk to lie in. A few minutes later the steward came round with hot tea and a bun. I must admit it was the grandest cup of tea I had ever tasted! . . . Eight hours after picking us up the *Oxfordshire* steamed into Freetown. We found our lifeboat had, although heavily overloaded, sailed 520 miles [NE] in the thirteen days . . . We learned later that our second steward Ho Fook, who

had been missing . . . at the time of the sinking, was picked up in a delirious condition two days afterwards by one of the Blue Star steamers . . . he had been forty seven hours on one of the small rafts, without water and food. Sharks had tried to get him off . . . he carried the marks of their teeth on one of his thighs.

Two days after the sinking of the *Benvrackie* Schewe had torpedoed a sister-ship, the *Benvenue*, Captain J. Struth, bound for Bombay and Karachi. The torpedo struck at 19.11 on 15 May, exploding in the ship's magazine, killing one of the soldiers manning the port Bofors and one of the radio officers. It also sheared the propeller shaft, and the main engine raced furiously. She too went down by the stern, taking eleven minutes about it, just long enough for four lifeboats to be launched. By midnight cold, torrential rain and strong squalls were making the 'motion of the boats rough and violent'. Next morning an emergency radio transmitter was set up and a distress message sent. Struth made sail to the east but doused it in the late afternoon as one boat had fallen astern and was soon out of sight. A little later they were picked up by a British ship, the *English Trader*, but there was no sign of the chief officer's boat.

The survivors were taken to Freetown, where six days later the six British and eight Chinese survivors of the fourth boat arrived aboard a destroyer, having made good about four hundred miles before being rescued. Struth concluded his subsequent report by saying that he 'was blessed with a splendid crew, each one doing his part nobly . . .' William Thomson's Ben Line was a first-class cargo-liner company, on a par with Holt's Blue Funnel and Glen Lines for its training and morale, and inculcated that invaluable *esprit de corps* which distinguished such shipping companies.

The day after sinking the *Benvenue* Schewe struck at a homeward-bound ship, the 11,800-ton *Rodney Star*, another fine, fast refrigerated cargo-liner part-laden with general and frozen meat from Fray Bentos, Uruguay. The calm weather was marred by an early morning overcast, a residue from the night's torrential squalls. At 05.30 the *Rodney Star* was hit in No. 3 Hold, penetrated on its starboard side by *U-105*'s torpedo, which destroyed two of the three lifeboats in the starboard davits. The engines shuddered to a stop and the ship began to list. At 06.02 Captain S.J.C. Phillips ordered the ship abandoned. 'There was no fuss or bother, and within about ten minutes all the sound boats had been safely manned and lowered.' Hardly had they cleared the ship when Schewe, having worked round to her port side, fired a second torpedo, and half an hour later a third, this time into the starboard side, breaking the *Rodney Star*'s back. At 07.00 'the U-boat surfaced and opened fire, hitting the bridge. She fired seventy eight rounds in all, which seemed a waste of ammunition and effort, several shells bursting close to the boats. A little later a blinding rain squall came sweeping down from the westward; the four boats took the chance, hoisted their sails and made off. They had orders to steer north-east and soon lost sight of each other.' After six days Phillips's boat was seen by the destroyer *Boreas*, Lieutenant Commander D.H. Maitland-Makgill-Crichton; some others were recovered by a British ship, others still by a Vichy French vessel. These last were landed at Dakar but unlike the *Memnon*'s people escaped internment, being almost immediately exchanged for the crew of a Vichy French ship, the *Criton*, recently captured by the British.

Schewe, meanwhile, headed for L'Orient, and on passage *U-105* torpedoed the coal-laden *Scottish Monarch*; all but one of the crew were picked up. Oesten in *U-106* had escorted a German blockade-runner, the *Lech*, before being released to operate off the Cape Verdes, where in just over a week he sank the home-bound *Silveryew, Clan MacDougall* and, while he was on passage towards L'Orient, the *Sacramento Valley*. The *Silveryew*, loaded with pig-iron, manganese ore, kyanite ore (aluminium silicate) and kernels, was sunk on 30 May. She went down quickly. One of her apprentices, Keith Angus, recalled that it was evening:

I might have slept through if my chum hadn't rushed in and aroused me. By the time I staggered out on deck the 4-inch gun was just disappearing under water, and the engines were still pounding away, the torpedo having hit the bulkhead between the engine-room and the refrigerated hold and flooded the engine-room with ammonia gas as well as water. The black gang [firemen] dropped everything and decamped, and pushed off a life raft, the boats being gone, all but one which was dangling from one fall. I jumped onto the raft too, with seven or eight others, all engine staff but me and the Chinese carpenter. Rafts then were not the elaborate devices we had later, just four drums in a wooden frame. The painter had no quick release, it was just tied [on]. The raft floated, like the dropped toast, knot-side down and was being dragged along as the engineers tried to release it. I had a knife and began to cut the painter but the ship suddenly plunged and down everything went, and everybody [with it]. We came up again, the raft having broken its painter and preceded us, and crawled back aboard. After a bit we thought there must be a head fewer than previous so looked about and found a hand sticking out from under the raft, waving feebly. We dragged it out, the owner, the Junior Fourth [Engineer], a happy type from Belfast, wheezing, 'Aw, thanks boys. You know I *thought* I was a long time comin' to the sairface.' He had been trapped by the buoyancy of his life jacket.

After several hours, I noticed that the raft had less freeboard, but decided it would do no good to announce it. It transpired from later conversation that everyone had noticed it, and had thought as I had. The matter was resolved when the Third Mate, a Canadian like me, showed up out of the darkness, rowing the jolly boat single-handed, and took us off.

Only Captain J. Smith was lost; the 51 crew members eventually reached São Antonio, in the Cape Verdes.

This was also the refuge of Captain C.H. Parfitt and the 84 survivors from the *Clan MacDougall*, which was outward bound with a general cargo for South Africa. Two men died with her. The survivors from the coal-laden *Sacramento Valley*, owned by Reardon Smith's of Cardiff, were picked up by various ships and landed at Freetown for repatriation; three men went down with their ship.

In *U-38* on 4 May Liebe sank the ageing outward-bound Swedish cargo-liner *Japan*, with no loss of life. Next day he attacked the British motor-vessel *Queen Maud*, laden with coal and government stores bound for Alexandria. Captain R.J. McDonald and all but one of his men were rescued by a Portuguese ship and HMS *Dragon*. Having replenished from the *Egerland* a few days before her apprehension by the British, in the eight days between 23rd and 31st May Liebe sank the Dutch motor-vessel *Berhala*, the British Strick Line steamer *Tabaristan* homeward bound from Basra with pig-iron, groundnuts, general and manganese ore, the *Empire Protector* and the Norwegian cargo-vessel *Rinda*, completing his patrol by torpedoing the *Kingston Hill*, also bound for Alexandria with a mixed cargo of coal and stores. Captain Niven and about half his crew were killed.

Beginning his patrol near the Canaries, Schütze in *U-103* torpedoed the outward-bound Norwegian vessel *Polyanna*, then off Freetown and in quick succession he sank the former Danish but now British-registered *Samsö* on 1 May and the *Wray Castle* on the 3rd. The Lancashire Shipping's *Wray Castle* carried a full cargo of Mauritian sugar; her master, Captain G.T. Dobeson, was picked up with his crew and eventually landed at Freetown, but was destined for further employment before he was repatriated. On the 6th Schütze attacked the P&O cargo-liner *Surat*, Captain T.E. Daniel, sinking her and her cargo of pig-iron, peas and rape seed. The same day *U-103* torpedoed Elder Dempster's out-bound *Dunkwa*, with the loss of eight men and a cargo of government stores intended for Opobo, Nigeria. Moving north to the Cape Verde Islands and his own rendezvous with the *Egerland*, within three days Schütze sank two Ellerman liners, the *City of Winchester* and *City of Shanghai*. Both had left Britain in Convoy OB313, the former bound for Cape Town and Beira with a general cargo, the latter with a valuable cargo of government stores for Turkey by way of the Cape and the Suez Canal – an example of the excessive distances British ships were compelled to sail. Schütze's next victim was the Egyptian steamer *Radames*, torpedoed off the Liberian coast on the 20th, followed on the 22nd by the tanker *British Grenadier*. The tanker was in ballast, heading for Aruba from Freetown for fuel oil for the Royal Navy. On 24 May *U-103* despatched the Greek-flagged *Marionga*, and on the 25th the Dutch *Wangi Wangi*.

Reaching Freetown, Schütze sank the *Elmdene*, a tramp loaded with a valuable cargo of 5,000 tons of coal, 1,000 tons of munitions and a score of crated aircraft. Fortunately for Captain E. Fear the munitions did not explode, and he and his crew abandoned ship safely. Schütze was now short of fuel and the loss of the supply ships meant he was ordered to head home, picking up fuel at Las Palmas, but also to attack Convoy SL76 en route. Mistaking her for a ship from this convoy, Schütze torpedoed the Italian steamer *Ernani*, which had been heading for Bordeaux disguised as a Dutch vessel.

Having sunk the *Calchas* on 21 April, Hessler moved south of the Cape Verdes, where on the evening of the 30th a torpedo from *U-107* sent the Lamport & Holt liner *Lassell* to the bottom. As noted, her master, Captain A.R. Bibby, was among those picked up by the *Benvrackie*. The remainder, 17 crew and eight gunners under Chief Officer Underhill, were also picked up by a British ship, the Elder, Dempster liner *Egba*, outward bound for Freetown. Underhill and his people had been in their boat for eleven days.

Moving west to the rendezvous off St Paul's Rocks, *U-107* took aboard fuel from the *Nordmark* and, a week later, torpedoes from the *Egerland* before returning to Freetown, where in the small hours of 16 May Hessler began his run of sinkings, starting with the Dutchman *Marisa*. This was followed by the torpedoing of the British *Piako*, whose master, Captain B. Evans, had already been torpedoed once. The torpedo struck in the engine room and killed the duty watch, wrecking the starboard boats and inflicting tremendous damage on the *Piako*, which immediately began to sink with her vital cargo of 10,100 tons of frozen meat and butter and 1,500 tons of zinc. Ten of her people were lost, and although Evans and 64 men were rescued by HM Sloop *Bridgewater*, several had been severely wounded in Hessler's attack.

Hessler next sank the Harrison liner *Colonial*. She had been the commodore's ship in the out-bound Convoy OB318, and in addition to Captain J. Devereux and his crew of 92, Commodore W.B. Mackenzie and his six staff were among those rescued by the ancient British battleship

Centurion, a relic from the First World War, much reduced in her armament and commanded by Lieutenant Commander R. W. Wainwright, who
landed them at Freetown. Hessler added to his laurels by next sinking the
Greek steamer *Papalemos*, followed by the *Sire*, a Canadian-registered ship
in ballast. Captain J.T. Bennett and all but three of his crew were also landed
at Freetown, from the corvette *Marguerite*. The same corvette picked up the
survivors from the *Alfred Jones*, thought by Hessler to be a decoy-ship; she
was in fact the commodore's ship from the dispersed Convoy OB320, and
in addition to her master Captain H. Harding and his crew had on board
Commodore G.T.C.P. Swabey and his staff, all but 14 of whom were saved.
Like the *Alfred Jones*, the *Adda*, Hessler's next target, was also owned by
Elder, Dempster and had been the commodore's ship, in her case in OB323.
As a liner she was carrying 266 passengers, mostly service personnel bound
for Freetown. Although Captain J.T. Marshall, 145 crew, five of the
commodore's staff and 264 passengers survived, Commodore W.H. Kelly,
seven crew and two passengers were lost with the ship. Withdrawing to
replenish *U-107*, Hessler encountered and sank the Greek *Pandias* close to
the rendezvous. The supply ships had by this time themselves been sunk,
however, so Hessler headed for home, having completed the most viciously
successful patrol any U-boat was to achieve during the war, his fourteen
victims totalling 86,699 tons at a cost of some 128 lives. His father-in-law
must have been gratified.

The authorities at Freetown were well-nigh overwhelmed by the numbers
of survivors, and every effort was made to repatriate them as swiftly as
possible in the hope that they would avoid catching malaria or Freetown's
second novelty, syphilis. But not only humans proved an embarrassment to
the naval officers aboard the *Edinburgh Castle*, which formed the headquarters of the naval authorities in Freetown; there was also an ex-Vichy
war-prize, the steamship *Criton*, intercepted and captured by the Armed
Merchant Cruiser HMS *Cilicia* for carrying war contraband.

Built by Gray's of West Hartlepool in 1927, the *Criton* had been owned
by the Compagnie de Navigation d'Orbigny, of 81 rue Taitbout, Paris. Her
gross tonnage was 4,564 and she had been employed on a Europe-to-South
America service before the war. Her designed speed was 10 knots, but as
events were to show her boilers were incapable of providing steam for this
speed – indeed, she proved incapable of making 8, for she had been sabotaged by her crew before being captured. She was ill-equipped, and infested
with cockroaches, the bane of the sailor in tropical latitudes. However, with
tonnage short and British losses mounting, she was ordered back to Britain,
and a scratch crew of volunteers from among the multitude of survivors

was put under the command of Captain Dobeson, former master of the *Wray Castle*. Along with Dobeson went a former Ben Line officer named Chalmers as mate, a Mr N. Clear as chief engineer, some of the released prisoners from Dakar, including the *Memnon's* two radio officers, Whalley and Johnson, and as second mate Mr 'Newman', formerly of the *Tewkesbury*. Other 'Distressed British Seamen' made up most of the crew, though it proved necessary to recruit the firemen locally, an expedient Mr Clear considered dangerous. As the *Criton* was a war-prize she should have had a proportion of naval personnel on board, but only the officer appointed to command the naval detachment arrived, a sub-lieutenant named Stretton. In addition to her red ensign aft she also flew the white ensign from her foremasthead, a somewhat obscure indication that she was a war-prize but not as yet cleared by a prize court, and thus inhabited a shadowy region of unspecified status. Once manned, *Criton* was moved upstream to Pepel, where she loaded a full cargo of iron ore and a third radio officer, R. Carter, joined the ship.

The *Criton* joined two dozen other merchantmen in Convoy SL78 which left Freetown on 18 June. It was soon apparent that she could not maintain station, and she straggled. Dobeson was furious when he received a condescending message from the AMC *Esperance Bay* escorting the convoy. Protesting that he had forecast the *Criton's* inability to maintain convoy speed and demanding an escort, he was told 'No escort I'm afraid. You'd better run along now. Good luck.'

As she was 'running along' that night, a stowaway was discovered; the young black man would have done better to remain at home, for the following morning, as the *Criton* limped south, she was intercepted and followed by a Vichy French warship. This fired a shot over her and ordered her to stop and not use her radio, to which Dobeson agreed, to the frustration of Whalley and Johnson in the radio room and in the teeth of Chalmers's outright disagreement. The impasse between Dobeson and Chalmers was terminated when the French warship persuasively raked the *Criton* with machine-gun fire, a circumstance that caused such alarm among the native firemen that they immediately rushed the lifeboats. Suffering from severe strain and faced with a *fait accompli*, Dobeson ordered the ship abandoned. This was a disorderly event, but Third Mate Christie and Second Mate Newman managed to launch the boats despite the panic among the firemen. In boarding Newman's boat Dobeson fell and injured himself, sending him into shock, and Newman had some difficulty getting away from the ship's starboard side as the French warship on the port side opened fire with her main gun and some of her shells passed right through the *Criton*, endangering Newman's boats on the unengaged side. The French commander afterwards apologised for this, claiming to have thought that the boats had got clear, but in the confusion of leaving the wretched vessel ten men were killed, and Dobeson was found to be badly injured.

Having sunk the *Criton* the French picked up her shaken survivors, and after landing they were taken to Konakri in French Guinea, where they were incarcerated in a camp containing other British merchant seamen, but segregated from them in a special compound surrounded by barbed wire. Again, conditions were deplorable; it was July, and at that season of the year the humidity was some 95 per cent, the daytime temperature averaged 28° C, and torrential rain flooded the palm-roofed mud huts, so that the compound was awash with rainwater and sewage. Many inmates of the camp were sick, and the local hospital was full. Several attempts to escape to the coast, steal a fishing boat and get away to Bathurst were foiled, and in due course Dobeson and his motley crew were arraigned before a court martial presided over by an admiral. Dobeson refused to acquiesce to the suggestion that he had ordered the *Criton* to be scuttled, a requirement presumably designed to cover the embarrassment of the Vichy authorities over having sunk a former French vessel; the outcome of his intransigence was that the members of the *Criton*'s crew were, like Captain Fryatt in the First World War, condemned as *franc-tireurs*, or pirates. The presence of a very junior British naval officer exacerbated the situation, for the court chose to interpret it as sinister in light of the *Criton*'s unresolved status as a claimed war-prize. Consequently, in late September all the officers were sent to Timbuctoo except the hospitalised, who included the fourth engineer, the third radio officer, and Sub-Lieutenant Stretton, who went to join Crabb at Koulikoro. Those remaining in Konakri, once released from hospital, continued to make escape attempts, and were moved to Kankan as a disincentive.

Those taken to Timbuctoo were subjected to a worse ordeal. Their journey began with an uncomfortable two-day sojourn on a narrow-gauge railway which took them to Kankan, from where they were moved by lorries to Bamako. Here they rested before the lorries then carried them to the headwaters of the river Niger, where they were ordered into a barge secured alongside an ancient paddle steamer. The steamer had two barges lashed on each side: the two to starboard contained ammunition, the inner port barge contained wood fuel for the vessel's steam-engine, the outer the British prisoners. They were five days on the river, stung to distraction by mosquitoes, until they disembarked near Kabara, to the south-east of Timbuctoo, then endured a five-day march across the desert to their new camp. Later they were moved back to Kankan, where they joined their former shipmates.

At Kankan the camp leader was Peter Johnson. Johnson was only 17 and he had been voted to command by his peers 'for two reasons. One, his ability to speak French, and more essentially for his fairness to all Ranks and Ratings when distributing Red Cross parcels and daily rations.' These men were to remain imprisoned for 18 months in conditions of terrible privation, the vindictive hostility of the Vichy authorities a consequence of the British raids on Dakar earlier in the war. By contrast, the helpless merchant seamen received kindnesses from the rank and file of their guards, and Johnson discovered that a number of the younger commissioned officers among these wished to escape their colonial exile and join the Free French forces under de Gaulle. Not before there had been several tense incidents under a regime which consisted of such petty tyrannies as the withholding of medicines and Red Cross parcels, clothing and footwear did release come, when the Allies invaded French North Africa in 1942. As Mr Clear reported, towards the end of their ordeal

the French Authorities had ordered my native firemen to perform menial duties for pro-British French Europeans who had just been interned with us. Peter [Johnson] refused to allow this. The whole camp was lined up, now numbering over one hundred men, and the guards [were] ordered to open fire. This the European sergeant refused to do. Peter informed the French Commanding Officer that he would take no responsibility as to what would happen if his guards did open fire. He was immediately personally attacked by the French Native Sergeant. At once the camp, almost to a man, moved to his assistance. Peter, quickly realising a potential riot [was about to break out] . . . ordered everyone to 'Stand back'. The potential riot quelled, Peter and the French Lieutenant retired to the Lieutenant's quarters to discuss matters . . . At the time it was generally thought that Peter's quick action and firm order [was] very commendable, and [taken] at great personal risk.

The *Criton's* crew were undoubtedly exceptionally badly treated by the Vichy French as compared with other merchant prisoners. Johnson, a minor at the time, never received any recognition for his part in this sorry tale. After the war the French government made an *ex-gratia* payment to the British in compensation, though unaccompanied by any formal apology. To rub salt into the wound, Attlee's Labour Government failed to make any attempt to pass the money on to its intended recipients. On his way home by sea Johnson himself wrote a full report which, as recalled by Clear, 'was sighted by British Military Intelligence in the West Indies, American Security in New York and finally confiscated on board by a

Lieutenant from MI5 before he [Johnson] left the ship in Liverpool. In addition the Lieutenant informed him that he was to write no more reports and that included even writing one for his own employers [Alfred Holt & Company].'[19]

By early May 1941 the new arrangement of providing a constant escort throughout a convoy's passage was getting under way. Convoy HX125 left Halifax on the 6th accompanied by the battleship *Revenge*, the AMC *Ascania* and the long-ranged sloops *Aberdeen*, *Banff*, *Culver*, *Fishguard* and *Hartland*. But that was not all. Matters in the northern margins of the Western Ocean were about to have a far-reaching effect upon the war in the greater part of the Atlantic. The Enigma decrypts proved themselves invaluable and the British secured a further advantage in May when intercepted meteorological observations from the *München* in the sub-Arctic enabled them to fix her position by radio-location. A powerful force was sent to capture her, and the cruisers *Edinburgh*, flying the flag of Vice Admiral Holland, *Manchester* and *Birmingham*, attended by the destroyers *Nestor*, *Somali*, *Bedouin* and *Eskimo*, closed the *München* in poor visibility off Jan Mayen Island on 7 May. *Somali*'s boarding party secured cipher equipment which was hurried south aboard the *Nestor* and finally delivered to the code-breakers at Bletchley Park. In due course its fruits reached the cryptanalysts at the Admiralty.

That same day, after the Germans had spent a fruitless week searching the North West Approaches, both Convoy HX122 and Convoy SC29 were located, the first by a Kondor, the second by *U-95*. Dönitz was unable to reinforce *U-95*, however, and both convoys escaped damage. But at noon the Admiralty intercepted a 'first sighting' report on a line of bearing that suggested it referred to Convoy OB318.

Late that afternoon at about 17.30, further to the north-west off Iceland, the escort to westward-bound Convoy OB318 changed over when Commander Baker-Creswell's 3rd Escort Group arrived from Hvalfjord to relieve Commander Bockett-Pugh's 7th Escort Group. With Baker-Creswell's three destroyers *Bulldog*, *Amazon* and *Broadway* came the AMC *Ranpura*, while Bockett-Pugh's corvettes *Auricula*, *Primrose*, *Nasturtium*, *Marigold* and *Dianthus*, along with the sloop *Rochester*, remained with OB318 in the absence of Baker-Creswell's, which were on their way. In fact what the Admiralty had intercepted was *U-95*'s 'first sighting' report on SC29, and in interpreting it to refer to OB318 they ordered an evasive alteration of course which probably contributed to its betrayal, for its funnel smoke was seen to the eastward by Kapitänleutnant Kuppisch in *U-94*.

Kuppisch dived at 20.00, intending to slip under the leading escorts and attack that night in the by now classic manner: from inside the columns of merchant ships, amid the roiling wakes and steaming hulls, all of which would confuse the escorts' defence. He did not reckon on Baker-Creswell's sonar operator picking up his echo at about 21.00, or on being followed by *Bulldog* as he penetrated the screen. He nevertheless succeeded in torpedoing two ships in the central columns, the *Eastern Star* and the *Ixion*. The *Eastern Star* was a standard-built vessel dating from the First World War and, although nominally British, belonged to a Norwegian company and was Norwegian-manned. She caught fire and burned rapidly, though her crew appear to have escaped unharmed, being rescued by the *Nailsea Manor*, a tramp nominated as rescue ship to the convoy. Kuppisch's second victim was another Blue Funnel liner, loaded with alcohol and general cargo bound for New York. The torpedo hit the *Ixion* aft, filling the air with the smell of whisky. Having inspected the influx of water into the engine room, Captain W.F. Dark ordered his people into their boats and they lay-to, watching *Ixion* as she sank at 02.45. Five boat-loads of her people were picked up by the *Nailsea Manor* while the sixth, including Dark, was rescued by the corvette *Marigold*.

In the meantime *Bulldog*, joined by *Rochester* and *Amazon*, had been subjecting Kuppisch to a pounding. It lasted four long hours, damaging *U-94* and driving her off, but despite it she was not compelled to return to base.

During the next day, the 8th, the rest of Baker-Creswell's warships arrived to relieve those of the 7th Escort Group, which rejoined Bockett-Pugh who was now heading east with Convoy HX123. The newly-joined corvettes were *Aubrieta*, *Hollyhock* and *Nigella*, and HM Trawlers *Angle*, *Daneman* and *St Apollo*. Unknown to Baker-Creswell, OB318 was still under surveillance, this time by Lemp in *U-110*, who had been directed towards the contact by Kerneval. Lemp summoned Oberleutnant Schnee in *U-201* and they conferred together on the surface ahead of the convoy. They agreed to attack next morning, Lemp first and Schnee half an hour later, having concluded that the bright moonlight expected that night would make a surface attack dangerous.

At about noon on the 9th, as the convoy approached the vicinity of Cape Farewell, Lemp torpedoed two British steamships, the *Esmond* and the *Bengore Head*. The former was in ballast and all hands were rescued; the latter, a much smaller vessel, lost one man when she sank with her cargo of coal and binder-twine. The convoy swung through an emergency turn to port, so that Schnee attacked its rear, torpedoing the *Gregalia* and severely damaging the *Empire Cloud*. The *Gregalia* was in ballast and no one was killed, all being rescued by ships in the convoy, while the *Empire Cloud*, although abandoned, was later reboarded, salvaged, and towed to the Clyde.

But Lemp's luck had run out; he was attempting to sink a third vessel, a tanker, when his periscope was spotted, drawing upon him the ire of Baker-Creswell in *Bulldog*, with *Broadway* and *Aubrieta* coming up fast. All three escorts obtained sonar contacts and *Broadway* lobbed one depth-charge into the sea before Lieutenant Commander V.F. Smith in *Aubrieta* systematically counter-attacked with several charges. The effect was devastating. Having first plunged to about a hundred metres of her own accord, *U-110* then broke surface, a fractured valve having admitted compressed air into her ballast tanks. On his conning tower Lemp was confronted by the three British ships, all firing at him. In a hail of shot and torn steel he ordered *U-110* abandoned. In the confusion the scuttling charges were not set, nor was Lemp's order to open all the ballast tank vents obeyed.

Nevertheless all hands escaped, the last man leaving as the water rose up the U-boat's conning tower. Intending to ram, Baker-Creswell noted that the U-boat seemed reluctant to sink, and decided instead to attempt to board her. Taylor of the *Broadway* had already closed the U-boat and dropped two shallow-set depth-charges, and their explosions may have added to the panic on board. He fouled *U-110* and damaged the thin, susceptible plating of his ex-American 'four-stacker', rupturing ten oil tanks and a magazine and fouling the port propeller. Seeing his U-boat failing to sink and a whaler being lowered from the *Bulldog*, Lemp vainly tried to return, calling upon his first watch officer to help, but he was too late. Some of his crew later maintained that he was shot by the boarding-party, who recognised him as they pulled past in the whaler; others claimed that he threw up his hands and surrendered. Given the difficulty of recognising even the notorious assassin of the *Athenia* among the heads bobbing obscurely amid the waves in those dramatic circumstances, the second version seems more likely.

Neither Baker-Creswell nor Taylor appears to have made much effort at the time to rescue the Germans. Smith had drifted away with his sonar under urgent repair, after the completion of which he rescued the men from the *Esmond*. Meanwhile Sub-Lieutenant D. Balme had the *Bulldog*'s whaler pulled over *U-110*'s casing and the nine heavily-armed British naval seamen jumped aboard. To Balme's astonishment the hatches were dogged, but down below the lights were still on. There was no flooding, nor any evidence of chlorine. He signalled his findings to his commander, and Baker-Creswell ordered Taylor to provide an engineering party capable of getting the U-boat's engines going while he took *Bulldog* close enough to get hold of a wire Balme's party had found lashed on the U-boat's forward casing. Balme went below again in a 'deathly silence' to discover 'this typewriter thing. We pressed a few buttons which lit up [different letters] in a rather odd way.' It was an Enigma machine. Balme formed a chain of men and passed out of the boat all official documents, including the code books and the 'typewriter thing', all set for a transmission. The 'telegraphist [Alan Long was curious and] . . . sent it up the hatch.'

As Baker-Creswell tried to tow the U-boat and the engineering party failed to start her engines, *Aubrieta* arrived and began to rescue the German seamen, hurrying them below to keep them from contact with the angry survivors from the *Esmond*. Operations were suspended for a while when a sonar contact was made and attacked, but it proved spurious. Baker-Creswell then ordered *Aubrieta* to return to the convoy and transfer prisoners to *Amazon*, thus ensuring that none but naval personnel should witness the anticipated salvage of *U-110*. Once she had been looted – the haul included several fine pairs of Zeiss binoculars, six sextants made by Plath of Hamburg, and Lemp's *Ritterkreuz* – *U-110* was secured and *Bulldog* began to tow her to Iceland, escorted by the damaged *Broadway*, but after about a hundred miles her bow reared up and she sank, 'a bitter blow' for Baker-Creswell. The crews of *Bulldog*, *Broadway*, *Aubrieta* and *Esmond* were afterwards sworn to secrecy regarding the event, a vow which appears to have been impeccably honoured for many years. Oddly, none of the Germans knew the U-boat had been boarded, a fiction Baker-Creswell maintained as he went from Hvalfjord to Scapa Flow. The capture of *U-110*'s Enigma machine and the *München* within days of one another provided access to much information emanating from Dönitz's operational headquarters at Kerneval.

Despite the secrecy, those concerned were rewarded. Baker-Creswell was promoted and he and Smith received the Distinguished Service Order from King George VI. Balme, Taylor and Dodds, the *Broadway*'s engineering officer, received the Distinguished Service Cross. There were Distinguished Service Medals and Mentions-in-Dispatches for several of the ratings, and the King remarked ambiguously that it 'was perhaps the most important single event in the whole war at sea'. Perhaps; certainly it had about it all the ingredients of Churchill's pertinent summary of the struggle for supremacy on the Atlantic as 'a war of groping and drowning, of ambuscade and stratagem, of science and seamanship'.

Convoy OB318 had meanwhile continued to the westward, oblivious of the drama it was leaving astern. Its ships had drama enough of their own, for *U-201* was still in contact. The *Amazon* found her by sonar and, calling in *Nigella* and *St Apollo*, subjected her to four hours of depth-charging which damaged but did not destroy her. It did however drive Schnee off, and the convoy proceeded until the small hours of 10 May, when Kapitänleutnant Wohlfarth sighted it and made a surface attack in *U-556*. Wohlfarth's torpedoes hit but only damaged the British steamer *Aelbryn*, which limped back to Reykjavik; they entirely missed the *Chaucer*.[20] Renewing the action in a second attack, *U-556* sank the Belgian ship *Gand* and the British steamer *Empire Caribou*. Only one man was lost from the *Gand*, but Captain B.E. Duffield and 33 men went down with the *Empire Caribou* and her cargo of Boston-bound chalk.

12

'We are a seafaring race'

Bismarck

B Y 13 MAY Dönitz had succeeded in organising a patrol line off Cape Farewell which consisted of *U-74, U-93, U-94* again ready for action, *U-97, U-98, U-109, U-111* and *U-556*, denominated the *West* Group. That day Gysae, in *U-98*, sighted and attacked the former Bibby liner *Shropshire*, now HM Armed Merchant Cruiser *Salopian*, which had detached from Convoy SC30 when east of Cape Farewell and was on her way back to Halifax. Some six torpedoes were fired into the ship before she foundered. Ropner's grain-laden tramp *Somersby* had straggled from the same convoy and was herself torpedoed by *U-111* (Kleinschmidt). Captain J.W. Thompson and his crew were rescued by the Greek steamer *Marika Protopava* which had also dropped behind SC30.

On the 19th Kuppisch sighted Convoy HX126 to the south of Cape Farewell. The escort to the 29 ships was pitiful at the time, consisting only of the AMC *Aurania* and the submarine *Tribune*, neither of which inhibited Kuppisch. Having reported the convoy to Kerneval he torpedoed another two grain-filled British steamers, the *Norman Monarch* at about midnight, followed some hours later by the *Harpagus*. Captain J.V. Stewart had hove the *Harpagus* to, to recover Captain T.A. Robertson of the *Norman Monarch* and 47 of his crew, but Robertson, 19 of his crew and all six of his naval gunners were lost with the *Harpagus*. Of Stewart's people, 25 crew, three passengers and four gunners were killed, the remnants of both ships' companies being pulled out of their boats by the escorts that later arrived from Iceland.

Kuppisch lost contact after this attack, but mayhem was not long postponed. Wohlfarth in *U-556* fired at, and damaged, the Eagle Oil tanker *San*

Felix, then hit and sank another tanker, the *British Security*, before torpedo-ing the *Darlington Court*, a grain-laden tramp-ship owned by Haldin & Phillips. The *British Security* had 11,200 tons of benzene and paraffin (kerosene) in her capacious tanks, and in the inferno all hands perished. The master of the *Darlington Court*, Captain Hurst, and about a third of his crew took to the boats. That evening Kuppisch was in touch once more and *U-94* sank the Norwegian tanker *John P. Pedersen*, loaded with 9,000 tons of fuel intended for the British army.

Gysae manoeuvred to fire at Donaldson Brothers' *Rothermere*, which was a comparatively new steamer. Carrying a cargo of steel and paper she settled fast, taking her master, Captain G. McCartney, and 20 men with her. The remaining 34 crew and a single passenger were later rescued by the Icelandic merchantmen *Bruarfoss*.

Because the through-escort policy had been only partially implemented Convoy HX126 had lacked anti-submarine cover, and by posting Kuppisch on the 41st meridian Dönitz had been able to intercept and attack it with impunity, just to the west of its rendezvous with the 12th Escort Group, a powerful force of five destroyers, four corvettes and two trawlers under Commander C.D. Howard-Johnston in *Malcolm*. The convoy commodore was expecting the arrival of these faster destroyers, but by the morning of 21 May the damage had been done and the convoy was in disorder, having made collective emergency turns and individual evasive manoeuvres through the night.

In the confusion of avoiding periscopes on the one part, and coping with misses and misfires on the other, it was impossible for either side to keep an accurate tally. Both Wohlfarth and Kleinschmidt were credited with torpedoing the *Cockaponsett*; although loaded with steel, trucks, general and 250 tons of TNT she did not explode but allowed her crew to escape in their boats. After the main convoy had passed, Kleinschmidt certainly found the *Barnby* astern of her station and attacked her. The torpedo from *U-111* killed two men in the engine room and consigned 7,250 tons of flour to the sea-bed. Captain A.J. Gale and his men took to their boats and landed on the Icelandic coast. The last U-boat to contact the convoy was *U-93*, Kapitänleutnant C. Korth, who in the early hours of the 21st fired a torpedo at the Dutch tanker *Elusa*. Although she was not sunk immediately three men were killed and, rather unusually, her cargo of diesel ignited.

Korvettenkapitän Fischer in *U-109* failed to make contact with HX126 on 20 May but sighted Convoy OB322 to the north of HX126 and sank the British tramp steamer *Marconi*. She was in ballast, and although 22 men were lost, Captain F.E. Hailstone and the remnant of his crew were found by the American patrol vessel *General Greene* and landed at St John's, New found land. These heavy losses prompted the Commander-in-Chief, Western Approaches, Admiral Sir Percy Noble, to order the rescue ship *Hontestroom* to detach from OB322 and search for survivors. Among those she picked up were Captain B. Green and all 40 of the crew of the *Cockaponsett*, a dozen from the *Darlington Court* and 16 from the *John P. Pedersen*.

Arriving on the scene to find his charges spread widely, Howard-Johnston set about re-forming the convoy. The appearance of the 12th Escort Group's five destroyers was reported to Kerneval, whereupon Dönitz ordered contact broken off, leaving *U-111* to transmit dummy signals to foster the belief that he was still harrying the convoy. In rounding up the scattered merchantmen Commander J. Bostock of the ex-American destroyer *Churchill* approached the *Elusa* and in a heavy sea managed to rig a jackstay and swing the members of her Dutch crew to safety. Next day Howard-Johnston ordered Lieutenant Commander D.A. Rayner of HM Corvette *Verbena* to extinguish the fires aboard the *Elusa*, then tow her towards a safe haven until salvage tugs should relieve him. As he approached the tanker, Rayner saw a surfaced U-boat coming towards him beyond the *Elusa*. He engaged with gun-fire and increased speed, intending to ram, but the U-boat crash-dived under the wreck. Receiving Rayner's signal aboard *Malcolm*, Howard-Johnston sent Bostock's *Churchill* to assist. Meanwhile Rayner had a sonar contact which he depth-charged, but since he had no deep-water charges he was unable to achieve anything, the U-boat having submerged a long way. The *Verbena* and *Churchill* made several attacks, frustrated by *Churchill's* 'obsolete type of American asdic [sonar] . . . which . . . was nothing like as efficient as our own British machines'. However the U-boat, thought to be Kentrat's *U-74*, received a sufficiently heavy pounding to cause her to abort her mission. Like the others of the *West* Group except *U-111* she was now ordered to the east, to support what the Germans had confidently denominated Operation RHEINÜBUNG.

Unable to achieve anything in the way of submarine-killing or salvage, Rayner and Bostock eventually withdrew towards Iceland. On their way they became aware of events of some moment occurring over the horizon to the east. The radio traffic increased, and at 10.00 they heard the disastrous news that the battle-cruiser HMS *Hood* had been sunk. They then intercepted transmissions from the cruisers shadowing the *Hood's* persecutor. Something big was clearly afoot: 'Just before lunch we could see a big ship on the horizon hurrying to the south; but she was hull down and difficult to identify.'[1] She was the *Bismarck*.

Operation RHEINÜBUNG never enjoyed more than sceptical approval from Hitler. He had been unimpressed by Lütjens's previous much-lauded 'achievement', and was unsurprised when the *Scharnhorst* and *Gneisenau* were bombed by the Royal Air Force in Brest. On 5 May he had travelled to Gotenhafen to inspect the Kriegsmarine's impressive new battleships *Tirpitz* and *Bismarck*. It is said that he countered Lütjens's exposition of the capital ships' virtues by remarking upon the dangers of enemy aircraft-carriers and their torpedo-bombers. With the intention of repeating Lütjens's earlier enterprise, Raeder nevertheless assigned the *Bismarck* and the heavy cruiser *Prinz Eugen* to a new raid on British commerce, again placing the two heavy ships under Lütjens's flag. The *Bismarck* moved to Kiel and the Seekriegsleitung made complex dispositions of supply ships and alerted Dönitz to the operation, calling in the assistance of his U-boats. Grossadmiral Raeder then took the unusual step of launching Operation RHEINÜBUNG before informing Hitler, which he did at a routine meeting on 22 May.

The British Admiralty learned of the sortie on the 21st. The intelligence services were alerted by an increase in radio traffic, the source of which was confirmed when a reported sighting of the squadron in the Kattegat by the Swedish cruiser *Gotland* was passed to London by Captain Denham, the British naval attaché at Stockholm.[2] A high-flying photo-reconnaissance Spitfire then located the two warships in the Kors Fjord. The following day, 22 May, an RAF Maryland found the fjord empty, just as German aerial reconnaissance was reporting that all the British Home Fleet's capital ships were at their moorings in the Orkneys. But the Commander-in-Chief of the Home Fleet, Admiral Sir John Tovey, had a direct telephone link from his flagship to the Admiralty, and the overcast skies had misled the German reconnaissance: in fact, Tovey had ordered one of his heavy battle-squadrons to sea early that morning. It consisted of the elderly battle-cruiser *Hood*, flying the flag of Vice Admiral Lancelot Holland, the brand-new battleship *Prince of Wales*, and six destroyers, *Achates*, *Antelope*, *Anthony*, *Echo*, *Electra* and *Icarus*. Tovey was to follow with his flagship, the battleship *King George V*, the carrier *Victorious*, the Second Cruiser Squadron of *Galatea*, *Aurora*, *Hermione* and *Kenya* under Rear Admiral A.T.B. Curteis, and the destroyers *Active*, *Nestor*, *Inglefield*, *Intrepid* and *Punjabi*. A second battle-cruiser, the *Repulse*, was ordered to cover Convoy WS8B, a small military convoy of fast merchant ships destined for the Mediterranean with vital stores for Malta.

Oblivious to this mobilisation of force, Lütjens headed north-west, intending to round Iceland to the north and descend into the North Atlantic and pounce upon the British convoy route by way of the Denmark Strait. To cover this eventuality Tovey had his routine cruiser patrols watching the Iceland–Faeroes Gap and the Denmark Strait itself, supported by flying-boats of Coastal Command. In addition to WS8B and HX126 there were at the time several other convoys at sea: HX127 was six days out of Halifax, with SC31 just ahead of it; from the east, OB323 and OB324 were also closing the area; in all, a total of 191 merchantmen were at sea in the North Atlantic.

At 19.22 on 22 May, as it swept down the Denmark Strait from the north amid scattered ice floes, snow squalls and fog banks, Lütjens's battle-squadron was seen and shadowed by the cruisers of the First Cruiser Squadron, *Norfolk* and *Suffolk*, patrolling off Straumness, Iceland under the flag of Rear Admiral W.F. Wake-Walker. With *Bismarck* leading *Prinz Eugen*, the German ships were spotted by Able Seaman Newall aboard *Suffolk*. Having reported this sighting to the Admiralty, Captain R.M. Ellis kept in touch with the enemy by means of his new radar while taking advantage of the mist and fog along the Greenland ice-edge. British air patrols had been frustrated by the weather, so the message from Ellis electrified the Admiralty. It failed to reach Tovey, but he did hear Wake-Walker's contact signal an hour later, when *Norfolk* reported having exchanged fire with *Bismarck* in a brief engagement at 20.30 that left Wake-Walker's flagship undamaged. 'In spite of steaming at high speed through rain, snow, ice-floes and mirage effects . . . [the two cruisers] held on, the *Suffolk* on the enemy's starboard quarter and the *Norfolk* to port.'[3] From the B-Dienst team on board *Bismarck* Lütjens knew he was still being followed; but he calculated that he could throw off the pursuit and disappear into the vastness of the ocean ahead of him. By midnight he had succeeded.

Vice Admiral Holland was by then off Reykjanes, the south-west tip of Iceland. He was also in a difficult position, aware of what was at stake and what was expected of him. The design of his flagship *Hood* was flawed, for while the armament of a battle-cruiser matched that of a battleship, her armour was sacrificed to obtain her high speed. The *Hood* was moreover an old ship with obsolete internal sub-divisions, and the refit to improve her deck armour, approved in March 1939, had never been carried out, though time had been found to update her anti-aircraft armament. By an extreme contrast her consort was a new ship, so new that although she had been reported as fit for service, problems were being experienced with the innovative quadruple mountings of eight of her heavy-calibre 15-inch guns. The manufacturers, Vickers Armstrong, still had technical staff on board trying to rectify the faults. By flying his flag in the prestigious *Hood*, which led the *Prince of Wales* and thus invited the attention of the enemy at the head of the line, Holland had only compounded these disadvantages.

Gun-for-gun, Holland possessed the advantage, if he could but use it quickly and decisively – but in *Bismarck* Lütjens had a flagship which possessed the merits of a modern battleship with a higher speed and a more weatherly design than the *Prince of Wales*, and while as a cruiser the *Prinz Eugen* was not comparable with either of her opponents, she was a new and fast ship, able to give considerable support. Both German warships were fully worked up for their operation, and they also possessed stereoscopic range-finding controls, which had proved superior to the British coincidental system a generation earlier, at Jutland.

By the early hours of 24 May a fresh northerly wind had dispersed the mists. The *Bismarck*'s radar had been damaged in the short action with *Norfolk* by her own gun-concussions, so Lütjens had ordered Kapitän zur See H. Brinckmann of the *Prinz Eugen* into the lead, and at 05.35 the cruiser's radar located Holland's capital ships. Holland was not using radar, lest its radiation be detected; fatally, when he caught sight of the enemy at 05.49 he ordered his squadron's fire to be concentrated on the leading ship. This was queried by Captain J.C. Leach aboard *Prince of Wales*, where the inferiority of the leading German ship was recognised at once, but it was already too late. During the preceding hours Holland had already made a number of decisions which events were to reveal as having further compromised him, among which were a slowing of his two capital ships, and an instruction to Wake-Walker to deal with the *Prinz Eugen*. They were to avail him nothing, and the first only served to deliver him onto all the guns his enemy could bring to bear.

With only their forward turrets able to engage, at about 05.55 the British ships opened fire at a range of some 11 miles, Holland giving a last-minute order to shift target to the second ship, the *Bismarck*. Where the *Hood*'s shells fell is unknown; they certainly did no damage to the enemy, whose superior gunnery control quickly found the range of *Hood*. Within six minutes 'There was an explosion of quite incredible violence . . .', wrote the gunnery officer aboard the *Prinz Eugen*. 'Through huge holes opened up in the grey hull, enormous flames leapt up from the depths of the ship . . .' The plunging German shells had penetrated the thin 3-inch deck armour and exploded in one of *Hood*'s magazines. 'An ash-coloured pall of smoke' rose in two columns above 'a kind of incandescent dome'.

Out of HMS *Hood*'s company of 1,419 men, only three escaped death as she blew in two and sank in seconds.[4] Leach had to alter course to avoid the wreckage as he engaged; moreover, the *Prince of Wales*'s gunnery compared poorly with the rapidity with which the Germans found the range of the British. Exposed to the full concentration of Lütjens's fire, *Prince of Wales* suffered a hit amidships and a second on her bridge. Here only Captain Leach and a signals rating were left alive, while battle damage combined with the defects in her gun turrets to reduce the new battleship's capacity to strike back. Making smoke, Leach turned away. He now had only two guns capable of retaliation, and they were in his after quadruple turret. Fearing the worst, he was relieved to be informed by his gunnery officer that Lütjens was not in pursuit, but instead 'decamping'.

Having struck this mighty blow Lütjens saw his immediate task as escaping the vengeance of Tovey, for he knew well enough that the Royal Navy would hunt him to the ends of the earth. Not that his orders from Raeder gave him any latitude; a disappearance into the Atlantic and a subsequent resumption of operations against British trade was his only realistic option, despite the pleas of his flag captain, Lindemann. The news of the loss of 'the beautiful *Hood*', described by Churchill as 'one of our most cherished naval possessions', struck deep in London, prompting that apocryphally growled order 'Sink the *Bismarck!*'[5]

Sir John Tovey scarcely needed to be told. He was already troubled by the restraint he had felt obliged to exercise out of respect for the vice admiral's seniority and experience; he felt he should have insisted that Holland reverse his order of sailing and place the *Prince of Wales* ahead of the vulnerable *Hood*. As Tovey steamed west, Wake-Walker pursued Lütjens's squadron and renewed contact, while Admiral Sir James Somerville in distant Gibraltar was ordered to head north-west with Force H.[6] Other dispositions were also made, including the despatch of the battleship *Revenge* to join Convoy HX128.

In fact, *Bismarck* had suffered damage from a few fateful hits by the *Prince of Wales*. When Rayner and Bostock saw the great ship sweep past, her fuel system was damaged and her range thereby curtailed, circumstances that induced Lütjens to order Lindemann to head for Brest, and to detach Brinckmann and the *Prinz Eugen* on a solo raiding sortie. When the news of the damage to *Bismarck* reached Berlin and Kerneval, Dönitz offered his help. Lütjens requested that a trap for his pursuers be set 360 miles south of Cape Farewell, through which he proposed the *Bismarck* should lead Wake-Walker. Dönitz obliged, directing the U-boats lately engaged with HX126 to divert and directing a second group to form another such trap 400 miles west of L'Orient. By the evening of 24 May he had deployed 'all available' (fifteen) U-boats in the two areas.

With Wake-Walker still in contact at the extreme range of *Suffolk*'s radar, late on the evening of the 24th Tovey ordered the *Victorious* to fly off her torpedo-carrying Swordfish biplanes. Nine took off, led by Lieutenant Commander E. Esmonde,[7] and using their simple radar sets prepared to make their first attack – on *Norfolk*; they were dissuaded from this course of action by signal, and sent on the correct course to locate *Bismarck*. Next they overflew three American vessels on Neutrality Patrol – the *Modoc*, *Northland* and *General Greene* – before, close to the limit of their fuel, they finally spotted through breaks in thick low cloud the hurrying shape of the German battleship. Esmonde's Swordfish attacked through a hail of anti-aircraft flak and one achieved a torpedo strike on the *Bismarck*'s armoured side. It did little or no damage in itself, but as she manoeuvred to avoid the Swordfish the temporary repairs to her damaged fuel system tore away. Sea-water poured into the *Bismarck*'s hull and oil leaked out, leaving a tell-tale slick trailing astern of her.

Shortly afterwards, during the small hours of the 25th, *Bismarck*'s echo faded from *Suffolk*'s radar. To make matters worse, the low scud that had hampered the Swordfish in locating their quarry was the beginning of a depression: bad weather was breaking.

A greater depression was gathering in London. The hours ticked past. Both *Ramillies* and *Revenge* were diverted from their convoys, and in addition to Tovey's detachment of the Home Fleet from the north-east and Somerville's Force H from the south-east, the battleship *Rodney* with a screen of destroyers – on her way to refit in the United States and escorting the troopship *Britannic* – was also ordered to the mid Atlantic. Lütjens too was depressed, quite unaware that the British had lost him. With *Prinz Eugen* detached under cover of the deteriorating weather, he now broke radio silence to transmit a series of signals to Berlin. One erroneously reported the continuing presence of the British, a longer one concerned the superiority of British radar over German, the problems with *Bismarck*, and Lütjens's own consequent intentions. As soon as his transmissions were intercepted at listening stations in Britain the Admiralty obtained a radio fix on his position and the bearings were passed to Tovey aboard *King George V*. Tovey was plugging south-west into a head sea, his flagship swept from end to end by green water. Because they lacked fuel, he had sent his destroyers to Iceland for bunkers; two were fitted with new radio direction-finding equipment, and their presence with that equipment might have prevented the error that now occurred.

Tovey had had the foresight to arrange with the Admiralty that any such radio-detected information be transmitted to him as raw data – radio bearings only, not a position in latitude and longitude. At the Admiralty, Lieutenant Commander P. Kemp had plotted the fix, but it was not of good quality: with no confirming cross-cuts from either Iceland or Gibraltar, the two intersecting bearings were at too shallow an angle for a positive location. Given the distances involved the capacity for error was signifi-cant, but at the very least, as Kemp realised, the bearings definitely showed that *Bismarck* was south and east of her previous reported position. The doubts Kemp and his superior Rear Admiral Clayton felt would, they thought, be tempered by confirmation from Tovey's own destroyers; since Tovey himself was maintaining radio silence, they did not know he was without them.[8]

The doubtful quality of the fix was further compounded by the fact that Kemp had plotted the bearings on a gnomonic chart, one which from the nature of its projection shows radio bearings in a straight line, and it is sometimes said that in receiving the bearings Tovey's staff distorted them by making an error in interpreting the half-convergency correction necessary to the application of the data to a Mercator chart of the sort used for ordinary navigation, on which the bearings would have been subject to curving. This was not the case: an error was in fact made in plotting on the gnomonic projection.[9] The effect of this mistake was to convince Tovey that *Bismarck* had moved not south but north, and he altered the course of his squadron accordingly.

The confusion and conflicting opinions given rise to by the errors of the Admiralty plotters have tended to obscure the folly displayed by Lütjens in breaking radio silence. He seems to have resigned himself to the role – and the fate – of an officer who is dutifully obedient to the end, without considering the options a man of more initiative might have perceived as being open to him. Nor was his the only indiscretion: Bletchley Park deciphered a personal message from a Luftwaffe officer in Athens who had a relative aboard the *Bismarck* and wanted to know where the battleship was bound; incredibly, Berlin told him.

In London on Sunday 25 May it was becoming increasingly clear to those involved that the *Bismarck* was heading for France. Submarine patrols were ordered to the Bay of Biscay, and Coastal Command was ordered to fly patrols out into the South West Approaches. Among these was a new American-built flying-boat, Catalina Z from No. 209 Squadron. Although commanded by Flying Officer D.A. Briggs of the Royal Air Force, it was actually flown by an American pilot, Ensign L. Smith, who was inducting the British aircrew in their new aeroplane and at the same time, on secret orders from Washington, soaking up operational experience. This was an additional patrol, suggested personally by the Commander-in-Chief of Coastal Command, Sir Frederick Bowhill, a former merchant naval officer.

Lütjens, meanwhile, had been informed by Berlin of the Seekriegsleitung's assessment that he had shaken off the pursuit, and Lindemann stood his ship's company down from the action-stations at which they had been for 36 hours. It was Lütjens's birthday, on which he received congratulations from Hitler and Raeder.

Next day, Monday 26 May, the *Bismarck* was seen by Smith from Briggs's Catalina Z through a rent in the clouds: the grey battleship was indeed heading for France. Furthermore, a French source had informed London that the dockyard at Brest were expecting *Bismarck* on Wednesday.[10] But with British warships widely scattered and several running out of fuel, the hoped-for concentration of interdicting force seemed doubtful of achievement. Lütjens was still 600 miles short of his objective, but he would soon run under German air cover, and escape. A gloomy assemblage of senior officers waited at the Admiralty while the situation was reassessed. Only Somerville's Force H coming up from the south – *Renown, Ark Royal, Sheffield* and the destroyers *Faulknor, Foresight, Foxhound, Forester, Fury* and *Hesperus* – posed any sort of threat, but it was still some distance off, and hampered by the bad weather. Nevertheless, just after noon, in appalling seas, her deck swept by a lashing rain, the *Ark Royal* flew off a patrol of 'Stringbags'. The slow Swordfish biplanes fought their way north, buffeted by strong winds, until through the low scud they saw the grey shape of a large ship heading east.

At 13.15 Somerville detached the cruiser *Sheffield* to try to make contact, and ordered Captain L.E.H. Maund of *Ark Royal* to prepare a strike force. The carrier's flight-deck pitched in the heavy seas as she turned into the wind and 14 torpedo-armed Swordfish lumbered down the deck, to be flung into the air or to drop over the bow and climb laboriously out over the breaking, spray-torn wave-crests; it was 14.50. An hour later, guided by their primitive radar sets operated in open cockpits, the Swordfish located an echo and attacked through the cloud, flattening out over the heaving grey sea and heading for the indistinct silhouette of a large warship. Alerted to the incoming attack by radio, Captain C.A.A. Larcom realised what must have happened, and as all 14 torpedoes dropped from the Swordfish and plunged towards the *Sheffield* he took swift evasive action.

The *Sheffield* emerged unscathed, but whether or not it was because Larcom had successfully combed all the tracks of the torpedoes, existing doubts about how well the magnetic proximity-firing pistols in the British torpedoes worked were enough to ensure that when the circumstances became known aboard *Ark Royal* and orders were given for a second wave to be prepared, their torpedo warheads were fitted with contact pistols instead, and set for a shallow run. Fifteen Swordfish from Nos 810, 818 and 820 Squadrons, led by Lieutenant Commander P.T. Coode, took off into the evening sky at 19.10. Coode's task was first to find *Sheffield* and then, relying upon her guidance, to attack *Bismarck*. It was past 20.45 when in 'low rain cloud, strong wind, stormy seas, fading daylight and intense and accurate gunfire' those archaic aircraft attacked the most advanced battleship then in existence. In the poor flying conditions all pretence at co-ordinated attack was thrown aside. Over the ensuing 38 minutes the two-man aircrews individually 'pressed in most gallantly and two of the thirteen torpedoes released found their mark. One hit was on the armour belt and . . . had little effect. The other was right aft, damaged the *Bismarck*'s propellers, wrecked her steering gear and jammed her rudders. It was this hit which sealed her fate.'

That torpedo strike transformed the situation; there was a flurry of activity in the Admiralty and the signals that flew from Whitehall drew upon the scene the first of *Hood*'s avengers, the 4th Destroyer Flotilla. This had been detached from Convoy WS8B and sent to replace Tovey's missing screen but its commander Captain P. Vian had in his typical fashion taken the initiative, disregarding his orders. His presence on the trail of Lütjens, while it deprived Tovey of a destroyer screen, ensured that contact would not be lost during the hours of darkness. For his part, the Commander-in-Chief had swung round and was now heading to intercept the *Bismarck*.

Vian harried his gigantic enemy aggressively throughout the night, at considerable risk to his small ships even though the damage to her stern had left *Bismarck* hardly manageable and her speed greatly reduced. Between 01.20 and 07.00 on 27 May the British destroyers *Zulu*, *Maori* and *Sikh* all fired torpedoes while the Polish destroyer *Piorun*, relishing the opportunity to create a diversion, engaged the German battleship with her inferior guns. At daylight, with the weather too bad for flying operations, Tovey warned Somerville to keep clear. He had been joined by *Rodney*, Captain F.H. Dalrymple-Hamilton, with the destroyers *Mashona*, *Somali* and *Tartar*, and other British men-of-war were closing in, the incorrigible *Norfolk* from the north-west and another cruiser, the *Dorsetshire*, from the south. Tovey waited for full daylight, and at about 08.50 the first salvos were fired at a range of 8 miles. *Bismarck* fired back and almost hit *Rodney*, but the accuracy of her gunnery waned as she was pounded by British ships slowly closing the range. At 10.15, with the *Bismarck* on fire, Tovey broke off the action; he was desperately short of fuel. He ordered the cruisers to sink the *Bismarck* with torpedoes; the *Dorsetshire* and *Norfolk* obliged, and at 10.36, her Swastika ensign still flying, Lütjens's flagship went down.

Some 110 survivors were picked up by *Dorsetshire* and *Maori*; several claimed their ship had been scuttled, not sunk by the British; it did not greatly matter.[11] Convoy WS8B escorted by two cruisers, *Cairo* and *Exeter*, and three destroyers had already crossed astern of *Bismarck*'s track, and all other convoys at sea were safe from what proved to be the last sortie by a German capital ship. As for her consort, the *Prinz Eugen* refuelled from the supply ship *Spichern* and cruised to intercept merchantmen between 26 and 29 May until Brinckmann, bedevilled by engine trouble, decided to make for Brest, arriving there unmolested on the forenoon of 1 June. The Luftwaffe took revenge by sinking the *Mashona* and damaging *Maori*, but the loss of the *Bismarck* was undeniably a severe blow to Germany.

Although Lütjens had obeyed his orders to the last, he had effectively destroyed not just the *Bismarck* but the future of the Kriegsmarine's surface ships. In mid June the *Lützow* made a sortie, but she was sighted and hit by a torpedo from an RAF Beaufort. Putting back to Kiel, she spent six months undergoing repairs. German heavy warships, the *Tirpitz* in particular, continued to cause anxiety at the Admiralty, but in fact they spent much of the rest of the war in the fastnesses of the Norwegian fjords 'like chained dogs'.[12] Hitler turned a deaf ear to all Raeder's pleas to employ them, and the Grossadmiral's star began to wane. Vizeadmiral Dönitz seized the day. He began to push the cause of the U-boat arm of the Kriegsmarine with ever-increasing fervour, clamouring for more new submarines, accelerated research and development of a new and faster type, and priority in dockyard facilities for the repair and refit of those already in commission.

As Force H returned to Gibraltar it was spotted by one of a group of Italian submarines that were patrolling this area full of British shipping in the hope of attacking OG and HG convoys or any other likely targets. Their success was only partial and included one innocent Portuguese trawler and a Royal Fleet Auxiliary tanker, the *Cairndale*, sunk by the *Guglielmo Marconi* on 30 May. Called to assist by his colleague Terra of the *Velella*, who had located the outward-bound Convoy OG63 as it swung east from its long detour into the Atlantic during the night of 5/6 June, Capitano di Corvetta P. Pollina was also responsible for sinking the British tramp *Baron Lovat* owned by 'Hungry' Hogarth's of Glasgow. Pollina also attacked the small Swedish merchantman *Taberg*, which was in ballast, killing 15 of her crew. Captain J.N. Garrett and the crew of the *Baron Lovat* were picked up by HM Sloop *Wellington*, Lieutenant Commander W.F.R. Seagrave, and landed at Gibraltar. Terra and Capitano di Fregata Roselli-Lovenzini of the *Eno* both reported hits, but only one further ship from the convoy was sunk, the small British ship *Glen Head*, which was bombed by a Kondor later in the day and may have been damaged by an earlier torpedo hit. That same night Capitano di Fregata Petroni in the *Veneiro* attacked the homeward-bound HG64 routed south of OG63, claiming two hits. For the most part the ready availability of escorts in the approaches to Gibraltar meant that punishing counterattacks met all submarine actions, though further south and west off the Azores, Capitano di Fregata Longanesi-Cattani had, as noted earlier, successfully attacked Convoy SL76.

In the aftermath of the pursuit of the *Bismarck*, intelligence derived from Ultra, made to look wherever possible like the result of assiduous, radarassisted searching, enabled the British to round up most of the German supply vessels intended to support both Lütjens's foray and Dönitz's U-boats. Beginning with the loss of the *Egerland* on 5 June, the most dramatic attack of this offensive yielded the 10,000-ton tanker *Belchen*. She was caught on her station off Cape Farewell by the cruisers *Aurora* and *Kenya* in the very act of refuelling Korth's *U-93*, and forced to scuttle. The bunker lines were thrown clear and Korth submerged, surfacing later to rescue all the *Belchen*'s 50 crew. He then used their presence aboard *U-93* as a pretext for not attacking or shadowing a convoy, conduct which earned him a sharp reprimand from Dönitz.

Thanks to the capture of Lemp's *U-110* and her Enigma machine, all British convoys could now be routed round known U-boat concentrations, for at the Admiralty Winn and his deputy Beesly knew 'the exact numbers of U-boats at sea . . . the contents of their own signals . . . [and] the instructions constantly being pumped out to them by Dönitz'. By late June 1941 Dönitz was a frustrated man: despite the number of U-boats he had in the Atlantic, he was again not receiving reports of convoy sightings.

With the merchant seamen this absence of action scarcely registered. Threat seemed to lurk everywhere, magnified by men's imaginations into an ocean infested with U-boats, and the widespread nature of Dönitz's dispositions was such as to fuel these fears. Attacks made on shipping off the Cape Verdes, off Freetown, in the North West Approaches, off Cape Farewell and off Iceland, though a few were made by the raider *Atlantis*, continued to account for dozens of merchantmen and to foster the notion of German superiority. The nights were short and most convoys avoided the lurking groups of U-boats, but even in June the North Atlantic is not warm, and only a few hours in a lifeboat was a chilling and demoralising experience. Nevertheless, the same day the *Bismarck* sank saw also a quieter triumph: HX129 became the first eastbound convoy to be provided with an anti-submarine escort throughout its entire passage.

There were other corresponding if small consolations: *U-147* was sunk on 2 June by *Wanderer*, Commander A.F.StG. Orpen and *Periwinkle*, Lieutenant Commander P. MacIver, escorting Convoy OB329 in the North Atlantic; and *U-138* was sunk in the Straits of Gibraltar on the 18th by *Faulknor*, Captain A.F. de Salis, *Fearless*, *Forester*, *Foresight* and *Foxhound*. On the 27th while escorting Convoy HX133 the corvettes *Celandine, Nasturtium* and *Gladiolus* sank Wohlfarth's *U-556*, one of ten U-boats gathered to annihilate the convoy. Two days later *U-651*, another of the U-boats attacking HX133, was despatched by the destroyers *Malcolm* and *Scimitar*, the sloop *Speedwell* and the corvettes *Violet* and *Arabis*. Yet over a period of six weary days five ships were lost from HX133, of which Kapitänleutnant P. Lohmeyer of *U-651* was responsible for two.[13] The Italians too paid for their limited success, for off Gibraltar the *Wishart* destroyed the *Glauco*. Furthermore, to the triumph of ransacking Lemp's *U-110* could now be added that of the capture of the weather-reporting trawler *Lauenburg* by a boarding-party from the destroyer *Tartar*.

Following the seizure of the German weather-reporting trawler *München* in May,[14] which occurred just before Lemp's *faux pas*, a second, highly secret operation was set up in June. Led by Rear Admiral Burrough in the cruiser *Nigeria*, three destroyers located the *Lauenburg* off Jan Mayen Island in the Arctic Ocean. Among the boarding-party was Lieutenant Allan Bacon, an intelligence officer of the Volunteer Reserve whose duties were intimately connected with the Enigma secret, and the material captured, in particular the codes for the following month of July, was of 'inestimable value'. 'After 1 June 1941 the code-breaking picture changed overnight. All of a sudden Bletchley Park could read [German] naval Enigma messages almost as quickly as the Germans.'[15]

And the Americans were being drawn inexorably into the battle: on 14 June the United States Navy extended its neutrality sweeps east, from the 30th to the 26th meridians, and American battleships patrolled the area in a formidable expression of sea-power which offered a tempting target to at least one U-boat commander.[16] At the same time the cruisers and destroyers of Task Force 3 under Rear Admiral J.H. Ingram, USN were operating out of Recife and Bahia as far south as the 20th parallel, courtesy of the Brazilian government. Beyond these strictly neutral deployments, more material aid was also forthcoming in the form of additional escort vessels. Both Admiral King and Secretary Knox were aware of the deficiencies in both the British and the Canadian navies, deficiencies made acute by the westward extension of German submarine operations. The inadequacies of the 'Flower'-class corvettes and the rotten state of the ex-American destroyer escorts were already apparent. The British were preparing replacement classes of an improved corvette design, the 'Castle'-class, and new, more sophisticated frigate classes, but the combined production rate of all British imperial resources was about eight vessels per month. The head of the British Supply Council in the United States, Rear Admiral J.W.S. Dorling, was pushing for a faster escort to be funded under the Lease-Lend arrangements. It was felt that American yards could produce ten vessels a month along with additional minesweepers and rescue tugs.

These were momentous events and presaged much, but so too did Berlin's ill-conceived designs. On 21 June 1941, the invasion of the Soviet Union was initiated. The demands this was to make on Great Britain's sea services have already been touched upon; and while it presented Dönitz with fresh opportunities, it also extended his own operations. The additional burden upon the British was intensified by the presence of German capital ships in Norwegian waters and German aircraft on Norwegian soil. Though many merchantmen had first to cross the Western Ocean before joining PQ convoys bound for the Soviet Union, the maritime war in the Arctic was not part of that in the Atlantic. Ships bound for Russia detached off Iceland and proceeded under escort to the Arctic convoy assembly-point in the Hvalfjord, and although on 19 July the United States Navy undertook to escort merchant shipping of any nationality to Iceland, thus providing a measure of relief to the overstretched Royal Navy, this new factor represented one more consideration in the growing complexity of the war, one more demand upon British resource.

In July Winston Churchill, aware of this increase and of the effect upon morale of German successes, sent a message to the men of the Merchant Navy appealing to their patriotism and sense of history. 'We are', he wrote, 'a seafaring race and we understand the call of the sea. We account you in these hard days worthy successors in a tradition of steadfast courage and high adventure, and we feel confident that the proud tradition of our Island will be upheld wherever the ensign of a British merchantman is flown.' Unlike his high words of praise for 'the Few' and his blood-and-guts promise of universal conflict if Britain were to be invaded by the Germans uttered the previous year, these sentences have been forgotten, eclipsed long since by succeeding events; but that he felt compelled to utter them is one further measure of how, at the time, the Merchant Navy was holding the line.

In July and early August 1941 there was something of a hiatus in the German offensive in the North Atlantic, largely because Ultra intelligence enabled convoys to detour to avoid waiting groups of U-boats. Statistical calculations indicate that about 1.5 million tons of shipping were thereby saved, but assertions that for three weeks in July and ten days in August no convoys were seen by U-boats in the North Atlantic are misleading, particularly if they are taken to imply that no merchantmen were sunk. The number of U-boats at sea had increased, and they continued to prey on British and Allied shipping throughout this period *and* to attack convoys. Some vessels, such as T. & J. Harrison's *Designer*, sank with heavy loss of life: Captain D.A. McCullum and 66 of his crew were killed, only 11 rescued by a Portuguese sailing vessel.

During July alone German and Italian submarines accounted for 16 merchant vessels and their activities included several group attacks on HG and OG convoys – seven vessels from Convoy OG69 were torpedoed off the Spanish coast – but these attacks were largely unsuccessful from the German point of view. German raiders continued their dirty work, the *Orion* sinking the tramp *Chaucer* west of the Cape Verde Islands on 29 July. In the same area a U-boat sank T. & J. Harrison's *Auditor*, Captain E. Bennett. She had sailed in Convoy OB337 bound for Cape Town with a cargo consisting of general and army stores, and after the convoy was dispersed on 27 June had followed an independent route provided at the Ocean Convoy Conference at Oban. Captain Bennett was to proceed due south from dispersal until he was close to the coast of Brazil, when he was to head across the South Atlantic towards the Cape. But on 4 July at moonset, about 02.00, the ship was shaken by a violent explosion in No. 4 Hold which carried away No. 4 Boat on the deck above. By virtue of a half-hourly update of the ship's position Chief Radio Officer H. Walker was able to send a distress message immediately, using the emergency transmitter because the main aerial was gone and much of the radio room was a shambles.

The second radio officer, George Monk, was fitting the emergency radio in No. 1 Boat when it was lowered, which meant he had to climb up the boarding ladder to transfer to his correct boat on the port side of the ship. On the boat deck under a starlit sky he met Captain Bennett, who had exchanged his uniform for a suit to avoid attracting attention to his rank – many masters feared being singled out and taken prisoner, as had happened on a few occasions. 'Go and get your Chief,' Bennett instructed him. 'She's going fast.'

In the radio room Walker was still transmitting and asked Monk to get his coat from his cabin, a deck lower. Here Monk heard the sea

pouring into the engine room below, just like the sound of a large waterfall. On returning to the radio office we checked that the code books had been thrown overboard . . . The only boat still alongside was No. 1, the Captain's. I went [back] down the ladder followed by my Chief and the Captain . . . When about eighty yards off and about fifteen minutes after the torpedo hit, the *Auditor*'s bow rose up until vertical; then she sank slowly into the Cape Verde Basin, some 3,000 fathoms below. Besides wreckage floating around, all that was left of a fine ship were a number of large crates [of] deck cargo and the three boats.

A little later the sound of diesels was heard; it was the *U-123* cruising around. Obviously [Kapitän] Leutnant Hardegen wanted to make sure that the *Auditor* had sunk but he did not contact us.

The crew in No. 1 Boat consisted of Captain Bennett, Chief Engineer D.C. Smith, Chief Steward R. Doyle, Extra Third Officer H. Procter, Walker and Monk, the gunner and 15 men – 22 souls in all. No. 1 was a standard wooden lifeboat with a length of 27 feet, a beam of 8 feet 3 inches and a depth of 3 feet 3 inches. 'When launched it leaked considerably,' Second Radio Officer Monk recalled.

As the voyage progressed the timbers tightened but it never became water-tight, and so it was necessary to bail regularly. Of course, when the seas fresh-ened we shipped water and bailing was vital but we always had water in the boat.

The equipment comprised . . . a rudder and tiller, eight ash oars and rowlocks, a sea anchor, a bailer, a spirit compass, ropes necessary for sea anchor and sailing, one large water beaker and one smaller one plus a dipper, distress flares, and a radio transmitter (but no receiver). In addition, there was a large quantity of ship's biscuits (inedible) and a case of small tins of condensed milk. There was, of course, a [mast and] sail.

At the time of the sinking the sea was moderate, but when the boat pulled clear of the *Auditor* the motion was such that many of the crew became violently seasick. This rapid motion – rolling and pitching – lasted the whole time we lay at [our] sea anchor. The seasickness added to the miseries of the situation, as all were more or less still shocked by the torpedoing . . . Fortunately, there were no serious injuries, but some had bruises and cuts from sliding down ropes. Sadly, some of the Lascars were only scantily dressed; the weather in these latitudes was cold at night and quite warm during the day. One of the Lascar crew, a fireman, was missing . . . [presumed] killed when the torpedo exploded.

At daybreak, the three lifeboats came together and put out sea anchors. Captain Bennett was determined that we must obey Admiralty instructions, which were to remain in the position in which we were torpedoed to await rescue. At the Convoy Conference Masters were advised that provided a SSSS message had been transmitted, a vessel would be sent to rescue the crew within two days.

During the morning of the first day Captain Bennett discussed our situ-ation, and it was evident that if there was no rescue we would set sail for the Cape Verde Islands. Years ago he had called at these Islands and remem-bered that one or two of them had mountains rising to over 10,000 feet, and therefore could be seen for a good distance. The alternative was to sail for South America, a much longer distance. The position of the Islands was not known as we had no charts . . . I always bought a Shipping Pocket Diary each year. As Captain Bennett was talking, I suddenly realised that my diary for 1941 – as luck would have it – was in my coat pocket. I remembered there was a page which listed all the major bunkering ports and their posi-tions. Quickly, I looked up this page and the position for St Vincent, C.V.I., was given. Now we had the data to prepare a chart. This I did, using a piece of paper taken from my wallet and the lines on my Marconi Pay Book which I had in my [emergency survival] 'Hammer Bag'.

Now that we had the direct course to the C.V.I.s it was given to the four

Deck Officers. They were to work out the course we were to sail to make the Islands, taking into account all the variables such as currents, winds, drift of boat . . . Later all four advised their course to which the Captain added his own. He then took the mean of the five courses and said that is the one to steer . . . my diary . . . was possibly a life-saver as all three boats made it to the Islands.

I think the first day was one spent coming to terms with our traumatic situation. If we were not rescued it would mean a 600-mile voyage to the islands. If we missed the islands what should we do? Should we sail east for the African coast, bearing in mind that the winds would be against us? Or should we sail for South America some 1,500 miles distant? No, that would be impossible as our meagre rations would only last for fourteen days. By that evening all the crew were very thirsty and hungry, but our next ration would not be until noon on the second day. Urinating was other problem, it was a painful process due to the violent motions of the boat.

As there was no rescue on the second day, it was decided that we must depart from our 'sea anchorage' the next morning. And so, fifty four hours after our ship sank, each lifeboat set sail independently for the islands. During the time we laid at sea anchor my Chief and I transmitted our distress message several times at the twice hourly 'silence periods' [when all shipping main-tained mandatory radio silence on 500 kiloherz in order to facilitate the inter-ception of weak distress signals], but as the MoWT had not supplied us with a receiver, we did not know if any ship was calling us.

On the third morning we got under weigh, and by dusk the Chief Officer's [Mr H.T. Wells] boat was well ahead; the Second Officer's [Mr D.O. Percy] boat could just be seen astern of us. As we were now sailing at around 2.5 knots the motion of the boat was much easier. We climbed the swells, had a quick look around the horizon, and then dropped into the valley. Often when in a valley, fish could be seen swimming well above us. Watches had been set, and steering was spread between the Captain, the Extra Third Officer, the Chief Engineer, my Chief and myself. As our Lascars would not keep look-out watches, it was left to the Europeans to do this work and issue the rations. As the compass had no light we steered at night by the stars. Thirst and hunger were getting worse. The days were warm and everyone got sunburnt as there was little protection. The nights were cold and, no doubt, they felt very cold due to our lack of food. Also, as the wind seemed to increase at dusk, we were often drenched in spray and became thoroughly wet, and could not dry out until next day. Most of each night was spent with spasms of shivering. Also, at night our mouth and tongue became thickly coated with white slime. I found it best to wash this away in the morning with sea water, but had to be careful not to swallow any. Another problem was that there was no space to lay out flat, and so I spent the thirteen and a half days sitting on the side benches, except for the time I was at the tiller.

On the eighth day Captain Bennett estimated that we had sailed 300 miles. All were suffering severely from thirst and hunger and our rations were doubled to 6 ounces of water and 2 teaspoonfuls of condensed milk a day. These rations would just about sustain life. Everyone was well and cheerful except for the Extra Third Officer who had been badly sunburnt and was weak. He tried to throw himself over the side, but we caught him just in time, and made him stay under the thwarts for the rest of the voyage.

By this time we were getting the feel of lifeboat voyaging, and the manner in which it stood the battering of the seas was a wonder to all. Of course, we were steering South East and taking full advantage of the North East Trade winds which continued to give us a speed of about 2.5 knots. However, on the thirteenth day at daybreak we sighted the island of São Antonio, about 35 miles distant, on our port beam. It was then necessary to alter course to ENE and start tacking. During the day our mast came down three times. This was due to it coming out of the step in the keelson. It was difficult to repair as we had no tools except a knife. At this time the boat was taking a terrific hammering from rough seas . . . The thirteenth day of our voyage proved to be the most traumatic because lifeboats were not built to . . . [beat to windward] but we had to force our boat to do just this. All through the day we shipped a lot of water and bailed continuously. As the seas were rough, the boat was not easy to handle when tacking. Also the crew were now in a weakened state which did not help. However, it's surprising what strength one can find when land was in sight . . .

Compelled to resort to their oars for three hours, an agony in their weakened state, they were seen and met by two boats which 'had brought out two carafes of fresh water. How good it tasted. The boats, manned by fishermen, took our ropes and towed us for the last 2 miles to the village of Tarrafal on the island of São Antonio.'

They found that Second Officer Percy had arrived two days earlier, and later rejoined the remainder of the crew on São Vincente, where the Chief Officer's boat had turned up; here they also met the survivors of the *Clan MacDougal* and the *Silveryew*. But even now their ordeal was not quite over: 'All our crew were warned against eating any solid foods when they landed. It was essential to keep to liquids for a few days so that the body can adjust to normal living.'

*

The losses sustained by the British mercantile marine had not quenched the defiant spirit which had animated several masters in their early encounters with German U-boats. On the forenoon of 6 July the Ellerman liner *City of Auckland* was outward bound for Australia with a general cargo, heading south some three hundred miles west of Madeira. German-built at Bremen in 1914 as the *Weissenfels*, she had been acquired by Ellerman's subsidiary Hall Line in 1921. As a coal-burner she was prone to make smoke, and her service speed was 11.5 knots. Steaming independently, that morning she was zig-zagging when her mastheads were sighted from the conning tower of *U-109*, a Type IXB U-boat on her second war patrol. Captain E.J. Myles and his officers had no idea of the proximity of the U-boat. Kapitänleutnant H. Bleichrodt began to pursue in wide semicircular curves, keeping only the trucks of the liner's mastheads in view above the sharp horizon edging the calm sea. Such were the length and angle of the *City of Auckland*'s zig-zags that it was some hours before the U-boat had worked up to a suitable position to submerge preparatory to making an attack. Just as Bleichrodt was about to do so the *City of Auckland*'s lookouts spotted *U-109*. Called to the bridge, Myles swung his ship away, frustrating Bleichrodt and prompting one of his crew to condemn *U-109* as crapulous: 'much too slow under water, exactly the same as in the last war'.

Bleichrodt was obliged to begin his stalking all over again, troubled by the knowledge that a sharp lookout aboard the *City of Auckland* had spotted the *U-109*'s periscope feathering the surface of the placid sea. It was two hours before he could surface and use the U-boat's superior speed to resume the pursuit properly, but the international distress frequency remained quiet, so he determined on a night attack. Finally, at about 01.30 on the 7th, the general cargo-liner lay dark in the glittering track of the westering moon ahead of the surfaced U-boat.

Two miles from his quarry, Bleichrodt fired a torpedo which missed, though it ran its course. An hour later, a second torpedo was fired; it too missed its target. Concerned by the approach of dawn, Bleichrodt made a third approach within half a mile of the *City of Auckland*. Again he attacked, and again he missed. A fourth torpedo also failed to hit the ship, which to those in the U-boat seemed to be adjusting her speed. Having checked their instruments and firing data, Bleichrodt and First Watch Officer Schwartzkopf concluded that the *City of Auckland* must have been aware of the approach of the torpedoes, a supposition apparently confirmed by the variations in her bow wave which showed that her speed was being altered; equally, however, this could be taken to suggest that she was fitted with hydrophones, and was therefore a naval auxiliary, a judgement that seemed confirmed when they realised that the ship had not transmitted any submarine alarm. Bleichrodt eventually concluded that his intended victim 'could be a U-boat trap'.

According to *U-109*'s senior telegraphist Wolfgang Hirschfeld, the conduct of the *City of Auckland*'s master was considered 'cocky' and caused Bleichrodt to regard his opponent as a '*Schwein*', particularly when the steamer again increased speed. Bleichrodt followed suit, clearing away his deck gun and engaging when he was within range. A hit was seen aft, then the steamer made smoke, 'confirming' the theory that she was a Q-ship. She also now transmitted a submarine attack signal, along with her position. Having fired 35 rounds and seen his target wreathed in smoke – it was in fact her own funnel smoke – Bleichrodt ordered a cease-fire and slowed *U-109* to a stop.

Bleichrodt was taking stock when, to the consternation of all on the conning tower and casing of the U-boat, the *City of Auckland* was seen heading towards them. Bleichrodt ordered full speed and turned away. The *City of Auckland* swung to open her arcs of fire and 'suddenly there was a belch of lightning flashes', whereupon 'a salvo screamed overhead' which those in the U-boat judged to be 'a broadside with medium calibre guns'.

With his gun crew tumbling below Bleichrodt now ran east as a second 'salvo' flew overhead, and for an hour his puissant symbol of the Reich fled from a British merchantman. As the moon set to provide a brief period of darkness before dawn, Bleichrodt determined on a 'crafty manoeuvre': he would turn away, allowing the pursuing cargo-vessel to overtake him, and then fire the two stern tubes at her. Switching to silent electric power Bleichrodt swung *U-109*'s head to starboard, and it was then he discovered that he had been pursued by a chimera – for Captain Myles, having driven off his tormentor, had sensibly resumed his voyage. The *City of Auckland* was incapable of the 14 knots Bleichrodt and Schwartzkopf had thought she was making, an estimate as wildly unlikely as the 'salvo' they thought had been fired from a cargo-liner with a 4-inch anti-submarine weapon, a 12-pounder and a handful of primitive machine-guns.[17]

The effect of this extraordinary episode was more psychological than material, though Bleichrodt did arrive in Cadiz on 21 July to refuel *U-109* and 'for emergency repairs'. The suggestion that she had suffered at the hands of what Bleichrodt took to be a Q-ship revived fears left over from the First World War, since the Germans remained unaware that the tactic had long since been abandoned by the British. The most charitable explanation of Bleichrodt's reaction to Myles's aggressive conduct is as an effect of the extreme anxiety attributed to him by Hirschfeld.[18]

Although the overall number of sinkings by U-boat had eased, the shortage of Allied shipping remained acute and the situation was aggravated by the often poor quality of what remained. One of the former American First World War standard ships, the 5,135-ton *Macon*, built in 1919, had suffered successive breakdowns and twice returned to Liverpool before she finally sailed in late January 1941. Under Elder, Dempster management the *Macon* was loaded with general cargo for West Africa and joined Convoy OB290. 'Well out into the Atlantic, the ship broke down again and we lost the convoy. At this stage there was no alternative but to proceed on the voyage and hope for the best. We had several more breakdowns but eventually managed to reach Ponta Delgada in the Azores where steam power finally failed,' Fourth Officer William Close wrote. 'In looking back I marvel that the ship survived thus far. By day clouds of dense black smoke were a common occurrence, and by night showers of sparks [rose] from the funnel. It was decided to re-tube the boilers in the Azores, with a new set brought from the United States which took two months, their fitting taking a further two . . .'

The *Macon* finally sailed on 22 July; two days, 300 miles and one further breakdown out of Ponta Delgada she was torpedoed by the Italian submarine *Barbarigo*, Capitano di Fregata Murzi. It was a clear calm night. Close was on watch

on the starboard side of the bridge and the torpedo struck the port side . . . a loud explosion and hatch boards falling all around. The two port boats were wrecked . . . but everyone, except two men, got away without too much difficulty in the two starboard boats. The Chief Officer and one fireman were missing. The fireman was killed in the stoke-hold and we thought the Chief Officer had fallen down the hatch that had the covers blown off. I was in a boat with the Master [Captain A. English] and nineteen others, and the Second and Third Mates were in the other boat with a similar number. We pulled away from the ship which did not sink, but was set on fire by shellfire from the submarine. They did not appear to see us although we saw them. We believed later from pictures shown to us that the sub was Italian. The two boats became separated, and the Master decided to try and sail back to the Azores, although this was against the prevailing winds. Apart from the Master and myself, no one had any experience of small-boat sailing . . . The weather was generally good and I do not recall actually living in the boat as an unbearable hardship. Water was the greatest concern and I constantly thought of spring wells and running water . . . The thought that we might not be picked up or make land and that we might die in the boat was one I did not dwell upon. I can remember thinking that it would cause great distress at home and that surely Providence would not allow this to happen, though towards the end I was beginning to lose this confidence.

We lost two men after about a week. Both became subject to delusions and one died in the boat. The other made some remark about going out for a while and stepped over the side before anyone could stop him. I was sailing the boat at the time and began to go about, but the Master said to carry on as the man in his disturbed state would affect others, which was a difficult decision but probably the right one.

We did sight one ship, a neutral, in daylight, but although we burned flares she did not see us. About 22.30 on the tenth day I was sailing the boat and sighted a darkened ship. We burned flares and were quickly picked up by HMS *Londonderry*, a convoy escort. We were extremely fortunate as the escort was well away from the convoy on the outside wing.

I think that had we not been rescued about that time things could have got much worse. We were still in fairly good shape but had started to reduce the water ration, and another ten days would have been serious indeed. We had made good about 120 miles towards the Azores which was less than half the distance, so the prospect of making land safely was remote.

Landed at Freetown, Close went home in another of Elder, Dempster's ships, in which he stood a watch. 'I did not suffer any ill effects and after about a month at home I went back to sea again.'

The *Macon*'s other boat encountered the *Clan Macpherson*, which took the survivors to Cape Town before repatriating them.[19]

Close and his companions were fortunate in the clemency of the weather and in sighting *Londonderry*. Such experiences had become commonplace as ships continued to be sunk. Through those 'quiet' ten days of August there were attacks on several convoys; one on SL81 involved the sinking of five merchantmen, another on ON5 accounted for the Canadian corvette *Picotee*. The breaking of the Kriegsmarine's codes had done nothing to impair the ability of the Luftwaffe to act as Dönitz's lookouts. Kondors vectored several U-boat groups onto convoys, though not with invariable success, for the Germans missed Convoy SL80.

This particular group of U-boats was directed to operate against the next convoy, SL81, consisting of 18 merchantmen coming north from Freetown, following monitoring of their radio traffic by the B-Dienst service. One of the merchant vessels in convoy was the *Maplin*, formerly the Morant Steamship Company's *Erin*, requisitioned in 1939 as an Ocean Boarding Vessel and later converted to a CAM-ship. With a catapult rigged over their forecastle capable of launching a Mark 1 Hurricane on a single, one-way trip, these 'Catapult Armed Merchantmen' were a primitive attempt to deal with the threat posed by the long-range FW200 Kondor. As *U-204* sighted the convoy and vectored in eight U-boats on 3 August, a Kondor appearing from 1 Kampfgeschwader 40 invited retaliation and was shot down. The U-boats were no more successful, kept away by an aggressive defence on the part of the 7th Escort Group. This was led by Commander A.F.StG. Orpen in the destroyer *Wanderer*, supported by the *Campbeltown* and *St Albans* (both ex-American destroyer-escorts) and the corvettes *La Malouine*, *Campanula*, *Bluebell*, *Hydrangea*, *Wallflower*, *Carnation*, *Heliotrope* and *Zinnia*. *Wanderer*, *St Albans* and *Hydrangea* sank *U-401*, killing Kapitänleutnant Zimmermann and all 43 of his crew.

The other U-boats remained in contact and succeeded in penetrating the defence that night, whereupon Kentrat in *U-74* torpedoed but did not sink the United Africa Company's *Kumasian*. After midnight she was hit by a second torpedo fired by Kell from *U-204*. Captain W.E. Pelissier and all but one of his crew were recovered from the water by *La Malouine*, Lieutenant V.D.H. Bidwell. Meanwhile *U-372* (Neumann) sank Ellerman's Papayanni liner *Belgravian*. It was Captain R.S. Kearon's second sinking of the war. Neumann also sank Ropner's tramp *Swiftpool*. Loaded with iron ore she foundered rapidly, only two men surviving as Captain H.R. Clark and 41 others went down with her. The survivors from all three ships were picked up by Lieutenant Commander R.E. Sherwood's *Bluebell*. Two further ships were lost to *U-75* (Ringelmann), J. & C. Harrison's *Harlingen*, Captain J. Willingham, and Lyle Shipping's *Cape Rodney*, Captain P.A. Wallace. The latter seems to have fallen behind the convoy when she was struck, and an attempt was made to salvage her, for she was taken in tow by the Dutch tug *Zwarte Zee* but foundered a few days later. *Hydrangea* and *Zinnia* picked up survivors from Ringelmann's attacks.

Kondors continued to sink Allied shipping, but their attacks were not always successful. Bound to New York from Lisbon with a cargo of cork the tramp *Briarwood* was well-armed for the times with 'the usual 4-inch, five light machine-guns and a 40mm Bofors. Lord knows how [Captain] Lawrence wangled such luxury . . .' recalled Keith Angus, who with four other Canadians was on his way home, by way of New York, after being torpedoed in the *Silveryew*. He had just completed his apprenticeship, and with his fellow survivors had been asked to undertake lookout duties.

It was warm summer weather, so why not? Thus I found myself on the monkey's island one afternoon when this four-engined monster loomed out of the east and bore down at us at sea level [from] astern . . . Quaking at my first close range air attack, I cocked my stubby Hotchkiss, the instinct to bolt repressed only by [the consideration] 'where to?' The second mate fired the PACs [wire-trailing rockets designed to inhibit low level air attacks], but one of the rockets failed and the whole apparatus came down again, enveloping the Bofors in festoons of wire . . . The FW dropped its bombs close aboard but Lawrence had gauged his own move perfectly and they landed where the poop had been a second before. Jerry nonetheless swept us from end to end with cannon and machine-gun [fire]. The cork on deck absorbed most of it, and there were only a couple of minor injuries. I shot off a clip from the Hotchkiss but the aircraft was over and past in an instant . . . Happily the FW called it off and departed.[20]

Less fortunate was the *Empire Hurst*, sunk by a Kondor off Cape St Vincent homeward bound with a cargo of iron ore from Spain.

On 4 August Churchill embarked in the battleship *Prince of Wales*, and in Placentia Bay, Newfoundland on the 9th he met President Roosevelt for the first time. The previous month American forces had relieved the British garrison in Iceland, further material aid to ease the pressure on the British; now, at a series of meetings held aboard HMS *Prince of Wales* and the USS *Augusta*, the two leaders and their staffs formulated the Atlantic Charter which established eight principles for future world order. As a statement of American intent they must have been clear to Berlin. Most significant to the struggle then in train on the high seas was the principle of freedom of navigation.[21]

In Churchill's entourage was Sir Dudley Pound, the First Sea Lord, and he met three American admirals who were to play a critical role in the months ahead: Admiral Harold Stark, the Chief of Naval Operations, Admiral Ernest King, then Commander-in-Chief, Atlantic Fleet, and Rear Admiral Richmond Turner, Director of the War Plans Division. Pound liked Stark, who transferred to London in April 1942, and managed to establish a rapport with King, a difficult Anglophobe who replaced Stark as Chief of Naval Operations. As far as the maritime war was concerned, the meeting merely ratified many of the arrangements already made during the secret staff conferences that had been held in Washington in the first quarter of the year, headed on the British side by a former and the incumbent Director of Plans, Rear Admiral R. Bellairs and Captain V. Danckwerts. On the assumption – accurate, as it proved – that Japan would enter the war on the side of the Axis, the fundamental decision was made that the secret Allies would defeat Germany first. Pound, writing to Cunningham, Commander-in-Chief, Mediterranean, remarked that 'They are longing to get into the war but I don't think there is much sign of America coming unless there is some incident.'

Nevertheless, the Americans were doing all they could, short of war, and Roosevelt's ban had immediately reduced the amount of oil available to the Japanese who depended on it. As a direct consequence of the Placentia Bay agreement the United States' Atlantic Fleet undertook the escort of all trade convoys in the western Atlantic as far east as the Mid-Ocean Meeting Point, or MOMP, off Iceland. This considerably eased the burden on the Royal Navy, whose escort forces at this time amounted to 250 destroyers of all classes, 99 corvettes and 48 sloops, to which could be added a number of trawlers and large yachts fitted for anti-submarine duties. Significantly, the first escort aircraft-carrier, HMS *Audacity*, was just coming into commission.

Churchill's return aboard the *Prince of Wales* was marked by one incident of note. Having been diverted to avoid German submarines, the battleship caught up with and steamed close to Convoy HX143. Visibly moved by the slow convoy of 73 laden merchant ships, Churchill ordered the *Prince of Wales* turned back through the convoy to repeat the experience. It came as a shock to those in the merchantmen, ignorant of all but their immediate surroundings. As one Bank Line officer recalled,

> We were on the starboard wing, keeping station to fog buoys for some time. The fog cleared a little and . . . the Indian lookout in the starboard cab came running at me pointing . . . there emerging from the light fog on the starboard quarter was a battleship!
>
> She seemed huge and infinitely menacing but since the convoy was holding its course . . . and we had no orders I assumed that she was friendly . . . She came up on the starboard wing with no more than a cable [one-tenth of a nautical mile: 600 feet] between us . . . My old cap and stained duffle coat were in sharp contrast with the impressive array of gold braid, full uniform, collars and ties. The officers looked cool and competent and the whole effect of this magnificent vessel was exciting and impressive . . .[22]

The increasing importance of air-power over the ocean, as marked by the commissioning of the *Audacity*, had long been understood in principle. But there remained, despite the delivery of new American Catalina flying-boats, a shortage of long-range aircraft capable of oceanic operations. As autumn approached, Sir Frederick Bowhill was relieved as Commander-in-Chief, Coastal Command by Sir Philip Joubert de la Ferté, a somewhat 'acrimonious' figure who twice before the end of the year requested that Bomber Command attack U-boat pens on the Atlantic coast of France. The second of these requests was rebuffed on the basis that since 'conditions at sea had so much improved', it was essential that the Royal Air Force's heavy bombers be deployed on 'the air offensive to which we must look to winning as opposed to not losing the war'. It will remain an open question whether switching the Royal Air Force's limited resources to more specific targets like the U-boat pens at La Pallice, L'Orient and St-Nazaire would have won the war more quickly.

The secret of Ultra was not widely known, but its effect on statistics quickly became apparent, articulated in that phrase 'conditions at sea had so much improved'. The creation and maintenance of an impression of overall success depended upon continuing success in code-breaking and cryptanalysis.

Germany's own cryptanalysts, the B-Dienst service, were able to detect convoys, if not precisely locate them. In early August 1941 Dönitz assembled groups of submarines to attack a homeward-bound and an outward-bound convoy, but his U-boats had no luck; the outward convoy was not seen at all. It should have been otherwise, for by 10 August Dönitz was able to summon no fewer than 21 U-boats on the great-circle route to the south-west of Iceland, but although a few minor triumphs were scored, including the independently-steaming Panamanian merchantman *Longtaker*, sunk off Reykjanes by Korvettenkapitän Schuch in *U-38*, he had rather the worst of it during August in the northern part of the Atlantic. Thanks to Ultra decrypts and the prescience of Rodger Winn at the Admiralty, the west-bound convoys ON6, ONS7, ON8 and ONS9, and east-bound HX144, HX145 and SC40 were all routed clear of the gaggle of U-boats lying in wait. On 25 August, moreover, Kapitänleutnant J. March's *U-452*, on her first war patrol, was spotted off the south coast of Iceland from Catalina *J* of No. 209 Squadron. Attacked by Flying Officer E.A. Jewiss, who called in HM Trawler *Vascama*, the U-boat was destroyed with the loss of 42 men. The Royal Air Force achieved further success on the morning of the 27th, when a patrolling Hudson from No. 269 Squadron sighted *U-570*. Kapitänleutnant H-J. Rahmlow was also on his first war patrol, and like March had left for the Iceland grounds from Trondheim. As she tried to join the U-boats directed to attack HX145 after a B-Dienst location report *U-570* was making heavy weather of it on the surface, so Rahmlow decided to submerge and rest his inexperienced crew for a brief period. Two hours later he surfaced to pursue his orders, but Squadron Leader J.H. Thompson's Hudson was overhead at that fatal moment, armed with depth-charges, and dropped all four close to the U-boat. The state of morale aboard *U-570* must have been poor, for within a few minutes, as Thompson flew round again and raked the wallowing U-boat with machine-gun fire, a lamp flashed and a white flag was hoisted. Rahmlow asked to surrender, and in response to dire threats from Thompson promised not to scuttle. Thompson summoned help from Hvalfjord and settled down to circle his captives.

In due course Jewiss arrived in Catalina *J* and took over from Thompson, and in the early evening HM Trawler *Northern Chief*, Lieutenant Knight, arrived on the scene. The weather was still poor the next morning when HM destroyers *Burwell* and *Niagara* and the trawlers *Kingston Agate, Westwater* and *Windermere* turned up. Having fired a line across to the U-boat by means of a Coston gun, Lieutenant H.B. Campbell from the *Kingston Agate* and two ratings hauled themselves across in a rubber dinghy, towing a heavy line with them. Scrambling aboard the U-boat's wet sea-washed casing they shackled this onto *U-570*'s stern. Campbell then supervised the removal of Rahmlow and his men, who had had plenty of time to drop their Enigma machine and its code books overboard and wreck a good deal of the submarine's more sensitive equipment. In the midst of this operation an aircraft from the RAF manned by a Norwegian crew flew over and dropped two depth-charges, adding to the general confusion. Once the crew, less one man who had been killed, had been shifted aboard Campbell's trawler and the U-boat had been secured, Campbell and Knight took her in tow for Iceland. The line parted several times and *Kingston Agate* was ordered to detach, leaving Knight to take in the prize alone, but *U-570* was successfully beached at Thorlakshafn with little ill effect. By 9 September she had been towed into Hvalfjord, inspected, and renamed HM Submarine *Graph*; on the 29th she sailed for Britain, arriving at Barrow-in-Furness on 3 October where she was refitted and then subjected to extensive trials in the Clyde area. She impressed British naval architects, who borrowed ideas from her construction to incorporate in British submarine design.[23]

These were real achievements and 'led to a surge of optimism and to some premature conclusions'[24] in London regarding the outcome of the struggle for mastery of the Atlantic supply route, but they were only tactical successes. In fact there had been a decrease in German air activity against the coastal convoys in the North Sea, almost entirely as a consequence of the massive offensive Germany had launched against Soviet Russia, combined with further diversions of her forces to Greece and North Africa. These actions were also, of course, depleting British naval resources too, and far from any 'corner' having been 'turned' it was soon apparent that a long struggle lay straight ahead.

There was one glimmer of hope, however, though the British had no way of knowing it at the time. Dönitz was worried about the possible compromise of Enigma signals following the capture of *U-570* and at the end of August he asked Admiral Erhard Maertens for an assessment. Maertens confirmed that a danger of compromise did indeed exist, but concluded that the U-boat's crew had probably done everything required of them, in destroying both equipment and code books. They had, so Maertens claimed, tried to convey as much in a message stating that they were having trouble reading incoming signals, messages which they should have easily received.

In any case, Maertens assured his chief in a final flourish, a new *Stichwort* or keyword was coming into use on 1 November, which would remove all anxiety. Despite this assurance, on 11 September Dönitz ordered 'random super-encyphering' for the positional prefixes used by Befelshaber der U-boote and the operational U-boats on the German grid map of the Atlantic Ocean, hoping thereby to introduce a further hurdle in any potential analysis by enemy radio intelligence.

The worry that continued to dog Dönitz might well have consumed him had he known of a visit Churchill made to Bletchley Park on 6 September following which Alan Turing and Hugh Alexander, two of the brilliant young decrypters working in Hut 8, wrote to Churchill on 21 October 1941 of their frustration at not getting their hands on mechanical equipment that would enable them to break the codes faster, their current rate being delayed by 'at least twelve hours every day'. The impact of such delay upon the fortunes of seamen in the Atlantic may be well imagined. Next day, 22 October, Churchill wrote one of his 'Action this day' memoranda, instructing General Ismay to 'Make sure they [the denizens of Hut 8] have all they want on extreme priority and report to me that this has been done.' What emerged from this was the world's first practical use of a computer.

Even before Churchill's visit to Bletchley, however, the British had again been rousing German suspicions. On 4 October a second series of interceptions of German supply ships began when the *Kota Pinang* was attacked west of the Spanish coast; on 22 November a rendezvous between *U-126* and the *Atlantis* was 'discovered' by the cruiser HMS *Devonshire*; later the cruiser *Dorsetshire* captured the *Python*. Hut 8 could read transmissions to the Kriegsmarine's surface units, and although Dönitz's alteration of the initial positional prefixes used by the U-boat arm caused a brief flurry of alarm the problem was shortlisted and Churchill was informed that 'The difficulties regarding the U-boat ciphers have been resolved.' An increase in the success of his own operations did much to soothe Dönitz's fears, as did a reassurance from Maertens of 24 October 1941 that 'The acute disquiet about the compromise of our Secret Operations cannot be justified. Our cipher does not appear to have been broken.'

Others were less certain; B-Dienst initiated an enquiry which did not report its findings until 18 March 1942. In it, the interceptions of the *Atlantis* and *Python* were characterised as 'remarkable', and suspicions were expressed 'that the loss[es] . . . could only have happened because of treason or through the cipher used by the radio service not being kept secret . . .' Admiral Fricke, heading the enquiry, nevertheless concluded reassuringly that the German system was 'superior to that used by any other country', adducing in support of this view that none of the movements of the newly-commissioned battleship *Tirpitz* had attracted the attention of the British. In fact this was due to no failure of intelligence, but to Britain's inability to decode that intelligence fast enough: but the illusion was maintained, and indeed appeared to be confirmed by the total humiliation of the British when in February 1942 the *Scharnhorst, Gneisenau* and *Prinz Eugen* broke out of Brest and made their way east up the English Channel without serious molestation. With the wisdom of historical hindsight, it is possible to see this event as a heavily disguised blessing.

13

'Cries for help could be heard'

Bluebell

D ESPITE THE PROMISE of American assistance in escorting convoys and the rapid expansion of the Royal and Royal Canadian Navies, the optimism felt in London and elsewhere in 1941 proved premature as summer turned to autumn. The concentration of U-boats in the 'Atlantic Narrows' had persuaded the Trade Division at the Admiralty to abolish the short OB convoys, and in July a new series of outward convoys was instituted complimentary to the SL series coming up under escort from Freetown. These constantly-escorted OS convoys were made possible by the gradual augmentation of his forces available to Sir Percy Noble as Commander-in-Chief, Western Approaches: however, they still contained vessels bound for the West Indies and the Panama Canal which had to detach in the South Western Approaches.

Dönitz too was receiving continuing reinforcements, and was now able to muster enough worked-up submarines to operate against all three major convoy routes: the trans-Atlantic HX/SC great circle, the Britain-to-Gibraltar OG/HG loop, and the longer SL/OS tracks. Operations against the first and last also exposed outward-bound merchantmen in the ON series, while special convoys, usually trooping operations under the prefix WS, received attention whenever opportunity offered.

As well as the intelligence-gathering of the B-Dienst operators, the Germans could rely upon a more romantic source where departures from Gibraltar were concerned: spies. From the waterfront at Algeciras or a vantage-point on Cape Tarifa any surface formation of British shipping, mercantile or naval, entering or leaving the Straits of Gibraltar during daylight could be clearly observed. Preparatory movements in Gibraltar prior to the hours of darkness were evidence enough, however, amply confirmed by the empty berths or moorings in the British enclave readily observable from Spanish soil.

It was agents that alerted Kerneval to the departure of Convoy HG67 on 18 July. A group of Italian submarines was gathered to attack but they had little success, and the four German U-boats directed to operate against the 27-strong convoy failed to locate it. A similar lack of success accompanied an attempt to strike outward-bound OG69 and homeward-bound SL80 when 15 U-boats received bearings from Kondors circling OG69. Contact was lost briefly on 26 July but regained that afternoon when seven German and two Italian submarines were given the position by Kondors.

Only two U-boats struck merchant ships that night, *U-79* (Kaufmann) and *U-203* (Mützelburg). Kaufmann sank the small British freighter *Kellwyn* of Swansea shortly before midnight on the 26th. Laden with coke bound for Lisbon she took her master Captain A. McLean and 13 men to the bottom with her. Kaufmann escaped serious damage from a counter-attack by HM Corvette *Rhododendron* and then, after injudiciously surfacing too soon, by her sister-ship *Pimpernel*. Also bound for Lisbon, carrying 2,806 tons of coal, the *Hawkinge*, Captain W.A. Isaksson, fell victim to a torpedo fired from Mützelburg's *U-203* early on the 27th. A similar number of lives were lost from the *Hawkinge*, but the survivors from both ships were recovered by the escorts. The U-boats fired at other vessels but without causing losses. German contact was also made with the outward Convoy OS1, west of OG69 and bound for Freetown, but temporarily lost with OG69 and then regained by a pair of FW200 Kondors which homed four U-boats onto the convoy. Just before midnight *U-126* (Bauer) sank Ellerman's Wilson liner *Erato* with a cargo largely composed of naval and military stores bound for Gibraltar. Bauer also struck the small Norwegian tramp *Inga I* owned by Johan Eliassen of Bergen with the loss of three men. Then, in the early hours of the 28th, Kapitänleutnant Bartels in *U-561* succeeded in torpedoing the small British steamer *Wrotham*, owned by the same company as *Hawkinge*. Captain J.G. Davies and all his crew were rescued by the escorts.

Bartels also fired at a tanker in the convoy, but to no effect. Convoy OG69 was now on the parallel of Cape Finisterre, labouring southwards with Kondors and six U-boats, *U-68*, *U-79*, *U-126*, *U-203*, *U-331* and *U-561*, intermittently hanging onto its flanks. That night Mützelburg struck again, sinking the Swedish steamship *Norita*, owned by Nordström & Thulin of Stockholm, with the loss of two men, and the British *Lapland*, owned by the Currie Line of Leith. Although her crew escaped, she took a cargo of exported tinplate and general to the sea-bed with her. Mützelburg claimed to have fired at other vessels, including the *Rhododendron* as she picked up

Captain J.S. Brown and the crew of the *Lapland*. Kapitänleutnant von Tiesenhausen attempted to attack in *U-331* but was driven off by the escorts.

By now agents' reports had indicated the departure of HG68, and the crossing-point of the two convoys was approaching. HG68 had drawn with it some U-boats and two Italian submarines, and on the following night both OG69 and HG68 suffered alarms and several torpedoes were fired, but both escaped further destruction. The loss of seven merchant ships from OG69 was bad enough, however. The escort group, consisting of several newly worked up corvettes, had unsuccessfully counter-attacked the enemy in their turn, and though they had located Mützelburg and dropped a considerable number of depth-charges, they had not nailed him.

In an almost contiguous action west of Ireland on the 26th against Convoy ON1, which had Macintyre's 5th Escort Group to protect it, Oberleutnant zur See Schüler in *U-141* had torpedoed and sunk the steamship *Botwey*. She was in ballast, and all her company were picked up by the rescue ship *Copeland*. Schüler also fired at and damaged, but did not sink, the British steamer *Atlantic City*. One of the new, British-built emergency standard ships then entering service, the *Atlantic City* was not, like her sister 'Empire' ships, built to the account of the Ministry of War Transport, but had been built under licence to the same wartime specifications for a private owner, in her case Reardon Smith's of Cardiff, as a replacement for lost tonnage. She was initially abandoned but afterwards reboarded and brought safely into port, and survived the war. Her predicament brought the wrath of Macintyre upon *U-141* and HMS *Walker* subjected Schüler and his company to a 20-hour pounding from which they were fortunate to escape.

A vigorous defence kept at bay the nine U-boats and three Italian submarines which Kerneval directed against Convoy HG69 as soon as the Germans learned of its departure from Gibraltar on 9 August. No ships were lost from the convoy, but the enemy's surveillance operation brought them into contact with other vessels, and in this otherwise frustrated operation collateral damage was suffered by the *Empire Hurst*, a brand-new emergency-built collier owned by the MoWT and managed by Smith, Hogg & Company, which was outward bound off Cape St Vincent on 11 August when she was bombed by an FW200 Kondor from Kampfgeschwader 40. Three days later, on the 14th, the 2,500-ton Yugoslavian steamer *Sud*, owned by Oceania Shipping of Susak, was steaming independently on passage to the west of Oporto. She was an ancient ship, having been built in 1901, and was capable of only 7.5 knots. Remarkably, she survived Capitano di Corvetta Pollina's cannonade fired from the *Guglielmo Marconi*, though her crew took to their boats. Abandoned, the *Sud* floated until Kapitänleutnant Bauer found her four hours later and sank her with a torpedo from *U-126*.

Meanwhile, on 13 August, two days after HG69 reached Liverpool, Convoy OG71 consisting of 21 merchantmen left the Mersey. The commodore was embarked aboard the Yeoward Line's *Aguila*, which also had on board more than 90 service personnel on their way to Gibraltar, 20 of them young women of the Women's Royal Naval Service, better-known as 'Wrens'. The convoy was accompanied by the 5th Escort Group which at the time comprised the sloop *Leith*, the Norwegian-manned ex-American destroyer-escort *Bath*, the anti-submarine trawler *Lord Nuffield* and the corvettes *Bluebell, Campanula, Campion, Hydrangea, Wallflower* and *Zinnia*. On 17 August Dönitz received a sighting report of the convoy from a Kondor of Kampfgeschweder 40 and immediately alerted seven of the U-boats which had been involved with Convoy SL81, directing them to assemble off Bloody Foreland. The ambush was duly formed, *U-75, U-83, U-106, U-201, U-204, U-559* and *U-564* lay in wait, and that evening Oberleutnant Schnee made contact. He maintained station in *U-201* throughout the following day, during which time Dönitz added *U-552* to the pack as she left St-Nazaire for her fifth war patrol. An attempt by Junkers Ju88s to attack the convoy *en masse* was broken up, but Schnee and the aircraft reports enabled *U-559* (Heidtmann) and *U-204* (Kell) to join *U-201*, and that night the three attacked.

Despite the season the weather was cold and windy, with gale-force winds during much of the convoy's outward passage. In these conditions Schnee moved in after midnight and sank the *Aguila*, with fearful loss of life. The master Captain Firth and six of his crew plus two passengers and one naval signaller were rescued from the cold sea by the *Wallflower*, Lieutenant Commander I.J. Tyson, and a further six crew by the tug *Empire Oak*, but Commodore P.E. Parker, a retired vice admiral, four of his staff, five gunners, 58 crew and 89 passengers were lost, a total of 157 souls.[1]

Kell struck simultaneously, firing at several targets and torpedoing HNorMS *Bath*, Kaptein-löytnant F. Melsom, which had earlier been engaged in an attack on a sonar contact. Struck by two torpedoes she went down fast, taking Melsom and most of his crew with her.[2] Kell's second hit was MacAndrews' former fruit-carrier *Ciscar*, bearing a cargo of military stores for Gibraltar. Thirteen of her men died, but Captain E.L. Hughes and 34 survived to be rescued by the British ship *Petrel*. Finally, before daylight forced the U-boats to break off the action, Oberleutnant zur See Heidtmann torpedoed the steamship *Alva* which was bound to Lisbon with a full cargo of 2,300 tons of coal. One man in the engine room died, but Captain C.S. Palmer and his 24 men were quickly picked up by the *Clonlara*.

These attacks and the loss of the *Aguila* augured badly for a convoy which was largely composed of ships carrying military stores and service personnel to Gibraltar by way of the Tagus, so that although OG71 shook off its tormentors on the 20th with the 5th Escort Group attacking sonar contacts thought to be *U-106*, the Admiralty reinforced the escort with the destroyers *Gurkha* and *Legion*. On the 21st OG71 was again spotted from a Kondor but again lost, until after another aerial sighting Oberleutnant Suhren in *U-564* saw it to the west of Portugal on the afternoon of the 22nd and vectored in Schnee again. Schnee had not been far from the tail of the convoy, and by this time *U-552* (Topp) was closing it too. Towards midnight Suhren and Schnee moved in for the kill. Suhren struck the *Empire Oak* and *Clonlara*, both loaded with survivors from the *Aguila* and the *Alva*. The *Empire Oak* was a tug managed by the United Towing Company on behalf of the MoWT and was on her way to Gibraltar to assist with ocean salvage. Her master Captain F.E. Christian and seven of her crew were picked up by the *Campanula*, Lieutenant Commander R.V.E. Case, but the few survivors from the *Aguila* were lost with her. The Irish ship *Clonlara*, belonging to the Limerick Steamship Company and loaded with 1,000 tons of best Welsh steam-coal bound from Cardiff to Lisbon, lost six of her own people plus all those pulled out of the sea from the *Alva*. Captain J. Reynolds and just half a dozen of his men were recovered by the *Campion*, Lieutenant Commander A. Johnson.

The small British motor-coaster *Stork*, owned by the General Steam Navigation Company of London, had loaded a full cargo of cased motor spirit in Preston on Government account. This highly flammable and dangerous cargo ignited when Schnee's next torpedo struck, and although three men escaped to be rescued by *Wallflower*, Captain E.A.M. Williams and 18 men died in the fire. Schnee also hit the steamer *Aldergrove*, Captain H.W. McLean. Owned by the Grove Line of Glasgow and loaded with 2,650 tons of patent fuel intended for Lisbon, she sank taking a naval rating embarked as a passenger with her. McLean and his men were taken to Gibraltar aboard *Campanula*.

Suhren also hit and damaged the Norwegian *Spind*, owned by Jacob Salvesen of Farsund. Burning, she fell astern of the convoy and was abandoned, her crew being picked up by the escorts. Topp found her on fire and finished her off with a torpedo and gunfire from *U-552* in the small hours of the 23rd. Suhren, meanwhile, had kept up with the convoy and fired ineffectively at several more merchantmen. Before the action was broken off as dawn lightened the sky he torpedoed the corvette *Zinnia*, Lieutenant Commander C.G. Cuthbertson. The torpedo must have struck her magazine, for she disintegrated with a tremendous explosion.

Both Italian and German submarines were directed against Convoys HG71 and HG72 but failed to locate either, and in the process, on 8 September, the *Baracca* was depth-charged to the surface by HMS *Croome*, raked by gunfire and rammed.

Meanwhile, during the last week of August in the North West Approaches Dönitz had gathered his customary pack of U-boats, eight on the 23rd when *U-143* (Gelhaus) sank the small Norwegian steamer *Inger* off the Butt of Lewis. That same day, led by its commodore embarked in the *Henry Stanley*, the 33 vessels of Convoy OS4, which included the rescue ship *Perth*, left Liverpool and made for the North Channel. Clearing the Irish coast in heavy weather it was spotted on the morning of the 26th by Oberleutnant zur See Schüler in *U-141*; fortunately, Coastal Command aircraft patrolling above the convoy compelled him to submerge and he lost contact. That afternoon, however, Kapitänleutnant Paulshen in *U-557* saw the merchant ships and began to stalk. By that night he had worked his way into an attacking position, whereupon he quickly sank four ships: the Norwegian *Segundo* in ballast at a cost of seven dead; the British *Saugor* with a general cargo and the loss of more than 30 souls; the British steam tramp *Tremoda*, loaded with military stores, with the loss of 32 men; and the British steam tramp *Embassage*.

James Norse's *Saugor* was bound for Calcutta under the command of Captain J.A.A. Steel and among her general cargo carried military aircraft. Her two dozen survivors, who included Steel, were picked up by the rescue ship. Captain J.S. Bastian was among the dead when the Hain Steamship Company's *Tremoda* went to pieces in the heavy seas after being severely damaged by the torpedo's explosion. The remaining crew, 21 men, were in the water for some time before the Free French sloop *Chevreuil* scooped them up and carried them to Jamaica. The *Embassage* had aboard 8,500 tons of general and military cargo, including aircraft and lorries loaded in Leith. She was to have picked up a bulk-cargo of iron ore at Pepel in West Africa for her homeward lading, but hit by two torpedoes this Hall Brothers' tramp foundered while at full speed, taking her master Captain E. Kiddie and 38 men to the bottom. *Embassage*'s three survivors, the bosun and two seamen, endured a four-day ordeal clinging to an upturned boat until they were rescued by HMCS *Assiniboine*.

Paulshen followed OS4 throughout the hours of daylight, bringing up *U-71*, *U-558* and *U-751*. Two U-boats had been spotted on the 27th from the convoy as it ploughed through continuing heavy weather, a westerly gale kicking up a rough sea and a moderate swell, but they were driven off by the destroyer *Walker* and the sloop *Bideford*. At 14.00 on the 28th, with OS4 about 330 miles west of the Fastnet Light, a bright flutter of bunting flying from the signal halliards of the *Henry Stanley* broke through the gloom of an occasional rain squall and gave permission for some of the ships, those heading not for West Africa but for the Caribbean and the Panama Canal, to detach.

Among these was the large fast cargo-liner *Otaio*, owned by the New Zealand Shipping Company of London. Working up to full speed, Captain G. Kinnell took her out of the convoy in company with several other ships from which she soon drew ahead. At 15.40, when she was still within sight of the convoy, two torpedoes slammed into her port side, one into No. 5 Hold, the second into the engine room. They had been fired by Kapitänleutnant G. Krech in *U-558*. The ship took on a very heavy list: with most of the engine-room watch killed and the port engine and auxiliary generators destroyed, the starboard engine continued to drive the *Otaio* so that she swung round to head east, at the same time sinking by the stern. The refrigerating engineer had been working in the compressor compartment in the upper engine room when the first torpedo struck, and in the few seconds before the second impact had made for the ladder to the upper deck. In the second explosion he was severely burned and almost lost his sight, but he made the boat deck in one piece. The sixth engineer had also been in the upper part of the engine room, and found himself swimming before he managed to reach the door to the open deck. He saw nothing of the third or the ninth engineers, or of the two greasers who had each been attending a diesel engine.

Kinnell was now obliged to order his ship abandoned, in most disagreeable circumstances. With a lowering crew of two men No. 3 Boat was being launched when it was lifted by a sea: the mousings slipped from the hooks, and the falls disengaged; the painter parted and the boat drifted uselessly astern: Nos 1 and 2 Boats were lowered into the water, but as No. 4 was passing the damaged area of her hull the *Otaio* rolled and the gangway gallows swung outboard, damaging the boat's side. Some men managed to scramble back on deck, but the next moment a swell lifted the lifeboat, and again, one mousing slipped prematurely, a fall disengaged and the end of the boat dropped, throwing several poor souls into the sea. One steward was drowned and the fourth officer lost a finger. Others escaped on the sole raft they could clear away and launch. Four engineers, two greasers, the steward, two seamen, the galley boy, one gunner and a radio officer were lost but Kinnell and 57 men escaped in the appalling conditions. They were quickly picked up by Lieutenant Commander S. G. W. Deneys in HMS *Vanoc*, who had detached from the convoy in response to Kinnell's distress call. The difficulty of launching a boat in heavy weather from a listing ship with residual way on her can scarcely be exaggerated, though the premature unhooking of the falls was an unfortunate and avoidable occurrence.

Nevertheless, Kinnell's tribute to his ship's company was glowing and he singled out his four apprentices for especial praise.

The action was broken off shortly after this. The U-boats had regrouped off the North Channel by the end of the month, but although Gelhaus sighted Convoy ON12 on the 30th, *U-141* was driven off by the 3rd Escort Group. Only Schüler had any success, sinking two fishing vessels before ending his patrol.

As these events were going on, two factors had initiated a wide search operation. A British merchant ship reported 'a *Hipper*-class' cruiser at large, and Ultra intelligence seemed to confirm the sighting. Capital ships, cruisers and destroyers from both the British and American navies were involved, and alarm warnings were transmitted to several convoys then at sea. The merchant ship's report turned out to be spurious, and the Ultra decrypts were found to refer to an auxiliary cruiser, the *Orion*, and some Axis blockade-runners, which all arrived safely in the Gironde between 20 August and 10 September.

Among the escorts receiving notice of this putative predator were two American groups shepherding merchantmen to Iceland, and they and others were re-routed a few days later on 27 August when Ultra decrypts indicated a concentration of U-boats to the south-west of Iceland. Eastbound Convoys HX146 and SC41 and westbound Convoys ON10 and ONS11 were also diverted to avoid the 14-strong group, which Kerneval had code-named *Markgraf*. One of these, *U-652*, was located and attacked by a British aircraft, but escaped destruction. She went on to counter-attack the American destroyer *Greer* which was coming up on her way to Iceland and which Oberleutnant G-W. Fraatz assumed had attacked him.

Fraatz's two torpedoes missed, but this was the sort of unprovoked attack on American ships that Hitler had been so anxious to avoid, and had expressly forbidden his U-boat commanders to engage in. Although in this instance it did not prove *casus belli*, it had a sufficient effect, for as a consequence Roosevelt ordered the United States Navy to 'shoot on sight'.

Dönitz redeployed the *Markgraf* U-boats further west but another re-routeing diverted the following HX147, though Korvettenkapitän H. Förster in *U-501* succeeded in sinking a Norwegian straggler from SC41, the *Einvik*, off Iceland on 5 September. Frustrated by this lack of success Dönitz decided to spread the *Markgraf* submarines, but his orders were intercepted and decrypted, and a whole series of Anglo-American naval movements thereby evaded detection. These included Convoys HX148, ON(S)12 and SC43, along with a powerful United States task force covering nine troop transports conveying a brigade of the United States Army to relieve the marines garrisoning Iceland. In the appalling weather various alarums raised around the task force included several entirely spurious 'contacts' which were vigorously attacked by the American destroyers escorting the troop ships.

While these evasions were almost entirely successful a tragic exception occurred in the case of SC42, which lost no less than a quarter of its 65 ships as the *Markgraf* boats widened their net, a triumph that seemed to confound any suspicions on the part of the BdU staff at Kerneval that the failures elsewhere were other than circumstantial. Convoy SC42 left Sydney, Cape Breton Island on 30 August, steaming at a speed of 7.5 knots, its multiple cargoes totalling half a million tons of supplies. It met heavy weather and was hove-to for two days until the wind eased on 7 September. From the Western Ocean Meeting-Point eastwards it was escorted by the Canadian 24th Escort Group, consisting of the destroyer *Skeena*, Lieutenant Commander J. Hibbard, and the corvettes *Orillia*, Lieutenant Commander W.S. Briggs, *Alberni*, Lieutenant Commander G.O. Baugh, and *Kenogami*, Lieutenant Commander R. Jackson.

Having received orders to divert from its planned track, the convoy was off Cape Farewell by sunrise on 9 September. Two ships had dropped astern because of engine trouble, and two torpedo tracks were seen from one of them, the *Jedmoor*, which raised the alarm but was not hit. First to be lost was the *Empire Springbuck*, a standard emergency-built steamer from the First World War. She had been bought from the Americans, renamed under British MoWT ownership and placed under the management of W.A. Souter & Company of Newcastle-upon-Tyne, a company experienced in tramping. Carrying explosives and steel, she had come within the sights of *U-81* as Kapitänleutnant F. Guggenberger approached the convoy and was hit by a salvo of torpedoes. The *Empire Springbuck* blew up, her explosive cargo counter-mining after the torpedo strikes, broke in two and sank within seconds, killing Captain W. O'Connell and all 41 souls on board.[3]

Later that afternoon, as the *Jedmoor* resumed her station, SC42 closed the southern extreme of Greenland and was sighted by Oberleutnant E. Greger in *U-85*. Although his initial approach was unsuccessful his contact reports alerted others of the dispersed group, homing them in. Guggenberger came up from the south, Schultze joined in *U-432*, and from various distances and over the next five days *U-43*, *U-81*, *U-82*, *U-84*, *U-105*, *U-202*, *U-207*, *U-372*, *U-373*, *U-433*, *U-501*, *U-552*, *U-572*, *U-575* and *U-652* all harried SC42 with varying degrees of success in the the course of one of the major convoy battles of the war. Although these U-boats did not attack simultaneously, the massing of resources they exemplified threw into sharp relief the weaknesses of a dissipated, distracted and dispersed escort. In provoking the British Admiralty to review its anti-submarine tactics, the tragedy that ensued proved a pivotal event.

The Admiralty's plan to divert the convoy to the southward was frustrated by a severe depression lurking there which would have destroyed the convoy's cohesion, rendering its constituent parts vulnerable to attack. The proximity of the Greenland coast and the field of loose pack-ice which came down the east coast and doubled Cape Farewell, posing a considerable nuisance to ships trying to maintain a tight formation, seemed to obviate a move in that direction, but the convoy commodore nevertheless swung SC42 north. The mass of ships headed up the east coast of Greenland into the Denmark Strait in an attempt to work round an estimated eight U-boats close to the east, to which Hibbard and his colleagues, including Commodore Mackenzie of the Royal Naval Reserve in W.J. Tatem's Cardiff-registered tramp *Everleigh*, had been alerted by Admiralty signal.

The German assault began shortly after dusk when with a dull roar a torpedo from *U-432* (Schultze) slammed into the deeply-laden Bright Navigation Company's tramp *Muneric*, which was lying fourth in the extreme port column. With 7,000 tons of iron ore in her holds she 'sank like a stone', taking with her Captain F. Baker, 60 crew and two wretched stowaways. The port escort, the *Kenogami*, turned outwards, increased speed and began to run down the torpedo track as a second torpedo passed along her own starboard side. At the same instant Jackson's lookouts reported the U-boat making off on the surface at high speed. Outrun by Schultze, Jackson opened fire with his 4-inch gun, but ceased when ordered to rejoin the convoy: the commodore and other merchantmen had spotted two more U-boats. A few moments later in the gathering gloom a fourth was seen running down between the columns of ships.

Events now moved apace as eight U-boats engaged the convoy with swift and devastating results. Guggenberger's *U-81* failed in an attack at this time, but within minutes of *Kenogami* putting her helm over to resume her station, two more merchant ships had been sunk. The first occurred when the tramp *Baron Pentland*, lying in the central rear of the convoy, was hit by the initiator of the 'Greer' Incident', Oberleutnant zur See G-W. Fraatz in *U-652*. The Hogarth tramp began to founder and was abandoned by Captain Campbell and his crew; being loaded with timber, she settled until the cargo bore up on the deckheads and then wallowed astern of the convoy. Fraatz also hit the laden British tanker *Tahchee*, an elderly 1914-built vessel of 6,508 tons owned by the Standard Transportation Company of Hong Kong. Damaged and immobilised, but not sinking, she fell out of her station as the second vessel in the fourth column, leaving SC42 to plough on to the north, heading for higher latitudes.

As the long sub-polar twilight faded, a 'high, white moon silhouetted the vessels'. Frequent sightings of surfaced U-boats between the columns led to bursts of fire from the lighter armaments of several merchant ships, while 'the corvettes and the destroyer did what they could with scramble nets . . .'

As midnight approached, a thick band of overcast was observed approaching the moon, and the order was passed by Mackenzie to prepare to execute an emergency turn in an attempt to ruin the approaches of the U-boats. Shortly before the executive signal was made another U-boat was seen on the surface, attracting fire from the closest ships. Hibbard turned *Skeena* and began to chase the U-boat down one interval between the columns when his quarry turned and, cutting across the adjacent line, sped down the next interval in the opposite direction before crash-diving. In attempting to pursue Hibbard almost collided with one of the merchant ships, and was obliged to go full astern to avoid it as the convoy, in obedience to the commodore's executive order, turned to port.

Not long afterwards the convoy resumed a course of NNE. The manoeuvre had failed to throw off the stalking Germans, for about two hours later, at 02.10 on 10 September, the Dutch tramp *Winterswijk* was hit by a torpedo from *U-432*. It was Schultze's second kill of the night. Stationed in the port rear of the convoy and loaded with over 4,200 tons of phosphates, the *Winterswijk* sank quickly. Twenty men died with her, thirteen survived in that freezing sea. Schultze had fired a salvo, for almost simultaneously the small timber-laden Norwegian vessel *Stargaard*, well ahead in the extreme port column, received a torpedo in her engine room and began to settle.

After failing in his first attack, by 02.45 Guggenberger was in a position on the far side of the convoy to line up *U-81* on the former Danish motorvessel *Sally Maersk* leading the extreme starboard column, the twelfth. Although Danish-manned, the ship was managed by the Moss Hutchinson Line of Liverpool on behalf of the MoWT. The torpedo struck her at 02.47, whereupon Captain J.K. Lindberg and all his crew of exiles took to the boats as their grain-laden home sank beneath the indifferent Atlantic.

Kapitänleutnant S. Rollman in *U-82* had made an attack on the *Skeena*, but missed his target. However, when the convoy made another short dogleg at about 05.00, this time to starboard, he was in a position to fire at and hit the Catapult Armed Merchantman *Empire Hudson*. This ship, leading the second column, commanded by Captain J.C. Cooke of the Silver Line on behalf of the MoWT, was brand-new, a product of the Sunderland Yard of J.L. Thompson who were then pioneering the partial prefabrication methods used in standard-ship construction (of which more later). She was loaded with more than 9,500 tons of grain and bore a Mark 1 Hurricane fighter on its catapult over her forecastle. Four men lost their lives, but Cooke and the rest, including the two pilots and aircrew, were picked up by merchant ships in company.

As daylight increased the U-boats withdrew, but the Admiralty continued to transmit U-boat alarms and at 11.43, just as the ships of the convoy prepared to signal their individual noon positions to the commodore, the Albyn Line's *Thistleglen*, leading the ninth column, was struck by a torpedo from *U-85* (Greger) and settled quickly, borne down by 5,200 tons of steel and 2,400 tons of pig-iron. Her engine-room watch were killed, but Captain G. Dodson, most of his crew and all the ship's gunners were rescued by a ship in convoy. Oberleutnant Greger's periscope had been seen from *Skeena*, and Hibbard made an attack. Then Baugh in *Alberni* came up and gained a contact and was joined by Jackson in *Kenogami*, which like her sister-corvette had been picking up survivors astern of the convoy. Air bubbles and some oil were seen rising to the surface of the sea, but his increasing distance from the convoy prompted Hibbard to return to his defence station. It was not in fact the 'probable kill' they had hoped it was, but Hibbard's escorts had succeeded in damaging *U-85* badly enough to force Greger to break off the operation and head for St-Nazaire.

In the early afternoon further evasive alterations of course were made in response to Admiralty warnings and a sighting of U-boats from a Catalina of No. 209 Squadron based in Iceland. The flying-boat had attacked a surfaced U-boat, *U-501*, so as day shaded imperceptibly into night again, renewed attacks were anticipated. Hibbard's defensive preparations were now somewhat compromised by the lack of *Orillia*, which had been working astern of the convoy picking up survivors, including those from the abandoned but still floating *Baron Pentland*, and was now attending the wallowing *Tahchee*. As the corvette struggled east towards Iceland with the tanker in tow, Hibbard was reinforced by the two Canadian corvettes *Chambly*, Commander J.D. Prentice, and *Moosejaw*, Lieutenant F.E. Grubb, which had been carrying out training exercises off the Greenland coast.

This fortuitous relief proved timely. As the two corvettes approached the convoy shortly before 21.00, the British tanker *Bulysses*, lying third in the tenth column, fired the rockets indicating she had been hit. Bound from New York to the oil refinery at Stanlow Port in Cheshire with a cargo of 10,500 tons of gas-oil, the Anglo-Saxon Petroleum Company's ship neither blew up nor sank rapidly, enabling Captain B. Lamb and most of his crew to escape. They were quickly picked up by the Finnish vessel *Wisla*, which was lying at the rear of the same column in the convoy.

Prentice and Grubb were heading for the area neck-and-neck when at 21.19 more rockets rose, this time from the *Gypsum Queen*. Stationed at the head of the eighth column, she had been on the commodore's starboard beam. Captain A.J. Chapman and 25 of his crew were later recovered by the Norwegian vessel *Vestland*, stationed towards the rear of the same column in the convoy, but ten men were lost with the ship, together with her cargo of 5,500 tons of sulphur from New Orleans.

Both *Gypsum Queen* and the *Bulysses* were victims of Rollman in *U-82*, and he now withdrew as *Chambly* and *Moosejaw* closed the scene. As Chapman and his men were bundling into their boats, *Chambly* quickly gained a sonar contact, though it was not Rollman, but Korvettenkapitän Förster in *U-501*. His sole success had been the sinking of the *Einvik* on the 5th, in which he had expended six torpedoes and 40 rounds of ammunition. These facts may be pointers to Förster's mental state, for his behaviour now was extraordinary. As *Chambly* dropped a pattern of five charges, he decided to surface. As *U-501* rose almost under *Moosejaw*'s forefoot, the men closed up round the corvette's 4-inch gun opened fire at maximum depression; the gun promptly jammed, and Grubb closed to ram. A moment later Förster put the helm hard over as the corvette struck the U-boat a glancing blow, slewing her round so that the two vessels were parallel, and in contact. The proximity of the corvette's deck with his own conning tower seems to have prompted Förster to leap aboard the *Moosejaw*. That he managed it astonished all witnesses, both Canadian and German, but as Grubb later stated, 'he did not get wet'. Fearful of being boarded in force, Grubb hauled off, whereupon the German submarine appeared to get under way again. Seeing his commander abandon ship, First Watch Officer Albring had ordered the secret equipment smashed. Using the U-boat's superior speed, he might have escaped, but Grubb, ringing on his own engines, now rammed properly. Several of the U-boat's crew, out on the casing in the wake of Förster's bizarre departure, made for their own deck gun, 'but a round or two from *Moosejaw*'s . . . discouraged that attempt'.

By this time *Chambly* had come up in the semi-darkness, and *U-501* was ordered to stop her engines. When this had been complied with, a boarding-party was sent by boat under Lieutenant E.T. Simmonds. An attempt to salve the U-boat was thwarted when she sank, with the loss of one of the boarding-party: Albring had ordered her scuttled as *Chambly* lowered her boat.[4] In the confusion, as Germans and Canadians alike jumped into the sea, 12 of the U-boat's crew drowned; 46 joined their commander as prisoners-of-war.[5]

Meanwhile the convoy had continued, and the nightmare of the previous evening had been repeated, although this time the greater defence was put up by the merchantmen themselves as they fired at the surfaced U-boats in their midst. The toll might have been far worse had all torpedoes fired actually damaged their targets. Lüth in *U-43* had four failures in a salvo of six, with two misses; Kapitänleutnant Linder in *U-202* missed with five torpedoes in his first attack, though he claimed to have sunk an escort. Mechanical problems dogged Schewe in *U-105*, as they did Kapitänleutnant Hinsch in the new *U-569*.

For the Allies, the early hours of 11 September were bad. At 00.45 Ropner's tramp *Stonepool*, having escaped Dau's *U-42* in the first weeks of the war, was finally sunk by *U-207*. She was leading SC42's column eleven when Oberleutnant F. Meyer's torpedo sent the ship and her cargo of oats and grain, topped off with army trucks, to the bottom with the loss of her master, Captain A. White, and 31 men. Half a dozen survived, to be picked up by the *Kenogami*. Minutes later Meyer hit another ship, the second Moss Hutchinson cargo-liner to be lost from SC42. The *Berury*, Captain F.J. Morgan, was lying next but one astern of the *Stonepool*, loaded with military stores, and all but one of her crew were rescued by the corvettes. Meyer struck once more before dawn, damaging the small ex-Danish but Canadian-flagged and -manned *Randa*, which had moved up into *Bulysses*'s station in the tenth column. Then for a while there was a lull in the sinkings but a welter of near-confusion as merchantmen sporadically opened fire on conning towers and the escorts probed for echoes or hunted surfaced sightings as they rejoined the convoy.

Shortly after 02.00 the night was again blown apart by torpedo explosions when two vessels were hit more or less simultaneously. Rollman was continuing his predations, his salvo severely damaging the Swedish ship *Scania*, lying in column four. She dropped back through the convoy as the sound ships steamed past her, her timber cargo keeping her afloat and enabling all her crew to escape, to be recovered from their boats by the corvettes. The *Scania* wallowed derelict until, hours later, she was sunk by Linder in *U-202*. The other ship to be hit, the *Empire Crossbill*, was immediately astern of the *Scania*. She was another old ex-American standard vessel from the previous war, loaded down with 6,686 tons of steel, and in the darkness she steamed straight under, taking with her Captain E.R. Townend, 37 crew, ten gunners, and a passenger who was apparently tending a small consignment of 'relief goods'. Twenty minutes later another explosion in the second column pronounced the end of the small Swedish timber-ship *Garm*, hit by a torpedo from Schultze's *U-432* with the loss of six hapless, neutral Swedes.

The Admiralty was by now thoroughly alarmed at the events taking place around SC42, and as the U-boats withdrew in daylight a pair of Catalinas arrived from Iceland to provide air cover, and more reinforcements were on their way. First on the scene were the corvettes *Mimosa* (Free French), *Gladiolus* and *Wetaskiwin* (Canadian), and two anti-submarine trawlers which had been diverted from Convoy HX147. Later in the forenoon the Royal Navy's 2nd Escort Group arrived from Convoy ON13. The group's destroyers had first raced to Hvalfjord to refuel before heading west to relieve Hibbard's beleaguered force. The senior officer was Commander W.E. Banks in the elderly destroyer *Douglas*, and with him were HM Destroyers *Veteran, Leamington, Skate* and *Saladin*. As he took up his station Banks was informed by one of the Catalinas that a U-boat had been seen surfaced ahead of the convoy. *Leamington* and *Veteran* were immediately ordered to proceed ahead, and at 15.00 they spotted Meyer's hitherto successful *U-207*.

Meyer's crash dive was made too late; at 22 knots the destroyers closed the swirl of water betraying the U-boat's rapid descent and were instantly in sonar contact. In three controlled attacks they rained 21 depth-charges down upon *U-207*, and although neither warship was credited with accounting for her, she was never heard from again.

That night Convoy SC42 passed into fog, and although some of the U-boats maintained a tenuous contact, the augmented escort proved too much for them. Fraatz in *U-652* made one last but abortive attack, and Schewe is thought to have struck at an independent or straggler. The trawler *Windermere*, also diverted from ON13, had been rounding up a straggling vessel, and these two rejoined that night, further beefing up the escort and frustrating Oberleutnant Uphoff in *U-84* and Lüth in *U-43*.

Next morning Hibbard in *Skeena* led *Kenogami* and *Alberni* off to Hvalfjord to refuel and were replaced by the Canadian destroyers *St Croix* and *Columbia*, which themselves had been withdrawn from SC41 and HX147, respectively. *U-373, U-432* and *U-433* remained in contact, though the following night of 12/13 September was again foggy and no attacks were made. After daylight Banks's destroyers were withdrawn to refuel again, relieved by a group of three American warships, USSs *Hughes, Sims* and *Russell*. Although five U-boats were still searching for the convoy, the poor visibility that was making station-keeping very difficult within SC42 denied them a sight of their quarry.

The complexities of convoy management were immense. The weakening of the defence of ON13, which was by now relying upon three corvettes and two trawlers,[6] meant that it too had to be re-routed, north of SC42. At the same time as SC42 continued on its painful way east, a small United States task force on its way home from reinforcing the Iceland garrison had to be routed to the south.

Hibbard rejoined SC42 later on the 13th, bringing with him five merchant ships on passage from Iceland to Britain, and HMCS *Chambly*; the United States warships were withdrawn on the 14th. Topp in *U-552* was in brief contact with some of the escorts before Dönitz ordered the operation broken off. It was not yet quite over, however; on the afternoon of the 16th, to the north-west of St Kilda, as Convoy SC42 lumbered south-east heading for the North Channel and the relative security of the Irish Sea, the Runciman-owned British tramp *Jedmoor* fell astern again. She was seen by Gysae in *U-98*. Closing her, he succeeded in firing a torpedo which hit forward of her bridge. Loaded with 7,400 tons of iron ore from Santos, the *Jedmoor* sank in two minutes, her stern rearing high in the air and 'the ore cargo rattling down inside the holds'; only five of her crew escaped, two being picked up by the British merchantman *Campus*, which lowered a lifeboat, three by the Norwegian *Knoll*, both of which had also fallen astern of the ill-starred convoy. Captain R.C. Collins and 30 crew were taken to their deaths by their ship as she plunged under the grey waters of the Atlantic. Finally, on 19 September, far astern of SC42, the derelict *Baron Pentland* was sunk by Neumann in *U-372* as other following convoys were being subjected to attack.

It had been a dismal episode; Hibbard's Canadian 24th Escort Group were much criticised for recovering survivors instead of pursuing the defence with greater vigour, but it was a failure that owed more to the imperfections of foresight than to the inadequacies of a very new and inexperienced navy. More to the point, the Royal Canadian Navy had secured its first kill of a German submarine, by two corvettes with green crews, though Commander Prentice himself was an experienced retired officer who had returned to duty in his country's hour of need. Furthermore, in latitudes above 61° North it was an important factor that few of the survivors from the torpedoed merchant ships had had to spend more than an hour or two in their boats.

The Admiralty requested that the Canadians increase the size of their escort groups to six men-of-war, but because they had not enough destroyers to provide more than one to each group the slow 'Flower'-class corvettes had perforce to deputise. Requests to Washington for assistance from the United States Navy – now, under the terms of the Placentia Bay agreement, responsible for the defence of convoys out to the Western Ocean Meeting-Point – were met with a curt refusal from Fleet Admiral Ernest King. He was not a man to learn from others' mistakes, nor to fall over himself to assist either the Canadians or the British.

As the *Markgraf* U-boats clung to the flanks of SC42 its 55-ship successor, SC43, passed unmolested across the Atlantic between 5 and 20 September. But the respite did not last, and Convoy SC44, which left Sydney on the 11th, was less fortunate. The convoy escort was nominally the Canadian 23rd Escort Group, but at this time it contained elements of the 15th and was led by the British destroyer *Chesterfield*. The corvettes involved were the British *Honeysuckle* and HMCSs *Agassiz, Levis* and *Mayflower*.

Against it a force of nine U-boats, code-named *Brandenburg*, was being mustered off Cape Farewell and one, *U-94*, located and sank three stragglers from westbound Convoy ON14 on 15 September, a heartening omen for Kerneval.[7] Consisting of 54 merchantmen under Commodore Robinson, Convoy SC44 had passed the southern point of Greenland when it was sighted by Kentrat in *U-74*, and although radio interference hampered German attempts to concentrate the *Brandenburg* U-boats, *U-94*, *U-373*, *U-552* and *U-662* joined Kentrat, attacking the convoy on the night of 19/20 September.

Shortly after midnight two torpedoes from *U-74* struck HMCS *Levis* on her port side, and although they caused extensive damage the warship remained afloat for five hours, prompting Lieutenant Commander G.H. Stephen of the *Mayflower* to attempt her salvage. Seventeen men had been killed, but 40 were removed by the *Mayflower* and her sister *Agassiz*. Meanwhile, having disposed of the flank guard, Kentrat penetrated the convoy and turned his attention upon the CAM-ship *Empire Burton*, under the command of Captain J. Mitchell, a Common Brothers master acting on behalf of the MoWT. All hands, including the half-dozen airmen, were rescued by the *Honeysuckle*, but almost 10,000 tons of wheat went to the bottom of the Atlantic.

Also loose among the convoy was Topp's *U-552*. Within a short space of time he had sunk the British tanker *T.J. Williams* belonging to the Anglo-American Oil Company with the loss of 10,036 tons of petrol and 17 lives. Captain R.T.C. Wright and 20 men were fortunate enough to escape the flames and were picked up by Lieutenant Commander G.W. Gregorie's *Honeysuckle*. Topp's next attack, against the Panamanian-flagged *Pink Star*, was equally successful; 11 died, and her general cargo was lost. Before dawn Topp had also torpedoed the Norwegian motor-tanker *Barbro*, which was carrying 9,000 tons of petrol. This caught fire, and in the blaze all 34 men of her company perished most horribly.

Kentrat and Oberleutnant Hamm in *U-562* made further attempts to approach SC44 but the escort was progressively reinforced, first by the Free French corvette *Alysse*, then by the Canadians *Arrowhead* and *Eyebright*, and finally by an American destroyer flotilla consisting of USSs *Winslow, Truxtun, Bainbridge, Overton* and *Reuben James*. Finally the motley escort was relieved and the British 3rd Escort Group took over for the remainder of the passage.

On 22 September, after breaking off the operation, Hamm in *U-562* sank the Danish-manned 'British' steamship *Erna III*, dispersed from ON16; Captain K.C. Sorensen and all his company were lost. Before completing his patrol, in an attack on westbound ONS19 Hamm also sank the CAM-ship *Empire Wave*, with heavy loss of life.

On her way back to Bergen, Ites's *U-94* encountered the Eagle Oil Company's tanker *San Florentino* on 1 October in mid Atlantic, 1,200 miles ENE from Newfoundland and not far from the position in which her sister-ship *San Demetrio* had been shelled by the *Admiral Scheer*. The *San Florentino*, in ballast and on her way to Venezuela for a cargo of Admiralty fuel, had 'become separated' from ONS19. Ites fired a salvo of torpedoes at her, causing severe damage; he then surfaced and, finding the vessel reluctant to sink, began to shell her. Captain W.R. Davis had not immediately abandoned ship but had ordered his crew to action stations. Down aft Second Officer G. Taylor, seeing the surfaced U-boat, opened fire with the poop gun and kept *U-94* at bay for some hours. Eventually Ites withdrew, but returned the following day to find the *San Florentino* still afloat, whereupon he fired a second salvo of torpedoes at the tanker, breaking her in two. Davis ordered the crew to the boats and Taylor and 21 men escaped in No. 3 Boat. No. 1 Boat was badly damaged but floated on her buoyancy tanks, offering some support to most of the remainder of the crew. Third Officer G.D. Todd and Able Seaman T. Clayton were trapped aboard the forward section of the ship and clung on as it reared up and stood vertically in the rough sea cut up by a strong westerly wind. For nine hours the survivors in the lifeboats were tossed about and soaked through. Captain Davis and 22 of his crew had perished in Ites's attacks, but the 35 survivors in the two boats were rescued by the westbound Canadian corvette *Mayflower*. The remains of the *San Florentino* had to be sunk by gunfire from Baugh's Canadian corvette *Alberni* once she had rescued Todd and Clayton, who had to slide from their perch high on the ship's forecastle down the fore-topmast stay and into the water. They had been clinging on for 13 hours. Taylor was afterwards awarded the George Medal and the Lloyd's War Medal for bravery at sea.

Other *Brandenburg* U-boats also struck at vessels straggling from Convoy ONS19, south of Greenland about six hundred miles east of Cape Race. On 2 October Kapitänleutnant G. Heydemann's *U-575* sank the Dutch motor-vessel *Tuva* and *U-431* (Dommes) torpedoed the British cargo-liner *Hatasu*. Owned by Moss, Hutchinson of Liverpool, the *Hatasu* was in ballast and sank rapidly, drowning Captain W.J. Meek and 39 of her crew. Nine men escaped death in a lifeboat commanded by the ship's carpenter, W. Manning. It was his second such experience in four months, and in the week before he was rescued he suffered so appallingly from immersion foot as to end his sea service. Manning and his companions 'all had periods when our minds seemed to wander, and we imagined we could see . . . all sorts of good food'. In response to survivors' complaints about how inconspicuous lifeboats were at sea, those of the *Hatasu* had been fitted with yellow covers and supplied with yellow flags. Manning's boat flew its flags and was spotted and its occupants rescued by the American destroyer *Charles F. Hughes*, then on her way to Reykjavik.

Hamm's destruction of the *Empire Wave* caused the death of Captain C.P. Maclay, his 19 crew, and nine airmen. The survivors, 23 of the ship's crew under Chief Officer J. Cameron, six gunners and two airmen, took to their boats but had far greater difficulty attracting attention. Their ship was not only a CAM-ship but another of J.L. Thompson's brand-new Sunderland-built standard cargo-vessels, yet even so she did not have the bright boat equipment carried by the *Hatasu*. After five days in cold, wet conditions her survivors saw two aircraft, but without rockets or flares were unable to attract their attention. After 14 days they spotted a third aircraft. By this time they were in sight of Iceland, and when next morning another aircraft flew over them on her way out to patrol the ocean wastes, Cameron ordered his companions to take to the oars, in the hope that the splashes would catch the eye of an observer. They were saved, it seems, when they used the tin lid of the medicine chest as a heliograph in a patch of pallid sunshine and were spotted at last by an American aircraft which directed an Icelandic trawler, the *Surprise*, to their assistance.

Reviewing the losses sustained by SC42 and SC44, one Admiralty Board member insisted that 'every single surface ship and every long-range aircraft we can possibly muster' should be assigned to the Atlantic campaign. Referring to the short-lived optimism of midsummer, he added, 'Any suggestion that the corner has been turned is not supported by facts.' Joubert de la Ferté renewed his plea to Bomber Command to target the German submarine bases on the Biscay coast of France, and a half-hearted acquiescence resulted in the inadequate bombing of one only, at L'Orient.

Convoy operations to the west of the 22nd meridian, which passes almost exactly through Reykjavik, were by now fully vested in the United States Navy controlled from Washington, with Rear Admiral Bristol's Task Force Four taking over the running of the faster HX and ON convoys between Halifax/Sydney and Hvalfjord. The slower SC and ONS convoys now came under Rear Admiral Murray's eleven Canadian escort groups. The slightly smaller yet more vulnerable and, as far as the Germans were concerned, more accessible area to the east of 22° West remained under Admiralty control from London. To this end the Royal Navy now had three main bases: Greenock on the Clyde, Liverpool on the Mersey, and Londonderry on Lough Foyle. At Greenock were based the 3rd, 4th and 11th Escort Groups, working out of the James Watt Dock. The first of these groups had a small and the second a strong contingent of Free French corvettes, and the third comprised two Polish destroyers. Based on Liverpool's Gladstone Dock were the all-Royal Navy 5th, 6th, 9th, 10th, 36th, and 37th and the combined British and Norwegian 7th Escort Groups. Working out of Lough Foyle came the 1st, 2nd, 8th, 12th, 40th, 41st, 42nd, 43rd and 44th. Those with high numbers were made up of sloops, the 9th, 10th, 11th and 12th were all-destroyer groups, all 'Hunt'-class ships; the remainder were composed of a small number of destroyers with supporting corvettes – in all, some 150 men-of-war, in addition to the 40-odd making up the eleven Canadian escort groups. On the face of it, it was a redoubtable force, but many of its elements, and particularly the Canadians, were not merely inexperienced in anti-submarine warfare and the tedious business of convoy escort, but strangers to the marine environment itself.

With Rear Admiral Ingram's American Task Force Three carrying out patrols between Trinidad, Recife and a point to the south-west of the Cape Verde Islands, United States participation in the Battle of the Atlantic was increasing. On 17 September the United States Navy took an active part in convoy support for the first time when Captain M.L. Dayo's American 1st Escort Group (USSs *Ericsson, Eberle, Upshur, Ellis* and *Dallas*) took over from the local Canadian escort and accompanied the 50-strong Convoy HX150 to the Mid-Ocean Meeting Point, where on the 25th it was handed over to a British group after a five-hour delay during which appalling weather held up the westbound ships they were escorting. HX150 arrived in Liverpool three days later, its only loss the *Nigaristan* which caught fire and had to be abandoned. Her crew of 63 were rescued during a gale, with a heavy sea running, by the USS *Eberle*, Lieutenant Commander E.J. Gardner, in a feat of seamanship which drew warm praise from the convoy commodore, Rear Admiral E. Manners. On parting, the American captain and British admiral exchanged signals. Manners thanked Dayo for his efficient escort; Dayo responded: 'As in the last war I know our people will see eye-to-eye.'

In a similar way, the 60 ships of Convoy SC45 were taken over on 18 September at the Western Ocean Meeting Point by the Canadian 14th Escort Group, which handed over to the British 2nd Escort Group at the MOMP after covering the westward movement of Convoy ON18. This convoy was then taken over by Captain F.D. Kirtland's American escort group (*Madison, Gleaves, Lansdale, Hughes* and *Simpson*) to be handed over to the Western Local Escort at the WOMP on 1 October. Over the same period ONS19, the fate of whose stragglers has already been related, was covered by the British 4th Escort Group as far as the MOMP and from there by the Royal Canadian Navy. American co-operation also ensured that the best efforts would be made to fly air patrols from Iceland and from

Argentia in Newfoundland throughout the coming winter. These complex and costly arrangements were to prove initially vulnerable, but ultimately of vital importance. They were, however, only part of the battle.

Elsewhere that early September conditions tended to benefit those at sea in the Atlantic. Dönitz deployed two groups of U-boats in the North West Approaches, but poor visibility frustrated their chances of attacking several convoys, including SL84 and OG73, despite aerial location by Kondors and occasional sightings from single submarines. Minor successes included Kapitänleutnant T. Fahr's on the second anniversary of the outbreak of the war when *U-567* sank the British-flagged *Fort Richepanse*. Under the command of Captain C. Draper of Canadian Pacific Ltd., who managed the vessel on behalf of the MoWT, this former French fruit-carrier was on an independent passage from Montreal towards Liverpool with a general cargo, including eggs and mail. She also bore a dozen passengers. Thirty-five of her crew, five of the passengers and Draper were lost, the remaining 15 crew and seven passengers being rescued by the Polish destroyers *Piorun* and *Garland*.

The homeward-bound HG72 was vigorously defended by Captain de Salis's 36th Escort Group, which kept four Italian submarines at bay west of Gibraltar, while other meditated attacks in the choke-point off Bloody Foreland were broken up by poor visibility and Coastal Command attacks on *U-95* and *U-561*.

A group of U-boats deployed between the Azores and St Paul's Rocks, against which the Admiralty had sent the large submarine *Clyde*, was no more successful in fulfilling its intentions, although Kapitänleutnant W. Kleinschmidt's *U-111*, working towards the Brazilian coast on 10 September, torpedoed the Dutch motor-vessel *Marken*, owned by Ruys & Sohnen of Rotterdam. All hands survived, which was not the case with Furness, Withy's Prince Liner *Cingalese Prince*, Kleinschmidt's last victim, which he sank ten days later.[8]

Torpedoed at 04.30 on the morning of 20 September when just south of the equator and passing 25° West, the *Cingalese Prince* was on an independent passage from Bombay towards Liverpool, with stops at Cape Town, Trinidad for bunkers, and Halifax. Here, deep-laden with 11,156 tons of mixed cargo which included large quantities of manganese ore and pig-iron, she was to join an HX convoy. When the torpedo struck Chief Engineer R.H. Wilson was asleep, and he awoke to complete darkness. The ship's list prevented him finding the torch he habitually kept by his bunk. 'The inrush of water', he later reported formally, 'had caused the vessel to heel over to starboard and my table and chair had been upset.' Jumping out of bed, he was disoriented:

My room, in which I had lived for eleven years except for periodical leave, was completely strange to me and I kept stumbling over things . . . I eventually groped my way into my office . . . and managed to put my hands on a [boiler] suit . . . first putting on my lifebelt. After trying to get my legs into the sleeves of my overall, I eventually managed to get it on.

Everything seemed to be deathly quiet, there was no vibration of the ship and no lights anywhere except for a few hand torches, and I surmised that she had been hit in the engine room. I ran along the alleyway and opened the door. There was complete quietness down below, except for the noise of rushing water. Even then I did not know just where the ship had been hit but learned afterwards that both torpedoes had struck on the starboard side . . . in Nos 5 and 6 Holds. The starboard propeller shaft tunnel was . . . badly damaged and the water was reaching the engine room through the watertight door, the inrush must have been so great that no time was available to shut the door . . .

Wilson's first concern was for his men.

I . . . endeavoured to find out how many of the staff could be accounted for, the affair having occurred shortly after the change of watches . . . In the messroom I saw all three of them, the 8–12 watch were by then all turned-out and getting dressed by the light of torches in the alleyway, so that was six accounted for. I saw the Engineer Officer who was in charge of the watch at the time of the torpedoing but he was some distance away from me and apparently did not hear my query as to whether the other two on watch with him had happened to get out of the engine room. Neither could anybody else give me any information of them . . . and in addition to them I had not seen either of the two Electricians.

By this time we were all making our way to the boat deck and when I got out on deck the after deck was practically awash and it was apparent that she was not going to float very much longer, though fortunately she was keeping on an even keel, though well down by the stern. I passed along the port side of the boat deck and there saw the Chief Officer trying to get the port aft boat away. It was very dark and there was a certain amount of confusion, quite unavoidable I'm quite sure. A number of men had got into the boat before starting to lower away and just as I was passing I heard a kind of swishing sound. Looking round I saw the boat hanging in a vertical position by the forward boat falls and a lot of men must have been spilled out into the water. It appears that the aft falls had been slacked away before the belly bands had been cast adrift and when they had been cut the boat just took charge. An endeavour was made to slack off the after falls but this could not be done quickly enough . . . I . . . discovered that a similar accident had happened to the forward boat on [the starboard side] . . . The [remaining] starboard aft boat was being lowered by the 2nd Officer and there were about 20 (approx.) men in it . . . By this time the forward weather deck was not very far off being awash and it was quite clear that she was just about done for and I had to act quickly. I tried to reach one of the man ropes hanging down from the davits but could not do so . . . [Then] the ship gave a lurch and one of the ropes swung in towards me. I grabbed this and slid down into the boat which was then water-borne, and only about 10 feet below me. The after falls were adrift but there was some unrecognisable person trying to get the forward falls adrift. The patent releasing gear didn't work – perhaps there was still a certain amount of way on the ship which was keeping too much strain on the falls for it to work. There did not appear to be more than eight men, all natives, in this boat and while the man trying to get the forward falls adrift was still busy on them, I endeavoured to induce some of the natives to get the lashings off one or two of the oars, but without exception they all appeared too dazed to do a thing . . . None of us had a knife but I managed to get one of the lashings off. Then I happened to look forward and saw the man who had been busy on the boat falls disappearing over the side and a further glance . . . showed me that the ship was going down stern first and at the same time heeling over towards our boat. I distinctly saw the funnel coming down towards me and decided it was time I got out of the boat – and did so.

Almost instantly, it seemed to me, I was caught in the swirl and turmoil of the ship going down, but luckily I did not get entangled in any ropes. I have no idea how far I went under but I swallowed a lot of water and my head and chest seemed to be bursting. Then I felt the pressure easing and my head came above water. A short distance away I could see a bulky object floating and struck out towards it, found it to be a raft and clambered on. There were already a few men on it and in the course of the next minute or so, a few more came alongside and were helped aboard. A cry for help was heard not very far away and a man was seen clinging to a piece of wood. The raft drifted down towards him and he was pulled on by the Bosun and myself. It turned out to be the Second Officer, Mr Jowett, and he was in a completely exhausted condition. From the time of the impact of the first torpedo until the ship sank could not have been more than five minutes.

Cries for help could be heard all around us; there were some very strong swimmers amongst the ship's crew and I cannot imagine why more did not manage to get on to one of the rafts which were later found to be floating

in the vicinity. The last man to reach our raft was the ship's carpenter . . .
Mr Jowett, after he had recovered from his immersion and shock, told me
he had had the same trouble in getting his boat falls adrift and one was still
connected when the ship started settling and he gave orders for all the men
in his boat to jump for it.

A count of the men on our raft disclosed us to be sixteen all told,
just three members of the ship's white crew and three DEMS gunners, the
remainder being Malay seamen and Indian greasers. As daylight began to
break, a vessel of some kind was seen making its way towards us and our
hopes rose at the chance of a speedy rescue. Unfortunately, the shape soon
disclosed itself to be a submarine and he stopped close alongside us and asked
all particulars of the ship. Where from, name, nationality, where bound, description of cargo, was the Captain saved, had any of the ship's lifeboats managed
to get away, were there any Officers on the raft? To this latter question I
answered 'No'. I had taken the precaution of taking off my lifebelt before he
got too near, for it had Chief Engineer stencilled across it. I saw no point in
refusing to answer any of his questions, particularly as one man had a machine-
gun trained upon us all.

He then circled round but some little while later came close to us again,
told us there was another raft with a few survivors on, some distance away.
I asked him if there was a rescue ship in the vicinity. He answered that he
could not use his wireless but the first 'free' ship he saw he would give them
our position . . . I assumed he meant neutral. The Commander was quite
young – middle 20s I should think – and a number of his crew who were
congregated around the conning tower had some among them who could
not have been more than sixteen to seventeen years of age. The Commander
asked me if we had plenty of 'pwowisions' (provisions), also if we would like
some chocolate, cigarettes and a bottle of brandy. A tin containing the cigarettes and chocolate was then handed over, also a bottle of French Cognac;
the chocolate was also of French make. At the time these articles were being
passed across to us, at least two of his crew were taking ciné-Kodak pictures
of us on the raft. The Commander then told us to make our way towards
the West, circled around once again, submerged . . .

By this time the sun was getting up and drying out our wet clothing[;]
not one of us being anything but sketchily clad, we were pretty cold and
darned miserable . . . There were three empty rafts close around us, so we
got the paddles adrift and by means of some laborious and strenuous work,
got all three collected and tied up in a line astern of the big raft, which was
rather crowded, so some of the men were transferred to the rafts astern.

We then set about taking stock of our resources in the way of water and
food . . . enough we reckoned to last 30 days . . . We were in the Equatorial

Current and the 2nd Officer expressed the opinion that, with a bit of luck, we might eventually drift into the track of vessels bound to or from the North and South Americas and be picked up. He computed the rate of drift at about 2 miles per day and we settled down to make the best of it. The days were very hot with a burning sun, but the nights were quite chilly . . . a heavy dew fell which, no doubt, helped out our meagre water ration. Everybody was stiff and cold when daybreak came . . . Fortunately for us, the weather kept fine all the time and a gentle breeze blew steadily, in more or less the direction we wished to go.

The whole time we were on the raft, day and night, we were constantly surrounded by sharks of different species . . . The water was very phosphorescent and their movements were easily followed. Very often they would come tearing towards the raft, then just before reaching it would turn over and scrub their belly on the side, no doubt to try and get rid of the parasites which grew on them.

They caught and ate one of these sharks, the meat of which was quite white and firm,

and from the appearance of the men, they quite enjoyed it. For myself, I found it quite palatable but I only chewed the juices out of it, not swallowing the meat. By this time, the tenth day on the raft, some of the natives were showing signs of having just about had enough of it and one confessed to having been drinking salt water, in spite of the strictest warnings . . . men were told off to keep watch on him that he didn't drink any more.

Some painful cases of sunburn were also showing up now, myself among them. The left side of my face just under the eye, the back of my neck, legs and feet, were badly blistered and swollen. Count of the days was kept in the good old-fashioned manner by cutting a notch in one of the planks each day and on the evening of the eleventh day on our floating home we all settled down as usual, wondering no doubt if the following day would be the one for our rescue. I had been *quite* sure in my own mind right from the beginning, that we would be picked up. About 1 a.m. of the twelfth day, the lights of a steamer were sighted. Seeing that she was lit up argued that she was most probably a neutral vessel. But neutral or not, there was a chance of being rescued.[9]

The ship was the Spanish-registered *Castillo Montjuich*. She lowered a boat, and within half an hour Wilson and his shipmates 'were safely aboard and thankful for it'. Landed at São Vicente in the Cape Verde Islands, they were not quite the only members of the crew of the *Cingalese Prince* to be rescued – one officer was picked up by the sloop *Londonderry* and a seaman by her sister-ship *Weston* – but they were few enough. Captain J. Smith, 48 crew and eight DEMS gunners perished with the ship and her valuable cargo.

14

'The sky was alight with star-shells'

Avoceta

FURTHER ACTION ON the United Kingdom–to–Gibraltar route began on 20 September when Kapitänleutnant J. Mohr in *U-124* reported the southward-steaming Convoy OG74. Covered by the 36th Escort Group led by Lieutenant Commander White in HM Sloop *Deptford*, supported by five corvettes and the Armed Ocean Boarding Vessel *Corinthian*, OG74 was also accompanied by the newly-commissioned rescue ship *Walmer Castle*, Captain G.L. Clarke, and an escort-aircraft-carrier, HMS *Audacity*, Commander D.W. Mackendrick. Unlike the rather extemporised Merchant Aircraft Carrier, or MAC ship, the escort-carrier was a properly commissioned man-of-war with an effective complement of aircraft. HMS *Audacity* was the former German war-prize *Hanover*, which had had her superstructure razed and a wooden flight-deck fitted. From this flew six robust, American-built Grumman Wildcats, which the British renamed Martlets.

The convoy itself was composed of two dozen merchant ships, and once Mohr had reported it Kerneval ordered a second U-boat, Schnee's *U-201*, to join forces. Schnee's submarine was spotted, strafed and forced to submerge by a Martlet flying an air patrol from *Audacity*. The Martlet's report brought *Deptford* and *Arbutus* to the scene, driving Schnee off for the time being.

Mohr next made an approach during the dark hours of the evening of the 20th in deteriorating weather, torpedoing first the small British cargo ship *Baltallin*, owned by the United Baltic Corporation and loaded with government stores for Gibraltar. Mohr's second attack was against the *Empire Moat*, managed by the tramp owners Watts, Watts & Company of London on behalf of the MoWT. Flying light in ballast this 3,000-ton standard small tramp-type was a new ship, recently built by Lithgow's on the Clyde. All hands including her master Captain J.F. Travis were picked up by *Walmer Castle*, which attended them before falling back to the position of the *Baltallin*'s boats, where she rescued Captain C.W. Browne and all but seven of his crew. By now Clarke's vessel was well astern of the convoy, and in trying to catch up the *Walmer Castle* was attacked after daylight on the 21st by a Kondor from Bordeaux-Mérignac. After strafing *Walmer Castle* three times, wounding Clarke as he strove to avoid her fire, the Kondor bombed the rescue ship, setting her on fire and causing considerable loss of life among the ship's own company and the 81 survivors then on board. Clarke was finally killed along with his engine-room staff, who died amid the shambles of wrecked machinery. As she lay stopped and on fire the *Walmer Castle*'s boats were lowered as a futile attempt was made to extinguish the blaze and rescue some of the survivors from incineration.

In answer to the *Walmer Castle*'s distress signal Commander White ran *Deptford* back through the convoy, and with the corvette *Marigold* succeeded in rescuing the remaining people, before *Marigold* sank the *Walmer Castle* by gunfire. Meanwhile a second Kondor which had made its appearance was chased, attacked and shot down by a Martlet from *Audacity*. This was rather too little, too late, and neither compensation for the loss of a valuable rescue ship after a mere week in commission nor help to those for whom she had proved no safe refuge.

The bad weather during the 21st had split the convoy, and White decided to cover four Lisbon-bound merchant ships laden with full cargoes of coal which had become detached but remained not far astern. Leaving the main body of OG74 under the escort of *Audacity, Pentstemon* and the other corvettes, White was unable to provide adequate cover, even with the help of *Marigold*. Both Mohr and Schnee were already in contact and the latter rapidly torpedoed three of the four British steamers, the sister-ships *Runa* and *Lissa* and the Currie liner *Rhineland*. Loss of life from all three vessels was severe, *Deptford* picking up only Captain H. McLarty and eight men from the *Runa*.

The presence of the two escorts did however dissuade the U-boats from further attacks, and they withdrew; but by now the homeward-bound Convoy HG73 had left Gibraltar and Kerneval directed the U-boats to join three Italian submarines already lying in wait for the 25 vessels which had set out on 17 September.[1] Escorted by a scratch group led by the elderly destroyer *Vimy* supported by eight corvettes, HG73 also contained a rather superior CAM-ship, the former Bank Line *Springbank*, which had been converted into a Auxiliary Fighter Catapult Ship. She was a commissioned warship equipped with a heavy anti-aircraft armament in addition to her catapult-launched Fulmar fighter. The convoy commodore was Rear Admiral Kenelm Creighton, who joined the small 3,000-ton passenger-cargo Yeoward liner *Avoceta*. Loaded with a general cargo and mails, she had arrived at Gibraltar after evacuating from the Riviera coast British subjects who had made their way out of Occupied France. Most of them 'were foreign women who had married men of British citizenship. They had been stranded without means of livelihood in France . . . The enemy soon began to appropriate . . . [their allowances] and so forced these people to clear out and claim their rights . . . They were a mixed company . . . had no use for England, whom they blamed for the war and the position in which they now found themselves. Few could even speak English. On board *Avoceta* there were now 128 of these people including sixty small children and babies.'[2]

Passing through a fleet of Spanish trawlers which Creighton was convinced passed details of the convoy to the enemy, HG73 headed west, hoping to lose itself in the vast wastes of the Atlantic ocean. Although the convoy was only proceeding at 7 knots, Creighton soon found that he was 'saddled', as he put it, with a 'lame duck'. His signaller called up the ship in question and received no reply. Urging the errant master to increase speed, he finally asked: 'What is the matter?' The reply 'Nothing . . . but there soon will be if any more bloody silly signals are made' failed to rile Creighton as it would have done earlier in the war, for he had been an admiral in another life.

There were some brief skirmishes on the convoy's periphery; on the night of the 21st/22nd the approaching Italian submarine *Luigi Torelli* was located, depth-charged and damaged by the *Vimy*. On the 23rd the *Leonardo da Vinci* made contact and remained close to the convoy for some hours, but without penetrating the screen. Next day HG73 was flown over by a Kondor. The *Springbank* promptly opened fire and launched her Fairey Fulmar, but the Kondor escaped by flying off at wave height and the Fulmar pilot was obliged to ditch, or try for Gibraltar. He chose the latter and succeeded, leaving the convoy with nothing to counter the Kondor that appeared the next morning. U-boat warnings too now began to arrive from London, but 'For everyone in HG73 the most frustrating factor of all during this time was to see the Focke-Wulf swooping about for hours on end like a great vulture waiting for the kill.' In the escorts, meanwhile, problems were being experienced with the primitive radar sets, so that the precise location of the shadowing U-boats was uncertain.

By the night of the 24th the convoy was well out into the Atlantic, somewhere north-east of the Azores and steaming north. During the early hours of the 25th *U-124* (Mohr) attacked and sank the *Empire Stream*, a sister-ship of the *Empire Moat*. Most of her crew were saved by the corvette *Begonia*, but six men and a pair of stowaways went down with the ship and her cargo of 3,730 tons of potash. The following day was filled with tension, especially among the wretched evacuees aboard the *Avoceta*, despite the assurances of a Catholic priest who was with them that their supplications would be met by a caring Deity.

Shortly after moonset at 23.30 on 25 September, Kapitänleutnant R. Mützelberg used his slight advantage of submerged speed to bring *U-203* into the convoy from astern at periscope depth. Firing four torpedoes, he waited only to see a sheet of flame roar up the side of the Norwegian tramp *Varanberg* before diving to avoid detection. Laden with more than 4,000 tons of iron ore, the Norwegian settled quickly, taking 21 men to their deaths and leaving six to swim away from the plunging hull. But the salvo's second torpedo hit the *Avoceta*, making the ship leap in the water and settle quickly by the stern. 'The vicious scream of escaping steam smothered some of the unearthly gargling sounds coming from the drowning and the tearing squeals of those trapped in the scalding agony of the engine room.' In no time the bow had risen, and launching the boats proved impossible. 'There was complete pandemonium; the thunderous bangs and crashes of furniture and cargo being hurled about below decks all mingled with the ghastly shrieks of the sleeping people waking to their deaths. As the bows went higher, so did the shrieks . . .'

Commodore Creighton clung to a stanchion 'feeling sick and helpless as . . . the children were swept out into the darkness below by the torrent of water which roared through the smoking room.' He was dragged down: 'I felt curiously as if I was pleasantly drunk . . . This was displaced by a sharp pain in my chest caused by the pressure of water from being forced so deep. The only way to stop this agony was, it seemed to me, to expel the remaining air in my lungs, swallow water and become unconscious and drown as soon as possible. I was about to do this when the pain suddenly eased. I looked up and saw the stars . . .' Below and around him 47 crew and 76 passengers gave up the ghost.

Struggling to a raft, shocked and deafened, Creighton saw the glare from the star-shells fired by the escorts in an attempt to spot the surfaced submarines; but Mützelberg, submerged, had not finished with them yet. As the commodore, the ship's master Captain H. Martin, 21 crew, five naval staff and a dozen passengers awaited their fate, the last two of *U-203*'s torpedoes slammed into the side of the British steamship *Cortes*. Owned by Macandrews & Company of London, the ship was loaded with a general cargo which included cork and potash. She also carried six passengers; none of them, nor Captain D.R. MacRae nor his 35-man crew survived, even though a handful escaped at the time to be picked up by the General Steam Navigation Company's *Lapwing*.

Mohr now struck again, hitting first the *Lapwing*'s sister-ship *Petrel*, steaming in an adjacent column. Despite having a part-cargo of cork, she did not take long to sink, though Captain J.W. Klemp and all 30 men were picked up by his colleague Captain T.J. Hyam of the *Lapwing*. Similarly loaded with cork and some pyrites, she was Mohr's next victim as she got under way after recovering Klemp and his men from the water. Hyam and 25 of his crew died in the carnage. Eight of her crew took to the boats with the survivors from *Petrel*, and after a long passage under Klemp, who was awarded a Lloyd's War Medal for his courage and leadership, they landed at Slyne Bay in Co. Galway on 9 October.

The more fortunate were rescued by the corvettes. Creighton, five of his staff and others who had survived the sinking of the *Avoceta*, including Captain Martin, 21 crew and a dozen passengers, were picked up after three hours in the water by *Periwinkle*, Lieutenant Commander P. MacIver. One of Creighton's staff supported a female passenger for almost the entire time, while Chief Officer M. Robertson also supported a woman for several hours: both men were afterwards awarded the Royal Humane Society's bronze medal. Once aboard *Periwinkle* Creighton, unable to hear anything because of damage to his ears, told MacIver to instruct the vice commodore to take over the convoy.

During the day which followed, as the survivors gradually recovered from the shock of explosions and immersion, HG73 was overflown by Kondors busy homing-in U-boats. A further attack on the night of the 26th/27th was inevitable. Again *U-124* and *U-201* came up, Mohr torpedoing a second Macandrews ship, the *Cervantes*, loaded with potash and cork. Captain H.A. Fraser, 30 of his crew and a single Distressed British Seaman were picked up by an escort.

Later that night Schnee made contact again and fired a torpedo at the *Springbank*, so severely damaging her that once Captain C.H. Godwin and 200 survivors had been evacuated by the corvettes *Hibiscus* and *Periwinkle*, she was sunk by gunfire from *Jasmine*. Schnee continued his work of destruction, torpedoing the Norwegian cargo-ship *Siremalm* which, laden with iron ore, drowned all 27 of her company in seconds.

The German submarines and aircraft maintained contact throughout the 27th, but by now HG73 was heading up towards the South West Approaches. After its mauling it was under Admiralty orders not to circumnavigate Ireland but instead to negotiate a passage through the minefields and proceed directly to Milford Haven. As the convoy came under British air cover Coastal Command struck one retaliatory blow, bombing and damaging *U-205*, which although vectored onto HG73 had played no active role in the attacks on it. Finally, that evening, *U-201* sank the elderly British cargo ship *Margareta* (she had been built in 1904). There were no fatalities, Captain H. Pihlgrenn and his crew being taken up by *Hibiscus*. By now Schnee and Mohr had expended all their torpedoes. From Dönitz's point of view, the operations against OG74 and HG73 had been as successful as those against SC42 and SC44.

Creighton remained aboard *Periwinkle* until she reached Liverpool, where Admiral Noble held an enquiry. 'No one had been looking forward to this . . .' Creighton admitted. 'But Admiral Noble was imperturbable as ever; nothing could move or dishearten him. He did his utmost . . . by saying that the enquiry was not being held to pin blame on the commanding officers of the escorts for their failure to drive off the U-boats . . . But he wanted to discover what lessons had been learnt and what improvements could be made . . .'

Creighton held his own private vigil, mourning the loss of his 19-year-old telegraphist, a Canadian volunteer; he also ruminated upon the fate of 'the old Chief Engineer of the *Avoceta*. Forty years of his life had been spent at sea . . . It was pathetic to see the lonely life he led – small photographs of his wife and family the only decoration in his cabin . . . It was a solitary life for a married man and hard on his wife and children . . . After leaving his home port he never went ashore again until he got back. This time he had not returned. And I picture him in the hour of disaster making his way to the engine room where the sea swept him up to his last home.'

An Irishman by birth, like many citizens of Eire serving in merchant ships Creighton inveighed against the indifferent attitude of the de Valera government. 'One factor which made the Gibraltar–Liverpool route so dangerous was the neutrality of Eire . . . although they knew that any attempt by the Germans to invade their land would be met by the RAF and the Navy . . . If we had been allowed the use of the southern Irish ports many hundreds of lives would have been saved. Escorts could have gone out to reinforce convoy protection . . . and the reach of Coastal Command [could] have been extended to cover a far wider area . . . This supposedly Christian country was entirely dependent on British ships to bring the coal, oil and countless different manufactured goods to her shores.'[3]

For some time the British had been concerned about the best means by which to make good the losses of merchant bottoms. The expedient of purchasing First World War standard tonnage from the United States Reserve Merchant Fleet was not only expensive but unsatisfactory, since many of the ships so acquired were slow and in a poor state of repair, adding to rather than solving the problems of convoy management. It was besides a finite resource, and it was clear that neither this measure nor the charter market – where risk was exceeding the likelihood of profit, and compensation for losses was inadequately persuasive – could provide the tonnage

Britain needed to win the war. Both the British Ministry of War Transport and the nascent American authorities were coming to realise that *they* would have to *own* the tonnage in which the sinews of war were conveyed across the Atlantic: the term 'Merchant Navy' would thereby acquire a more than merely evocative ring.

Straitened though the British were both physically and fiscally they put in hand a new programme of ship-building in which techniques of partial pre-fabrication and unitised construction were pioneered; this would reduce costs, and also the need for specialised training for crews, who would become accustomed to a standard ship-type. This emergency programme had been initiated by the foresight of the Sunderland builders Joseph L. Thompson, which during the worst of the Depression had modernised their yard on the river Wear and in 1935 built the coal-burning *Embassage* for Hall Brothers of Newcastle-upon-Tyne. This 9,300-ton ship was followed by two dozen sisters, and it was her design that was taken up by the MoWT when they were faced with those crippling losses in the North Atlantic.

The first of the new breed of standard-ships to be built under the Ministry's aegis was the *Empire Liberty*, 7,157 gross tons, capable of carrying 10,000 tons deadweight at a speed of 11 knots from a modest power output of 2,500 indicated horse-power. She was followed by a variety of 'types', not all coal-burning, which provided replacements for tramps, small cargo-vessels and tankers. They were not built in huge numbers until after 1943, but their gradual appearance from 1941 rewards began to provide the answer to enemy attrition. Such were the *Atlantic City, Empire Moat* and *Empire Stream*, whose losses, along with that of the *Embassage* herself, have been noted.

The major problem confronting Britain was the paucity of space in her mercantile ship-building yards, which by reason of their location were incapable of expansion. The yards were also hampered by lack of investment and out-of-date working practices, but most significant was the fact that they were largely committed to producing corvettes, whose design and equipment had deliberately been chosen so that mercantile yards could churn them out. It was almost inevitable, therefore, that those in whom responsibility for repairing the damage done to Britain's worn-out merchant fleet was vested should look across the Atlantic. Canada was one place where space and opportunity existed, and Canadian yards began turning out British-designed standard-ships. Just as British-built vessels of this type had names prefixed by 'Empire', the Canadian-built and -manned vessels were named after parks, while those built in Canada for the MoWT were called after forts. Yet Canada was unable to fund or to build enough ships, and it was to the United States that Britain was compelled to turn in her hour of extreme need.

Initially the United States' merchant fleet was in as deplorable a condition as Britain's. Moves to rebuild it after years of depression had begun with the Merchant Marine Act of 1936 and the consequent formation of the United States Maritime Commission. It was clear long before the Japanese attack on Pearl Harbour that even a European war would affect the patterns of global trade and impact restrictively upon America, so that the United States would require a better merchant fleet than it had at the time.[4] Significantly, in addition to expressing a desire to have 'a new, modern and efficient merchant marine', the 1936 Act stated explicitly that 'such [a] fleet should be capable of serving as naval or military auxiliary in time of war or national emergency'.

In 1936 there had only been ten shipyards and 46 slipways capable of building a hull of 400 feet, the standard ocean-going length for a vessel capable of lifting 10,000 deadweight tons. The American solution as envisaged at that time was to plan over a decade for an annual production rate of 50 vessels divided between three classes of freighter and a high-speed oil-tanker type. The concept of 'standardisation for individualists' – that is, individual ship-owners – was a bold one, but entirely in tune with the American way, and provided for a modicum of tailoring to ensure fitness-for-purpose. Events in Europe accelerated the original programme, so that in the summer of 1939 the schedule was doubled, then doubled again in August 1940. By this time the value of the turbine-powered 'C'-Type freighters produced by the Commission's 19 contracted shipyards had been proven: one had crossed the Atlantic at no less than 17 knots, while in November 1940 the first of the Commission's all-welded hulls had been built, showing a saving of over 500 tons in weight and materials.

Despite these measures replacement was slow, and the bulk of the United States merchant fleet, both privately- and government-owned (in the form of the reserve fleet), remained more than 20 years old. Britain was now beginning to make new demands on the Americans, and in September 1940 a British Shipping Mission arrived in the United States. It was led by Cyril Thompson, a member of the family of Sunderland shipbuilders, and he took with him the plans of the SS *Dorington Court*, a derivative of the *Embassage* and sister of the *Empire Liberty*, built for Haldin & Philipps's Court Line in 1939.

The chief of the United States Maritime Commission, Admiral Land, was not impressed by the 'simple and slow' design, but thought the British should be permitted to commission the 60 ships they wanted from American yards – until it was discovered that there was not enough capacity in the traditional yards, and that if the British wanted their ships they would have to be of the new all-welded construction and built in newly established yards.[5]

In the event, two 30-ship contracts were awarded to the Todd Shipyards Inc. and Henry Kaiser's yards, with additional equipment provided by a combination of engineering companies known as Six Services Inc. By January 1941 Land and his Commission were reassessing their own plans in the light of their failure to deliver sufficient ships, and it had become obvious that the British programme focused on numbers rather than the American programme focused on quality was the only solution in the short term. For a while argument vacillated between the revival of a First World War American design and Thompson's concept: in the end, time and American pragmatism decided in favour of the latter. It was at least proven, and lent itself readily to all-welded construction. The Americans put their collective shoulder to the wheel, and the first of the 'Oceans', *Ocean Vanguard*, American-built for British manning, was named by Land's wife on 15 October 1941.

The policy for the building of American and British tonnage was announced in February, and Roosevelt's description of the new ships as 'dreadful-looking objects' caught the headlines. They were also referred to as 'ugly ducklings', and one American newspaper proclaimed that 'sea scows with blunt bows will carry the tools to Britain'. Sensitive to the poor propaganda value of this dismal image, Land rechristened them the 'Liberty fleet' and declared 27 September 1941 as 'Liberty Fleet Day'. There was a multi-layered subtlety at work here, for in addition to the obvious contemporary significance of what history now knows as 'Liberty ships', the first one, launched that day, was named after the rebellious Virginia lawyer who in 1775 had cried 'Give me liberty, or give me death' – a gentle guying of the British. On the day following the *Patrick Henry*'s launch at the Bethlehem Fairfield Yard in Baltimore the second Liberty ship, *Star of Oregon*, was launched on the Pacific coast: the two ships were delivered to the Maritime Commission on 30 and 31 December 1941, respectively, though neither sailed on her maiden voyage for some weeks.

Construction time was quickly whittled down thanks to the innovative methods pioneered in particular by Cyril Thompson (who went on to help extend production in Canada) and Henry Kaiser, an engineer who specialised in prefabrication and mass production. The average assembly time of the components, which were manufactured all over the United States, was 42 days, but the fastest building time achieved was that of the *Robert G. Peary*, launched from the No. 2 Yard of the Permanente Metals Corporation on 12 November 1942, just four days and fifteen and a half hours after the keel had been laid. The vessel was fitted out and ready to proceed to sea under her steam reciprocating machinery just three days later.

By September 1942, the time of the crisis in the war at sea, American shipyards were capable of producing three Liberty ships per day. It is perhaps worth noting here that although 11 million tons of merchant shipping were produced during 1942, 8 million of them in the United States, Axis forces were destroying more, almost 12 million tons. The Allied output proved sustainable, however, an achievement that owed much to the sheer size of America, where huge yards with many slipways could be laid out on virgin sites. Kaiser's particular genius, which had taken him from a small photographic shop in New York to the construction of the Hoover, Bonneville and Grand Coulee dams, lay in his ability to site his various works and yards in apparently unfavourable places. Ignorant of the technicalities of ship-building tradition, Kaiser brought practicality and common sense to the resolution of problems and delighted in eschewing nautical terms in favour of the every-day and familiar. It was as well, for many of the people who did the work of prefabricating some of the 30,000 parts of these ships across 32 states had never even seen the sea. Initiative was another characteristic that marked Kaiser's approach: when doubts were expressed as to the availability of supplies of iron ore for steel production, he ordered local prospecting, whereupon ore was discovered in the State of Utah.

While the Americans named their freighters, like their destroyers, after prominent heroes (the *Star of Oregon* was an exception), those Liberty ships completed to Britain's account were prefixed 'Sam', not a reference to Uncle Sam but an acronym for a 'single accommodation block amidships', unlike the British-designed 'Parks' and 'Forts' which used a split superstructure. Other modifications reduced the numbers of curved plates involved in the construction, so that in the Liberty ship in its purest form only two plates, one either side of the forefoot, required the complex process of heating and power-pressing.[6]

After the amendment of the American Neutrality Law on 13 November 1941 all American war-built emergency standard shipping was also fitted with a proper armament. The work could not be carried out immediately, but all pretence that merchantmen were anything other than auxiliaries in the war had by now been abandoned, and the principle was embraced universally. In addition to their 4-inch anti-submarine stern gun, most carried a 12-pounder anti-aircraft gun, supplemented by Bofors, Oerlikon, Hotchkiss or Marlin high-angle mountings. Tankers and the later, faster turbine classes of freighters were to follow in due course, but these first ships 'built by the mile and sawn off by the yard' had a dramatic impact on Allied fortunes at sea. Although the programmes did not run without hitches and shortages, in the main they were highly efficient. The watch-words were speed, standardisation, and interchangeability. When Canadian hulls were short of engines, for example, engine parts constructed ahead of schedule for American vessels were sent north from the United States, and later some American-built Liberties incorporated Canadian-made components.

In February 1942, with the United States fully embroiled in the war, the American Maritime Commission disappeared to be replaced by the War Shipping Administration, operating on similar lines to the British Ministry of War Transport. Like their British allies, American ship-owners became agents of the United States government.

As the war progressed the emergency merchant ship-building programme continued in British yards, but by mutual agreement Britain concentrated on warships, leaving the bulk of mercantile construction to the apparently infinite capabilities of the Americans.

The *Patrick Henry*, the *Star of Oregon* and the *Empire Liberty* were small enough compensation. In the central Atlantic Narrows, to the north-east of Rear Admiral Ingram's patrolling cruisers of Task Force Three, Dönitz's U-boats, led by his son-in-law Korvettenkapitän G. Hessler in *U-107*, attacked Convoy SL87 as it headed north during late September 1941 on its way from Freetown to Liverpool. A small convoy of 13 ships escorted by the 40th Escort Group, SL87 was west of the Canaries when the *Silverbelle* was hit by torpedoes from *U-68*, Korvettenkapitän K-F. Merten, on the evening of the 21st. Hessler's first attack was frustrated by malfunctioning torpedoes and then aborted as *U-107* suffered an engine failure. The following night the steamer *Niceto de Larrinaga* and the motor-vessel *Edward Blyden* were both torpedoed by Kapitänleutnant W. Winter of *U-103*. Survivors were picked up by Lieutenant Commander W.J. Moore, now in command of HM Sloop *Bideford*. During daylight on the 23rd Kapitänleutnant G. Müller-Stockheim attacked in *U-67* and torpedoed the *St Claire II*. This vessel capsized quickly, dragging all her lifeboats down and preoccupying the escorts in assisting her while the U-boats withdrew. Finally, on the morning of the 24th Hessler, his engine repaired and now on his mettle, sank the *John Holt*, the *Lafian* and the *Dixcove* in a spectacular hat-trick that delighted his distant father-in-law.

Most of the lost vessels had been loaded with such West African produce as palm oil, copper and cocoa beans, though the *Niceto de Larrinaga* carried 2,000 tons of manganese ore and the *Silverbelle* 6,000 tons of phosphates. Loss of life was not heavy, though 13 of the *St Clair II*'s people were killed. The attrition rate of seven ships out of a convoy of eleven was high, however, especially given the strength and experience of the escort: the three British sloops *Bideford, Lulworth* and *Gorleston* (the latter two were ex-American Coastguard 'Cutters'), two Free French vessels, the sloop *Commandant Duboc*, and the corvette *Gardenia*. For some reason none of these had refuelled at Freetown, and the *Commandant Duboc* had to return there with the *Silverbelle*'s survivors. Nor were the escorts in a particularly high state of efficiency. According to Moore, all the commanding officers were exhausted from lack of sleep and the *Gardenia* 'was not much good', while during the operation 'nobody had so much as sighted a U-boat'.

When they arrived at Londonderry a preliminary investigation was held aboard the sloop *Egret* and its findings precipitated a formal Board of Enquiry, held on 17/18 October under the presidency of Captain Howson, an officer on Noble's staff at Derby House. Presented with Howson's findings, the Commander-in-Chief was uncharacteristically furious; no counter-attack had been organised by the Senior Officer in command of *Gorleston*, and he had diverted his own ship and *Gardenia* to concentrate on a futile attempt to save the *Silverbelle*. Noble removed the wretched man from command of an escort group, and circulated a report of his misdemeanours to all forces under Western Approaches Command as a warning.

After their actions against SL87, *U-67* and *U-68* moved towards a rendezvous with *U-111*, a plan complicated by one of *U-67*'s crew suffering the agonies of gonorrhoea and requiring proper medical attention. The outcome of the rendezvous was touched upon in chapter 14, and culminated when the British submarine *Clyde* made her attack on the U-boats in Tarafal Bay in the Cape Verdes. Of the others, in defiance of Hitler's orders *U-66* under Korvettenkapitän R. Zapp sank the Panamanian-flagged but American-owned tanker *I.C. White* to the east of Recife on 26 September, and Kapitänleutnant E. Bauer's *U-126* sank the American freighter *Lehigh* west of Freetown a month later. Bauer had also sunk the British tramp *Nailsea Manor* off the Cape Verdes on 10 October on his way south, and on the 20th, the day after he despatched the *Lehigh*, he torpedoed the tanker *British Mariner*. She had just left Freetown to collect a cargo of Venezuelan boiler oil for the local escort force. The three men on duty in the engine room were killed outright, but rescue was at hand in the form of the Dutch tug *Donau* and HM Salvage Tug *Hudson*, the latter of which picked up Captain Beattie's crew. The *British Mariner* was towed into Freetown where, although considered a constructive total loss and thus unfit for sea-service, she was used as an oil-storage hulk.

Bauer continued to operate off the West African coast. On 13 November he sank the 'British' cargo ship *Peru* on her way to join a convoy from Calcutta with a mixed cargo of general, pig-iron and groundnuts. Captain C.V. Frederiksen of the Danish East Asia Company was, like his ship, an exile; he and his crew were rescued from their boats by the South African tanker *Uniwaleco*, a converted whale-factory ship, and later landed at Freetown. Bauer then moved south, operating with another Type IXC U-boat, Merten's *U-68*. On 22 October Merten approached St Helena and sank the British naval oiler *Darkdale*, then went on to sink the tramp *Hazelside* nine hundred miles west of Walvis Bay on the 28th before moving closer and torpedoing the *Bradford City* on 1 November. The last was the second ship of that name and was on her way to the Middle East with a military cargo.

Both Merten and Bauer now became involved in the British interceptions of the German raider *Atlantis* and the supply ship *Python*, alluded to earlier. Mertens refuelled *U-68* from Rogge's *Atlantis* off St Helena on 13 November, the same day that Bauer sank the *Peru*. It was Bauer's turn to rendezvous with Rogge early on the 22nd and as *U-126* and the raider lay hull to hull, connected by the oil-fuel hose, the water-pipe and a chain of men bantering as they passed dry stores down into the U-boat, Bauer went aboard the *Atlantis* to breakfast with Rogge. Suddenly the superstructure of a British cruiser made its appearance and a spotting aircraft was seen approaching. The *U-126*'s first watch officer promptly cast off all lines and hoses and dived, hoping that in approaching to determine the raider's identity, the British cruiser would offer herself as a suitable target. But Captain R.D. Oliver of HMS *Devonshire*, not satisfied with the answer given his interrogating signal, opened fire from a range of ten miles.

The *Atlantis* was doomed, and quickly reduced to a foundering state. Rogge, his crew, and his hapless guest Bauer took to the raider's boats while Oliver, aware of U-boats operating in the vicinity, steamed away. *U-126* came back to the surface and Bauer rejoined her, along with 55 men from the *Atlantis*, including some wounded; 52 men kitted out in life-jackets made themselves comfortable on the U-boat's casing, while the remaining 201 were towed astern in four lifeboats. Rotating those in the boats, Bauer made his way to a rendezvous with the *Python*, which they reached during the night of the 23rd/24th, whereupon Rogge and his men clambered aboard the supply ship and Bauer headed for L'Orient, arriving there on 13 December.

The *Python* now steamed to a new rendezvous 800 miles south of St Helena where she was due to meet *U-68* and *U-A* on the night of 30 November/1 December. The two U-boats began refuelling at daylight, whereupon another British cruiser again interrupted the proceedings. HMS *Dorsetshire*, Captain A.W.S. Agar, VC, rapidly sank the supply ship and departed. The *Python* was swiftly abandoned and her company plus that of the *Atlantis*, 414 in all, were taken aboard the two submarines or towed astern in boats or on rafts. Following radio contact with Kerneval they met

U-124 and Clausen's *U-129* on the 5th. Both U-boats had come south as escorts to the *Python*, and on the way Mohr's *U-124* had sunk the British cruiser *Dunedin* off St Paul's Rocks and the American freighter *Sagadhoc* off St Helena. Kapitänleutnant N. Clausen had been less successful, and *Python*'s predicament now curtailed his third war patrol; oddly enough, the circumstances almost exactly replicated those of his second patrol, when as escort to the supply ship *Kota Pinang* he had been obliged to rescue *her* survivors after she was shelled by HMS *Kenya* west of Cape Finisterre on 3 October.

Having redistributed the men in *Python*'s lifeboats, the four submarines continued north until 16 December, when they rendezvoused with the Italian submarines *Luigi Torelli, Enrico Tazzoli, Giuseppe Finzi* and *Calvi*. When the survivors had been divided between the eight submarines all made for France, the rescued having travelled more than five thousand miles.

From the Allied perspective, the battle for the North Atlantic went well during the first part of October. The complex British, American and Canadian escort arrangements dovetailed with a nicety that must have gratified the planners. The 44 eastbound merchantmen of HX151, followed by the 61 of SC46 (which lost three ships to collision or wrecking), swapped their escorts with those of the westbound ON20, followed by ONS21, Hamm's sinking of the *Erna III* being the only loss to mar the lull after the attacks on SC44. The British 6th took over SC47 from a Canadian Escort Group, passing on their own charges, Convoy ON22, to an American force. In the same way Convoys HX152 and ONS 21, ONS 22 and ONS23 passed near the MOMP, the east-bound Halifax convoy almost losing a straggler, the former Norwegian whale-factory ship *Svend Foyn* of 14,795 tons. She fell foul of Kapitänleutnant J. von Rosenstiel in *U-502* and was damaged as a consequence, though she afterwards made Iceland. From there, 79 black British Honduran timber-workers, being taken as labourers to Britain, continued their interrupted passage in the rescue ship *Zaafaran*.

Not that this lack of enemy action reduced the apprehension of danger. It was ever-present, particularly aboard the merchant ships, which received no reassurances and were not informed of signals indicating the likelihood or otherwise of the presence of enemy submarines, as received aboard the busy escorts. The constant and debilitating demands of the apparently simple but grindingly wearing job of keeping station were bad enough, but the task had its own inherent dangers. An encounter with an unlit vessel on a reciprocal course could end in near-tragedy. Typical was the experience of the Ellerman & Papayanni cargo-liner *Castilian* which was leading the extreme port column of a convoy on a night of 'pitch darkness and poor visibility'. At 22.00 'the Master had come up to the chartroom to write up his night orders', and Third Officer Cooper 'could see a shadow in the darkness'. His report continued in staccato style:

> I asked the lookout if he could see anything. He could not, but I was sure and it appeared to be getting bigger. Shouted to the Master asking if I could switch on the navigation lights as I feared we were on a collision course. The answer was yes, so I switched on. The shadow did likewise . . . Yelled to the helmsman 'Hard a-starboard', blew a blast on the whistle [indicating an alteration of course to starboard, thereby] causing pandemonium in the convoy. Nearly had a heart attack when the approaching ship swung to port [it being the convention under international regulation that vessels approaching end-on should give way to starboard]. Our bows touched and with an almighty crash we were alongside of each other . . . She was a tanker, light ship . . . [and] we were low in the water. Had to look up to the bridge to exchange names and companies. The Master told me to sound round. Found we were not making water [although] there were a lot of rivet heads on our foredeck from the *Athelprince* [and] they looked new. Found out when we got home she had [just] been repaired after being struck with two torpedoes.[7]

October 1941 saw a concentration of effort by Dönitz with a mixed force of German and Italian submarines operating west of Gibraltar against convoys running between Liverpool and The Rock. Having sunk the Free French corvette *Fleur de Lys* from the escort of OG75, Kapitänleutnant H. Opitz in *U-206* was one of these; he reached the rendezvous early and sank the British tramp *Baron Kelvin* off Tarifa Point on 17 October while lying in ambush for HG75. Twenty-six men were killed, but her master Captain W.L. Ewing and a dozen of his men reached Gibraltar. Opitz was not the only U-boat early on the rendezvous. After secretly refuelling from the *Thalia* lying in Cadiz, Kell's *U-204* attacked a target on the opposite side of the strait off Cape Spartel on the 19th. She was the motor-tanker *Inverlee*, Captain T.E. Alexander, almost at the end of her independent passage from Trinidad with 13,880 tons of fuel oil for the naval vessels at Gibraltar. Alexander and 21 of his men died, a further 21 being rescued by naval vessels which rushed to the scene. As the destroyer *Duncan* picked up these men assisted by HM Trawlers *Haarlem* and *Lady Hogarth*, the corvette *Mallow*, Lieutenant W.R.B. Noall, and the sloop *Rochester*, Commander C.B. Allen, hunted *U-204* and destroyed her with depth-charges.

Despite these alarums, Convoy HG75 sailed as planned. Made up of 17 merchant ships, it was escorted by the 37th Escort Group consisting of the sloop *Rochester*, the corvettes *Campion*, *Carnation*, *Heliotrope* and *La Malouine* and the Free French *Commandant Duboc*, to which local support was added by a formidable group of destroyers led by *Cossack* and consisting of *Lamerton, Legion, Duncan* and *Vidette*. The enemy were in almost immediate contact: Kapitänleutnant W. Flachsenberg in *U-71* brought up *U-206* and *U-564* (Suhren), but none were able to penetrate the strong escort. On the night of 23/24 October, when the convoy was standing out into the Atlantic miles to the south-west of Cape St Vincent, these three U-boats were joined by *U-563*. Commanded by Oberleutnant K. Bargsten, before midnight she torpedoed and damaged the *Cossack*, Captain E.L. Berthon, and in the hours that followed the *Alhama*, a small ship laden with Spanish produce – tartaric acid, cork, onions, wine and general – from Seville and Valencia. Captain A. Cameron and his crew were rescued by the *Commandant Duboc* and later transferred to British destroyers. An effort to tow *Cossack* back to Gibraltar was sustained for three days before the destroyer foundered.

Meanwhile Suhren had joined Bargsten and torpedoed and sank two ships, the *Carsbreck* and the *Ariosto*. The former was carrying iron ore loaded in Almeria and sank quickly, taking Captain J.D. Muir and 23 of his crew to their deaths, the remainder being rescued by the escorts. The *Ariosto*, owned by Ellerman's Wilson Line, was the commodore's ship. She had loaded a cargo of general, ore and cork in Lisbon before arriving at Gibraltar and embarking Commodore F.L.J. Butler and his staff. Captain H. Hill, the commodore and 40 crew, naval staff and passengers were rescued, but six men were lost.

For a few hours the Germans lost contact with HG75, until first a Kondor and then *U-71* regained it. The Italian submarine *Ferraris* was bombed and damaged by a Catalina from Gibraltar, then finally sunk after a gun-duel with the destroyer *Lamerton*. During the succeeding hours the *Guglielmo Marconi* succumbed to some unknown fate, but by the night of the 25th/26th two more U-boats, *U-83* and *U-563*, had found HG75. The former torpedoed the auxiliary fighter catapult ship *Ariguani*, which by now bore some of the *Carsbreck's* survivors; she was at first abandoned but afterwards reboarded and towed back to Gibraltar.

Attacks by *U-563* and *U-564* during the following night failed, but by the 28th, with the convoy to the east and north of the Azores, Schultze had caught up. In a final flourish he attacked in *U-432*, sinking the steamship *Ulea*. Under the command of Captain F.O. Ambrose, she bore three passengers and a cargo of 2,400 tons of copper pyrites; Ambrose, his passengers and 15 of his crew drowned, but the remaining five were scooped out of the water by two corvettes. Having exhausted their torpedoes the three U-boats still in contact broke off the action and headed for their French bases, leaving the convoy to continue its passage in relative peace.

In the first fortnight of November Dönitz formed a new group to operate off Spain against HG76. Kerneval expected it to depart from Gibraltar about the 1st but nothing was seen of it by the searching Kondors from Bordeaux-Mérignac flying low over the sea off the Iberian peninsula. They were ordered to switch their focus to the northbound Convoy SL91 which the B-Dienst service had located at sea, but this too eluded its hunters. Meanwhile Lüth's long-range *U-43* was also ordered towards Gibraltar, and on passage sighted Convoy OS12 off the Azores on 28 November. Lüth attacked in the early hours of the following morning, torpedoing the Bank Line tramp *Thornliebank*, which was on Government charter, bound for the Middle East and loaded with a large quantity of explosives. The detonation that resulted caused slight damage to *U-43* but instantly killed Captain S. Letton and his crew of 74 men. Lüth withdrew and two days later, when he came in sight of a straggler from the same convoy, he sank her. She was the Ropner tramp *Ashby*, sailing in ballast. Captain T.V. Frank and 16 men were killed, but 33 made it in their boats to Fayal. Still off the Azores, on 2 December Lüth fired at a tanker; she proved to be an American, the *Astral*, owned by the Socony-Vacuum Oil Company Incorporated of New York. Loaded with 11,950 tons of gasoline, she went up in a sheet of flame, incinerating all 37 souls on board. Lüth and *U-43* eventually arrived in the Gibraltar area too late to take part in the attack on HG76.

The final quarter of 1941 was characterised by bad weather in the North Atlantic. While this made difficulties for the ships in convoy, it also tended to make visual location by U-boats almost impossible. Contact was often intermittent, therefore, and even the plodding progress of a convoy occasionally outran a labouring U-boat. Convoy OG75, for instance, though constantly located by Kondors and shadowed by a large group of submarines, made Gibraltar with the loss of only one ship, the corvette *Fleur de Lys*, torpedoed in the very approaches to Gibraltar by Opitz in *U-206*, as already noted. Out in the Atlantic, however, a convoy battle began involving the 50-strong SC48 and the troop convoy TC14, then making their way across the Western Ocean along with HX153.

The first merchantman to be attacked was the *Vancouver Island*, Captain R.C. Stonehouse, one of several vessels which had dropped astern of SC48 in the appalling weather; she was sunk with all hands and 36 passengers by *U-558* on 15 October, with her valuable cargo comprising 3,132 tons of general, 751 tons of aluminium, 993 tons of copper, 450 tons of zinc, a quantity of steel, and 357 tons of asbestos. The same day, at the southern extremity of Dönitz's patrol line, Korvettenkapitän K. Thurmann saw SC48's smoke from the conning tower of *U-553* and made a swift approach after transmitting a sighting report. Shortly afterwards the British motor-vessel *Silvercedar* and the small Norwegian steamer *Ila* were sent to the bottom by Thurmann with considerable loss of life. He was driven off by a destroyer, though not before he had attempted to torpedo her, and dropped astern to shadow. Meanwhile four U-boats were trying to catch up with the convoy, and a further four were moving ahead of it. One of these was *U-568*, and in the small hours of the 16th Kapitänleutnant J. Preuss struck the *Empire Heron*, Captain J.D. Ross. Loaded with sulphur, she foundered with all hands, leaving HMS *Gladiolus*, arriving to search in vain for survivors, to drive off Preuss.

Concerned about the concentration of U-boats mustering against SC48, the Admiralty assessed the situation in the light of Ultra decrypts. While several escort forces *could* be brought to the assistance of SC48, timing was the critical factor. The decision was therefore made to disperse westbound Convoy ON24 and transfer its escort groups to reinforce the Canadian corvettes *Westaskiwin*, Lieutenant Commander G. Windeyer, and *Baddeck* and the British *Gladiolus* and Free French *Mimosa*, then covering SC48. The escort transferred from Convoy ON24 consisted of an American destroyer group under Captain L.H. Thebaud which had just relieved the British 3rd Escort Group. Baker-Creswell's 3rd – *Bulldog, Amazon, Richmond, Georgetown, Belmont, Heartsease, Angle, St Apollo* and *Warwick* – was, with the rescue ship *Zaafaran*, ordered to refuel at Reykjavik and join SC48 with all despatch, while the corvettes *Veronica* and the Free French *Lobelia* were summoned from the screen of ONS25. Three destroyers, *Highlander, Broadwater* and *Sherwood*, on their way to relieve the Canadian escort to the troop convoy T14, were also ordered to the scene, while the Canadian corvette *Pictou*, which had fallen astern of ONS21, was diverted to the now closer SC48.

While these arrangements were under way Thebaud left ON24 and proceeded directly to SC48 with the destroyers *Plunkett, Livermore, Greer, Decatur* and *Kearny*, joining the handful of beleaguered corvettes at noon on the 16th. Thebaud was now in nominal command of a multinational force of American, British, Canadian and French warships in which the British and Free French corvettes, though the most junior, were the most experienced. The night which followed was dark and windy. American destroyers, unblooded, unequipped with radar and ill-prepared, were no better than Old World corvettes at discovering the U-boats that lurked beyond the convoy perimeter. Undetected on sonar or radar or by eye, Thurmann's *U-553*, Krech in *U-558* and Schultze's *U-432* took up attacking positions outside the screen. At 22.00 Thurmann torpedoed the Panamanian steamer *Bold Venture*, causing the deaths of 17 men. The escorts, hitherto steaming in rigid formation, now broke station to fire star-shell and drop depth charges indiscriminately. In a night of utter confusion the merchant ships did their utmost to preserve the convoy formation as the escort thrashed about.

At 23.15 *U-558* hit two tankers stationed in the centre of the nine columns, the British *W.C. Teagle* loaded with 15,000 tons of fuel oil and the Norwegian *Erviken* carrying 10,800 tons of heavy oil. Twenty-six Norwegians were killed outright: a dozen were picked up by the escorts in the coming hours. Captain H.R. Barlow and 39 men perished in the freezing water as the *W.C. Teagle* burned and slowly foundered.

Krech renewed his attacks at about 02.00 on the 17th, sinking the small Norwegian steamship *Rym*, while Schultze's *U-432* struck at the Greek tramp *Evros*, killing all but two of the 32 on board, and then at the Norwegian motor-tanker *Barfonn*, killing 14 and leaving 26 to swim for their lives until they were picked up. A burning tanker threw the USS *Kearny* into sharp relief just as Lieutenant Commander Danis brought her up short when a corvette dashed across her bow in pursuit of a U-boat – or a chimera. Thurmann caught sight of her, took her for a British 'Tribal'-class destroyer and fired a salvo of torpedoes from *U-558* into her starboard side, damaging her badly. Finally, as the U-boats withdrew, Krech appears to have fired at a corvette which had dropped astern to pick up survivors. Neither the precise fate of *Gladiolus* nor the author of her sinking is clear, but she disappeared in the confusion.

Dawn was now approaching, and the first of the reinforcements were arriving. These were the destroyers *Highlander*, Commander Voucher, *Sherwood* and *Broadwater*. The last was assigned to join the search for survivors and soon located and recovered ten men from the *W.C. Teagle*, while Radio Officer N.D. Houston was picked up by the *Veronica*. Voucher now relieved Thebaud, who proceeded with three of his destroyers to Hvalfjord to refuel. Escorted by the *Greer*, the wounded *Kearny* limped along under her own power with 11 men dead and two dozen wounded, a potent and rousing symbol of America's plight in her 'actions short of war' operations. During that forenoon a Catalina flew in a consignment of plasma supplied by the cruiser *Wichita* then at Hvalfjord and dropped it by parachute close to the *Kearny*. The Catalina was part of an air patrol which successfully forced the half-dozen U-boats still trailing SC48 to submerge.

They were not deterred, however, and the following night four – *U-73*, *U-77*, *U-101* and *U-751* – attempted to attack. Only one succeeded: Mengersen's *U-101* torpedoed the former American four-stack destroyer HMS *Broadwater*. There was heavy loss of life, including the survivors from the *W.C. Teagle*; Houston, picked up by *Veronica*, was therefore the sole member of her crew left alive. It was a dismal conclusion to a bungled operation. Much had been lost: in addition to the oil in the tankers, copper, steel and cotton had gone to the abyss in the *Bold Venture*, 7,673 tons of sulphur in the *Empire Heron*, 9,300 tons of rock phosphate in the *Erviken*, 7,000 tons of iron ore in the *Evros*, timber in the *Rym*, steel and general in the *Silvercedar*. And while the escorts had done their best, the *Zaafaran* failed to arrive to help drag survivors from the water. Worse, however, was one of the 'fundamental lessons' learned in this action; the United States Navy's official historian put it thus: 'Indiscriminate depth-charging was countermanded, as more embarrassing to floating survivors than to the enemy.' The euphemism was, and remains, unfortunate.

The fact was that SC48 lost almost one ship in five to a handful of U-boats which without much effort had penetrated the convoy's defences. It was a statistic sobering enough to attract the attention of those in the Admiralty Trade Division, the Submarine Tracking Room, and Derby House.

Hitler now caused the U-boats to be diverted to other tasks, and there was a lull in German operations against convoys. A sortie by the *Admiral Scheer* was aborted, but not before U-boats had been deployed in anticipation. They were also sent to the Mediterranean against an anticipated British invasion of Algeria, and a number were assigned to escort blockade-runners, mercantile commerce-raiders, or prizes in or out of the danger areas west of France. Dönitz, lamenting, flew to Berlin to remonstrate that all these diversions were 'most injurious to our cause'. When it was dispersed, part of the force intended to cover the *Admiral Scheer's* Arctic sortie was directed to mount an attack on Allied shipping by a deep penetration of the waters off Newfoundland, but this too was cancelled when Dönitz was once again compelled to divert most of his submarines to the Mediterranean.

Nevertheless, there were U-boats working as far west as the Belle Isle Strait between Newfoundland and Labrador, where their intercepted radio transmissions facilitated the diversion of convoys. The only German dividends were two sinkings, that of the British cargo-liner *King Malcolm* off Cape St Francis on the morning of 31 October by Oberleutnant U. von Fischel's *U-374*, and of the steam tramp *Larpool*, sunk by Oberleutnant A. Schlieper in *U-208* east of Cape Race in the small hours of 2 November. Captain J. Wilson and all 37 men of the *King Malcolm* were lost with their full cargo of potash, while Captain C. Patten and five of his men from the *Larpool* got ashore in a boat at Burin, Newfoundland; 11 were rescued by the Canadian corvette *Bittersweet*, and 22 perished.

Meanwhile the HX and SC convoys ploughed doggedly through the foul autumnal weather, almost undisturbed by enemy action. Although Dönitz mustered several groups against them, effective contact was not made. Only Topp, in U-552, succeeded; but the manner in which he made a direct attack on Convoy HX156 at daybreak on the morning of 31 October was highly prejudicial to the interests of his masters in Berlin.

At the time the 43 merchantmen, steaming at 9 knots, were defended by five American destroyers under Commander R.E. Webb. One, nearest to Topp on the port flank of the convoy, picked up a radio transmission, presumably Topp's contact report to Kerneval. With her helm hardly put over to turn onto the bearing to investigate, the destroyer's progress was arrested as a torpedo slammed into her port side. The explosion must have counter-mined her forward magazine, for the forward part of the ship disintegrated. The after section remained afloat for approximately five minutes, then it sank. As it did so, the increasing water pressure activated the hydrostatic firing mechanisms of her armed depth-charges, and survivors swimming for their lives were killed. Only 45 of her 160 company were picked up; not one officer survived. Topp had sunk the USS *Reuben James*.

The sinking of this American destroyer was an important event, playing into the hands of both Roosevelt and Churchill, eroding the confidence of Nazi sympathisers in the United States, and inclining public opinion to swing increasingly behind the President. For Admiral Bristol, the loss of one of his ships was seen as inevitable, a mere matter of time after the damage to the *Kearny*. For Dönitz, exculpating Topp, it was a matter of logic: 'If Germany were not to abandon altogether her Atlantic operations . . . and if the United States persisted in its active intervention . . . contrary to international law, such incidents as the torpedoing of the *Kearney* [*sic*] and the *Reuben James*, were bound to recur repeatedly.' In his memoirs Dönitz went on to quote Bristol's chief, Fleet Admiral King: 'Whatever might be thought from the point of view of international law the US Navy had adopted a realistic attitude towards events in the Atlantic.'[8]

Topp and Endrass in U-567 maintained contact with HX156 and made several unsuccessful attempts to attack. On the same day U-96, trying to join them, encountered instead the outbound OS10 and sank the Dutch freighter *Bennekom* with the loss of eight lives. Much U-boat energy was expended during this almost fruitless phase. Kentrat's U-74 was on her way home after her sixth war patrol; despite an attack on ON28 some five hundred miles west of Ireland she had sunk nothing, and on 1 November Kentrat, low on fuel after a patrol of more than 1,600 miles, headed for St-Nazaire. That same day the newly built Federal liner *Nottingham* sailed from Glasgow on her maiden voyage. She had been built by Alexander Stephen & Sons at Linthouse on the Clyde, and was to proceed independently to the St

Lawrence under the command of Captain F.C. Pretty. He had won a Distinguished Service Cross in the First World War when serving as a lieutenant in the Royal Naval Reserve, and in September 1940 he had managed to fight his bombed ship, the *Cornwall*, from Alexandria to Malta, for which he had been appointed OBE. His new ship's company consisted of 61 officers and ratings, including five naval gunners. She also bore a passenger, Captain A.G. Cooper of the Port Line, who was travelling to take up a position in the British Ministry of War Transport in Montreal.

On the evening of 7 November the *Nottingham* transmitted a distress message indicating that she was under attack from a submarine; her reported position was some 550 miles to the south-east of Cape Farewell. It was the last anyone heard of her: she had met her nemesis in the person of Kapitänleutnant E-F. Kentrat of *U-74*.

This was a period during which the Admiralty, using intelligence derived from Ultra decrypts, managed by deft re-routeing of convoys to avoid the wolf-packs Dönitz contrived to assemble out of the remnant of his scattered forces. Those at Kerneval were concerned that the effectiveness of the U-boat arm seemed to be waning, casting grave doubt on its future. Matters had begun to go badly for German arms in Russia, and the strategists in Berlin were beginning to doubt the wisdom of allowing Dönitz a free hand, arguing that a diversion of resources and manpower eastwards would more speedily achieve the war objectives of the Reich. Dönitz strenuously opposed this line of thinking, arguing in his turn that a continuing submarine offensive against Great Britain, in constantly threatening, if it did not materially reduce, the import flow, required the British to tie down immense forces in containing it. Pointing to the losses on the Eastern Front and the successes against several SC convoys, the Befelshaber der U-Boote passionately emphasised the low cost of this achievement – only a handful of U-boats lost to an enemy whose efforts to fight an anti-submarine war were not proving particularly effective. With an anticipated output of more U-boats in the coming months, Dönitz was confident he possessed the means of achieving victory in the west. This was before the action surrounding HG76.

During this comparatively quiet period in early November, with many U-boats diverted to the Mediterranean, a mighty assembly of American and British merchantmen, the former temporarily transferred to the British registry, all screened by a heavy escort, effected the transport of about 20,000 British and Commonwealth troops on their way east by way of the Cape of Good Hope.

Twelve merchant ships were lost from Convoys SC52, SC53, SC57 and SC58, and one straggler from HX166 was sunk before the turn of the year,[9] but for weeks there were no casualties in the westbound ON series, though the heavy westerly gales persisted, forcing no fewer than 26 ships to fall out of formation from Convoy ON37 in November. Bad weather also caused the single loss from SC58, the Norwegian freighter *Nidardal*, laden with sulphur, which foundered in heavy weather south-west of Rockall on 16 December. The escorts also received punishment; the Canadian destroyer *St Laurent*, escorting ON33, suffered structural damage from heavy green head-seas in early November, and later that month damage to the American destroyer *Du Pont* in a collision with a Norwegian cargo vessel necessitated a two-month sojourn in a Boston shipyard.

During the twelve weeks of the last quarter of the year gales were recorded on 53 days, 17 of them in November, and including winds over Force 10 (storm force, approaching that of hurricane velocity); paradoxically, the horrendous weather also contributed to the fact that ship losses for November were the second lowest since the outbreak of war. But even when the winds abated the residual swell was heavy and lasted for days, making life difficult for those rolling about in the little escorts. The convoys could not take up kinder, more southerly routes, since the poor fuel capacities of the escorts permitted only the shortest, great-circle route to be followed.[10] Nor did the warships' anchorages offer much of a refuge at the end of a passage: the holding ground at Hvalfjord was particularly poor, and anchor watches were times of constant vigilance and occasional stressful activity when ships dragged their anchors and threatened their neighbours.

The first significant check on Dönitz's U-boat arm occurred in late December, after the Japanese attack on Pearl Harbor and while the German staff were preparing plans for Operation PAUKENSCHLAG, or 'drumbeat', the deployment of German submarines on the eastern seaboard of the United States. This check was centred upon Convoy HG76, for which Dönitz had prepared an ambush in November.

In fact HG76 did not sail until 14 December, when it threw its assailants off the scent by beginning its passage south-west, along the coast of Morocco, before heading west. HG76 was accompanied by a strong defence force to which the escort-carrier *Audacity* had been assigned. The senior officer of this, the 36th Escort Group, was a man whose influence upon the outcome of the Battle of the Atlantic was to be profound: Commander F.J. Walker, then in command of HM Sloop *Stork*. The other units in the group were the sloop *Deptford* and the corvettes *Convolvulus*, *Gardenia*, *Marigold*, *Pentstemon*, *Rhododendron* and *Vetch*. In addition to the *Audacity*, Commander D.W. MacKendrick, Walker was also supported by the destroyers *Blankney*, *Exmoor* and *Stanley*, and by an independent hunting group detached from

Admiral Somerville's Force H at Gibraltar and tasked to clear the convoy's passage. This comprised the destroyers *Gurkha, Foxhound, Croome* and the Australian *Nestor*.

Convoy HG76 was overflown by air patrols, and that afternoon a Sunderland from No. 202 Squadron sighted a U-boat, causing her to dive and alerting the destroyers from Force H. It was *Nestor*, Commander G.S. Stewart, which located the U-boat and began a depth-charge attack that destroyed Kapitänleutnant B. Hansmann and the 50 young crew-members of *U-127* on her first war patrol.

Convoy HG76, consisting of 32 merchantmen under Commodore Fitzmaurice, proceeded undetected throughout the 15th. About noon the next day German aircraft located it, whereupon *U-67, U-108, U-107* and *U-131* were homed-in and made contact. Various attempts to close with the merchant ships were frustrated by the air patrols and the aggression of the escorts, and on the 17th a Martlet from *Audacity*, ranging out to twenty miles from the convoy, spotted *U-131* and strafed her, compelling Baumann to dive. The Martlet's pilot called up assistance; five escorts arrived, and *U-131* was subjected to a depth-charge attack by *Pentstemon* and *Stanley*. With *U-131* damaged, Baumann sought escape by going deeper, but he was unable to remain submerged, and two hours later he resurfaced.

Stanley, Pentstemon, Stork, Blankney and *Exmoor* all approached Baumann as he tried to escape on the surface, but he was again attacked from the air. Manning their anti-aircraft gun, Baumann's men shot down a Martlet from No. 802 Fleet Air Arm Squadron from the *Audacity*, killing the pilot, Sub-Lieutenant G.R.P. Fletcher. It was the first instance of a U-boat shooting down an aircraft, but it did little for Baumann's chances. He was soon under fire from the pursuing destroyers, which had seen the aeroplane fall and now engaged from a range of seven miles. In twenty minutes *U-131* had sustained eight direct hits and was a shambles; Baumann ordered her scuttled, losing one man, before he and the rest of his crew were taken prisoner.

Walker picked up Fletcher's body and it was buried at sea the following day, by which time a second U-boat had been forced to scuttle. Under the command of Kapitänleutnant W. Heyda, *U-434* had come down from the north after the *Admiral Scheer's* sortie was aborted, refuelled from the German supply-ship *Bessel* in Vigo harbour, then made contact with HG76 on the evening of the 17th after seeing the end of Baumann from a distance. At about this time Korvettenkapitän K. Scholtz, who had on the 12th sunk the Portuguese neutral *Cassequel*, made an attack in *U-108*, but it failed, and it was Heyda who was spotted at daylight on the 18th by the lookouts aboard *Stanley*. Increasing speed and heading for *U-434*, some five miles distant, Lieutenant Commander D.B. Swan's destroyer was missed by a torpedo fired at him by Heyda. He then circled the spot where he thought Heyda had dived, from a suspicious oil slick lying on the surface of the sea. Gaining a sonar contact, Swan dropped two depth-charges and was joined by Thorburn in *Blankney*, who fired more. With both warships harrying *U-434*, one of the charges was close enough to detonate a torpedo in one of the U-boat's stern tubes. Water began to flood the U-boat, Heyda blew all tanks and *U-434* rose, to remain on the surface just long enough for all but three of her 45-man crew to get out and be picked up by *Stanley, Blankney* and *Exmoor*.

As HG76 proceeded west towards the Azores, two FW200 Kondors were shot down by Martlets from *Audacity* during the day, and that night *U-107* and *U-67* were frustrated in their attempts to strike at the convoy; but in the early hours of the following morning, the 19th, *U-574*, on her first war patrol under Oberleutnant D. Gengelbach, fired a spread of torpedoes at HMS *Stanley*. *U-574* had been brought back from the Cape Race area (see below) and she too had refuelled from the *Bessel*. During the dark evening of the 18th Gengelbach had made a surface attack on but missed the *Convolvulus*, attracting the attention of that corvette, her sister *Pentstemon*, and the *Stanley*. For two hours the British ships sought the U-boat but she escaped and they withdrew, hurrying off to regain their respective stations. Gengelbach brought *U-574* up to the surface and pursued. As he approached in the darkness the lookouts aboard *Stanley* saw her, but it was too late, and a torpedo slammed into the destroyer, blowing up her magazine and tearing the ship apart in a sheet of blinding flame.

Aboard *Stork*, Walker too was aware of the U-boat, and turned towards her astern of the main body of the convoy. As she dived Walker's operators detected her and he made two attacks, forcing *U-574* to the surface where *Stork* swung under full helm to ram. Gengelbach tried to turn inside the sloop and the two vessels circled one another, the *Stork's* gunners unable to depress their weapons and reduced to swearing and shaking their fists at the enemy until Walker, his machine-guns having finally raked the conning tower, was able to bring *Stork* in to ram the U-boat, half rolling her over. As *U-574* was carried past them by her momentum, *Stork's* depth-charge crew dropped a brace of charges over her stern on shallow settings, almost destroying the U-boat. Gengelbach and 27 of his men were killed, while 18 were picked up, prisoners-of-war, some by *Samphire*.

One of *Samphire's* company wrote: 'Action stations about 4 a.m. and I saw things I shall remember as long as I live. When I got on deck the sky was alight with star-shells . . . Guns blazed and depth-charges were [being] fired and I wondered what was going to happen. Eventually we heard men calling in the water and . . . we lowered boats and picked up thirteen Germans from the sub which *Stork* had rammed. We then heard that the

Stanley had been torpedoed (she must have gone down in a couple of minutes) and we went to pick up survivors . . .' Later he wrote: 'Have been on guard over the prisoners again today. They don't seem bad fellows but you [*sic*] got to keep your eye on them. Some of them are quite young . . .'

As this incident was occurring astern of the convoy Scholtz succeeded in manoeuvring into a position from which to torpedo and damage the British steamship *Ruckinge*, loaded with a mixed general cargo. She was abandoned and her crew were picked up by the *Stork*, while *Ruckinge* heself was sunk by gunfire from the corvette *Samphire*, which had arrived too late to search for survivors.

That afternoon two more Kondors were shot down by the *Audacity's* fighters but Scholtz remained in contact, along with *U-107* and several other U-boats. Aircraft and the corvettes *Marigold* and *Samphire* again prevented close approaches, but during the night of 21/22 December Endrass and Bigalk both penetrated the defences, the former, in *U-567*, torpedoing the Norwegian freighter *Annavore* which, loaded with 4,800 tons of iron pyrites, took 34 men to the bottom, only four escaping.

At about 20.30 Bigalk in *U-751* had meanwhile fired torpedoes at the *Audacity*, hitting her and bringing her to a stop. Closing his quarry, Bigalk fired two more and the carrier began to sink. *U-751* was detected by a corvette but succeeded in escaping, and Bigalk withdrew, to make a propaganda broadcast after his return to St-Nazaire on Boxing Day.[11]

After *Audacity* went down Endrass made another attack, but had to pay for his success: *U-567* was quickly located and counter-attacked by *Deptford*, Lieutenant Commander H.C. White, and *Samphire*, Lieutenant F.T. Renny. At first White thought Endrass had escaped and he withdrew when he lost contact, following *Samphire* back towards the convoy; but then there were two sudden detonations, and nothing further was heard from Endrass or his crew. White's return to station was marred by a minor collision with *Stork's* stern in the darkness. The impact killed two German prisoners held below-decks and added to Walker's depression, as he blamed himself for the loss of *Audacity*. Only the appearance of an 'American-built Liberator aircraft of RAF Coastal Command' cheered him, providing the air cover they had been deprived of by the loss of the escort carrier. It 'played a significant part in the final series of counter-attacks, which eventually freed the convoy from further pursuit'.[12]

The last of the enemy were driven off by *Vetch* and the reinforcing destroyers *Vanquisher* and *Witch*, which joined Walker's force early on 23 December. It had been a memorable action, and although two men-of-war had been sunk, only two merchant ships had been lost, at a cost of five U-boats. Walker's achievement had been won at some cost but it provided a glimmer of hope.

For those involved, Christmas Day 1941 'didn't seem like it . . . we have run out of spuds . . . What a trip this is. It's getting everybody on edge and can you wonder at it . . . I think the worst is over . . . I'm longing for a restful sleep with no fear of a tin fish hitting you any minute.' *Samphire*, along with the rest of Walker's 36th Escort Group, berthed on 27 December; she had expended all but six of her 'nearly one hundred' depth-charges.[13]

PART FOUR
January–July 1942

WEAKNESS IN
DEFENCE

15

'Presented to us on a plate'

Liberty ship

THE JAPANESE ATTACK by carrier-borne aircraft on American warships at Pearl Harbor on Sunday 7 December 1941 owed much to two British precedents. The first was a pre-emptive strike by a powerful British force on the Danish capital, Copenhagen, in 1807, the purpose of which was to deny Napoleon the use of the Danish fleet; significantly, it was made without any declaration of war. The second was the British Fleet Air Arm's attack on the Italian Fleet at Taranto in June 1940.[1]

The attack on Pearl Harbor brought to a head the policies of both Roosevelt and Churchill, for at a stroke the American people were outraged. Where the capture of the United States merchant ship *City of Flint* by the *Deutschland* in December 1939 had entrenched the isolationists and strengthened the hand of those pressing for the Neutrality Act, the wholesale bombing of United States battleships was seen without equivocation as *casus belli*. It meant that Great Britain would no longer bear the brunt of the war, and while the participation of the United States Navy, in its own version of 'phoney war', had already proved of the utmost importance in easing the Royal Navy's burden, it was felt that its wholehearted support would prove decisive.

But while the Grand Strategists in London might breathe a sigh of relief, those more intimately concerned with grey-water strategy had a crisis yet to face, and for those involved with tactical action at sea there were months of steadfast attrition by the enemy to come. All the benefits of Ultra decrypts notwithstanding – and they could be intermittent, and fail at critical moments – the ability of the German's B-Dienst service to read British naval signals and monitor British naval movements was fatal to the Allied interest. From 1934 the B-Dienst under Kapitänleutnant Heinz Bonatz had maintained a close watch on British and French developments, and by the summer of 1939 some five hundred operators in sixteen stations were engaged in this task.

The British Admiralty used two encrypting mechanisms, the Naval Cypher for operational signals and the Naval Code for administrative purposes, which in due course included ship movements. Both used numerical encoding, and were then super-encyphered by means of complex tabulations which changed regularly. But the Naval Code had been used before the war without this latter refinement, and it had been easy to break by comparing the encoded reports emanating from merchant ship movements with accounts of their passages published by Lloyd's of London. At the time of Mussolini's invasion of Ethiopia the Admiralty had begun to super-encypher the Naval Code in the same way as the Naval Cypher, and this had enabled the B-Dienst cryptanalyst Wilhelm Tranow to crack the latter by way of the former. By the time of the Norwegian Campaign of 1940 Tranow and his colleagues could expect to read up to half the Allies' radio traffic, enabling the German navy to evade British concentrations.

By March 1940 the British Merchant Navy Code too had been cracked with the aid of captures made in Norway and by German commerce-raiders at sea. These successes were short-lived, however, for in August the Admiralty introduced new code books, posing the B-Dienst cryptanalysts a new challenge. But by January 1941 about a fifth of the new Naval Cypher and about a quarter of the new Naval Code, as well as the super-encrypting techniques, had been penetrated. This was invaluable to the Kriegsmarine's operations, of course, and even the introduction of a third Naval Cypher in June 1941 only stalled the Germans for a while, since Tranow had broken it too by the end of the year.

By the beginning of 1942, therefore, B-Dienst were able to read 'important information like the departure signals from New York, the route and route-change orders, and finally even the daily U-boat situation reports of the Admiralty'. This was made possible by the use of Hollerith machines, which helped to 'strip' the super-encypherments. It was such a time-consuming task that only about a tenth of intercepted signals were usually available in time to be used by Dönitz and Godt at Kerneval, but even delayed decrypts had their value, for example in analysing the timetables of the convoys and their changes. Such analyses were of great importance during the German attacks on convoys between November 1942 and March 1943.

From the time of the sinking of the *Athenia* and the directing of *U-31* to the interception of Convoy OB4 in the South West Approaches in September 1939, Dönitz had had the benefit of this signals intelligence. Against this, the British had the ability to intercept tactical U-boat traffic at sea by means of radio direction-finding stations, and when information thus acquired was added to the Ultra intelligence, convoys could be routed to evade the lurking 'wolf-packs' of grouped U-boats. The loss of initiative imposed when the approach of naval escorts forced a local tactical group commander to submerge persuaded Dönitz that tactical operations were best directed from Kerneval.

When a contact to a convoy was established and the U-boats began their attacks and sent a great amount of radio signals, the [U-boat] Command was happy to have all the information and saw no danger in this signalling because the enemy in any case did then know that U-boats were in contact. This was a great mistake. The [British] Admiralty realised by a close observation of the German signal procedures the great importance of the contact signals and forced the development of an automatic high frequency direction-finding set [HF/DF, known colloquially to the Royal Navy as 'Huff-Duff'] for small escorts. After [each of] the escort groups were equipped with at least one HF/DF set from mid-1942, more and more contacts to [sic] convoys did not lead to successful [German attacks] . . . because the first contact-holder was forced to submerge to an escort running down the [radio] bearing.[2]

Radio Direction Finding, like signals intelligence and ship-building on a Protean scale, had its effect on the outcome. The fact that a submerged U-boat was effectively knocked out of an attack led the Germans to seek the development of submarines with a high under-water speed, while the British development of radar was a cause of such extreme anxiety that fear of it blinded German analysts to their enemy's deadly use of direction-finding. In February 1942 Dönitz, constantly nagged by doubts about the security of Enigma-transmitted messages, introduced a new, four-wheeled Enigma machine. This, with its associated new code books, blacked out Bletchley Park for eleven months and led the Admiralty's Operational Intelligence Centre to admit on 9 February that 'little can be said with any confidence in estimating the present and future movements of U-boats'.

Nor was this all the new Allies were up against. While the help of the United States in the Battle of the Atlantic was welcome, it also initially gave the British cause for grave anxiety, and Dönitz was quick to exploit the cause. It was simple: despite its 'operations short of war' experience in the Atlantic, despite its rather smug contemplation of its struggling naval partner, the

United States Navy foolishly failed to introduce the convoy system on its home coast.

Whatever the reasons for this blunder, the consequences were deplorable; not least because the Americans also refused to black out the coastline of the eastern seaboard. The consequence was a great loss of lives, ships, raw materials and manufactured goods, not all of them American, or confined to American interests. The intransigence of the new Commander-in-Chief of the United States Navy, 63-year-old Fleet Admiral Ernest King, is usually held to have been at the root of this wanton perversity.

On 21 December 1941, ten days after Hitler's declaration of war on the United States, King relinquished command of the Atlantic Fleet to Admiral R.E. Ingersoll and assumed his new and supreme office. His influence over the conduct of the war in the Atlantic continued, however – not, according to the official historian, 'from any desire to retain power, but because Cinclant (Commander in Chief, Atlantic) as a floating command lacked the necessary communications and other facilities to direct so complicated a war as this was becoming in the Atlantic'. In fact King's new post incorporated that of Chief of Naval Operations, which automatically involved him personally. But as Samuel Morison concedes, King's 'decisions were made quickly and without consultation; when anyone tried to argue with [him] beyond a certain point, a characteristic bleak look came over his countenance as a signal that his mind was made up and further discussion was useless.'[3] The reality was rather more complex.

The failure of the United States Navy to form convoy along its Atlantic and Caribbean coasts remains a scandal, but also something of a mystery. Much has been made of King's responsibility for it, yet before he hauled down his flag as Commander-in-Chief of the Atlantic Fleet – notably, three weeks before Pearl Harbor – he was well aware of the vulnerability of the shipping that travelled up and down America's east coast. As well as shipping on passage to Britain from the Caribbean (and the Pacific, via the Panama Canal) by way of the convoy assembly ports of Canada, an immense amount of purely American coastal trade was involved, which included much of America's domestic oil. King was particularly sensible of this last, and also well aware of the vulnerability of all ships to submarine attack: *Niblack* and *Greer* had both been in action with U-boats, the *Kearny* had been damaged and the *Reuben James* sunk while under his overall command. With this in mind, in a letter to Rear Admiral A. Andrews, in charge of the Eastern Sea Frontier, on 17 November 1941 he had made some preliminary moves to initiate the establishment of convoys. 'I am told', King had written, 'that organizations of the necessary scope and size and readiness do not exist. May I therefore suggest that steps be taken at once – if not already under way – to get the indicated convoy ports [Boston, New York and Hampton Roads] organized, to which end it would be well to have first hand knowledge of how Halifax is organized and managed.' Andrews responded testily that such port operations were already in place and that two dummy convoy exercises had been held; they had been confused and unsatisfactory.[4]

Yet, tragically, the matter was delayed, compromised less by intransigence than by simple inertia. The most charitable explanation is that King, having had power concentrated in his hands by Presidential decision, became too much preoccupied with the establishment of the American/British Joint Chiefs of Staff and the formulation of grand strategy to take much interest in a theatre that was now devolved to Ingersoll and subordinate admirals like Andrews, concerned with the operational areas of the Eastern and Gulf Sea Frontiers. But there is a lingering whiff of perversity about King, a characteristic of his arrogance, womanising and drinking, and neither this nor his apparently 'near-psychotic' Anglophobia nor his contempt for the British and their Royal Navy as a weak and spent force can be entirely ruled out as explanations for his failure to follow up these matters, especially from his position of supreme control as well as supreme responsibility.[5] American citizens serving as volunteers in the Royal Navy and sharing British anxieties found King's decision inexplicable, and in wardrooms his reported assertion that 'inadequately escorted convoys were worse than none' was greeted with derision by battle-chastened young officers from backgrounds as diverse as Threadneedle Street and Wall Street.

Nevertheless, among other things the modifications King suggested for the North Atlantic route did seem to embody a release of American escorts for the duty of convoy escort along the eastern seaboard, and surely no Anglophobia, however psychotic, can have impelled him to consign American merchant seamen – his own countrymen – to untimely deaths. It is most likely that King suffered from a complaint regrettably common among most senior admirals on both sides of the Atlantic: a failure to appreciate the true worth, as an asset, of a merchant marine and its socially obscure human members – until it was almost too late.

King concerted revised operations for trans-Atlantic convoys with the First Sea Lord, Sir Dudley Pound, who had accompanied Churchill to Washington in late December for a meeting of the Combined Chiefs of Staff, but he took no action to compel local authorities to black out the coast. As a consequence of this neglect, the U-boat commanders arriving off America in the New Year as part of Operation PAUKENSCHLAG found it a matter of comparative ease to surface at night just outside the shipping lanes and torpedo merchantmen (some of which still themselves exhibited navigation lights) silhouetted against the backdrop of coastal lighting. It was three long and terrible months before a blackout was imposed, and then, incredibly, it aroused vociferous local complaints about the ruination of the tourist trade.

No wonder the Germans regarded this period as their 'Second Happy Time'. Kapitänleutnant P. Cremer, arriving off the United States coast in the spring of 1942 in *U-333*, had this to say:

> We had left a blacked-out Europe behind us. Whether in Stettin, Berlin, Paris, Hamburg, L'Orient or La Rochelle – everywhere had been pitch dark. At sea we tried not to show any light, even hiding the glowing ciga-rette in the hollow of the hand when smoking was allowed on the bridge. Not a ray of light came through the conning tower hatch. Yet here the buoys were blinking as normal, the famous lighthouse at Jupiter Inlet was sweeping its luminous cone far over the sea. We were cruising off a brightly lit coastal road with darting headlights from innumerable cars. We went in so close that through the night glasses we could distinguish equally the big hotels and the cheap dives, and read the flickering neon signs. Not only that: from Miami and its luxurious suburbs a mile-wide band of light was being thrown upwards to glow like an aureole against the underside of the cloud layer, visible from far below the horizon. All this after five months of war!
>
> Before this sea of light, against this footlight glare of a carefree new world, were passing the silhouettes of ships recognisable in every detail and sharp as the outlines in a sales catalogue. Here they were formally presented to us on a plate: please help yourselves! All we had to do was press the button.

This again was a scandal. And there had been more. Despite attempts by the Germans to leak information suggesting a concentration of U-boats in the North West Approaches to the British Isles, Rodger Winn had presciently divined Dönitz's purpose and on 2 January 1942, the day that the first U-boat struck, he had almost exactly second-guessed Dönitz's precise dispo-sitions. Winn's assessment was transmitted to Washington and was forwarded to the Atlantic Fleet.

Since 1918 the United States Navy had, like the Royal Navy, largely ignored anti-submarine warfare and the defence of merchant shipping. It, and the associated American Coast Guard, were chronically short of escorts, and to assist them the British transferred 22 anti-submarine trawlers together with their experienced crews (though they did not arrive in American waters until 1 March). They were to be followed by a number of corvettes to be transferred to and manned by the United States Navy. The Americans were also short of aircraft, but an attempt to retain for home use aeroplanes made in the US but destined for the RAF was rejected by the desperate British, who traded their trawlers instead. Air cover on the American coast was provided by a small number of Army Air Force aircraft, which soon gained a reputation, with the Germans at least, for ineffectiveness, although they repeatedly reported successful attacks on surfaced U-boats during daylight. Initially nine planes made twice-daily sweeps over the coast between Maine and Florida. 'That was all.' By April the numbers had grown, and swiftly: there were soon 19 bases along the Atlantic seaboard from which 84 Army and 86 Navy aircraft operated. During the same period anti-submarine patrols were maintained by a handful of small craft, gradually augmented by the experienced British trawlers.

But 55 merchant vessels were sunk on this coast in January 1942 and a similar number were lost in February, many of them tankers. In March, of the total tonnage of shipping sunk, over half were loaded tankers. Many of them were coming north from the Gulf of Mexico and the Caribbean, bound for Halifax or Sydney to join HX or SC convoys; others were part of the American domestic distribution system.

As some compensation for the lack of organised convoys, mine-protected anchorages were established within the deep inlets that seam the east coast of the United States. With vessels encouraged to make daylight hops, a passage between, say, New York and Jacksonville in Florida could be made in four days. As elsewhere, the U-boat commanders discovered the choke points where they might most advantageously lie in ambush, and while many vessels used the alternative route offered by the extensive canal system inland of the exposed coast, many more were too large to do so and were caught off Cape Hatteras. Further south, southbound vessels passing close inshore to avoid the northward set of the Gulf Stream found themselves silhouetted against the glare of brightly-lit Miami.

Anything more than a look at the opening of the war on the American coast and in the Caribbean is outside the scope of this work; suffice it to say that the depredations of Dönitz's U-boats significantly affected the supply of *matériel* and oil over the so-called 'Atlantic Bridge', which for this reason proved the weak point in the flow of imports towards Britain. That this interdiction was achieved by a mere handful of submarines – initially only five Type IX U-boats, followed by seven Type VIIs sent to the nearer waters off Newfoundland – simply attests to the vulnerability of independently-steaming merchant ships. It was an old lesson learned anew, and it was costly in terms of human life. It was also damaging to morale, reinforcing the merchant seaman's opinion that no one gave a damn for him. It was not an encouraging atmosphere in which to expose the as yet largely unblooded American Mercantile Marine.

Although the Japanese had informed neither Germany nor Italy of their intention to attack the United States at Pearl Harbor, Dönitz was able to take swift advantage of the situation thanks to a contingency plan formulated while the United States Navy was gradually involving itself in the defence of British convoys during the 'operations short of war' phase. Both Dönitz and Raeder had concluded that a war in the Pacific would divert American attention away from the Atlantic at the very moment when, if Germany were to immediately declare war upon the United States, American shipping would lose its neutral immunity and become exposed to legitimate attack. They were not aware of the 'defeat Germany first' principle established between Churchill and Roosevelt, though it is a curious fact that in preparing a report for Hitler on 12 December Raeder had asked his staff to consider a question put forward by the Führer as to whether there was any possibility that 'the USA and Britain will abandon East Asia for a time in order to crush Germany and Italy first?' Raeder's conclusion had been that such a policy would endanger British India, and was therefore unlikely. He had also emphasised his opinion that as a result of the Japanese action the Americans would withdraw both men-of-war and merchant vessels from the Atlantic, and that 'the strain on British merchant shipping will increase'. Raeder, keen to occupy Dakar as a German naval base, had also noted that Britain's quondam ally Amiral Darlan 'has offered to give the German Navy information which he possesses concerning the disposition of British naval forces due to his knowledge of British intelligence methods in the past'. Unsurprisingly, Hitler sanctioned acceptance of the offer, and a conference followed.

As for Dönitz in distant Brittany, he had noted in his War Diary two days after Pearl Harbor that 'The attempt must be made . . . to strike a blow at the American coast with a drumbeat.' In view of Berlin's insistence that many U-boats remain in the Mediterranean, the outcome fell short of Dönitz's expectations, but from the Allied standpoint it was bad enough, and swept away at a stroke the optimism engendered at the Admiralty by America's entry into the war. The failure of the Americans to introduce convoy immediately on their eastern and Gulf coasts caused much genuine anger and distress in London: the first drumbeat was sounded by Hardegen in *U-123*, who struck not an American but a British ship.

Alfred Holt's Blue Funnel liner *Cyclops* had been used in the Norwegian campaign and in the evacuations from the Atlantic coast of France in 1940.

By January 1941 she was on her way home from Hong Kong, having left there not long before the Japanese arrived. Dating from 1906, she was one of Holt's older steamships, but with a deadweight of 12,390 tons, and built to Holt's exacting specifications, she remained a valuable vessel. The *Cyclops* had completed her loading in Auckland, New Zealand before crossing the Pacific and passing through the Panama Canal, entering the Caribbean on 2 January. Heading for Halifax to join an HX convoy, she was 125 miles south-east of Cape Sable, zig-zagging at a speed of 12.5 knots, by the evening of the 11th. In addition to some 7,000 tons of mixed general cargo, Captain L. W. Kersley had in his charge a crew of 55, six gunners, one Distressed British Seaman and some 78 passengers, many of them apparently Chinese, travelling to Britain to escape the situation in the Far East. Possibly many were connected with shipping, either as seafarers or as members of the considerable corps of Chinese wharfingers, tally clerks and stevedores employed by Holt's at their wharves in Hong Kong and China.

At 19.45 that evening a torpedo struck the ship's starboard side aft, between Nos 6 and 7 Holds, killing two men. Kersley at once ordered the lifeboats manned and a distress message transmitted. In the gloom of the gathering night the crew began to evacuate the ship. Mr A. Harrison, the chief engineer, reported afterwards on 'the cool courage and efficiency of Captain Kersley' as he and his officers carried out an inspection to see if the *Cyclops* might be saved. As they were doing so a second torpedo slammed into the vessel from the port side, under the bridge, and she began to settle. Close to the after rafts at the time, Chief Officer J. Simpson managed to release them, but he, Kersley and the others were obliged to jump into the freezing sea, to either scramble onto the rafts, or be hauled into the boats. There was heavy loss of life during the night as about forty of *Cyclops*'s crew and some 46 passengers fell victims to the slow horrors of hypothermia, so that it was a much reduced ship's company who were rescued next day by the Canadian minesweeper *Red Deer*.

Hardegen had in fact been on his way further south, and in the succeeding days he sank the American-owned, Panamanian-flagged tanker *Norness*, then south of Rhode Island the British tanker *Coimbra*, blown up in a ball of flame which consumed all but six badly burned men. He next attacked but failed to sink the American coastal tanker *San José*, off Atlantic City. She appears to have been in collision with another vessel, the *Santa Elisa*, which caught fire and limped into New York. On the 19th, between Cape Hatteras and Roanoake Island, Hardegen sank three more vessels, one American steamship, the *City of Atlanta*, an unidentified vessel thought at first to have been the *Brazos* (which was actually sunk in a collision earlier with the British escort-carrier *Archer* then working-up in the Caribbean), and the

Latvian *Ciltvaira* of Riga. That same day, with *U-123* in shallow water, Hardegen engaged the Seminole Steamship Company's *Malay* with gunfire, damaging her but being chased by the Norwegian whale-factory ship *Kosmos II*, her master perhaps thirsting after vengeance for his enforced exile. Calling for assistance from the shore, the *Kosmos II* kept up her hot if lumbering pursuit while Hardegen's crew feverishly repaired a defective diesel engine and eventually managed to outrun the large factory ship two hours later. It is an indication of how unprepared the Americans were that no aircraft arrived in time to catch *U-123* on the surface. Hardegen had his revenge, too, for he sank the Norwegian motor-tanker *Pan Norway* on his way back to L'Orient, during which passage he also destroyed the British Royal Mail liner *Culebra* with the loss of all hands. Both of these actions were by gunfire.

At this stage of the war, it was to Hardegen's credit that two days later he intercepted the Greek steamship *Mount Aetna*, owned by the Atlanticos Steamship Company of Athens. She was under a Swiss charter and there-fore technically a neutral, and he requested that she pick up the survivors from the *Pan Norway*.

Hardegen had certainly opened the campaign with as loud a drumbeat as his Commander-in-Chief could have desired, and he was not alone. In addition to *U-123* Dönitz had deployed *U-66* commanded by Korvettenkapitän R. Zapp, who struck off Cape Hatteras, where ships were obliged to conform to international regulations and burn bright navigation lights. On the night of 18/19 January Zapp first torpedoed the American steam-tanker *Allan Jackson*; 35 of her 48 men died in the fierce flames that consumed her. Next was the Canadian passenger-liner *Lady Hawkins*, bound south from Halifax and Boston to Bermuda with 212 passengers and 3,000 tons of general cargo. In the explosion and the wreck of the sinking ship Captain H.O. Giffen, 86 of his crew, two DBSs and 162 passengers died. The survivors, 21 crew and 49 passengers under the *Lady Hawkins's* chief officer Mr P.A. Kelly, who was later awarded Lloyd's War Medal for his outstanding leadership, endured five appalling days in the boats before being picked up by the American vessel *Coamo*, which landed them in Puerto Rico.

In the next few days Zapp sank two more American ships, the *Norvana* which was lost with all hands and a cargo of sugar and the ore-loaded *Venore*, and the British tanker *Empire Gem*. Commanded by Captain F.R. Broad, this last was a new, war-built 'Ocean'-standard type, based on a Shell design popularly known as the 'three twelves' because their deadweight tonnage was 12,000 and their service speed was 12 knots at a modest fuel consumption of 12 tons per day. Full of petrol and with 920 tons of machinery bound for Britain, the *Empire Gem* was heading to join a convoy at Halifax; instead she blew up with the loss of all but her master and one radio officer.

Dönitz's offensive now gathered momentum all along the coast from Canada to the Gulf of Mexico and the Caribbean. In the weeks to come German submarines destroyed a greater tonnage than they had at any other time or in any other place – about 100,000 tons in the first two weeks and in February and March a quarter of a million, of which almost one-fifth were tankers. The two next war patrols of *U-66* illustrate the point: on the first of these, between 21 March and 27 May, she was deployed in the Caribbean. Here she sank the Greek steamer *Korthion* off Barbados, the Dutch steamship *Amsterdam* and the Panamanian motor-tanker *Heinrich von Riedemann* off Grenada, the American steamer *Alcoa Partner* and the Panamanian motor-tanker *Harry G. Seidel* off Curaçao. Two more motor-tankers, the Norwegian *Sandar* and the British *George W. McKnight*, were attacked: the former sank off Tobago, the latter, a straggler from Convoy ON87, was towed into Port of Spain and later repaired. On her next patrol *U-66* was commanded by Kapitänleutnant F. Markworth. She sailed from L'Orient on 23 June and operated among the Caribbean islands until she ran very low on fuel. To enable U-boats to operate in distant waters the Germans had developed the Type XIV U-boat, a large submarine tanker, and Markworth bunkered from one of these: *U-462* lay west of the Azores at this time, refuelling nine U-boats for further operations, and five, Markworth's among them, to enable them to return to France. During this war patrol *U-66* sank the Yugoslavian steamer *Triglav* before laying mines off the Leeward Islands which damaged two British motor-torpedo boats. In July and August Markworth sank the Brazilian steam ship *Tamandaré* and the British freighter *Weirbank* off Tobago, attacked a Polish merchant ship and, operating next off Guyana, sank the American steamer *Topa Topa*, the Panamanian motor-vessel *Sir Huon*, the American steamer *West Lashaway* and the Canadian tanker *Winamac*, with heavy loss of life. On his way towards *U-462*, Markworth sank the Swedish East Asia Company's motor-cargo-liner *Peiping*.

In this frenzy of destruction the American merchant seaman experienced what his counterpart in the British and other Allied mercantile marines had been enduring for two and a half years. When Markworth's torpedoes slammed into the *Topa Topa*'s side at about 01.00 on 29 August, the explosion detonated petrol in her Nos 2 and 5 Holds, and the ammunition stored in the ship's after magazine. As she was engulfed in fire three lifeboats escaped and lay in the vicinity for twelve hours. Surfacing and approaching the boats, Markworth learned that Captain C.E. McCoy was dead. He took the chief mate on board *U-66* for questioning, then released him back to his boat. The following evening the survivors were picked up by the British cargo-liner *Clan Macinnes*.

On 30 August the steamer *West Lashaway*, on a passage from Takoradi to New York with a cargo of cocoa beans, was hit by Markworth's torpedoes when 350 miles east of Trinidad. The ship's lookouts spotted their approaching tracks and the helm was put hard over in an attempt to avoid them, but they struck amidships. The explosions stopped the *West Lashaway*'s engine, blew up her bridge and damaged the starboard boats. The ship listed heavily to starboard and sank rapidly; there was time neither to lower boats nor to send a distress message. The survivors managed to get away on four rafts, which stayed together until they were separated by bad weather. Two were never seen again, a third was sighted by a West Indian fisherman who rescued its single occupant, an able seaman. The fourth raft was seen by an aircraft on 13 September and food parcels were dropped, one of which burst, throwing the contents into the water, where sharks swiftly consumed them. The other parcels provided much-needed nourishment in the form of pemmican, chocolate, and condensed milk. Bottles of malted milk broke on impact. The survivors' hopes were raised and the next day a destroyer, thought to have been the USS *Barney*, was seen. It remained in sight for hours, then disappeared before passing very close in the darkness, but the 19 wretched merchant seamen under the third mate were unable to attract its attention. Their next encounter was with a British destroyer, HMS *Vimy*, which was seen approaching with a small convoy of four ships. To the consternation of the *West Lashaway*'s men she opened fire on them, letting off some sixteen rounds before they lowered their makeshift sail and the British realised their error in having taken the raft's silhouette for a submarine. The *Vimy* picked them up and later transferred them to one of the transports she was convoying, the Dutch liner *Prins Willem van Oranje*, from where they were landed at Barbados. Since abandoning ship they had lost the master, Captain B. Bodgen, and a naval gunner.

Such was the baptism of fire undergone by the American Mercantile Marine, and much of the blame for it has been laid at the door of Fleet Admiral King. British commentators have emphasised his Anglophobia, but much of what is perceived as his anti-British sentiment seems based on his refusal to acquiesce in the proposal put forward by Churchill and Pound that all convoy escorts should come under a single, over-arching authority: that of Admiral Noble, the British Commander-in-Chief, Western Approaches, Liverpool. King utterly rejected the notion. Here one might perceive if not Anglo- then Xenophobia: he did not wish for either British or Canadian officers to be commanding convoy escorts on the American coast. The stand he made on this point might have been reasonable had the United States Navy moved more actively towards the establishment of even the most rudimentary convoy system; as it was, he merely appeared perverse and arrogant. Criticism in high places in Britain of American lack of success at submarine-hunting and a corresponding playing-up of Britain's greater experience did not help. Nor was it entirely candid: while the Royal Navy had had some considerable early successes against submarines, and one or two victories since, they were by no means the consummate masters of anti-submarine warfare they liked to imagine, and at this time were arguably inferior to the enemy they were engaged with, as their own statisticians demonstrated weekly.

King rejected a further attempt to impose a unitary command on the Atlantic at a second, dedicated convoy-conference in Washington on 22 January, but accepted the ten corvettes the British had hoped would 'bribe' him to agree to it. Eight corvettes were now being completed every month, and the British offered these too, in the hope of speeding up the United States Navy's dilatory efforts to protect British and Allied merchantmen running along the American coast.[6]

In the event this conference succeeded in establishing a three-part command structure, and adopted King's own suggestions about a re-routeing further south. The high-latitude, great-circle passage was 'rapidly becoming untenable' because operational difficulties caused by the weather led to delayed or missed rendezvous. Neither Argentia Bay nor Hvalfjord were ideal as escort support bases, but the latter continued to be important in particular for the mustering of ships from North America destined to join convoys to North Russia.

These arrangements were not concerted without rancour: once back in London, Pound cabled his disquiet about King's dilatory implementation of convoy on the American coast; and while King had allocated ten destroyers to the task, Pound wanted to double the number. The differences between the two admirals gave rise to misunderstanding and mistrust. It was an unfortunate and unforgivable situation, but one to be expected of King, a man without a shred of humility. It may be that he was congenitally incapable of handling a matter of this sensitivity with the requisite tact and diplomacy; he might however have considered a little more the plight of the men of the Allied mercantile marines now ploughing their solitary and vulnerable passages along America's glittering nocturnal coastline. And if that level of compassion was beyond him, he might simply have considered the impact on his own country of the loss of *American* ships and *matériel* sunk by the Germans, and acted more decisively. Whichever way analysts of the situation cut the pack, it was an inglorious moment for Allied naval history.

In the midst of these deliberations the incompetence of the British was apparently exemplified in the humiliating 'Channel Dash' of February, in which the German capital ships in Brest broke back to Germany through the English Channel. Roosevelt, in papering over the cracks of this fiasco and perhaps intending to mollify the sensibilities of the hard-pressed British with words of encouragement, cabled these comforting words: 'I am more and more convinced that the location of all the German [capital] ships in Germany makes our joint North Atlantic naval problem more simple.' As events played themselves out, while the threat of the *Tirpitz* in Norway had a dire effect on Convoy PQ17, as far as the Atlantic was concerned the German exploit did indeed prove a strategic bonus for the British.

The cost of the failure to introduce convoy in American waters was enormous, but the end result of the joint Anglo-American deliberations was beneficial, culminating in a practical structure in which most trans-Atlantic convoys were to be routed further south to avoid the worst weather. Six short-ranged Canadian escort groups of the Western Local Escort Force would shepherd convoys 1,100 miles east to the longitude of Cape Farewell (45° West, the West Ocean Meeting Point, or WESTOMP). From here 14 longer-ranged escort groups, five American, five British and four Canadian, of the Mid-Ocean Escort Force would take convoys over and cover their progress to the East Ocean Meeting Point, or EASTOMP, on the 22nd Westerly meridian. This lay south of Reykjavik, from where a separate group of American escorts would shuttle between the EASTOMP and Hvalfjord, taking care of the merchant ships bound first for Iceland and then for the Soviet Union in PQ, and much later JW, convoys. The remaining trans-Atlantic ships, bound for Britain, would be taken over by British escort groups, assuming responsibility from the EASTOMP to the Clyde, Loch Ewe and Liverpool; from these points the ships would be dispersed to local ports or re-routed by the coastal convoy network round the north of Scotland and down the North Sea coast – a Royal Navy responsibility, of course. Such coastal passages bred a separate but integrated and equally complex convoy system. They were horribly exposed to air and surface attacks by fast torpedo-boats and destroyers and also to mines, more lethal in many ways than the ocean passages of the Atlantic. This dangerous extension completed the voyages of many merchantmen.

Such an arrangement of mid-ocean escort changes, largely for the slow SC and ONS convoys, allowed the various groups of the Mid-Ocean Escort Force, once relieved of their charges, to run ahead and refuel, in the east at Londonderry in Northern Ireland, in the west, for the Canadians at St John's in Newfoundland and for the Americans at either Portland or Boston. Fast HX convoys would have an American escort all the way to the EASTOMP, where the British would take over, with the American warships going on to take bunkers in Northern Ireland before picking up a faster westbound

ON convoy. A schedule of boiler-cleaning, routine dockings and repair periods was to be established, much of it based on Boston but with considerable support provided by the efficient engineering and other facilities rapidly burgeoning in British ports. Furthermore, in Londonderry and off the Ulster coast the United States Navy would be able to take advantage of British anti-aircraft and anti-submarine training facilities, the latter using British submarines in a live role. Compared with Iceland, Ulster offered the Americans greater freedom and a pleasanter landscape, an intangible but significant bonus: two days of work-up training after a period of repair and recreation there rapidly brought American escort standards up to those of their more experienced Allied colleagues.

The constantly-increasing number of warships allocated to these tasks soon amounted to an immensity of men and warships. Moreover, as time passed the types of escort involved became less a matter of expediency as the lessons of war were translated into improved design and adaptation. In due course the basic 'Flower'-class corvette was replaced by the larger 'Castle'-class, and the faster and more sophisticated frigates of the 'River', 'Bay' and 'Loch' classes. The early use of fleet destroyers and hurried conversions of elderly destroyers to LREs (Long Range Escorts), both British and American, were superseded by a more suitable 'destroyer escort' type based on an American model. To these were gradually added escort-carriers and an increased number of rescue ships, and there were other warships whose contribution is too readily eclipsed by the more familiar corvette, destroyer and frigate. Particularly fine service was rendered by British ocean minesweepers which, equipped with sonar, became effective proto-frigates, while American Coast Guard cutters under both the white ensign and the Stars and Stripes were particularly able ships, not least for their sea-keeping qualities and the comfort they afforded their crews.[7]

But in those early weeks before these arrangements were in place, matters were very different. In the three-part command structure that eventually emerged from the haggling between Pound and King, strategic command of the American areas was to come under Admiral Bristol, USN, the Canadian under Admiral Murray, RCN, in Ottawa, and the British under Noble. Pound had bowed to King's claim that American control over the western Atlantic was a satisfactory *fait accompli*, but was careful to reserve his position. 'We will do all we can to make the scheme work,' he said in a signal to King, 'but I must be free to reopen [the] question should I consider our trade is suffering.'

The misperceptions that bedevilled relations between these two able if flawed commanders-in-chief arose in part from the fact that King had two other concerns: the Pacific, and troop convoys. Ten British and four American destroyers were immediately assigned to troop convoys and these, as far as the Americans were concerned, formed part of Admiral Ingersoll's command. The first had already left: NA1 was a small convoy of two British troop-ships and two British destroyers which had sailed from Halifax on 10 January bound for Londonderry. These convoys, outside the scope of this work, really began to get under way on a significant scale in February 1942, when Convoy AT1 left New York on the 19th. It consisted of 15 ex-passenger liners escorted by 18 warships, and initiated a series of convoys (AT from New York, AN from Halifax) designed to slowly build up Allied Forces first for the amphibious invasion of Vichy French North Africa, then for Italy, and ultimately for the final offensive against German Occupied Western Europe. Their significance for the mercantile or trade convoys was that they drew off a large number of fast fleet destroyers that were serving as escorts, leading to the assertion that under King 'all of the American destroyers were withdrawn immediately [on the entry of America into the war] for service in other theatres'. The truth is that the United States Navy's 'defense of American troop shipping [i.e., Atlantic troop convoys] was one of the un-alloyed victories of World War II'.

While this 'unalloyed victory' owed much to an overwhelming escort and a high average speed, which almost entirely eliminated the threat from enemy submarine attack (although Rollman in *U-82* succeeded in sinking the ex-American four-stack destroyer HMS *Belmont*, escorting NA2, on 31 January 1942), there was something else: the troop convoys had the benefit of heavy air cover, including dirigibles flown over the western Atlantic by the Unites States Coastguard, at each end of the convoy route. Air cover remained inadequate as far as the trade convoys were concerned, a particu-lar disadvantage at this stage of the war, when what has become known as 'the Battle for the Air' began in Britain.

It will be recalled that Coastal Command's Commander-in-Chief, Sir Philip Joubert de la Ferté, had in 1941 twice petitioned the Air Ministry to bomb the U-boat bases on the Atlantic coast of France. His request was denied, apart from a token response which led London to conclude that the concrete pens under which the U-boats sheltered were impregnable. In February 1942, just before the infamous 'Channel Dash' of the *Scharnhorst, Gneisenau* and *Prinz Eugen*, the British Air Ministry produced a Bombing Policy which required all available bombers to be deployed over Germany. This resulted in a long and acrimonious struggle between those responsible for the trans-Atlantic war and those favouring an aggressive bombing offen-sive against Germany of which the outcome – the denial of resources to the struggle in the Atlantic, a fundamental part of Britain's grand strategy – must be attributed to Churchill's pugnacity. However much what happened ı the Atlantic might trouble the great man's sleep, it was to him an absolute nperative that Britain should be able, and should be seen to be able, to rike back at her enemy. At a time when the war in the Mediterranean, ıe only other theatre which might yield Britain a small dividend of success, ʹas going badly, British bombing raids on Germany seemed to offer a righter alternative. Nevertheless, the failure to allocate substantial air assets ı ɔ the Atlantic can be said unequivocally to have cost the Allies dear in ı ıen, ships and *matériel*.

Admiral Pound had demanded several squadrons of long-range Wellington bombers to attack U-boats coming and going across the surface transit routes in the Bay of Biscay, together with 81 long-range American Liberators to close the air gap in the North Atlantic. He wanted Coastal Command's strength to stand at 1,940 aircraft, rather than its current 519, and he wanted operational control over those aeroplanes to be vested entirely in the hands of those responsible for the war at sea. In this the First Sea Lord had the full support of Joubert de la Ferté, who cut to the heart of the matter and courageously questioned the very doctrine of bombing Germany. On 3 March, having canvassed the opinion of the Naval Staff, he laid before the War Cabinet Defence Committee his own paper outlining 'Air Requirements for the Successful Prosecution of the War at Sea' in which he admirably summed up the facts: 'If we lose the war at sea, we lose the war. We lose the war at sea when we can no longer maintain those communications which are essential to us.' The air marshal went on to state in essence that excessive losses of war *matériel* and fuel at sea would preclude offensive military and air-borne operations of *any* sort. Whether or not this was an absolute truth is disputable; what is indisputable is that the threat to the import flow was serious enough to cause deep concern to those responsible for its defence.

On 8 March the Air Staff riposted, claiming that the bombing campaign against Germany 'could best contribute to the weakening of the U-boat offensive' by destroying the means by which the Germans produced U-boats. They also asserted that it would be 'unsound at any time' to divert bombers 'to an uneconomical defensive role'. The notion that to use bombers to protect Britain's primary supply line would be 'unsound' because it was both 'uneconomical' and 'defensive' is extraordinary, but it was based upon a supposition that the bombing offensive envisaged would enable the RAF 'to deliver a heavy and concentrated blow against Germany *when German morale is low* [my italics: RW] and when the Russians are in great need of our assistance'.

The matter came to a head ten days later when the War Cabinet Defence Committee met and General Sir Alan Brooke tabled a paper advocating an

Army Air Force operating under War Office control, leaving the Royal Air Force free to operate an offensive bomber fleet.[8] What ever the merit of the idea, resources were quite inadequate to implement it, and it served only to fuel the battle for the air, which raged on for twelve long months. Pound, already worn down by the constant nagging pain of an arthritic hip, was also suffering from the first signs of the brain tumour that killed him nineteen months later. His opposite number on the Air Staff, Air Chief Marshal Sir Charles Portal, whose 'intellectual capabilities, integrity and moral courage' appeared impressive, weighed heavily against him in Cabinet debates, and he had considerable influence over Churchill. Unfortunately, if he failed to grasp what was going on in the Atlantic, there is evidence that his appreciation of the potential effectiveness of the RAF's bombing offensive was equally skewed.

In April Mr Justice Singleton was appointed to the War Cabinet to investigate the likely outcome of an 'air attack on Germany at the greatest possible strength during the next six, twelve and eighteen months . . .' Singleton did not think the air offensive 'ought to be regarded as of itself sufficient to win the war *or to produce decisive results*' [my italics: RW], a conclusion confirmed by events.

Singleton's deliberations were ignored, adding to the frustration of Pound and Joubert de la Ferté. On 10 May Pound reiterated his plea for long-range aircraft 'capable of locating and attacking targets at sea with success', a point that he repeated in his own hand, hinting that Bomber Command's abilities were a good deal less than they were cracked up to be.

Anxiety over this fundamental and entirely British dispute was creeping outside Whitehall. Disquiet was expressed by Admiral Stark, since 30 April America's chief naval envoy in London, with his headquarters at 20 Grosvenor Square. He was a tactful man and enjoyed the complete confidence of his British counterparts, particularly of his British personal liaison officer, Vice Admiral Geoffrey Blake, with whom he worked closely. Blake was already an Assistant Chief of the Naval Staff, and may well have been the informant to whom Stark was referring when in early June 1942 he let it be known to King that an un-named British admiral had admitted to him that the Admiralty was unable to get any help 'unless the RAF sees fit to give it to us. They are fighting their own war, and it can't be done by bombing Germany alone.'[9] The matter had been simmering for some time.

Noble's eventual successor as C-in-C, Western Approaches, Admiral Sir Max Horton, had long since turned down command of the Home Fleet on the grounds that it lacked supporting air-power, and at Western Approaches Command itself the ocean-plot displayed the evidence – and the consequences – of lack of air cover with blinding clarity. The man who had taken over the Home Fleet, Admiral Sir John Tovey, now came forward to support Pound. 'The situation at sea had now become so grave', Tovey wrote, 'that the time had come for a stand to be made, even if this led to Their Lordships taking the extreme step of resignation.' Tovey added that he had the support of his predecessor, Sir Charles Forbes, and of Sir Andrew Cunningham, then Commander-in-Chief, Mediterranean but eventually Pound's successor as First Sea Lord.

The minutes of a Chiefs of Staff meeting held on 16 June 1941 record Pound as having declared that 'The present threat to our sea . . . communications, on the security of which our existence and ultimate victory depends, calls for an immediate increase in the strength of the land-based air forces working with the Navy.' Unfortunately, Churchill was in Washington, so Rear Admiral Brind and Air Vice Marshal Slessor, both Assistant Chiefs of their respective staffs, were deputed to confer. Their recommendation was for 54 long-range aircraft to be made available for operations over the Western Approaches, the Bay of Biscay, and in support of Tovey's Home Fleet; and that two squadrons of Lancaster bombers should be immediately transferred from Bomber to Coastal Command. Their conclusions were dismissed by Portal, now supported by Bomber Command's new Air Officer Commanding, Sir Arthur Harris, who threw fuel on the flames: 'If we decide on the wrong course, then our air power will . . . become inextricably implicated as a subsidiary weapon in the prosecution of vastly protracted and avoidable land and sea campaigns.'

There is a whiff of intrigue here, in the employment of that gobbledy-gook phrase 'inextricably implicated as a subsidiary weapon'. The sea campaign might well prove to be 'vastly protracted', but how on earth was it 'avoidable'? Harris's assertion presumably rested upon the perceived success of an overwhelming use of high explosive, for it was made in the light of the terrible thousand-bomber raid on Cologne of 30/31 May, which in Harris's words 'had proved beyond doubt in the minds of *all but wilful men* [my italics: RW] that we can even today dispose of a weight of air attack which no country on which it can be brought to bear could survive. We can bring it to bear on the vital part of Germany. It requires only the decision to concentrate it for proper use.' The best that can be said of this assessment is that it is evidence of Harris's belief that a total concentration of Bomber Command's resources might achieve a quick and absolute victory. It does however also display Harris's lack of appreciation of the war in the Atlantic, for in it he anathematised Coastal Command as 'an obstacle to victory'.[10] Unfortunately, there was on the face of it some justification for Harris's offensive remark, for during the first half of 1942 Coastal Command's sorties over the Bay of Biscay had yielded not one successful strike as against 265 unopposed U-boat passages to and from L'Orient and St-Nazaire.

For many convoys at sea, the reality verged upon the pathetic. Writing of the Gibraltar route when he served in the 40th Escort Group, Lieutenant Commander W.J.Moore recalled that

> At 10.30 a long range Focke-Wulf appeared in the clear blue sky, circling serenely around the convoy at . . . 5,000 feet. The Sunderland flying-boat which had joined us earlier had not the speed to do anything about it and neither the corvettes nor *Folkestone* possessed any A/A guns. Some of the ships in the convoy loosed off a few rounds, more of a token gesture than anything, but the plane kept well out of range of their weapons. After half an hour of this frustration the great bird swooped low over [a] . . . small steamer which was straggling a couple of miles astern of the main body, scoring an accurate hit with a bomb and setting her on fire − a nasty sight. After a second bombing run the enemy flew off to the southward . . .

That the FW200 Kondor could act with such impunity despite the presence of a Coastal Command Sunderland, and that the best anti-aircraft guns were fitted to the merchant vessels in convoy, are facts which speak for themselves. Those at the Admiralty responsible for high policy were only too well aware of them, and they were the basis of Pound's plea for more capable, radar-equipped aircraft.

It was while this distracting furore was raging that poor Pound made his fatal decision over the Russia-bound Convoy PQ17. To what extent it affected him must remain conjectural, but his order to scatter PQ17 had wide consequences, not least among his War Cabinet colleagues, whose perceptions of the Royal Navy's competence they undeniably influenced. In a Royal Navy operation which for the first time included major United States warships under British operational command, Convoy PQ17 was to all appearances abandoned by its ocean escort. Pound anticipated an attack by a heavy squadron centred on the new and formidable German battleship *Tirpitz*, but his personal decision to withdraw the escort and a covering force of cruisers to meet the threat was based upon faulty intelligence and a misappreciation of the actual situation. The threat never materialised, and the result of Pound's decision was the destruction of the greater part of the convoy by U-boats and aircraft whose crews could scarcely believe their good fortune.

Sadly, its effects went far beyond the loss of men, ships and cargoes: they were felt by the Royal Navy, whose sense of having let down their merchant charges was profound; by the Americans, who viewed the affair as proof of the Royal Navy's incompetence and degeneration; by the Chiefs of Staff in London, who saw it as evidence of Pound's failing powers; and by Churchill, who had travelled from Washington to Moscow and was dining with Stalin when the news arrived. He suffered the mortification of being constrained to submit to Stalin's taunting that the Royal Navy did not know how to fight.

Finally but not least among the effects of this notorious blunder was that upon the morale of the Merchant Navy, whose faith in the ability of the Royal Navy to protect it was already shaky, and for whom such a whole-sale sacrifice of British, American, Russian and other nations' merchant seamen seemed to represent an equally wholesale belittling of their own efforts and sacrifice. The patronising attempt made to influence the minds of survivors when they were finally brought home was a lasting humilia-tion. When the majority of these men arrived in Glasgow in the ships of westbound Convoy QP14, many of them still in oily clothes, they were not allowed to go home immediately but were herded into St Andrew's Hall and addressed by Philip Noel-Baker, Labour MP for Derby and Parliamentary Secretary to the Ministry of War Transport responsible for the welfare of merchant seafarers and Llewellin's successor at the MoWT. 'We know what the convoy cost us,' he tactlessly informed the assembled weary seamen. 'But I want to tell you that . . . it was well worth it.' This crass, stupid and insen-sitive platitude was greeted by a howl of derision.

Sir John Tovey, aware of the damaging impact of Pound's error, to his credit did rather better. When the American cruiser *Wichita* arrived back at Scapa Flow he boarded her and addressed to her ship's company a personal apology for the circumstances which had led to the deaths of so many American *merchant* seamen.[11]

At the time, such were the tonnage losses on the American coast that those attributable directly to the mismanagement of PQ17 did not stand out from the statistical morass.[12] With Stalin's unjust sneer at the Royal Navy's pusillanimity ringing in his ears, Churchill returned to London to solve the riddle with which the Chiefs of Staff confronted him. On 21 July he decided in favour of the case made by Portal and Harris over that made by Pound, now so discredited, and his fractious admirals. Bomber Command was to be *increased* from 32 to 50 squadrons and, to add insult to injury, two of them were to be *withdrawn* from Coastal Command. On 25 July, three weeks after the scattering of PQ17, when losses in the Atlantic had grown appallingly, Joubert de la Ferté sent another cutting memorandum to Pound: 'The immense quantities of material and valuable lives lost in the sinkings are quite irreplaceable.'

The seemingly endless broadsides of this fruitless squabble thundered on, distracting Pound from his operational duties. What is beyond all debate is that between the Scylla of Fleet Admiral Ernest King's failure to implement convoy on his homeland's coast in the first weeks of 1942, and the Charybdis of Churchill's bellicose determination to strike retaliatory blows at the heartland of the German Reich, merchant ships, their cargoes and crews were destroyed by a gleeful enemy. Even with the wisdom of hindsight, one cannot escape the conclusion that this was a wanton sacrifice.

16

'All who were ever found'

Maimoa

IN THE FIRST weeks of PAUKENSCHLAG five U-boats sank numerous ships. Off Nova Scotia Bleichrodt's *U-109* despatched the British ships *Thirlby* and *Tacoma Star* and the tanker *Montrolite*. Loss of life from the last two was heavy, amounting to all hands in the case of the Blue Star liner, which had already been severely damaged in the blitz on Liverpool. Bleichrodt had been refuelled by *U-130* and on his way back to L'Orient he engaged the Greek tramp *Halcyon*, shelling her heavily before the Dutch-built former cargo-liner sank. Folkers's *U-125* sank the American freighter *West Ivis* off Cape Hatteras with the loss of all hands, and Korvettenkapitän E. Kals, having escaped an aerial depth-charge attack by the RCAF off Cape Breton Island on 12 January, worked his way south sinking the Norwegian cargo-ships *Frisco* and *Alexandra Höegh* and the tanker *Varanger*, the Panamanians *Friar Rock* and *Olympic*, and the American tanker *Francis S. Powell*.

The second wave of Type VII submarines deployed by Dönitz in the waters off Newfoundland suffered just like their prey from the bad weather prevailing over the extreme northern latitudes of the North Atlantic, and Dönitz allowed them to move their operations southwards as fuel and opportunity offered. Recalling the period, *U-333*'s commander Peter Cremer wrote: 'North Atlantic winter! In such weather waging war stops of its own accord because everyone has enough on his hands without it – even when we unexpectedly sighted a tanker about 3,000 metres away. I tried to keep contact . . . it being impossible to attack straight away because of the high seas and colossal swell. Wind Force 10. At one moment the tanker was on a mountainous wave, the next she had disappeared into the valley. Then I lost sight of her altogether. Snowfall and visibility between 1,000 and 100 metres.'[1]

Aboard the targets hunted by Cremer and his colleagues it was little better. 'In three days of pitching into a head sea and swell we went forward less than one hundred miles,' wrote Second Mate Fyrth of the steam-tramp *Baxtergate*, deep-laden with a full cargo of steel billets. The ship was ill-found and the crew had complained about the standard of the lifesaving equipment. The master, 'a fine seaman, but in all other respects a most miserable bastard', had not wished to cross his owners and the ship sailed in poor but not untypical condition. As they headed east in convoy with *Baxtergate* leading the outer port column, Fyrth was on watch when, quite suddenly,

I thought I was in a dream! Everything familiar ahead had disappeared! There were no ships, no horizon, no scudding clouds. Instead there was a huge wall of green, far higher than the thirty-five-foot height of the bridge. Looking up to the top of the wall there was a breaking mass of white water towering above me with spume blown away by the wind . . . I dashed back into the wheelhouse.

'Get down flat on the deck!' I shouted to the apprentice [on the wheel], and we both lay on the deck as the wave hit the bridge. I went out [onto the bridge wing] in time to see the last of our lifeboats smashed to pieces. There was some broken woodwork on the port side of the bridge . . . but no windows had broken. I waded through water pouring down the ladders and looked over . . . at the foredeck. One of the life-rafts had been washed out of the rigging and was swilling about in the water on the deck. Then I looked at No. 1 Hatch.

Things could have been worse, but not much . . . In one corner the [hatch]boards had been displaced . . . and the tarpaulins were badly torn. We must have taken a good deal of water and when the next sea hit us we were going to take a lot more . . .

The galley had been flooded and water had entered the engine room by way of the skylight on the boat deck. The master was missing, and one of the DEMS gunners had injured his leg after being washed along the deck.

Right aft there was one of the life-rafts from the mainmast rigging, together with some wreckage from the smashed lifeboats. I looked underneath and saw a horribly mangled mass of flesh. I had found the Captain.

The Old Man had been in the accommodation alleyway through the engineers' quarters when the sea hit us . . . Bits of clothing confirmed what had happened.

On the bridge the mate hove the ship to and 'very slowly the rest of the convoy moved away . . .'

Having moved the master's remains into the saloon, the mate decided to send out a plain-language distress message. This was heard by another tramp in a similar predicament, and loaded with iron ore. The SOS had another, quite unforeseen consequence, for

> when the news reached the owners they immediately stopped our allotment notes, that is the proportion of pay sent directly each month to wives and relatives. Even after more than forty years this is a piece of meanness I find hard to forgive. The money was only paid the month after it had been earned and in fact should have been paid the day after we were in distress. It would eventually have to have been dispensed, but I suppose the owners thought they would have the benefit . . . for some months . . . As it was . . . our relatives thought we were lost at sea.

The *Baxtergate* shipped green seas over her bows for five days. 'Everybody fell back into routine tasks to stop them from thinking that perhaps the end result would be futile. The end of the gale was most spectacular. The howling wind, the high seas, and the flying spray simply went roaring away to the south-west horizon, and we were left with a heavy swell and a light breeze blowing from southwards. With the other damaged ship we decided to make for Iceland and a corvette from the convoy came back to escort us.' In Iceland an inquest was held, at which it was concluded that the master's death was accidental, 'with a rider that as the convoy was deliberately . . . taken through the storm to evade the enemy, it should be considered death through enemy action', thus enhancing his widow's pension.

Eventually the *Baxtergate* reached home. In addition to the loss of her master, two of her company had mental breakdowns 'so complete that they would never go to sea again'. But she had 'brought ten thousand tons of steel for the war effort across the Western Ocean in mid winter . . .' Soon afterwards, Fyrth concludes, 'this company and several other small lines were put under the more direct control of the Ministry of War Transport . . . it was a sort of victory.'[2]

Dönitz's decision to move his submarines south came in the light of such reports as Cremer's. Under Kapitänleutnant W. Schulte, *U-582* also encountered savage cold, high winds and heavy seas, snow squalls and frequent fogs on the Grand Bank off Newfoundland. Schulte's 'bag' was one ship, the British tanker *Refast*, a veteran of the First World War which had started life as the American *Gulflight* and enjoyed the distinction of having been the first American ship to be attacked by a German submarine before the United States declared war in 1917.

Another U-boat, *U-701* (Degen), lost her second watch officer overboard on passage. Some, such as *U-87*, struck lucky on passage, encountering independents, or stragglers from ON and ONS convoys. *U-87* sank the *Cardita* outward bound, then the Norwegian tanker *Nyholt* off Newfoundland after she had crossed in ON52. Degen also encountered a lone ship, the Hogarth tramp *Baron Erskine*, Captain G.S. Cumming, which had straggled from SC62. Loaded with a full cargo of phosphates from Tampa, Florida for Liverpool, she went down with all hands. But that was the extent of his success. Kapitänleutnant F. Praetorius in *U-135*, equally ill-rewarded, had reached Cape Race before locating a target, the Belgian ship *Gandia* which had straggled from ON54, while *U-84* and *U-86* had no success at all and *U-203* sank only four small vessels.

Several, however, succeeded in justifying their long passage by sinking or damaging two or three merchantmen. Kapitänleutnant J. Oestermann in *U-754* torpedoed two Greek ships, the *Mount Kitheron*, from which twelve out of 36 men lost their lives, and the *Icarion*, which lost a third of her crew of 29; and two Norwegian vessels, the *Belize* and the *William Hansen*. Half the crew of the latter survived, but all hands were lost with the former, only a water-logged lifeboat being found by the Canadian corvette *Spikenard*. Korvettenkapitän K. Thurmann torpedoed the ballasted British tanker *Diala* off St John's while she was heading south from the dispersal of Convoy ON52 and completed his patrol by sinking the Norwegian tanker *Inneröy* off Sable Island on 22 January. Then, after a patrol off Norway, *U-553* returned to the Newfoundland area on 3 May. After a number of encounters with Canadian forces during which Thurmann succeeded in penetrating the St Lawrence River, he sank the British cargo ship *Nicoya* and the Dutchman *Leto* within the estuary. On his way home, off Cape Sable on 2 June he sank the British motor-vessel *Matawin*, one of Elder, Dempster's cargo-liners on government service. She bore 7,000 tons of military stores and a handful of United States army personnel, bound from New York to Alexandria. All were rescued by a Norwegian freighter and an American Coast Guard cutter. Thurmann was now desperately short of provisions, and on the following day he discovered an empty, abandoned lifeboat, from which he helped himself to some emergency rations. He made a final attempt to locate a reported HX convoy, but was sighted by an American flying-boat which depth-charged him and drove him off.

One or two other U-boats attacked trans-Atlantic convoys directly as they approached the Newfoundland coast from the sea. Oberleutnant zur

See L. Forster's *U-654* had had an unsuccessful patrol, but on returning met and attacked Convoy ONS61 about 680 miles east of Cape Race. Forster fired a salvo of torpedoes and succeeded in so severely damaging the Free French corvette *Alysse* that although there was a struggle to save her by towing, she foundered on 10 February. At the same time Oberleutnant E. Greger in *U-85* had also attacked ONS61, but achieved no success until the evening of the 9th when he torpedoed the *Empire Fusilier*. A captured Italian ship, she was in ballast, and nine men were lost with her.

Greger left for his second war patrol on 21 March, and on 10 April off Cape Hatteras is thought to have sunk the Norwegian *Chr Knudsen* before proceeding to operate in shallow water off Roanoke Island, where on the night of 13/14 April *U-85* lay in ambush, awaiting passing shipping.

As she was on her way south to take up an anti-submarine patrol, the USS *Roper*'s recently-fitted British-built Type 286 radar revealed the echo of a small target ahead. It could have been a fishing boat, except that the sonar operators next reported the noise of racing screws. *Roper*'s captain, Lieutenant Commander H.W. Howe, turned *Roper*, increased her speed, and began to run down the bearing. Turning away, Greger did likewise in an attempt to outrun his pursuer since he was unable to submerge in a bare 100 feet of water, frequently altering course, and firing a torpedo from his stern tube. Howe clung on to the radar target and held his hand until he was close upon the echo, whereupon he turned his searchlights on, to see *U-85*'s conning tower a dull gleam in the night. The Americans opened fire with the *Roper*'s 3-inch forward gun and her machine-guns, securing a direct hit. It is thought that Greger ordered *U-85* to be scuttled; she was certainly settling as *Roper* raced onwards and Howe's men continued to fire, strafing the U-boat's casing as it filled with men spilling out of the conning tower. As *Roper* passed through the German seamen in the water Howe's depth-charge crews went into action, and as she turned and repeated her run over the position of the U-boat, 11 depth-charges exploded among Greger's wretched crew, who cried out to be saved. None were. Greger and 16 men went down in their steel coffin and 29 bodies were recovered but two, too fearfully mangled to warrant retrieval, were left to the gulls. Greger's *U-85* was the first U-boat to fall victim to the United States Navy.

In addition to the Newfoundland area, Dönitz had also made a direct assault on the trade routes of America's Eastern Sea Frontier, initially sending out five of the longer-ranged Type IX U-boats, *U-103*, *U-106*, *U-107*, *U-108* and *U-126*. First to arrive had been *U-103*, now under Kapitänleutnant W. Winter, who off the Delaware River on 2 January had sunk the American tanker *W.L. Steed*. It was midday, with a cold north-westerly wind kicking up a rough sea, and the ship began to settle forward as fire consumed her cargo of South American crude oil. The boats had been lowered and had worked clear of the tanker when *U-103* surfaced and began to shell her. A little later she exploded and sank. Although all four boats escaped, by the time No. 2 Boat was picked up by the British tramp *Hartlepool*, only the chief and second mates remained of the 15 men originally in her. The chief mate died of hypothermia in hospital in Halifax. Two of the five men in No. 3 Boat survived, rescued by HMCS *Alcantara*, and No. 4 Boat was sighted by the British steamer *Raby Castle* ten days later, by which time only the second engineer was still living, the other 13 having succumbed to exposure; sadly, he did not live to be landed and was buried at sea. No. 1 Boat, with Captain H.G. McAvenia and three others aboard, was never seen again. While these non-combatant Americans were dying of cold, Kapitänleutnant Winter was busy moving south and sinking more vessels, the Panamanian *San Gil* on the 4th and then two more American tankers, one on the 4th and one on the 5th, both belonging to the Mobil Oil Corporation.

The *India Arrow* was sunk on the 4th; at about 19.00 a torpedo strike sent a curtain of fierce flames into the air as the cargo of diesel took fire, burning the after lifeboats. As the forward bulkhead ruptured, the engine room flooded and the ship's after section rapidly filled, and burning oil poured out over the surface of the sea. Although the tanker sank in ten minutes, Winter felt it imperative to surface and shell her forward part, endangering those still trying to escape. The midships boats in davits on the bridge superstructure were lowered, but No. 2, on the port side, was fouled as the *India Arrow* sank. Dragged down with the ship, all but two of the 20 men in the lifeboat were drowned.

No. 1 Boat was in a similar position but was successfully disentangled, and Captain C.S. Johnson and 11 of his crew managed to hoist sail and get away. The following day they twice signalled approaching ships but these, suspicious that what they were seeing might be a ruse by a German submarine, turned away. Fortunately, Johnson and his handful of survivors were eventually picked up and brought ashore by two New Jersey fishermen out in a small boat.

The *China Arrow* was torpedoed on the morning of the 5th, appropriately enough off the Winter Quarter lightvessel. Bound to New York with a cargo of fuel oil loaded at Beaumont, Texas, she was struck by two torpedoes which blew the deck off three tanks and set their contents ablaze. The chief engineer managed to fight his way aft past the flames roaring upwards from the blazing tanks and activate the ship's steam smothering apparatus. Meanwhile, having given orders for the boats to be lowered, Captain P.H. Browne and his radio operator were transmitting a distress message when

Winter surfaced and began shelling the ship. Incredibly, three boats got away with all hands. The weather being moderate, Browne lashed them together to avoid separation and they were all rescued by the USCG cutter *Nike*.

Kapitänleutnant H. Rasch, now in command of *U-106*, began his predations on 24 January with the sinking of the *Empire Wildebeeste* off New York, then moved slowly south, torpedoing the British Harrison liner *Traveller* two days later, followed by the American tanker *Rochester*, the Swedish ship *Amerikaland* off Cape Hatteras and the New Zealand Shipping Company's *Opawa* off Bermuda on 6 February. With a cargo containing 600 tons of explosives, the *Traveller* was lost with all hands: the *Amerikaland* lost 29 of her 40-man crew; and the *Opawa* suffered the loss of 55 men, although Captain W.G. Evans and 14 men were rescued by a Dutch freighter, the *Hercules*.

The *Opawa* was a large ship, built in 1931 and with a service speed of 16 knots. She had been zig-zagging in accordance with Admiralty orders and was at the point of altering course when Rasch's torpedo hit her. She had loaded 4,000 tons of copper and 2,000 tons of sugar in Australia before completing her loading in New Zealand, where she had picked up a further 300 tons of butter, 262,120 lamb and sheep carcases and 1,533 bales of prime wool. Evans was thus responsible for an exceedingly valuable cargo and *Opawa* was laden to her marks when she departed Port Lyttleton. She passed through the Panama Canal and was bound for Halifax, where had· all gone well she would have picked up a fast HX convoy.

In the event, at 06.00 on 6 February, with 430 miles to run before reaching Bedford Basin, she took a torpedo in the fuel tanks forward of the engine room. Her engines were stopped, her steering gear jammed and her wireless transmitter shattered, all internal systems failed. With several fires burning, the *Opawa* described a half-circle and then lay stopped, down by the head. Those on the control platform in the lower engine room died while others, working higher, escaped to join the rest of the ship's company mustering on the boat deck. As the bow slowly sank and the ship listed and then swung upright again, the boats were all launched and the living were evacuated. About 08.00 Evans decided to put back to the ship 'to see if we could send another distress message on the emergency [wireless] set, salvage a set of navigational tables and a Nautical Almanac and, perhaps, get some warm clothing for the men, some of whom were very scantily clad. When we attempted to approach the ship, however, the U-boat surfaced and started firing shells into her . . . He had to fire between sixty and seventy rounds . . . before she showed signs of sinking. The *Opawa* was well ablaze amidships. The U-boat then ceased fire and passed ahead of the ship as if to read her name. It then moved off in a southerly direction without trying to contact the lifeboats. Five minutes later, the *Opawa* turned slowly on to her port side and sank quietly, bows first.'

Evans decided to head south, for the warmth of Bermuda. 'We were 400 miles from land and it was bound to be cold up north . . . and most of the men had few clothes . . . We all shaped course south-south-west. The wind veered during the afternoon and the best that could be made was west-south-west. There was heavy rain all day and everybody was soaked to the skin.' In the variable conditions and heavy sea they made little progress in the coming hours. It was the familiar story: the boats lost contact, and next morning Evans's was alone. In it he had the fourth officer, the first radio officer, two apprentices, the chief, fifth and ninth engineers, the chief electrician, two able seamen, one ordinary seaman, one naval gunner, an assistant steward, and the steward's boy.

Having reefed sail, they found they could make good a course of south-east, but at noon the wind shifted so they decided to head west and try to intercept a ship steaming north. By sunset the wind had forced them to take another reef. By 03.00 the next morning they were in a full gale, and had been pooped. All attempts to heave-to failed as the sea-anchor could not be made to sink and drag the boat's bow round head to sea. 'We then lashed a galvanised bucket to a fifty-foot rope and put that over the bows. It worked like magic . . . I am convinced this bucket saved the boat . . .' The exhausted men tried to grab some rest despite the appalling rolling. Next day the gale abated but a high sea continued to run until the following afternoon, when it blew up again and heavy rain fell. 'The men began to complain of swollen feet and knees . . .' Evans had found that to start with all hands lacked any appetite, 'but on the second day I had to give a little [food and water] to a few of the men. On the third day everybody had a drink and some food and by the fourth day everybody was craving . . . I allowed each man two dippers of water each measuring half a pint and on this allowance we had enough water to last twenty-five days. Many of the men could not eat the food after the fourth day and during this day our hands, feet and knees became very painful. We dried them and rubbed them with oil supplied, but I personally did not think the oil did any good. Some of the men suffered great pain in their feet which became swollen to nearly double their normal size.'

Attempts were made to make way, and the following afternoon they saw a ship and burned flares, but to no avail. Towards sunset, however, the *Hercules* hove in sight. During the seven days they had been in the boat they had been continuously wet. Evans was later appointed OBE and Fourth Officer R.C. Downie MBE, and apprentice P. Luard was awarded the BEM, with Able Seamen Fisher and Levine earning official commendations for good service. It is clear from these acknowledgements that considerable seaman-ship skills had been necessary to save the boat. Of the *Opawa*'s other boats, no trace was ever found. Clearly they had not had the luck or the skill to survive the onslaught of successive strong gales or the fearful tumbling of breaking seas.

In a reverse progress to that of *U-106*, *U-107* had worked her way north under Kapitänleutnant H. Gelhaus, who had replaced Dönitz's son-in-law Hessler. On 31 January, off Bermuda, Gelhaus sank the British tanker *San Arcadio*, Captain W.F. Flynn, with heavy loss of life, then on 6 February he torpedoed the American freighter *Major Wheeler*, which was lost with all hands and a full cargo of Puerto Rican sugar bound for Philadelphia. Finally Gelhaus reached Cape Sable, where on the 21st he torpedoed and damaged the Norwegian motor-tanker *Egda*. Meanwhile Korevettenkapitän Scholtz in *U-108* was at work off Cape Hatteras, sending the British *Ocean Venture* to the sea-bed with a cargo of foodstuffs and aircraft on 8 February. In the next three days he sank two Norwegian ships, the *Tolosa* and the *Blink*, both with heavy loss of life. Off Bermuda he sank a Panamanian-flagged ship, the *Ramapo*, and returning by way of Sable Island he sank the British Royal Mail liner *Somme* on the evening of the 18th. The weather was very bad and had boats been launched, their chances of survival would have been slim. An elderly ship, the *Somme*, loaded with general cargo, could only make 10.5 knots, and had been included in Convoy ONS62, from which she had dispersed on her way to Bermuda. Captain C.C. Prosser and all 47 of his crew were killed.

The last of the long-ranged U-boats deployed in the opening rounds of Operation PAUKENSCHLAG was Bauer's *U-126*. He was sent further south, to open the offensive along America's southern littoral and operate off the Greater Antilles. Here, on 2 March, he began by sinking the Norwegian ship *Gunny*, followed by the American ships *Mariana, Barbara, Cardonia, Texan* and *Olga*, and also damaging the *Halo* and *Colabee*; the *Halo* was afterwards sunk by *U-506* on 20 April and the *Colabee* beached and eventually salvaged. Bauer also struck two Panamanian-registered vessels, sinking the *Hanseat* and damaging the tanker *Esso Bolivar*.

So much for the opening tattoos of 'Drumbeat'. That they affected ships convoyed safely across the Atlantic and then left to their own devices as well as hitting ships coming north to join convoys at Halifax was further evidence of the American navy's neglect of the first principles of trade protection.

As for the trans-Atlantic convoys, despite the weather and the diversion of German submarines to the exposed eastern coast of America, they had not been running entirely unscathed. Convoy ON55 had lost the Norwegian steamer *Ringstad* and most of her crew to Cremer's *U-333* as she made heavy weather across the Atlantic in the first days of the new year. This U-boat, of which there is more to relate, had also sunk a straggler from SC63. With a full cargo of wheat, the *Caledonian Monarch* had fallen behind the convoy, which was later scattered in heavy weather. She was torpedoed south of Iceland on 18 January and went down with all hands in a gale. Reflecting on his kill, Cremer smugly admitted that 'with the damage inflicted I could see that the U-boat had already almost paid for itself'.

By 22 January, the day Thurmann sank the *Inneröy* off Sable Island, Cremer was off Cape Race, where he torpedoed the Greek tramp steamer *Vassilios A. Polemis* which had been part of Convoy ON53. 'The ship broke in two . . . the funnel tipped over onto the bridge and in ten minutes the Greek had disappeared.' Cremer surfaced and 'for the first time', seeing the survivors, he 'experienced the misery of shipwrecked crews. In one of the boats a man with burns lay across a thwart.' To his credit, Cremer passed bandages, burn dressings, biscuits and cigarettes to the men in the boats. 'After we had seen them step the mast and set sail we gave them a course for Halifax – about 250 nautical miles.' Of her crew of 33, 12 were rescued by their fellow-countrymen aboard the *Leonidas N. Kondylis* and landed at Halifax.

Convoy HX168 was west of Rockall on 11 January when it found an unwelcome visitor in its midst. Lüth, having lost his way in *U-43*, surfaced in the middle of the convoy, then hurriedly submerged again and shadowed until he fell in with the Swedish steamer *Yngaren*, which he sank with the loss of all but two of her 40-man crew. Then, shortly after midnight on the 14th, off the Iceland coast, he encountered ON55 and promptly sank three ships, the Greek steamers *Cheop* and *Maro*, and the *Empire Surf*.

In addition to the *Refast* sunk by Schultze in *U-582* and mentioned earlier the convoy following, the slow ON56, lost two tankers, the British *Athelcrown* and the Norwegian *Leiesten*, to *U-82* (Rollmann) the day before he sank HMS *Belmont*, escorting the troop convoy NA2. Rollmann now headed for home, but on 6 February when north of the Azores he sighted the ships of the outward Convoy ON18. He began to shadow, but on the following day *U-82* was detected by the radar of HM Sloop *Rochester*, Commander C.B. Allen, who immediately attacked in company with the corvette *Tamarisk*, Lieutenant N.C. Dawson. Rollmann and his crew perished as *U-82* was pulverised by depth-charges.

In the first quarter of 1942 it looked as though Topp was aspiring to Kretschmer's mantle. His Type VIIC *U-552*, had been part of the second wave of U-boats sent to Newfoundland and had sunk the British cargo ship *Dayrose* and the American *Frances Salman* in January, then returned to France before making her next crossing as part of the fourth beat of Dönitz's drum in early March. Topp torpedoed but did not sink the Dutch tanker *Ocana*, whereupon her master retaliated and attempted to ram *U-552*. Topp eventually set her on fire, compelling a handful of the courageous Dutch, eight out of 57, to abandon her. She burnt out and survived as a derelict until mid April, when the Canadian minesweeper *Burlington* sank her.

Off Chincoteague Inlet in Virginia, late on the evening of 3 April, *U-552* attacked the coal-laden American coaster *David H. Atwater*. Under cover of darkness but in very shallow water Topp engaged this small vessel with his deck-gun, raking her with machine-gun fire as the crew tried to get away in their boats. Observing distant gunfire, the United States Coast Guard Cutter *Legare* raced to the spot, only to find the mast trucks of the *David H. Atwater* breaking the surface of the sea. Of her 26 men, all that remained were three bodies and three survivors. One of her two lifeboats was riddled with machine-gun holes.[3]

Topp went on to sink two tankers, the *Byron D. Benson* and the *British Splendour*. The former, an American vessel owned by the Tidewater Associated Oil Company, a subsidiary of Getty Oil, was attacked off North Carolina on the evening of 4 April. By this time some attempt was being made to provide convoy, for she was in company with another tanker, the *Gulf of Mexico*, and they were escorted by a mixed force consisting of the American naval destroyer *Hamilton*, the Coast Guard Cutter *Dionne* and the British A/S trawler *Norwich City*. She was full of Texas crude oil and her No. 7 Tank exploded in flames, destroying her bridge. This prevented her from being stopped and she followed a curve to starboard, spilling burning oil into the sea. Twenty-seven men managed to escape in the boats, but Captain J. McMillian, all three mates, the radio operator, a steward and two seamen in No. 2 Boat were consumed in the blaze.

The tanker *British Splendour* was also under escort, that of two Royal Navy A/S trawlers, *St Zeno* and *Hertfordshire*, but these did little good on 7 April when Topp struck again. Although they picked up Captain J. Hall and 40 of his men, a further 12 were missing as the cargo of 10,000 tons of benzene went up in a fire-ball.

Topp's tonnage total rocketed with his next targets, the Norwegian whale-factory ship *Lancing* and the American tankers *Atlas* and *Tamaulipas*. The difficulties confronting the crews abandoning these burning tankers were formidable, with the ships themselves on fire and blazing oil spreading out over the sea. His men found it difficult to breathe as they strove to pull their lifeboats through just such an inferno so Captain H. Gray of the *Atlas* ordered them to dive overboard and try to duck and swim through the slick with the hope of finding breathable air between the patches of flaming oil. Remarkably, several did so, and survived. Off Cape Lookout in North Carolina the *Tamaulipas* was more fortunate when she was struck in the first minutes of 10 April. Although her back was broken by the exploding torpedo, all but two of her 37-man crew escaped, to be rescued by the A/S trawler *Norwich City*, again serving as coastal escort.

Cremer, having 'fulfilled' his 'quota' of three sinkings with that of the *Ringstad* out of ON55 on 24 January, set *U-333* on her homeward course. On the afternoon of the 31st the U-boat was west of the Bay of Biscay when a steamer was sighted and confirmed to be British. The mean of her zig-zag heading persuaded Cremer that she was making for the Irish coast; he decided to attack, but was uncertain of the outcome. Hearing the vessel transmitting a distress signal in English and frustrated by the onset of fog, Cremer eventually fired his last torpedo into what he thought to be a British vessel named *Brittany*. In fact she was a German blockade-runner called *Spreewald* on her way home from Dairen, in the Japanese puppet-state of Manchukuo, where she had been languishing for two years. Loaded with a valuable cargo of much-needed commodities including rubber, quinine and wolfram (tungsten), the *Spreewald* had made a rendezvous with the *Kulmerland*, one of the supply ships tending the Kriegsmarine's surface-raiders. From her she had taken aboard 300 British prisoners-of-war, victims of the *Kormoran*.

The day of her fatal encounter with *U-333*, the *Spreewald* was supposed to have met *U-575* for an escort across the Bay of Biscay and into the sanctuary of an Occupied French port. The commander of *U-575*, Kapitän-leutnant G. Heydemann, asserted that his submarine had been in the correct position, while the *Spreewald* was thought to have been miles distant from the rendezvous. She also failed to transmit the correct identification signal. Realising what had happened, Dönitz, Godt and their staff mustered nine U-boats, including Cremer's, and organised an intensive search, which went on until 4 February. At first only *U-105* had any success, picking up 24 Germans and 58 of the 300 British merchant seamen aboard the *Spreewald*, but by the 4th 'almost all those involved were saved'. Having ordered that no survivor must know that the *Spreewald* had been sunk by a German submarine, Dönitz charged Cremer with disobedience, damaging military property, and manslaughter. His son-in-law Hessler 'was able to lay the blame on the *Spreewald* for failing to report her position and thus disobeying orders', however, and thanks to him Cremer was acquitted. As for the British crews of *Kormoran*'s victims, they were transported to the prisoner-of-war camp at Milag Nord in northern Germany.

Even as the German submariners enjoyed their second 'Happy Time', numerous convoys were passing across the Atlantic with little intervention from the enemy. Indeed, the United States Navy's official historian goes so far as to say that 'so few submarines were contacted . . . that the merchant seamen became careless about making smoke and showing lights'. Commander R. W. Hungerford, senior officer of the American A5 Escort Group and commanding the USS *Bristol*, reported that smoke from Convoy HX179 'was frequently visible over 30 miles after the weather cleared on 17 March'.[4] This was yet another typical instance of a naval officer reporting upon merchant ship-management which he imperfectly understood, on a par with all the epithets about poor station-keeping and the whole gamut of naval opprobrium. Like their Royal Navy brethren before them, the officers of Uncle Sam's navy had now to learn not only that station-keeping was extremely difficult for a merchant ship never designed for such a thing, but that in the matter of making smoke, the age of the ship, the state of her boilers and the quality of her fuel had more to do with it than any 'carelessness' on the part of her firemen, whose interests scarcely lay in advertising their presence to the enemy. These apparently self-evident truths notwithstanding, their masters were constantly being urged not to make smoke, and as repeatedly adjured their chief engineers to do their best. That these men in their turn ruled a most turbulent work-force may be judged from the evidence of Apprentice R.M. Dunshea of Shaw, Savill & Albion's 8,011-ton steam cargo-liner *Maimoa*.

Built in 1920, the *Maimoa* was a coal-burner 'driven through the water by a great deal of hard manual labour on the part of the stoke-hold crowd . . . Each [fire]man [had] to feed his three furnaces with two tons of coal each four-hour watch, as well as slicing and raking the fires to ensure good consumption. At the beginning of each watch ash-pits had to be cleaned. A stokehold was a dirty and unpleasant place of work . . . the firemen and [coal-]trimmers were a rough lot . . . Each watch [was] accommodated in a single, badly ventilated room in the fo'c's'le . . . At sea with a seven-day week they had no diversions. In port they usually sought solace in dockland hostelries.' In such establishments 'many seafarers fell foul of the ladies . . . [t]he effects manifesting themselves a few weeks [later].' Returning to their ship, these men 'proclaimed in four letter words their refusal to serve England's cause'. Yet they did, despite conditions that were appalling enough in peace time and which in war put them in a submerged 'front-line' that, being out of sight, has been put out of mind. In the event of their ship taking a torpedo amidships it was those in the boiler and engine rooms who were most likely to perish. Moreover, if they escaped drowning, being burned by hot coals or oil fuel or scalded by steam, they were likely to arrive on deck in the cold darkness of an Atlantic night dressed only in the singlet and trousers suitable to their usual place of work.[5]

It is quite clear from the number and classes of ships that became stragglers, many of which were not the rust-bucket tramp-ships of popular imagination but vessels belonging to liner and oil companies with high operating standards, that something other than incompetence and 'carelessness' was at work. The truth was that the ships, many of them already ageing in 1939, were suffering from lack of maintenance, and in the exacting environment of the North Atlantic under wartime conditions were simply wearing out.

So for a few weeks, although merchant ships continued to be lost if they straggled, few succumbed if they managed to cling on to their stations in a convoy.[6] The same could not be said of the escorts, for in addition to the loss of the Free French corvette *Alysse*, the Canadians had lost the *Spikenard*, senior escort of Convoy SC67, and the British the *Arbutus*. The latter had been the only casualty from Convoy ONS63, sunk some three hundred miles west of Rockall on 4 February by Kapitänleutnant H. Zetzsche in U-591. Six days later Zetzsche was on weather-reporting duties when he saw SC67. Calling in U-136 to assist, he began to stalk the convoy.

SC67 had left Canadian waters in thick fog and on the evening of the 10th was south of Iceland. The night was pitch dark, a gale was blowing and a heavy sea was running when on the port flank of the convoy the corvette *Chilliwack* gained a sonar contact: Lieutenant L.F. Focall attacked. The other escorts suddenly saw what they thought was a single explosion in the convoy.

On the starboard wing the leading escort, HMCS *Spikenard*, Lieutenant Commander H.G. Shadforth, was zig-zagging when the Norwegian cargo ship *Heina*, loaded with general cargo, was hit by Zetzsche's torpedo. From the rear of the convoy the corvette *Dauphin* increased speed and moved to assist the *Heina*'s people, becoming engrossed in this task for the next two hours. Meanwhile the escort immediately astern of *Spikenard*, HMCS *Louisburg*, having a moment before the *Heina* was hit spotted a torpedo track, spent the next ninety-odd minutes attacking a contact. From the port quarter of the convoy the corvette *Shediac* arrived close to *Dauphin*, when she was ordered by Lieutenant MacNeil to search for a possible second victim. The other escort, the corvette *Lethbridge*, remained on station on the convoy's port flank. Attempts made to contact *Spikenard* by short-range radio telephone produced no responses, which was put down at the time to the frequent failures experienced with this VHF equipment. While all the escorts were preoccupied no further importance was attached to this circumstance, and it was not until daylight revealed no sign of the senior officer's ship that doubts about *Spikenard*'s whereabouts began to trouble Shadforth's colleagues. Even then, it was thought 'that she might be somewhere over the horizon looking for the British local escort which was expected'.

About 11.00 the British escort arrived without *Spikenard*, and the corvette HMS *Gentian* was despatched to search to the west along the convoy's route. 'After several hours of hunting, *Gentian* came upon a Carley float with eight survivors of *Spikenard*'s crew: all who were ever found.'[7]

The Canadian corvette had been hit by a torpedo from *U-136*, Kapitänleutnant H. Zimmermann, which had destroyed the bridge and much of her starboard forecastle and ignited 'several drums of petrol stowed beside the mast'. The fierce flames from these had made an impenetrable wall of fire, barring the path of the men trying to escape from the inferno below as the corvette began to dive. As she sank her whistle sent a long piercing shriek into the night and then, as her hull began its descent into the abyss, either a boiler or a fused depth-charge exploded, killing or maiming men in the sea above her. Only minutes before *Dauphin* approached the oil-soaked survivors of the *Heina*, all of whom she picked up, a short distance away in the howling darkness *Spikenard* had foundered.

It was a black moment for the Royal Canadian Navy, attracting further adverse comment upon its abilities and reinforcing the jibe that its units were only fit for picking up survivors. That they had failed to achieve even this in *Spikenard*'s case only rubbed salt into open wounds. The tragedy arose from the fact that the Canadian navy was being compelled by circumstances to expand too rapidly, forced to recruit farm-boys more used to the wide spaces of the prairies than the turbulent wastes of the ocean, who after perhaps literally only a few days of working-up into a wartime ship's company had to confront a practised enemy.

Zimmermann went on sink the *Empire Comet*, a new X-Type standard tramp built under the emergency war programme by the MoWT and placed under the management of Dodd, Thompson's Scottish Steamship Company. She had joined Convoy HX174 after making the passage from Bombay with a mixed cargo including manganese ore, groundnuts, linseed and the all-important tea. Having straggled, she was torpedoed on 17 February with the loss of Captain H.R. Willis and all hands. Another escort lost at this time, though in entirely different circumstances, was the American Coast Guard Cutter *Alexander Hamilton*, sunk by Kapitänleutnant E. Vogelsang in *U-132*. Vogelsang had aimed his torpedoes at the broken-down American transport *Yukon* as she was being patiently dragged towards Iceland by the cutter, but they missed and hit the towing vessel instead. The U-boat was counter-attacked by the USS *Stack*, and although Lieutenant Commander I. Olch failed to destroy *U-132*, he inflicted enough damage to terminate Vogelsang's crowing and send him back to La Pallice.

Convoy HX174 also lost one vessel, the Norwegian steamship *Anderson*, which went ashore and was wrecked on Eastern Head, Newfoundland, and its predecessor HX173 lost the Russian freighter *Divinoles* after a collision with the Norwegian tramp *Havprins*. This convoy was also attacked by Bigalk in *U-751* on 2 February, shortly after it left Halifax. He damaged but did not sink the Dutch motor-tanker *Corilla* but his torpedoes drew the attention of an escort and shore-based aircraft which drove him off. He did not go far, however, for on the 4th he lay off Hunt's Point where he torpedoed the *Silveray*, which was on her way south, having just left Convoy ON55 as it dispersed off Halifax. Most of the *Silveray*'s company were quickly recovered by a USCG cutter and a fishing boat. Once again Bigalk's audacity provoked an intensive search and once again he escaped, to sink the *Empire Sun*, a CAM-ship laden with 9,000 tons of grain and due to join a convoy at Halifax the next day. Having now expended all his torpedoes Bigalk next fought a short gun-duel off Sambro Light with an unidentified vessel, but since the weather was bad he did not press the attack, heading instead for St-Nazaire. The next deployment of *U-751* was further south. Refuelling from a U-tanker, Bigalk attacked and sank the American fruit-carrier *Nicarao* off the Bahamas, breaking her back so that she sank in minutes and most of her crew had to jump for their lives. Moving into the Caribbean, his last success was the freighter *Isabella*, torpedoed and shelled off Navassa Island, Haiti at 04.40 on 19 May. Bigalk returned to St-Nazaire before sailing again on 14 July for *U-751*'s seventh war patrol. It was to be her last. Crossing the Bay of Biscay she was spotted to the north-west of Cape Finisterre and attacked by two British aircraft, a Lancaster bomber from No. 61 Squadron, Flight Lieutenant P.R. Casement, and a Whitley medium bomber from No. 502 Squadron. Under Admiralty pressure both aircraft were on temporary loan to Coastal Command, and it was Casement's first anti-submarine patrol. Dropping depth-charges the two aeroplanes destroyed the U-boat, killing all 47 men in her crew – and making a salient point as to the effectiveness of aircraft over this important transit area that was not lost on those who had co-opted their invaluable services.

At the end of January 1942 the British deployed their first ship-borne radio direction-finding set, aboard the sloop *Culver*. As part of the 40th Escort Group, *Culver* sailed in company with the homeward-bound Convoy SL98, leaving Freetown on 15 January. By the 31st SL98 was north of the Azores, where it was sighted by the lookouts aboard *U-105*. Bleichrodt had been outward-bound from L'Orient when earlier that day he had been ordered to the position of the sinking *Spreewald*. Having been the first U-boat to recover survivors – 82 Germans and their British prisoners – he had turned back towards the Breton coast to disencumber his submarine of his unwanted guests when the convoy was seen. Bleichrodt attacked and sank the *Culver*, stirring up a hornet's nest among the other sloops, *Londonderry, Lulworth, Landguard* and *Bideford*. They counter-attacked, and *U-105* was damaged, but avoided destruction. In unimaginably overcrowded conditions that must have been worse for the helpless British prisoners, Bleichrodt that night headed for home.

Three weeks later the radio direction-finder fitted aboard the rescue-ship *Toward*, Captain A.J. Knell, proved useful to the American A6 Escort Group attending Convoy ONS67, though not decisively so. The new long-range *U-155* was outward bound for the American coast on her first war patrol when she sighted the convoy about 600 miles ENE of Cape Race. Korvettenkapitän A. Piening transmitted the usual signal to Kerneval and this was intercepted aboard the *Toward* by her 'Huff-Duff' officer, Mr C.S.C. Nixon, at 17.30 on 21 February. Informed of this, the senior officer commanding the escort, Commander A.C. Murdagh aboard USS *Edison*, ordered the destroyer *Lea* to run down the bearing. Meanwhile the remaining escorts, the American destroyers *Nicholson* and *Bernadou* and the temporarily attached Canadian corvette *Algoma* went to action stations. The *Lea* was not equipped with radar and 'returned in less than an hour without a contact . . . what followed showed the unwisdom of making so brief an investigation'.

Meanwhile, on receipt of Piening's signal Kerneval had called in five U-boats, and these were on their way when after eight hours of quiet, at 03.05, there were sudden explosions within the perimeter of ONS67 as two vessels were hit by torpedoes fired from *U-155*. The first to be sunk was the ballasted British motor-tanker *Adellen* which went down with the loss of 36 men, though Captain J. Brown and 11 men escaped, being picked up by the *Algoma* and afterwards transferred to the *Toward*. The second ship hit was the small Norwegian steamer *Sama*. Laden with china clay, a commodity used in the armaments industry, she sank rapidly with half her crew, the survivors being rescued by the *Nicholson*.

During the day that followed Murdagh ordered two of his destroyers to sweep astern of the convoy to deter U-boats from following and working into a position to attack, but by the following night the German re-inforcements had arrived from other points of the compass. Of the five boats ordered to intercept the convoy, *U-158, U-558* and *U-587* were by then in contact, and they first struck at 00.30 on the 24th, making a second attack about 02.30 and finally breaking off the action at daylight. Four ships were lost despite the launching of snowflake rockets which, burning an illumi-nating powder above the merchant ships, enabled them to themselves engage any submarines observed on the surface inside the convoy's formation.

Fresh out from Helgoland, Kapitänleutnant E. Rostin was on his first war patrol in command of another new Type IXC U-boat, *U-158*, when he hit and damaged the 'Ocean'-type tanker *Empire Celt*. She was being managed on behalf of the MoWT by Sir James German.& Company of Cardiff, and in ballast. Rostin's strike left her badly damaged and settling in the water, with six men killed. The decision was made to abandon her and Captain E. McCready and a score of survivors were rescued. Meanwhile Rostin had attacked but failed to sink the British tanker *Diloma*, which survived the war. Kapitänleutnant G. Krech in *U-558* had better luck. Attacking first just after midnight, he began a day's work which saw five ships sent to the bottom. Three of them were tankers, two British, the *Inverarder* and the Shell motor-tanker *Anadara*, and the third a Norwegian, the *Finnanger*.

Although all hands escaped from the *Inverader*, the entire ship's company of the *Anadara* were lost as the U-boat shelled her after she had fallen astern of the convoy and failed to sink swiftly enough for her assailant. All the Norwegians aboard the *Finnanger* were also lost. Krech then torpedoed and damaged another Norwegian tanker, the *Eidanger*, but there was no loss of life as the escorts scurried round picking up the survivors. His strike at the British tramp *White Crest* with her full load of Welsh steam coal for Buenos Aires was a grim triumph, however. Captain G. Joures and his ship's company of 40 souls were murdered as their laden vessel drove under.

After daylight Convoy ONS67 ploughed on to the westward, leaving a trail of derelict wreckage astern. Then, shortly after noon, Nixon aboard *Toward* reported more U-boat radio traffic and again obtained a radio-bearing. Murdagh directed *Lea* and *Nicholson* to investigate and the two destroyers increased speed and turned back to the east. A little later, look-outs aboard the *Nicholson* spotted two U-boats about twenty miles astern of the convoy. Murdagh was rattled enough to seek permission from Washington to either disperse the convoy or execute a major alteration of course. It took more than *seven hours* for Washington to react, by which time it was dark, and almost too late. Fortunately, however, the convoy received permission to alter course rather than disperse, and swung away. As the escorts zig-zagged along the flanks of the thirty-odd ships still in company, *Edison* made a sonar contact and then spotted a surfaced U-boat just before it crash-dived. Murdagh made six depth-charge attacks which were not fatal to the U-boat but deterred her from a further approach. Returning to station, *Edison* sighted another surfaced submarine, but it too escaped. By now Murdagh's aggressive tactics were working, throwing off the convoy's pursuers or forcing them down and robbing them of their initiative. Far astern during the afternoon, while Murdagh waited for Washington's permission to alter the convoy's course, Krech had sunk the *Eidanger*.

The derelict *Empire Celt* drifted for a month before being sent to the bottom on 25 March, it is thought by Borcherdt in *U-587* as he made his way towards St-Nazaire. Three days later Borcherdt's lookouts spotted the fast troop convoy WS17, and his reporting signal was monitored by Huff-Duff. Within a short space of time *U-587* was under attack from four escorts, HMSs *Grove, Aldenham, Leamington* and *Volunteer*. There were no survivors, and the British were rightly convinced that in Huff-Duff they possessed a vital and decisive new weapon in their armoury.

Rostin went on to sink several vessels on the east coast of America, where it remained open season, but the lesson of ON67 had been learnt by the United States Navy. The loss of so many ships out of ONS67 had been a blow to their prestige, an experience too closely mirroring that of the British and Canadians. The prolonged delay in receiving permission to make a tactical course alteration was ridiculous and clearly hampered Murdagh, who on the evidence of his aggressive actions when left to himself was a competent senior officer. In the debriefing that followed common sense prevailed, and it was agreed by the Commander-in-Chief's staff that such decisions were best left to the man on the spot. The value of radio direction-finding and radar was a clear and unambiguous lesson, as was 'the urgent need of a definite doctrine for depth-charge attacks, and better training in following up underwater sound contacts'.

It was all basic stuff, and even for the Americans the war was months old. In ON67 alone it cost the lives of 123 Allied merchant seamen for them to learn these lessons.

The methods by which the Battle of the Atlantic was eventually won were in fact already in place, and being used, albeit imperfectly. Apart from the indisputable if erratic advantages of Ultra decrypts and the emerging perception of the importance of maritime air cover, there were solid and tactically useful weapons for those actually in charge of convoy escort at sea. Improvements in sonar technology and techniques, the latter the fruit of hard-won operational experience, along with the introduction of Huff-Duff radio direction-finding, were beginning to be seen as war-winning weapons. Other significant if incremental advantages were slowly accruing in the Allies' favour, not least that of the short-range VHF radio telephone which allowed the senior officer quick and unambiguous command and control of his escort force.

And there was radar. Although the principles and possibilities of radio detection of an object were understood by the mid 1930s and all the soon-to-be belligerent powers busied themselves developing a method of radio location, different emphases had placed different advantages in the hands of those powers. For example, German preoccupation with control of naval gunnery, though it had its proven usefulness, was in the long run less beneficial than the British concern with pure location, born out of a justifiable fear of aerial bombing, a threat taken very seriously after the Munich crisis.

In the event the successful development of what became known as radar – an acronym deriving from 'Radio Direction And Range' – hinged on the production of short-wave transmissions, to provide useful definition, and high-power emissions, to provide an equally useful operational range. While metric radar was quite possible, what was desirable was a shorter wave length of somewhere between 3 and 10 centimetres. Moreover, if equipment capable of operating on these shorter wave lengths could be produced in a small enough size by production-line methods, it could be fitted to small ships and even to aircraft. Such economies of scale in both the actual and metaphorical sense seemed at first to be a Grail beyond the reach of science. The Americans had made some progress with a 'Klystron' valve which by raising the frequency of the radio emission generated a wave of less than a metre, but it was incapable of dealing with the power needed to meet the requirement of useful range. Then in 1940 scientists at Birmingham University in Britain made the break-through with the 'Magnetron', a 'cavity resonator' which transmitted a high enough frequency to produce the required short wave at a power output which suddenly made all things possible. Early Magnetron sets were made in Britain, but it was clear that mass production would be best undertaken in secret in the United States, and a Magnetron was flown across the Atlantic. Production of a device which would give the operator 'eyes' in all conditions of visibility, and in all but the worst of sea states, got under way. For many months the early radar sets proved unreliable, frequently breaking down and susceptible to vibration from the discharge of weapons or to violent movement arising from the motion of a ship in a heavy sea. But improvements followed, and in time radar proved a decisive weapon in its own right.[8]

The refinements in sonar went hand-in-hand with those in depth-charge launching. From the beginning it had been recognised that during the last moments of an attack on a submarine, as the escort closed above its target's position and before depth-charges could be fired out over the escort's quarters and stern, sonar contact was lost. In these critical last moments of an attack, a cool U-boat commander had just enough time to take evasive action. What was required to eliminate that opportunity was a weapon which could be fired ahead of the attacking escort while she still retained her enemy within the sonar beam, enabling depth and range to be more precisely predicted. By the autumn of 1941 experimental work had produced a multiple mortar which threw 24 spigot-bombs charged with high explosive and a contact fuse *ahead of the escort*. Initial tests were not promising, however, for in the first trials the forepart of the participating destroyer was severely damaged, and it was some time before what was called 'Hedgehog' became a truly effective weapon. Although it was always susceptible to the launching vessel's motion in a heavy sea, it was capable of striking an enemy submarine 230 yards in advance of her attacker, giving the U-boat commander no warning of the impending attack and thus depriving him of his last-minute side-slip.

'Hedgehog' entered service in January 1942, fitted to the destroyer HMS *Westcott*. The following month she was escorting the Union Castle liner *Llangibby Castle*, then engaged in trooping. Off the Azores on 16 January the *Llangibby Castle* was attacked by two U-boats: *U-581* had no success, but *U-402* under Korvettenkapitän F.S. von Forstner torpedoed and damaged the liner and she was taken into Horta for urgent, emergency repairs. When these were completed she sailed with three escorts sent to bring her home and was again attacked by the two U-boats, which had lain in wait, and by a third, *U-572*, Kapitänleutnant H. Hirsacker, which had joined them. As they attempted to sink the transport they were counter-attacked by the *Westcott*, Commander I.H. Brockett-Pugh using his new-fangled Hedgehog bombs to deadly effect. *U-581* was destroyed with the loss of four men, and Kapitänleutnant W. Pfeifer and all but one of the remainder were made prisoners-of-war.[9]

But, since the moral is to the material as three is to one, it was upon the quality of the manpower ranged against Dönitz's young submariners that the British and their Allies had to rely. In the critical eighteen months between December 1941 and May 1943 Dönitz made the most of the principle that attack makes less demand than defence on resources, since the point of attack is at the discretion of the attacker and a local superiority is always possible, even at a time of overall strategic inferiority. Only slowly were the Allies able to master his attrition of their resources. While merchant seamen were sent across the Atlantic to take over the new Liberty ships 'welded up very quickly by teams of newly trained [female] typists!', the inexperienced officers and ratings drafted to the increasing number of escorts rolling down the slipways on both sides of the Atlantic were undergoing an increasingly rigorous induction of their own.

From his headquarters aboard HMS *Western Isles* 'the Terror of Tobermory', as Commodore G. Stephenson was by now familiarly known throughout the Allied navies, was busy turning similarly inauspicious material into fighting seamen. 'These fellows', he said later with characteristic emphasis, 'had absolutely no knowledge of the sea and, in a *fortnight*, had to learn what it had taken me between *five and ten years* to learn!' While

Stephenson's reputation has perhaps garnered much in the telling, his assessment of his task was no exaggeration. He achieved remarkable results, largely because 'the Admiralty never interfered and this remarkable and ageing man invented the method himself. It relied upon four priorities which acknowledged that the task ahead was formidable and that what counted was a consistency of quality which would meet the threat wherever it was encountered. The first priority "was *Spirit* . . . the determination to win. Next came *Discipline*: it's no good being the finest men in the world if you are not going to obey orders. Third – *Administration*: making sure the work of the ship was evenly divided; that meals were in the right place at the right time; that the whole organisation of the ship was both stable and elastic. Then, lastly . . . *Technique* – how to use the equipment."'

Stephenson and his staff achieved a series of miracles in working-up ships for active service by means of a remorseless programme based upon 'Close-Order Drill', the inculcation of instant and unquestioning obedience to orders which at one and the same time broke the civilian mind-set and replaced it with the enormous gratification of a job well done as part of a team. It was not a perfect system, but it was an effective one, and to a certain extent Stephenson tailored it to individual ships, adopting a subtly different approach when dealing with vessels manned by, for example, ex-trawlermen from that he used with one full of 'Hostilities Only' ratings, who might have been anything from car salesmen to Classics graduates. He was also sensitive to national differences, for in addition to British and Canadian escorts, *Western Isles*'s staff trained French, Dutch, Norwegian, Polish and Greek ships. Dutch submarines joined the British 'boats' sent to act as U-boats in the anti-submarine attack exercises, while Stephenson's own facility in French enabled him to establish a warmly appreciated *rapport* with the men of the Free French navy.

At heart a kindly man, Stephenson could also be ruthless. From time to time he removed a commanding officer from his ship without reference to the Admiralty, and on one occasion he recognised the symptoms of battle fatigue and insisted that the officer should have proper leave. A French corvette commander, Jean Levasseur, remembered Stephenson as a 'demon of a man, as sharp as a needle, [who] judges you rapidly and rarely makes a mistake. The extreme conscientiousness with which he takes his responsibilities forbids him to send into action any ship that has not every chance of winning. His eyes, sometimes twinkling, sometimes serious, soon discover your weak points and he sets to work to correct them.'

When promoted to command *Bideford*, Lieutenant Commander W.J. Moore underwent the ordeal soon after Stephenson had taken post. Stephenson was, Moore wrote afterwards, 'the ideal man for the job. He terrified the incompetent and lazy, but was a good friend to those who tried hard. Many commanding officers had come to be grateful for his help in bringing their ships to peak efficiency before facing the enemy and for the uncompromisingly high standards he insisted on . . . Nothing that happened in the miniature fleet anchorage passed unnoticed. From the moment a new ship arrived off the harbour entrance until she departed with his blessing, ready for action, her people were given little rest.' Moore concludes shrewdly: 'There were no shore distractions and no wives at hand to take men's minds off the job.'

Stephenson's quick-fire disaster scenarios demanding instant response from a ship's company might be applied at any time during any 24 hours. The man seemed tireless, as did his staff. Even on Christmas Day, exercises followed a brief relaxation over the festive board. Harbour evolutions were followed by four days of exercises at sea with a submarine and other corvettes. The ships under training 'practised manoeuvring, towing, boarding, sub-hunting . . . each ship with a nurse, a staff-officer from *Western Isles*.' The work-up culminated with a 'hectic inspection' by Stephenson personally. Under such tutelage a ship either flourished or failed; most rose to the occasion, and Stephenson is owed an immeasurable debt for his part in the outcome of the struggle for mastery of the Atlantic supply line.[11]

But while Stephenson could turn out a ship's company capable of executing the basic duties of a convoy escort, he could not do everything. What was lacking was that 'urgent need of a definite doctrine for depth-charge attacks, and better training in following up underwater sound contacts' that had been identified in Murdagh's debriefing.

The question had already been raised on the eastern side of the Atlantic. In the Atlantic Committee meetings Churchill himself had asked the pertinent questions as to whether the sonar system worked properly, whether depth-charges were inefficient and, most perspicacious of all, 'What do the escorts actually *do* when the convoy is attacked?' The answer to that was rather woolly and enveloped in much bluster about increasing speed and investigating, but essentially what they did depended upon the style and experience of the senior officer of the escort. To some extent the establishment of escort groups had led to the development of ideas about what procedures should be followed, but they were too vague and varied to be universally effective and could be useless when escorts were transferred from one group to another for operational reasons – which in effect simply meant in order to make up the numbers. The most frequent answer returned by escort commanders was more likely to take the form of another question: 'What *can* you do, other than keep a sharp lookout?'

All this was clear evidence of the way the Royal Navy of the inter-war years had neglected the practice of anti-submarine warfare and convoy defence. It was a particularly shocking revelation after months of vicious war at sea.

Following some deliberation the task of sorting the mess out was delegated to an officer who was shoving paper around in the Admiralty. While in command of a destroyer shortly before the war, Commander Gilbert Roberts had been invalided out of the service with tuberculosis. The outbreak of hostilities found him deeply frustrated, even volunteering for the police as a Special Constable, but his persistent applications to the Admiralty finally bore fruit and he was recalled, to be given an administrative post in Whitehall. A little later he was sent to Portsmouth barracks, where in the wake of Dunkirk and the losses of the *Royal Oak* and *Courageous* a large number of virtually idle seamen were waiting to be drafted to new ships. Roberts turned them into an Anti-Invasion Battalion and commanded them until January 1942, when Churchill catechised his naval adviser, Vice Admiral C.V. Usborne, about a suitable man to sort out the escorts. Usborne bethought himself of Roberts, recalling his valuable work earlier in his career during two years at the navy's Tactical School, where Roberts had constantly harped on about trade protection and commerce warfare, and had as constantly been ignored.

Usborne sent for him and told him: 'Time is not on your side, Roberts. You must devise convoy protection tactics. You must find methods of attacking and sinking the U-boat. You must train the escort commanders . . .' It was an awesome charge and a daunting task, but the upshot of the meeting was that Roberts was sent to Liverpool, where on the top floor of Derby House he set up the Western Approaches Tactical Unit. His arrival was met with dispiriting indifference by Noble though his Chief-of-Staff, Commodore J.M. Mansfield, proved helpful, providing personnel, including a number of Wrens. Roberts set about extemporising a 'tactical-teacher', painting a grid on the floor representing a convoy's defence area, and upon it a number of screened 'stations' representing each escort's position, indicating just how limited and circumscribed each one's view of what was happening would be at sea.

Roberts also gleaned what information he could from the anti-submarine staff officer, Commander C.D. Howard-Johnston, former commander of the 14th Escort Group. Faced with one particular query Roberts telephoned the Admiralty, and by chance was put through to Admiral Horton, then in charge of the Royal Navy's submarines and shortly to take over Western Approaches from Noble. A former submariner with a formidable reputation, Horton was able to reassure Roberts that German tactics undoubtedly relied upon attacking from inside the perimeter of the convoy's defence, a fact which by then should have been self-evident from the reports of dozens of senior officers of convoy escorts, let alone from the debriefings of masters of merchant ships containing incontrovertible evidence of it.[12]

Roberts also interviewed a number of escort commanders himself, to determine what *they* did when a convoy they were engaged in protecting came under submarine attack. Among these was Commander J.D. Prentice, a former Royal Navy officer who had retired to Canada to become a cattle rancher, and then by virtue of his previous experience was swiftly elevated to the command of a Canadian Escort Group. This be-monocled officer had applied ranching techniques to the problem, directing part of his group to close up with the convoy while others moved round the perimeter to deter U-boats as they approached. There was a certain logic to Prentice's method, but a more promising solution had been devised by Commander F.J. Walker, who had commanded the successful and aggressive defence of Convoy HG76 mentioned earlier. He was another officer hitherto passed over for promotion to captain for reasons of 'unsuitability'; but Walker, unde-terred, had devoted much time and thought to the tactical dilemma posed by U-boat attacks. He went on to prove himself outstanding, the Royal Navy's most competent U-boat hunter, with a reputation that became rapidly and widely respected among merchant seamen.

Walker's basic method, once adopted and promulgated as standard 'best practice' by Roberts, underpinned the whole Allied anti-submarine counter-offensive. It was based upon a set of standard manoeuvres which were initi-ated by a single code-word transmitted over the short-range VHF radio telephone. The first code-word was 'Buttercup', and on receipt of it all escorts moved outwards firing star-shell, forcing any U-boats to submerge, thus reducing their speed and manoeuvrability, and enabling the escorts' sonars to locate them. From this simple beginning a series of co-ordinated manoeuvres could be developed. 'Raspberry' was the order for a counter-attack on a U-boat after it had struck at a merchantman from inside the convoy. In this manoeuvre, while the senior officer's escort maintained a questing zig-zag across the 'bow' of the convoy, the flank and rear escorts turned to concentrate upon the now submerged U-boat as it tried to sneak out of the rear of the convoy, masked by the sinking merchantman and the rescue operation around it. Other manoeuvres followed, each dealing with a specific tactical variation, including extended searches for U-boats reported shadowing a convoy. To these basics sophistications were added and the escorts developed a casual argot of their own which would be incompre-hensible even if intercepted by the enemy. Preceded by a nickname for each escort as daft as 'Buttercup' or 'Raspberry', these instructions covered such eventualities as despatching a corvette to search for survivors, or a move of station to cover a part of the convoy exposed by the detachment of its regular escort.

In addition to Roberts's Tactical Unit, which was initially intended for commanding officers, there were shore training establishments for the development of anti-submarine warfare skills in their officers. One such was HMS *Nimrod* at Campbeltown on the Mull of Kintyre in Scotland, commanded by Captain Addis. Attached to it were three sonar-equipped motor-yachts, *Shemara*, *Tuscarora* and *Carina*, two anti-submarine whalers, *Bulldog* and *Spaniel*, and several submarines, including *Oberon*. Much later in the war more advanced training was given at HMS *Osprey* at Dunoon on the Clyde, while a second tactical training school was set up in Londonderry.

Roberts, a man with 'the talent to acquire knowledge, whether verbal or from a report or ... handbook, and retain this information', was quick to perceive the virtues of Walker's methods and to embrace the comments of other Group commanders. He equally quickly worked out new tactics, in which successive courses of senior officers were inducted over the months to come. Like Walker at sea, Roberts ashore in Liverpool exhausted himself in rising to each new challenge, but the Western Approaches Tactical Unit proved as invaluable a weapon in the defeat of Dönitz's submarines as the rather inauspicious-looking *Western Isles* at Tobermory.[13]

17

'The cruel sea'

U-boat *U-510*

ON COMPLETION OF each week-long course at the Western Approaches Tactical Unit, Roberts sent the participating officers back to sea with a short summing-up. What they were engaged in, Roberts said, was 'the war of the little ships and the lonely aircraft, long, patient and unpublicised, against our two great enemies, the U-boat and the cruel sea.'[1] It was also the war of an even more unpublicised section of the maritime community: the Allied merchant fleets, for whom the next eighteen months were to prove the most terrible.

But as Stephenson and Roberts wrought their particular magic and, with a slowness painful for the merchant jacks who paid what Kipling called 'the price of Admiralty', improved the quality of those defending convoys, their enemy began to suffer from the strains of war. To a degree, the Kriegsmarine's U-boat arm was a victim of German manufacturing success. By early 1942 U-boat production was so good that Dönitz was faced with the problem of a growing manpower shortage, particularly of men suitable as senior watch officers and U-boat commanders. At the same time, the Luftwaffe possessed too many, so the expedient was adopted of transferring some of this super-fluity to the Kriegsmarine to supply Dönitz's shortfall. Though it was not immediately apparent, this marked the beginning of a decline in the quality of U-boat officers which as it worsened and was subjected to slow but increasing attrition by the Allies made its own contribution to the final outcome. This is not to say that any particular watershed was reached at this time but, like the shifting tides in the war of technology which was another factor in the struggle for supremacy in the Atlantic, a gradual erosion of tech-nical competence and aggressive spirit had been set in train. In the months to come, however, it was entirely eclipsed by the numbers of U-boats becoming operational, and at the same time the widespread adoption and refinement of the group attack or *Rudeltaktik* continued to confront escort commanders with what appeared at times to be an insuperable challenge.

In the first half of 1942 Dönitz deployed wave after wave of U-boats along the east coast of North America. Refuelling unimpeded from U-tankers, from store-ships like the *Charlotte Schliemann* in Puerto de la Luz, Las Palmas and from Spanish vessels such as the minelayer *Marte* and the sailing ship *San Miguel*,[2] the young men of the Reich's submarines sated themselves with the work of destruction. Between late January and early March five Type XI U-boats – *U-106*, *U-107*, *U-108*, *U-124*, *U-128* and *U-332* – sank 26 vessels and damaged others seriously enough to force their withdrawal from service for repairs. Their own losses were minimal: on 6 February Rollmann's *U-82* on her way home from the American coast ran across Convoy OS18 and was sunk by HMSs *Rochester* and *Tamarisk*; similarly, having encountered ON72, *U-503* (Gericke) was sunk on 15 March by a Hudson covering the convoy. But during the five weeks that followed, more U-boats arriving fresh from their French bases sank a further 44 merchantmen and damaged still more.

A paucity of destroyers led the United States Navy to introduce shipping-lane patrols, a system thoroughly discredited during the First World War that proved no better now. It cost the lives of all but 11 ratings aboard the blithely-patrolling destroyer *Jacob Jones*, sunk on the 'calm moonlit night' of 28 February south of Atlantic City by Korvettenkapitän E-A. Rehwinkel in *U-578*. As the German offensive moved south, curling round Key West and focusing on choke-points like the Florida Straits, off the Mississippi Delta, and the Yucatan Strait between Cuba and the Main, it proved even more ineffective.[3]

So desperate was the situation that Roosevelt himself suggested the United States Navy should resuscitate another First World War expedient – the decoy, or Q-ship. King did not try to counter the presidential initiative, and in conditions of woefully lax security several vessels were prepared in the US Navy's yards. Most failed in their role of enticement though one, the ancient 3,200-ton steamship *Carolyn*, converted to the USS *Atik* at Portsmouth, New Hampshire, achieved a brief notoriety. At sunset on the evening of 26 March, about 270 miles east of Cape Hatteras, the *Atik* encountered a surfaced U-boat. It was Hardegen's *U-123*, on her ninth war patrol and her second in American waters. Hardegen had already sunk the American tanker *Muskogee* and the 'Ocean'-type tanker *Empire Steel*, both loaded with inflammable products and both lost with appalling effects upon their crews.

Having shadowed his quarry for some hours, about midnight Hardegen fired a torpedo which struck the *Atik* amidships. He then watched the ship being 'abandoned' by what was called 'the panic party', who sent an SOS and aped what was popularly held to be the stereotypical conduct of a merchant crew escaping a doomed ship. Hardegen approached on the surface, unwilling to sacrifice another torpedo as he had been having trouble with them since leaving L'Orient. As Lieutenant Commander H.L. Hicks saw what had now become *his* quarry approaching, the naval crew threw aside the mask. The *Atik*'s false bulwarks fell away and a medium-calibre gun, laid on *U-123*, opened fire. Unfortunately the shells fell wide, and although *U-123* was raked by machine-gun fire which killed a cadet, Hardegen engaged with his deck gun before diving, 'feeling', he afterwards admitted, 'like a schoolboy'. He moved out of range of the depth-charges with which Hicks was peppering the sea and made another approach at about 04.00. The presumption is that Hicks had meanwhile picked up his boats and 'the panic party'. At very short range Hardegen fired a second torpedo, which sank the *Atik*. She settled slowly and then blew up. All hands must have been killed, for no one was found by American ships searching the area that forenoon.

Hardegen continued his war patrol by damaging three American tankers, the *Liebre, Oklahoma* and *Esso Baton Rouge*, then sank the United Fruit Company's *Esparta* and so severely damaged the tanker *Gulfamerica* that after drifting as a derelict for six days she sank. Loss of life was heavy, for Hardegen shelled the vessel as the crew made to abandon her. Callous conduct such as this caused great grief to American seafarers. The following day the USS *Dahlgren* based at Jacksonville in Florida attacked Hardegen, but her commander was no match for his opponent and *U-123* escaped, to sink the American freighter *Leslie* off Daytona Beach late the next day. Two hours later, just after midnight, Hardegen, having run out of torpedoes, surfaced and shelled the neutral Swedish motor-vessel *Korsholm*. The ship blew up, killing about a third of her company. By the 17th Hardegen was heading for home when, 300 miles east of Cape Hatteras, he found the *Alcoa Guide* and attacked on the surface at night, *U-123*'s deck gun opening fire at about 21.50.

Captain S.L. Cobb was on the starboard bridge wing dumping his confidential books when a shell-burst blew him onto the deck below. He landed on a derrick winch, receiving serious injuries. He and a wounded seamen were put in a lifeboat. In a brief interval as *U-123* circled, the crew abandoned the *Alcoa Guide* and her cargo of US army stores bound for Guadeloupe. The majority of the men were picked up later by an American destroyer, but Cobb and the seaman had died, and four more men perished on a raft found by the British steamer *Hororata* on 16 May, sixty miles to the west; one still clung to this precarious life-saver.

Hardegen had long since headed for France.

The eleven-month intelligence blackout that followed the introduction of the new Enigma M4 cypher machine to U-boats on 1 February almost entirely obscured their movements from the British Admiralty. What little Bletchley Park was able to glean came from radio transmissions by small German surface escorts to U-boats leaving the Biscay bases and heading across the Bay, which used the Kriegsmarine's main code system and the older machines.

It was soon clear from the depredations of Hardegen and his kind that the Germans were reacting with wicked glee to the stimulus of the opportunities the Americans gave them. Within a week of United States troops occupying Curaçao and Aruba on 11 February, Dönitz's planned Operation NEULAND began. By directing several U-boats to the vital areas from which Allied shipping sailed unprotected, and in particular targeting oil ports, Dönitz hoped to inflict major damage on Allied supplies. Korvettenkapitän Hartenstein lay off Aruba in *U-156* and torpedoed three tankers, sinking one, the British-flagged *Oranjestad*, with the loss of half her crew. He escaped from an attack by an American aircraft from the 29th Bomber Squadron, but his attempt against shipping at the Shell oil terminal at Largo went disastrously wrong when his gun was fired before the tompion had been removed from its barrel. The U-boat was obliged to head for Martinique and hand her badly-wounded second watch officer to the Vichy French at Fort de France, having buried one of the gun's crew on passage. Hartenstein then sank the homeward-bound American freighter *Delplata* without loss of life, and the British tanker *La Carrière*, 15 of whose men were killed. Having exhausted his torpedoes but repaired his deck gun's breech, Hartenstein shelled and sank the British steamship *Macgregor* and her cargo of coal.

He also attacked the American Texaco tanker *Oregon* taking a cargo of fuel oil to the United States naval base at Melville, Rhode Island. The survivors believed they were being attacked by two submarines as fire was opened on the *Oregon* early on the morning of 28 February. The shells began to hit and started fires on the bridge and poop, the two accommodation areas. Captain I.C. Nilsen ordered the ship abandoned, and as members of the crew attempted to launch No. 4 Boat on the port quarter they came under machine-gun fire. As Nilsen, his chief and second mates, radio operator and cook were lowering a forward lifeboat they too were machine-gunned and killed. The third mate, chief and third engineers and one engine-room hand were compelled to jump over the side as the tanker was subjected to a protracted bombardment. One of these men said that 'while he was struggling in the water one of the subs attempted to run him over'.

One boat escaped with 26 of the *Oregon*'s 36-strong complement to land at Puerto Plata in the Dominican Republic on 4 March. The four men in the water managed to lash the wreckage of two lifeboats together and were rescued from this precarious refuge on the afternoon of the 5th by the passing tanker *Gulfpenn*.

Hartenstein's *U-156* was the first of the NEULAND U-boats to return to France. Her cruise had been fairly typical. That of *U-67* (Müller-Stockheim) which began off Curaçao was similar, resulting in the sinking of two tankers, the *J.N. Pew* and the Panamanian *Penelope*. Captain T.E. Bush of the *J.N. Pew* and 32 of his 36-strong crew died as the first of three torpedoes set the amidships accommodation ablaze early on the evening of 21 February. Although the ship went down in less than a minute the two after boats were launched, but No. 3 capsized, leaving 11 men to cling to it throughout the night. It was righted the following morning, but the fresh water had been lost and one by one in the following three weeks the men perished. The single survivor, a mess-man, was spotted by a patrolling aeroplane which directed the Panamanian-flagged *Annetta 1* to his position, and he was saved on 14 March. No. 4 Boat got away with only two men aboard, the chief steward and the pump-man. These two stalwarts reached the Colombian coast on 25 February and were befriended by the indigenous people, who helped them the 35 miles to Riohacha, from where they were taken to Baranquilla.

Like Hartenstein's *U-156*, *U-67* had also been attacked from the air by an aeroplane from the 29th Bomber Squadron, but escaped damage. She had joined forces with *U-502* in an attempt to shell Aruba but they were foiled by a blackout and the vigorous action of local patrol craft. Prior to this, Kapitänleutnant J. von Rosentiel's *U-502* had operated off Maracaibo, sinking two British tankers, the *Tia Juana* (a sister-ship of the *Oranjestad*) and the *San Nicholas*, along with the Venezuelan *Monagas*. Seventeen men of the *Tia Juana* and seven from the *San Nicholas* were killed. After her abortive attempt to bombard Aruba, *U-502* sank the Norwegian tanker *Kongsgård* and the Panamanian tanker *Thalia*, and damaged the American steamship *Sun*. Elsewhere in the West Indies, *U-161* (Kapitänleutnant A. Achilles) audaciously entered Port of Spain, Trinidad and damaged the American Matson Line's cargo-ship *Mokihana*, which was lying at anchor with lights burning. He then torpedoed and damaged the tanker *British Consul*, which sank in the shallow water (and was afterwards raised, only to be sunk on 19 August off Boca Grande in Trinidad by *U-564*). Having fired at his targets, Achilles brazenly proceeded out of the port with his own navigation lights on. Off Port of Spain two days later he sank the British tanker *Circe Shell* after an abortive first attack, following which *U-161* was herself attacked by a Royal Navy Albacore flying from Piarco in Trinidad. The Albacore's inadequate anti-submarine bombs merely shook the U-boat.

On 23 February Achilles attacked a second Matson Line ship, the *Lihue*. The vessel was 275 miles west of Martinique, bound from New York to the Persian Gulf with war materials. She did not sink immediately, but an attempt by the USS *Partridge* to tow her ended in failure. Enduring another air attack, this time by a Boeing B18, Achilles then sank the British whale-factory ship *Uniwaleco* west of St Vincent. This vessel, the 1905-built former *Sir James Clark Ross*, was still being used as a tanker, having in her whale-oil tanks some 8,800 tons of fuel oil bound from Curaçao to Freetown for naval use there.

Two days later, on the night of 9/10 March, Achilles took *U-161* into Port Castries, St Lucia and attacked shipping lying alongside, hitting two British vessels, the *Umtata* of Bullard King's Natal Line, and the Canadian-owned *Lady Nelson*. Both were severely damaged (they were repaired and re-entered service, but the former was sunk by *U-571* in July that year). Achilles had not yet finished, and on 14 March, west of Trinidad, he torpedoed and sank the small British-Canadian merchantman *Sarniadoc*, running in ballast from Georgetown in British Guiana to St Thomas in the Virgin Islands. Captain W.A. Darling and all 18 of her crew were killed. On the following day *U-161* encountered the American lighthouse tender *Acacia* going about her lawful occasions, and sank her with gunfire.[4]

The last successes of the NEULAND U-boats were those of Clausen's *U-129* off Guiana. Near Trinidad and Tobago in the Windward Islands between 20 February and 3 March Clausen sank four vessels: the Norwegian steamer *Nordvangen* went down with all hands; the Canadian tramp *George L. Torain*, which was loaded with bauxite, with her master Captain J. Allan and 14 of her crew; the American *West Zeda*, in ballast, with no loss of life; and the Canadian-registered *Lennox*, also loaded with bauxite, but from which the majority of the crew were rescued by the British tanker *Athelrill*. Shifting westward to Paramaribo, Clausen torpedoed and sank the Panamanian-registered *Bayou* and two American ships, the *Mary*, which was loaded with a Lend-Lease cargo bound for the British in the Middle East, and the *Steel Age*. Aboard the *Mary*, one able seaman was killed in the explosion caused by the torpedo but the remaining 33 men under Captain S. Broadwick escaped in two lifeboats. They made a voyage of 540 miles in the six days following the destruction of their ship, being picked up by the *Alcoa Scout* less than forty miles from Georgetown in British Guiana. Only one man survived the sinking of the *Steel Age*. Owned by the Isthmian Steamship Company of New York, the freighter was hit on the starboard side and sank within two minutes. Jumping overboard, the solitary able seaman was dragged out of the water by Clausen's men and returned with them to France, to be sent to the prison camp at Milag Nord. He cannot have enjoyed the attack to which the U-boat was subjected as she crossed the Bay of Biscay on her return to L'Orient on 1 April, when Flight Sergeant V.D. Pope bombed and damaged *U-129* in his Whitley bomber, on loan from No. 502 Squadron to Coastal Command.

German losses in the Caribbean continued to be light, though on 13 June the USCG Cutter *Thetis* sank the Type IXC *U-157*. Korvettenkapitän W. Henne was on his first war patrol. Just after midnight on 11 June he had torpedoed the American tanker *Hagan* off Cayo Guajaba, Cuba. Armed and with a 'naval armed guard' of six men,[5] the *Hagan* and her 22,000 barrels of blackstrap molasses sank rapidly, carrying six men to their deaths and leaving three more injured among the 38 survivors who managed to launch the amidships lifeboats. They did not go unavenged, however, for *U-157* was spotted from the air later that same day and badly shaken by four depth-charges dropped from a B18. Forced to dive, the U-boat was next seen from a civil aircraft, but United States Navy planes reacting to the reports failed to locate her. Next morning, however, another B18 sighted her heading west, just before Henne dived again. By now all available American forces were hurrying towards her reported position, and that afternoon she was seen again by an A29 of the USAAF.

Then, early on the 13th, she was located by the *Thetis*. The flag officer responsible for the Gulf Sea Frontier, Rear Admiral J.L. Kauffman, had concluded from his recent experience in Iceland that the patrol system might be made more efficient by the introduction of 'killer groups' of surface warships which 'would go out on any favorable contact and stick to it until they scored'. He had initiated such a concentration of force immediately upon learning of the *Hagan's* loss, but despite being provided with the radar-equipped B18s for night operations, his forces had not brought Henne to account in all the hours since *U-157* had first been seen in the Old Bahama Channel on the 10th. Henne had made a successful transit of the Florida Strait and was almost into the wider waters of the Gulf of Mexico before Lieutenant N.C. McCormick's cutter caught her south-west of Key West. One of the 'killer group' based at Key West, *Thetis* attacked at 15.50 and dropped seven depth-charges. Other vessels arrived and joined in, but it was McCormick's initial attack that sent Henne and his 51 men to their deaths.

Kauffman's instinct, like that of Captain Walker, was right, but the resources committed to this hunting of a single U-boat were disproportionate in terms of the overall threat to merchant shipping on the American coast, and the experiment was not repeated. It was clear, however, that the attachment of independent groups of anti-submarine warships to the protection of a convoy was a different matter. Such 'support groups' were assigned to the cover of ocean convoys a year later, but in the spring and summer of 1942 there were not enough such vessels available, and the damage being done to dispersed merchant shipping made triumphs like this one insignificant.

In April Korvettenkapitän W. Kölle sank five ships off the Greater Antilles. On his way from Kiel to L'Orient he had attacked Convoy HX175 and fired no fewer than 14 torpedoes, all of which failed to hit their targets, a fact which was attributed to the misalignment of U-154's torpedo control system when it was examined at L'Orient. Whether or not Kölle should have reverted to visual methods, and whether or not his failure to do so attests to his lack of operational experience, once arrived off Puerto Rico he had no trouble rapidly sinking two 'tank-ships'. Both his victims were American, both were converted freighters, and both bore cargoes of molasses. The *Comol Rico* had loaded at Humacao, Puerto Rico, bound for Boston. By mid afternoon on 4 April she was 225 miles north of San Juan when the watch saw torpedo tracks approaching. The helm was put over but the torpedoes blew the side of the ship in and destroyed the engine, throwing parts of it up into the air. The three men in the engine room were killed outright and the ship sank forty minutes later, the survivors being picked up after three days.

The following day U-154 attacked the *Catahoula*. Kölle's first torpedo caused an explosion which flooded the engine room, ruptured a cargo tank and wrecked a section of the deck and catwalk. Although No. 4 Boat and a life-raft were destroyed, Captain G.B. Johanesen ordered the ship abandoned, and as the crew ran to the remaining boats Kölle surfaced to survey the damage. The armed guard had fired on U-154 before escaping. As the boats were being lowered Kölle fired a second torpedo, whereupon the *Catahoula* rolled over to starboard, crushing Nos 1 and 3 Boats and dragging them down with her as she capsized. Only No. 2 Boat and a raft remained, the former with 25 survivors, the latter with 13, most of whom had initially been in No. 1 Boat. The three men in the engine room had been killed when the torpedo struck, five more men were drowned in the swamped boats, and the third mate, the pump-man and a seaman were lost during the attack. The survivors were recovered by the destroyer USS *Sturtevant* on the morning of the 6th.

By this time Kölle was on his way south-west, passing through the Mona Passage into the Caribbean. Here, off Jacmel on the south coast of Haiti, on the morning of the 12th he sank the American general cargo-vessel

Delvalle. Owned by the Mississippi Shipping Company of New Orleans, the *Delvalle* was on a voyage from there towards Buenos Aires with five passengers and a general cargo. Warned by a radio signal from a passenger aircraft at 10.00 on 11 April that he was being tailed by a surfaced submarine, Captain E.F. Jones had ordered a sharp lookout kept astern, and at 17.30 a periscope was sighted. Jones abandoned his zig-zag, ordered the fullest possible speed and swung round to ram his persecutor, but Kölle ran deep and Jones was obliged to make off. Built in 1919, his ship was capable of 13 knots, but it was not enough to out-run *U-154*. With a surface speed of 17 knots, she was able to work up abeam of the *Delvalle*, and at 00.30 on the 12th she fired two torpedoes. These hit the *Delvalle* on her starboard side and she began to list and settle. Seven minutes later a third torpedo hit her and she 'sank gently about fifteen minutes' later. There was time to abandon her without panic, but even so Jones lost his doctor and a seaman.

On the following day the newly-built British 'Ocean'-type tanker *Empire Amethyst* was also heading south from New Orleans, where she had loaded a cargo of 12,000 tons of petroleum spirit, and was taking a somewhat circuitous route home, bound for Freetown to join an SL convoy. Having passed the Yucatan Strait Captain G.D. Potter shaped his course north of Jamaica, and on the morning of 13 April was heading east past Navassa Island off the extreme west of Haiti's southern peninsula enclosing the Gulf of Leogane. Potter, his ship and 40 of his men were incinerated when the *Empire Amethyst* was hit by Kölle's torpedo. Only five men survived to be picked up by the Norwegian tanker *Innerøy*, then on her way to Halifax.

Kölle dodged north through the Windward Passage between Haiti and Cuba and by the 20th he lay off Caicos, where he attacked the Canadian steamship *Vineland*. Fortunately the vessel was in ballast, and although she was subjected to a torpedo strike and then a surface shelling, only one man was killed and Captain R.A. Williams and his men afterwards landed on Turks Island. Kölle returned to L'Orient but was back in the Caribbean in June. Having sunk a fishing boat off the Yucatan peninsula, *U-154* was surfaced on the 13th when an approaching aircraft forced her to crash-dive, abandoning Mechaniker Bahmer who was squatting on a bucket on the casing, relieving himself. By the time *U-154* reached 80 metres Bahmer's absence from his action station had been reported to Kölle, who returned to periscope depth and observed astern a circling flock of gulls. Finding the air clear of quartering aeroplanes, Kölle brought *U-154* to the surface and motored towards the discommoded and indignant Bahmer, who was hauled aboard by his shipmates while an officer fired his Luger at an approaching shark. After this incident Kölle discovered that he was trailing oil, evidence of his presence which would be highly visible from the air. Kerneval at first refused him permission to return to France, but Dönitz relented. Kölle refuelled from the U-tanker *U-463* west of the Azores in mid August and reached L'Orient on the 23rd after an 81-day patrol which had yielded a single Panamanian fishing vessel, the *Lalita*. Unsurprisingly perhaps, Dönitz removed Kölle from further operational duties.

After a successful patrol in the previous December as part of the initial PAUKENSCHLAG operation, by mid April Korvettenkapitän E. Kals's *U-130* was off Trinidad, working her way into the Caribbean. He sank the Norwegian motor-vessel *Grenager* with no loss of life on the 11th and damaged the tanker *Esso Boston* so badly that she had to be beached and was afterwards declared a total loss. Kals approached Captain J.L. Johnson in his boat, and having obtained the name of the tanker and her cargo – crude oil – he offered the American seamen food and water. Thereafter Kals's luck ran thin. On the night of 18/19 April he began to bombard the Shell oil terminus at Bullen Bay, Curaçao, but the responding shore guns drove him off. He was subsequently unable to find further targets, and headed east.

During this period Italian submarines were operating to the east of the Antilles. In the *Luigi Torelli* Capitano di Fregata de Giacomo sank two ships, one of which was the Blue Star Line's *Scottish Star*. The torpedo explosion on the evening of 19 February killed the duty watch in the engine room and the ship settled fast. The boats were launched, but Captain E.N. Rhodes was obliged to jump for his life and swim to the nearest lifeboat. Surfacing and firing into the sinking ship, di Giacomo made no effort to succour those he had rendered homeless, leaving them to make the best of it. Three boats were found by HMS *Diomede*, which had received the *Scottish Star*'s distress call; the fourth made the six hundred miles to Barbados under Chief Officer M.C. Watson, landing on the 27th.

The *Giuseppe Finzi* under Capitano di Fregata Giudice sank three vessels, including the British tanker *Melpomene*, Captain Henney, on 6 March. The ship was in ballast and no one was lost, but the torpedo explosion had wrecked her aerials, so the survivors were fortunate in being rescued by the American freighter *Idaho*. The Harrison liner *Daytonian* was sunk by torpedo and gunfire from the *Enrico Tazzoli*, Capitano di Fregata Fecia di Cossato, on 13 March. Only one man was killed, Captain J.J. Egerton and the rest of his crew being picked up from their boats by the Dutch tanker *Rotterdam* and landed two days later at Nassau in the Bahamas. This submarine also sank the British tanker *Athelqueen* and four other merchantmen, while the *Morosini*, Capitano di Fregata Fraternale, sank three ships, among them Christian Salvesen's tanker *Peder Bogen* on her way from Trinidad to join a convoy at Halifax. She went down with 14,000 tons of fuel oil intended for the Royal Navy. Aboard the *Leonardo da Vinci*, Capitano di Fregata Longanesi-Cattani sank two ships before moving to the West African coast where he sank four more, two of them British. The United Baltic Company's cargo-vessel *Chile*, Captain N.E. Bom, was loaded with pig-iron, cotton-seed and groundnuts, and five of her crew were killed. Longanesi-Cattani also sank the Clan liner *Clan Macquarie*, which unusually for such a vessel was in ballast on her way to New York from Bombay and Durban.

Having taken a prominent part in the rescue of the *Python* survivors in the previous December, Korvettenkapitän K-F. Merten's *U-68* was back in the Central Atlantic by early March, and on the 3rd sank the Blue Funnel liner *Helenus* which was east of Freetown homeward bound from the orient laden with a full general cargo that included consignments of copper, sisal fibres, tea, rubber and cinnamon. Merten's two torpedoes tore open her starboard side, stopping the ship and causing her to list heavily. A deck-boy and all four men in the stoke-hold had been killed and the starboard boats were destroyed. Captain P.W. Savery ordered the port boats lowered but one was overset, so that the remaining 76 crew and their ten passengers were obliged to cram into Nos 2 and 4 Boats. As the *Helenus* sank, with boats still alongside her, Merten surfaced and motored round before heading off to the south-east without hailing the survivors. Meanwhile Chief Officer R. Fountain had succeeded in salvaging a waterlogged boat, so Savery redistributed the survivors and took stock of all recoverable food from the rafts floating close by. At this point a ship appeared. It was the Watts, Watts tramp *Beaconsfield* – but such was the rumoured extent of German evil and cunning that her master, suspecting a trap, manned his guns and zig-zagged away. In fact, he had himself earlier been attacked by Merten, but had avoided the torpedo fired at him. As soon as he was certain of having escaped he swung round, and at 18.00, as the sun set, approached the *Helenus*'s boats and signalled what Savery's officers read as 'There is a submarine about, lower your sails'. Anticipating immediate succour they doused the sails, where-upon the *Beaconsfield* turned away at full speed.

Later an aeroplane flew overhead, in response to the *Helenus*'s distress signal received at Freetown, then flew over the retreating *Beaconsfield* and signalled her; in due course the tramp returned to the wallowing boats and effected the long-overdue rescue. It transpired that her master had prefixed his signal with the word 'if', but this had been lost on those receiving it as they bobbed helplessly upon the ocean. Reporting later on the conduct of his people, Savery wrote that 'the behaviour of every member of the crew was exemplary in every way: the passengers (who included two women) also behaved very well.'

Merten went on to sink six more vessels, the Strick liner *Baluchistan* off

Liberia on 8 March and, in the same area a week later, the tramp *Baron Newlands*. Moving to Cape Palmas, *U-68* next torpedoed the British ships *Île de Batz*, *Scottish Prince* and *Allende* and, off Monrovia on the 30th, the *Muncaster Castle*. Six men of the *Allende* were killed outright, but Captain T.J. Williamson and his 32 fellow survivors were unfortunate enough to land at Taba on the Côte d'Ivoire, where they were interned at Bobo Dinlassu by the Vichy French authorities. The *Muncaster Castle*, a sister-ship of the *Wray Castle* whose master had subsequently commanded the ill-fated *Criton*, was loaded with 3,000 tons of government stores bound for Colombo in Ceylon. She was also carrying 265 passengers, largely service personnel, and 13 naval ratings as part of her complement of 82. Five of the crew and 19 passengers were lost before the survivors were rescued by the corvette *Aubrieta* from the local escort force and the tramp *Ann Strathos* of Athens, to be landed at Freetown. The *Muncaster Castle*'s master, Captain H.W. Harper, was afterwards awarded Lloyd's War Medal for bravery at sea.

Operating in conjunction with Merten, Kapitänleutnant A-O. Loewe in *U-505* sank four ships, despite a formidable attack by a corvette on 28 March which Loewe evaded by diving deep. His victims were William Thomson's Ben liner the *Benmohr*; the Norwegian motor-vessel *Sydhav*, half of whose 24 crew perished; the American freighter *West Irmo*, whose bow was blown off and which sank after an attempt to tow her stern-first by HMS *Copinsay*; and the Dutch *Alphacca*, a third of whose crew lost their lives.

The *Benmohr*'s crew, having taken to their boats on the night of 4 March, managed to keep together, and on the morning following the sinking of their ship were seen by a Sunderland from No. 95 Squadron based at Freetown. This landed on the sea and taxied towards them. Captain D. Anderson commanded a crew of 27 British and 29 Chinese, all of whom crammed into the flying-boat, which succeeded with some difficulty in taking off, and landed them at Freetown. They were in Glasgow by the 22nd, one of the fastest repatriations of a merchantman's crew on record. Although the *West Irmo* lost none of her crew, she was carrying 55 African stevedores, ten of whom were killed as they sat on No. 1 Hatch on the evening of 3 April.

Kals was back on patrol in the Atlantic Narrows in *U-130* in early July, firing at Convoy SL115's escort, HMS *Lulworth*, on the 14th, only to be counter-attacked and forced to run. On the evening of the 27th, to the south-west of the Cape Verde Islands, he did however torpedo the Norwegian motor-tanker *Tankexpress* which was acting as an auxiliary for the Royal Navy. The same day the British tanker *Elmwood* was sunk west of Freetown; she was a brand-new ship loaded with 7,000 tons of military equipment. Her master, Captain L.J. Herbert, and 50 men escaped in one lifeboat, landing at Freetown; the second officer's boat with 11 men on board reached the coast further south, at Bissao in Portuguese Guinea, on 11 August; and the chief officer and 18 people were rescued by the American Liberty ship *Davy Crockett* and landed at Cape Town.

Having been refuelled by *U-116*, Kals sank the British-registered, Danish-manned *Danmark* at the end of the month, without loss of life, and the Norwegian *Malmanger* in early August. The latter was another Norwegian tanker being used as a naval auxiliary; 18 men were killed in her destruction, two were made prisoner, and a further 14 survived after a spell in the boats. Three further vessels were sunk before Kals completed his patrol in late August. One was yet another Norwegian tanker being used as a British naval auxiliary, the *Mirlo*, sunk without loss of life; the others were the British Blue Star Line's *Viking Star* and the tramp *Beechwood*. Captain S.J. Dring of the *Beechwood* became Kals's third prisoner, and was obliged to sit out the war in Milag Nord. The ordeal endured by the crew of the *Viking Star* is detailed in chapter 18.

The damage inflicted by these and other attacks was immense, mainly in the material but also in another sense. The mounting losses of American merchant seamen were not widely disclosed, and much could be masked beneath the murmurs about British incompetence that blew south-west on the winds of rumour from the Barents Sea where Convoy PQ17 had met its fate. What was of greater immediate moment was the damage inflicted on the mercantile marines of neutral countries – not the neutral nations of Europe, who whether they liked it or not were bound by ties of geography and politics, but the neutral nations of Central and South America. Apart from those flying the flag of Panama, which were usually beneficially American-owned, merchantmen wearing the ensigns of Argentina, Brazil, Chile, Colombia, Cuba, Dominica, Honduras, Uruguay and Venezuela were among those sunk. The Chilean-flagged *Tolten*, for example, was torpedoed and sunk by *U-404*, Korvettenkapitän O. von Bülow, just 30 miles off the Ambrose lightvessel in the very approaches to New York. Only one man survived. Several of such countries had ties with Germany, and strong elements in their social fabric that were sympathetic to Fascism.[6]

However, in January 1942 the Brazilian authorities, reacting to FBI pressure, rounded up six spy-rings operating inside their borders that had been passing information about shipping movements to Berlin. Concerned about their losses of merchant vessels, seven of which had been sunk between February and April, the Brazilians began to arm their merchantmen, and at the end of May announced that their military aircraft would attack Axis submarines. Dönitz found this an insufficient deterrent: five more Brazilian-flagged vessels were sunk in mid August, with heavy loss of life. Brazil severed relations with the Axis powers as a consequence, and on the 22nd President Vargas declared war against Germany and Italy.

Germany's commerce-raiders continued to be active during the first half of 1942. One of the captures of the *Atlantis* in the Indian Ocean in 1941 had been Bank Line's *Speybank*; having been sailed as a prize to Bordeaux, she was there converted to a U-boat supply ship, commerce-raider and minelayer, and left La Pallice on 21 January to head south. She was renamed *Doggerbank* – a neat twist – and was able to masquerade as her sister-ship *Levernbank* when challenged first by a South African aircraft off Cape Town, then by the light cruiser *Durban*. Passing his ship off as the *Inverbank* the following day when intercepted by the Armed Merchant Cruiser *Cheshire*, Kapitänleutnant Schneidewind was able to lay mines off Cape Agulhas, on the threshold of the Indian Ocean. Schneidewind had been prize-master of the *Speybank*, and as a merchant mariner with experience of the Indian route he was well able to exploit his various aliases. Considering the concentration of British shipping off the Cape of Good Hope, which included trooping movements made by major liners such as both the *Queen Elizabeth* and the *Queen Mary*, Schneidewind's mission was not particularly successful. It nevertheless caused great anxiety, and considerable resources had to be diverted to mine-sweep these liners in and out of South African ports. It also inspired the initiation of a new procedure for warships that required them to report any suspicious vessel to the Admiralty, whereupon the true position of the ship whose identity was being claimed would be verified.

The *Doggerbank*'s first victim was a Dutch vessel, the *Alcyone*, from Convoy OS19. Subsequent reports of mines being seen and of the fouling of one on the paravane of the British Shell tanker *Mactra* alerted the naval authorities at Cape Town, who promptly mobilised the local mine-sweeping force. These mines also damaged the British cargo-ship *Dalfram* and then, on 15 May, the destroyer depot-ship HMS *Hecla*. That same day, the Peninsular and Oriental Steam Navigation Company's cargo-liner *Soudan* also struck a mine, rapidly filling and sinking. Three lifeboats were launched and all 100 people escaped in them. The boats remained together for the first night and then, with the dawn, they headed for land. Two were quickly picked up but the third, under the second officer and with 31 souls on board, was at sea for six days in the heavy weather prevalent in that quarter in the autumn, during which the lifeboat lost half her stern-post. Unable to attract the attention of two aircraft, the survivors signalled passing ships, only for them to sheer away. They were finally closed by the *Clan Murray* on the morning of the 22nd but found themselves the object of continuing suspicion. The Clan liner circled them for twenty minutes, her guns trained on their battered craft, before the master ran alongside and took them aboard. 'They were clothed, fed and warmed, and as they realised they were safe, the reaction set in and some of them slumped down in a corner of the saloon and wept.'

Far to the north and west the *Doggerbank* had meanwhile met and stored the German blockade-runner *Dresden*, and a month later replenished the raider *Michel* before transferring most of her supplies to the tanker *Charlotte Schliemann*, which had finally left the shelter of the Canaries. Schneidewind embarked 177 British Merchant Navy prisoners captured by various raiders and held aboard the store-ship. The *Doggerbank* then steamed to Japan by way of Batavia, arriving in Yokohama on 19 August, when she handed over her prisoners-of-war to the Japanese. Her end is not without interest. Having loaded a valuable cargo of oils and rubber in south-east Asian ports under Japanese control she sailed for France, intending to run the British blockade; instead on 3 March 1943 she was torpedoed by *U-43*, in another case of mistaken identity between German warships and one not, in the circumstances, without its irony. Oberleutnant zur See H-J. Schwantke reported sinking a Blue Star or Union Castle liner off the Canaries, but these were vessels distinctly unlike a quondam Bank Line ship. Hit by three torpedoes, the *Doggerbank* sank swiftly, and only 15 men escaped to seek refuge in a small Japanese dinghy. Schneidewind was among them, subject to all the privations and horrors of their circumstances, and according to the sole survivor, a man named Fritz Kürt, he shot four of the crew before putting himself out of his misery. Kürt himself was picked up unconscious by the Spanish ship *Campoamour* on 29 March 1943.

In the spring of 1942 the *Michel*, having been replenished by the *Doggerbank*, sank two tankers, one of which was the British Anglo-Saxon Petroleum Company's *Patella* with the death of three men on 18 April. A few days later, at about 05.30 on 1 May and some 720 miles south-west of St Helena, the *Michel* signalled the British cargo-liner *Menelaus* to stop, and not to use her radio. Her master, Captain J.H. Blyth, was on his way from Durban to Baltimore; he ordered his chief engineer, Mr J. Blackstock, to increase from the ship's service speed of 14.5 knots to the fastest the *Menelaus*'s turbines were capable of. The radio officers aboard the *Michel* simulated a British coastal station at the Cape, politely acknowledging the *Menelaus*'s signal, but this had no effect. Probably the British radio-operators, familiar with the distinctive 'signatures' of the Cape operators, were not deceived. The *Michel* opened fire as Blyth turned away, but the shells fell short. Under Second Engineer A.A. Ritchie and the senior fireman Chen Sung Yung, meanwhile, the *Menelaus* had managed an additional knot, when a torpedo-boat (it was commanded by Leutnant Krink) flying the white ensign was seen approaching at 35 knots. The fact that her crew were wearing duffle coats on the Tropic of Capricorn gave them pause, however, and persuaded Blyth and his mate, Mr B.L. Brind, that things were not what they seemed.

The *Michel* herself was now only six miles astern of them, and hoisting out a second fast boat. Fortunately Kapitän zur See von Ruckteschell did not launch his second torpedo-boat, and at about 07.20 Blyth succeeded in combing the track of one of the two torpedoes launched at him by the first. Though it misfired the second torpedo actually hit the *Menelaus*, for as Blyth swung the ship 'a low rumbling noise was heard on the *Menelaus's* port side, just below the bridge, and the vessel vibrated with shock or impact'.

As he took avoiding action, Blyth was subjected to a second salvo from the *Michel*; this also fell short, and von Ruckteschell slowed to recover his torpedo-boat. The *Michel* was now having trouble with her own engines, and von Ruckteschell was obliged to abandon his chase, allowing the Blue Funnel liner to escape. He had in fact been in sight of the *Menelaus* for some hours, and indeed had sent one of his torpedo-boats to attack her in the darkness of the previous night. In the light of this abortive attack and the second the following day Krink was relieved of command of the *Michel's* auxiliary, and ordered to be dismissed from the ship when she reached a German port. (Shortly after the war, before his trial for war crimes, von Ruckteschell remarked to an American reporter: 'if you meet the Captain of the Blue Funnel liner *Menelaus*, give him my compliments. He was the only man who outmanoeuvred me and got away.')

The *Thor*, Korvettenkapitän G. Gumprich, was also at large in the South Atlantic, having sailed from the Fatherland on 14 January. After a sortie into the Antarctic Ocean where Gumprich failed to locate the southern whaling fleet, he refuelled from the supply vessel *Regensburg* some thousand miles west of the Orange River in South Africa, then on 23 March fell in with the Greek steamer *Papasitikos*. Removing her crew, he sank her with a torpedo. A week later, on the afternoon of 30 March, he came in sight of the Denholm tramp *Wellpark*, then 700 miles south-west of St Helena on her way from St John's to Alexandria with a military cargo. Captain Cant was surprised to hear an aircraft overhead, given his distance from land. The approach of an Arado seaplane trailing a wire and grapnel which carried away the *Wellpark's* radio aerial prompted Cant to ring the alarms. A distant ship was seen to be closing and Cant sent his men to action stations, managing to drive off the Arado as he turned his stern to the approaching enemy. The chase lasted seven hours, then Cant's men engaged briefly with their 12-pounder as the *Thor* found the *Wellpark's* range with her second salvo. Thereafter the *Wellpark* was subjected to a fierce shelling. Within minutes she was taking direct hits, and Cant ordered his ship abandoned. Seven of her 48 men were killed before her crew were taken prisoner.

Two days later, on 1 April, about 475 miles WSW of St Helena, the *Thor* sighted the Watts, Watts tramp *Willesden*, Captain Griffiths, which was also on her way to Alexandria, though from New York. Gumprich trailed his victim for twelve hours before the raider's Arado seaplane tore down the tramp's aerial and dropped two bombs. Gumprich's guns began a cannonade which expended no fewer than 128 rounds, setting fire to a deck cargo of oil drums and destroying the *Willesden*'s bridge. She returned fire, but was doomed. With her bosun killed and six men wounded (four of whom afterwards died), Griffiths had no alternative but to abandon her. The remaining 42 of her crew became prisoners-of-war, joined on the 3rd by the Norwegian crew of the *Aust*, which like the *Willesden* had been attacked by the Arado and then shelled.

On 10 April the *Thor* intercepted Ropner's tramp *Kirkpool*, bound from Durban towards Montevideo laden with coal and labouring along in heavy seas some 240 miles north of Tristan da Cunha. The *Kirkpool* had been seen on the *Thor*'s radar and shadowed all day, so that it was late and the short winter twilight was closing down a day blighted by low visibility by the time Gumprich decided to attack. The *Thor* appears to have closed her quarry before opening fire and almost immediately shooting away her wheel and wrecking her steering, when *Kirkpool*'s involuntary turn persuaded the Germans that her master intended to ram their ship. The *Kirkpool* was soon on fire and her chief engineer recalled 'a boy of seventeen snatching two minutes to get down on his knees and say a prayer . . . and . . . Indian firemen sitting in a circle in the fire-glow of a burning and sinking ship appealing to Allah.' Captain Kennington could do little but order his ship abandoned, but Gumprich felt threatened by the perceived intention to ram and fired a torpedo. The *Kirkpool*, still under way though ablaze from end to end, drove under while her crew jumped into the sea. Sixteen men were lost, the others hoped for the best. 'I felt so tired,' Chief Engineer C. Burley wrote afterwards, 'real tired, and cramp was getting into my legs, and the thought came to me [that] all I had to do was to let go and end it, it seemed so easy, but somehow, someone somewhere seemed to always want attention, especially . . . two wounded men, and we were a sorry lot of fourteen of us on [hatch] boards, [with] a rough sea, a burning ship astern of us, nothing else in sight . . . and possibly a thousand miles from anywhere and a black night.'

To his credit, Gumprich remained in the area for three hours searching for survivors, many of whom were saved by the small red lights now regularly attached to the new standard life-jackets being supplied to British merchant ships. Kennington, Burley and 28 men survived, to be taken east with the others as *Thor* moved into the waters of the Indian Ocean, where she captured or destroyed five more vessels before proceeding to refit in Japan.[7] Here her prisoners, British, Dutch, Norwegian and Greek, were landed into the custody of the Japanese, who incarcerated them in camps at Kawasaki and Yawata. They were used at Kawasaki as forced labour, discharging ships, working in factories or on the railways, and treated not as military personnel but as despicable civilians. Cant of the *Wellpark*, who was 37, became senior officer of the 160 or so British merchant seamen interned there, and was greatly respected. At Yamata, on the island of Kyushu near Nagasaki, the prisoners were made to work in the steelworks. They were ravaged by dysentery: of the 1,200 held at Yamata, '400 died from disease aggravated by beatings'. Others died shortly after their liberation in 1945.

Until the United States Navy introduced a comprehensive, 'interlocking' convoy system along the entire American east coast, the first of which took effect in mid May 1942, Dönitz continued to capitalise upon the advantages surrendered to his U-boats there, leaving the trans-Atlantic trade convoys largely unmolested. During March, 450 merchant ships crossed the Atlantic in 19 convoys without loss, and between mid May and midsummer there were no losses from HX and SC convoys bound for Britain. Although U-boats picked off stragglers and the sea accounted for two founderings, there was only one vessel lost to the enemy out of this convoy series and that was the *Denpark*. Another of Denholm's tramps and loaded with manganese ore, she was part of SL109, ships from which picked up 25 of her company. In an attack on the convoy 220 miles north-west of the Cape Verde Islands by three U-boats,[8] only Kapitänleutnant U. Heyse succeeded in penetrating the screen. The *Denpark* had been bound from Takoradi by way of Freetown to the Clyde, and thence to Workington, when she was hit by *U-128*'s torpedo. She went down quickly, taking Captain J. McCreadie and 20 men with her.

The complementary OS convoy series did suffer some losses. On 21 May, when outward bound for the Caribbean, *U-159*, Kapitänleutnant H. Witte, attacked Convoy OS28 to the east of the Azores and sank two vessels. One, the British *New Brunswick*, a First World War standard-built steam-ship, now under the management of Elder, Dempster Ltd., was loaded with government and military stores, including 20 aircraft. Accompanying vessels and escorts picked up Captain C.M. Whalley and all but three of his crew. Heyse's second victim, in the early hours of that same morning, was the smaller British naval oiler *Montenol*. The Royal Fleet Auxiliary was in ballast, bound for Freetown, and so severely damaged by Witte's torpedo that she had to be sunk by gunfire by HM Corvette *Woodruff*. Lieutenant Commander W.F.R. Seagrave's sloop *Wellington* picked up Captain E.E.A. Le Sage and all except the three-man engine-room watch who had been killed in the attack.

A loss was inflicted on Dönitz in mid July when Zimmermann's *U-136*, taking part in a group operation against Convoy OS33 in which six vessels were sunk, was herself sunk by the Free French destroyer *Léopard*, the sloop *Pelican* and the frigate *Spey*. Convoy SL115 was also attacked by the Italian submarine *Calvi* (Longobardo). Located by the sloop *Lulworth*, Longobardo was obliged to surface after a depth-charge attack and fought a gun-duel with the British sloop. Having missed the *Lulworth* with two torpedoes, the *Calvi* later sank while *Lulworth* was engaging *U-130* nearby. After the attack on OS33 the group moved east and sank six more merchantmen off Freetown, while further south still von Ruckteschell's *Michel* was carrying on her dirty trade, sinking the American tanker *William F. Humphrey*.

Hit with 'at least sixty shells, plus hundreds of rounds of machine-gun fire' and three torpedoes, the *William F. Humphrey* sank stern first. Four men were killed in the attack but the *Michel* picked up 29 more, all of whom were eventually imprisoned in Japan, where three died. Captain R. Schwarz, eight of his seamen and two of his armed guard avoided apprehension and drifted away on rafts. Next morning they found and boarded the tanker's No. 2 Lifeboat and set sail for the coast of Africa, eight hundred miles to the east. On 22 July, six days later, they were taken aboard the Norwegian cargo ship *Triton* and landed at Freetown, where several needed urgent medical treatment.

The former American vessel *Empire Hawksbill*,[9] now managed on behalf of the MoWT by Sir Walter Runciman & Company, was part of Convoy OS34 when she was torpedoed and sunk by Suhren's *U-564*, which had previously had a successful cruise on the American coast sinking a number of tankers, including the neutral Panamanian *Lubrafol* and the Mexican *Potrero del Llano*. On her next patrol in the Caribbean she was called up by *U-126*, on her way home with all her torpedoes expended, when, north of the Azores, Kapitänleutnant E. Bauer saw OS34. Early the following morning, 19 July, Suhren sank the *Empire Hawksbill*, killing Captain H.T. Lamb and his entire crew. He then torpedoed Haldin & Philipps's motor-vessel *Lavington Court*. This new tramp-ship was loaded with 6,000 tons of military and naval equipment destined for the Middle East. Six of her crew and one soldier were lost, though Captain J.W. Sutherland and the majority were rescued by Seagrave's *Wellington*. An attempt to salvage the *Lavington Court* ended unfortunately on 1 August when she sank under tow, two-thirds of the way between the Azores and the Fastnet lighthouse.

It was the west-bound convoys that suffered most during this period of spring and high summer. There was an attack on ONS76 on 19/20 March by four U-boats. In *U-507* Kapitänleutnant Schacht found his torpedoes deficient, but in the early morning of the 25th, at 01.50, Oberleutnant zur See O. Ites in *U-94* fired two torpedoes at the tanker *Imperial Transport*, part of ONS76. It will be recalled that this vessel had endured a similar ordeal in February 1940, when she was towed in and beached at Kilchattan on the Isle of Bute. Once more she proved her durability: thought to be sinking, she was ordered abandoned, but at daylight Captain W. Smail, still in command of the tanker, with the same chief engineer, Mr C. J. Swanbrow, and others of her crew scrambled back aboard, leaving the comparative safety of the Free French corvette which had picked them up earlier. Although she was holed and badly flooded forward there was some prospect of again saving the *Imperial Transport*, so while the French warship left with 45 of the tanker's survivors, Smail and a number of his crew joined a salvage party put aboard by a British corvette.

The 16 mixed mercantile and naval salvage crew withdrew from the *Imperial Transport* for the night, but at daylight on the 26th they returned, and by trimming the vessel Swanbrow succeeded in making the hand-operated fuel feed pump work, and steam was soon raised; meanwhile other necessary repairs were effected. 'Steam was raised by 11.30 . . . auxiliary machinery was started and the engine room and pump room bilges were being pumped . . . The steering control gear was changed from telemotor to direct control. At [14.15] the auxiliary compressor was started and the air reservoirs were filling. At [15.15] the chief engineer reported to the master that the engines were ready for starting. At [15.30 the] vessel got under way at 50 revolutions per minute . . . On March 27th, at 00.30 the ship took a list to port, and was righted by trimming No. 5 Tank.'[10] In due course full telemotor steering was re-established, and although Swanbrow was compelled to use salt water as feed water, the weather was moderate enough to enable him to increase speed. By the afternoon of the 29th land was in sight, and the *Imperial Star* entered St John's under her own power. This staunch vessel went on to survive the war.

This was a small enough triumph, however. Convoy ON92 lost seven of its 41 vessels, the British ships *Batna*, laden with coal, *Cristales* with general and china clay, the CAM-ship *Empire Dell* in ballast, and the *Llanover*, also flying light; also torpedoed were the Greek *Mount Parnes*, the Panamanian *Cocle* and the Swede *Tolken*. All but the *Batna, Cocle* and *Tolken* were sunk by *U-124* (Mohr), the remainder being the responsibility of Ites in *U-94*. Mercifully, only seven men died from all seven vessels. The escort had been provided by the 'American' A3 Escort Group consisting of the destroyer

Gleaves under Commander J.B. Heffernan, the USCG Cutter *Ingham* and the HMCSs *Algoma, Arvida, Bittersweet* and *Shediac*. Attached was the rescue ship *Bury*, Captain L.E. Brown, fitted with HF/DF equipment. Insufficient use appears to have been made of the bearings supplied by the *Bury*, which may account for the poor performance of the escorts. The *Bury* herself did fine work among the sinking merchantmen, rescuing 178 survivors.

Escorted by the British 7th Escort Group, Convoy ONS94 lost two Greek ships to those two old enemies, the weather and the sea state. They had made their way across the turbulent North Atlantic and were almost within sight of their dispersal point in Cape Cod Bay when the *Anna Mazaraki* was driven ashore and wrecked on East Bar, Sable Island, and the *Emmy* suffered the same fate after driving ashore in Morien Bay, Cape Breton Island.

Having failed to attack ON96 because of the terrible weather, a westerly storm of high winds and high seas, both Ites and Mohr ambushed Convoy ON100 on 9 June. The convoy consisted of 38 vessels, many of which were in ballast, and was accompanied by the Rescue Ship *Gothland*. Cover was provided by the C1 Escort Group, led by the Canadian destroyer *Assiniboine*, Lieutenant Commander J.H. Stubbs, and supported by the British corvettes *Dianthus* and *Nasturtium* and the Free French corvettes *Mimose* and *Aconit*. Later, on the 11th, Commander Prentice arrived in the Canadian corvette *Chambly* with the *Orillia* in company, and by the time the U-boats had broken off the action on the 13th HM Corvettes *Bittersweet* and *Primrose* had also come up.

In the early hours of the 9th Ites torpedoed the *Mimose* and then, 24 hours later, sank the *Ramsay* and *Empire Clough*. The latter, on her maiden voyage, was a brand-new ship only recently completed at John Readhead's yard at South Shields. She had been placed by the MoWT under the management of the Larrinaga Steamship Company of Liverpool and was in ballast, bound for New York. Although five men were lost with her, her master Captain F. de Bastarrecha and 43 men were rescued, the majority by the corvette *Dianthus* and a dozen by the Portuguese fishing schooner *Argus*, which landed them on the Greenland coast, from where they were taken by US naval patrol boat to the American mainland. Such a dispersal of a crew was always a problem for the authorities responsible, but at least most of the *Empire Clough*'s crew were alive. Those aboard the tramp-ship *Ramsay* were far less fortunate, for although Captain B.F.R. Thomas and seven men were soon picked up by the corvette *Vervain*, 40 men were lost with *Ramsay* as she sank rapidly, her empty holds quickly filling with water as she steamed along. For these gallant actions, Ites was awarded a *Ritterkreuz*.[11]

The only other ship actually in the main body of the convoy to be lost had already been accounted for by Mohr, who had torpedoed the Watts, Watts tramp *Dartford* in the small hours of 12 June. Captain S. Bulmer and 29 men were lost with her, for although the *Gothland* was on the scene, Captain J.M. Hadden was only able to find 17 men. Another of the five U-boats operating with Mohr and Ites, *U-569*, torpedoed and damaged the British steamer *Pontypridd* of Cardiff, which was then straggling astern of the convoy. She was also in ballast but did not sink immediately, enduring an attack by Ites before Kapitänleutnant H-P. Hinsch returned in *U-569* to administer the *coup de grâce*. The tramp's master, Captain H.V.B. Morden, was taken prisoner to La Pallice and sent on to Milag Nord. The other 42 men were taken up by the *Chambly*.

The men of this U-boat group[12] were still eager to exercise their *Rudeltaktik* in mid June when they ran into ONS102. Dönitz ordered them to attack, but the escort was strong. Commander P.R. Heineman now commanded the A3 Escort Group, which was made up of the USCG Cutters *Campbell* and *Ingham*, the US destroyer *Leary*, the Canadian destroyer *Restigouche* and HMC Corvettes *Collingwood, Rosthern, Mayflower* and *Agassiz*. The rescue ship *Perth* was also in company; like the *Restigouche* she was fitted with HF/DF, and good use was made of their bearings in driving the U-boats off. Both *U-94* and *U-590* were echo-located, attacked with depth-charges and damaged, though without fatal consequences. The USS *Leary* escaped five torpedoes fired at her by *U-406* (Dieterichs) on the 17th but on the following day Mohr, still shadowing the convoy, torpedoed the American freighter *Seattle Spirit*. She was commanded by Captain E.W. Myers, former master of the *Robin Moor*, and was returning from Murmansk after a voyage to Russia as part of PQ15 outward and QP12 homeward. Mohr's torpedo blew in the shell plating in way of the engine room, which immediately flooded, drowning the watch and causing her boilers to explode. One more man died after jumping into the sea, but the rest were saved by HMCS *Agassiz* and *Perth*, the *Seattle Spirit* being sunk by *Agassiz*'s guns that afternoon when it had become clear the ship could not be salvaged.

Elsewhere that spring Walker's escort group was patiently developing its tactics. Back on 10 April, after landing agents in Iceland, Kapitänleutnant K. Lerchen in *U-252* had sunk the small Norwegian ship *Fanefield*, which had just left Isafjörd, with the loss of all hands. The U-boat was on her way from Helgoland to a French base when she met Convoy OG82 on the night of 13/14 April. Lerchen shadowed the 17 merchantmen, but on the following evening his conning tower 'painted' a response on the plan position indicator of the 10-centimetric radar aboard the *Vetch*, part of Walker's 36th Escort Group assigned to cover OG82. At 7,000 yards' range Lieutenant

Menzies turned *Vetch* and worked her up to full speed, firing snowflake to illuminate his target and dodging the two torpedoes Lerchen fired at him as *U-252* dived. A little later Lerchen came back to the surface, hoping to be covered by the darkness; instead he found himself once again ahead of *Vetch*. Menzies again increased speed, but Lerchen's nemesis was now approaching in the form of HM Sloop *Stork*. Commanded by Walker himself, *Stork* joined *Vetch* in shelling *U-252* until she dived again, whereupon *Vetch* obtained a sonar contact and depth-charged her. Walker followed suit and dropped two patterns before Menzies made a second attack, followed by a final bombardment from *Stork*.

The expenditure of 51 depth-charges resulted in débris and human remains, 'a revolting mixture of oil, wood, blood, and guts . . . and a human heart and lungs complete but penetrated by splinters', floating to the surface in the slick left by the submarine concussions: *U-252* and all 44 souls aboard had died for the Reich.

Walker's group were next in action while providing the escort to the homeward convoy HG84 which left Gibraltar on 10 June. After the disastrous attempt against HG76 the previous December Dönitz had stayed his hand from sorties against convoys west of Gibraltar, a decision reinforced when in an attack by *U-71*, *U-93* and *U-571* on HG78 on 15 January, *U-93* was sunk by the destroyer *Hesperus*. Although only six men died, Oberleutnant zur See H. Elfe and 40 more were made prisoners-of-war. His force was reported to be small, but Walker's robust defence of OG82 and the loss of *U-252* combined with the loss of Rollmann in *U-82* to persuade Dönitz that the British were running lightly-escorted dummy convoys as U-boat traps. The Britain–Gibraltar run was still vulnerable, however, and as the pressure built up on U-boats operating in the far west he began to think that an attack west of Gibraltar after five months' respite was likely to find the escorts complacent. Accordingly, having received intelligence from Algiers on 9 June that a convoy was preparing to depart, he directed a pack of U-boats on passage to American waters to concentrate against it before refuelling from a U-tanker and resuming their westward courses. This convoy was HG84.

Among the 23 merchantmen were the rescue ship *Copeland* and the *Empire Morn*, a standard, emergency-built cargo-vessel completed in 1941 by Thompson's at Sunderland and fitted as a CAM-ship. The convoy, with Commodore H.T. Hudson aboard Macandrew's *Pelayo* leading the centre column, stood out into the Atlantic, heading west in a strong westerly wind and heavy sea and swell. The visibility was excellent, and on the 11th, as three ships joined from Lisbon, the ominous rumble of a Kondor's engines was heard and the first FW200 was seen on the horizon, intermittently hidden in the clouds. Walker held his hand, and it was not until noon on the 14th that he ordered the *Empire Morn* to launch her fighter, hoping thereby to deprive the Germans of intelligence some hours before, in his estimation, they were likely to attack. His instinct proved sound. From the forecastle of the *Empire Morn* the Mark 1 Hurricane was rocketed skywards but failed to inflict any damage on the Kondor, which flew off, obscured by cloud, leaving the Hurricane pilot to ditch in the hope of rescue. He was not disappointed, for he landed close to *Stork*, whose sea-boat quickly fished him out of the water.

The ace had been played, and Walker's prescience was confirmed. Dönitz's prepared ambush of eight U-boats – group-named after the dead hero Endrass and intended to avenge his loss in the area the previous December – was under orders to attack that night, and at 16.00 *Copeland* intercepted a U-boat sighting report being transmitted to Kerneval from a position astern of the convoy.

The Kondor's signal had alerted Topp, and *U-552* was soon joined by *U-89* and *U-132*, with *U-437* not far away. The *Endrass* group was a mixture of the experienced and the green: with Topp in *U-552* were Vogelsang in *U-132*, Flachsenberg in *U-71*, Uphoff in *U-84* and Heydemann in *U-575*, but Schendel in *U-134*, Lohmann in *U-89* and Schulz in *U-437* were scarcely blooded.

Walker turned *Stork* back though the convoy, picked up *Gardenia*, and followed *Copeland*'s HF/DF bearing. They soon saw the enemy, but the range was too far and the sloop and corvette were rolling too much to hope for a hit as the U-boat turned away and made a run on the surface. Soon afterwards she dived, and half an hour later *Stork* had echo-located her. She was Vogelsang's *U-132*.

The convoy ploughed on, now heading north and with a greater concentration of U-boats off its starboard bow. Only *Convolvulus* was still acting as close escort, since Lieutenant J.A. Halcrew in *Marigold* was investigating a second reported U-boat, Lohmann's *U-89*.

Pressed for time as the convoy drew away from him, Walker made five depth-charge attacks on Vogelsang before *Gardenia* caught up with him, by which time *Stork*'s stock of depth-charges was depleted. For the first time he now employed the form of 'creeping' attack that in due course he made so successful. Well aware of the opportunity for evasion afforded by the inevitable loss of sonar contact in the last, crucial moments of an attack, Walker slowed *Stork* and, echo-locating *U-132* himself, vectored *Gardenia*'s commanding officer over her. It ought to have been a resounding success, yielding up the gruesome remains that were the only evidence acceptable to an Admiralty sceptical about claimed U-boat kills, but in fact one of

Gardenia's depth-charges exploded prematurely, damaging the corvette's stern. The wreckage was cleared away and the attack repeated, but the action was inconclusive. It was now 22.00. Learning that *Convolvulus*, like *Marigold*, had left the vicinity of the convoy to track down a U-boat, Walker left *Gardenia* still in contact and headed for HG84.

The five-columned convoy was intact despite its exposure, and by midnight *Stork* and *Convolvulus* were back on station and *Marigold* was returning to hers. The vigorous actions of the small escort, of which only *Stork* possessed a slight advantage in speed over a surfaced U-boat, had kept the enemy away – all, that is, except one. Topp had evaded close attention, but when he received relocating signals transmitted by *U-437*, which had been driven off by *Convolvulus*, he headed towards HG84 from a position ahead of the advancing mass of shipping. Walker was covering the vulnerable rear of the convoy: for once he had got it wrong.

Topp now put in an extraordinary performance which began at about 01.00 when, undetected, *U-552* moved in and fired a full salvo of four bow and one stern torpedoes at a range later thought to have been about 3,000 yards. Three of the weapons failed or missed but the rest struck three ships, Moss Hutchinson's *Etrib*, the commodore's ship *Pelayo*, and the Norwegian tanker *Slemdal*. The confusion caused by these almost simultaneous acts of destruction allowed Topp to withdraw and reload. In the rear of the convoy at about 04.00 *Stork's* lookouts located another U-boat and Walker dropped a pattern of depth-charges, thought he had achieved a kill, and moved away as reports reached him that U-boats had been seen on the starboard bow of the convoy. This was where the mass of the *Endrass* group were still located, seeking a weakness in the convoy's defence.

Even as *Stork* changed station Topp struck again from within the convoy. Again he fired a full salvo, again two failed to find targets or malfunctioned, but at 04.30 two struck home. In a blinding flash and with a concussion that caused every vessel in the convoy capable of doing so to illuminate her surroundings with snowflakes, the *Thurso* blew up. An instant later a torpedo exploded on Ellerman's *City of Oxford*.

As Walker fulminated on the bridge of *Stork*, in the light of the snowflakes' glare *Marigold* and *Copeland* tried to rescue those hapless individuals cast into the water by Topp's first attack. The *Etrib* had been carrying a load of fruit, fruit-pulp, wine and cork, and Captain McMillan and 42 of his 48 men were picked up by the corvette, afterwards transferring to the *Copeland*. Captain W.J. Hartley's rescue ship hauled Captain R.H. Williams of the *Pelayo*, 26 of his crew and three of the commodore's staff out of the water, but Commodore Hudson, a veteran of PQ12, two of his staff, three DEMS gunners and 11 of the *Pelayo's* crew were killed. All hands aboard the *Slemdal*, which was acting as a Royal Navy Auxiliary, were rescued, but by this time Topp's second attack was under way. The *Thurso*, owned by Ellerman's Wilson Line, had been one of the three vessels joining HG84 from Lisbon. Why she should have blown up is unclear, for her cargo consisted of 850 tons of general cargo and mails. Captain W. Walker and 28 crew were picked up by *Marigold*, but 13 men were killed. Only one man died aboard the *City of Oxford*, which was carrying a cargo of cork and iron ore; Captain A. Norbury and 42 men found refuge aboard the *Copeland*.

Walker was furious. He had asked for air cover, but none had been forthcoming. He had one disabled corvette, the *Gardenia*, which was incapable of exceeding 10 knots, while another, *Marigold*, was encumbered with 172 survivors. Even so, the aggression of his corvettes had kept the remainder of the U-boats at bay. Topp's *U-552* had endured a depth-charge attack and sustained serious damage. Flachsenberg's *U-71* had also received a pummelling, and while Heydemann in *U-575* had fired a salvo of four torpedoes at overlapping targets, all had missed or misfired. Although Walker could not know it, only Topp had eluded his thinly-spread resources, and if *U-552* had struck at his charges with devastating effect, *Stork* and her three corvettes had successfully defended them against greater numbers.

As *Stork*, *Marigold* and *Copeland* effected a redistribution of survivors astern of the convoy, a lookout aboard the corvette spied a U-boat and Hartley took off after it. He was unsuccessful, however, and had to abandon the chase to rejoin the convoy and take up his night station before darkness. The submarine remained at the extreme of visible range of the convoy throughout the day in consequence, transmitting a homing signal. There was every prospect of the following night being bloodier than its predecessor.

That evening, the 15th, an RAF Liberator arrived and Walker directed it to attack the trailing U-boat. This it failed to do, though it transmitted a report claiming success. Darkness fell and the Liberator withdrew as *Gardenia* regained station, *Stork* took up her night position in the convoy's rear and *Marigold* and *Convolvulus* moved into their respective starboard and port flank stations. 'The night was full of false alarms and sightings.' There was much scurrying about, though only *Convolvulus*, the sole escort still with a full inventory of depth-charges, was actually in contact with a U-boat. No attack matured, and not long after daylight a Catalina arrived, circling the convoy and deterring any enemy from making a close approach. Later that afternoon a Whitley bomber came on the scene and Walker, ever restless, transferred depth-charges by boat from *Convolvulus* to *Stork*, a difficult task at best, but evidence that the secrets of Walker's growing success were attention to detail, and no opportunity wasted.

In addition to the aircraft, surface assistance now arrived in the form of HM Destroyer Wild Swan and the new 'River'-class frigates Rother and Spey, then on their way to Gibraltar. These did not stay long with HG84, but their mere presence gave the U-boat commanders the excuse to claim that the escort was 'strong'. More Allied aircraft appeared too: Lancaster bombers, Boeing B28s, and Catalinas. On 17 June Dönitz, having just acquired his own reinforcements of some Junkers Ju88 dive-bombers, sent them out to help their colleagues. They attacked a fleet of Spanish trawlers and the Wild Swan, sinking the British destroyer and four trawlers, but not before the Wild Swan had shot down several of their number. The destroyer Vansittart later picked up 133 of Wild Swan's company, and 11 Spanish fishermen.

As HG84 approached the Irish coast, Hudson medium bombers arrived and the convoy was given constant air cover. This and the fact that the weather had fined away, falling to a calm with good visibility, gave Dönitz his excuse to break off the action. He was disappointed, despite Topp's success, for U-552 and U-71 had to return to France for repairs and replenishment. Walker did not know it, but he had won a small victory which, though not without its cost in both men and ships, exemplified the technical advantage slowly gathering in the Allies' favour. In addition to the obvious success of the long-range aircraft, elements such as Huff-Duff, Type 271 radar and shallow-set depth-charges, combined with Walker's style of convoy defence – including his pioneering creeping attack – played important parts in the mounting challenge to the Befelshaber der U-boote.

Dönitz appreciated little of this. He was however already concerned about the increasing dangers to which his submarines were exposed as they crossed the Bay of Biscay, hence his persuasive success in wresting 24 Ju88C6s from Reichsmarschall Goering, and his orders for all U-boats to be fitted with defensive anti-aircraft machine-guns. He was concerned too about the existence of what he called 'an enemy surface-location device' which seemed to confer almost magic powers on British aircraft. Several of his U-boats had suffered night attacks by aircraft using a powerful searchlight to illuminate their target. This, the Leigh light, gave the British and their Allies one more incremental advantage, as the superiority Dönitz's submarines had enjoyed ever since the occupation of France's Biscay bases was slowly eroded.

On 6 July a Wellington from No. 172 Squadron armed with radar and a Leigh light sank U-502 on her way back from a war patrol, and on the 12th U-159 was likewise damaged. Five days later a Whitley from No. 502 Squadron and a Lancaster of No. 61 Squadron sank the outward-bound U-751, while a Wellington of No. 311 (Czech) Squadron RAF so damaged U-106 that she was forced to return to her base.

On 19 July Dönitz withdrew the last seven U-boats from the American east coast. Frustrated at last by the introduction by the Americans of convoys, they found themselves bereft of targets. Two were lost, one returned to base, and the remaining four moved north towards Nova Scotia, where Vogelsang's U-123 had some successes in the Gulf of St Lawrence with the sinking of several ships.[13] In the last few days of July his submarine was one of three U-boats that attacked Convoy ON113, and he sank the *Pacific Pioneer*. She was in ballast and all hands escaped, as they did from the *Empire Rainbow* which was sunk by Jeschonneck in U-607.[14] The third U-boat was Topp's U-552; having damaged the tanker *British Merit*, he struck at the British tramp *Broompark*, torpedoing her with the loss of four men, including Captain J.L. Sinclair. Her damaged hull was taken in tow by the American passenger-vessel *Cherokee* until she sank five days later, on 1 August. Her survivors were rescued by HMCS *Brandon*.

German operations continued in the Gulf of Mexico and the Caribbean, though U-153 was sunk off Panama on 13 July, and they obtained two small successes in the North Atlantic against independently-sailing or straggling merchant ships. Kapitänleutnant J. Oestermann in U-754 sank the 12,435-ton *Waiwera* north of the Azores on 29 June. Eight lives were lost when the Shaw, Savill & Albion liner went down with a valuable cargo of 13,000 tons of butter, tea and meat, 2,100 bags of mail, and 20 passengers. Captain C.M. Andrews and most of his people were picked up by a Norwegian ship, the *Oregon Express*. Oestermann went on to contact and shadow Convoy ON113 a month later. He was spotted by a covering Hudson of No. 113, Royal Canadian Air Force, flown by Squadron Leader N.E. Small, which took U-754 by surprise on the surface and depth-charged her before banking round and machine-gunning the conning tower. Oestermann dived, but an hour later an explosion brought oil and muck to the surface, sufficient evidence that the U-boat had been destroyed.

That last day of July saw another U-boat destroyed. In the Azores, 160 miles east of Santa Maria, U-213 encountered a convoy whose escort echo-located her. Oblerleutnant zur See A. von Varendorff and 49 men were sent into the abyss by the sloops *Rochester*, Commander C.B. Allen, *Erne* and *Sandwich*.

But the real battle was still to come.

PART FIVE

August 1942–May 1943

GREY DAWN
BREAKING

18

'It was a rare event . . .'

Laconia

THE COMING TEN months saw the climax of the Battle of the Atlantic. During the first half of this critical period the Germans enjoyed a run of successes but, fatally based as they were upon the miscalculations of Hitler, they were the last fruits of Dönitz's ambitions. In his beloved submarines' final months of apparent victory, the German admiral expended what remained of his best commanders and crews. Moreover, although German ingenuity continued to produce innovations potentially dangerous to the Allied cause, the reserves of expertise, determination and drive behind them were dwindling.

One U-boat commander who after the war confessed to having been broken by the British in captivity denied that it was as the result of any kind of duress, sadly explaining that he had lost his faith in a German victory when he was taken to dinner in London by his captors. He had been convinced by his masters that the city had been laid waste by the Luftwaffe, and the revelation that this was a palpable untruth changed his attitude at a stroke.[1]

Such a profound and individual revelation was denied the great mass of men who made up the crews of the British and Allied merchant vessels. *Their* faith was undergoing a crisis of a different sort as misunderstandings, exaggerations and downright lies continued to spread in ever-widening ripples from the Barents Sea. They spread slowly but insidiously and, it has to be said, unsupported by much evidence, yet appealing to a body of men who believed themselves to be as hard done by now as they had been in the Depression. Seen in very general terms, the morale of the Merchant Navy slid into a war-weariness that reached its nadir in 1944, even as the fortunes of the Allies were climbing towards an assurance of victory. It was of such moment as to stimulate government efforts to combat it and to take more care of its existing merchant sailors, and hurriedly train more to man the newly-built merchant ships.

Individual examples of personal heroism, tenacity, devotion to duty and 'getting on with the job' were of course as manifest as ever. There was even the occasional ray of sunshine, as in July 1942 when a small group of merchant seamen were removed from the Milag Nord prison camp at Westertimke near Bremen and exchanged for their German counterparts on a rank-for-rank basis.[2] These men were predominantly victims of German commerce-raiders. At Milag Nord, where Captain A. Hill, lately commander of Brocklebank's *Mandasor*, was for some time the senior officer, in conditions of moderate privation senior officers set up courses for the younger seamen and built training models that enabled them to study for their able seamen's qualifications, while apprentices, cadets and junior mates could prepare for and sit the written examinations for their certificates of competency as second mate, first mate, even master. The Germans also allowed one of the first-class libraries circulated to British merchantmen by the Seafarers' Education Service to be sent in by way of Switzerland, the protecting power. Milag Nord even boasted a small orchestra led by some musicians off the liner *Orama*, which also supplied the camp's British master-at-arms, a mercantile rank found only aboard passenger-liners, for the regulation of their large crews.[3]

Among the incarcerated seamen were a number of Indian lascars whom the German authorities attempted to suborn and to use as agricultural workers. The lascars, whose All India Seamen's Federation had declared in 1941 that they were 'bringing food and transporting war materials in the face of the danger from enemy submarines . . .' and that they 'wanted to be useful in this fight against the forces of evil', were seen by their captors as amenable to separation from enforced loyalty to their imperial masters. This assumption proved ill-founded; on one occasion when a work party returned to the camp after gathering nuts, the lascars 'once down into their barracks . . . disgorged chickens, eggs, potatoes and everything in high glee.'

Hill, whose crew had been largely composed of Indians, also reported that an attempt to shift a large number of lascars to another site failed when they 'refused to enter the trucks, sat down in the road and dared the Germans to shoot them'. This defiance, already familiar as a tactic of Indian non-violent protest, led to their return to Milag Nord the same evening.[4]

A few Indians collaborated, joining the Indian Legion, and four British seafarers volunteered for the British Frei Korps, while Chinese seamen were sent to work in a tank factory near Hamburg. Milag Nord was the chief but not the only prison camp occupied by merchant seamen. In other camps, 'neutral' Irish nationals serving in the British Merchant Navy had a hard time.

The American interlocking convoy system introduced in July 1942 dove-tailed into the slow SC/ONS and fast HX/ON series, providing regular links with Boston and New York. The new convoy routes then led south to locations off Key West (the NK/KN series), or to Guantanamo Bay (the NG/GN series). From these two dispersal-cum-rendezvous points, feeder convoys ran to the ports of the Gulf of Mexico, to Colon at the northern end of the Panama Canal, to the oil ports of Venezuela, to Trinidad and then on down the Brazilian coast to Recife and Rio de Janeiro. In the succeeding months there were variations and additions to these,[5] but the principle of co-ordinated convoy had been established, and while the gathering naval resources assigned to the task came under King as both Commander-in-Chief, United States Fleet and Chief of Naval Operations, they were actually controlled by the Convoy and Routeing Section, an American equivalent of the British model upon which it was based.

An important feature of the development of this rationalisation was the shifting of the terminus for the Halifax and Sydney convoys to New York, 'which then became the greatest *entrepôt* of shipping in the world'.[6] The prefix HX remained, and the first convoy to sail from New York was HX208, which departed for Liverpool on 17 September with 59 merchantmen, none of which was lost in convoy.

By the end of the summer of 1942 the number of U-boats under Dönitz's command was edging towards the four-hundred mark, with some 50 per cent actually operational and supported by a commissioning rate of between 59 per quarter in July 1942 and 71 per quarter the following year. To oppose them the Allies now had 26 escort groups which were increasingly assisted by independent support groups, while a steady augmentation of aircraft numbers in the British and Canadian air forces ensured growing air cover. In addition to airborne radar, the Leigh light and improved air-borne depth-charges significantly increased the capabilities of the aircraft in service. But since neither the Hudson, Wellington and Whitley bombers nor the Catalina and Sunderland flying-boats in service with either Coastal Command or No. 1 Group of the RCAF possessed sufficient range, the air-gap remained. Significant deficiencies also continued on the American coast, where a mixture of United States Army and Navy aircraft was initially supplemented by civilian patrols and it was not until midsummer of 1943 that the entire littoral was covered by US naval aircraft.

Despite the fact that it was operating under incomplete air-cover, the interlocking convoy system robbed Dönitz of most of his initiative on the American coast, and the operation of individual U-boats in such distant waters proved uneconomic. He therefore switched the focus of German effort back to the North Atlantic, well aware of the continuing Allied weakness in the air-gap south of Cape Farewell and the potential harvest still to be reaped in the old U-boat stamping grounds off Nova Scotia. Here, as July turned into August and the 41 vessels of Convoy ON115 ploughed west in the custody of the Canadian C3 Escort Group, Dönitz's submarines continued their dirty work.

The senior officer of C3 was Lieutenant Commander D.C. Wallace, RN aboard HM Canadian Destroyer *Saguenay*. In support Wallace had another destroyer, HMCS *Skeena*, and the corvettes *Galt, Sackville, Wetaskiwin, Agassiz* and *Louisburg*. In the last days of July they had succeeded in defending the convoy against five U-boats, destroying *U-588* in the process.[7] On 1 August, as ON115 approached Cape Race, a new group of U-boats was cobbled together and given the name *Pirat* by Dönitz's staff. It included Jeschonneck and Topp, and they sighted the convoy on the 2nd. By this time the cohesion of Wallace's group had been undermined by the detachment of the destroyers for refuelling, and a little later the *Wetaskiwin* was sent off on a hunt and failed to rejoin the convoy. However, the remaining corvettes were reinforced by two destroyers, the Canadian *Hamilton* and the British *Witch* from the Western Local Escort Force.

Topp remained in contact, and on the morning of the 3rd he attacked, hitting two ships, the British tanker *G.S. Walden* and the Belgian-flagged *Belgian Soldier*: both were damaged, and both survived. Lieutenant A.H. Easton, RN in HMCS *Sackville* counter-attacked and depth-charged *U-552*, but Topp was wily: he released some oil, broke off operations, and stole away. His apparent loss caused mourning in Germany and at Dönitz's headquarters, until *U-552* turned up off St-Nazaire on 13 August.

The remaining U-boats resumed their attack on the night of the 3rd/4th, and shortly after midnight Oberleutnant Jeschonneck in *U-607* struck the damaged *Belgian Soldier* and sent her to the bottom, killing 21 of her company of exiles. The last kill was made by *U-553*, on her way to the West Indies but summoned to the scene by Topp's report. Commanded by Korvettenkapitän K. Thurmann, she sank the Royal Mail liner *Lochkatrine*, Captain P. Cooper. This ship sank with the loss of the one passenger she was carrying and eight of her crew. Despite the hour, the remaining 17 passengers and 64 crew were picked up by the escorts. By now the convoy was meeting the fogs and mists of the Grand Banks, and although several attacks were mounted, none succeeded.

A significant weakness in the capabilities of the escorts lay in the short range of many, particularly the destroyers. Since these were invariably the ships commanded by the escort's senior officer, their removal from a convoy screen was a significant weakening of its defence. The Royal Navy, blessed with the legacy of world-wide bunkering stations, had never, prior to the Battle of the Atlantic, had to take the question of refuelling at sea as seriously as current circumstances clearly dictated it must. Various methods were now experimented with, most usually that of lying astern of an 'oiler', but numerous accounts tell of the difficulties involved, which ranged from doing so in conditions dictated by the sea-state to a lack of standard couplings. In due course these confusions were overcome and tankers acting as naval auxiliaries were routinely attached to trans-Atlantic convoys. As usual, too, good sense and good seamanship prevailed – but the matter should have been resolved sooner.[8]

The decision made by Dönitz to return to his old hunting-grounds had an immediate impact, resulting in a ferocious series of actions around Convoy SC94 which left Sydney on the last day of July. Under a commodore embarked in the Hain tramp *Trehata* it consisted of 30 ships with a convoy speed of 7.5 knots. Escort was provided by a mixed group of British and Canadian warships which made up the nominally 'Canadian' C1 Escort group. Although the destroyer HMCS *Assiniboine*, Lieutenant Commander J.H. Stubbs, was among these, the senior officer was Lieutenant Commander Ayer of the British corvette *Primrose* and the remainder consisted of the British corvettes *Nasturtium* and *Dianthus*, and the Canadians *Battleford, Chilliwack* and *Orillia*. At the time none were fitted with HF/DF equipment, and only *Nasturtium* possessed the efficient Type 271 centimetric radar, though *Assiniboine* had Type 286.

Against these Dönitz mustered a group of eight U-boats east of the Newfoundland Bank. The number of U-boats engaging SC94 subsequently varied as the action progressed and Kerneval despatched outward-bound submarines to the battle. As SC94 emerged from the mists of the Grand Banks it was Kapitänleutnant G. Kelbing in *U-593* who first made contact and upon whose summons Kerneval acted. Submarines up to three hundred miles distant raced towards Kelbing, who launched the offensive on 5 August with *U-595*, Kapitänleutnant J. Quaet-Faslem, in support. The convoy had by this time passed Cape Farewell and was in the air-gap when Kelbing torpedoed Hudig & Pieters's tramp *Spar*, formerly of Rotterdam. The three men on watch in her boiler and engine room were killed as she sank with 4,900 tons of general cargo. In response *Nasturtium* and *Orillia* counterattacked, and drove Kelbing and his colleague off for a while.

Quaet-Faslem returned to the attack, choosing the *Assiniboine* as his target in the darkness of the early morning of the 6th. His torpedo exploded either prematurely or at the end of its run, and Quaet-Faslem found himself the centre of unwelcome attention from *Chilliwack* and *Primrose*, who got in some shots before *U-595* dived. The two corvettes then subjected her to so punishing a depth-charging that Quaet-Faslem, although he remained in contact for some time and made another attack, was eventually compelled to retire to Brest. The same day Kapitänleutnant B. Hackländer's *U-454* entered St-Nazaire, also too badly damaged to continue operations, having been echo-located and violently depth-charged by *Dianthus*.

Unaware of her own escape, *Assiniboine* herself located another submarine, Kapitänleutnant R. Lemcke's *U-210*, pounding her with such accuracy that Lemcke was forced to the surface, where a short-ranged and bloody fire-fight ensued. The *Assiniboine*'s first shot punctured a fuel tank, preventing *U-210* from diving, and Lemcke tried to escape in an adjacent patch of fog, unaware that Stubbs had him on radar. The two were soon so close as to be firing at point-blank range, Lemcke trying to keep within the destroyer's turning circle. German shells ignited the destroyer's bridge, killing one Canadian seaman, the youngest on board, and wounding 13 others before Lemcke and five of his own men were killed by a direct hit on *U-210*'s conning tower. With this wrecked, the wounded first watch officer, G. Göhlich, tried to dive and fired a torpedo before Stubbs moved in to ram. Dropping more depth-charges on a shallow setting as he twice slammed into the U-boat, Stubbs killed five men before finally sinking the U-boat. *Dianthus*, arriving out of the mist, assisted Stubbs in picking up 37 sailors as prisoners-of-war. The entire action had taken less than forty minutes.

The escort had driven the enemy off, but *Assiniboine* was now so badly damaged by her contact with *U-210* that Stubbs was compelled to withdraw, significantly weakening Ayer's defence. Meanwhile, from signals made by Quaet-Faslem as he retreated Kerneval was able to order more U-boats to the scene and these closed on the slow mass of eastbound merchantmen during 7 August. The first attack came that afternoon when Kapitänleutnant E. Mengersen happened upon a group of ships which had straggled and now lay astern of the main body. None of his torpedoes found their target, nor did those from Kessler's *U-704* that same evening, nor those from Bauer's *U-660* a few hours later. At noon on the 8th two more U-boats, *U-597* and *U-605*, fired at the stragglers, but their torpedoes also failed, and matters looked inauspicious until a few hours later *U-176* and *U-379* made almost coincident assaults on the convoy itself.

On the 4th, on his way to the rendezvous, Korvettenkapitän R. Dierksen in *U-176* had sunk the British Union Castle Line's 1939-built refrigerated fruit-carrying cargo-passenger-liner *Richmond Castle*. Now, reaching SC94, he rapidly added three more vessels to his tally, torpedoing in quick succession the commodore's vessel *Trehata*, the *Kelso*, and the *Mount Kassion*.

The convoy, unused to daylight attacks, endured an afternoon of confusion. The *Trehata* was laden with 3,000 tons of steel and 3,000 tons of foodstuffs, and took Captain J. Lawrie and 19 of her crew with her. Lawrie had won the Distinguished Service Order twice and the Distinguished Service Cross once since the beginning of the war; the convoy commodore, former Vice Admiral D.F. Moir, was also a holder of the DSO, and was among those killed, along with four of his staff and a naval gunner, as the *Trehata* sank. The survivors, 25 in all, found refuge aboard the accompanying Norwegian cargo-vessel *Inger Lise*. The *Kelso*, one of Ellerman's Wilson Line, was lost with 2,620 tons of general cargo and 2,000 tons of ammunition. Her master and crew were luckier, though all on watch in the engine room were killed as Dierksen's torpedo pierced the *Kelso*'s hull. Captain A. Hinchcliff and the remainder were rescued by the *Battleford*. Dierksen's third target, the Greek freighter *Mount Kassion*, bore 9,700 tons of general cargo, but her crew escaped without loss.

As these three vessels were in their death throes, Kapitänleutnant P-H. Kettner, on his first war patrol in *U-379*, fired a salvo of torpedoes which struck two steam-ships, the American *Kaimoku* and the British *Anneberg*. The former, belonging to the Matson Navigation Company of San Francisco, commanded by Captain T. Cunningham and laden with United States Army stores, lost her assistant engineer and his three firemen as they stood their watch in the boiler room. Their shipmates were pulled from the sea by the *Battleford*. The *Anneberg* was a small and ancient vessel, built in 1902 and full of 3,200 tons of pulp.[9] A former foreign-flagged ship, she was under the management of Gardiner, James & Company of Glasgow on behalf of the MoWT and in the charge of one of their masters, Captain C.L. Bullock. Although torpedoed she took some time to sink, and was despatched by *Dianthus*, which was joined by *Nasturtium* and *Primrose* in picking up her crew.

The explosions resulting from the attacks by these two U-boats caused consternation as five ships settled in the convoy and their consorts were obliged to swung out of line to avoid hitting them as the escorts went into action. In the welter the men on several other vessels became infected by the panic of uncertainty amid a growing expectation of imminent death. Not all those aboard the merchantmen were battle-hardened seafarers, and the crews of the *Empire Moonbeam* (the last vessel to be completed at the Hong Kong & Whampoa Dock Company's yard before the Japanese occupied the Crown Colony), the ageing American-built *Empire Antelope* and the *Radchurch* all abandoned their ships in the conviction that they had been torpedoed. 'It was', the official historian Roskill records, 'a rare event for British merchant seamen to act in such a manner.' Captains W.J. Slade and W.G.S. Hewison afterwards persuaded their crews to reboard their vessels and continue the voyage, but Captain J. Lewin of the *Radchurch* was not only unable to prevent his crew taking to their boats but afterwards failed to cajole them into following the example of the others in rejoining, once the true state of affairs had become clear. Perhaps the fact that the *Radchurch* was an old and rotten ship had something to do with it. British-built in 1910 and originally owned by an Italian company under the name *Istina*, by 1939 she had been acquired by the Oceania Shipping Company of Susak, Yugoslavia. Lately she had been taken over by the MoWT and placed under the management of a Cardiff-based tramping firm, Evans & Reid, in their subsidiary the Strath Steamship Company. Perhaps, too, it had something to do with her lading, a full cargo of iron ore. In the confusion two men were lost, unnecessary casualties compounding a reprehensible incident.

While this crisis in labour relations was going on the *Dianthus*, having plucked a few men from the sea and despatched the foundering *Anneberg*, resumed her own station. A little later her lookouts spotted two surfaced U-boats, and Lieutenant Commander C.E. Bridgeman opened fire with *Dianthus*'s 4-inch gun. Both targets submerged, but after casting about for some time in the gathering darkness the corvette's lookouts again spotted a U-boat and star-shell was fired over her, forcing her to seek concealment under water once again. Now the *Dianthus*'s operators obtained a sonar echo and Bridgeman went tenaciously in quest of its source. Within minutes depth-charges had blown Kettner's *U-379* back to the surface in the glare of another burst of star-shell. With all his guns now blazing at the U-boat, Bridgemen dropped more shallow-set charges, then swung round and rammed the forepart of *U-379*, riding over her pressure hull and lobbing five more depth-charges over as she did so. Kettner was now compelled to scuttle and abandon his submarine under a withering fire from *Dianthus*, while Bridgeman crashed his corvette remorselessly into the dying U-boat's pressure hull. Just after midnight *U-379* sank. Only five Germans were taken prisoner before Bridgeman, anxious about the crippled state of *Dianthus* and the presence of other U-boats, ordered a Carley raft thrown over the side for the benefit of any further survivors before turning for home.

Meanwhile the *Radchurch* drifted astern of the convoy, only her master still aboard. When it became clear that the crew would not return, Captain Lewin was taken off and the ship abandoned. Later, on the 9th, Dierksen found her again, took her for a mere straggler, and fired torpedoes from *U-176*'s bow tubes, finally sending her to the bottom.

The behaviour of the three crews was embarrassing, but the incident was swiftly relegated to the periphery of events as later on the 8th the escort received the welcome reinforcements of two destroyers, the Polish *Blyskawica* and HMS *Broke*, Lieutenant Commander Layard, who became senior officer. *Broke* was fitted with HF/DF equipment, so with an air escort due from Northern Ireland in the form of a long-range Liberator from No. 120 Squadron and a Catalina stretching down from Iceland, Layard's warships were drawn away to attack contacts astern of the convoy itself, which was left in the hands of Ayer in *Primrose*. The American Catalina assisted in tracking contacts, reporting a surfaced U-boat to the northward. Layard brought it to the attention of the *Blyskawica*, which 'streaked away to hunt it'. It was during this period of activity that Quaet-Faslem made his last attack, firing unsuccessfully at *Broke*.

Unfortunately, a number of newly-arriving U-boats still lay ahead of SC94 and several made abortive attacks. Ayer counter-attacked one, forcing her down and away from the immediate vicinity of the merchantmen, and it was not until the afternoon of the 10th, as SC94 approached Rockall, that submerged daylight attacks secured any further successes for the Germans. These were made by *U-438* and *U-660*, which again struck with near-coincidence in both timing and targets.

Kapitänleutnant R. Franzius in *U-438* torpedoed first the Greek freighter *Condylis*, sending 7,000 tons of grain and vehicles along with nine men to the sea-bed, and then the *Oregon*, which took more than 8,000 tons of general and 11 men with her. Both vessels had also been hit by torpedoes from *U-660*, and Kapitänleutnant G. Baur went on to torpedo the *Empire Reindeer* with her general cargo, and the timber-laden *Cape Race*. Captain W.E. Bacon and all his men from the former and Captain J. Barnetson and his crew from the latter, which included a dozen survivors from the *Port Nicholson*, like Captain S. Edmonson and his crew from the *Oregon* and the men from the *Condylis* were rescued by the escorts.

As the convoy moved under the air-umbrella Western Approaches Command sent more aircraft and five fresh escorts to deter the enemy, so Dönitz broke off the action. In addition to his loss of three U-boats, seven were limping home damaged or destitute of torpedoes.[10] Berlin exaggerated the tonnage sunk and minimised German losses, which Dönitz and his chief-of-staff Godt justified with rather limp exculpation. What they had achieved 'in spite of the strength of the escort' was 'the deciding factor which justifies the continuation of our war on convoys', Dönitz wrote, falling back upon the consolation to be derived from the improved rate of U-boat construction 'thanks to an increase in labour available for work in the home dockyards'. He also looked forward to the greater things expected of the new Type XXII submarine, with its high underwater speed. 'The Walter boat', Dönitz wrote in a memorandum to Raeder on 24 June 1942, 'would instantly render all but wholly ineffective the enemy's defensive measures . . .'[11]

As long as Britain and her Allies lacked sufficient numbers of similarly fast, responsive escorts, Dönitz might have been right. Currently, the Type VII and IX U-boats, once driven off, had great difficulty regaining an attacking position on even a 7.5 knot convoy. But the Type XXII was not after all available in time, or in sufficient numbers. What was more to the point, there were no Kretschmers left to man them.

Seeking a measure of comfort in the destruction of three U-boats, the Admiralty analysts chalked up a minor triumph, but the severe damage to *Assiniboine* and *Dianthus* was enough to keep them out of action for some time to come. The truth was that the inadequate speed of the 'Flower'-class corvettes, combined with the lack of centimetric radar and HF/DF radio-location equipment in *all* the escorts engaged, and the costliness of the tactic of ramming, meant that the mixed bag of warships that had made up the variable escort of SC94 was in itself a weakness. Dönitz's perception of its strength was based solely upon its numbers, not upon its cohesive quality. And while the defence it rendered was individually creditable, the loss of ten merchantmen – a *third* of Convoy SC94's strength – was again a serious blow, and not merely on the material front.

The failure of morale among the crews of three ships was a serious business, and caused a ripple of concern in high places. In the aftermath of the PQ17 débâcle, in response to a question from the Parliamentary Secretary about the general morale of merchant seamen, the Deputy Director of the MoWT stated in mid 1942 that it 'had not so far been affected, and the only thing one can say with conviction on the subject is that it is admirable and indeed wonderful'. Indeed; and against the steadfast performance of the mass of men engaged in their dangerous occupation, this transient weakening must be regarded as a temporary aberration, a psychological response to the near-intolerable pressure suffered by men denied the catharsis of counter-attack enjoyed by their naval cousins. A year earlier the Ministry had circulated the officers' and seamen's unions with a questionnaire intended to winkle out a notion of the merchant seamen's state of mind. 'Everyone was willing to answer the inessential questions. They grumbled about food; they realised, they said, what it would mean if Britain were defeated; they had not been approached by enemy agents . . . The rest was silence.' As the official historian Miss Behrens comments: 'There were many thousands of serving officers and men in the Merchant Navy and even if there had been a general answer to the question of what they felt, it was not to be discovered, for men in these circumstances do not generally talk.'[12]

Not, at least, to government snoops. Nevertheless, officials of the MoWT mounted an enquiry into the conduct of the errant crews of the *Empire Antelope*, *Radchurch* and *Empire Moonbean*.

With two escorts *hors de combat* and 11 merchantmen lost, the attack on SC94 boded ill from the Allied perspective. Dönitz was still clearly in a position to inflict major damage, and the principal supply route upon which Great Britain relied for survival was again under strain. Moreover, while the convoys of the North Atlantic could be attacked at the root at far less risk, with an increasing number of U-boats operational Dönitz was also able to turn his attention towards those vulnerable concentrations of shipping in the South Atlantic as vessels headed alone for the convoy mustering ports.

And losses elsewhere were significant. In early August, off Trinidad, German submarines sank several tankers. On the 3rd a triple strike from *U-108* blew Anglo-Saxon Petroleum's *Tricula* in two and cost her master Captain O.E. Sparrow, one passenger and 45 of his crew their lives. Eagle Oil's *San Emiliano*, loaded with high octane spirit and hit by *U-155*, disappeared in a sheet of flame which killed Captain J.W. Tozer and 39 men; a handful were picked up, several severely wounded, while outstanding bravery earned Apprentice D.O. Clarke a posthumous George Medal, and Chief Radio Officer D.W. Dennis a George Medal. Off Haiti 19 days later a second Eagle Oil tanker, the *San Fabian*, was sunk in convoy.

Korvettenkapitän A. Piening of *U-155* enjoyed a remarkable third war patrol. Prior to sinking the *San Emiliano* he had torpedoed eight vessels, including two Brazilian merchant ships, the *Barbacena* and the *Piave*.[13] He went on to sink the Dutch ship *Strabo* before several air attacks by British and American bombers compelled him to return to France, dodging along on the surface.

Having sunk the Norwegian tanker *Arthur W. Sewall* on the evening of 7 August, Bleichrodt in *U-109* destroyed another British tanker, the *Vimeira*, off Sierra Leone on 11 August. Fortunately for most of her people she contained a cargo of low-octane fuel oil, but even so her chief officer and six men were killed in the attack. Captain N.R. Caird, who had endured one sinking the previous November, was taken prisoner and eventually sent to Milag Nord after an uncomfortable 52 days spent cooped up in *U-109* as Bleichrodt's 'guest', while 20 survivors were picked up and landed a few days later at Takoradi. A further 17 were taken aboard the corvette *Crocus* and transferred to the British ship *Sylvia de Larrinaga* which in her turn was sunk by the Italian submarine *Reginaldo Giuliani*. While 29 survivors from the *Sylvia de Larrinaga* were rescued by the *Port Jackson*, it seems that those originally from the *Vimeira* had to spend a further 29 days in their boat before being discovered.

The *Reginaldo Giuliani*'s commander, Giovanni Bruno, was responsible for a number of gruelling boat voyages. Alfred Holt's Blue Funnel liner *Medon* was in ballast, bound from Mauritius to New York, when she was torpedoed midway between Freetown and Trinidad at about 03.50 on 10 August. With her main shaft broken, her engine seized and an enemy submarine shelling her, Captain S.R. Evans decided to order the crew into the boats, lie off, and await events. Four of the *Medon*'s six boats were launched, and evacuated all but one of the ship's crew. Third Mate E.G. Painter took No. 4 Boat back to the stern when an army gunner who had broken his leg appeared on her poop. He was persuaded to jump into the sea, from which Painter picked him up and then went in search of the doctor. At daylight Second Mate J.F. Fuller, the chief radio officer, the carpenter and an able seaman from No. 3 Boat reboarded the ship. While Mr C.W. Paterson, the carpenter, sounded the wells, the chief radio officer transmitted another distress message and stores, water, blankets, a sextant, chronometer and charts and Fuller's wild-fowling piece were passed down into No. 3 Boat, now joined by Painter in No. 4. Fourth Engineer Harris assisted the Sparks to coax the main transmitter into life again. Those on board had begun to launch the ship's No. 3 Boat, the only one powered by motor, when they came under shell-fire from Bruno, who had surfaced to inspect his handiwork. Although she was flooded aft, *Medon*'s engine room and forward holds were intact. Alarmed by the submarine's menacing presence, Fuller now ordered everyone back into the boats, which they had hardly regained when Bruno fired another torpedo into the *Medon*'s port side. With her engine room now flooding fast the ship slowly stood on her stern and sank, whereupon the *Reginaldo Giuliani* submerged and disappeared. Fuller now decided to abandon the motor-boat as of little use.

Meanwhile Captain Evans in No. 1 Boat had been conferring with the chief officer, Mr G. Edge, in No. 2. They decided to sail south to clear the easterly drift of the Equatorial Current before heading west, hoping to make the coast of South America under the influence of the south-east trade winds before coasting to British Guiana, about 1,200 miles distant, using a westerly coastal current. This decision had been communicated to Painter, but Fuller was in ignorance of it: he was some distance from the other boats by the time he got clear of the ship, and headed west directly.

With a visibility limited to their individual horizons, it was inevitable that the boats should soon become separated. Evans's No. 1 Boat was on passage for eight days before it was sighted and its occupants rescued by the Panamanian-flagged *Rosemount* on her way to Cape Town. Edge and his 13 men were less fortunate. Having been sunk when in the *Teiresias* off St-Nazaire in June 1940, Edge had equipped all the boats with care, but he did not have the benefit of the navigational kit salvaged by Fuller and was reduced to estimating his longitude by the sun's rising and setting, helped by a reliable wristwatch. He allotted rations on the basis of a 45-day voyage, and also extemporised a spar-deck by spreading the boat's bottom boards over the thwarts and covering these with life-jackets and spare clothing, giving the off-duty men a degree of comfort at night and sparing them having to sleep in the ever-present bilge water. Heavy rain squalls provided them with ample fresh water, but in between them they began to burn under the hot sun. The wind was light and unfavourable, with the trades precious little in evidence, and on the fourteenth day, 'after a hellish night of heavy rain and heavy seas', Edge decided to reduce rations in the hope of further eking out their stores, a measure agreed to by those on board. The Chinese refused to take part in the daily exercises Edge urged on all hands, smiling with their customary politeness at the antics of the European *fan kwei*.

Three days later the mast broke, and they had some difficulty re-rigging the boat. It was clear to Edge that they were making no westward progress, and that morale was beginning to suffer. Death was discussed by both Chinese and Europeans, a coincidence Edge recorded as odd. As the light airs that beset them continued, he tried to maintain spirits by encouraging the men to tell stories, but they fell silent. On the twenty-fourth day and again on the twenty-seventh Edge further reduced the rations. Weakness and lassitude began to affect them all. The rain continued and their water supplies remained healthy, but their 'stomachs were . . . painfully empty'.

At 21.00 on the thirty-fifth day in the boat, Midshipman Brookes at the helm spotted a light. To their 'indescribable joy' it proved to be the Portuguese steamer *Luso*. As she was skilfully manoeuvred by her master, Captain Botto, Edge sent four men to the oars to close the distance, and all No. 2 Boat's crew clambered up a pilot ladder without assistance to a warm welcome. They had all lost weight – an average of two stones – but the greatest affliction suffered was constipation, which in one case lasted 37 days and eventually required an enema. The lifeboat was discovered to have travelled almost six hundred miles to the SSE, quite at odds with Edge's supposition.

Second Officer Fuller, in No. 3 Boat, was best provided for in terms of navigational equipment, and for the first few days was in a similar condition to No. 2. On the twelfth day he ordered a cut in rations, and although a large ship was seen on the evening of the sixteenth, the burning of flares only prompted the vessel to turn away fearing a U-boat's ruse. Fuller was able to obtain reasonably accurate positions, and they observed an eclipse of the moon on 26 August. Subjected to light airs or calms and the unwelcome attentions of a whale, they got out the oars and pulled the boat for some hours. Another large ship ignored their signals, and when Fuller shot a large fish, it was swallowed by the trailing sharks before they had a chance to grapple it, discouragements that persuaded them to make another reduction in rations. On the morning of 13 September they were seen and rescued by the Ropner tramp *Reedpool*, Captain W. Downs, aboard which they enjoyed 'hospitality and care in keeping with the highest traditions of seamen and the sea'. After 36 days the boat had made 313 miles to the southward, and there was a difference of only 7 miles between Fuller's calculated position and that of the *Reedpool*.

Unfortunately, the *Reedpool* herself was torpedoed on 20 September, 240 miles south-east of Trinidad. Downs lost six of his men, and was taken prisoner by Kapitänleutnant W. Henke aboard *U-515*. The remainder of the *Reedpool*'s crew plus the *Medon*'s survivors took to the only undamaged lifeboat, some fifty men in what must have been very crowded conditions. Happily their ordeal was short, for the following day they were taken up by the schooner *Millie M. Masher*, Captain F. Barnes, and landed at Georgetown, British Guiana on the 24th.

No. 4 Boat under the third mate had the benefit of extra food and Painter's sextant, but with neither chronometer nor nautical almanac the only thing he could calculate with any approximation of accuracy was their latitude. They also had the ship's doctor on board, transferred from Edge's boat to tend the injured gunner. As they set course for the south-west Painter's men had greeted their first night with a sing-song, but they too suffered the frustration of light winds and calms, and were deterred from pulling by the slight progress achieved. After a few days Painter decided to head north and seek the north-east trades, and on the sixth day they picked up a north-easterly breeze which gave them about 4 knots to the north-west. Eight or ten such days of steady wind, Painter noted, would see them on the coast – but before long they saw a ship and made signals to attract attention. She proved to be the Norwegian cargo-liner *Tamerlane* belonging to Wilhelmsen, a commercial rival of Holt's. The *Tamerlane* swept down on them at speed in order to check that they were indeed distressed mariners before rounding-to with a derrick over her side. Captain Krafft's men picked up the injured gunner in a stretcher on the derrick runner, followed by the *Medon*'s survivors and their boat. Painter discovered that he had made only 40 miles to the south-west of the *Medon*'s last position, but his ordeal ended happily with 'excellent food' where 'cheerful and laughing goodwill abounded'.[14]

Bleichrodt also sank several other vessels in the same area. The British cargo-vessel *Ocean Might*, Captain W.J. Park, was torpedoed off Takoradi, loaded with military stores bound for the Middle East. Most of her crew landed at Ningo on the Gold Coast, some 35 miles east of Accra. Then, shortly before midnight on 6 September, Bleichrodt hit Blue Star's *Tuscan Star*. The vessel was loaded with 7,300 tons of frozen meat and homeward bound from Buenos Aires by way of Freetown, where she was to join a convoy. The ship was making 13.5 knots when suddenly two torpedoes blasted their way into the engine room and No. 5 Hold, killing 40 of her crew, eight gunners and three passengers. The ship rapidly settled, with a heavy starboard list developing. Captain E.N. Rhodes ordered her abandoned, and within ten minutes the 48 remaining crew and 22 passengers were in the boats, only one of which had been damaged in the explosions. Four minutes later the *Tuscan Star* plunged to the bottom.

After a while the survivors became aware of the rumble of a diesel engine in the darkness; then they were illuminated by searchlight as the bulk of *U-109* loomed out of the night. A voice speaking in English, probably Bleichrodt's, asked the usual questions about the ship's name, cargo and ports of departure and destination before the submarine disappeared. A little later it returned, and the same officer announced that they had picked up Second Radio Officer Gill from the water and intended taking him prisoner to Germany. It seems that Bleichrodt had spotted women and children among the huddled survivors in the third officer's boat. He ordered her alongside and had some food and water passed down into it before apologising: 'I am sorry, but I have to do my duty.'[15]

This lifeboat was found to be leaking, and in order to lighten it the women and children were transferred into Rhodes's boat. At daylight they set sail, driven north at about 3 knots by a southerly breeze. A southerly swell caused sea-sickness among many of the passengers, but all hands were given their rations of water, pemmican, biscuits, chocolate and malted milk tablets. The boats became separated in the night: Rhodes's was sighted by the Orient liner *Otranto* the following afternoon and its occupants were taken to Freetown; the other boats 'also reached safety'.[16]

Bleichrodt completed his patrol by sinking the British tramp *Peterton*, outward bound for Buenos Aires. Once again he took a prisoner, this time the ship's master, Captain T.W. Marrie, who like Gill was duly interned in Milag Nord. Twelve of the *Peterton*'s crew were rescued by the *Empire Whimbrel* and returned to Buenos Aires, but 22 were adrift in their boats for 49 days before HM Trawler *Canna* from Freetown found them. Eight men died in the attack or in the boats.

A few days earlier, on 25 August, Lord Vestey had lost another of his meat-laden Blue Star liners homeward bound from Buenos Aires, the *Viking Star*, mentioned in chapter 17. Like the *Tuscan Star* after her, she had been approaching Freetown to join a convoy. The afternoon was fine, with a moderate sea kicked up by a fresh breeze from the SSW. At 16.50 the *Viking Star* was hit by torpedoes from *U-130*, the explosions smashing the port side, fracturing steam pipes, inundating the main deck with water and destroying two lifeboats. The *Viking Star* immediately listed to port and the order was given to abandon ship, probably by Chief Officer F. MacQuiston, whose watch it was: Captain J.E. Mills was killed in the attack and it is not known whether he reached the bridge after the torpedoes hit his ship.

It was clear to MacQuiston that no time was to be lost. Immediately some rafts were flung overboard and the starboard boats were lowered down the side, riding on their skids against the increasing list. One of these, 'fairly full of men, cast off and drifted away . . .' Third Officer Rigiani, having grabbed a sextant from the chart-room and rapidly checked for anyone left on board, slid down a lifeline into the second boat. This was also full of men, but in the rush the bung had not been inserted and it was 'filled to the thwarts with water and useless', so the men transferred to a nearby raft, which became so overloaded that it threatened to capsize. Rigiani abandoned this and swam to the first boat away, astern of which its occupants had tied another raft. Some organisation now manifested itself, with MacQuiston and Second Officer F. Jones in the first boat and Rigiani on the raft explaining the predicament of the second. MacQuiston's boat was pulled over and the stores removed from the waterlogged lifeboat, but while this was in progress they were concussed by a further explosion. Looking up they saw the *Viking Star* break her back; both bow and stern 'reared themselves out of the water and disappeared . . .'

Having watched their own ship sink, they now sat helplessly as a U-boat motored towards them on the surface. Before them was a 'big man with a red beard' who spoke a little English. This was Korvettenkapitän Kals, who having asked the customary questions then boasted tactlessly of the number of ships he had sunk, before *U-130* moved away into the twilight.

With darkness falling, MacQuiston took stock: he had more than thirty men in the lifeboat with a further 13 on two nearby rafts, and by means of a torch he had determined that more were adrift on other rafts in the distance. During the night the weather deteriorated, and at daylight the two trailing rafts were lashed together. Since they had signalled to a Sunderland the previous afternoon they assumed that they were close enough to Freetown to be in the air-patrol area, and that it would be best to sit tight. Nothing was seen that day but some smoke on the horizon.

On the rafts Rigiani, fearing the worst, planned for a 25-day voyage and issued rations to his 13 men accordingly. One of the rafts was awash but the other rode correctly, and between them they had a fair supply of food, water and equipment. Their rations, issued at dusk and dawn, were a spoonful of pemmican, one Horlick's malted milk tablet, one piece of chocolate, and half a dipper of water. The men detailed to keep a lookout did so on the waterlogged raft, where their bodies, chilled down, soon began to suffer the effects of immersion, but this allowed the others to rest on the better raft.

In a worsening sea, difficulty was experienced with the rafts alternately bumping and tugging at their lashings to the lifeboat. The decision was made to separate, with MacQuiston going for help. Hoisting sail he set off to the north-east with 36 souls, making good progress during the 27th and 28th despite a heavy, breaking sea. In the pitchy darkness of the 29th, at about 03.00, the boat was suddenly lifted on a huge sea. Three curling wave crests dashed over her as she was caught in a breaking surf. All aboard were flung out, and in a roil of water, confusion, equipment and bad language cast upon a sandy shore. Salvaging what they could, they managed to drag the heavy boat up the beach and bail it out. MacQuiston, Jones and the others found themselves on the coast of Sierra Leone near Bonthe, and in due course managed to reach safety.

Rigiani's rafts were less tractable, and he and his men were at the mercy of the wind. If it held steady, 'there would be a chance to hit land before the Guinea current swept us around the bulge of Africa and into the Gulf of Guinea', Rigiani noted with impressive sangfroid. 'This course was materially assisted by energetic paddling to keep the wind astern . . . The knowledge that the land lay some 150 miles to the eastward was of great assistance to our spirits, despite the fact that many were suffering from open wounds . . . with little or no clothing to protect them from the alternate heat of the sun and the extreme chill of frequent rain squalls, and the accumulating and depressing ordeal of spending every other six hours sitting in salt water. Each morning and evening the food ration was issued and the men tackled it with gusto. Occasionally a fish was caught . . .'

On one occasion a ship was seen, but to no avail. On 30 August the small sharks which had been keeping them company were joined by some larger species which 'came too close for comfort . . . and once a large whale broke surface within fifty feet . . . With nightfall came wind. The sea became fiercer. We heard an aeroplane overhead . . . but had no means of attracting attention.' On the evening of the 31st they sighted another raft, and when it was still in sight next day they paddled for four hours to get alongside it, finding a man named Boardman clinging to it quite alone. They lashed the three rafts together, cheered by the augmentation to their rations, though disappointed that the flares, red lights and medical kits were soaked through. Rigiani dressed Boardman's salt-water boils: 'All hands were suffering from this same painful ailment and could not bear to be touched in certain parts of their bodies.'

Then, '[d]uring the afternoon [of 1 September] land was sighted far away to the eastward, and all hands paddled enthusiastically towards it for the rest of the day and during the night', but next morning, after a boisterous night of heavy rain and swell, the land had vanished. With the wind still from the south-west they paddled gallantly on, and at 21.00 saw a flashing light, though they could make nothing of it. But on 3 September their fortitude paid off: 'With daylight we observed a hump of rock, apparently an island with a lighthouse on it, away to the south-east, distant about nine or ten miles . . .' They continued paddling, cutting the third raft adrift to 'facilitate progress. The men were now very weak from exhaustion, but they kept gamely on, and in the late afternoon we were rewarded by seeing . . . a line of low land . . . to the eastward from north to south, distant about five miles. A double issue of food and drink put new energy into us, and we paddled on through the night . . .'

They were far from safe, however, for '[a]t about midnight the heavy swell changed into long rollers, and I realised that we were close to the land. After another hour we suddenly heard the roar of surf and found ourselves in very heavy breakers. A dark line of land was visible ahead. We made an attempt to coast in on the breakers; but the sea was too high and I realised that it was essential to keep offshore until morning. By now the breakers were continually surging over the rafts, and all hands were in danger of being washed off.' An attempt to fight the onshore drift failed, and '[s]uddenly a very high breaker tossed the raft completely over and all hands were swept off. Luckily everyone managed to clamber back; but we lost everything except the food in the locker and some of the water. For the rest of the night we clung to the rafts and by the mercy of God were not swept by any more breakers.'

The following morning, with the land a tantalising half-mile away, they broke up the second raft to improvise paddles, consumed a ration issued by Rigiani, and then paddled like demons. For an hour they worked their craft inshore, and then a breaker capsized them again. They were not far from the beach, and since they could all swim Rigiani told them to make the best of their way ashore. The beach shelved steeply and there was an undertow, but Rigiani floundered ashore, followed by most of the others. Perversely, the raft was flung among them in the surf. As they recovered they became aware that they had lost one man: Boardman was never seen again.

In due course they were discovered by some local people who treated them with great compassion, told them they were on the Liberian coast, and took them to their settlement. Next day they began a seven-hour trek along the shoreline and then inland towards the village of Latia, which lay on a river. En route they met another castaway who had been washed ashore, Chief Radio Operator Sullivan, the solitary occupant of a fourth raft. From Latia Rigiani was able to send a message to a Dutch merchant at Cape Mount, the nearest town, and about midnight a launch belonging to Pan American Airways arrived to take them onwards. Arriving at the Dutchman's house they were not only afforded medical relief and food but discovered that the *Viking Star*'s chief and second engineers and one of her refrigerating engineers were already accommodated under the trader's roof.

MacQuiston was appointed MBE for 'his leadership and skill' in bringing 'thirty six people to safety, and his efforts [which] led to the early rescue of other survivors'. Young Rigiani sadly received no acknowledgement of his own outstanding determination and leadership, but his well-written account is a moving document of an ordeal such as was suffered, with variations in detail, by many other survivors.[17]

Another Blue Funnel liner, the motor-vessel *Myrmidon*, was lost in the same area to Kapitänleutnant E. Würdemann in *U-506* on 5 September. This ship had the misfortune to be sunk in Liverpool docks by an aerial mine in March the previous year, and had then detonated a mine in the Mersey without suffering much damage. She had left Freetown, heading south for Cape Town and Bombay in a three-ship convoy escorted by the destroyer *Brilliant* and the boom-defence vessel *Fernmoor*. Shortly after midnight on the 5th, with the convoy off Cape Palmas in the Gulf of Guinea, two torpedoes were seen, their trails revealed by bioluminescence in the tropic sea. They passed astern of *Myrmidon* and the officer of the watch had hardly had time to breathe a sigh of relief before a third slammed into the ship's port side and she stopped and began to settle. The *Myrmidon*'s ten boats were quickly and efficiently launched, evacuating all 116 of her crew and 129 passengers, before the ship sank by the head. Captain A.M. Caird kept the boats together and before daylight they had all been picked up by *Brilliant*, which proceeded to Pointe Noire in French Equatorial Africa. Finding the prospects of travelling further from there poor, Caird persuaded Lieutenant Commander A.G. Poe to take all the survivors to Banana, at the mouth of the Congo River. Caird had served in destroyers in the previous war and was full of praise for Poe's men, especially the cook, who 'managed to provide three meals a day for 421 persons from a small galley'. From Banana the passengers were sent to Cape Town by train, while the *Myrmidon*'s crew returned to Freetown by sea.

A few days later, on 13 September, Würdemann sank the neutral Swedish Johnson liner *Lima* off Monrovia with the loss of three dead. He then became one of several Axis submarines caught up in an extraordinary and contentious episode.

Owned by the Cunard-White Star Line, the 19,695-ton passenger-liner *Laconia* was steaming north-east of Ascension Island on 12 September, heading home from Egypt under the command of Captain R. Sharp. In addition to a ship's company of 463 officers and ratings, the *Laconia* bore 80 civilian passengers, among them women and children, 'service families evacuated from danger zones [and] a few nursing sisters', and 286 British 'army, navy and Royal Air Force personnel from Malta and the Middle East'. There were also 1,793 Italian prisoners-of-war guarded by 103 Polish soldiers, lately themselves prisoners of the Russians, liberated by the events of the previous summer. The Italians, captured in the Libyan desert, had been embarked in *Laconia* after a staging break at Cape Town. Although no longer the Armed Merchant Cruiser she had been earlier in the war, *Laconia* still carried some at least of her previous armament, and was painted the standard grey of most merchantmen and troopships. But she was now only capable of about 12 knots, not the 16 of earlier years.

That same day, 12 September, Korvettenkapitän Hartenstein, on his way south in *U-156* bound for operations in the South Atlantic, came in sight of the *Laconia*. He trailed her all day, working into a position to attack, and that evening he closed her as she loomed large in the darkness. He had already sunk the homeward-bound *Clan Macwhirter* with the loss of her master, Captain R.S. Masters, ten men and a cargo of 2,000 tons of manganese ore, 3,500 tons of iron ore, 3,500 tons of linseed and a quantity of general cargo, all loaded in India. Now he torpedoed the *Laconia*.

Aboard the *Laconia*, one sitting of dinner had just finished. As the second torpedo slammed into the liner and she began to list, the passengers 'stumbled over fallen doors, broken woodwork and shattered glass to our lifeboat stations. And there we waited. The torpedoes had hit the engine room; and the mainmast, the wireless transmitter and some of the lifeboats had been carried away. The list made it very difficult to swing out the remaining boats; moreover it was a dark night, and a fairly heavy sea was running. The second torpedo had apparently burst among the prisoners, and panic and turmoil were following. They rushed their Polish guards, they streamed up the stairs, they stormed the lifeboats or leaped into the sea' – possibly because, as it was afterwards alleged, their guards had closed water-tight doors on some of the compartments; this would account for the high number of Italian fatalities.

One of the nursing sisters, Miss Doris Hawkins, waited with others 'for what seemed an age; really it was only for about fifteen minutes. Then we were told that our lifeboat had been blown away . . . There was no one to direct us . . .' Miss Hawkins lost the baby in her care as the lifeboat into which she finally clambered capsized in the water from the indisciplined press of humanity crammed into it. She was obliged to struggle for her life from the embrace of an Italian soldier who clung to her desperately, finally surfacing just in time to see 'the ship rear half out of the water, and then she sank like a great monster, hissing and roaring – an awe-inspiring sight . . .' Captain Sharp, 138 of his crew, 551 passengers and 1,378 prisoners either went down with the *Laconia* or died in the tragic aftermath.

The *Laconia* herself had not yet finished with those in the sea. 'There was a loud explosion which I was told later must have been the bursting of the submerged boilers; whatever the cause, the explosion through the water was terrific. I felt a sickening pain in my back, while Squadron Leader [H.R.K.]Wells, who had been facing the explosion, seemed to curl up just as we reached . . . [a] raft.' Miss Hawkins, Wells and a naval lieutenant named Tillie got onto a raft already supporting 'nine or ten Italians.'

'Later we put the Italians on another raft, to which some more of their compatriots were clinging, then all who remained were British. In the water we had swallowed a good deal of thick oil from the wreck, as well as sea, and in turn we were all violently sick. Our hair and faces were thickly covered with oil. We were cheerful, even optimistic. I remember . . . Wells saying: "This is a lie – it can't have happened to us!" – and so it seemed – unreal, fantastic. We felt detached from it all.'[18]

As he brought *U-156* closer to examine his handiwork Hartenstein may well have had similar sentiments. What he saw through his glasses made him realise the scale of the incident, manifested by the numbers of people in the water. On Miss Hawkins's raft the men took it in turns to sit beside her. Tillie, who had so cheerfully encouraged the others, suddenly died, and they discovered that he had quietly bled to death.

Meanwhile *U-156* nosed forwards, moving towards the boats and rafts and the men thrashing and cursing in the water. Then, to his astonishment, Hartenstein heard cries for help, not in English, but in Italian. The enormity of what he had done provoked him to a humane response: he ordered his crew onto the casing to rescue as many as possible.

Throughout the long night Miss Hawkins froze atop her raft, also hearing the cries for help in Italian. 'Sometimes our raft overturned and we were all flung off into the water; each time it was more difficult to get back for our limbs were stiff and our fingers numb from clinging on so tightly. When at last dawn came there was a fairly high sea; only occasionally', she remarks, emphasising the small compass of the survivors' world, 'did we glimpse any other raft or lifeboat, as we rose on the crest of a wave.'

The sun came up, and warmed them; then it burned them, and they were stung by jellyfish. They saw *U-156* and Wells tried to swim towards her, but the U-boat moved away. At dusk they saw a second submarine. It 'cruised around and then submerged. The sun set; we began to dread a second night. Suddenly the first submarine turned and came straight towards us. German sailors threw us a lifeline, and we were all taken aboard.'

Hartenstein had reported the incident to Kerneval, then began broadcasting in English, the international language of the sea, on the 25-metre distress frequency: 'If any ship will assist the shipwrecked *Laconia* crew I will not attack her, provided I am not attacked by ship or air force. I [have] picked up 193 men 4° 52' South, 011° 26' West.' Hartenstein's operator transmitted this repeatedly.

Dönitz received the news just after midnight on the 13th. Hartenstein told him 'Ship unfortunately carrying 1,800 Italian prisoners of war. So far 90 rescued,' then concluded by requesting instructions. Dönitz ordered those of Hartenstein's colleagues heading for operations off Cape Town to assist. In his memoirs he sanctimoniously claimed that he did so knowing that he was contravening one of the principles of maritime warfare 'accepted by all nations . . . that the exigencies of action take precedence over all rescue operations . . .', adding for good measure that he knew 'of no case in which the British or American Navy have acted otherwise than in accordance with this principle'. With the German–Italian alliance under strain Hitler approved, provided the Cape Town operations were not adversely affected and the U-boats ran no risk to themselves. The Befelshaber der U-boote also ordered any submarines off Freetown to assist, thus involving Würdemann's *U-506* and Schacht's *U-507*, along with the Italian submarine *Comandante Cappellini* (Revedin), which arrived on the scene on the 15th and 16th. Dönitz also asked the colonial authorities in Vichy French West Africa to help. The Cape Town-bound U-boats found nothing, leaving *U-506* and *U-507* and the Italian submarine to go to Hartenstein's aid. Meanwhile, the transmissions had been intercepted at Freetown, and the British merchantman *Empire Haven* and the Armed Ocean Boarding Vessel *Corinthian* were soon on their way towards the scene.

As relief approached, *U-156*, with almost two hundred survivors down below and 70 more on the casing, patiently towed four laden lifeboats. Other boats and rafts lay in the vicinity. When *U-506* arrived on the night of the 14th/15th, Würdemann relieved Hartenstein of 132 of his guests. Schacht, approaching the scene on the afternoon of the 15th, encountered four of *Laconia*'s lifeboats and removed the women and children, passing comforts to the men remaining and taking them in tow. Later Schacht took up a further 164 Italians, and two British officers who were carried back to France as prisoners-of-war. The three U-boats (the *Comandante Cappellini* had relieved Hartenstein of the Italians aboard *U-156*, then apparently gone in search of more of her countrymen) now headed at slow speed for a rendezvous arranged with the Vichy French warships, the lifeboats bobbing in their wakes. Mercifully the sea state remained calm and fair progress was made. Hartenstein was approaching the rendezvous, expecting the others later, when, half an hour before noon on the 16th, the Americans arrived.

A four-engined Liberator flew over *U-156*, on the conning tower of which Hartenstein had displayed a large white sheet with a red cross painted on it. An hour later a second Liberator roared in, flying at a height of '80 metres slightly ahead of the [U-]boat and dropped two bombs . . . While the tow with [*sic*] four lifeboats was being cast off, the aircraft dropped a bomb in the middle of the latter. One boat capsized . . .'[19]

It was a shambles. Another aircraft arrived and dropped bombs, 'one of which . . . exploded directly under [the] control-room [of *U-156*]. Conning tower disappeared in a mushroom of black water. Control-room and bow compartment reported taking in water . . .' The clipped notes of Hartenstein's War Diary are augmented by Miss Hawkins's later description of her plight: 'Six bombs were dropped, and each was a very near miss. The submarine shivered and shook, and one end compartment was damaged. It was a dreadful sensation; we knew that one direct hit could send us to the bottom. The explosions through the water were tremendous.'

The American aircraft had been 'unequivocally ordered to sink the submarine'[20] they had discovered, and on reporting the attack Hartenstein, Würdemann and Schacht were ordered by Dönitz to abandon their enterprise. Schacht passed the location of other boats to the commander of the Vichy French minesweeper *Annamite*. Hartenstein, 'genuinely distressed', was compelled to divest himself of his guests and manoeuvred *U-156* 'fairly close' to two of the remaining three lifeboats, after which Miss Hawkins and the others 'found ourselves once again swimming for our lives'.

It took Miss Hawkins, Wells and their companions almost an hour to reach the lifeboat, and Wells so exhausted himself that he died a few days later. Miss Hawkins and a female colleague found themselves with 64 British and two Polish survivors in a single, overcrowded boat. At dusk Revedin arrived, took all the Italians from the three boats into *Comandante Cappellini* and 'remained to watch over us all night'.

The 68 souls remaining 'were to be companions for many long and bitter days. Most were destined not to survive the dreadful journey in that boat.' There was no ship's officer, but the *Laconia*'s doctor, a young man named Geoffrey Purslow, had some knowledge of sailing, so he and a lieutenant colonel took charge. The rations were sparse, especially the water, which amounted to only fifteen gallons and was doled out at the rate of two ounces an evening, and they were without mast, spars or rudder. They managed to improvise a rig from the oars and blankets, however, and headed NNE, where, 600 miles away, land lay. They were cold at night, and they were occasionally soaked as water broke over the boat. 'The days passed in dreadful monotony.'

Meanwhile, though Hartenstein had abandoned the mission, Würdemann and Schacht, overloaded with survivors, disobeyed Dönitz's order and made the rendezvous with the Vichy warships, transferring the wretched survivors, irrespective of nationality, into the cruiser *Gloire*, the sloop *Dumont d'Urville* and the minesweeper *Annamite*. On the way to the rendezvous on the 17th *U-506* was again attacked by an American aeroplane, but Würdemann had all the survivors towing astern in their lifeboats and simply cut them adrift, enabling him to dive and escape an aerial depth-charging. Surfacing afterwards, he picked up the tow again and continued towards the French ships. Schacht's *U-507* was also attacked as she made for the rendezvous, though Revedin seems to have escaped. In total the French warships embarked one naval officer and 178 ratings, 17 army officers and 87 soldiers, nine RAF officers and 70 airmen, 80 merchant officers and 178 seamen, one Polish officer with 69 men, and 50 women and children. The precise number of Italians saved seems uncertain, but some 1,350 were lost out of 1,793.

Divested of their wretched encumbrances, Schacht and Revedin headed for home. Having done his best to ameliorate the sufferings of others Würdemann ended his patrol by returning to his proper business, sinking the former Danish- but now British-flagged *Siam II* (originally named *Siam*, and owned by the Danish East Asiatic Company of Copenhagen). Captain A. Larsen and all his crew were rescued by the P&O cargo-liner *Nagpore*.

But all was not yet over for everyone from the *Laconia*. The survivors in Miss Hawkins's boat knew from Hartenstein that he had arranged a rendezvous with the Vichy French, but he had also told them that they would not make it and were unlikely to reach land. Then an American plane had flown over them, its signal lamp winking, and at first they were confident that rescue could not be far off; but it was not to be. Miss Hawkins remained confident despite the situation, marvelling at the beauty of the sea, profoundly moved by the evidence of teeming life in the tropical water. She later recorded, too, how the *Laconia*'s practical fourth engineer, William Henderson, worked tirelessly for their comfort and any amelioration of their hardships he could devise. He fashioned a new rudder, and took the lead in pumping the damaged and leaking boat. Then, 'one morning we found that he was no longer breathing'.

Their worst deprivation was of water, their worst suffering the unimaginable torture of thirst:

After a time we could quite easily bear the lack of food, but the lack of water tried us sorely. When each water ration was passed along, everyone peered at it with longing . . . When we received our precious drop, we took a sip, ran it round our teeth and gums, gargled with it and finally swallowed it. We repeated this until not a drop nor a drip was left clinging to the little biscuit tin from which we drank. After five minutes we could not tell that we had had any . . . Our pores closed up completely after a few days, and we did not perspire at all, in spite of the intense heat. Our nails became brittle and broke easily . . . we became a little light-headed, and were unable to sleep, but dozed lightly, and dreamed always of water . . .

They lost weight, the men's beards grew, and their salt-water sores became infected. Fingers and toes became septic, boils appeared, and Miss Hawkins's own eyes became inflamed and infected. She and Purslow did their best for their comrades, keeping wounds open and draining pus using a pen-knife primitively disinfected in sea-water. Miss Hawkins's fellow nurse, whom she identifies merely as 'Mary', died at dawn on 26 September and they shipped her over the side, attempting to sing 'Abide with Me' through their swollen throats.

Others too began to die. Their tongues grew hard and dry, their lips cracked, they had difficulty talking. The small water ration made the consumption of what food there was difficult. Inevitably, there was bickering over small things: the position of one person in relation to another, a contact that hurt a neighbour, the division of a flying fish. They became wildly excited when they saw a ship, but when it did not respond to their signals the depression that followed was terrible. The lieutenant colonel rallied them with a pep-talk. Then Purslow's left hand and his right foot began to swell. Miss Hawkins opened them with a razor blade. The discharge from his hand was promising, but his leg showed the red lines of deep infection, and his glands began to swell ominously. Septicaemia had set in and he lay inert, unable to speak. He was now a danger to them all. With a huge effort he told them he could no longer compromise those who were left, and with a 'Good-bye' went overboard.

Despite all this they had managed to maintain a course, sometimes under a fresh wind and with a heavy sea running, so that it was with the greatest difficulty that the boat was held to her heading. After about 21 days at sea they ran out of water. Next morning there was a downpour; their joy was immense, and they were able to eat their rations. Two men developed severe glandular swellings, but with six gallons of water collected matters seemed better. Then on Thursday 8 October one of the seamen saw what he took to be a ship. It was land.

They did not make it ashore that day, and an offshore breeze carried them seaward the following night, but the next morning a flying-boat flown by Group Captain A.G. Store saw them. They were 60 miles south of Monrovia, and that evening they were finally 'washed up on the sand by two great rolling waves . . . anywhere else for miles on either side we should have been dashed against rocks . . . Sixteen survivors out of our original sixty-eight. We had travelled over 700 miles in our open boat. The senior surviving Englishman was a sergeant of the RAF; of the officers there was only the stolid Polish cadet', who alone appeared unaffected by the incident. Soon afterwards they were taken up by some kindly Liberians who had been anxiously watching the boat offshore for two days.

In due course they made their way to a town known as Grand Bassa, where Dutch traders were established. Even after landing death stalked them, as one of the men suffering from glandular swelling died from gas-gangrene. A naval trawler arrived and they were embarked for Freetown, later transferring to a destroyer. While on passage to Freetown she attacked a submarine contact – the only occasion, according to Miss Hawkins, when she knew real terror. After several weeks in hospital she and her fellows were sent home in another troopship. The voyage was a nerve-racking experience, but they arrived safely in England in early December.

During his trial at Nuremburg the *Laconia* incident formed part of the indictment against Dönitz, on the grounds that after it he had ordered his men to offer no succour whatsoever to the crews of any ships they sank. The seizure of masters and chief engineers remained a standing order, and survivors might be picked up for interrogation in order to aid operations, but that was all. Dönitz ended his infamous so-called '*Laconia* Order' with a final harangue to his men: 'Be severe. Remember that in his bombing attacks on German cities the enemy has no regard for women and children.' He was let off the hook by Admiral Chester Nimitz of the United States Navy, whose affidavit stated that American submarines 'as a general rule . . . did not rescue enemy survivors . . .'

The conduct of American aircraft, it would seem, was little different.

19

'Conduct beyond the call of duty'

Viscount

SINCE GERMAN SUBMARINES had now extended their operations over the whole of the Atlantic Ocean and the Caribbean Sea, their presence was perceived as ubiquitous. And although they inflicted grievous wounds on ships in convoy off the Antilles, the United States, with the assistance of British and Canadian warships, was increasing its dominance of its coastal waters, and during August several U-boats were lost in the Atlantic theatre.[1] The raiders *Stier* and *Michel* were still active, each sinking British cargo-vessels.[2] Elsewhere other damage was inflicted on the British merchant fleet,[3] but Dönitz's main target remained the trade convoys of the North Atlantic. More than a dozen U-boats, some lately deployed against SC94 and others reinforcing them, were sent to search for Convoy SC95, detected by the B-Dienst service. In support were two U-tankers, *U-174* and *U-462*.

The 41 vessels of Convoy SC95 had left Halifax on 4 August covered by the nominally American escort group A3, which in fact consisted of warships from the United States Navy and Coastguard as well the British and Canadian navies, led by the USS *Schenk*.[4] All went well until the 14th, as the convoy reached the Rockall Bank and four ships detached for Reykjavik. At 01.40 the following morning this section, escorted by the US Coastguard Cutter *Campbell*, was attacked by *U-705*. Kapitänleutnant K-H. Horn torpedoed the American freighter *Balladier* which was loaded with general cargo, steel pipes and timber and owned by the Parry Steamship Company of New York. The *Balladier* 'sank . . . in seven minutes' with the loss of 12 killed, including her master.

The *Campbell* 'was steaming well ahead' of her charges 'and made no responses to signals from the small convoy that a ship had been torpedoed'.[5]

Two of the merchant ships carried on in the escort's wake. Only the American freighter *Norluna*, alerted to the presence of men in the water by the life-jacket lights and flares set off by the *Balladier's* floundering crew, stopped and hauled them out of the freezing sea. In the darkness they left one dead man in a lifeboat, and two of those rescued later died, probably from hypothermia. When he arrived at Reykjavik the *Campbell's* commander seems to have reported that both the *Balladier* and *Norluna* had been torpedoed, for the 'naval authorities expressed surprise when the *Norluna* arrived next day'.

One other vessel from SC95 was lost, the neutral Swedish passenger-cargo-vessel *Suecia* owned by the Johnson line of Stockholm, which had fallen astern of the main convoy and was sunk by *U-596*, Kapitänleutnant G. Jahn, on the 16th with the loss of 12 of her company.[6]

The German U-boats lost contact with SC95 and were directed instead towards the slow westbound ON122, which had been sighted from *U-135* on 22 August. Three dozen merchantmen were escorted by the B6 Escort Group led by Lieutenant Commander Waterhouse in HMS *Viscount*. The old destroyer had recently been converted into a long-range ocean escort, and fitted with Type 271 radar and HF/DF equipment and one of the new forward-firing 'Hedgehog' anti-submarine mortars.[7] *Viscount* had with her a mixed force of Norwegian and British corvettes, *Acanthus, Eglantine, Montbretia* and *Potentilla*, and a rescue ship, the former railway steamer *Stockport*.

Kapitänleutnant Praetorius's *U-135* was soon joined by Baur's *U-660*, lately engaged with SC94, and other U-boats were on their way. All through the 23rd and 24th Praetorius and Baur tried to keep contact with ON122, but were located by *Viscount's* HF/DF and prevented from approaching close enough to attack. That night, a black night of wind and rain, more U-boats arrived. Three managed to evade Waterhouse's guard and strike the convoy. Shortly after midnight Schütze in *U-605* fired a salvo, torpedoing two ships in ballast, the British *Sheaf Mount*, with the loss of her master Captain R.S. de Gruchy and 30 crew, and the ancient Latvian steamer *Katvaldis*. Built in 1907, the *Katvaldis* was now, under her sixth name, re-registered as a British ship and commanded by her Latvian master, Captain I. Lejnieks. Her crew were picked up by the *Stockport* and clambered up nets suspended from booms while Captain T.E. Fea's motor-boat was launched to recover a handful of men from the *Sheaf Mount*.

As *Stockport* went about her business, the Norwegian corvette *Eglantine* went about hers, echo-locating *U-605*, damaging her and obliging Schütze to retire to Brest. By now Dierksen and Franzius were on hand. A near simultaneous attack was launched by *U-176* and *U-438*, and both hit their targets. Franzius may have fired at the *Empire Breeze*, but Dierksen's torpedoes certainly sank her. A standard cargo ship of 7,454 tons, she had been built by Thompson's of Sunderland for the MoWT and placed in the hands of J. Denholm of Glasgow. Fortunately only one man was lost, while Captain R. Thomson and 47 men were taken out of their boats and landed at Dunmore in Eire by the neutral Irish ship *Irish Willow*. Franzius's torpedoes also hit the small Norwegian steamer *Trolla*, killing five of her 22-man crew.

Meanwhile *Viscount* and the Norwegian corvette *Potentilla*, having located a suspicious echo, pounded *U-256*, forcing Kapitänleutnant O. Loewe to withdraw for repairs. On his way home, while surfaced crossing the Bay of Biscay, Loewe was sighted and bombed, first by an RAF Whitley from No. 502 Squadron and then by a second from No. 51 Squadron. So badly damaged was the U-boat that Loewe transferred 30 of his crew to the homeward-bound *U-438* and struggled into L'Orient. *U-256* remained in dockyard hands for over a year.

At the same time as the attempt was being made on SC95, on another part of this vast battlefield a second group of six U-boats was being directed towards the homeward-bound Convoy SL118 from Kapitänleutnant G. Feiler's *U-653*. In the ensuing action off the Azores several ships were sunk. Oberleutnant G. Remus had been the first to shadow in *U-566*, and though he was initially frustrated by the activity of the escort, which in addition to the Armed Merchant Cruiser *Cheshire* consisted of the sloops *Folkestone, Gorleston* and *Wellington* and the corvette *Pentstemon*, was finally the first to strike. After dark on the evening of 17 August Remus sank Wilhelmsen's *Triton*, loaded with wheat, wool and general cargo, without loss of life. During the following hours more U-boats converged on SL118, and 24 hours later Kapitänleutnant G. Reeder fired a four-torpedo salvo from *U-214* and hit three ships. He sank the Dutch general cargo-vessel *Balingkar* with the loss of one man and hit British India's *Hatarana*, leaving her so battered that she had to be sunk later by the *Pentstemon*, while a third torpedo damaged HMS *Cheshire*.

By this time SL118 was moving under air cover, the deterrent effect of which the Germans found increasingly intimidating. That same day Liberators from Culdrose in Cornwall reached the convoy. Aircraft *F* of No. 120 Squadron, Coastal Command, flown by Squadron Leader T.M. Bulloch, which had damaged *U-89* two days earlier, strafed and bombed Feiler's *U-653*, forcing her away from SL118. The circling Liberators deterred the U-boats from any further action, and also Cremer in *U-333*. Shortly afterwards he was depth-charged by two of the escorts but escaped. To Dönitz he carried the hint of an Allied device capable of detecting a U-boat on the surface, with a range beyond that of radar as calculated by the Germans at the time: he had spotted the curious aerials of the HF/DF short-wave detectors borne aloft by one of the sloops.[8]

Next day, therefore, only Kapitänleutnant H. Dieterichs's U-406 remained in a position to attack, and on the afternoon of the 19th she torpedoed the City of Manila, heading for Glasgow from Bombay and Cochin with a general cargo that included pig-iron and groundnuts. Only one man was lost, Captain A.S. Reay and the rest being rescued by the sloop Gorleston, the US Coastguard Cutter Itasca and the merchantman Empire Voice.

Having been joined by U-406 and U-107, Reeder and Remus were again in action a few days later, attacking the following convoy, SL119. Kerneval also directed U-68, U-156, U-172 and U-504 from the South Africa-bound Eisbär (Polar Bear) group to join in. On 26 August Hartenstein's U-156 torpedoed and sank a straggler, the Clan Macwhirter, an ageing ex-American vessel, untypical of the Clan Line, loaded with 2,000 tons of Indian manganese ore, 3,500 tons of linseed, 2,200 tons of pig-iron and a part general cargo. Captain R.S. Masters and ten crew were lost, the remainder being picked up by the neutral Portuguese sloop Pedro Nuñes and landed at Funchal.

Despite these successes the Seekriegsleitung were not happy about the diversion of the Eisbär U-boats towards SL119 and they over-rode Dönitz's staff, leaving the original U-boats to attack the convoy. By the 28th, when SL119 was roughly on the parallel of Lisbon, only one of these was able to reach the merchant ships through the escort's screen. Remus took U-566 in close and sank the Dutch freighter Zuiderkerk, though without loss of life, and another Ellerman liner, the City of Cardiff, with a total loss of 18,500 tons of general cargo. Captain R.L. Stewart and most of his crew were picked up by the sloop Rochester, though 21 died.

Throughout this period U-604 was stationed in a reconnoitring position on the mid Atlantic route, and here had sunk the Dutch freighter Abbekerk. Not far away a group of U-boats was being directed towards Convoy SC97, and Kapitänleutnant H. Höltring of U-604 joined his colleagues. Owing to the presence of American aircraft flying south from Iceland, the operation was not a success. The 58-strong convoy, escorted by the Canadian C2 escort group,[9] was sighted by Kapitänleutnant K. Rudloff, U-609, who submerged and attacked immediately. He succeeded in torpedoing two ships, the Norwegian motor-vessel Bronxville and the Panamanian Capira. Although Rudloff made a second attempt to hit the convoy, as did other U-boat commanders, the escorts were too active, and after 1 September air cover proved too daunting, so the Germans gave up.

These U-boats then mustered west of Lisbon and U-107 sank two British tramp ships, the Hollinside and Penrose, on 3 September, the third anniversary of the outbreak of war. Both vessels had been part of an unescorted group of five vessels on their way to join an HG convoy at Gibraltar. They were heading south, close along the Portuguese coast, when Gelhaus struck. Three men were lost from the *Hollinside*, the survivors from both ships being rescued by Spanish trawlers. Gelhaus and his colleagues then refuelled off the Cape Verdes before dispersing, some to operate off Freetown.

The increasing domination of the airspace over the Bay of Biscay by Allied aeroplanes was beginning to impact significantly upon Dönitz's operations. Even as some of his U-boats dithered ineffectually off Lisbon, others, transiting the Bay, were under regular attack. Royal Air Force Whitleys so badly damaged *U-256* that she had to be rebuilt, while Australian and Polish aircraft caught the Italian submarine *Reginaldo Giuliani*, damaging her, killing her commander Raccanelli, and driving her into the Spanish port of Santander. Then, also on the third anniversary of the war's beginning, when homeward-bound after her first war patrol during which she had operated against SC94 and SC95 (from which she sank the *Balladier*), *U-705* (Horn) was sunk by Whitley *P* of No. 77 Squadron with the loss of all on board.

Convoy ON127 left Liverpool the following day bound for New York. It consisted of 34 ships, escorted by the C4 group under Lieutenant Commander A.N. Dobson in HM Canadian Destroyer *St Croix*, with another destroyer, the *Ottawa*, and the corvettes *Amherst, Arvida, Sherbrooke* and *Celandine*, the last of which was British. The 13 U-boats mustering against ON127 first made contact on 9 September but then lost it until noon the next day, when Oberleutnant H. Hellriegel in *U-96* again sighted the convoy. Moving into a firing position submerged, Hellriegel sank the Belgian cargo ship *Elisabeth van Belgie*, a very elderly steamer belonging to the Compagnie Royale Belgo-Argentine, with the loss of a single life. Hellriegel also torpedoed two tankers, neither of which sank. One, the Norwegian motorship *Sveve*, which was serving as a naval oiler, had to be shelled by the escorts after her crew had been evacuated safely; the other, the British *F.J. Wolfe*, was able to continue her passage with ON127.

The pace quickened during the night of 10/11 September when several attacks were made, and though a number of torpedoes missed, *U-659* (Stock) struck the British tanker *Empire Oil* late on the 10th. It took a second torpedo, from *U-584* (Deecke) four hours later, to sink her, and all her company were picked up by the escorts. Next to go, torpedoed by von Bülow in *U-404*, was the Norwegian tanker *Marit II*, also being used as a naval auxiliary. She was followed by another Norwegian tanker, the *Fjordås*, which fortunately remained afloat and struggled back to the Clyde. Other U-boats suffered misses or misfirings, and Hellriegel added lustre to his laurels by surfacing and opening fire upon a trawler that had unwittingly strayed into the vicinity of the convoy.

While all this was going on the escorts were wrestling with what appears to have been a wholesale failure of their radar sets. It was not until the attacks were renewed on the 11th that they had any effect upon the convoy's tormentors, when *U-659* received damage from a depth-charge attack, forcing Stock out of the fight.

It was little enough. Late that day the predators moved in again, first blood going to Kapitänleutnant J. Deecke in *U-584* when he damaged the Norwegian *Hindanger* so badly that she had to be sunk by the corvette *Amherst*. Then Kapitänleutnant K. Hause of *U-211* torpedoed the tanker *Empire Moonbeam* (whose crew had temporarily abandoned her during the troubled passage of SC94), and the British whale-factory ship *Hektoria*, acting as a tanker though she was at the time in ballast. Neither sank immediately, but they fell astern, and both were later sent to the bottom by torpedoes from *U-608*, Kapitänleutnant E. Struckmeier. Captain Hewison and most of the company of the *Empire Moonbeam* were taken up by the *Arvida*, as were Gjertsen and his crew from the *Hektoria*. Von Bülow returned to the attack and *U-404* damaged yet another valuable though empty Norwegian tanker, the *Daghild*, but she too was able to continue her passage. Other torpedoes missed, including one aimed at *Ottawa* from *U-92* (Oelrich).[10]

Throughout the daylight hours of the 12th the U-boats were prevented from drawing close, and during darkness they failed to outwit the defence, but next morning the Panamanian-flagged *Stone Street*, which had straggled, was torpedoed and sunk from *U-594* by Kapitänleutnant F. Mumm. That night the British destroyer *Witch* and the Canadian *Annapolis* joined the escort from Canada, but Kapitänleutnant H. Walkerling evaded detection in *U-91* and fired at HMCS *Ottawa*. It was a foul black and windy night, presaging a winter of ferocious gales, and the convoy was already in the grip of the Labrador Current. At first the corvette seemed relatively safe, then a second torpedo broke her apart and she foundered rapidly. Those who escaped the sinking struggled in the water. One of these was her captain, Lieutenant Commander C.A. Rutherford, who gave his life-jacket to a rating. He was lost, together with 109 of *Ottawa*'s company and the survivors from the *Empire Oil*.

On the forenoon of the 14th the welcome drone of covering aircraft arriving from Newfoundland was heard overhead. Convoy ON127 stretched to the south, and on the 20th arrived at New York. On its way it ran into the east-bound Convoy SC100, and one of its ships, the *Empire Soldier*, sank in collision with the damaged tanker *F. J. Wolfe*.

Having been driven off SC99, the U-boats now followed the fortunes of SC100, which had left Halifax on 12 September. It was a relatively small convoy of 20 ships, but had a large covering force, for attached to the American A3 Escort Group were a number of warships on their way to take part in Operation TORCH, the invasion of Vichy French North Africa. The weather was bad, however.

The convoy was directed away from the first known concentration of U-boats only to encounter a second, the 10-strong *Pfeil* (Arrow) group deployed in its path by Kerneval. Despite the conditions, by the 20th Kapitänleutnant G. Jahn had managed to work into a position to torpedo the *Empire Hartebeeste* and her cargo of 4,000 tons of steel, 1,000 tons of canned goods, 2,000 tons of vehicles and timber. Happily, Captain J.F. Travis and all his men were picked up by two Norwegian ships in the convoy, the *Rio Verde* and *Norhauk*.

By the 21st the wind had risen to hurricane force, inhibiting the pursuit of SC100; some U-boats turned their attention to coastal convoys, and those who clung to SC100 were unable to press home any attacks until the convoy was south-west of Iceland on the 23rd. Kapitänleutnant A. Brandi was one of these tenacious opportunists, and sank the tanker *Athelsultan*. Selected as flagship for the convoy commodore, she was loaded with 13,250 tons of molasses and alcohol. As *U-617*'s torpedo slammed into her and the *Athelsultan* began to sink Captain J.D. Donovan distinguished himself, and was later awarded a Lloyd's War Medal. He and a handful of his men were recovered from a heavy sea and swell by the escorts, but Commodore N.H. Gale, a reserve officer, along with his staff, the naval gunners and 36 crew were lost.

As the convoy passed on Brandi hit a straggler labouring astern of the main body, the wheat-laden British tramp *Tennessee*. Captain A.H. Albrechtsen and 14 of his crew died. Brandi then attacked the Belgian steamer *Roumanie*. All but one of her 43-strong company were killed, the single survivor being dragged from the water and taken prisoner by Brandi's sailors. Brandi next sighted Convoy ON131, in the charge of C3 Escort group led by Lieutenant D.C. Wallace in the *Saguenay*. In addition to the *Skeena* and the corvettes *Agassiz, Galt, Sackville, Wetaskiwin* and the British *Anemone*, Wallace could call upon an additional HF/DF set aboard the convoy commodore's vessel, the steamer *Cairnesk*. Gathering the widely-scattered U-boats on Brandi's signal, Kerneval ordered an interception, not appreciating that Wallace, using Admiralty intelligence, was able to evade them. Foiled, they were dispersed to refuel from the U-tankers *U-118* and *U-116* off the Azores.

It was at this time that New York became the western terminus for trans-Atlantic trade convoys, with HX208 leaving on 17 and SC102 on 19

September. The interval for departures was extended from a weekly to an eight-day cycle, and the Western Ocean Meeting Point was shifted from 52° West to the 46th meridian. The Local Western Escort Force now comprised 22 corvettes, seven large minesweepers of the 'Bangor' class, and five destroyers. At the same time there were now sufficient resources for the formation of the first support group under Commander Walker. Misnamed the 20th Escort Group, it was to be short-lived because a month later its ships were required for Operation TORCH, but it sailed as a reinforcement to the B6 Escort Group attending westbound Convoy ON132, and was the welcome harbinger of better days: all 37 merchant vessels arrived safely at New York on 8 October.

Another nail was driven into the enemy coffin by the destruction of the commerce-raider *Stier*, in circumstances of great gallantry. The presence of raiders and increasing numbers of U-boats in areas where trade was conducted without the benefit of convoy had added greatly to the risks undergone by merchant ships, particularly in the South Atlantic, where losses had been appreciable.

In June the *Stier* had apprehended the American tanker *Stanvac Calcutta*, whose master and naval armed-guard commander had concerted an aggressive course of action to be followed in the event of a challenge. When ordered to heave-to, therefore, Captain G.O. Karlsson turned away, unmasking the after 4-inch gun with which Ensign E.L. Anderson immediately opened fire. Before his gun sights were destroyed and he himself received a facial wound, Anderson had succeeded in knocking out one of the *Stier*'s four port side guns. Eventually *Stanvac Calcutta* was shelled, torpedoed and sunk, her survivors, Anderson among them, being taken to imprisonment in Japan aboard the *Charlotte Schliemann* as related earlier.

After disposing of his prisoners Korvettenkapitän H. Gerlach resumed his cruise, making a rendezvous 650 miles NNW of St Helena with the *Michel* on 24 September. Next day his crew replenished their stores from the blockade-runner *Tannenfels*. The weather was windy, wet and misty, but the two ships remained in company until the 27th, when at 08.52 they suddenly saw a vessel coming up from the south-east, less than a mile away.

This was the Liberty ship *Stephen Hopkins*, which had been launched from Kaiser's yard at Richmond, California in June and was on her maiden voyage, having been ordered first to Australia and from there taken a cargo of grain to South Africa. On her way across the stormy southern Indian Ocean she had received a battering from the prevailing westerlies, enduring winds of Force 9 to 11. From Cape Town she was proceeding in ballast towards Paramaribo for a cargo of bauxite when, emerging from a mist patch, Captain P. Buck found his ship in the presence of the two strangers.

Immediately the *Stier* flashed the command to 'Stop at Once'. Buck put his helm hard over and turned away, seeking the shelter of the rain and mist, ringing the alarms, and keeping his stern to the enemy.

Although she was a newly-built vessel the *Stephen Hopkins* had not received any of the up-to-date weaponry fitted to her later sisters. Like her British cousins she had perforce to fight for her life with a 4-inch low-angle 'anti-submarine gun of First World War vintage'. In addition she had two 37-millimetre anti-aircraft weapons and six machine-guns. *Stier* by herself out-gunned her, despite the damage inflicted by the *Stanvac Calcutta*, and in addition the *Tannenfels* bore an armament similar to that of the Liberty ship.

Buck's manoeuvre prompted a quick response from the two German vessels, both of which opened an all-calibre fire upon her. Undeterred by these odds, Ensign K. Willett's armed guard ran to their posts, supported by their merchant shipmates. Among those assigned to the after gun were Cadet-Midshipman E. O'Hara, who oversaw ammunition-loading, and Cadet-Midshipman A. Chamberlin, who acted as spotter.

As the Germans opened fire, shell splinters and shrapnel began to shower the American ship's decks, while the machine-guns from both the *Stier* and the *Tannenfels* swept her with a storm of lead. On gaining his post Willett received a shrapnel wound in his stomach, but the short range at which the two parties had discovered one another – possibly less than 1,000 yards – enabled his gun crew to hit the *Stier* with their first shot, which struck the rudder and jammed the *Stier's* helm. The second passed through her shell-plating and severed a fuel feed pipe in the engine room. While this robbed Gerlach of the power to manoeuvre and fire a torpedo, it did nothing to stop the shells from his heavy guns slamming into the frail plating of the *Stephen Hopkins*, or to prevent Kapitän Haase's machine-gunners from raking the Liberty ship from the *Tannenfels*, destroying her radio room while the operator was sending a distress signal. The *Stephen Hopkins* was now on fire in several places, including her engine room, where one shell had hit and blown up the starboard boiler, her port boats had been shot to pieces, and she had slowed to a stop, the sea pouring into her stricken hull. Buck reluctantly gave the order to abandon her.

Second Mate J.E. Lehman, in charge of the anti-aircraft guns, poured a rapid fire into the *Stier* with some effect, but he and his gunners in the forepart of the ship were hit as the *Stephen Hopkins* slewed round and broached-to in the rough sea. Chief Mate R. Maczkowski, 'who was shot high in the chest and in the left forearm, continued to direct and rally his men . . .' On the poop the 4-inch gun continued firing. Ensign Willett, bleeding to death from his stomach wound, received additional injuries as his men fell about him. A shell blew up the ready-use ammunition locker, hurling Willett to the deck of the gun-tub while rapid machine-gun fire drove the last few men away from their weapon. Not receiving any further requests for ammunition, young O'Hara climbed to the gun from his post below and, finding five rounds remaining, single-handedly loaded, aimed and fired at the *Tannenfels*. He is alleged to have scored five hits, evidence of the short range at which this intense action took place.

Seeing the enemy still firing from the stern, the *Stier's* gunners concentrated on the *Stephen Hopkins's* poop, and a few seconds later O'Hara had fallen among his fellows.

Young Chamberlin managed to report to Buck as the master ordered his ship abandoned. Mustering what remained of his men, and still under fire, Buck and Second Engineer G. Cronk attempted to lower No. 1 Boat and launch life-rafts, but a shell burst among them and two men were killed; despite this, Cronk and the steward continued until the boat reached the water. As Cronk jumped after it, Buck appears to have gone to join a raft. Beyond a glimpse of him clinging to one, nothing further is known of him. Chamberlin left the ship from the poop but failed to clear the wreck. Of the 41 merchant seamen and 15 armed guard, 37 were lost in the action or in the foundering of the ship.[11]

But the damage the Americans had inflicted on the *Stier* was fatal. Twenty minutes after the encounter, she too was on fire. Gerlach ordered her crew to abandon her after setting scuttling charges. Taking to the water, 325 of her company were hauled aboard the *Tannenfels* before the charges blew and the *Stier* followed the *Stephen Hopkins* on the slow journey to the bottom. With Gerlach and his men safe, Kapitän Haase headed for Bordeaux.

Struggling aboard his lifeboat, Cronk took charge. He was the senior surviving officer, and for two hours he paddled round picking men out of the water. Streaming the boat's sea-anchor they remained in the vicinity until noon the next day, but no further survivors were seen, only a rough and wreckage-strewn sea. With little more to guide them than the certainty that the continent of South America lay to the westwards, Cronk and his men hauled in the sea-anchor and set sail to the north-west, their most advantageous heading in the prevailing wind. There were 19 men in the boat, one of whom had a piece of shrapnel dug out of his shoulder; in the ordeal they were now compelled to endure, four more died of wounds or privation. Early on the morning of 27 October, after a voyage of 31 days, Cronk and his shipmates drove No. 1 Boat up onto the sandy beach close to the Brazilian village of Barra do Itapbopoana. Ten crew and five naval armed guards were all that remained of the *Stephen Hopkins's* crew of 56.

The defence of the *Stephen Hopkins*, brief, but courageous against all odds, is rightly one of the famous exploits of the war and established her men in the pantheon of American gallantry. Gerlach reported that his opponent had been 'a patrol vessel, or even an armed merchant cruiser';[12] Fleet Admiral King's spokesman extolled the action as one of 'extraordinary heroism . . . in keeping with the highest tradition of American seamanship', concluding that the ship's company's 'fearless determination to fight their ship . . . until . . . [she] was rendered useless, aflame and in a sinking condition, demonstrated conduct beyond the call of duty.'

But if such heroism eroded the utility of commerce-raiders in the South Atlantic, Dönitz was able to counter by substituting the four long-range Type IX U-boats of the *Eisbär* group, which by early October were arriving there after their aborted diversion against SL119. On their way they had been refuelled south of Ascension by *U-459* (Wilamowitz-Möllendorff), and *U-68* had sunk the British tramp *Trevilley* and the Dutchman *Breedijk*. The *Trevilley's* master Captain R. Harvey and his chief engineer were taken out of the boats, then transferred to *U-459* for eventual internment at Milag Nord.

The four original U-boats in the *Eisbär* group, *U-172, U-159, U-68* and *U-504*, had now been joined by a fifth, *U-179*, and all were in position off Cape Town by the night of 7/8 October. Merten in *U-68* had been on the coast for five days, reporting back to BdU as he penetrated Table Bay and photographed the anchorage. Emmermann's *U-172* was fitted with a Metox set, a device capable of detecting radar transmissions from other vessels, and he too made a reconnoitring sortie, writing afterwards that 'the picture which the town and harbour presented was so beautiful and peaceful that we stayed a few hours on the surface and called the crew up one by one to the bridge to enjoy the sight . . . [of the] brilliantly illuminated city.' He then quietly submerged, still observing the movements of shipping in the 'brilliant sunshine on the roadstead, the sea as smooth as a mirror, only a strong swell making it difficult to keep the U-boat at a steady depth.'

The southerly movement of the *Eisbär* U-boats had been noted in the Admiralty Tracking Room in London, from where Admiral Tait, Commander-in-Chief, South Atlantic, had been urged to try to organise merchantmen into small convoys, no matter how weakly escorted. Tait had insufficient resources even for this, however, and in any case it would have achieved little, for what no one on the Allied side knew was that the U-boats were not intended to operate as a *Rudel*, or group, but individually. After delivering a demoralising attack on Table Bay, they were to target widespread independently-sailing merchantmen, among them a preponderance of valuable passenger-cargo-liners. Known as 'the Tavern of the Seas', the Cape Town area was a focus for shipping routes, and the U-boats' initial success was spectacular, achieving their objective. The handful of Royal Navy destroyers and small South African warships available did their best and were quick to respond, supported by Ventura aircraft of the South African Air Force, but they could only be reactive, operating after a merchant ship had reported an attack. They did, however, enjoy one early triumph.

This was the destruction of *U-179*, which under Korvettenkapitän E. Sobe was on her first war patrol and had not been diverted against SL119. On the afternoon of 8 October, as the U-boats began operations Sobe had submerged *U-179* after a Ventura was seen approaching about sixty miles west of Cape Town. A few hours later, before dark, Sobe observed a ship through his periscope; 40 minutes later he was in position, and fired at her. The torpedo struck the *City of Athens*, but another aircraft was seen and Sobe dived to 80 metres.

Outward bound, the *City of Athens* had left Glasgow and was on her way to Alexandria by way of Takoradi and Cape Town with almost 6,000 tons of government stores and eight Admiralty staff officers. Once she had been hit Captain J.A. Kingsley ordered her abandoned, and although she quickly sank her six lifeboats were launched and then reported by a Ventura flying low over the scene. The air was filled with distress calls from other ships under attack in the offing and the naval vessels were already responding to a situation of mounting crisis.

Lieutenant Commander M.W. Tomkinson in HMS *Active* was diverted from another distress call to the boats of the *City of Athens* and all but one of her crew were taken aboard the destroyer. It was now 23.30, and Tomkinson received a report that the radar had an echo 2,500 yards away to the south-east. A few minutes later a sonar contact followed, and then a visual sighting of

a large U-boat . . . stopped, presumably charging her batteries. Speed was increased to 25 knots and course altered slightly to bring U-boat broader on the beam. At 800 yards the target was illuminated by searchlight, and fire was opened by B gun . . . The U-boat dived . . .

Active altered towards and steadied on a course about 5° ahead of U-boat's conning tower. The U-boat passed down the [*Active's*] port side at close range and was attacked with a 10 charge pattern fired by eye, set to 50 and 150 feet. The charges are reported to have burst all round the U-boat, the swirl and bubbles caused by its diving still being clearly visible. The depth-charge party reported that the U-boat was blown to the surface as a result of the attack and then disappeared, but this cannot be confirmed. No contact was obtained in spite of a search carried out throughout the night. A large patch of diesel oil came to the surface . . . No wreckage was found.

Emmermann's *U-172* was not far away, and he was in no doubt: he 'clearly' heard 'the sounds of another U-boat being sunk'. Sobe and his 60 men were dead.

Despite their best endeavours this was the only retaliation the forces in South Africa were able to inflict upon the *Eisbär* U-boats as they continued their orgy of destruction, for the Germans had no intention of concentrating off Table Bay and spread out to operate individually.

Korvettenkapitän K-F. Merten's *U-68* sent four ships to the bottom when he struck on 8 October. First was the Greek tramp steamer *Koumoundouros*, followed by the Dutch cargo-liner *Gaasterkerk*, the American tanker *Swiftsure*, and the British Royal Mail liner *Sarthe*.[13] Next day he sank a second American ship, the *Examelia*, laden with Indian manganese ore, jute, burlap and hemp. Eleven men were killed in the torpedo explosion which destroyed lifeboats and caused such extensive damage that the *Examelia* sank in seven minutes, taking one of the lifeboats down with her as she capsized and overturning another.[14] Merten then went on to torpedo the Belgian ship *Belgian Fighter*, a war-built standard ship manned by exiled members of the Belgian merchant service. On the 29th, low on fuel, he headed for L'Orient, and by 6 November was about five hundred miles south of St Helena when he sighted the Ellerman liner *City of Cairo* and torpedoed her.

Captain W.A. Rogerson was on a passage from Bombay and Cape Town home with a hundred passengers and a general cargo that contained pig-iron, wool and silver bullion. Merten appears to have suffered some pangs of conscience, perhaps fearing a second *Laconia* incident, for he surfaced, and after apologising gave the boats a compass-bearing for St Helena. One hundred and four people died as the *City of Cairo* sank, and the diverse fates of the survivors stand as evidence of the capricious nature of personal luck. The majority, more than two hundred, were eventually picked up and landed safely by two British cargo-liners, the *Clan Alpine* and the *Bendoran*. Those rescued by the Ben liner had been 13 days in their boat, by which time 'the skins of the Europeans were so burned . . . that at first I thought the boat contained only Asiatics,' reported the *Bendoran's* master, Captain W.C. Wilson, who had been peering through his binoculars at the boat as he slowed his ship. He picked up 48 women, children, servicemen, and lascar sailors. Interestingly, he reported that the recovery rate of the women and children rescued was faster than that of the men.

Two more of the *City of Cairo's* survivors were taken aboard a Brazilian corvette and landed at Recife, but three were rescued by the German blockade-runner *Rhakotis*, on her way from Japan to Bordeaux – all who were left after 36 days in an open boat. One was 'a quiet English girl', a twenty-year-old passenger who had distinguished herself in the lifeboat not only in tending the injured but in handling the tiller; the other two were the chief quartermaster and a steward. All three were at risk when the *Rhakotis* was intercepted and destroyed by the British cruiser *Scylla* off Cape Finsterre on 1 January 1943. During the action the young woman was killed but the two men found themselves back in the Atlantic until they were rescued a second time, by *U-410*, landed at St-Nazaire and sent to Milag Nord.

The other *Eisbär* boats wrought similar havoc. Hours before Merten's attack Kapitänleutnant C. Emmermann of *U-172*, having concluded his ruminations on the tranquil state of the Cape shoreline, had on 7 October sunk the American freighter *Chickasaw City*. Next day he sank the Panamanian motor-vessel *Firethorn* and the Greek steamer *Pantelis*. But Emmermann had attracted the notice of the South African Defence Force, and was in his turn attacked by patrol craft from Cape Town. Escaping serious damage, he waited for his next chance. This came on the morning of the 10th, when in the strong winds and heavy seas for which the area was well known he torpedoed the Orient liner *Orcades*. The peace-time passenger-liner was homeward bound as a troop-ship from Suez to Britain. Captain C. Fox had aboard 723 servicemen, a general cargo of 3,000 tons and a large crew, in all more than 1,300 souls. The *Orcades* was hit by two torpedoes, and Fox ordered the ship abandoned and the boats lowered. One capsized and all 38 aboard were drowned, but the rest escaped to be picked up by a Polish vessel, the *Narwik*. Fox and a party of 52 volunteers attempted to get the damaged *Orcades* back to Cape Town and were under way when Emmermann sent three more torpedoes into her: she went down in three minutes. In addition to those lost in the lifeboat, several men were killed in the engine room during the second attack, but Fox and his party escaped and were also picked up by the *Narwik*.

On his way across to the Brazilian coast where he was ordered to operate for the second half of November Emmermann sank two more British ships, the *Aldington Court*, Captain A. Stewart, and *Llandilo*, Captain W.R.B. Burgess. Although he allowed survivors onto the U-boat's casing while their lifeboats were baled out and they were afterwards picked up by other ships, loss of life was heavy. On his new patrol ground 250 miles north-west of Parnaíba, he torpedoed a third victim, the *Benlomond*, Captain J. Maul.

The *Benlomond* was in ballast, on passage for Paramaribo, a mustering port for American coastal convoys which thereafter headed onwards under escort to New York. Shortly before noon on 23 November there was a terrific explosion in the vicinity of the *Benlomond*'s engine room. Second Steward Poon Lim was in his cabin and rushed up to the boat deck, taking his lifebelt and donning it as he went. On the boat deck he found two officers trying to launch a lifeboat, but they were suddenly overwhelmed by a sea which swept them away. Poon too was dragged down, until the buoyancy in his lifebelt brought him gasping to the surface; surrounded by wreckage he grasped a plank of wood, worried about sharks. After what seemed an age he saw a life-raft bobbing some distance away and swam towards it. Once he had gained a footing he looked around and saw another raft, recognising its occupants as the gun's crew. They waved and tried to paddle closer, but to no avail. Poon also heard some cries for help, but he saw no one else, and the rafts drifted further apart.

Then he saw a submarine, which his description of it and of the emblem on its conning tower suggested might have been an Italian but was unlikely to have been Emmermann's *U-172*. Poon called to the men cleaning its gun and they waved him away. Resignedly he took stock: he had food and water for about fifty days, and was in an area often subject to heavy tropical rainfall. In the weeks to come he saw many ships in the distance, and let off flares on several occasions. Like Cape Town the area was a focal point of Allied merchant shipping, yet none stopped to pick up the Chinese steward.

Poon, a man of determination and self-discipline, set himself a rigorous programme, carefully rationing himself from the six boxes of hard-tack, two pounds of chocolate, ten small cans of pemmican, one bottle of lime juice, five cans of evaporated milk, and ten gallons of water. He was able to supplement his meagre diet with an occasional fish and sea-bird. Stranding the raft's lifeline to make a fishing-line, he patiently dug a galvanised nail out of the raft and fashioned a hook with his teeth. This was baited with ship's biscuit mixed with water and left to dry. His first fish was small, and he prudently used it as bait to catch a larger quarry. He managed to grab seagulls when they alighted on his raft and, once, upon his shoulders. He sliced up the birds with a knife made out of a pemmican can. His thin cotton shirt and shorts soon rotted and he was burnt rapidly, his skin erupting in blisters, to some extent soothed by the fuel oil with which he was covered. Until the 100th day, he was lucky enough to be able to top up his water, extemporising a funnel from his lifebelt, but after that it stopped raining regularly. As his water ran out, he began to despair of surviving. Then it rained again, and on the 120th day an aeroplane flew low over him, rocking its wings in the international signal of recognition. Poon's spirits rose accordingly, but successive aircraft of the Brazilian air force were unable to locate him, and he again began to decline. By the 130th day he was so weak that he could no longer help himself, and lay inert upon the raft. Three days later he was found by a fisherman: he was only ten miles from the Brazilian coast, near Salinas, and was landed at Belém. Once ashore he astonished his benefactor by consuming hot red peppers by the handful.

To the equal astonishment of Poon's doctors at the Beneficienza Portuguese Hospital, who apart from malnutrition diagnosed only a slight stomach disorder, the stoical if shrivelled Chinaman was restored to full vigour in a little over a fortnight and able to report the loss of the *Benlomond* with almost all her company to the British consul at Pará. As this official himself reported to the MoWT, Poon deposed that 'he was alone on the life-raft and he declares that he always was'. Poon Lim was later appointed MBE and received the insignia from King George VI at Buckingham Palace.[15]

As for Emmermann, before refuelling and heading for his base he sank one more ship off St Paul's Rocks. This was the American freighter *Alaskan*, also on her way to join a convoy at Paramaribo and loaded with chrome ore. As her crew abandoned the ship, Emmermann surfaced and shelled her, then withdrew Captain E.E. Greenlaw from his lifeboat and questioned him about routes used by merchantmen. Before letting him go, Emmermann is reported to have apologised: 'Sorry we sank you, but this is war. Why don't you tell America to get out of it?' Greenlaw afterwards made a 40-day boat voyage before finding help.

Kapitänleutnant H. Witte was also in action on 7 October off Cape Town as *U-159* sank the British steam-ship *Boringia*. Owned by the United Baltic Corporation of London, the *Boringia* was a long way from her normal stamping-ground, carrying a cargo of potash, cotton and gum from Haifa to Britain. Captain S.H.K. Kolls and 31 of his crew were killed. Early the next morning 28 were picked up by the *Clan Mactavish*, but the Clan liner was then herself torpedoed as she lay stopped, waiting for the *Boringia's* boats to close her. Seven more of the *Boringia's* crew died, along with 53 from the *Clan Mactavish*, among them her master, Captain E.E. Arthur. The ship sank with a load of copper bound from Beira to Britain. Those left of the two ships' companies were rescued by the British ship *Matheran* and landed at Cape Town.

On the 9th Witte sank the American cargo-vessel *Coloradan*[16] and escaped unscathed a depth-charge attack by a South African aircraft. Moving her hunting ground further south and east, by the end of the month she had sunk a further three British ships, the *Empire Nomad*, Captain J.T. Nelson, the *Ross*, Captain J. Dodds, and the *Laplace*, Captain A. MacKellan. All were loaded with valuable cargoes.

A month later, during the evening of 7 November, Witte made a surface attack on another American vessel, the *La Salle*, Captain W.A. Sillars, 350 miles south-east of the Cape of Good Hope. The *La Salle*, according to Emmermann, simply 'atomised' as his torpedo struck her. The warhead exploded in the *La Salle*'s cargo of ammunition, sending a 'pillar of flame hundreds of metres high. For minutes, splinters rained down on my deck, wounding three men on bridge watch.' For safety reasons the *La Salle* had been routed from New York to Cape Town by way of the Panama Canal and the South Pacific. Due at Cape Town on 1 November, she had already been posted missing. Her detonation was heard by the keepers at Cape Point lighthouse more than three hundred miles away.

A week later Witte found another target, the large six-masted American schooner *Star of Scotland*, in ballast between Cape Town and Paranagua. It was early in the forenoon when a shot plunged into the sea ahead of the sailing-vessel. The second fell short but the third hit, starting a fire and destroying the radio-shack. All except Captain C. Flink left the vessel, the chief mate falling into the sea and drowning in the process. Witte circled in U-159, approached, and questioned the men in the boat. Meanwhile Flink launched a second boat, placing in it 'the ship's accounts, sextant, binoculars and the chronometer'. Witte's men promptly confiscated Flink's boat and looted the schooner of three boatloads of supplies, taking Flink aboard the U-boat. Witte intended to make him prisoner, but Flink successfully argued that with the mate dead no one else was capable of navigating the survivors in the boat. Witte extracted from Flink a promise that he 'would not command another ship sailing against Germany', whereupon he was given some black bread and cigarettes before they parted company. The *Star of Scotland* finally sank eight hours after the initial shelling, and Flink began a 1,040-mile passage to Santa Maria lighthouse on the Angolan coast, where he landed on 1 December.

At about the same time Witte, who had headed for St Paul's Rocks, was refuelling U-159 from U-461. He then maintained a patrol between the isolated seamounts and the Brazilian main, and in three days he sank as many British ships. The first was the Ellerman liner *City of Bombay*, Captain F.W. Penderworthy, which was on an outward voyage from Liverpool to Karachi by way of Trinidad and South Africa, loaded with a cargo of military stores and a handful of service personnel. The weather was kind and all but ten of the 130 on board escaped, to be rescued by other ships, 12 by the *Star of Suez*.

Witte began to stalk this vessel, and two days later, on 15 December, fired a torpedo at her. Owned by the Red Rose Line of Alexandria and managed by Watts, Watts & Company, she sank with the loss of two men in the engine room. Next day Witte struck at the Cardiff tramp *East Wales*, sending to the bottom her cargo of coal and military stores destined for the forces fighting in the Western Desert. Captain S.A. Rowland and 16 men were lost. Witte now headed for L'Orient.

The fourth of the original *Eisbär* U-boats, *U-504*, was commanded by Korvettenkapitän F. Poske, who launched his attack south of Cape Town on 17 October before moving north-east towards Durban. He sank the *Empire Chaucer*, a new standard-built freighter managed for the MoWT by Tatem of Cardiff and on her way home from India with general cargo, mail, pig-iron and tea. Although only the three men in the engine room were killed, Captain R. Jennings and his crew were widely dispersed in the aftermath. Jennings and 11 men were picked up by a sister-ship, the *Empire Squire*, which carried them to Trinidad; another 15 spent 23 days in an open boat before the Royal Mail liner *Nebraska* found them and landed them at Cape Town; a further 14 made a two-week voyage and landed at Bredasdorp, near Simonstown.

Off East London on 23 October Poske next sank the *City of Johannesburg*, Captain W.A. Owen, followed on the 26th by the American *Anne Hutchinson*[17] and, on the 31st, by two more vessels, the British *Empire Guidon* to the east of Durban and the *Reynolds* off Madagascar. After this foray into the Indian Ocean Poske turned back, and on 3 November, before he too headed for France, fired his last two torpedoes at the Brazilian-registered steamer *Porto Alegre* east of Port Elizabeth.

Despite the loss of Sobe's *U-179* the *Eisbär* operation was a success for Dönitz, demonstrating what he might have achieved had he possessed larger and longer-ranged submarines at the beginning of the war. The vulnerability of Britain's dispersed shipping and its high value were in clear evidence off the Tavern of the Seas during the southern-hemisphere summer.[18]

The submarine seen by Poon Lim on 23 November may have been the Italian *Leonardo da Vinci*, Capitano di Corvetta Gazzana-Priaroggia, which had sunk four ships earlier in the month when operating off the Cape Verde Islands, before moving towards the Brazilian coast near Recife. A fifth target, the Dutch steam-ship *Frans Hals*, evaded her torpedo and opened fire on the surfaced submarine, forcing her to dive. Also patrolling off the Cape Verdes at this time was Korvettenkapitän R. Dierksen in *U-176*. At 15.00 on 25 November he fired a spread of three torpedoes at a cargo-ship with the distinctive profile of a Blue Funnel liner which he had been stalking since 02.00. The torpedoes missed but the premature detonation of one alerted the second officer on watch on the *Polydorus*, and Captain H. Brouwer was quickly on the bridge, his crew going to their action stations and clearing away the *Polydorus*'s armament. The ship was owned by Alfred Holt's Dutch subsidiary, the Netherlands Ocean Steamship Company, and had sailed as part of ON145, dispersing from the convoy and heading as an independent for Freetown laden with military stores. She had aboard a mixed crew of Dutch, British and Chinese.

Astern of him Brouwer saw the surfacing U-boat, and increasing speed he headed east. After dark he altered course, but Dierksen kept *Polydorus* in sight in the bright moonlight. With an advantage in speed of 3 knots, Dierksen was able to close his objective, and at 21.00 he opened fire. Brouwer responded with Oerlikons, dropped smoke floats and tried to increase his own speed further. Although one shell hit the engine-room skylight the damage was not serious and Brouwer was able to run into the cover of a rain shower, after which, heading east, he carried out a series of zig-zags. Dierksen nevertheless caught up, and at dawn fired a second torpedo from a submerged position. Fortunately Brouwer's lookouts spotted the incoming track and full starboard helm was applied, the laden cargo-liner heeling as she swung away, and the nearest torpedo passed ahead of *Polydorus*. Down below Chief Engineer E.J.V. Beymerwerdt and his assistants raised steam pressure to 250 psi, 'a difficult process as several near-misses had caused leak-ages in our settling tanks and bunkers'.

Dierksen, having fired several more torpedoes, now surfaced a mile and a half on *Polydorus*'s port beam, intending to engage again with his gun. Hardly had he opened fire when the *Polydorus* responded, and Brouwer extended the range to 5 miles as a thirty-minute gun-duel ensued. Under Second Mate B. Salomons the 4-inch poop-mounted gun 'kept regularly firing at the enemy with splendid stubbornness'. At about 07.30 Dierksen turned towards his quarry, whereupon Brouwer swung *Polydorus* away and again dropped smoke floats. At 08.15 *U-176* reappeared clear of the smoke and sent a few more shells after the *Polydorus* before slowing down and breaking off the engagement.

Brouwer was not deceived by this feint and once he was out of sight decided to run to the north-westwards, assuming that his opponent would try to work ahead of his own intended track. Inspecting his ship, Brouwer found two lifeboats wrecked and some superficial damage from heavy- and light-calibre weapons. After dark the *Polydorus* was gradually swung round to resume her passage towards Freetown, and at 03.00 on the 27th was 740 miles due west of her destination. Suddenly two torpedoes struck her port side.

Dierksen had maintained contact by hydrophone, and had resighted *Polydorus* in the moonlight shortly after midnight. His War Diary notes that the Dutch radio-operator was transmitting Brouwer's SSSS signal even as the ship was sinking and the crew were abandoning her in four boats in good order. Shortly afterwards *U-176* surfaced and motored towards them, stopping near No. 1 Boat and asking for the master. Brouwer, who had removed his epaulettes, answered that the captain was not present. Having ascertained a few details Dierksen sheered off, leaving the men in the boats to watch the death throes of their ship, which sank 'in a cloud of dust' at 05.00 leaving them feeling 'very lonely'.

Brouwer now set about consolidating his position. One Chinese fireman had sadly died of his injuries soon after leaving the ship, otherwise all 80 hands were present, and they and the stores were put in the three best boats, Nos 1, 6 and 7. This, which took most of the day, included an officers' conference held aboard an RAF launch which had torn clear of its lashings on *Polydorus*'s deck where it had been part of her cargo. After a night's rest, sail was hoisted at 09.00 on the 28th and the 'very well equipped fine strong boats' headed south-east, experiencing no difficulty keeping in touch. Shortly after midnight they sighted the lights of a neutral ship and burnt flares, whereupon they were taken aboard the Spanish steamer *Eolo*, whose master Captain Urgelles did everything possible for his Dutch guests. Brouwer and his men were landed on 5 December at Las Palmas. Their ship had endured the longest chase by a submarine of the entire war, a 50-hour epic recognised much later by Queen Juliana and the Dutch government.

It was also off St Paul's Rocks that the actions of *U-174*, Fregattenkapitän U. Thilo, brought Dönitz's sortie into the South Atlantic to an end. Between the last day of October and 15 November Thilo sank five vessels, among them the Dutch ship *Zandaam*, which was carrying home survivors from several American ships sunk by his colleagues operating off Cape Town.[19]

The *Eisbär* U-boats had achieved a notable victory against targets that proved almost helpless against their onslaught. But they had not won the war at sea; that was still being fought out in the North Atlantic as winter closed its grip upon the grey wastes of the northern latitudes.

20

'The . . . courage of ordinary people'

Stentor

OCTOBER 1942 PROVED bloody enough, yet the full onslaught of the U-boats in the North Atlantic was frustrated by bad weather and the corruption of sighting signals by poor atmospherics, and several were destroyed, mostly by Catalinas,[1] but these events did little to ease the burden borne by the merchant ships and their crews. Heavy weather might inhibit an attack, but a U-boat could sink below the turbulent surface and her crew sit out a gale in bearable if mephitic discomfort, while their enemies on the surface were subject to all the violence the ocean could muster against them. The men in the escorts fared worst: most of the merchant seamen were inured to the caprice of the sea.

Even the sub-tropical waters of the Atlantic Narrows, where in late October Kerneval deployed the *Streitaxt* (Battle-axe) group, could prove unpleasant. Apart from stragglers, there were no losses from the OS convoy series between July 1942 and March 1943, but the same could not be said of the laden northbound ships of the complementary SL convoys against which the *Streitaxt* U-boats were now mustered. The 42 ships of Convoy SL125 left Freetown on 16 October.[2] By the time it arrived at Liverpool on 9 November it had lost 13 of its ships in an ambush off the Canaries.

Because of demands elsewhere its escort was inadequate, consisting initially of HMSs *Petunia*, Lieutenant Commander J.M. Rayner, and *Woodruff, Crocus, Cowslip, Copinsay*, and *Juliet*, and the Free French Sloop *Commandant Drogou*. The salvage tug *Salvonia* was also in the convoy. That evening, as *Petunia's* radar set failed, Commodore Reyne in the P&O cargo-liner *Nagpore* reported to Rayner that the master of *Hopecastle* had obtained on 437 kilocycles a radio-bearing of a U-boat towards the north. Next day, as attempts were made to repair *Petunia*'s radar, the tanker *Alexandre André* and the *Pinto* and *Lafonia* fell out of line, and *Copinsay* and *Commandant Drogou* were left to screen them. Later the *Copinsay* was detached to recover survivors from the *Oronsay*, which had been sunk earlier by the Italian submarine *Archimede* while on an independent passage.

On the 19th smoke was seen on the horizon and three merchant ships, the *Président Doumer*, the Norwegian heavy lift ship *Belnor* and the British *Ardour* joined the convoy with their escort, the sloop *Bridgewater*. The *Anglo-Maersk* appeared to have straggled during the night, however, and was no longer in her station. In the course of the next few days several minor incidents occurred. The American-flagged *West Kebar* left to proceed independently to the Caribbean (but was afterwards sunk by *U-129* off Barbados on the 29th), the *Germa* had steering problems, and the *Bridgewater* left the escort for other duties. On the evening of the 23rd the *Commandant Drogou* and the *Snowdrop* arrived escorting the *Bothnia, Mano* and *Calgary* which joined the convoy, after which the two escorts left and returned to Freetown.

Then on the 26th Kapitänleutnant W. Witte in *U-509* sighted and subsequently torpedoed the British-flagged ex-Danish tanker *Anglo-Maersk*, which had not straggled at all but instead had 'romped' 60 miles ahead of SL125. On receipt of Captain K.N. Valsberg's distress signal Rayner sent the *Juliet* and the *Salvonia* ahead to assist, but although the *Anglo-Maersk* did not sink immediately, she was given the *coup de grâce* by Höltring in *U-604* some hours later as he sought the main body of the convoy. Meanwhile the escorts refuelled from the tanker *British Ardour*, and Rayner received warnings from the Admiralty that there were U-boats in his vicinity.

By the evening of the 27th, when SL125 was spotted by *U-409* which then closed in with Witte's *U-509, U-203, U-604* and *U-659*, the escort had been reduced to four vessels, the corvettes *Petunia, Woodruff, Crocus* and *Cowslip*. By the time it was dark enough for a surface attack the visibility was still good, though a low swell presaged a coming gale. Witte ran into the approaching convoy and at around 19.30 fired several torpedoes, the opening rounds of what was to be a run of spectacular destruction. One torpedo struck the Blue Star liner *Pacific Star*, another the Blue Funnel liner *Stentor*.

The *Pacific Star* was hit on her starboard bow and No. 1 Hold rapidly flooded. For a while Captain G.L. Evans was able to maintain his station, but his ship gradually lost speed as water drove into her hull and her bow sank. In response the escorts carried out the 'Raspberry' counter-attack procedure and *Woodruff* dropped one depth-charge, but without effect. Rayner was quite unaware that *Stentor* had also been hit. Meanwhile, aboard the *Pacific Star* tanks were trimmed to keep her head up, but during the night the wind freshened from the north-west, compounding Evans's problems, and by 02.00 the next morning the convoy was out of sight. Evans altered course for Gibraltar, which brought the rising wind and sea onto the port beam and eased the situation a little, but with conditions deteriorating further he decided to try for the neutral Canaries. The *Pacific Star* limped along with the wind astern and a heavy, quartering sea. One after lifeboat was torn out of the davits, and at 17.00 on the 28th the bulkhead between Nos 1 and 2 holds collapsed, and the ingress of water could not be stemmed by the pumps.

Evans ordered a distress message transmitted and the ship abandoned, advising his officers to remain near the ship. It says something for their seamanship that the *Pacific Star* was evacuated without loss of life, but at dawn next morning only Evans's and the second officer's boats were in sight of the ship. Any thoughts of reboarding the *Pacific Star* evaporated as they watched the sea break over her waterlogged hull. Evans could only hope that the arrival of another vessel might enable him to save his cargo (frozen Argentine beef), and he clung on in that hope until the morning of the 30th. 'The weather was still bad . . . and in view of the condition of the men in the boats we had to leave her and make for the land. The vessel was settling down as we left.' Evans was appointed OBE for his persistence and seamanship. He commended his radio officer, Mr J. D. Dempster, who 'was a great help to me all the time, and was a fine fellow.'

The boats landed at Santa Cruz, Las Palmas in the Canaries, and the men were repatriated via Gibraltar in Spanish ships. Evans reported hostility on the part of the Spanish authorities, though 'the ordinary man-in-the-street is very much on our side'. The captain was interrogated 'by both the Captain of the Port and the Military Commissar. The former asked me to complete a questionnaire' giving details of the force of the escort, the disposition of the ships in the convoy, the nature of the cargo, what in Evans's opinion was the state of the naval war, and had he 'seen any damage during the war to ports and installations?'

Meanwhile SL125 had ploughed on. The morning following *Pacific Star*'s loss, *Woodruff* signalled *Petunia* that *Stentor* had also been lost during the night and that 'when last seen SS *Pacific Star* was still under way'. *Woodruff* also reported that she had picked up 200 survivors from the *Stentor* 'including the master but [Vice] Commodore Garstin was missing'.

Unusually, instead of an experienced master aboard his own ship acting in the capacity of vice commodore, this convoy had a specially-appointed vice commodore. Garstin was a retired captain from the Royal Indian Navy and his ship, the *Stentor*, had been leading the ninth of SL125's eleven columns. He was on the bridge at the moment of the torpedo strike, which burst in one of the *Stentor*'s deep tanks with a thump. The ship had been loaded with West African produce in Lagos and the tank contained flammable palm oil, which was thrown up and over the bridge, where it 'erupted into a huge fountain that shot high in the air. It was on fire when it came back down,' recalled Yeoman of Signals G. Clarke. It poured over the accommodation which instantly burst into flames, searing Garstin, who was last seen being led away to the ship's doctor.

'The whole of the bridge structure and Nos 1 and 2 lifeboats . . . were ablaze,' wrote Radio Officer Borrer. 'Topping this awesome picture, on the monkey island, surrounded and illuminated by the flames, were the third and fourth mates (Mr C.R. Hearne and Mr G.D. Lewis) busily throwing overboard live ammunition from the Oerlikon gun locker, regardless of the imminent fate of the ship.'

The *Stentor*'s own commander, Captain W. Williams, ordered the boats launched and the ship abandoned. In addition to her crew of 121, *Stentor* had aboard 125 passengers who included civilians, service personnel and a dozen nursing sisters, one of whom, Joan Hunter-Bates, later recalled the 'seventy-five to a hundred faces on the main staircase, stoically waiting their turn to ascend to safety or to death. There was no pushing or shoving, just the plain, solid courage of ordinary people . . . To get out onto the [boat] deck . . . I had to duck through a doorway of fire, for the bridge was ablaze. [*Stentor*] was going down bows first . . .'

Only four boats had been lowered when the ship began to rear up. From the water Borrer now watched 'the ship upended as though on an axis. The stern rose high in the air and I could see the funnel horizontal against the darkening sky. The ship seemed to hang in this position for a few seconds before starting to slide slowly beneath the sea.' Most, like Miss Hunter-Bates, had to 'jump into the water. When I surfaced again I was covered in oil . . .'

After about two hours the corvette *Woodruff* appeared and took aboard the survivors from the boats, but then Lieutenant F.H. Gray shouted out into the darkness that he had a sonar contact and must investigate it, and would return to the area. This was cold comfort for those left clinging to rafts or swimming in the water, but in due course the *Woodruff* did indeed loom out of the night again, and recovered all those remaining. In addition to Garstin, Captain Williams, the first, third and fourth mates, the doctor and 17 crew, three soldiers, four nurses and 16 civilian passengers lost their lives. The report from *Woodruff* that Gray had picked up the ship's master was an error, and the man probably referred to was the holder of another unusual appointment to the *Stentor*, a staff captain whose duties were to deputise for the master in dealings with the passengers.

The man in question, Captain W. B. Blair, had been dragged down with the ship, but was able to surface safely. The second officer, Mr R.H. Carruthers, slid down a slack boat-fall at the last moment, to drop into the sea. Doctor W. Chisholm remained tending the blinded vice commodore until it was too late and he went down with the *Stentor*, being awarded a posthumous Albert Medal.

Meanwhile Rayner had oiled *Petunia* from the *British Ardour* in the difficult conditions of a low north-westerly swell. It was not until the late afternoon that he learned the *Pacific Star* was sinking and her crew taking to the boats, and also that the Spanish steamship *Jalerva* and an unidentified Portuguese ship were going to her assistance. Beyond that, it was 'not known if they picked up any survivors'. It seems they did not.

As night fell the weather remained cloudy, with a fresh breeze, moderate to good visibility, a moderate sea and a low swell. At 19.00 Rayner received a report that 'a ship in one of the starboard columns had been torpedoed'. Again he carried out the 'Raspberry' procedure, 'entirely without results'. The victim was the *Hopecastle*, which had been badly damaged by Witte in *U-509* and lay stopped, five of her men dead. The ship next astern, the *Tasmania*, had slowed to manoeuvre and began picking up survivors, including Captain D. McGilp and 20 of his men; 19 others were obliged to make a boat voyage to Funchal in the Canaries. The *Hopecastle* had sailed from Cochin with a general cargo including magnesite and ilmenite, the precious black ore in which titanium is found.

After completing her part in the counter-attack *Crocus* dropped back to screen *Tasmania*, and it was just as they were rejoining the convoy, about 03.10 on the morning of the 29th, that Witte struck again, damaging the *Nagpore*, which a moment afterwards was hit by Kottmann in *U-203* and broke in two.[3] Within seven minutes she had sunk. She had been carrying Commodore C. N. Reyne and his staff, one of whom was killed, as was the *Nagpore*'s master, Captain P.E. Tonkin, and 18 of his own crew. Reyne, his five surviving staff, five gunners and 24 crew were picked up by HM Corvette *Crocus*, but Lieutenant J.F. Holm failed to locate one boatload, who under Fourth Engineer J. Marshall were obliged to endure a 14-day boat passage before landing at Puerto Orotava in the Canaries.

Marshall's No. 4 Boat had had her rudder smashed in leaving the ship and the gale that was hampering the *Pacific Star*'s crew swept also over them. They had seen a German supply-ship and had been interrogated from a U-boat she was replenishing, but had been left alone to pursue their lonely passage. On the 30th Marshall wrote: 'Constant bailing out of water. Did not dare hoist sail as storm terrific.' They suffered days of such conditions, constantly massaging their feet to prevent rot, and burning flares when they sighted ships, only to be ignored.

Rayner had by now ordered the senior rear commodore, Captain W.A. Haddock, master of the *Empire Cougar*, to assume responsibility for the convoy and speed was reduced from 7 to 6 knots to allow *Crocus* and *Tasmania*, doing 10 knots, to catch up. He was told that *Hopecastle* was still afloat, but reassured that her confidential books had been destroyed. Reyne, aboard *Crocus*, told Rayner that he had seen a U-boat on the surface on the starboard side of the *Nagpore* and thought it probable that the U-boat had then escaped at speed through the convoy. It was a conclusion Rayner had also come to, and explained the ineffectiveness of 'Raspberry' as a tactic to nail the predator.

By this time the weather had deteriorated, and *Cowslip*'s attempt to oil was terminated abruptly when the hose parted. The experience of the night was now telling elsewhere, for 'the *Esperance Bay* had been sighted ahead of the convoy . . . and it was assumed that she had bolted when the U-boat attacked. *Esperance Bay* did not rejoin . . . and was not seen again.' This ship, thought by other vessels in the convoy to have been sunk, was carrying home many of the survivors stranded at Freetown. Other vessels were struggling, the *Dundrum Castle* having trouble keeping station with the *Lynton Grange* edging past her as she fell back. The Royal Mail liner *Brittany* also had difficulties, and seemed to Third Officer P. Dudley aboard the *Dundrum Castle* to be 'an exceptionally windy sort of bird'.

In view of the overall situation and his paucity of capable anti-submarine escorts, Rayner now designated HMS *Kelantan* as rescue ship; he also re-deployed his corvettes for the coming night, with *Petunia* ahead, *Cowslip* astern and *Woodruff* and *Crocus* on the port and starboard flanks respectively. At 18.55, as SL125 approached the vicinity of Madeira, an alarm was raised in the rear of the convoy and *Petunia* doubled back through the columns, her 4-inch gun's crew 'at some hazard from fire from Merchant ships as they concentrated at the perceived position of a U-boat, but nothing was located' other than the straggling tanker *Bullmouth*.

It was a night of confusion that only partially resolved itself at daylight, and the exact details defied resolution until after the war. It seems certain that the fire of the merchant ships was not the nervous wild-fire implied by Rayner in his Report of Proceedings, for Witte had been among them on the surface, damaging the *Corinaldo*. *Cowslip* made for the stricken ship, hoping to catch her attacker; instead she came upon the *Corinaldo*'s crew, and was picking them up when a big explosion was heard.[4]

At daylight on the 30th there was no sign of *Bullmouth*, no sign either of *Kelantan* or *Corinaldo*. Kapitänleutnant H. Kottman, having finished off both the *Nagpore* and the *Hopecastle*, had also despatched the *Corinaldo*. The ship had received further damage from *U-659* (Stock), but had proved difficult to sink. Seven officers and three men went down with her cargo of frozen meat, Captain W. Anderson and 49 men being picked up by *Cowslip*. The *Bullmouth*, which was in ballast, seems to have been hit by a torpedo from Oberleutnant H-F. Massmann's *U-409*, but she did not finally sink until a second torpedo from *U-659* despatched her. Only the chief officer and five seamen survived, landing by boat at Bugio near Maderia; Captain J.W. Brougham and 49 men died, unknown to Rayner, who now designated the *Mano* as rescue ship.

At sunset, just as Rayner was deploying his screen for the night, the *Président Doumer*, leading column four, was torpedoed on her starboard side and burst into flames. In the glow of the fire a U-boat was seen and Rayner, asking for maximum speed and firing high explosive and star-shells, drove at her. 'By this time the convoy was firing snowflakes and the U-boat was clearly seen travelling through the starboard columns of the convoy at very high speed . . . The chase was continued clear of the convoy then the U-boat[,] which had gained rapidly throughout, was lost, despite the star-shells . . . Accurate shooting', Rayner reported, 'had been impossible', partly because of the passing merchantmen, but also because of 'the violent movement of the ship due to prevailing weather . . . Whilst the U-boat was being chased through the convoy, HMS *Cowslip* was ordered by R/T to make for the starboard quarter of the convoy at full speed to intercept. HMS *Cowslip* [which was having boiler problems and could make little more than 9–10 knots] carried out this order but failed to make contact . . .' A corvette, even at full speed, was no match for a surfaced U-boat.

Poor Rayner's cup of misery now filled to overflowing, for the night was one of intense darkness with occasional very heavy rain squalls which reduced visibility. In a rising north-westerly wind and sea, without radar, he found it 'extremely difficult to keep in touch with the situation'. Rayner thought the enemy had sunk 'at least five ships' and *Cowslip* was left astern to do what she could, as Witte initiated yet another round of destruction. His next victim was the Royal Mail liner *Brittany*, which had taken aboard a cargo of hides, rice and cotton in Buenos Aires. She appears to have hauled out of her column as the attack developed, and when hit sank quickly. Two torpedoes struck her, the second killing crew and passengers as they mustered at their stations. Great difficulties were experienced getting the boats clear as the *Brittany* capsized in their midst. Both Captain W. W. Dovell and Chief Officer A. K. Lynton were commended, while Third Officer L. A. Cook was appointed MBE. Despite the rough sea Captain Dovell and 39 men were picked up by *Kelantan*, and only 14 were lost.

The following day was to prove even more disastrous. A further 69 men died with the *Président Doumer* which had been hit by a torpedo from

U-604. This former French Messageries Maritimes passenger-liner, still under the command of Capitaine J.P. Mantelet but under British Bibby Line management for the MoWT, was carrying 62 service personnel and a large crew. Mantelet and 260 drowned with their ship, the 85 survivors being picked up by ships in convoy and *Cowslip*. Kapitänleutnant H. Höltring next struck the British tramp *Baron Vernon*, Captain P. Liston. Although she was loaded with ore, all hands had time to escape and were picked up by a sister-ship, the *Baron Elgin*.

Having damaged the *Bullmouth*, Massmann attacked the general-cargo-carrying *Silverwillow*. Again the ship did not sink, and was considered 'definitely salvable'. *Cowslip* stood by for a while, but she was overloaded with survivors and Rayner was anxious to have her back with the main body. The *Silverwillow* was not finally abandoned by Captain R.C. Butler and all but five of his men until 5 November, when they were taken off by the patrol vessel-cum-rescue ship *Kelantan*, herself striving to catch up with the convoy. Even then *Silverwillow* remained waterlogged but afloat for a further six days.

Convoy SL125 was now in disarray. Rayner still thought the *Baron Vernon* was afloat and in company with her sister-ship the *Baron Elgin*, and 'that they, together with the SS *Amstelkerke* [*sic*], went ahead independently at the time of the attack'. The last vessel from SL125 to be sunk by the *Streitaxt* group was the *Tasmania*, torpedoed first by *U-659*, Kapitänleutnant H. Stock, on the 30th. Yet again the vessel was only damaged, and was despatched in the early hours of the 31st by *U-103*, Kapitänleutnant G-A. Janssen, a recent arrival with the group. Janssen claimed another strike and it may have been the Norwegian ship *Alaska*, which was damaged and detached from the convoy to head for Lisbon.

By now SL125 was receiving reinforcements. The convoy ought already to have had air support, but this had been prevented by the bad weather. However, the corvettes *Spiraea* and *Coltsfoot* arrived at 01.54 on the 31st, and when Haddock suggested to Rayner that they should all make for Gibraltar to reorganise, Rayner demurred: the previous night's experiences, bad though they had been, had sharpened them all up, and a destroyer was expected. With that the new commodore was content. 'Your message gratifying,' Haddock replied when informed. 'Trust all goes well tonight.'

That morning the ships re-formed on a narrower front of six columns, *Crocus* refuelled, and HMS *Ramsey*, Captain R.B. Stannard, VC, arrived to take over command of the escort; he also reported U-boats ahead of the convoy. *Ramsey* heeled as she swung round and Stannard ordered Rayner to join him, and they hurried ahead to force the U-boats to dive. This was the last SL125 heard of the enemy, though there was one final alarm on the following day. The escorts suffered several breakdowns, one of which deprived them of the services of *Ramsey*, and they were subjected to another gale, which blew for five days and disorganised the convoy again, but on the 5th the destroyer *Saladin* arrived. SL125 was now under the umbrella extended by Coastal Command's single but effective squadron of Liberators, and their presence dissuaded Dönitz from continuing an action with which he was otherwise delighted.

So, paradoxically, was the British Admiralty. Convoy SL125's original commodore, the former Vice Admiral Cecil Reyne, 'a tough, hard-bitten seaman of the old school', told Stephen Roskill soon after his return that 'It is the only time I have been congratulated for losing ships.' Reyne had been lucky to escape with his life, for he had been struck by wreckage and hauled unconscious onto a raft by the *Nagpore*'s third officer, Mr S.W. Walter. Despite their latitude it was bitterly cold, and it was four hours before he and others were finally taken aboard *Crocus*.

Once he was back in London, Reyne's 'sardonic sense of humour' had been provoked by the delight felt in the Admiralty that Dönitz's attention had been so focused on SL125 that he had missed the opportunity to act against the movement of thousands of troops into the Mediterranean for Operation TORCH. A partial disguise had been effected by some of the vessels bound for Gibraltar and the Mediterranean in support of TORCH sailing ostensibly as part of OS and SL convoys. The critical factor, as Dönitz noted in his Memoirs, was that 'the landing in North Africa was quite unexpected by the Axis Powers'. He later deployed U-boats west of the Strait of Gibraltar and these sank Allied ships, both merchant and naval and including the escort carrier *Avenger*, but it was too little, too late, and they had no strategic impact. Though not actually intended as a decoy, SL125 had served as one. According to Churchill, 'in the circumstances' the loss of 13 merchantmen 'could be borne.'

Unaware of the strategic implications of their sacrifice and fuming over the men, ships and cargoes the enemy had destroyed, the merchant masters coming ashore after SL125 were strident in their criticisms. Staff Captain Blair of the *Stentor* complained about the weakness of the escort, as did another Blue Funnel master, Captain H.C. Skinns of the *Ville de Rouen*, a French prize under Alfred Holt's management, who in emphasising the loss of life spoke of 'hundreds in the water'. Others inveighed against the choice of the *Nagpore* as the commodore's ship. An ageing vessel nominally capable of 11.5 knots, she was unable to exceed 7 in the heavy weather encountered, causing several masters in faster ships to argue that they had all been held back by her. The charge that the very name 'P&O' implied a comfortable billet for an elderly admiral was clear, but in fact the varied vintage of the famous company's black-hulled cargo-ships gave the lie to this myth.

In the wake of the unpleasant mutterings about PQ17, there was just enough truth in the suggestion to lend colour to the rumour that Convoy SL125 had been deliberately sacrificed to distract German forces. In a letter written on 14 November 1942 to Alfred Holt & Company Reyne said: 'whether or not Convoy SL125 was "left to the wolves" the fact remains that, thankfully, the convoys of Operation TORCH reached their destinations unmolested by U-boats.' While this is not evidence that such an undertaking was intended, it is evidence that such a perception was abroad, and in wartime notions like this gain a life of their own. There was no doubt, however, that it was another occasion on which at the very least the Merchant Navy felt it had been under-supported, under-valued, and therefore too easily abandoned to satisfy the wolves. It was all of a piece with the self-deprecating jest that if you turned the 'MN' badge upside-down it read 'NW' – meaning, of course, 'Not Wanted'.

Wanted or not, the 35 merchantmen of Convoy HX209 left New York on 24 September and picked up the six-strong British and Norwegian B4 Escort Group at the new Western Ocean Meeting Point, almost immediately running into bad weather. Only one ship was damaged by the enemy, the American *Robert H. Colley*, a tanker loaded with fuel oil from Venezuela. In the late afternoon of 4 October, when the convoy was labouring in a heavy sea some three hundred miles SSW of Reykjavik, she was struck by a torpedo forward. The damage caused her to break in two, and during the hours of darkness the forward section sank. Two after lifeboats and two rafts were launched from the stern section and 11 men got away in the heavy seas, never to be heard of again. Captain J.J. McCaffrey, 20 crew-members and eight naval gunners were lost. Thirty-three men remained aboard on the after section until the next day, when the corvette *Borage* manoeuvred alongside and, in a fine display of seamanship, took them off before shelling the remains of the ship until she sank.

The U-boats, struggling against the weather and experiencing difficulties in homing-in on convoys without stirring up the increasingly efficient escorts or having to take cover from reconnoitring aircraft, found easier pickings among the slower SC convoys. Several concentrated against Convoy SC104 of 47 ships which sailed from New York on 3 October. Chief among these was *U-221*, on her first war patrol and commanded by Kapitänleutnant H. Trojer. By 8 October a number of scattered U-boats had been re-deployed as the *Wotan* group and were sent after SC104. They sighted the convoy on the night of 12/13 October in the air-gap south of Cape Farewell.

In the early hours of the 13th Trojer moved in, and in two separate attacks sank three of the five ships he was to account for that day: the Norwegian freighter *Fagerstein* and her cargo of steel and timber, killing 19 of her crew; the British tramp *Ashworth* which, loaded with bauxite, swiftly took Captain W. Mouat and his crew of 48 to their deaths; and the Norwegian *Senta*, which also sank with all hands.

A second successful member of the group was *U-607*, Kapitänleutnant E. Mengersen, which also penetrated the escorts' screen shortly after midnight on the 13th to sink the Greek-flagged *Nellie*. Laden with steel and timber, the tramp took 32 of her 36 crew to their deaths. Mengersen was counter-attacked by HM Destroyer *Viscount*, however, and suffered some damage.

Some hours later Trojer struck again, sinking the American freighter *Susana*. The crew tried to launch their boats in the heavy seas and one got away, but most of the men had to jump into the freezing sea. Fortunately the British rescue ship *Gothland* was on hand, and Captain J.M. Hadden skilfully manoeuvred to pick up 21 men from the boat and the sea, though the *Susana*'s master and 38 men were lost. Trojer followed this by an attack on the British whale-factory ship *Southern Empress*, which like her sisters had been commandeered as a tanker. She was one of two such ships in the convoy and had on board 11,700 tons of fuel oil and a deck cargo of 21 invasion barges. Captain O. Hansen, 23 of his crew, a score of Distressed British Seamen and four gunners were lost as the huge ship sank; the survivors were picked up by the escorts and later transferred to the second factory ship, the Norwegian *Suderøy*.

During these strikes Commander Heathcote's B6 Escort Group was busy keeping the other U-boats at a distance. Heathcote in the destroyer *Fame* had with him the *Viscount* and the Norwegian corvettes *Acanthus, Eglantine, Montbretia* and *Potentilla*. At one point *Eglantine*, Lieutenant Commander Voltersvik, caught sight of *U-258* and shelled her.

In the small hours of the 14th Kapitänleutnant K. Baberg in *U-618* worked his way into the convoy and sank the *Empire Mersey*, a MoWT ship under the management of Larrinaga & Company. Her cargo of government stores was lost along with 16 men, including her master, Captain F. de Bastarrechea. The 39 survivors were picked up by *Gothland*, which was next called up to pluck from the sea 21 survivors from the Yugoslavian ship *Nikolina Matkovic*. Fourteen of her crew were lost along with her cargo of sugar and timber after she was torpedoed by *U-661* under the command of Oberleutnant E. von Lilienfeld.

During the night of 14/15 October Mengersen closed to attack again but was echo-located by the Norwegian corvette *Acanthus*, Lieutenant Commander Bruun. Forced to dive under a hail of depth-charges, *U-607* was damaged and driven off, to limp home to St-Nazaire. But under cover of darkness von Lilienfeld made another approach in *U-661*. He was first driven off by *Montbretia*, Lieutenant Commander Söiland, but was incautious enough to resurface and was located by *Viscount*'s radar. Lieutenant Commander Waterhouse ran down the bearing, ramming *U-661* at 26 knots, ending her first war patrol and the lives of all her crew.

During the forenoon of the 15th *Fame* and *Acanthus* drove off *U-258* and *U-599*, and that afternoon *Acanthus* depth-charged *U-442*. By now aircraft had arrived overhead, Liberator *H* of No. 120 Squadron, Coastal Command bombing *U-615* and forcing *U-258* to dive. By the following morning only *U-258* was in contact with the convoy, but the presence of British Liberators and American Catalinas inhibited the others until about noon. At midday Oberleutnant O. Römer approached the convoy to make a submerged attack in *U-353*. This U-boat was echo-located by the sonar operators aboard *Fame*, enabling Commander Heathcote to carry out a depth-charge attack which forced Römer to the surface. The destroyer promptly rammed *U-353*, then withdrew as the U-boat's crew began to pour out of her conning tower and onto the casing. As the two columns of the convoy passed, one on either side of the foundering U-boat, the merchant ship's gunners took advantage of this rare opportunity and fired on their enemy. A little later Heathcote sent his sea-boat over and some documents were removed from *U-353* before she sank.

Both Heathcote and Waterhouse now had to withdraw their damaged destroyers, leaving SC104 in the hands of the four Norwegian corvettes. A final approach was made by *U-571* (Möhlmann), which had just arrived on the scene, but she was driven away by gunfire and depth-charges from *Potentilla*. Thus, battered but unbowed, SC104 arrived in Liverpool on Trafalgar Day, 21 October 1942.

The next major action resulting in losses surrounded Convoy HX212, the 45 ships of which had left New York at midnight on 17/18 October.[5] The convoy commodore was former Vice Admiral W. de M. Egerton aboard the *Jamaica Planter*, who exercised the convoy in an emergency turn, a standard procedure once a convoy had settled down. Under cover of the local western escort, led by Commander R. Sorenson of the Royal Norwegian Navy in the ex-American *Lincoln*, and of an air umbrella which was in sight 'pretty continuously', some of the merchantmen practised firing their 4-inch guns. On the 21st two of the merchant ships collided and one, the American *Matthew Luckenbach*, sank; the other, the *Yacapa*, had to be sent in to Halifax for repairs. Egerton quickly became dissatisfied with the performance of the American *Barnhill* as convoy guide, the leader of the extreme starboard column upon which the others kept station. She was 'N[o] B[loody] Good', in his estimation, so he replaced her with the British Shaw, Savill liner *Coptic*.

At noon on the 23rd the ocean escort took over. Nominally the American A3 Group, it consisted of the US Coast Guard Cutter *Campbell*, the USS *Badger*, the British corvette *Dianthus* and the Canadian corvettes *Rosthern, Ville de Quebec, Summerside, Trillium* and *Alberni*. Several American merchantmen detached for St John's with Sorenson's departing men-of-war, and Egerton signalled a change of course by sound signal, recording that the convoy's response was 'quite good'. Next day they ran into fog and one or two ships began to straggle, while another made excessive smoke; her master reported that her coal had been supplied at North Shields, but did not know the name of the supplier; that such details were considered important indicates the seriousness with which fuel quality was regarded. It was that afternoon that from the Submarine Tracking Room in London the first reports reached the convoy informing them of the proximity of enemy U-boats.

Next day, Monday 26 October, there was a 'moderate northerly gale', during which the tanker *Laurelwood* was obliged to slew out of station and heave-to while her crew secured some of the stock of spare depth-charges she was carrying, which threatened to break loose. Unknown to anyone, Kapitänleutnant G. Seibicke had spotted HX212 from *U-436* and was just then calling in other U-boats attached to the *Puma* group, one of several Dönitz had gathered to operate against the convoys then transiting the North Atlantic. During the following day Egerton was busy with the routine duties of his charges, signalling changes in destination to the merchant ships which were to disperse to the Clyde, Belfast and Oban as well as Liverpool. Then, at 23.10, with HX212 in the mid-Atlantic air-gap, the enemy struck.[6]

In rapid succession Seibicke torpedoed the *Sourabaya*, the *Frontenac* and the *Gurney E. Newlin*. The *Sourabaya*, Captain W.T. Dawson, was another whale-factory ship turned into a tanker by the British and loaded with fuel oil. Almost all the crew escaped, being picked up by the escorts or a Canadian ship, the *Bic Island*. The Norwegian tanker *Frontenac* survived, though damaged, but the *Gurney E. Newlin* was not so lucky. She was a newly-built American tanker with 12,000 tons of petrol and paraffin in her tanks. Seibicke's torpedo struck her in the engine room, killing the three men on watch but not setting her cargo on fire, so the remaining 57 were able to escape in the boats and were also rescued by the *Bic Island*. The tanker herself remained afloat, drifting astern of the convoy as it steamed onwards, on a collision course with 'three neutral ships with all lights burning'. At 00.10, with an unknown number of U-boats hanging on his flanks, Egerton was obliged to execute two emergency turns which the convoy, steaming at 9.5 knots, carried out without further incident.

The weather remained 'squally with frequent showers of rain or hail' as a second U-boat attacked. This was *U-606*, Oberleutnant H. Döhler, and his target was another factory ship-cum-tanker. Not only did the Norwegian *Kosmos II* bear 21,000 tons of crude oil but her extensive accommodation contained a number of servicemen, so she had 150 people on board. Her cargo did not ignite, but in the confusion as the ship was abandoned and left astern, a third of these men lost their lives.

During the day the *Bic Island* rejoined the convoy with her harvest of survivors. Meanwhile the American escort commander, in Egerton's deprecating words, 'went off chasing subs' which were now reported ahead of the convoy by a Liberator of No. 120 Squadron from Iceland. The heavy weather and the proximity of the enemy, combined with a lack of suitable vessels, meant that – to Egerton's annoyance – two salvageable tankers full of white oils were drifting in the wake of HX212. Later that day Döhler, having passed through the convoy, sent the *Gurney E. Newlin* to the bottom.

At 02.20 on the 29th, under the fitful and ominous light of the moon as it emerged periodically from the clouds, with the air full of the howling menace of the now north-easterly gale driving vicious hail squalls over heavy, breaking seas, another U-boat joined the fray. Kapitänleutnant Graf von Soden-Fraunhofen in *U-624* fired at the American tanker *Pan New York*, loaded with 12,400 tons of petrol. The cargo took fire and smoke was drawn into the accommodation by the ventilation fans as the blazing spirit spilled out over the sea, the ship slowing, broaching, and rolling heavily. The *Pan New York* had already lost three of her lifeboats in the breaking seas and it was now impossible to lower the remaining No. 2.[7] She was equipped with rafts but these could not be unlashed, since they would only drift to leeward on a sea aflame with burning petrol, so the remaining 15 of her crew huddled on the poop. At daylight 13 of them jumped into the water one by one and were picked up by the *Rosthern*. Two others did the same, both wearing life-saving suits, a new innovation, but only one was picked up by the *Summerside*, so that Captain H.V. Thompson, 26 crew and 16 of her Naval Armed Guard were lost.

Throughout these attacks Egerton manoeuvred the convoy imperturbably, the moonlight from time to time augmented by snowflakes thrown up by the escorts in an attempt to deter the U-boats from surfacing inside their screen. Despite this, three hours later Oberleutnant H-C. Kosbadt in *U-224* torpedoed the *Bic Island*. In addition to her own crew she had on board 73 men from the *Sourabaya* and 45 from the *Gurney E. Newlin*, so loss of life was heavy. The *Bic Island* seems to have been gallantly attempting to pick up more men, probably from the *Pan New York*, a task at which Captain H.V. Thompson and his crew were clearly adept.[8]

Having escaped counter-attack by the escorts, the U-boats passed clear of the convoy and later that day *U-624* sank the still-floating *Kosmos II*. But contact had not been lost and that evening Seibicke was back. *U-436's* torpedo hit the British tramp *Barrwhin*, Captain T.S. Dixon. Loaded with grain and military stores, she also had on board survivors from other ships, 12 of whom, with 12 of her own crew, were lost in the incident. In appalling conditions the survivors were picked up by a Canadian corvette. It was indeed 'winter, North Atlantic'.[9]

The gale blew itself out overnight and 30 October dawned 'fine and clear'. The convoy speed of 9.5 knots was too much for the new *Fort à la Corne* and Egerton was displeased with another new guide, the *Ocean Courier*, which was half a mile astern of the main body at 07.30 that morning, and went so far as to note the name of her officer of the watch, but these were details. Egerton was mindful of the convoy's morale the following day as HX212 prepared to split up. His yeoman sent a personal signal to all ships that the 'conduct of the convoy had been excellent under very trying conditions', and at noon all ships lowered their ensigns to half-mast in honour of their dead. Next morning, with Malin Head distant 35 miles to the SSE, the convoy dispersed, three ships bound for the east coast heading for Oban. Later, off the Mull of Kintyre, seven headed for the Clyde, the remainder standing through the North Channel, bound for Belfast or Liverpool.

In his report Egerton reserved his main criticisms for the convoy organisation and the escort. Having informed Their Lordships that snowflake was ineffective in high winds, he added that the 'moon is decidedly a factor to be reckoned with', and, mindful that his losses in tankers had been excessive, that 'important ships should be stationed in the half of [the] convoy nearer [the] moon, or the south side going east.' As for the Senior Officer of the Escort, the captain of the *Campbell* who had acted cavalierly in the case of the *Balladier* noted earlier, Egerton thought that he had made 'excessive use of radio telephony throughout the voyage. In fact he was scarcely ever silent', adding that if the enemy was able to obtain radio bearings of such transmissions, 'he had excellent opportunities. Apart from this, the way R/T was used must have had the effect of preventing commanding officers of escorts [from] attending to their proper work. Had I been one myself,' Egerton trenchantly commented, 'my [radio] set would have had a bad breakdown.'

Egerton also thought that the 20 miles' distance at which the *Campbell* operated from the convoy when 'sub-hunting' made his own routine 'night intentions' signal to the American cutter interceptable by the enemy, as he was unable to use a visual lamp. Moreover, the weather had prevented the refuelling of *Badger*, which lacked the endurance of the other escorts, and deprived them of her services sweeping astern of the convoy to deter a shadower. Egerton concluded that 'in whatever manner the shadowing was done it was a very creditable piece of work from the enemy's point of view.'

Dönitz strove to deploy his U-boats into the path of each convoy as it moved in the wake of its predecessor, but with only limited success. They continued to pick off stragglers and sink 'independents'[10] throughout the period, however, suffering some losses themselves, and they were sinking merchantmen with ruthless efficiency in the Caribbean, off Trinidad, off the shoulder of Brazil, and in the Gulf of St Lawrence.

Kerneval's next major assault in the Western Ocean was focused on Convoy SC107, which was reported on 30 October by Kapitänleutnant H. Schneider in *U-522* while it was being handed over to the Canadian C4 ocean escort off Cape Race. Its 41 ships had left New York on 24 October. Before it arrived at Liverpool on 10 November it had lost more than a third of them.

The C4 Escort Group was led by Lieutenant Commander D. W. Piers in the Canadian destroyer *Restigouche*. He was supported by the Canadian corvettes *Algoma, Amherst* and *Arvida*, plus the British *Celandine*. In addition SC107 had with it a rescue ship, the *Stockport*, and the convoy commodore was former Vice Admiral B.C. Watson, embarked in the P&O's *Jeypore*. For a few hours Piers kept in company the British destroyer *Walker* and the Canadian corvette *Columbia*, both from the local escort force.

As the convoy stretched out across the Grand Bank on the 30th, the first skirmishes took place: Senkel's *U-658* was seen on the surface, attacked and sunk by a Canadian Hudson of No. 145 Squadron, and *U-520* (Schwartz-kopf), on her first war patrol, was also depth-charged to destruction by a Digby of No. 10 Squadron of the Royal Canadian Air Force. Having reported the convoy, Schneider attempted to sink the *Columbia* but failed, and in making another approach next day was driven off by the escort. Kapitänleutnant K. Bargsten was forced to dive *U-521* and lose contact by another of No. 145 Squadron's Hudsons.

Thus deterred, the U-boats withdrew, as did *Walker* and *Columbia*, but at Kerneval B-Dienst intercepts revealed the intended track of SC107 and Dönitz was able to make alternative dispositions. By 1 November a new patrol line, touchingly named the *Veilchen* or 'Violet' group, had been deployed. This initially consisted of three U-boats, *U-381*, *U-402* and *U-704*, all of which closed with the convoy but were located and promptly driven off by the *Restigouche* and *Celandine*. So far, so good, but more U-boats were on their way, and the first three had not given up. Just after dark *U-71* approached on the surface, but was located by radar and driven off; *U-89* also closed the convoy but Korvettenkapitän D. Lohmann declined to attack. Not far off, *U-84* was also on her way to the area.

The weather remained bad, with strong winds and heavy seas hampering both sides in their respective objectives, so that it was shortly after midnight on 2 November before the first attack developed. When it did so, it was conducted to deadly effect. With great skill Korvettenkapitän Freiherr S. von Forstner manoeuvred *U-402* into the convoy and fired a salvo of torpedoes, hitting five ships and sinking four of them. The crisis erupted in moments, the first torpedo sending the British *Dalcroy* and her cargo of steel and timber to the bottom. Captain J.P. Johnson and his crew took to their boats and were all rescued by the *Stockport*. Captain T.E. Fea's rescue ship was soon in great demand elsewhere as a second torpedo exploded in the Greek-flagged *Rinos*, loaded with a general cargo and vehicles, killing eight men. Next to be hit was the *Empire Leopard*, Captain J.E. Evans. Loaded with zinc concentrate and munitions, she sank rapidly, taking 37 men with her and leaving only three for Fea's *Stockport* to recover from the cold Atlantic.

Loaded with general cargo, the *Empire Antelope*, whose crew's behaviour on a former occasion had been less than creditable, was struck almost simultaneously. Captain W.J. Slade and all hands escaped and they too found sanctuary aboard the *Stockport*. Von Forstner's last torpedo damaged but did not sink the *Empire Sunrise*. Again all hands, including the master Captain A. W. Hawkins, were plucked from the water by the rescue ship. The *Empire Sunrise* and her cargo of steel and timber were sunk astern of the convoy three hours later by *U-84*, Kapitänleutnant H. Uphoff.

Kapitänleutnant Schneider had again come up with SC107 and now he too joined in the work of destruction. In his initial attack he struck first the British tramp ship *Hartington*, damaging her so that she was afterwards an easy target for *U-438* and *U-521*, before she took her full cargo of wheat and six tanks on her deck down with her. Captain M.J. Edwards and 23 men were lost, 24 being rescued by an escort. Schneider's next torpedo exploded in the British cargo-vessel *Maritima*, Captain A.G. Phelps. She was largely loaded with general cargo but a consignment of explosives detonated, the ship sank in four minutes, and Phelps and 31 men were blown to pieces. *Arvida* picked up the remaining 27 as a third torpedo from *U-522* slammed into the Greek-flagged *Mount Pelion*. Loaded with general and vehicles she sank with seven of her crew.

By this time Piers's escort had been reinforced by the Canadian corvette *Moosejaw*. Prior to despatching the *Hartington*, Bargsten in *U-521* had just missed the *Moosejaw* as both corvette and U-boat approached the convoy; Korvettenkapitän H-J. Hesse in *U-442* also failed to score, though his torpedoes exploded near the Greek ship *Parthenon*. Schneider in *U-522* then went for her late that afternoon under water, sinking her and killing six of her crew.

One vessel, the *Hatimura*, an elderly 1919-built standard ship, had dropped astern of the main body with engine trouble, but after sunset a thick mist enveloped both the straggling ship and the convoy, the members of which streamed their fog buoys and, lookouts alert, threw off their tormentors for a few hours. Moreover, not far away Convoy HX213 was proceeding comparatively unmolested, and on orders from Western Approaches Command the destroyer *Vanessa* was detached from her escort to further reinforce that of SC107.

On the morning of the 3rd the mist lifted fitfully. Commodore Watson had executed several zig-zags to throw off pursuit, but as time passed and SC107 resumed its mean course nine U-boats glimpsed the convoy and began to work into position to resume their offensive. Several approaches were made but were frustrated by radio interceptions, and *Celandine* and *Vanessa* were kept busy. Franzius in *U-438* got close; then, about midday, Kapitänleutnant K. Bargsten worked *U-521* into a firing position and sank the American tanker *Hahira* with three torpedoes. The ship was severely wrecked by the explosions and fire broke out in her cargo, so Captain J.B. Elliott ordered her abandoned. Three men were lost, the rest being succoured aboard the *Stockport*, which was unsuccessfully fired at by Franzius as she lay stopped astern of the convoy hauling aboard the *Hahira*'s crew. At roughly the same time Schneider's *U-522* loosed torpedoes at *Restigouche* which also missed.

That evening, after night had fallen, Lohmann, having run *U-89* ahead of the convoy, brought her back into contact and fired at the Dutch vessel *Titus*, a general cargo-ship belonging to the Royal Netherlands Steam Ship Company. The torpedoes exploded so close to the *Titus* that her crew thought she had been hit and had begun to abandon ship before they realised their error. They reboarded her and soon afterwards caught the convoy up, their absence hardly noticed in the mayhem by then prevailing.

Lohmann's second salvo had hit the *Jeypore*. Captain T. Stevens, Commodore Watson and all but one seaman were picked up by two American naval tugs crossing the Atlantic with the convoy, the *Uncas* and *Pessacas*; they were all later transferred to the *Stockport*, fortunate in their escape because the *Jeypore*'s general cargo included explosives and these had detonated, started a fire and set the whole forepart of the ship ablaze within minutes. The *Jeypore* went down by the head, watched by her crew as they reached the safety of the tugs' decks. 'Within a few minutes there was [another] sudden burst of flame from her, and when this had died down only a blur of smoke remained.'

Midnight approached as the convoy nervously settled down again. Just as the vice commodore took charge the darkness was again rent by a detonation as the Dutch ship *Hobbema* was hit by a torpedo from Vogelsang's *U-132*, which had caught up from the west. The attack killed 28 men. A second torpedo from the salvo sank the *Empire Lynx*, laden with a general cargo. Captain T.H. Muitt and all his hands escaped into the boats, to be picked up by the *Titus* as she rejoined the convoy. The Dutchman was to render a further service too, so her crew's hasty reaction to *U-89*'s torpedoes suggests the guiding hand of Providence.

Vogelsang next fired at the British India *Hatimura*, which had dropped out of the convoy on the 2nd. The vessel had been employed for some time on the Indian coast and had only just been armed in New York prior to joining SC107. After this work had been carried out she was loaded with 8,950 tons of general cargo, which euphemism covered TNT and incendiary bombs. The first torpedo to hit her caused a deluge on the bridge and damage 'enough to sink the vessel', a slightly premature judgement. Captain W.F. Putt had ordered his crew into their boats and four of the six had been launched and manned when a second torpedo struck the *Hatimura*, further damaging her amidships and injuring Putt. In the evacuation of the ship the elderly purser fell into the water and was lost, as were a Chinese steward and an Indian saloon servant. Some men were picked up by the two American tugs; others found a refuge aboard the obliging *Titus*, whose crew thereby further expiated their earlier precipitate conduct.

In the ultimate fate of the *Hatimura* there lies something of a mystery, for it is supposed that she received a final death wound from Hesse's *U-442* three hours later, and he certainly fired at her burning hull. Either at this moment or, perhaps more likely, as she sank, the trinitrotoluene in her holds exploded with a tremendous concussion the effects of which were felt in the convoy, by now some miles away. Hesse escaped, but Vogelsang's *U-132* was never heard of again and the German staff at Kerneval made the presumption that his U-boat was destroyed by the *Hatimura* acting as an immense depth-charge.

On the following day, 4 November, unsuccessful attacks were made by *U-71*, *U-438* and *U-442*. By now the numbers of survivors dispersed throughout the convoy were causing Watson some anxiety, and arrangements were made to detach the *Stockport*, *Uncas* and *Pessacas*, along with the damaged *Titus*, towards Iceland under the escort of the *Arvida* and *Celandine*. In exchange the USS *Schenk* and *Leary*, together with the US Coast Guard

Cutter *Ingham*, were sent out from Reykjavik as reinforcements. These warships had not arrived late that evening when Lohmann managed to penetrate the depleted screen and fire at the *Daleby*. Another of Ropner's tramps, the *Daleby* sank with a cargo of grain and motor parts, allowing time for Captain J.E. Elsdon and his 46-man crew to take to their boats. With the *Stockport* absent they were left astern, but luck had not entirely deserted them and they were spotted and taken aboard the Icelandic trawler *Bruarfoss* to join the other survivors at Reykjavik.

Next morning eight U-boats remained in the vicinity of SL107, but the appearance of air patrols acted as a deterrent. The aircraft were directed by Piers to fly down radio bearings taken aboard *Restigouche*, and Lohmann was caught on the surface by Squadron Leader T.M. Bulloch flying a Liberator of No. 120 Squadron. Bulloch dropped depth-charges on the submerging *U-89*, damaging her.[11]

Kerneval ordered the operation broken off next day as the *Veilchen* boats sent in their claims, which included the sinking of a destroyer and a corvette, presumably connected with the near-misses on *Restigouche* and *Moosejaw*. Four days later, on 10 November, the main body of SC107 arrived at Liverpool.

By this time Convoy ON144 of 28 ships was already three days into its passage in the opposite direction. Just as Operation TORCH had sapped the supply of escorts for trade convoys, Dönitz's attempts to attack the new supply line to the ports captured by the Allies in North Africa reduced the number of U-boats available in the Atlantic. Those that could be were sent out from French bases to reinforce those still at sea and capable of remaining operational. A total of nine such U-boats now formed the *Kreuzotter* (Viper) group and were ordered into the air-gap astride the great-circle route between Cape Race and Malin Head. Here they ambushed ON144.

The claims sent in to Kerneval were encouraging – 15 merchant ships sunk, plus two destroyers and a corvette, Bargsten apparently particularly successful in *U-521*. In fact he had hit nothing, and the actual tally was one corvette, the Norwegian-manned *Montbretia*, sunk on 18 November by *U-262* (Franke), and five merchantmen. Two had been sunk the previous day, the 17th; they were the Greek tramp *Mount Taurus*, in ballast and torpedoed by *U-264* (Looks) with the loss of two men; and the coal-laden *Widestone*, hit by *U-184* (Dangschat) with the loss of Captain W. Storm and all 41 of his crew.[12] The 18th saw the torpedoing of the American fruit-carrier *Parismina* of Boston, hit by *U-264*. In ballast, she went down quickly, drowning Captain E.T. Davidson and 21 hands. Kapitänleutnant Ulrich Graf von Soden-Fraunhofen then torpedoed the tanker *Président Sergent*, a former French prize being operated by the Shell Oil Company. She was in ballast and did not sink at once, though 20 of her crew were lost. She was under the command of Captain P.G.G. Dove, who had been captured by the *Admiral Graf Spee* when his coastal tanker *Africa Shell* had been sunk in the Mozambique Channel in the first months of the war, and she also carried Commodore J.K. Brooke. These officers, the naval staff, seven DEMS gunners and 24 crew were picked up by the rescue ship *Perth*, Captain K. Williamson, which had been attached to the convoy. The abandoned tanker sank seven hours later. Von Soden-Fraunhofen also damaged the American freighter *Yaka*, which was in ballast; all hands escaped to be scooped up by the escorts, the *Yaka* being subsequently despatched by Schneider in *U-522*.

ON144 arrived at New York on 27 November, leaving Dönitz to conclude bitterly that 'all the attacks were made from too great a range, and it seems that the torpedoes did not hit but exploded at the end of their runs. In all cases, due to the excessive range and rather poor visibility, no ships were observed to sink . . .'

After the action several U-boats were desperately short of fuel and waited on the rendezvous with main engines and auxiliaries stopped, rolling agonisingly in the prevailing bad weather. Heavy seas also hampered their refuelling when the U-tankers finally found them. 'Sometimes the only workable method . . . in rough weather was to float over five-gallon drums. It was all very unpleasant.'[13]

For a week or two, Allied trans-Atlantic convoy losses were low. ON145 of 35 ships which crossed westbound between 9 and 25 November lost one, the *Empire Sailor*, Captain F.W. Fairley, to *U-518* (Wismann). She was carrying general cargo and ammunition, and 22 men were killed. Eastbound SC109 also left on 9 November and also lost one ship, to *U-43* (Schwantke). The American tanker *Brilliant* was damaged on the 18th but actually lost when under tow on the 25th. Convoy HX217, which left New York on 27 November, arrived at Liverpool on 14 December minus two of its 26 ships. Both were British, the *Empire Spenser*, Captain J.B. Hodge, a brand-new tanker full of benzene sunk on 8 December by *U-524* (von Steinaecker); and the freighter *Charles L.D.,* Captain D.E. Canoz, sunk the next day with heavy loss of life by *U-553* (Thurmann). The rescue ship *Perth* was in attendance and picked up the survivors from both vessels.

By now the winter furies had tightened their grip on the Western Ocean. In attempting to attack HX217 in stormy conditions two U-boats were in collision: Trojer's *U-221* ran into Gilardone's *U-254* on 8 December, causing extensive damage. Gilardone resurfaced but found he could not dive again. Four of his crew jumped overboard and were picked up by Trojer, but Gilardone was compelled to remain on the surface and endure an attack by the ubiquitous Bulloch, whose Liberator depth-charged

U-254 and sank her with the loss of her commander and the remaining 40 crew members.

The gales were unrelenting and furious. Heavy swells built up over miles of storm-swept fetch, compounded by enormous breaking seas. With a long 'period' these could culminate in successive tumbling crests which descended from waves thirty or forty feet high and a quarter of a mile apart. The ships' hulls, wracked by stresses, heaved up and pounded into the troughs, laden vessels wallowing, their decks swept by green water, those in ballast light and unmanageable, the wind catching under the flare of their bows and threatening to blow them off course. A moment later their sterns would lift and their screws thrash the air, engines racing and their entire sterns shuddering.

In such extreme conditions the air becomes full of spray and as the wind speed increases still further, and at 65 knots reaches hurricane force, the crests are blown off, streaming to leeward, so that the 'air' seems to contain more atomised sea-water than oxygen, and hits human skin like buckshot.[14]

Convoy ON152 ran into such conditions in mid December, losing two ships to the violence of the sea. Neither the American *Maiden Creek* nor the Greek *Oropos* could keep up with the convoy, although it was itself hove-to and barely making headway. Both straggled and foundered alone and unsupported, with the loss of all hands.

The following westbound convoy, ON153, of 43 ships, attracted attention from the U-boats that had missed its predecessor in the westerly storm. Two ships were sunk from the convoy itself on 16 December, the Belgian *Émile Francqui* by *U-664* with 46 killed and the Norwegian *Bello*, in ballast, with the loss of those in the engine room, hit by *U-610*. Then the following day *U-211* torpedoed and sank the escorting destroyer *Firedrake*.

While ON153 steamed into New York on the last day of 1942, astern of it raged one of the fiercest convoy battles of the war.

21

'This does not look at all good'

Whimbrel

THE ATTACK ON Convoy ON154 was a crucial action occurring at a critical time. Notwithstanding diversions to the Mediterranean Dönitz's resources had now increased dramatically to some 365 submarines, of which about 200 were fully operational. Enough were available for group operations in the Atlantic to render the Allied rerouteing of convoys useless. Churchill's description of the war as one 'of groping and drowning, of ambuscade and stratagem, of science and seamanship' became increasingly apt as it moved towards its climax.

Of groping and drowning much evidence has been adduced, but there was one vital incident to which these words applied most aptly, though it was more a matter of opportunism than ambuscade, fought out in a distant corner of the eastern Mediterranean. While the B-Dienst service had been coolly intercepting the Royal Navy's operational radio signals, the British decrypters at Bletchley Park had spent months in the dark, groping intellectually as others groped for a life-raft at sea. The so-called 'Triton' code seemed impenetrable; and then, on 30 October 1942, five destroyers and a Wellington bomber attacked and forced U-559 to the surface. In the face of overwhelming odds Kapitänleutnant H. Heidtmann ordered his submarine scuttled and abandoned, but before she sank Lieutenant Commander P.C. Egan, commanding HM Destroyer *Petard*, had despatched a boarding-party under Lieutenant F.A.B. Fasson. As they pulled alongside U-559 they knew exactly what they were looking for. Scrabbling in the interior of the submarine as water poured into her, they seized the Enigma encoding machine and its accompanying code-books and passed them into the boat. As they continued their search, Fasson and Able Seaman C. Grazier became trapped, and were drowned, but their loot was flown to England and in December the 'Triton' code was broken at Bletchley Park: the blackout in signals intelligence that had hampered operations since the previous February was finally lifted.[1]

Shortly before the flow of information resumed a change of Commander-in-Chief had taken place in Liverpool. Sir Percy Noble's contribution to victory has been eclipsed by the achievements of his successor at Derby House, yet the weapon handed to Sir Max Horton, who has made a brief appearance in this history as Flag Officer, Submarines, had been fashioned by Noble. In setting up at Liverpool and elsewhere at a time of dire shortages of ships, men and equipment the organisation that Horton inherited, Noble's achievement was prodigious. Sir Percy was 'a determined and fastidious leader, his single-mindedness masked by warmth, charm and good looks to a degree unusual in an admiral'. His apparent hostility to Roberts notwithstanding, and making use of the training methods of both Roberts and Stephenson along with the rapidly increasing number of escorts, Noble strove during the closing weeks of his tenure to form support groups on the model that Walker had briefly commanded immediately prior to Operation TORCH. The intention was that these support groups, with long endurance, would be switched to augment the escort of any convoy under attack by a group of U-boats. Noble also initiated the conversion of the old 'V'- and 'W'-classes of destroyers to long-range escorts as they were refitted, and the commissioning of the first escort-carriers capable of providing a convoy with local air cover. The first of these small aircraft-carriers was allocated to Operation TORCH, so they were yet to impact on the battle in the Western Ocean, but they were to hand, and Horton eagerly employed them and all the other developments when he took office on 19 November. It was a dire moment, for the U-boats were inflicting the worst losses yet experienced by Allied convoys in the North Atlantic.

Horton, like Dönitz, was a First World War submariner, a man of ruthless determination and tremendous strength of character. To keep fit he played golf every possible afternoon, but as night fell he was to be found at his post in Derby House. He and his colleague in Coastal Command, Air Marshal Sir Leonard Slatter, oversaw events as they transpired upon that immense battle-ground lying far to the westward under the night sky. Unmarried, totally committed, Horton missed nothing; he was a master of detail capable of handling the big picture and of fighting the political battles that went with competing for scarce resources. Forbidding in aspect, he possessed a deeply spiritual side to his private character that spoke of a sensitivity to which few were made privy. Tough, forceful and intolerant of fools, he respected those who stood their ground. He could win loyalty with the twinkle of an eye, as he did that of Lieutenant Commander Moore. Taking command of the new sloop *Whimbrel*, Moore found him 'as charming, understanding and alive as his predecessor'.

Not all succumbed to his charm. Although he was as one with his fighting officers, the new Commander-in-Chief bore irascibly upon his staff, who found his smile 'catlike' and his methods feline. Prior to the war Horton had earned a reputation among the midshipmen in his flagship for an almost obsessive intolerance, but much of this was now absorbed and softened on a daily basis by his very able female flag-lieutenant, Third Officer Kay Hallaran of the WRNS. Nevertheless, there were times when, 'according to his signals officer, Edwards, [he] tended to take his frustrations out on his staff, the animosity getting to the point that it became impossible to find golfing partners for the Admiral.'[2]

But unlike many of his contemporaries he was fascinated by, and personally mastered, technical details. On the day he took over at Derby House he visited Roberts and the Tactical Training School. Horton asked Roberts abrasively what he *thought* he accomplished. Roberts, 'with a touch of heat' and no doubt recalling Noble's lukewarm reception, told the new C-in-C what he was *trying* to do. Next morning Horton put himself through Roberts's course, after which the two men got on well. On one occasion the former submariner handled the attacking 'U-boat' and was sunk three times. No one dared tell Horton he had theoretically been blown to pieces by a third officer Wren 'in command' of the convoy's defence, but the experience proved to him the value of Roberts's endeavours. Horton had a similar encounter with Rodger Winn at the Admiralty, complaining that he had insufficient knowledge of the information upon which Winn made his amazing assessments to determine what value to place upon them. Winn invited him to visit the Admiralty and do the job temporarily himself. Horton agreed, but after three hours during which he was utterly bemused by the nature of Winn's raw material he confessed himself out of his depth. Recognising that there was something almost preternaturally prescient about Winn's divinations Horton, who in general disliked the familiar use of Christian names, shook his hand and said, 'Goodbye, Rodger, I leave it to you.' His robust interference would have intimidated a lesser man.

Horton was able to capitalise on his predecessor's patient groundwork, without which his task would have been far more difficult. As it was, at his desk overlooking the plot of Western Approaches Horton proved himself a disciple of Admiral Jackie Fisher, under whose influence he had spent his formative years, in believing with Fisher that 'moderation in war is imbecility'. He had arrived in the nick of time.

Grand strategy though TORCH was, it complicated Horton's task. Not only must an additional number of escorts he found to cover the additional convoys demanded by the military operations, and not only did this mean a consequent weakening of the numbers available to cover the regular trade convoys, but the consumption of fuel by the armies landing in North Africa, combined with an increase in U-boat strikes, particularly against tanker traffic in the Caribbean, meant that a fuel crisis loomed.

So despite everything, Horton's immediate problem was lack of escorts; he was so concerned by this deficiency that the day he took command he informed the Admiralty that he deplored the loss of *Fame* and *Viscount*, rendered *hors de combat* as a result of ramming U-boats. A week later he was at the Admiralty securing an assurance that Noble's pleas for more long-range aircraft would be honoured. Churchill was quickly convinced that successful convoy defence required proper co-ordinated air and sea support, and Horton immediately sought to close the air-gap and increase the air offensive against U-boats crossing the Bay of Biscay. In the event Coastal Command's long-range Liberators were withdrawn for upgrades in their radar and fuel systems, a necessary temporary weakening in defence that was in part covered by American assistance.[3]

On 25 November Horton submitted an assessment of 'The Escort Group System' in which he pointed out the failure of convoy defence when 'escorted by a collection of ships strange to one another, untrained as a team and led by an officer inexperienced in convoy protection'. This was Horton cutting straight to the bare bones, and he would accept no half-measures: 'Until', he went on, 'each group is led and manned by competent officers, and until it has attained a high degree of group efficiency and is completely equipped with the latest devices, heavy losses will continue.' Most important, in Horton's analysis, was the retention of experienced escort commanders who 'should not be removed from their groups on promotion, since their loss must entail a falling off of efficiency which may well be measured in many thousands of tons of shipping sunk . . .'

Nor did Horton forget the necessity of resting the crews of escorts after the rigours of a hard-won crossing of the Western Ocean.[4] In due course his philosophy led to an increase in the size of trans-Atlantic convoys and sailings at slightly longer intervals, for he argued that it was as easy to defend a convoy of 60 ships as it was one of 40. More, he thought, would become unwieldy, but a one-half increase in capacity was manageable. As for the support groups, as they became available they would be used regularly to beef up the escort as each convoy ran through the shrinking air-gap. 'I feel very strongly that the solution of the German U-boat menace will be found only by the development of highly trained Support Groups working in co-operation with an adequate number of very long range aircraft.'

Horton felt that he could not wait until enough new warships had been commissioned, as was originally intended, and decided to reduce each escort group by one ship, thus releasing 16 from which to organise four support groups immediately. 'It is, of course,' he went on, revealing the ultimate isolation of high command, 'a gamble that I must be sure will succeed, because to weaken the close escorts without gaining a dividend would be a fatal blunder.'

At the time of the submission of his Report the new Commander-in Chief had presided over the nadir of the war in the Atlantic, which began its sharpest descent with the mauling of ON154. This convoy, once again under Commodore W. De M. Egerton in the *Empire Shackleton*, supported by a vice commodore, Captain W. Evans, master of the *Fort Lamy*, consisted of 45 merchantmen. Among these were the *Ville de Rouen, Zarian, King Edward* and *Lynton Grange*, all recently members of SL125. There were also the special service ship HMS *Fidelity*,[5] aboard which a company of Royal Marines were embarked, the rescue ship *Toward* and the tanker *Scottish Heather* to refuel the six warships of Canadian C1 Escort Group. Led by Lieutenant Commander G.S. Windeyer in the destroyer HMCS *St Laurent*, this consisted of the corvettes *Chilliwack*, Acting Lieutenant Commander L.F. Foxall, *Napanee*, Lieutenant S. Henderson, *Kenogami*, Lieutenant J.L. Percy, *Shediac*, Lieutenant J.E. Clayton, and *Battleford*, Lieutenant F.A. Beck. At the convoy conference the briefing officer had apologised to the assembled masters for the lack of escorts. 'We did not think much of this,' recorded Captain Skinns of the *Ville de Rouen*, 'because there were over forty ships in the convoy.' The sense of foreboding must have been palpable.

The main body of Convoy ON154, accompanied by the Canadian corvettes, had left Liverpool Bay on 18 December 1942. Aboard the *Empire Shackleton*, Captain H. Ellington-Jones, Commodore Egerton and his staff went through their familiar drilling of the ships as they approached the North Channel and the rendezvous off Malin Head. Here the sections from the East Coast and the Clyde joined and by this time, early on the 19th, the convoy was already pitching into a rough head sea with a strong breeze sweeping in from the westward under a low overcast. The only brightness was from the two-flag signals each merchantman flew as her station number. Slowly in the heavy sea they formed their columns up, the newly-joined ships enlarging the convoy so that it expanded to a twelve-column front that extended for some five miles. With about four ships in each column the depth was about a quarter of that, and once each had jostled into station Egerton hoisted the convoy speed signal: K8 – 8 knots. As an outward convoy, ON154 contained ships destined for ports spread across the free world. About its flanks steamed the small shapes of its corvettes.

The escort still awaited the arrival of two destroyers. The *St Laurent* was then at Moville on Lough Foyle near Londonderry, where her bow was being repaired after a minor collision with the fleet oiler, and she herself was waiting for the return of her radio direction-finding officer, in quest of some spares for his defective equipment. The second destroyer, the ex-American four-stacker *Burwell*, was declared unfit owing to engine trouble and failed to join. Windeyer left Moville at 22.15 that evening lacking both a working HF/DF set and its operating officer. He caught up with ON154 at about 10.30 the following morning, the 20th, and steamed up the centre to run alongside *Empire Shackleton* and exchange signals with Egerton.

'December 21st was a featureless kind of day, one of the many that crept into a voyage and out again, leaving no trace of its having been except a cross on the calendar.'[6] The only manifestation of life beyond the bounds of the convoy as it headed west over the grey and heaving sea was a Sunderland that flew over just at dusk. That night the wind freshened and the conditions worsened, causing the officers on watch in the merchant ships to have trouble keeping their immediate neighbours in sight, making the job of maintaining station increasingly difficult. Next day the ships were hove-to, barely moving, and the convoy was disintegrating by degrees as each ship individually fought its traditional battle against the sea, U-boats forgotten. Windeyer recorded that *St Laurent* was hove-to and had 'lost touch with convoy'.

The dawn of Christmas Eve brought a moderation and the merchant ships again hoisted their station numbers and, increasing speed, worked their way back together. By 11.00 a few had reformed, while 'Far away astern, several [more] ships were creeping up, some shepherded by escorts. At 15.00 hours, now with good visibility, all ships seemed to be back on station. To the west, away ahead of the convoy, silhouetted by a low, lemon sunset lay *St Laurent* . . .'

As the watches changed at midnight and the relieved wished the relievers a happy Christmas, Convoy ON154 was back in formation. Ahead lay *St Laurent*, with *Chilliwack* and *Battleford* each guarding a 'bow' of the convoy. Astern on the port 'quarter' steamed *Kenogami*, with *Napanee* on the opposite starboard station and the *Shediac* between them. Beneath and around them, their sonars probed the dark waters.

The Befelshaber der U-boote at Kerneval had been frustrated in attacks against HX218, ON152 and ON153. On the 23rd, 18 U-boats already on patrol were formed into two groups, *Spitz* (a type of dog) and *Ungestüm* ('impetuous'). Alerted by B-Dienst intelligence, they were seeking the next westbound convoy and 'covered a relatively wide area in mid Atlantic'.

During the forenoon of Christmas Day the *Scottish Heather* dropped to the rear of ON154 and attempted to refuel *St Laurent*. In the heavy swell securing a line proved difficult, and the operation was aborted. Meanwhile a Christmas dinner was served up in warships and merchantmen alike; with full bellies and the convoy back in formation, morale was high. Next morning the wind had veered into the north and dropped to a fresh breeze. Another attempt was made to fuel *St Laurent*. After half an hour the lines and hoses parted, but Windeyer's destroyer had managed to take aboard almost 100 tons. It was just as well: ON154, now heading south-west, had long since passed the 20th meridian and was approaching the air-gap. To the north-west the most southerly U-boat of the *Spitz* group, *U-664* commanded by Oberleutnant A. Graef, caught sight of the convoy and reported it. Kerneval ordered him to keep contact and transmit the homing signal, then broadcast his location to the 18 submarines of the combined *Spitz* and *Ungestüm* groups, concluding: 'Do not attack. Await further orders.' Five hours later, after Korvettenkapitän W. Hermann of *U-662* had reported being in sight of the convoy, Kerneval ordered all U-boats to 'Await darkness and attack without further orders.'

In London the Submarine Tracking Room realised that an ambush was being prepared for ON154 and, copying the signal to Derby House, warned Windeyer and Egerton. In the fading daylight a string of bunting rose above the *Empire Shackleton*'s bridge: 'Convoy close up.' No one in any of the merchantmen needed an explanation. Nor did they have long to wait. At about 20.30 that evening the first snowflake was sent up, followed by others fired indiscriminately by most of the merchantmen. The convoy was bathed in 'scores of scintillating lights' as the flares descended on their tiny parachutes, provoking Egerton to transmit a radio signal to 'Cease firing snowflakes.'

At 21.45 HMCS *Shediac* reported seeing a submarine and *Toward*'s HF/DF operators reported strong radio activity, a report which Windeyer received after he had left station to investigate *Shediac*'s sighting. At 23.10, as he hunted on the port wing of the convoy, Windeyer's lookouts shouted a torpedo alarm and the destroyer dodged the track, the torpedo exploding harmlessly at the end of its run.

It was the discovery of Hermann's *U-662* that had triggered the initial firing of the snowflakes, and he had had to crash-dive. His second attack had resulted in the unexpected encounter with *Shediac*, after which he had escaped on the surface and then made a third assault, on the approaching *St Laurent*, and dived after firing at the destroyer. The failure of two torpedoes was a bitter disappointment, and as the noise of the *St Laurent*'s engines died away *U-662* surfaced again. Also closing in was *U-356*, Oberleutnant G. Ruppelt, which had homed-in on *U-664* whose presence had probably served to add to the wild shower of snowflakes thrown up by anxious merchantmen.

Unknown to the U-boats, the escort had already been weakened. The *Shediac* had been detailed to stand by the *Norse King*, which had just reported engine trouble, hoisting the two red lights that indicated she was 'not under command', and was already falling back through the ranks of the convoy. At midnight Egerton carried out the first of two pre-arranged course alterations, to be executed as *Empire Shackleton* blew her siren. Each ship followed her next-ahead round to starboard, repeating this twenty minutes later. As it happened, though these manoeuvres drew the convoy away from Hermann, they closed the distance with Ruppelt. Having swung away from the first eruption of snowflakes above the convoy, which threatened to reveal his presence, Ruppelt had remained on the surface and, using his full speed of 17 knots, now found himself advantageously placed as ON154 obligingly approached him. At about 01.30 on the 27th he began to stalk a ship, and ten minutes later he fired. Within seconds one torpedo struck home, whereupon Ruppelt, aiming across the heads of the starboard columns, fired a second salvo from both bow tubes. He was already withdrawing ahead of the convoy at full speed when one of the salvos exploded; the other missed. Then he dived.

The first torpedo from *U-356* slammed into the after starboard side of the *Empire Union*, leading column twelve. The vessel slewed to port and heeled over, water pouring into the almost empty Nos 4 and 5 Holds. The *Empire Union* began to settle as Captain H.A. MacCullum fired his snowflakes and ordered a distress signal transmitted on his radio and the engines stopped. The single red light indicating a torpedoed vessel was switched on, and the crew began mustering at the boats.

The conditions for launching were poor. Darkness, sea, swell and fear combined to make a perilous situation deadly. On the port side, both Nos 2 and 4 Boats unhooked themselves from the falls as they rose and fell alongside. Seeing this, one man, thought to have been the second engineer, slid down the falls, but with the toggles drawing out of, or being pulled from, their painters the boats fell astern and the poor man found nothing at the bottom and fell into the sea. The two port boats were now adrift, each with only a couple of men in it. Swimming to the ship's side the second engineer found a lowered boarding ladder, clambered up to the boat deck, and ran to No. 1 Boat on the starboard side. He found it already lowered and full of men. Scrambling down its boarding ladder he fell back into the sea between the boat and the ship's side. Other men were in the water, one of whom was lost; the chief engineer was hauled into No. 1 Boat. Also on the starboard side, No. 3 Boat was lowered properly under the supervision of the second mate, who climbed down to join the score of men already aboard. The purser was picked up by those in No. 3 Boat and ten seamen escaped on a Carley raft from the starboard foremast rigging, leaving the master and chief steward on board.

By now both after holds were flooded and the bulkhead between them was ruptured, as was the shaft tunnel, through which water was filling the engine room. It was now 50 minutes since the ship had been hit, and the convoy was several miles away. Those in the boats watched the dark mass of the bow rear up; the red light above the bridge was extinguished and, with a deep and disturbing rumbling, the *Empire Union*, a war prize, went to the bottom. She took Captain MacCullum, the chief steward, a gunner and a greaser with her.

Only seconds after *Empire Union* had veered off course Ruppelt's second torpedo had struck the *Melrose Abbey*, Captain F.J. Ormrod, at the head of column ten. Her crew were already rushing to action stations as the *Melrose Abbey* was hit just forward of the bridge in the starboard side, in way of No. 2 Hold. Debris was flung high in the air and she broke up, her extremities rising, her cargo of coal falling out through the bottom. Men rushed to the boat deck. Third Engineer C. McLeod fought his way out of the engine room scalded by steam escaping from fractured pipes. Others had on only singlets and cotton trousers as they jumped into the water. One boat was launched from the starboard side, into which eight men scrambled, but it was found to have been damaged by the torpedo impact. Others made for the rafts, and two were thrown over the side for some of the survivors to cling to as complete darkness followed the extinguishing of a last snowflake. Then the bulk of the ship disappeared, with the loss of six men.

In the following hour those left freezing but alive in the water or shivering uncontrollably in the boats were picked up by the *Toward*, skilfully manoeuvred among them by Captain G.K. Hudson. She was screened by HMCS *Napanee*, sent thither by *St Laurent*. In the rough sea they failed to reach one man, possibly Chief Engineer Mudie, and he was left to his fate. Hudson, seeing more red lights and flares, then picked up the survivors from the *Empire Union*.

Windeyer, meanwhile, had taken up *Napanee*'s station on the convoy's starboard quarter. He now received the welcome news that both *Shediac* and *Norse King* were catching up with the convoy. Ruppelt had spotted *Toward* and *Shediac* as he sought to re-engage, and filling *U-356*'s ballast tanks sufficiently to submerge most of her hull, he sneaked inside the *St Laurent*'s guard. Shortly after 04.00 he fired another salvo of torpedoes, then swung round and moved up inside the extreme starboard column at full speed, concealed by the darkness and the confusion attending the explosion of the torpedo he had just fired. Ruppelt then boldly crossed between the ships until he was in a position to attack the leading ship in the eighth column and fired yet again, before turning and almost running into the *Battleford* as she swept across the head of the convoy firing star-shell; then he escaped by running back through the advancing convoy.

This daring assault had not gone undetected. The *St Laurent*'s radar had alerted Windeyer to the presence of a rogue echo within the convoy, confirmed by the brilliant flashes of the torpedo strikes. As *Battleford* swung to port to intercept, Windeyer had brought *St Laurent* into the body of the convoy at 20 knots, ordering his forward gunners not to fire and risk hitting a merchantman as he did so. His lookouts soon spotted *U-356* and a moment later the destroyer's 20-mm Oerlikons raked her with rapid fire. Seizing a chance, the gun-layer at B-gun fired a round of flashless cordite, blinding Windeyer on the bridge. The last sight of *U-356* was her periscope close ahead of the *St Laurent*. As the destroyer passed over her a shallow-set depth-charge attack was made and the sonar operators reported a roar. Six minutes later a contact was obtained almost a mile astern, and Windeyer pounced. A ten-charge pattern, set between 50 and 140 feet, was thrown over the side. Eleven explosions were counted, the last of which was very loud, the sonic wave hitting the *St Laurent*'s hull with such violence that it tripped breakers off the main switchboard in her engine room. As Windeyer made another attack a large oil slick was seen, after which all contact was lost. Ruppelt and his crew were dead.

He had done his damnedest, though; behind him three of his torpedoes had hit their targets. His first had been the Rotterdam Lloyd cargo-liner *Soekaboemi*, on her way to India with a general cargo. After the shock of the blast at 04.10, Captain A. van der Schoor de Boer Haijo and his chief officer inspected the damage and the chief engineer went to have a look at the engines. No. 1 Hold was filling and the ship was going down by the head, so the master ordered the crew to the boats. The abandonment was as difficult as those from the two British ships, attended by confusion, lifeboats slipping their falls and their painters, and men disappearing in the water in the darkness. All were taken aboard boats or rafts, except one man who was lost. The vessel had a few passengers and one huddling in a boat, a 19-year-old British radio officer on his way out to join a ship in India, asked the Dutch second mate how far the nearest land was. 'Two miles,' was the reply, 'straight down.'

Ruppelt's final torpedo, fired at the leading ship in the eighth column at about 04.15, had hit the *King Edward*, which was flying light and had had a particularly difficult time in the bad weather. Now as the explosion flung her into the air men reacted under the powerful motive of self-preservation. The distress signal was transmitted, the confidential books dumped, and then Captain J.H. Ewens ordered her abandoned. The boats were launched in good order and the men were boarding them when the sea, working on the hull, found its way to the boilers, which erupted with a tremendous roar, blowing the bottom out of the ship and folding her in half. Below them, as they desperately tried to work the boats clear of the foundering wreck, the water glowed. Ewens got No. 1 clear but the mate was less successful and No. 2 Boat was drawn back over the *King Edward* as the bow section went down with a hissing and roaring, blasting aloft air, steam, dust and debris. No. 2 Boat was caught under the forestay, which sliced downwards, capsizing her and tossing the men into the sea. When she had gone the cloud of dust dispersed in the wind, leaving one boat full of men, two rafts onto which a further handful clung, and a cluster of wretches bobbing in the waves, some illuminated by the faint red gleam of their life-jacket lights.

Ewens picked up five men and these were all taken aboard the *Toward* when she arrived on the scene later that morning. Hudson had also gathered in some of the survivors from the *Soekaboemi,* while *Napanee* had the remainder. Of the *King Edward*'s people, two more found clinging to the keel of the capsized No. 2 Boat, plus three found in the sea, were also hauled aboard the *Napanee*. Twenty-three men were dead.

The Dutch ship was still afloat and her master wished to reboard and try to get her back to Britain. To exiles such as he their ship was even more of a home than was the case with British seamen, but permission was refused by Windeyer and Haijo was compelled to remain sadly on the *Toward*. It was 08.30 when the rescue ship and the corvette left the detritus of two ships and the floating hulk of the *Soekaboemi* behind them. By then the convoy was 35 miles away.

Within the convoy itself the remaining ships closed up their stations, and aboard *Empire Shackleton* Egerton and his staff assessed the night's damage. After a brush with a U-boat at dawn came the first new Admiralty warning of enemy submarines 'in your area'. Throughout the coming hours, during which *Napanee* and *Toward* strove to catch up, they flooded in. The rescue ship's HF/DF operators were also monitoring U-boat transmissions and warning Windeyer of their presence, and in addition the two vessels relayed signals informing ON154 of the imminent arrival of two destroyers – gullible if honest responses to a ruse of Windeyer's whereby he was transmitting plain-language messages to 'mythical supporting destroyers' in the hope of thus masking the escort's fundamental weakness.

Just before sunset *Chilliwack* was ordered to refuel from *Scottish Heather*, which slowed down to accommodate the corvette, and later *Kenogami* dropped back to stand by another merchantman with engine trouble. Thus at twilight the convoy's screen consisted of only *Shediac* on its port bow, *Battleford* to starboard and *St Laurent* still on its starboard quarter. The air was thick with apprehension.

Far astern *U-441*, one of the hunting pack, in attempting to regain contact and making 15 knots on the surface in a choppy head sea, came in sight of the abandoned *Soekaboemi* and torpedoed her. Kapitänleutnant G. von Hartmann watched her mast trucks disappear and then headed south-west after ON154. The convoy was now steering SSW, and as darkness fell *Chilliwack* was completing her fuelling 15 miles astern. Just before leaving *Scottish Heather* she fought a brief engagement with a U-boat on the surface. The U-boat in question was *U-225*, which had heard the slow pulses of the tanker and her suckling corvette on hydrophone. Oberleutnant W. Leimkühler approached, only to be met by a barrage of fire from the *Chilliwack*. He thereupon disappeared into the darkness, but his presence had caused the master of the tanker to zig-zag. Having been reassured by Lieutenant Foxall that he had driven the U-boat off, the *Scottish Heather* resumed a direct course towards the convoy; it would take her five hours to catch it up.

Having thrown off the *Chilliwack*'s pursuit and heard her disappear into the night, Leimkühler made a second attempt to get within range of the *Scottish Heather*. At 20.40 the silhouette of the tanker loomed in his attack periscope and he fired a salvo of torpedoes. Although laden with fuel oil for the escorts, she did not catch fire or explode, but she was badly wounded in her starboard side. At the midships accommodation only No. 1 Boat could be launched and this was got away with the master and mate in it. They began collecting up the men forced to jump directly into the cold and choppy sea. On the poop the second and third mates were lowering Nos 3 and 4 Boats. Having launched No. 3, Second Officer J. Crook clambered back on board and, consulting with the third mate and some engineers, decided that the ship might be saved and called for volunteers from both after boats: No. 3 was eventually cast off and No. 4 was left towing astern. Crook had mustered a party consisting of Third Mate J. Gorst, Sixth Engineer G. Allan, two able seamen, three gunners, the cook, a greaser and a galley-boy. The *Chilliwack* had seen the torpedo strike but now, reassured by Crook, wished them good luck and steamed away, regaining her screening station on the convoy by midnight. *Scottish Heather* was left alone with her skeleton crew.

Shortly afterwards *Napanee* and *Toward* rejoined the main body as ON154 continued on its way. In the early hours of the 28th there were some brief contacts with U-boats probing the defences, and at one point as the wind dropped the convoy was shrouded in fog. Then *St Laurent* went in pursuit of a radar contact and sighted a U-boat in the moonlight. Attacking with depth-charges as the radar 'paint' faded, indicating that the U-boat was diving, Windeyer missed, turned and made a second approach. Amid the explosion of depth-charges a larger detonation was heard. Followed as it was by the appearance of oil, it led to the conclusion that *St Laurent* had sunk her quarry. Later, at 03.15, *Chilliwack* also optimistically reported a direct hit on a U-boat.

During the daylight hours of the 28th Egerton once more reorganised his charges. The *Toward* was voicing concerns as to her ability to provide for the 164 survivors she was harbouring, but Windeyer thought the situation would ease when they received a welcome *genuine* reinforcement of two destroyers, *Milne* and *Meteor*, the next day. Egerton nevertheless ordered all ships in the rear to pick up survivors. Two of the escorts were also causing Windeyer a headache. Both *Battleford* and *Shediac* were running low on fuel, and during the afternoon the 'reserve tanker', the *E.G. Suebert*, dropped astern to succour the corvette. *Shediac* secured astern of the tanker, allowing herself to be towed as the operation proceeded, but Windeyer was worried about the rising sea-state and the heavy but steady strain on the towline and therefore forbade this, ordering Lieutenant Clayton to maintain way himself. It was not a sensible move; the now erratic load on the tow-wire caused it to part, and with it the hose. *Shediac* was still low on fuel, and had to remain with the tanker as she sought to regain her station in column seven before dark.

That same day those in the *Scottish Heather*'s No. 1 Boat, having spent an uncomfortable night, pulled long at the oars, expecting any moment to sight the rescue ship. After several hours they saw not the *Toward* but their own ship, under way towards them. As the sea washed in and out of her midships starboard cargo tanks, Crook bought the labouring tanker down towards the boat, and before darkness they had recovered their shipmates. Rather than try to regain the convoy and the U-boats circling it, they decided to put the tanker about and head for home.

As darkness once again closed over the convoy and the *E.G. Suebert* and *Shediac* regained their stations, a signal was received indicating that *Milne* and *Meteor*, though due to arrive next afternoon, would not stay long: they too were short of fuel. Throughout the day Admiralty signals had repeatedly warned of a gathering of the enemy. This was largely thanks to Kapitänleutnant H. Purkhold, who had maintained contact in *U-260* and transmitted homing signals. As night fell the escorts and U-boats began a series of surface clashes and under-water encounters. At one point four U-boats were in sight from *Battleford's* bridge alone.

The bright moonlight encouraged Windeyer to try another tactic and he closed the *Fidelity*, requesting that one of her two Kingfisher seaplanes be hoisted out and lowered to take off and maintain an air patrol over the convoy during the night. Her commander, Langlais, agreed but the first attempt failed because of the rough sea. A second attempt in which the seaplane was lowered into the smooth water caused by the *St Laurent's* wake as the destroyer steamed ahead of the *Fidelity* seemed successful. The seaplane, her engine already running, was unhooked and her throttle opened, but the sea conditions were quite inappropriate for such a venture, and as she bobbed and rolled her wing dropped, and she was instantly capsized. Pilot and observer escaped to cling to the floating wreck, then the observer was swept away. Seeing the disaster, Windeyer swung *St Laurent* round and after some anxious moments recovered the pilot, but it was more than an hour before the observer was located – an hour during which the *St Laurent* had been absent from her station guarding the convoy.

As this drama was taking place astern of the convoy, *U-203* (Kottmann), *U-435* (Strelow) and *U-591* penetrated the screen and the convoy columns to fire torpedoes. Kottmann and Strelow missed as snowflakes burst above the merchant ships. Catching sight of the dark shapes of the conning towers and the low hulls with white water washing along their flanks flitting in and out of view as they broke away ahead of the convoy, the merchant ships' gunners fired their Oerlikons.

A little later Kapitänleutnant H. Zetzsche brought *U-591* to attack from the starboard bow. He struck the *Norse King* before escaping at speed through the steady columns of the convoy. He was followed by Leimkühler in *U-225*, who fired at the *Melmore Head* as she avoided the *Norse King* ahead of her, the torpedo striking her starboard bow. Leimkühler dodged round the stern of the Norwegian tanker and straightened up to fire two torpedoes at the *Ville de Rouen*, fourth in column nine, before turning to break out ahead of the convoy at full speed. One torpedo missed, but the other struck the former French ship in her starboard side, in way of No. 2 Hold.

The Belfast-owned and -registered *Melmore Head* had been third in column eleven, and Captain W.J. Leinster's quick reaction in avoiding the *Norse King* was a consequence of his anxiety about his own tramp's station-keeping. Astern of him all the ships in the following column also dodged the stricken Norwegian as Egerton forbade the firing of more snowflakes. The *Melmore Head* had hardly resumed her course when she too was hit, the torpedo destroying the bulkhead between Nos 1 and 2 Holds and admitting tons of water into the empty ship. Still under full power she drove under, Leinster shouting the order to abandon ship as his crew began to dive overboard. Only one boat, No. 4, was launched, largely thanks to the speed with which the third officer's boat crew disengaged their gear. Less than three minutes after being struck *Melmore Head* sank, taking 14 men with her. The third officer paddled his boat round on the dark water with only two men at the oars as the rest of the column thrashed past in the wild darkness, picking up Leinster and 30 more shipmates. They were still searching when they met another boat.

This was from the *Ville de Rouen*, which had gone to action stations as Kottmann and Strelow made their abortive attack. Captain H.C. Skinns was on the bridge when the lookout shouted 'Here comes ours, sir!' A second later, at 20.05, the torpedo struck. The engines were stopped and the lifeboats manned, but Skinns passed word that they were not to be lowered and the mate was to report damage. Three of the boats had been lowered without orders, however, and although one remained alongside, Skinns found that most of his crew were in them; they knew the ship to be loaded with high-explosive ammunition as well as the rather unusual consignment of a prefabricated bow intended for a damaged destroyer in South Africa.

Apart from the three deck officers on the bridge with Skinns, the chief and fourth engineers, one British seaman and two Chinese were the only others left aboard. Having briefly restarted the engines, Skinns then stopped them again and decided to leave the ship until moonrise or daylight. In the boats he would have a chance to encourage his men. Reluctantly he and those with him slid down the lifelines and boarded No. 1 Boat, which had a motor. Once all the lifeboats had been rounded up and their occupants more evenly divided between them they lay-to, until at 22.15 another torpedo, fired from *U-662*, Korvettenkapitän W. Hermann, caused the *Ville de Rouen* to sink rapidly. Skinns took his other boats in tow and then rounded up all the boats he could find from the ships that had been sunk. In due course they were picked up by the *Shediac*.

While this was in train Windeyer, having finally located the *Fidelity's* seaplane observer, was bringing *St Laurent* up astern of the convoy. He anticipated that he would catch U-boats escaping from the rear of the merchant ships' ranks; instead he found boats and rafts filled with survivors. At this point his sonar operators echo-located a target and *St Laurent* attacked a contact on the convoy's port quarter. On the opposite diagonal *Battleford*, her radar defunct, was firing star-shells, while the tracer-fire from the merchantmen was clear evidence of U-boats still active within the convoy. On the starboard quarter of the convoy, *Napanee* had attacked a surfaced U-boat as it headed into the convoy, forcing it to dive. Carrying out a depth-charge attack, Lieutenant Henderson reported a heavy explosion which shook his corvette.

It was now about 20.45. In the lead of the vulnerable eleventh column the *Empire Wagtail*, an ageing ex-American freighter full of coal, was torpedoed by Purkhold in *U-260*. The cargo must have been wet when it was loaded and the ship's holds full of gas in consequence, for the torpedo caused an immense explosion and *Empire Wagtail* simply disintegrated, instantly killing Captain G. Almond and his entire crew.

At about this time Langlais reported engine trouble aboard the *Fidelity*, and the special service ship slowed and dropped astern. Hard-pressed, Windeyer ordered *Shediac* to cover her, thus exposing the port bow of the convoy, but instructed *Chilliwack* to cover the port flank.

Having escaped ahead of the convoy after his failed attack, at about 21.00 Kottmann was able to resume operations on the relatively unscathed and exposed port side of ON154. At 21.15 he ran in between columns two and three, turned *U-203* under the stern of the *Debrett* in column two and fired at the first two vessels in column one. Both his torpedoes missed. Meanwhile *Chilliwack* was engaging a U-boat off the port side, close to where Kapitänleutnant H. Dieterichs in *U-406* was also approaching. At 21.20 Dieterichs aimed at the exposed flanks of the second and third vessels in the first column. His torpedoes missed their marks, but one crossed the intervening gap and struck the port side of the *Lynton Grange*.

Dieterichs then slowed *U-406*, and as the third ship in the outer column one slid into view he fired again. The torpedo ran its course and exploded against the port side of the *Zarian*, penetrating the ship's side, bursting in the engine room and destroying the port boats in their davits. Swinging round, Dieterichs now found another target, illuminated by the blazing *Zarian*, and she too received a torpedo before he turned and withdrew at speed. The *Baron Cochrane*, Captain L. Anderson, had been hit in the engine room but was safely abandoned by all except two of her crew as the convoy passed on.

Loaded as she was with army stores and 3,000 tons of ammunition bound for the Middle East, it was a mercy that the *Lynton Grange* was hit in No. 1 Hold, which was devoid of high explosives. Nevertheless, as the ship's bow sank Captain R.S. Griggs ordered her evacuated and the confidential books jettisoned. By 21.30 all hands had abandoned the vessel, despite the fresh south-westerly breeze, the sea, and the swell. Aboard the *Zarian*, Captain W.E. Pellisier also gave the order to abandon ship. Difficulty was experienced getting the lee boats off the burning ship's side as she drifted downwind. None of the three ships, the *Ville de Rouen, Lynton Grange* or *Baron Cochrane*, was actually sunk by their attackers, and all were left derelict far astern of the convoy. This was now in a whirl of confusion, Windeyer suffering from information overload as signals came in from escorts, torpedoed ships, and vessels reporting themselves hit though the concussions heard were actually reverberations from torpedo strikes upon their near neighbours.[8] Merchant ships were also passing on torpedo-track sightings in an endeavour to assist the escorts to catch the predators, while the *Toward* simultaneously reported numerous HF/DF bearings and the *Fidelity*, fitted with sonar and HF/DF, sent in her own intercepts. Overburdened with her human lading, *Toward* took no further part in rescue operations, but only one of the rear rank of merchant ships stopped to pick up survivors as Egerton had ordered. As for the escorts, they were bereft of any co-ordinated response, being kept fully employed by a constant stream of sightings from their own lookouts.

At 22.15 Leimkühler renewed his attack from the exposed port bow. He sighted the leading ship of the first column and *U-225* was headed obliquely across the advancing front of the convoy. Selecting the leader of column six, Leimkühler fired. His target was Egerton's *Empire Shackleton*, a new standard cargo-ship built in 1941. The torpedo blew the hatch boards off No. 1 Hatch and flooded the ship's hold. The men ran to their stations and No. 4 Boat was rapidly lowered with a cadet, five sailors and five naval gunners and signalmen in it. Towing alongside as the ship steamed on was dangerous, and someone cut the painter. The boat fell astern as the mass of the *Empire Shackleton* disappeared into the night. Cadet S.W. Dean and his astonished crew were spotted by the *Calgary*, which was slowed down while her crew threw nets and ladders over the side of their ship. Dean and his men worked frantically at the oars and brought their boat alongside, scarely needing the exhortations to get a move on. Within a few moments the *Calgary* was on her way again.

Having hit the *Empire Shackleton*, Leimkühler took *U-225* under the stern of the third ship in the sixth column, the *Esturias*, then overtook the convoy in the interval between that column and the seventh. As *U-225* came back up towards the head of ON154 the vessel that had occupied the station astern of the commodore's ship was offset to starboard, offering Leimkühler a new target. As he slowed and slewed to port to line up his tubes, he received machine-gun fire from the large Belgian Petrofina tanker *Président Franqui*, and he retaliated. His torpedo blasted its way into the empty forward cargo tanks, which apparently were gas-free. As the *Président Franqui* slowed down, Nos 3 and 4 Boats on the poop were lowered without orders. Seeing this from the bridge amidships, Captain G. Bayet ordered them kept alongside, but the starboard boat was cast off and the port one left the ship to pick up two men who had jumped into the sea. Neither boat made any effort to return to the ship, so Bayet decided to make for the Azores. Leimkühler remained in pursuit.

By 23.00 that night, to Windeyer's chagrin, the convoy had lost nine ships. With the victims either embarking on a solo struggle for self-preservation or about to be despatched in its wake, Convoy ON154 had lost something of its cohesion and also its commodore, though Captain Evans in the *Fort Lamy* had taken over that task. Rummaging among the debris and detritus, the boats, bodies and rafts of their handiwork, the U-boats of the *Spitz* and *Ungestüm* groups, many of which had not actually attacked ON154, went about their murderous business under cover of the night's shroud. The *Lynton Grange* was sent to the bottom by *U-628* (Hasenschar) with an immense explosion as her load of ammunition detonated. The *Zarian* was sunk by Zetzsche in *U-591*, taking with her two crated Spitfire fighters intended for Egypt, and the *Baron Cochrane* was sunk by Schroeter in *U-123*. The single boat-load of survivors from the Hogarth tramp watched resentfully as their ship sank, and then joined the two boats from the Houlder Brothers' liner. It was barely midnight and bitterly cold, the air clear under an overcast sky, and the sea was running under the impetus of a strong south-westerly breeze at heights of six or seven feet, heavy enough to make life in the crowded boats and on the wave-swept rafts barely tolerable. A surfaced U-boat rushing back towards the distant glow of the action almost ran down the *Zarian*'s lifeboat. For some of her men it was the third time they had been torpedoed.

It had been reported to Windeyer that the HF/DF vectors indicated the U-boats had broken off their attacks and were now astern of the convoy, and at about 23.00 he had ordered Lieutenant Percy to join him. HMCSs *St Laurent* and *Kenogami* then carried out a search over an area ten miles astern of the convoy. As he concluded this operation without having either struck a U-boat or rescued any survivors, Windeyer became anxious about the continuing detachment of the *Shediac* as cover for the *Fidelity*. He knew that the special service vessel was unique in possessing anti-torpedo netting, and he was concerned not only about the missing element in the escort but about the fuel state of the *Shediac*. Langlais, with Gallic sangfroid, declared that he could manage on his own, and *Shediac* was ordered to head back towards the convoy thirty miles away, keeping a lookout for survivors. Langlais stopped and deployed his nets; later, with his repairs completed, he got under way at slow speed and headed south for the Azores.

Far away to the east the Admiralty tug *Eminent* was ordered out of Gibraltar to *Fidelity*'s assistance, and from Derby House Horton, appalled, ordered the escort of Convoy KMS4, a series initiated to support Operation TORCH, to relinquish two warships to search for survivors from ON154. At 05.06 the destroyers HMS *Viscount* and HMCS *St Francis* were ordered to comply.

At 02.00 on the 29th Clayton began a long zig-zag across the track of the convoy, every available man lining *Shediac*'s rails as lookouts. After an hour they picked up the chief officer's No. 4 Boat from the *Ville de Rouen* and half an hour later they came across Captain Skinns in his motor-boat towing three others bearing his own and the men from the *Melmore Head*. All were taken aboard the *Shediac*. Two hours after this a raft with Captain Ellington-Jones and six of his men from the *Empire Shackleton* was encountered, and some time later still a boatload of people from the *Président Franqui* were scrambling over the corvette's rail. Clayton then headed his overcrowded little warship for the convoy.

After the *Empire Shackleton* was hit, Ellington-Jones too had decided that he would make for the Azores in the hope that he might save his ship, her cargo of general, ammunition and aircraft, and those of his crew who remained with him. Having agreed the plan with Egerton and informed Windeyer to this effect, he had headed for the archipelago. In less than an hour he had run foul of the U-boats astern of the convoy and was attacked and damaged by Schroeter in *U-123* and then hit by a torpedo from Strelow's *U-435*. With *Empire Shackleton* doomed Ellington-Jones gave the order to abandon her, and he himself, four seamen and two DEMS gunners were those found by *Shediac*. Egerton and about 50 men in two other lifeboats had lost contact in the darkness.

At 07.30 that same morning the destroyers *Milne* and *Meteor* arrived on the scene from Gibraltar and found the *Baron Cochrane*'s boat. With *Meteor* screening her, *Milne* stopped and fished them up. A few minutes later they came upon the *Lynton Grange*'s survivors, then the *Zarian*'s. Hauled aboard by 08.15, Third Officer H. Revely 'walked aft' and 'noticed for the first time since that awful crash the night before, that my stomach muscles were relaxed. On reaching the companionway down to the wardroom I paused and looked astern. In the receding distance the lifeboat and raft bobbed to the surface, then disappeared and rose again. A momentary nostalgia crept over me as the thought came to my mind that they had sustained me through the long arduous night. My gaze became unseeing and when I refocused my eyes both raft and boat had disappeared from view.'

Having discovered that the *Fidelity* was heading for the Azores under her own power and that in any case the *Eminent* was going to her assistance, the *Milne* and *Meteor* headed west, to reinforce the C1 Escort Group around ON154.

*

Bayet's *Président Franqui* had meanwhile proceeded independently until 06.30 that morning, when a torpedo hit aft, wrecking the steering and damaging the auxiliary boiler. *U-225* surfaced and passed across her stern so close that the third officer could not depress the 4-inch poop gun sufficiently for it to bear. Leimkühler then disappeared until 09.30, when two U-boats were seen; one was his *U-225*, the other *U-336* commanded by Kapitänleutnant H. Hunger, who by mutual consent was to sink the tanker. Hunger fired three torpedoes, all of which proved dud. Leimkühler then fired, forcing the *Président Franqui* to stop, and Bayet finally abandoned his ship. Two more defective torpedoes were fired before *U-225* finally despatched her, one more tanker that proved the durability of her design. Then *U-336* approached the lifeboats, and in excellent English asked for the ship's master. The unfortunate Bayet was taken prisoner while the survivors, 26 of the original 32-man crew under Chief Officer M. A. Lagay, set out for the Azores.

That afternoon *U-435*, having missed the *St Laurent* the night before, was astern of the convoy. At about 14.30 Strelow's lookouts reported a ship. It was the *Norse King*, the first merchantman to have been disabled and now a drifting derelict. Closing her, he fired a torpedo at 15.07, shortly after which she sank with her cargo of coal. Although she had remained afloat for hours after her torpedoing, all 35 of her company died.

Some miles to the south-east, through the periscope of *U-615*, Kapitänleutnant R. Kapitzky was surveying a mysterious vessel which seemed stopped, with boats clustered about her. He thought her reminiscent of a decoy or 'Q'-ship and cautiously approached her at periscope depth. The wind had dropped and the sea was slight as Kapitzky observed this oddity. She was of course the *Fidelity*, also struggling towards the refuge of the Azores. Aboard her Langlais had decided to hoist out the motor-torpedo boat he had on his foredeck and carry out an anti-submarine screen during the hours of darkness as the *Fidelity* steamed slowly towards safety. She was unable to make more than a few knots, hampered as she was by her defects and her nets, which Langlais had decided were best left hanging from their booms. Then at 12.30 he hoisted out the one remaining of his two seaplanes and this took off with a roar, to return shortly afterwards with a report that two submarines were not far away, along with some lifeboats. Both seaplane and MTB remained close to the *Fidelity*, which was again suffering engine trouble. An attempt to send the MTB towards the reported lifeboats was frustrated by a failure of her main engine, and instead Langlais sent off two landing-craft, also part of his bizarre ship's equipment.

They returned some hours later with about fifty survivors from the *Empire Shackleton*, including Commodore Egerton. These men struggled aboard and the landing-craft were recovered. Shortly afterwards darkness fell. It was now that the watching Kapitzky approached. Firing all four bow tubes at the suspicious ship without effect, he then swung *U-615* and discharged a stern tube. A Belgian officer commissioned into the Royal Navy as 'Lieutenant J.H. O'Neill' was still in the MTB astern of the *Fidelity*, and saw *U-615* surface on the ship's port quarter. In response Langlais fired a pattern of depth-charges, but to no effect. It was a dark night, and the U-boat crash-dived. At about 21.00, following a second sonar contact, Langlais fired another load of charges. 'O'Neill' had engine troubles of his own and dropped astern, and at daylight there was no sign of the *Fidelity* from the MTB. With little fuel, no mother ship and defective engines, 'O'Neill's' position was un-enviable. He and his second-in-command, Sub-Lieutenant M.J. Pollard, RNVR, decided to make for Britain under sail using the prevailing south-westerly wind, which was again freshening. Late that night, extemporising a rig out of blankets and canvas and a leeboard out of the cabin sole, *MTB 105* and her four-man crew headed north-east.

As for the *Fidelity*, having failed to sink her Kapitzky withdrew, so that it was Strelow who encountered her in *U-435* and sank her in the late after-noon of the 30th. The full truth of her sinking never fully emerged, even after the war, although Strelow's War Diary survived when *U-435* was sunk the following June. The survival of *Fidelity*'s seaplane crew and 'O'Neill' and his men seemed to suggest there was more to the plain fact of her sinking than was apparent at the time. Strelow reported three to four hundred people drowning about her as she sank. Among these must have been Egerton, who had been commodore of eight ocean trade convoys, two of which, HX212 and ON154, were badly mauled. The men of T Company, 40 Commando, Royal Marines added to the number of the dead.

The Admiralty mounted a search for the *Fidelity* that involved six warships and lasted until 11 January 1943. No survivors were found. Strelow's report to Dönitz elicited from his superior the query 'whether their [the survivors'] destruction can be counted upon?' Strelow avoided making a direct reply, and returned to the scene at daylight. The mystery of the loss of the *Fidelity* lies in the fact that nothing, not even a corpse in a life-jacket, was ever found.[9]

As the wreckage was being mopped up on the 29th, ON154 continued to the west. During the morning *Shediac* made a sonar contact, attacked, and claimed a kill. It was as unfounded as the others. Only one U-boat, Ruppelt's *U-356*, was actually 'killed' during the entire action. After some evasive alter-nations of course in response to more Admiralty submarine warnings, the afternoon brought the welcome sight of *Milne* and *Meteor* finally approaching from the east. They had unknowingly passed only 15 miles north of the *Fidelity* some hours earlier. As they neared ON154 they too gained a contact and attacked, but without any apparent result apart from driving off their quarry. During the late afternoon and early evening several torpedo tracks were reported, and by now more reinforcements were being diverted from elsewhere. *Fame* was being sent from ON155, USSs *Dallas* and *Cole* were sailing from Argentia, HMCSs *Arrowhead, Chicoutini* and *Digby* were also on their way. At 17.30 *Napanee* finally succeeded in topping up her bunkers from the *E.G. Suebert*, but this did not greatly ease the situation, for just after midnight on 30 December *Battleford* and *Shediac*, the latter desperately short of oil, detached for the Azores, while *Milne*'s Captain M. Richmond signalled the 'Commander-in-Chief, Western Approaches, repeated Admiralty' that '*Milne, Meteor,* and *Napanee* must retire to fuel PM today, 30.12.42.'

Before leaving he assessed the situation as 'extremely black' and 'ordered the commodore to do an emergency turn to starboard after dark and told SS *Calgary* a 15 knot ship carrying women and children, and SS *Advastun* to escape if in their judgement they had an opportunity.'

Richmond's gloom proved ill-founded. Before dark *Viceroy* and *St Francis* arrived, and after twilight had faded the siren blasts from *Fort Lamy* signalled the emergency turn. There were to be no further attacks. The B-Dienst service had warned Dönitz of the strengthening of the escort and he withdrew his U-boats, sending many to refuel from *U-117* west of the Azores.

Fuel was now an acute problem for the escorts which had left the convoy. *Meteor* ran out 5 miles short of Ponta Delgarda and had to be towed in; *Milne* arrived all but empty. Further astern, *Battleford* was towing in the *Shediac*. The small Portuguese town, where the British and German viceconsulates occupied adjacent premises on the main street, was swamped.

Meanwhile, as the old year ended Convoy ON154 continued its passage. It was a tradition for a ship's most junior officer to ring the New Year in with sixteen bells, and a few ships observed it. On the morning of 1 January Windeyer permitted the *Fanan* and *Ungeni* to increase speed and proceed ahead to their destinations. An hour or so later HMS *Fame* arrived, and then in the afternoon Windeyer handed the escort over to the USS *Cole*. *St Laurent* was herself short of fuel, and headed for St John's.

Far to the east and south the search for *Fidelity* went on. From the 31st onwards warships arrived in the area in which it was erroneously thought she had been sunk. By the 3rd it was being combed by the *Milne, Meteor, Shediac, Battleford, Prescott* and *Woodstock*. The last-named had already picked up 'O'Neill' and his men from *MTB 105*, along with the Kingfisher seaplane's crew who had been rescued by the MTB. *Prescott* had picked up

Chief Officer Lagay and more survivors from the *Président Franqui*. Lagay afterwards reported 'bad and riotous' behaviour among the survivors from his vessel. Water had been 'filched', others had malingered to avoid rowing, and his orders for 'general safety were not carried out and were answered by scoffs or insulting language. A Belgian Marine [had] hit the Chief Officer on the head with a whisky bottle.' It was a dismal end, a disintegration arising from defeat.

On 2 January the tanker *Scottish Heather* reached the Tail o' the Bank anchorage in the Clyde, a gaping hole in her starboard side. On the evening of New Year's Eve the Nazi defector William Joyce, known as Lord Haw Haw, had broadcast the news of the destruction of Convoy ON154, mentioning among the ships sunk the tanker *Scottish Heather*, and the crew's relatives had already received the 'missing at sea' telegrams. But Second Officer Crook, already appointed MBE for making a thousand-mile, 28-day boat voyage after the *Athelknight* was torpedoed in the Caribbean, had brought his ship into a safe haven. For his further outstanding conduct he was awarded the George Medal and Lloyd's War Medal.

What was left of Convoy ON154 arrived in New York on 12 January.

The survivors landed at Ponta Delgarda on São Miguel in the Azores were well treated. Accommodation and clothing were arranged by the consul, and while some were hospitalised, others were sent to hotels or to stay aboard the Belgian ship *Katanga*, in port for repairs. 'During our stay', Apprentice W.A. Bishop of the *Lynton Grange* wrote, 'we were given every possible help and shown great kindness and generosity, both by the local population and by the officers and crew of the *Katanga* . . .'

On 6 January 1943 the troopship *Llangibby Castle* entered port, specially tasked to embark the survivors from ON154 and others who had landed in the Azores. 'We left next day and disembarked at Liverpool on 12 January. Here we felt unwanted and a nuisance to local officialdom whose manner in dealing with most of the survivors was most condescending and ungracious. It felt degrading to be treated like criminals because we had no papers, money, decent clothing, etc. One would almost believe that the largesse they were distributing was from their own pockets rather than an entitlement . . .'

Those aboard the little *Toward* had similarly enjoyed precious little succour. The 19-year-old British radio officer who was a survivor from the *Soekaboemi* recorded that after being picked up by the rescue ship 'the following ten or twelve days were the most miserable I spent at sea. I admired her master, and the crew did all they could but the facilities were hopeless to the task [of accommodating 164 survivors, after which the ship was considered full] . . . We understood comforts in the way of clothing were kept on board

but unless you arrived "starkers" [i.e., naked] not so much as a handker-
chief was issued . . .' Many men slept on deck and 'during the first few days
morale was at a low ebb despite chats given by the master [Captain G.K.
Hudson]. Although I owe everything to the *Toward* and her crew, I can
never forget the misery, largely infectious and encouraged by the poor
catering, from which point of view it was more like a floating lost dogs'
home . . . She was just not equipped to deal with such a situation.'[10] It was
15 January before these wretches landed at Halifax. As for *Toward* herself,
she was sunk while homeward bound as rescue ship to Convoy SC118.

Most of Third Officer Revely's four weeks of survivor's leave was spent
in obtaining a new seaman's identity card, clothing coupons, compensation
for lost gear such as a sextant, nautical tables and binoculars, and generally
're-equipping' himself. He spent 'over £100' and received £64 in compensation, the maximum allowed. Nor did it help when, kitted out in his new
uniform, he was grilled by two CID officers who accused him of imper-
sonating an officer in the Merchant Navy. He subsequently joined the
Lagosian, and on 28 March 1943 was sunk off the Canaries.

The year had ended badly for the Allies. The situation in the Atlantic was
dire, losses having been, in Roskill's words, 'little short of catastrophic: for
they amounted to no less than 1,664 merchant ships totalling 7,790,697
tons', most of which, some 1,160 ships, or 6,266,215 tons, had been sunk
by enemy submarines. British imports had been reduced by a third of the
peace-time requirement, to some 34 million tons. So concerned had
Churchill become that on 4 November he formed a new Cabinet Anti-
U-Boat Warfare Committee, taking the chair himself.

By December only 300,000 tons of available bunker fuel remained in
the entire country, with consumption running at 130,000 tons a month.
The Admiralty possessed a reserve of one million tons, but that was intended
for an emergency. 'An ample reserve of fuel on this side of the Atlantic is
the basis of all our activities,' the First Sea Lord informed Churchill, and
when given the figures for the oil stocks in December he minuted it: 'This
does not look at all good . . .'

To ease the situation the trade convoy cycle was extended from eight to
ten days and the escorts thus released were assigned to bring special convoys
of tankers from Aruba on a twenty-day cycle. The first of these was designated TM1.

22

'Stay tough!'

Storaas

THE GROWING CRISIS in supplies, reminiscent of that of 1917, was exacerbated by the demands for fuel oil, both black and white, following the Allied invasion of North Africa in November 1942. This prompted the despatch of TM1, composed of nine British and Norwegian tankers, from Trinidad to the Mediterranean. The convoy sailed on 28 December 1942.[1] The Commodore was Captain A. Laddle, master of the Shell tanker *Oltenia II*, and the escort was provided by the B5 Escort Group led by Commander R.C. Boyle in the destroyer *Havelock*, supported by three corvettes, *Pimpernel*, *Godetia* and *Saxifrage*.

Only *Havelock* and *Saxifrage* were fitted with HF/DF and *Havelock*'s set was defective; *Godetia*'s radar broke down on 2 January 1943, and *Pimpernel*'s suffered a reduction in efficiency after the 8th. The escorts were returning from a six months' deployment in the West Indies and although they were worked-up, they 'possibly lacked the finer edge which would have been expected of a front-line Western Approaches Group. They had been painted plain grey at the request of the [American] Eastern Sea Frontier Commander, New York, so were without the normal Western Approaches protective camouflage and this is considered materially to have assisted the U-Boats to sight and avoid them. In any case there had been no time to change their appearance.'[2]

Convoy TM1 sailed from Port of Spain on 28 December 1942, heading north-east for Gibraltar. Initially the escort lacked *Godetia* but air-cover was provided by a Catalina, which early the next morning reported a U-Boat on the surface, some twenty miles astern of the convoy. The flying-boat attacked with depth-charges and 'Mousetrap' bombs, forcing the U-boat to dive and evade *Godetia*, which searched the area as she caught up with the convoy. The U-boat was probably *U-514*, on her way home from the Caribbean; but whoever she was, she informed Dönitz of an eastbound convoy composed solely of tankers. He immediately redirected a strong group of U-boats code-named *Delphin*, bound for Brazil with a U-tanker in support, to intercept TM1.

After their initial scare the convoy, unaware of the building threat to its security, enjoyed three quiet days, but its modest speed of 8.5 knots was reduced by head winds and sea, to which had to be added the contrary ocean current. Once again attempts to refuel the escorts were frustrated by imperfect techniques and poor fittings, though some success was achieved from the *Cliona*. On the afternoon of 3 January, when TM1 was about 1,050 miles east of Trinidad, an Admiralty signal warned of another U-boat in the vicinity of the convoy, and later a signal from the American naval command ordered a more southerly route, putting the convoy on a course a little north of due east. At dusk a U-boat was sighted in the distance, and at 21.35 *Havelock* echo-located a contact three miles ahead of the convoy.

Boyle had increased speed to close this when a second U-boat was detected on radar, and at 21.46 the officer of the watch aboard the *British Vigilance* caught sight of the dark shape of a submarine ahead. An instant later the tanker staggered as she was struck by a torpedo. Her cargo, 11,000 tons of petroleum, burst into flames, filling the night with light and illuminating *U-514*, a Type IX C U-boat, speeding down her port side.

In attempting to escape through the convoy Kapitänleutnant H-J. Auffermann was fired upon as *U-514* ran the gauntlet of the guns of all the tankers whose fields of fire were not masked. The second ship in column three, *Empire Lytton*, tried to ram *U-514*, and claimed 'about 200 hits with both Oerlikons at a range of between 100 and 300 yards before the U-Boat disappeared into the darkness'. The crew working *Oltenia II*'s 4-inch gun also claimed a near-miss.

Boyle ordered the escorts to carry out the standard 'Raspberry' counter-attack, 'without positive result, although *Pimpernel* sighted a disturbance on the convoy's starboard quarter which may have been the U-Boat diving, but no contact was made.'

Aboard the blazing *British Vigilance* Captain E.O. Evans, who was vice commodore, gave the order to abandon ship, and along with 26 of his men he went over the side to find refuge aboard the *Saxifrage*, which picked them up as the disappointed escorts resumed their stations. The hulk of the BP tanker drifted astern, burnt out and lay derelict for three weeks until it was sunk on the 24th by *U-105* (Nissen). Somewhere aboard her were 27 incinerated corpses.

The presence of U-boats increased Boyle's anxiety. The *Havelock's* HF/DF set was again operational but he was concerned about the escorts' fuel state. Fortunately some oiling was carried out on 5 January and offensive sweeps were made, but there were neither sightings nor sonar contacts until the evening of 8 January, when at 21.35 *Havelock*, well ahead of the convoy on its port bow, obtained a radar response between herself and TM1. Ringing for full speed, Boyle applied full helm and *Havelock* raced to the attack, sighting a U-boat on the surface. Determined to ram before the enemy submerged, he was frustrated by the sight of the U-boat's conning tower disappearing in a smother of white water. Nevertheless, a moment later his operators reported a sonar contact and as he ran over his target and dropped a five-charge pattern there were other explosions as first the *Albert L. Ellsworth*, leading the first column, and then *Oltenia II*, leading the sixth, were torpedoed. Less than five minutes had passed since *Havelock* first gained a radar echo; already the Norwegian-flagged *Albert L. Ellsworth*, on charter to the Admiralty with fuel for naval units in the Mediterranean, was in flames and dropping astern through the ranks of the convoy, which wove round her as her crew dashed for their boats. The commodore's ship 'sank in two minutes, dragging the survivors down with it'.

Both ships had fallen victim to Kapitänleutnant G. Siebicke in *U-436*, one of the 16 U-boats now forming the enlarged *Delphin* group. Once again the escorts counter-attacked, Boyle getting a radar response at 1,000 yards. Firing a star-shell revealed a U-boat in the act of submerging. At 21.47, having picked the enemy up on her sonar, *Havelock* attacked with a fourteen-charge pattern. At 22.10 another echo was attacked with a five-charge pattern. Contact was then lost, but an underwater explosion was heard shortly afterwards. Further searches astern of the convoy proved fruitless, however: Boyle found no other evidence of human remains than survivors from his charges. Screened by *Saxifrage*, *Havelock* pulled 43 men from the *Oltenia II* and all hands from the *Albert L. Ellsworth* out of the water. By 23.12 the rescue work was finished, and both vessels rejoined the convoy. Captain Laddle and 16 officers and ratings were lost from the Shell tanker. Although he had never previously acted as commodore, Laddle's 'signals invariably showed a thorough appreciation . . . and . . . his method of conducting the convoy could not have been bettered,' Boyle later reported, regretting the loss of 'this most gallant master'.

In the event Siebicke was able to finish off his handiwork, for the following evening he came across the still-burning *Albert L. Ellsworth*, and shelled her until she sank.

Following these losses, Captain J.D. Miller of the *British Dominion*, which was now leading the second column, had become commodore. Meanwhile

Pimpernel, Lieutenant Commander F.H. Thornton, had detected another U-Boat on the convoy's starboard quarter and ran towards her, firing her 4-inch gun. The U-boat submerged and a ten-charge pattern was dropped at 22.33 hours, whereupon *Pimpernel*'s sonar operators reported another loud underwater explosion. Neither *Pimpernel*'s action nor *Havelock*'s, so optimistically reported, yielded a kill, but by 02.00 on the 9th all escorts were back in their defence stations.

As the minutes ticked by other contacts were made, and by 05.15 a new attack had matured, despite the vigilance of the escorts. Penetrating the screen *U-575*, under Kapitänleutnant G. Heydemann, torpedoed the leading ship in column nine, the Norwegian *Minister Wedel*, and then her fellow-countryman the *Norvik*, second in column seven.[3] Both tankers caught fire, but did not sink. As *Havelock* and *Saxifrage* doubled back to counter-attack, Heydemann dived, receiving depth-charges from both destroyer and corvette. Again a loud explosion was reported, and Boyle remained close to the two burning tankers in the hope that the attacking U-boat would return to finish off her victims.

Simultaneously *Pimpernel* and *Godetia* were engaging other contacts on the port side of the convoy, which was proceeding ENE at 9 knots, but this action did not prevent Korvettenkapitän H-J. Hesse in *U-442* from firing at the *Empire Lytton* at about 04.10. Although she was carrying 12,500 tons of highly inflammable aviation spirit the *Empire Lytton* did not catch fire immediately. The torpedo hitting her passed right through her, only seven feet from her bow, blowing the top off No. 1 Tank as it did so. This tank was singular in that it contained a consignment of heavy oil, which did not immediately ignite but was flung over the whole forepart of the ship. The chief officer, Mr A.J. de Baughn, was overcome by the fumes, and the oil soaked the boat falls and then spilled out over the sea as it caught fire. Captain J.W. Andrews ordered his ship abandoned. Because of the saturated state of the ropes, lowering the midships lifeboats was impossible, so he made for the poop.

'Almost the entire crew aft [emerging from the engine room and poop accommodation] had got into a panic, jumped into the port [after No. 4] boat and lowered [it] into the water while the ship still had considerable way on her, causing the boat to break open and throw them into the sea [which was] heavily coated with oil fuel.' Andrews, in his boat, reported picking up 11 men, including his chief officer 'who unfortunately showed little signs of life. The boat was then too overloaded to take any more aboard, although I saw ten or twelve men still in the water . . .'

Boyle, still close to the *Minister Wedel* and *Norvik*, was diverted to pursue a sonar contact and attacks were carried out until the echo faded, whereupon

Havelock then returned to the two casualties to find *Norvik* with her back broken. The master of the *Minister Wedel* thought his ship could be salvaged. He had lost none of his men and convinced Boyle of the possibility of saving the tanker, but Boyle was now receiving news of 'six or seven' U-boats in the vicinity of the convoy. He had little option; after their crews had been removed, both *Norvik* and *Minister Wedel* were shelled by *Havelock*. The *Norvik* was left burning furiously but *Minister Wedel* seemed little damaged. Meanwhile, Lieutenant N.L. Knight's *Saxifrage* was rescuing Captain J.W. Andrews and the 33 survivors from the *Empire Lytton*. Signalling to Boyle, Knight transferred de Baughn to *Havelock*, but Boyle's surgeon-lieutenant pronounced him dead as both escorts hurried back to rejoin the convoy.

The *Norvik*, two of whose crew had been killed, and the *Minister Wedel* had both been torpedoed by Kapitänleutnant H. Schneider in *U-522*. Further skirmishing occurred and at 14.30 the bubbling trail of a torpedo was seen from the Norwegian tanker *Vanja*, which altered course to avoid it, while a periscope, spotted from the *British Dominion*, was sprayed with 20-mm Oerlikon shells. On the point of being overwhelmed, all the warships did their best. Lieutenant Commander A.H. Pierce was particularly active, engaging *Godetia* in several counter-measures, and none of the U-boats were able to press home their own attacks. By 15.30 they had withdrawn to await the onset of darkness, leaving Boyle and his colleagues to contemplate the wreck of the convoy, now reduced to a mere third of its original strength, the three tankers *British Dominion, Vanja* and *Cliona*.

During the night *Havelock* and *Saxifrage* obtained several HF/DF bearings indicating U-boats ahead and astern of the convoy, but surprisingly no attacks materialised, and at dawn the remnant three tankers were still in station, outnumbered by their escort. By noon it appeared to the Admiralty's Submarine Tracking Room that only one U-Boat remained in contact, with a further four within 90 miles and another four or five within 150 miles – an assessment that was to prove flawed. Nevertheless, as the convoy steamed north-east and approached Madeira during the sunlit hours of 10 January, the lack of action seemed heartening. Unfortunately the sun set in a blaze of glory, the convoy and its defenders 'strikingly silhouetted against the Western sky'.

A diversionary alteration of course to the ESE was made after dark, to no avail. The alarm was given by Knight, stationed on the convoy's starboard quarter in *Saxifrage*, who attacked a sonar contact with a ten-depth-charge pattern at 19.23. Twenty minutes later, after a brief and inconclusive engagement, *Saxifrage* gave up and headed back to her defence station. Then at 23.30, the enemy having remained quiet in the interim, TM1 swung back towards the north-east. Eleven minutes later three torpedoes hit *British Dominion* on her port side. Carrying 9,000 tons of 'aviation spirit [, she] burst into violent flames which brightly illuminated the area for a considerable distance all round'. In the stark light of the blazing tanker a U-Boat was clearly visible between *British Dominion* and *Vanja*. The *Vanja* altered course to port and opened fire on the U-Boat with her 4-inch gun and her machine-guns. Hits were claimed, but little damage was achieved; Kapitänleutnant Schneider escaped, taking *U-522* clear of the retaliating escorts.

Boyle immediately ordered a 'Raspberry' response, and as the escorts swung round firing star-shell, no fewer than three U-Boats were sighted in the course of the next minutes. Those in the *Havelock, Saxifrage* and *Pimpernel* all sighted *U-522*, which dived out of sight at 23.43. Pierce in *Godetia* had seen a second U-boat, and in attacking drove her under. Boyle's star-shells had illuminated a third U-Boat, which also crash-dived as *Havelock* approached at speed. She was quickly echo-located and attacked with a fourteen-charge pattern. After this she was heard blowing tanks, and within two minutes a large underwater explosion was heard. Further attacks were made on the spot, but by 00.39 on the 11th all contact had been lost.

The damage had been done. Aboard the *British Dominion* 37 men were already dead but her master, Captain J.D. Miller, 'by superb seamanship, managed to get a boat away with the surviving [15] crew members', which in due course were picked up by *Godetia*.

At daylight the Australian destroyer *Quiberon* joined the escort and a Catalina appeared overhead. Later in the day two more destroyers, *Penn* and *Pathfinder*, reinforced the escort, but it was far too late. Of the nine tankers that had set out from Trinidad, only the *Vanja* and *Cliona* reached Gibraltar on 14 January 1943.[4] Not far away, under the shadow of The Rock, the other ships' survivors trooped disconsolately ashore. The conduct of Convoy TM1 had been a disaster.

Unusually, the Germans thought they had inflicted less damage than was the case, their estimate of the convoy's size being 15 tankers. Their assessment of its defenders was more telling. 'The convoy escort', Hessler wrote afterwards, '. . . was unpractised and lacked perseverance.'[5] This indictment was matched by one aimed at the attacking U-boats: 'Preoccupation with torpedoed tankers and enemy depth-charge attacks soon caused many . . . to drop astern, so that after the second day only four boats were still in touch, and the pursuit was abandoned on the 11 January near Madeira.' That preoccupation resulted in the death-blow being administered to the four drifting, burnt out-wrecks as Hesse sank the *Empire Lytton* on the evening of the 9th,[6] Schneider sank the *British Dominion* during the forenoon of the 10th, and other U-boats accounted for the *Norvik* and the *Minister Wedel*.

Curiously, that none of the successful U-boats long survived their encounter with TM1 has been advanced as a vindication of the fate of the convoy and the inadequacies of its escort. Boyle had done his best, but that best had been limited by the forces available to him and, to a lesser but significant extent, by the difficulties the British were still experiencing in refuelling at sea. The destruction of Convoy TM1 has almost escaped the notice of history, for it lacks the crackling political repercussions and allegations of incompetence attached to PQ17, yet the matter was regarded as serious enough for the Admiralty to order an enquiry into the conduct of the convoy, and it was held at Gibraltar amid disturbing rumours of treachery.

With Captain W.G. Parry of the battle-cruiser *Renown* in the chair, the board considered 'The behaviour of *Vanja*[, which had given] rise to a certain amount of suspicion. Her station-keeping was deliberately bad, and every time a ship was torpedoed, she was well out of the way . . . The W/T Operator of *British Dominion* reported that he had heard homing signals on 500 kcs thought to have come from *Vanja* . . .' Chief Officer G. Alvik of the *Norvik*, himself Norwegian, also mentioned having heard, presumably from his own ship's radio operators, that homing transmissions had been picked up on the same frequency. These were grim allegations, the suggestion that *Vanja* was manned by Quislings and actively informing the enemy of TM1's position an accusation of horrid implication against her Norwegian crew. Captain Andreasson, *Vanja*'s master, had been 'rather upset at receiving a signal from SoE [Boyle] deploring his station-keeping', though this circumstantial fact is quite inconsistent with accusations of treachery. In the event the contention was resolved by the evidence of Captain Randall of the *Cliona*, who deposed that *Vanja*'s poor station-keeping was 'easily . . . attributable to the difficulty she was having with her Diesel engines', which were suffering from a cracked cylinder.

Parry and his board accepted the allegations against the *Vanja* as bordering on the paranoid; besides, there were other matters to consider, including indiscipline aboard *Empire Lytton*, a charge which if adjudged the fault of Captain Andrews might cost him his certificate of competency. Andrews robustly complained that he 'had never sailed with such a bad crew. Their behaviour when the ship was torpedoed was disgusting . . .' Thus was displayed the consequence of the MoWT despatching crews mustered by means of the common Pool, which denied masters any choice of men, as was customary in peace time. Andrews considered 'some disciplinary action should be taken', and intended 'reporting [the matter] to my owners'. He was also anxious that no taint should attach to his officers, whose conduct he described as 'splendid'.

Parry's conclusions dismissed the notion that *Vanja*'s poor station-keeping was deliberate, and he did not consider the indiscipline in *Empire Lytton* attributable to the master or his officers. Instead, he and his board were quite clear that the fault lay with the weakness of the escort, which the failures of the radar sets in *Pimpernel* and *Godetia* had only made worse.[7]

The heavy loss of fuel, men, and ships of a type that even Hessler conceded possessed a great capacity for survival, was an Allied defeat of some magnitude. But the horror of it could be sunk with the convoy's ships. Neither its British and Norwegian survivors nor its casualties enjoyed the cachet of military status, and TM1 was not the first convoy to have been exposed to the enemy by a weak escort. The survivors could be subsumed in other ships; the dead were irretrievably lost.

In the northern part of the Atlantic the strong winds and heavy seas of January and early February 1943 hampered the U-boats, and their potential was further circumscribed by the difficulties of position-fixing in poor visibility and under overcast skies, so that the sharing of precise locations for convoy interceptions made a group attack a matter of difficulty. Despite this the U-boats had some successes during January, Heydemann's *U-268* attacking HX222 on the 17th and sinking the large Panamanian-registered tanker *Vestfold*. In addition to more than 17,000 tons of oil and 19 men, she sank with three landing craft on her deck. HX223 also lost a tanker, the Norwegian *Nortind*, with 11,000 tons of oil and her entire crew. She had straggled and was torpedoed by Kapitänleutnant R. Manke in *U-358* on 26 January. At 03.20 on 2 February, after shadowing for three days in a heavy westerly gale, Kapitänleutnant M. Teichert in *U-456* attacked HX224 and damaged the American Liberty ship *Jeremiah van Rensselaer*. Her crew panicked and abandoned her in disorder, capsizing two boats and leaving one man behind, though he was taken off by a corvette before the ship was sunk by the gunfire of an escort. Despite being holed in Nos 1 and 4 Holds the ship might have been saved. Loss of life was heavy: the rescue ship *Accrington* picked up 24 men, but 46 died in the confusion, most of them drowned. Perhaps more might have survived had Captain Webb not been among the dead but able to retain control of the crew; sadly, however, the inglorious end of this ship is evidence that in finding scratch crews for their new tonnage the Americans too were having manning problems. The curtain was not rung down on this tragedy until a week later, when the Free French corvette *Lobelia* picked up two corpses from a drifting life-raft marked *Jeremiah van Rensselaer*.

Following the convoy, Teichert torpedoed the British tanker *Inverilen* 24 hours later, killing Captain J. Mann and 24 of his crew, 16 being picked up by the corvette *Asphodel*. Another U-boat in Teichert's *Landsknecht*

(Mercenary) group, *U-632*, encountered a straggler. The Bowring tanker *Cordelia* was on Admiralty charter, laden with 12,000 tons of fuel oil for the Clyde. Captain E. Marshall and all except one of his crew were lost. The sole survivor was hauled aboard *U-632*, where under interrogation he 'carelessly' revealed to Kapitänleutnant H. Karpf that HX224 was being followed by the slower SC118.[8]

The consequence of this revelation put a smile back on the face of Grossadmiral Dönitz, for not only had the bad weather frustrated his plans but several of his submarines, including Heydemann's *U-268*, had been lost to Allied aircraft.[9] In addition to commanding the Kriegsmarine's U-boats Dönitz had now succeeded Raeder as Commander-in-Chief of the entire German naval service. Ever on the lookout for an interception, on receipt of Karpf's intelligence he did not hesitate.

Allied merchant ship losses in the higher latitudes of the North Atlantic had dropped dramatically in the bad weather, though the sea had levied its own toll. In January the rescue ship *St Sunniva*, a ferry built for the Aberdeen-to-Shetland service but sailing in support of Convoy ON158, foundered with the loss of 64 dead; it was thought she capsized after being overwhelmed by icing. Convoy ON160 lost the former French cargo-ship *Ville de Tamatave*, under British MoWT management. Her last report indicated that her rudder had been smashed in heavy seas, and she took all 88 of her company to the bottom. In addition to Heydemann's strike, HX223 had suffered a further loss of a loaded tanker, the Norwegian *Kollbjorg*, which broke in two; only those men left on the after part survived, the 12 isolated forward being drowned.

The information let slip by the wretched survivor from the *Cordelia* suggested that SC118 would follow in the wake of HX224, and it was thought by German intelligence that it would 'consist of many ships with cargoes for Murmansk'. Dönitz, acting upon Karpf's report, summoned a group of 20 U-boats to ambush it.[10]

Convoy SC118 was large, 61 merchant ships escorted by Lieutenant Commander F.B. Proudfoot in the destroyer *Vanessa*, leading the B2 Escort Group which comprised HM Destroyers *Vimy, Witch* and *Beverley* and the corvettes *Abelia, Campanula, Mignonette* and *Lobelia*, along with the American Coast Guard Cutter *George M. Bibb*. Numerically it was an impressive if mixed force, but its regular senior officer, Commander D. Macintyre, was absent: his destroyer *Hesperus* required extensive repairs after ramming *U-357*, further eloquent testimony to the desperate and counter-productive nature of this extreme tactic. If this were not enough, Proudfoot was but newly-promoted into *Vanessa*.

Quite apart from the unspeakable folly of the *Cordelia*'s chief engineer airing his views about convoys, probably picked up in his conversations with Captain E. Marshall, the mercantile service made its own contribution to the horrors ahead. On the night of 3/4 February a bored lookout on the Norwegian steamship *Annik* carelessly set off a snowflake rocket. It was observed 20 miles away.

Lying ahead of the convoy on 4 February, some 1,250 miles to the south of Cape Farewell in *U-187*, Kapitänleutnant R. Münnich saw the flare. His sighting report was intercepted by *George M. Bibb* and the HF/DF operators aboard the rescue ship *Toward*. Without orders, Lieutenant Commander R.A. Price increased speed and took the four-stacked *Beverley* from her flanking position at 22 knots, followed soon afterwards through the heavy swell by Lieutenant Commander J.N. Knight in *Vimy*. Münnich dived, but he was on his first patrol in *U-187*, and he was about to be outclassed: Price and Knight nailed *U-187* with their sonars and pounded her with depth-charges, consigning Münnich and eight of the crew to their deaths. From the wreckage they plucked 45 prisoners.

In the hours of the following night five U-boats closed the convoy, probing the screen unsuccessfully, chattering among themselves apparently oblivious to the exposure, and consequently being driven off by the active escort, working at times 20 miles from the convoy. The commodore meanwhile made an alteration in the convoy's course which seriously disturbed the ships' cohesion: a radio failure resulted in Proudfoot not being informed, so while the port three columns maintained the original course, the remaining eleven turned to starboard. It was two hours before the three prodigal lines of ships were swung onto a converging course to unite them with the main body, but fortunately this bifurcation of the flock confused the wolves more than the sheepdogs. In the midst of the disturbance the American transport *Henry R. Mallory* was found by the *Lobelia*, herself engaged in rounding up the errant merchantmen, to be astern of her station. She refused to answer *Lobelia*'s signals.

Kapitänleutnant K. Rudloff in *U-609* and Kapitänleutnant H. Franke in *U-262* now attacked the detached ships. The *Lobelia* succeeded in keeping Rudloff at bay but it is thought that Franke, attacking on the other side, sank the Polish steamer *Zagloba*. The *Beverley* and *Vimy* were soon on the scene, and as she withdrew *U-262* was depth-charged and damaged by *Lobelia* and the two destroyers. Rudloff too attracted Knight's attention, and *Vimy* fired depth-charges at *U-609*. Meanwhile in the rear of the convoy, coming up from the west, Kapitänleutnant G. Poel in *U-413* sighted a straggler, the American freighter *West Portal*, which he sank at 13.00. Her distress calls were monitored by *Vanessa*, but she was lost with all hands.

There were other stragglers and one broken-down ship, the Greek *Polyktor*. It was a situation to tax the escorts, and Proudfoot in particular, though the principal sections of the convoy had re-formed by dawn on the 5th. One frustrated corvette, rounding up a sluggish merchant ship incapable of making the convoy speed in the rough sea, sent 'Hebrews 13 verse 8'. Referring to his Bible, the master of the merchant ship read: 'Jesus Christ [,] the same yesterday, and today, and forever.'

In London the officers manning the Submarine Tracking Room at the Admiralty became concerned by the apparent numbers of U-boats converging on SC118. Consequently, during the afternoon of the 5th, as the *Witch* detached to refuel, the escort was reinforced from Iceland by three American warships, the destroyers *Babbitt* and *Schenk*, and the Coast Guard Cutter *Ingham*. Though the last of these had a defective sonar, the augmentation prevented Rudloff from regaining touch, and it was the following morning before a new contact signal was made by Kapitänleutnant H. Wolff from *U-465*. Happily this was intercepted, and the submarine was bombed by Liberator *X* of No. 120 Squadron, Squadron Leader D.J. Isted, whose presence overhead in the thinning cloud cover deterred other U-boats from making a close approach. To augment this, *George M. Bibb* and *Ingham* were ordered to take station as stern guards in order to deter close shadowing. Among the trailing U-boats Kapitänleutnant R. von Jessen's *U-266* sank the *Polyktor*, picking up as prisoners the master and chief engineer and leaving the remainder to their inevitable fate.

But Rudloff clung on, earning from Dönitz both approbation and exhortations to 'Operate ruthlessly to relieve the Eastern Front!' – where the Wehrmacht had been repulsed at Stalingrad on 2 February. Ominously, after dark on the 6th *U-609* was being joined by other U-boats. The defence was equal to the challenge, however, and *Vimy, Abelia, Lobelia* and *Babbitt* counter-attacked, Knight severely damaging *U-267* and compelling her shaken commander, Kapitänleutnant O. Tinschert, to creep away at 400 feet.

Meanwhile Franke penetrated the defence and fired at a target, but his torpedoes missed or misfired and he was damaged in a depth-charge counter-attack by Capitaine de Corvette P. de Morsier in *Lobelia*. Franke surfaced and ran away at top speed. De Morsier was joined by Lieutenant H.H. Brown in *Mignonette* for a while as the U-boats relentlessly probed the convoy's screen and *Abelia* attacked a U-boat, forcing her to dive. But strong as the escort was, it was outnumbered. As she sought to regain her station *Lobelia* encountered the damaged *U-262* astern of the convoy. Thus far the fight had been fierce and both sides had been equally active, the advantage lying initially with the escort. But the defence of one flank of the convoy necessarily left the other exposed, and SC118 was about to suffer accordingly.

As the hours ticked away and the merchant ships steamed steadily east in good order, two U-boats were in close contact. Moving up shortly after midnight, when his superiors ashore were despairing of any submarines penetrating the escort's screen, Korvettenkapitän Freiherr S. von Forstner took *U-402* through the gap in the starboard screen undetected and made the first of several murderously efficient forays, repeating his performance against SC107 the previous November.

The flank guards were absent and *George M. Bibb* was chasing a Huff-Duff contact 15 miles south of the convoy, while *Mignonette* had turned to investigate another astern. Unfortunately, Brown had been joined by Lieutenant Commander B.A. Royes in *Campanula*, and von Forstner seized his moment. His first victim was the poorly-equipped rescue ship *Toward*, which caught fire and quickly took 46 men, including her entire medical staff, to the bottom; Captain G.K Hudson and 27 survivors were picked up by the *Mignonette*. By then von Forstner had swung and fired his stern tubes, striking the American tanker *Robert E. Hopkins*. Von Forstner dropped back to reload, but his diversion had enabled his colleague Kapitänleutnant W. Sträter to bring *U-614* close to the port side and torpedo the British tramp *Harmala*, which had fallen out of station. Loaded with ore, she settled quickly, her master Captain H.C.Walker and two-thirds of his crew going with her, leaving the pitiful remnant for *Lobelia* to fish out of the water. In the confusion of *Harmala*'s sinking two more escorts swept across the rear of the convoy as *Schenk* eagerly increased speed to ram a U-boat that turned out to be the *Campanula* hunting *U-614*.

Meanwhile de Morsier's radar had picked up a contact and he rang for full speed. The *Lobelia*'s stern settled as she ran down the bearing. Ahead in the darkness Rudloff turned *U-609* away, but a star-shell from *Lobelia*'s gun illuminated him and he crash-dived, swinging to starboard after submerging. De Morsier's sonar operator detected the U-boat's turn and *Lobelia* lobbed a ten-charge pattern before hurrying out of the way of the detonations. De Morsier had the helm over to run back and repeat the process when the sonar operator reported a rumbling. Then they could all hear the noise of the underwater explosion, followed by a gigantic air bubble amid the pallid disturbance left by the depth-charges. Rudloff's *U-609* was finished.

As *Lobelia* completed her work of destruction, *Abelia* on the port bow of the convoy chased off another U-boat, but SC118 was now exposed across its entire rear and von Forstner, the tubes of *U-402* recharged, renewed his assault. Heading for a large tanker, he sank the *Robert E. Hopkins*, Captain R. Blanc. Loaded with British naval bunker oil, the American tanker took two torpedoes, the second of which caused the boilers to explode, and devastating damage. Of the 67 souls on board, a quarter were lost; the *Mignonette* recovered the shaken majority. At 03.40 von Forstner hit a second tanker, the Norwegian *Daghild*, leaving her afloat but damaged and immobile. Dropping back in expectation of a counter-attack, von Forstner experienced none, reloaded and increased speed again. Two hours later he fired and hit the British motor-vessel *Afrika*, and with satisfaction watched her settle. The *Afrika* was loaded with a large military and general cargo of 7,000 tons and 5,000 tons of steel. Captain E.B. Jensen and 22 men went down with their ship, the rest being picked up by the corvettes *Mignonette* and *Campanula*. As he veered away von Forstner caught sight of a large vessel in the squally night and closed her to half a mile. Lining up, he fired a single torpedo.

The *Henry R. Mallory* of New York was a passenger-vessel and as a war transport was carrying 494 people, the majority of them American naval, army and marine personnel intended for the Iceland garrison; she was loaded with military stores, vehicles, mail and foodstuffs. Her master, Captain H.R. Weaver, had just been promoted, having been her chief mate, and her crew lacked training – a common circumstance in the American mercantile marine, since the demand for experienced seamen outstripped supply. Boat-drills had been carried out but they had been perfunctory, and the lifeboats were not swung out; moreover, although the crew was at action stations, including a large armed guard and 16 lookouts, many of her passengers had turned in.

The *Henry R. Mallory* had been a poor station-keeper, partly at least because the ships both ahead and astern were so erratic that constant adjustments of her engine revolutions had been necessary. In the confusion of the night action, with low cloud and snow squalls reducing visibility, Weaver had unwisely hauled out of line and dropped astern, where he maintained a perfect convoy speed of 7 knots, without zig-zagging. Earlier, he had ignored *Lobelia*'s signals that his ship was a sitting duck.

Von Forstner's single torpedo smashed into No. 3 Hold, wrecking the marines' messdeck and the refrigerating plant, then blew the boards off No. 4 Hatch and wrecked two boats. Choking ammonia fumes filled the fore part of the ship and broken companionways inhibited escape, starting a panic. 'We were all helping each other,' one survivor recalled, 'then I saw a bayonet come out. I grabbed a rope and climbed it hand-over-hand.' By contrast, half-sleeping men in other parts of the ship thought the bump no more than a heavy sea.

Quite what happened on the bridge is unclear. No distress signals were transmitted, no red light was hoisted, no snowflakes were fired. Worst of all, there were no orders. Weaver certainly lost his life, and may already have been dead, killed in the blast, but for some time the ship remained steady, and abandonment was in the hands of individuals. A rough sea was running, rough enough to bewilder an untried and inexperienced crew. Only five of the undamaged nine lifeboats were lowered, and of these several had their plugs out or were swamped. One capsized, and one was so severely over-loaded as to be unmanageable. Many rafts were thrown overboard, but many more remained lashed in their places as the *Henry R. Mallory* suddenly began to list and sink. With no supervision from her officers and crew, panic begot disaster. There were some heroic episodes: the single Filipino crew member, a steward, was last seen calmly waking army officers still in their bunks.

The sea was littered with wreckage, debris, boats, rafts and men shouting for rescue from the cold, cold sea. Half an hour later all was silent. The only survivors sat huddled dejectedly in boats or on rafts. With the escorts occupied and SC118 about 15 miles to the east, they had little chance.

Searching astern of the convoy for survivors from the *Toward*, the *Schenk* reported small red life-jacket lights in the water, presumably those of the *Henry R. Mallory's* survivors, but Proudfoot ordered the American destroyer to rejoin the screen: the rescue work would be carried out by the slower corvettes. *Lobelia* was assigned to the task, although she was even further astern and it would be some time before de Morsier reached the survivors' position. Since Proudfoot's primary duty was to protect the convoy, and the faster destroyer was of more immediate value in this, his decision, given *Lobelia's* position, is understandable. This was not however the view of Commander R. Raney in the *George M. Bibb*, who had been chasing a radio bearing to the south-west of the departing convoy, and by great good fortune for the survivors happened to spot a red flare away to the north-west. It was about 07.00 when Raney came across a boatload from the *Henry R. Mallory*, and the full extent of the tragedy became clear.

Stopping to recover these men, Raney reported to Proudfoot what he had learned, but he too was ordered to return to the convoy screen and to leave lifesaving to the corvettes. Raney ignored the order; he was nomin-ally senior to Proudfoot, whom he knew to be only the acting commander of the B2 Escort Group, and the *George M. Bibb* was merely attached to B2, not a permanent member. While there was an understanding that, irre-spective of his substantive rank, the designated escort commander retained tactical control of any situation, Proudfoot *was* British: it may be that old antipathies were stirring in Raney. It is, however, equally probable that the *George M. Bibb's* commander realised that these fortuitously discovered survivors were American service personnel, and bent to his compassionate task. The *George M. Bibb's* men pulled 202 of the total of 267 survivors from the freezing sea, and *Ingham* picked up a further 24 when Proudfoot ordered her to sweep fifty miles astern of the convoy and sink any derelicts. In executing this task, and before she encountered the remnants of the *Henry R. Mallory*, *Ingham* had found the wreckage of von Forstner's next victim.

Proudfoot's anxiety to bring up *George M. Bibb* and *Schenk* to stop the hole in his rear defences was a consequence of the continuing destruction of Convoy SC118. At about 06.10 von Forstner, still unmolested, returned to the attack and torpedoed the Greek tramp *Kalliopi*. Loaded with 6,500 tons of steel and timber she sank quietly and without protest, and some of her crew escaped. When Captain A.M. Martinson arrived on the scene of the disaster in *Ingham*, the day was drawing on. Boats paddled among the floating corpses in a rough sea that capsized 'a British corvette's' small sea-boat. The rescue work went on for several hours, disturbed by one sonar contact, until it was 'getting dark, and the ocean was gray and lonely'. Night had fallen by the time *Ingham* picked up her last boat.

Several U-boats were still in closer contact with the badly shaken convoy than several of its escorts. One, making an approach, was seen close under the bow of the Greek freighter *Adamas*, which altered course to port and ran foul of the brand-new Liberty ship *Samuel Huntington* in the adjacent column; the Liberty ship's bow drove into the hull of the veering tramp. Thinking his ship torpedoed, the *Adamas's* radio-operator transmitted a distress signal, and the commodore ordered an alteration of course while the escorts fired star-shells in response. The *Adamas*, her engine and boiler rooms flooding but her screw still turning, drove across the convoy, adding to the confusion until she stopped twenty minutes later, rolling in a heavy sea churned by the wakes of the vanishing convoy.

The widely-scattered escorts caught up, rescuing survivors as they came and occasionally firing upon one another in the darkness. The *Babbit* rescued some of the *Adamas's* crew and *Lobelia* came across others, and put a depth-charge aboard to sink her. The detonation cracked the *Lobelia's* own thrust block, and the gallant little corvette wallowed in the sea until the destroyer *Vimy* came back to take her in tow. De Morsier and his crew had achieved much in three days of ceaseless action, damaging several U-boats and sinking one, and rescuing nearly seventy merchant seamen; but her disablement only compounded the escort's disarray, and von Forstner's tenacity was pitiless. Shortly before midnight he struck again, torpedoing the British tramp *Newton Ash*. Captain J. Purvis and all but four of her hands were lost with her and her cargo of 6,500 tons of grain and military stores.[11]

How many escaped this ship is unclear. Picking up the *Newton Ash's* survivors was *Ingham's* task as she finally rejoined the convoy. As a relent-less flow of sonar alarms was received Martinson must have been sorely-pressed, torn between his need to recover the merchant seamen, his duty to preserve his ship, and his desire to strike back at the enemy. Nor did the sea mitigate its indifference. One boat was smashed against the cutter's side as she drifted to leeward, crushing a group of men in the water between boat and ship.[12] Of the estimated two dozen in the boat, only three were actually hauled aboard *Ingham*. One man, wearing on his sleeve the four gold rings of senior rank, simply sank. After moving away in response to a sonar contact, Martinson made one final pass and hauled a single Cockney seaman out of the last boat. He broke down on deck, then pulled himself together and thanked his saviours.

Mercifully, not only had von Forstner by now expended all his torpedoes but *U-402* was suffering from engine defects, his crew were showing signs of exhaustion, and the presence of Allied aircraft prevented him from shadowing SC118 on the surface. Receiving his reports, Dönitz's congratulations were accompanied by exhortations: 'Stay there, hold contact . . . Depth-charges also run out. Stay tough. This convoy very important.' With *Vimy* committed to towing *Lobelia* and *Babbit* almost out of fuel Proudfoot was desperate, but at last SC118 was coming under the umbrella of aircraft flying from Northern Ireland.

Von Forstner broke off contact the following forenoon, but the battle was not quite over. Teichert had also clung on until the last moment in *U-456* and had made an attack which had been frustrated by *Beverley*, while far, far astern Oberleutnant Reisener sent a torpedo from *U-608* into the drifting and derelict hull of the *Daghild*, finally sending her to the bottom. The other U-boats half-heartedly trailing SC118 were driven off by aircraft: *U-135* was damaged by a Liberator of No. 120 Squadron and *U-614*, in making an attack on the *Lobelia* under tow, was bombed by a Fortress of No. 206 Squadron. In one last vicious aside, while homeward bound Teichert sank a small coaster off Ireland.

But if the U-boats had given up, the Atlantic had not. Convoy SC118 still had some 450 miles to run before reaching the North Channel. On 10 February, as the *Ingham, George M. Bibb* and *Schenck* headed north with the portion of the convoy destined for Iceland and thereafter Murmansk, the wind began to pipe from the south-west. For four days all the ships laboured in quartering seas with a wind that rose above hurricane force to scatter the convoy over a wide area. *Ingham* had the whole of her No. 4 gun sponson torn away by a green sea, while *Vimy*'s salvage of *Lobelia* became a minor epic.

SC118 was a hard-fought action in which the defence acquitted itself well initially and most of the escorts kept the convoy's defence a priority throughout the action. The temptation to hunt twenty miles from the convoy was understandable, but a mistake, and one not justified, in the final analysis, by the number of enemy submarines destroyed. Despite the presence of a large number of U-boats only one actually penetrated the defence, at a point where no defence existed, and thereafter inflicted a disproportionate amount of damage. The unfortunate loss of *Toward* at the beginning of the action had the effect of diverting too many escorts to the recovery of survivors, and this in turn exposed the rear of the convoy to von Forstner's opportunism. This was a weakness that could only compound itself. Nor, sadly, were the rescue attempts that caused the weakness even hugely successful, as men were abandoned to their deaths by escorts suddenly reacting to sonar alerts. In respect of the *Henry R. Mallory*, some blame for the heavy loss of life must be laid at the doors of those both ashore and afloat who were responsible for her management. The liner had been included in SC118 rather than HX224 only because she was bound for Reykjavik and the earlier, faster convoy contained no other vessels for Iceland.

All in all it was a sorry tale. Dönitz called it 'perhaps the hardest convoy battle of the whole war', extolling the virtues of his commanders and their 'determination and self-control', an encomium hard to stomach when applied to the initiators of terror and destruction. And what of those who held their course and station, passive perhaps, but no less imbued with steadfastness? They attracted no decorations like the *Ritterkreuz* awarded to Freiherr Siegfried von Forstner.

In addition to the complications inherent in his elevation to the chief command of the German navy, Dönitz found that what he called 'this game of chess' had become 'more complicated ... Under the command of Admiral Horton the British anti-submarine forces made great improvements, not only in material and technical means, but also and most particularly in tactical leadership and morale. As an outstanding submarine captain of the First World War . . . Horton was better qualified than anyone else to read the mind of German U-boat Command.'[13]

Horton had the support of an able staff led by Commodore A.S. Russell, while Engineer Rear Admiral Sir Henry Wildish and Rear Admiral (S) H.R.M. Woodhouse headed his engineering and supply sections. Subsidiary departments dealt with health, administration, and the secretariat. His chief liaison officer with the merchant service was his Convoy Secretary, Mr William S. Wellings, a co-opted member of the Elder, Dempster Company's shore staff who, quartered in the Royal Liver Building, was important enough to warrant an armed naval sentry on his outer office door.

In January, Derby House received a visit from the Minister of Aircraft Production, Sir Stafford Cripps, who was a member of Churchill's

Anti-U-Boat Committee. He and Horton concurred over the absolute necessity of obtaining long-range aircraft to cover the convoys. These, the two men agreed, were 'the absolute solution to the U-boat menace', and 39 were expected soon. Supply from America was slow and delayed, and although Cripps had taken steps to modify some 16 Hudsons from Bomber Command, Horton expressed his impatience, and his desire for 50 or 60. Cripps informed Horton 'that the Admiralty had never made a clear and detailed case for V[ery] L[ong] R[ange] aircraft. They had simply asked for more aircraft for Coastal Command without giving detailed reasons and it was mainly owing to their not making out a clear and definite case that the Navy had not done better in the past in regard to its suitable aircraft.' He added that it was not until he himself had suggested it that it began to be taken seriously.

In fact a year earlier, in February 1942, the Admiralty had made a cogent case for 36 Liberators and 54 B-17 Fortresses, repeating the request in May and again in June. Whether or not Cripps's assertion now was an example of political disingenuousness, a bid for Horton's good opinion, or pure self-conceit is irrelevant. It was a sad fact that the long and so-called air-war, the details of which have been touched upon, simply failed to take account of events in the Atlantic, and that the diversion of air assets to the bombing campaign was in some part paid for by the heavy losses of merchant shipping, much *matériel*, and the lives of many wretched merchant seamen.[14]

Cripps shared the view of the Merchant Navy that stigmatised it as a service of bumblingly amateur sea warriors. Picking up a suggestion from Lawrence Holt, senior manager of the Blue Funnel and Glen Lines who was himself punctilious in the training of his crews, Cripps suggested to Horton 'that perhaps greater security in the convoys would be obtained by instruction of the masters by naval officers in regard to station-keeping, manoeuvring, necessity to show no lights, etc.' Horton's response was not short on acid – 'I told him that British masters of merchant ships knew their job pretty well at this state of the war and hardly required instruction in first principles. In fact I suggested they would probably resent it' – only somewhat neutralised by the explanation that 'Cautions with regard to all these matters were given them before every convoy sailed.'[15]

The provision of aircraft was outside Horton's immediate control; improving the navy's ability to protect convoys was not, and he remained concerned by the poor performance still being put up by escort groups, particularly the rapidly mobilised and inexperienced Canadians. In February 1943, as a supplementary training arm to Stephenson's at Tobermory and Roberts's Tactical Training Unit upstairs in Derby House, he created an advanced training facility at Larne in Northern Ireland which was based upon HMS *Philante*, formerly a private motor-yacht (and, after the war, the

Royal Norwegian Yacht *Norge*). Commanded by Captain A.J. Baker-Creswell, whose duty, as Training Captain, was to induct escort groups in active training exercises, the *Philante* played the part of 'the convoy'. With the assistance of Coastal Command aircraft and opposed by two submarines acting as 'U-boats', each escort group was exercised for two days prior to taking a convoy west. In this way Horton 'drove and drove and drove at training; shore training at their bases, sea training with *Philante*, and sea and air training all the time, even when with the convoys . . .'

Up the Dock Road in Gladstone Dock on the Mersey, Horton's escort and support groups were not far away from his headquarters at Derby House and the Naval Control of Shipping based nearby in the Liver Building. On the Clyde they used the James Watt Dock at Greenock and occupied quay space at Moville on Lough Foyle. At each of these bases, back-up staff capable of providing repair and replenishment facilities kept the small, storm-battered warships as nearly in the condition Horton required as circumstances permitted, while their crews enjoyed liberty and rest prior to their work-up for the next convoy.

As for the merchantmen, the increasing assignment of naval and army gunners was improving the ability of these mundane workhorses to fight back, while more and more of them were having their hulls degaussed – magnetically 'wiped' – to reduce their vulnerability to the magnetic mines many of them would encounter if bound to England's east-coast ports by way of the north of Scotland and the North Sea.

Nor were the men of the merchant service themselves left out of this regime, for more and more were being sent to the gradually improving gunnery schools established in all major ports, to hone the skills required for their ancient anti-submarine artillery and to enable them to take advantage of the increasing number of Oerlikons slowly being fitted to merchant ships. They became better able to support the fully-trained service gunners drafted aboard their ships, and in thus improving their ability to fight back, achieved a measure of psychological rehabilitation.

Coincidentally, the German U-boat offensive was at this time at its most effective. Its numerous submarines were ably directed by the Befelshaber der U-Boote supported by the B-Dienst service, then also at the zenith of its achievements.[16] But increasingly effective Allied air cover and the air offensive over the Bay of Biscay, which began in earnest on 4 February, were concentrating German attacks on the North Atlantic air-gap[17] and attacks on convoy routes elsewhere, other than to and from Russia or associated with military operations in the Mediterranean, were slowly abating. If the main target area was the vulnerable section of the trans-Atlantic lifeline, other U-boats nevertheless kept up the ruthless battle against ships sailing independently to the convoy mustering ports, and losses of valuable ships, cargoes and men continued.

On the day that von Forstner opened the offensive against SC118, in the Mediterranean off Algiers *U-77* sank two freighters, *Empire Banner* and *Empire Webster*, in a convoy bound from the Clyde to Bona. Two other British merchantmen, the *Baltonia* and the *Mary Slessor*, also in convoy and heading homeward from Gibraltar, were lost shortly after departure to submarine-laid mines. And before SC118 had arrived in the Irish Sea two more had been sunk off Cape Agulhas, the *Queen Anne* and the *Helmspey*, by *U-509* and *U-516* respectively.

As will appear, the likelihood of survival following a torpedoing was not much improved, and long boat voyages were still being made, like that of the four boats from the British Blue Funnel cargo-liner *Rhexenor* in early February. But the rate of retribution was increasing: in the days following the loss of the *Helmspey* three U-boats were destroyed by British aircraft of Coastal Command, two off Portugal and one in the dreary waters south-east of Cape Farewell.[18]

Few were in a position to perceive the approaching climax, but as early as 8 February Rodger Winn, with his accustomed prescience, was reporting to his superiors in the Admiralty an increase in the numbers of U-boats reporting defects shortly after departing on a war patrol. In Winn's judge-ment this did not necessarily indicate a drop in maintenance standards, but more likely marked a lowering of morale. The establishment of a defect list provided a U-boat commander and his crew with excuses upon which to fall back if the pressures upon them at sea became too great to bear. But as von Forstner had demonstrated, if a confident and numerous escort could but be diverted, one determined and skilful predator could outwit it.

There was as yet little in the way of encouragement for the men manning the merchant ships. Their perceptions were limited to their own immediate horizon, which might be empty, but equally might conceal a sly enemy beneath the grey sea. The merchant jack derived his understanding from what he saw about him: the snowflakes, the alarms; the explosions; the wild-fire of Oerlikons within the convoy; the distant dash of escorts, their worrying absence over the horizon, and the crumps of depth-charge attacks. 'The North Atlantic', one veteran remarked ruefully, 'was full of dead whales.' Such psychological pressures were immense, and invariably enhanced by the enforced helplessness of their passive victims.

And there was that remarkable, intuitive bush-telegraph that had its origins in rumour and speculation born of dread, but which often proved remarkably accurate in the long run and may have owed much to the gossip of the lonely radio-officers and W/T operators. These often very young men sat for hours encapsulated in their headphones listening to the SSSS signals pouring in from across the vast wastes of the ocean, often tricked by atmospheric conditions into believing the enemy to be closer than he was.

So, as the ships of SC118 began to break bulk and discharge their cargoes, the following convoys, SC119 and HX226, were evasively routed round concentrations of U-boats, largely in response to Ultra intelligence, as were the westbound ON166 and ON167. Although it offered an economically less important target than the eastbound convoys, ON166 had attracted attention, and even as German radio-intercepts were monitoring transmissions from Allied aircraft covering its debouchment into the Atlantic, U-boats were moving against it. In the lulls between gales many had been, and were to be, sustained by the two submarine tankers, *U-460* and *U-462*, stationed some five hundred miles north of the Azores. On the forenoon of 20 February, as it steamed along the southern route passing the 50th parallel in longitude 28° West, Convoy ON166 was spotted by Kapitänleutnant H. Höltring in *U-604*.

Led by Commodore Magee, this convoy consisted of 48 merchant ships under the protection of the rather mixed A3 Escort Group commanded by Captain P. Heineman of the United States Navy who was aboard the United States Coast Guard Cutter *Spencer*. Effectively he was a flag officer, since the *Spencer* had her own Coast Guard captain, Commander H.S. Berdine. Also in company was a second Coast Guard cutter, the *Campbell*, and with her five corvettes, the British *Dianthus* and the Canadians *Chilliwack, Dauphin, Rosthern* and *Trillium*. For the first three days of the passage, once clear of Malin Head ON166 had endured atrocious Western Ocean conditions which had disrupted the cohesion of the convoy. By the time that Höltring came in sight of the convoy the weather had eased, but nine vessels were straggling astern.

As the gale blew itself out and darkness fell, Heineman began to receive reports of HF/DF intercepts. He despatched his ships to run down the bearings and in the hours ahead drove off six U-boats; *Spencer* herself detected Höltring ahead of the convoy by radar and forced *U-604* down with a depth-charge attack. The night of 20/21 February was encouraging, but the day and night which followed opened a running engagement that was to cover a thousand miles of ocean. Even before darkness fell the U-boats had closed in, two of them securing their first victim that afternoon. Kapitänleutnant R. Münnich in *U-187* and Oberleutnant H-J. Bertelsmann of *U-603* both fired at the Norwegian tanker *Stigstad*. The three men on duty in the engine room were killed but the *Stigstad* took a quarter of an hour to sink, enabling the remainder to escape by way of a corvette.

As dusk fell and the alarms increased, the escorts worked outwards on their deterrent duty, running down bearings, so that only four of them were in close touch when the next merchantman was torpedoed. The *Empire Trader* had been built for Shaw, Savill & Albion's New Zealand service in 1908 as the *Tainui*.[19] A fine twin-screw steamer in her day, by 1939 she was worn out and had been sold to the breakers, only to be reprieved. She was handed back to her old owners to be managed on behalf of the MoWT under her new name and was commanded by Captain E.T. Baker, who had been nursing her through the gale. Not yet back in her station, she was hit by a torpedo from Kapitänleutnant A. Oelrich's *U-92* and settled but did not sink. Baker determined to save the *Empire Trader* as she wallowed astern of the convoy, and Heineman assigned *Dauphin* to stand by her. Captain T.E. Fea of the rescue ship *Stockport* also dropped back to take aboard some of her crew, but after releasing non-essential men Baker decided to head east under *Dauphin*'s escort. Unfortunately the rescue attempt failed as *Empire Trader* settled and finally had to be abandoned, Baker and his men being taken aboard *Dauphin* as she hurried to rejoin the convoy.[20]

Oelrich next stalked the large Norwegian whale-factory ship *N.T. Nielsen Alonso* and fired both bow tubes at her, killing the three men on watch below but failing to sink the empty extemporised oil-tanker. Heineman ordered the *Campbell* to her assistance and she took 50 men out of their boats, only to discover as she sped back towards the convoy that the Norwegian master had neglected to jettison his confidential books and convoy instructions. Commander J.A. Hirshfield put his helm over and ran back towards the *N.T. Nielsen Alonso*. Korvettenkapitän A.M. von Mannstein had brought *U-753*, one of the U-boats driven off the previous night, close enough to finish off the *N.T. Nielsen Alonso*. His torpedo set the factory ship alight, and Hirshfield, seeing this as *Campbell* approached, judged the breach of security was no longer important. By this time the *Campbell* was upwards of forty miles astern of ON166; as Heineman recalled his widely dispersed pickets and in response Hirshfield raced *Campbell* back to her station, she had three encounters with U-boats.

During the daylight hours of the 22nd the Admiralty Submarine Tracking Room had warned Heineman of mounting evidence of a major attack in the coming night, hence his recall order. Among those affected was Captain Baker, most of whose 106-strong ship's company had been taken off the *Empire Trader* and transferred from *Dauphin* to the rescue ship *Stockport*. He was now compelled to abandon the old liner and join Lieutenant Commander R.A.S. MacNeil in *Dianthus* as the corvette was ordered to shell the former *Tainui*. Meanwhile, the Polish destroyer *Burza* had been ordered to join Heineman from the escort of ON167, away to the east.

From astern she came up with the still-burning *N.T. Nielsen Alonso* and subjected her to a short but fatal bombardment before, soon after dark, taking up a station on the convoy's port flank. She had hardly reached it when the first attack of the night came.

Oberleutnant zur See H. Döhler had been trailing ON166 all day, aware of the weakness of the dispersed defence. Bringing *U-606* close he fired and hit three ships, two Americans, the *Chattanooga City* and *Expositor*, and one British, the *Empire Redshank*. Both *Burza* and the corvette *Chilliwack* responded, the corvette picking up a sonar contact as Döhler swung away to the south, delivering a depth-charge attack and then losing the echo. But as Lieutenant L.F. Foxall broke off, *Burza*'s sonar detected *U-606* and Kapitan F. Pitulko[21] fell upon the Nazi enemy with all the ardour of the dispossessed. Pitulko subjected *U-606* to a number of depth-charges as Döhler took her into a steep dive below the 200-metre limit. Damage was extensive, exacerbated by the great depth, with oil pipes fracturing, a crack in the hull developing and chlorine filling the U-boat. Döhler, an inexperienced commander with a crew whose morale was dubious, gave the order to blow tanks and *U-606* rose to the surface. As she breached, her conning-tower hatch jammed. With *Burza* in the offing it was Hirshfield in *Campbell* who was her nemesis, and his own. Having seen the surfacing U-boat, *Campbell* drove in to ram, her guns firing. But she did not hit the U-boat squarely, and as two depth-charges were being lobbed over the stern the big cutter grazed down the U-boat's side. *U-606*'s hydroplane sliced into the *Campbell*'s side like a can-opener, admitting water into her engine room. Then the U-boat drifted astern, illuminated by *Campbell*'s searchlight. The firing of the cutter's guns ended only when the water in her engine room caused the generators to short-out.

Döhler meanwhile, having reached the deck by way of the forward torpedo hatch, opened the conning tower from the outside and ordered his men on deck. Shortly afterwards he was blown into the sea by a shell-burst, after which *U-606*'s crew surrendered. *Campbell* was also badly damaged and flooding. As the German crew's morale finally collapsed a rescue operation took place in which only a dozen survived as the U-boat sank.[22] Hirschfield's men, meanwhile, had set about heeling their ship, jettisoning fuel and getting a collision mat over the hole.[23] Three hours later *Burza* arrived to screen *Campbell*, but she was short of fuel and the next day had to divert to St John's without even turning aside to pick up survivors spotted by air patrols; she did however carry with her the 50 men from the *N.T. Nielsen Alonso*, taken off *Campbell*.[24] In her place *Dauphin* began to tow the *Campbell* towards a safe haven, but she was eventually hauled into St John's by the tug *Tenacity*.

Most of the recipients of *U-606*'s torpedoes had been picked up. The torpedo that hit the *Chattanooga City* had fractured her propeller shaft and so damaged her plating that after lifting bodily in the water, the Isthmian steamer began to sink. Captain R. Forbes and all hands escaped in the boats and were hauled aboard *Trillium* three hours later. The *Expositor*, Captain J. Klepper, was also severely battered: Döhler's torpedo destroyed three boats, blew in a boiler, and filled the accommodation with scalding steam. Six men died as the rest scrambled aboard the remaining boats and a raft. Of the 48 men picked up by *Trillium*, two died of their wounds. As for the *Expositor*, she wallowed in the convoy's wake until sunk later that day by *U-303*. Döhler's third victim, the *Empire Redshank*, the former American standard-ship *Braddock* built in 1919, was immobilised and abandoned by Captain J.H. Clinton and all hands, who in due course were also picked up by the *Trillium*. Lieutenant P.E. Evans, finishing his assigned task of rescue, fired several shots into the *Empire Redshank* and completed her destruction.

Heineman's depleted escort group was increasingly hampered throughout the succeeding hours. During the early hours of the 23rd the convoy had also lost another supporting vessel. Earlier that day, striving to catch up with ON166 after standing by the *Empire Trader*, the *Stockport* had been torpedoed by Höltring, still trailing the convoy in *U-604*. There were no survivors. The little London & North Eastern Railway Company's steamer, built in 1911, had sunk with her master, Captain T.E. Fea, his merchant naval crew of 51, nine naval gunners, 6 naval HF/DF staff and at least 91 of the survivors she had been tasked to rescue.

During the same period, Kapitänleutnant H. Hasenschar in *U-628* attacked ON166 and fired at two tankers, damaging them both. The Norwegian tanker *Glittre* did not sink but she was immobilised, her engine-room crew dead; the remainder took to the boats. The second was the *Winkler*, Panamanian-registered but beneficially owned in Philadelphia. She seemed capable of steaming and her master, seeing *U-628* surface, put his helm over and rang for full speed in an attempt to ram the U-boat. As the tanker swung, her gun's crew got in several shots, claiming a hit on the conning tower. As Hasenschar took to the depths, *Winkler* ranged up alongside the *Glittre*'s Norwegians in their boats and her master offered to pick them up. His offer was turned down; they would take their chances. The *Winkler* headed back for the convoy, but before she could resume her station she was hit by *U-223*. Kapitänleutnant K-J. Wächter sent *Winkler* to the bottom, only 19 of her people being rescued by *Dianthus*. This corvette also took up the *Glittre*'s survivors, and within three hours Bertelsmann had fired two more torpedoes from *U-603* into *Glittre*, finally sinking her.

As dawn began to lighten the eastern sky on the morning of the 23rd, Kapitänleutnant S. Hesemann in *U-186* penetrated the screen and fired at two targets. One torpedo hit the American freighter *Hastings* in No. 5 Hold and blew in all her after bulkheads, flooding her two after holds and her engine room. Nine of her crew were lost as Captain R.O. West ordered his men into the boats. In seven minutes their ship was gone, and within half an hour of the strike they were being hauled aboard the *Chilliwack*, who had hurried up to locate their attacker. Hesemann had also hit the *Eulima*. The British Shell tanker was not mortally hurt, and although she fell astern and out of her station, Captain F.W. Wickera considered she might be saved.

These disasters notwithstanding, the escort had not been idle. Several U-boats fired torpedoes at them and Heineman and Berdine in the *Spencer*, working across the front of the convoy, had made numerous depth-charge attacks on sonar contacts. As Hesemann hit the *Hastings*, the *Spencer* was in contact with a U-boat and damaged *U-454*, forcing Kapitänleutnant B. Hackländer to the surface. The attack had drawn *Spencer* far from the convoy, however, and Heineman broke off the action without further harrying Hackländer.

Heineman's problems were now compounded; the weather remained poor, with too heavy a sea running for him to be able to refuel his ships from their auxiliary oiler. At this point MacNeil, himself rejoining after the abortive attempt to succour *Empire Trader* and acting as rescue ship, reported that *Dianthus* was chronically short of fuel. Heineman was compelled to detach her to steam directly to St John's, where she arrived burning all surplus oils available on board.

Hesemann, meanwhile, had avoided detection and let the convoy pass above him. As the main body drew away and he returned *U-186* to periscope depth, he saw his wounded victim and, awaiting his moment, fired into her again. This time there was no doubt: the *Eulima* sank, taking Wickera and 61 men with her. Three survived. Hesemann picked up Third Officer J. Campkin, landing him at L'Orient bound for Milag Nord, while two other officers were pulled aboard Massmann's *U-409*. Unlike Hesemann, Hasenschar had remained in close touch in *U-628*, and on the 24th he fired at the fine 11-knot Norwegian cargo-vessel *Ingria* of Bergen. This ship was also hit by Kapitänleutnant B. Zurmühlen in *U-600*, but sank slowly enough for all hands to escape and seek refuge aboard a corvette.

By now the convoy was approaching soundings on the Grand Bank, but it remained in some disarray. One straggler was the Liberty ship *Jonathan Sturges*, which at around midnight was hit by two torpedoes from *U-707*. Oberleutnant G. Gretschel's U-boat was in pursuit of ON166 after refuelling from *U-460* east of Newfoundland, and it was her only contact with the convoy. The new, all-welded *Jonathan Sturges* was almost severed forward of the bridge, and Captain T. Leerburg gave immediate orders to abandon her. Two lifeboats got away with 36 men, and one of them met a boat from the Dutch cargo-liner *Madoera* which contained only a handful of men. Some of the American seamen joined the Dutch, and both boats were picked up on 12 March by the USS *Belknap*.

The *Madoera* had been damaged by a torpedo from *U-653*, Kapitänleutnant G. Feiler, but the Dutch vessel, although partially abandoned, had not sunk and was eventually towed into St John's. Meanwhile the *Jonathan Sturges's* second boat, which had initially contained 17 men under Captain Leerburg, was not found until it had been adrift for an excoriating 41 days. Only five men remained alive, two of the Liberty ship's crew and two from her naval Armed Guard.

On the 25th, as ON166 moved into the mists hanging over the shoaling waters of the Grand Bank and Heineman's A3 Escort Group was relieved by the Local Western Escort, the U-boats began to lose contact. The operation was broken off with a Parthian shot fired from *U-628* by Hasenschar. He sank the almost new cargo-liner *Manchester Merchant*. The big, empty ship went down in a minute and a half, drowning 35 men, though Captain F. Struss and 31 others were dragged from the freezing sea by HMS *Montgomery* and HMCS *Rosthern*.

The attack on ON166 was a victory for the Germans; the sole mitigating factor for the Allies was that only the *Empire Trader* had carried any cargo, a small consignment of 990 tons of chemicals. It was cold comfort for Heineman and Horton, none the less; colder still for the American crew of the *Jonathan Sturges*, still bobbing astern, dying slowly in the convoy's wake.

23

'Fireflies in the water'

Lulworth

With the month's losses at more than sixty merchantmen, Horton was very sensible that the escorts were being beaten. As a submariner himself, he also knew that the attrition rate would have been worse if the Germans had pressed their attacks with greater vigour. What Winn had divined by analysis, Horton may have known in his bones: that the U-boats were lacking *edge*. The Commander-in-Chief, Western Approaches sensed that the decisive moment was at hand, and champed for the means to seize it and stem the haemorrhage of men and *matériel*.

He plied the Admiralty with requests to hasten the long-promised delivery of escort-carriers and he harried his departmental heads, now coping with a large number of escorts damaged by the weather and by incautious contact with the enemy. But most ardently he pressed for more new anti-submarine vessels to augment his rapidly coalescing support groups. These were gradually entering service, vessels vastly more sophisticated than the stop-gap corvettes. In early 1943 Lieutenant Commander W.J. Moore took command of the new sloop *Whimbrel*, which he later recalled as 'a very complex ship, with her formidable A/A armament of six 4-inch guns and associated fire control system, two twin Bofors guns on stabilised Hazemeyer mountings, Denny brown stabilisers, paravanes, the latest type of radar, HF/DF and Asdics (sonar), plus all the usual depth charges . . . a speed of 20 knots and a complement of 250 officers and men . . .'

At the time Horton's predecessor, Sir Percy Noble, was in America attending an Atlantic Convoy Conference in Washington chaired by the United States Naval Commander-in-Chief, Admiral King, at which he represented Horton's interests with great ability. Among the many differences between the Allies there was at least a '[m]utual understanding of the air problem . . . recommendations were made for a redistribution of available aircraft and . . . to convert a quota of bombers for anti-U-boat duties. *If a decision to this effect could have been taken a year earlier, many ships with their priceless cargoes would have been saved* [my emphasis: RW].'

But even as Horton groped for dominance, he knew it could not be achieved overnight, and if February was bad, with its new intelligence blackout due to the German's introduction of their M-4 cypher machine, March was worse. The Admiralty's Submarine Tracking Room was stifled from 8 March to the 19th, when Bletchley Park's ten senior cryptographers working on the German naval Enigma traffic finally broke the so-called 'Shark' code; his escorts were defective from battle and bad-weather damage; and word of terrible losses running through the docks of the kingdom was rattling the nerves of ill-informed merchant seamen.

February had ended with more gales. Winds blew at storm force for days on end, humping up huge seas with half a mile between their crests. Even an eastbound convoy could find such a quartering blow disruptive. When Heineman's A3 Escort Group, hardly recovered from its ordeal with ON166, took over the escort of SC121 on 4 March, it was to find the convoy bereft of the Local Western Escort, its senior officer alone in HMS *Witherington* ten miles astern of the merchantmen, and SC121 on the point of disintegration in the appalling weather. Heineman requested Commodore H.C. Birnie to re-form from fourteen columns to eleven, to enable his six escorts to make a fist of their defence. Birnie, worried about the ships' station-keeping, suggested waiting until the weather moderated; reluctantly, Heineman concurred. He had more pressing problems. Heavy aeration under the warships' tossing hulls reduced their sonar ranges, while blinding snow-squalls cut visibility, and the sea-clutter inevitable with a heavy sea reduced the effectiveness of their radars. Such weather might have been expected to deter the U-boats, but the only effective electronic counter-measure, HF/DF, was indicating several of them on the flanks of SC121. By daylight on 6 March Heineman's group consisted of *Spencer*, the USS *Greer* and the corvettes *Dianthus, Dauphin, Rosthern* and *Trillium*. Also in company was the rescue ship *Melrose Abbey*.

That night *U-230* penetrated the convoy and torpedoed the Ellerman & Papayanni liner *Egyptian* with her cargo of West African oilseed, palm oil and tin ore. Adjacent merchantmen opened fire on the U-boat as it was seen within the convoy and snowflake rockets were fired, but Kapitänleutnant P. Siegmann ran clear. Heineman was unaware that any vessel had been hit, and it was not until Lieutenant R.J.G. Johnson of *Rosthern* reported lights astern of the convoy and steamed to investigate that it became apparent that another merchant ship, the *Empire Impala*, had slowed to attempt the rescue of the *Egyptian*'s crew. Quite how many men Captain T.H. Munford's act of compassion saved is uncertain; quite how difficult it was in the heavy seas then running may be guessed at; but the consequence was that the *Empire Impala* failed to catch up with the main body of the convoy.

It was a paradox that often the merchantmen, even within the protective pale of the convoy, were closer to the enemy than the escorts. Captain R. Coates of the *Kingswood*, lumbering through the black night and the gale, saw a U-boat wake so close that he turned the bluff bow of his tramp-ship to ram. Over the roar of the wind and the breaking waves Coates heard the evading helm order shouted below him in German as the two vessels passed within feet of one another. His gunners engaged, but by then the U-boat was astern, lost in the darkness amid the heaving black seas.

During the early forenoon of the 7th Kapitänleutnant H. Zetzsche in *U-591* torpedoed the *Empire Impala*. Only three of *Egyptian*'s men, having found a refuge on board her, were again hauled out of the vile sea by *Rosthern*; Munford and 40 of his hands aboard *Empire Impala* perished, along with Captain D.V. Murphy and 45 men from the *Egyptian*.

As the daylight hours wore on and SC121 passed the meridian of Cape Farewell, several sighting and sonar contacts with U-boats were made by the escorts, and at one point the merchant ships in the rear of the convoy opened fire on a conning tower. Alerted to events, Horton ordered the American vessels *Ingham* and *George M. Bibb* to sail from Reykjavik and reinforce Heineman. The *Ingham*, having had her sonar dome repaired in the British floating dry-dock at Hvalfjord, lost it again as she pounded south to join SC121. Other escorts were suffering from the usual crop of defects induced by heavy weather, and Heineman's burden was increased by the alarming number of stragglers, which now included the Canadian corvette *Trillium*, and one romper, another Ellerman ship, the *Guido*. On 8 March, as Zetzsche continued his destruction of stragglers in the rear of the convoy by sinking the Yugoslavian *Vojvoda Putnik* with the loss of all hands, Möglich in *U-526* torpedoed the *Guido* in full view of Heineman and Berdine in *Spencer*. The Coast Guard cutter attempted to counter-attack, but lost contact. Instead she picked up Captain G. Mussared and all but ten of his crew, at the cost of an engine put out of action for two hours as a loose rope was cleared from a condenser intake.

That afternoon, when *George M. Bibb* and *Ingham* joined the escort, the U-boats were still concentrating against the straggling merchantmen in the rear of the main convoy, and sunk several. Again a number of the merchant ships opened fire with their guns, and one almost succeeded in ramming a U-boat, while the escorts continued their own aggressive counter-moves, *Spencer* driving off *U-229*. But that night was to prove disastrous. Oberleutnant H-F. Massmann in *U-409*, still with the tanker *Eulima*'s officers on board, torpedoed the American freighter *Malantic*, whereupon part of her cargo of 8,000 tons of explosives counter-mined.

Badly burned, Captain E. Knowles ordered the *Malantic* abandoned in the surviving port boats. Four hours later the *Melrose Abbey*, covered by the *George M. Bibb*, found one man in the water and Captain Knowles's boat with ten men in it. The second cook held her alongside the *Melrose Abbey* as his shipmates climbed up her scrambling nets, but when it came to his turn he lost his grip and fell into the sea. One officer went in after him, but it was too late. Knowles then told *Melrose Abbey*'s master, Captain R. Good, that there was another boat in the offing, but when this was located it capsized, trapping several men. The remaining ten were hauled aboard the rescue ship with great difficulty.

Massmann also hit the tanker *Rosewood*, acting as oiler to the escorts, but Captain R. Taylor continued in station for a while, until the stresses on the *Rosewood*'s hull proved too much and she began to break up. The night had now become chaotic. The escorts fired snowflakes, but in the heavy sea all that could be seen were the single red lights being hoisted aloft as merchantmen reported being hit by torpedoes. With *Melrose Abbey* and *George M. Bibb* still astern tending to the *Malantic*'s boats, Heineman lost *Dauphin* to the duty of rescue ship.

Among the convoy's columns Oberleutnant R. Schetelig in *U-229* fired a salvo of torpedoes, hitting three ships, the *Nailsea Court*, the *Bonneville*, and the *Coulmore*. The British tramp *Nailsea Court* was carrying a valuable cargo including copper, nickel ore and asbestos; almost all hands were lost, including the master, Captain R.J. Lee, only three men being picked up by *Dauphin* and, later, one by *Melrose Abbey*. The *Bonneville* was a Norwegian freighter carrying Commodore Birnie, his staff and a military cargo; as she began to settle, her crew abandoned her. The third ship, the *Coulmore*, while damaged and stopped, was not in a sinking condition, but in the confusion the crew had lowered boats and rafts. Approaching her as *Dauphin* went about her work of rescue, the *Greer* requested permission to pick up survivors. Heineman ordered *Greer* to leave this task to *Dauphin*, but to screen her. Unfortunately the corvette now suffered a failure of her steering gear.

The rescue operation, difficult enough in the prevailing conditions, was further hampered by breakdowns. Despite their best intentions, the ships engaged in this task rolled down upon the lifeboats and life-rafts, upsetting or damaging them; men within sight of succour fell back into the sea cold and exhausted. Only seven men escaped from the *Bonneville*, whose master died near a raft with Birnie. At the height of the shambles *Spencer*'s radio failed, so that Heineman lost control of the tactical situation. *George M. Bibb* and *Melrose Abbey* finally arrived, releasing *Dauphin* and *Greer*, but the damage had been done. As *Greer* steamed back towards the convoy she again came upon the *Coulmore*. *Coulmore*'s forepeak had a hole in it, but she was otherwise afloat and in no danger of sinking. It appeared that of two boats lowered, one had drifted away and the second had capsized, losing 14 men. Raney's *George M. Bibb* located one raft upon which clung seven freezing survivors. His final task before returning to SC121 was to search for the *Rosewood*. She had broken in half and both parts remained afloat, miles apart. *George M. Bibb*'s shelling put paid to her; Captain Taylor and his 40 men were gone. On Raney's return his lookouts again spotted the *Coulmore*, lying a-hull and rolling in the hollow of the sea. Raney reported her position and she was afterwards salvaged and towed into port, to survive long after the war.

Grindingly bad weather and poor maintenance had undoubtedly exacerbated the escort's difficulties, but they were no excuse: the escort had been inadequate to the challenge, and the consequent losses had been immense because in addition to the ships mentioned, others had been torpedoed straggling astern of the convoy. One of these was the *Fort Lamy*, sunk with her military cargo by *U-527* (Uhlig): of her crew only 12 were found by the corvette *Vervain*, after 12 days adrift. Another, the *Empire Lakeland*, had been torpedoed by *U-190* (Wintermeyer) with the loss of all hands and her cargo of general and frozen foodstuffs. Both theses ships sank on 8 March. On the 11th the Swedish *Milos* was sunk with all hands and a cargo of steel and timber by *U-530* (Lange); and the *Leadgate* was sunk by *U-642* (Brünning) on the 13th. It was a sad, sad tally – but the fate of SC121 was overshadowed by another convoy battle already raging.

While an attack on HX227 yielded only two stragglers, and Dönitz's numerous U-boats missed several east- and westbound convoys, the story changed on 10 March. There was no Enigma-derived Ultra intelligence available to the Admiralty in the continuing blackout that followed the introduction of the Enigma's fourth rotor; in contrast, B-Dienst had a firm grip on affairs and had been able to advise Dönitz's staff of another laden eastbound convoy. Then came a sighting signal from Kapitänleutnant H. Hunger in *U-336*: Convoy HX228 had been located.

Consisting of 59 merchantmen under Commodore J.O. Dunn aboard the *Tetela*, plus the Royal Fleet Auxiliary tanker *Orangeleaf*, HX228 was escorted by Commander A.A. Tait's B3 Escort Group. From *Harvester* Tait commanded three other destroyers, HMS *Escapade*, ORPs *Garland* and *Burza*, HM Corvettes *Orchis* and *Narcissus*, and the Free French corvettes *Aconit*, *Roselys* and *Renoncule*. This convoy was also joined by the American 6th Support Group, commanded by Captain Short in the escort-carrier USS *Bogue* with the destroyers and cutters *Belknap, Osmond* and *Ingham*. However, a serious error was made in deploying the *Bogue* in the centre of the convoy, where it was thought she would be well protected – but where she was unable to manoeuvre. This was something of an egregious blunder, for experience of operating carriers in support of convoys was not wanting, having by this time been obtained by the Royal Navy in the Mediterranean. When deployed in the rear of the convoy – not the centre – they not only had room to manoeuvre but deterred U-boats from approaching that vulnerable area, and blocked their traditional escape route. The USS *Bogue*'s presence with HX228 seems to have been to little effect, and flying operations were further hampered by the bad weather.

Nevertheless, although some 18 U-boats were being mustered to attack, Hunger had already received unwelcome attention from an Avenger flying an air patrol from the *Bogue*. But in two attacks the aircraft's bomb release gear had failed and *U-336* had escaped, only to be driven off a second time on the 10th. HX228 was now however in the periscope sights of Oberleutnant A. Langfeld, who began to stalk it in *U-444*.

Kapitänleutnants F. Deetz in *U-747* and H. Trojer in *U-221* had also located the convoy. Trojer had a few days earlier sunk the solitary Norwegian motorvessel *Jamaica* far to the west of Ireland, and he was to be the first to attack HX228. At about 21.30, from a surfaced position inside the convoy and undetected in the darkness, he fired a salvo, claiming an unsubstantiated hit. His second salvo was aimed at two merchantmen leading a column. He sank both. The leading ship was the British fruit-carrier *Tucurinca* now carrying a general cargo including food and mail, and ten Canadian air force officers. Only the third engineer was lost, Captain J.A. Moore and 77 officers and men being rescued by *Roselys*. Trojer's second torpedo struck the American freighter *Andrea F. Luckenbach*, immediately astern of the *Tucurinca*. Two torpedoes detonated a cargo of explosive ammunition in the freighter's stern, which 'disintegrated ... in flames and a vast cloud of smoke. Hundreds of steel plates flew through the air like sheets of paper ...' killing 11 of her armed guard closed up round her stern gun and 11 men accommodated in her poop. Her engine stopped, the *Andrea F. Luckenbach* began to settle by the stern and Captain R. Neslund ordered her abandoned. Two lifeboats got away, other men jumped into the sea and clung to wreckage or, most extraordinarily, some bomb cases which had been part of her cargo. In due course they scrambled up the side of the *Orangeleaf*.

Shortly afterwards, at 23.30, Langfeld fired at the *William C. Gorgas* from *U-444*. Captain J.C. Ellis's Liberty ship was carrying a cargo of explosives, food, steel, landing craft and two naval motor-patrol boats. Langfeld's torpedo destroyed the engine room and the vessel listed and began to settle, although she did not sink immediately. About twenty minutes after being hit Ellis ordered his crew into the boats and personally supervised the escape of 51 men. Deetz in *U-757* was also at large among the merchantmen and fired at the Norwegian *Brant County*. Her holds contained a general and military cargo, including 670 tons of TNT which blew up with such force that 35 of her crew were killed instantly, and both *U-757* and *U-221* were damaged. According to Dunn, she '[b]urst into flames . . . like an inferno and lit everything up like daylight. I could see the whole convoy and [the] escorts ahead and on both wings.'

Retribution of a more specific sort was bearing down on the predators as Tait swung *Harvester* and brought her down through the convoy, illuminating the sea with snowflake flares. Seeing the destroyer approaching as he sought to steal out through the rear of HX228, Langfeld dived. But Tait's accurate depth-charge attack prevented his escape and *U-444* surfaced, to be rammed by *Harvester*. The destroyer rode up over the U-boat and became locked as *U-444* fouled *Harvester's* extended propeller-shafts. For ten long minutes the two vessels wallowed together in the darkness, the high-pitched shriek of grinding steel piercing the night as Tait and his men tried to disentangle their ship and Langfeld ran his engines full astern. Finally the two separated, Tait drawing *Harvester* away on one propeller driven by a wounded shaft.

Unlike his colleague Deetz had escaped as the convoy passed, and shortly after midnight on the 11th saw the dark loom of the wallowing *William C. Gorgas*. Although *U-757* was damaged Deetz torpedoed her, the TNT exploding with a terrible concussion which blew the bow off the Liberty ship, sinking her about an hour later.

As *Harvester* strove to catch up the convoy, the French corvette *Aconit*, sent to her assistance, came upon *U-444* on the surface. Capitaine de Corvette Levasseur rang on full speed and rammed the U-boat, sending Langfeld and his crew into the abyss. Tait rejected *Aconit's* assistance and ordered Levasseur to rejoin the convoy escort, arguing that her presence there, even with a damaged bow, had the priority. *Harvester* was making the best of her way to the rear of the convoy when at about 07.00 she came in sight of the two lifeboats and rafts of the *William C. Gorgas*. She needed little checking to slow down and recover the Americans, after which she continued her painful progress. Then, at about 11.00, *Harvester's* remaining shaft sheered, she came to a standstill, broached, and lay rolling in the trough of the heavy sea. Tait's distress signal had Levasseur reversing his course, but it was too late, and Tait paid a heavy price for the damage inflicted upon *U-444*, and his concern for HX228: at 13.06 the *Harvester*, wallowing and helpless, was hit by two torpedoes fired by Kapitänleutnant H. Eckhardt from *U-432*, skulking in the convoy's wake.

With the extreme rolling of the stricken destroyer no boats could be launched, and officers, ratings and the rescued merchant seamen jumped over her rails. *Aconit*, her mangled bow pushing a huge bow wave before her as she breasted the lumpy sea, was within sight of the column of smoke the explosion threw up and received Tait's last signal. At her best speed the corvette closed the scene and Levasseur, picking up a sonar contact, vigorously attacked *U-432*, pounding the U-boat with depth-charges. Eckhardt was beaten: *U-432* surfaced and was shelled. For the second time that day, *Aconit* drove her bow into a U-boat. Eckhardt and half his crew went down with their submarine but a score of survivors were taken aboard *Aconit*, along with the remnants of *Harvester*'s and the *William C. Gorgas*'s people. Both Tait and Ellis were among the missing.[1]

Two U-boats, *U-590* and *U-440*, remained in contact with HX228 until the early hours of 12 March, but under the leadership of *Escapade* the escort drove them off, and the convoy arrived in the Irish Sea three days later. It was some comfort, perhaps, that ON170, escorted by Commander D. MacIntyre's B2 Escort Group, completely outwitted five U-boats by brilliant use of HF/DF intercepts; and that ON171, escorted by the B1 Escort Group and routed far to the north on the great-circle route under Cape Farewell, had also passed unmolested. This was indeed a double relief, for ON168 and ON169 had suffered terribly from straggling in appalling weather that also prevented the escorts from refuelling. The British ships *Empire Light* and *Baron Kinnaird* had both been torpedoed, as had the American *Rosario* and the Panamanian *H.H. Rogers*, while the Liberty ship *Thomas Hooker* broke in two and foundered after her welded hull failed.

Before either SC121 or HX228 had reached their destination, within 24 hours of each other, three following convoys had left New York: SC122 on 5 March, HX229 on the 8th and HX229A on the 9th. Like most trade convoys in the slow series, Convoy SC122 was composed of many vessels making only a part of the long voyage. Of those which left New York, five were bound for Halifax or St John's, while a further seven would detach for Iceland during the passage.[2] Other ships would join it from Halifax, two of which were also bound for Iceland. With nine vessels for Reykjavik, those heading for Britain amounted to 38 from New York, 11 from Halifax and one from St John's.[3] With them went the rescue ship *Zamalek*.

Among the nominally British-flagged vessels were exiled Norwegian tankers and former French vessels, and the overall mixture of ships was eclectic. The commodore was embarked in the *Glenapp*, one of several valuable cargo-liners in the convoy, while the flour-laden *Ogmore Castle* had been built as a War-Emergency standard-ship a generation earlier and could do no more than 8.5 knots. Marginally faster and a little newer was the *Carso*, an ex-Italian ship salvaged from the bottom of Mogadishu harbour and repaired; she was manned by a crew scraped together from survivors at Cape Town consisting of British officers and lascar ratings. At the other end of the spectrum was the brand-new *Fort Cedar Lake*. Supposedly capable of 12 knots, she was suffering from engine trouble, hence her assignment to a slow convoy. She also had other problems.

Standing-by as their ship was completed in Canada, and later during her loading, her 'crowd' could not resist the lure of alcohol, and caused her master and the local authorities great problems. The *Fort Cedar Lake* suffered from a steady haemorrhage of deserters, including two men who ran on the eve of sailing. So increasingly desperate to man its merchantmen was the MoWT that situations like this rose in proportion as time passed. Young and inexperienced crews who lacked the steadying influence of older hands gained the British Merchant Navy a bad reputation in certain quarters.

Convoys HX229 and HX229A were made up of faster liners and freighters carrying higher-value cargoes, in contrast to the homogenous bulk ladings of SC122. There were also the tankers with their loads of black and white oils: six sailed in SC122, ten in HX229, eleven in the trans-Atlantic portion of HX229A. At least two of these, the *Svend Foyn* and *Southern Princess*, were capacious converted whale-factory ships.[4] HX229A also left New York with detachments bound for Halifax, St John's and Iceland, but these were smaller than those assigned to the SC convoy. All HX229's 40 vessels were bound directly for Britain and included, in addition to one 'Fort'-class and two newly built 'Empire'-class vessels, eight Liberty ships.[5]

Of the others involved, two refrigerated cargo-liners, Donaldson's *Coracero* and Royal Mail's *Nariva*, had both loaded boned carcases in the Rio de la Plata. To avoid the U-boats off the Brazilian coast they had headed south, doubled Cape Horn, and proceeded north to the Panama Canal before picking up the American navy's interlocking convoy system in the Caribbean in order to reach New York safely.

For the men aboard this multitude of ships assembling off Sandy Hook, the attractions of New York were expensive but wonderful, a sybaritic contrast to the dismal grey wastes of the North Atlantic in early spring, or the gloomy blackout of the bombed ports awaiting them on the further shore. New Yorkers made them welcome; in addition to the bars, clubs, strip joints and traditional watering-holes of the merchant jack, including the Stage Door Canteen, after which a Liberty ship was later named, there were the British Merchant Navy Officers' Club, the British Apprentices' Club, Dutch and Norwegian Seamen's Clubs, Seamen's Missions, and the general hospitality of the American Legion. Few places did more to make the merchant seafarer feel his contribution to the war effort was properly appreciated. As for the masters, mates and engineers taking over Canadian- and American-built ships, whatever the shortcomings of their green crews might be, most of them, used to the profligate, wasteful and dilatory methods of their native land, found that the specially-trained, new-to-the-task work-forces in the building yards of the New World could put a ship together in exemplary fashion. Moreover, such ships, though built hurriedly and under wartime restrictions, provided facilities only to be dreamed of in the scrimped tramps they replaced.

But once aboard, the grim imperatives of the sea-life impinged, even in the assembly anchorages. Ice-floes slid down the Hudson River, fogs lay cold over the flat, grey water, and when the wind blew and ships began to move in the crowded roads, anchors dragged and minor collisions were not infrequent. It was this congestion that decided the naval authorities to split HX229 in two, despite the shortage of escorts due to necessary repairs, and the notion that large convoys were advantageous. Tentative steps had been taken to sail HX228 as a very large convoy, but the exercise had been only partially successful.[6]

All three convoys had commodores with merchant service backgrounds who had long been commissioned in the RNR. Formerly of the Booth Line, Commodore S.N. White boarded the *Glenapp* in SC122; Commodore M.J.D. Mayall, previously a Canadian Pacific master, joined the Norwegian-flagged *Abraham Lincoln* in HX229; and Commodore D.A. Casey, once of the Royal Mail Line, took passage in the *Esperance Bay* to lead HX229A. The usual appointments of vice and rear commodores were made from among the experienced masters available in each convoy.

In addition to their cargoes, many of the ships carried passengers, ranging from servicemen to government contractors and from female Red Cross personnel *en route* to Iceland to British children being brought home from Burma and Malaya, all now under Japanese occupation. More than a hundred 'DBSs', Distressed British Seamen, all of them convoy survivors, were put aboard the *Svend Foyn*.

The pre-sailing conferences, by now a routine ritual, had thrown up the usual arguments about the lack of escorts and the time zone, or zones, in which operational orders would be given, countered by the customary warnings about the dire consequences of making smoke and keeping poor station. The day SC122 left New York was unpleasant, with 'scudding cloud . . . a yellow hazy sun' and a rough, 'dirty brown' sea. The following morning the first ship dropped out: the 1903-built *Georgios P.* was unable to make 7 knots in the freshening southerly wind which kicked up an uncomfortable, quartering sea. By the next day, 24 February, a gale was blowing and station-keeping became difficult for all, particularly for the Royal Navy tank-landing craft assigned as column leaders. White soon sent them to fend for themselves in the convoy's rear, supplying them with a rendezvous position, as was customary so that ships separated in bad weather could reassemble easily. Stragglers began to drop out of the convoy. Among these were the *English Monarch* and *Clarissa Radcliffe*. The latter ship, commanded by Captain S. Finnes, was never seen again and is believed to have been sunk as she made her way independently across the Atlantic, possibly by *U-663* (Schmidt) on 18 March.

Following SC122, the faster Convoys HX229 and HX229A dodged the gale but were smothered by fog and soft snowfalls. Such conditions also complicated station-keeping, and when the weather cleared only a handful of ships remained in formation. Only the elderly *Clan Matheson* was unable to maintain convoy speed, however, although the tankers *Sunoil* and the *Southern Sun* failed to rejoin at the next rendezvous. Captain R.J. Parry of the *Clan Matheson* was the convoy's vice commodore, so Mayall nominated Captain B.C. Dodds, master of the *Nariva*, to supersede him.

After SC122 and HX229A had taken up the east-bound ships joining from Newfoundland, both convoys headed out across the Grand Banks. One trans-Atlantic vessel to drop out of HX229 at this point was the new Liberty ship *Stephen C. Foster*: ominously, her welds were failing. It was now that the Local Western Escort handed over to the Ocean Escort.

Once each of the three convoys had picked up its Ocean Escort off Cape Race it would stretch north, reaching higher latitudes than the great-circle route demanded, but reducing the air-gap. HX229A, being the most valuable, would be routed on the most northerly course, SC122 on the most southerly, to reduce the distance she must slowly travel. Ocean escort for SC122 was provided by Commander R.C. Boyle's B5 Escort Group, consisting of *Havelock, Swale* (a new 'River'-class frigate), the corvettes *Buttercup, Godetia, Lavender, Pimpernel* and *Saxifrage*, the British armed trawler *Campobello* and the American destroyer *Upshur*. HX229 was now defended by the B4 Escort Group under Lieutenant Commander G.J. Luther in *Volunteer*, together with the destroyers *Witherington, Beverley* and *Mansfield*, and the corvettes *Pennywort* and *Anemone*.

There had been some problems organising these escorts. B4 was a hurriedly-formed scratch group under an inexperienced senior officer. Although he was an anti-submarine specialist who had been attached to the Home Fleet, Luther had only been involved in one previous convoy escort across the Atlantic, and that had been devoid of U-boat alarms. Fortunately Luther's *Volunteer*, although she was an old 'V'-class destroyer, had been converted for long-range escort duties and had good communications equipment. But she was also the only vessel in HX229 fitted with HF/DF, and without a second cross-bearing, while enemy radio transmissions might be detected, they could not be fixed. Finally, the decision to split HX229A from HX229 meant that its escort, Commander J.S. Dalison's 40th Escort Group, had had to be hurried across the Atlantic to St John's to refuel in anticipation of taking it over. Dalison's force consisted of the sloops *Aberdeen*, *Hastings*, *Landguard* and *Lulworth*, and the new frigates *Moyola* and *Waveney*.

As time passed the two HX convoys gradually caught up with SC122.

The U-boats breaking off operations against SC121 and HX228 almost all had enough fuel to stay in theatre and were turned about in two groups, *Stürmer* and *Dränger*. Meanwhile B-Dienst decryptions were yielding valuable intelligence to Dönitz and his staff and a third group, *Raubgraf*, vainly searching for ON170, stumbled upon what they thought was SC122. The *Raubgraf* U-boats were rapidly reinforced by the others and the first attack was made on the morning of 16 March. As the most easterly submarines rushed west to join the attack, that same night a second convoy was reported ahead of the engaged one and it was realised that this second one was SC122, and the first-attacked was in fact HX229. The plot showed that with a speed differential of 1.5 knots, the faster HX229 was overhauling SC122. Although their courses were neither parallel nor converging, and this would pose something of a problem to the U-boats homing in, the convoys nevertheless 'formed a common objective' for all U-boats in the general area. Moreover, no action was taken against ON172, which was known to have sailed and which was, in fact, closer to most of the *Stürmer* U-boats. The consequences of these details were cumulative: the enemy were able to muster almost forty submarines against a mass of Allied merchant shipping.

Convoy SC122 had in fact been routed north of its intended track by the Americans in order to avoid a detected concentration of U-boats, the *Raubgraf* group, thought to have extended further south than it did. Ironically the *Raubgraf* boats also contacted ON170 and in foul weather a brief engagement was fought, resulting in the torpedoing of one ship. This encounter betrayed the true position of the U-boats, and SC122 and HX229 were consequently diverted east: still some way to the westward, HX229A was ordered north, towards the Davis Strait. B-Dienst deciphered this traffic, and after no further success against ON170, on the afternoon of the 14th the *Raubgraf* boats swung south-east, to make contact early on the 16th.

The weather remained foul, a south-westerly gale humping up heavy seas over a swell. During the 15th Boyle failed to top up *Havelock's* fuel, and the small Icelandic freighter *Selfoss* and the smaller A/S trawler *Campobello* lost contact with SC122. The *Selfoss* made her destination, but *Campobello* had sprung a leak in way of her bunkers. The ingress of water was too great for her pumps to cope with so she dropped astern, signalled her plight to Boyle, and drew her fires before the water reached her boilers. The *Godetia* was sent back to evacuate her crew and to sink her. Later Boyle requested that the American Coast Guard Cutter *Ingham* and USS *Babbitt*, due to rendezvous with SC122 and pick up the escort of the Iceland-bound merchantmen, should depart early and reinforce his escort.

Slightly further south, the faster HX229 had the worst of the weather, passing through the centre of the depression around midnight amid high, confused waves and a swiftly veering wind. Several of the ships in convoy took aboard punishing green seas, some were pooped, others had their boats damaged. Aboard the New Zealand Shipping Company's *Tekoa*, as Captain A. Hocken recalled, after three days of fog came the gale in which 'at times the cabins were knee deep in sea-water'. In the squalls of snow and rain, the visibility was 'as thick as a hedge'.

Worst of all, Luther had been deprived of an escort, the destroyer *Witherington*, which suffered structural damage and hove-to, thus losing contact with HX229. He had also lost the Liberty ship *Hugh Williamson*, which became detached; proceeding independently, she eventually arrived safely at her destination.

Towards dusk the weather began to moderate. SC122 had by now passed out of the worst of it, and out of danger from the *Raubgraf* group, shortly to encounter HX229. It was, however, heading for other U-boats, and the Admiralty, about to assume responsibility for the convoys' routeing, had decided that further evasion would be counter-productive, and they should be fought straight through the enemy concentration and brought under the air-umbrella as soon as possible. It seemed like the lesser of two evils, but by ill-luck the game was quickly given away. As she withdrew to the nearer of the U-tankers off the Azores, having lost five men overboard in the heavy weather, low on fuel and suffering from engine defects, U-653 almost ran into HX229. Oberleutnant Fraatz called up the *Raubgraf* pack of eight U-boats. It was the only part he played in the battle that was to follow, but it was fateful.

Ahead and to the north of HX229, still thought by the Germans to be SC122, was the slow convoy itself, and ahead of SC122 the *Stürmer* and

Dränger groups of 28 U-boats lay in wait. Two more were completing their fuelling and were ordered to move north, while a further seven were awaiting replenishment from either *U-463* or *U-119*. *Volunteer*'s solitary HF/DF did not pick up *U-653*'s contact signals but a British shore-station did, and the Admiralty informed Luther that HX229 was being shadowed. By dawn on the 16th other U-boats were in distant contact, so the evasive alteration of course to the north-east had no effect on the outcome. Nor did *Volunteer*'s final interception of a second transmission from *U-653*, except to divert *Mansfield* on a wild-goose chase to the northwards of SC122, which now made a right-angled, 'eight-point' turn to starboard to head ESE. HX229 slowed down to allow two stragglers to catch it up and resume their stations. From his own and Admiralty radio intercepts Luther was aware that he was surrounded, and this tightening-up was a prudent measure. However, he failed to inform Lieutenant Commander L.C. Hill of the alteration of course to the ESE, so that it was the 17th before *Mansfield* rejoined the convoy.

During that afternoon, as Commodore Mayall instructed the rear ships in each column to act as rescue ships for the vessels ahead, Luther made an abortive attempt to refuel *Volunteer* from the *Gulfdisc*, but the swell remained too heavy. Aboard the warships, commanding officers passed the word that 'two wolf-packs' were in contact with the convoy, and that a busy night lay ahead of them. On the merchant ships it was a matter of inference: Able Seaman H.J. Brinkworth aboard the *Nariva* told his shipmates that the flag signal 'TS' flown from a destroyer meant U-boats were in the area. Elsewhere, on the Dutch tanker *Magdala*, loaded with 10,000 tons of aviation spirit, Radio Officer J.F.J. Van Dongen died of a heart attack. Before darkness fell, bringing with it a mood of deep apprehension, HX229 had resumed a north-easterly course and passed under Admiralty control. It was now heading directly for home.

The night that fell was almost ideal for exploiting the *Rudeltaktik*, the group attack, given the weak state of Luther's escort. Although a heavy sea and swell were still running and a strong wind had got up again, the visibility was clear, with a moon near the full. The gaps across the broad front of Convoy HX229 were inviting, and Luther had moved *Volunteer* to port of the convoy's centre line, expecting attack from the north. No one saw, and no radar detected, Bertelsmann run *U-603* in on the surface, heading for the high-number columns on the convoy's starboard side.

His salvo missed the two leading vessels in the outer column but hit the Norwegian motor-vessel *Elin K.* leading the next, striking her in her after hold and inflicting a mortal wound. Captain R. Johannessen ordered her abandoned as she settled rapidly, and two boats got away. Although the *Elin K.* had displayed the red light and rocket indicating she had been hit, neither the designated 'rescue' ship, the Dutchman *Terkoelei*, nor Luther himself seems to have realised she had been sunk. In fact she went down so fast that she was probably submerged by the time the *Terkoelei* swept past. Nevertheless, the signals were observed from the *Pennywort*, which rounded-to and rescued all the *Elin K.*'s people. A full cargo of wheat and manganese ore had been lost in this first attack, and with the delay of the *Pennywort* HX229 was even more exposed, since only *Volunteer, Beverley* and *Anemone* were left to provide defence.

It was approaching midnight when Kapitänleutnant H. Manseck attacked from the starboard beam, hitting the Dutch *Zaanland* and the American Liberty ship *James Oglethorpe*. Captain G. Franken of the *Zaanland* knew his ship was sinking, and the boats were launched in conditions far from ideal but typical of the North Atlantic. Having lowered his, Second Officer Mr J. Wassenaar climbed down into it where it tossed violently alongside the *Zaanland*. Here he struggled to disengage the fall blocks. 'One moment there was slack in the boat falls, the next moment they were dangerously tight ... One moment our eyes were level with the ship's railing, the next moment we saw the boot-topping flash past us. When we got our after block free, it started to swing dangerously over our heads ... Disengaging the forward block was impossible and, in the end, we cut the falls ...' *Zaanland* 'sank very quickly, stern first ... With her bows high in the air, we heard a rumble like thunder – probably the boilers crashing through the bulkheads – we saw sparks on the forecastle probably caused by the anchor chains running away and then it was all over.'[7] Last to leave his ship, Franken found himself immersed in boiler oil, which he swallowed, and although he was picked up by Wassenaar it was not without hazard, for a Liberty ship kept steaming in circles through the position of the *Zaanland*'s four boats.

This was the *James Oglethorpe*, whose young, totally green crew's conduct was in marked contrast to that of the *Zaanland*'s tough and experienced Dutchmen and their well-disciplined evacuation: the abandonment of the *James Oglethorpe* was marred by panic. Newly-built and carrying her first cargo of steel, cotton and foodstuffs in her holds, she bore on her exposed decks aircraft, tractors and trucks. The ship was hit in No. 1 Hold, where the cotton caught fire as the ship took a turn out of line at 8 knots. To the horror of Captain A.W. Long, 43 of his crew made for the boats, and without orders began lowering them. With way on the vessel this could only end in disaster, and one boat, its falls cut prematurely, threw 11 men into the sea. Two other boats escaped with 30 men, who were picked up by *Pennywort*, but by this time the *James Oglethorpe* was steaming in circles, endangering her own and the *Zaanland*'s boats, until Long got her under command again and sent his second mate forward to fight the fire. This was doused, and Long decided it best to head west for St John's and join the next east-bound convoy. By this time *Pennywort* was on the scene, having picked up *Zaanland*'s men, along with the frightened Americans from the Liberty ship. Learning of Long's decision Lieutenant O.G. Stuart asked these men, now aboard his corvette, to return to their own vessel, but they refused, and *Pennywort* was ordered to rejoin the screen. Stuart and Long parted company.

In addition to *Pennywort, Beverley* had briefly dropped back to pick up survivors after completing the counter-attack ordered by Luther. Turning to regain station in the van himself, Luther ordered *Beverley* back into hers. As *Volunteer* crossed the rear of the convoy, Luther saw in the moonlight another stricken Liberty ship. This was the *William Eustis*, four of whose boats, along with some life-rafts, were bobbing round the wallowing vessel. Since none of the merchant ships were obeying the order to act as rescue ships, poor Luther now had to decide whether to stop to pick up these Americans, or to attend to the convoy, which at this moment was devoid of any escort whatsoever. He stopped and threw his scrambling nets over the side. His crew were horrified to see the Americans coming aboard complete with suitcases and peeling off rubber survival overalls to reveal 'what looked like complete Sunday suits . . .' To compound matters, the master admitted he had abandoned ship without destroying his confidential books, and the chief engineer expressed an opinion that if *Volunteer* were to wait until morning, there might be a chance of saving the *William Eustis*. Luther was obliged to waste further time sinking this brand-new Liberty ship and a valuable cargo of 7,400 tons of sugar. He threw depth-charges at her, full speed was rung on, and *Volunteer* disappeared after HX229. In fact the *William Eustis* did not sink: Luther's depth-charges were no more fatal than the torpedo fired into her by Kapitänleutnant S. Strelow from *U-435*.

Anemone, meanwhile, had sighted a submerging U-boat and ran over her, dropping depth-charges and shaking her own hull to such an extent that her radio-telephone and radar were rendered useless. Lieutenant Commander P.G.A. King persisted and made five attacks, seeing *U-89* again on the surface, but he failed to sink her and she escaped destruction.

Incredibly, during the period that HX229 was without naval escort no U-boat attacked, though four were in a position to do so. The panicky response to torpedo attack evinced by green American crews hurriedly trained and quickly promoted to man the new Liberty ships was happily matched that night by a corresponding failure of will on the part of several U-boat commanders. But other U-boats were arriving, and while *Volunteer* was attending the *William Eustis* and *Mansfield* caught up with the convoy to join *Beverley*, they renewed the assault.

To what extent the masters within the convoy realised they were bereft of cover is uncertain, but Captain R.McKinnon of the *Harry Luckenbach* had seen several torpedo tracks pass his ship in her station at the head of the starboard column. Since these had hit vessels on his port quarter he could have had little doubt where the attack came from or what the actual target had been, so he increased speed, drew ahead, and began to zig-zag in self-defence.

As midnight passed, Lieutenant Commander R. Price in *Beverley* took temporary command of the immediate escort. He was informed that *Mansfield* was without effective radar, and the *Harry Luckenbach* was off station; reprimanded, McKinnon resumed his post. About forty minutes later two torpedoes fired by Kapitänleutnant H. Hungershausen from *U-91* struck the American freighter, which was badly damaged and began to sink rapidly. Having sent up his rocket, lit the red light and transmitted his distress message, McKinnon gave the order to abandon ship. In five minutes the *Harry Luckenbach* had gone, but three boatloads of survivors were apparently spotted from *Beverley* as she swept down the starboard flank of the convoy. Price, hunting *U-91*, was hard-pressed, and the convoy's security came first. Signalling Luther, he turned back to the weakly defended convoy, assuming that the escorts coming up astern would deal with the *Harry Luckenbach*'s boats. As *Volunter* hurried back to resume command of the escort, Luther's lookouts spotted the boats and passed the duty to *Anemone*. The corvette failed to find them, though they were seen from *Pennywort*, which was also trying to catch up, after an absence of six hours, and was already loaded with 108 survivors.

Lieutenant Stuart, unable to get through to Luther because of the increased defence traffic on the radio telephone, assumed 'that these lifeboats contained the crew of a salvageable merchant ship which had been abandoned too soon and that the men in the lifeboats could reboard their ship'.[8] It is possible that the boats were also spotted by the *Abelia*, one of three warships (the others were HMS *Highlander* and HMCS *Sherbrooke*) steaming at full speed from St John's to join the escort and under orders to do so with all despatch. If so, it was the last time anyone saw McKinnon and his crew; they were abandoned to their fate, and the total loss from their ship amounted to 80 officers and ratings. Driven as he was by the harsh imperatives of the action, Luther's decision to concentrate his forces on HX229 was entirely understandable, but the *assumption* that these merchant seamen had abandoned ship prematurely was unfortunate. Alas, the rapid expansion of the American merchant marine was exacting an appalling price.

The early hours of 17 March ticked by, and it was about 03.00 before *Volunteer* resumed her post, the first of the errant escorts to do so. The lull had merely marked a lack of success on the part of the U-boats, however, *Beverley* having had a narrow escape from four torpedoes fired from Oberleutnant S. Koitschka's *U-616*. Moments after Luther had relieved Price, *U-600*, attacking from ahead and on the surface, fired a salvo that hammered three ships. Kapitänleutnant B. Zurmühlen's torpedoes destroyed three bulk-heads in the *Irenee Dupont*, flooding two of the freighter's three forward holds and breaching the engine room. The ship's head drove down as she lost way and water poured over her foredeck, convincing Captain C. Simonsen that she was going down. The order to abandon ship was followed by a panic. One lifeboat was overset and one life-raft was let go and drifted away, while others could not be released, compelling most of the crew to leap into the cold sea.

Zurmühlen's second victim also drove down by the head, and also remained afloat. The Royal Mail passenger-cargo-liner *Nariva*, loaded with her frozen meat, was hit forward. An enormous hole was blasted in her side, so large that as the crew abandoned ship one life-raft was washed into it as the *Nariva* rolled down, and then washed out again as she rolled away. These men were picked up by Second Officer G.D. Williams as he and the other officers kept their boats close by the wallowing hull. Captain B.C. Dodds was hopeful of reboarding at daylight if the vessel remained afloat, and dawn was not now far off.

The third vessel to be hit was the *Southern Princess*. Although loaded with the low-grade fuel oil that was normally difficult to ignite, substantial quantities of gas had built up in the ullage and this caused a secondary explosion, lighting the gases evaporating off the oil and rapidly spreading round the ship from the ruptured tanks. The heat could be felt aboard the ships in adjacent columns as they passed but, as was so often the case with tankers, although four men were lost, the size of the vessel enabled Captain H. Neilson, 66 of his crew and 27 of the convoy survivors sailing as passengers to escape into the boats. The blazing tanker acted as a beacon to U-boats in the offing as *Anemone* arrived to save Neilson and his men.

Captain Hocken in *Tekoa*, the last vessel in her column, was the only master to obey Commodore Mayall's injunction to act as rescue ship. He was imbued with a strong sense of duty, and had told his crew he intended to do what he could if any fellow merchantmen were sunk. As the *Irenee Dupont* was hit, Hocken swung *Tekoa* out of line: 'Fellows were floating about, the red lights on their life-jackets like a carpet of fireflies in the water. Some men were whistling quite chirpily and others were shouting like mad. We ... drifted among them ... We had ropes with bowlines and we would drop a bowline over a man and then five or six of my men would haul him up. It was dark, but the men made darker blobs in the water and . . . A ship on fire (the *Southern Princess*) several cables' lengths off lit things a bit too. We were four hours picking chaps up . . . 146 altogether.' Most were from the *Southern Princess*, but 51 belonged to the *Irenee Dupont,*' which lay 'like a ghost ship, low in the water forward'.

Thirteen men, including a passenger, were missing from the *Irenee Dupont*, which did not sink. As she lost way the buoyancy in her forward hold had reasserted itself and she was left wallowing behind the convoy, heavily down by the head, her code books and diplomatic mail still on board. Quite when Simonsen himself left her is uncertain,[9] but some time later *Anemone*, having picked up survivors from the *Southern Princess*, fired into her and dropped a depth-charge close by. This failed to sink her wounded hull, in which lay 3,200 tons of oil and 5,800 tons of general and military cargo.

HMS *Mansfield* was also in the vicinity and picked up 20 of the *Irenee Dupont*'s people, unaware than she herself had been the target of an abortive attack by *U-228*. In *Anemone* Lieutenant Commander King decided to stand-by the *Nariva*, but prevailed upon Captain Dodds to leave his boats and board the corvette. As a reserve officer from the Orient Line, King understood Dodds's predicament. Later in the morning they would see what could be done to save *Nariva*. As the corvette and the derelicts were left alone, the *Southern Princess* slowly rolled over, her deck cargo of locomotives and landing-craft breaking adrift from their lashings as she capsized. After she had gone her oil slick continued to burn. Seeing *Mansfield* and *Tekoa* increase speed and head east, Kapitänleutnant Christophersen drove *U-228* after them.

During the last hours of the night Commodore Mayall, frustrated by a deafening silence from the escorts after the torpedoing of the *Southern Princess* and uncertain of the fate of the vice commodore, had only the haziest notion of what was transpiring. He 'considered the U-boats were either spread out on our line of advance or were relaying along it. Something had to be done to try and shake them off.' Accordingly he ordered two emergency turns and the entire convoy wheeled simultaneously to port, except for one vessel which almost rammed Mayall in *Abraham Lincoln* before conforming. Mayall then resumed the convoy's course at about the same time as Luther – getting to grips with the situation after *Volunteer*'s extended absence – began a series of outward drives culminating with the firing of single deterrent depth-charges intended to intimidate the U-boats and keep them at a distance. As Price conducted one of these firings, *Beverley*'s radar gained a contact: it was *U-228*, briefly silhouetted against the burning oil from the *Southern Princess*. Price slowed his speed and allowed Christophersen to approach, but the destroyer was seen and *U-228* submerged, then turned tightly away. Price picked up a sonar contact and dropped seven charges set for different depths, but Christophersen went deep and ran silent, evading further detection and compelling Price, aware of the paucity of HX229's escort, to break off his chase.[10]

A grey daylight now washed into the sky. The merchant ships of both SC122 and HX229 stood out against the eastern horizon. Well astern of the latter convoy, surfacing on the heaving grey seas, Kapitänleutnant Hungershausen in *U-91* came across the Liberty ship *James Oglethorpe*, trying to return to St John's, and fired three torpedoes at her. They hit her in the engine room and after holds, sending her rapidly to the bottom with Captain Long and his remaining 30 loyal hands.

With the coming of the day the merchant officers checked their cruising sheets and 'marked off the unfortunate missing numbers and that, with a short prayer, was that'. Mr MacLellan, Mate of the *Baron Stranraer*, admitted to 'an intense feeling of helpless anger that good men and ships would be seen no more and, eventually, a guilty sense of relief that "we were still afloat".'[11] But not, perhaps, for long: with their customary enthusiasm for rumour the merchantmen's crews seized upon the notion that 'the convoy was to be sacrificed for bigger things'. As for the escort, Luther considered that the mood of his warships was 'rather embittered' with the taste of defeat 'by pure weight of numbers'.

Far astern Captain Dodds, along with his second officer and chief engineer, was rowed across to the *Nariva* in *Anemone*'s little sea-boat. 'She looked a bit pathetic,' recalled Second Officer Williams, 'bows deep in the water and the foredeck awash as she rose and fell in the heavy swell. I noted . . . there was still a wisp of steam and smoke pouring out of the funnel. The surface of the sea all around . . . was littered with still frozen carcases.' While Williams and Chief Engineer Brophy were busy discovering the boilers to be red hot, empty of water and full of steam, King was obliged to ring on full speed as a torpedo was seen approaching. After conducting an unsuccessful search for *U-616*, King returned to find Dodds and his party back in *Anemone*'s sea-boat. The state of *Nariva*'s boilers was such that salvage was only feasible by means of a tug towing her stern-first. The delay inherent in such a plan, which would involve *Anemone* standing-by, was not viable, and reluctantly Dodds and King decided to leave her. A few shots were fired ineffectually into the liner, and a depth-charge was dropped alongside, also to little effect. The same procedure was carried out alongside the *Irenee Dupont*, with the same result. In the end, it was

Hungershausen in *U-91* who sent both derelicts and the *William Eustis*, also still afloat, to the sea-bed.

The night had been little better for Commander Boyle's B5 Escort Group guarding SC122. Kapitänleutnant M. Kinzel had penetrated the convoy's outer defence in *U-338*, dodging the new frigate *Swale* hunting ahead of the starboard flank. Kinzel sent a sighting report and then attacked, firing first his bow and then his stern tubes. Having hit four ships he immediately dived, allowing the convoy to pass above him. Attacking obliquely across the convoy's front, Kinzel had hit the *Kingsbury* and the *Alderamin*, the leading ships in columns three and four, and the *King Gruffydd* astern of the *Kingsbury*. The fourth torpedo missed its intended target but buried itself within the convoy, striking the *Fort Cedar Lake*.

Ordering his crew to the boats, Captain W. Laidler of the *Kingsbury* waited on the bridge while Radio Officer King finished sending his distress message. With him was Able Seaman S. Ward, who had been on the wheel. The boats succeeded in getting clear of the sinking tramp, which had loaded bauxite and West African produce in Port Harcourt and now began to settle quickly by the stern. Four men, including Ward, were lost, Laidler and King escaping at the last minute on a raft which was whirled about in the maelstrom of the *Kingsbury*'s death-throes.

Astern of her the *King Gruffydd* sank with equal speed and heavy loss of life. In addition to iron ore and 500 tons of tobacco, she carried 493 tons of high explosives, a fact which further sped the hands to their stations when Captain H. Griffiths ordered his ship abandoned. One watch were trapped in the forecastle and their screams pierced the night as Second Officer F.R. Hughes dumped the code books, a dutiful delay which cost him a dry embarkation in the lifeboat he ought to have commanded. Leaving Captain Griffiths on the bridge, Hughes jumped into the water, struggled to his boat and was towed away from the ship, which reared up and sank. The sea was bitterly cold.

The *Alderamin* was a Dutch vessel from which only the motor-lifeboat escaped. Two of her lifeboats had been destroyed by the torpedo explosion and a third capsized on launching, but the motor-lifeboat had been manned by the chief engineer and the lowering crew. Rather than wait for those handling the falls and the other hands to scramble down the boarding ladder or slide down the lifelines, the chief engineer had the boat cast loose and motored clear of the ship into the night. The remainder took to the hurriedly launched life-rafts, or jumped into the sea.

Captain C.L. Collings of the *Fort Cedar Lake* had been in despair of his drunken and ill-disciplined young crew, but after the torpedo hit and with the ship burning, 'they were very steady and obeyed all orders'. The ship did not sink immediately, however, and Collings, conscientious master in the service of the Hain Steamship Company that he was, took with him when he left the vessel the chief steward's accounts for canteen sales – accounts that were rendered in full before final payment of crew wages. It was a suitably cold night for such revenge upon his wayward and troublesome hands.

In the rear of the convoy, Captain O.C. Morris brought the *Zamalek* to a stop and, lying a-hull, began the wearying work of recovering survivors. Griffiths and 23 men from the *King Gryffydd* had been lost, but 25 were picked up. One of the *Kingsbury*'s boats turned turtle after banging up against the *Zamalek*'s side, and by the time they reached the scrambling nets the chief engineer and a passenger were so cold that they could not cling on, and fell back to their deaths. In contrast, everyone from the *Fort Cedar Lake* was recovered by the rescue ship, leaving their own vessel burning. She was sunk later that same day by *U-665*.[12]

With the *Zamalek* busy it was *Saxifrage*, standing by to help, that was assigned the duty of picking up the *Alderamin*'s crew. Fifteen seamen were lost, and three of those saved died later of hypothermia. The Dutch master, Captain C.L. van Os, insisted on being the last to be taken up, and swam indefatigably round ensuring that no one had been left behind. At a consequent Extraordinary Board of Enquiry held in October, the chief engineer's conduct was examined. The wretched man candidly confessed to his terror and after being deliberated by the Board the matter was dropped.

On the forenoon of 17 March Dönitz sat gleefully in his new headquarters in Berlin, taken up when he superseded Raeder. His staff rapidly and correctly concluded that there were two convoys, and realised which was which. Exhortatory messages were sent, and the remaining unengaged U-boats from the *Stürmer* and *Dränger* groups were ordered to close in on the two convoys, now little more than a hundred miles apart.[13] In Liverpool, in the absence of Horton in London, Air Vice Marshal Slatter mustered what support he could by way of Liberators from Iceland and Northern Ireland, aware that HX229 was still within the air-gap. One Liberator was already on its way towards SC122. Provision had also been made for the Iceland-bound portion of SC122 to continue on to Britain instead, with the two American Coast Guard cutters *Ingham* and *Babbitt* remaining with them as reinforcements to Boyle.

In the Atlantic the weather was moderating: the wind had dropped, and with it the sea. Now only the occasional snow-squall drew its soft grey curtains across the undulating swell. Although *Zamalek* and *Saxifrage* were well astern of SC122, *Godetia* was in the process of catching up, and the Liberator arrived from Aldergrove, 900 miles away. It had missed the convoy in the last hours of darkness, but in over-shooting had discovered *U-439*, one of several shadowing submarines. Flying Officer C. Burcher's depth-charges did no material damage, but dissuaded Oberleutnant H. von Tippelskirch from approaching. Burcher then began an air patrol, during which he attacked one more U-boat and forced others down. The Liberator was not able to remain with SC122 for long, but quite apart from its work of intimidation, its appearance gave a boost to those in the ships below. The strong head-winds at high altitude delayed the aircraft coming from Reykjavik, so that after Burcher's disappearance SC122 was again without air-cover.

As the deck officers throughout the convoy took their noon sights, the enemy reappeared on the port flank. Lieutenant A.M. Larose put *Godetia's*[14] helm hard over to avoid a torpedo which ran obliquely across the first column and struck the Panamanian *Granville*, bound notionally for Iceland with a military cargo and leading the second line of vessels. A second torpedo, glimpsed as it bounded free of the wave crests, tracked across the convoy and only missed the Dutchman *Parkhaven* because her helm was put over in time. Commodore White took the convoy through an emergency turn to starboard as the *Granville's* crew rushed to their only boat left after the explosion, but this capsized on hitting the water. Life-rafts were flung overboard as a part-cargo of cased petrol caught fire and began to burn, while the ship's hull showed signs of breaking in two. Reduced to clinging onto the upturned boat, Captain F. Matzen watched as his ship split in the centre and her bow and stern rose briefly skywards before both ends sank with a roar. Twelve men were found to have drowned when the Danish master mustered the survivors aboard the *Lavender*, whose executive officer Lieutenant W. Weller had dived into the water to save the rapidly-weakening second mate. Sadly the officer, Mr C. Micallef from Malta, died before he could be resuscitated and was buried that afternoon. The *Granville* was Kinzel's fifth victim; this time he was counter-attacked by HMS *Godetia* and the USS *Upshur*, but he escaped.

The convoy now welcomed the arrival of the Liberator from Iceland, which had put down Kapitänleutnant R. Bahr's *U-305* ten miles short of SC122. But it was not relieved in the last hours of daylight, allowing the U-boats to work up close unobserved, in preparation for the night.

During the early forenoon of 17 March Commodore Mayall had re-formed HX229, reducing from eleven to nine columns. Aboard *Volunteer*, Luther had had one piece of good news: he had been ordered to refuel *Mansfield*, which should have turned back to St John's on crossing the 35th meridian, and to keep Lieutenant Commander Hill's destroyer with him. On the other hand, *Pennywort* was still absent after her rescue work and would not rejoin until twilight, for she had assumed that HX229 had reverted to a NNE'ly heading, rather than the ENE'ly course along which it was steaming. But the enemy were gathering, guided by Bertelsmann's homing signals from *U-603* which attracted the reinforcements of the *Stürmer* and *Dränger* groups. Long before *Pennywort* reappeared at 10.30 that morning, HX229 was again bleeding.

Hardly had the Dutch-flagged *Terkoelei* gained her new station leading the outer starboard column when she burst into 'a cloud of smoke, spray and pieces'. An instant later, even as she turned to avoid it, a torpedo hit the Donaldson liner *Coracero*. Precisely which U-boats hit which ships is disputed, but *U-384* seems to be the strongest contender for the destruction of the *Coracero*. The *Terkoelei*, a German prize taken in Sourabaya, was loaded with mail, zinc and wheat, and manned with a mixed crew of Dutch officers, Javanese ratings and British gunners. Of the four boats that escaped from the sinking ship, two, were trapped as she capsized, and loss of life was heavy. The *Mansfield* arrived among the carnage to rescue the survivors, one of whom, after considerable efforts to get him aboard, died on the destroyer's deck. She also recovered the *Coracero*'s people. Like *Nariva*, the *Coracero* had been loaded with frozen Argentinian meat, and it appeared that like her she would drift astern unless sunk. But just as Hill manoeuvred to fire a torpedo, she gave up the ghost. Captain R.C. Young had lost five of his men, mostly in the *Coracero*'s engine room. One, a trimmer signed-on as 'J.J. Elder', turned out to be 14-year-old Robert Yates, who had run away to sea and a life of adventure.

This attack put paid to any idea of refuelling *Mansfield*, and while Luther requested reinforcements, Captain Nancollis of the *City of Agra* sought permission of the commodore to proceed independently. The Ellerman liner was capable of at least 13.5 knots, but Mayall dismissed the notion. It proved a wise decision. Within minutes *Beverley* was stretching out ahead of the convoy, where two U-boats had been detected. Price made a series of six attacks and drove his quarry deep, but the failure of a heavy Mark X depth-charge marked the end of his attack. The U-boat, *U-530* (Lange), had however been so damaged by depth-charges and water pressure that her patrol was over.

Towards late afternoon the appearance of a Liberator cheered them all; soon afterwards a second was in sight. It was in fact the aircraft designated to provide cover to SC122, but that convoy's loss was HX229's gain. The flights out to the convoy and the endurance of these aircraft set records at the time. Several U-boats were sighted and attacked from the air, but the Liberators' depth-charges were soon expended and they were reduced to strafing. Finally they headed for home, one leaving the impression aboard *Volunteer* that a U-boat was only five miles away. Luther was alarmed, but soon after dark *Volunteer, Beverley* and *Mansfield* had been rejoined by *Anemone* and *Pennywort*. *Mansfield* could stay only until the next day, for her failure to refuel at sea in the inclement conditions meant that she had to press on to Londonderry at 12 knots. However, that night, contrary to all expectations, HX229 was not molested. Instead, only 80 miles ahead, SC122 was bearing the brunt of a vicious attack. The two convoys were just over half-way across the Atlantic.

The second U-boat to dodge *Swale, U-305,* fired a salvo of torpedoes across the bow of SC122 at about 20.15 that evening. Kapitänleutnant R. Bahr struck the British cargo-liner *Port Auckland* and the tramp *Zouave*. The *Port Auckland* had completed loading her cargo of 8,000 tons of frozen meat and 1,000 tons of general in Brisbane, and after crossing the Pacific and passing through the Panama Canal had embarked ten airmen before leaving Halifax. Now Captain A.E. Fishwick lost eight crew in the attack, mostly in the engine room, which was inundated by the impact of the torpedo. 'The engines had stopped themselves as the water came pouring in . . . everything was in utter darkness.' The ship was rolling so heavily that it was possible to almost step into the lifeboats as they rose up the ship's side. 'In the circumstances it was quite remarkable that exactly 100 people embarked in three lifeboats with no one being injured or even falling into the ditch!'

Captain W.H. Cambridge's *Zouave* was loaded with iron ore from Pepel, and she sank rapidly. Twelve men were lost, but Cambridge and the remaining 29 were picked up by *Godetia* – standing in for *Zamalek*, still miles astern of the convoy – which also rescued Fishwick, his 99 crew and ten passengers. With *Campobello*'s men, Larose was now playing host to 165 survivors. He made one sally at a radar target but *U-305*, running on the surface, turned away, leaving Bahr able to fire another torpedo into the *Port Auckland* and ensure her sinking.

Snow-squalls and a rising wind from the north made for a bleak dawn on the 18th. Bahr was still in contact with SC122 and transmitting homing signals, but five sorties flown by Liberators of No. 120 Squadron kept the U-boats away throughout the day. Occasionally the escorts left the convoy to investigate contacts, but no decisive actions were fought, though Kinzel's *U-338* was damaged and forced to withdraw, as was Bahr, *U-305*'s batteries being exhausted. SC122's only casualty was the *Empire Morn*, compelled to drop astern with engine trouble. Boyle did not detach an escort to stand by her.

Convoy HX229 had no benefit from air-cover during the gale-swept 18th. The best that could be said was that two of the aircraft out looking for the convoy did attack U-boats in the offing. Commander Day, B5's regular senior officer in *Highlander*, which with *Abelia* was on her way to reinforce Luther, was unable to home on *Volunteer*. Meanwhile a sea that just failed to sweep overboard the rating responsible for decoding did wash the code books out of his hands, making a bad situation worse.

As Luther struggled, Kapitänleutnant Trojer lay in the grain of the convoy in *U-221*, and at about 14.00 he attacked from ahead, running down between columns two and three. His first torpedo struck the American Liberty ship *Walter Q. Gresham*; she had already lost a lifeboat and its davits during heavy weather on the 15th, and now Trojer's torpedo tore off her screw and smashed a hole in her side, so that her part-cargo of dried milk washed out into the sea.

Aboard the *Canadian Star* in the adjacent column, Third Officer R.H. Keyworth saw the attack and the U-boat's periscope an instant before Trojer's torpedoes hit his own ship. Keyworth had been in the act of putting the helm over as the two torpedoes arrived, one blasting its way into the engine room and exploding against one of the main engine cylinders, the other blowing in the shell plating in way of No. 5 Hold. The blast from the first destroyed the lifeboats swung out on the port side, tore part of the chart room away and wrecked much of the midships accommodation. Captain R.D. Miller, 'an exceptionally fine seaman . . . [whose] quiet cool behaviour set a magnificent example', ordered the *Canadian Star* abandoned. The ship was settling fast by the stern and Chief Officer P.H. Hunt supervised the launching of the starboard boats and the mustering of the 24 passengers. Conditions were bad, with the immobilised ship rolling in the heavy seas. The lowering crew lost control of No. 3 Boat, which ran away and hung by its forward fall, flinging several passengers, including women and children, into the sea. When the boat was lowered on the forward fall, it promptly capsized. 'No. 1 Boat was then launched with as many people as the davits would support, and orders were given by the Captain to man and launch the starboard rafts. All four starboard rafts were successfully launched and saved many lives, while No. 3 Boat was . . . righted and manned with the Third Officer in charge.'

The *Canadian Star* reared up vertically and remained thus for five minutes before she went down. Second Officer W.A. Clarke-Hunt escaped on a raft but Captain Miller went with her, as did her carpenter, who deliberately 'walked right into the path of a wave pounding across the afterdeck'.

The chief officer recorded that 'Practically the whole crew were accommodated in the two boats and the rafts, and the large loss of life was due to the weather. No. 1 Boat picked up all they could until it was overcrowded. No. 3 Boat capsized twice and many more were lost . . . The rafts that were properly manned stood up in the weather, while the ones with few people in them were capsized by the tops of the waves, causing loss of life.' Clarke-Hunt had 'twenty-two men on a ten-man raft, most of [whom] had to hang on the side . . . We lost six of these fairly quickly; you would see them getting cold, a certain look came into their eyes and then they just gave up. The army officer who had seen his wife and child [fall from No. 3 Boat] was the first to go . . . Only nine of us were eventually picked up.' Keyworth's boatload was reduced to five persons before *Anemone* and *Pennywort* arrived to pick up the survivors two hours later. Chief Engineer E.G. Buckwell and a woman passenger died after rescue.

These two corvettes also rescued Captain B. Miller, 65 crew and two passengers from the *Walter Q. Gresham*. Twenty-seven men were lost, one of them the radio operator, whose would-be rescuers were unable to get a firm grip of him. The difficulties of picking up sodden, oil-soaked men – and some women – chilled to the bone, already suffering from hypothermia, trauma and poisoning by oil were productive of horrific scenes, only compounded by the delay in helping them.

Luther had taken *Volunteer* right through the survivors in his hunt for the attacking U-boat, an 'appalling dilemma which a brave, decent and humane young captain had to face and decide on in about five minutes – the survivors or the submarine? We wallowed past them, the captain shouting from the loud-hailer, "We'll be back."' Aboard *Volunteer* the survivors from the *William Eustis* 'seemed angry and resentful' as they watched their colleagues drift forlornly astern.[15]

When the corvettes did undertake the rescue work, the naval sailors were helped by the survivors of other vessels already on board. But it was really too late. Having performed prodigies in twice righting a capsized boat, Third Officer Keyworth had watched the men, 'one by one, their eyes glazing . . . eventually losing their grip and being washed up and down the boat and eventually out of it altogether.' Then he too began to get a 'feeling of cosiness'. Such a feeling generally brought with it hallucinations of home, and a loss of consciousness that usually proved fatal.

The 'survivors or submarine' dilemma, by no means an unusual one in that long battle, had a poignant twist in Luther's case, for he went to his grave, not long after the war, convinced that he had made the wrong decision and blaming himself for the deaths of the 57 people killed by Trojer.[16]

It cannot have helped Luther that Commander Day now arrived in *Highlander*, critical of the convoy's averaged position, which was in error owing to the prevailing conditions, and making light of its difficulties. Day was also irritated that Luther had detached two escorts for the rescue operation. Contacting Mayall, he ordered the convoy to alter course after dark and alter back again later in the night, so that dawn on the 19th would find HX229 back on its rhumb line and the U-boats left astern. This decision of Day's unwittingly headed HX229 directly into the U-boats mustering in the rear of SC122.

The master of the *Mathew Luckenbach*, Captain A.H. Borden, was determined to leave the convoy and take advantage of his ship's 15-knot speed. Convincing the naval guard commander and finding his decision endorsed by all hands, who signed a declaration to that effect, he rang on full speed. Day spotted the *Mathew Luckenbach* beginning her romp and surged alongside in *Highlander*, but Borden was having none of it and drew away into the night. He too was heading not for the open ocean but for the wolves astern of the slow convoy ahead.

Once again the wind went down with the sun and the cloud thinned, revealing bright moonlight – good conditions for the surfaced U-boats. About two dozen of these were still in the vicinity, the majority in the dead and shrinking waters between the two convoys. The HF/DF operators aboard *Zamalek* and the escorts were now aware of the gathering storm, and to Day's relief *Pennywort* and *Anemone* closed up with HX229 shortly before midnight. Three hours later King's corvette was back in the thick of things, reporting a U-boat astern, in the path of the moon, which Day sent *Anemone* and *Volunteer* to hunt down. Their objective, *U-615*, escaped damage, but collateral wounds were inflicted upon *U-440* and *U-134*. Then Kapitänleutnant K. Hartmann fired into the port flank from *U-441*, claiming several hits but missing with all torpedoes, and Day's lookouts alerted him to a further U-boat, so close to *Highlander* in the convoy's van that they could see her commander staring through his Zeiss binoculars. Day increased speed but muffed his approach and, failing to gain a sonar contact, dropped no fewer than ten speculative depth-charges. He managed to shake von Tippelskirch's *U-439*, but was unaware that *Highlander* had escaped three torpedoes fired from *U-609*.

Returning to HX229 from the rear once again, King's *Anemone* encountered two U-boats in the convoy's wake, their conning towers dark against the dawn. King had only two depth-charges left and sought to engage with his single 4-inch gun, but both submarines dived as they saw the corvette coming up in the darkness astern.

Similar events had been taking place around SC122, but towards 05.00 only *U-666* was still in a position to attack. From the starboard flank Kapitänleutnant H. Engel fired at and hit the Greek tramp *Carras*, loaded with wheat. Captain D.C. Mazavinos ordered her abandoned at once and *Zamalek* was promptly on the scene, picking up all hands. An attempt to save her was mishandled: the naval salvage tug *Saucy* and the corvette *Jonquil* left Londonderry and searched for her for some days before it was discovered that *Buttercup* had shelled her. In fact, *Carras* had then drifted astern, still floating, to be despatched by *U-333*, now commanded by Oberleutnant W. Schwarff.

Soon after dawn *Ingham* arrived from Iceland. Dawn also brought retribution to the romping *Mathew Luckenbach*, which ran into *U-527*, Kapitänleutnant H. Uhlig, and was torpedoed for her temerity. His engines were undamaged, but Captain Borden abandoned ship. Although Nos 2 and 4 Holds were full of water and wheat and the ship sat very low in the water, she might have been salvaged. Borden and his men were picked up by *Ingham* and Captain Martinson called for volunteers to return aboard to save the old vessel, but none were forthcoming. Borden's chief mate, a former seaman in the Imperial German Navy, observed gloomily that the crews of the U-boats were 'very efficient'; it may be imagined what influence he exerted in these proceedings.

Martinson withdrew, and *Mathew Luckenbach* was finally sunk by *U-523*.

As the two convoys moved steadily ENE a considerable number of aircraft were being brought into action, and during the forenoon of the 19th a B-17 Fortress from No. 206 Squadron flown by Pilot Officer L.G. Clark dropped through a snow-squall astern of SC122 – and therefore ahead of HX229 – to discover *U-384* on the surface. Four depth-charges stove in the U-boat; Oberleutnant H-A. von Rosenburg-Gruszcynski and 47 men were killed. Another attack by a second Fortress severely damaged Engel's *U-666*, driving her out of the action. Sunderlands were also successful in forcing U-boats away from their intended targets, not least one which frustrated Kinzel, who was working *U-338* into a position to torpedo the straggling *Empire Morn*.

As darkness fell the wind died completely. When the moon eventually rose it was above an oily sea undulating with a low, residual swell. The calm night and clear air gave maximum visibility as first *Abelia* and then *Babbitt*, arriving from Iceland and after an encounter with *U-109*, reinforced Day's escort of HX229. The excellent visibility persuaded Flying Officer Esler of

No. 120 Squadron to remain above the convoy for a further two hours, and at least one U-boat was forced under as the Liberator roared overhead. That day and the next found Coastal Command's wandering aircraft attacking several U-boats, causing damage but making no 'kills'.

As SC122 and HX229 ran in under the air umbrella, Dönitz called off the operation. Although they had inflicted such damage that, according to a later British Admiralty assessment, 'The Germans never came so near disrupting communication between the New World and the Old as in the first twenty days of March, 1943', the *Raubgraf, Stürmer* and *Dränger* groups were battered. The German Commander-in-Chief, however, was already beginning to assemble a new *Seeteufel* (Sea-Devil) group, south of Iceland, to intercept the next westbound convoy. It also lay in the way of HX229A.

This fast convoy of crack ships, forced up into the jaws of the Davis Strait, had worked through new ice-floes, low rounded growlers of old ice awash and dangerous in the fogs, and bergs and ice-islands of rafted and homogenised ice compacted over years of elemental travail. Two of the escorts, *Aberdeen* and *Waveney*, had their shell plating pierced, and five merchantmen had turned back for St John's after sustaining serious damage. One, the 14,795-ton *Sven Foyn*, struck an iceberg and was immobilised on 19 March. The sloop *Hastings* was left to stand by her, and both vessels were surrounded by ice and briefly beset. That night a gale blew up but had exhausted itself by morning, when a glassy calm fell and two vessels arrived to take off the crew and the large number of DBS survivors the former whale-factory ship was carrying in her large accommodation. Captain F. Thompson refused permission for anyone to leave his ship, however, even though there was no heating aboard her: he was determined that the Coast Guard cutters in attendance could and should tow her clear and salvage her. The *Hastings*'s commander, Lieutenant Commander L.B. Philpot, a former merchant officer, was angry with Thompson, but the latter was adamant. Unfortunately another gale blew up in the night and, quite suddenly, the *Sven Foyn* foundered. *Hastings* and the American Coast Guard cutters *Algonquin, Aivik, Modoc* and *Frederick Lee* picked up 152 of the 195 known to have been aboard her; Captain Thompson was not among them, having paid the price of his dogged intransigence.

Convoy HX229A had pressed on, meanwhile, *Hastings* being replaced by the American cutter *George M. Bibb*, sent from Iceland. Having been apprised by the Admiralty of the presence of the *Seeteufel* U-boats, the fast convoy was routed evasively and reached Liverpool on 26 March, three days after the remnants of HX229 and two after SC122. These had traversed the final five hundred miles without interference, though not without trouble. Ordered to clean up their quarters aboard *Anemone*, the oily survivors of one British merchantman refused, arguing that they were not going to work without being paid. It was an old and bitter wrangle, out of which the stubborn merchant seamen emerged with little credit, but it was evidence of the collective mind-set. Lieutenant Stuart, RCNVR, in command of *Pennywort*, did not hesitate to lock up some American survivors who demanded extra pay for helping to clean the corvette before she entered port. Most, of course, did what they could, led by the exemplary Norwegians and Dutch. Many wrote testimonials of gratitude, or subscribed to gifts for their rescuers.

To relieve the strain on their catering staffs and facilities the little warships loaded with survivors proceeded ahead of the main body, as did the over-crowded *Zamalek* and *Tekoa*, most to discharge their human load at Gourock on the Clyde.

Of those merchantmen that arrived in SC122 one more was to be sunk, as she headed south down the east coast of Scotland. This was the ore-laden Swedish vessel *Atland*, which as the proceeded in a coastal convoy in company with her station-mate *Carso* from SC122 was rammed by her and foundered with the loss of 19 men.

In the aftermath of the action, assessments and evaluations were made at several levels. Luther was summoned by Horton but emerged from his inter-view unscathed. No naval officers were either decorated or reprimanded. It was all in the day's work. As Commodore Mayall recorded in his report, 'apart from U-boat attacks the voyage had been fairly average'. A few merchant officers were awarded decorations. Captain R.D. Miller of the *Canadian Star* won a posthumous commendation, while his chief and third officers, Hunt and Keyworth, were appointed MBE. Hocken of the *Tekoa*, on the other hand, received only two letters of approbation, one from the Admiralty Trade Division, the other from the Honours and Awards Section. These were grudging acknowledgements, and a contrast with the award to the American merchant seamen, *en masse*, of a battle star. With individual exceptions like that of Captain Ellis of the *William C. Gorgas*, the Americans' performance had not been brilliant. It may be that Fleet Admiral King, characteristically, considered it no worse than that of the British navy. Aware of the perception that many American merchant seamen had been aban-doned in their extremity, he put an abrupt end to escort groups of mixed British and American vessels.

Of the merchant crews, the army and naval gunners, and the passen-gers, a quarter had been lost in the 22 vessels sunk. Most of the damage had been inflicted by a minority of the U-boats within operational range of the convoys. By contrast, the escorts had lost one man, swept overboard from the *Mansfield* on the last leg of her run for fuel.

Any analysis of the actions around HX229 and SC122 will throw up the question of why the Admiralty did not divert some of Boyle's force to assist Luther. SC122 was never under the same pressure, though intercepts and decrypts doubtless indicated a similarly large number of U-boats mustering around the periphery of both. Nor was there any doubt by this stage of the conflict that air power was the key to victory, whether flown from escort-carriers or shore bases. The diversion of the first escort-carriers to other operations cost many men, and some women, their lives. Horton, famously, when confronted by Churchill with the apparent failure of the escorts, asked for fifteen more. Churchill responded sharply that admirals always wanted more ships. But Horton got them, and within weeks had transformed the war in the Atlantic.

24

'The decisive factor'

California Star

DURING THE PASSAGE of the two beleaguered convoys, other events of moment had been taking place in the Atlantic. In high northern latitudes, steaming at 30 knots, the new Cunard liner *Queen Elizabeth* had made one of her fast independent passages with 15,000 American troops on board, while far to the south a drama of another kind was in progress, also involving a laden and requisitioned passenger-liner.

In November 1942, the SL series of convoys had been suspended after SL125 to avoid confusion with American military convoys sailing in support of the invasion of North Africa. Until their resumption the following spring all merchant ships arriving in Freetown proceeded to Cape San Roque on the shoulder of Brazil before heading north to join SC and HX convoys at New York. When the series resumed towards the end of March, SL126 lost four British ships, but thereafter only two more ships in SL convoys were destroyed by the enemy.[1] Many vessels sailing independently were sunk by Axis submarines, however, often with heavy loss of life.

Typical of these was the *California Star*, which had passed through the Panama Canal on her way to Liverpool from Australia and New Zealand with a full cargo of refrigerated food and a handful of passengers. On the fine, clear evening of 4 March she was about 380 miles north-west of Flores in the Azores, steaming at 16 knots in a light southerly breeze with Chief Officer J. Davis on watch when the darkness was sundered by two immense and simultaneous explosions as two torpedoes struck the starboard side of No. 3 Hold.

Immediately all the internal lights went out. The off-duty watch struggled into warm clothing and Mr Robert Stewart, the senior radio officer, transmitted a submarine attack distress message as Captain S. Foulkes arrived on the bridge, relieved Davis and ordered him to clear away the life-rafts forward. Second Officer Cameron Stewart and Third Officer Rackham went to the boat deck, mustered the crew and lowered the undamaged starboard boats. Having assessed the state of the *California Star*, Foulkes ordered Chief Engineer Kilpatrick to get his men out of the engine room and Stewart to keep transmitting. By this time No. 4 Boat had been lowered and manned and was pulling away from the ship in the charge of the second officer. Reaching the boat deck to find that Rackham had gone to clear the after rafts away, Foulkes supervised the lowering of No. 2 Boat. This was half-way down when a third torpedo hit the *California Star* right below the boat in the falls, shattering it and killing all its occupants. Fifty yards away, No. 4 Boat was almost overset by the blast wave. Above, Foulkes and the lowering party were blown off their feet. Foulkes did his best for them and then, seeing that Rackham was launching the after rafts, returned to the radio room, to learn that Stewart had made nine transmissions and received no reply. The deck inclined steeply as *California Star*'s bow dipped and Foulkes told him to leave and save himself. As Stewart went aft, Foulkes jumped straight over the side and swam for a small light he could see. This was on a life-raft from the foredeck and on it were Chief Officer Davis, the third radio officer and two DEMS gunners. Hardly had Foulkes been hauled out of the water when a fourth torpedo slammed into the dark shape of the *California Star* as her stern began to lift clear of the water.

'It was very dark,' gunner W.W. Mackintosh in No. 4 Boat recalled, 'but we could just make out the ship going down.' From the life-raft Foulkes and Davis now saw the dark loom of a conning tower and heard the low rumble of a diesel engine. The two officers tore off their uniform jackets and lay with the two gunners in the well of the raft with the cover pulled over them as *U-515* passed by. They went unobserved as Kapitänleutnant W. Henke approached No. 4 Boat. 'The submarine came alongside us with two German sailors in oilskins on deck and covering us with machine-guns. Someone . . . shouted in broken English from the conning tower wanting the name of the ship and to take the Captain . . .' Second Officer Cameron Stewart was removed into the U-boat before she disappeared into the darkness, 'leaving us to do the best we could'.

The purser took charge of the 24 men, and as daylight grew in the eastern sky they closed with some rafts, on one of which they discovered Captain Foulkes, Davis and the gunners. There were four rafts in all, upon which clung another 28 men, and they were lashed together and towed astern of No. 4 Boat, but no progress could be made and there were too many men to accommodate in the lifeboat. After conferring, the master and chief officer decided that Foulkes would make for the Azores in No. 4 Boat, leaving Davis to keep up morale on the rafts until rescue arrived. All the provisions that could be spared were placed aboard them and the ship's doctor, Erik Pedersen, transferred to one to tend a severely injured man who could not be moved. Hoisting sail, the lifeboat set off, leaving those on the rafts 'at the mercy of the winds whichever way they blew'.

Foulkes had only enough water for a two-ounce ration per day, and after four days the wind freshened, the sea rose and the survivors began a constant round of bailing. The galley boy, who 'hadn't much constitution', died on the tenth day, just before they raised the Azores. 'Most of the crew', Foulkes afterwards reported during his debrief at the Admiralty Trade Division, 'behaved very well[;] there were four men, however, who refused to do anything, they would not bail or look-out, and even stole the fresh water from the forward tank.'

Foulkes's boat's crew landed on the eleventh day at Larges das Flores, where they found the islanders kindness itself. Foulkes arranged for the *California Star*'s last position to be cabled to the Admiralty in order that a rescue operation could be mounted and the rafts located. Most of the survivors from No. 4 Boat were badly constipated, necessitating purging, and some, like Mackintosh, found that their toes and fingers ached. 'It reminded me of when I went snowballing as a boy.' He had been taken in by a devout couple, and 'every morning' the English-speaking husband, José Pimental Soares, 'went down to the sea and brought back a bottle of sea-water and massaged my hands and feet in it,' easing the gunner's ailment. In due course 'a tailor made them all a suit' and their names were cabled home. Then they were put aboard a Portuguese ship and taken to Lisbon, from where Mackintosh and the other DEMS gunners were flown home in a Liberator while the merchant seamen 'were all sent to Gibraltar to pick up various ships'.

Of the 70 souls on board the *California Star*, only Foulkes's party lived. Forty-eight crew and gunners and four of the seven passengers died, for despite a search the four rafts were never seen again. Pedersen and Radio Officer Stewart received posthumous commendations.

Henke's expenditure of torpedoes had been excessive and the destruction of the *California Star*'s No. 2 Boat wanton, turning an act of war into an act of murder. He went on to sink six more merchantmen – three British, one Dutch, one Norwegian and one Vichy French – before returning to L'Orient, whence Second Officer Cameron Stewart was sent to Milag Nord.[2]

If numbers increase the magnitude of a tragedy, that which befell the Canadian Pacific Company's *Empress of Canada* was a greater. The liner was on her way from Durban to Britain by way of Takoradi. Like the *Laconia* before her, she had among her 1,536 'passengers' about five hundred Italian prisoners-of-war as well as British, Greek and Polish soldiers. Captain G. Gould's crew consisted of 320 officers and ratings and 44 naval gunners. On 14 March the *Empress of Canada* was 73 miles south of the Equator, north-east of Ascension, when she was hit by torpedoes from the Italian submarine *Leonardo da Vinci*, Capitano di Corvetta G. Gazzana-Priaroggia. Listing over, she filled slowly, giving Gould and his crew the opportunity to abandon her in good order. They had considerable difficulty, however, in lowering some of the boats against the list, and while the Italian prisoners behaved well, though they were reluctant to leave the ship and take to the comparatively insubstantial safety of the boats, the Greeks and Poles were nervous. Gould's subsequent report made a point of the fact that all the Greek and most of the Polish officers survived.

Gazzana-Priaroggia fired a second torpedo which exploded under a lowered lifeboat as the escaping seamen and soldiers climbed down the ship's side into it. As well as the deaths it caused in the lifeboat, this second torpedo settled the *Empress of Canada*'s fate. The *Leonardo da Vinci* surfaced and took up a number of survivors, including an Italian doctor, before disappearing to the south-east, but 348 'passengers' and 44 of the ship's company were lost, most trapped below or destroyed by Gazzana-Priaroggia's second torpedo. Gould reported that while they were in the water or on rafts '[a] lot of people were bitten by sharks . . . Several . . . were suffering from barracuda bites; I think the sharks are worse, but the barracuda are more annoying as they bite slowly.' Gould himself was not bitten even though he spent two hours swimming about, and attributed his immunity to the fact that he was 'smothered by oil which probably kept [the sharks] away, as they don't like the taste of it.'[3]

In due course a rescue operation was mounted from Freetown and the destroyer *Boreas*, the corvettes *Petunia* and *Crocus*, and the Ocean Boarding Vessel *Corinthian* succeeded in saving Gould, 1,188 military passengers, 26 of the gunners and 273 of his ship's company.[4]

Gazzana-Priaroggia's submarine was sunk some weeks later off the Azores, but not before he had sunk the *Lulworth Hill*, on 19 March. A newly-built tramp, she was on passage from Mauritius to Britain via Freetown with a cargo of 413 tons of rum and no less than 11,000 tons of sugar. On the evening of the 18th she was about a thousand miles west of Loanda, in Portuguese West Africa, when a torpedo track passed her stern. Gazzana-Priaroggia surfaced and the *Lulworth Hill*'s gun opened fire, driving him down. Captain W.E. McEwan turned away and increased speed. During the night the *Leonardo da Vinci* chased the *Lulworth Hill*, whose crew prepared the boats for an evacuation. At 03.40 Gazzana-Priaroggia's second attack succeeded. Carpenter K. Cooke wrote:

> The deck was a scene of pandemonium ... Figures dimly seen ... ran desperately to their boat stations, only to find, as I did, that to continue farther towards the boat deck was impossible. Shouts of 'Jump, for God's sake, jump!' were coming from ... everywhere.
>
> Groping my way through thick wraiths of hissing steam, I discovered that the poor old girl had been cut clean in two ... The forward part was already upending and ready to plunge beneath the waves. I could see figures ... running up the sloping deck and leaping overboard ... Shouts, screams, and curses filled my ears as the bows dived ... Beneath me I felt the after part, too, begin to tilt. I scrambled aft ... when I reached the taffrail ... I gazed at the water [far] below me ... the huge twin propellers were still turning ... and deterred me from the leap ... Then with a tiny tremor ... the ship began to take her dive ... My fear of being sucked under with the dying *Lulworth Hill* overcame my fear of the revolving propellers ... I shut my eyes and over I went.

The *Lulworth Hill* had sunk in 90 seconds.

The *Leonardo da Vinci* surfaced among the wreckage and survivors, taking prisoner a DEMS gunner named Hull. Some time later Cooke was hauled, exhausted, onto a raft; it was the beginning of a 50-day ordeal. McEwan and 42 men were killed. Of 14 men who got away on two rafts under the mate, Mr B.E. Scown, five were minors – three boys and two apprentices. All 14 were cut and bruised, but the second engineer was badly injured. They anticipated being rescued, since the radio officer had the previous evening transmitted a message that they were under attack, but after a week the ravages of exposure under a tropical sun were beginning to tell. They began to sail north and east. As one of the boys began to fail and Scown to hallucinate, Cooke recorded events on scraps of sailcloth. The mate died on the afternoon of 6 April, the nineteenth day on the raft.

The desire for water became intense and some of the men drank seawater, rapidly becoming delirious and even violent; many 'gave up hope and lost the urge to struggle on for their lives'. Three days later Deck Boy Fowler expired, and thereafter death was a daily visitor. So was a cortège of sharks, 'six to eight any time you look'. On the 13th Cooke lamented the death of 18-year-old Apprentice J. Arnold, one of four who had given up the ghost the previous day: 'He was a good, kind lad. What an officer he would have made! ... The sort who had a helping hand and a kind word for everybody.' Arnold's last words had been: 'I have been talking to God. Some of you are going to be saved.' That day too the second engineer died: 'a likeable, reserved man, who, considering the enormity of his suffering, had complained very little.'

By the 21st, the thirty-fourth day on the raft, only Cooke, Chief Steward Platten and Able Seaman C. Armitage remained alive. They eked out their provisions in a heat so appalling that they 'could not move, think, look or breathe without heavy effort'. Platten died in the night. 'His quiet personality had done a lot towards keeping order and sanity on the raft. On the *Lulworth Hill* he had been known as "Fair Play" Platten because of the equity of his dealings with officers and men. No mess-table went short of food through any fault of his.'

On the 25th Cooke and Armitage ate the last of the hard ship's biscuit; they now had only a daily ration of two ounces of Bovril pemmican, eight Horlick's malted-milk tablets, five squares of chocolate, and a little water. On 30 April, the forty-third day on the raft, they saw four aircraft, but received no indication that they had been spotted, though they had fired smoke floats and, after painfully deciphering the instruction book, activated their portable radio. 'We are', recorded Cooke painfully in his canvas diary, 'both very ill.' Aeroplanes were seen on 1 May, and more the next morning. Then one spotted them and dropped four packages; they could only reach two. They were still adrift on the 4th when they had to cut their daily water ration to four ounces. On the 5th an aircraft dropped a message, but still no rescue appeared and morale, previously sustained by expectation, sank: the world of normality seemed to have turned its face against them.

In addition to being sunburnt and covered in salt-water boils, bruised and sore from constant bony contact with the raft's structure, Armitage was now nursing a hand seared from igniting and holding up flares. Dropped overboard, a piece of bloody dressing extemporised from a kapok life-jacket stirred the trailing sharks to a terrifying frenzy. The largest persistently hit the raft with its lashing tail.

That afternoon they were picked up by HMS *Rapid*. Machine-gun fire deterred the sharks as Cooke looked up speechlessly and found himself 'gazing at a pleasant, weather-beaten face under a capful of gold braid': it was Lieutenant Commander M.W. Tomkinson. Then 'agile ratings tumbled down the netting, and . . . carried [us] on board the destroyer.' The Royal Navy did its liberal best for its poor sister-service. One 'tough-bitten' petty officer looked at the two men and remarked: 'I've heard they starve you blokes in the "Merch", but I never knew they did it as proper as that!'

There was more than a hint of unintended truth in the comment. Cooke and Armitage were in due course repatriated, and were awarded both the

George Medal and Lloyd's War Medal. Sadly, Armitage became epileptic after his ordeal, and did not long survive it.[5]

The statisticians evaluating the effects of Dönitz's offensive calculated that during the first three weeks of March 1943 shipping – half a million tons of it – was lost at approximately twice the rate at which Allied tonnage was being built. In a visit to Horton at Derby House Lord Hall, Financial Secretary to the Admiralty, let the Commander-in-Chief know that Their Lordships were secretly of the opinion that the convoy system should be abandoned and the merchant ships left to make the best of their way across the Western Ocean independently.[6] That ancient and fallacious school of thought based on the specious but attractive notion that the Atlantic was vast and that, left to their own devices, enough merchantmen would probably make it across was a spectre that would not die. Such a wanton disregard of the realities of the situation was contrary to all Horton's instincts and would play into the hands of German submariners willing to attack single, unprotected merchantmen where they were less enthusiastic about taking on a well-managed escort group – and this at a time when, at long last, the support groups were to hand, as were the escort-carriers (albeit one, HMS *Dasher*, had blown up on trials in the Clyde when aviation spirit ignited).

In the light of subsequent events and the speed with which the situation was utterly reversed, it is hard to appreciate why the Admiralty were considering this. The question whether the morale of the Allied merchant services involved, principally the American and British, would stand such a volte-face was one ignored by the Admiralty staff. The American merchant service, expanding exponentially in terms of both manpower and ships, remained green and inexperienced in convoy, too subject to the erratic conduct of men taking shelter behind union-driven demands for 'danger-money' and 'double-overtime' when any unusual circumstances arose. It is unlikely that without naval protection it would have ever begun to supply Britain, even supposing its political masters and naval colleagues had agreed to do so. And while the British 'Merchant Navy' and its exiled Allies would have fought on, they too were different people from those they had been in 1939.

Their organisation had been radically overhauled and rationalised since their welding into the 'Fourth Arm of Defence', but they had taken enormous punishment. Morale had been subject to a heavy erosion afloat; their joint sacrifices, they felt, were still barely comprehended by their fellow countrymen ashore, many of whom seemed to be doing very-nicely-thank-you out of black-market profiteering in commodities men died for in the cruel sea. Moreover, the British merchant service was also expanding, recruiting inexperienced youngsters to man the emergency tonnage being built largely in Canada and the United States, young men like those assigned to the *Fort Cedar Lake* whose early conduct had been so reprehensible. The old traditions derived from company loyalty, a contemptuous toughness bred in the poor bones of hard-bitten professional seafarers – these had suffered from the 'attrition of war, were watered down by the new drafts. Such a change in quality was inevitable with such an augmentation in quantity, but to rely upon this quality would at best have been to rely upon an uncertainty, quite apart from any broader strategical considerations.

Horton can have had no doubts about the folly of Hall's expressed presumption, and probably responded with forthright candour. He was well able to gauge the impact of such a decision upon Fleet Admiral King in Washington, to say nothing of the dire consequences that would flow from it. Besides, he was now optimistic, and his optimism was grounded in fact. If HX229 and SC122 had been 'sacrificed to bigger things', as many of the merchant seamen involved thought was the case, the bigger things in question had not been some extension of grand strategy elsewhere in the world; nothing could be bigger than the Battle of the Atlantic, as the First Sea Lord, Sir Dudley Pound, had pointed out when he said that loss of the conflict over the Western Ocean meant loss of the war. But Horton could not bring his new weapons to bear until they were ready, and what the immolation of those merchant seamen and ships of SC122 and HX229 had bought him was time – invaluable time.

Much of the opposition confronting the Allied forces had been produced by a small number of determined U-boat commanders, rather than the mass of U-boats lying in wait for the convoys. There was a perceptible waning in German aggression generally, due to a number of factors, predominantly a failure in that essential 'ability of the commander' which, as Dönitz had pointed out in 1940, 'will always be the decisive factor'.[7] In addition to the burn-out of experienced commanders, attrition forced the Germans, like the Allies, to rely on 'green' men. Dönitz had been driven to the expedients of sending officers out on war patrol without prior command experience, and of transferring surplus manpower from the Luftwaffe. German method failed to produce the necessary officers for their abominable task, however, while British method succeeded admirably. Moreover, by the end of March 1943 Horton had mustered five support groups that were now ready to join their battered colleagues in the Atlantic.[8]

Despite the exhaustion of his commanders and the state of many of his submarines, by 20 March Dönitz was in receipt of further radio intercepts that gave a precise position for a westbound convoy on the following day. ONS1 was the first of a new series of slow convoys running concurrently with the ON series, and the position betrayed to BdU was the rendezvous for ships joining it from Reykjavik. The *Seeteufel* (Sea-Devil) group was made up from a few former *Stürmer* U-boats reinforced by others from France. Its spearhead was to be Kapitänleutnant H. Pich, who was ordered to take *U-168* to the rendezvous, to make contact with ONS1 and to shadow it. Both *U-168* and her commander were on their first Atlantic war patrol, and Pich failed to sight any of the 34 vessels making up ONS1, so the extending patrol line was in turn moved westwards in expectation. By the 26th the U-boats lay along a line running SSE from Cape Farewell where it was further extended by the *Seewolf* group, a huge number of U-boats spread over 800 miles of open water.[9]

Commander Heathcote's B6 Escort Group was spotted briefly from *U-306*, but there were no further developments against ONS1. It was almost inconceivable that more than thirty U-boats disposed over such an area should fail to intercept at least one convoy. However, such large numbers could not themselves go undetected, and on 25 March *U-469* was sunk on her way to station by a Fortress from No. 206 Squadron of Coastal Command, while two days later another Fortress sank *U-169*.

Meanwhile, on the afternoon of the 26th the 45 ships of SC123 had been seen from *U-564* and reported by her commander, Oberleutnant H. Fiedler, who assumed it to be headed west. Convoy SC123 was escorted by MacIntyre's B2 Escort Group,[10] reinforced by the all-American 6th Support Group which consisted of the escort-carrier *Bogue*, Captain G.E. Short, USN and two destroyers, USSs *Belknap* and *George E. Badger*. *U-415* and *U-663* also arrived, but none of the three U-boats was able to mount an attack, being forced away by the Grumman Wildcats flown from the *Bogue*.

On the same day that *U-169* was sunk, Kapitänleutnant R. Bahr in *U-305*, at the most northerly end of the *Seewolf* line and roughly one-third of the way along the combined groups from the north, caught sight of HX230, which had been routed north of the perceived concentration. Dönitz immediately ordered some 22 of the nearest U-boats to attack.

The 41 vessels of Convoy HX230 had left New York on 18 March under Commodore I.W. Whitehorn in the *Pacific Shipper* and, proceeding first through dense fog, picked up an ocean escort of Commander E.C. Bayldon's B1 ships, the destroyers *Hurricane*, *Rockingham* and *Watchman*, the frigate *Kale* and the corvettes *Dahlia*, *Meadowsweet*, *Monkshood* and *Wallflower*. Refuelling the escorts from the *Esso Charleston* proved the by now customary mixture of success and farce. By the 27th not only had Bayldon been reinforced by Captain McCoy's destroyers of the 3rd Support Group, *Offa*, *Obedient*, *Oribi*,

Orwell, Onslaught and *Icarus*, but the weather had deteriorated dreadfully. The south-westerly wind rose first to storm force and then, throughout the 28th, reached Force 12, with hurricane-strength winds in excess of 65 knots. Inevitably, HX230 broke close formation and spread out, three ships straggled, and 'several . . . [were] experiencing difficulties with deck cargoes'. One, the *Baronesa*, had some of her deck cargo torn free and swept overboard, and the American *John Eaton* had all her lifeboats stove-in.

Of the submarines sent against HX230 only *U-260* (Purkhold), *U-415* (Neide), *U-591* (Zetzsche), *U-610* (von Freyberg-Eisenberg-Allmendingen) and *U-631* (Krüger) were able to get anywhere near it to join Bahr's *U-305*. In the spume and spindrift of the storm Korvettenkapitän Purkhold worked close to a merchantman on the late afternoon of the 28th and decided to attack on the surface before darkness fell. 'With the very heavy sea running there is very little likelihood of her sighting me. Spray has reduced visibility to something between one and two miles.' Purkhold's attack failed, and by 22.00 he had given up. 'To remain on the bridge was impossible. On the bridge the CO and the watch, after half an hour . . . were half-drowned. In a very short period 5 tons of water were shipped through the conning tower hatch, the voice pipe and diesel air intake. The [target] ship was running directly before the storm.' Purkhold turned away 'with a heavy heart'.

He was not alone; Dönitz had been notified of the presence of the escort carrier *Bogue* attending SC123, and Short's 6th Support group remained in the air-gap as HX230 passed through. Dönitz let the U-boat commanders at sea know that the sinking of the *Bogue* was of particular importance 'for the progress of convoy operations'. The sea conditions broke up the U-boat attacks, but Dönitz 'was surprised to learn that the extremely bad weather did not interrupt the intense enemy air activity'. The support group and the escort group deterred any close approach to HX230, and there was now a shift in the Germans' targets: 'Though it [the bad weather] prevented the aircraft from making accurate attacks on our [U-] boats, their mere presence caused the [U-] boats to move eastwards even more slowly than *the stragglers they were trying to attack*' [my emphasis: RW].

One of these stragglers was the American Liberty ship *William Pierce Frye*, which was having engine and steering problems in the heavy sea on the same day that Purkhold was stalking an unidentified merchantman. That morning two torpedo tracks passed close past the vessel and Captain M. Scherf cracked on 12.5 knots in an attempt to regain the shelter of the convoy some thirty miles away, but seven hours later, now 16 miles astern of HX230, the *William Pierce Frye* was hit by a torpedo from *U-610* fired by Kapitänleutnant Freiherr von Freyberg-Eisenberg-Allmendingen. The force of the explosion was largely absorbed by the wheat in No. 1 Lower Hold, but four minutes later a second torpedo blasted its way into the engine room and within six minutes the *William Pierce Frye* had vanished. She had been heavily laden, carrying a mixed cargo of wheat and explosives, her capacious decks bearing five landing-craft. One of these tore free of its lashings and provided a refuge for seven men who, having jumped overboard, swam to it. One lifeboat was thought to have been lowered, despite the heavy roll and list of the vessel, but no trace of her or the 12 men aboard her was ever found. The men on the landing-craft, five sailors and two naval guardsmen, were rescued five days later by the British destroyer *Shikari*. Captain Scherf was lost with his ship.

By 29 March HX230 was approaching Rockall and a strong air escort was present from Northern Ireland, supplementing the heavy surface cover. March continued to roar out like a lion, the weather remaining bad. All but one vessel from HX230 had won through, however. Behind it laboured the following 33 laden ships of SC124, while going west and routed well clear, the 41 vessels of ON174 headed for New York. Neither was in contact with the enemy.[11]

The Allied appraisal said of *Bogue*'s air cover over HX230 that it 'came not a moment too soon, for convoy losses in the [air-] gap were mounting. With end-to-end air cover, the convoys could now take a more southerly route.' Horton also minuted Bayldon's report that his escort group was the first 'to be reinforced by a Support Group of Home Fleet Destroyers and the results are encouraging'. Bayldon's *Hurricane* had, with *Rockingham*, got into close surface contact with one U-boat and failed to sink it 'due to the inadequacy of our weapons'. Bayldon properly declined to ram, on the grounds that such action would incapacitate *Hurricane* and reduce the effectiveness of his ability to protect the convoy. The staff assessment conclusion that Bayldon's escort group had failed to 'kill' any U-boats prompted the Commander-in-Chief to comment that it was 'impossible and undesirable to lay down rigid instructions and every case must be judged on its own merits'. With one straggling exception, Bayldon had nevertheless brought in his convoy safely.

HX231 was less fortunate. The convoy had left New York on 25 March, led by Commodore Sir Charles Ramsey, a retired admiral, whose pendant flew in the Blue Funnel liner *Tyndareus*. It was a large convoy of 61 vessels, occupying a front of 8 miles, and it became disorganised in fog on the Grand Bank. By the time it was picked up by Commander P. Gretton's B7 Escort Group it had been routed north, into cold and heavy weather. With the wind in the higher latitudes usually blowing from the north and west, spray froze on the upper works and had to be broken off with picks and shovels. Aboard the P&O cargo-liner *Shillong* the port lifeboats on the weather side had become so encrusted that the davits bent and the boats were brought inboard and lashed on deck from where, it was hoped, they would float free if they were needed. Life-rafts had been swept away and the main mast, its steel brittle in the extreme cold, had simply carried away, compelling Captain J.H. Hollow to haul out of line and slow down while all hands turned-to to clear away the dangerous wreckage.

Other ships were in similar straits and Ramsey was having trouble with ice on his flag halliards. Gretton's group, consisting of the frigate *Tay*, the destroyer *Vidette* and corvettes *Alisma, Loosestrife, Pink* and *Snowflake*, had chivvied most of the merchantmen, including *Shillong*, back into station by nightfall on 30 March. The group was aware of the presence of U-boats, and had one brush with the enemy on the afternoon of the 4th. For all its busy shepherding, B7 was relatively unblooded, and too small to guard such a large convoy as HX230, but that day Gretton received a signal that Captain Scott-Moncrieff's 4th Support Group was hurrying to his assistance for the transit of the air-gap. Before sunset, however, two U-boats had been spotted ahead of the convoy, and the atmosphere was ominous.

The *Shillong* had long since resumed her station at the head of the twelfth column when, at 22.15, a torpedo slammed into her port side just forward of her boiler room. Oberleutnant W. Winkler in *U-630* had fired it, and the *Shillong* began to settle by the head. She was well loaded with 3,000 tons of general cargo and grain, plus 4,000 tons of zinc concentrates. On the bridge the watch officers, the third officer and a cadet, attempted to release the distress signals and switch on the red light indicating a hit, but 'the chart room was a shambles. All the concrete [reinforcing] around the plating had fallen down in the concussion, both doors had been blown in and the settee hurled across the chartroom. The book case and echo sounding gear had crashed to the deck, and the chronometer cases were smashed. It was impossible to find flares or matches amid the debris.' At this point Captain Hollow ordered Cadet Clowe to dump the confidential books and then to take to the boats.

On the starboard side of the boat-deck the naval gunlayer, Petty Officer Hadley, Cadet Francis, the third engineer, a gunner and three Lascar seamen lowered No. 3 Boat, Francis ensuring that, despite the heavy downward pitch of the deck, the falls kept the boat horizontal. In the boat Cadet Coleman had taken charge. Meanwhile Clowe had left the bridge with the third officer, but by now the water was rising fast, and with half a gale blowing a heavy sea, thick with flotsam, washed the third officer away. Clowe retreated and then dived clear, later scrambling aboard No. 3 Boat. He was followed in his dive by Hadley and Francis, who made for a raft upon which perched twenty or thirty survivors. But this was repeatedly swamped and capsized by the wind and sea until only nine men remained clinging to it: Hollow, his chief officer and third engineer, Cadets Francis and Moore, Hadley, another gunner, and two lascars.

It was only now, as the *Shillong* went down, that the convoy became aware of the presence of the enemy and fired snowflakes. The pitiful survivors saw a corvette not far away illuminated by the eerie light and blew their whistles and shouted, but to no avail. They 'huddled together . . . in the bitter cold. The wind whistled through their teeth and the sea drenched them as it smashed up through the slats or broke over them. It seemed impossible to be so cold and yet live.'

Not all did. That night Hollow, his chief officer, Francis and one lascar all died. At dawn the remainder broached the provisions, Moore improvising a water dipper from his life-jacket light. As the daylight grew they spotted No. 3 Boat and attempted to paddle towards her. Seeing their plight, Cadet Coleman manned his oars and picked up the handful of men and their provisions off the raft. He told them that during the night those in the boat had spoken with an escort – it appears to have been Gretton's *Tay* – which was hunting U-boats but promised to return and pick them up. It never did. Gretton had in fact sent *Pink* back to search for survivors, but she had found nothing.

There were now 38 men in *Shillong*'s No. 3 Boat. At first they rode head to sea to the sea-anchor, and when that carried away they rigged the boat's sail as an extemporised drogue. They were now threatened by flotsam from the wreck of their own ship: the steel-bound wooden hatch-boards were a particular menace, and threatened to stove-in the boat. Fending off with a boat-hook, Third Engineer Macrae sat in the bow, exposed to the icy wind, clad in a boiler suit and patrol jacket sodden from his night's ordeal on the raft. When they had cleared the wreckage Macrae came inboard, sat quietly in the bow sheets and shortly afterwards died. Although they tried to man the oars, the cold was biting, affecting the lascars terribly. One seacunny or quartermaster assisted with the bailing until he too succumbed to hypothermia. Next day the drogue carried away and Coleman sank into a coma and died. Clowe took charge of the boat, which was short of potable water. His crew dwindled as the remaining three lascars perished. Moore and a gunner named Barnes began to make a jury sail, but they were growing increasingly feeble. Clowe cut his hand badly and had to have a tourniquet applied, and the third radio officer was unfit for duty. This left five gunners and Cadet Moore to man the oars as they strove to keep the boat head-up, into the wind and sea.

On the fourth day the weather moderated briefly and they had a respite from pulling, but it did not last long. More men were failing, and those in reasonable condition were complaining of intolerable thirst and painful feet. By noon on the seventh day the weather had eased again so they ceased pulling and, with a south-easterly breeze, set their scrap of sail on the boat hook. They sailed for four hours under bright moonlight until, once again, the sea got up and they put out the oars. They could now hardly cope with the influx of water, and at this juncture the radio officer gave up the ghost. It became imperative to rig another sea-anchor, and they managed to fabricate a drogue from the bottom boards. When the boat was riding more easily they bailed it again and, as if in reward for their fortitude, saw a Catalina and succeeded in attracting its attention. But no ship arrived, and a further night was spent at the oars as the boat continually fell off the wind and the sea rose again. The delay seems to have been caused by the necessity to divert the rescue ship *Zamalek* from Convoy ON177, which was then westbound some miles away. Of the 78 men aboard *Shillong* when she was torpedoed, only Cadets Clowe and Moore and DEMS gunners Hadley, Barnes, Stevens, French and Theobald remained alive. But the sea had not finished with them. Gangrene had attacked them: Moore, Hadley and Theobald each lost both legs; Barnes had his feet amputated; and Moore lost most of his fingers. Only Clowe, French and Stevens eventually left hospital as God had made them. Hadley, an older man, commented in a written report that Moore and Barnes had been outstanding: 'These chaps would have a go at anything.' In his Report of Proceedings Gretton attributed these losses 'directly' to HX231 having had no rescue ship in attendance.

When *Shillong* sank, Gretton's counter-measures were 'hampered by three foreigners in the starboard wing column who decided to break out of the convoy, thereby wasting the precious time of the *Tay* who chased them without success.'[12] In the chaos caused by this indiscipline Oberleutnant H. Eckelmann slipped under Gretton's guard and shortly after midnight, passing *U-635* down between two columns, fired at the fourth ship in column four.[13] Nineteen men were lost with the *Waroonga*, a British India cargo-liner from Australia carrying eight passengers, three Distressed British Seamen and 8,500 tons of general cargo, among which were 1,500 tons of tinned meat, 5,000 tons of dairy produce and several score bags of mail. As the torpedo struck and the snowflake rockets went up, the whole ghastly panorama was given added lustre by the aurora which began its fantastical, numinous dance across the northern sky. The *Waroonga* had been struck aft in No. 4 Hold, and Captain Charles Campbell Taylor considered that since the space was full of butter and cheese the ingress of water was not likely to be excessive, and the *Waroonga* could continue in station, pumping out her No. 4 bilges.

She was still afloat at dawn and, 'given the chance of the weather improving, there seemed good prospects of making port'. Taylor's optimism was short-lived; by noon the engine room bulkhead was weeping. Ramsey signalled that *Tay* would stand-by, and would not let Taylor down. 'I liked the last bit,' Taylor reported candidly. '. . . it bucked me up considerably. It was a queer feeling I had all this time; I felt that everybody on board was watching me, and I hoped that we would be able to pull through. I was on deck all the time . . .' In fact Gretton had dropped *Tay* back 'to discuss the situation over the loud hailer. She was keeping perfect station and all hands were extremely cheerful. Indeed, from the port side the only sign of trouble was a knot of men huddled in the lee of a deck house, each with his little bag of belongings. On the starboard quarter, however, there was a hole through which a car could have been driven. The Master wished to transfer all men not required for steaming the ship, to an escort, but the sea was becoming rough, making boat work difficult and lengthy.'

At nightfall the weather worsened. The *Waroonga* was now wallowing heavily aft and it was clear that she was foundering. With the water swirling about her after deck Taylor gave the order to abandon ship, remaining on the bridge 'feeling rather lonely . . . but all was going as we had practised hundreds of times before, there was no panic and everybody was being quietly efficient. It was dark, cold and blowing hard.'

Gretton had characterised daylight boat operations as 'difficult and lengthy' and now it was dark – and now the *Waroonga* was sinking. Only those with practical experience of lowering boats from large ships in mid ocean can truly appreciate the realities of a situation like this, so commonly faced by thousands of merchant seamen since September 1939. To lower any boats at all in any wind above a gentle breeze bespoke a skill and certainly a daring outside the run of ordinary events. Even more remarkable was the seamanship required in heaving a laden merchantman to and picking up boatloads of survivors, but that was what Captain T.A. Morasson of the new Liberty ship *Joel R. Poinsett* accomplished. He took up some of the 112 souls escaping in the *Waroonga*'s boats, which Taylor rightly considered 'dangerous work and bravely done'. Those lost, who included five passengers and one of the Distressed British Seamen, were in the chief officer's boat which was swamped and overset, evidence of the sea conditions prevailing at the time.

Early next morning Gretton became aware that in addition to his three missing 'foreigners' another American ship, the tanker *Sunoil*, was straggling well astern with engine trouble. Meanwhile Oberleutnant R. Schetelig in *U-229* had encountered the Swedish *Vaalaren*, one of Gretton's wandering 'foreigners' that had broken out of the starboard wing the previous afternoon. The *Vaalaren* had been in several mid-Atlantic convoys, but now she disappeared; there were no survivors. Nor was the straggling *Sunoil* long alone: Kapitänleutnant G. von Hartmann's *U-563* found her zig-zagging and torpedoed her that morning. On receipt of Captain S.B. Hegglund's report that he had engaged *U-563* with his stern gun Gretton sent *Vidette* back to assist and to attack the U-boat. *Vidette* searched, but Lieutenant Commander R. Hart found no trace of the *Sunoil* or her boats and could not linger, being under strict orders to return to his station by nightfall. The *Sunoil* was sunk by Lange's *U-530* later in the day, though exactly when she had been abandoned is unclear, for no one lived to tell. Another of the wanderers, an American Liberty ship, returned to the fold later in the day.

With *Pink* back by noon and a promise of air cover arriving from Iceland that afternoon, the convoy altered course from NNE to east. 'The weather had become perfect with a calm sea and good visibility, and the U-boats were chattering like magpies all around the horizon,' wrote Gretton, 'our HF/DF operator reporting one bearing after another.' Gretton was tempted to move out of the screen before *Vidette* had returned as a Liberator attacked a U-boat ahead of the convoy and requested assistance to kill it. As *Tay* sped off 'there was an explosion and we saw an enormous column of water rising from a ship in the centre of the convoy.' This was the tanker *British Ardour*, second in column six, acting as the escorts' oiler. She caught fire and Captain T. Copeman ordered the crew into the boats. All hands escaped, to be picked up by *Sunflower*, Lieutenant Commander J. Plomer, but the *British Ardour* was still afloat and was despatched by Hart on *Vidette*'s way to catch up with the convoy before dusk.

Shortly after dark the U-boats began closing in. HM Corvette *Loosestrife* reported a contact but then, to Gretton's displeasure, bungled her counter-attack. This was the first of eleven separate enemy probings of the escort, but Gretton's loss of the *British Ardour* and her fuel-oil had persuaded him not to let his escorts distance themselves for long or too far from the convoy. Several of the escorts had brushes with U-boats; *Tay* depth-charged *U-635*[14] and almost collided with a Prince Line vessel which veered out of station with failed steering gear.

During the 6th Scott-Moncrieff's Support Group arrived, rather later than planned, and the Home Fleet destroyers were kept busy among the contacts now astern of the convoy, which was out of immediate danger. It only remained for the corvette *Alisma* to recover the 54 survivors from the Dutch-flagged *Blitar*, third of the 'foreigners' romping ahead of the convoy. A single overcrowded lifeboat was found, a further 26 men had lost their lives. The *Blitar* had been torpedoed by Kapitänleutnant H. Karpf in *U-632* in the early hours of that morning, but Karpf did not survive the day, being depth-charged west of Rockall by a Liberator from No. 84 Squadron flown by Flight Lieutenant C.W. Burcher.

The alarums of the night of 6/7 April were inconclusive, and air cover during the following day proved a strong deterrent. The U-boats broke off the action, and as *Tyndareus* led the columns through the North Channel, Gretton's escort group turned away for Lough Foyle and the berths at Londonderry. He went aboard *Loosestrife* and *Snowflake* on arrival there and spoke with some of the survivors. Taylor of the *Waroonga* impressed him by remarking that he 'had better be thinking of getting . . . another ship.'

The Germans now turned their attention to the following convoys but failed to attack SC125, largely because of the presence of a British support group. Instead the assembled U-boats, reformed into the *Adler* (Eagle) group, moved south-east to intercept HX232. Contact was first made with westbound ON176, however, and a portion of the *Adler* submarines were ordered to attack. During a night assault in the early hours of 11 April Kapitänleutnant S. Lüdden in *U-188* sank the ex-American destroyer HMS *Beverley*, one of the B4 escorts of ON176.

The main attacks on ON176 and HX232 came 24 hours later. From ON176 the *Lancastrian Prince* was lost to von Bülow in *U-404*; she was in ballast and foundered rapidly, downing Captain F.R. Elliott and all hands. In HX232 Reardon Smith's tramp *Fresno City* was hit by a torpedo from Hartmann's *U-563* but was actually sunk by a later one fired from *U-706* (Zitzewitz). Although laden with 3,000 tons of manganese ore and 6,000 tons of general and military cargo, the *Fresno City* floated long enough to allow Captain R.A. Lawson and his entire crew to escape. Hartmann also sank the Dutch-flagged *Ulysses*, which went down without loss of life, and the *Pacific Grove*, Captain E.W. Pritchard. Eleven men were killed from the latter, a Furness Withy general cargo-liner, although all her 16 passengers were rescued by the corvette *Azalea*, Lieutenant G.C. Geddes, acting as rescue ship.

In German terms these achievements were paltry, given the high numbers and dispositions of U-boats at sea in the North Atlantic. Dönitz attributed the lack of success to the weather and to the augmentation of Allied convoy defences, especially in terms of increased air cover, which was not only accounting for a rising number of U-boat 'kills' but 'prevented many of the U-boats from gaining a position ahead of the convoy from which to launch their attacks'. And while Gretton admitted in retrospect to deficiencies in the defence of HX231, Dönitz failed to acknowledge that most successful attacks were the work of a handful of U-boat commanders, and that while their extended dispositions caused many to fail to close with a convoy, there were others who failed to press home a promising approach. With an HX convoy steaming at 9 knots a U-boat had only one realistic chance of doing this, and even those that did, firing multiple salvos, frequently claimed far more strikes than they accomplished. To this lack of *élan* on the part of the Germans must be added the Allied triumph in directing convoys clear of U-boat groups. All these circumstances combined to ensure that the German U-boat offensive had, by the spring of 1943, passed the high-water mark.

Evidence that the ebb was already under way came in mid April with an attack on HX233, which had left New York on 6 April. Comprising 54 merchantmen led by Commodore O.H. Dawson aboard the Lamport & Holt liner *Devis*, its ships, like those in all these convoys, carried a mixture of military hardware, food, oil, and economically necessary raw materials. Many ships carried mixed general cargoes along with explosives and bombs. Grain and wheat filled many holds while timber was stacked and lashed on deck – a dangerous cargo liable to be washed overboard in heavy weather, leaving a vessel to list helplessly. No fewer than 20 tankers were included; some, such as the *Velma* and *British Pride*, second and third vessels in column three, carried fuel for the British Admiralty, while the Norwegian *Norsol*, lying third in column nine, carried highly inflammable aviation spirit. Of the cargo-vessels, several were emergency war tonnage: nine were Liberty ships, one was the Canadian-built, British-manned *Fort Rampart*; the *Empire Wordsworth* was a British-built tanker. The second 'Empire' vessel was the *Empire Pakeha*, one of the former Shaw, Savill & Albion liners which had previously served as a dummy battleship. Her master, Captain H.C. Smith, now acted as vice commodore to HX233.

The convoy's ocean defence was provided by Captain Heineman's A3 Escort Group led by the American Coast Guard Cutters *Spencer* and *Duane*, one of the last of the mixed groups that fleet Admiral King so fervently wanted abolished. The corvettes were HMSs *Bryony, Dianthus* and *Bergamot*, and the Canadians *Wetaskiwin* and *Arvida*, which in the absence of a rescue ship was to double in that capacity. The Canadian destroyer *Skeena* later reinforced Heineman.

HX233 was ordered along the southern route, roughly along the latitude common to Cape Sable and Cape Finisterre, until two-thirds of the way across, when course was altered to north-east at about noon on 16 April. That morning one U-boat, *U-262*, had been driven off, but during the afternoon and evening it became apparent from HF/DF intercepts that a number were gathering. As was usual, none of the merchant ships were informed of this impending danger, though Dawson would have been aware of it. That night Oberleutnant H. Bruns regained contact in *U-175* and homed in Kapitänleutnant H. Hasenschar's *U-628*. At about 05.00 on the 17th, with HX233 steaming over a calm sea ruffled by light airs about 660 miles WSW of the Bishop Rock light, Hasenschar attacked the vessel leading the second column. This was the *Fort Rampart*, whose master Captain W.H. Stein had distinguished himself in Russia when his previous ship, the *Empire Starlight*, had been subjected to concentrated attacks by German aircraft.[15]

The torpedo blew the *Fort Rampart*'s rudder and propeller off, destroyed the after crew's accommodation and admitted sea-water into the after holds. The transfer of shock through the part-welded hull caused major cracks to open up further forward. The extensive after deck cargo of timber had been disturbed, and Stein can have been in little doubt that his ship was doomed when he assessed the damage after dumping the confidential documents. Although the red light signalling a hit was hoisted the rockets were useless, and several of the escorts had no idea a ship had been torpedoed. Stein and two seamen roused out the dazed men of the watch below and, with the ship settling fast, gave the order to abandon her.

Four boats were lowered and all except six men escaped safely. By 07.15 they had been taken aboard the *Arvida*, one of the few vessels either in or escorting the convoy which seemed aware of the *Fort Rampart*'s plight. Even the vice commodore, who afterwards reported sighting the red lights, seems not to have informed Dawson at the time. The *Fort Rampart*, having a considerable quantity of timber below decks, remained afloat for some time. Seeing her reluctance to sink, Stein proposed that the *Fort Rampart* be salvaged, and upon the arrival of Captain McCoy's 3rd Support Group an hour or so later the destroyers *Penn* and *Panther* were ordered to assess the possibility. By the time they approached, however, the *Fort Rampart* was hit by another torpedo from Hasenschar's U-boat, with *U-226*, Oberleutnant A. Gänge, astern of the convoy hoping to pick off stragglers, also claiming a hit. As *Penn* and *Panther* closed with the derelict she broke in two. *Panther*, having a weak sonar contact, fired depth-charges which damaged *U-628* and drove Hasenschar out of the action.

This was the only loss suffered by the ships in Convoy HX233 to enemy action, and was at least in part mitigated by the destruction of *U-175* later that same day by Commander Berdine in the *Spencer*. However, three days later the Liberty ship *James Fenimore Cooper* was in collision with *Lena Luckenbach* during the dark hours of early morning. The elderly *Lena Luckenbach* appears at some time to have been reassigned from leading a column to its rear, probably because of difficulties in station-keeping and steering, placing her adjacent to the Liberty ship with which she later came into violent contact. Although neither vessel was sinking, the *Lena Luckenbach* was severely damaged forward and settled heavily by the head, persuading her ship's company otherwise. They consequently abandoned her in a great hurry and, contrary to orders from the corvette *Dianthus*, they did so without leaving a small salvage party aboard, thus presenting the crew of the *Bergamot* with considerable difficulties when they arrived later in the day to pass a tow in rough seas. This difficult operation was completed successfully, but there was insufficient catenary or 'sag' in the tow-line to absorb shocks and, to the frustration of *Bergamot*'s crew, a sudden sheer parted the hawser. The weather had greatly improved by the time the Admiralty tug *Growler* arrived to complete the task at 07.30 on the 21st and the *Lena Luckenbach* was beached in Kames Bay, from where she was in due course repaired and returned to service.[16]

Collision, always a hazard at sea but particularly in convoy, accounted for no fewer than eight more merchantmen before the HX series ended in 1945,[17] compared with six sunk by U-boats while actually in convoy over the same period. One of those torpedoed in convoy was in HX234, against which several U-boats were directed. The *Amerika*, Captain C. Nielsen, was torpedoed by Kapitänleutnant C. von Trotha in *U-306* on 22 April in a daylight, underwater attack. A large vessel owned by the British United Baltic Corporation, the *Amerika* was carrying a valuable cargo and more than fifty Canadian air force personnel. Loss of life was severe, some 86 souls altogether, including 37 of her passengers.

However, the U-boats continued to reap a grim harvest among the stragglers. Von Trotha found one the following day. The new Liberty ship *Robert Gray* had fallen astern of HX233 ten days earlier. Von Trotha sank her south of Cape Farewell with the loss of Captain A.R. Lyngby and all hands. No further attacks could be made on the main convoy because of fog and snow-squalls, and the presence of American Catalinas flown from Greenland. When the weather cleared on the 23rd, Liberators of No. 120 Squadron of Coastal Command flying from Iceland provided air cover. One, flown by Flying Officer J.K. Moffatt, caught *U-189* with two fatal depth-charges, sending her to the bottom with all her crew.

On her way to intercept HX234, Kapitänleutnant K. Neide's *U-415* was one of five U-boats diverted to attack the westbound convoy ONS3 which had also been routed north and lay some forty miles south of Cape Farewell on the morning of 21 April.[18] Neide's attack first hit the United Africa Company's *Ashantian*, which was in ballast and bore the convoy commodore, Vice Admiral J. Elliot. He and Captain Charles Carter Taylor, together with 14 crew, were killed, though 50 crew, naval gunners and the commodore's staff were picked up by an escort, HM Trawler *Northern Gift*. The *Northern Gift* also joined the corvette *Poppy* in rescuing Captain W.B. Johnston and all but two of the crew of the Watts, Watts tramp *Wanstead*, which was hit by Neide's second torpedo. The ship did not sink immediately and Lieutenant N.K. Boyd attempted to despatch her from *Poppy*. These escorts were also able to rescue 39 men from the *Scebeli*, a fine, fast Norwegian fruit-carrier from Sandefjord which was torpedoed by Kapitänleutnant H. Fiehn in *U-191*, killing two men.

Dönitz had considerable forces at his command, but he was aware that many of the U-boats currently in the Atlantic were low on fuel or torpedoes. He must also have sensed that matters were approaching a climax, and that he must seize the moment or lose the initiative altogether. He therefore diverted a number of Type IX U-boats from operations in distant waters, where pickings were becoming lean, to reinforce the offensive in the North Atlantic, and instructed the French bases to turn round incoming submarines with more despatch.

The next westerly convoy, ONS4, consisting of 32 ships escorted by MacIntyre's B2 Escort Group, was steaming west concurrently with ON179 of 51 ships covered by Lieutenant Commander Chavasse's C2 Escort Group. In the vicinity was the 5th Support Group under Captain E.M.C. Abel-Smith in the British escort-carrier *Biter*, whose Swordfish aircraft of No. 811 Squadron, Fleet Air Arm, flew effectively deterrent air patrols. On the afternoon of 23 April MacIntyre's *Hesperus*, joined by the corvette *Clematis*, destroyed Fiehn and *U-191* using a one-ton depth-charge and her forward firing 'Hedgehog' anti-submarine mortars: there were no survivors. On the 24th *U-710*, on her very first Atlantic patrol, was sunk off Iceland by a Liberator of No. 206 Squadron; all her men were killed. Next day one of *Biter*'s Swordfish homed the *Pathfinder* onto a contact, and in a two-hour attack Commander E.A. Gibbs forced *U-203* to surface, shelling her as she appeared. Kottmann and all but 11 of his men were captured.

At the rear of these complex convoy movements was ONS5. The turning-point had arrived.

25

'With the precision of a battle-fleet'

Gharinda

ALLIED LOSSES OF merchant ships had dropped dramatically during April after the dreadful attrition of March, but at the beginning of May 1943 the German submarine presence in the North Atlantic was at its greatest: 60 U-boats extended in four long patrol lines. Even if the Allied monthly 'kill' rate of 15 U-boats was sustained, the threat posed remained formidable, at least in theory. In fact the advantages accruing to the Allies were now gaining almost daily momentum. During May a change in Allied codes choked off the flow of B-Dienst intelligence to Dönitz, while the introduction of support groups and closure of the air-gap by escort-carriers was the decisive feature of the campaign. Much of the speed of this change in fortunes was due to Horton. 'He was that *rara avis* among Admirals,' wrote Commander R.A.B. Phillimore, a staff officer of the Fleet Air Arm, 'a technician who had completely mastered the . . . devices brought in to . . . the battle against the U-boats . . . He was a man of immense drive who refused to accept . . . delays and objections to any scheme on which he had made up his mind . . . It seems incredible . . . that only eight weeks elapsed to introduce a new weapon [anti-tank rockets adapted for firing at U-boats], get aircraft fitted with it, crews trained in its use, and get a kill with it in mid-Atlantic. Max Horton was the only man in the country who could have done this.' His was what an admirer called 'the master hand'.

This was in evidence as April ended and May began. When Ultra decrypts enabled Derby House to re-route SC127 and HX235, avoiding the *Amsel* (Blackbird) and *Specht* (Woodpecker) groups totalling 30 U-boats. Horton next turned his attention to a 16-strong U-boat group known to Dönitz as the *Star* (Starling) group, lying in ambush for ONS5 midway between Reykjanes and Cape Farewell.

The passage of Convoy ONS5 began on 21 April when the main division left Liverpool. Joined by the Clyde and Belfast portions, it emerged into the North Atlantic to meet its ocean escort, Gretton's B7 Escort Group, off Oversay at 14.00 next day. Gretton had returned to the ageing destroyer *Duncan*, which had been refitted during the passage of HX231, when he had been in *Tay*. The refit had not extended the *Duncan*'s range by the addition of extra fuel capacity, which was to prove a liability as the destroyer 'had a bad reputation for oil consumption', but it had provided 'Hedgehog' and the 'monstrously big [one-ton] depth charge which was discharged from a torpedo tube'. *Duncan* also bore the latest sonar, radio, radar and HF/DF equipment, while her crew had received a thorough work-up at Tobermory. Gretton himself had had to endure a post-mortem analysis of the defence of HX231 and an interview with Horton.

Before departing on its next task, the group had undergone the now routine exercise off Northern Ireland with the *Philante*, her accompanying elderly submarines and aircraft. With a new commanding officer in *Loosestrife* and the addition of two veteran anti-submarine trawlers to act as rescue ships and additional escorts, Gretton pronounced himself satisfied with the state of his escort group. In addition to *Duncan*, *Loosestrife* and the trawlers *Northern Gem* and *Northern Spray*, B7 consisted of *Tay*, *Snowflake*, *Sunflower* and *Pink*.

When fully formed Convoy ONS5 consisted of 45 merchantmen; 30 were British, four American, three Norwegian, two Dutch, two Greek, and one each flying the ensigns of Poland, Yugoslavia, Denmark and Panama.[1] Most were tramps, but in addition to the tankers, two of which (the *British Lady* and the *Argon*, owned by the Socony-Vacuum Oil Company of New York) acted as oilers, there were several fine and weatherly cargo-liners. Commodore J. Brooks, leading the sixth of twelve columns in the Norwegian tramp *Rena*, was a captain in the naval reserve and therefore understood the difficulties of manoeuvring merchant ships in convoy. This was just as well since most were in ballast – 'flying light' – and awkward to handle when station-keeping in heavy weather. And as ONS5 ploughed west it was clear that the weather was going to be appalling, and that the actual speed of this 'slow' convoy would be far below the planned 7.5 knots.

With a violent head wind and heavy sea, ONS5 was soon struggling to maintain any significant headway, and the frequent sight of two vertical red lights marking a ship as 'not under command' indicated the difficulty many masters were having holding on. On the 26th two vessels ran foul of each other and the more severely damaged of the pair was detached without escort to Iceland, where she arrived safely, undetected by the enemy in the poor visibility caused by the gale. Coming the other way, *Vidette* arrived from Reykjavik with three merchant ships, one of which was the *Gudvor*, bringing the convoy up to its full strength as it reached high latitudes, passing the 62nd parallel and approaching the southern end of the Denmark Strait.

Leaving his corvettes to act as sheep dogs, Gretton initially minimised *Duncan's* fuel consumption by placing her in the heart of the convoy astern of the *Argon*, but the next day a moderation in the weather allowed *Duncan* and *Vidette* to refuel from the *British Lady* while Iceland-based Hudsons maintained an air patrol overhead. The weather continued reasonable on the 28th, though visibility was only some three miles. At noon radio intercepts indicated a U-boat ahead of the convoy and Gretton increased to full speed, taking *Duncan* out to the west of ONS5 but finding nothing. As he returned to station, ordering Lieutenant Commander R.E. Sherwood in *Tay* to take over the hunt, Gretton experienced again 'that horrible sinking feeling' of foreboding.

The bad weather had hampered the U-boat commanders, making astro-navigation impossible and dead reckoning increasingly unreliable as it degraded over time. However, Oberleutnant E. von Witzendorff, stationed at the northern extremity of the *Star* patrol line in *U-650*, had sighted ONS5, and although he was driven off by Catalinas flying from Greenland he managed to call up five other U-boats, all of which either saw or attempted to attack the convoy that night.[2]

Just before dark *Duncan's* lookout spotted a U-boat, but with a fresh breeze blowing and the ships labouring through a heavy swell the conditions were against Gretton leaving his station. Anticipating an attack from the south, he prepared for the coming night by withdrawing *Tay* from her fruitless search and placing all his escorts on the convoy's port flank. Not long after nightfall *Sunflower* spotted a U-boat and opened fire, forcing it to submerge, whereupon Lieutenant Commander Plomer depth-charged her before being recalled to his post; Gretton was determined not to have his escorts lured too far from the convoy. At 23.30 *Duncan's* radar picked up a response and, as the detected U-boat submerged, Gretton fired depth-charges. He could not linger, for his radar had located yet another, running down-wind towards the convoy. *Duncan* was swung head to sea and increased speed, 'sending spray over the mast and drenching the guns' crews and everyone on the bridge . . .', but 'the U-boat dived quickly, making our depth-charge attack of doubtful accuracy'.

With the depth-charge crews trying to reload while slithering about on the sea-swept quarterdeck as the destroyer pitched and rolled, for the benefit of his crew Gretton kept up a running commentary on the loud-hailer: 'There is nothing worse than working on blindly, literally in the dark as to what is happening.' Having dropped another pattern, Gretton had turned to take up *Duncan*'s station on the port quarter of ONS5 when another sighting was reported between her and the convoy. *Duncan* was now running down-wind and came close to her objective, but the U-boat again dived and Gretton 'dropped an accurate pattern over the swirl of the conning tower'. Now, to his amazement, 'yet another U-boat was picked up on its way to the convoy'. But as *Duncan* turned towards it, it too disappeared. During the night both *Snowflake* and *Tay* had also been in action but without positive results, though the integrity of the convoy defences remained unbreached. In the face of an unusually determined and well co-ordinated assault by an estimated four U-boats, this was something.

At daybreak the weather again improved. As *Tay* fell back to discourage shadowing with a sweep astern of the convoy, a torpedo struck the *McKeesport* lying second in the fourth column on her starboard bow. The explosion cracked several bulkheads and affected her steering gear, but emergency steering was connected, and although he was overtaken by the ships astern, Captain O.J. Lohr kept his vessel going. The perpetrator was Kapitänleutnant W. von Mässenhausen in *U-258*, which was located by the sonar aboard *Northern Gem* as she closed the damaged freighter. Gretton was reluctant to weaken his screen and *U-258* escaped immediate attack, but later that day at dusk she was sighted, depth-charged and damaged by an American Catalina flown from Iceland by Lieutenant W.A. Sherlin. The *McKeesport* steamed on for a further 45 minutes but then took on a sudden list to port and, as her bulkheads failed, sank further by the head. Lohr now ordered her abandoned and 'great difficulty was encountered in lowering the boats because of the list . . . [They became] entangled in the life nets . . . thrown over the side for the men to climb down . . . One net had to be cut to clear a lifeboat, one man had to be cut down from a net and hoisted onto a raft.' All 68 of her crew were pulled aboard the *Northern Gem* an hour later, but one seaman died of hypothermia next day.[3] Sherwood was sent to sink the derelict, but by the time *Tay* reached her position, the *McKeesport* had vanished.

It was now that Horton reinforced Gretton's escort with McCoy's 3rd Support Group. McCoy himself sailed as soon as possible, *Offa* leaving in company with *Impulsive*, while *Penn* and *Panther*, then at St John's, were instructed to catch him up. Detached in Iceland, the destroyer *Oribi* was ordered to join forthwith. Meanwhile Gretton tried to use the daytime to refuel *Duncan* and *Vidette* 'but the weather had got worse again and it seemed too risky . . . [The weather also] prevented any air-cover being provided.'

Throughout the greater part of the day it blew hard, heaping up heavy, breaking seas which the escorts shipped green; *Sunflower*'s bridge flooded to waist height, while the midshipman in the crow's-nest above reported it full of sea-water.

As so often happens, the gale died with the day, and the night of 29/30 April 'was reasonably quiet. One rather half-hearted attack was driven off . . . but prospects were gloomy because it was a long way to go to Newfoundland, the weather forecast was shocking, and the convoy seemed to get slower and slower.'

Gretton's comments on the weather are worth quoting. It was 'astonishing even for the North Atlantic . . . Uniformly bad throughout . . . with short spells with no wind but with big swells, sandwiched in between the gales . . .'[4] Nevertheless, *Oribi* had now joined company, and during a moderation that forenoon Gretton ordered her to fuel from *British Lady*. Once again lack of expertise in replenishing at sea wrecked the gear, denying *Vidette* and *Duncan* the opportunity to follow suit. *Duncan*'s lack of bunkers was to prove significant as the weather proceeded to grow steadily worse.

During the night that followed, as the convoy staggered to windward in extreme conditions, *Snowflake* and *Sunflower* warded off an attack and *Duncan*, in support, suffered slight damage to her stern from one of her own depth-charges. Next day, May Day, the wind was at hurricane force. The entire convoy was hove-to in monstrous seas, visibility limited by flying spume, station-keeping gone to the devil, and the vessels gradually dispersing in their struggle to stay together. Two, unable to sustain any headway, put their helms up and headed down-wind for the shelter of Iceland's Hvalfjord. Gretton did his best, hove-to 'reasonably close' to the *Rena*, from where he watched 'the convoy melting away before our eyes'. One Liberator appeared, 'a magnificent effort', but it brought the news that although no U-boats were in sight, ice-bergs, growlers and floes lay 30 miles ahead of *Duncan*.

Despite her recent refit *Duncan*'s wracked hull was now suffering from bunker leaks into her forward boiler room, causing Gretton concern about her fuel stock as well as about the scattered state of his charges and the proximity of the Greenland pack-ice. As the wind dropped on the morning of 2 May the escorts began the slow business of rounding up the convoy, helped by another Liberator. One vessel, the Blue Funnel liner *Dolius*, was hove-to, her master steering with the engines as her engineers strove to repair her failed steering gear in trying conditions. That a breakdown like this should have occurred in such a well-found vessel, fitted with hydraulic steering gear, speaks volumes for the severity of the conditions. That evening, with the *Dolius* under command again, Captain G.R. Cheetham cracked on speed to catch up with the convoy.

As ONS5 slowly re-formed it passed through light pack-ice and Gretton hoped to use the effect this had on reducing the swell to refuel, but the attempt failed 'owing to the continual twisting and turning of the tanker as she avoided the ice'. By noon, as they cleared the floes, the wind was getting up again, but the greater portion of the convoy was in sight, the ships struggling to regain their stations. Stragglers apart, a separate detachment of five merchantmen had reformed on *Pink*, and that afternoon McCoy arrived with his four destroyers, *Offa, Impulsive, Panther* and *Penn*.

As they gathered their charges and concerted their defence, neither Gretton nor McCoy knew that Dönitz had already broken off the action against ONS5 in order to concentrate against SC128, far to the south-west. Here, the previous night, the escorts had carried out a ruse, detaching and firing flares to throw the questing U-boats off the scent by pretending that SC128 was some miles east of its real position. Wrestling with this tactical problem in Berlin and realising the deception, Dönitz and his staff redeployed the available groups off Newfoundland, ordering the *Star* U-boats down from the north-east as reinforcement and intending to renew their interception of SC128. By 4 May 27 German submarines were moving against SC128, and that afternoon smoke was seen heading for the centre of the new patrol line. This was not SC128, however, and the westbound convoy was quickly assessed by Befelshaber der U-Boote as ON180. It was, in fact, the much-delayed ONS5.

The night had been quiet 'except for the wind which continued to blow very hard indeed', but by the morning of 4 May *Duncan's* fuel was so low that Gretton had no option but to turn over command of the close escort to Lieutenant Commander R.E. Sherwood of HMS *Tay* and head for St John's. The fuel state of Captain McCoy's destroyers was also giving cause for concern, and that day his support group was reduced to *Offa* and *Oribi*, the latter having arrived from Iceland in the interim. *Northern Gem* also detached with her load of survivors. However, Horton had ordered Commander G.N. Brewer's 1st Support Group to sail from St John's to assist. This group consisted of the sloop *Pelican*, the frigates *Jed, Wear* and *Spey*, and the former American Coast Guard Cutter *Sennen*.

That afternoon a Canadian flying-boat at the extremity of its endurance attacked a surfaced U-boat and damaged *U-438*. A short time later a second Catalina spotted a U-boat surfaced astern of the main body of ONS5 and depth-charged her, and at about the same time a U-boat was also attacked by *Vidette*: *U-630* was not heard from again.[5] Other U-boats were driven off by the escorts and *U-270* was damaged as ONS5 began to encounter wraiths of fog and a few 'bergy-bits' drifting down from the Davis Strait.

Aboard the shadowing U-boats a signal was received from Dönitz. The

Grossadmiral was aware that the coming night was the last opportunity for the 41 U-boats he had gathered to attack ONS5. His exhortation suggests that he had also divined the weakening of resolve permeating his men: 'You are better placed than ever before . . . Don't overestimate your enemy, but strike him dead.'

As darkness fell that increasingly foggy evening, ONS5 consisted of 31 merchant ships covered by McCoy's two destroyers, Sherwood's frigate *Tay*, the destroyer *Vidette*, and the corvettes *Sunflower*, *Snowflake* and *Loosestrife*. The *Pink* and her five charges *Gudvor*, *Omega*, *Director*, *Dunsley* and *Nicholas* lay far astern, while six more straggling merchantmen and HM Trawler *Northern Spray* were trying to catch up, having become separated in the bad weather.

Aboard the Newcastle tramp *Wentworth*, Able Seaman P.J. Cottgrave spent five shillings on 200 cigarettes and bought a tin of sweets from the ship's slops store. Emptying the sweets, he stuffed the tin full of cigarettes, 'hammered the lid on to make it watertight' and added it to the small canvas bag which contained his identity papers and lived in his coat pocket. Then he lay on his bunk and waited for eight bells and his turn on watch. Such small, personal and preparatory rituals were enacted hundreds of thousands of times throughout the war by the men who lived with a constant uncertainty and an omnipresent sense of imminent disaster.

The night that followed was a confusing swirl of action as the escorts, with the benefit of radar, deflected a stream of attacks and took devastating counter-measures, but the screen was nevertheless penetrated and murder was done among the merchant ships. At 23.06 Kapitänleutnant H. Looks in *U-264* blew the stern off the American Moore-McCormack freighter *West Maximus*. Two boats were immediately lowered and several men abandoned ship without orders, whereupon Captain E.E. Brooks shouted to them to lie off and await events while he tried to salvage the ship, but two hours later a second torpedo slammed into her amidships, destroying her engine room, rupturing her fuel tanks, throwing oil everywhere and killing six men. Brooks ordered the crew away, and as they slithered across the oily decks a third torpedo struck, sinking the *West Maximus* in ten minutes. Another man was drowned before the survivors were taken up by the *Northern Spray*, which arrived on the scene about 07.00.

Around midnight Looks also hit J. & C. Harrison's tramp steamer *Harperley* which bore a cargo of 6,000 tons of exported coal. Captain J.E. Turgoose and the majority of his crew escaped to be picked up by the *Northern Spray*, though ten were lost in the attack. Looks had, of course, retired beneath the passing ships.

Shortly after midnight the *Bristol City*, Captain A.L. Webb, laden with china clay and a general cargo of manufactured goods, was sunk by Kapitänleutnant R. Manke in *U-358*. A third of her people were lost, but Webb and the remainder were picked up by *Loosestrife*. At 03.15 Manke fired again, at the *Wentworth*, severely damaging her. Captain R.G. Phillips ordered her abandoned and his crew took to the boats. It was 'very, very cold'. In due course they were hauled aboard *Loosestrife*. Lieutenant Commander Stonehouse failed to sink the tramp, but left her low in the water, drifting forlornly behind the convoy.

Here, where there were no escorts, another action was under way, for hunting among the stragglers in the rear of ONS5 were several U-boats. One, probably Kapitänleutnant O. Curio's *U-952*, torpedoed the former French vessel *L'Orient* then manned and managed by the Cardiff tramp-owners Radcliffe, Evan Thomas & Company and commanded by Captain W.J. Manley. She was in ballast and sank with all hands sometime late on the 4th or possibly after midnight on the 5th.[6] Oberleutnant G. Gretschel in *U-707* torpedoed and sank another straggler, the *North Britain*, early on the 5th. A 1940-built tramp, she bore a part-cargo of firebricks and bagged fireclay loaded in Glasgow. Gretschel hurried after the convoy leaving Captain J.L. Bright and 34 hands to their deaths, for only 11 freezing men were later dragged aboard the *Northern Spray*.

Hasenschar's *U-628* was another U-boat coming up from astern. In the early hours of the 5th he fired at and damaged a second Harrison tramp, the *Harbury*. Captain W.E. Cook and most of his crew were picked up by the *Northern Spray*, though seven men died with their ship. The *Harbury* was seen at first light by Looks in *U-264*; he fired at her, sending her to the bottom. Hasenschar had in his turn fallen back, and despatched the derelict *Wentworth* later that day. But the initiative was not exclusively in German hands. The corvette *Pink* was still shepherding her clutch of five merchantmen, and during the forenoon she echo-located a U-boat. Lieutenant Atkinson attacked *U-192* persistently until Oberleutnant W. Happe and his crew had been hunted to destruction.[7]

Dönitz was eager to press his advantage in numbers and clearly willing to risk losses, but there is something of an air of desperation about his instructions to his commanders to risk detection by aircraft rather than lose contact with ONS5. During the forenoon Oberleutnant O. Staudinger worked *U-638* into a position to strike at the *Dolius*, leading the second column. It was 10.40 and nine men on day-work had just left the engine room for their morning 'Smoke-O' when a torpedo opened the engine room to the sea, flooded the ship and killed the three watch-keepers. Such a bold act invited immediate retribution, and Staudinger was counter-attacked by *Loosestrife* as *Sunflower* 'left the convoy and came across to stand by her'. As the boats pulled away from the sinking *Dolius* two men were discovered to be still aboard. Third Mate T.K. Haworth put back alongside to take them off, discovering them to be DEMS gunners, one of whom was mortally wounded. Meanwhile Lieutenant Commander Stonehouse's corvette *Loosestrife* pounded *U-638* and all aboard her to destruction, while Cheetham and his British and Chinese crew were taken aboard Plomer's. In *Sunflower* they were recipients of 'magnificent efforts for our comfort during our enforced stay', and gained an unfamiliar perspective of the battle as the corvette continued with her anti-submarine duties.[8]

That afternoon, as the sun began to wester, wraiths of fog began to form. The wind had now fallen and the sea quickly dropped away. Astern of the main body of ONS5 the American freighter *West Madaket*, Captain H. Schroeder, which had been on her own since parting company with ONS5 during the gale on 2 May, now caught up with the five vessels under *Pink's* protection. But despite the approach of the corvette, which was in the process of returning to her charges after sinking *U-192*, her luck had run out: also close by were Gretschel's *U-707* and Kapitänleutnant J. Deecke's *U-584*, intent upon catching up with ONS5. Both appear to have fired torpedoes, for two strikes from opposite sides slammed into the *West Madaket's* after hold, which flooded, settling her by the stern and wrecking her steering gear. All hands evacuated the ship, getting clear in the lifeboats and scrambling aboard *Pink* as she came up to help. *Pink's* ratings were amazed by the suitcases the Americans had with them, a contrast to the modest 'scram-bags' usually borne by British and other Allied merchant seamen.

Early in the evening and by now far astern of ONS5, Hasenschar in *U-628* despatched the derelict *Wentworth*. As darkness fell and the fog thickened the number of U-boats still in touch with the main body of the convoy remained overwhelming, and the escorts were kept in a state of perpetual reaction to radar and sonar contacts. It was inevitable that their defence would be breached, and once again it took only one determined penetration to do immense damage.

Firing a spread of four torpedoes from *U-266* across the vessels leading the extreme starboard columns, Oberleutnant R. von Jessen sank three vessels. The Strick liner *Selvistan* was hit in No. 5 Hold by two torpedoes and settled fast, drowning six men as she sank. Von Jessen's largest victim was the worn-out British India liner *Gharinda*, described by her chief officer as 'the wreck of the British India fleet', an emergency standard-ship built in 1919. She was holed forward at about 17.30 and the blast blew off the hatch covers, which fell back on the bridge and deck. 'The ship seemed to lift out of the water,' recalled Frank Fox, her senior radio officer, 'and went down by the bow but the bulkhead between the first and second holds held back the water and the ship settled herself' without a list. After sending a distress signal to the commodore on low power and disposing of his codes Fox grabbed his scram-bag and a blanket and made for the boat deck. Here Captain R.R. Stone's officers had lowered all but one boat, No. 5, which 'nose-dived into the sea with the ship's papers'.

Stone himself got away in the motor-boat, observing as he went that, 'although the rudder and propeller were out of the water', the *Gharinda* had not sunk; he determined to return with a small crew and save the ship. After about an hour *Tay* swept up and hove-to, her crew throwing scrambling nets over and 'yelling at us to hurry because they were a sitting target.' Fox remembered that he 'felt petrified trying to grip the net with my hands and plimsoles [*sic*] from a pitching lifeboat with some twenty feet of net to climb . . .' The *Gharinda*'s entire British and Indian crew were hauled over *Tay*'s rail and Fox found himself in the frigate's wardroom, in which 'there were already thirty to forty survivors . . . some of whom had been in the water and some who were injured. How anyone who had been in the water could have survived the near freezing temperature, I don't know . . . Most of them were shivering uncontrollably although it was warm . . .'

The hospitality was greatly appreciated. On *Tay*'s bridge Sherwood managed to persuade Stone that at the height of an action during which he had at one point had seven U-boats in sight, thoughts of saving *Gharinda* were out of the question. Ominously, the barometer was also falling again. Stone reluctantly agreed.

The vigilant watch aboard the small Norwegian tanker *Bonde* had spotted *U-266*'s periscope among the convoy and had opened fire with their Oerlikons, but 'then there was an explosion and [the *Bonde*] . . . seemed to jump in the water,' recalled Captain Gates of the *Baron Graham*. 'When the smoke and spray had cleared away, the *Bonde* was already standing on her end with her bow . . . vertically out of the water.' A moment later she had gone, leaving only 12 of her 38 men to be rescued by *Tay* as the frigate caught up after attending the *Gharinda*'s people.

Sherwood, the commander of the escort, was not only junior to McCoy and, when he arrived, Brewer, but a reserve officer. By the sensible convention mentioned earlier, however, Sherwood remained in tactical control of his convoy's defence, giving orders to the senior officers in command of the support groups acting with him by means of 'suggestions'. Throughout this period of intense activity, although ONS5 did suffer losses Sherwood's B7 Escort Group, assisted by McCoy's two destroyers and now, on the morning of 6 May, reinforced by Brewer's 1st Support Group from St John's, kept up a spirited defence. Moreover, they exacted a savage revenge: six U-boats were attacked and sunk during the action, with a further dozen suffering damage, some, like *U-533* which was rammed by *Sunflower*, severely. In addition to the loss of *U-630*, *Pink*'s destruction of *U-192* and *Loosestrife*'s despatch of *U-638*, on 6 May *Vidette* sank *U-125*. Folkers had been rammed earlier by Commander J.C.A. Ingram in *Oribi* in a joint attack with Lieutenant H.G. Chesterman's *Snowflake*, but had escaped under cover of a rain squall. Then Lieutenant Hart attacked with depth-charges and 'Hedgehog', finishing *U-125* off with *Vidette*'s gunfire. Ingram's *Oribi*, again with *Snowflake*, sank *U-531* (Neckel) and Brewer's *Pelican* sank *U-438* (Heinsohn). Others were fatally engaged soon afterwards.

The attrition rate among the U-boats was now rising fast. During the morning of 7 May, in an interception of the homeward bound SL128, located in mid Atlantic by German aerial reconnaissance the previous day, both *U-456* and *U-230* were attacked by air and surface escorts. Covered by four corvettes, the 48-strong convoy suffered only one casualty, the Greek steamer *Laconikos* heading the fourth column. Korvettenkapitän D. Lohmann in *U-89* fired at the Blue Funnel liner *Idomeneus*, Captain W.F. Dark, but her lookouts spotted the torpedo tracks and her helm was put over, so that it was the *Laconikos* that was sunk by default. Eleven Greeks survived but 23 of her crew were killed; loaded with 5,200 tons of manganese ore, she sank rapidly. That same day, however, *U-447* (Bothe) operating nearby was depth-charged and sunk by two Hudsons from No. 233 Squadron. *U-456* and *U-230* were also attacked from the air, and as the operation was broken off in deteriorating visibility, Dönitz ordered *U-89*, *U-456*, *U-230* and *U-753* to head north to intercept HX237.

Having attacked ONS5, von Jessen's *U-266* was one of several U-boats sent to attack SC129. The convoy was covered by Macintyre's B2 Escort Group of the *Hesperus*, *Whitehall*, *Vanessa*, *Campanula*, *Clematis*, *Gentian*, *Heather* and *Sweetbriar*. Two merchantmen were lost from SC129, both sunk by von Forstner in *U-402* in an attack on the night of 11/12 May. The British tramp *Antigone*, Captain F. Williams, loaded with 7,800 tons of grain and general and 250 vehicles, went down with three of her crew on 11 May. No lives were lost from von Forstner's second victim, the Norwegian *Grado*, which sank with 1,000 tons of steel and 3,000 tons of timber. Survivors were picked up by Captain R. Good's rescue ship *Melrose Abbey*.

Macintyre counter-attacked, taking *Hesperus* in a sweep across the rear of the convoy, and encountered not *U-402* but Wächter's *U-223*. Forcing her down, Macintyre depth-charged *U-223* until Wächter was compelled to surface, whereupon he fired five torpedoes at *Hesperus*. He missed, rang on full speed, and tried to ram the destroyer. Macintyre opened fire and in turn tried to ram, but Wächter took evasive action, ordering his men to prepare to abandon ship. Incredibly, he managed to slip away in the confusion, but two of his men, one badly wounded, had gone overboard. Even more incredibly, the unwounded man was found a few hours later by *U-359* (Förster) when she surfaced to recharge batteries; a couple of days later he was put back aboard *U-223*.

On the 12th no fewer than 11 U-boats were milling about the convoy seeking an opening, but a bold alteration of SC129's course and energetic action on HF/DF bearings on the part of the escorts kept them at bay. During this activity Macintyre 'killed' *U-186* (Hesemann), and the next morning aircraft flying from *Biter* provided the final blow.

On the night of 14/15 May von Jessen, who had worked ahead of SC129, was located on the surface and attacked by a Halifax of No. 58 Squadron. Wing Commander W.E. Oulton dropped the first homing torpedo to be used operationally, and destroyed *U-266*.

Meanwhile, prior to Abel-Smith's move to assist SC129 with the 5th Support Group led by *Biter*, an action had developed round HX237, which was approached by Lohmann and his colleagues on 12 May. *U-89* was seen 6 miles ahead of HX237 from a Swordfish of No. 811 Squadron of the Fleet Air Arm flying from *Biter*. The Swordfish attacked, but with uncertain results, and called up assistance. It was soon relieved by the destroyer *Broadway* and the frigate *Lagan* of the C2 Escort Group. Captain Chavasse, who had been fighting off approaches by *U-359* and *U-403* in the preceding days, now attacked and sank *U-89*. *Biter* had lost one Swordfish, shot down by *U-230* whose commander, Kapitänleutnant P. Siegmann, had obeyed Dönitz's injunction to remain surfaced and in contact – but this was a costly strategy. Although Kapitänleutnant M.M. Teichert in *U-456* had sunk the *Fort Concord* earlier that morning, his submarine was spotted and so severely damaged by another of the new homing torpedoes, dropped from a Liberator of No. 86 Squadron flown by Flight Lieutenant J. Wright, that Teichert could not dive. *U-456* was at the mercy of the destroyers *Pathfinder* and *Opportune* of the 5th Support Group, which now arrived on the scene and effected Teichert's end.

The *Fort Concord*, loaded with a full cargo of grain and a deck cargo of military supplies, had straggled in the inclement weather and was lost with her master Captain F.P. Ryan and 36 of her company. Chief Mate J.B. Tunbridge, 17 crew and one Distressed British Seaman were taken out of their boats by the Canadian corvette *Drumheller*, part of Chavasse's C2 Escort Group. None of HX237's main body was attacked, but the weather had caused other vessels to drop astern. That same day, 12 May, Trojer in *U-221* torpedoed the Norwegian tanker *Sandanger* with the loss of half her 40-man crew. Bertelsmann was also in pursuit of HX237, and that morning *U-603* had been located by one of *Biter's* Swordfish and endured a depth-charge attack by *Pathfinder*. Bertelsmann escaped by running west and later came across another Norwegian ship trying to catch up with the convoy. The motor-vessel *Brand* was sunk with the loss of her engine-room watch, the survivors being rescued later by an escort.

On the following day two Sunderlands of No. 423 Squadron called up the escort and Chavasse sent the *Lagan*, Lieutenant Commander A. Ayre, and *Drumheller*, Lieutenant Commander P. Denny, to deal with *U-753*. Subjected to depth-charge and 'Hedgehog' attacks, Korvettenkapitän A.M. von Manstein and all his men were killed. It was at this point that Dönitz broke off the attack and Horton, sensing victory, swiftly ordered Abel-Smith to take *Biter* and the 5th Support Group to the assistance of Macintyre and SC129.

While ON184 made an unmolested passage outward-bound, *U-640* located and called up reinforcements to attack ONS7. Despite a tenacious shadowing, during which the escorts constantly harried Oberleutnant K-H. Nagel, the convoy lost only one vessel, and Nagel's *U-640* was caught and sunk off Cape Farewell by an American naval Catalina from VP 84 Patrol Squadron based at Reykjavik. It was Nagel's first Atlantic war patrol, and he and all 49 of his men were killed.

Nevertheless, Nagel's summons had mustered 23 U-boats, and Dönitz formed them into two groups. The most northerly of the U-boats, *U-657*, commanded by Kapitänleutnant H. Göllnitz, attacked ONS7 on the night of 16/17 May. ONS7's 40 merchantmen were escorted by Lieutenant Commander J. Jackson's B5 Escort Group, which included the frigate *Swale*, the destroyer *Volunteer* and the corvettes *Buttercup, Godetia, Lavender* and *Saxifrage*; the rescue ship *Copeland* and trawler HMS *Northern Wave* were also with ONS7.

Shortly after midnight Göllnitz sank the *Aymeric*, an elderly former American Emergency-built freighter dating from 1919 and now under the management of Andrew Weir's Bank Line. In ballast, she sank quickly, taking 53 men to the bottom of the Atlantic. Captain S. Morris and 24 crew, including most of her DEMS gunners, were taken aboard *Copeland* or *Northern Wave*. Curiously, the *Aymeric's* original name had been *War Nemesia*; she was an ugly, undistinguished Allied vessel that during her obscure life had flown both the Stars and Stripes and the red duster. Not only did her sinking mark the end for Göllnitz, who was killed an hour later by Jackson in *Swale*, but she was the last merchantman from a trans-Atlantic convoy to be sunk for four months.

That day *U-646*, chasing ONS7, was sunk by an Iceland-based Hudson from No. 269 Squadron flown by Sergeant F.H.W. James. Two days later another from the same squadron, piloted by Flying Officer J.N.F. Bell, 'killed' *U-273*. Both were on their first Atlantic war patrols under junior commanders.[10]

Horton had 'got Dönitz where I want him'. Nemesis had indeed arrived.

After the battering it had received covering ONS5, Gretton's B7 Escort Group patched itself up alongside the inadequate repair ship *Greenwich* at St John's and was ready just in time to sail to the rendezvous with Convoy SC130. The 37 loaded ships had left Halifax on 11 May under Commodore J. Forsythe, a captain in the naval reserve. The *Zamalek* lay in the rear ranks as rescue ship and the requisitioned ex-Danish tanker *Bente Maersk* was to act as oiler. On meeting SC130 off Cape Race at dawn on the 15th, Gretton signalled that he had a 'most pressing private engagement to keep at St Mary's, Cadogan Square, two days after [the convoy] was due to arrive'. Forsythe replied 'that he had a golf match that same day and would do his best'.

After this bonhominous exchange, reality set in. A fog lay over the sea, but the majority of the merchant ships were ancient coal-burners and made too much smoke for Gretton's liking, even in that merciful shroud. Nor could most of them do the 7.5 knots required of the convoy orders. The new vessels suffered from their own disadvantages. Bent on chivvying the poor station-keepers, Gretton swept *Duncan* up alongside a new Liberty ship lying astern of the convoy and remonstrated through his loud-hailer. 'Listen here, Captain,' the master replied, 'not one of my officers has ever stood a watch before and I cannot stay up here all the time.' To his credit, Gretton recorded that 'we felt very ashamed of our language'. The inexperience of the new breed of hurriedly-produced American merchant mates was as much a problem as the ancient ships that were the consequence of a lack of pre-war investment in new tonnage on the part of their British allies.

Such general difficulties were explicable and excusable, as irksome for those aboard the merchant ships as for the naval officers responsible for their safe conduct, and had of necessity to be borne with fortitude. Individual acts of indiscipline were different. After nightfall, in thick fog, as the look-outs aboard the vessels in convoy watched the fog buoys of the ship ahead, *Vidette* located an iceberg on her radar. Gretton ordered her to stand by it and divert the approaching columns round it using her searchlight and sounding 'U' in morse on her siren, the international signal indicating that a vessel is 'standing into danger'. By this means SC130's vulnerable formation negotiated the berg safely. However, before the night was over a Hong

Kong-registered British ship, the *Tamara*, pulled out of the convoy with neither orders nor explanation, a discourtesy Gretton resented. That she returned safely to Newfoundland was cold comfort.

By the time the fog had cleared on the morning of 16 May, Gretton's force was up to strength. With *Duncan* he again had *Tay*, the British corvettes *Sunflower, Snowflake, Pink*, and *Loosestrife*, the Canadian *Kitchener* and HM Trawler *Northern Spray*. In perfect weather he topped some of them up from the *Bente Maersk*. All hands, including Gretton himself, were busy reducing her top-weight by chipping copious layers of paint off *Duncan's* over-adorned steel upperworks while the old destroyer took station in the centre of the convoy to save fuel. Past worries over good visibility were lifted by the comforting roar of covering aircraft, even though '[r]elations between the air force and the navy in Newfoundland were not as good as they ought to have been ...' The men of the navy had, however, done their best, 'with gin and good fellow-ship, to put things right during our stay at St John's.'

Next day a sick American seaman was transferred from a tanker to the *Zamalek* for surgery and on the 18th, in continuing perfect weather, the remaining escorts took on fuel, despite the lack of air cover that day. One merchant ship that developed engine trouble on the 19th was detached with *Northern Spray* in support to make the best of her way east, clear of SC130. That night the HF/DF reports indicated the presence of U-boats and *Vidette* was sent down one bearing, but without any contact being made. SC130 executed an emergency turn and at 01.00 Gretton himself made a sally along a radio-bearing. 'It was a bright moonlit night with a calm sea, and the U-boat must have seen us coming ...' Once again there was no contact, but *Duncan* dropped some deterrent charges. After a while SC130 resumed its course. Then, before dawn, Gretton and Forsythe took the ships through a series of alter-courses to step aside from U-boats waiting in the grain of the convoy, HF/DF fixes indicating their positions along the original track. Daylight also brought the sight of a distant Liberator of No. 120 Squadron attacking U-boats, of which six or seven were forced to dive and one was damaged. Further west, a Liberator caught *U-258* on the surface, lying in wait ahead of SC130. Squadron Leader T.R.E. Proctor's attack condemned von Mässenhausen and his 49 men to die for their Führer.

Sallies by the escort during the day also caused damage. *Duncan* relieved *Snowflake* of a target and attacked Kapitänleutnant Graf W-H. von Pückler und Limpurg's *U-381*, which had penetrated the convoy. Gretton drove her down until SC130 had passed over her, whereupon *Duncan* 'settled down to hunt', finally sinking her with 'Hedgehog'. Sherwood's *Tay* was also in action, damaging *U-952*, and other U-boats were attacked by *Pink* and *Snowflake*, though they outran the corvettes on the surface.

At noon the 1st Support Group arrived, consisting of the frigates *Wear, Jed, Spey* and the ex-American cutter *Sennen*. They mopped up the rear, attacking *U-954* after Kapitänleutnant O. Loewe had fired torpedoes at the frigates. Lieutenant Commander R.C. Freaker in *Jed*, supported by *Sennen*, sank her with 'Hedgehog' and depth-charges. Among her 47 dead was Dönitz's younger son Peter, *U-954*'s second watch officer; it was his first war patrol. Gretton, meanwhile, blocked an attack by *U-707* (Gretschel) and forced her out of the action. Three Liberators from Iceland joined the escorts in the constant work of foiling approaches or keeping at a distance a dozen U-boats. Although SC130 was the main target, BdU was aware of other convoys at sea, thanks to B-Dienst decrypts. HX239 was not far away, nor was ON184, which in addition to the C1 Escort Group had Captain Short's powerful American 6th Support Group centred on the escort-carrier *Bogue*. Early on 22 May, with the wind rising from the east, one of *Bogue*'s Avengers attacked a surfaced U-boat. It was *U-468*, effecting repairs and unable to submerge. Oberleutnant K. Schamong fought off the Avenger with flak, completed his repairs and vanished.

That afternoon, with an easterly gale now blowing, *Bogue*'s Avengers found another target, scoring several hits and so damaging *U-569* that she dived steeply, rose on her side, submerged again and then surfaced on an even keel. By this time the Canadian destroyer *St Laurent* had been called up from HX239's escort. Lieutenant Commander G.H. Stephen was in the act of lowering his whaler in heavy seas when Oberleutnant H. Johannsen ordered his men onto the casing and *U-569* was scuttled. About half her crew were lost, but Johannsen and 24 men were taken prisoner. *U-569* was the first U-boat to be destroyed by aircraft flown from an escort-carrier.

SC130 had in the interim been making good progress. Having beaten off the first attacks on the 19th, Gretton relinquished *Kitchener* to join ON184 and refuelled *Duncan* and *Vidette*, accomplishing the latter while the entire convoy carried out an alteration of course. Forsythe and the merchant ships were executing these with such confidence as to prove SC130, despite the initial misgivings, to be generally well-disciplined. The diversionary step-aside tactic exposed the U-boats to HF/DF fixes as they mutually expressed their frustration by radio, enabling Gretton and his staff to vector air support to attack them.

Dönitz now broke off operations against SC130 and concentrated against the 42 ships in HX239. But Horton had augmented the convoy's ocean escort of the B3 Group with the 4th Support Group[11] and, moreover, had fortified Scott-Moncrieff's destroyers, *Milne, Matchless, Eclipse* and *Fury*, by the addition of the newly-commissioned escort-carrier *Archer*. It was Schamong's misfortune that *U-468* had hardly resurfaced after his escape from *Bogue*'s Avenger than he encountered *Archer*'s anachronistic Swordfish. Once again Schamong's anti-aircraft gunners threw up their flak, deterring the biplane and enabling *U-468* to escape before *Milne* could reach her.

The air cover and the activity of the escorts and supporting groups prevented any U-boat from coming within striking distance of HX239 throughout 23 May. Of those German commanders still in touch, Kapitänleutnant K-E. Schroeter's *U-752* was lying in the offing that morning when he was attacked by a Swordfish from *Archer*'s No. 819 Fleet Air Arm Squadron. With depth-charges falling round *U-752*, Schroeter crash-dived, resurfacing about an hour later only to be observed by another of *Archer*'s Swordfish. This one was armed with Horton's specially adapted anti-tank rockets, and Sub-Lieutenant H. Horrocks fired eight of them at the crash-diving U-boat. The last pair penetrated *U-752*'s pressure hull forward of her conning tower, flooding her and forcing Schroeter to abort his dive. German seamen emerged to man their guns, Horrocks called for fighter assistance, and a few minutes later a Martlet from *Archer*'s No. 892 Squadron arrived. She strafed *U-752* and her machine-guns killed Schroeter and several of his men, driving his demoralised gunners below. The chief engineer set scuttling charges and the crew began to leave *U-752*. Schroeter's first watch officer called for three cheers from the conning tower, and went down with the nose-diving U-boat. Called up from the B3 Escort Group, the destroyer *Escapade* arrived to fish 13 prisoners out of the water.[12]

In Berlin Dönitz received the news of his bereavement and his other less personal losses with dismay. He had tried to whip his commanders into action, telling them that if any of them thought 'that fighting convoys is no longer possible, he is a weakling and no true submarine captain', a message that must have been received with incredulity. His order to fight it out on the surface when attacked by aircraft had been accompanied by an exhortation to 'Be tough! Get ahead and attack. I believe in you.' That too, must have had a demoralising effect on those at sea, betraying either a lack of trust on the part of their leader, or Dönitz's realisation that his forces were no longer capable of the task.

There can be little doubt of Dönitz's deep anxiety following the failure of his offensive against HX237 and SC129. 'Once again we must question how it was possible for the enemy to learn of our dispositions,' he agonised at the time. The Kriegsmarine had lost 33 U-boats during May, and with them 1,600 officers and ratings. The tally included one submarine tanker, nine Type IX and 23 Type VII U-boats. On 24 May, as an attack against SC131 failed, largely frustrated by *Bogue*'s aircraft and Captain Short's tactical mastery, Berlin transmitted a signal ending the submarine offensive in the

North Atlantic for the time being. Efforts were to be concentrated in the less effectively defended areas off Dakar and Freetown, in the Caribbean, east of Trinidad and off the Brazilian coast. The withdrawal was, of course, only a temporary measure, pending the upgrading of the U-boats' anti-aircraft defences with new radar detection equipment, new torpedoes and other technological advances, which in due course included the *Schnorkel* mast and the Walther Type XXII U-boat. 'Operations', Dönitz afterwards wrote, 'could only be resumed if we succeeded in radically increasing the fighting power of the U-boats. This was the logical conclusion to which I came, and accordingly I withdrew . . .' Much later he realised the true significance of what had happened: 'We had lost the Battle of the Atlantic . . .'

The statistical evidence Godt and the staff produced in support of Dönitz's decision to withdraw was persuasive. Heavy losses were only acceptable if 'the amount of shipping sunk is proportionate. In May, however, the ratio was one U-boat to 10,000 gross tonnage of enemy shipping, whereas a short time ago it was one U-boat to 100,000 tons of shipping.' U-boat losses had 'therefore reached unbearable heights'.

At Derby House, Horton's assessment was less emotional – 'the returns show an ever-increasing toll of U-boats and decreasing loss of merchant ships in convoy . . .' – and while he praised the work of the Allied fighting services, he accorded those more passive warriors their obscure but fair share of glory: 'Quite apart from the spectacular kills which have been achieved by the Escort Groups and Support Groups, many notable victories have been achieved by the safe and timely arrival of a number of convoys in the face of heavy enemy air attacks . . .'

The main body of Convoy SC130 approached the Mersey on 26 May 1943. It had broken up in the North Channel a few hours earlier, one portion detaching for the Clyde, a second to head north up the Minch for 'north-about' passage to the east coast of Britain. Commodore Forsythe led those columns of salt-stained, grey-painted merchant ships that were Liverpool-bound past the Bar lightvessel toward the low coast with its irregular, jagged skyline marking the great port. Bright spots of signal flags passed orders up and down those lines of laden vessels and they made their last manoeuvres together. SC130 was 'the last convoy to be seriously menaced', and despite its inauspicious beginning among the fogs of the Grand Bank it arrived off the Mersey able to acquit itself 'with the precision of a battle-fleet'.[13]

CONCLUSION

'Full of agonized bewilderment'

City of Marseilles

DÖNITZ HAD LEFT a handful of operational U-boats at sea transmitting radio signals over a wide area. Horton was undeceived, and knew he had at last achieved the upper hand. In the last days of May he had deployed Walker's 2nd Support Group, *Starling, Wren, Woodpecker, Cygnet, Kite* and *Wild Goose*, to cover the passages of ONS8 and HX240. The first, 52 vessels under the protection of the C4 Escort Group, and the second, 56 ships under the C5 Escort Group, steamed across the Western Ocean with neither sight nor sound of a U-boat, though Walker's sloops carried out a prolonged creeping attack of fifteen hours' duration on *U-202* (Poser), sinking her as she surfaced for lack of air just after midnight on 1 June.

There was no enemy action in the North Atlantic until 19 September, when Dönitz returned to the offensive. In the interim numerous HX and SC convoys bore their cargoes eastwards, linking up with the Russian spur which supported the Red Army and the Soviet ally on the Eastern Front. A corresponding number of ON and ONS convoys travelled the other way, in ballast or loaded with those British exports essential to fund the war. Alongside these unglamorous 'trade-convoys' the fast liners made their trooping runs, while the military convoys to the Mediterranean sustained the Allied thrusts into the under-belly of Hitler's Fortress Europe following the invasion of Sicily and Italy later in the year.

If May 1943 was the turning-point in the struggle to dominate the Atlantic, it was not the end of the war. Hundreds of merchant ships were yet to be sunk and thousands of merchant seamen were still to die, and in due course the merchant navies of the Allies had their part to play in Operation NEPTUNE and the assault of D-Day, but the up-swing in Allied fortunes marked a corresponding change in the Allied mercantile sea services. From roughly the summer of 1943 the numbers of emergency, standard-built vessels – of which the Liberty ship has become the best-known – slowly grew to outnumber the relics of a former age, and with them came an augmentation of manpower, new blood without the grim baggage borne by the old. The British mercantile marine had indeed been transformed into a formidable 'Merchant Navy', but the hard-bitten and surprising dignity engendered in the old guard by the pressures of adversity was often absent from the new. Incidents like the disgraceful behaviour of the crew of the *Fort Cedar Lake*, though infrequent, continued to blight 'the Merch'. Rapid expansion and indiscriminate conscription took no notice of suitability, alcohol was too often freely available, and the prospect of death remained a potent motive for excessive behaviour, particularly ashore, where it irked the authorities. There remained some residual justifications. Although the MoWT had introduced legislation to end the abuse by which a seaman's pay stopped at the time of a sinking, it prevailed even in 1943. Repatriated after the sinking of the *Wentworth* in ONS5, Able Seaman P.J. Cottgrave found that his wife had visited the owner's offices in Tyneside to obtain her monthly allotment of her husband's pay on 5 May, the day the *Wentworth* went down. Dalgleish's clerk announced that the ship had been lost: that month's allotment was forfeit. The National Union of Seamen was no more helpful. Meanwhile Cottgrave had arrived in Montreal where he and the others received 'survival pay of £24 that was for everything we had lost . . . So we got onto them about allotments and got no reply.' Others received tax demands for the periods they were off pay: it was hardly surprising they capsized their 'MN' badges and thought themselves 'Not Wanted'.

It was not treatment calculated to encourage Jack, but the merchant seaman knew no other employment so he went back to sea and back to grumbling. According to one young officer, there was a collapse of morale in 1944, due largely to war-weariness, of which the piece-meal evidence of indiscipline in both the Royal and the United States Navies in the Pacific in 1945 was probably a further indication, all evidence that long service at sea was an excoriating experience for most individuals, and unsuitable for vast numbers of hostilities-only conscripts.

The quality of the merchant seaman cannot be judged by broad generalisations any more than by the misdemeanours of a minority. The dog already had a bad name, and there were sufficient instances of gross misconduct to maintain it. Young men who entered the 'Merchant Navy' with only unemployment as their experience of the world, to whom even the paltry wage of a merchant seaman was comparative riches and the unbridled licence of the waterfront an opportunity too good to miss, could easily

come unstuck. But often the raw material was of the worst kind. The protag-
onists of the most notorious episodes were only merchant seamen by *force
majeure*. The infamous conduct of the British crew of the *George Washington*
was largely a consequence of the fact that the Ministry of War Transport,
so desperate were they for manpower, had released a group of prisoners on
the condition that they assume the mantle of merchant seamen. It was true
that many had at one time or another been to sea – but so had many
working-class men in Glasgow: it did not make them seafarers in the true
sense of the word. In another such extreme example, during an engagement with a German naval force in the Barents Sea the firemen aboard the
Empire Archer, the commodore's ship in Arctic Convoy JW51B, broached a
part-cargo of rum and fell to fighting with knives. Not only had these men
been released from Barlinnie Gaol, they had been offered a *douceur* of £100
to serve at sea, which can scarcely have endeared them to the steadier
'Company' or regular Pool men who formed the majority of ratings.

Nor were these men as biddable as the authorities would have liked.
Writing aboard the *Empire Faith* waiting to lead Convoy HX225 out of
Bedford Basin in March 1943, Commodore R.H.C. Mackay recounted how
the ship's master, short of a quartermaster, had sought one among the 400
seamen then in Halifax on the Pool's books. Curiously, when he called for
a suitable man, not one would admit to being able to steer.

With their appallingly tough lives of unremitting toil, shovelling
hundreds of tons of filthy coal in the heat of a boiler-room, raking and
slicing, often watch-on and watch-off, firemen generally had the worst
reputation. It was one frequently justified, for the case of the Shaw, Savill
& Albion liner *Ceramic*, whose 'stokeholds were manned by hard-case
firemen who sailed together in feuding family groups' was not an unusual
one.[1] Commodore Mackay was not impressed by excuses; smoking and
poor steaming were 'more a matter of discipline than fuel. Firemen just
keep peacetime routine, fill up at the beginning of the watch and then
take it easy.' This was unjust; there was a false allegation against a fireman
in the *Gloucester City* accused of 'deliberately disobeying orders' and
causing his ship to drop astern, but there are references enough to poor
coal to raise more than a suspicion that the demand on coal stocks led to
the use of poor-quality fuel. This was the case aboard the Union Castle liner
Dundrum Castle in Convoy SL125. She had bunkered with coal from the
mines at Wankie in Rhodesia, and her engineers claimed that it 'glowed
red then turned to ash giving no heat in the process'.[2] The fireman from
the *Gloucester City* was, like any individual master, officer or ship under a
cloud, referred by a convoy commodore to the Ministry of War Transport
for investigation. Enquiries often went to considerable lengths to determine

why a ship was smoking, a radio officer was poor at his job, or a deck officer was unfamiliar with convoy procedure. Commodores complained that masters often failed to digest their paperwork, regarding the convoy conference as a sufficient briefing, while their mates complained that 'the Old Man keeps everything locked up'.

Episodes like these grew in the telling, as such news will, adding little lustre to the Merchant Navy's laurels. What is never emphasised in the repetition of these tales is their positive side. In the case of *Empire Archer*, for example, the ship's own officers suppressed the miscreants, knives and all.[3] As Third Officer Arthur Bird of the *Australind* commented: 'Merchant Navy Ship-Masters and Officers were accustomed to commanding respect and obedience by strength of character reacting on the general good sense of their crews. The Articles gave them little support', less still once they had been broken by sinking and technical 'discharge at sea'. Sir Kenelm Creighton, it will be recalled, had said much the same, and Mackay was told by one chief engineer that 'it was not like the navy', that he could 'give orders but [could] not be sure they [would] be carried out', while another said he ran his engine room on his personality.

Indeed, as a sociologically identifiable group the officer corps of the mercantile marine has attracted little interest and less praise. In fact it did a difficult job efficiently and acquitted itself well. One commodore who in 1943 moaned that 'station-keeping does not improve', also admitted that 'it is impossible to keep proper station with half your rudder out of water and racing screws'. Sadly, good behaviour attracts no attention, for it is expected, while the follies of others act like a magnet upon iron filings.

Captain T.A. Kent, master of the *Diomed* which flew Commodore R. Fitzmaurice's broad pendant in HX217, 'hardly left the bridge during the voyage and by his endurance and assistance in correctly navigating the convoy contributed to [its] . . . safety . . . This officer has had his previous ship [the *Talthybius*] sunk by bombs under him in Singapore and was torpedoed twice in the last war[. R]ecognition of his services on this occasion would', Fitzmaurice thought, 'be appreciated by the Merchant Service.' Kent was torpedoed again the following September in the *Phemius*, and by the end of the war had been appointed OBE for meritorious sea service.

Extreme circumstances brought out not only the best but often the worst in people, as in the case of the four contemptible creatures in Captain Foulkes's lifeboat from the *California Star*. Certainly the Merchant Navy provided a refuge for a number of men who chose it in preference to any of the armed services. Paradoxically, the worst-behaved men on board were occasionally the naval or army gunners, who seemed uncomfortable under the relaxed discipline prevailing aboard merchant ships, which lacked the rigour of military oversight. One private soldier of the Maritime Regiment of Royal Artillery deposited his account of his experiences in the Imperial War Museum; it is a shamelessly pointless, endless chronicle of drinking and consequent disgrace. Captain A. Cromarty of the *Holmpark* complained that during a 16-day passage in his lifeboat, one gunner spent his time stirring up the Arab members of the *Holmpark*'s crew, 'under the impression, I think, that they were not doing enough work whilst he was doing too much, whereas it was the other way round. Several times I told him to "shut up", and on one occasion it became necessary to threaten him with an axe.'[4]

Among the Indian lascars, Chinese seamen, Somali firemen or any other of the disperate nationalities to be found aboard British merchant ships, the standard of conduct was, if anything, marginally less extreme. Occasional 'trouble' was experienced but, as several masters readily attested, the behaviour of their so-called 'native' crews was not merely exemplary, but outstanding. In respect of firing boilers, one master stated that 'We have no trouble, it's a native crew and they are very careful.' Usually, though not always, a distinction in conduct might be drawn between the tramp-ship, with its uncaring tradition of poor pay and conditions, and the cargo-liner or tanker, whose men felt they owed an allegiance to their owners and therefore functioned better as a 'ship's company' and not a mere 'crew'.

But the seafarer was, as Admiral Napier had long ago complained, 'the devil in harbour'. Seamen in trouble ashore and hauled before a magistrate usually pleaded guilty and assured the court that their intentions were not evil. On Merseyside, 'if a seaman expresses his willingness to go back to sea next day, the Bench and the Magistrates' Clerk are usually quite impressed and the result is a moderate penalty.' At sea, a ship's master had recourse only to the official 'logging' procedure, deducting one or more day's pay, according to the offence. In the main it was sufficient, and in the main the men of the merchant service did their duty.

The reputation of the merchant seaman swung between the extremes of the fractious, intractable social dreg and the heroic figure as portrayed in propaganda posters or evidenced by the simple patriotism of Frank Laskier as broadcast on the BBC. Both were a distortion: the former a disingenuous characterisation of a plain, hard-bitten man, the latter a rather cynical manipulation intended to muster public admiration for the benighted merchant jack. Studying merchant seafarers closely, the retired army officer Owen Rutter was able to bring a more objective eye to bear. They 'lived tough lives . . . improvident and thriftless by standards ashore . . . They have also been, and still are, impatient of discipline and tenacious of their rights, and ready to combat any infringement of their independence . . . taking service when they will, leaving it when they feel inclined . . . They may be led, but they cannot be dragooned.'[5]

There was heavy loss of life in the Royal Navy, but a proportionately greater risk was run in the civilian sea-service. If a merchant seaman's ship was sunk, he had a 46.3 per cent chance of surviving the ordeal.[6] Analysis suggests that while relatively few men were killed by the impact of a torpedo in the hull of a merchantman, more than a quarter of those still alive after that disastrous moment then perished in the chaos of escape, during the act of abandoning ship, or in the sea. Only 6 per cent of those who made it onto a raft or into a lifeboat died, but the statistic is skewed by the fact that, as the patient reader will have remarked, most on rafts or in boats were relatively quickly picked up if a vessel was sunk within or close astern of a convoy. A prolonged boat voyage increased the chance of death exponentially over time.

Most of those who died in the period between being sunk and gaining some form of tenuous safety lost their lives through a failure of survival equipment, from hypothermia, or from trauma. Obviously a slow sinking in daylight in the tropics offered better prospects than having to abandon an ore-laden tramp off Cape Farewell in midwinter, but even in the most auspicious circumstances stoicism, a good supply of clothing, and sound leadership and seamanship could prolong life. A memorandum issued as a guide to survival in 1943 clearly stated that: 'Experience has shown . . . that the . . . chances of survival, of those adrift depend upon the frame of mind of the boat's company.'[7]

The degree to which such advice was helpful depended upon the level of disruption caused to a ship's company through enemy action. Boats might well be provisioned and equipped with the maximum of forethought, drills held and all hands practised in their duties, but if the boats or their launching gear were damaged, if the evacuation procedures were rendered impossible or the fragile command structure was fractured by death, then the carefully rehearsed procedures rapidly disintegrated. The three or four deck officers usually had several tasks to perform before taking command of their lifeboats, and often they arrived on the boat-deck to see their charges already sea-borne.

Very often a torpedoed vessel was a straggler, bereft of the mutual support of other vessels in her convoy and without much prospect of succour from an escort or rescue ship. The knowledge that they were aboard a straggler tended to work upon men's minds, as did the increased risk of being torpedoed. When the terrible moment came, accompanied perhaps by darkness and cold, the shock of sudden immersion could be cataclysmic, a panic-inducing reverse of the comforting notion most men clung to: that 'it will not happen to me'.

The stark details of some survivors' reports scarcely convey the bleakness of the moment: 'It was bitterly cold,' recalled Chief Officer E.W. Bushen of the *Dayrose*, sunk on 14 January 1942, 'the temperature of the water being 33° F [0° Celsius]. It was snowing with the wind force 6–7 all that night.' The difficulties of abandoning a ship are readily obvious to any seafarer, and what truly astonishes is the fact that so many lifeboats *were* lowered successfully, often in such poor conditions as Bushen adumbrates.

Once a ship had been abandoned rescue was never guaranteed, even, as has been repeatedly described, when the Royal Navy was present. One 23-year-old corvette officer recalled an incident in January 1941:

> . . . we were returning alone to Belfast. A few hundred miles west of Ireland we came across a lifeboat full of men. Our Captain said that he was under orders not to stop because a large ship stopped in the water would be a sitting duck to a U-boat. We passed as close as we could to the lifeboat to tell the men that help would be coming, and we notified the Admiralty of their position. But it was heart-breaking to see the distraught faces of those men, who were committed to at least another winter's night in an open boat (and we did not know how long they had been in that boat). It must have appeared to those men to be an act of cruelty. The scene became etched in my memory.[8]

The great oceanic battlefield still lies to the west of these islands, yet it bears no record of those whose bones lie beneath its surface and is troubled only by the great winds that scour its surface.[9] Men and women still traverse it, but none possess it now, any more than it was held by either contending party in the Second World War. But between September 1939 and May 1943 the men of the British and exiled merchant services, latterly joined by those of the mercantile marine of the United States of America, maintained the long supply line upon which the survival of Britain and opposition to Nazi Germany depended.

Churchill himself had in the inter-war years been fooled into thinking that the Royal Navy had mastered the submarine, but when shortly before the outbreak of war the Parliamentary Secretary for the Admiralty claimed that science had achieved this domination, he presciently warned that 'we have this measure of the submarine, this superiority, *only* if there is an abundance, a super-abundance, of destroyers and other small craft available'. That 'super-abundance' did not manifest itself before 1943; until then not only the supply line but the battle-line itself was held by a Merchant Navy whose men have been described as 'full of agonized bewilderment'.

The strategic value of the asset which by 1943 had been accepted as a true Merchant Navy had long before been appreciated by the nineteenth-century American naval officer and historian, Captain Alfred Mahan. Mahan had written that: 'Britain . . . will depend as far ahead as we can see, not on the Royal Navy, but on the merchant ships that actually carry [the] basic requirements, both in peace and in war.'

Alas, that it should have been so quickly forgotten. In the years succeeding the war, after a brief boom, the British-manned and British-owned merchant fleet has all but vanished from the oceans of the world. Those merchant seamen, reported by Admiral of the Fleet Lord Chatfield, who reversed their 'MN' badges in token of them being 'Not Wanted' were ultimately proved correct.[10]

NOTES

INTRODUCTION: 'THIS NATION OWES THESE PEOPLE A GREAT DEAL'

1. See Woodman, *Arctic Convoys*.

2. When in the face of the rise of Fascism an urgent ship-building programme was initiated in the mid 1930s, Britain was unable to respond fully. Though she was in receipt of German reparations, in addition to returning to the gold standard Britain had been obliged to service the debt to the United States she had incurred during the First World War. By contrast, France and Belgium used reparations to modernise their steel industries. Germany, in receipt of American loans and in return for unfulfilled undertakings, rebuilt her own industrial power-base.

3. Despite the so-called 'miracle' of Dunkirk in which the British Expeditionary Force was evacuated from France in the spring of 1940, the British army lost all its equipment, exacerbating the demand for all forms of armaments.

4. Stewart, *The Sea Our Heritage*, p. 83.

5. Captain Edgar May, 'A Memoir', in *Journal of the Honourable Company of Master Mariners*, Vol. XVIII, Spring 1993, No. 213.

6. Creighton, *Convoy Commodore*, p. 54.

7. R.M. Dunshea, Imperial War Museum, 81/45/1.

8. Generally such 'small' vessels were not designed for oceanic service, but in peace time plied the short-sea trades.

CHAPTER 1: 'WE WERE UTTERLY MISERABLE'

1. Captain George Russell, 'Six Years on the North Atlantic, 1939–45,' *in Journal of the Honourable Company of Master Mariners*, Vol. XVIII, Summer 1993, No. 214. For loss of *Vardulia*, see Alan Villiers, *Posted Missing* (Hodder and Stoughton, 1956), p. 230.

2. John C. Coullie, 'Account of experiences during the loss of the *SS Athenia*', IWM P284.

3. Certain liners had been selected by the Admiralty on the grounds of speed, range and hull strength for arming with medium-calibre armament, usually 6-inch guns. These vessels were then manned by naval crews, though many of the ship's original complement, particularly in the engineering department, were retained as naval reservists. As an extemporised form of warship known as Armed Merchant Cruisers (AMCs) such ships were used for ocean patrol

work and convoy escort. Despite the obsolescence of their guns and their general unsuitability for the exigencies of war, AMCs nevertheless acquitted themselves well.

4. H.W. Swindley, Letter to friends dated Toronto, 20 September 1939, IWM P284.

5. Mr Copeland's report is in the National Archive (PRO) ADM 199/2130. See ch. 3.

6. Ironically the *Knute Nelson*, owned by Fred Olsen & Co. of Oslo, later fell to the Germans when Norway was occupied and was sunk by a mine in September 1944. Of the other rescuing ships, the *City of Flint* is mentioned in ch. 4.

7. The British called these three vessels 'pocket-battleships' after seeing the *Admiral Scheer* at a pre-war review. It was clear that with their six 11-inch guns they were intended to pack as much power as the German designers could fit into a hull that did not break the restrictions imposed upon them under the Treaty of Versailles and the Washington Naval Treaty of 1922. They were intended as prestigious heavy cruisers, and the Germans classed them as *Panzerschiffen*, or 'armoured ships'. The propaganda effect of her possible loss prompted Hitler to order the renaming of the *Deutschland*: she became the *Lützow* (see ch. 4).

8. Dönitz, *Memoirs*, p. 51.

9. Warlimont, *Inside Hitler's Headquarters*, p. 31.

10. Renamed *Crown Arun*, she was placed under the management of the Ministry of Shipping. She was torpedoed, shelled and sunk a year later by *U-99* when straggling from Convoy HX72. All the British crew survived.

11. Hessler, *German Naval History, U-boat War in the Atlantic*, p. 1. The Types I (an early unsuccessful type of which only two were built) and IX were of 700 tons displacement, the Type VIIs, the backbone of the U-boat arm, of 500. Although the early VIIAs suffered from a lack of range, later modifications, the VIIB and VIIC, were much more successful. The other 30 operational submarines were of the 250-ton coastal Type IIs. The U-boat's principal weapon was the torpedo, supplemented by a deck gun. It was with this latter that she was supposed, under the Prize Rules, to compel a merchant ship's crew to abandon ship, saving the torpedo for the *coup de grâce*.

12. Dönitz, p. 42.

13. *Ibid.*, p. 37.

14. Some ship-building was suspended, including two of the proposed four aircraft carriers being built at Kiel. The keel of the *Graf Zeppelin* and the *Peter Strasser* were laid in 1936 and the former was later launched, complete with flight-deck, but neither was ever completed.

15. See ch. 11.

16. Hessler, *op. cit.*, p. 40.

17. Like his colleagues in disguised merchant raiders, Kapitän zur See Hans Langsdorff of the *Admiral Graf Spee*, commerce-raiding in the South Atlantic and Indian Oceans, practised warfare under the Prize Ordinance in the early months of the war.

18. Roskill, *The War at Sea*, Vol. 1, p.103, and Dönitz, op. cit., p. 35.
19. Dönitz, op. cit., pp. 56–7; but he is mistaken in claiming that this occurred in 'early October'. Wynn, *U-boat Operations*, Vol. 1, p. 4, says the *Gun* was sunk on the 27th but Swedish records state it that occurred on 30 September, the day after she sailed from Gothenburg. She was the fourth *neutral* Swedish vessel to be sunk. *U-3* returned to Kiel on 3 October.
20. Lord Lee of Fareham, speech 22 December 1921, quoted in G.H. & R. Bennett, *Survivors*, p. 2.
21. *Führer Conferences on Naval Affairs*, p. 39.
22. *Ibid.*, p. 39: information revealed by Dönitz's Chief of Staff, Admiral Godt, and included by the editor. Also Vause, *Wolf: U-boat Commanders in World War II*, p. 40.
23. *Führer Conferences*, p. 46.

CHAPTER 2: 'ENGAGED IN A PERILOUS OCCUPATION'

1. Conversation with the distinguished submariner Vice Admiral Sir Ian McGeoch, KCB, DSO, DSC. Curiously, and although he later eulogised the big-gun cruiser, on 10 August 1914 Dudley Pound noted in his diary the need to use aircraft to locate submarines. See Brodhurst, *Churchill's Anchor*, p. 22 *et seq.*
2. This was the first U-boat to be destroyed in action and her 44 survivors were captured; for some time they were held in the Tower of London. The following year two of them were shot while attempting to escape.
3. Little was really understood about the effects of hypothermia until proper studies were carried out after the war. At the time it astonished many rescuers that despite being placed in hot baths or warm blankets, survivors continued to deteriorate until they died. Only later was it understood that once the body's core temperature has been reduced beyond a certain limit, recovery is impossible in battlefield conditions. To this must be added the traumatic impact of shock. Alcohol, thought to be a specific against exposure on account of its apparent warming effect, and an invariably acceptable restorative after trauma, when taken in even modest amounts under such conditions dilates the capillaries, accelerates the onset of hypothermia, and significantly decreases the chances of survival.
4. The National Archive (PRO) ADM 199/2130, Captain T. Georgeson.
5. *Ibid.*, Captain Thomas Prince. Also A.D. Divine, *Merchant Navy Fights*, p. 13 *et seq.*
6. Charlton, McCallum & Company of Amen Corner, Newcastle-upon-Tyne, were typical of the remnant of the small, tramp-ship-owning companies of which there had been hundreds before the First World War. Their Charlton Steam Shipping Company owned only three ships in 1939, the *Hazelside*, *Hollinside* and *Homeside*. The *Hazelside* was replaced by a ship of the same name which was in turn torpedoed by *U-68* in October 1941. The *Hollinside* was torpedoed in convoy by *U-107* in September 1942.

7. On 13 September a report was received in London from Amsterdam that in mid Atlantic the *Bremen* had changed her flag-state from Germany to Italy. She took refuge in the Soviet Russian port of Murmansk along with eighteen other German merchantmen and thereby eluded the Home Fleet's first sweep. On 12 December she was sighted off Helgoland returning to the Elbe from Russia by HM Submarine *Salmon*, Lieutenant Commander Bickford, who surfaced and ordered her to 'stop instantly'. *Bremen* took no notice and Bickford was compelled to dive deep as a Dornier flying-boat approached. During the period of Soviet–Nazi *rapprochement* the Russians had under the mutual Non-Aggression Pact supported a number of German vessels, including the commerce-raider *Komet*, which was assisted by Russian ice-breakers through the Kara Sea and the North East passage to debouch into the Pacific by way of the Bering Strait.

8. Martin Doughty culled this for his excellent study *Merchant Shipping and War*, attributing it to a quote in an unpublished D.Phil. thesis by Brian Ranft, 'The Naval Defence of British Seaborne Trade, 1860–1905' (Oxford, 1967). The pronouncement is valuable in that – as a direct consequence of their private employment – the opinions of few merchant service officers have been recorded. This source is said to have been 'prominent'.

9. A few converted and specially equipped merchant ships were commissioned at the beginning of the Second World War as 'Q'-ships, but they did not last and were soon returned to trade.

10. During the American War of Independence a Franco-Spanish fleet entered the Channel unopposed by the Royal Navy's Western Squadron and caused a very real invasion scare. The enterprise was ruined by scurvy in the enemy fleet.

11. See Ronald Hope, *New History of British Shipping*, p. 350.

12. See Course, *Merchant Navy*, p. 274.

13. *Ibid.*, p. 274. A merchant seaman off articles could earn nothing more until he was re-engaged, so he could afford little time at home but was compelled to return to sea as soon as possible in order to support his family.

14. The Admiralty also had to deal with a similar situation in the disciplined ranks of the Royal Navy when in September 1931, prompted by the world financial depression of 1929–31, Their Lordships abruptly announced a 10 per cent reduction in the pay of the lower deck. This provoked the men of the Atlantic Fleet to refuse to take their ships to sea from their anchorage at Invergordon. Normally acquiescent and biddable, the ratings of the Royal Navy were the antithesis of the most extreme forms of organised labour to be found in the desolate stoke-holds of merchantmen. 'What worried these moderate men [of the Atlantic Fleet] . . . was, in the simplest possible terms, the prospect of any [pay] cut at all. They lived at the very edge of the margin between reasonable existence and poverty. The economists' calculations about the cost of living were beyond their comprehension. They knew the price of bread and eggs and new blankets. They were quietly and very humanly worried about what would happen to their homes' – a particular anxiety of men compelled to dwell so distantly

and for so long from their families. As a consequences, 'many decent men were driven to distraction by anxiety about their homes . . . [and] swept off their feet by this anxiety'. No similar cuts were imposed upon the army or air force, a discrimination not lost on the sailors, and clear evidence that 'The real moral issue . . . [lay] in the failure of successive Boards of Admiralty to maintain a reasonable interest in the backgrounds and the home conditions of the men on the lower deck.'

Fortunately, after a few days of confrontation during which the 'mutiny' thoroughly rattled the Establishment, the Admiralty were compelled to relent and the men's pay was restored, though with a singular lack of magnanimity, for the vindictive wrath of dismissal and obloquy was visited upon the identifiable ring-leaders.

See Divine, *Mutiny at Invergordon*, p. 198 *et seq*.

15. See Hirson and Vivian, *Strike Across the Empire*; also Hope, *New History of British Shipping*, ch. 20. Wilson survived, to die a Companion of Honour and a CBE, while his union, re-formed as the National Union of Seamen, continued to represent its members for many years with varying degrees of success. The subsequent seamen's strike of 1966 is held by many authorities to have marked the beginning of the end for the British merchant fleet.

16. See Hope, *op. cit.*, p. 375. I recall that even in 1960 the Chinese accommodation in Alfred Holt's *Glenartney*, built in 1940, lacked doors to the crew's lavatories.

17. *Ibid.*, p. 378.

18. *Ibid.*, p. 379. This marked a significant decline since about 1900, when British-flagged vessels had made up half the global merchant fleet. There was a similar decline in exports, significantly of coal, which had been about 77 million tons in 1913. Oil imports were however increasing, from 1.7 million tons in 1913 to 11.1 million tons in 1938.

19. One of HMS *Worcester*'s students is better known to history as Admiral Togo, victor of the Battle of Tsu-Shima in the Russo-Japanese War of 1903–5.

20. For a long time experience in sail was required of a potential officer, but though sailing vessels still made up a considerable proportion of the British merchant fleet in 1914 it was decided about 1917 that there was no commercial future in sail.

21. Even in February 1941 the BBC were still broadcasting references to the 'British Merchant Marine': see Hardy, *Everyman's History*, Vol. 1 (1948), p. 325.

22. Creighton, *Convoy Commodore*, p. 55 *et seq*.

23. The previous day Liebe had stopped but released a French vessel, the *Pluvoise*, whose master had transmitted a submarine alarm, provoking Dönitz to reinforce his hands-off order to his commanders in the field.

24. Captain Parsloe of the *Anglo Californian* engaged a U-boat and Captain Bisset-Smith of the *Otaki* engaged the raider SMS *Moewe*. The special warrant was ignored throughout the Second World War, the highest decoration for valour given to Merchant Navy personnel being the George Cross, a civilian deco-

ration, even when earned in the face of the enemy, as in the case of Captain Dudley Mason of the tanker *Ohio* during Operation PEDESTAL, August 1942.

25. That same day, 6 September, the Germans made their first air raid on Britain.

26. Dönitz, *Memoirs*, p. 56.

CHAPTER 3: 'THE SAFETY OF OUR TRADE . . .'

1. Although asdic/sonar was undoubtedly a war-winning weapon, initially its efficiency was grossly over-estimated and its deficiencies under-appreciated. Among others, Churchill himself seems to have been deluded chiefly by a demonstration off Portland in which the attacking destroyers had no trouble in echo-locating an obliging submarine by its means. He was manifestly pleased by the result, which was witnessed by Captain Maurice Underwood, RN, who related an account of it to the author in 1994. For the 'flogging' of logs and reports, see Mars, *Court Martial*; for the 'Cinderella' status of anti-submarine warfare, see Whinney, *U-Boat Peril*.

2. For Dudley Pound, see ch. 1, n. 1.

3. The National Archive (PRO), CAB.4/25, C.I.D.1276-B, Annex 1, 2 July 1936. para 20, quoted Doughty, *Merchant Shipping and War*, p. 47 *et seq.*

4. *Op. cit.*, p. 9.

5. Although it has long been appreciated that commercial shipping earns money at sea and loses it in port, and seafarers, ship-owners, naval architects and builders have historically made every effort to improve the speed and reliability of passage-making, it is only comparatively recently that the industry as a whole has sought a comparable efficiency in the speed of cargo-handling and in turn-round time in port.

6. Behrens, *Merchant Shipping and the Demands of War*, p. 24.

7. The *Schnellboote* were the equivalent of the British fast motor-torpedo or gun-boats, and were known to the British as 'E-boats'. Developed by the Lürssenwerft, they could achieve high speeds of around 40 knots in moderate sea conditions powered by 20-cylinder Daimler-Benz V-form engines. Confusingly, the Kriegsmarine also possessed small destroyers which literal translation renders into 'torpedo-boats', as well as larger destroyers also capable of mine-laying. This is another neglected area of the maritime war, and the interested reader is recommended to consult J.P. Foynes's self-published *Battle of the East Coast*, 1939–1945 (1994).

8. Roskill, *War at Sea*, Vol. 1, p. 6 *et seq.*

9. Broadly, the Vice Chief had special responsibility for Intelligence, Planning and Communications, together with hydrography and fleet navigation. The Second Sea Lord was responsible for personnel and manning of the Royal Navy, the Third and his deputies tended naval construction, research and weapons development, the Fourth stores and victualling, and the Fifth the Fleet Air Arm. There were also a Civil Lord responsible for civil works and labour, a Parliamentary Secretary who dealt with contractual and purchasing matters,

and a secretariat headed by a Permanent Secretary. The whole came, of course, under Winston Churchill, First Lord of the Admiralty, a political appointee and Cabinet member. The administration of the Controller of Merchant Shipbuilding and Repairs lasted until the end of 1944.

10. The revised title for the Assistant Chief of Naval Staff (Trade). Before November 1942, the Trade Division had no plot combining the dispositions of convoys, independent merchantmen and warships (ADM1/14194).

11. Conversation in 1992 with the late Peter Kemp. Kemp was an admirer of Pound and, having recounted Pound's nightly visits, added: 'Cunningham [Pound's successor] never did such a thing!'

12. Stock, C., 'A Worm's Eye View from the Admiralty, 1943–45', from the *Seven Seas Club Magazine*, Vol. 79, No. 6, p. 10.

13. Conversation with Mrs Rosemary Sherbrooke, summer 1993.

14. Watt, *In All Respects Ready*, p. 27 et seq.

15. Schofield, *British Sea Power*, p. 185.

16. It was a routine of normal trading practice for ship-masters to visit consular officers to report their arrival or departure, and to 'note protest' – that is, to make a formal declaration that their ships had encountered exceptional heavy weather, such as a hurricane or typhoon, so as to offset insurance claims for cargo damaged by 'Act of God' rather than from their own neglect of seamanlike precautions. On rare occasions a master might also request a British consul to convene a Naval Court to try a serious offence allegedly committed by a member of his ship's crew.

17. By the end of the war the DEMS Organisation fielded some 24,000 men and the Maritime AA Regiment, later the Maritime Regiment of Royal Artillery, about 14,000. The presence of gunners did not automatically improve the defensive capability of a merchant ship. During a practice shoot aboard the *Empress of Australia* in the Gulf of Aden, the recoil from the first discharge of her 4.7 inch gun was insufficiently absorbed by the weapon's mechanism and the deck house upon which it was mounted – which was the ship's hospital – collapsed. The liner, carrying troops to India, entered Bombay with the humiliating wreckage on her poop.

18. Dreyer was a highly distinguished officer who came within a whisker of becoming First Sea Lord. He was removed from the Admiralty Board following Invergordon mutiny. Upon the outbreak of hostilities he volunteered for convoy service and served as a Commodore, 2nd Class, RNR before taking up his new and influential appointment.

19. The *Royal Ulsterman*, loaded with ammunition, was ordered to Norway during the disastrous Anglo-French intervention of 1940. Unwilling to proceed, her crew refused duty and were replaced by naval personnel.

20. Doughty, *Merchant Shipping and War*, p. 42. Statutory control was provided for under the Royal Prerogative and the Defence of the Realm Act.

21. By their occupation of Norway the Germans in turn acquired the Norwegian 'Homefleet' of 833 small vessels (totalling 675,000 tons). Of these, 172 were lost to British or Russian action, with a loss in lives of 639 Norwegian seamen,

392 Norwegian nationals caught on board as passengers, and an unspecified number of German military and naval personnel.

22. Doughty, *op. cit.*, p. 105.

23. Watt, *op. cit.*, p. xvii. Watt mentions in particular the desertion of twenty men from the 1918-built Greek freighter *Michael L. Embiricos* in Halifax, Nova Scotia.

24. All captured prizes and many vessels built under the emergency building programmes were given names beginning with the word *Empire*.

25. Burn, *Fighting Commodores*, quoted p. 32. In addition to standard 'Trade' convoys, Goldsmith also commanded a number of military convoys.

26. The National Archive (PRO), ADM 199/718.

27. Hague, *Allied Convoy System*, p. 30 *et seq.*

28. From papers of Captain T. Speakman, then Chief Officer of the *City of Yokohama*, convoys OB230 and SL71.

CHAPTER 4: 'THE NIGHT WAS MONSTROUS WITH THREAT'

1. The *Bremen* returned to Bremerhaven, where it was intended she should act as a military transport for the invasion of England, but on 16 March 1942 she was deliberately set on fire and burnt. She was later stripped to the water-line, and her remains were finally broken up in 1953.

2. The job was not without hazard: the ex-trawler *Northern Rover*, for example, converted into an Armed Boarding Vessel, was torpedoed by *U-59* at the end of October. But Horton's biggest problem was the weather, and the heavy seas that swept his low-freeboard and obsolete 'C'-class cruisers from one end to the other, keeping their crews perpetually damp. Many were later rearmed as anti-aircraft cruisers.

3. This destruction of the German merchant fleet was not, of course, carried out exclusively by the Northern Patrol. In the South Atlantic, for instance, off the Rio de la Plata on the first day of the war the German cargo ships *Olinda* and *Carl Fritzen* were scuttled after being stopped by the British cruiser *Ajax*, while two days later the *Inn* was sunk off the Brazilian coast by HMS *Neptune*.

4. Bekker, *Hitler's Naval War*, p. 37 *et seq.*

5. Von Lückner had acquired the admiring soubriquet 'The Sea Wolf', a term which underwent a transformation in the Second World War.

6. Gray, *Hitler's Battleships*, p. 36 *et seq.* The B-Dienst (to give it its full name, Funkbeobachtungsdienst) operators were civilians in the service of the Kriegsmarine's Intelligence Division. They had broken British naval codes as early as 1936, and Berlin had little trouble passing on Admiralty signals to its operational chiefs afloat or ashore.

7. The receipt, with Langsdorff's mimeographed signature, was sold at auction in London in January 2003.

8. Roskill, *War at Sea*, Vol. 1, p. 70. Roskill mistakenly states that the *City of Flint* actually arrived at Murmansk.

9. For *City of Flint*'s fate, see ch. 22, n. 6.

10. Bekker, *op cit.*, p. 41.

11. Churchill, *Second World War*, Vol. 1, *The Gathering Storm*, p. 464.

12. Force H comprised the cruisers *Shropshire* and *Sussex*; Force I the carrier *Eagle* and the cruisers *Dorsetshire* and *Cornwall*; Force L was at Brest with the French battleship *Dunkerque*, the carrier *Béarn* and the cruisers *Montcalm, Gloire* and *Georges Leygues*; Force M (Dakar) the cruisers *Dupleix* and *Foch*; and Force N (West Indies) the British carrier *Hermes*, the French battleship *Strasbourg* and the British cruiser *Neptune*.

13. Schull, *Far Distant Ships*, p. 16 et seq.

14. I make no claim to the absolute accuracy of such figures and do not wish to trouble the reader with overmuch numerical data, save to indicate trends. I have here used Roskill's figures from Appendix R, *War at Sea*, Vol. 1.

15. Dönitz, *Memoirs*, p. 63, and Blair, *Hitler's U-boat War, The Hunters*, p. 110 et seq. Several U-boats were to be lost in this manner. On 24 October 1939, for example, *U-16* also struck a mine and was stranded on the Goodwin Sands.

16. Divine, *The Merchant Navy Fights*, p. 65. The title is slightly misleading, for this is an account of the exploits of the tramp-ships belonging to Sir R. Ropner & Co., of West Hartlepool. For *Stonepool's* fate, see ch. 13.

17. Dönitz, *Memoirs*, p. 62; Blair, *Hitler's U-Boat War, The Hunters*, p. 113. Furious at the torpedo failures, Sohler broke radio silence to complain. Dönitz, equally angry, ordered that the magnetic pistol-fired torpedo, which was more effective than the contact-pistol type because it exploded beneath the target's hull, was not to be used. Reversion to the more primitive contact-type put Dönitz's U-boats 'back to where we were in 1914–1918'.

18. Kerr, *Business in Great Waters*, p. 33.

19. German radar was primitive and was limited to enabling gun control to be achieved in the dark or in low visibility. Neither side had an effective operational electronic surface search capability at this stage, though Langsdorff, for instance, had a primitive *Seetakt* set in the *Admiral Graf Spee*.

20. The crew of the *Bertha Fisser* had attempted to scuttle her and, glad of the practice, '*Chitral* put seven rounds into her just before dark fell [on the 20th] and the blast of the guns shattered the windows in the Iceland [*sic*] village of Hoefn and even in farms six miles from the shore.' Having caught fire the *Bertha Fisser* grounded on the rocky coast, where she broke her back.

21. Typically, the ship-owner's employees engaged under the T124 and T124X articles as RN personnel made up one-fifth of the *Rawalpindi's* crew. Of these, six survived and five had been taken prisoner aboard *Scharnhorst*. The remainder of the crew were regular and reserve naval officers, petty officers and ratings, or conscripted 'HO' (Hostilities Only) ratings.

22. Konteradmiral K. Fricke, the Kriegsmarine's Chief of Operations, is alleged to have remarked that 'Battleships [the Germans considered the *Scharnhorst* and *Gneisenau* to be fast battleships, while because of their 11-inch-calibre guns the British rated them as battle-cruisers] are supposed to shoot, not lay smoke-screens!' Marschall vigorously repudiated the implied charge of not having done his utmost, if not of outright cowardice.

23. 'Taffrail' (pen-name of Captain Taprell Dorling, DSO, R.N, F.R.Hist. S.), *Blue Star Line*. The Blue Star Line was owned by the Vesteys and intended originally to service their Argentine beef interests. By this time Blue Star ships traded world-wide, operating refrigerated cargo and cargo-passenger-liners.

24. Although a shipping company supplied a ship with a pair of chronometers and perhaps three or four pairs of binoculars, most officers had their own glasses and were expected to provide their own sextants (see ch. 1). Such instruments were always stowed on the bridge ready for use.

25. The *Port Chalmers* was destined to be the commodore's ship in Operation PEDESTAL relieving Malta in August 1942; see Richard Woodman, *Malta Convoys* (John Murray, 2000).

26. It appears that Langsdorff had been very annoyed with his boarding officer for failing to secure a supply of fresh meat from the *Tairoa*, and that only afterwards, when a receipt was made out in German and English, did he learn the actual cargo of the ship. Copies of the receipt are reproduced in Shaw, Savill & Albion's privately published and circulated war history, *The Flag of the Southern Cross*, written for the company by the well-known author and master mariner Frank Bowen in 1947.

27. Taprell Dorling, *Blue Star Line*, p. 26.

28. This was complex, and lies outside the scope of the present work, but the Germans wanted time to effect repairs to the *Admiral Graf Spee*, Britain wanted her sent to sea, while France and the United States wished for her to be interned for the duration of the war. As to the final exchange of gunfire, evidence from Capitan de Navio F. Fuentes of the Uruguayan cruiser *Uruguay* which put to sea and witnessed the events suggests that *Achilles* was culpable. It is unlikely that this unduly troubled Captain W.E. Parry and his Kiwi crew.

29. Other dispositions included the carrier *Ark Royal*, battle-cruiser *Renown* and cruiser *Neptune* being ordered to join Harwood's blockade, with the carrier *Eagle* and the cruisers *Cornwall* and *Gloucester* covering any possibility of escape to the Indian Ocean.

30. See Gray, *Hitler's Battleships*, p. 60 *et seq.*

31. Through the patronage of Churchill, who favoured admirals who had proved their aggressive fighting qualities, Harwood was unwisely promoted into Cunningham's shoes as Commander-in-Chief, Mediterranean, in 1943. He was not a success.

32. Quoted in Taprell Dorling, *op. cit.*, p. 29.

33. The *Altmark*, renamed the *Uckermark*, was intended to support the *Gneisenau*, *Scharnhorst* and the merchant raider *Michel*, but blew up and sank in Yokohama in September 1942.

34. Whether or not anybody, rescuers or rescued, actually cried out 'The Navy's here!' seems unsubstantiated. It is curious that so traditionally 'naval' an author as 'Taffrail' should not have mentioned it, had it been remembered by the Blue Star officers whose ordeal he was chronicling.

35. The naval slang for cocoa well laced with sugar.

CHAPTER 5: 'QUITE ENOUGH DISASTER'

1. Matthes's *U-44* was sunk off the Shetlands on her next patrol by HMS *Fortune*. Matthes and his 46 men were all killed.

2. The early OA series of convoys formed in the Thames Estuary and The Downs and combined a coastal and oceanic element. They proceeded down-Channel, the coastal element departing off Land's End and heading north, having picked up ships from ports such as Southampton and Falmouth as it passed. In the South West Approaches the ocean portion would combine with an OB convoy from the Irish Sea and proceed to the ocean dispersal point. However, ships bound for the Mediterranean or southwards would remain in company as a 'G' series, hence OA80G/OG16. The practice ceased after the Fall of France in May 1940.

3. The *Langleeford* had collided with and sunk another vessel off the Smalls lighthouse the previous November.

4. The *Leo Dawson* belonged to the Beverley Steamship Company of Newcastle-upon-Tyne, a small, two-ship company that specialised in the carriage of coal to South America. In fact she was on this occasion carrying iron ore, and sank very quickly.

5. Finland was then fighting for her life against Nazi Germany's Soviet Russian ally. This 'Winter War' ended when the Treaty of Moscow was signed between Finland and the USSR on 12 March 1940. In July 1941, when Hitler invaded Russia and turned Stalin from friend to implacable enemy, Finland joined the Axis. In 1939 the Finnish merchant marine still possessed ten ocean-going sailing vessels of British or German manufacture.

6. She was to serve as an Admiralty oiler attached to the Royal Fleet Auxiliary service, and was sunk in January 1943.

7. It is thought that after leaving Helgoland *U-54* hit a British or a German mine.

8. The *Imperial Transport* was nominally owned by the Empire Transport Company, a single-ship subsidiary of Houlder Brothers which were, in turn, part of the Furness Withy Group.

9. A 'donkeyman' was a senior engine-room hand responsible for the secondary 'donkey' boiler which provided steam for the vessel's auxiliary machinery, such as windlass, deck winches, etc.

10. The after part was taken to Greenock, dry-docked and repaired, then anchored while a new forepart was built. The two halves were then married at Elderslie. For the further adventures of this remarkable vessel, see ch. 17. Smail, Swanbrow and others of the crew were awarded civil decorations for brave conduct. See Houlder Brothers, *Sea Hazard, 1939–1945*.

11. Dönitz, *Memoirs*, p. 32, *et seq.*

12. See Roskill, *Merchant Fleet in War*, p. 29 *et seq.* Roskill erroneously attributes *Pyrrhus's* loss to Hartmann's *U-37*. Spencer's report is highly critical of the commodore's decision to slow the convoy, while the commodore criticises the escort as inadequate in strength and performance.

13. The *Banderas* had been built in 1899.

14. These were valuable because they were unique to the German naval codes and had not been part of the Enigma reconstruction passed to the British by Polish patriots. In May, during the Norwegian campaign, three Wehrmacht and Luftwaffe Enigma machines were captured and sent to Bletchley Park.

15. As part of this, British troops occupied the Danish Faeroe Islands at the invitation of the governor.

16. An old sailor's couplet runs: 'From Padstow Bar to Lundy light / A sailors' grave by day or night.'

17. She was sunk by the cruiser *Devonshire* off Ascension in November 1941.

18. The first *Western Isles* proved unsuitable and was later replaced by an Isle of Man packet temporarily given the same name. *Philante*, formerly the millionaire yachtsman Tommy Sopwith's motor-yacht, was used for operational training and occasional convoy escort in the Western Approaches (see convoy diagram).

19. See Captain W.J. Moore, DSC, RD, 'Tales of a Rocky,' unpublished typescript in the Imperial War Museum.

20. Albert Victor Alexander was MP for the Hillsbrough division of Sheffield and later created 1st Viscount (1950) and then Earl (1963) Alexander of Hillsborough. He was a popular First Lord, good at exhorting the Fleet. Sir Guy Jarrett, his Private Secretary for most of the war, considered that his speeches on behalf of the navy made a major contribution to the war effort, for they led to many villages and towns 'adopting' ships and providing material support and comfort to the Royal Navy.

21. Roskill, *War at Sea*, Vol. 1, p. 232.

22. *Ibid.*, p. 235.

23. Churchill, *Second World War*, Vol. 2, *Their Finest Hour*, p. 172.

CHAPTER 6: 'THIS IS A THING TO DO NOW'

1. The shortfall of anti-aircraft weapons had been foreseen, and the order for 1,500 of their 20-mm guns was placed with the Oerlikon-Bührle Company just before the outbreak of war. The Oerlikon's chief advantage was that it was light, simple to operate, and fired an explosive shell. The gun-mounting consisted of a simple pedestal, and one gunner aimed and fired using a simple drum magazine capable of 600 rounds per minute. Although many merchant ships, especially the standard types including the Liberty ships, were fitted with permanent gunpits, a movable version for temporary installation in merchant ships was fitted to augment the fixed armament when a vessel was wanted for a special operation as a military transport.

2. At the end of 1938 the Italian merchant fleet consisted of 830 steamships grossing 2,500,000 tons, 320 motor-vessels grossing 680,000 tons, a grand total of 3,180,000 tons. By comparison, France possessed 1,120 vessels of 2,845,000 tons and Germany 2,350 ships totalling 4,209,000. The total for the British Empire, including those vessels employed exclusively on the Canadian Lakes, was 9,050 ships grossing 20,500,000 tons.

3. See Hough, *Former Naval Person*, p. 131. The Naval Intelligence Officer was probably Lieutenant Commander Peter Kemp. Churchill took over from Earl Stanhope, a 'weak and ineffective' First Lord.

4. *Ibid.*, p. 133.

5. *Ibid.*, p. 135.

6. Roskill, *War at Sea*, Vol. 1, p. 134.

7. Even at this time Churchill was still writing that a battleship was 'absolutely proof against air attack'. In addition to Pound, one of those still persuaded of the invulnerability of the battleship was the Deputy, later Vice, Chief of the Naval Staff, Rear Admiral Tom Phillips, a man many believe to have been highly flawed. Phillips lost his life when the almost new battleship *Prince of Wales* and the battle-cruiser *Repulse* were sunk by Japanese aircraft off Singapore in 1941. The carrier assigned to Phillips's Force Z had been delayed in joining his flag by a grounding in the West Indies. The Royal Navy's *Fighting Instructions* of 1938 'was written on the basis that the naval war would be little different from 1914–18 . . . [and] would be fought with battleships in line of battle'.

8. The East Coast convoys and the series run to Norway before 1940 are outside the scope of this work.

9. The number of Italian submarines in the Atlantic theatre rose to 26 in November 1940 but their lack of aggression led Dönitz to 'dispose the German U-boats . . . without considering [the use he might have made of] the Italians' and this in turn led to their reduction to 10 by May 1941: Roskill, *War at Sea*, Vol. 1, p. 347.

10. Apart from the ships destroyed by Admiral Somerville at Oran and Dakar, a French battle squadron remained in quietly suspended animation under the guns of Cunningham's British Mediterranean Fleet at Alexandria, and several powerful units were isolated in French colonies.

11. Van der Vat, *The Atlantic Campaign*, p. 126.

12. Captain C.F.H. Churchill's 'Report of Proceedings', 17 July 1940, IWM 65/24/1–2[2].

13. Broome, J., *Convoy is to Scatter* (William Kimber, 1972), p. 79.

14. Mars, *Court Martial*, p. 37 *et seq.*

15. The others were *Carinthia, Scotstoun, Andania, Laurentic, Forfar* and *Patroclus*.

16. Houlder Brothers, *Sea Hazard*, p. 20 *et seq.*

17. The *Havildar* was drydocked at Elderslie and placed in the hands of Messrs Barclay, Curle & Company. A hole had been blown in her starboard side which measured 68 feet by 42 feet, exposing No. 4 Hold to the sea and buckling her main deck. Temporary repairs were effected in one week, after which she was moved to Meadowside Drydock and D. & W. Henderson rebuilt her wounded side. She re-entered service in the following January, loaded a cargo for Chittagong to the account of 'Paddy' Henderson's, and survived the war.

CHAPTER 7: 'IT'S ONLY A TORPEDO'

1. See *Two Survived*, (as narrated to) Guy Pearce Jones.
2. The former King Edward VIII had been sidelined and appointed Governor of the Bahamas after his abdication.
3. Tapscott died in 1963. The *Anglo-Saxon*'s jolly-boat is preserved in the Imperial War Museum, London.
4. The *Empire Dawn*'s master, Captain William Scott of Carlisle, also gave evidence against von Ruckteschell. The *Michel* attacked at night without warning and caused 22 casualties out of a crew of 44 (Reuter's).
5. Karl Muggenthaler, *German Raiders of World War II*, quoted in Slader, *Fourth Service*, p. 127: 'it was an impression many frightened survivors in many wars, shocked by their ordeal, ducking from flying fragments of steel and deadly ricochets, retained even after much of their hatred had worn off, but it was one usually impossible to substantiate.'
6. Roskill, *War at Sea*, Vol. 1 p. 358.
7. Hessler, *U-Boat war in the Atlantic*, p. 49.
8. Captain E. May, *Journal of the Honourable Company of Master Mariners*, Vol. XVIII, Spring 1993, No. 213, p. 1009 *et seq.*
9. Schull, *Far Distant Ships*, p. 49 *et seq.* The *Margaree* (ex-HMS *Diana*) had just been taken over from the Royal Navy. She had sailed from Londonderry on 20 October 1940 and was lost at about 01.00 on the 23rd. The *Port Fairy*, 8,337 tons, built in 1928, survived the war and was scrapped in the mid 1960s. The clause 'in this case' indicates the prevailing attitude of the time regarding merchant ships.
10. The *Ville de Mons*, independent, and the *Titan*, out of Convoy OA207.
11. To demonstrate that the real nature of the struggle was wider than the Atlantic itself, the Larrinaga Steamship Company lost a second ship that same night. The *Minnie de Larrinaga* was discharging a cargo of grain in the London Docks when she was sunk by the Luftwaffe. The ship caught fire and burned out; she was later refloated and sunk as a blockship in Dover harbour.
12. Dönitz, *Memoirs*, p. 105.
13. All Kapitänleutnants, except Stiebler and Lüth, who were Oberleutnants.
14. Cooper's Report is in the Imperial War Museum, Misc 593.
15. Other information is taken from *Atlantic Ordeal, The Story of Mary Cornish*, written by Elspeth Huxley after interviewing Miss Cornish. The Children's Overseas Resettlement Scheme did not allow parents to accompany the children, so volunteers were called for, the intention being to return them by sea to Britain, ready to accompany another shipment. Those aboard the *City of Benares* included two young priests, a parson's son and, among the larger number of women, a female doctor, an artist, a nurse, three teachers and a musician, Mary Cornish, aged 41. Only four survived. Miss Cornish, Fourth Officer Cooper and Assistant Steward Purvis were all awarded the British Empire Medal in March 1941. By comparison with Cooper's official report, Huxley rather dramatises the 'threat' posed by the lascars and, unlike Cooper, makes absolutely no mention of the sick lascar who died on board HMS *Anthony*.

16. This was the third of Nisbet's tramps to be sunk, and the company became managers on behalf of the Ministry of War Transport.

17. See Roskill, *Merchant Fleet in War*, p. 56 *et seq*. One of *Eurymedon's* radio officers was an Irishman, Eric Ranalow, who wrote afterwards in *A Corkman at Sea*: 'The German possession of the French naval bases on the Bay of Biscay for four years and Ireland's refusal to allow the Allies use of her western and southern coastlines, contributed immensely to the Allied losses in the Atlantic. It was largely due to the Allied bases in Northern Ireland and Iceland that the one remaining route to Britain [through the North Channel] was kept open.' I am indebted to Mr Ranalow for permission to quote from his book.

18. Miss Drummond served at sea from 1922 to 1962. Although employed by Blue Funnel and British India, both blue-chip companies in their day, she was constantly and deliberately failed when she sat for her Chief Engineer's Certificate of Competency. To become Chief Engineer, therefore, she secured a Panamanian certificate, and served in flag-of-convenience vessels owned by Chinese interests in Hong Kong.

19. Dönitz, *Memoirs*, p. 105.

CHAPTER 8: 'RULERS OF THE SEA'

1. Dönitz, *Memoirs*, p. 108.

2. Roskill, *War at Sea*, Vol. 1, p. 350.

3. Rayner, *Escort*, p. 64 *et seq*. Rayner was afterwards the first RNVR officer to command a destroyer, the *Shikari*, and in her was later the senior officer of 21st Support Group. He twice won the Distinguished Service Cross.

4. See Harling, *Steep Atlantick Stream*.

5. Captain W.J. Moore, DSC, RD. Unpublished typescript 'Tales of a Rocky', Imperial War Museum. The Extra Master Mariner's Certificate of Competency was a grade higher than was judged necessary to command a merchant ship. It took the vocational qualification into the academic field and was, for a while, held to be the equivalent of a degree. It was normally only acquired by officers intending to take up a second career as an official of one of the government's regulating bodies, as an Examiner of Masters and Mates, a Hull Surveyor, or a marine lawyer. Post-war, Moore returned to Holt's employment and commanded several Blue Funnel liners, including their training ship *Diomed*.

6. *Ibid.*, p. 33.

7. *Ibid.*, p. 60.

8. Kippins was to earn the DSC and the OBE before the end of the war.

9. Oerhn had sunk four other ships, *Georges Mabro*, *Samala*, *Heminge*, and the tanker *British Consul*. He had also despatched the derelict *Corrientes*, torpedoed by *U-32* on 26 September.

10. Captain W. Armstrong of the *Sandsend* and all but five of his crew were picked up by the corvette *Hibiscus*.

11. Dönitz, *Memoirs*, p. 106.

12. Quoted in Williams, *Battle of the Atlantic*, p. 94.

13. *Ibid.*, p. 99, Frank Holding quoted.

14. See Hessler, *U-Boat War in the Atlantic*, p. 52 *et seq.*

15. *Ibid.*, p. 54.

16. Schulz had been previously depth-charged: when his cook pointed out that both attacks had occurred when chocolate pudding was on the dinner menu, he banned it.

17. Quoted in Thomas, *The Atlantic Star*, p. 49.

18. Third Radio Officer Gerald Whitehead of the *Caprella*, quoted *ibid.*, p. 49. By this time three radio officers were being assigned to merchant ships in order to maintain a 24-hour radio watch in place of the limited, zone controlled watch routine of peace time.

19. See Blair, *Hitler's U-Boat War, The Hunters*, p. 203.

20. The Italian submarines were a disappointment. They suffered from a major design flaw in that when they were operating on the surface, air for their diesels had to be drawn through the conning-tower hatch – a drawback in the heavy seas of the Atlantic. They also lost 17 boats, mostly in the Mediterranean in the first five months after June 1940.

21. The epic work undertaken by the Polish destroyers was awe-inspiring, and they formed a fully integrated arm of the Royal Navy. *Burza* means 'squall'. See Divine, *Navies in Exile*, pp. 1–45.

22. *U-31* had been sunk in the Jade Estuary after being bombed by an RAF Blenheim in March 1940 when on trials after a refit; all on board were killed. She was the first U-boat sunk by an aircraft. Raised and repaired, she became Prellberg's command. She therefore also had the curious distinction of being the only U-boat to be sunk twice.

23. Correspondence with the author. Third Officer, later Captain, J.R. Cooper was from a seafaring family. His widowed mother had five sons in the Battle of the Atlantic. Ronald Cooper was Fourth Officer of the *City of Benares* and was quoted earlier; Arthur Cooper was Chief Engineer of the *Empire Sailor*, lost when she was sunk by a U-boat on 21 November 1942; a third, Norman Cooper, having survived the sinking of the *Albuera* attacked by an E-boat in the English Channel, died as Third Engineer when the *Benvorlich* was sunk in March 1941 by a Kondor. The Coopers also had a half-brother, Jack Smith, who was lost on 18 April 1945 as an Able Seaman aboard the *Empire Gold*, sunk by *U-1107* west of the Bay of Biscay.

24. See 'Report of an Interview with Mr Charles Pollard, Chief Engineer, and Mr Arthur G. Hawkins, Second Officer, of the M.V. "San Demetrio"', recorded at the Shipping Casualties Section of the Trade Division of the Admiralty, 20 November 1940. Two accounts of the *San Demetrio*'s salving have been published, an autobiographical work by the Shetland fisherman, Callum Macneil, the other a war-time (1942) HMSO publication; see Bibliography. Broadside to the wind, the *San Demetrio* would make up to 4 knots in leeway, against leeway of about

1 to 1.5 knots made by a lifeboat lying to a sea-anchor. This different rate of drift explains the 'disappearance of the tanker'.

Curiously, although the Commissioners for Irish Lights had their head-quarters in Dublin they were funded by 'lights dues' levied on shipping using British and Irish ports which were then distributed to the CIL as one of the three General Lighthouse Authorities for Britain and Ireland (the other two being Trinity House and the Commissioners for Northern Lighthouses). At this time, expenditure on Irish lighthouses exceeded receipts from Irish light dues.

25. See papers of W.T. Brookes, Imperial War Museum 89/3/1.

CHAPTER 9: 'ONE OF THE FINEST BITS OF SEAMANSHIP'

1. A romper was the antithesis of a straggler, a ship which had become separated from and run ahead of its convoys. *Planter* seems to have been one such, running ahead of Convoy SL53 from Freetown, Sierra Leone.

2. Taken at Calcutta on 10 June 1940, this Italian ship was allocated the name *Empire Inventor* but was sunk before she could assume it, and the name was reallocated.

3. See Saunders, *Valiant Voyaging*, pp. 167, 168, 172–177.

4. Wynn, *U-Boat Operations*, Vol. 1 p. 34 says this was the Belgian-flagged *Ville d'Arlon*, 7,555 tons.

5. Kretschmer sank one more ship, the Dutchman *Farmsum*, before narrowly avoiding defeat. Surviving a depth-charge attack with luck and a considerable amount of damage, *U-99* returned to L'Orient on 12 December and did not sail again until February 1941, on her eighth and last cruise.

6. Captain Rice and Chief Engineer Mr A.G. Johnson were appointed OBE; Chief Officer Mr G.A. Shepherd and Carpenter Mr W. Patterson were offi-cially commended for good service. The *Orari* was fully repaired and survived the war after taking part in Operation HARPOON, a vital military convoy to Malta in June 1942.

7. *The Diaries of Sir Alexander Cadogan*, ed. D. Dilks (1971). Cadogan was head of the Foreign Office.

8. The National Archive (PRO), ADM 205/7.

9. In addition to sinking or capturing merchant ships, German raiders laid mines off Cape Town, Auckland, Sydney and Melbourne, where they knew British ships would be concentrating as they approached those ports.

10. See Laskier, *Log Book*, p. 71.

11. The *Eurylochus*'s position was 8° 15' North 025° 04' West, and Caird's signal was monitored in Freetown. One AMC, HMS *Bulolo*, and two cruisers were sent in an unsuccessful search for the *Kormoran*.

12. After the rescue Laskier encountered a BBC reporter named Terence de Marney who was making a series of recordings in Britain's blitzed ports. In the Seaman's Home in Liverpool's Canning Place (a former women's prison) he heard of

Laskier, and the result of their meeting was that Laskier made a series of short broadcast monologues about life and war at sea from the perspective of the merchant seaman. They were thought to be scripted, but were in fact off-the-cuff. Although coloured and somewhat inaccurate (Laskier thought the *Eurylochus* had been shelled by the *Admiral Scheer*) they were very popular, and were transcribed and published by Allen and Unwin in 1941 under the title *My Name is Frank*, which was how the otherwise anonymous Laskier had made himself known to his listeners. After recovering from his amputation and pneumonia, Laskier went back to sea as an A.B. Gunner. His unflattering autobiography, *Log Book*, was published in 1942.

13. See Lane, *Merchant Seamen's War*, p. 251 *et seq*.

14. Following its establishment for this purpose, Aberdovey subsequently became the first of the Outward Bound schools set up by Laurence Holt and Otto Hahn.

15. Roskill, in his account of the attack in *A Merchant Fleet in War*, draws on *The Raider 'Kormoran'* (Kimber, 1959), and also expresses surprise that the Chinese crew were not taken aboard the *Bulolo*, which had a naval surgeon and, as a Burns Philp cargo-passenger-liner, also a 'hospital'.

16. See the *London Gazette*, 11 December 1945.

17. Roosevelt also learned the importance of air power from a USN analysis of the Norwegian débâcle.

18. *Journal of the Honourable Company of Master Mariners*, Vol. XVIII (Summer 1993), No. 214.

19. See 'A Seaman's War', unpublished typescript by a deck officer, Patrick Fyrth, Imperial War Museum 88/42/1.

20. See 'A Sailor's Reflections, 1939–1941, 70,000 miles with convoys at 6 or 7 knots', Rear Admiral Thring. Typescript in the Imperial War Museum.

21. The official position of the sinking places the *Gairsoppa* about 95 miles southwest of Mizen Head, other accounts 200 miles further out into the Atlantic. The latter is more consistent with a voyage of thirteen days' duration, even at the slow rate of progress to be expected of a ship's lifeboat. See Saunders, *Valiant Voyaging*, p. 37 *et seq*.

22. The *Clea*, *Arthur F. Corwin* and *Black Osprey*. Metzler's *U-69* also sank the *Empire Blanda* out of HX107. She was loaded with scrap, and all hands were lost.

23. See Dönitz, *Memoirs*, p. 140.

CHAPTER 10: 'THERE WAS A TERRIFIC EXPLOSION'

1. The *Aikaterini*, the *King Robert* and the *W.B. Walker*.

2. Bristol's Chief-of-Staff, sent to Britain to arrange matters, tried unsuccessfully to wrest an Irish base from the de Valera government. See Morison, *History of United States Naval Operations*, Vol. 1, *The Battle of the Atlantic, 1939–1943*, p. 49 *et seq*. Twenty-seven warships in groups of nine made up the flotillas. Bristol flew his flag in the destroyer-tender *Prairie* at Norfolk, Virginia.

3. See Kerr, *Business in Great Waters*, p. 134.

4. See *The Ben Line*, prepared by William Thomson & Co. (owners of the Ben Line), Thos Nelson, 1946.

5. 'Report of an Interview with Captain L.A. Church, Master of the S.S. "Franche Comté", 4 April 1941'. This vessel was owned by the Société Française de Transports Pétroliers, but had been taken under British management and manning by the MoWT.

6. Two other tankers from HX114 were lost before they reached their final destinations, the Norwegian-flagged *Hidlefjord*, with the loss of 29 men who perished amid 10,600 tons of burning petrol, and the British tanker *San Conrado* which, laden with heavy fuel oil, took none of her crew with her. Both were in a coastal convoy bombed by aircraft from Kampfgeschwader 27 off the Pembroke coast after HX112 had dispersed off Liverpool.

7. There was an unsuccessful hundred-bomber raid on Brest at the end of March, but on 6 April 1941 four RAF Beaufort torpedo bombers were despatched to attack *Gneisenau* anchored in the roads. The battleship was not anchored in open water, but Flying Officer K. Campbell and his three-man crew flew in almost at sea level in defiance of heavy anti-aircraft fire, 'hopped' the obstructing breakwaters and loosed his torpedo seconds before the Beaufort was torn to shreds. The torpedo blew off the *Gneisenau's* stern; she required emergency repairs in dry dock, where she was further bombed a few nights later. In view of Raeder's orders that Lütjens should avoid the heavy-calibre guns of British battleships at all costs, there was a certain irony in this twist to the tale of German capital ship mismanagement.

8. The *Zamalek* held the record for most rescues (665 survivors) and participated in Convoy PQ17 to North Russia, including its tragic aftermath. Her master, Captain Morris, served throughout the war and earned the DSO, an unusual honour for a Merchant Navy officer.

9. The *Kormoran's* boarding party removed from the *Agnita* 'a very fine chart' of the swept channels into Freetown, copies of which were made and passed to the next U-boats succoured by the raider.

10. See Turner, Gordon-Cumming and Betzler, *War in the Southern Oceans*, p. 73.

11. Remarks by Vice Admiral Sir Ian McIntosh in McVicar's obituary. William McVicar, a son of the manse, went to sea aged 17. He was 26 at the time of *Britannia's* sinking.

12. Between 23 and 31 March the west-bound tankers *Chama* and *Agnete Maersk* were sunk by *U-97* (Heilmann) and *Veniero* (Petroni) respectively, the west-bound tramp *Koranton* was sunk by *U-98* (Gysae) after straggling from SC25, and *U-48* (Schultze) attacked Convoy HX115 and sank the *Hylton* (Captain W.E. O'Connell and Commodore Sir C.G. Ramsey). Metzler's *U-69* sank the westbound *Coultarn* out of OB302. Operating off the Cape Verde Islands, *U-106* (Oesten) sank the *Eastlea* with the loss of all hands, and off Freetown Convoy WS7 was attacked by *U-124* (Schulz) who sank the Natal Line's *Umona* with heavy loss of life. One boat containing one gunner and one passenger was adrift for thirteen days.

13. The participants were interviewed by the author Richard Hughes and gave him the basis of his novel *In Hazard*. Evans, while widely praised for saving his ship, was censured by his owners, Alfred Holt & Company, for the loss of the vessel's blue funnel! He was born at sea in the cabin of his father's barque, then off the coast of Chile: 'Chile' was his third Christian name.

14. See Kerr, *Business in Great Waters*, p. 65 *et seq.*

15. Quoted by Roskill, *Merchant Fleet in War*, p. 119 *et seq.* It was Holt's practice to call their apprentices 'midshipmen'.

16. The Dutchman *Saleier*, the Belgian *Ville de Liège* and the Swede *Venezuela*.

CHAPTER 11: 'THE END WAS TERRIBLE AND VIOLENT'

1. The 'B' stood for 'British'. They were complemented by Canadian escort groups which bore the prefix 'C'. The 'Escort Group' should not be confused with the much later introduction of the independent 'Support Group', which was not attached to a specific convoy but was directed to the assistance of anyone in the vicinity under attack.

2. These Hudsons carried a pair of homing pigeons in case of being forced to ditch before a position signal could be transmitted.

3. The subject of keeping destroyers in the Orkneys while convoys were being mauled in the North Atlantic was debated in the House of Commons after the war. See *Hansard*, Navy Estimates Debate, 18 March 1947.

4. Successive British governments denied veterans of Arctic Convoys any official campaign medal separate from the Atlantic Star, the campaign medal for the Battle of the Atlantic. The most recent, and probably final, rejection was made by Defence Minister Geoffrey Hoon in the spring of 2003.

5. And, it has to be said, admirals on both sides of the North Sea would have been justified in their faith in the efficacy of the big gun in German hands. Given the effectiveness when they were brought to battle of both *Bismarck*, a fully-fledged battleship, and *Scharnhorst*, a light battleship which was better armoured than the battle-cruiser the British contemporarily classed her as, it is inconceivable that Lütjens could have failed to out-fight and out-manoeuvre the slow 'R'-class battleships or the unmodified *Malaya* acting as ocean escorts to convoys.

6. Peter Le Quesne Johnson when Purser of the MV *Glenlyon* to the author when Fourth Officer of the same vessel in 1964.

7. See Roskill, *Merchant Fleet in War*, p. 110 *et seq.* A Foreign Office official, upon learning of landings on the coast of Vichy French Senegal, made the astonishing comment that 'merchant seamen must be very ignorant to make their landings there'.

8. As mentioned in ch. 10, *U-105* and *U-106* had pioneered this double-patrol system with Schulz in *U-124*. Having replenished from the *Kormoran*, Schulz remained in theatre until the end of April, and sank a number of British and Greek ships, though he was absent from the climax of the actions.

9. On the same day near St Paul's Rocks, off the shoulder of Brazil, the raider *Kormoran* sank the Harrison liner *Craftsman* on her way to Alexandria via the Suez Canal. She too was carrying Admiralty stores, an example of the steady attrition of military cargoes as well as of British imports and exports achieved by the Germans.

10. See Roskill, *Merchant Fleet in War*, p. 121 *et seq*.

11. See Bennet, *Survivors*, p. 178, *et seq*.

12. Even in the 1960s lifeboat biscuit remained hard and rather unpalatable, its successful mastication requiring considerable quantities of saliva. Compared with ship's biscuit made to the Royal Navy's recipe in the Napoleonic War, it was slightly less hard, but also less flavourful. The issue of fishing tackle, sanctioned by the Chamber of Shipping in October 1942, was not universal in British ships even as late as 1944.

13. The most primitive form of astro-navigation is called Parallel Sailing. In this, the navigator knows the latitude of his destination, and by sailing north or south onto it, may then cast east or west until he finds his refuge. From the altitude, or angle above the horizon, of the Pole Star, Polaris, an approximation of the observer's latitude can be determined with relative ease.

14. See Behrens, *Merchant Shipping and the Demands of War*, Chapter VII and Appendix XXX. It should be remembered that the term 'merchant seaman' was generic, and included officers. In addition to the dead and disabled, and those in the RNR, it was estimated that fewer than a thousand had been taken prisoners-of-war, and that these men were almost all captured by surface raiders. Some foreign seamen employed in British ships before the war left the merchant service when hostilities began, but there was a small gain from seamen recruited in Newfoundland. Significantly, the above figures do not include apprentices, cadets, or deck or galley boys, many of whom joined the Merchant Navy after the outbreak of war but who were all minors, many below 'military' age.

15. Most of the German supply ships scuttled themselves rather than be captured with their Engima machines and codes. Among them were the tankers *Belchen* off Greenland, the *Gedania* and the *Gonzenheim*. The *Gedania* was due to relieve the *Egerland* and did not scuttle, but engaged the destroyer *Marsdale*. On board was found a rich haul of intelligence material which, *inter alia*, enabled aircraft from the carrier *Eagle* to intercept and bomb the homeward-bound German freighter *Elbe* off the Azores in early June.

16. See Harling, *Steep Atlantick Stream*, p. 114 and 162.

17. Private interview with the author.

18. Captain R.S. Craston of the *Ena de Larrinaga* was awarded the Lloyd's War Medal for bravery at sea.

19. Information kindly supplied by Bernard de Neumann and George Monk; a 'Statement concerning Mr P. Le Q. Johnson: Radio Officer Merchant Navy', made on 19 October 1968 by Mr N.T. Clear, Chief Engineer of the *Criton* and the British Petroleum Tanker Company; and from P. Le Q. Johnson's papers (89/5/1) in the Imperial War Museum, which include a long memoir and

detailed records of rations issued at Kankan. Having sailed with Peter Johnson I knew something of these events but, characteristically, little of the detail. There are two war graves at Timbuctoo, those of Chief Engineer William Souter, who died aged 60, and Able Seaman John Graham, who died at 23. Both men belonged to the *Allende*, sunk by *U-68* in March 1942. Fourth Officer Eric Casson of the *Memnon* later joined the RNR and acted as a Japanese interpreter. At the end of the war he returned to sea with Holt's and rose to become Chief Officer, but afterwards took Holy Orders and became a very popular padre of the Anglican Missions to Seamen. One other member of *Memnon*'s crew, Midshipman Curtis, went back to sea, to be sunk twice more.

20. See ch. 12.

CHAPTER 12: 'WE ARE A SEAFARING RACE'

1. See Rayner, *Escort*, p. 92. Rayner appears to confuse HX126 with SC31 and SC30, to which the *Salopian* was escort.

2. See H. Denham, *Inside the Nazi Ring* (John Murray, 1984), p. 84, *et seq.*

3. Roskill, *War at Sea*, Vol. 1, pp. 397–8.

4. They were picked up later by the destroyer *Electra*.

5. According to his own account, when he heard of the loss of the *Hood*, Churchill went to see Roosevelt's envoy Averell Harriman and told him 'The *Hood* has blown up, but we have got the *Bismarck* for certain,' after which he went back to bed.

6. Somerville's flagship the battle cruiser *Renown*, the cruiser *Sheffield* and the carrier *Ark Royal*, with destroyers.

7. Esmonde was killed in a strike from Manston in Kent on the *Scharnhorst*, *Gneisenau* and *Prinz Eugen* when they made their Channel Dash from Brest back to Germany in February 1942. He was awarded a posthumous Victoria Cross.

8. In fact one of these destroyers had suffered engine trouble and returned to Scapa Flow soon after leaving, and aboard the second the D/F equipment was defective.

9. Only afterwards did Captain F. Lloyd, Master-of-the-Fleet and Tovey's chief navigator, find out what had happened, by using spherical trigonometry rather than physical plotting; this is impractical for quick results, as the calculation is time-consuming. See Kennedy, *Pursuit*, note 2, pp. 221–2.

10. This was Lieutenant de Vaisseau J. Philippon, who was working in the Brest dockyard. See Kennedy, *Pursuit*, pp. 124–7. His intelligence actually arrived too late to be of operational value, but it did confirm the deductions based largely on the interpretation of the Operational Intelligence Centre at the Admiralty. See Beesly, *Very Special Intelligence*, p. 86 *et seq.*

11. The rescue operation was curtailed by the presence of U-boats.

12. Although never afterwards a real threat to convoys in the North Atlantic, they were to prove a thorny problem for those going to and from North Russia

and had an impact, if obliquely, on morale among merchant seamen in the aftermath of Convoy PQ17. See R. Woodman, *Arctic Convoys, 1941–1945* (John Murray, 1994).

13. HX133 lost the *Grayburn*, *Brockley Hill*, *Maasdam* (Dutch), *Malaya II* and *Soloy* (Norwegian). Lohmeyer sank the first two.

14. After the mauling of Convoy SC26 on 2–4 April 1941, the brilliant young Harry Hinsley, working in Naval Intelligence, deduced that transmissions from isolated German weather-reporting trawlers were probable evidence that they carried Enigma machines. Operation EB, consisting of a force of cruisers and destroyers under the ill-fated Holland in *Edinburgh*, was set up as target-specific. It was accompanied by Jasper Haines, an officer from OIC who was privy to the secret. *Somali* under Caslon, with his executive officer Lieutenant Sir Marshall Warmington leading the armed party, boarded the *München* on the afternoon of 7 May. The Enigma machine and associated material were soon afterwards at Bletchley Park, but the next month's codes were not secured. To cover the seizure a communiqué was issued which stated that 'One of our patrols, operating in northern waters, encountered the *München*, a German armed trawler. Fire was opened, and the crew of the *München* then abandoned and scuttled their ship. They were subsequently rescued and made prisoners', thus (it was hoped) diverting German suspicious that secret material had been seized.

15. Of the eight vessels despatched in the ambushes set up to destroy German supply ships between 3 and 21 June, six were sunk as a direct consequence of Enigma-derived intelligence. During the next three weeks a further seven supply- and weather-reporting vessels were disposed of. Although these operations were disguised as far as possible, the Admiralty had to curtail further action in order to protect their source. The greatest anxiety in Berlin was caused by the capture of the *Gedania*, but this was entirely circumstantial, the consequence of an encounter with the destroyer *Marsdale*. Two of the *Marsdale*'s seaman were afterwards captured by the Germans following the abandonment on 11 July of the Armed Ocean Boarding Vessel and ex-Ellerman liner *Malvernian*, to which vessel they had been transferred. See Sebag-Montefiore, *Enigma*, p. 179 *et seq*.

16. On 19 June 1941 Kapitänleutnant Mützelburg sighted the American battleship *Texas* and her destroyer screen in the Denmark Strait about ten miles inside Germany's declared war zone. *U-203* pursued the American squadron for 140 miles without being able to manoeuvre into a firing position, much to Hitler's relief: he feared a provocative incident which would bring America into the war.

17. See Hirschfeld, *Secret Diary of a U-Boat*, p. 58–64.

18. See Blair, *Hitler's U-Boat War, The Hunters*, p. 327.

19. William Close, Imperial War Museum, 89/5/1.

20. K.C. Angus, correspondence 13 November 1995. Although born in the prairies, Angus had been sent to Britain in 1937 to complete his education aboard HMS

Conway. Of the gulf separating Royal Navy and merchant officers he writes: 'Its basis lay, I think, in their inability to see us as civilians. My ship once shared a drydock with a destroyer in Liverpool. Drydocks provide washing and toilet facilities on shore – you can't discharge water and waste into a drydock – well, you *can*, but at the risk of being lynched. The Liverpool facilities were filthy. Efforts to persuade the dock officials to clean them were fruitless. The destroyer's first lieutenant visited me [Angus was by then Chief Officer, and therefore equivalent in rank] and proposed that we form working parties to clean them ourselves. I pointed out that my crew worked under Articles of Agreement, a contract setting forth their duties. Cleaning shore toilets was not in the deal, and were I to *order* it they not only could, but undoubtedly would, lawfully decline . . . The lieutenant plainly didn't know what I was talking about. To him, officers ordered, the men did. He departed mumbling about discipline and, I fear, thinking the worse of me.'

21. The other seven were: 1 No territorial aggrandisement; 2 No territorial changes without the consent of the people concerned; 3 National self-government; 4 International economic co-operation; 5 Improved labour standards, economic advancement and social security for all; 6 Freedom from fear and want; and 7 General disarmament after the war. These subsequently formed the basis for the establishment of the United Nations' Charter.

22. See 'Spunyarns', unpublished typescript by Captain R.E. Bayly, IWM 87/2/1.

23. HMS *Graph* sailed on operations in September 1942 and made one unsuccessful attack on *U-333* in the Atlantic. She was placed in reserve in the following year, then sent for scrap in 1944. On the way she broke her tow and was wrecked on Islay. She was finally broken up in 1947. Rahlmow was sent to a prison camp containing Luftwaffe captives but his first watch officer, Leutnant B. Berndt, was tried by a Court of Honour at Grizedale Hall POW Camp in Cumbria, not far from Barrow where *U-570* then lay. The court was presided over by Kretschmer (who was later interned in Canada) and found Berndt guilty; honour would be restored if he were to escape, go to Barrow and destroy *U-570*. Berndt escaped but was recaptured and was being returned to Grizedale Hall when he made a run for it. He was shot, and died in a farmhouse before medical help arrived. He was buried with full military honours. Later Rahlmow joined Kretschmer in Canada, where it seems he was ostracised.

24. Roskill, *War at Sea*, Vol. 1 p. 467.

CHAPTER 13: 'CRIES FOR HELP COULD BE HEARD'

1. The fate of the WRNS particularly affected the first lieutenant of the *Campanula*, Nicholas Monsarrat. He omitted any mention of it in his small wartime publication *H.M. Corvette*, but drew upon it in his *magnum opus*, *The Cruel Sea*, published in 1951.

2. Frederick Melsom was a submariner who when the Germans invaded his homeland the previous spring had sunk his submarine, the *B.1*, in the Ofotfjord,

raising it again during the brief Anglo-French occupation of Narvik and taking it to Trömso, a symbol of the renascent Royal Norwegian Navy. Eighty-two of the *Bath*'s crew were lost. See Divine, *Navies in Exile*, p. 46 *et seq.*

3. Guggenberger and *U-81* went on to sink the carrier *Ark Royal* off Gibraltar two months later. O'Connell had been sunk five months before when in command of the *Hylton* in HX115.

4. Förster defended his conduct on the grounds that he was intending to 'negotiate the surrender of the crew'. He was afterwards imprisoned at Grizedale Hall, where an attempt was made by Kretschmer to have him tried for cowardice by a Court of Honour, like Rahlmow and Berndt, but the British moved him elsewhere.

5. While British intelligence officers marvelled at the lack of experience in Förster's crew and his own comparative maturity – he was 36 and as a Korvettenkapitän relatively senior – most of the crews of the two corvettes 'had never been to sea before', hence their working-up off Greenland.

6. HM Corvettes *Abelia*, *Anemone* and *Veronica*, and HM Trawlers *Vizalma* and *St Zeno*.

7. Oberleutnant O. Ites of *U-94* sank the British steamships *Newbury*, Capper, Alexander & Co., cargo of 6,800 tons of coal for Buenos Aires, Captain T. Pryse and all 44 crew killed, and *Empire Eland*, MoWT, managed by Douglas & Ramsay of Glasgow, bound for Mobile in ballast, Captain D.C. Sinclair and all 37 hands lost; and the Greek steamer *Pegasus*, 16 killed and 13 survivors after shelling.

8. HMS *Clyde* unsuccessfully attacked *U-68* and *U-111* when they were transferring stores in Tarafal Bay, Cape Verde Islands, and the British submarine was in collision with *U-67* in a ramming attempt that misfired. *U-67* was severely damaged but *Clyde* only slightly so, though she was compelled to make for Gibraltar. *Clyde*'s exploits also provided fuel for the debate over the possible compromise of Enigma outlined at the end of ch. 12. On her way back to L'Orient *U-111* was echo-located and depth-charged by HM Trawler *Lady Shirley*, Lieutenant Commander A. Callaway, and forced to the surface. The U-boat's deck gun was hit by the *Lady Shirley*'s first shell and *U-111* sank shortly afterwards with the loss of Kleinschmidt and seven crew. Forty-four men were taken prisoner by Callaway and landed at Gibraltar.

9. See 'Report of Mr R.H. Wilson, Chief Engineer of the "Cingalese Prince"', Imperial War Museum, 20/9/41.

CHAPTER 14: 'THE SKY WAS ALIGHT WITH STAR-SHELLS'

1. These were the *Luigi Torelli*, *Morosini* and *Leonardo da Vinci*. A fourth Italian submarine, the *Alessandro Malaspina*, failed to make the rendezvous.

2. Creighton, *Convoy Commodore*, p. 127 *et seq.*

3. Creighton concludes this by saying: 'Many of the young men of Eire to their credit paid no heed to the policy of their government and flocked to England

in their thousands to fight with their traditional courage in every arm of the British forces.'

4. After the emergency construction programmes of 1917–1920, when some 2,500 merchant ships had been built, the American ship-building industry had rapidly declined. Between 1922 and 1937 only *two* bulk dry cargo vessels were built in American yards, though a number of tankers and 29 cargo-passenger-liners were constructed under an earlier Merchant Marine Act of 1929.

5. Welding was already established as a ship-building technique. The Royal Navy had had its first all-welded vessel, the minesweeper *Seagull*, for some time, and ships built in British yards before the war often combined riveting with welding. There were some problems of integral strength associated with early welding, which did not always survive the wracking stresses on a hull working in the Atlantic Ocean, but they were overcome during the building programmes initiated at this time. Significantly, it was far easier to train welders than riveters.

6. Other American innovations included refrigerators and running water in the crew accommodation, facilities which especially under the stress of war the British thought unnecessary for their seamen. Although they were intended to be expendable, the Liberty ships proved unexpectedly durable and many lasted until well after the war. As late as the 1960s they were tramping the oceans of the world, most under Greek, Panamanian or Liberian flags. Some were cut in two and lengthened by the fitting of an extra hold, others in Italian ownership were fitted with Fiat motor engines. *Empire Liberty* herself became the Blue Funnel liner *Mentor*, for like other British ship-owners Alfred Holt had to make good his war losses as best he might until new post-war tonnage had been constructed. The standard 10,000-ton 'Liberty' cargo remained the common unit for commodity-trading on the mercantile exchanges of the world for even longer than the ships remained at sea, and it was Thompson's Sunderland yard that produced the standard SD14 tramp-type 'Liberty' replacement in the late 1960s before the final death knell was rung over British ship-building.

7. Correspondence with Captain J.R. Cooper, former third officer of the *Castilian*, December 2000.

8. Dönitz, *Memoirs*, p. 193. The Grossadmiral ends this passage in a pleasing display of Nazi dissembling: 'Notwithstanding the fact that it was *we* who declared war [on America], the International Tribunal at Nuremburg found that Germany *had not waged a war of aggression* against the United States – nor against Britain or France.'

9. Lost from SC52 were: *Marouko Pateras* (Greek), wrecked with a full cargo of sugar; *Empire Energy*, wrecked with a full cargo of maize; *Empire Gemsbuck*, lost with 6,200 tons of general; *Everoja*, sunk by *U-203* with a full cargo of wheat; *Flynderbourg*, sunk by *U-202* with a timber cargo and three men killed; and *Gretavale*, sunk by *U-202* with a cargo of steel and vehicles, 42 dead. From SC53 the *Empire Dorado* was lost after a collision with the *Thedmitor*; her cargo was fruit and copper. Convoy SC53 also lost two stragglers, the Panamanian steamers

Meridian and *Crusader*, to Bartels in *U-561*. From SC57: *Kirnwood*, with a full cargo of grain and 12 dead; *Kurdistan*, with food and steel, ten dead; *Star of Luxor* (Egyptian), with 7,000 tons of general and government stores. All these were sunk by *U-130*, Korvettenkapitän E. Kals, when the convoy was in the North West Approaches under British escort. The straggler from HX166 was the *Scottish Trader*, loaded with a general cargo; she was sunk by *U-131*, Korvettenkapitän A. Baumann, who was on his way south to join a U-boat group mustering to attack HG76. Captain G.R.J. Harkness and all hands were lost.

10. A great-circle route is a straight line between two points on the earth's surface, and hence the shortest distance between them. On a Mercator projection of the North Atlantic in which the meridians are conventionally shown as parallel lines rather than lines converging towards the poles, a great-circle route appears as a curve bowing up towards the nearer pole, hence most convoys' proximity to the tip of Greenland and the suitability of the southern entrance to the Denmark Strait as an interception point for the U-boats. Steering along a great-circle course means that instead of holding to one compass heading a series of alterations of course has to be made.

11. The Germans claimed to have sunk nine merchant ships with a total tonnage of 37,000 tons, and that *Audacity* was a 'Formidable'-class aircraft-carrier of 23,000 tons.

12. Quoted in *The People* newspaper, Sunday 4 January 1942.

13. Quotes from papers of Richard Bird, a Hostilities Only seaman aboard *Samphire*. Bird was afterwards commissioned into the RNVR.

CHAPTER 15: 'PRESENTED TO US ON A PLATE'

1. Another curious fact is that it was after an incursion into Japanese waters by a frigate of the Royal Navy during the latter part of the Napoleonic War that the shogunate government of the country, having visited a terrible punishment upon the hapless local authorities and the population surrounding the harbour of Nagasaki, determined that Japan should no longer ignore sea-power and should acquire a navy. See C. Northcote Parkinson, *War in the Eastern Seas, 1793–1815* (Allen & Unwin, 1954), p. 307.

2. I am indebted to Professor Doktor Jürgen Rohwer for kind permission to quote and to use material from his paper on *German Naval Intelligence in World War Two* delivered to the Naval Historians' Group in London on 21 October 1997.

3. Morison, *History of United States Naval Operations in World War II*, Vol. 1, p. 115.

4. Quoted by Blair, *Hitler's U-Boat War, The Hunters*, p. 457 *et seq.*

5. See Van der Vat, *The Atlantic Campaign*, p. 233 *et seq.* As Van der Vat points out, Eisenhower thought matters might have proceeded more smoothly had Ernest King been shot; on the other hand, having become a pilot at the age of 48, King was instrumental in ensuring that the United States Navy possessed very fine carrier-borne aircraft.

6. The Americans saw these ten corvettes as a *quid pro quo* for the ex-Coastguard cutters that were commissioned into the Royal Navy as 'Captain'-class escorts.

7. The long (327 feet) 'Treasury'-class cutters, six of which were attached to escort groups, were very fine, weatherly ships, a factor which improved the fighting efficiency of their better-accommodated crews.

8. Assessments of the purpose of air power among influential military figures were then being debated. The following is not without interest: '. . . a powerful article in the *News Chronicle* by Admiral of the Fleet Sir Roger Keyes begging for a revival of the Royal Naval Air Service [a naval air force as opposed to a mere Fleet Air Arm] . . . If the Navy is allowed to evolve it (he contends), it can give a complete answer to the torpedo-bomber versus warship question, and so maintain British sea-power as the first bulwark of political liberty over the whole world. The Admiralty control of Coastal Command is at present little more than nominal, while the Fleet Air Arm itself has been shamefully starved of machines and personnel.' Private diary entry by D.R. Woodman, Thursday 18 December 1941.

9. Stark Papers, quoted Brodhurst, *Churchill's Anchor*, pp. 265–6.

10. Webster, C. and Frankland, N., *The Strategic Air Offensive Against Germany, 1939–1945*, Volume 1, p. 340.

11. See Woodman, *Arctic Convoys*, chs 12 and 13. Churchill also made an attempt to mitigate the effects by addressing some of the destroyer complements involved.

12. In the period from January to August 1942 between 60 and 108 Allied merchant ships were sunk per month. This amounted to some four million tons destroyed by U-boats, and an incalculable loss of cargoes and seamen.

CHAPTER 16: 'ALL WHO WERE EVER FOUND'

1. Cremer, *U-333*, p. 61.

2. See 'A Seaman's War', unpublished typescript by Patrick Fyrth in the Imperial War Museum, IWM 88/42/1. Fyrth goes on to say that Messrs Turnbull, Scott & Co. 'gained a reputation for being quite a good company. The next generation, so I hear, are now highly respected members of the shipping community.' Elsewhere he points out that not all tramp-ship owners were exploitative capitalists, citing one vessel that was run on short commons because she was the only estate left to a widow who had, of sheer necessity, to employ an agent and master capable of making a sufficient return to support her and her family.

3. Moore, *A Careless Word*, p. 70, and elsewhere. I am indebted to Captain Arthur Moore for his assistance in sending me a copy of his invaluable and detailed work, which is a handsome tribute to the American Merchant Marine and from which most of the details pertaining to American merchantmen have come.

4. See Morison, *History*, Vol. 1, *Battle of the Atlantic*, p. 119.

5. See R.M. Dunshea, IWM 81/45/1. The *Maimoa* herself had in fact been

captured by the auxiliary cruiser *Pinguin* and sunk in the Indian Ocean on 20 November 1940. All her 87 crew were taken prisoners-of-war.

6. Stragglers excepted, losses out of SC convoys at this time were negligible. Apart from the *Heina* in SC67 they amounted to only two other ships, the American *Independence Hall* and the British *Empire Lotus*; neither was to the enemy. The first was a 1920-built freighter belonging to Moore McCormack which broke in two during heavy weather on 7 March when off Cape Sable. Captain E.A. Curot, his chief and second mates, one radio operator and three able seamen were lost off the forward section; an oiler, a wiper and the chief cook were lost from the after part. All nine of her naval 'armed guard' and the remaining 28 of her crew were rescued by HMS *Witch*. The British destroyer had two boats capsized in the rescue and lost one of her own men in the attempt. The *Independence Hall* had sailed the previous day but the convoy had run into fog and heavy weather. She soon lost contact and, carrying thirteen battle tanks on her decks, was probably heavily stressed. At the time of the breaking-up the third mate was administering medical attention to the bosun, who had been injured in the head by a swinging davit he was attempting to secure. The *Empire Lotus* disappeared a week later, foundering with all hands, yet one more victim to the seaman's ancient enemy, the cruel sea.

7. Schull, *Far Distant Ships*, p. 101 et seq. Schull assumes the *Heina* was a tanker; she was in fact a 4,028-ton general-cargo motor-vessel owned by Mowinckels Rederi of Bergen, built in 1925.

8. An early British-made centimetric radar had been installed at Pearl Harbor by the end of 1941 but on Sunday 7 December its readings were ignored. For the full story of naval radar, see Howse, *Radar at Sea*.

9. One officer is supposed to have swum ashore and made his way back to Germany, where on receipt of his report certain modifications were made to the glands in the pressure hull of the Type VIIC U-boat.

10. Captain R.E. Bayly, Imperial War Museum, IWM 87/2/1.

11. Stephenson was knighted in 1943 and awarded the Légion d'honneur with Rosette in 1948. See Baker, *Terror of Tobermory*.

12. See Williams, *Captain Gilbert Roberts RN*, p. 91. Roberts's biographer makes much of this 'revelation'. Roberts had no doubt appreciated that this German tactic was a possibility but was ignorant of it as a certainty, and was not given much time to sift information before his Tactical School was expected to be up and running, hence his query to the Admiralty.

13. Roberts, unlike Walker, survived the war, but at one time during the struggle his weight dropped to eight stone. He was appointed CBE for his fundamental contribution. In 1965 he was the recipient of a letter from Garter King of Arms informing him that he was to be appointed a Knight Bachelor. It turned out to be a mistake; Roberts received neither apology nor explanation.

CHAPTER 17: 'THE CRUEL SEA'

1. Roberts's words impressed one young officer of the Volunteer Reserve in particular. Lieutenant Nicholas Monsarrat used the phrase for the title of his seminal post-war novel of the Royal Navy's part in the Battle of the Atlantic.

2. See Morison, *History of United States Naval Operations in World War II*, Vol. 1, fn. 22,. 129.

3. During May, June and July of 1942 the following Allied and Neutral merchant ships were sunk in these areas: the Gulf of Mexico: *Las Choapas*, *Tuxpam*, *Cadmus*, *Gundersen*, *Moira*, *San Blas*, *Oaxaca*, *Carrabulle*, *Amapala*, *Torny*, *Mentor*, *Empire Mica*, *Joseph M. Cudahy*, *Ogontz*, *Hampton Roads*, *Lalita*, *Baja California*, *Norlindo*, *Hermis and Tuapse*, with the *E.P. Theriault* damaged; off the Mississippi Delta: *Heredia*, *Service Toledo*, *Shéhérazade*, *Hamlet*, *Gulf Prince*, *Halo*, *David McKelvey*, *Gulf Oil*, *Gulf Penn*, *Benjamin Brewster*, *Virginia*, *Rawley Warner*, *Bayard*, *Robert E. Lee*, *Alcoa Puritan* and *Ontario*; nine other vessels were attacked and damaged, but not sunk. In the Yucatan Strait losses were: *Elizabeth*, *Clare*, *Nidarnes*, *Suweid*, *Tillie Lykes*, *Tela*, *Crijnssen*, *Rosenbourg*, *Knoxville City*, *Samuel O. Brown*, *Castilla*, *Hector*, *William J. Salman*, *Mercury Sun*, *Calgarolite*, *Comayagua*, *Tuscaloosa City*, *Green Island*, *Allister*, *Bushranger*, *New Jersey* and *Tachira*, with a further three damaged. In the Florida Strait the following were sunk: *Port Antonio*, *Faja de Oro*, *George Calvert*, *Nicholas Cuneo*, *Managua*, *Andrew Jackson*, *Millinocket*, *Onondaga*, *J.A. Moffet Jnr*, *Sama*, *Umtata* (mentioned in main text), *Portrero del Llano*, *Lubrafol*, *Ohioan*, *Amazone*, *Halsey*, *La Paz*, *Ocean Venus* and *Laertes*, with three damaged.

4. President Roosevelt incorporated the Bureau of Lighthouses into the United States Coastguard on 1 July 1939, thus conferring war status on the otherwise pacifist lighthouse tenders and, with the Bureau's self-propelled lightvessels, doubling the size of the USCG fleet at a stroke. See D. Peterson, *United States Lighthouse Service Tenders, 1840–1939* (Eastwind Publishing, Annapolis, 2000).

5. The 'naval armed guard' was the American equivalent of the British DEMS system.

6. Chile is a case in point. The Chilean army had been trained on the German model, wore 'Prussian' field grey and Wehrmacht-style uniforms. Her navy, on the other hand, having been established by Almirante Cochrane, tenth Earl of Dundonald and a brilliant former British frigate captain, was modelled upon the British Royal Navy and staunchly observed British traditions. After the war many former German servicemen, especially Luftwaffe pilots, settled in Chile.

7. Among which were James Nourse's *Indus*, which fought a fierce gun-duel in which half her crew were killed, and the Dutch tanker *Olivia*, which was set on fire. Many of her crew were burnt to death or drowned, others were picked up, and one boat escaped to land on Madagascan soil. Burley's account is in the Imperial War Museum, IWM 91/31/1.

8. The other two were *U-126* and *U-161*. Heyse had sunk three tankers off the Bahamas on his previous patrol, the Americans *Pan Massachusetts* and *Cities*

Service Empire and the Norwegian *O.A. Knudsen*. After the abortive attack on SL109 the three submarines operated unsuccessfully off Brazil before moving into the Caribbean, where *U-128* sank five more ships.

9. Earlier in the year, the *Empire Hawksbill* had been in collision with and sunk the *Brynymor* while both ships were preparing to sail from Liverpool in Convoy ON76.

10. See Houlder Brothers' *Sea Hazard*, p. 49. Those decorated for their part in the February 1940 salvage of the *Imperial Transport* were Smail, Swanbrow (Commended), Second Engineer A.J.J. Broom, and Fourth Engineer K.H. Malins (MBE), Donkeyman G.H. Coles (BEM) and Donkeyman G. Andrea (Commended). In the second salvage in March 1942 the salvage team again consisted, in addition to the master and chief engineer, of Broom and Malins, Coles and Andrea. Smail and Swanbrow were both appointed OBE for their part in the second operation.

11. Ites and most of his crew were later captured when *U-94* was sunk in the Caribbean in August 1942.

12. The others were *U-96*, *U-406* and *U-590*.

13. *U-215* and *U-576* were lost and *U-402* returned to France. Those sent north were *U-89*, *U-132* (Vogelsang, despite damage inflicted by Walker's 36th Escort Group, had not returned to France as he might have done after the action against HG84), *U-458* and *U-754*.

14. All three vessels were in ballast. The *Empire Rainbow* was a tramp under Ropner management on behalf of the MoWT, the *Broompark* was owned by Denholm's of Glasgow, and the cargo-vessel *Pacific Pioneer* by Furness, Withy & Company.

CHAPTER 18: 'IT WAS A RARE EVENT . . .'

1. An account of this admission was rendered privately to the author by a well respected authority, a former officer of the RNVR, who was on cordial professional terms with the German naval officer in the post-war maritime world.

2. See Taylor, *Prisoner of the 'Kormoran'*, an account of the experiences of W.A. Jones, a cook on the Australasian United Steam Navigation Company's steam ship *Mareeba*, 3,472 tons. Jones was born in Manchester, enlisted as a drummer-boy in the Lancashire Fusiliers and saw active service in the First World War. After this he went to sea in the merchant service, settling in Australia, though he remained at sea until 1939 in trans-Pacific and Australasian coastal routes.

3. The *Mandasor* was sunk by the *Atlantis* off the Seychelles on 24 January 1941; the *Orama*, owned by the Orient Line and employed trooping during the ill-fated Norwegian campaign, was hit by the cruiser *Admiral Hipper* and the destroyers *Hans Lody* and *Karl Galster*.

4. Both quotations are from Captain A. Hill, *Some Experiences of SS 'Mandasor' and her Crew during the World War* (Edinburgh, 1947), pp. 77–81. In 1943 Hill was replaced by Captain R.S. Finlay-Notman of the *Athelfoam*. For full details of Milag Nord, see Thomas, *Milag: Captives of the Kriegsmarine*.

5. There were, for example, only 17 TE convoys from Trinidad eastwards, and they were discontinued in September 1942.

6. Roskill, *War at Sea*, Vol. 2, p. 107.

7. Confusingly, commanded by Kapitänleutnant Viktor Vogel and sunk by Lieutenant Commander G.S. Windeyer, RCN in *Wetaskiwin* and Lieutenant Commander K.L. Dyer, DSC, RN of *Skeena*.

8. The Royal Navy's now well-publicised and practised ability to refuel, swap personnel and replenish stores and ammunition at sea by jackstay transfer with vessels lying in line abreast derives from their enforced adoption of the United States Navy's practice, an example of one lesson which went from west to east, rather than the other way round.

9. I am uncertain of her original nationality. Formerly named *Farmsum*, she should not be confused with the 1929-built Dutch *Farmsum*, a straggler from OB252, sunk by Kretschmer in *U-99* on 7 December 1940.

10. *U-71*, *U-254*, *U-593*, *U-595*, *U-597*, *U-607* and *U-704*.

11. Dönitz, *Memoirs*, p. 236.

12. Behrens, *Merchant Shipping*, pp. 176–7.

13. The others were the Norwegian *Bill*, from the boats of which he captured one officer, the American steamer *Cranford*, the Dutch-flagged *Kentar*, the British cargo-liner *Clan MacNaughton*, the British *Empire Arnold* and the Dutch motor-vessel *Draco*. Piening also took a prisoner out of the *Empire Arnold*, and rendered her wounded survivors a measure of medical attention. *U-155*, a Type IXC U-boat, reached L'Orient on 15 September.

14. Mr F. Fuller, later a master in the Blue Funnel Line, was afterwards (1960) Warden at the Outward Bound Sea School at Aberdovey. Both Painter and Edge also afterwards commanded Blue Funnel liners.

15. Taprell-Dorling, *Blue Star Line*, p. 106.

16. The numbers lost from the *Tuscan Star* are confusing. Taprell-Dorling's some-what casual account draws only on Rhodes's own report made at the time, and claims that only nine were killed, and that only the master's boat was relieved by *Otranto*. Other sources state that 51 were killed, and put the total number of survivors at 62: this tallies with the complement of 88 crew and 25 passengers.

17. Rigiani's account is quoted by Taprell-Dorling, pp. 99–105. In addition to Captain Mills and Boardman, six others were killed in the loss of the *Viking Star*. Rigiani reported the survivors he brought in as himself and Sullivan, along with Fourth Engineer D.P. Lennon, Chief Steward C. Hill, Lamptrimmer T. Hewett, Able Seamen J. Daintith, W. Kaye, E. Kitchen, J. Hitchin and P. Quirke, Greaser L. Lipton, and Deckhands J. Lynch and J. Holmes. The total saved were MacQuiston and 36 in the lifeboat, Rigiani's 13, and the three engineers.

18. See Hawkins, *Atlantic Torpedo*.

19. Hartenstein's War Diary, quoted by Van der Vat, *Atlantic Campaign*, p. 293.

20. *Ibid.*, p. 293.

CHAPTER 19: 'CONDUCT BEYOND THE CALL OF DUTY'

1. In the West Indies in August U-boats sank a considerable number of ships including the *Treminnard*, *Empire Corporal*, *Michael Jebsen*, *Empire Cloud*, *British Consul*, *Cressington Court*, *Amakura*, *Fort La Reine*, *San Fabian*, *Winamac*, and the British-flagged schooner *Vivian P. Smith* of 130 gross tons which Kapitänleutnant B. Zurmülen destroyed by gunfire from *U-600*. A US Coastguard aircraft sank *U-166* (Kuhlmann). Off Haiti the *Empire Bede* was so damaged by a torpedo from *U-553* that she had to be sunk by the corvette *Pimpernel*. Of the submarines sunk, two were in the Bay of Biscay, *U-578* and *Morosini*, destroyed by the RAF on the 10th and 11th; *U-464* off Scotland by a USN Catalina on the 20th; and two in the Caribbean, *U-654* by USAAF aircraft and *U-94* by HMCS *Oakville* and a US aeroplane.

2. Respectively, the *Dalhousie* in the South Atlantic on 9 August and the *Arabistan* off St Helena on the 14th.

3. Off Freetown the *City of Wellington* was torpedoed by *U-506*. She was an Ellerman ship carrying general cargo, including consignments of chrome and copper ores. This company suffered savage losses in the autumn of 1942.

4. The others were USCG Cutters *Campbell* and *Spencer*, HMC Corvettes *Bittersweet*, *Trillium*, *Collingwood* and *Mayflower*, HM Corvettes *Snowflake* and *Wallflower*.

5. Moore, *A Careless Word*, p. 27.

6. The USN official historian, Samuel E. Morison, mentions severe losses being suffered in SC95 (see *History of United States Naval Operations in World War II*, Vol. 1, p. 105). The context suggests he may be confusing it with its predecessor, Convoy SC94.

7. Towards the end of the war the 'Hedgehog' was replaced by the more effective and powerful 'Squid' mortar.

8. See Cremer, *U-333*, p. 121, *et seq*.

9. Actually a mixed group: HM Destroyers *Burnham* and *Broadway* and HMC Corvettes *Brandon*, *Dauphin*, *Drumheller* and *Morden*.

10. The other U-boats engaged against ON127 were: *U-91*, *U-92*, *U-211*, *U-218*, *U-380*, *U-404*, *U-407*, *U-411*, *U-584*, *U-594*, *U-608* and *U-659*.

11. The *Stephen Hopkins* is reported to have fired 35 rounds with her 4-inch gun in the 20 minutes the action lasted, 15 of them hits. A Liberty ship was later named after Captain Paul Buck, and an American destroyer-escort after Ensign Kenneth Willett.

12. By 'patrol-vessel' he probably intended a reference to the Armed Ocean Boarding Vessels commissioned by the British as naval auxiliaries in 1939, which were often similar in size and armament to AMCs. From her vigour in returning fire Gerlach thought that the *Stephen Hopkins* bore one 6-inch and six 4-inch guns, and perhaps he had never before seen the high freeboard of a Liberty ship in ballast. Since the entire incident was over and the *Stephen Hopkins* had sunk within half an hour, in murky conditions, not too much should be made of this oft-repeated assertion of his.

13. Only five men were lost with the *Koumoundouros*, none with the Dutchman or the British ship, and none from the *Swiftsure*, though she caught fire and the crew attempted to extinguish it. Sixteen died when the *Zaandam*, a Dutch vessel in which they were being repatriated, was in turn torpedoed and sank. Eight survivors spent five days in a lifeboat before being rescued, seven others made a boat voyage to the Brazilian coast.

14. Of the *Examelia*'s 40 survivors, 21 were also lost with the *Zaandam*, 14 were picked up by another ship, and five made the long voyage to Brazil.

15. Much was made of Poon Lim's story at the time, and it furnished copy for numerous magazine articles. It is said that Poon Lim afterwards tried to enlist in the United States Navy but that he was rejected as medically unfit because of flat feet. Poon Lim's remarkable exploit is usually cited as the longest boat-voyage by a merchant seaman, but was in fact surpassed by that of two Indian survivors from the *Fort Longueuil*, torpedoed in the Indian Ocean off the Chagos Archipelago by a Japanese submarine on 19 September 1943. The two seamen, Mohamed Aftab and Thakur Miah, drifted 3,400 miles and landed on an Indonesian island, only to be taken prisoner by the occupying Japanese. They had been at sea for 135 days.

16. Some of her survivors were among those lost in the sinking of the *Zaandam*. The *Coloradan* had a ton of gold in her strong-room.

17. The *Anne Hutchinson* broke in two, and although her forward section was towed into Port Elizabeth, she was declared a total loss.

18. As a measure of the relentless losses of valuable British ships, on 9 October, in the Atlantic Narrows, the Italian submarine *Archimede*, Capitano di Corvetta Saccardo, had sunk another large troop-ship, the Orient liner *Oronsay*, Captain N. Savage; off Ascension on the 10th the Canadian Pacific liner the *Duchess of Atholl*, now also a troop-ship, had been torpedoed by *U-178*, Kapitän zur See H. Ibbeken, before he moved south-west to sink six British, Norwegian and American vessels off South Africa: and Holt's lost another Blue Funnel cargo-liner, the *Agapenor*, south of Freetown on the 11th, sunk by *U-87*, Kapitänleutnant J. Berger.

19. See note 13 for the fate of the *Zandaam*'s survivors. The others were the British *Marylyn* and *Elmdale*, the American *Alcoa Rambler* and the Norwegian *Besholt*. Among the *Leonardo da Vinci*'s victims was the British *Empire Zeal*. One of her survivors, a deck apprentice, wrote: 'There is something dreadfully tragic about watching one's ship go down. We all sat still in the boats and watched our ship, our home, dip its bow beneath the waves then saw its stern lift high up with the propeller and rudder showing, then within seconds everything slid below the surface, gone, gone forever. For many minutes we just sat there. We looked around us and saw sea, sea, sea, nothing else . . .' After being spotted by a Catalina, they were picked up by the USS *Winslow*. He concludes: 'Some will be interested to know that our homeward voyage was made as Distressed British Seamen. We became DBS from the moment the ship went down, and for the record our pay stopped then. Mind you mine was only sixteen shillings and eight pence per month plus a £5 per month war bonus, so I did not miss much . . .'

CHAPTER 20: 'THE . . . COURAGE OF ORDINARY PEOPLE'

1. Those lost to British and American aircraft were *U-253* (Friedrichs), *U-582* (Schulte) and *U-619* (Makowski).

2. As a convoy of note, the stations of the merchant ships in eleven columns were: Column 1: *Germa, Sembilan, King Edward;* Column 2: *Zarian, Empire Cougar* (joint Rear Commodore), *Baron Elgin, Baron Kinnaird, Calgary*; Column 3: *Baron Vernon, Anglo-Maersk, Alaska, West Kebar* (independent), *Mano*; Column 4: *Tasmania, Président Doumer, Bullmouth, Bothnia, Lafonia*; Column 5: *Marquesa, British Ardour* (joint Rear Commodore), *Alexandre André*, the Auxiliary Patrol Vessel HMS *Kelantan*; Column 6: *Nagpore* (Commodore), *Amstelkerk, Belnor, Bornholm*; Column 7: *Esperance Bay, Hopecastle, Tynemouth, Welsh Trader*; Column 8: *Pacific Star, Corinaldo, Ville de Rouen, Empire Simba*; Column 9: *Stentor* (Vice Commodore), *Debrett, Guinean, San Francisco*; Column 10: *Silverwillow, Brittany, Dundrum Castle, Pinto, Lynton Grange*; Column 11: *Henry Stanley, Clan Murray*, station vacant, HM Tug *Salvonia*. The tanker *British Ardour* acted as oiler to the escorts. The appointment of two rear commodores is of interest.

3. Kottman had served in the *Admiral Graf Spee* during the action off the Rio de la Plata and had escaped internment when the *Graf Spee's* crew were detained in Uruguay in 1940. He had returned to Germany by way of Vladivostok and the trans-Siberian railway during the period of *rapprochement* between Stalin and Hitler.

4. Lieutenant Commander J.M. Rayner, RNR, 'Report of Proceedings, Convoy SL125', The National Archive (PRO), ADM 199/1210.

5. Convoy ON132 lost one ship, the *Millcrest*, after she collided with the *Empire Lightning* on 7 October with the death of one man; and ON139 lost two British-flagged ships, the Shell tanker *Donax*, Captain J.M. Cuthill, and the *Winnipeg II*, Captain O.F. Pennington, both sunk on 22 October by *U-443*, Oberleutnant K. von Puttkamer. The latter was carrying 68 passengers, but there was no loss of life from either vessel.

6. Egerton gives the position of the attack as Latitude 54° 20' North, Longitude 031° 40' W. See '1942 Diaries of Vice Admiral W. de M. Egerton', Imperial War Museum, p. 186.

7. The practice of swinging lifeboats outboard in readiness for emergency launching undoubtedly cut down the time necessary to escape from a sinking ship and saved many lives. But it left them vulnerable to being hit by heavy seas, a circumstance compounded by their buoyancy, which made them react to rather than resist any sea engulfing them, straining their lashings and eventually tearing them free or smashing them up. Hanging outboard, they were also vulnerable to torpedo-blast.

8. Several authorities cite her as a straggler and therefore not strictly 'sunk in convoy', but there is absolutely no evidence of this in Egerton's account. He says she was torpedoed 'port side forward' and gives no indication that she was other than with the convoy at the time of her being hit, though probably in a rear station.

9. Many classes of cargo-vessel had their freeboards increased during the North Atlantic winter and were prohibited from loading a cargo that depressed them excessively. Their load-lines, the so-called 'Plimsoll marks' cut into and painted onto their sides, included one water-line, higher than those for 'Summer', 'Salt Water' and 'Fresh Water', which denoted 'Winter North Atlantic' (WNA).

10. Among the latter was the large Elder, Dempster passenger-cargo-liner *Abosso*, which was torpedoed by Heydemann's *U-575* north-west of the Azores on 29 October. Captain R. W. Tate, 166 crew and 173 passengers were lost, the 53 survivors being picked up by the sloop *Bideford*, Lieutenant Commander W.J. Moore, RNR.

11. Bulloch had previously attacked Lohmann's *U-89* off the Azores on 16 August. At this time No. 120 was the only RAF Squadron equipped with the highly effective long-ranged Liberator.

12. This was *U-184*'s first war patrol, and her only success. After pursuing the convoy on the 19th Kapitänleutnant G. Dangschat and his 49-strong crew vanished the next day from an unknown cause. The U-boat was a Type IX C-40.

13. The words are those of Fregattenkapitän Gunther Hessler, tasked by the Allies to write an operational history, *The U-boat War in the Atlantic* (see Bibliography). The quotation is from page 68. As related in an earlier chapter, Korvettenkapitän Hessler had commanded *U-107* in 1941 on the most successful war patrol of any U-boat and afterwards served on the staff of the Befelshaber der U-Bootes.

14. This is no exaggeration. In addition to service elsewhere in the world, I spent a winter in the North Atlantic in Ocean Weather Ships, former 'Castle'-class corvettes, collecting data. Wind speeds in a normal 'gale' of 35 to 40 knots frequently gusted to 70 plus, while extreme conditions of 90 to 100 knots were quite common. Wave heights and periodicity were then difficult to measure, but I have known plating to be set in and a ship's bridge to be entirely engulfed, so that a foot of water afterwards sloshed about the wheelhouse and forced its way into the accommodation below through the ventilation trunkings. I would not claim these circumstances to be in any way exceptional, and other mariners can give evidence of far worse circumstances.

CHAPTER 21: 'THIS DOES NOT LOOK AT ALL GOOD'

1. The other destroyers were *Pakenham* (Captain E.K.B. Stevens), *Dulverton* (Commander W.N. Petch), *Hero* (Lieutenant Commander W. Scott) and *Hurworth* (Lieutenant D.A. Shaw).

2. Horton was a highly complex man. For many years he kept up a liaison with a lady 'companion'. Having hauled down his flag on 15 August 1945 he visited Germany to see the effects of Allied bombing, after which he went to Padua and Assisi in Italy, entering spiritual retreat. He enjoyed good food and wine and was devoted to the opera, but was depressed by the condition of Britain in the post-war world. He retired after the war and died on Monday 30 July 1951, asking after news of the submarine *Affray* which had sunk in scandalous

circumstances in the English Channel. I am indebted to the late Charles Owen for details regarding Horton and Noble, and for a full appreciation of the former.

3. See Churchill, *Second World War*, Vol. IV, *The Hinge of Fate*, p. 114. Horton secured an agreement that seven new Coastal Command squadrons would be deployed thus: one *very* long-ranged squadron stationed in Northern Ireland, another in Iceland and a third in Newfoundland; two long-ranged squadrons available for the Biscay offensive, another for reconnaissance over Biscay and one more for reconnaissance over the Western Approaches.

4. Sub-Lieutenant R.C. Bird, RNVR of HM Corvette *Samphire* reported that at this time RN crews began to receive lectures on current affairs.

5. A former French steamer, *Le Rhin*, she had been commissioned into the RN and her Franco-Belgian crew of escapees from Nazi and Vichy rule had been given false names and identities. HMS *Fidelity* was on her way to the Far East to carry out a maritime guerrilla war, having aboard T Company of 40 Commando Royal Marines. She was commanded by a flamboyant and very tough intelligence officer with maritime skills named Claude-André Costa. He had been commissioned as Lieutenant de Vaisseau Peri and never sailed without his gun-toting mistress, Madeleine Guesclin, an equally tough character. Costa/Peri and *Le Rhin* had carried out one successful raid in May 1940 when her crew penetrated Las Palmas and attached limpet mines to the German supply ship *Corrientes*. After the Fall of France *Le Rhin* arrived in Britain and Costa metamorphosed into Commander Jack Langlais, Guesclin into First Officer M.V. Barclay, WRNS, and *Le Rhin* into HMS *Fidelity*, armed and fitted out with two seaplanes and a launch. Thereafter Langlais and his ship seemed long on promise but short on delivery. The Far East appeared an appropriate place for the Admiralty to despatch her, to raid the Japanese-held coasts of former French Indo-China. However, the value of this extraordinary vessel was doubtful.

6. An irresistible quotation that accurately sums up a typical day of foul weather in the Western Ocean. It is taken from Henry Revely's fine detailed account of *The Convoy that Nearly Died*, p. 48. Revely was Third Officer of the United Africa Company's *Zarian*.

7. She had a small cargo of 940 tons of general and government stores.

8. The *Fanan*, *Dundrum Castle*, *J.M. Bartelmi*, *Empire Geraint* and *Jasper Park* either reported themselves, or were reported by other vessels, as having been hit, such was the confusion of the night action.

9. Although little concrete evidence exists to suggest that U-boat commanders callously eliminated merchant seamen, and only Heinz Eck was actually convicted of such a war crime, and although there are many recorded occasions on which these officers materially assisted survivors, there seems little doubt about Hitler's views. At a conference on Monday 28 September 1942 attended by Hitler, Raeder, Keitel, Dönitz and others he expressed the opinion that it was 'very much to our disadvantage if a large percentage of the crews

of sunken merchant ships is able to go to sea again in new ships.' An abstract of this conference is given in *Führer Conferences on Naval Affairs*, p. 294 *et seq.* Hitler's method of rule – giving a nod to his satraps, rather than a written order – may be noted here. It remains doubtful whether Dönitz took this 'legitimised' hint, though he does seem to have told his commanders a month later 'that the manning problem was the Achilles heel of the Allied merchant service and that the time had come to wage "total war" on ships and crews'. One might argue that this was standard Nazi exhortation at a time when extra endeavour was required, and it has to be said that Eck and his accomplices went to their deaths denying that they had received orders to massacre the survivors from the SS *Peleus*, sunk on 13 March 1944. But a contrary viewpoint might be argued with equal validity, given the fact that Strelow's U-boat was alone. The complete absence of corpses or flotsam is unusual, though not unique.

10. Albert Hawling, quoted by Revely, *op. cit.*, p. 159, on his way to India to join a ship, afterwards travelled instead from Halifax to Vancouver to join a newly-built 'Fort'-class vessel.

CHAPTER 22: 'STAY TOUGH!'

1. These were: British: *Oltenia II* (Commodore), *British Dominion* (Vice Commodore), *British Vigilance*, *Empire Lytton* and *Cliona*; Norwegian: *Vanja*, *Minister Weddel*, *Albert L. Ellsworth*, and *Norvik* (see note 3).

2. See Captain R.S. Allen, 'The Saga of Convoy TM1', in *Journal of the Honourable Company of Master Mariners*, No. 213, Vol. XVIII, Spring 1993.

3. The *Norvik*, though Panamanian-flagged, was beneficially owned in Norway by Johan Rasmussen & Co. of Sandefjord.

4. *Cliona* went on to Algiers where she delivered her cargo of Admiralty fuel, while *Vanja* discharged into a tank farm at Oran. Both ships survived the war.

5. See Hessler, *U-Boat War in the Atlantic*, p. 79.

6. Hesse's *U-442* was sunk by a Hudson off Lisbon attacking Convoy KMS9 on 12 February 1943, with no survivors.

7. National Archives (PRO), ADM 199/719, Convoy TM1.

8. The survivor, allegedly her chief engineer, was landed at Brest on 14 February and sent to Milag Nord. On her next patrol *U-632* was sunk by an RAF Liberator from Northern Ireland.

9. Others were *U-225* (Leimkühler), *U-529* (Fraatz) and *U-623* (Schröder). Other U-boats were lost elsewhere in the Atlantic, most to aircraft.

10. These were: *U-89*, *U-135*, *U-187*, *U-262*, *U-266*, *U-267*, *U-402*, *U-413*, *U-438*, *U-454*, *U-456*, *U-465*, *U-594*, *U-608*, *U-609*, *U-613*, *U-614*, *U-624*, *U-704* and *U-752*.

11. It was customary by this time to load military items – anything from trucks, jeeps and guns to crated aircraft – on the decks of tramps carrying bulk cargoes in their holds. They might be lost, but the loss of such small parcels was preferable to the loss of dedicated ships carrying a greater value of such hardware.

For all that, the consequences of the loss of staples like grain were no less serious.

12. The notion that a ship gives a safe lee into which a boat may pull is a misapprehension. A vessel may make up to 4 knots to leeward, creating a nasty 'slop' into which a boat will have difficulty pulling and which will affect its motion. (Paradoxically, a greater 'smooth' is left to windward, due to the upwelling from the downwind progress of the hull.) Once close alongside on the leeward side, this motion will pin a boat against the much larger hull drifting down on top of her, often with serious consequences. When abandoning ship, such pressure on leeward boats made escaping from a ship's side difficult. See R. Woodman, 'Sea-boat Seamanship', in *Seaways, The International Journal of the Nautical Institute*, August 1997, p. 3 *et seq*.

13. Dönitz, *Memoirs*, p. 317.

14. Cripps's visits took place on 9 and 10 February. It is perhaps significant that a few days earlier, on 5 February, Air Chief Marshal Sir Philip Joubert de la Ferté had been relieved as C-in-C of Coastal Command. Like Noble and his own predecessor Sir Frederick Bowhill, he was one of those who, in John Terraine's words, 'preside over bad times, weather the worst storms, but do not remain in command when the change of fortune comes'. Terraine (*Business in Great Waters, The U-boat Wars, 1914–1945*, Leo Cooper, 1989, p. 522 *et seq*) charges him with a lack of aggression that was not shared by his successor, Air Marshal Sir John Slessor. Slessor, on the other hand, 'never really understood the significance of Coastal Command's rôle' in the Battle of the Atlantic. 'His heart was in the bombing campaign.'

15. Horton's account of Cripps's two visits is given in Chalmers, *Max Horton*, pp. 174–7. When Cripps returned the next day Horton produced an American officer who explained many of the difficulties of operating even long-range aircraft over the Atlantic from bases in remote places. The Greenland base, Cripps was informed, 'was much easier to get away from than to find'.

16. Beesly, *Very Special Intelligence*, p. 160.

17. Centimetric radar was now available for fitting to Coastal Command aircraft; all escorts had been fitted with it, and according to Beesly (p. 146) it was 'probably the most decisive single British development in the U-boat war'.

18. These were *U-442*, *U-620* and *U-529*.

19. On the outbreak of war three other old Shaw, Savill & Albion Company vessels, the *Pakeha*, *Mamari* and *Waimana*, were purchased by the Government and converted into dummy warships, the *Mamari* to resemble the carrier *Hermes*, the others to look like *Royal Sovereign*-class battleships. Anchored in the Firth of Forth, their purpose was to deceive German aerial reconnaissance. They were later sent to be restored to refrigerated cargo-liners, but the *Mamari* was wrecked on passage. Since 1936 the Shaw, Savill & Albion Company had been part of the Furness, Withy Group, and had been owners of the Aberdeen & Commonwealth Line, owners of *Jervis Bay*, since 1932.

20. The precise number of survivors from the *Empire Trader* is unclear. No one

seems to have been killed in the initial attack and some may have been taken off by *Stockport*, but the subsequent loss of this ship confuses the issue.

21. The rank 'Kapitan' in the Polish navy was roughly equivalent to the Anglo-American Lieutenant Commander.

22. Döhler had been elevated directly from second watch officer to command, and Allied debriefing officers assessed his U-boat's survivors' morale as 'the worst we have encountered in any U-boat to date'.

23. Part of a warship's standard damage control kit, a collision mat was a large wire-reinforced mat of interwoven coir fibres. When spread outside a ship's shell-plating over a hole, water-pressure clamped it against the hole, greatly reducing the ingress of water and often permitting pumps to cope and further temporary repairs to be effected.

24. The *Burza* arrived at St John's with more than four hundred on board. Her fresh water had been contaminated by sea-water and her food stocks were very low.

CHAPTER 23: 'FIREFLIES IN THE WATER'

1. Roskill quotes an assessment of Tait as 'an outstanding leader of a group of British, Polish and Free French escort vessels'. James Ellis had served as chief mate of the freighter *Bellingham*, owned by the Waterman Steamship Corporation of Mobile, Alabama, during the disastrous passage of PQ17. Returning from Russia in Convoy QP14 the *Bellingham* had been sunk in the Barents Sea, but Ellis had survived to be appointed master of the *William C. Gorgas* under Waterman's management. Offered a place on a life-raft by a seaman, Ellis declined, and was not seen again.

2. Those bound for Iceland were: from New York: American: *Cartagao* and *Eastern Guide*; Icelandic: *Godafoss*; Norwegian: *Askepot* and *Gudvor*; Panamanian: *Granville* and *Alcedo*. From Halifax: Icelandic: *Fjallfoss* and *Felfoss*.

3. Those bound for Britain were: from New York: American: *McKeesport* and *Vistula*; British: *Aymeric, Baron Elgin, Baron Semple, Baron Stranraer, Beaconoil, Benedick* (oiler for escorts), *Boston City* (Vice Commodore), *Bridgepool, Carso, Christian Holm* (reserve oiler for escorts), *Clarissa Radcliffe, Dolius, Empire Dunstan, Empire Galahad, Empire Summer, English Monarch, Filleigh, Fort Cedar Lake, Glenapp* (Commodore White), *Gloxinia, Historian, Innesmoor, King Gruffydd, Kingsburg, Losada, Orminster, Shirvan* and *Vinriver*; Dutch: *Alderamin* and *Kedoe*; Greek: *Carras* and *Georgios P.*; Panamanian: *Bonita*; Swedish: *Atland*. There were also two large naval landing-craft, *LST 305* and *LST 365*. Those from Halifax were: British: *Badjestan, Drakepool, Empire Morn, Helencrest, Ogmore Castle, PLM13, Port Auckland* and *Zouave*; Dutch: *Parkhaven*; Swedish: *Porjus*; Yugoslavian: *Franka*; plus the British *Reaveley* coming from St John's.

4. *Southern Princess* was in fact reverting to her original configuration, having been built for the Eagle Oil Company as *San Patricio*.

5. These were: American: *Gulfdisc* (oiler for the escorts), *Harry Luckenbach, Mathew*

Luckenbach, Hugh Williamson, Irenée Dupont, James Oglethorpe, Stephen C. Foster, Walter Q. Gresham, William Eustis, Daniel Webster, Jean, Kofresi, Margaret Lykes, Pan Rhode Island and *Robert Howe*; British: *Canadian Star, City of Agra, Clan Matheson* (initial Vice Commodore), *Cape Breton, Antar, Coracero, Luculus, Nariva* (Vice Commodore), *Nebraska, Nicania, Tekoa, San Veronico, Kaipara, Southern Princess* (reserve oiler for escorts), *Regent Panther, Fort Anne, Empire Cavalier* and *Empire Knight*; Dutch: *Magdala, Terkoeli* and *Zaanland*; Norwegian: *Abraham Lincoln* (Commodore Mayall) and *Elin K.*; Panamanian: *El Mundo* and *Belgian Gulf*.

Convoy HX229A's British-bound portion from New York consisted of: American: *Esso Baytown, Henry S. Grove, John Fiske, Pan Florida, Pan Maine, Southern Sun, Southern Oil, Pierre Soule* and *Socony Vacuum*; British: *Fort Drew, Empire Nugget, Tactician, Svend Foyn* (Vice Commodore), *Esperance Bay* (Commodore Casey), *Clausinia* and *Daphnella*; Panamanian: *Franz Klasen, Michigan* and *Orville Harden* (oiler for escorts).

Those from Halifax to Britain were: Belgian: *Belgian Airman*; British: *Akaroa, Arabian Prince, Bothnia, City of Oran, Fresno Star, Tudor Star, Port Melbourne, Manchester Trader, Taybank, Lossiebank, Norwegian, Tahsinia, Tortugero* and *Ribera*; Dutch: *Ganymedes*; Panamanian: *Rosemount*; with the American-flagged *Lone Star* joining from St John's.

Of the Iceland portion only one, the *Empire Airman* (British), made it; the other two, the *North King* (Panamanian) and *Shickshinny* (American), straggled and returned to St John's.

6. The British Admiralty's Operational Research Section headed by Professor P.M.S. Blackett had produced evidence based on the 'elementary mathematical fact' that 'whereas the area of a convoy is proportional to the square of its dimensions, the length of perimeter to be occupied by the escorts is proportionate only to the length of the radius'. Blackett also demonstrated that by cutting the number of convoys and increasing them in size, the escort size could also rise. By increasing the escort from six to nine warships, losses fell by a quarter. Most tellingly, the provision of air cover reduced the losses by about 65 per cent.

7. The boot-topping was a narrow band of paintwork between the light and loaded water-lines. The quotation is from Middlebrook, *Convoy*, p. 175. For a painstaking account of the actions surrounding Convoys HX229 and SC122, Mr Middlebrook's study cannot be bettered. For a highly detailed analysis, Dr Jürgen Rohwer's *The Critical Convoy Battles of March 1943*, is of enormous value. I gratefully acknowledge my debt to both authors.

8. Middlebrook, *Convoy*, p. 186.

9. *Ibid.*, p. 188.

10. A staff assessment considered that Price should have remained longer than the hour he did, a rather unfair judgement, particularly as he had effectively knocked Christophersen out of the action.

11. Quoted by Middlebrook, *op. cit.*, p. 202.

12. This was *U-665*'s first and only patrol. Oberleutnant H-L. Haupt and his crew were lost when *U-665*, on her way back to Brest, was depth-charged by an RAF Whitley bomber commanded by Pilot Sergeant J.A. Marsden. The despatching of the derelict *Fort Cedar Lake* was their only achievement.

13. By an odd coincidence, while these events were taking place Horton was at the Admiralty in London, attending Churchill's now regular Anti-Submarine Committee meetings, and the same day the Atlantic Convoy Conference was also sitting in Washington, with Sir Percy Noble representing British interests.

14. Although Larose was commissioned into the Royal Naval Reserve and *Godetia* was one of His Majesty's Ships, Larose and his crew were all exiled Belgians, part of the Force Belge, whose members received little recognition and no promotion, despite the fact that her executive officers were drawn from the Schelde pilot service and all were very experienced sea-officers with Belgian merchant command qualifications.

15. Quotations from Middlebrook, *op. cit.*, p. 247 *et seq.*, and Taprell Dorling, *Blue Star Line*, p. 138 *et seq.*

16. Trojer earned the *Ritterkreuz* by this day's work. He was killed six months later on 27 September 1943 when *U-221* was depth-charged by a Halifax of No. 58 Squadron. Before *U-221*'s fatal last dive, her gunners shot the aircraft down, killing two of its aircrew. Flying Officer E.L. Hartley and his five survivors were adrift for eleven days before being picked up by the destroyer HMS *Mahratta*. Trojer and his 50 crew died in the dark depths of the Atlantic.

CHAPTER 24: 'THE DECISIVE FACTOR'

1. The four lost in SL126 were *Empire Bowman* and *Nagara* to *U-404* (von Bülow), *Empire Whale* (with heavy loss of life) and *Umaria* to *U-662* (Müller). One further British ship, the *Urlana*, was wrecked on the Isle of Skye in September. The two later sinkings were the Greek *Laconikos* in May and the Norwegian *Hallfried* in November, both with considerable loss of life.

2. Many early Merchant Navy POWs were kept at Stalag XB at Sandbostel. In September 1941 a party was sent to Westertimke and began converting an abandoned Luftwaffe air station into Milag Nord with its adjacent Marlag Nord for Royal Navy prisoners. By early 1942 all merchant prisoners, including Dutch and Norwegians, and some passengers, had been transferred from Stalag XB to Milag Nord, where they were under Kriegsmarine command.

3. Quoted Bennett, *Survivors*, p. 131 *et seq.*

4. The corvettes each picked up 348 survivors, thought to have been the record. They were all landed at, and repatriated from, Freetown. HMS *Corinthian* was a 1938-built, requisitioned Ellerman, Papayanni liner.

5. See Cooke, *What Cares the Sea?* At the time he wrote, Cooke thought the *Lulworth Hill* had been sunk by a U-boat. His sail-cloth diary is in the Imperial War Museum.

6. Roskill, *War at Sea*, Vol. 2, p. 367: 'It appeared possible', Roskill records the Naval Staff assessing, 'that we should not be able to continue [to regard] convoy as an effective system of defence.'

7. Dönitz, 20 October 1940, quoted in Mulligan, *Neither Sharks Nor Wolves*, p. 158.

8. Roskill itemises these at this particular time as: 1st Support Group, Commander G.N. Brewer, HM Sloop *Pelican*, HM Frigates *Sennen*, *Rother*, *Spey*, *Wear* and *Jed*; 2nd Support Group, Captain F.J. Walker, HM Sloops *Cygnet*, *Starling*, *Wren*, *Kite*, *Whimbrel*, *Wild Goose* and *Woodpecker*; 3rd Support Group, Captain J.A. McCoy, HM Destroyers *Offa*, *Obedient*, *Oribi*, *Orwell* and *Onslaught*; 4th Support Group, Captain A.K. Scott-Moncrieff, HM Destroyers *Inglefield*, *Eclipse*, *Impulsive*, *Icarus* and *Fury*; 5th Support Group, Captain E.M.C. Abel-Smith, HM Escort-Carrier *Biter*, HM Destroyers *Obdurate* and *Opportune*; 6th Support Group, Captain G.E. Short, USN, USS *Bogue* (Escort-Carrier), USSs *Belknap* and *George E. Badger*. The British destroyers were on temporary loan from the Home Fleet, and by July Horton had twelve Support Groups under Brewer (*Pelican*, 1st SG), Walker (*Starling*, 2nd SG), McCoy (*Offa*, 3rd SG), Scott-Moncrieff (*Milne*, 4th SG), Birch (*Nene*, 5th SG), Short, USN (USS *Bogue*, Escort-Carrier, 6th SG), Durnford-Slater (*Pheasant*, 7th SG), Rayner (*Shikari*, 21st SG), Majendie (*Fowey*, 37th SG), Christie (*Enchantress*, 38th SG) King (*Rochester*, 39th SG) and Dallison (40th SG).

9. The following U-boats were directed to form these two groups: *U-84*, *U-86*, *U-91*, *U-134*, *U-188*, *U-260*, *U-257*, *U-305*, *U-306*, *U-333*, *U-336*, *U-373*, *U-415*, *U-440*, *U-441*, *U-523*, *U-526*, *U-527*, *U-530*, *U-564*, *U-572*, *U-590*, *U-591*, *U-592*, *U-610*, *U-615*, *U-618*, *U-631*, *U-632*, *U-641*, *U-642*, *U-663*, *U-666* and *U-706*.

10. HM Frigate *Whimbrel*, HM Destroyers *Vanessa* and *Whitehall*, and HM Corvettes *Clematis*, *Gentian*, *Heather* and *Sweetbriar*.

11. SC124 was escorted by the Canadian C3 Group, ON174 by the British B3 Group. Waters and Dönitz both mention, *en passant*, that the commodore's ship of HX230 capsized and sank with all hands. This is incorrect; Commodore Whitehorn's Report is in ADM199/576 in the National Archives, and Furness, Withy's *Pacific Shipper* survived the war.

12. See Gretton, *Convoy Escort Commander*, p. 121 *et seq.*

13. Some sources state that *U-635* accounted for the *Shillong* and *U-630* the *Waroonga*. Since both U-boats were destroyed on these their first Atlantic patrols it becomes an academic question. I have followed Wynn and Tennant in this, but other sinkings are confusing, not helped by the exaggerated claims submitted by U-boat commanders.

14. Gretton mentions this as a sinking, but Wynn states that Eckelmann's *U-635* was sunk by a Liberator from No. 120 Squadron flown by Flying Officer G.L. Hatherley. This view is supported by Rohwer, who also states that *U-527* was rammed and damaged by a destroyer. This may have been the close encounter recorded by Gretton which he states was with *U-635*. The confusion inherent in these accounts attests to the uncertainty of battle conditions.

15. See Woodman, *Arctic Convoys*, p. 109 *et seq.*

16. For a very detailed account of the passage of HX233, see Haskell, *Shadows on the Horizon*.

17. These were the American vessel *J. Pinkney Henderson*, the British *Empire Ibex*, *Empire Manor*, *Elisabeth Dal* and *Jamaica Planter*, the Norwegian *Santos*, and the Panamanians *El Almirante* and *J.H. Senior*.

18. This routeing was as a result of Ultra decrypts and was intended to avoid contact with any U-boats.

CHAPTER 25: 'WITH THE PRECISION OF A BATTLE-FLEET'

1. The disposition of this convoy was as follows: Column One: British *Bristol City*, American *West Madaket*, British *Harperley* and *Temple Arch*; Column Two: British *Dolius*, American *West Maximus*, Dutch *Bengkalis* and British *Lornaston*; Column Three: British *Ottinge*, *Baron Graham*, *Wentworth* and *L'Orient*; Column Four: Norwegian *Fana*, American *McKeesport*, British *Director* and Yugoslavian *Ivan Topic*; Column Five: British *Losada*, *British Lady*, *Baron Elgin* and *Empire Gazelle*; Column Six: Norwegian *Rena* (Commodore) and American *Argon*; Column Seven: British *Empire Advocate*, *Merton*, *Campus* and *Cydonia*; Column Eight: British *Penhale*, Norwegian *Bonde*, British *Harbury* and Polish *Modlin*; Column Nine: British *North Britain*, *Omega*, Danish *Borkholm* and British *Baron Semple*; Column Ten: British *Yearby*, *Selvistan*, *Mano* and Dutch *Berkel*; Column Eleven: British *Gharinda*, *Commandant Dorise* (formerly French-registered), Greek *Agios Georgis* and British *Dunsley*; Column Twelve: British *Empire Planet*, Panamanian *Isobel* and Greek *Nicholas*. The third and fourth stations in column six and the fourth in column twelve were vacant.

2. These were *U-258*, *U-378*, *U-386*, *U-528* and *U-532*.

3. Once the core of the human body has been significantly reduced below blood temperature, reversal may prove impossible despite every effort, and hypothermia, then known as 'exposure,' will prove fatal.

4. Post-war experience on Ocean Weather Station *Alpha* in the approximate position of ONS5 at the southern end of the Denmark Strait bears this out. In latitudes around 60° North it is common for a sequential series of intense yet discrete depressions, known as a 'family', to pass rapidly through a given point. Very high south-westerly winds veer and then drop, backing and freshening as the next depression moves quickly in at speeds of 20+ knots. However, the heavy swell generated by this energy has no time to drop away, and the motion of the ships would have been unremitting.

5. The destruction of *U-630* was attributed to Squadron Leader B.H. Moffitt in a Catalina flying-boat from No. 5 Squadron RCAF until 1991, when an Admiralty reassessment awarded the 'kill' to Lieutenant R. Hart in *Vidette*. *U-630*'s commander was Oberleutnant W. Winkler. The more likely victim of Moffitt's Catalina appears to have been *U-209*, Korvettenkapitän H. Brodda, which was attacked on the 7th and not heard of after the 9th (see Wynn, *U-Boat Operations* Vol. 1, p. 153, and Vol. 2, p. 95). Blair, in *Hitler's U-boat War*, Vol.

2, is unclear (see pp. 283 and 291). The original Admiralty assessment attributed the loss to *Jed* and *Sennen* on the 19th.

6. Credits for some of these sinkings are too contradictory to be reliable. *U-125* (Folkers) and *U-732* (Carlsen) are also contenders, but the bare fact is that *L'Orient* was lost with all hands. She was originally British-built in 1921 and owned by the Compagnie du Chemin de Fer de Paris à Orleans.

7. Some authorities credit *Loosestrife*, the Admiralty credit *Pink*: see *The Defeat of the Enemy Attack on Shipping, 1939–1945*, App. 2 (iii), p. 258.

8. Captain Cheetham and Chief Engineer T.R. Jones were repatriated by bomber, flying from Montreal. Mr G. McMechan, the chief officer, and the majority of the *Dolius's* crew re-embarked in *Sunflower* and witnessed the passage of SC130.

9. Sherwood was awarded an immediate Distinguished Service Order by radio signal for his defence of ONS5. While the attack was in progress, convoys ON180 (65 ships), ON181 (44 ships), ON182 (56 ships), ONS6 (31 ships), HX235 (36 ships) and HX236 (46 ships) crossed the Atlantic unopposed.

10. *U-646* was commanded by Oberleutnant zur See H. Wulff and *U-273* by Oberleutnant zur See H. Rossmann, who did not immediately dive but engaged Bell with machine-gun fire, throwing up a heavy flak as the Hudson dropped four depth-charges.

11. These were the destroyers *Keppel* (Commander M.J. Evans) and *Escapade*, the frigate *Towy*, the British corvettes *Orchis* and *Narcissus* and the Free French corvettes *Roselys*, *Lobélia* and *Renoncule*.

12. A further four were later picked up by *U-91*. North-east of the Azores, the same day saw the 'killing' of the Italian submarine *Leonardo da Vinci* by the destroyer *Active* and the frigate *Ness*. On 26 May in the Bay of Biscay the frigate *Test* and the corvette *Hyderabad* destroyed *U-436*, on the 28th an RAF Liberator sank *U-304* off Cape Farewell, and on the 31st in the Bay *U-563* and *U-440* were sunk by Coastal Command. From now on the 'kill' rate was steady.

13. Gretton's finale to his 'Report of Proceedings' in the National Archives (PRO) ADM199/575.

CONCLUSION: 'FULL OF AGONIZED BEWILDERMENT'

1. See Lane, *Merchant Seamen's War*, p. 151.
2. Correspondence with Peter Dudley, third officer of the *Dundrum Castle*.
3. See Woodman, *Arctic Convoys*, p. 326.
4. The National Archives (PRO), ADM 199/142.
5. See Rutter, *Red Ensign*, p. 195.
6. *The Hazards to Men in Ships Lost at Sea, 1940–44* was published in 1956 by the Medical Research Council from data gathered in the war from 448 sinkings.
7. Medical Research Council War Memorandum No. 8 (1943), *A Guide to the Preservation of Life at Sea after Shipwreck*, p. 4.
8. Private correspondence with Sir Barry Sheen, QC.
9. Precisely how many *Allied* merchant seafarers died in the Battle of the Atlantic

remains open to debate, and the matter has no prospect of so-called 'closure'. The generally accepted figure of *British*-registered seafarers lost is around 35,000, though the real number is almost certainly larger.

10. Quoted by Ivor Halstead in the Introduction to his book *Heroes of the Atlantic* published by Lindsay Drummond in 1941. In context with his comments this makes sad reading.

SELECT BIBLIOGRAPHY

(Place of publication London, unless otherwise stated)

I HAVE REFERRED TO all the following books to a greater or lesser degree in the writing of this work. All are commended to those who wish to pursue elements of this vast and pelagic campaign further; for a powerful evocation there can be none better than that of Nicholas Monsarrat in *The Cruel Sea*, the reading of which was, in its navigational sense, my own point of 'departure'.

Aiken, Alexander, *In Time of War, The history of TSMV 'Glenearn'*, published by the author, Glasgow, 1980

Armstrong, W., *Freedom of the Seas*, Jarrolds, 1943

——*Battle of the Oceans*, Jarrolds, 1943

Baker, R., *The Terror of Tobermory*, W.H.Allen, 1972

Battle of the Atlantic, An Anthology of Personal Memories, Picton Press, Liverpool, 1993

Beesly, P., *Very Special Intelligence*, Greenhill Books, 2000

Behrens, C.B.A., *Merchant Shipping and the Demands of War*, HMSO, Second Amended Edition, 1956

Bekker, C., *Hitler's Naval War*, Macdonald, 1974

Bennett, G.H. and Bennett, R., *Survivors, British Merchant Seamen in the Second World War*, The Hambledon Press, 1999

Bird, A.E., *Farewell Milag*, Lietratours, 1995

Blair, C., *Hitler's U-boat War: The Hunters, 1939–1942*, Weidenfeld and Nicolson, 1997

——*Hitler's U-boat War: The Hunted, 1943–1945*, Weidenfeld and Nicolson, 1999

Blake, George, *The Ben Line, 1825–1955*, Thomas Nelson, 1956

——*B.I. Centenary, 1856–1956*, Collins, 1956

Bone, D.W., *Merchantmen Rearmed*, Chatto and Windus, 1949

Bowen, Frank C., *The Flag of the Southern Cross, 1939–1945*, printed by the Shaw, Savill & Albion Company for private circulation, Liverpool, 1947

Brodhurst, R., *Churchill's Anchor: Admiral of the Fleet Sir Dudley Pound*, Leo Cooper, 2000

Brodie, M. (ed.), *A World Worth Fighting For*, Gooday, 1990

Broome, J., *Convoy is to Scatter*, William Kimber, 1972

Burn, Alan, *The Fighting Commodores*, Leo Cooper, 1999

Bushell, T.A., *Eight Bells: Royal Mail Lines War Story, 1939–1945*, Trade and Travel, 1950

Carse, R., *There go the Ships*, William Morrow, New York, 1942

Chalmers, Rear Admiral W.S., *Max Horton and the Western Approaches*, Hodder and Stoughton, 1954

Cherry, A., *Yankee RN*, Jarrolds, 1954

Churchill, W.S., *The Second World War*, 6 volumes, Penguin, 1985

Cooke, K., *What Cares the Sea?*, Hutchinson, 1960

Course, Captain A.G., *The Merchant Navy: A Social History*, Muller, 1963

Creighton, Sir Kenelm, *Convoy Commodore*, Futura, 1976

Cremer, P., *U-333, The Story of a U-Boat Ace*, Triad Grafton, 1986

Divine, A.D., *The Merchant Navy Fights* (a war history of Sir R. Ropner's tramps), John Murray, 1940

Divine, D., *Navies in Exile*, John Murray, 1944

——*Mutiny at Invergordon*, Macdonald, 1970

Dönitz, Admiral Karl, *Memoirs: Ten Years and Twenty Days*, Cassell, 2000

Doughty, M., *Merchant Shipping and War, A Study in Defence Planning in Twentieth Century Britain*, Royal Historical Society, Studies in History Series, No. 31, 1982

Drummond, C., *The Remarkable Life of Victoria Drummond, Marine Engineer*, The Institute of Marine Engineers, 1994

Dunmore, S., *In Great Waters*, Pimlico, 2001

Edwards, Bernard, *The Merchant Navy Goes to War*, Robert Hale, 1989

Elphick, R., *Life Line: The Merchant Navy at War, 1939–1945*, Chatham, 1999

Franklin, G., *Britain's Anti-Submarine Capability 1919–1939*, Frank Cass, 2003

Führer Conferences on Naval Affairs, 1939–1945: *see* Showell

Gleichauf, J.E., *Unsung Sailors: The Naval Armed Guard in World War II*, Naval Institute Press, Annapolis, Maryland, 1990

Gorley Putt, S., *Men Dressed as Seamen*, Christophers, 1943

Gretton, P., *Convoy Escort Commander*, Cassell, 1964

Grey, E., *Hitler's Battleships*, Leo Cooper, 1992.

Grove, E. (ed.), *The Defeat of the Enemy Attack on Shipping, 1939–1945* (a revised edition of the Naval Staff History, vols 1A and 1E), Ashgate, for Navy Records Society, 1997

Hague, A., *The Towns*, World Ship Society, Kendal, 1988

——, *Sloops, 1926–1946*, World Ship Society, Kendal, 1993

——, *The Rescue Ships, 1940–1945*, World Ship Society, 1998

——, *The Allied Convoy System, 1939–1945, Its Organisation, Defence and Operation*, Chatham Publishing, 2000

Halstead, I., *Heroes of the Atlantic*, Drummond, 1941

Hardy, A.C., *Everyman's History of the War at Sea*, 3 vols, Nicholson and Watson, 1948–1955

Harling, R., *The Steep Atlantick Stream*, Chatto and Windus, 1946

Haskell, W.A., *Shadows on the Horizon, The Battle of Convoy HX233*, Chatham Publishing, 1998

Hawkins, D.M., *Atlantic Torpedo*, Gollancz, 1943

Heal, S.C., *A Great Fleet of Ships: The Canadian Forts and Parks*, Vanwell, Ontario, 1999

Hessler, G., *The U-Boat War in the Atlantic*, MoD (Navy), HMSO, 1989

Hirschfeld, W., *The Secret Diary of a U-Boat*, Orion, 1997

Hirson, B., and Vivian, L., *Strike Across the Empire*, Clio Publications, 1992

HMSO, *British Vessels Lost at Sea, 1914–1917 and 1939–1945*, facsimile edition, Patrick Stephens, Wellingborough, 1988

Hope, R., *A New History of British Shipping*, John Murray, 1990

——, *Poor Jack*, Chatham, 2001

Hope, S., *Ocean Odyssey: A Record of the Fighting Merchant Navy*, Eyre and Spottiswoode, 1944

Hough, R., *Former Naval Person: Churchill and the War at sea,* Weidenfeld and Nicolson, 1985

Houlder Brothers, *Sea Hazard (1939–1945)* (an unattributed company history of Houlder Brothers), 1947

Howarth, S. and Law, D. (eds), *The Battle of the Atlantic Conference Papers*, Greenhill, 1994

Howse, D., *Radar at Sea*, Macmillan, 1993

Hudson, J.L., *British Merchantmen at War: The Official Story of the Merchant Navy, 1939–1944*, HMSO, 1944

Hurd, A., *Britain's Merchant Navy*, Odhams, 1943

Huxley, E., *Atlantic Ordeal: The story of Mary Cornish*, Chatto and Windus, 1941

Jackson, I., with Todd, I. and Ormerod, J., *Three Boys in a Ship*, privately published, 1999

Jordan, Roger, *The World's Merchant Fleets, 1939*, Chatham Publishing, 1999

Kennedy, L., *Pursuit: The Chase and Sinking of the 'Bismarck'*, Collins, 1974

Kerr, George F., *The Ben Line, A Merchant Fleet at War, 1939–1945*, (unattributed company war history, probably written by George Kerr), Thomas Nelson, 1946

——*Business in Great Waters: The War History of the P&O, 1939–1945*, Faber and Faber, 1951

King, E.J., and Whitehill, W.M., *Fleet Admiral King*, Eyre and Spottiswoode, 1953

Knox, C., *Atlantic Battle*, Methuen, 1941

Jones, D.E.C., *The Enemy we Killed, My Friend,* Gomer, 1999

Laird, Dorothy, *Paddy Henderson: The story of P. Henderson and Co. 1834–1961*, George Outram, Glasgow, 1961

Lane, T., *The Merchant Seamen's War*, Manchester University Press, Manchester, 1990

'Lanyard', *Stand by to Ram!*, Crosby Lockwood, 1943

Lash, Joseph P., *Roosevelt and Churchill, 1939–1941*, André Deutsch, 1977

Laskier, F., *My Name is Frank: A merchant seaman talks*, Allen and Unwin, 1941

——*Log Book*, Allen and Unwin, 1942

Lennox Kerr, J., *Touching the Adventures of Merchantmen in the Second World War*, Harrap, 1953

Lenton, H.T, *British Escort Ships*, Macdonald and Janes, 1974

——*British and Empire Warships of the Second World War*, Greenhill Books, 1998

Macintyre, D., *The Battle of the Atlantic*, Pan, 1969

——*U-Boat Killer*, Corgi, 1976

Macneil, C., '*San Demetrio*', Angus and Robertson, 1957

McBrearty, R.F., *Seafaring 1939–45 As I saw it*, Pentland Press, 1995

Mars, Alastair, *Court Martial*, William Kimber, 1954

Middlebrook, M., *Convoy: The Greatest U-Boat Battle of the War*, Cassell, 2003

MoD (Navy), *German Naval History: The U-boat War in the Atlantic, 1939–1945*, facsimile edition, HMSO, 1989

Moore, A.R., *A Careless Word . . . A Needless Sinking*, American Merchant Marine Museum, New York, 1993

Morison, S.E., *History of United States Naval Operations in World War II*, Vol. 1, *The Battle of the Atlantic, 1939–1943*, Little, Brown, repr. 1993

Mulligan, T.P., *Neither Sharks nor Wolves*, Chatham, 1999

Osborne, R. (ed.), *Conversion for War*, World Ship Society, Monograph No. 8, Kendal, 1983

Pearce Jones, G., *Two Survived*, Hamish Hamilton, 1941

Ranalow, E., *A Corkman at Sea*, privately published, n.d.

Rayner, D.A., *Escort*, William Kimber, 1955

Revely, H., *The Convoy That Nearly Died*, William Kimber, 1979

Rinman, T., and Brodefors, R., *The Commercial History of Shipping*, Rinman and Lindén AB, Gothenburg, Sweden, 1983

Rohwer, J., *The Critical Convoy Battles of March 1943*, Ian Allan, 1977

—— and Hummelchen G., *Chronology of the War at Sea, 1939–1945*, Greenhill, 1992

Roskill, Captain S.W., *The War at Sea*, 4 vols, HMSO, 1954–1961

——, *A Merchant Fleet in War: Alfred Holt & Co, 1939–1945*, Collins, 1962

Rutter, O., *Red Ensign: A History of Convoy*, Robert Hale, 1942

Sargent, R.S., *Seaways of the Empire: Notes on the Geography of Transport*, A. & C. Black, 1930

Saunders, Hilary St George, *Valiant Voyaging, A Short History of the British India Steam Navigation Co. in the Second World War, 1939–1945*, Faber and Faber, 1948

Schofield, Vice Admiral B. B., *British Seapower: Naval Policy in the Twentieth Century*, B.T. Batsford, 1967.

Schofield, Vice Admiral B.B., and Martyn, Lieutenant Commander L. F., *The Rescue Ships*, William Blackwood, 1968

Schull, J., *The Far Distant Ships: An Official Account of Canadian Naval Operations in the Second World War*, published by Authority of the Minister of National Defence, Ottawa, 1950.

Seabag-Montefiore, H., *ENIGMA: The Battle for the Code*, Phoenix, 2000

Smith, G., *The War at Sea: Royal and Dominion Navy Actions in World War 2*, Ian Allan, 1989

Showell, Jak P. Mallman (Foreword), *Führer Conferences on Naval Affairs, 1939–1945*, Greenhill Books, 1990

Slader, J., *The Red Duster at War*, William Kimber, 1988

——*The Fourth Service – Merchantmen at War, 1939–45*, Robert Hale, 1994

Stewart, Jean Cantlie, *The Sea Our Heritage*, Rowan, Keith, Banffshire, 1995

Syrett, D. (ed.), *The Battle of the Atlantic Signals Intelligence: U-boat Situations and Trends, 1941–1945*, Ashgate, for the Navy Records Society, 1998

——The Battle of the Atlantic Signals Intelligence: U-boat Tracking Papers, 1941–1947, Ashgate, for the Navy Records Society, 2002

Taprell Dorling, Captain H., The Blue Star Line: A Record of Service, 1939–1945, published by the company, date unknown (1948?), Liverpool

Taylor, James., Prisoner of the 'Kormoran', Harrap, 1945

Tennant, Alan J., British and Commonwealth Merchant Ship Losses to Axis Submarines, 1939–1945, Sutton Publishing, Stroud, 2001

Tennyson, Jesse, F., The Saga of the 'San Demetrio', HMSO, 1942

Thomas, D., The Atlantic Star, 1939–45, W.H. Allen, 1990

Thomas, G., Milag: Captives of the Kriegsmarine, Merchant Navy Prisoners of War, The Milag Prisoner of War Association, n.d.

Thornton, R. H., British Shipping, Cambridge University Press, 1939

Trevor-Roper, H.R. (ed.), Hitler's War Directives, 1939–1945, Pan Books, 1966

Turner, L.C.F., Gordon-Cumming, H.R., Betzler, J.E., War in the Southern Oceans, 1930–1945, Oxford University Press, Cape Town, 1961.

Van der Vat, D., The Atlantic Campaign: The Great Struggle at Sea, 1939–1945, Hodder and Stoughton, 1988

Vause, J., WOLF: U-boat Commanders in World War II, Airlife, 1997

Warlimont, General W., Inside Hitler's Headquarters, 1939–45, Presidio Press, California, 1964

Waters, J.M., Bloody Winter, Naval Institute Press, Annapolis, 1967

Waters, Sydney D., Ordeal by Sea: The New Zealand Shipping Company in the Second World War, 1939–1945, published by the Company, 1949

Watt, Cdr F.B., In All Respects Ready, Totem Books, Ontario, 1986

Whinney, Captain R., DSC and two bars, RN, The U-Boat Peril, Arrow Books, 1989

Williams, A., The Battle of the Atlantic, BBC, 2002

Williams, Mark, Captain Gilbert Roberts RN and the Anti-U-boat School, Cassell, 1979

Winton, J. (ed.), Freedom's Battle, Vol. 1: The War at Sea, 1939–1945, Hutchinson, 1967

Woodman, R. Arctic Convoys, 1941–1945 (John Murray, 1994)

Wynn, K., U-boat Operations of the Second World War, 2 vols, Chatham Publishing, 1997

Young, John M., Britain's Sea War: A Diary of Ship Losses, 1939–1945, Patrick Stephens Ltd, Wellingborough, 1989

Yule, H. and Burnell, A.C., Hobson-Jobson: The Anglo-Indian Dictionary, Wordsworth, 1996

ACKNOWLEDGEMENTS

I SHOULD LIKE TO thank Roderic Suddaby and the staff of the Imperial War Museum Department of Documents for their help, and the following copyright-holders for their kindness in permitting me to quote from material held in their name at the Imperial War Museum: Mrs F. Ashmore, Mr W.A. Bishop, William Close, Commander Neil Churchill, Mr David Egerton, Angela Fox, Mrs Barbara Fyrth, Julian Moore, Eric Ranalow, Mary Roper, Commander E.T. Thring and Mr H.F. Watson.

Among others who helped with the preparation of this work I wish express my gratitude to Mr A.C. Douglas, editor of *Sea Breezes*, for promulgating my request for information, and to Keith C. Angus, Bernard Ashton, Ernest Ashworth, Lieutenant Commander Richard Baker, H. Barnes, Captain J. Bax, Captain Eric Beetham, Richard Bird, W.F. Bishop, Captain Malcolm Borland, Captain Graeme Boxall, Ron Bramall, Ian Browning, David Charteris, David Craig, Captain J.R. Cooper, Richard Cornish, Brian Coulton, D.C. Dawson, W.C. Dawson, Captain Peter Dudley, Peter Eagleton, George Fletcher, Frank Fox, Captain Lennart Granqvist, Michael Grey, W.A. Haskell, J.E. Hefford, Alan Hope, Dr Ronald Hope, Barry Johnson, Professor Alston Kennerley, Professor Tony Lane, the late Captain C.W. Leadbetter, John Long, Captain P.H. King, the late Charles Owen, Captain Niall M. Macfarlane, Brian McManus, the late John McNaught, Mervyn Manson, Ian A. Millar, George Monk, Captain A.R. Moore, Captain Harry Mowat, J.Gordon Mumford, Professor Bernard de Neumann, A.P. Nolan, John Page, John Persson, Mike Richey, Professor Dr Jürgen Rohwer, Commander Morin Scott, Sir Barry Sheen, Charles Stock, Commander Neville Towle, the late Commodore John Wacher, and Captain Gwilym Williams, who all, in one way or another, aided me materially in my task by forwarding information, advice, opinion or permission to quote from their own books or reminiscences.

My thanks also go to the staff of the National Archives at Kew, to Captain Peter Adams, editor of *The Journal of the Honourable Company of Master Mariners* and to The Master, Wardens and Court of the Honourable Company of Master Mariners, for permission to quote from the *Journal* and to use illustrations from the Honourable Company's collection. A particular thanks to John Morris for his excellent drawings, and to Eric Grove who kindly read the typescript and made several helpful suggestions.

To those whose contribution has not been acknowledged through my inability to trace them, or the current copyright-holder, I offer my sincere apologies. If they wish to receive acknowledgement, I should be happy to oblige in any subsequent edition of this book.

My grateful thanks to Gail Pirkis and John Murray for their help and encouragement at the inception of the project, to Roland Philipps and Caro Westmore for their kindness and diligence during the process of production, to Mark Robinson for some helpful suggestions as to structure and especially to Liz Robinson for her assiduous, thoughtful and painstaking editing, to Douglas Matthews for the Index, and to Barbara Levy for her assistance as my agent. The debt that I owe to my wife Chris, whose contribution has been enormous, is beyond my powers of expression.

For those errors and omissions which inevitably creep into a work of this complexity despite the best efforts of its author, I offer my apologies.

Richard Woodman
Harwich, 2004

INDEX

Richard Woodman's acclaimed book *Arctic Convoys* is
also available in John Murray paperback

Arctic Convoys 1941–1945

During the last four years of the Second World War, the Western
Allies secured Russian defences against Germany by supplying
vital food and arms. Few are aware of the courage, determination
and sacrifice of the Allied merchant ships, which withstood
unremitting U-boat attacks and aerial bombardment to maintain
this lifeline. In the storms, fog and numbing cold of the Arctic,
where the sinking of a 10,000 ton freighter was equal to a land
battle in terms of destruction, the losses sustained were huge. Told
from the perspective of their crews, this is the inspiring story of
the long-suffering merchant ships without which Russia would
almost certainly have fallen to Nazi Germany.

'An admirable work of scholarship . . . It is also a gripping
narrative, filled with stories of bravery, self-sacrifice and sheer
doggedness which at times defy credibility'
John Keegan, *Daily Telegraph*

'For sheer heroism and brazen drama the icy saga
Woodman tells is hard to beat'
Frank McLynn, *Literary Review*

ISBN 0 7195 6617 7
£9.99

Order your copies now by calling Bookpoint on 01235 827720 or
visit your local bookshop.